CURRENT BIOGRAPHY

JANUARY 1962
VOL. 23   NO. 1

18

Editor: Charles Moritz

PUBLISHED BY THE H. W. WILSON COMPANY, 950 UNIVERSITY AVE., NEW YORK

CONTENTS   *Page*   *Page*

ABOUT THIS PUBLICATION

Current Biography (published every month except August) presents articles on people who are prominent in the news—in national and international affairs, the sciences, the arts, labor, and industry. Sources of information are newspapers, magazines, books, and, in some cases, the biographees themselves. It should be pointed out, however, that these are objective rather than authorized biographies. At the end of the year the articles in the monthly issues are cumulated in one alphabet, revised, and printed in a single volume known as *Current Biography Yearbook.*

Authorities for biographees' full names, with some exceptions, are the bibliographical publications of The Wilson Company. When a biographee prefers a certain name form, that is indicated in the heading of the article: for example, MACMILLAN, (MAURICE) HAROLD means that he is usually referred to as HAROLD MACMILLAN. When a professional name is used in the heading, as, for example, GLENN FORD, the real name, in this case GWYLLYN SAMUEL NEWTON FORD, appears in the article itself.

The heading of each article includes the pronunciation of the name if it is unusual, date of birth (if obtainable) and occupation. The article is supplemented by a list of references to sources of biographical information, in two alphabets: (1) newspapers and periodicals and (2) books.

References to newspapers and periodicals are listed in abbreviated form. For example, "Sat Eve Post 217:14+ S 30 '44 por" means *Saturday Evening Post,* volume 217, pages 14 ff, September 30, 1944, with portrait. For full names, see the section "Periodical and Newspaper Designations," which is included in all *Current Biography* Yearbooks and in the January issue each year. Obituary notices appear for persons whose biographies have been published in *Current Biography.*

An index to names that have appeared this year is to be found at the back of this issue.

NOTE: Authors whose biographies do not appear in *Current Biography* may usually be found in *Twentieth Century Authors,* Kunitz & Haycraft, 1942, H. W. Wilson Company, or in the FIRST SUPPLEMENT (1955). Authors of books for young people are included in *The Junior Book of Authors* (Second Edition, Revised) edited by Kunitz & Haycraft, 1951, H. W. Wilson Company. Musicians whose biographies do not appear in *Current Biography* may usually be found in *Living Musicians,* compiled and edited by David Ewen, 1940, H. W. Wilson Company, or in its FIRST SUPPLEMENT (1957).

KEY TO PRONUNCIATION

ā	āle	N	Not pronounced, but indicates the nasal tone of the preceding vowel, as in the French *bon* (bôN).	û	ûrn; French eu, as in *jeu* (zhû); German ö, oe, as in *schön* (shûn), *Goethe* (gû'tĕ)
â	câre				
ă	ădd				
ă	ăccount				
ä	ärm				
à	àsk				
à	sofà	ō	ōld	ŭ	tŭb
		ô	ôrb	ŭ	circŭs
ē	ēve	ŏ	ŏdd	ü	Pronounced approximately as ē, with rounded lips: French u, as in *menu* (mē-nü); German ü, as in *grün*
ĕ	ĕnd	oi	oil		
ē	makēr	o͞o	o͞oze		
		o͝o	fo͝ot		
g	go	ou	out		
ī	īce				
ĭ	ĭll	*th*	*then*	zh	azure
		th	thin	′ =	main accent
K	German ch as in *ich* (ĭK)	ū	cūbe	″ =	secondary accent

CURRENT BIOGRAPHY

JANUARY 1962

AMINI, ALI (ä-mē'nē) June 1907- Premier of Iran; lawyer; economist; diplomat

Address: b. Présidence du Conseil des Ministres, Ave. Kakh Carrefour, Tehran, Iran; h. Park Aminol-Dowleh, Tehran, Iran

Representing the "revolution from above," the Premier of Iran, Dr. Ali Amini, has been called "an outspoken critic of past regimes." He was appointed by Mohammed Riza Shah Pahlevi to succeed Jafar Sharif-Imami on May 5, 1961, following student demonstrations that threatened to erupt into revolution. A wealthy lawyer and economist, Amini once served as Iran's Minister of Finance and Minister of Justice, and he was largely responsible for negotiating the agreement that ended the dispute between Iran and foreign oil companies in 1954. He later served as Iranian Ambassador to the United States.

As Premier, Amini has ruled by decree, pending revision of Iran's electoral system. Despite great obstacles, Amini has met with some success during his first few months in office in his war against corruption, and has eased Iran's financial difficulties by means of economy measures and foreign loans. For the benefit of Iran's 16,000,000 peasants, he has initiated a two-year land redistribution program. "Reform and good health —in every field of national life" is his announced goal.

Destined to inherit rich agricultural estates near the Caspian Sea and to become one of Iran's twenty largest landholders, Ali Amini was born at Tehran in June 1907. He is related to the old Qajar dynasty, which was overthrown by Riza Pahlevi, the father of the present Shah, in 1921. After completing his primary and secondary schooling in his native city, Amini went to France in April 1925 to study law at the University of Grenoble. He later attended the University of Paris, where he received his doctorate in law and economics from the Faculty of Law in 1931. His thesis, *L'Institution du Monopole du Commerce Exterieur en Perse*, dealing with Iran's foreign trade during and after World War I, was published in Paris in 1932.

Upon his return to Iran in 1931, Amini was appointed an alternate judge of the Court of First Instance. Subsequently he served on one of the penal branches of the Court of Appeals at Tehran. In 1933 he joined the staff of the economic section of the Ministry of Finance, and later he was appointed assistant director of the Opium Administration Monopoly. In the middle of 1934 Amini was appointed assistant director of the Customs Administration, and in 1936 he became director general. He was named economic director general of the Ministry of Finance in 1938.

Wide World

ALI AMINI

In 1940 Amini was elected a deputy from Tehran to the Majlis, or lower house of the Iranian parliament. In the same year he was appointed undersecretary to the Minister of Finance and, later, Deputy Prime Minister. In 1943 Premier Qavam-es Sultaneh was so impressed by his capabilities that he made him his own undersecretary. Re-elected to the Majlis in 1945, Amini was active in the furtherance of Iran's first Seven Year Development Plan, approved by parliament early in 1949.

During the early 1940's Amini went to India to study its wartime economy. In 1949-50 he was Iranian representative to the Opium Commission at Ankara and Geneva, and in 1950-51 he was chairman of the Iranian delegation to the Commission on Narcotic Drugs of the United Nations Economic and Social Council. He has also served as president of the Exchange Control Commission, and as governor of the Industrial and Mining Bank of Iran. Amini was chairman of the Iranian commission that negotiated a commercial treaty with the Federal Republic of Germany in 1949-50. In June 1950 he was appointed Minister of National Economy in the cabinet of General Ali Razmara.

In March 1951 Premier Razmara was assassinated by a religious fanatic who belonged to a sect that wanted to cancel foreign aid agreements and nationalize the oil industry. The Premier had not yielded to nationalist pressure to move

AMINI, ALI—*Continued*

against the foreign control of Iranian oil. A new government, headed by Hussein Ala, resigned late in April 1951, and Dr. Mohammed Mossadegh, the leader of the National Front coalition, became Prime Minister. On May 2, 1951 an oil nationalization act went into effect, and in October the Anglo-Iranian Oil Company withdrew its technical staff from the huge refinery at Abadan. But Iran was unable to staff oil operations adequately or to dispose of more than a trickle of her petroleum on the world market. As the oil royalties ceased, Iran's financial condition grew rapidly worse. By August 1953 the treasury was empty.

In August 1953 Mohammed Riza Shah Pahlevi dismissed Mossadegh and appointed General Fazlollah Zahedi as Prime Minister. Mossadegh was subsequently arrested and imprisoned. Amini was named Minister of Finance in Zahedi's cabinet, and in this capacity he headed the Iranian mission, which in April 1954 began to negotiate a settlement of the oil controversy. On August 5, 1954 an agreement was reached whereby oil operations were taken over by an international consortium consisting of the Anglo-Iranian Oil Company and several other foreign companies. Although Mossadegh supporters considered the consortium's profits too high, Amini convinced the Shah and the parliament that the settlement was the best attainable. Oil company officials regarded Amini as a hard bargainer, and one offered him a position, which he turned down.

When ill health forced Zahedi to resign as Premier in April 1955, Amini was retained as Finance Minister by his successor, Hussein Ala. A month later, the Shah (who regarded Amini as the most suitable man to reorganize the Justice Ministry) appointed him Minister of Justice. In November 1955 Amini was named to replace Nasrollah Entezam as Iranian Ambassador to the United States. It has been said that this appointment was made because Dr. Manouchehr Eghbal, who basked in the favor of the Shah, and who was to become Premier in 1957, wanted Amini out of the country. Although he was well-liked in Washington, Amini was recalled in 1958, partly because he had publicly advanced the view that poverty in the midst of plenty would cease if the oil-producing nations of the Middle East, including Iran, would share their wealth with the less fortunate Middle Eastern countries.

On returning from Washington, Amini was often ignored by the Shah, although it has been said that he was closely watched by police during this period. He ended two years of political inactivity when he ran as a candidate of the Independent party in the election to the Majlis of August 3, 1960. When he subsequently charged that the election had been rigged in favor of the victorious National party of Eghbal, the Shah voided the election and appointed Jafar Sharif-Imami as Premier.

For a time Iran seemed to hover on the brink of revolution, especially when demonstrations by 30,000 students and teachers in Tehran led to the resignation of Premier Sharif-Imami in May 1960. Fearing that his regime might follow the fate of the governments of Syngman Rhee in South Korea and Adnan Menderes in Turkey,

which had been brought down by student revolts, the Shah decided to carry out the revolution from above. For this task the Shah went beyond Iran's two-party system to choose Amini, who was appointed Premier on May 5, 1961.

In accepting the appointment, Amini declared that the Shah "must reign but not rule." Subsequently, in reply to Amini's insistence upon freedom to make his own decisions, the Shah dissolved the parliament, enabling Amini to govern by decree. In a broadcast to the people on May 8, 1961 Amini referred to the great financial and economic difficulties resulting from the waste of natural resources, the disregard of financial laws, and the misuse of government funds by "incompetent and traitorous" officials.

Amid growing opposition and clamor for free elections, Amini, like "a man with his finger in the dike," made almost daily speeches to win support. During his first few months in office he took stern measures to stem corruption and to restore economic health. He arrested a number of prominent Iranians for graft, including the "Queen of Caviar," a court favorite. He has greatly limited luxury imports and foreign travel, reduced bank credits, and banned foreign showgirls and cabaret performers. Several expensive building projects were cancelled, and steps were taken to reduce prices in Tehran's bazaar. Iran has received emergency advances from the United States and the consortium, and has negotiated a $50,000,000 loan with West Germany. Construction has been started on the great Dez River Dam. Amini has affirmed Iran's ties with the Western nations and has resisted pressure by the Soviet Union aimed at forcing Iran to abandon its membership in the Central Treaty Organization (CENTO).

Amini has taken steps to revitalize the civil service and has campaigned against illiteracy. He has doubled the salaries of teachers, and made the leader of the teachers' strike his minister of education. For the benefit of the peasants, Amini has initiated a two-year land redistribution plan. Under this program large estates would be broken up, and no individual owner would be permitted to hold more than 875 acres of irrigated, or 1,750 acres of dry, farming land. Any excess acreage would be sold by the government to small farmers on an installment basis. Although Amini's policies have met with widespread criticism because of their restrictions upon civil liberties, one economist has said that his harsh measures have "restored sanity to the economy."

By the middle of November 1961 rumors were circulating in Tehran that the Shah was about to oust Amini or at least demand that his government be reconstituted. Unwilling to make the sacrifices that Amini demanded, the old conservatives and members of the National Front greatly stiffened their opposition to his measures, and there was more than one indication that Amini was nearing the end of his term in office.

Of medium height and build, Amini has soft, graying hair, a prominent nose, large, protruding eyes, and a "puckish smile." Described as a "technician rather than a crowd-pleaser," he speaks in a low voice and uses gestures for emphasis. His French is fluent, and his English adequate. He often works eighteen hours a day.

Amini and his wife Batol (or Batool) reside in a villa in Tehran with a large Persian garden. They have a son, Faridun, who works for an oil company. In June 1961 they adopted a foundling infant whom they named Khodadad (Gift of God). In his free time, Amini enjoys working in his garden, and he has reserved one of the many farms he owns for his personal management.

According to Claire Sterling, Amini is "so very rich as to be beyond corruption; and though he is called a conservative, he thinks of himself as a Franklin D. Roosevelt—a man who is trying to save his class from itself by figuring out what an enlightened revolutionary would do and doing it" (*Reporter*, August 17, 1961).

References

N Y Herald Tribune p6 My 6 '61 por
N Y Times p2 My 30 '61 por
Newsweek 57:41+ Je 26 '61 por
International Who's Who, 1960
Middle East, 1961

BIDDLE, ANTHONY J(OSEPH) DREXEL Dec. 17, 1896-Nov. 13, 1961 Diplomat; during part of World War II was United States Ambassador to governments-in-exile of several European countries; Ambassador to Spain (1961); retired from the Army in 1955 in rank of brigadier general after serving on staffs of SHAEF and SHAPE. See *Current Biography* (March) 1941.

Obituary

N Y Times p39 N 14 '61

BRIDGES, (HENRY) STYLES Sept. 9, 1898-Nov. 26, 1961 United States Senator from New Hampshire since 1937; chairman of the Appropriations Committee (1947-48, 1953-54); senior Republican Senator in point of service and a leader of the party's conservative wing. See *Current Biography* (March) 1948.

Obituary

N Y Times p1+ N 27 '61

CHANCELLOR, JOHN (WILLIAM) July 14, 1927- Journalist; television personality
Address: b. National Broadcasting Co., 30 Rockefeller Plaza, New York 20

One of television's most prized and demanding assignments—serving as host of the National Broadcasting Company's *Today* show—went in July 1961 to a young newsman who had gained his reputation covering gangland shootings in his native Chicago, racial violence in Little Rock, and political developments in Moscow. When John Chancellor took over the spot relinquished by Dave Garroway, NBC transferred control of *Today* to its news department, promising to strengthen the program's emphasis on national and international affairs. Although Chancellor insists that he is primarily a newsman, he has discovered that two hours of exposure every weekday before a television audience of some 4,000,000 families have transformed him into a national personality.

JOHN CHANCELLOR

John William Chancellor was born in Chicago, Illinois on July 14, 1927, the only child of E. M. J. Chancellor and Mollie (Barrett) Chancellor. He was educated at DePaul Academy, which he left at the age of fifteen, according to an article in *Look* magazine (October 24, 1961). He had a series of "oddball jobs"—hospital orderly, carpenter's assistant, chemical tester, parker of trailer trucks, job agency interviewer, and deckhand on an Illinois River boat. He entered the United States Army in 1945 as a private and served as a public relations specialist until 1947, when he was discharged with the rank of T/5.

After attending the University of Illinois Chicago undergraduate division briefly, Chancellor joined the staff of the Chicago *Sun-Times* in 1948 as a copyboy. He subsequently became a reporter, rewrite man, and feature writer. His beat ranged from the Rocky Mountains to the Appalachians and from Canada to the Gulf of Mexico. In 1950 he joined the staff of WNBQ, the National Broadcasting Company outlet in Chicago, where he tracked down stories in an unmarked mobile unit equipped with a flashing red light and siren, chasing police calls. "For a long time," Chancellor recalls, "the police thought we were from the fire department, and the firemen thought we were the police. It helped."

Once, while lying face down in a Chicago street as police bullets whined overhead, he made a tape recording of the capture of a killer. For this achievement he won the national Sigma Delta Chi award for outstanding reporting in 1955. On another occasion he reported on a fire blazing in an oil refinery, continuing the broadcast while debris fell all around him. In 1958 he won a Robert E. Sherwood Award from the Fund for the Republic for a television documentary that he had filmed about the plight of white Southern migrants in unfriendly Northern cities. "When we weren't in a light plane in a thunderstorm," Chancellor has said, "we were passing a big truck on a small curve. We learned to

CHANCELLOR, JOHN—*Continued*

process films in bathtubs, to broadcast from telephone booths, to do our laundry on airlines. I was never happier."

During the 1956 contest for the Presidency, Chancellor covered the Democratic and Republican primary campaigns, served as a television floorman at the Chicago and San Francisco conventions, and accompanied Adlai E. Stevenson around the United States. On Labor Day in 1957 he was sent to cover the opening of the school term in newly desegregated Central High School in Little Rock, Arkansas, leaving for the plane in such a hurry that he was dressed in a sport shirt and slacks. He remained in Little Rock for eight weeks—long enough for him to acquire new clothes and new honors for his reporting about Governor Orval E. Faubus and the school integration story.

Chancellor received his first assignment overseas in early 1958, when NBC News assigned him to its Vienna bureau. On his way to Austria he covered events in Paris, Rome, and Tunis, and the Algerian revolt that once more installed General de Gaulle in power. Later in the year he spent several months reporting on the civil war in Lebanon. Transferred to the London bureau, he covered the wedding of Princess Margaret from a roost near Westminster Abbey. From time to time he left London to make a film at the Khyber Pass, to join a camera crew in a jeep traveling through Pakistan, and to circle the Mediterranean for three months while directing David Brinkley's "Our Man in the Mediterranean." In 1960 he was assigned to cover the abortive summit conference in Paris.

In April 1960 Chancellor was assigned by NBC News to Moscow, where he covered such important events as the trial of the U-2 pilot Francis Gary Powers and the space flight of Yuri Gagarin. Summoned back to the United States by NBC in the fall of 1960, he helped to cover the Presidential campaigns. He journeyed with the candidates and fired questions at them during their debates and on *Meet the Press*. On the night of election he manned the Midwest desk at NBC election headquarters. According to a *Time* writer (July 14, 1961), Chancellor "outdid Huntley and Brinkley in sagacity and was one of the few commentators who kept saying all night long that the result would be close."

In June 1961 Chancellor reported on the meeting in Vienna between President John F. Kennedy and Premier Nikita S. Khrushchev. He then returned to New York City for a week's tryout as host and moderator of NBC-TV's *Today*, after Dave Garroway had decided to withdraw from the program for personal reasons. Chancellor's cordiality and dry wit, coupled with his professional skill in reporting and interpreting the news, prompted NBC executives to name him as permanent host of the program. He accepted, although he was reluctant to leave his key assignment in Moscow and expressed his wariness about becoming another "character" on television.

Over the ship-to-shore telephone from the *Queen Mary* Chancellor had told Marie Torre of the New York *Herald Tribune* (July 12, 1961): "In some ways, I feel as if I'm returning to New

York for reassignment. Know what I mean? 'Today' is going to be a news game, supervised by newsmen, produced by newsmen, and interpreted by newsmen. Though they call me Garroway's replacement, the concentration will not be on one dominant personality but on a corporate personality—Edwin Newman, Frank Blair, and me. I think this is all to the good. I don't mean to knock Garroway, but the new format will have the look of a younger generation—the New Frontier, if you will."

The dry humor and quick wit that Jack Gould of the New York *Times* (July 18, 1961) had hailed in a review of Chancellor's work on *Today* were apparent in an article that Chancellor wrote for *Show Business Illustrated* (October 17, 1961). In it he described the *Today* program as being "as well established as Harvard University or Mrs. Grass's Noodle Soup—and it contains elements of both. It has been on the air for nearly 10 years, a kind of commuter service ferrying what must by now be nearly a billion people from seven o'clock to nine o'clock in the morning. It is full of news and entertainment and interesting guests and occasional jokes, and the very best thing I can say about it is that on most days it is a pleasant and informative program to watch."

Others in authority agree with him. Jack Gould maintains that *Today* is more regularly viewed by Washington officials than any other offering on television. When Newton N. Minow, the chairman of the Federal Communications Commission and a friend of Chancellor, was asked to give an example of a television program that did not belong to the "wasteland," he named *Today* as the first example that came to his mind.

Another friend is Robert (Shad) Northshield, once a night caption writer on the Chicago *Sun-Times* when Chancellor was a copyboy there, and now the producer of *Today* at Chancellor's request. The two men have introduced several changes into the show. *Today* is now broadcast "live" every morning Monday through Friday from 7 to 9 A.M. Eastern time, rather than recorded on tape the previous afternoon, as it was done under Garroway. In another innovation Chancellor covers major national and international stories on the spot rather than from behind his desk at NBC.

John Chancellor married Barbara Upshaw, a graphic designer, in 1958. They have two children: Laura Campbell, born in Vienna, and Barnaby John, born in London. His previous marriage, in 1950 to Constance Herbert, ended in divorce. By that marriage he has a daughter, Mary Catherine. Chancellor wears glasses, stands six feet in height, and weighs about 190 pounds. According to a New York *Post* writer (July 30, 1961), his NBC colleagues view him as "charming, eclectic, gentlemanly, impossibly energetic, an excellent bar companion, a people collector, old-fashioned," and as "an eager beaver who doesn't give a damn."

A man without hobbies, Chancellor once defined happiness as "a matter of balancing one's curiosities." Interested in virtually everything (except women's fashions), he sees nothing unusual in the diversity of his absorptions. "I'm a reporter," he told Bob Williams of the New York

Post (July 30, 1961), "and a reporter couldn't afford not to be interested in anything. Supposing somebody handed you an assignment slip to go and interview this funny doctor who plays an organ and is planning to set up a hospital in Africa?" He was one of nine NBC newsmen who contributed chapters to *Memo to JFK,* which was published by G. P. Putnam's Sons in the fall of 1961. His clubs are the National Press Club in Washington, D.C., and the Overseas Press Club in New York City. *Today* under John Chancellor, he hopes, will "send a fellow off to work with something to think about."

References

N Y Post Mag p2 Jl 30 '61 por
N Y Times II p13 Ag 13 '61 por
Time 78:72+ Jl 14 '61 por

CHESHIRE, (GEOFFREY) LEONARD Sept. 7, 1917- Social worker; former aviator

Address: b. 7 Market Mews, London W. 1, England; h. Cavendish, Suffolk, England

During World War II, Group Captain Leonard Cheshire established a reputation both as a London playboy and as an ace in the Royal Air Force. At the end of World War II he became known as the only British military observer at the atomic bombing of Nagasaki. Since then he has acquired a different kind of reputation, based on his establishment of the Cheshire Foundation Homes for the Sick. Begun in 1948, the homes, now numbering over thirty, have spread beyond the United Kingdom to Ireland, India, Malaya, Nigeria, and Jordan. The Cheshire Homes are places where the chronically ill or disabled who do not need hospital care and who still have much of life before them can live in ordinary surroundings and play as active a part as possible.

Geoffrey Leonard Cheshire was born in Chester, England, on September 7, 1917, to Geoffrey Chevalier Cheshire and Burella Primrose Eleanor (Barstow) Cheshire. The Cheshires, landowners in the county of that name for centuries, produced many lawyers in the nineteenth century. Leonard's father was Vinerian Professor of Law (as well as bursar of Exeter College) at Oxford University and is the author of several textbooks on property law, some of which have become standard throughout the English-speaking world. Leonard has a younger brother, Christopher.

When Leonard was one year old, the Cheshire family took up residence in North Oxford. He studied for two years at Miss Owen's school in Oxford before joining, at the age of eight, the sons of other dons at Dragon School, also in Oxford. In 1929 Leonard and his brother helped their father build at Cothill, about ten miles from Oxford, a large house called Grey Walls into which the family moved in November of the same year. The following year Leonard, previously a day student, became a boarder at Dragon School. The Cheshire brothers also spent periods of their childhood with their grandmother at Pau, France.

In September 1931 Leonard went on scholarship to Stowe School, Buckingham. Undistin-

LEONARD CHESHIRE

guished in his studies and mediocre in sports, he worked hard at both, became captain of lawn tennis, a prefect, and head of Chatham, his residence hall. T. H. White, the novelist, who taught him English, found his essays refreshing. "He was one of the few children of fourteen or so who could actually *tell* you that he liked to lie on his back in a hayfield, smelling clover, and wondering what it would be like to fall upward into the clouds," White has said.

After gaining his higher certificate in classics at Stowe in 1935, Cheshire spent four months in Germany before entering Merton College, Oxford University, in 1936, to study jurisprudence—somewhat reluctantly. "It was at Oxford I started not to work," Cheshire has said. He set himself a modest scholastic goal, devoted himself to speeding in his Alfa-Romeo, gambling on dog races, late night carousing, and escapades generally. He took second class honors in the School of Jurisprudence examinations in July 1939.

A member of the Oxford University Air Squadron and the Royal Air Force Volunteer Reserve, Cheshire had actually been looking forward to World War II. He qualified for his wings in the Royal Air Force on December 15, 1939. Assigned to 102 Squadron of the Bomber Command, he took off on his first operational mission as an acting pilot officer in a Whitley bomber on June 9, 1940. While in 102 Squadron he won his first command as well as the D.S.O.—a citation to which were later added two bars, as well as the Distinguished Flying Cross (1941) and the Victoria Cross (1944).

Early in 1941 Cheshire was transferred to 35 Squadron, and in September 1942 to 67 Squadron. In April 1943, with his rank raised to group captain, he was assigned to supervision of training at Marston Moor RAF Station. Impatient of desk work, he voluntarily dropped back to wing commander in rank in 1944 in order to take command of 617 Squadron. With 617 he developed a method of pinpoint bombing that

CHESHIRE, LEONARD—*Continued*

crippled Hitler's flying bombs and rockets at their source. After he completed his hundredth mission in 1944, Cheshire was assigned for a few months to the Calcutta headquarters of the Eastern Air Command, then, in 1945, to the British Joint Staff Mission in Washington, D.C.

On the sunny morning of August 9, 1945, Cheshire flew over Nagasaki, Japan, in the nose of an American B-29 minutes after that city of 100,000 men, women and children had been turned at one atomic stroke into a mass of dead, dying, and writhing humanity. His romantic view of war had hardened into a destroy-and-survive perfunctoriness in his missions over Europe. The most destructive European raids, however, paled in comparison with this horror.

Interpretations of the effect of the Nagasaki bombing on Cheshire vary. Soon after the raid Cheshire himself said of it: "Something had happened which altered our fundamental concepts of life." In November 1945 he said: "The necessity of ending war is a biological necessity. It is a choice between survival and extinction." A close associate writing on his behalf in July 1961 listed "Nagasaki" as one of the major influences in his life.

In January 1946 Group Captain Cheshire was discharged from the RAF with a disability pension for psychoneurosis. He leased a town house in Kensington and devoted himself full time to the life of a London playboy. At the same time, however, through lectures and a fortnightly column in the *Sunday Graphic,* he began to attract attention to himself as the champion of veterans maladjusted to the postwar world.

After revolving various schemes for colonies in which veterans could put to peacetime constructive use some of the camaraderie they had experienced in war, Cheshire began two communities. They failed. In 1948 he was in the process of closing down the second of the community sites—a twenty-five room house, Le Court, at Liss in Hampshire, which he had bought from an aunt—when his attention was called to the plight of Arthur Dykes, an ex-colonist at Le Court, who was hopelessly ill of cancer and whose bed at Petersfield Hospital was needed for cases more amenable to medicine. After searching in vain for congenial quarters for the dying Dykes, Cheshire took him to Le Court and nursed him until he died. In the meantime other old and infirm persons began gaining admission to Le Court simply by knocking on the door. By Christmas 1949 there were thirty-two patients and a growing staff.

In obviously deteriorating health since the end of the war, Cheshire in 1951 turned over Le Court to trustees and found temporary respite in a research position at the Vickers-Armstrong plant in Cornwall. (In 1954 the old building at Le Court was replaced by a new building financed largely by the Carnegie United Kingdom Trust. It now limits inmates to those under forty.)

Near his home at Tredannack on Lizard peninsula in Cornwall, Cheshire noticed some abandoned aircraft huts. Granted a monthly tenancy by the Air Ministry, he repaired the huts, called them St. Teresa's, and began to move in the chronically ill. (The people of Cornwall have since replaced the huts with a new home at Long Rock, Penzance, Cornwall.) To accommodate a patient at St. Teresa's whose problems were mental rather than physical, Cheshire in 1952 opened another home in Cornwall for the mentally ill. (The latter home was the forerunner of the present Miraflores—for rehabilitating ex-mental patients—in Wimbledon, and Hawthorn Lodge—for mentally handicapped children—in Dorchester.) In the same year Cheshire left Vickers-Armstrong to devote himself to the Cornwall homes.

Later in 1952 Cheshire was stricken with tuberculosis and hospitalized for more than two years. From his bed in Midhurst Sanitorium in 1954 he founded St. Cecilia's home in Bromley, Kent for the very ill and especially the old, and began thinking about the foundation of St. Bridget's in East Preston, Sussex for chronically ill but ambulatory patients between the ages of thirty and sixty.

In addition to Le Court, St. Teresa's, St. Cecilia's, St. Bridget's, Miraflores, and Hawthorn Lodge, by late 1961 there were fifteen Cheshire Foundation Homes for the incurable and homeless sick in the United Kingdom, and nine others being planned. In Eire there was one; in Nigeria one; in Jordan one, and another planned; in Malaya two; in India seven, and two others planned. A central Trust presides over the homes in the United Kingdom and similar trusts have been set up in some of the other countries. Each home has in addition an autonomous local managing committee for home policy. Support comes largely through voluntary help and subscriptions. The majority of the homes accommodate at least thirty patients.

Cheshire is five feet ten and one-half inches tall and weighs 140 pounds. He has brown hair, heavy eyebrows, sharp hazel eyes, a pouting smile, and a crisp, precise voice. His great capacity for leadership is more charismatic than administrative. An agnostic until the end of World War II, he has been a Roman Catholic since December 1948. He traces the story of his conversion in "My Quest for Certainty" in *Where Dwellest Thou?* (Gilbert Press, 1956), edited by John Anthony O'Brien. He has also written *Bomber Pilot* (1942), *Pilgrimage to the Shroud* (1955) and *The Face of Victory* (1961), all published by Hutchinson.

Cheshire's marriage in July 1941 to American actress Constance Binney, a divorcée, and therefore invalid in the eyes of the Roman Catholic church, was dissolved by civil divorce in 1951. On May 4, 1959 Cheshire married Margaret Susan Ryder, who since World War II had been working for relief of concentration camp victims, refugees, and stateless or homeless persons. In 1958 the Ryder activities had become amalgamated with the Cheshire Foundation. The Ryder Cheshire Mission for the Relief of Suffering has homes or centers in Germany, Poland, England, and India. Cheshire is a member of the RAF Reserves Club, London, and the Marylebone Cricket Club. He holds an honorary M.A. degree in jurisprudence from Oxford University. His recreation is photography.

CHESHIRE, LEONARD—*Continued*

References

Boyle, Andrew. No Passing Glory (1955)
Braddon, Russell. New Wings for a Warrior (1954)
Catholic Who's Who, 1952
Hughes, Cledwyn. Leonard Cheshire V. C. (1961)
Who's Who, 1961

DOWNEY, SHERIDAN Mar. 9, 1884-Oct. 25, 1961 Former Democratic United States Senator from California (1939-50); sponsored bills on reclamation, pensions, old-age insurance, and Civil Service. See *Current Biography* (October) 1949.

Obituary

N Y Times p33 O 27 '61

DRYFOOS, ORVIL E(UGENE) Nov. 8, 1912
Newspaper publisher

Address: b. New York Times, 229 W. 43d St., New York 36; h. 1010 Fifth Ave., New York 28

The New York Times

ORVIL E. DRYFOOS

When Orvil E. Dryfoos succeeded his father-in-law, Arthur Hays Sulzberger, as publisher of the New York *Times* on April 25, 1961, he continued the close family control of a newspaper that has come to be regarded as something of a public institution. In 1935 Sulzberger succeeded his own father-in-law, Adolph S. Ochs, as publisher of what is perhaps the best edited and most influential newspaper in the United States. Sulzberger once cautioned his son-in-law: "Remember that none of it would have happened that way except for the fact that I was sensible enough to marry the boss's daughter, and you were too." Dryfoos became assistant to the publisher of the New York *Times* in 1943, vice-president and director in 1954, and president and director in 1957.

Orvil Eugene Dryfoos was born in New York City on November 8, 1912, the eldest son of Jack A. Dryfoos, who was in the textile business, and Florence (Levi) Dryfoos (now Mrs. Myron G. Lehman). He has two brothers, Donald and Hugh Dryfoos. He attended the Horace Mann School, a private preparatory school in New York City, where he belonged to the soccer, tennis, and swimming teams. He also wrote a sports column, called "The Dug-Out," for the Horace Mann *Record,* the school newspaper. After he graduated from Horace Mann in 1930, he entered Dartmouth College, where he majored in sociology and received the B.A. degree in 1934. At Dartmouth he was active in sports and worked on the college yearbook. His first job was with Asiel & Company, New York City stockbrokers. Three years later, as a partner in Sydney Lewinson & Company, he purchased a seat on the New York Stock Exchange, where he was an active trader from 1937 until the end of 1941. He gave up his seat on the New York Stock Exchange in 1949.

When he was once asked to list the factors that helped to influence him in the choice of his life work, Dryfoos wrote simply: "Marriage to the daughter of the publisher of the New York *Times.*" The marriage took place on July 8, 1941; his bride, Marian Effie Sulzberger, is the oldest child of Arthur Hays Sulzberger. On January 2, 1942 Dryfoos came to the New York *Times* and began the same kind of apprenticeship that the late Adolph S. Ochs had given his own son-in-law, Arthur Hays Sulzberger—a training course in the responsibilities shouldered by the publisher of the New York *Times.*

His first desk at the New York *Times* was in the city room, from which, as a cub reporter, he was sent out to cover local news stories. In 1943, after having worked in the city room and on the make-up desk, Dryfoos was appointed assistant to the publisher and intensified his training in every department of the newspaper. At the same time, under Sulzberger's vigilant eye, he began to take on executive tasks of increasing importance and responsibility. In April 1957 he was named president of the New York Times Company and its various subsidiaries, including the Interstate Broadcasting Company, Inc., which operates radio stations WQXR and WQXR-FM; the Times Neediest Cases Fund, the newspaper's annual Christmas appeal in behalf of local city charities; and the New York Times Building Company. Sulzberger assumed the title of board chairman and remained as publisher. Four years later he retired as publisher.

The newspaper that Dryfoos took over as publisher is at the crest of its prestige and influence. In making a survey of the New York press, a writer for *Time* magazine (July 14, 1961) described the *Times* as a paper "that is constantly finding so much more news fit to print that it is now in a class all by itself." It is also the fastest-growing newspaper in New York, with an average weekday circulation up more than 200,000 (to 744,763) in the past decade alone. Its Sunday circulation reached a record high of 1,400,826 in 1961, and its advertising volume of nearly

DRYFOOS, ORVIL E.—_Continued_

62,000,000 lines in 1960 set a record not only for the _Times_ but for all daily newspapers in New York.

Yet the newspaper's margin of profit remains astonishingly low. On total operating revenues of $112,149,302 in 1960, net operating income amounted to only $348,051, less than half of one week's payroll. In fact, most of the profits for the year came from dividends of $1,304,341 distributed by Spruce Falls Power and Paper Company, Ltd., of Canada, in which it holds a substantial minority interest and of which Dryfoos is a director. The New York _Times_ makes no attempt to be the most profitable newspaper in the United States; furthermore, according to the company's 1960 report, the paper had printed 602 texts of speeches, Presidential conferences, documents of public interest, and the like. "The cost of these news activities further reduced the 1960 profit," the report observed, "but we believe they were a good investment in our product."

The reproduction of the documents was also part of the _Times'_ continuing campaign to help create an informed public opinion on the issues of the day. In an address at the twenty-fifth reunion of his class at Dartmouth, in 1959, Dryfoos emphasized the newspaper's function as a continuation of the educational process and told his fellow alumni: "The press, it seems to me, makes our twenty-five-year-old degrees negotiable in today's world."

Orvil E. and Marian Dryfoos have three children: Jacqueline Hays, Robert Ochs, and Susan Warms Dryfoos. They live at Fifth Avenue and 82d Street, and Dryfoos walks the two and a half miles from his home to his office daily. The family also has a summer home, Rock Hill, on Rockrimmon Road in Stamford, Connecticut, adjacent to the home of Mr. and Mrs. Arthur Hays Sulzberger. Mr. Dryfoos is Jewish; he is a member of Temple Emanu-El in New York City. A man of medium height and weight (five feet eight inches, 157 pounds), Dryfoos has gray eyes and brown hair. Although he has given up tennis, he still indulges in golfing and trout fishing on weekends. He is a fan of the New York Yankees. His clubs are the Dutch Treat Club in New York City and the Century Country Club in White Plains, New York.

A trustee of the Baron de Hirsch Fund, Dryfoos is also a member of the board of governors of the Hundred Year Association of New York, and a member of the boards of directors of the Bureau of Advertising of the American Newspaper Publishers Association, the Fifth Avenue Association, the New York Convention and Visitors Bureau, and the New York World's Fair 1964-65 Corporation. He sits on the board of trustees of Dartmouth College, which awarded him an honorary M.A. degree in 1957; on the board of lay trustees of Fordham University; and on the board of trustees and executive committee of the Rockefeller Foundation. He belongs to the American Australian Association, the Council on Foreign Relations, the France-America Society, the Japan Society, Inc., the Pan American Society of the United States, the Pilgrims of the United States, and the Deadline Club, the New York City professional chapter of Sigma Delta Chi.

In an article in _Times Talk_ (the monthly newspaper published for the 5,000 employees of the _Times_) shortly after he retired, Sulzberger remarked that the New York _Times_ had never had a publisher who possessed all the attributes required for the position, although his son-in-law had some of them. "He is much too nice a fellow to have too many of the traits I've outlined because he's a real human being," Sulzberger observed. "I had nothing to do with choosing him to be the father of my oldest grandchildren," he added, "but he's very satisfactory that way and I have no doubt he will fill his new job just as well."

In filling the job, Dryfoos keeps a close watch on the news contents of the New York _Times,_ despite the heavy responsibilities on the business side of the paper that the position of publisher carries. He attends the daily news conference of _Times_ editors and, when he cannot be present, telephones to learn which stories will appear on the first page of the next morning's edition. A sketch of Dryfoos in the New York _Times_ (April 26, 1961) on his appointment as publisher noted that he "is not known as a 'driving' executive although he can be firm when necessary. He prefers to vest responsibility in competent men and let them carry out the duties to which they have been assigned."

As publisher of the New York _Times,_ Dryfoos has a standard of excellence to maintain not only in the eyes of readers in New York, Washington, and around the world but in terms of the tradition established by Adolph S. Ochs. It is the responsibility of the New York _Times,_ Ochs wrote in his will, to be "an independent newspaper, entirely fearless, free of ulterior influence, and unselfishly devoted to the public welfare without regard to individual advantage or ambition, the claims of party politics, or the voices of religious or personal prejudice and predilection." Orvil E. Dryfoos is determined to meet that responsibility. In a personal statement on the New York _Times_ editorial page on his first day as publisher, he wrote: "I pledge that my associates and I will maintain vigilantly the high standards set by our predecessors."

References

N Y Times p30 Ap 26 '61 por
Who's Who in America, 1960-61

DUNHAM, FRANKLIN May, 17, 1892-Oct. 27, 1961 Educator; educational director of the National Broadcasting Company (1931-41); chief of the radio and television services of the United States Office of Education since 1945. See _Current Biography_ (January) 1942.

Obituary

N Y Times p88 O 29 '61

EINAUDI, LUIGI Mar. 24, 1874-Oct. 30, 1961 Italian statesman; economist; journalist; Governor of the Bank of Italy (1945-48); Minister of the Budget (1947-48); President of the Italian Republic (1948-55). See _Current Biography_ (July) 1948.

Obituary

N Y Times p31 O 31 '61

FERGUSON, ELSIE Aug. 19, 1885-Nov. 15, 1961 Actress; first starred in Channing Pollock's comedy *Such a Little Queen* (1909) in New York; most successful stage roles included those in *The Strange Woman* (1913) and *Varying Shore* (1921;) appeared in several silent motion pictures; retired from the stage in 1929. See *Current Biography* (February) 1944.

Obituary

N Y Times p39 N 16 '61

GREENEBAUM, LEON C(HARLES) Dec. 30, 1907- Business executive
Address: b. Hertz Corp., 660 Madison Ave., New York 21; h. 895 Park Ave., New York 21

In 1907 a New Yorker named Charles L. Greenebaum bought a horse and wagon and went into the trucking business, establishing a company that he later named Metropolitan Distributors, Inc. On January 1, 1961 his son, Leon C. Greenebaum—born the same year that the business was founded—was designated chief executive officer of the world's largest car and truck renting and leasing company, the Hertz Corporation. Leon Greenebaum had joined Hertz as a director when it acquired Metropolitan Distributors in early 1955; he became board chairman the following year. During his first five years at Hertz, operating revenues soared from $39,000,000, in 1955, to $125,000,000, in 1960.

Leon Charles Greenebaum was born in New York City on December 30, 1907, the son of Charles Leon and Estelle (Schoeps) Greenebaum. After attending local public schools, including Townsend Harris High School (a school for intellectually gifted boys), he entered Dartmouth College in New Hampshire, where he earned the B.S. degree in 1927. Upon graduation, he joined Metropolitan Distributors at the bottom, starting as a maintenance man in the company garage. After a year, he was promoted to dispatcher and then spent another year learning office routine. He was named assistant treasurer in 1930 and vice-president in 1931 and became president of the firm in 1936.

During the next nineteen years, Metropolitan expanded under Greenebaum's leadership into the largest truck leasing firm located in any one city in the United States, supplying trucks to more than 900 customers. A company policy instituted by Greenebaum was to supply no drivers except in special cases. In this way the firm using the trucks could concentrate on close control over drivers and routes, relying on Metropolitan for maintenance.

Metropolitan Distributors was acquired by the Hertz Corporation in January 1955 in a major business deal that laid the foundations for Hertz's further remarkable growth. One of the assets that Hertz took over was the management experience and skill of Greenebaum, who was elected a Hertz director and vice-chairman of the board in February 1955. He is considered, Alexander R. Hammer wrote in the New York *Times* (December 25, 1960), "not only an excellent administrator but a first-rate negotiator and expert in financial matters, especially those concerned with acquisitions and expansions."

Conway Studios Corp.
LEON C. GREENEBAUM

The Hertz Corporation had developed from a company that Walter L. Jacobs, a Chicago automobile dealer, had founded in 1918 under the name Rent-A-Car, Inc. In 1925 he sold his business to John Hertz, who made it part of his Yellow Truck and Coach Manufacturing Company. After General Motors Corporation acquired Hertz' company in 1926, Jacobs became general manager of the GM subsidiary Hertz Driv-Ur-Self System, Inc. The Omnibus Corporation bought the company from GM in 1953 and in November 1954 was reorganized as the Hertz Corporation, with Hertz as honorary chairman, Benjamin Weintraub as chairman, and Jacobs as president.

Working closely with Jacobs, Greenebaum concentrated on formulating plans and procedures for the company's expansion. It was he who directed the organization and subsequent development of the company's foreign operations through the formation in 1957 of its international subsidiary, jointly owned with the American Express Company. The firm, called Hertz American Express International Ltd., features a plan under which a traveler can drive a Hertz car to any United States airport, board a plane, and pick up another Hertz auto at the terminal abroad. The Hertz-American Express venture has grown rapidly, with volume for 1960 exceeding $8,000,000, a gain of 50 per cent over 1959. The international company operates in forty-five countries and is expected to represent an increasing part of the corporation's future business.

Greenebaum believes that American thinking is gradually changing from the concept of ownership to that of use—not only of motor vehicles but of more and more kinds of equipment. A recently inaugurated venture based on this conviction is the Hertz Rent-All Corporation, formed during the latter part of 1960. This new wholly owned subsidiary entered the field of retail rental of party supplies, hospital and sickroom equip-

GREENEBAUM, LEON C.—*Continued*

ment, and other merchandise. A nationwide chain of Hertz-owned-and-licensed outlets is planned. Hertz is also exploring the possibility of renting boats, works of art, and a variety of other items.

The year 1960 also saw the organization of Hertz Equipment Leasing Corporation, for leasing of industrial and commercial equipment; and the Electric Coin Processing Corporation, which leases equipment for collecting, sorting, and authenticating coins from parking meters and vending machines. Hertz has also formed its own insurance firm—Atlantic National Insurance Company—specializing in rented and leased vehicle underwriting.

But Hertz's main business is the renting and leasing of cars and trucks. Biggest income-producer is the rent-a-car division, which in 1960 grossed more than $59,000,000—topping, for the second time, revenues from truck leasing, which totaled $54,000,000. Yet Greenebaum believes that the potential has barely been tapped: more than 90 per cent of America's 85,000,000 licensed drivers have never rented a car from Hertz. Car leasing revenues have also grown rapidly and in 1960 totaled nearly $11,000,000. Another mark of progress has been the annual rise in the average number of Hertz-owned vehicles. In 1960 this figure (including vehicles of licensees) stood at nearly 68,000 cars and trucks, as compared to 12,150 in 1954. This huge fleet was operated from more than 1,700 locations in more than 1,100 cities around the world—an extensive network developed over a period of some forty years.

Expansion-minded Greenebaum is convinced that the potential markets are almost limitless in the service industry, of which Hertz is the acknowledged national and international leader. In May 1961 he told stockholders that he expected record-breaking revenues in the vicinity of $140,000,000 for 1961, and at another time he forecast Hertz revenues of $200,000,000 by the end of 1964. In other business affiliations Greenebaum is president of the Coe Realty Corporation and the Ryma Corporation and a director of Halero Truck Sales Corporation and Motorways, Inc.

Leon C. Greenebaum has been married to the former Myra Cole since May 21, 1948. Greenebaum's son by a previous marriage, Charles L. Greenebaum, is an assistant vice-president and director of Hertz real-estate operations. Mrs. Greenebaum has a son by a previous marriage, Tony, who is employed by the Atlantic National Insurance Company, a Hertz subsidiary. A pastel self-portrait of Mrs. Greenebaum hangs opposite her husband's desk at the company's new world headquarters on New York's Madison Avenue. The company moved there in 1960, consolidating offices previously located in seven separate buildings in New York and Chicago.

According to the way of thinking at Hertz, the individually owned car has lost most of its weight as a status symbol and status is now achieved by, among other things, a backyard swimming pool larger or more ornate than the neighbor's, a custom-built stereo high-fidelity unit, and European travel. By his own standards, Greenebaum is a man of status. Many of the rooms in his fifteen-room Park Avenue apartment

are wired for stereophonic sound, and he has traveled widely, having made more than twenty trips to Europe visiting the company's offices abroad. His travels leave little time for playing the piano, one of Greenebaum's favorite forms of relaxation, or for romping with Coco, his French poodle.

At Hertz, Greenebaum is known for his pleasant manner and ready smile. He drives himself hard and expects equally high performance from his men. A tall, athletic-looking man, he was once an occasional golfer and now prefers deep-sea fishing as a sport. In college he was a member of the swimming and water polo teams. One of his favorite subjects in college was English, and he still enjoys writing his own speeches. "Anything that appears over my signature was written by me," he told a New York *Times* interviewer.

Active in Dartmouth alumni affairs, Greenebaum has served as one of the national officers of the Dartmouth Alumni Association and belongs to the Dartmouth College Club in New York. He is also a member of the Empire State Club in New York; Old Oaks Country Club in Purchase, New York; Hollywood Golf Club in Deal, New Jersey; and Society of Automotive Engineers. He is president of the Charles and Estelle Greenebaum Foundation, Inc.

References

N Y Times III p9 D 25 '60 por
Who's Who in America, 1960-61
Who's Who in Commerce and Industry (1961)

GUINZBURG, HAROLD K(LEINERT) Dec. 13, 1899-Oct. 18, 1961 Publisher; co-founder (1925) and president of the Viking Press; president of the American Book Publishers Council, Inc. (1956-58). See *Current Biography* (July) 1957.

Obituary

N Y Times p35 O 19 '61

HARRIS, HARWELL HAMILTON July 2, 1903- Architect; educator

Address: b. 3603 Lemmon Ave., Dallas 19, Tex.; h. 3525 Turtle Creek, Dallas 19, Tex.

His fidelity to the principle that buildings must meet the needs of people has enriched the work of Harwell Hamilton Harris with an individuality and freshness that survive the passing fashions in modern American architecture. Both his residential and nonresidential designs, mainly carried out first in California and then in Texas, shun the fads and clichés of the moment in responsiveness to basic social changes in patterns of living, technology, and aesthetic values. Combining his private practice with educational activities, he directed the School of Architecture at the University of Texas from 1951 to 1955 and has taught at Columbia and other universities.

California, one of the most important centers of architectural development in the United States, is the birthplace of Harwell Hamilton Harris and was for many years his home. The son of an architect, he was born to Frederick Thomas and May Julia (Hamilton) Harris on July 2, 1903 in Redlands. He attended San Bernardino High School in California, where he was the school's newspaper correspondent for the San Bernardino *Sun.* His other activities outside the classroom centered on debating, track, and photography.

At Pomona College in California, which he entered after graduating from high school in 1921, Harris worked as a reporter on the college newspaper. Leaving Pomona in 1923, he studied at the Otis Art Institute in Los Angeles until 1925 and later at the Los Angeles College of Engineering. Sculpture was his chief interest at the art institute, and he regards his study of sculpture and his two and a half years (1926-29) of practice in sculpture as a preliminary to architecture. "I now feel that architecture and sculpture—and I should probably include the other arts as well if only I knew them—are structurally alike," he commented a decade later (*Architectural Forum,* March 1940). "Each is a rhythmic organization into which one projects oneself."

The shift from sculpture to architecture resulted largely from Harris' discovery of the work of Frank Lloyd Wright. In his own designs Harris has frankly used methods developed by Wright, and it is significant that he began his career in architecture as an associate, from 1929 to 1932, of Richard J. Neutra, an Austrian-born Californian architect who helped lead the movement that adapted European ideas to Wright's organic and humanistic architecture.

In 1933 Harris began a private practice in Los Angeles that continued until 1951. His early work, largely residential, gained for him within less than a decade a secure place among the contributors to an advanced type of domestic architecture that flourished in California and shortly came to be admired throughout the world. One of its foremost concerns was for the actual living patterns of the inhabitant of a house, and the finest California houses are, in fact, expressions of a way of life.

Very early in his career Harris discovered that with each new client he made further explorations in architecture because he confronted a new set of requirements in designing a home to answer the individual needs of its owner. Harris has emphasized that unpretentiousness is a principal characteristic of his work: "As a background to living, a house succeeds only to the extent that it helps the occupant to be most himself."

Like Wright and Neutra, Harris paid careful attention to achieving unity between the interior and immediate surroundings of the building, and he became adept in designing houses that took advantage of California hillside sites. Many of his houses had terraces and balconies and made provisions for private outdoor living areas. The garden, just as much as the furnishings of the home, grew out of a single conception.

In the Wright tradition, also, Harris respected the inherent characteristics of his building materials and skillfully employed available and economical materials, favoring wood and glass. He let the grain and color of wood create his pattern while he accommodated his use of wood to modern power tools. A distinctive detail of his

HARWELL HAMILTON HARRIS

houses was likely to be clerestory lighting, and a more general feature was cellular composition, which he described as "the development of a characteristic cell, and the growth through simple addition of cells."

As early as 1934 an honorable-mention award in *House Beautiful* had brought Harris' work to national attention. In April 1942 his designs were among those of six architects selected by the San Francisco Museum of Art in an exhibition of contemporary domestic architecture, an exhibit that also included the work of Wright and Neutra and that some critics thought represented the best domestic architecture of the day. The Museum of Modern Art in New York City included his work in its exhibition in 1943 (and again in 1953) of forty or more most significant buildings of the preceding decade.

The house that Harris built in 1941 for Weston Havens of Berkeley, California, overlooking San Francisco and the Golden Gate Bridge, was described in Wayne Andrews' *Architecture in America* (Atheneum, 1960) as "one of the great houses of the twentieth century." Other notable examples of his domestic architecture in California are the Birtcher House (1942), the Johnson House (1947), and the English House (1950).

During his eighteen years of practice in California, Harris also acquired a distinguished reputation in nonresidential architecture, with his buildings for the Chadwick School in Palos Verdes and the Treanor Equipment Company in Delano, among others. In 1950 he became design consultant to the National Orange Show in San Bernardino, and one of the halls that he designed for the National Orange Show, the Feature Exhibits Building, was pictured in the exhibit of American architecture at the American National Exhibition in Moscow during the summer of 1959.

Harris left California in 1951 to serve as director of the School of Architecture at the Univer-

HARRIS, HARWELL HAMILTON—*Cont.*

sity of Texas in Austin, a position in which he remained until 1955. His earlier experience in education had included lecturing at the University of Southern California in 1945 and 1946. He was visiting critic at Yale University in 1950 and 1952 and at the University of Minnesota in 1955. During 1960-61 he held the post of adjunct professor and graduate design critic at Columbia University, commuting between New York and Dallas.

After Harris had resigned from the University of Texas, he practised for about a year (1956-57) at Fort Worth with the firm of Harris & Sherwood. In 1958 he opened his office in Dallas. Among his varied undertakings since his move to Texas have been designs for the State Fair House (1954); a special project for the Homestyle Exhibition in Grand Rapids, Michigan (1956); the American Embassy in Helsinki, Finland (begun in 1957); and the First Unitarian Church, Dallas (1961-62). An achievement of some importance in the history of architecture in the United States was Harris' remodeling in 1958 of the Security Bank & Trust Company of Owatonna, Minnesota, which had been designed by famed American architect Louis Sullivan in 1908.

Harris' designs have been published extensively, in architectural books and magazines in the United States, Europe, South America, and Japan. His own articles have appeared in *California Arts & Architecture, Journal of the American Institute of Architects, House Beautiful,* and other periodicals. Among the more recent exhibitions that have included his work are the American Institute of Architects Centennial Exhibition, National Gallery of Art, Washington, D.C. (1957); Triennale Fair, Milan, Italy (1957); and the American Federation of Arts traveling show (1960). He belongs to the American Institute of Architects, Texas Society of Architects, Chaparral Club in Dallas, and Tau Sigma Delta. He is a Protestant and a Republican.

Harwell Hamilton Harris married Jean Murray Bangs, a social worker, on February 23, 1937. A trim man, with blue eyes and brown hair, Harris is five feet eight inches tall and weighs 140 pounds. He swims for exercise and enjoys music, opera, the theater, and motion-picture photography.

References

House B 87:54 Jl '45

American Architects Directory, 1958
Who's Who in America, 1960-61

HARTLE, RUSSELL P(ETER) June 26, 1889-
Nov. 23, 1961 United States Army officer; commanded the 34th National Guard Division, the first American contingent sent to Europe in World War II; retired in 1946 in the rank of major general. See *Current Biography* (June) 1942.

Obituary

N Y Times p31 N 24 '61

HEINEMAN, BEN W(ALTER) Feb. 10, 1914- Railway executive; lawyer
Address: b. Chicago & North Western Railway Co., 400 W. Madison St., Chicago 3, Ill.; h. 1126 E. 48th St., Chicago 15, Ill.

When the Chicago attorney Ben W. Heineman became chairman of the Chicago & North Western Railway Company in April 1956, that Midwestern rail system, the country's ninth longest, was among the most distressed in the troubled industry. He has since then made an exceptional record in the transportation field by his rehabilitation of the railroad and by justifying his faith, against a current trend, in a commuter passenger service as a source of revenue. Within five years a commuter deficit of as much as $2,000,000 a year was wiped out and a slight but growing profit was attained.

Ben Walter Heineman was born on February 10, 1914 in Wausau in central Wisconsin, where his grandfather, Benjamin Heineman, an immigrant from Germany, had established a lumber business in 1869. He is the only son of Walter Benjamin and Elsie Brunswick (Deutsch) Heineman, who also had three daughters. His father was a prominent Republican, serving on the party's state committee and as vice-treasurer of Herbert Hoover's 1928 Presidential campaign. He prospered in the family lumber business until the Depression: in 1930, after going bankrupt, he committed suicide.

In 1930, also, Ben W. Heineman graduated from high school in Wausau and entered the University of Michigan. Accepted by the Northwestern University Law School at the end of his junior year at the University of Michigan, Heineman left Ann Arbor in 1933 without waiting to qualify for his bachelor's degree. He collaborated with J. P. Vail, Jr., on a highly regarded analysis of the Johnson Act published in the *Illinois Law Review* in June 1935. The following year he was one of the top ten receiving the LL.B. degree from Northwestern University.

For five years beginning in 1936 Heineman practised with the Chicago law firm of Levinson, Becker, Peebles & Swiren, specialists in corporate work. During this period he contributed papers on priority of jurisdiction and on the Securities Act to the *Illinois Law Review.* Because of blindness in one eye, he was permanently deferred for World War II military service. He spent two war years, from 1941 to 1943, as assistant general counsel with the Office of Price Administration in Washington. There, in charge of the court review section, he wrote the rules for the OPA's emergency court of appeals.

The State Department then assigned him to several months' service in North Africa in 1943 as legal adviser and assistant director of the North African Economic Board in Algiers. He was also a member of General Dwight D. Eisenhower's civil affairs staff and assistant to the ambassador to the French government and helped to negotiate the first lend-lease agreement with France. Declining a State Department assignment in London, he returned to Chicago, and in 1944 he joined his colleague, Max Swiren, in the new partnership of Swiren & Heineman, specializing in corporation law.

Ben Heineman's impressive thirty-page article "A Law Revision Commission for Illinois," published in the *Illinois Law Review* (January-February 1948), was the outcome of his membership in the administrative law section of the Illinois State Bar Association. In 1949 he began two years of service on the Illinois Administrative Practice and Procedure Commission; then, in 1950, as chairman of the Chicago Bar Association's committee on the uniform commercial code, he participated for the first time in the National Conference of Commissioners on Uniform State Laws with Respect to the Uniform Commercial Code.

When Adlai E. Stevenson, then Governor of Illinois, asked Heineman in 1951 to serve as a special assistant district attorney in the investigation of a cigarette-tax fraud, he accepted the challenging assignment and spent about a year helping to break up the ring of racketeers. Self-described as an "independent Democrat," Heineman was active in 1952 in raising funds and organizing citizens on the Pacific Coast for Stevenson's first Presidential campaign.

The sequence of events leading to Heineman's position as railroad executive started in 1950, when he negotiated an out-of-court settlement of dividend-payment claims brought by certain stockholders of the Chicago Great Western. "The case," Carl Rieser commented in *Fortune* (September 1957), "brought Heineman renown as one of the few lawyers who had ever won a dividend case."

Three years later (1953) he joined the Chicago investor Franklin Lyons and other dissatisfied stockholders in the Minneapolis & St. Louis Railroad to force representation on the board of that line, long dominated by Lucian C. Sprague. A bitter proxy fight ended with the retirement of Sprague in May 1954 and the election of Heineman as chairman of a newly created executive board.

The modern accounting methods introduced by Heineman in his two years as M. & St. L. chairman resulted in increased earnings. But his plans for expansion by acquiring the Toledo, Peoria & Western and the Monon Route railroads were frustrated when the Pennsylvania and Santa Fe railroads bought control of the T.P. & W. Meanwhile, in August 1954, Lyons had induced Heineman to accept the chairmanship of the Four Wheel Drive Auto Company in Clintonville, Wisconsin, manufacturer of heavy-duty road equipment. After modernizing the company over a period of three years, Heineman resigned in July 1957 in favor of Lyons.

Heineman had therefore had considerable managerial experience when in 1955 he became the leader of a Chicago and Cleveland group engaged in heavy buying of shares in the Chicago & North Western Railway Company. By February 1956 Heineman and his associates controlled about 550,000 of the North Western's 1,729,447 shares, or enough to threaten a proxy fight. This was avoided when it was agreed later in the month that Paul E. Feucht, the railroad's president, would retire and that Heineman would become chairman of the board and chief executive officer.

BEN W. HEINEMAN

In order to give his full time to the management of the Chicago & North Western, after taking office on April 1, 1956, Heineman resigned from the Minneapolis & St. Louis Railway and ended his law partnership. He also brought in the former Illinois Central railroadman Clyde J. Fitzpatrick as president of the company. The nation's ninth largest rail system, the 7,857-mile Chicago & North Western extends from Chicago north to Duluth and west to Lander, Wyoming. Passenger deficits, light traffic on branch lines, truck competition, and high operating costs had almost bankrupted the railroad. Heineman at once began a long-range program of managerial reorganization and equipment modernization. According to *Time* (December 15, 1958), during his first two years at North Western, "he also became the foremost critic of union featherbedding in rails, trimmed his own payrolls from 26,300 to 18,500—but was a shrewd enough labor negotiator to avoid a full-scale strike."

While, however, earnings rose in 1958, the railroad lost $2,000,000 on commuter service. Heineman was not convinced that a commuter deficit was inevitable, as he made clear in a speech on October 17, 1957. Citing "sheer economic waste" as the real trouble with the railroad business, he pointed out that "in commuting we can move 48,000 riders by rail in one hour on one passenger line compared with 6,720 by bus and 2,250 by automobile on one express lane."

To reduce his line's existing commuter deficit, Heineman closed down twenty-three unneeded Chicago suburban stations, overhauled the ticket-checking system, and raised fares by 24 per cent. At the same time, while other lines were seeking to discard all commuter, and even all passenger, service, Heineman and Fitzpatrick set in motion a $43,000,000 modernization program designed to give Greater Chicago the "finest commuter service in the world." Trains were speeded up, and two hundred air-conditioned, two-level coaches

HEINEMAN, BEN W.—*Continued*

were ordered, all of which were to be in service by June 1961. By the end of 1959 the C. & N.W. was making a profit of an estimated $30,000 on its commuter operations.

In another development under Heineman, the C. & N.W. secured an entrance to St. Louis through acquisition of the Litchfield & Madison Railway in 1957. Other railroads with which he is associated are the Chicago, St. Paul, Minneapolis & Omaha Railway (chairman); Indiana Harbor Belt Railroad (director); and the Packers Car Line (director). He is a director of the Association of American Railroads and has served on various committees of that organization and of the Association of Western Railroads.

Heineman is also a member of the board and executive committee of the American National Bank and Trust Company of Chicago. He is a Fellow of the American Bar Foundation and a member of the American Judicature Society; the American Law Institute; and the American, Illinois, and Chicago bar associations; and the Phi Delta Phi law fraternity and the Order of the Coif. His social fraternity is the Zeta Beta Tau, and his clubs are the Standard, Quadrangle, Executives, and Columbia Yacht. Lawrence College in Appleton, Wisconsin awarded him an honorary LL.D. degree in 1955.

Ben W. Heineman and Natalie Goldstein, then a medical social worker, were married on April 17, 1935 and have two children, Martha Brunswick and Ben Walter, Jr. The Heinemans' faith is the Jewish. "He dislikes dining away from home except for the most pressing reason. . . ," Carl Rieser wrote in his *Fortune* article on Heineman. "Every summer he packs his wife and teen-age daughter and son aboard a rented sailboat and cruises off Cape Cod for five weeks. He also likes to ride, ski, go skeet shooting."

References

Fortune 56:170+ S '57 pors
Time 70:72 D 15 '58 por
U S News 48:95 D 20 '57 por
International Who's Who, 1961-62
Poor's Register of Directors and Executives, 1961
Who's Who in America, 1960-61
Who's Who in Railroading in North America (1959)
Who's Who in the Midwest (1958)

JOHN, AUGUSTUS (EDWIN) Jan. 4, 1879-Oct. 31, 1961 British painter and etcher; noted for his portraits of Shaw, Yeats, and other celebrities; also famous as a nonconformist. See *Current Biography* (October) 1941.

Obituary

N Y Times p 1+ N 1 '61

KENNELLY, MARTIN H(ENRY) Aug. 11, 1887-Nov. 29, 1961 Former Democratic Mayor of Chicago (1947-55); head of several business firms, including a warehouse and trucking company. See *Current Biography* (December) 1949.

Obituary

N Y Times p37 N 30 '61

KIPLINGER, W(ILLARD) M(ONROE) (kĭp'lĭng-ẽr) Jan. 8, 1891- Publisher; journalist
Address: b. Kiplinger Washington Editors, Inc., 1729 H St., N.W., Washington 6, D.C.; h. 6609 River Rd., Bethesda 14, Md.

> NOTE: This biography supersedes the article that appeared in *Current Biography* in 1943.

Although W. M. Kiplinger turned over the presidency of Kiplinger Washington Editors, Inc., to his son Austin in July 1959, he remains chairman of the board and still takes a major hand in the writing of the Kiplinger Washington Letter, which he established in 1923. This newsletter, sent weekly to subscribers by first-class mail, had in 1960 a circulation of about 200,000 copies, far exceeding that of any other specialized report to businessmen. Kiplinger is also executive editor of the monthly *Changing Times*, one of several other lucrative enterprises of Kiplinger Washington Editors, whose estimated gross totaled about $10,000,000 in 1960.

Besides writing numerous articles on economic trends for newspapers and nationally circulated magazines, Kiplinger is the author of five books, of which *Washington Is Like That* (1942) is probably the best known and *Your Guide to a Higher Income* (1959), the most recent. Kiplinger once expressed his philosophy of investment as follows: "You may think you have no money, but you may have a little saved up and available for investment. Investment is like seed corn. A little makes a lot next year, and much more a few years later."

Willard Monroe Kiplinger, who was named after the temperance leader Frances Willard, was born to Clarence E. and Cora (Miller) Kiplinger on January 8, 1891. His birthplace is Bellefontaine, Ohio, where for two generations the family had operated a carriage-building business. When Willard was ten years old, he moved with his parents to Columbus, Ohio, where he later attended North High School.

In high school Kiplinger edited the school paper *Polaris* and, subsequently, at Ohio State University he was one of the first two students to enroll in the School of Journalism started under Professor Harry Franklin Harrington. He was advertising manager and later editor of the college newspaper the *Lantern* and helped to form the Ohio State University chapter of the Sigma Delta Chi journalism fraternity. After winning membership in Phi Beta Kappa, he graduated with the B.A. degree in 1912.

As a reporter on the *Ohio State Journal* for two years beginning in 1912, Kiplinger wrote the "Grandfather's Column," which has been described as "containing news of earlier days such as the invasion by the telegraph lines from the East and the use of brick for paving roads." He was also one of the *Journal* staff who reported on the Columbus flood of March 1913, making a perilous trip through the city to compile a list of names of the 100-odd victims. He also covered city hall for the *Journal* and admittedly ignored the principle of unbiased reporting when he conducted a crusade against loan sharks in Ohio.

Kiplinger joined the Columbus bureau of the Associated Press in 1914, and after covering the

Ohio State Legislature for two years, he was transferred to the Washington bureau. "Unlike most young AP men of the time," Kenneth Gale Crawford wrote in the *Saturday Evening Post* (January 25, 1947), "Kiplinger was more interested in what the Government was doing on the economic and social fronts than in who was to be elected to what." He was mainly occupied from 1916 to 1919 as a financial writer and editor and during World War I made a notable scoop with a complete list of newly appointed state directors of the War Savings Drive.

Leaving the Associated Press in 1919, Kiplinger became a specialized reporter in politico-economics for the National Bank of Commerce. As such he established a query service to answer questions of clients about what was happening in Washington. This led to his borrowing $1,000 from the Riggs National Bank to start the Kiplinger Washington Letter, which first appeared in September 1923.

Unlike the rival Whaley-Eaton letter, it was colloquial and staccato in style, mimeographed on two sides of legal-size paper (later, four pages of facsimile typewriter script), with "flag words" underscored and a controversial amount of prophetic opinion. "That violated all rules of newswriting," Kiplinger told Washington newsman Truman R. Temple thirty-seven years later, "but I felt a reporter couldn't tell everything if he were restricted to the facts, and I still think so. I was young and full of prunes in those days, but this was an obsession with me" (*Washington Evening Star*, September 29, 1960).

It had been Kiplinger's experience that "men in public life would often give you a straight story in private, then reverse their field in their pro forma public statement." His newsletters, accordingly, have never quoted a source, and have abounded in off-the-record comment indicating trends. Not until after the stock market crash of 1929, when inside tips on Washington policy became of increasing importance to businessmen, did the Washington Letter begin to pay its way. Kiplinger had meanwhile met his payroll with signed articles in the New York *Times Magazine, Nation's Business,* and other publications.

Kiplinger had supported Hoover's policies, but was without rancor toward Franklin D. Roosevelt. "Although generally classified as a moderate conservative," Kenneth Crawford wrote in 1947, "he favored such New Deal experiments as AAA and NRA. . . . In so far as his social sympathies show through his letter and his talk, they are with the middle classes, particularly with the professional brain workers."

Letting his clients know what they may expect, explaining the significance for them of a particular trend, is an important aspect of Kiplinger's service. Not always accurate in his forecasts, he reiterated in 1936 the prediction that the Roosevelt-Landon Presidential race would be close and during the Truman administration went astray on the President's attitude toward extension of O.P.A. On the other hand, he published details of the Marshall Plan four months before public announcement.

By the summer of 1946, the circulation of the Washington Letter was estimated at about 125,000 a year and its annual gross at $2,250,000.

W. M. KIPLINGER

(In 1960 the circulation was around 200,000 and the gross around $4,000,000.) Special fortnightly Kiplinger Tax and Agricultural Letters were being circulated when *Kiplinger Magazine,* at first oriented toward businessmen but later given a family appeal, appeared in January 1947. John Denton, its managing editor, and Kiplinger's son Austin, its executive editor, failed to agree on administrative matters; and in March 1948, after Denton resigned, the elder Kiplinger took major responsibility for the policy of the magazine, which then adopted *Changing Times* as its main title.

Changing Times, which carried no advertising, had a circulation of approximately 50,000 in 1948 when, on the day following Truman's victory over Dewey in the Presidential election, it came out with an article," What Will Dewey Do?" based on the assumption that Dewey had been elected. Candidly admitting the enormous blunder, Kiplinger set out to restore the consequently declining circulation of his publications. He did so with such success that by 1951 the Kiplinger enterprises were ready to move into their new ten-story, $2,000,000 headquarters in Washington, and by 1953 the circulation of *Changing Times* rose to 200,000 (seven years later it reached 800,000.)

Also in 1953 a newsletter explaining United States trends to foreign businessmen, made its appearance. Originally it was called Overseas Postscript and is now the Kiplinger Foreign Trade Letter. A Florida Letter and a Book Club were also added to the Kiplinger group of publications. When Austin Kiplinger took over the presidency of Kiplinger Washington Editors, Inc., in July 1959, his father continued as chairman of the board and as editor in chief of *Changing Times*. With its May 1961 issue the magazine took as a subtitle *The Kiplinger Service to Families.*

As early as 1935 a pamphlet-length work by Kiplinger and Frederick Shelton entitled *Inflation*

KIPLINGER, W. M.—*Continued*

Ahead! What To Do About It (Simon & Schuster) was published in book form. In 1942 Kiplinger's *Washington Is Like That* (Harper), for which his son Austin helped in the research, reached the bookstores and the best-seller lists. Reviewing it for the *Saturday Review of Literature,* Duncan Aikman thought it "on the whole . . . the best guide book to the business of government in the United States yet written," although Clifton Fadiman commented in the *New Yorker* that because Kiplinger had "put in everything" his book was "formless and in part trivial." Among his later books are *Kiplinger Looks to the Future; Boom and Inflation Ahead; And What You Can Do About It* (Simon & Schuster, 1958) and *Your Guide to a Higher Income* (Simon & Schuster, 1959).

Willard Monroe Kiplinger has married three times. His son Austin and his daughter Jane Ann are the children of his marriage to Irene Austin Kiplinger, which began on June 28, 1914 and ended in divorce in April 1926. He married Leslie Jackson on June 13, 1926, and they were divorced in May 1931. Peter, the son by his second marriage, was killed in motorcycle accident in 1958. On May 18, 1936 Kiplinger married his secretary, LaVerne Colwel; they have a daughter, Bonnie Susan.

Ohio State University awarded Kiplinger an honorary LL.D. degree in 1937. He is a trustee of the National Press Building in Washington and of the Greater Washington Educational TV Association, Inc., and a member of the job opportunities committee of the Federal City Council. He belongs to the Kenmore Country Club and to several Washington clubs, including the Cosmos and National Press. His faith is the Unitarian. He is about six feet tall and has been described as "aggressively unostentatious" and as "abstemious . . . but not a teetotaler." As a hobby, he enjoys gardening on his fifteen-acre estate in Bethesda, Maryland.

References

Newsweek 29:50 Ja 6 '47 por; 41:86+ F 16 '53 por
Sat Eve Post 219:28+ Ja 25 '47 pors
Time 62:44 Jl 27 '53 por
Washington (D.C.) Evening Star S 29 '60 por
Author's & Writer's Who's Who (1960)
International Celebrity Register (1959)
Who's Who in America, 1960-61

KOESTLER, ARTHUR (kĕst'lẽr) Sept. 5, 1905- Author

Address: b. c/o A. D. Peters, 10 Buckingham St., London W.C. 2, England; c/o Macmillan Co., 60 5th Ave., New York 11

NOTE: This biography supersedes the article that appeared in *Current Biography* in 1943.

Perhaps more than any other living writer, Arthur Koestler embodies the dilemma of man in the twentieth century because his work intensifies the social and moral clashes of the age, the ideological and military conflict between totalitarianism and freedom, and the struggle of antagonistic forces like science and religion, action and contemplation. The title of his recent *The Lotus and the Robot,* which records his search for Far Eastern solutions to Western perplexities, reflects an antithesis apparent also in the titles of *Darkness at Noon* (his best-known novel), *The Yogi and the Commissar, Arrival and Departure, Promise and Fulfillment,* and several of his other books.

Koestler also often handles his subject matter with an antithesis between scientific detail and sweeping generalization. He is a former Communist, Hungarian-born and Austrian-educated, who first made a name as a German-language journalist and science editor. His writing retains a fondness for scientific terminology and an immediacy of firsthand reporting. Almost all of his work has been published by the Macmillan Company.

The only child of Henrik K. Koestler, an Hungarian industrialist and would-be inventor, and his Viennese wife, Adele Koestler, Arthur Koestler was born in Budapest on September 5, 1905. In his autobiographical *Arrow in the Blue* (1952), he has described at length his guilt-ridden, lonely, and introspective childhood in Budapest and later in Vienna. He was reared bilingually, learning to speak both Hungarian and German. At school he was interested almost exclusively in mathematics and science, and for recreation he played chess.

Graduating from a boarding school in Baden, near Vienna, in 1922, at sixteen Koestler entered the Technische Hochschule, or Polytechnik, a school with university status. Although his parents were Jewish, he had been brought up, as he relates in *Arrow in the Blue,* "in an assimilated environment without roots in Judaic tradition" and he was not attracted to Judaism. But at the university he became so deeply absorbed in the Zionist movement that in April 1926 he left Vienna without taking his degree and set out for Palestine.

Koestler says that he began his career as a manual laborer, picking up stones on a farm at Heftsebā. In the Middle East for the next two years, he almost starved to death and worked as a lemonade vendor, a tourist clerk, a land surveyor's assistant, and an editor of a Cairo weekly paper before he found a promising job in journalism. In 1927 he was hired as correspondent in Jerusalem for the German Ullstein Verlag, traditionally liberal publishers of a number of influential newspapers, including *Vossische Zeitung* and *B.Z. am Mittag,* and of books and magazines. He covered a seven-country beat in the Middle East, writing about three articles a week for Ullstein publications.

In July 1929 Ullstein transferred Koestler to Paris as its foreign correspondent, but about a year later called him to Berlin to become its science editor and adviser and subsequently made him also the foreign editor of *B.Z. am Mittag.* During the summer of 1931 he took part, as the only newsman, in the arctic expedition of the *Graf Zeppelin.* Although he was now a busy and prosperous journalist, he suffered a feeling of intellectual stagnation and an acute awareness of a false personality.

Just before the end of 1931, on December 31, foreseeing the onrush of the Nazi tide, Koestler joined the Communist party. He had earnestly studied Communist literature, and as a resident of Germany in the 1930's, he felt compelled to choose between fascism and Communism. Along with five other prominent former Communists, he has explained in *The God That Failed* (Harper, 1950) why he was attracted to Marxism. He left Germany in July 1932 for the U.S.S.R., where he spent a year as a guest of the Soviet government. In *The Invisible Writing* (1954) he carries his autobiography through his seven years in the Communist party.

Unable and unwilling as a Communist to return to Germany, Koestler found a temporary home in France, where he occupied himself in free-lance journalism and underwent his apprenticeship in novel writing. At the outbreak of the Spanish Civil War in 1936, he went to Spain as a correspondent for the London *News Chronicle*. His articles about the extent of German and Italian military aid to Franco made him hunted as a spy, and he was captured by the fascists in February 1937 and condemned to death. But in May the British Foreign Office arranged for his release. Koestler's stirring account of his three-month nightmarish ordeal in Spanish prisons was published in *Spanish Testament* (1938) and in the briefer *Dialogue With Death* (1942).

Well over a year before the August 1939 Russo-German nonaggression pact, Koestler had left the Communist party. Signs of his disillusionment appear in his first novel, *The Gladiators* (1939), which tells the story of Spartacus and the Servile War in 73 B.C. Having gone to Paris in 1938 to edit the German-language *Zukunft* (Future), an anti-Hitler, anti-Stalin weekly, he was arrested as a refugee at the beginning of World War II and imprisoned at Le Vernet. His experiences at this notorious French detention camp are the subject of *Scum of the Earth* (1941).

Koestler was released from Le Vernet in January 1940, again through British intervention, and arrived in England the following fall, after having joined the French Foreign Legion in a futile attempt at earlier escape from France. In the spring of 1941 he enlisted in the Pioneer Corps of the British Army, and upon his discharge about a year later, he was employed in the British Ministry of Information.

Some years earlier, in France, Koestler had worked on a novel about the Moscow trials of 1937, drawing for many details upon his own suffering as a prisoner. *Darkness at Noon* (1941) dramatizes with subtle psychological insight the tragedy of Commissar Rubashov, an old Bolshevik imprisoned by a new generation of Communists and persuaded to confess to crimes against the state of which he is innocent. Praised in many countries for both its craftsmanship and its insight into the workings of the totalitarian mind, the novel established Koestler's international reputation. In the United States it was a Book-of-the-Month Club selection, and later Sidney Kingsley used it as the basis of his play *Darkness at Noon*, produced on Broadway in 1951.

Darkness at Noon, which was translated into thirty languages, was the last book that Koestler wrote in German. Among his early books written in the English language were the antitotalitarian

ARTHUR KOESTLER

Arrival and Departure (1943), a political novel about the psychiatric problems of a European Communist who has escaped from Nazi torture; and *The Yogi and the Commissar* (1945), a collection of essays dealing among other subjects with the role of the intelligentsia, book reviewing, social change, and moral aspects of revolution and war.

Koestler's interest in Zionism had faded after he left Palestine in 1929, but it was revived by the Nazi treatment of the Jews during World War II. His novel *Thieves in the Night* (1946) is a powerful depiction of the Jewish struggle to resettle Palestine in the late 1930's. Just after the partition of Palestine in 1948 and in the midst of fighting between the Jews and Arabs, Koestler visited Israel and soon afterward gave an on-the-spot report of the tragic conflict in *Promise and Fulfillment* (1949). He also analyzed the economic, political, and emotional factors involved in the Jewish-Arab-British relationship between 1917 and 1949. In the London *Times Literary Supplement* (October 28, 1949), *Promise and Fulfillment* was recommended as "one of the best books that has yet appeared on Jewish Palestine."

In another book that Koestler published in 1949, *Insight and Outlook*, he explored his theories about the common foundations of science, art, and social ethics. Despair and pessimism pervaded his novel *The Age of Longing* (1951), with its grim picture of the Paris international intelligentsia, and his book of essays *The Trail of the Dinosaur* (1955), with its apprehensions of the extinction of mankind.

Even when he tries to be dispassionate, Koestler usually does not conceal his personal involvement in his subject. In writing *Reflections on Hanging* (1957), he openly admitted to "a vested interest in capital punishment," since he had been under the sentence of death in Spanish prisons. First syndicated in the London *Observer*, his book stimulated the movement in England in 1955 for the abolition of the death penalty. (In

KOESTLER, ARTHUR—*Continued*

1956 the House of Commons ended the death penalty, except for murderers under life sentence convicted of new killings.)

The wealth of facts that Koestler has acquired in his lifelong preoccupation with science informs *The Sleepwalkers; A History of Man's Changing Vision of the Universe* (1959). Through his account of the discoveries of Copernicus, Kepler, Tycho de Brahe, Galileo, and Newton, he examines the part that man's creative faculty has played in the construction of cosmological systems.

During 1958 and 1959 Koestler made what he regards as a pilgrimage to India and Japan to try to find out whether the East could offer a cure for the spiritual ailments of the West. His study of the cultures of the two widely divergent Asian countries, detailed in the *The Lotus and the Robot* (1961), led him to conclude that "to look to Asia for mystic enlightenment and spiritual guidance has become as much of an anachronism as to think of America as the Wild West." He gained an intensified awareness and respect for Europe's sustaining self-regeneration, its "unique history—its unity-in-variety in Space, and continuity-through-change in Time."

Although Koestler's more recent books have not stirred readers with the dramatic impact of *Darkness at Noon,* he has remained one of the significant writers of his generation. His personal tone and his centrality, which for some critics weaken his treatment of such subjects as Communism and Zionism, often lend his writing vibrancy and brilliance. Martin Greenberg, in reviewing *The Lotus and the Robot* for the *Reporter* (March 30, 1961), makes a restrained evaluation of Koestler's work as a whole: "He has given the time back to us in books that lie somewhere between literature and journalism. One remembers them with pleasure for their lucid, lively, forthright prose and unsolemn seriousness, but they are touched with the inescapable vulgarity of the science popularizer that Koestler started as . . . and has never ceased being."

Since World War II Koestler has been a British subject; he lives mainly in England and contributes to the London *Observer* and other periodicals. He travels, however, from country to county as much now as in the past and spends considerable time at his mountain hut in the Tyrol. He first visited the United States in May 1948, on a lecture tour for the International Rescue and Relief Committee, and he wrote *Arrow in the Blue* while living at Island Farm, near New Hope, Pennsylvania, and in Fontaine le Port, France.

In 1935 Arthur Koestler married Dorothy Ascher, from whom he was divorced in 1950. Later in 1950 he married his secretary, Mamaine Paget. Once stocky, Koestler now weighs 140 pounds; he is five feet eight inches tall and has blue eyes and brown hair. He is a member of the P.E.N. club in England and a Fellow of the Royal Society of Literature. Throughout his life he has found recreation in chess. In his leisure he also turns to mountain climbing and canoeing, and he is said to be an expert on fine wines.

When asked recently to name his religious and political affiliations, he disclaimed attachments.

Koestler excites controversy, but perhaps not many of his readers would disagree about the import of his observation in *Arrow in the Blue,* "What I have written may be regarded as the chart of an experimental neurosis produced in the laboratory of our time."

References

Atkins, John. Arthur Koestler (1956)
Author's & Writer's Who's Who (1960)
International Who's Who, 1961-62
Koestler, Arthur. Arrow in the Blue (1952); The Invisible Writing (1954)
Twentieth Century Authors (First Supplement, 1955)
Who's Who, 1961
Who's Who in America, 1960-61

LEWIS, JOHN (AARON) May 3, 1920-
Composer; pianist; arranger; musical director
Address: b. MJQ Music, Inc., 881 Tenth Ave., New York 19

A leading exponent, composer, and performer of the so-called "third stream" of jazz, in which classical and jazz elements intermingle, John Lewis is a classically trained musician whose work has been influenced not only by Dizzy Gillespie and Charlie ("Yardbird") Parker, but also by Bach, Haydn, and Mozart. According to jazz critic Whitney Balliett, Lewis has "pointed the way toward the use of classical forms—the fugue, the rondo, and episode—while maintaining, through some memorable improvisations and a frequent use of the blues, direct contact with the fundamentals of jazz." In recent years Lewis has been chiefly known as musical director of the Modern Jazz Quartet, a group that he helped to found in 1952 and in which he plays the piano.

John Aaron Lewis was born in La Grange, Illinois, on May 3, 1920 into a family of mixed Indian and Negro origin that had lived in New Mexico for four generations. When he was seven months old his parents returned to Albuquerque, where his maternal grandfather owned a hotel, and it was in Albuquerque that Lewis was raised. Both of his parents were musical: his mother, a singer, had studied with the daughter of the famous contralto Ernestine Schumann-Heink and his father, an optometrist, played the piano and violin. Lewis began lessons on both these instruments when he was seven.

Despite parental objections, Lewis managed to hear many of the great jazz musicians of the 1930's, most of whom toured the Southwest. He was most impressed by Duke Ellington, the jazz musician to whom he is now most often compared, because Ellington had somehow escaped being labeled as an entertainer and had been accepted as a creative musical talent.

Not until he heard the "modern jazz" of Charlie Parker and Dizzy Gillespie, however, did Lewis decide to become a jazz musician himself. During his final year at the University of Mexico he switched his major subject from anthropology to music, but before he could get his degree he was drafted into the United States Army in 1942. He served in the musical branch of Special Services for three years and there met the drummer Kenny Clarke, who later helped to launch him on his jazz career.

After his discharge from the Army in 1945 Lewis moved to New York City, where he joined the big band of Dizzy Gillespie as an arranger and pianist. During this period he made arrangements of "Two Bass Hit," "Emanon," "Stay On It," and "Minor Walk," later recorded on long-playing discs that Gillespie made for RCA Victor and Rondo-lette. He also began to compose, and his first major work, *Toccata for Trumpet and Orchestra*, was introduced by Gillespie at a Carnegie Hall concert in September 1947.

After completing a European tour with the Gillespie band, Lewis remained in Paris for two months to work with Tony Proteau's ensemble. When he returned to the United States in October 1948 he joined the Illinois Jacquet band for a period of eight months. He then played and recorded with Lester Young and Charlie Parker and served as soloist and arranger for the influential "chamber jazz" recordings that Miles Davis made for Capitol Records in 1949 and 1950. Some of his work from this period, notably the arrangements for "Move," "Budo," and "Rogue," has been reissued in Miles Davis' Capitol album *Birth of the Cool*.

When he first arrived in New York City, shortly after World War II, Lewis had enrolled at the Manhattan School of Music. During the years that followed he continued his education in classical music, despite his growing reputation as a jazz musician, studying everything from simple theory to advanced orchestration and composition. He even studied voice and for some time sang with the Schola Cantorum, a choral group. He earned two degrees from the Manhattan School of Music and later returned there to teach piano and theory.

After completing his formal studies, Lewis returned to the jazz scene with fresh ideas about the presentation of music. He felt he needed a stable group with which to work—and one that could perform his compositions in public. When Milt Jackson and he founded the Modern Jazz Quartet in 1952, he realized his ambition. The Modern Jazz Quartet, which developed out of scattered performing dates that its members had played during 1951, began with John Lewis as pianist, Milt Jackson as vibraphonist, Kenny Clarke (a war-time friend of Lewis) as drummer, and Percy Heath as bassist. The Modern Jazz Quartet is a co-operative group, in which the players split the profits and share the responsibilities. Since its inception, however, Lewis has been its principal composer and unquestioned artistic director and leading creative force. Moreover, his delicacy of touch and sure sense of rhythm as a pianist have contributed a great deal to the success of the Modern Jazz Quartet.

Although it was established in 1952, the Modern Jazz Quartet did not perform regularly until August 5, 1954, when it began its first engagement at New York City's Birdland. In the meantime, Lewis worked with Ella Fitzgerald and in early 1954 toured the United States and Australia as her accompanist. Since 1954 the Modern Jazz Quartet has grown in popularity both in the United States and abroad, and it has absorbed all of Lewis' energies.

JOHN LEWIS

During its 1957 tour of Great Britain and the Continent, the Modern Jazz Quartet played eighty-eight concerts in four months. Speaking for Italian jazz enthusiasts, Arrigo Polillo, editor of *Musica Jazz*, wrote: "The MJQ was triumphantly received. I think that no other jazz group has ever impressed the Italians as much as this one." The Modern Jazz Quartet is the first jazz group to have appeared at such major classical music festivals in Europe as the Donaueschingen Festival of Contemporary Music in Germany and the Maggio Musicale Fiorentino in Italy. Since the late 1950's the Modern Jazz Quartet has enjoyed such prestige in the United States that it has dispensed with night club engagements and has restricted its appearances to formal concerts.

The continued existence of the Modern Jazz Quartet with only one change of personnel in a decade—when Connie Kay replaced Kenny Clarke on drums in 1955—has engendered a reciprocal composer-performer relationship unique among contemporary jazz groups. Gunther Schuller, the young classical composer and critic of jazz, has written of the Modern Jazz Quartet: " 'Music which is *both* created by the players *and* fully shaped by the composer.' These words, written . . . about Duke Ellington and his orchestra, apply with equal accuracy to the Modern Jazz Quartet and its composer John Lewis. Though the Quartet is guided and dominated artistically by John, each player in it is able to contribute creatively—one is tempted to say compositionally—to the final result in a manner almost nonexistent in jazz since the great days of the Ellington band."

Lewis' earliest compositions for the Modern Jazz Quartet were "Vendome," "Versailles," and "Concorde"—fugal pieces inspired by his love of Paris. "The Queen's Fancy," which he wrote about the time of the coronation of Queen Elizabeth II, was inspired by music written for Queen Elizabeth I. "Django," one of his most popular and most moving works, is an elegiac

LEWIS, JOHN—*Continued*

piece for the late French gypsy guitarist Django Reinhardt. "Django" illustrates the way in which Lewis and the Modern Jazz Quartet work together. After having improvised on "Django" for more than seven years, the Modern Jazz Quartet is still experimenting with new approaches to the composition.

On his trips to Italy, Lewis became fascinated with the theater of the Italian Renaissance and, starting with "Fontessa" in 1955, began to compose pieces based on the characters of the *commedia dell'arte*. Later he added "La Cantatrice" and "Harlequin," creating a group of compositions called *The Comedy*. Louis Johnson, the choreographer, used these pieces as the groundwork for a ballet that met with much acclaim in Paris.

One of the first composers of the new jazz to write for films, in 1957 Lewis produced the score for the French film *Sait-On Jamais*, released in the United States as *No Sun in Venice* in 1959. The English musician and critic Max Harrison has observed of Lewis' film music: "Partly through the sheer expressiveness of the MJQ's playing, and partly through the appositeness of Lewis' ideas, whenever music is present it enhances the atmosphere and underlines the prevailing mood." The six set pieces that make up this score have become a standard part of the repertoire of the Modern Jazz Quartet. Early in 1959 Lewis wrote the musical score for a United Nations short subject on the world-wide refugee problem, entitled *Exposure*. Later that year he completed work on the score for *Odds Against Tomorrow*, which represented a major advance in the use of jazz in motion pictures.

Lewis has blended the talents of jazz and classical musicians, both in recordings and on the concert stage. He was the prime mover in organizing the short-lived Jazz and Classical Music Society, which made a successful Town Hall appearance in November 1955. In February 1958 he made an RCA Victor recording called *European Windows*, conducting thirty-two members of the Stuttgart Symphony and four jazz musicians in six of his compositions. In September 1959 the Modern Jazz Quartet joined the Beaux Arts String Quartet in a Town Hall recital during which they played two compositions that had been written for them jointly. Whitney Balliett of the *New Yorker* (October 3, 1959) thought the Modern Jazz Quartet, on its own, behaved "as if it had just been excused from Sunday school," and suggested that the group "stay in its own backyard, where there is enough weeding to be done."

In 1958 and 1959 Lewis served as music director of the Monterey (California) Jazz Festival and in 1960 he won the *Metronome* poll as the year's best arranger. Much of his work has been published by MJQ Music, Inc., a publishing company devoted to the publication and dissemination of editions of jazz material, of which he is president. Since 1957 he has headed the faculty of the Music Inn School of Jazz at Lenox, Massachusetts. There for three weeks each summer, students from all over the world work under a faculty consisting of some of the best musicians in jazz, including Dizzy Gillespie,

Oscar Peterson, Jimmy Giuffre, Max Roach, J. J. Johnson, Bill Russo, and members of the Modern Jazz Quartet. Lewis believes that this type of school is needed to replace the jam session. "When I was coming up," he says, "there were older, very good musicians who weren't so busy making money they had time for young people like I was then. That doesn't exist anymore."

If musical temperaments may be classified as either classic or romantic, that of John Lewis is definitely on the romantic side. Leonard Feather has noted in the *Encyclopedia of Jazz* (1960): "He knows exactly what he wants from his musicians, his writing and his career, and achieves it with an unusual, quiet firmness of manner, coupled with modesty and a complete indifference to critical reaction." He impressed even the reserved English with his reticence, independence, and reserve. An arranger who has worked with Lewis has referred to his lack of temper and "Gandhi approach." Lewis wears a well-trimmed beard that goes well with the so-called "mortician's uniform"—striped trousers and a black jacket—of the Modern Jazz Quartet.

References

    Hi Fi 10:54+O '60 por
    Feather, Leonard. Encyclopedia of Jazz
    (1960)

LOEB, JAMES (ISAAC), JR. Aug. 18, 1908-
United States Ambassador to Peru; journalist

Address: b. United States Embassy, Lima, Peru; h. U.S. Residencia, Avenida Arequipa, Lima, Peru

The United States Ambassador to Peru, James Loeb, Jr., is a former teacher of Romance languages who was selected for his post not only because he knows Spanish, but also because he speaks the language of political, social, and economic reform that is current in President Kennedy's "Alliance for Progress" program of aid to Latin-American countries. Active in liberal causes in the United States for more than twenty years, and a confidant of leading South American political and labor figures, Ambassador Loeb is sensitive to the impatience of many of the nations south of the border for the kind of American help that will enable them to raise living standards and develop their economies.

James Isaac Loeb, Jr., was born in Chicago, Illinois on August 18, 1908, the son of James I. and Viola (Klein) Loeb. He has a brother, Theodore, and sister, Virginia (now Mrs. Herbert Van Straaten). His father was in the insurance business. Jim Loeb graduated from Deerfield-Shields High School (now called Highland Park High School) in 1925. He then entered Dartmouth College, where he majored in English, was active in dramatics, served as manager of the college yearbook, and was elected to Phi Beta Kappa. He received the B.A. degree, *cum laude,* in 1929.

That year, Loeb has recalled, was "a fabulous year *not* to join my father's insurance business." He spent the next year studying in France and Spain (he maintains that he learned French by playing bridge) and returned home to enter Northwestern University with a fellowship in

French. He received his M.A. degree at Northwestern in 1931 and served as a Fellow and
later as an assistant instructor in the university's
Romance languages department. In 1936 the
Ph.D. degree was conferred upon him with
highest honors. His doctoral dissertation was entitled, "Public Attitudes Toward Tragedy in
Eighteenth Century France."

Moving to New York City, Loeb was appointed
an instructor in French and Spanish at Townsend
Harris High School, where he taught from 1937
to 1941. In May of 1941 he helped Reinhold
Niebuhr and other intellectuals found the Union
for Democratic Action (UDA), an organization
whose chief purpose was to stem the tide of
isolationist sentiment then current among many
American liberals. Loeb subsequently became
executive director of this organization. Rejected
for military service for reasons of health, he
worked in New York and Washington as the
director of the UDA until 1947. In that year the
Union for Democratic Action was changed into
Americans for Democratic Action (ADA). Its
founders included liberal Congressmen, labor
leaders, former New Deal officials, business and
academic leaders, writers, and clergymen. Eleanor
Roosevelt, Walter Reuther, and Arthur Schlesinger, Jr., were among the founders of ADA.

Loeb was named national director of ADA with
headquarters in Washington, D.C. Under his
direction it developed into a nationwide, independent, anti-Communist political organization of
45,000 members, "dedicated to . . . making liberalism a more effective force in the United
States." He helped to plan and execute the
ADA's three-point program, calling for the
formulation of liberal foreign and domestic
policies consistent with the realities and needs of
American society; the enlisting of public understanding and support for these goals; and positive
efforts to put these policies into effect by down-
to-earth political action through the two major
political parties. By its own admission, ADA has
most often found itself in agreement with the
liberal wing of the Democratic Party.

While he was on a tour of the United States
for ADA, Loeb first met Hubert Humphrey, then
Mayor of Minneapolis. Humphrey became one
of the national leaders of ADA and worked
closely with the organization's director. "I still
remember walking down the aisle with Humphrey
at the 1948 Democratic convention after he'd
made his civil rights speech and the Southern
delegations were walking out," Loeb told Joseph
Wershba of the New York *Post* in an interview
(May 10, 1961). "There was so much tension in
the air that I thought someone would really take
a shot at Hubert."

That same summer Loeb appeared before the
platform committee of Henry A. Wallace's Progressive party and branded the party's program as
Communist-dominated. He challenged the Pro-
gressives to "oppose the police state and totalitarian dictatorship everywhere in the world—
whether in Mississippi, in Spain, in China, or in
the Soviet Union and its satellites."

In 1950 while serving with ADA, Loeb was one
of the organizers of the Inter-American Association for Democracy and Freedom, founded in
Havana, Cuba. Through this body, of which he
is still a member, Loeb came to know many

JAMES LOEB, JR.

of Latin-America's young political reformers.
One of them, who became his good friend, was
a Venezuelan exile named Rómulo Betancourt,
now President of Venezuela.

The following year Loeb became consultant to
Charles Murphy, then special counsel to President Harry S. Truman. Loeb's service as a White
House aide in 1951-52 also included a period as
an executive assistant to W. Averell Harriman,
who was then a special adviser on foreign affairs
to President Truman. In 1952 Loeb was executive
director of the national Harriman-for-President
Committee. He also served as a special assistant
to Harriman in 1958, when the New York
Governor ran, unsuccessfully, for re-election
against Nelson A. Rockefeller.

On June 1, 1953, Loeb and Roger W. Tubby,
a former press secretary to President Truman,
entered the newspaper publishing field when they
purchased the *Adirondack Daily Enterprise,* published in Saranac Lake, New York. Joseph
Wershba in the New York *Post* (May 10, 1961)
has described the *Enterprise* as "an oasis of
Democratic thought in a rock-ribbed Republican
area." In September 1960 Tubby and Loeb
purchased a weekly, the Lake Placid (New York)
News, thus forming what Loeb has described as
"the smallest newspaper chain in America." One
factor inhibiting the growth of the "chain" has
been the recent absence of the two owner-editors
from their newspapers. Since February 1961
Roger W. Tubby has been Assistant Secretary of
State for Public Affairs. On April 7, 1961 President John F. Kennedy designated Loeb as United
States Ambassador to Peru, succeeding Selden
Chapin.

Loeb's appointment to the post as envoy to
Lima was considered an especially significant
recognition of his personal qualifications for the
position, because he had worked for Senator
Humphrey against Kennedy during the Democratic primary campaign in the spring of 1960.
In the late fall of 1961 Loeb drew both praise

LOEB, JAMES, JR.—*Continued*

and censure when he wrote an open letter addressed to Mario Samame Boggio, the rector of the Peruvian National School of Engineering, in which he criticized Peruvian intellectuals for not publicly condemning the resumption of nuclear weapons testing by the Soviet Union.

On November 23, 1932 James Loeb, Jr., married Ellen Katz. They have two children, Peter, a student at Harvard, and Susan, who is attending high school in Peru. Jim Loeb is six feet two inches tall, weighs 160 pounds, and has green eyes and brown hair. He has been described by Joseph Wershba as a "free-gaited, Lincolnesque man with an easy-going exterior and a churning, socially conscious interior." He has written many articles for such liberal magazines as the *Nation, New Republic,* and *Commonweal*. Loeb is a member of the Rotary Club of Saranac Lake and the Saranac Lake Chamber of Commerce. He is a member of the Jewish faith. Tennis and baseball are his favorite recreations.

In criticizing past United States policy toward Latin America, Loeb has said that it has often lacked a sense of timing. He noted that the tragedy of the ill-fated Cuban invasion of April 1961 was that it came at a time when there seemed to be a "new impulse" coming from the United States. "Latin America remembers the Good Neighbor policy—and they remember it with fondness," Loeb told Joseph Wershba. "And I think that Latin America feels that when President Kennedy comes with offers of help—he means it."

References

N Y Post p52 My 10 '61 por
N Y Times p4 Ap 8 '61 por

McCLINTIC, GUTHRIE Aug. 6, 1893-Oct. 29, 1961 Broadway producer and director; directed over ninety stage productions, including *The Old Maid* (1934), *High Tor* (1937), and numerous plays in which his wife, Katharine Cornell, appeared. See *Current Biography* (May) 1943.

Obituary

N Y Times p29 O 30 '61

McCRACKEN, JOAN Dec. 31, 1922-Nov. 1, 1961 Dancer; actress; became an "overnight success" in *Oklahoma!* (1943); appeared in several other musicals, including *Me and Juliet* (1953), and in dramatic roles on Broadway as well as in motion pictures. See *Current Biography* (June) 1945.

Obituary

N Y Times p37 N 2 '61

MACY, JOHN W(ILLIAMS), JR. Apr. 6, 1917- United States government official

Address: b. United States Civil Service Commission, 8th St. and F St., N. W., Washington 25, D.C.; h. 3508 Lowell St., N. W., Washington, D.C.

The chairman of the United States Civil Service Commission, John W. Macy, Jr., is President John F. Kennedy's principal adviser on questions involving government personnel. Macy began his career in government service in 1938 as an intern with the National Institute of Public Affairs, and has served in various administrative positions with the Social Security Board, the War Department, and the Atomic Energy Commission. In 1953 he became executive director of the United States Civil Service Commission, the highest nonappointive position in the Civil Service system. He served as executive vice-president of Wesleyan University in Middletown, Connecticut, from 1958 until 1961. On March 6, 1961 he was sworn in to succeed Roger W. Jones as chairman of the Civil Service Commission.

John Williams Macy, Jr., was born in Chicago on April 6, 1917 to John Williams Macy, an advertising executive, and Juliette (Moën) Macy. He has two brothers, Bradford, and Francis Underhill. Another brother, Lawrence Shaw, is deceased. John was reared in Winnetka, Illinois, where he received his secondary education at the North Shore Country Day School. He played football, baseball, and basketball, was active on the school newspaper, and developed an extracurricular interest in opera. After graduating from high school in 1934, he entered Wesleyan University in Middletown, Connecticut, where he majored in government. He was elected to Phi Beta Kappa, won a Thorndike scholarship, and was a Rhodes Scholar nominee. Macy served as editor of the college newspaper, president of the dramatic club, manager of the soccer team, and was a member of the glee club and choir. After graduating with a B.A. degree in June 1938, he did some postgraduate work at the American University in Washington, D.C.

Macy entered government service in 1938 as a participant in the administrative intern program of the National Institute of Public Affairs. From June 1939 until 1940 he was administrative aide with the field operations division in the office of the executive director of the Social Security Board. He became an administrative assistant in the civilian personnel division of the War Department in November 1940 and was promoted to assistant director of this division in 1942.

In 1943 Macy enlisted in the Army Air Force as a private and subsequently rose to the rank of captain. His service in the Air Force included duty as personnel staff officer with the Air Transport Command and as staff adviser with the military advisory group in China. While he was a second lieutenant in the Air Force, Macy worked with Frank Pace, then a first lieutenant, who later became Assistant Secretary of the Army and now is board chairman of General Dynamics Corporation. In 1946 Macy was discharged from the Air Force and returned to his position as assistant director of civilian personnel in the office of the Secretary of War.

The Atomic Energy Commission sent Macy to Los Alamos, New Mexico, on a ninety-day assignment in June 1947. He stayed on in New Mexico until 1951 as director of organization and personnel in the Santa Fe operations office. His duties included the function of town manager of a city with a population of 13,000. In August 1951, while he was executive officer of the atomic tests at Las Vegas, Nevada, he was drafted by

Secretary of the Army Frank Pace to serve as a special assistant to the Under Secretary of the Army.

In August 1953 Philip Young, the chairman of the United States Civil Service Commission, selected Macy to be the executive director of the commission, the highest career position in the federal merit system. During his tenure as executive director, Macy was responsible for implementing many desirable changes and reforms in the Civil Service system. Under his leadership, plans for world-wide extension of the Civil Service system were formulated, a career-conditional appointment system was established, and the government's college recruiting program was revitalized. Many new fringe benefits for federal employees were added to the government's personnel system. The executive director encouraged giving recognition to employees for superior performance on the job and for money-saving suggestions.

Macy participated in the Sixth American Assembly, which met at Arden House in Harriman, New York in October 1954 to consider ways and means of improving the federal Civil Service system and of enhancing the President's relations with the various government agencies. Among the proposals that grew out of the panel discussions and workshops at this conference were suggestions that the President exercise greater leadership over personnel management of the federal government, especially with regard to the loyalty-security program, and that Congress should not go beyond promulgating broad statements of policy with respect to personnel administration.

On January 31, 1958 Macy resigned as executive director of the Civil Service Commission. It has been speculated that he resigned because he was dissatisfied with the policies of the Eisenhower administration. Not long afterward, he became executive vice-president of Wesleyan University at Middletown, Connecticut. In January 1959 Macy announced a plan under which Wesleyan was to be divided into separate colleges, corresponding somewhat to the British system prevailing at Oxford University. Among his other duties at Wesleyan was teaching a class in public administration that dealt with the American Presidency. In teaching this course in 1960-61, he emphasized the problems occurring in the change of administrations after a national election. While at Middletown, Macy was also active in community affairs, and he headed fund-raising campaigns that raised large sums for the United Fund and the Middlesex Memorial Hospital Building Fund.

President-elect John F. Kennedy designated Macy for the post of chairman of the Civil Service Commission on January 4, 1961. Upon learning of his appointment, Macy praised outgoing chairman Roger W. Jones and said that he intended to build on the foundation that Jones had laid. On March 2, 1961 Macy's appointment was confirmed by the Senate, and on March 6 he was sworn into office.

The United States Civil Service Commission, created by an act of Congress approved on January 16, 1883, is the central personnel agency of the federal government. The purpose of the act was to provide (in the parts of the govern-

JOHN W. MACY, JR.

ment service covered by its provisions) a merit system under which appointment would be made on the basis of fitness, without regard to political or religious considerations. The principal functions of the Civil Service Commission are to provide for examinations to test the fitness of applicants for positions under the competitive service; to provide qualified personnel to government agencies upon request; and to administer the various laws and regulations relating to the Civil Service. The Commission consists of three members, including the chairman, appointed by the President of the United States. In 1960 there were 2,398,705 employees under the United States Civil Service.

Macy favors a strong Civil Service system with a close relationship to the White House. He advocates greater efforts on the part of the government to attract civil servants of the highest possible caliber, and he encourages a "close, working partnership between education and government." He has called for the preservation of the political neutrality of the service and the assurance that advancement be based on merit alone; the guarantee of equal opportunities for all candidates and employees, regardless of race, creed, or sex; and the development of a climate conducive to high-quality performance. He has emphasized the need for salaries and benefits for government employees commensurate with those prevailing in private industry, and he has advocated Congressional approval of legislation, sponsored by the Kennedy administration, to set up more than 1,000 new top-level Civil Service jobs.

In an address before members of the American Society for Public Administration on April 6, 1961, Macy asked for "greater creativity, bold new programs, imagination, and innovations." He underlined the need to "combat overcautiousness and conformity among employees and to create a climate in which ideas will flourish." He called upon civil servants to "combat confusion and

MACY, JOHN W., JR.—*Continued*

waste" and to "fight mediocrity in all forms through the pursuit of excellence." In November 1961 he noted, however, that the administration's goals for better management and better personnel do not necessarily mean any great increases in the size of the Civil Service staff. "High quality of personnel, not high quantity, must be our goal," he said.

Since 1954 Macy has served on the board of trustees of Wesleyan University. He was national president of the American Society for Public Administration in 1958-59 and was vice-chairman of the Connecticut Economic Planning and Development Committee in 1960. He is a member of the Phi Nu Theta fraternity and of the University Clubs of Washington and New York City.

Macy has received several high honors and awards. In 1957 he was one of ten men in the federal career service who received the award of the National Civil Service League. In 1958 he received the Stockberger Award of the Society for Personnel Administration and the Commissioner's Award of the United States Civil Service Commission. Both the Secretary of the Army and the Secretary of the Air Force conferred upon him the Distinguished Civilian Award in 1958.

John W. Macy, Jr., married Joyce Hagen on February 12, 1944. Before their marriage Mrs. Macy was employed as an intelligence analyst. They have three children: Thomas Lawrence, Mary Derrick, and Susan Bradford. Macy is six feet one inch tall, weighs 178 pounds, and has gray hair and brown eyes. For relaxation he likes to read, swim, and play tennis. He has been described as a person who "bounces through a typical eleven-hour day (which he denies is overwork) with zip and zest." He is a Democrat and a member of the Episcopal Church.

In trying to improve the quality of Civil Service personnel, Macy has constantly appealed to college graduates to make the federal service their life-time career. He feels that the prestige of the service has been steadily increasing and that "public employment is now generally recognized to be as honorable a calling as anyone could choose." Macy once asked: "Where else can you find a career in which your horizons will not be bounded by the interests of one company, or one industry, or one city, state, or region, but will reach from border to border and even beyond?"

References

Hartford Courant Mag p3 F 5 '61 pors
Look 21:80 My 14 '57 por
New Frontiersmen (1961)
Who's Who in America, 1960-61

MARTIN, EDMUND F(IBLE) Nov. 1, 1902-
Steel company executive
Address: b. Bethlehem Steel Co., 701 E. 3d St., Bethlehem, Pa.; h. 1220 Prospect Ave., Bethlehem, Pa.

Bethlehem Steel Corporation, the second largest steel-producing enterprise in the world, elected its fifth president—Edmund F. Martin—on July 28, 1960. He succeeded Arthur B. Homer, who became chairman of the board and remained the chief executive officer. Martin joined the Bethlehem Steel Company in 1922, the year in which he graduated from Stevens Institute of Technology. He was general manager of the company's Lackawanna, New York plant from 1950 until 1958, when he was named vice-president in charge of steel operations. Bethlehem, with an annual steelmaking capacity of 23,000,000 tons and assets of $2,274,957,167 (in 1960), ranks in size below only the United States Steel Corporation among the giants of the industry.

Edmund Fible Martin was born in Chicago, Illinois on November 1, 1902, the son of Albert and Bettie Garth (Fible) Martin, both originally Kentuckians. His father practised law in Chicago. The boy attended grammar schools in Hinsdale, Illinois and University High School in Chicago, from which he graduated in 1918. Deciding to become a mechanical engineer, he enrolled at Stevens Institute of Technology in Hoboken, New Jersey, where he was elected to Tau Beta Pi, the honorary engineering fraternity. After earning the M.E. degree in 1922 he became a member of the first class in Bethlehem Steel Company's "Loop Course" for college graduates.

On completing this management training course, Martin was assigned to the roll shop of the Saucon division of the Bethlehem plant at Bethlehem, Pennsylvania, where he worked first as a repairman helper, then as a tool grinder, and later as a draftsman. In 1924 he was promoted to foreman of the twelve-and eighteen-inch mills at Saucon. Two years later he became foreman of the forty-two- and forty-eight-inch mills, advancing in 1927 to the post of assistant superintendent in these mills.

In the following year he was appointed department superintendent, a position he held until 1939 when he was made superintendent of the Saucon division, where he remained through World War II. During that period Bethlehem Steel Company's shipbuilding division built 1,127 fighting and cargo vessels and converted, serviced, or repaired over 37,000 ships, while its plants produced 73,000,000 tons of steel.

Martin was transferred to the company's Lackawanna, New York plant near Buffalo in 1946 as assistant general manager and four years later was appointed general manager. During his twelve years at the Lackawanna plant he was active in many civic organizations: director of the Buffalo Chamber of Commerce and Buffalo Redevelopment Foundation, member of the Community Chest board and the Buffalo and Erie County Planning Association, and vice-president of the Associated Industries of New York State. He also served on the executive board of the Citizens Appeals Review Committee and was a delegate to the Council of Social Agencies.

Returning to headquarters in Bethlehem in 1958, Martin was made vice-president in charge of steel operations of the Bethlehem Steel Company, the principal subsidiary of Bethlehem Steel Corporation. On July 28, 1960, when Arthur B. Homer was elected chairman, Martin was elected to succeed him as president of the corporation and of Bethlehem Steel Company.

The Bethlehem Steel Corporation is the holding concern for the family of companies developed from the Bethlehem Steel Company, which was found by John Fritz in South Bethlehem,

Pennsylvania in 1899 and taken over by Charles M. Schwab in 1903. The corporation, with its shipbuilding subsidiary, was incorporated in 1904. Eugene Gifford Grace became president of the company in 1913 and of the corporation in 1916. Homer succeeded Grace in 1945.

In addition to its steel plants and thirteen fabricating works, the corporation has nine shipbuilding and ship repair yards and twenty-one other manufacturing units. Its steel plants products include: ferromanganese, coal chemicals, blooms, billets, slabs, bars, carbon, alloy and special steels, structural shapes, tin mill products, sheets and strip, tool steels, plates, rails, pipe, wire, wire rods, concrete-reinforcing bars, and steel piling.

Over the past five or six years the United States steel industry has spent some $7 billion in a modernization program to improve efficiency in steelmaking. Among the projects that Bethlehem Steel completed in 1960 were facilities for increasing the production of expanded pipe and a reinforcing bar mill at the Steelton, Pennsylvania plant; the rebuilding of a battery of coke ovens at the Sparrows Point, Maryland plant; remodeling the 134-inch plate mill at the Johnstown, Pennsylvania plant; and building four piers and a high-water bulkhead for ship repairs at San Pedro, California. The corporation also set up technical and commercial research facilities at its new research center in Bethlehem, pioneered in the production of hardened steel rolls from vacuum-degassed steels, and introduced the new products Bethalume and Bethnamel.

Contrary to the steel industry's expectations of an increased demand for steel in 1960, there was a downward turn after the first quarter of the year. By that time the backlog of demand resulting from the 116-day strike of the United Steelworkers of America in 1959 was largely satisfied, and both distributors and consumers of steel began to reduce inventories. "As a result of a general softening of economic conditions," the corporation's 1960 annual report pointed out," requirements for steel products were gradually reduced in such important areas as construction, heavy machinery, and containers. Moreover, the increase in the proportion of compact cars produced by the automotive industry considerably lessened the steel requirements in this area." Nevertheless, Bethlehem produced 15,941,104 net tons of ingots in 1960 and reported total revenues of $2,208,954,823.

Bethlehem's 1960 report predicted that the entire steel industry in 1961 would produce between 95 million and 100 million tons of steel. Despite a fourth-quarter drop of 13 per cent in production, the corporation expected an increase in the first quarter of 1961. This increase, however, did not occur, and the report for the first quarter of 1961 (issued April 27) showed that steel production (ingots and castings) totaled 2,963,690 net tons as compared with 5,584,295 net tons during the first quarter of 1960. Nevertheless, quarterly dividends of 60 cents per common share were paid on March 1 and on June 1, 1961.

Because of the efficiency resulting from its recent modernization, Bethlehem is able to show a profit even though it is not operating at full capacity and has had to pay steadily increasing

Hesselbein Studios
EDMUND F. MARTIN

wages. In 1960 it employed 138,344 workers at a cost of $945,732,419. During early 1961 it was expected that the steel industry would ask for a steel price rise to correspond to wage increases, but in June 1961 large producers, including Bethlehem, disclosed that they had made a 10 per cent cut in the price of steel cable.

Martin's organization and club memberships include the Bethlehem Club, Newcomen Society, American Iron and Steel Institute, Association of Iron and Steel Engineers, and Bethlehem Chamber of Commerce. He is a member of the board of trustees of Stevens Institute of Technology and holds an honorary D.Eng. degree from the University of Buffalo, conferred in 1961.

Edmund F. Martin and Frances Taylor were married on November 27, 1926. They have two daughters, Caroline Bettie and Barbara Taylor (Mrs. Robert C. Stout). Martin is an ardent golfer, having learned the game at the age of nine. He was formerly the club champion at Saucon Valley Country Club. He has brown eyes and brown hair, stands six feet one inch tall, and weighs 185 pounds. He is a Republican and a Presbyterian.

References

Who's Who in America, 1960-61
Who's Who in Commerce and Industry (1961)

MEERLOO, JOOST A(BRAHAM) M(AURITS) (mâr'lō yōst) Mar. 14, 1903- Psychiatrist; psychoanalyst; author; lecturer

Address: 300 Central Park West, New York 24

The Dutch-born psychoanalyst Dr. Joost A. M. Meerloo, now practising in New York City, is an authority on totalitarian thought control and the techniques of brainwashing. In his books and articles he has scrutinized the mind in captivity and the process of menticide (a word that he

J. Schneider

DR. JOOST A. M. MEERLOO

coined) that thrusts it into prison. His theory that anyone can break down in the hands of an enemy who uses the strategy of menticide was accepted by American military courts in trials of servicemen charged with collaborationism during the Korean War. Dr. Meerloo is now examining the implications of his theory of mental contagion and the subtle ways in which a technological culture exerts pressures on the minds of men.

He has more than an academic interest in totalitarianism, having witnessed Nazi methods of mental torture and having experienced enforced interrogation at first hand. He came to the United States in 1946 after imprisonment by the Nazis and a harried escape to Great Britain. During World War II he served in the Netherlands army-in-exile as chief of the psychological department.

Joost Abraham Maurits Meerloo was born on March 14, 1903 at The Hague, the seat of the Netherlands government, the youngest of the six children of Bernard Meerloo, a businessman, and his wife, Anna (Benjamins) Meerloo. He is the only surviving member of his family; his three sisters and two brothers were victims of Nazism. The boy was educated in local schools at The Hague and was an excellent student. From early childhood he wanted to study medicine. When he finished the requirements leading to the baccalaureate in 1921, he matriculated at the University of Leyden. Beginning in 1924, Meerloo served for three years as a medical resident at the university hospitals in Leyden. After receiving the M.D. degree in 1927, he decided to undertake advanced study in psychiatry and psychoanalysis.

During the seven-year period of Dr. Meerloo's psychoanalytic education, he served as a physician in mental institutions. After completing an eight-month assignment (January to August 1928) at the Maria Oord sanitarium in Gennep, Meer-

loo was appointed an assistant psychiatrist at the Provincial Hospital in Santpoort. He left there in 1930 for an academic grand tour of Europe, studying with distinguished professors in Paris, Zurich, Berne, and London. When he returned to Holland in the late months of 1930, Meerloo was named to the post of psychiatrist and chief of a department at the Maasoord Psychiatric Hospital in Rotterdam. In addition to performing his medical duties, Dr. Meerloo taught clinical psychiatry to the students and residents at the hospital, conducted a postgraduate course for doctors, and lectured in social psychology at the People's University in Rotterdam. Dr. Meerloo also broadened his research activities while in Rotterdam (1930-34) and his findings provided the basis for more than forty papers and a book, *The Action of Barbituric Acids* (Amsterdam, Paris Publishers, 1932). The volume was originally presented as a dissertation for a Ph.D. degree at the University of Utrecht in 1932.

When Dr. Meerloo returned to The Hague in 1934 he began his private practice, simultaneously holding the post of psychiatric consultant to government agencies and to the Netherlands Royal Court. In 1939 he was called up in the reserves, but before Holland fell to the Nazis in May 1940, he published a psychiatric interpretation of those cataclysmic times: *Homo Militans, the Psychology of War and Peace in Man* (The Hague: Servire, 1940) and *The Psychology of Pain and Sorrow* (N. H. Uitgevers, 1940). Until his own imprisonment in 1942 Dr. Meerloo used his psychiatry to treat the victims of Nazi mental torture. Thus he was introduced to the totalitarian technique of "killing the mind" and underwent those personal and professional experiences that became the basis for his life's work.

The doctor escaped from a Nazi prison to England in 1942. There he joined the Netherlands Army-in-Exile as a colonel and chief of the Psychological Department. He recorded his experiences in psychological warfare in *Total War and the Human Mind; A Psychologist's Experiences in Occupied Holland* (International Universities Press, 1945). From 1944 to 1946 he served as High Commissioner for Welfare for the Netherlands government and adviser on welfare problems to UNRRA and SHAEF.

Dr. Meerloo immigrated to New York City in 1946 and immediately published *Aftermath of Peace; Psychological Essays* (International Universities Press), which studied fear, hatred, and treason during wartime and their effects on displaced persons, war orphans, and former members of the underground, and outlined a program for waging the peace. Within two years he fulfilled all the requirements for a license to practise as a psychiatrist in New York State. Dr. Meerloo maintains a private practice in New York. Since 1949 he has been a member of the teaching faculty in psychiatry at Columbia University and a lecturer in social psychology at the New School for Social Research in New York City. In 1950 he was also appointed a lecturer in psychotherapy at the Institute for Psychotherapy in New York.

The recognition accorded to Dr. Meerloo as an authority on the problems of thought control, brainwashing, and mental coercion has been based on his research and extensive writings. His

Delusion and Mass-Delusion (International Universities Press, 1949) is a monograph that introduced the word "menticide" into the English language—a term that describes the destruction of the human mind or soul. His *Patterns of Panic* (International Universities Press, 1959) is a description of panic, the varieties of individual reactions to it, and the self-destructive tendencies of mankind.

The book that brought critical acclaim to Dr. Meerloo and prompted one critic to call him the "passionate spokesman for the democratic practice of life" was *The Rape of the Mind* (World, 1956), an examination of the robot personality in the totalitarian state and the techniques of thought control. Dr. Meerloo presents the thesis that "today a man is no longer punished only for the crimes he has committed. Now he may be compelled to confess to crimes that have been conjured up by his judges, who use his confession for political purposes. . . . We must understand what impels the false admission of guilt [and] take another look at the human mind in all its frailty and vulnerability."

Other social phenomena have interested Dr. Meerloo. He has attributed the "Kilroy was here" fad to the enlisted man's hostility to his officers, and has analyzed the hula hoop craze, rock 'n' roll, and juvenile anti-Semitic hate campaigns. He has become an authority on mass communication and mass persuasion. Dr. Meerloo has decried the use of advertising experts in planning political campaigns, lest "unknowingly we may become opinionated robots, though we still have the illusion of being original and individual."

In addition to his longer works, Dr. Meerloo has written more than three hundred articles for scholarly and popular periodicals. Two other books for which he is well known are *Communication and Conversation* (1952) and *Two Faces of Man* (1954), both published by International Universities Press. He has a distinguished reputation as an editor, and in 1960 he supervised *Child Family Digest, Psychoanalysis and Psychoanalytic Review* and *Médecine et Hygiène* (Geneva, Switzerland). Since 1928 his book reviews have appeared in professional journals and the scholarly press.

Dr. Meerloo is a Fellow of the American Academy of Psychoanalysis, American Psychiatric Association, and the Royal Society of Medicine (England). Included among his many professional and medical memberships in the United States and abroad are the Medical Association and the Association for Psychiatry and Neurology in the Netherlands; the British Psychological Society; the American Medical Association; American Board of Psychiatry and Neurology; Association for the Advancement of Psychotherapy; American Psychosomatic Society; Menninger Foundation; American Association for the Advancement of Science; and the Center for the Psychological Study of War and Peace. He also serves as a consultant to the United States Navy and the Air Force and to the United Nations Commissioner for Refugees. He is chairman of the psychological department of the Civil Defense Research Association. In 1934 he received an award from the University of Amsterdam for a study of insulin treatment and the Netherlands

Government decorated him with the Distinguished Service Cross in 1943. In 1961 the American Association for Social Psychiatry gave him a peace award for his "unselfish concern and dedication to the welfare and preservation of mankind."

Scholarly and self-effacing in manner, Dr. Meerloo stands five feet seven inches in height, weighs 168 pounds, and has green eyes. His first marriage, on May 16, 1928, to Elisabeth Johanna Kalf ended in divorce in May 1946. He married Louisa Betsy Duits, a physical therapist, on May 7, 1948. He looks upon writing and his practice as his true hobbies, but he also enjoys mountain climbing and music. Dr. Meerloo was naturalized as an American citizen in 1950. He is a Democrat.

Reference

Who's Who in the East (1959)

MOORE, CHARLOTTE EMMA *See* Sitterly, C. M.

OLAV V, KING OF NORWAY July 2, 1903-
Address: Royal Palace, Oslo, Norway

When King Olav V succeeded his father, King Haakon VII, to the throne of Norway on September 21, 1957, he was already an experienced ruler. As Crown Prince, he had led his country's military resistance to the Nazi occupation during World War II. In 1955, when his aging father had become unable to continue as active ruler for reasons of health, Olav served as Norway's regent. Since becoming King, Olav has proved a popular monarch and has championed his country's deep-seated love of democratic freedom.

Not a Norwegian by birth, King Olav V was born on July 2, 1903 in Sandringham, England, the only child of Prince Carl, or Charles, of Denmark (the second son of the Danish monarch Frederick VIII) and Princess Maud of England (the youngest daughter of King Edward VII). He was christened Alexander Edward Christian Frederick.

Olav V was not destined at birth to become King of Norway, which at that time was still annexed to Sweden. In 1905 the Norwegian Storting (parliament) decided to establish an independent kingdom and gave King Oscar II of Sweden the opportunity to name a Swedish prince to Norway's throne. When he proved unwilling to do so, the Storting decided to choose a Danish prince in order to re-establish the ancient Danish line of the Norwegian monarchy. Prince Carl was selected, but made his acceptance conditional upon the consent of the people.

In June 1905 the Norwegian people approved the selection of Prince Carl as King of Norway. Upon assuming the throne, Carl became King Haakon VII of Norway, and his son's name was likewise changed to Olav, a royal name famous in the heroic days of the Vikings. Thus, at the age of two, Olav was brought to Norway as heir apparent to its throne.

(Continued next page)

OLAV V, KING OF NORWAY

Olav began his education with private tutoring at the Royal Palace in Oslo in 1911. Two years later, in keeping with the democratic principles of Norway's royal family, Olav was sent to Halling, an Oslo public school, where he received no special considerations because of his royal blood. Elected president of Halling's student body, he was removed from the position when his fellow students disagreed with one of his decisions.

In 1921, after graduating from Halling's secondary school with the rating of Very Satisfactory, Olav entered the Norwegian Military Academy, from which he graduated in 1924. The next stage in his education took him to England, where he studied economics, political science, and political economy at Balliol College, Oxford. Finally, he attended the Norwegian War College, graduating fourth in his class.

Meanwhile, Olav was also preparing for his succession to the Norwegian throne. At the age of eighteen, he had begun sitting in on cabinet meetings, over which the King presided. He also learned to perform the ceremonial duties attendant on being a Crown Prince, such as presiding at official functions. In 1924, when he attained his majority, he swore his formal oath of allegiance to the Norwegian constitution.

On March 21, 1929 Olav married Princess Märtha, the daughter of Prince Carl and Princess Ingeborg of Sweden. The nationwide celebrations that attended the marriage had a political as well as a personal basis, for the wedding symbolized the reconciliation of Norway and its former conqueror, Sweden. Crown Princess Märtha and the Crown Prince had three children, Princess Ragnhild Alexandra (now the wife of a commoner, Erling Lorentzen); Princess Astrid Maud; and Prince Harald, now the Crown Prince.

With his wife, Crown Prince Olav made extensive state tours, both of his own land and of foreign countries. In 1939 the royal couple visited the United States on a two-and-one-half-month tour and were given a warm reception both by the public and by government officials, including President Franklin D. Roosevelt. Since that time, Olav has continued to visit the United States and has proved himself a sympathetic friend to this country.

In World War II, when German forces suddenly attacked Norway on April 9, 1940, Prince Olav was well prepared to take the lead in his country's resistance efforts. Aside from his academic military studies, the Prince had the qualification of active training with the Norwegian armed forces and had risen to the rank of General of the Army and Admiral of the Navy.

Although Olav offered to remain in Norway during the Nazi occupation, the Norwegian government refused the offer and in June 1940 insisted that the Crown Prince flee with the other members of the royal family. Thus, with his father and the government-in-exile, Olav departed for England, while his wife and children accepted President Roosevelt's offer of sanctuary in the United States.

On December 23, 1940 Olav traveled incognito to the United States to spend Christmas with his wife and children who were living at a private estate in Maryland. The Prince expressed his belief that the Nazi invaders would eventually be expelled and also reported that the Germans were removing from Norway large amounts of food that his country could ill spare.

Throughout the war, Olav continued to visit the United States and Canada on lecture tours and official missions. He spent most of his time, however, in England, where he and King Haakon directed the Norwegian resistance movement and became the symbols of Norway's fight for freedom. On July 1, 1944 the exiled Norwegian government in London appointed Olav Commander in Chief of Norwegian Forces for Liberation.

At the time of the liberation of Norway, Prince Olav was the first member of the royal family to return home. On May 13, 1945, wearing the battle dress of a Norwegian general, he arrived in Oslo and was given a tumultuous welcome by the largest crowds in the city's history. One of his statements on that occasion was the announcement that the Norwegian High Court would exact the death penalty for all Norwegian traitors, possibly about 2 per cent of the population.

As King Haakon's age and infirmity made it more difficult for him to bear all the burdens of his position, his son came more and more to assist him in affairs of state. During Norway's postwar reconstruction, Olav was kept busy presiding over the dedication ceremonies of newly built roads, bridges, and industries. In 1955, when King Haakon fractured a thigh and became confined to a hospital, Olav took over the rule of his country in the capacity of regent.

When King Haakon VII died on September 21, 1957, Olav V automatically succeeded him as constitutional monarch, submitting to a special meeting of the cabinet a written oath of fealty to the Norwegian constitution. On January 20, 1958, he repeated the oath orally before the Storting. There was no formal coronation to commemorate his accession to the throne. One of his official functions as king is to serve as head of Norway's Evangelical Lutheran Church, the national church of his country. Crown Princess

Märtha did not live to become Queen of Norway; she died on April 5, 1954.

King Olav V has always been an ardent sportsman. He began to ski at the age of three and eventually became an expert ski jumper. Despite his mother's protests, he was for years a successful participant in the Holmekollen ski jumping contests. Also an expert yachtsman, he has won many prizes in Norwegian and foreign regattas and in 1928 sailed his yacht *Norna* as Norway's representative at the Olympic Games in Amsterdam, winning the gold medal in the six-meter class. At Oxford, he also excelled as a fencer.

Athletic in appearance, too, King Olav V is six feet tall and solidly built. He has a ruddy, jovial face and sandy hair that is now receding. His Norwegian speech is marked by a pronounced Oslo accent. Although his rather shrill voice has prevented him from attaining distinction as a speaker, his informal, democratic ways have established him as a favorite with the people of his country. In October 1961 the United Nations High Commissioner for Refugees awarded King Olav V the Fridtjof Nansen medal, given for outstanding services on behalf of refugees.

References

N Y Herald Tribune p2 S 22 '57 por
N Y Times p12 S 22 '57 por
U S News 43:17+ O 4 '57
International Who's Who, 1961-62
Who's Who in America, 1960-61
World Biography (1954)

OZBIRN, CATHARINE (FREEMAN) *See* Ozbirn, Mrs. E. L.

OZBIRN, MRS. E. LEE Nov. 24, 1900(?)- Organization official

Address: b. General Federation of Women's Clubs, 1734 N St., N.W., Washington 6, D.C.; h. Skirvin Tower, Oklahoma City, Okla.

The president of the General Federation of Women's Clubs, Mrs. E. Lee Ozbirn, heads what has been described as the largest group of organized women in the world. Pledged to an action program of "responsible, responsive citizenship for survival," Mrs. Ozbirn has sounded a call for "all-out action on public issues." Long active in club work and community causes, notably with the American Cancer Society, Mrs. Ozbirn was chosen in June 1960 to succeed Miss Chloe Gifford for a two-year term as president of the G.F.W.C.

Since taking office Mrs. Ozbirn has been speaking throughout the United States and abroad, expressing her earnest conviction that "at no time in the history of our country has our way of life been on trial as it has today." To encourage citizenship responsibility she has mapped out strategy with the aid of several universities for an extensive program of adult education. Mrs. Ozbirn wants to make the Federation's membership of some 11,000,000 women in fifty countries "the best informed, best organized, best educated force for good in the world."

Mrs. Ozbirn was born Catharine Freeman, in Era, Texas, about the turn of the century. She gives her birthday as November 24. Her father, Dr. Wiley Howell Freeman, was a "horse and buggy doctor" and also a businessman with large landholdings in Oklahoma and Texas. Her mother, Laura (Seagraves) Freeman, a native of Kentucky, also came from a family of physicians. Katie Freeman had one brother, Dr. I. S. Freeman, who is no longer living; and one sister, now Mrs. Eunice Miller. After receiving her early education in private schools, she attended secondary school at Ward-Belmont, an exclusive school for girls in Nashville, Tennessee, and was valedictorian of her graduating class. She then entered the University of Oklahoma, where she majored in English and participated in social and community activities. After receiving the B.A. degree in 1921 she took additional graduate work in business administration at the university. She was married to E. Lee Ozbirn on November 24, 1923.

Mrs. Ozbirn began her women's club service in the small town of Sentinel, Oklahoma, "vitalizing small tasks given her until they seemed important ones," and developing executive ability on local and state levels. She became a member of the board of directors of the G.F.W.C. in 1940 and has promoted its civic and educational projects. She was state president from 1940 to 1943; general federation director in 1943-44, chairman of the extension division from 1944 to 1947, and chairman of the public affairs department from 1952 to 1954. In 1958 she was elected first vice-president of the G.F.W.C.

Because of her interest in medicine, fostered by her father's career as a physician, Mrs. Ozbirn early participated in the work of health and welfare organizations in Oklahoma City, and subsequently became active in the American Cancer Society. Working through the General Federation of Women's Clubs, Mrs. Ozbirn launched a campaign to "Conquer Uterine Cancer by Early Examination," in co-operation with Dr. G. N. Papanicolaou, whose discovery of early diagnosis of uterine cancer by means of the "smear test" or "Pap test" has been used by doctors in co-operation with the American Cancer Society. "Through a dynamic, persistent and fearless program of public education," Mrs. Ozbirn has said, "the G.F.W.C. has encouraged women to obtain uterine tests, thereby detecting the disease at an early stage, and thus saving thousands of lives." Mrs. Ozbirn served as vice-president of the American Cancer Society for two terms, from 1955 to 1957. In 1958 she was elected an honorary life member of the board of directors.

At the sixty-ninth annual convention of the General Federation of Women's Clubs, held at Washington, D.C. in June 1960, Mrs. Ozbirn was the unopposed choice for the presidency, succeeding Miss Chloe Gifford for a two-year term. Founded in 1890, the General Federation of Women's Club is an international organization with a membership of some 11,000,000 women in fifty countries. Included in its membership are some 850,000 women in 15,500 clubs in the United States. The purpose of the G.F.W.C. is "to bring into communication and to unite the women's clubs and like organizations throughout the world for the purpose of mutual benefit, and

Chase, Ltd.

MRS. E. LEE OZBIRN

for the promotion of their common interest in educational, industrial, philanthropic, literary, artistic, and scientific culture."

In her inaugural address, delivered on June 17, 1960, Mrs. Ozbirn said: "As we plunge into the 'soaring sixties'—and what could well be the 'sobering sixties of great decisions'—never before have our opportunities been *greater,* never before have our challenges loomed quite so large as in this most demanding of all decades." She announced that she would emphasize Western Hemisphere solidarity during her administration, and she proposed round-table discussions and town hall meetings to enlighten the community on the vital issues of the day. She urged clubwomen to re-examine and re-evaluate organizational problems, to lay aside old rules and customs, and to unite to meet the present challenges and threats to democracy.

Among the projects and activities undertaken by the G.F.W.C. under Mrs. Ozbirn's presidency are fellowships and scholarships for foreign students, community improvement contests, research in family living, and women's club conferences in Canada and Latin America. One project, personally planned by Mrs. Ozbirn, provides for a series of seminars on community improvement, to be held in five areas in co-operation with adult education leaders at six universities. She mapped out her strategy with the guidance of two faculty members at the Oklahoma University School of Continuing Education. Questionnaires were sent to every state governor, senior United States senator, and state university president for views on what the country's major issues are, for discussion by state G.F.W.C. members.

Speaking at the seventieth annual convention of the G.F.W.C. at Miami Beach, Florida, in June 1961, Mrs. Ozbirn asserted that clubwomen as a group were potentially more powerful than the atom bomb. "Women *must* get their teeth into vital issues if they are going to measure up

to their potential," she said. With reference to the G.F.W.C.'s current program of "Western Hemispheric Solidarity for Survival," Mrs. Ozbirn announced a new "Dollars for Scholars" program, under which the graduate education of eleven Latin-American women was being sponsored at a cost of $30,000. The program is expected to cost a quarter of a million dollars eventually. The convention passed resolutions expressing support of the United Nations, the North Atlantic Treaty Organization, and the Organization of American States.

After the Miami convention, Mrs. Ozbirn led a group of 144 clubwomen on a thirty-day good will tour covering several Latin-American countries. Upon their return, the participants organized themselves into the "Ozbirn Hemisphere Solidarity Club," with the purpose of keeping alive interest in their Latin-American neighbors and fostering the Federation's Latin-American educational program.

While serving as president of the G.F.W.C. Mrs. Ozbirn lives at the Federation headquarters, 1734 N Street, N.W., Washington, D.C. She supervises a staff of thirty-five, attends meetings of many governmental agencies as the Federation's representative, is hostess to national and international dignitaries, and is a traveling ambassador. The Queen of Denmark and the Queen of Thailand have been among her guests.

Mrs. Ozbirn has been chosen as one of the five most important women in Oklahoma. In 1951 she received the American Cancer Society award, the first lay person in her state to be so honored. In 1952 she received the outstanding community award from both the Quota International and the Soroptimist Club. The Oklahoma City Chamber of Commerce awarded her a citation in January 1961 in appreciation of her interest and participation in civic affairs.

The organizations and committees in which Mrs. Ozbirn has been active include the President's national advisory committee of the White House Conference on Aging, the American Heritage Foundation, National Bible Week, the national advisory committee of the Office of Civil and Defense Mobilization, Radio Free Europe Fund, National Farm-City Committee, and many others. She has served as a consultant for the Children's Bureau with the United States Department of Health, Education, and Welfare and as a member of the board of directors of the Woman's Medical College of Pennsylvania. She has also been on the board of CARE and of the National Multiple Sclerosis Society. In January 1961 she was elected to the board of directors of the National Recreation Association. Mrs. Ozbirn is a Democrat and a member of the Christian Church. Her club memberships include the Cosmopolitan (Sentinel, Oklahoma), Twentieth Century (Oklahoma City), Chautauqua (New York City), and the P.E.O. sisterhood.

Catherine Freeman and E. Lee Ozbirn were married on November 24, 1923. Mr. Ozbirn, who died on October 13, 1954, was a landowner and real-estate operator. Their daughter, Lé Kathrin, is the wife of Lewis H. Bond, Jr., who is president of the Fort Worth National Bank at Fort Worth, Texas. Mrs. Ozbirn has three granddaughters. A diminutive dynamo, Kate Ozbirn is five feet one inch tall and weighs 110 pounds. She has brown hair and brown eyes. Her colleagues have noted her enthusiasm for difficult tasks. Mrs. Ozbirn lives by this creed: "We make our lives significant only as we give ourselves to something that outlasts us."

Reference

Who's Who of American Women (1961-62)

RABAUT, LOUIS CHARLES Dec. 5, 1886- Nov. 12, 1961 United States Representative from Michigan (1935-47 and since 1949); prominent in the House Appropriations Committee; known as both a New Deal and a Fair Deal Democrat. See *Current Biography* (January) 1952.

Obituary

N Y Times p31 N 13 '61

RANDOLPH, JENNINGS Mar. 8, 1902- United States Senator from West Virginia; educator

Address: b. Senate Office Bldg., Washington 25, D.C.; h. 206 Davis Ave., Elkins, W.Va.; 4608 Reservoir Rd., N.W., Washington 7, D.C.

The senior Senator of West Virginia, Jennings Randolph, who was first elected to the United States Senate in November 1958 to fill the unexpired term of the late Matthew M. Neely, in 1960 was chosen by the voters of his state for a full six-year term. Although he declines to be pigeonholed as either a liberal or a conservative, Randolph has generally voted along liberal lines as a member of the House of Representatives from 1933 to 1947 and as a Senator. He considers himself a Jeffersonian democrat.

Beginning his carer as a journalist, Randolph subsequently became a college teacher and administrator, and in 1932 he was elected as one of the youngest members of the Seventy-third Congress. From 1947 until his election to the Senate in 1958, Randolph served as an official with Capital Airlines. He sponsored the Civil Aeronautics Act and much other legislation relating to aviation.

Jennings Randolph was born in Salem, in Harrison County, West Virginia, on March 8, 1902, the son of Ernest and Idell (Bingman) Randolph. He has one sister, now Mrs. Ernestine Carr. He was named after the noted statesman and orator, William Jennings Bryan. Receiving his early education at public schools in Salem, he graduated from Salem Academy in 1920. He then entered Salem College. During his senior year he was president of the West Virginia Inter-collegiate Press Association. After getting the B.A. degree in 1924, Randolph became a reporter on the staff of the Clarksburg (West Virginia) *Daily Telegram*. In 1925 he took a job as associate editor of the *West Virginia Review*, published at Charleston. In 1926 he joined the faculty of Davis and Elkins College at Elkins, West Virginia. He became head of the department of public speaking and journalism and remained in this position until 1932.

Wide World

JENNINGS RANDOLPH

In 1930, at the age of twenty-eight, Jennings Randolph campaigned as a Democrat against Frank L. Bowman, the incumbent Republican representative in Congress for the Second West Virginia District, but he was defeated. In 1932 he again contended for Bowman's Congressional seat, which he won in November in the Democratic landslide that carried Franklin D. Roosevelt to the Presidency. He was introduced to the outgoing Congress by Representative Ruth Bryan Owen of Florida, daughter of William Jennings Bryan.

Re-elected to the six Congresses that followed, Randolph was named to the House Civil Service Committee in his second term. He became its chairman in 1945, retiring as chairman of the District of Columbia Committee to take that post. He also served as assistant majority whip and on House committees on Labor, Roads, and Expenditures in the Executive Departments. He belonged to the Mines and Mining Committee and was chairman of its subcommittee on coal.

As early as March 1940 Randolph offered a House resolution proposing that the British West Indies and British Honduras be ceded to the United States as part payment of war debts. In August 1943 he urged that negotiations be started with Denmark for the acquisition of Greenland, for its strategic value and its importance to aviation. Randolph was a sponsor of the Civil Aeronautics Act of 1938, and he has been the author or co-sponsor of other measures relating to aviation, including provisions for federal aid to airports, civil pilot training, and air mail pick-up. He helped to establish National Aviation Day and the National Air Museum. From 1942 to 1945 he served as counselor for the National Aeronautical Association, and in May 1944 he organized the first Congressional flying club.

A strong supporter of New Deal domestic legislation and of the Truman administration's

RANDOLPH, JENNINGS—*Continued*

European aid policies, Randolph in 1945 voted for the extension of price controls, for the continuation of subsidies under the Reconstruction Finance Corporation, for the government reorganization bill, and for the anti-poll tax bill. On the other hand, he voted against the extension of the Trade Agreements Act. He voted in favor of the establishment of a permanent House Committee on Un-American Activities. In 1946 he voted for the Employment Act, for continued rent and price controls, for the extension of the military draft, and for the loan to Great Britain. He opposed the Case strike-control bill, but supported President Harry S. Truman's emergency strike-control bill. He consistently sponsored legislation calling for the merging of the armed services under a single department of defense.

Defeated for re-election to Congress in November 1946, Randolph was in 1947 named assistant to the president and director of public relations for Capital Airlines, and held this dual position until his election to the Senate in 1958. Meanwhile, until 1953, he continued to occupy the chair in public speaking at Southeastern University in Washington, D.C., to which he had been appointed in 1935, and from 1952 to 1958 he served as dean of that university's school of business administration. He also served, from 1948 to 1958, as a faculty member of the Leadership Training Institute in Washington, D.C.

From 1947 to 1949 Randolph was chairman of the Aviation Planning Commission in Washington, D.C., and from 1953 to 1956 he was a director of the Washington Board of Trade. (He had previously served as chairman of its world trade committee.) In May 1953 he was elected chairman of a panel set up by the Department of Commerce to study federal aid to airport construction. Meanwhile, Randolph continued to play an active role in Democratic politics. He served as a delegate-at-large from West Virginia to the Democratic National Conventions of 1948, 1952, and 1956, and he was a member of the subcommittee of the convention resolutions committee that drafted the Democratic national platform of 1956.

Elected to the United States Senate on November 4, 1958 to fill the unexpired term of the late Matthew M. Neely of West Virginia, Randolph polled 64.4 per cent of the vote in his contest with Republican candidate John D. Hoblitzell, Jr., who was the interim appointee of Governor Cecil Underwood. Seated in the Eighty-fifth Congress on the following day, Senator Randolph thus gained seniority over newcomers to the Eighty-sixth Congress.

In the Eighty-sixth Congress, Randolph was assigned to the Senate Labor and Public Welfare Committee, the Public Works Committee, and the Select Committee on Small Business. In the spring of 1959 he joined with Senators John F. Kennedy of Massachusetts and Wayne Morse of Oregon in a drafting of a section in the Kennedy labor bill designed to speed up union elections. In May 1959 he proposed legislation to carry on the federal highway program without resort to increased gasoline taxes. In October 1959 he accused the Eisenhower administration of weakness in handling the problem of chronic unemployment, and in February 1960 he called Republican farm proposals "a patchwork affair." Commenting in March 1960 on the dual launching of Atlas and Titan missiles, Senator Randolph said: "I am thinking of the constructive work that the people of West Virginia could do with the money spent on even one of these expensive duds that aim for outer space and then flop in the ocean."

In the key voting during the Eighty-sixth Congress, Randolph in 1959 voted in favor of foreign aid appropriations, liberalizing veterans' pensions, and overriding the President's vetoes on the Housing Act and the public works appropriation bill. He opposed the McClellan amendments aimed at strengthening existing labor legislation, and he voted against confirmation of Lewis L. Strauss as Secretary of Commerce. In 1960 he voted against efforts to weaken proposed civil rights legislation and against the attempt to reduce the number of workers to be covered under proposed minimum wage legislation. He supported salary increases for federal employees and medical aid to the aged under Social Security, and he voted to override the Presidential veto on the Area Redevelopment Act.

On November 8, 1960 Randolph was elected to a full six-year Senate term, defeating the Republican candidate, Governor Cecil Underwood, and polling 55.3 per cent of the votes cast. In the Eighty-seventh Congress he served on the Senate Post Office and Civil Service Committee in addition to committees earlier assigned. He was also chairman of the subcommittee on public buildings and grounds of the Public Works Committee, and he was chairman of the subcommittee on relations of business with government of the Select Committee on Small Business.

In the voting on key issues in 1961 Randolph generally supported the policies of the Kennedy administration. He voted for the administration's depressed areas bill, the housing bill, emergency extension of unemployment insurance, minimum wage legislation, and federal aid to schools. He strongly opposed aid to parochial schools. In June 1961 Randolph headed a group of sixty-three Senators who offered a study resolution calling for a special national study of fuels and energy to forestall an "energy gap."

A contributor to magazines, Randolph wrote a newspaper column, "Washington Week by Week," while he was a member of the House of Representatives. He is now associate editor and co-owner of the Elkins, West Virginia, newspaper, the *Randolph Enterprise-Review*. With J. A. Bell, he is the co-author of a guide to public speaking, published in 1939 under the title *Speaking That Wins* and reissued in 1951 as *Chairman, Ladies and Gentlemen*. Randolph wrote the chapter on federal airport legislation in Lucien Zacharoff's symposium, *Vital Problems of Air Commerce* (Collins, 1946).

Randolph is a member of Tau Kappa Alpha (the honorary forensic fraternity), the Speech Association of America, and the American Platform Guild, and he is a former Redpath Chautauqua lecturer. His fraternal organization is the Loyal Order of Moose. His memberships also include the Elkins Rotary Club and the Tygart

Valley Lions Club; the Elkins and West Virginia Chambers of Commerce; the American Federation of the Physically Handicapped; the West Virginia Press Association; and the American Academy of Political and Social Science. He is a member of the board of governors of the National United Service Organizations, and he is a trustee of Salem College and of Davis and Elkins College. Randolph has also served as counselor, treasurer, and vice-president of the National Aeronautic Association; as treasurer of the American Road Builders Association; and as chairman of the air panel of the Transportation Association of America.

In 1939 Davis and Elkins College conferred an honorary LL.D. upon Randolph, and in 1940 he received an honorary D.Lit. degree from Southeastern University. He also holds an honorary Doctor of Aeronautical Science degree, awarded to him by Salem College in 1943. He received the Randolph County Civic Merit Award in 1948; the Outstanding Service Award from the National Federation of the Blind and Blinded Veterans Association in 1956; and the West Virginia Son of the Year award from the West Virginia Society of the District of Columbia in 1960.

On February 18, 1933 Jennings Randolph married Mary Katherine Babb of Keyser, West Virginia. They have two sons: Jennings Randolph, Jr., a businessman and broadcaster in Clarksburg, West Virginia; and Frank Babb Randolph, a student at American University in Washington, D.C. Randolph is a member of the Seventh Day Baptist Church. Of portly build, he is five feet ten inches tall and weighs 208 pounds. He has been described as a "skillful speaker, with a genial approach, a firm handshake, and a trace of the snake-oil vendor" (*Time*, October 17, 1960).

References

N Y Times p24 N 6 '58 por
Biographical Directory of the American Congress, 1774-1949 (1950)
Congressional Directory (1961)
Who's Who in America, 1960-61
Who's Who in United States Politics (1952)
Who's Who in World Aviation and Astronautics (1958)

RAYBURN, SAM(UEL TALIAFERRO) Jan. 6, 1882-Nov. 16, 1961 United States Representative from Texas since 1913; first elected Speaker of the House in 1940; served as Representative and Speaker longer than any other man in American history; permanent chairman of the Democratic National Conventions of 1948, 1952, and 1956. See *Current Biography* (March) 1949.

Obituary

N Y Times p 1+ N 17 '61

REYBOLD, EUGENE Feb. 13, 1884-Nov. 21, 1961 United States Army officer; chief of the Corps of Engineers (1941-45); directed the construction of the Pentagon; retired in 1946 in the rank of lieutenant general. See *Current Biography* (June) 1945.

Obituary

N Y Times p33 N 22 '61

RUSSELL, JAMES S(ARGENT) Mar. 22, 1903- United States Navy officer; NATO commander

Address: b. Navy Department, Washington 25, D.C.; h. 7738 Walnut Ave., S.W., Tacoma 99, Wash.

One of the top commands of the North Atlantic Treaty Organization (NATO) is held by veteran United States naval airman Admiral James S. Russell. He was appointed in August 1961 to assume command on January 1, 1962 of Allied air, sea, and land forces in the Mediterranean and southern Europe. Russell, an authority on carrier aircraft warfare, once headed the Navy's Bureau of Aeronautics and is also former Vice-Chief of Naval Operations. As Commander in Chief South (CINCSOUTH), he succeeds Admiral Charles R. Brown in one of four commands subordinate to General Lauris Norstad, Supreme Allied Commander, who selected Russell with the approval of the United Kingdom, France, Italy, Greece, and Turkey.

The main influence in his choice of the Navy as a career, James Sargent Russell has said, is the fact that his boyhood home (and lifelong legal residence) is a seaport. He was born on March 22, 1903 in Tacoma, Washington to Ambrose James Russell, an architect, and Loella Janet (Sargent) Russell. He attended Tacoma's De-Koven Hall Boys School and the Stadium High School, where his favorite extracurricular activity was swimming.

World War I was still in progress when Russell graduated from high school in 1918. He tried to enlist in the Navy, but was rejected when it was discovered that he was underage. Joining the Merchant Marine instead, he spent the next four years either at sea or as a student at the United States Shipping Board Navigation School at the University of Washington in Seattle. He was appointed to the United States Naval Academy at Annapolis, Maryland in the summer of 1922 and graduated with the B.S. degree and an ensign's commission on June 3, 1926. At the Naval Academy he won the Daughters of the American Revolution Sword for Seamanship, a varsity letter in gymnastics, and class numerals in swimming.

Ensign Russell served aboard the battleship *West Virginia* until August 1928, when he entered the Naval Air Station at Pensacola, Florida for flight training. At the completion of the course in May 1929 he was designated a naval aviator and two months later was promoted to lieutenant (j.g.). He returned to the USS *West Virginia* as a member of the air unit, and he later also served as a patrol squadron gunnery officer for six months, before being sent back to Annapolis in June 1932 as a "general line" student at the Postgraduate School of the Naval Academy.

In a second year at the graduate school Russell studied aeronautical engineering. He then en-

ADM. JAMES S. RUSSELL

rolled at the California Institute of Technology in Pasadena, where he received his M.Sc. degree in aeronautical engineering in 1935. The title of his master's thesis was "Static Stability in Aircraft as Affected by Running Propellor." After a tour of duty as engineering officer of Bombing Squadron Five-B, he served for three years aboard the USS *Yorktown*. In June 1939 he was assigned to the aircraft-carriers desk of the Navy Department's Bureau of Aeronautics.

When the United States entered World War II in December 1941, Russell was in command of Patrol Squadron 42. Leading his squadron in the early Aleutian campaign, from February to October 1942, he established his wing's first base at Cold Bay. He also led the first naval air unit to operate out of Nome and made many fog-enveloped patrols over the upper Bering Sea. He won the Distinguished Flying Cross for "heroism and extraordinary achievement" against enemy Japanese forces during those eight months. He was also awarded the Air Medal and the Legion of Merit, and Patrol Squadron 42 received the Navy Unit Commendation.

The Navy recalled Russell to Washington in the fall of 1942 to direct the military requirements division of the Bureau of Aeronautics. He had risen gradually through the ranks and held a captaincy when he was returned to the Pacific in August 1944. As chief of staff to the commander of Carrier Division 2, a fast carrier task group, he co-ordinated all components of his group into one striking force, operating at Palau, Iwo Jima, and Okinawa. His "courage, inspiring leadership under aircraft bombing and suicide attack" won him a Gold Star in lieu of a second Legion of Merit.

From the end of the war in the Pacific in September 1945 to March 1946 Captain Russell served with the Air Technical Intelligence Group in Japan and as a member of the naval analysis division of the Strategic Bombing Survey. He also

commanded USS *Bairoko* for about a year before he returned to Washington in June 1948 as head of the weapons branch of the Atomic Energy Commission.

Russell conceived the basic plan for Task Group 7.1, Joint Task Force Seven, Operation Sandstone, and, as commander of Task Group 7.1 (the USS *Albemarle*) from February to June 1948, was responsible for conducting the test program. In this mission, states the citation accompanying his Gold Star in lieu of a third Legion of Merit, he "contributed directly to the successful scientific completion of the Atomic tests at Eniwetok and thereby to the national security."

Another position that Russell filled for the Atomic Energy Commission was deputy director of the military application division, from July 1948 to January 1951. He spent the following year in the Mediterranean as commanding officer of the attack carrier *Coral Sea*, functioning as a unit of the Sixth Fleet. Then recalled to the Office of the Chief of Naval Operations, he served first as head of the military requirements and new developments branch and later, after his promotion in July 1953 to rear admiral, as director of the air warfare division. From May 1954 to March 1955 he commanded successively the Anti-Submarine Carrier Division 17 and the Attack Carrier Division 5 in the Far East.

The Navy Department's Bureau of Aeronautics, of which Russell became chief in March 1955, is responsible for the design, development, and material effectiveness of Navy and Marine Corps aircraft. It therefore fell to him, in October 1955, to explain to investigators for a House of Representatives Armed Services subcommittee why sixty F-3H Demon jet fighter planes had been powered with engines of insufficient thrust. These planes, ordered in 1951, had been grounded after eleven crashes in which four pilots were killed. Russell explained that the Navy had taken calculated risks under the pressure of the emergency in Korea and that efforts were being made to forecast aircraft performance with greater accuracy. "In this day of rapid technological progress," he pointed out, however, "we must venture into the unknown."

In November 1956 Russell announced that the Navy would go ahead with production of Seamaster jet bombers despite the failure of two experimental models and also that a combination rocket-jet plane was being built. The Collier Trophy awarded annually "for the greatest achievement in aviation in America," was presented in December 1957 jointly to Russell and Charles J. McCarthy and his associates in Chance Vought Aircraft, Inc., of Dallas, for their conception in 1952 and later development of the supersonic Crusader Navy fighter, the first carrier-based aircraft to fly at over 1,000 miles an hour.

Along with his promotion to vice-admiral in the summer of 1957, Russell received an appointment to the posts of Deputy Commander in Chief of the United States Atlantic Fleet and chief of staff and aide to the Commander in Chief. In July 1958 he was promoted to full admiral and at that time succeeded Admiral Harry D. Felt as Vice-Chief of Naval Operations in Washington. Addressing a reserve officers' convention in October 1960, Admiral Russell said that the concept of a "single service" was "not a panacea for whatever evils are allegedly besetting the military services. . . The answer is, instead, mutual respect, understanding and a close co-operation among the present military services."

General Lauris Norstad announced in August 1961 the appointment of Admiral Russell as Commander in Chief of Allied Forces in southern Europe, to become effective in January 1962. When he left his post of Vice-Chief of Naval Operations in November 1961, he was decorated with the Distinguished Service Medal for demonstrating ability "of the highest caliber" during his three years in that office. Russell's new headquarters are in Naples, Italy.

James S. Russell and Dorothy Irene Johnson of Hoquiam, Washington, daughter of the late United States Representative Albert Johnson, were married on April 13, 1929 and have two sons, Donald Johnson and Kenneth McDonald. Admiral Russell is five feet ten and a half inches in height and weighs around 175 pounds. His eyes are blue, and his brown hair is now turning to gray. Russell mentions tennis, swimming, and sailing as favorite recreations. He is a Fellow of the Institute of Aerospace Sciences (as an associate Fellow he was honorary chairman of the 1957 national aviation meeting) and a member of the Naval Institute. His church is the Episcopal.

References

Navy 2:5 Ag '59 por
Officer 36:7 Ja '60 por
U S News 51:24 Ag 28 '61

American Men in Government (1949)
Navy Register, 1960
Who's Who in America, 1960-61
Who's Who in World Aviation and Astronautics (1958)

SHURLOCK, GEOFFREY M. Aug. 10, 1894- Motion-picture executive

Address: b. Motion Picture Association of America, Inc., 8480 Beverly Blvd., Los Angeles, Calif.

Probably the most powerful nongovernmental censor of motion pictures in the world is Geoffrey M. Shurlock, who since 1954 has been administrator of the Motion Picture Production Code, succeeding Joseph I. Breen. Shurlock grants the seal of approval to American motion pictures that, in his opinion, conform to the ethical standards of the Motion Picture Production Code. He came to his position after a long career in motion-picture production and regulation.

In 1934 the Motion Picture Association of America, Inc., originally known as the Motion Picture Producers and Distributors of America, began the practice of bestowing on American pictures, before their release, a seal of approval signifying that they conformed with the Motion Picture Production Code. The code itself dates back to 1930, and the movement for self-censorship in the American film industry dates back to 1922, when Hollywood executives responded to the widespread censorship of motion pictures by civic governmental boards.

Geoffrey M. Shurlock was born on August 10, 1894 in Liverpool, England. When he was seven years old, his parents left England for the United States and settled in San Diego, California. There Geoffrey was educated in private schools and specialized in music and foreign languages. His first professional contact with the motion-picture industry took place in 1922 (some sources give 1923), when he was hired as literary secretary to author Rupert Hughes, who was at that time associated in film production with the firm then known as the Goldwyn Company. In 1926 Shurlock joined Paramount Pictures as a story reader. He rose to the position of assistant to Benjamin P. Schulberg, then a vice-president in charge of production, and later was made the studio's scenario editor.

With the advent of talking pictures in 1929, Geoffrey M. Shurlock was made executive in charge of Paramount's foreign language productions and headed a studio unit sent to Paris for dubbing Paramount films. But Shurlock preferred California to France and returned to Paramount's Hollywood offices, again in the scenario department. He remained with Paramount until 1932.

In 1932 Geoffrey M. Shurlock began his association with the Motion Picture Producers and Distributors of America (popularly known as the "Hays Office" in honor of its first director, Will H. Hays). Shurlock's first position with what was to become the Motion Picture Association of America, Inc., was as a member of the studio relations committee, the forerunner of the Production Code Administration.

In 1930 the Motion Picture Producers and Distributors of America had adopted a formal code of ethics written by the Reverend Daniel Lord, a Jesuit, and Martin Quigley, a Roman Catholic publisher of a film trade paper. But the moral level of American movies had not risen as a result. On the contrary, Hollywood producers who wanted to attract impoverished Depression audiences and exploit the realistic possibilities of spoken dialogue often resorted to sensationalism in their pictures.

Adding to the distribution difficulties imposed by the lengthening list of civic film censorship boards, a committee of Roman Catholic bishops in 1934 established the National Legion of Decency and threatened the motion-picture industry with public censure for its promulgation of immorality. Hoping to stem the tide of protest by regulating the industry from within, the Motion Picture Producers and Distributors of America appointed Joseph I. Breen as first director of the Production Code Administration. Geoffrey M. Shurlock acted as his assistant.

Instituting the practice of awarding a seal of approval to morally acceptable films, Breen succeeded in enforcing the Production Code and thereby established the pattern of the Hollywood "family picture," morally unobjectionable but vulnerable to the charges of sentimentality and escapism. Breen remained the exacting ruler of the Production Code Administration until he retired in 1954, except for a one-year period in 1941-42, when he accepted a post with the RKO studios. Geoffrey M. Shurlock served as acting head of the Production Code Administration during this time.

(Continued next page)

Impact Photos, Inc.

GEOFFREY M. SHURLOCK

When Geoffrey M. Shurlock replaced Breen as Production Code Administrator in 1954, the motion-picture industry was being undermined by the soaring popularity of television. Forced to compete with free entertainment, Hollywood producers saw their solution to this competition in offering to the public themes and situations that could not be treated on the home screen. Reassured by the public's welcome of foreign films dealing with subjects considered taboo by the Production Code, Hollywood film makers were pressing for the freedom to create more adult film fare.

The producer and director Otto Preminger proved the most daring opponent of the Production Code Administration. In 1953 he released *The Moon is Blue*, a comedy about attempted seduction, although the Administration (under Breen) had denied it the seal of approval. In 1956 he again overrode the Administration (now under Shurlock) by releasing *The Man With the Golden Arm*, a drama about narcotics addiction, which had also been denied official approval.

When the Preminger films brought long lines to the box office, the Production Code Administration under Geoffrey M. Shurlock decided that the time had come to liberalize the Code. In December 1956 the Motion Picture Association of America announced that four formerly taboo subjects—narcotics, abortion, prostitution, and kidnaping—were now considered acceptable, if kept within certain limits. The former restriction against the depiction of miscegenation was discarded.

The liberalization of the Production Code illustrates one of Shurlock's fundamental beliefs—that morals in motion pictures only reflect the public's own standards. "The relaxation of movie morality," he has said, "has been much less than that of public morality. The movies are, to a large extent, based on those novels and plays that

have won the widest public approval. These books and plays did not come out of a vacuum. They reflected changes in public attitudes" (New York *Times,* February 12, 1961).

Shurlock and his organization have continued to exhibit a liberalism that was unheard of during the regime of Joseph I. Breen. In July 1961 the Production Code Administration reversed itself on *The Moon is Blue* and *The Man with the Golden Arm.* Shurlock said that *The Moon is Blue* should have been granted a seal when it was first released in 1953. Another epochal change in the Motion Picture Production Code was effected on October 3, 1961 when the board of directors of the Motion Picture Association of America, acting in response to a request from Shurlock, amended the code to enable film makers to treat the subject of homosexuality. Several movie makers had films in progress that dealt with that subject. In the more and more permissive climate of American movie making Shurlock continues to adhere to one basic tenet of the Motion Picture Production Code: "The sympathy of the audience shall never be thrown to the side of crime, wrongdoing, evil, or sin."

The change of attitude on the part of the movie industry toward controversial themes has aroused the ire of some religious and governmental groups. Geoffrey M. Shurlock has twice been summoned by Congressional investigating committees to answer questions about the possible harmful effects of films on the morals of American youth and the limits that the industry intends to impose upon the treatment of such themes as homosexuality on the screen.

Shurlock carefully plans his working day. Two of his six assistants go over the script of every Hollywood film, referring any questionable passages in important pictures to Shurlock himself. Shurlock and his team also attend a screening of the completed film and often pass judgment on segments of the film while it is still in production.

In addition to this direct scrutiny, Shurlock and his aides spend much time in discussing and arguing points of censorship with the film makers themselves. A vice-president of the Motion Picture Association of America as well as director of the Production Code Administration, Shurlock has traveled abroad on official business: to Europe in 1932, to Latin America in 1944-45, and again to Europe in 1956.

Geoffrey M. Shurlock has been described as "a small, roundish man of staccato speech and modest manner" (New York *Times,* February 12, 1961). The same source reports him as explaining that his solitary ways in the gregarious film colony result from his fear of being "sucked into personal relationships with the people whose work you have to judge." Shurlock has been a widower since 1953. He is an Episcopalian.

References

Life 48:79+ F 29 '60 por
Look 23:80+ S 29 '59 por
N Y Times II p5 O 24 '54
N Y Times Mag p15+ F 12 '61 por
International Motion Picture Almanac, 1961
International Television Almanac, 1961

SITTERLY, MRS. BANCROFT WALKER
See Sitterly, C. M.

SITTERLY, CHARLOTTE MOORE Sept. 24, 1898- Astrophysicist

Address: b. National Bureau of Standards, Washington 25, D.C.; h. 3711 Brandywine St., N.W., Washington 16, D.C.

One of the foremost authorities in the world on the composition of the sun is Dr. Charlotte Moore Sitterly, an astrophysicist with the National Bureau of Standards and the author of many works about solar and atomic spectra. She is engaged in completing the fourth volume of a compendium on atomic energy levels. Dr. Sitterly has also been working with Professor Marcellus Minnaert of the University of Utrecht on the revision of earlier editions of his work on the solar spectrum. Her interpretations have been recognized by scientists throughout the world as the most complete summary of atomic, spectroscopic, and solar spectrum data. Before joining the atomic physics division of the National Bureau of Standards in 1945, she had worked at the Princeton University Observatory.

Her efforts to keep astrophysicists supplied with laboratory data needed for the interpretation of the various spectra of celestial bodies have brought Dr. Sitterly international recognition. The most recent acknowledgment of her outstanding scientific achievements was made in February 1961, when the United States government named her as one of six women to receive the first annual Federal Woman's Award.

Dr. Sitterly is the former Charlotte Emma Moore, one of the six children of George Winfield and Elizabeth Palmer (Walton) Moore. She was born on September 24, 1898 in Ercildoun, in Chester County, Pennsylvania, in the heart of the Quaker country. Her father was superintendent of schools in Chester County and her mother was a schoolteacher. The parents imbued the children (three girls and three boys) with a love of learning. Charlotte was educated at the local public schools and at Coatesville High School. After she graduated in 1916 she matriculated as a mathematics student at Swarthmore College in Swarthmore, Pennsylvania, where she held a working fellowship, tutored students, and performed tasks for faculty members to help pay her expenses. These jobs did not prevent her from joining extracurricular activities, and she participated in the glee club, the hockey team, and the student government association (of which she was treasurer). She maintained a brilliant scholastic record, and when she graduated with a Bachelor of Arts degree in mathematics in 1920, she was elected to membership in Phi Beta Kappa.

Acting upon the suggestion of her physics professor at Swarthmore College, Dr. John A. Miller, Charlotte Moore decided on a career in astronomy. In 1920 she accepted her first job as a mathematics computer at the Princeton University Observatory. She worked with the eminent astronomer, Professor Henry Norris Russell, whose spectroscopic studies resulted in the development of a theory of stellar evolution. Charlotte Moore did research on atomic spectra and astrophysical

CHARLOTTE MOORE SITTERLY

problems, laying the foundation for her present studies of the solar and stellar spectra. Five years later she was appointed to a similar post at the Mount Wilson Observatory in Pasadena, California, where she collaborated with Dr. Charles E. St. John in the preparation of a monograph on the solar spectrum.

She returned to Princeton in 1928, but resigned the following year to pursue advanced study in astronomy. As a candidate for the doctorate at the University of California at Berkeley, she held the highly prized Lick Fellowship. She received her Ph.D. degree in 1931. Her thesis was concerned with atomic lines in the sun-spot spectrum.

After she completed her graduate studies in 1931, Dr. Charlotte Moore was appointed to the staff of the Princeton University Observatory as a research assistant, and in 1936 she became an associate. On May 30, 1937 Charlotte Moore married Dr. Bancroft Walker Sitterly, an astronomer and physicist, whom she met while working at the Princeton Observatory. In 1945 Dr. Charlotte Sitterly joined the National Bureau of Standards, a subsidiary of the United States Department of Commerce, as a physicist and astronomer in the spectroscopy section of the atomic physics division. She has had a major role in supervising a program that had as its main objective the preparation and compilation of tables of atomic energy levels as obtained from the analyses of optical spectra. Three volumes have already been published, and Dr. Sitterly has begun work on the fourth and final volume, which will be concerned with the extremely complex rare-earth spectra.

In conjunction with the material on atomic energy levels, Dr. Sitterly has prepared multiplet tables, which contain laboratory wavelengths of lines that are essential in the study of stellar spectra. The tables not only increase our knowledge of abundances of chemical elements in the stars, but are also important for a detailed study

SUGGS, LOUISE—*Continued*

Women's Open, Titleholders', and Saint Petersburg Open in 1959. She was the leading money winner in 1960, and her victories for that year included the Dallas Open, Trumbull Women's Open, San Antonio Civitan Open, and Triangle Round-Robin.

Her record in 1961 typifies the consistent excellence of her performance over the years. In January she scored 229 for three rounds to win the Sea Island (Georgia) Ladies' tournament by one stroke over Marlene Bauer Hagge and Ruth Jessen. In February she proved what she has long contended—that, given the equal opportunity to reach from tee to green in one shot, the women would "beat the stuffing" out of the men. Playing on the Palm Beach, Florida course, where holes vary in length from 108 to 215 yards, with all holes par-three, Miss Suggs shot a 156 for three rounds and beat out five other women and twelve male professionals for the title. The males included such illustrious players as Sam Snead, Lew Worsham, and Dow Finsterwald.

In March Miss Suggs won the Bradentown (Florida) Women's Open by two strokes with a score of 293. In April she was home first in the $10,000 Civitan Open at Dallas, Texas, the third time in succession that she won that tourney. In June she finished second to Mary Lena Faulk in the Triangle Round-Robin tournament, which she had previously won three times. Although she trailed behind in the United States Women's Open later in that month, she won the Kansas City Women's Open in August. In October she set a new record for women professionals when she won her forty-ninth professional tournament and her fifth victory of the season by winning the San Antonio Civitan Women's Open tournament.

In addition to playing professional golf, Miss Suggs designs women's golfing clothes. Her creations are on view in leading department stores. She is the editor and co-author with six other women professionals of a book, *Golf for Women* (Doubleday, 1960). She is now the resident professional at Castleview Course in Atlanta. She has served as president of the Ladies' Professional Golfers Association and is at present a member at large. In 1951 she was elected to golf's Hall of Fame.

Louise Suggs is unmarried. She is five feet five inches tall and weighs 135 pounds. When she began to play professional golf, she weighed only 115 pounds, but small though she was, she could hit the ball up to 236 yards. She can now drive a golf ball 260 yards. Her power derives from her arms, which she has strengthened by horseback riding, swimming, and bowling.

Writing in *Sports Illustrated* (June 19, 1961), Barbara Heilman describes Louise Suggs as a "*grownup*" and a "definitive loner," and notes that she occasionally alienates people by her forthrightness. She adds, however: "Fond of her or not, everyone respects her absolutely—personally and as a golfer." Although Miss Suggs told Barbara Heilman that she has no friends, her fellow professional golfer Ruth Jessen has said: "Louise is always doing things for you, and never lets you know she did." Traveling anywhere from 35,000 to 55,000 miles in a season, Miss Suggs is sometimes accompanied by her mother, but usually she drives alone. "I could team up with other girls, of course," she has said, "but I just can't stand gabbing females."

Off the course, Miss Suggs displays a warm smile, and she is an interesting and intelligent conversationalist. While playing, however, she becomes as hard as flint, especially in a close match. She has earned the affectionate nickname, Little Toughie. "Golf is very much like a love affair," she wrote in the introductory chapter to *Golf for Women*. "If you don't take it seriously, it's no fun; if you do, it breaks your heart. Don't break your heart, but flirt with the possibility."

References

N Y Times p46 D 14 '59 por
Sports Illus 14:60+ Je 19 '61 por

SWITZER, MARY E(LIZABETH) Feb. 16, 1900- Government official

Address: b. Department of Health, Education, and Welfare, Washington 25, D.C.; h. 422 Underhill Place, Alexandria, Va.

A "dedicated bureaucrat," according to her own description, Mary E. Switzer has served as director of the Office of Vocational Rehabilitation since 1950. She holds one of the highest appointive offices in the federal government ever given to a woman. Her directorship has been marked by an impressive growth in federal and state rehabilitation programs. Her work on behalf of the handicapped has earned her one of medicine's greatest honors, an Albert Lasker Award, and she is the first woman to have been thus honored.

Mary Elizabeth Switzer was born in Newton Upper Falls, Massachusetts, on February 16, 1900, the daughter of Julius F. and Margaret (Moore) Switzer. Raised and educated in the Boston area, she attended Radcliffe College, where she was the first undergraduate to major in international law. After receiving her B.A. degree in 1921 Miss Switzer moved to Washington, D.C. and, taking a job as assistant secretary with the Minimum Wage Board, embarked upon what was to become a lifetime of government service. In 1922 she joined the Treasury Department as a junior economist. She also served for a time as executive secretary of the Women's International League for Peace and Freedom.

During her early years in Washington Miss Switzer met Tracy Copp, a pioneer in aiding the handicapped. The older woman's dedication to her work, added to the opportunities that she afforded her young friend to view the problems of the disabled at firsthand, made Miss Switzer decide, "I'd like to get into this work if the chance ever comes."

It was some time, however, before Miss Switzer's career took her into the field of rehabilitation. She remained in the Treasury Department, where she was transferred to the chief clerk's office in 1924. From 1928 to 1933 she was in charge of press intelligence for the Secretary of the Treasury. During part of this period, from 1929 to 1933, she served also as assistant chief of the White House editorial reports service. In

1933 she was made assistant chief of the correspondence division with the office of the Secretary of the Treasury.

In 1934 Miss Switzer took a big step toward her goal when she was appointed assistant to the Assistant Secretary of the Treasury in charge of the Public Health Service, then a part of the Treasury Department. She held that position until 1939. From 1935 to 1938 she also served as assistant to the chairman of the interdepartmental commission to co-ordinate health and welfare activities. In that capacity she was instrumental in the establishment of the Federal Security Agency, which was set up in 1939 to concentrate on health and welfare programs. She joined the new agency as assistant to the Federal Security Administrator.

During World War II Miss Switzer represented the FSA on the War Manpower Commission, aiding in the development of the procurement and assignment service for physicians, dentists, veterinarians, sanitary engineers, and nurses. She also assisted the director of the War Research Service. For these services, she received the President's Certificate of Merit, the highest award given to a regular Civil Service employee.

On November 9, 1950 Miss Switzer was appointed to succeed Michael J. Shortley as director of the Office of Vocational Rehabilitation. The OVR was then under the Federal Security Agency and was subsequently transferred to the Department of Health, Education, and Welfare, when the latter was established in 1953. When Miss Switzer took over its leadership, the government's program of vocational rehabilitation was thirty years old. Begun in 1920 as an outgrowth of the rehabilitation services rendered to World War I veterans, the work of the OVR was still extremely limited in scope. During its first twenty-five years, the number of disabled rehabilitated annually averaged only 10,000. While interest in vocational rehabilitation was stimulated to some degree by the manpower shortages that accompanied World War II, the emphasis of the program, as late as 1945, remained on quick courses for the most promising individuals. Almost no aid was offered to the severely handicapped.

Soon after she took office, Miss Switzer recommended that a group of nongovernmental experts make an objective study of national needs and resources for rehabilitation. The study was undertaken and resulted in plans for the expansion of the national rehabilitation program, with its announced goal the rehabilitation of 250,000 persons a year. Thanks to Miss Switzer's efforts, this blueprint was embodied in the Vocational Rehabilitation Act of 1954. Passed unanimously by Congress, this legislation made possible an increase in the supply of rehabilitation personnel. It gave teaching grants to colleges and universities and fellowships to trainees, expanded facilities through the United States Public Health Service's program of grants for hospital construction, and intensified rehabilitation research through grants administered directly by the Office of Vocational Rehabilitation.

Vocational rehabilitation is that specialty within the general field of rehabilitation that aims at restoring the handicapped person to work. It is based on the principle that work is both a part of therapy and an end in itself. "Work," says Miss Switzer, "is not a separate compartment of a person's life. Work is the central structure which gives it purpose and meaning . . . [it] is even a factor in medical care and in the physical restoration of the disabled person, for it represents the *reason why* of rehabilitation."

Miss Switzer believes that "the ability to earn eliminates or reduces dependency and equalizes other opportunities for the disabled person to assume an accepted place in the community." Tnus, she sees vocational rehabilitation as fundamental to the democratic concept of equality of opportunity for all. By work Miss Switzer does not mean busywork or merely placing the handicapped in a few menial tasks, but "bringing the person to the highest and most productive place he can achieve." According to standards set forth in the Vocational Rehabilitation Act of 1954, a disabled person is not considered rehabilitated until he is employed to his *own* satisfaction, as well as that of his employer.

Since Miss Switzer has taken office, the number of persons returned to work annually has risen from 56,000 in 1950 to 88,275 in 1960, a record for the fifth consecutive year. Even more significant than numbers is the fact that the vocational rehabilitation program now reaches persons suffering from severe disabilities that would have caused them to be termed "infeasible of rehabilitation" as little as ten years ago. Those suffering from mental illness, mental retardation, and senility are also being added in much greater numbers than ever before.

Vocational rehabilitation has proved itself both socially and economically sound. According to Dr. Howard A. Rusk (New York *Times,* December 4, 1960), 88,275 persons were rehabilitated during the fiscal year that ended in June 1960, at a cost to the federal government of about $16,000,000. The annual earnings of these persons are estimated to have increased since rehabilitation from about $28,000,000 earned previously to about $171,000,000. Thus, within a few years, those rehabilitated will have repaid the government every dollar spent upon their rehabilitation, through the federal income taxes on their increased earnings. Furthermore, about one-fifth of the group currently employed were previously on public assistance, receiving relief payments totalling about $17,000,000 annually.

In addition, persons rehabilitated in 1960 will contribute about 132,000,000 man-hours of work annually to the nation's productivity. Over 14,000 of them are working in the professions and skilled trades, including such short-supply fields as engineering and medicine. By 1970 the United States government hopes to include all of its physically handicapped citizens in its rehabilitation program.

On August 23, 1960 the Eighth World Congress of the International Society for the Welfare of Cripples named Miss Switzer as a recipient of an Albert Lasker Award, citing her as "the prime architect of a workable rehabilitation service for the nation's physically handicapped." Modestly, she sees the award as a tribute to the whole department. "It's for 'we,'" she says, "not me." Asked what she planned to do with the $2,500 prize that accompanies the award, she replied:

Dept. of Health, Education &
Welfare—S. Stanton Singer

MARY E. SWITZER

"I'll use it for international travel in connection with rehabilitation work, to assure that I or someone else can attend various meetings which otherwise could not be attended."

Miss Switzer has received many other awards. In 1946 the Catholic Hospital Association cited her for "securing for the hospitals of the country one advantage after another." The Institute for the Crippled and Disabled presented her with its Friend of the Disabled Award in 1952, and in 1955 she received the President's Award of the National Rehabilitation Association. In 1956 the United States Department of Health, Education, and Welfare presented her with a Distinguished Service Award and she has also received, among others, the Distinguished Service Award of the United Cerebral Palsy Association, the Achievement Award of the Philadelphia Education Week for the Blind, and the AMVETS Silver Helmet Award.

In addition, Miss Switzer has been honored by several colleges and universities. She holds the degree of Doctor of Humane Letters from Tufts University, Gallaudet College, and Western College for Women. Adelphi College has awarded her the degree of Doctor of Laws and she also holds the degrees of Doctor of Humanities from Boston University, and Doctor of Medical Science from the Women's Medical College of Pennsylvania.

Miss Switzer belongs to many volunteer and professional organizations. She has served as president, for 1960-61, of the National Rehabilitation Association and as first vice-president of the American Hearing Society. She is a member of the board of directors of the Virginia Rehabilitation Association, the Association for Aid to Crippled Children, and the Woodrow Wilson

Rehabilitation Center Foundation. She is a trustee of the Menninger Foundation and of the Easter Seal Research Foundation, an advisory Fellow of the World Federation of Occupational Therapists, and a member of the steering committee of the First World Mental Health Year. In addition, Miss Switzer is on the national advisory council of the community services committee of the AFL-CIO, and she is on committees of the National Foundation and the International Society for the Welfare of Cripples. She is a trustee of Radcliffe College and a member of the board of overseers of Brandeis University. In her home town of Alexandria, Virginia she is a member of the board of health and a volunteer worker at the local hospital.

According to Miss Switzer, part of her job is "barnstorming the country, selling my wares." She has gone above the Arctic Circle as a missionary for rehabilitation and has traveled all over the world to take part in international conferences in the field of health. She was a representative of the United States at the First International Health Conference in 1946, which drafted the constitution of the World Health Organization. Miss Switzer feels that vocational rehabilitation is not only a collection of clinical procedures, but also "a philosophy and life of service." She believes that the community has a "moral responsibility to ensure that the opportunities that our country gives generally to all of us be available, too, for those among us whose lives would otherwise be limited by physical disability."

References

> Washington (D.C.) Post C pl Ag 24 '60
> por
> Who's Who in America, 1960-61
> Who's Who of American Women (1961-62)

TAYLOR, A(LBERT) HOYT Jan. 1, 1879- Dec. 11, 1961 Physicist; radio engineer; pioneered in the development of radar at the United States Naval Research Laboratory during the 1920's and 1930's; installed the first radar unit on a battleship (1938). See *Current Biography* (September) 1945.

Obituary

> N Y Times p43 D 13 '61

THURBER, JAMES Dec. 8, 1894-Nov. 2, 1961 Humorist and cartoonist long associated with the *New Yorker* magazine; famous for his drawings of men, women, and dogs; author of essays and short stories, including "The Secret Life of Walter Mitty," and about two dozen books, including *The Last Flower* (1939). See *Current Biography* (October) 1960.

Obituary

> N Y Times p 1+ N 3 '61

TOBIAS, CHANNING H(EGGIE) Feb. 1, 1882-Nov. 5, 1961 Social worker; minister of the Colored Methodist Episcopal Church; senior secretary of the colored men's department of the YMCA (1923-46); held important positions in the National Association for the Advancement of Colored People. See *Current Biography* (July) 1945.

Obituary
N Y Times p37 N 6 '61

VERTÈS, MARCEL Aug. 10, 1895-Oct. 31, 1961 Artist; book illustrator; designed sets and costumes for a number of motion pictures, including *Moulin Rouge* (1952); also worked in advertising art. See *Current Biography* (April) 1961.

Obituary
N Y Times p39 N 1 '61

WENNER-GREN, AXEL (LEONARD) June 5, 1881-Nov. 24, 1961 Swedish industrialist and philanthropist; founded the Electrolux Company (1921) to manufacture vacuum cleaners and later refrigerators; had extensive industrial holdings in Europe and North and South America. See *Current Biography* (October) 1942.

Obituary
N Y Times p 1+ N 25 '61

PERIODICAL AND NEWSPAPER DESIGNATIONS

ALA Bul—American Library Association Bulletin
Am Artist—American Artist
Am Pol Sci R—American Political Science Review
Am Sociol R—American Sociological Review
Ann Am Acad—Annals of the American Academy of Political and Social Science
Arch Forum—Architectural Forum
Art N—Art News
Arts—Arts (incorporating Art Digest)
Atlan—Atlan Monthly
Aviation W—Aviation Week

Bet Hom & Gard—Better Homes and Gardens
Bsns W—Business Week
Bul Atomic Sci—Bulletin of the Atomic Scientists

Cath Lib World—Catholic Library World
Cath N—Catholic News
Chem & Eng N—Chemical and Engineering News
Christian Cent—Christian Century
Christian Sci Mon—Christian Science Monitor
Colliers—Collier's (discontinued)
Cur Hist—Current History

Ed & Pub—Editor and Publisher

For Affairs—Foreign Affairs
Forbes—Forbes Magazine

Gen Army—Generals of the Army and the Air Force and Admirals of the Navy (discontinued)
Good H—Good Housekeeping

Harper—Harper's Magazine
House B—House Beautiful

Ind Woman—Independent Woman (changed to National Business Woman)

Ladies Home J—Ladies' Home Journal
Lib J—Library Journal
Life—Life
Look—Look

Macleans Mag—Maclean's Magazine
Mus Am—Musical America
Mus Q—Musical Quarterly

N Y Herald Tribune—New York Herald Tribune
N Y Post—New York Post
N Y Sun—See N Y World-Telegram
N Y Times—New York Times
N Y Times Bk R—New York Times Book Review
N Y Times Mag—New York Times Magazine
N Y World-Telegram—New York World-Telegram and Sun
Nat Bsns Woman—National Business Woman
Nat Geog Mag—National Geographic Magazine
Nature—Nature
New Repub—New Republic
New Statesm—New Statesman
Newsweek—Newsweek

Opera N—Opera News

Pan Am Union Bul—Bulletin of the Pan American Union (now Américas)
Pol Sci Q—Political Science Quarterly
Pop Sci—Popular Science
Pub W—Publishers' Weekly

Read Digest—Reader's Digest
Reporter—The Reporter

Sat Eve Post—Saturday Evening Post
Sat Night—Saturday Night (Canadian)
Sat R—Saturday Review (formerly Saturday Review of Literature)
Sch & Soc—School and Society
Sci Am—Scientific American
Sci N L—Science News Letter
Science—Science

This Week—This Week Magazine
Time—Time

U N R—United Nations Review
U S Dept State Bul—United States Department of State, Bulletins
U S News—United States News & World Report

Vital Speeches—Vital Speeches of the Day

Washington (D.C.) Post—Washington Post and Times Herald
Wilson Lib Bul—Wilson Library Bulletin

CURRENT BIOGRAPHY—VOL. 23. NO. 1

This is the index to the January 1962 issue. For the index to 1961 biographies, see December 1961 issue; for the index to 1940-1950 biographies, see 1950 Yearbook. For 1951-1960 index see CURRENT BIOGRAPHY Yearbook 1960.

CURRENT
BIOGRAPHY

FEBRUARY 1962
VOL. 23   NO. 2

Editor: Charles Moritz

PUBLISHED BY THE H. W. WILSON COMPANY, 950 UNIVERSITY AVE., NEW YORK

CONTENTS

ABOUT THIS PUBLICATION

Current Biography (published every month except August) presents articles on people who are prominent in the news—in national and international affairs, the sciences, the arts, labor, and industry. Sources of information are newspapers, magazines, books, and, in some cases, the biographees themselves. It should be pointed out, however, that these are objective rather than authorized biographies. At the end of the year the articles in the monthly issues are cumulated in one alphabet, revised, and printed in a single volume known as *Current Biography Yearbook*.

Authorities for biographees' full names, with some exceptions, are the bibliographical publications of The Wilson Company. When a biographee prefers a certain name form, that is indicated in the heading of the article: for example, MACMILLAN, (MAURICE) HAROLD means that he is usually referred to as HAROLD MACMILLAN. When a professional name is used in the heading, as, for example, GLENN FORD, the real name, in this case GWYLLYN SAMUEL NEWTON FORD, appears in the article itself.

The heading of each article includes the pronunciation of the name if it is unusual, date of birth (if obtainable), and occupation. The article is supplemented by a list of references to sources of *biographical* information, in two alphabets: (1) newspapers and periodicals and (2) books.

References to newspapers and periodicals are listed in abbreviated form; for example, "Sat Eve Post 217:14+ S 30 '44 por" means *Saturday Evening Post*, volume 217, pages 14 ff, September 30, 1944, with portrait. For full names, see the section "Periodical and Newspaper Designations," which is included in all *Current Biography* Yearbooks and in the January issue each year. Obituary notices appear for persons whose biographies have been published in *Current Biography*.

An index to names that have appeared this year is to be found at the back of this issue.

NOTE: Authors whose biographies do not appear in *Current Biography* may usually be found in *Twentieth Century Authors*, Kunitz & Haycraft, 1942, H. W. Wilson Company, or in the FIRST SUPPLEMENT (1955). Authors of books for young people are included in *The Junior Book of Authors* (Second Edition, Revised) edited by Kunitz & Haycraft, 1951, H. W. Wilson Company. Musicians whose biographies do not appear in *Current Biography* may usually be found in *Living Musicians*, compiled and edited by David Ewen, 1940, H. W. Wilson Company, or in its FIRST SUPPLEMENT (1957).

KEY TO PRONUNCIATION

ā	āle	N	Not pronounced, but indicates the nasal tone of the preceding vowel, as in the French *bon* (bôN).	û	ûrn; French eu, as in *jeu* (zhû); German ö, oe, as in *schön* (shûn), *Goethe* (gû′tě)
â	câre				
ă	ădd				
ă̄	ăccount				
ä	ärm				
å	åsk			ŭ	tŭb
à	sofà			ů	circŭs
		ō	ōld	ü	Pronounced approximately as ē, with rounded lips: French u, as in *menu* (mē-nü); German ü, as in *grün*
ē	ēve	ô	ôrb		
ĕ	ĕnd	ŏ	ŏdd		
ē	makēr	oi	oil		
		o͞o	o͞oze		
g	go	o͝o	fo͝ot		
		ou	out		
ī	īce				
ĭ	ĭll	*th*	*then*	zh	azure
		th	thin	′ =	main accent
K	German ch as in *ich* (ĭK)	ū	cūbe	″ =	secondary accent

CURRENT BIOGRAPHY

FEBRUARY 1962

ANDRIĆ, IVO (ăn-drēch ē-vō) 1892- Yugoslav writer

Address: h. Prizrenska 7, Belgrade, Yugoslavia

The Swedish Academy awarded the 1961 Nobel Prize for Literature to the Yugoslav novelist Ivo Andrić "for the epic force with which he has depicted themes and human destinies drawn from the history of his country." In announcing the award, the Academy singled out for special praise Andrić's *Na Drini ćuprija* (*The Bridge on the Drina*), a chronicle novel spanning over three centuries of Bosnian history. In the Yugoslav diplomatic service for two decades, Andrić was his country's minister to Berlin when he withdrew from the service in 1941. Devoting himself to writing, he published after World War II the series of novels that brought him fame in Europe and acclaim from French critics as "the Yugoslav Tolstoy." Since the war he has been active in Yugoslav politics in addition to writing, and he is now a deputy in the Yugoslav Parliament, representing his native district of Bosnia. His works, which place human problems in an epic context and use Bosnia as their setting, began to be published in English translation in 1959.

In addition to his novels, short stories, and novelettes, Ivo Andrić has written essays and poems. His work has been praised for its freedom from party lines, propaganda, and prejudice. Andrić is the first Yugoslav to win the Nobel Prize for Literature.

Of Serbian ancestry, Ivo Andrić was born in 1892 into the family of a poor artisan of Doc, a village near Travnik, in the northern part of Bosnia, which fourteen years earlier had been wrested from the Turkish Empire and placed under Austro-Hungarian control. His father died when Ivo was two, and the family was raised by his mother, a strict Roman Catholic in a country that was Turkish as well as Slav. Raised in Višegrad, he attended secondary school in Sarajevo, the capital of Bosnia, and studied philosophy and history at the universities of Zagreb in Yugoslavia, Vienna in Austria, Kraków in Poland, and Graz in Austria. He received his doctorate from the University of Graz in 1923, after having submitted a doctoral thesis on the cultural history of Bosnia.

A South Slav patriot, before twenty Andrić belonged to the Bosnian revolutionary youth organization which opposed the Hapsburg regime and sought unity and independence for the South Slavic peoples. A member of this organization assassinated Archduke Ferdinand of Austria in 1914, precipitating World War I. Because of his membership in the organization, Andrić was a

IVO ANDRIĆ

political prisoner for three years during the war. "I grew up inside during those years," he has said.

At the time of his imprisonment he had already published his first poems and articles and had translated Walt Whitman. In prison he read the works of Sören Kierkegaard, the Danish philosopher and writer on religion. The reading of Kierkegaard darkened his outlook and plunged him into a gloom that penetrated his writing for almost two decades. In *Ex Ponto*, a collection of his prison meditations published after his release, he wrote: "There is no other truth but pain, there is no other reality but suffering, pain and suffering in every drop of water, in every blade of grass, in every grain of crystal, in every sound of living voice, in sleep and in vigil, in life, before life and perhaps also after life." Like Kierkegaard, Andrić viewed the world as the dwelling place of terror and irrationality.

After World War I Andrić entered his country's diplomatic service and continued to serve as a diplomat after the Kingdom of the Serbs, Croats, and Slovenes became Yugoslavia in 1929. His diplomatic career during two decades took him to Rome, Bucharest, Trieste, Graz, Berlin, and elsewhere in Europe. During the early years of his foreign service career he published several short stories and novellas that were pervaded with a sinister sense of aboriginal evil in the

ANDRIĆ, IVO—*Continued*

world. The quantity of his writing diminished as his diplomatic responsibilities became heavier. In his last assignment he was Yugoslavia's minister to Nazi Germany. In 1941, after the Yugoslav cabinet repudiated an alignment with Germany against the Allies, Andrić left Berlin and returned to Belgrade only a few hours before the first bombs fell. The Germans were already occupying Yugoslavia.

During the occupation Andrić devoted himself to writing in his Belgrade apartment. He remained, under virtual house arrest, despite the bombardments of the city. "I looked out of my window and saw the people fleeing," he once explained. "They were all trying to save something, their lives, their children, some precious possession. I had nothing to save but my life and it was beneath human dignity to run for that."

By the end of the war he had written his Bosnian trilogy: *Gospodica* (Miss), *Travnička khronika (Bosnian Story)* and *Na Drini ćuprija (The Bridge on the Drina)*. The three novels were published in 1945. Writing in the New York *Times Book Review* (November 12, 1961), Joseph Hitrec, a Yugoslav-born novelist and critic, recalled Andrić's earlier work and found that an obsession with evil and guilt was still evident in the trilogy. Hitrec also detected new elements. "One is a deliberate reaching back for myth and the healing touch of legend—the childlike folktale with its promise of innocence. The other, more important one, is the discovery of permanent values in the legacy of the past," Hitrec noted. In his essay "Conversations with Goya," published in Yugoslavia in 1955, Andrić had explained: "Having long been puzzled by what took place around me, I became convinced . . . that it is futile and mistaken to seek meaning in the unimportant and yet apparently so important events occurring around us; that we should seek a meaning, instead, in the strata built up by the centuries upon the few great legends of mankind."

Na Drini ćuprija was translated from the Serbo-Croatian by Lovett F. Edwards and published under the title *The Bridge on the Drina* by George Allen & Unwin, Ltd., in London and by the Macmillan Company in New York in 1959. The Drina is the river that marks the dividing line between Bosnia and Serbia. The bridge is the one that the Turks built across the river at the Bosnian town of Višegard in the sixteenth century. The novel chronicles life and death in Višegard over a span of three and one-half centuries, up until World War I, using the bridge as a symbol of permanence, the river as a symbol of the restless flux of history. When Gabriel Pearson reviewed the book for the *New Statesman* (March 21, 1959), he was not the only critic who found the tragedy too diffuse; yet he had to recognize its control and panoramic power. For *The Bridge on the Drina* Andrić received Yugoslavia's highest literary award. The New American Library published a paperback edition of the novel in New York City in 1960.

Translated by Kenneth Johnstone, *Travnička khronika* was published in English in 1959, with the title *Bosnian Story*, by Lincolns-Prager, Ltd., in London and by the British Book Centre

(London House & Maxwell) in New York. The novel covers the seven years (1807-14) that French consul Jean-Baptiste-Étienne Daville spent in Travnik, Bosnia. The relationship between characters is more closely meshed than in *The Bridge on the Drina,* and in the rivalry between Daville and the Austrian consul there is a plot of sorts. Reviewing the book in the New York *Herald Tribune* (November 7, 1959), Maurice Dolbier wrote: "*Bosnian Story* makes demands on a reader that, when met, are handsomely rewarded."

Sources close to the Royal Swedish Academy of Letters were reported to have said that in 1960 Andrić lost the Nobel Prize for Literature to St.-John Perse by one vote. In 1961 the academy deliberated only ten minutes before choosing Andrić from among sixty-five nominees. It was the second year in a row that the award went to a writer who had been a former diplomat. The Royal Swedish Academy of Letters called Andrić "a master of the narrative art, who appeals to us from the depths of the tortured South Slavic soul."

When told of the award in Belgrade, Andrić asked: "Is it true?" When assured that it was true, he reportedly said: "I am very excited. I am very moved. Everything that I wrote, all my work, is the literature of our country and of myself. I am so proud to be regarded with this prize. I am a very, very happy man." It is said that he later drank a toast to Sweden in slivovitz (plum brandy). The award was presented to Andrić in Stockholm on December 10, 1961, on the sixty-fifth anniversary of the death of Alfred Nobel.

A modest, soft-spoken, and dignified man, Andrić still looks like a diplomat, particularly in his choice of wardrobe. His dark hair is turning gray. He wears glasses with heavy horn rims. With his wife Milica—a well-known Yugoslav painter and designer for the Belgrade National Theater whom he married in 1959—he lives in an unpretentious four-room apartment in downtown Belgrade. For several years he has represented his native district of Bosnia as a deputy in the Yugoslav parliament, and since World War II he has been associated with the Yugoslav Liberation Movement. He is president of the Federation of Writers of Yugoslavia. The Yugoslav government has awarded him its Prize for Life Work, given annually to statesmen, scientists, and engineers, but seldom given to writers. Andrić's pastimes include watching children in Belgrade play basketball and walking through the Bosnian countryside, listening to folk tales that sometimes find their way into his books.

References

    N Y Herald Tribune p19 O 27 '61 por
    N Y Times p8 O 27 '61 por
    N Y Times Bk R p2 N 12 '61
    N Y World Telegram p7 O 26 '61
    Newsday p42 O 27 '61 por
    Pub W 180:21 N 6 '61
    Sat R 64:25 N 11 '61 por
    Toronto Globe and Mail p11 O 27 '61 por
    Washington (D.C.) Post A p20 O 27 '61
      por

    International Who's Who, 1961-62

BALL, GEORGE W(ILDMAN) Dec. 21, 1909- United States Under Secretary of State; lawyer

Address: b. Department of State, Washington 25, D.C.; h. 3100 35th St., N.W., Washington, D.C.

In what has been characterized as the first great shakeup of the Kennedy administration, the President announced on November 26, 1961 the replacement of Under Secretary Chester Bowles, the second-ranking State Department officer, by George W. Ball. A Washington lawyer and specialist in international law and commercial relations, Ball had served since the previous January as Under Secretary of State for Economic Affairs.

The promotion of Ball to this position was described in a New York *Times* editorial (November 29, 1961) as "formal recognition not only of his ability as an administrator but also of the extreme importance the President is placing on a forward-looking foreign trade policy." Since 1945 Ball has worked with Jean Monnet, the architect of the European unification movement, and he is expected to play a major role in determining United States policy toward the European Common Market.

George Wildman Ball was born on December 21, 1909 in Des Moines, Iowa, one of three sons of Amos and Edna (Wildman) Ball. His father, a native of Devonshire, England, came to the United States at the age of five. His mother, a former schoolteacher, was a member of a family that moved from Ohio to Iowa after the Civil War. George received his early education in Des Moines public schools. At the age of eleven he moved with his parents to Evanston, Illinois, where he attended Township High School. After graduation in 1926 he entered Northwestern University, where he received the B.A. degree in 1930 and then went on to Law School, receiving the J.D. degree in 1933. While at Northwestern he contributed notes on accident insurance and other subjects to the *Journal of Air Law*. He is a member of Phi Delta Phi, the law fraternity.

Ball was one of several young graduates brought to Washington by Professor Herman Oliphant when the latter was appointed general counsel for the Farm Credit Administration under Henry Morgenthau, Jr., in 1933. In the following year Ball transferred with Oliphant to the general counsel's office in the Treasury Department. He found, however, that his responsibilities exceeded his experience, and he decided to get some experience in the private practice of law. Having been admitted to the Illinois bar in 1934, he returned to Chicago in the following year. For the next seven years he practised successively with two law firms, working primarily in the areas of federal taxation, corporate reorganization, and the reorganization of major railroads. Adlai E. Stevenson was a member of one of the law firms, and Ball and Stevenson formed an enduring friendship.

At the suggestion of Stevenson, who went to Washington in mid-1941 as special assistant to Secretary of the Navy Frank Knox, Ball returned to government service in 1942. Appointed to

GEORGE W. BALL

the staff of the general counsel of the Office of Lend-Lease Administration, he was soon advanced to associate general counsel, serving as legal adviser to the administrator, Edward R. Stettinius, Jr.

In 1943 Ball became associate general counsel for the Foreign Economic Administration, which combined the Office of Lend-Lease Administration, the Office of Economic Warfare, and other agencies concerned with foreign economic affairs. In 1944 he was invited by General Henry H. Arnold to become the civilian member of the Air Force Evaluation Board, studying the effects of tactical operations in Europe. Later in that year Ball was appointed director of the United States Strategic Bombing Survey, a civilian group established to assess the social, economic, and physical effects of the strategic air offensive against Germany. In the spring and summer of 1945 members of the group interviewed a number of surviving Nazi leaders, among them the former German minister of armaments, munitions, and production, Albert Speer. The report on the seven-day interrogation of Speer, on which Ball and John Kenneth Galbraith collaborated, appeared in *Life* magazine on December 17, 1945.

Ball returned to Washington in September 1945. In 1945-46 he served as general counsel for the French Supply Council, which was engaged in the acquisition of supplies for the rehabilitation of France. In July 1946 he became a founding partner of the law firm Cleary, Gottlieb, Steen & Ball, which subsequently established offices in New York, Brussels, and Paris, as well as in Washington, D.C. The firm represented American companies and individuals doing business in foreign countries. Having become acquainted, in 1945, with Jean Monnet, who originated the European unification movement, Ball worked closely with Monnet in establishing the Coal and Steel Community—the first step toward eliminating economic barriers between Western European na-

BALL, GEORGE W.—*Continued*

tions. For years Ball made monthly visits to Paris. He has crossed the Atlantic about 155 times by air and twenty times by ship.

As a member of his firm, Ball has represented the European Economic Community; the European Community of Atomic Energy; the European Coal and Steel Community; and the French manufacturers' association, the *Patronat*. The firm has also represented private interests in Venezuela and the Cuban sugar mill owners' and cane growers' association, but it has not had any dealings with the Castro regime of Cuba.

In the 1952 Presidential campaign Ball served as the national director of Volunteers for Stevenson, and in 1956 he was director of public relations for Stevenson and Kefauver. In 1960 he again supported the candidacy of Stevenson for the Democratic nomination for the Presidency. However, before John F. Kennedy was inaugurated as President, Ball and John Sharon, one of his law partners, organized task forces for the study of foreign affairs and edited their reports. Ball took charge of the groups on economic policy, balance of payments, outflow of gold, foreign aid, and commercial policy. Kennedy was greatly impressed with Ball's role in the preparation of the 200-page report delivered a week after the November election, and on January 11, 1961 he designated Ball as Under Secretary of State for Economic Affairs, the third-ranking post in the State Department.

During the hearings of the Senate Foreign Relations Committee on January 24, 1961 Ball was challenged by Republican Senator Bourke B. Hickenlooper of Iowa concerning a letter Ball had written to the New York *Times* during the 1960 campaign. In the letter Ball had expressed strong doubts as to the competence of Republican candidate Richard M. Nixon. Ball replied that the letter had been written in the spirit of political campaigning and was intended to counteract the strong emphasis that had been placed upon the Vice-President's political experience. Ball's nomination was subsequently confirmed by the Senate. Before he took office as Under Secretary of State for Economic Affairs, Ball ended all connections with his law firm.

In March 1961 Ball attended the London meeting of the Development Assistance Group, a subsidiary of the new Organization for Economic Cooperation and Development. There he suggested that future foreign aid should take into greater account the financial condition of recipient countries. He also proposed that industrial nations should accept a fair share of the cost of aid according to their ability to pay. In July 1961 Ball visited Hong Kong and urged that this British crown colony bring under control its high level of textile exports to the United States. Later in the same month he also headed the United States delegation to a sixteen-nation conference on textiles at Geneva, Switzerland, where an American proposal to freeze exports for twelve months at existing levels was unanimously accepted.

During the early months of the Kennedy administration Ball concentrated mainly on long-range questions of trade, anticipating the eventuality, hoped for by the administration, that Great Britain would join the European Common Market. When in the summer of 1961 Under Secretary Chester Bowles, the second-ranking State Department officer, was sent on a number of missions abroad, Ball became for all practical purposes the Under Secretary. His assignments included such problem areas as the Congo, the Dominican Republic, Korea, and Ghana, and soon about 70 percent of his work dealt with political problems.

Observers saw indications that Ball was being considered for the post of Under Secretary in the President's heavy reliance upon him in the formulation of a new foreign aid program and in the preparation of legislative proposals designed to give the White House greater authority to reduce tariffs. In the middle of November 1961 President Kennedy asked Ball to sit in on cold-war strategy talks with West German Chancellor Konrad Adenauer.

Ball delivered an important address, previously approved by the White House as representing the administration's trade policy, at the forty-eighth National Foreign Trade Convention in New York City on November 1, 1961. He criticized the view that every American industry must be protected against the adjustments required by competition, and maintained that the President should have broader powers to negotiate for reductions in tariffs and other restrictions on trade, to "meet the opportunity and the challenge of the European Economic Community."

When his appointment as Under Secretary of State was announced on November 26, 1961, Ball was attending meetings of the General Agreement on Tariffs and Trade (GATT) in Geneva, Switzerland. On December 5, 1961 he was sworn into his new office. When Secretary of State Dean Rusk left on a European mission the following week, Ball, as acting Secretary of State, was confronted with the problems involved in the United Nations military action in the secessionist Congo province of Katanga. "Our aim," he said on December 10, 1961 "is the consolidation of the country under a stable Government. . . . If Katanga is not peacefully integrated, the Congo will face civil war and anarchy, and be open to Communist penetration." Three days later he voiced United States opposition to a British proposal for an immediate cease fire in Katanga, which he did not regard as feasible until the minimum U.N. objectives had been attained. Replying to critics of U.N. policies in the Congo, Ball said in a speech in Los Angeles on December 20, 1961; "Peacekeeping is not necessarily wholly peaceful. But in this case it was necessary to prevent a civil war that would have made the past few days in Elisabethville look like a picnic."

Testifying before a subcommittee of the Joint Congressional Economic Committee on December 12, 1961, Ball proposed that the President be given authority to enter into linear agreements, lowering tariff barriers on some categories of commodities. He said that the United States should not join the European Common Market, but should instead seek a partnership that would be "dedicated not only to the parochial interests of its members, but to the expansion of relations with the rest of the world."

Ball has been active in the Council of Foreign Relations, and has attended a number of international economic conferences of the Bilderberg Group under the sponsorship of Prince Bernhard of the Netherlands. He is a part-owner of the *Northern Virginia Sun,* a liberal daily newspaper in Arlington County, Virginia. He has received the French Legion of Honor and the United States Medal for Freedom.

On September 16, 1932 George W. Ball married Ruth Murdoch of Pittsburgh, Pennsylvania. They have two sons: John Colin, who is a student of Arabic at the American University at Beirut; and Douglas Bleakly, a graduate of Wooster College in Ohio. Ball is six feet two and a half inches tall and weighs about 200 pounds. "The consensus of Ball's immediate staff in the State Department," wrote E. W. Kenworthy in the New York Times *Magazine* (December 10, 1961), "is that their boss is a bear for work . . . a bad relaxer, and a nuisance after hours and on weekends. . . . But he is no martinet: he rarely blows up." Ball writes his own speeches and has been known to spend an entire weekend in preparing for an important speech.

Frederic W. Collins in the *Christian Science Monitor* (February 6, 1961) described Ball as "a tall, incredibly energetic man with a somewhat quizzical outlook on life, a mind which seems to defy overload, and an apparently limitless variety of active interests." These interests include Democratic politics, history and economics (in which he reads widely), and carpentry, his hobby.

References

N Y Post p54 N 28 '61 por
N Y Times p20 N 28 '61 por
Newsday p30 N 28 '61 por
Who's Who in America, 1960-61

BARNSLEY, ALAN (GABRIEL) *See* Fielding, G.

BREWSTER, (RALPH) OWEN Feb. 22, 1888-Dec. 25, 1961 Republican Governor of Maine (1925-29); member of the United States House of Representatives (1935-41) and of the Senate (1941-53); chairman of the Special Senate Committee to Investigate the National Defense Program (1947). See *Current Biography* (May) 1947.

Obituary

N Y Times p25 D 26 '61

BUTLER, PAUL M(ULHOLLAND) June 15, 1905-Dec. 30, 1961 Lawyer; active for over twenty years in local and state politics in Indiana; Democratic committeeman from Indiana (1952); chairman of the Democratic National Committee (1954-60). See *Current Biography* (May) 1955.

Obituary

N Y Times p1+ D 31 '61

DUKE, ANGIER BIDDLE Nov. 30, 1915- United States government official

Address: b. Department of State, Washington 25, D.C.; h. 2400 Foxhall Rd., Washington, D.C.

Angier Biddle Duke, who since January 1961 has been chief of protocol for the State Department and the White House, brings to his post a lively social conscience and a wealth of experience in the diplomatic service in Argentina, Spain, and El Salvador and in the administration of aid to refugees. A practitioner of what Marguerite Higgins of the New York *Herald Tribune* has called "the art of preventive diplomacy," Duke stands upon as little ceremony as possible and hopes to introduce logic, simplicity, and dignity into protocol. He is also continuing his long campaign to prevent incidents of racial discrimination in the United States from defacing the American image abroad. His aim is "to put as much substance into international human relations as possible."

Heir to part of the tobacco fortune created by his grandfather, Benjamin N. Duke, who helped found the American Tobacco Company and Duke University, Angier Biddle Duke was born in New York City on November 30, 1915 to Angier Buchanan Duke, an executive of the American Tobacco Company, and Cornelia (Drexel Biddle) Duke. He has a brother, Anthony Drexel Duke. Angier Biddle Duke is a direct descendant of Nicholas Biddle, who was president of the Bank of the United States before the Jacksonian Era. He is also a nephew of Brigadier General Anthony Drexel Biddle, Jr., who was deputy chief of staff to Dwight D. Eisenhower during World War II. The boy's parents were divorced when he was six years old.

For his preparatory school education, Duke attended St. Paul's School in Concord, New Hampshire, where he managed the school hockey team. After graduating in 1934 he enrolled at Yale College, but left in 1937 at the end of his junior year. "I went to college during the Depression, when all values in society were being questioned," Drexel has recalled. In his opinion, college was not providing the answers he was seeking. After leaving Yale, he traveled around the world and after his return, worked briefly as a copywriter.

World War II provided him with some of the answers to his questions. "The experiences I had in the Army were my education," Duke has said. "Nothing so illuminating had ever happened to me before." He enlisted in the armed services in January 1941, entered Officer Candidate School a year and a half later, and served with the Air Transport Command in North Africa and Europe. By the time he was discharged in 1945 with the rank of major, he had experienced the satisfactions of leadership and had witnessed at firsthand the suffering of humanity. He landed in France shortly after D-Day and entered Paris with the troops that liberated the city. Arriving in Buchenwald the day after it was liberated, he shrank from the stacked corpses and from the stench of decay— a stench that he never forgot. But it was the survivors whom he most pitied.

(Continued next page)

United Press International Photo
ANGIER BIDDLE DUKE

Like many other veterans, Duke floundered about for a few months after the war ended, uncertain about what he wanted to do. He traveled in Latin America for a few months, then in 1945 founded Duke International Corporation, an organization engaged in managing foreign and domestic investments in a complex of activities that ranged from importing French films to founding a ball-point pen factory in Argentina. He held the post of president of Duke International Corporation until 1948.

Duke's fluency in Spanish and French, his extensive travel, and his experiences overseas during World War II were factors that contributed to his final choice of a career in the diplomatic service. Before World War II he had considered himself more or less a Republican; after the war he joined the Democratic party and gradually became active in New York politics. Encouraged and helped by Stanton Griffis, then the United States Ambassador to Argentina, he became a foreign service officer in 1949. After serving briefly in Washington, he went to the United States Embassy in Buenos Aires, Argentina as second secretary and consul. In 1951 he accompanied Griffis to Spain as special assistant to the Ambassador (a sort of social secretary).

When he was appointed Ambassador to El Salvador by President Harry S. Truman in 1952, succeeding Howard Tewksbury, who resigned, Angier Biddle Duke became the youngest Ambassador in the history of the United States. Some of the socialites who had lounged with him on the beaches of Southampton were skeptical, and one wit exclaimed, "From El Morocco to El Salvador!" Duke confounded them by working hard in El Salvador. He traveled widely, and his facile Spanish enabled him to use his office to promote goodwill not only at the governmental level, but also among the people. In paying him tribute, one Salvadoran newsman wrote: "He has dedicated more sewers, slaugh-

terhouses, and clinics than half-a-dozen politicians." Oscar Osorio, the President of El Salvador, often visited Duke unannounced and lunched with him. When the Republican administration took over after the 1952 defeat of Adlai E. Stevenson, Duke wanted to be kept on, but President Dwight D. Eisenhower formally accepted his resignation and he was succeeded by the former State Department press chief Mike McDermott.

A writer for *Time* magazine (May 25, 1953) described Duke as a diplomat "who has proved himself one of the best ambassadors the U.S. has ever sent to Latin America." In a letter to the editor of *Time* (June 15, 1953) Duke said that he would prefer to be regarded as "a friendly pleader for El Salvador's special role, not only as a nation sympathetic to our objectives, but as the showcase for a dynamic approach to the problems that are currently plaguing all Latin America."

It was in his work for the International Rescue Committee, a private, nonsectarian group helping political refugees from behind the Iron Curtain, that Duke addressed himself most directly to international problems. Elected chairman of its executive committee in June 1955, he went immediately to Vietnam to coordinate the relief work of the International Rescue Committee in the midst of the confusion and misery that followed in the wake of revolution and partition. Concerned that relief aid was not reaching the people, he formed the American Friends of Vietnam, a fund-raising organization subsidiary to the International Rescue Committee. In 1957 he returned to Vietnam to inspect the medical aid operation of the International Rescue Committee in Laos, and early in 1958 he organized "Medico," a branch of the International Rescue Committee designed to bring medical help to Africa and Asia. In recognition of his services to Vietnam, the Vietnamese government made him a Commander of the National Order of Vietnam.

In February 1956 Duke set up an emergency commission of the International Rescue Committee, headed by General William J. Donovan, which investigated an intensive Communist repatriation program in Western Europe. During the first week of the 1956 Hungarian uprising, Duke flew to Vienna to mobilize International Rescue Committee facilities in Vienna for all emergencies. His plane carried terramycin capsules for the wounded of Hungary. The committee's emergency campaign for Hungarian refugees raised almost $3,000,000. Upon his return from Austria and Hungary, Duke pronounced the Hungarian revolt "the most important political victory since the war against Russian communism." He said that the uprising had exposed the mockery of the Soviet peaceful co-existence theme and had changed the political climate of Europe for the next decade.

Under the auspices of the International Rescue Committee, Duke in October 1957 set up the temporary Zellerbach Commission to make a survey of the complexities of the refugee situation. In March 1959 the Zellerbach Commission submitted its final report embodying specific recommendations for an early solution of the European refugee problem. It recommended that the United States admit 50,000 refugees within the following two years in an international "crash" program. Campaigning for a more flexible immigration policy, Duke continued to work for a revision of the immigration laws as president of the American Immigration and Citizenship Conference.

Representing the city of New York, Duke attended the ceremonies accompanying the establishment of the independence of the Republic of Togoland on April 27, 1960. As a member of the foreign policy advisory committee of the Democratic advisory council, he subsequently visited and conferred with nationalist leaders in every West African state from Senegal to the Congo. In the autumn of 1960 he toured Panama, Costa Rica, Nicaragua, Honduras, and Guatemala on behalf of the New York 1964-65 World's Fair, heading a task force charged with presenting invitations to the various governments to exhibit at the Fair. Wherever they went, they encountered a cordial reception.

In 1960 Duke at first favored Senator Hubert Humphrey, Jr., for President of the United States, but when Humphrey was defeated in the West Virginia primary and withdrew from the contest, Duke switched his allegiance to Senator John F. Kennedy. He served as chairman of nationalities and intergroup relations for New York City, the first time he served in a political job not associated with the raising of funds. He also served as liaison between the reform group and the regular organization.

President-elect John F. Kennedy formally announced the appointment of Angier Biddle Duke as chief of protocol for the State Department and the White House, with the personal rank of Ambassador, early in January 1961. Duke was sworn in on January 24, 1961, succeeding Wiley T. Buchanan, Jr. His staff of twenty-seven is housed in brand-new offices on the ground floor of the State Department Annex.

Duke's task is to make sure that foreign diplomats and dignitaries are dealt with on the basis of rank and seniority. He is in charge of the social and diplomatic amenities and sees to it that diplomats are properly greeted on their arrival and properly treated on their departure. Duke sees his work as a "deepening" of the functions always associated with his post. He feels that an international agreement on a uniform standard of diplomatic rights and procedures is badly needed in modern times, and believes that he should be empowered to carry out any policy that will improve the nation's diplomatic position. In his opinion, the function and need of entertaining as an arm of diplomacy could stand review and redefinition. He also advocates the establishment of a social and cultural center in Washington, D.C. to bring the people of other nations into closer relationships with Americans.

Most of the recently established African republics are newly represented in Washington, D.C., and African diplomats often encounter racial prejudice in the nation's capital and other parts of the United States. Making these African diplomats the objects of his special concern, Duke and his staff help them to secure suitable housing, schooling for their children, and a courteous reception in restaurants and department stores.

His handling of a much publicized incident of discrimination in Hagerstown, Maryland on March 1, 1961 is a prime example of Duke's philosophy in action. Dr. William Fitzjohn, a diplomat from Sierra Leone, was refused service in a Howard Johnson restaurant. Instead of merely tendering an official apology, Duke immediately called the attention of the Mayor of Hagerstown to the damaging publicity abroad that had resulted from the incident. Dr. Fitzjohn was invited back to Hagerstown as the city's guest and the restaurant was desegregated. Duke would like to use his office to help remove racial barriers in general, not just those erected before African diplomats.

In August 1961 Duke quietly resigned from the exclusive Metropolitan Club in Washington, of which he had been a member for twenty years, in protest against its refusal to allow Negroes as guests. "It would be inconsistent with my duties, being the link between the diplomatic corps and the administration, to remain a member,' Duke said. Others who resigned that fall from the club were Attorney General Robert F. Kennedy and George C. Lodge, former Assistant Secretary of Labor.

The many committees on which Duke has served have included the Mayor's Puerto Rican Affairs Committee (New York City), the American Friends of Vietnam, the Emergency Committee for U.N. Action on Hungary, and the New York Citizens Committee for Kennedy and Johnson. He has been decorated with the Order of Honor and Merit by Haiti and with the Grand Cross of Merit, Order of Malta. He was given a distinguished service award by the American Veterans Committee in 1957 and by the World Affairs Council of Philadelphia in 1958. He is a trustee of Iona College in New Rochelle, New York, which awarded him an honorary Doctor of Laws degree in 1957. He belongs to the Council on Foreign Relations, the Foreign Service Association, the Pilgrims, the Sons of the American Revolution, and the Society of Colonial Wars. Among his clubs are the Racquet and Tennis Club in New York City and the Travellers Club in Paris.

Angier Biddle Duke married Priscilla St. George in 1938. He has a son, A. St. George Biddle Duke by that marriage, which ended in divorce. In 1940 he married Margaret Screven White. The marriage ended in divorce in 1952. In Mexico City on December 11, 1952 he married Maria-Luisa de Aranha, a member of the Spanish Basque nobility, whom he had met while serving in the diplomatic corps in Madrid. The couple lived with their children, Maria-Luisa and Drexel Dario, in a red brick house on Foxhall Road in Washington and maintained a summer home in Southampton, Long Island. Mrs. Duke was killed in the crash of a private airplane in New York City on July 18, 1961. Tall, slender, and aristocratic in appearance, Duke is six feet in height, weighs about 170 pounds, and has gray eyes and thinning brown hair. He prefers Continental tailoring. Born a Methodist, he was converted to Roman Catholicism on October 4, 1952.

Reference

Who's Who in America, 1960-61

EADY, SIR (CRAWFURD) WILFRID (GRIFFIN) Sept. 1890-Jan. 9, 1962 British government official; Joint Second Secretary of the Treasury (1942-52); after World War II led loan missions to the United States and Canada. See *Current Biography* (October) 1947.

Obituary

N Y Times p47 Ja 10 '62

FAIRLESS, BENJAMIN F(RANKLIN) May 3, 1890-Jan. 1, 1962 Chief administrative officer of the United States Steel Corporation (1938-55); president of the American Iron & Steel Institute (since 1955); spokesman of American steelmakers and from time to time a consultant to the United States government. See *Current Biography* (May) 1957.

Obituary

N Y Times p1+ Ja 2 '62

FIELDING, GABRIEL Mar. 25, 1916- Novelist; physician

Address: b. 10-11 Northumberland Court, Shepway, Maidstone, Kent, England; h. 374 Loose Rd., Maidstone, Kent, England

Untangling the threads of his youth, British physician Alan Barnsley, under the pseudonym Gabriel Fielding, has woven a literary fabric of which Whitney Balliett has said, "The reader sinks right into these dark, leisurely, disquieting, old-fashioned books where the bears bite and death really stings." The books are three novels about the Blaydon family, particularly young John Blaydon: *Brotherly Love, In the Time of Greenbloom,* and *Through Streets Broad and Narrow.*

Although the Blaydon novels are Fielding's most recognized works, both in England and the United States, they do not constitute all of his achievement. His other work includes the novel *Eight Days* and two books of poems. His first book, *The Frog Prince and Other Poems,* was published in 1952. A practising physician since 1943, Fielding has been a general practitioner since 1948. As writing has taken over more and more of his time, he has relegated to two colleagues an increasing share of his medical practice.

Gabriel Fielding was born Alan Gabriel Barnsley in Hexham, Northumberland, England, on March 25, 1916. He was the fifth of six surviving children—the first child had been stillborn—of George Barnsley and Katherine Mary (Fielding Smith) Barnsley. Although his ancestry on his father's side was partly Irish, he is mainly descended, through his father, from Derbyshire farmers. Reportedly, there is also Welsh blood in the family background. Fielding is said to be descended on his mother's side from Henry Fielding, the eighteenth-century novelist.

Fielding's well-to-do father was a clergyman of the Church of England—a "sporting parson," in Fielding's words. The father had been converted to High Church Christianity by the mother, a playwright and well-known breeder of whip-

pets. According to Evelyn Cavallo, in the *Critic* (December 1960-January 1961), Fielding's mother was both the "scourge and stimulus" of his childhood and early manhood. "She assumed an air of Scriptural rightness. . . . From this stemmed a whole network of exhortations and prohibitions. . . . It is not surprising that Fielding's revolt against the vicarage ethos was, at one time, total and committed." In 1961 the mother, an octogenarian, was working on an autobiography that Fielding planned to edit. "Until I have done that it would be most imprudent and very nearly impossible for me to convey a round picture of this remarkable, talented, occasionally wise, occasionally misguided, but never less than good woman," Fielding said in the late summer of 1961.

Reared in Sussex, in Yorkshire, and on the Isle of Anglesey, Fielding received his secondary education at the now defunct Grange School in Eastbourne (1925-1929) and at St. Edward's School, Oxford (1929-1931). At Trinity College in Dublin he won prizes in anatomy and biology and took his B.A. degree in 1939. He finished his medical studies at St. George's Hospital Medical School in London, earning in 1942 his membership in the Royal College of Surgeons (England) and his licentiate in the Royal College of Physicians (London).

In 1943 Fielding began his medical career as a lieutenant in the Royal Army Medical Corps. Raised to the rank of captain in 1944, he remained in the R.A.M.C. until 1946. Entering private practice as a general practitioner in January 1948, he opened an office in a former bakery shop on the edge of a Labor government housing project in Maidstone, Kent. He now works part time in a practice that he shares with two junior partners. Since 1948, as a part-time medical officer, he has attended the prisoners in H.M. Training Establishment in Maidstone. Evelyn Cavallo wrote of this experience: "As a prison doctor . . . his vision has been widened. Criminal psychology interests him deeply, and the manic and 'messianic' killer Horrowicz (who features in the novel *Eight Days*) is a character elaborated out of experience and observation."

From the age of six Fielding had been determined to become a writer. Too financially insecure to risk studying English at Oxford, he had instead decided on medicine, in which he was also interested. The decision had included the hope that medical practice might later allow him time to write. It has.

Hand and Flower Press published Fielding's first book, *The Frog Prince and Other Poems,* in 1952. During the eight years that followed he published another book of poems, *XXVIII Poems* (Hand and Flower, 1960), and four novels. One of the novels, *Eight Days* (Hutchinson, 1958; Morrow, 1959), based mostly, like the others, on his own experience, is a religious thriller about the eight-day vacation that William Chance, a prison doctor and convert to Roman Catholicism, takes in North Africa. During his holiday he finds that his new faith is being tested. "For all its concern with fraud and piety," William Bittner wrote in the *Saturday Review* (February 28, 1959), "*Eight Days* is pervaded with suspense."

It is for the other three novels that Fielding is best known: *Brotherly Love* (Hutchinson, 1954; Morrow, 1961), *In the Time of Greenbloom* (Hutchinson, 1956; Morrow, 1957), and *Through Streets Broad and Narrow* (Hutchinson, 1960; Morrow, 1960). These are genealogical novels, about a Blaydon family that bears striking similarities to the Barnsley family.

Brotherly Love—"the tightest and most subtle" of the three in the view of Whitney Balliett (*New Yorker*, September 23, 1961)—focuses on David Blaydon (whose prototype was Fielding's brother George Derek) and David's fatal clash with his mother's relentless driving of him into church and respectable marriage. The character who finally emerges as central, however, is John Blaydon. "Through the character of John Blaydon," Evelyn Cavallo observed, "Fielding was trying to understand himself; to seize, with a sense of exact location, the moods and masks of his former existence. And into this search he put all the concentration, the warmth of affection, the depth of insight, the color and humor of his vivid disposition."

John Blaydon's adolescence is the subject of *In the Time of Greenbloom*. The nightmare quality of these years in the boy's life is keyed by the rape-murder of his girl friend, Victoria. John's haunting grief, self-pity, and irrational feeling of guilt, mirrored and abetted by the external world, are finally partly dissolved by the gradual persuasion of Horab Greenbloom, Oxonian friend of an older brother. Some critics found the hero too whiny, others thought the style was too subtle. The critical consensus, however, was overwhelmingly eulogistic. Patricia Hodgart saw faults in the novel but was nevertheless convinced, by Fielding's "highly developed feeling for narrative, that his is a rare and unusual talent" (Manchester *Guardian,* June 19, 1956). Sylvia Stallings, writing in the New York *Herald Tribune Book Review* (June 9, 1957), said the novel was written "from a poetic vision that never loses sight of realism, even the realism of the psychologist and the social worker."

Through Streets Broad and Narrow follows John Blaydon through his medical studies at Trinity College in Dublin. A reviewer of the novel in *Time* magazine (May 23, 1960) said of Fielding: "His greatest strength—dramatic invention—contributes to his greatest weakness: overplotting." Peter Green in the *Saturday Review* (June 4, 1960) called the work "a brilliant, infuriating, awkward novel—rather like Blaydon's own character."

Whitney Balliett, writing in the *New Yorker* (September 23, 1961), assessed all three novels thus: "At first Fielding seems to handle words by the pound. Then one notices certain things: many of his characters, though barely touched upon, spring up three-dimensionally . . . ; his narrative strength occasionally outpaces us; we *see* some of his settings; his dialogue, unfashionably high-spirited and gabby, is effortlessly right. . . . All three books are episodic and fragmentary, and yet they are unbreakable wholes."

In 1961 Fielding announced: "I am currently writing my most difficult novel—and have been busy with it for the past two years: *The Birthday King*, a romance of about 150,000 words set in

GABRIEL FIELDING

Nazi Germany and covering the period between 1939 and 1946. This is the first time I have dared to break away from my own immediate experience in using material for a novel." Besides his novels and books of poems, Fielding has published short stories in anthologies and periodicals. He broadcasts talks and occasionally reviews books on the BBC Home Service.

Alan Gabriel Barnsley and Edwina Eleanora Cook were married on October 31, 1943. They have five children: Michael Fielding, Jonathan Milne, Mario Simon George Gervaise, Felicity Anne, and Mary Gabriel Elizabeth (in descending order of age). Lean and tall in appearance, Fielding stands five feet ten and one-half inches and weighs 159 pounds. His hair and eyes are brown. He has been a Roman Catholic since 1954. He has described his political affiliation as "Liberal—vaguely." He is reported to be a frank, curious, and—above all—warm person, hospitable and attentive to the needs of others. A spellbinding conversationalist, he is also a sympathetic listener, adept at putting others at ease, at drawing out the shy and reserved, particularly in private conversation. He has said that his favorite recreations are swimming, particularly in the sea; flying (he would like to own his own plane or glider); and "being invited out to dinner by 'interesting' people, which is to say wise, talkative people who do not drink very much before, during, or after they have talked."

Reference

Critic 19:19+ D '60-J '61

GILMORE, VOIT Oct. 13, 1918- United States government employee; lumberman

Address: b. United States Travel Service, Department of Commerce, Washington 25, D.C.; h. 700 E. Indiana Ave., Southern Pines, N.C.

The man selected by President John F. Kennedy to run the first government agency in

VOIT GILMORE

United States history designed to attract foreign visitors to American shores is a gregarious North Carolina lumberman who is himself a much-traveled American. Voit Gilmore, director of the United States Travel Service, brings to his newly created office broad experience as an airline representative, hotelkeeper, travel promoter, and public official. In addition, he is a close friend and political associate of Luther H. Hodges, Secretary of Commerce, under whose department the service was established in 1961 to promote international understanding—and attract enough foreign visitors to the United States to help redress America's unfavorable balance of trade.

Voit Gilmore was born on October 13, 1918, in Winston-Salem, North Carolina, the son of John Merriman Gilmore, a lumber dealer, and Helen (Hensel) Gilmore. After receiving his public schooling in Winston-Salem, Voit attended the Georgia Military Academy in College Park, Georgia for a year and then entered the University of North Carolina at Chapel Hill. As chairman of the university's Political Union, he once persuaded President Franklin D. Roosevelt to address the student body. The President, impressed with the young college politician and Phi Beta Kappa member, invited him to Washington to spend a few days at the White House. During one summer he was in Europe as a college exchange student in Denmark and Holland. This was his second trip abroad: he had earlier attended the Boy Scouts world jamboree in Budapest.

Upon graduating from North Carolina with a B.A. degree in journalism and political science in 1939, he won a Rockefeller scholarship to the National Institute of Public Affairs in Washington. During 1940 he served as secretary to Senator Josiah W. Bailey of North Carolina, chairman of the Senate Commerce Committee, which dealt, among other matters, with airline affairs. Gilmore attracted the attention of Pan American World Airways officials and took a job as assist-

ant to the manager of the airline's Eastern division in Miami, where he served in 1940-41.

In 1942 Pan American assigned him to Accra, Khartoum, and Cairo as personnel manager of Pan American Airways-Africa, Ltd. Gilmore's first government travel assignment came in 1943 when he was commissioned as an ensign in the United States Naval Air Transport Command and sent to Treasure Island in the South Pacific to join the staff of Admiral John W. Reeves, Jr. He served during the rest of World War II in Naval public relations in the Pacific. (Later, in 1958 and 1960, he made two trips to the South Pole as an observer for the Navy, traveling by helicopter, icebreaker, and sled. In 1958, also, he flew to the North Pole as an observer for the Air Force.)

Discharged from active service in 1946, Gilmore rejoined Pan American, which made him public relations director of the company's Pacific-Alaska division in San Francisco and Seattle. In 1947 he returned to North Carolina to look after the family lumber interests as vice-president of W.M. Storey Lumber Company in Winston-Salem. After he became president of the company in 1948, he transferred the business to the North Carolina resort town of Southern Pines, where he has a 450-acre tree farm. He is also vice-president of Highlands Builders Supply, Inc.

In Southern Pines, Gilmore opened in 1956 his first Howard Johnson's Motor Lodge & Restaurant, which he operates as president of the Holly-Redbud-Magnolia Corporation. In 1958 he became president of Western Hills-Hamore Corporations, operators of a similar motel in Winston-Salem, and he has since acquired a third Howard Johnson lodge and restaurant in Salisbury, North Carolina.

Another investor in Howard Johnson franchises was Luther H. Hodges, a candidate for lieutenant governor of North Carolina when Gilmore met him in 1952. Hodges was elected lieutenant governor and two years later, after the death of Governor William B. Umstead, unexpectedly became governor. "We moved into orbit together," Gilmore has recalled. Having quickly become prominent in the community life of Southern Pines, he served as chairman of the town's planning commission in 1952-53, councilman and mayor pro tem from 1953 to 1955, and as mayor from 1955 to 1957. On the state level, he was appointed in 1957 to the Board of Conservation and Development, of whose forestry committee he was chairman, and from 1957 to 1959 he was president of the North Carolina Travel Council, where he played a key role in raising tourism from the eighth-ranking to the third-ranking industry in North Carolina's economy.

During the 1960 Presidential campaign Hodges and Gilmore worked closely as chairman and co-chairman of Businessmen for Kennedy. Gilmore was also a delegate to the Democratic National Convention in Los Angeles. One of President Kennedy's first cabinet appointments was that of Governor Hodges as Secretary of Commerce. Not long afterward the President reactivated the "Visit the USA" campaign that President Dwight D. Eisenhower had initiated but that had failed to win Congressional approval. The United

States was then the only major country in the world that did not have an official tourist-promotion bureau.

Government interest in promoting travel to the United States was aroused when it was revealed that an important cause of the growing United States foreign trade deficit was that Americans traveling abroad spent some $2,600,000,000 in 1960 while foreigners visiting the United States spent only $900,000,000 here. The difference —some $1,700,000,000—amounted to nearly half of the total deficit in the United States balance of payments for the year.

To close the "tourist gap," Congress passed the International Travel Act on June 29, 1961 creating the United States Travel Service as part of the office of the Secretary of Commerce. Secretary Hodges turned to his North Carolina colleague to take charge, and Gilmore's appointment was announced by President Kennedy on July 18, 1961. He was sworn in by Secretary Hodges on August 15, 1961.

One of Gilmore's first acts was to launch a series of marketing surveys in Europe to determine what people thought was wrong with tourism in the United States. At the annual convention of the American Society of Travel Agents in Cannes, France in October 1961, Gilmore spoke of USTS plans to make it easier, cheaper, and more pleasant for foreign tourists to visit the United States by encouraging local communities to extend hospitality to foreign visitors; by stimulating restaurants and hotels to print menus, directories, and signs in foreign languages; by having multilingual police and taxi drivers at ports of debarkation; and by establishing information centers and readily accessible currency exchange facilities.

Gilmore expressed particular sensitivity to the need for putting a smile on the faces of United States customs men inspecting the luggage of foreign visitors, since officiousness has been a long-time source of annoyance to foreigners as well as returning United States residents. Another goal of the Travel Service is to make it less expensive for foreign tourists to cross the ocean and to travel within the United States.

The USTS was given an initial year's budget of $2,500,000, with future annual appropriations up to $4,700,000 under the Travel Act. Much of the first year's budget went to establishing a network of "Visit America" centers in London, Paris, Frankfurt, Caracas, Sydney, and Tokyo. The offices, standard in design, "will speak America the moment you walk in the door," Gilmore has said.

Gilmore's straightforward approach has made a striking impression on the leaders of the American travel industry, who he believes have a special and vital role in promoting tourism in the United States through more package tours, cheaper transportation, and greater stress on arousing the American public to its responsibilities in playing host to visitors from abroad. "Travel should be recognized in economic interchange of people, meeting and understanding each other," Gilmore has explained (*American Forests*, August 1961). "Our nation has overlooked too long the opportunity to tell its story to the world in the most practical manner—by

showing visitors our natural and man-made attractions and our way of life."

Among the organizations in his home state with which Gilmore is affiliated, as a director, are the Business Foundation of North Carolina, the Morse County Hospital, the North Carolina Medical Association of Chapel Hill, and the North Carolina Symphony Society. He is an honorary vice-president of the American Forestry Association. His fraternity is Chi Psi and his clubs are the Sandhills Kiwanis of Southern Pines (president in 1952-53), the Explorers in New York City, and the Bohemians in San Francisco. He is a trustee of the Consolidated Presbyterian College of North Carolina and is a deacon of the Brownson Memorial Presbyterian Church of Southern Pines. He belongs also to the Young Democrats of North Carolina.

Voit Gilmore and Kathryn Kendrick of San Francisco were married on January 21, 1945. Their children are Kathryn, Geraldine, Susan, and Peter. Gilmore is slender and tall (six feet two inches), and in his role of top salesman of American tourism he has the assets of an eager smile, an enthusiastic outlook, and an animated manner of speaking.

References

    Am For 67:15 Ag '61 pors
    Sat R 44:33 S 9 '61 por

    World Who's Who in Commerce and Industry, 1961

GORDON, LINCOLN Sept. 10, 1913- United States Ambassador to Brazil; educator; economist

Address: b. Department of State, Washington 25, D.C.

When President John F. Kennedy in August 1961 appointed the Harvard economist Lincoln Gordon as Ambassador to Brazil, he chose an expert in international business and economic relations, in the relations between government and industry, in the development of America's water and energy resources, and—in recent years —in Latin-American economic affairs. In addition to his teaching at Harvard Business School, where he had been William Ziegler Professor of International Economic Relations since 1955, Gordon has served as adviser, planner, and consultant for the United States government on matters of international economic programs and development of resources. On August 28, 1961 the Washington *Post and Times Herald* editorialized: "The nomination of Lincoln Gordon as our Ambassador to Brazil is a case of putting a good man in the right job." Gordon succeeds John M. Cabot in the post.

Lincoln Gordon was born in New York City to Bernard and Dorothy (Lerned) Gordon on September 10, 1913. His mother, who moderates youth forums for the National Broadcasting Company, formerly moderated the New York *Times* Youth Forum, which she founded. Lincoln Gordon attended the Ethical Culture School in New York City and received his diploma from the Fieldston School in New York in 1930. He then attended Harvard College, from which he graduated *summa cum laude* in 1933.

(*Continued next page*)

Warren Kay Vantine

LINCOLN GORDON

Awarded a Rhodes Scholarship, he studied at Balliol College, Oxford University for three years. He was granted a Ph.D. degree in 1936, after having submitted a thesis that was later published as *The Public Corporation in Great Britain* by the Oxford University Press in 1938.

After he returned from Great Britain, Gordon worked as instructor and faculty instructor in government at Harvard University, from 1936 to 1941. He took a leave from Harvard during World War II to serve the government, but came back as an associate professor of business administration in 1946-47. From 1947 to 1950 he was a professor of government and administration at the Harvard Graduate School of Business Administration and the Graduate School of Public Administration. He resigned from the faculty in 1950 to devote himself full time to posts in the United States government.

Gordon's connection with the federal government dates back to 1939, when he worked for a year as a research technician on energy and water resources with the National Resources Planning Board. In 1940 he became senior economic consultant to the National Defense Advisory Board. From 1942 to 1945 he held various posts—as economist, deputy director, and director—with the War Production Board, serving as program vice-chairman from May to November 1945. In 1946 and 1947 he was a member of the United States delegation to the United Nations Atomic Energy Commission. He was also a consultant during the immediate postwar years to the Army and Navy Munitions Board and to the State Department in its development of the European Recovery Program. During 1948 he worked on program co-ordination and trade policy for the Division of Economic Cooperation Administration in administering the European Recovery Program (Marshall Plan). In 1949 and 1950 he directed the program division, office of the special representative in Europe of the Economic Cooperation Administration.

In 1950 and 1951 Gordon was economic adviser to the special assistant to President Harry S. Truman; in 1951 he also served as alternate for the United States member of the North Atlantic Treaty Organization temporary council committee. During 1951 and 1952 he served as assistant director for programs at the office of the director for mutual security. From 1952 to 1955 he served at the American Embassy in London as United States minister for economic affairs and director of the United States operations missions to the United Kingdom.

Then, in 1956, Gordon acted as a consultant to the North Atlantic council committee of three on nonmilitary aspects of the North Atlantic Treaty Organization. Three years later he visited Argentina, Brazil, and Chile on an exploratory mission for the Ford Foundation. After he was elected President of the United States, John F. Kennedy appointed Gordon as a consultant to an interdepartmental task force on Latin-American affairs, headed by Adolf A. Berle, Jr. Having surveyed the relations between Latin-America and the United States, the group submitted its report in January 1961. It contained the germinal idea for the "Alliance for Progress" program.

Before he joined the interim task force for Latin America, Gordon in 1960-61 held a Harvard Corporation appointment as a research associate at the Center for International Affairs. In April 1961 he visited Brazil for the Inter-American Bank, and in August of the same year he attended the Inter-American Economic and Social Conference at Punta del Este in Uruguay, held in the interests of the Alliance for Progress. Gordon also accompanied Adlai E. Stevenson, the United States representative to the United Nations, on his goodwill tour of Latin America.

As a recognized expert on Latin-American, and particularly Brazilian, affairs, Gordon had been favorably viewed by the Brazilian government as the successor to John M. Cabot before President Kennedy nominated Gordon for the post on August 24, 1961. White House sources insisted that the appointment was routine, but Cabot— a career diplomat who had been the United States Ambassador to Brazil since July 1959— had in July 1961 drawn an implied rebuke from Jânio da Silva Quadros, then President of Brazil, for what Quadros termed "meddling" in Brazilian affairs. The ambassadorship, perhaps the most sensitive post in South America, was made still more so when Quadros resigned a few days after Gordon's nomination had been announced. He was replaced on September 7, 1961 by former Vice-President João Goulart, a man regarded by the United States as sympathetic to the Communist viewpoint. The United States Senate confirmed Gordon's appointment during the Brazilian crisis at the end of August, and he took up his duties as Ambassador at the beginning of October 1961.

During his busy career in government and teaching, Gordon has managed to set some time aside for the writing of scholarly books and articles. With Merle Fainsod he is co-author of *Government and the American Economy* (Norton, 1948). He contributed an article entitled "The Economic Recovery Program in Operation" to the *Harvard Business*

Review in March 1949 and another article called "Myth and Reality in European Integration" to the *Yale Review* in the issue of autumn 1955. Also in 1955 the American Foreign Service Association announced that his essay entitled "Organization for the Conduct of Foreign Policy," which appeared as the leading article in the August 1955 issue of *Foreign Service Journal,* had won the $1,000 grand prize in an essay contest sponsored by the *Foreign Service Journal.* More recently Gordon has contributed an article on "Private Enterprise and International Development" to the July-August 1961 issue of the *Harvard Business Review;* one on "Underdeveloped Countries and the World Economy" to the *International Yearbook* published by the *Cotton Trade Journal;* and one on "Economic Regionalism Reconsidered" to the January 1961 issue of *World Politics.* He has completed work on the manuscript of a book dealing with the impact of Brazilian government policies on United States manufacturing investments in Brazil.

Lincoln Gordon married Allison Wright of Brookline, Massachusetts on June 25, 1937. They have four children: Anne, Robert W., Hugh, and Amy. Only the youngest child, Amy, lives with her parents in their new home above Guanabara Bay in Brazil. The Gordons formerly divided their time between their home in Belmont, Massachusetts and their summer home at Georges Mill on Lake Sunapee in New Hampshire, where Mrs. Gordon sculpted and painted and Gordon played tennis and sailed. Gordon stands five feet eight inches in height, weighs about 160 pounds, and has gray hair. A biographical sketch in the New York *Times* (August 25, 1961) quoted one of Gordon's life-long friends as saying that he is a "very normal human being, who is never cross." The writer of the sketch described Gordon as being the kind of man "who cuts his own firewood with an axe and a chain saw." A lover of music, especially of string quartets, Gordon supplemented his basic knowledge of the piano by learning to play the 'cello during his assignment at the American Embassy in London. He is fluent in French and Portuguese. His political affiliation is with the Democratic party. Gordon belongs to the American Economic Association, the American Political Science Association, the Royal Economic Society, the Council on Foreign Relations, and the American Academy of Arts and Sciences.

References

N Y Times p10 Ag 25 '61 por
Who's Who in America, 1960-61

GUION, CONNIE M(YERS) (gī'ŏn) Aug. 29, 1882- Physician
Address: 147 E. 50th St., New York 22

In the struggle of women in the twentieth century to gain acceptance as doctors, Dr. Connie M. Guion's impressive list of "firsts" signifies major advancement. Her career as an internist, which spans a period of over forty years, has been closely connected with New York Hospital-Cornell Medical Center and has

Portrait by Molly Guion

DR. CONNIE M. GUION

combined care of patients with teaching and research. In 1961 Dr. Guion, who is regarded in medical circles as the dean of women doctors, could take pride in President John F. Kennedy's appointment of Dr. Janet G. Travell as the White House physician not only because Dr. Travell is one of her former students, but also because the appointment signals a marked decline in prejudice against women doctors.

Connie Myers Guion was born on a plantation in Lincolnton, North Carolina on August 29, 1882, the ninth child of Benjamin Simmons and Catherine Coatesworth (Caldwell) Guion. Her parents had been married during the Civil War and had twelve children, four boys and eight girls. Her father was a railroad executive and a farmer whose fortunes had suffered in the war. It was from her mother that she acquired an interest in medicine, as did three of her sisters who became trained nurses.

The Guion family lived on the plantation in Lincolnton until 1892, when they moved to Charlotte, North Carolina. Connie Guion went to public schools in Charlotte and later, with the financial help of an older sister, studied at Miss Kate Shipp's School in Lincolnton from 1898 to 1900. She also tutored two boys and in her spare time played tennis and collected stamps. Then after two years at Northfield Seminary in Northfield, Massachusetts, she enrolled at Wellesley College, Massachusetts on a scholarship. Chemistry and English literature were her major subjects, and tennis continued to be her favorite sport. She belonged to the Shakespeare Society and was custodian of The Barn, and she helped meet some of her expenses by tutoring in chemistry and working in a self-help dormitory.

Although Miss Guion was eager to prepare further for a career in medicine, her first concern was to help provide in her turn for the

GUION, CONNIE M.—*Continued*

education of her younger sisters. Accordingly, after Wellesley had awarded her the B.A. degree in 1906, she became an instructor in chemistry at Vassar College in Poughkeepsie, New York. Two years later she accepted a similar position at Sweet Briar College in Virginia, where she was promoted in 1910 to professor of chemistry and head of the department of chemistry.

In 1913, the year that she left Sweet Briar, Connie Guion graduated from Cornell University in Ithaca, New York with the M.A. degree, for which she had submitted the thesis *Purine Metabolism of the Racoon, the Opossum and the Rat.* She received her M.D. degree from Cornell Medical College in New York City in 1917, graduating at the top of her class and winning the Polk Prize for general efficiency.

Dr. Guion served her internship at Bellevue Hospital in New York from 1917 to 1919. When she rebelled against the twenty-four-hour ambulance duty required of interns and was told that the practice had been going on for a hundred years, she remarked tersely, "Well, the century's up" (*Look*, September 12, 1961). The shift was shortly afterward reduced from twenty-four to twelve hours. For a year after she had completed her internship she was assistant attending physician at the Cornell division of Bellevue Hospital. She was then associated with the New York Infirmary, as assistant attending physician from 1920 to 1926 and as attending physician and department director from 1926 to 1929, and with Booth Memorial Hospital in New York, as attending physician from 1920 to 1926 and subsequently as consulting physician.

In 1922 Dr. Guion helped to organize the Cornell Pay Clinic—an outpatient service organized like a doctor's office—which became part of New York Hospital-Cornell Medical Center in 1932. While she was holding the position of chief of the clinic from 1929 to 1953, she also served on the staff of the New York Hospital as assistant attending physician from 1932 to 1942 and attending physician from 1943 to 1950. Since 1950 she has been a consultant. In 1946 she became the first woman member of the hospital's medical board, and in 1951 she was the first woman to be made an honorary member of the board. Since 1926 she has also maintained a private practice, specializing in internal medicine. Her associates in her New York office are her niece, Dr. Parks McComb, and Dr. Artemis Pazianos, who had studied at Wellesley College on a Dr. Connie Guion scholarship and under Dr. Guion at Cornell Medical College.

The teaching phase of Dr. Guion's work in medicine had begun in 1919 when she was appointed to an instructorship at Cornell University Medical College. She was promoted to assistant professor of medicine in 1929 and to associate professor in 1936. Ten years later she was the first woman in the country to become a professor of clinical medicine.

During her many years of practice and research Dr. Guion has written a number of papers on various medical problems. On the subject of diabetes she is the co-author with Conrad Berens of "Sarcoma of the Choroid, An Unusual Complication of Diabetes Mellitus" (*Journal of the American Medical Association*, March 1924) and with Elaine P. Ralli of "Synthalin in Treatment of Diabetes" (*Journal of Laboratory and Clinical Medicine*, May 1929). Her work in thyroid diseases was reported in "Treatment of Diseases of the Thyroid Gland" (*Medical Clinics of North America*, September 1930), "Some Aspects of the Medical Treatment of Thyroid Diseases" (*Medical Women's Journal*, June 1935), and other papers.

Civic work has also been part of Dr. Guion's life. From 1942 to 1948 she was a member of the industrial council of the Department of Labor of the State of New York, and in 1948 she served as chairman of its medical appeals unit. She is a member of the advisory committee of the National Health and Safety Council of the Girl Scouts of America and a trustee of Sweet Briar College. Since 1940 she has been president of the Marie and John Zimmerman Fund, Inc., and since 1950 vice-president of the Joseph Collins Foundation. She is also a member of the fellowship grants committee of the American Association of University Women.

Two "firsts" head the list of Dr. Guion's honors. New York Hospital honored her by naming its new outpatients building after her. The Doctor Connie Guion Building, although still under construction in 1962, has been in use since the latter months of 1961. This is the first building to be named after a living woman doctor. Dr. Guion was also the first woman to win the annual award of distinction from Cornell University Medical College Alumni Association, an award she received in 1951.

Other honors accorded Dr. Guion include honorary D.Sc. degrees from Wellesley College (1950), Women's Medical College of Pennsylvania (1953), and Queens College in Charlotte, North Carolina (1957). Dr. Guion was also the recipient of the Elizabeth Blackwell citation of New York Infirmary in 1949 and the Northfield Award for Distinguished Service presented by Northfield School for Girls in 1951, and she was named Medical Woman of the Year in 1954 by the American Medical Women's Association.

A member of the New York Academy of Medicine, New York State Medical Association, and the Women's Medical Association of New York City, Dr. Guion also belongs to County Medical Society, Cornell University Medical Council, and Cornell Medical College Alumni Association (president in 1946-47). She is also a member of Phi Beta Kappa, Sigma Xi, and Alpha Omega Alpha, and the Shakespeare Society of Wellesley College, Wellesley College Alumni Association, and the Cosmopolitan Club of New York City.

Partly because of her distinctive hairstyle—she wears her white hair piled into a high crown on top of her head—Dr. Guion is known to her associates as "the Queen." She has blue eyes and is five feet three inches tall. A writer for the New York *World-Telegram and Sun* (April 18, 1961) was impressed by her "royal bearing . . . and the warmth of her personality and her genuine interest in the welfare of the human race." She is unmarried. Her church is the Episcopal and her political party the Republican.

Fishing and bird watching are now her favorite outdoor recreations, and in earlier years she enjoyed horseback riding as well as tennis. Her other pleasures, besides her lifelong hobby of stamp collecting, are a cocktail before dinner and the theater, and she admits to "looking" at television. "Evil and conflict have always been with us," she observed in an interview for *Look* (September 12, 1961). "It's mass communication that makes them seem worse."

References

Who's Who in America, 1960-61
Who's Who in New York, 1960
Who's Who of American Women (1958-59)

HALL, PETER (REGINALD FREDERICK)
Nov. 22, 1930- Theater director

Address: b. Royal Shakespeare Theatre, Stratford on Avon, England; Aldwych Theatre, London W.C. 2, England; h. 31 Montpelier Sq., S.W. 7, London, England; Avoncliffe, Stratford on Avon, England

Since launching the 101st season of the Royal Shakespeare Theatre (then the Shakespeare Memorial Theatre) at Stratford on Avon in 1960, the inspired young director Peter Hall has brought several invigorating changes to the world's most famous Shakespearean festival. In order to build a permanent, year-round company that could evolve an individual style, he established a London home of the Royal Shakespearean Theatre, at the Aldwych Theatre, for the presentation of both modern and Elizabethan plays, and at both the Stratford and Aldwych theaters he gave the stage a jutting apron. Some 360,000 theatergoers attend performances at Stratford during its April-November season; the Aldwych is open all year. Over the past seven years Hall has directed more than forty-five plays, including the London première of Jean Anouilh's *The Waltz of the Toreadors* (1956) and the Broadway production of *The Rope Dancers* (1957).

Peter Reginald Frederick Hall was born in Bury Saint Edmunds, Suffolk, England, on November 22, 1930, the only child of Reginald Edward Arthur Hall, a station master, and Grace Florence (Pamment) Hall. He graduated in 1948 from the Perse School in Cambridge, where he had been a student monitor, and then attended St. Catharine's College, Cambridge University. Specializing in English, he earned a number of scholarships and in 1953 received his M.A. degree with second class honors. From 1948 to 1950 he had also served in the education corps of the Royal Air Force as sergeant instructor in economics.

During his university years Hall produced and acted in some twenty plays and worked on the administrative committees of the Amateur Dramatic Society, the University Actors, and the

J. F. W. Cocks, Stratford-Upon-Avon, Warwicks

PETER HALL

Marlowe Society. In 1953 audiences in Windsor saw his first professional production. He later produced in repertory in Windsor, Worthing, and Oxford; staged two Shakespearean productions for the Arts Council; and was artistic director of the Elizabethan Theatre Company.

In January 1954 Hall became assistant director to John Fernald at the Arts Theatre in London, where subsequently, from January 1955 to July 1956, he was the director. Among his presentations at the Arts Theatre were Federico García Lorca's *Blood Wedding*, Carlo Goldoni's *An Impresario from Smyrna*, and Eugene O'Neill's *Mourning Becomes Electra*. He staged the London premières of Julien Green's *South* (March 30, 1955) and Samuel Beckett's controversial *Waiting for Godot* (August 3, 1955), as well as the first Eugene Ionesco play performed in England, *The Lesson* (March 9, 1955).

The first play that Hall directed on Broadway, and his thirty-first professional production, Morton Wishengrad's *The Rope Dancers*, opened on November 20, 1957. Brooks Atkinson praised Hall's direction for "the clarity, the force, the mood, the pressure that express the author's point of view" (New York *Times*, December 1, 1957).

Earlier in 1957 Hall had formed his own producing company, the International Playwrights Theatre, in London, which offered Tennessee Williams' *Camino Real* in April 1957 as its first presentation and George Tabori's riotous satire *Brouhaha* in August 1958 as its second presentation. In the interim, besides directing *The Rope Dancers*, Hall had staged the world première in May 1957 of the opera *The Moon and Sixpence* and the London première in early 1958 of Tennessee Williams' *Cat on a Hot Tin Roof*, starring Kim Stanley.

Since 1956 Hall had also been directing plays for the Shakespeare Memorial Theatre, including

HALL, PETER—*Continued*

Cymbeline in 1957. During the 100th season of Stratford's Shakespeare theater, which began in April 1959, he directed Charles Laughton as Bottom in a presentation of *A Midsummer Night's Dream* that broke with all non-Elizabethan traditions. His second play of the season for the Memorial Theatre was *Coriolanus*, which starred Sir Laurence Olivier in a notably vigorous production.

It had been announced at the opening of the 1959 season that in January 1960 Peter Hall would succeed Glen Byam Shaw as director of the Shakespeare Memorial Theatre. One of the first changes that Hall made was an alteration in the theater itself, which had been built with funds subscribed by English-speaking people all over the world and had been opened on April 23, 1932. In an effort to approximate Elizabethan design and to increase intimacy with the audience, Hall remodeled the proscenium stage to extend a fourteen-foot apron into the audience area.

When Hall presented *Two Gentlemen of Verona* at Stratford in April 1960 as his initial production as director, W. A. Darlington (New York *Times,* April 6) commented that it was a "slow, overloaded and complicated production that caused the actors to run continuous obstacle races among chunks of moving machinery. This made a disappointing start for Mr. Hall's much-heralded regime as director . . . it probably will turn out to be a prelude to better things." That this prediction was confirmed is evident from the success of subsequent productions in 1960. These included the comedies *Twelfth Night, Troilus and Cressida* (staged in a hexagonal sandbox), *The Taming of the Shrew, The Merchant of Venice,* and *The Winter's Tale.*

At the end of Stratford's 1960 season Hall took over control of the Aldwych Theatre and began to operate it on a year-round basis in conjunction with the Memorial Theatre, whose season runs from April to November. While the Stratford theater continues to present only Shakespearean plays, the Aldwych offers plays mainly by other writers, both contemporary and pre-twentieth century. Hall organized a troupe of actors, under a three-year-contract, to appear in productions at both theaters.

"Every actor longs for a lounge suit after a spell of wearing tights," Hall explained in an article that he wrote for the New York *Times* (December 11, 1960). ". . . Variety of work combined with artistic and financial security makes an attractive offer even if there's not much money in it. I also can offer the actor limited freedom . . . although the new Stratford contract gives me first claim on the actor's services for the next three years, he can spend as much as a third of his time working elsewhere. Not only will this stop his stagnating; it will also give him the opportunities to enjoy the big money of television and the films."

By working with the same performers over a long period of time, Hall hopes to develop a permanent company with a new and distinctive style recognizable as Stratford's. He has commis-

sioned new plays from John Arden, Peter Shaffer, and other writers and has encouraged dramatists to make a broad, or epic, use of the stage in treatment of contemporary themes.

The first production of Hall's company at the Aldwych was John Webster's *The Duchess of Malfi,* which opened on December 15, 1960 to much acclaim, with Dame Peggy Ashcroft as the Duchess. During 1961 Leslie Caron appeared in Jean Giraudoux's *Ondine,* and Christopher Plummer and Eric Porter co-starred in Jean Anouilh's *Becket.* Another 1961 production, John Whitings's *The Devils* (based on Aldous Huxley's *The Devils of Loudun*), was the first play commissioned especially for presentation by the Stratford-Aldwych company.

The Hollow Crown, an anthology compiled by John Barton about the Kings and Queens of England in their own words, played at Stratford in 1960 for one Sunday evening. Its success was so immediate that it was brought to the Aldwych Theatre in 1961; a shortened version was presented on the BBC-TV program *Monitor*; and the full-length version became part of the Aldwych repertory. The cast includes four readers, three singers, and one instrumentalist.

The Shakespeare Memorial Theatre was renamed the Royal Shakespeare Theatre in March 1961, and the company at Stratford and the Aldwych became the Royal Shakespeare Company. In late 1961 it was announced that the company would make its first tour of the United States during the following fall.

Commenting on the selection of Hall as the director of the Stratford festival, Harold Hobson noted in the *Christian Science Monitor* (September 2, 1959) that Hall was "one of the three most powerful directors in London," powerful both for artistic insight and for the rights he holds to certain plays. "Mr. Hall's most striking characteristic," Hobson went on to say, "is his rich sensitivity to the atmosphere and mood of a play. As Jean Anouilh said to me recently, Mr. Hall is one of the few directors who gets to the inside of a play and works outward."

One of the stars of Peter Hall's company is also his wife. He and French-born ballet dancer and actress Leslie Caron were married on August 6, 1956. They have two children, Christopher John and Jennifer Caron. Hall is slender, stands six feet two inches tall, and has dark-brown eyes and dark-brown hair. His hobby is music of all kinds. His club is the Garrick in London. Although he did not join the Committee of 100, which staged sit-down demonstrations in favor of nuclear disarmament, he said in a brief interview for the London *Sunday Times* (September 17, 1961) that his sympathies were with the committee: "Too many people in this country have a death-or-glory spirit. I think the Committee are making us aware of the dangers of brinkmanship."

References

N Y Herald Tribune IV p3 Ja 17 '60
N Y Times p16 Ag 31 '59
International Who's Who, 1961
Theatre World Annual (1961)
Who's Who, 1961

HART, MOSS Oct. 24, 1904-Dec. 20, 1961
Playwright; director; collaborated with George
S. Kaufman on several comedies, including *You
Can't Take It With You* (1936); wrote by himself *The Climate of Eden* (1952) and other
plays, as well as motion-picture scripts, winning
an Oscar for *Gentleman's Agreement* (1947);
directed *My Fair Lady* (1956) and other Broadway productions. See *Current Biography* (November) 1960.

Obituary
N Y Times p1 + D 21 '61

HILLYER, ROBERT SILLIMAN June 3,
1895-Dec. 24, 1961 Poet; novelist; essayist;
his many volumes of poetry include *Poems for
Music, 1917-1947* (1947) and *The Suburb by
the Sea* (1952); won the Pulitzer Prize for Poetry in 1934 and other important awards; taught
English literature at Harvard University for
almost twenty-five years (beginning in 1919)
and at the University of Delaware (since 1952).
See *Current Biography* (July) 1940.

Obituary
N Y Times p23 D 25 '61

**KELDYSH, MSTISLAV (VSEVOLODO-
VICH)** Feb. 10, 1911- Mathematician; physicist;
Soviet government official

Address: b. U.S.S.R. Academy of Sciences, B.
Kaluzhskaya 14, Moscow, U.S.S.R.

Elected president of the U.S.S.R. Academy of
Sciences on May 19, 1961, Professor Mstislav
Keldysh is a distinguished physicist and mathematician and a professor at the University of
Moscow. He is recognized in the Soviet Union
as a leading authority on space mathematics
and aerodynamics. Early in his career he directed research at a major Russian aircraft
development center, concentrating on such design problems as the dynamic properties of
wings, vibration, and landing year. As head of
a secret research institute during the 1940's he
took a leading role in spurring Soviet rocket
development. Keldysh has a reputation for his
theoretical studies in such fields as calculus
of variations and boundary-value problems.
More recently, as a director of several major
research institutes concentrating on mathematics
and mechanics, he has proved himself to be a
brilliant scientific organizer.

Mstislav Vsevolodovich Keldysh was born
into an intellectually prominent family on February 10, 1911 in Riga, a major seaport on the
Baltic and the capital of the Latvian Soviet
Socialist Republic. His sister is a mathematician
and his father, V. M. Keldysh, a civil engineer
with the Kuibyshev Military Engineering Academy and the Academy of Construction and
Architectural Sciences of the U.S.S.R., is noted
for his work in the development of reinforced
concrete.

After completing his lower school education,
Mstislav Keldysh studied in the department of
physics and mathematics at Moscow State University. Following his graduation in 1931 he

Wide World
MSTISLAV KELDYSH

joined the staff of the Central Aero-Hydrody-
namics Research Institute (CAHI), the major
aircraft development center in the Soviet Union.
During the early 1930's Keldysh did work on
the wave-motion theory, water impact theory,
and the theory of elastic oscillation in an air
stream. He indicated the course of his future
research in his early studies on the unsteady
motion of bodies in fluid and the aerodynamics
of compressible air.

While he was occupied with his work at
CAHI, Keldysh continued his graduate studies
in the evening at the Steklov Institute of Mathematics. In 1938 he received a doctor's degree
in advanced physics and mathematics. After he
completed his dissertation Keldysh was appointed head of a research unit engaged in
investigating the dynamic strength and vibration of aircraft. He completed an analysis of
vibrations in all parts of an airplane, the
wings, empennage (the tail assembly of an airplane comprising stabilizer, elevator, vertical fin
and rudder), and landing gear. Dr. Keldysh
formulated several theories that provided the
basis for developing methods to eliminate serious malfunctions in aircraft. He attributed the
origin of sudden vibrations in wings and
empennage to aerodynamic forces known as
flutter, a phenomenon that is now almost completely under control.

As a result of his research on sustained vibrations in pneumatic wheels, which he presented
in a monograph entitled "Shimmy in the Forward Wheel of the Tricycle Landing Gear," designers developed methods for eliminating these
tremors from the front wheel of a three-wheel
landing gear. Dr. Keldysh was the first to discover that some vibrations of the airfoil (any
surface of a plane, such as a wing or stabilizer,
designed to help in lifting or controlling the aircraft by making use of the air currents through
which it moves) produce thrust rather than

KELDYSH, MSTISLAV—*Continued*

drag. In a similar area of research related to the development of hydrofoil boats, Dr. Keldysh studied bodies striking water and investigated hydrofoils moving at a shallow depth in water.

Sometime during 1943 Dr. Mstislav Keldysh was selected to head the top secret "Russian Institute, Number 1" of the Ministry of Aircraft Industry. During the early years of the 1940's he concentrated on studies in the field of aerohydrodynamics, which deals with the forces in and motions of liquids, air, and other gases. Professor Keldysh made some important discoveries about fluid flow properties and was responsible for some significant research in rocket development. His studies provided the foundation on which the Soviet Union built its rocket and missile programs, achieving success with the satellite Sputnik in December 1957. Of particular significance also are Professor Keldysh's theoretical studies on the effect of fluid compressibility on lift. In this work he complemented the original theories elaborated by N. E. Zhukovsky, a pioneer in Russian aviation science.

In addition to his being recognized in aviation science, Dr. Keldysh is regarded in the Soviet Union as a mathematician of the front rank. Many mathematical techniques that he devised have proved their practical significance when applied to problems in physics and engineering. He has conducted fundamental research into the theory of functions of a complex variable and has worked on the potential theory, the approximate integral solution of differential equations, the degenerated elliptic equations under boundary conditions, and the theory of non-self-adjoint operators. In a more practical area Dr. Keldysh has taken the lead in introducing into the Soviet Union the concepts of computer mathematics, computer engineering, and some aspects of automatic control.

Since the 1950's, Dr. Keldysh has acted as a director of several major research institutes. These assignments have placed him in administrative work rather than in theoretical research, and have provided him with experience for his present position. The development centers under his supervision concentrated on studies in mathematics and mechanics and were responsible for solving important development problems in the area of special technology.

At a general meeting of the Soviet Academy of Sciences on May 19, 1961, Dr. Mstislav Keldysh was elected to the presidency by the unanimous choice of the delegates. In this policy position Keldysh will have a powerful voice in determining the future course of Russian scientific activity, since his organization virtually controls all the research institutes, laboratories, observatories, museums, and scientific committees in the U.S.S.R.

One of Dr. Keldysh's first official functions was to greet an all-union conference of scientific workers to disclose future scientific plans. He emphasized that full electrification, the main goal of the Soviet Union, commands a higher priority than rocket research. He told the space researchers that interplanetary travel and direct study of close planets had become a practical

certainty. Most important, Keldysh stressed that through the work of the Academy, which has been reorganized as a purely theoretical scientific body, "Soviet science must emerge to first place in the world."

Dr. Keldysh succeeded Aleksandr N. Nesmeianov, a chemist, who resigned after serving in the post for two five-year terms. Although Keldysh's election was reported in the Soviet press as a routine change at the end of a term of office, some Western authorities speculated that it was a maneuver by Premier Nikita S. Khrushchev to downgrade the Academy. The United Press International carried a news release that interpreted Keldysh's election as an obvious attempt to reorganize and modernize the Academy and to direct pure science toward practical results. Dr. Detlev W. Bronk, president of the National Academy of Sciences in the United States, disagreed with this point of view. He saw nothing unusual in Nesmeianov's resignation after so long a term of office and he did not think that the Russians intended to discourage pure science in favor of predetermined results. Supporting Bronk's opinion was Nicholas DeWitt of the Russian Research Center at Harvard University. In an article he wrote for *Science* (June 23, 1961), DeWitt explained that a debate over the management of all research and development programs in the Soviet Union has been raging since the 1950's. The issue, according to DeWitt, has been the presence in the Academy of a number of specialized research institutes, which tended to divert the Academy's attention away from its original function of conducting pure research to problems of technology and application. Part of Keldysh's job will be to implement the reorganization so that the direction of science and technology will be the responsibility of the newly established State Committee for Coordinating Scientific Research. Dr. Keldysh will direct the Academy to concentrate on "the most important long-run problems of science undergoing rapid development."

In addition to his being both a research scientist and academician, Dr. Keldysh has taught on the mathematics faculty of Moscow University as assistant professor (1932-49) and full professor (1949-61). He has been credited with organizing major schools of scientific research, and many of his students (who have become leading scientists in their own right) are now continuing his investigations in mathematics and mechanics.

A prominent scientific personality in the Soviet Union, Dr. Keldysh lectures frequently at conferences and university gatherings. His numerous articles and monographs have been published almost exclusively in the Soviet Union. He has written papers on the vibrations of wings with suspended attachments in air currents (1938); on the solvability and stability of the Dirikhle problem (1940); and on the representation of functions of a complex variable by series of polynomials in a closed domain (1945).

Dr. Keldysh is an active member of several scientific and technological societies in the Soviet Union. He was elected a corresponding member of the Soviet Academy of Sciences in 1943 and a full member three years later. He sat on the presidium (the ruling body) of the Academy from 1953 to 1960 when he was elected vice-president of the organization. Dr. Keldysh is also active on the presidium of the Committee for Lenin Prizes.

Stalin prizes were bestowed on Professor Keldysh in 1942 and 1946 for his work on aerodynamics and aircraft development. He holds a coveted Lenin Prize as well as five Orders of Lenin, three Orders of the Red Banner, and the title Hero of Socialist Labor. The last was conferred on him in December 1957 after the successful firing of the first Soviet satellite. Keldysh has been a member of the Communist party since 1949.

References

Nature 190:959+ Je 10 '61
N Y Times p9 My 20 '61 por
Science 133:1986+ Je 23 '61
Biographic Directory of the USSR (1958)
International Who's Who, 1961-62

KHOURI, FARIS EL- 1879-Jan. 2, 1962 Syrian statesman; professor of law at the University of Syria (1919-40); Prime Minister of Syria (1944-45, 1954-55); held other high government positions; head of Syrian delegation to the United Nations. See *Current Biography* (September) 1948.

Obituary

N Y Times p33 Ja 4 '62

LOBER, GEORG (JOHN) 1892-Dec. 14, 1961 Sculptor of conservative and realistic design; did the statue of Hans Christian Andersen in New York's Central Park; executive secretary of the New York City Art Commission (1943-60). See *Current Biography* (November) 1957.

Obituary

N Y Times p37 D 15 '61

LUTHULI, ALBERT JOHN 1899(?)- African liberation leader; former Zulu chieftain

Address: h. Groutville, Umvoti Mission Reserve, Natal, South Africa

The recipient of the Nobel Peace Prize for 1960, Albert John Luthuli, is a mission-trained leader of the liberation movement of Negroes in the Union of South Africa, president-general of the proscribed African National Congress, and a former Zulu chieftain. He was cutting sugar cane on his small farm, to which he had been banished by the government, when news of his honor reached him on October 23, 1961. Luthuli said, "The award is not just an honor to me but to all freedom-loving South Africans." The Nobel Peace Prize, amounting to over $43,000, is given annually by the Norwegian parliament to the person "who has done most or best to further brotherhood amongst the peoples." After having been delayed by the South African government, Luthuli finally received the Nobel Peace Prize for 1960 in Oslo, Norway in December 1961.

Wide World

ALBERT JOHN LUTHULI

At the same time announcement was made of the posthumous award of the Nobel Peace Prize for 1961 to Dag Hammarskjöld, the late Secretary-General of the United Nations. An editorial writer for the New York *Times* (October 24, 1961) commented: "Dag Hammarskjöld would have been proud to have his name joined in this award with Albert John Luthuli. . . . The Swedish diplomat and the African tribesman are united in life and death by their humility and their love of humanity."

A member of the African aristocracy, Albert John Luthuli was born about 1899 and grew up in the Groutville mission station in the Umvoti mission reserve on the coast of Natal near Durban, South Africa. His father was an interpreter at the local Congregationalist mission, which had been founded by Americans. His mother was a Gumede, a member of one of the most honored of Zulu tribes, and his uncle was the reigning chief of the Abasemakholweni tribe of Zulus.

Albert John Luthuli attended the local mission school and then went on to Adam's Mission Station College, the mission's secondary school, near Durban. After school hours the boy herded cattle along with other schoolchildren. His upbringing and mission training instilled in him profound religious convictions, a respect for Western civilization, and an awareness of the dignity of all mankind, regardless of color or creed. Luthuli became fluent in English and in 1921 he qualified as an instructor. He taught at Adam's Mission Station College for fifteen years, then in 1936 accepted a call to serve as chieftain of the Abasemakholweni tribe, consisting of about 5,000 members. The tribe elects its leader through a democratic process.

He governed in Groutville for seventeen years. He presided over the councils and beer drinks, quelled disturbances in the sugar fields, stepped up the yield of sugar, arbitrated disputes, im-

LUTHULI, ALBERT JOHN—*Continued*

posed fines, and enforced laws. At the same time he strengthened his ties with organized Christianity. He went to India in 1938 as a delegate to the International Missionary Council, representing the Christian Council of South Africa. At home he served as chairman of the Congregational Churches of the American Board, as president of the Natal Mission Conference, and as an executive member of the Christian Council of South Africa.

In 1946 Luthuli became a member of the Natives Representatives Council not long before its adjournment, and shortly thereafter joined the African National Congress. He was soon named president of the Natal Provincial Division of the African National Congress. In 1952 he helped to launch the "defiance campaign," sponsored by the Congress, in which thousands of Africans invited arrest in sit-in demonstrations protesting racial segregation in libraries, post offices, railway stations, and other public facilities. Because of his role in this nationwide display of passive resistance, Luthuli was summoned in October 1952 to the government's Native Affairs Department in Pretoria and warned that he must quit the Congress and abandon the defiance campaign or surrender his position as a tribal chief.

He accompanied his refusal to halt his Congress activities with a statement that a chief, by Zulu tradition, was first of all a leader of his people and only secondarily a functionary of the government. Eloquently summing up the determination of the Africans to win equality in their own land, he said: "I only pray to the Almighty to strengthen my resolve . . . for the sake of the good name of our beloved country, the Union of South Africa, to make it a true democracy and a true union, in form and spirit, of all the communities in the land."

In reply, the government deposed him as chieftain and prohibited him from visiting any of the major towns or cities of the Union of South Africa for twelve months. But in a gesture of support for their vanished chief, the tribal elders refused to name a successor to Chief Luthuli. That same year Luthuli became president-general of the African National Congress. A country chief when he went into the defiance campaign, Luthuli had emerged from it as a national public figure.

The following year a new government ban restricted Luthuli to his home at Groutville for two years. In December 1956 he was one of 156 African national leaders arrested on the charge of high treason. After detaining him for a year, however, the government dropped its charges against Luthuli and sixty-four others. He renewed his activities but in May 1959, he was banished once again to his small farm (this time for five years) under the Suppression of Communism Act and the Riotous Assemblies Act and forbidden from attending any meetings or gatherings—despite Luthuli's consistently anti-Communist and nonviolent record. Today he lives quietly in a simple five-room cottage of tin and concrete, filled with books on religion, philosophy, and politics, that he built himself

and that stands at the end of a rough, untarred road. Here he works each evening after his chores in the field are done.

Chief Luthuli believes that the African National Congress' chief weapons in its struggle against apartheid are economic. He particularly favors peaceful work stoppages or "stay-at-homes," since they have an immediate impact on the South African economy, which is based on the availability of cheap African labor. He has also called for economic boycotts of certain goods and services as another means of exercising economic pressure on the government.

In March 1960 Luthuli appeared in Pretoria as star defense witness in the treason trial for which he had originally been arrested in 1956, when a mass protest was launched against the hated "pass" system, which requires all black Africans to carry an identity card in moving about South Africa. On March 21 tragedy occurred when more than 250 Africans were shot —seventy-two fatally—while peacefully demonstrating in the town of Sharpeville. This massacre shocked the world. Luthuli publicly burned his pass in protest, for which he was fined $280, and called for a national day of mourning for the victims of the Sharpeville massacre. The government then declared a state of emergency, banned the African National Congress, and again arrested Luthuli. He was released on grounds of ill health (he has high blood pressure and once suffered a mild stroke) and returned to exile in Groutville.

In the face of the provocation and suffering —including physical beatings at the hands of white ruffians—that he has endured over the years, Luthuli still clings to his Christian convictions and he still advocates change without bloodshed in South Africa, if possible. For his continued policy of moderation and nonviolence, however, Luthuli has been criticized by some of his fellow Africans whose patience has run out. In 1959 the Pan-Africanist Congress was formed by younger and more militant members who broke away from the African National Congress and whose rallying cry is "Africa for the Africans."

In announcing its 1960 Peace Prize, the Nobel Committee said that Albert John Luthuli was being honored "because in his fight against racial discrimination he had always worked for nonviolent methods." The announcement was hailed abroad but denounced at home. The South African Broadcasting Corporation, owned and operated by the government, broadcast a scathing attack on him, and Senator Jan H. de Klerk, the Minister of the Interior, in reluctantly granting Luthuli a ten-day passport to accept the Nobel Peace Prize in Oslo, Norway, said: "The government fully realizes the award was not made on merit and must necessarily rob the Nobel Peace Prize of all its high esteem in the judgment of objectively minded people." Luthuli replied: "I am delighted that the government has given permission, but I deeply regret Senator de Klerk's uncalled for remarks about merit."

Luthuli had responded to the news of his honor with characteristic humility. "God has answered the call of the oppressed people of South Africa," he said. He expressed gratitude to the "many South Africans and friends abroad who have sympathized with the liberation struggle."

In the middle of December 1961 Luthuli finally arrived in Oslo with his wife, and he told reporters that he did not feel the biting cold because he was meeting "so many warmhearted people." Mr. and Mrs. Luthuli opened their many gifts in their hotel suite, went shopping, and relaxed by throwing snowballs outside the Storting (parliament). When he made his acceptance speech at a dinner held in the great hall of the University of Oslo, he was dressed in his tribal costume; a robe of blue and black, a leopardskin cap fringed with monkey tails, and a necklace made of the teeth of leopards. Luthuli said that he foresaw the end of the African revolution within the present generation and compared South Africa to "a hangover from the dark past of mankind, a relic of an age which everywhere else is dead or dying." Persisting, however, in the optimism he felt for the future of Africa in general, Luthuli said: "In a strife-torn world, tottering on the brink of complete destruction by man-made nuclear weapons, a free and independent Africa is in the making, in answer to the injunction and challenge of history: 'Arise and shine, for thy light is come.'"

Although he has never met an official of the government of H. F. Verwoerd, Luthuli remains the most influential figure among the 10,000,000 black Africans who comprise two-thirds of South Africa's population. Gray-haired, stockily built, and massively dignified, he is not tall but has the "large head, set majestically back on a strong neck" and commanding presence that South African novelist Nadine Gordimer has described as typical of the Zulu warrior in an article in the *Atlantic Monthly* (April 1959). According to Miss Gordimer, Luthuli also conveys "a sense of repose" and "a monumental quiet." He speaks English with an American accent, a by-product of his American mission education, and he has a fine singing voice with which he leads the singing of the African National Congress anthem "Mayibuye (Come Back) Africa," to the tune of "Clementine." By his wife Nokukanya he has a large family of sons and daughters; one of his daughters is a physician. After working at his small sugar cane trucking business, he likes to read and to listen to music on a stereo record player run by transistors. In summing up his credo, he once said: "I am no racist. South Africa is large enough to accommodate all people if they have large enough hearts."

References

Atlan 203:34+ Ap '59 por
Christian Sci Mon p1 O 26 '61 por
N Y Times p6 My 28 '59 por; p22 O 24 '61 por
Newsweek 58:51 N 6 '61 por
Time 18:26 N 3 '61 por
International Who's Who, 1961-62
Segal, Ronald. Political Africa (1961)

McCONNELL, F(OWLER) B(EERY) Dec. 4, 1894-Dec. 27, 1961 Business executive; began working for Sears, Roebuck & Company in 1916; became president in 1946 and chairman in 1958; retired in 1960; helped direct large expansion of the company. See *Current Biography* (July) 1952.

Obituary

N Y Times p23 D 29 '61

MARGAI, SIR MILTON (AUGUSTUS STRIEBY) (mär-gī') Dec. 7, 1895- Prime Minister of Sierra Leone; physician

Address: b. Prime Minister's Office, Freetown, Sierra Leone; h. The Lodge, Hill Station, Freetown, Sierra Leone

The Prime Minister of the new West African nation of Sierra Leone is Sir Milton Margai, a physician whose political activity and leadership were instrumental in his country's achievement of independence from Great Britain on April 27, 1961 and its membership in the Commonwealth of Nations. After serving for over twenty years as a medical officer for the Sierra Leone government, Dr. Margai retired in 1950 to take a more active part in politics and to bring about political cooperation between the Creole settler population of the colony and the natives of the protectorate. He became a Member of the Order of the British Empire in 1947 and was made a Knight Bachelor by Queen Elizabeth II in 1959.

Under British rule, Sierra Leone was divided into the colony and the protectorate. The colony, founded in 1787 and used for the settlement of liberated Negro slaves, had an area of 256 square miles and a population of 370,000 persons, mostly Creoles (descendants of the immigrant African settlers). The protectorate—the area of the hinterland where slavery was legal until 1927—came under British rule in the 1890's and had an area of 27,669 square miles and an estimated population of 2,130,000 persons. The colony had a literacy rate of 50 percent, while the protectorate, of which Sir Milton is a product, had a literary rate of 5 percent. Sierra Leone, now unified under one central government, is about the size of Ireland and has an estimated population of 2,500,000.

Milton Augustus Strieby Margai was born on December 7, 1895 in Gbangbatoke, Banta Chiefdom, in the southern part of the protectorate of Sierra Leone. He is the eldest son of M. E. S. Margai, a well-to-do merchant. His grandfather was a Mende warrior chief. The Mende tribe of the south and the Temnes of the north account for more than half of the population of Sierra Leone and are the most powerful of the twelve major tribal groups in the country.

Margai was raised in Bonthe and received his primary and secondary education in American-oriented schools. He first attended the Evangelical United Brethren School in Bonthe and then Albert Academy in Freetown, the major city in the colony and now the capital of Sierra Leone. Going on to Fourah Bay College in Freetown, he specialized in history and was granted the B.A. degree, the first awarded to a student from the

SIR MILTON MARGAI

questions affecting the protectorate. The district councils and the protectorate assembly were said to have evolved from proposals that Margai had originally made to the tribal chiefs.

In 1946 Margai joined the Sierra Leone Organization Society (S.L.O.S.), which he later headed. Originally founded to promote agricultural co-operation in the protectorate, the S.L.O.S. became a political organization to guard protectorate rights within the traditional framework, and to implement and improve the new constitution proposed by the British Governor, Sir Hubert Stevenson, in 1947. Margai also established the politically influential Sierra Leone *Observer,* the first protectorate newspaper, published at Bo and managed by himself and other members of the S.L.O.S.

Speaking in the protectorate assembly in 1950, Margai strongly endorsed the new constitutional proposals and moved for their early implementation. In 1951 the modified Stevenson constitution went into effect, giving the more populous but less developed protectorate a substantial share of the representation in the Legislative Council of Sierra Leone for the first time. To promote co-operation between the colony and the protectorate, Margai in 1951 founded the Sierra Leone People's Party (S.L.P.P.), merging the S.L.O.S. and the Freetown People's Party. Basically conservative in its outlook, the S.L.P.P. stood for moderate nationalism, political unification of the colony and the protectorate, and self-government within the British Commonwealth of Nations.

In the November 1951 elections the S.L.P.P. became the majority party in the Legislative Council. Along with five other S.L.P.P. members, Margai was appointed to the Executive Council, an embryo cabinet. In 1952 he unofficially took charge of the departments of health, agriculture, and forestry, and in 1953 he became minister of these departments. As leader of the majority party in the government, he was known informally as leader of government business.

In June 1954 Margai became chief minister while retaining the ministries of health, agriculture, and forestry. He was re-appointed chief minister and also became minister for internal affairs and development in 1957 after the first general elections ever held throughout the country had given twenty-seven out of forty seats in the legislative council to the S.L.P.P. The conservative and cautious policies of Dr. Milton Margai came to be strongly criticized by a faction led by his younger brother, Albert Michael Margai, a lawyer, who contended that the S.L.P.P. was coming too much under the influence of the Governor, Sir Maurice Dorman. Although in a bid for the leadership of the S.L.P.P. Albert Margai defeated his brother by one vote, Albert subsequently withdrew from the party to establish the more militant and dynamic People's National Party in September 1958.

protectorate. The college, established in 1827, was supported by the Church Missionary Society and became affiliated with the University of Durham in England in 1876.

For his medical education, Margai went to England to attend the King's College medical school at Newcastle-on-Tyne, a part of the University of Durham. There he received the B.S., M.A., and Bachelor of Medicine degrees, qualifying as a physician in 1926. He also attended the Liverpool School of Tropical Medicine. Returning to Sierra Leone, he engaged in private practice in Freetown and Bonthe in 1927-28.

In 1928 Margai entered government service as a medical officer. During his twenty-two years in this capacity, he served in all of the twelve districts in the protectorate except that of Koinadugu. He thus came to know the people and to inspire their respect as a leader and as a surgeon and expert on midwifery. Working through the Bundu—a women's secret initiation society whose chief aim is to prepare girls for womanhood—he instituted a campaign for instruction in pre- and post-natal care and child welfare, and undertook measures to increase literacy.

Margai took an interest in the training of Native Administration midwives and other staff, and he wrote a primer and a catechism on midwifery in the Mende language. In 1950 he retired from the government service as the senior medical officer at Bo, the capital of the protectorate. He continued his medical practice in private and opened a surgery and nursing home at Bo. He recently gave this home to the nation to be used as a Cheshire Home for the chronically ill.

Margai first entered politics in 1930, when he was elected to the Bonthe district council—the local government unit composed of representatives of the various chiefdoms in the district. Subsequently he represented the council as a non-chief member of the protectorate assembly, which up to 1957 functioned as an advisory body to the government on social, political, and economic

As a step in the direction of independence a new constitution was adopted on August 14, 1958, establishing an All-African Executive Council, presided over by the governor. The Legislative Council was replaced by a House of Representatives, and Margai was named Premier. He was knighted by Queen Elizabeth in 1959. Following the constitutional conference held at London in

April 1960, at which it was decided that Sierra Leone should attain independence in April 1961, Sir Milton's title was changed to Prime Minister. Meanwhile, in March 1960, Sir Milton led the movement to form a united national front of all parties—including the People's National Party—to work together toward independence.

On independence day, April 27, 1961, some 15,000 persons crowded into the Freetown sports stadium. The singing of the hymn "Lead, Kindly Light," was followed by the new national anthem of Sierra Leone. Fireworks accompanied the raising of the new green, white, and blue flag in place of the Union Jack. At the opening of the Sierra Leone Parliament, the Duke of Kent, representing Queen Elizabeth II, handed over the formal documents of sovereignty to Sir Milton Margai. Members of the All People's Congress party—a radical opposition group, which had broken with the united national front—were arrested under emergency measures for the duration of the festivities on charges that they planned to disrupt the independence celebrations, allegedly with aid from abroad. At a pre-independence banquet Sir Milton said, however, that his government would not repress "responsible criticism" and would welcome comments presented in a democratic manner.

The coalition government headed by Sir Milton includes his brother Albert Margai as Minister of Natural Resources. Sir Milton has indicated that his government would continue the program of development begun before independence, including the mechanization of agriculture, industrial growth, reforms in education and local government, improved medical services, and increased revenues from the major exports: diamonds, iron ore, and palm products. To implement this program, the Prime Minister is seeking investment capital from Great Britain, the United States, and other Western nations. He has said, however, that he is not interested in aid from the Soviet Union or Communist China.

Sierra Leone is a member of the Commonwealth of Nations and has established cordial relations with one of her neighbors, Liberia. Sir Milton is, however, apprehensive about possible infiltration and subversion from neighboring Guinea, which is oriented toward the Soviet Union. In May 1961 Sir Milton headed a delegation to the conference of heads of state in Monrovia, Liberia. On September 28, 1961 Sierra Leone was accepted as the 100th member of the United Nations, by unanimous vote of the General Assembly.

Sir Milton Margai is a member of the Evangelical United Brethren Church. In 1960 Durham University awarded him an honorary D.C.L. degree, and he was decorated by Liberia in 1961 with the Grand Cordon of the Order of Pioneers of Africa. His wife was a secretary and stenographer before their marriage. They have children and grandchildren. Sir Milton often dresses in a pink-striped *agbada*—the long gown worn by his countrymen. He is said to look like the late Mohandas K. Gandhi. Although he is of slight build, he is a man of considerable energy and still plays a vigorous game of tennis. He also enjoys music and plays the piano, the organ, and the violin.

Conservative in temperament and social outlook, Sir Milton has the medical man's distrust of hasty action and rash judgment. He is direct and to the point, and his speeches are devoid of rhetoric. Although he is advanced in years, he intends to continue to play an active political role. "I am not going to build something up, only to stand by and see some young men destroy it," he has said.

References

Christian Sci Mon p9 Ap 27 '61 por
N Y Times p4 Ap 28 '61 por
Toronto Globe and Mail p7 Ap 26 '61 por
Washington (D.C.) Post C p20 Je 29 '61 por
International Who's Who, 1961-62
Segal, Ronald. Political Africa (1961)
Who's Who, 1961

MELLERS, WILFRID (HOWARD) Apr. 26, 1914- Educator; musicologist; composer
Address: b. University of Pittsburgh, Pittsburgh, 13, Pa.

When funds provided by the A. W. Mellon Educational and Charitable Trust enabled the University of Pittsburgh to endow a chair of music in its new College of Academic Disciplines, a committee of scholars was appointed to select a music educator worthy of the post. The search for the first Mellon Professor of Music led the committee to England, where they chose Wilfrid Mellers for the position. In so doing, they honored his long experience as an educator, his proved intellectual abilities (not only in music but in literature and social studies), and his practical knowledge of music gained through a long career as a composer.

Wilfrid Howard Mellers was born on April 26, 1914 at Leamington Spa, England. He attended Leamington College before enrolling in Downing College, Cambridge University, in 1933. By the time he left Cambridge in 1939 with the degree of Master of Arts, Mellers had distinguished himself both in literature and in music, having taken a first in English before he decided to specialize in music. In his literary studies, Mellers came under the influence of the Cambridge literary critic F. R. Leavis.

In addition to his academic work at Downing College, Wilfrid Mellers studied musical composition privately, principally with Egon Wellesz, whose interest in the twelve-tone school of modern music left a permanent impression upon the younger composer. Mellers at this period also received a great deal of advice from another composer, Edmund Rubbra, with whom he shared a profound interest in Elizabethan poetry and its possible relationship to modern musical settings.

Wilfrid Mellers' first musical appointment, lasting from 1938 to 1940, was at Darlington Hall. From 1940 to 1946 he served as extramural lecturer in music at both Cambridge and Birmingham universities. In 1945 he returned to Downing College to accept the post of supervisor in English, at the same time lecturing

WILFRID MELLERS

there on music. In 1946 he was awarded the Mendelssohn Fellowship for Composition.

In 1948 Wilfrid Mellers left Downing College once again, this time to assume the post of staff tutor in music at the extramural department of Birmingham University. Eventually he rose to the position of senior lecturer at Birmingham, but in 1960 he left to accept the University of Pittsburgh's invitation to become the first Mellon Professor of Music.

An intrepid worker, Mellers was unabashed by the heavy schedule assigned to him at the University of Pittsburgh during his first academic year. This included three weekly lectures in a general course on the history of European music (offered to students not specializing in music), an advanced seminar in the music, poetry, and theater of the seventeenth and eighteenth centuries (offered to selected students from the departments of music, literature, and drama), eight public lectures dealing with American music, one of Mellers' favorite subjects, supervision of graduate studies in music, and lessons in composition. Mellers spent the academic year of 1961-62 on leave of absence in England.

In teaching general courses in music history, Mellers' pedagogic technique consists of concentrating upon one work or a small group of works exemplifying the major musical epochs. Playing the work at the piano, Mellers proceeds to analyze it and to place it in its historical context. He believes that this is the ideal way of teaching the history of music.

Despite his busy academic career, Wilfred Mellers has also succeeded in distinguishing himself as a writer on music and as a composer. In the former role, he contributed numerous articles to F. R. Leavis' journal *Scrutiny* and also served a term as music editor of that publication beginning in 1940. He has also published many studies in learned music journals and reference works, such as *Musical Quarterly* and the fifth

edition of *Grove's Dictionary of Music and Musicians,* as well as articles and reviews in such popular publications as the *Listener* and the *Spectator.*

Wilfrid Mellers' first published book was *Music and Society,* which, in its first English edition (Dobson, 1946), bore the subtitle *England and the European Tradition.* This highly praised study soon went into a second edition, published both in England (Dobson, 1950) and in the United States (Roy, 1951).

Reviewing the American edition of *Music and Society* for the *Saturday Review of Literature* (May 26, 1951), N. C. Carpenter wrote: "Illumined by remarkable erudition combined with deep musical sensitivity and literary artistry, this account of the evolution of English musical styles in relation to social concepts shows the importance of the social background in shaping British music and explains plausibly the flowering of this music at certain periods as well as the lack of a first-rate musical culture from Purcell's time until the present."

Mellers' second book, *Studies in Contemporary Music* (Dobson, 1948), was, like its predecessor, later released in an American edition (British Book Centre, 1950). Shortly thereafter, Mellers' *François Couperin and the French Classical Tradition* (Dobson, 1950; Roy, 1951) established the author as one of the world's leading experts on the music of France's classical period.

A reviewer for the London *Times Literary Supplement* (December 15, 1950) complained of Mellers' book on Couperin: "The voluminous information and the abundant reflections contained in this book do not make it an easy one to read." He went on to admit, however, that "Mr. Mellers has staked a new claim for English scholarship in this field, and if his book has some of the failings of its kind, it is nevertheless a remarkable achievement and provides a classical study of a composer and period wholly neglected in this country and insufficiently investigated elsewhere."

Mellers next published a short study entitled *Music in the Making* (British Book Centre; Dobson, 1953). He also wrote the third and fourth volumes of the series *Man and His Music* that Essential Books in the United States, Rockliff in England, and Smithers and Bonnellie in Canada began to publish in 1955. Mellers' two contributions, *The Sonata Principle* (from c. 1750) and *Romanticism and the Twentieth Century* (from 1800), virtually constitute a history of music from the middle of the eighteenth century to the present.

Wilfrid Mellers won recognition more quickly as a writer on music than as a composer. One reason for this is his great interest in vocal and choral music that often involve unusual combinations of voices and instruments and are therefore not suitable to most public concerts. Although his output includes orchestral pieces, chamber music, and works for solo instruments, the greater part of his work consists of music for the human voice.

Following World War II, Mellers renounced most of the music he had composed up to that time, and his new compositions began to find some favor with English audiences; public performances of his works became more frequent and numerous commissions began to come his way. In 1946, for example, the Institute for Contemporary Arts commissioned his Serenade for Oboe, Clarinet, and Bassoon; in 1947 his incidental music for Aeschylus' *Prometheus* was used in a Birmingham University production of the drama.

The year 1948 saw commissions by the Highbury Little Theatre for incidental music for Aristophanes' *Lysistrata,* and by Homerton College, Cambridge University, for the cantata *The Song of Ruth,* set to a libretto by R. J. White based upon the Biblical text in the Authorized Version. In the following year, the W. M. A. Singers commissioned and gave a London performance of his cantata *News from Greece,* with words by R. F. Willett.

Further commissioned choral works by Wilfrid Mellers include *Yggdrasil* (words by Christopher Harsall), commissioned and performed in 1951 at the Bryanston Summer School; *Nausicaa's Welcome* (words by R. F. Willetts), for the Attingham Summer School in 1952; and *The White Island* (set to poems by Robert Herrick) for the Stafford Women's Training College, also in 1952.

Despite his successes in the field of choral writing, Wilfrid Mellers considers himself above all a composer of operas. Mellers' operatic works include *The Tragicall History of Christopher Marlowe,* composed in 1950-52 to an R. J. White libretto but still unperformed, and a masque for puppets, *The Trial of the Jewelled Peacock,* a setting of George Moore's words for soprano, tenor, baritone, and chamber orchestra (1952). Another Mellers opera, *The Shepherd's Daughter,* has been given a public production that received enthusiastic notices.

Wilfrid Mellers and his wife, Peggy, have two daughters, Judith, born June 22, 1950, and Caroline, born November 11, 1954. Mellers' organizations include the Performing Rights Society and the Composers Guild of Great Britain.

References
> Manchester Guardian p6 Ag 25 '60 por
> Baker's Biographical Dictionary of Musicians (1958)
> Grove's Dictionary of Music and Musicians (1955)

MILLER, WILLIAM E(DWARD) Mar. 22, 1914- United States Representative from New York; lawyer; political party official
Address: b. House Office Bldg., Washington 25, D.C.; h. Lockwood Heights, Olcott, N.Y.; 6605 Radnor Rd., Bethesda 14, Md.

Republicans have pinned a large measure of their hope for victory in 1962 and 1964 on Representative William E. Miller, who was elected chairman of the G.O.P. National Committee on June 2, 1961. An orthodox, articulate, and frankly partisan Republican, he demonstrated his political craftsmanship, in organization and debate, as chairman of the House of Representatives Republican Campaign Committee in 1960. Miller who was first elected to Congress in 1950, represents a district of upstate New York, where he practices law.

WILLIAM E. MILLER

William Edward Miller was born on March 22, 1914 in Lockport, Niagara County, New York, where his father, Edward J. Miller, was employed as a janitor by General Motors. His mother, Elizabeth (Hinch) Miller, ran a milliner's shop. The boy attended St. Patrick's Roman Catholic Parochial School in his native city and graduated in 1931 from the Lockport High School. At Notre Dame University in South Bend, Indiana he majored in economics, was a varsity debater, and received his B.A. degree in 1935.

"Deep interest in law and desire to make a contribution to the cause of good government," Miller has said, determined the course of his career. In June 1938 he graduated with the I.L.B. degree from Union University's Law School in Albany, New York, where he had won the Benjamin Cardozo Prize for excellence in trial work. Later in the year he was admitted to the New York State Bar and was appointed United States commissioner for the western district of New York by Federal Judges John Knight and Harold Burke.

During the next four years, from 1938 to 1942, Miller divided his time between his work as commissioner and his private law practice in Lockport as the junior partner of the firm of Holley & Miller. In 1940, during the Willkie for President campaign, he was a member of the speaker's bureau of the Republican party.

Inducted into the Army as a private on July 1, 1942, Miller took basic training at Fort Meade, Maryland. In January 1945, after serving with the Military Intelligence Branch, he was selected for the Officer Candidate School of the Judge Advocate General Branch at Ann Arbor, Michigan. He graduated four months later, was commissioned a first lieutenant, and was assigned to the War Criminals Branch in Washington. In August 1945 he was selected as one of the assistant prosecutors under Supreme Court Jus-

MILLER, WILLIAM E.—Continued

tice Robert A. Jackson at the Nazi war criminals trials at Nuremberg.

After his discharge from the service in the rank of first lieutenant in early 1946, Miller resumed private law practice in Lockport and also accepted an appointment as assistant district attorney of Niagara County. On January 1, 1948 Republican Governor Thomas E. Dewey of New York named him district attorney of Niagara County—an appointment confirmed in the November election by a majority of over 13,000 votes. During Dewey's campaign for the Presidency, Miller served again as a member of the Republican speaker's bureau. Earlier in 1948 he had become the senior partner of the Lockport law firm of Miller & DeLange—a partnership that continued until 1953.

Miller was first elected to the House of Representatives in November 1950. At that time his district, covering Niagara County and part of Erie County, was the Forty-second New York Congressional District, but at the next biennial election it became the Fortieth District. Seated in the Eighty-second Congress in January 1951, he was assigned to the House Expenditures and Government Operations committees, but in October 1951 he was transferred from Expenditures to the Judiciary Committee, of which he is now the second-ranking Republican member. Some years later, for several sessions, the Judiciary was his only committee assignment, but in 1959 he was also named to the Committee on Un-American Activities.

Beginning with his first year in Congress, Miller sponsored legislation authorizing hydroelectric power development by private utilities at Niagara Falls, and in 1956 he vigorously opposed New York Senator Herbert H. Lehman's bill providing for development by the New York State Power Authority and giving public agencies and rural co-operatives priority over private groups in access to power. Lehman's bill was passed in the Senate, but in the House it was being held in the Rules Committee by Howard W. Smith of Virginia. Miller's opponents have alleged that when he heard that the bill was to be reported out of the committee, he took the floor to denounce a pending civil rights bill, even though he was a member of the Judiciary Committee, which favorably reported the bill, and subsequently the Rules Committee failed to clear the Lehman proposal. In 1957 Congress passed a bill providing for state development of Niagara power, but also containing the compromise that Miller wanted in favor of private interests.

In denying charges that he had moved to kill the civil rights bill in exchange for Southern help against the public power bill, Miller explained that he felt the civil rights measure would have given too much power to the Attorney General and the proposed Civil Rights Commission. He had earlier voted for all Republican-backed civil rights legislation and later he supported the bill that became the Civil Rights Act of 1960—making obstruction of court orders for school desegregation a crime, requiring preservation of voting records, and providing for court referees.

Representative Miller backed Dwight D. Eisenhower for the Republican Presidential nomination in 1952 and in succeeding years generally supported the Eisenhower program, including mutual security and renewal of the reciprocal trade agreements. Although once an opponent of the St. Lawrence Seaway, he voted in favor of that project in 1953, partly because of the benefits that it would bring Buffalo and partly because it was on the Eisenhower program.

On other key-vote issues, Miller opposed postponement of British debt payments (1957) and a freeze of farm price supports (1958). He voted for Alaska statehood (1958) and Hawaii statehood (1959), for the Landrum-Griffin labor reform bill (1959), for the minimum wage increase and an increase in postal and federal employees' salaries (1960), and against the $4.9 billion authorization for housing (1961) and the emergency educational bill (1961).

According to Congressional Quarterly charts, Miller scored zero in the number of times he voted in opposition to Republican-Southern Democrat coalition against Northern Democrats on roll-call votes in 1959 and 1960. In 1961 his conservative coalition opposition rose to 9 percent, but at the same time his conservative coalition support rose to 61 percent from 50 percent for 1959 and 1960. Examining his voting record before the 1960 election, Americans for Democratic Action scored him 22 percent on the number of times he had voted in accordance with its own views, and the AFL-CIO committee on political education gave him 10 percent. His percentage of agreement with Americans for Constitutional Action was 96.

In January 1960, with the support of Representative Charles A. Halleck, whom he had backed for Republican House leader the year before, Miller was elected chairman of the Republican Congressional Campaign Committee. He concentrated his efforts mainly on eighty districts (seventy of which had been lost by the Republicans in the preceding six years) where he believed his party's chances were good, and he traveled in thirty-four states on behalf of candidates. In October 1960, as the campaign closed, he accused the Democrats of emphasizing the religion of their Presidential candidate, Senator John F. Kennedy, "in ways they think will get him votes." This he described as "bigotry in reverse." Miller was given much of the credit for the twenty-two seats that the Republicans gained in the election. He himself was re-elected by 104,752 votes to 85,005 for his Democratic opponent.

Although partial to the conservative wing of the G.O.P., Miller had avoided involvement in ideological differences among Republicans. He was therefore politically acceptable to leaders of all sections of his party—former Vice-President Richard M. Nixon, New York Governor Nelson A. Rockefeller, and Senator Barry Goldwater of Arizona—and was elected unanimously on June 2, 1961 to succeed Senator Thruston B. Morton of Kentucky as chairman of the Republican National Committee. He is the forty-third chairman in the party's history and the second Roman Catholic to hold that office.

Miller's first task was to strengthen party organization in an effort to win the House of

Representatives for the Republicans in the November 1962 elections. He postponed discussion of the challenges that would come with planning for the national convention and Presidential campaign of 1964. As chairman, Miller has been notably diligent in attacking President Kennedy and Democratic policies, especially in Cuba and the Republic of the Congo, and in criticizing administration press and public relations practices.

The day after his election to the chairmanship Miller announced that he planned to open a new law firm in Buffalo on August 1, 1961 In July 1961 he and John W. Bailey, the Democratic National Chairman, were named to the board of trustees of the Citizenship Clearing House. Miller belongs to the Lockport Fraternal Order of Eagles and to other fraternal groups as well as veterans organizations. His clubs include the Lockport Town and Country and the Columbia Country.

William E. Miller and Stephanie Wagner were married on February 26, 1943; their children are Elizabeth Ann, Mary Karen, and William E., Jr. Trim and dapper, with a preference for Homburg hats and Chesterfield coats, Miller is five feet eight inches tall and weighs 140 pounds. He has hazel eyes and brown hair. In manner he is said to be brisk, aggressive, and scrappy, though even-tempered, and he has a gift for stinging words. Some political commmentators see his competitiveness reflected even in his hobbies—watching football and baseball games and playing golf and bridge.

U. S. Army

PAUL H. NITZE

References

Cong Q p933 Je 2 '61
N Y Post Mag p2 Je 11 '61 por
N Y Times p10 Ja 22 '60 por; p9 Je 3 '61 por
N Y Times Mag p26+ O 16 '61 por
American Catholic Who's Who, 1960 and 1961
Congressional Directory (1961)
Who's Who in America, 1960-61
Who's Who in New York, 1960

MOSES, ANNA MARY ROBERTSON Sept. 7, 1860-Dec. 13, 1961 Painter, better known as Grandma Moses; described as "an authentic American primitive"; began painting in her late seventies; noted for vivid, nostalgic rural scenes of upstate New York. See *Current Biography* (January) 1949.

Obituary

N Y Times p1+ D 14 '61

NITZE, PAUL H(ENRY) (nĭt'sĕ) Jan. 16, 1907- United States government official
Address: b. The Pentagon, Washington 25, D.C.; h. 3120 Woodley Rd., N.W., Washington 16, D.C.; Bel Alton, Md.

The appointment of Paul H. Nitze to the powerful and strategic post of Assistant Secretary of Defense for international security affairs, in December 1960, ended an eight-year hiatus in the public career of a government official of proved merit and capability. An investment banker before the war, Nitze had gone to Washington in 1940 as an expert in economics and had advanced to top policy-making positions in the State Department. He fell victim in 1953 to the political change in climate of the Eisenhower administration, but retained an importance in the field of defense and foreign policy as a writer, lecturer on international affairs, and educational organization official. Since taking office on January 29, 1961 he has been a key figure in co-ordinating the diplomatic and military policies of President John F. Kennedy's administration.

Paul Henry Nitze, the son of William Albert and Anina Sophie (Hilken) Nitze, was born in Amherst, Massachusetts on January 16, 1907. His family is of German Protestant stock, and both his parents were natives of Baltimore. His father, the noted philologist, was professor of Romance languages at Amherst College at the time of his son's birth; he later taught for many years at the University of Chicago. Paul Nitze's sister, Elizabeth Hilken, married Walter P. Paepcke, the founder of the Container Corporation of America.

For his college preparatory training, Nitze attended Hotchkiss School in Lakeville, Connecticut, and he then enrolled in Harvard University, where he became a member of the freshman crew and Hasty Pudding. He majored in economics and finance and received the B.A. degree *cum laude* in 1928. The following year, after a brief period of employment with the Container Corporation of America, he entered upon his career as "a Wall Street prodigy," to use his phrase, as a vice-president of Dillon, Read & Company, the New York investment banking firm of which C. Douglas Dillon, now Secretary of the Treasury, also became a vice-president, in 1938.

(Continued next page)

NITZE, PAUL H.—*Continued*

Nitze remained with Dillon, Read until he entered government service, with the exception of the years 1938 and 1939, when he headed his own firm, P. H. Nitze & Company, specializing in corporate reorganization. When in later years his shift from the Republican to the Democratic camp brought him the label of "ex-Republican," his response was, "I'm also an ex-Wall Street banker."

At Dillon, Read & Company, Nitze had met James V. Forrestal, who in 1940 accepted an appointment as Under Secretary of the Navy. Nitze left Wall Street that year to go to Washington as Forrestal's assistant, but in 1941 he was named financial director of the Office of the Coordinator of Inter-American Affairs, under Nelson A. Rockefeller. He became chief of the metals and minerals branch of the Board of Economic Warfare the following year and then moved in 1943 to the Foreign Economic Administration as director of the foreign procurement and development branch. From 1944 to 1946 he was vice-chairman of the United States Strategic Bombing Survey, performing a service for which President Harry S. Truman awarded him a Medal of Merit.

Economic problems grew increasingly important in United States postwar foreign policy, and in 1946 Nitze transferred to the Department of State as deputy director of the Office of International Trade Policy, where he helped develop the Marshall Plan (European Recovery Program). He was appointed in June 1948 as deputy to the Assistant Secretary of State for Economic Affairs and in August 1949 as assistant to George F. Kennan, director of the State Department's policy planning staff. Before the year was over he succeeded Kennan as director, thus becoming one of the country's top foreign policy makers. Besides helping to prepare the Congressional legislation responsible for the Marshall Plan, Nitze's larger assignments during the late 1940's included the shaping of NATO and planning the cold war strategy. In 1951 and 1952 he figured in resolving the British-Iranian oil dispute.

After the Republicans came to power in 1953, Nitze was considered for an influential post in the Defense Department, then under Charles E. Wilson, and reportedly was slated to succeed Frank C. Nash as Assistant Secretary of Defense for international security affairs. Republican Senators demurred, however. Although various names were mentioned in connection with the opposition, most political commentators believed that it was Senator Joseph R. McCarthy who fought the appointment of Nitze because he had served in the State Department under McCarthy's foe, Dean Acheson.

In December 1953 Nitze was elected president of the Foreign Service Educational Foundation in Washington, a privately supported organization that is financially responsible for the School of Advanced International Studies, which it co-administers with Johns Hopkins University. He also served as a research associate of the school's Washington Center of Foreign Policy Research and as a trustee of Johns Hopkins. In 1957 he was an adviser to the com-

mittee that prepared the Gaither report, which appraised the status of national defense. In the latter part of the 1950's he often lectured on foreign and defense policy, and besides contributing articles to *Foreign Policy*, the *Reporter*, the New York *Times Magazine*, and other publications, he often wrote policy papers for the Democratic National Committee. He is also the author of *U.S. Foreign Policy, 1945-1955* (Foreign Policy Association, 1956).

During the eight years of Republican administration, therefore, Nitze continued to be active in the fields in which his earlier government experience had made him an expert. In 1959 the Senate Foreign Relations Committee called upon him to make a report on the impact of long-range missiles and future weapons systems on United States foreign policy, and in 1960 he headed Kennedy's pre-election committee on national defense problems.

The position to which Kennedy appointed Nitze on December 24, 1960 was the same for which Eisenhower had considered him in 1953 —Assistant Secretary of Defense for international security affairs. In making his announcement Kennedy said that the office would have "broadened scope and influence" and that Nitze would play a key part in developing disarmament plans. Nitze's other responsibilities include his department's relations with the National Security Council and the State Department as well as the direction of military assistance programs. In one of his columns on changes in the Pentagon under Secretary of Defense Robert S. McNamara, Hanson W. Baldwin pointed out (New York *Times*, November 21, 1961), "Today strategy and strategic concepts are probably being influenced more by the office of Paul H. Nitze . . . and by the State Department, than by the Joint Chiefs of Staff."

Nitze's background has made him a strong proponent of bipartianship—disagreement when necessary, debate, a resolution that represents the most effective and unified national stand. His own position has been opposed to the Eisenhower-Dulles concept of massive retaliation. A further estimate of where he stands was made by a close observer and quoted in *United States News and World Report* (January 9, 1961), "The Stevenson group believes that Soviet Russia can be 'appeased,' while the Acheson group insists there cannot be a deal that is not iron-clad. Nitze is going to be on Acheson's side. He will work well with Rusk, pretty well with Bowles, and not at all with Stevenson."

One of the areas in which Nitze has since worked closely with Acheson is the Berlin crisis. Nitze is a member of the Berlin Task Force, which President Kennedy created in June 1961 to handle strategy in a possible showdown with Russia over Berlin. He agrees with Acheson's view that the objective of the U.S.S.R. in Berlin is to humiliate the West in the eyes of the world; and in September 1961 in an authoritative speech on military policy in the Berlin crisis Nitze said that Berlin was "the focus of a larger problem" and that Communist interference with the West's rights in Berlin would be considered "the straw that breaks the camel's back" in regard to the patience of the democracies.

Among Nitze's business interests are the Aspen Skiing Corporation, of which he is chairman of the board, and the Aspen Corporation, of which he is a director. (His brother-in-law, the late Walter P. Paepcke, did much to develop Aspen, Colorado and was the founder of the Aspen Institute of Humanistic Studies.) Nitze is also vice-president and director of United States Commercial Company and a director of Rubber Development Company and Technical Services, Inc.

Since December 2, 1932, Paul H. Nitze has been married to Phyllis Pratt, whose grandfather was an official of Standard Oil and founder of Pratt Institute. Her mother was a Republican Congresswoman from the Seventeenth ("Silk Stocking") District of New York. The couple have four children: Heidi, Peter, William 2d, and Phyllis.

Nitze is known as affable, self-effacing, and reserved, as a hard worker and tough-minded man of intellectual brilliance. His wide range of interests includes theology, philosophy, science, and history. He is also fond of music and plays the piano. Well-groomed and handsome, with gray hair and an athletic build, he is considered one of the most distinguished-looking men in government circles. Almost as vigorous physically as he is mentally, he enjoys skiing, hunting, and playing tennis, and he has a farm in Maryland where he raises tobacco and beef cattle.

References

Democratic Digest p18+ Ja-F '61
N Y Herald Tribune p9 D 25 '60
N Y Post Mag p2 Ja 1 '61 por
Time 77:22 Ap 7 '61
U S News 50:38 Ja 9 '61 por
International Who's Who, 1961-62
New Frontiersmen (1961)
Who's Who in America, 1960-61

STIKKER, DIRK U(IPKO) (stĭk′ĕr dĭrk ûp′kō) Feb. 5, 1897- Dutch diplomat and statesman

Address: b. Palais de l'OTAN, Porte Dauphine, Paris 16ᵉ, France; h. Hôtel George V, 29 ave. George V, Paris, France; "Villa Belfaggio," Menaggio-Loveno, Lago di Como, Italy

NOTE: This biography supersedes the article that appeared in *Current Biography* in 1950.

In the face of new Soviet threats in West Berlin, Dirk U. Stikker, who became the Secretary-General of the North Atlantic Treaty Organization (NATO) in April 1961, has warned the Soviet government not to underestimate the unity of the North Atlantic alliance or its ability to meet Communist military actions in Europe. His new position imposes on him a major responsibility for maintaining this unity and military capability. Since World War II Stikker, a successful banker and businessman in the Netherlands, has served his country as a legislator and political leader, as Minister of Foreign Affairs, as Ambassador to Great Britain, and as permanent representative to

DIRK U. STIKKER

NATO and to the Organization for European Economic Cooperation (OEEC).

Dirk Uipko Stikker, the son of Uipko Obbo and Ida (Meursing) Stikker, was born on February 5, 1897 in Winschoten, in the province of Groningen, the Netherlands. He attended the Gymnasium in Groningen and then entered the University of Groningen, from which he received the LL.D. degree in 1922.

Like his father, Stikker decided to make his career in banking, and he began as an employee of the Groningen bank. In 1922, after leaving the university, he became a member of the legal staff at the Twentsche Bank in Amsterdam, one of the largest in the Netherlands. His first executive position was that of manager of the Lissensche Bank Vereniging in Lisse. When the Twentsche Bank took over the Lisse bank, Stikker was made manager of its western section. He was subsequently transferred to the Leyden branch and, after four years there, to the Haarlem branch.

From 1935 to 1948 Stikker was managing director of Heineken's Brewery Company (Bierbrouwerij Maatschappij in Amsterdam. Responsible for the foreign interests of the company, he traveled widely to visit its overseas branches in Europe, the Near and Far East, the United States, and the West Indies. He also was a member of the board of directors of several leading banking and commercial enterprises, such as the Netherlands Bank, the Netherlands Trade Society, and the International Society of Brewers in Brussels.

Stikker's worldwide commercial interests are shown by his directorships at one time or another of the Koloniale Brouwerijen "Cobra" in Amsterdam; Heineken's Netherlands Indies Brewing Company in Sourabaya; Malayan Breweries, Ltd.; A.B.C. Brewery Company in Singapore; Société Anonyme des Bières Bomonti et Pyramides in Cairo; Meuse Breweries in Paris;

STIKKER, DIRK U.—*Continued*

Leopoldville Brewery in the former Belgian Congo; and several important Belgian breweries.

Meanwhile, in prewar years, Stikker had also become president of an employers' association that had worked closely with the Dutch labor unions in industrial matters and, like the unions, disbanded after the Nazi invasion of 1940 in World War II. During the German occupation of Holland he organized co-operative action between the unions of employers and those of workers, and, in the position of trustee or organizer, he helped to finance the resistance movement in Holland.

After the war, Stikker served in 1945 as a member of the purging council for industry and commerce, and in the same year he helped to establish and became president of the Netherlands Foundation of Labor, a national organization concerned with promoting co-operation between employers' associations and trade unions. His organization helped to eliminate the cause of economic disputes and greatly facilitated Dutch postwar rehabilitation. He also became president of the Central Social Association of Employers and of the Labor Board. His interest in labor-management relations led to his appointment as delegate to the 1946 conference of the International Labor Organization in Montreal. He participated also, as a member of the Netherlands committee, in the early work of the Food and Agriculture Organization.

Concerned with the re-establishment of Dutch government after the liberation, Stikker became a member of the National Advisory Committee of the Provisional Parliament. In 1946 he founded the Freedom party and served as its president for two years. When the party merged with other groups in 1948, he became president of the new People's Party for Freedom and Democracy (the Liberal party). This party favors free competition, and although it does not oppose social legislation, it opposes nationalization and restriction of free enterprise. From 1945 to 1948 he was president of the board of the *Algemeen Handelsblad,* a Liberal party newspaper in Amsterdam.

In 1946 Stikker was elected to represent the Freedom party in the First Chamber (senate) of the States-General (parliament) in the Hague. In the July 1948 cabinet reorganization, Willem Drees of the Labor party formed a coalition government in which Stikker became the Minister of Foreign Affairs. He was sworn into office on August 7, 1948 and remained in that post until September 1952. During these four years he had a major responsibility for guiding his country through the negotiations that granted Indonesia her independence from Holland and committed the Netherlands to the development of Western European union and to a North Atlantic community.

The Indonesians' desire for independence from the Netherlands after World War II had led to considerable fighting and occasional agreement. As Foreign Minister, Stikker negotiated with Indonesian representatives at 1948 and 1949 round table conferences. On December 27, 1949 the transfer of sovereignty to Indonesia was completed, but the question of the Netherlands

New Guinea (Dutch West Irian) remained a source of dispute between the two countries. In 1951 a seven-week cabinet crisis occurred when Stikker resigned over criticism of his offer to share with Indonesia the administration of the territory. Drees, in a new coalition cabinet, reappointed Stikker as Foreign Minister.

Meanwhile, to meet the problem of the postwar economic rehabilitation of Europe, the United States offered the Marshall Plan in 1947. The European Recovery Program countries established in 1948 the Organization for European Economic Cooperation (OEEC), designed to help the United States carry on its European aid program and to develop economic co-operation between the member countries (eventually eighteen European nations). Stikker was appointed the Netherlands representative to the OEEC Council and in February 1950 was made the political conciliator of the group. From late 1950 to 1952 he was chairman of the OEEC Council. In 1952 the Marshall Plan ended, but the OEEC continued to help promote economic co-operation among its members.

Other efforts toward promoting co-operation in Europe also gained from Stikker's participation. Along with the Foreign Ministers of the other four Brussels Treaty countries (Great Britain, France, Belgium, and Luxembourg), he agreed in January 1949 to organize a Council of Europe, envisaging a European federation. The European Coal and Steel Community came into effect in 1952 for the creation of a common market for the goods under its jurisdiction among Belgium, France, West Germany, Italy, Luxembourg, and the Netherlands.

Steps toward the creation of a North Atlantic community were taken in 1949. Stikker participated in the discussions leading to the pact for the North Atlantic Treaty Organization (NATO), and on April 4, 1949 he signed the treaty in Washington for the Netherlands. He also represented his country in the first meeting of the NATO Council in Washington and the September 1950 meeting in New York. In 1951 he agreed on the details of a European army project with the Foreign Ministers of West Germany, Italy, France, Belgium, Holland, and Luxembourg, and he signed for the Netherlands the European Defense Community treaty on May 27, 1952.

Later in 1952 a cabinet reorganization gave the Dutch government a new Foreign Minister, and Stikker was appointed the Netherlands Ambassador to the Court of St. James's; he remained there for six years. During part of this period he was concurrently the Netherlands Minister to Iceland (from 1954 to 1956) and then Ambassador to Iceland (from 1956 to 1958). In 1955-56 he was also chairman of the Netherlands delegation to the Economic and Social Council of the United Nations.

Moving from London to Paris in 1958, Stikker served for three years as the Netherlands permanent representative on the NATO Council and to the OEEC with the rank of ambassador. He presented his nation's views to these two organizations and led his national delegation of advisers and experts. During this period the OEEC had been adapting itself to the changing conditions of the European and world economic situation, and was planning for its successor, the Organization for Economic Co-operation and Development (OECD). The new organization went into effect in the fall of 1961, with the United States and Canada as additional members. Its purpose is to promote Atlantic economic co-operation among its twenty members and to co-ordinate aid to developing countries in Europe and in the rest of the world.

After the resignation of Paul-Henri Spaak as Secretary-General of NATO, Stikker was chosen to succeed him and took office on April 21, 1961. He thus became responsible for the organization of the work of the Council, permanent Council committees, and temporary working groups, with the assistance of the international staff secretariat. By the nature of his position he may also be the initiator of policies, a conciliator among the points of view of the fifteen member nations, and the spokesman for the entire group.

In his first year as Secretary-General, Stikker underscored the need to give NATO an independent striking force, to develop political consultations among the members, and to promote economic co-operation among them. He traveled to the capitals of the member nations for consultations with their government officials. He warned the Soviet government of NATO's strength and determination over the Berlin crisis—a warning backed by the build-up of NATO conventional forces in Europe to almost twenty-five divisions.

Stikker's articles and speeches have appeared in English in *Vital Speeches, Foreign Affairs, United Nations Bulletin,* and other publications. He has received decorations and awards from the governments of the Netherlands, Great Britain, Luxembourg, France, Venezuela, the Dominican Republic, Belgium, Brazil, and Iceland, and from the Holy See.

Dirk Uipko Stikker married Catharina Paulina van der Scheer on May 2, 1922, and they have two sons, Uipko Dirk and Allerd. Stikker combines an enormous capacity for work with a forceful and realistic approach to business and governmental problems. Genial and dapper, with graying blond hair and blue eyes, in manner and appearance he easily satisfies the popular notion of a diplomat. His homes are a Paris chateau and an Italian lakeside villa, and his recreational interests range from playing golf to listening to opera.

References

Christian Sci Mon p2 F 1 '61 por
N Y Post p64 Je 28 '61 por
N Y Times p4 F 11 '61 por
Newsday p50 Ap 19 '61 por
N U Bul 7:766 D 15 '49; 8:59 Ja 1 '50 por
International Who's Who, 1961-62
International Year Book and Statesmen's Who's Who, 1961
Who's Who, 1961
Who's Who in the United Nations (1951)
Wie is Dat? (1956)
World Biography (1948)

TEAGLE, WALTER C(LARK) May 1, 1878-Jan. 9, 1962 Industrialist; president (1917-37) and board chairman (1937-42) of the Standard Oil Company (New Jersey); exponent of liberal labor policies; director of the Federal Reserve Bank of New York. See *Current Biography* (June) 1942.

Obituary

N Y Times p47 Ja 10 '62

THANT, U (thŏnt ōō) Jan. 22, 1909- Acting Secretary-General of the United Nations; Burmese diplomat and civil servant

Address: b. United Nations Secretariat, United Nations, New York 17.

The Acting Secretary-General of the United Nations, U Thant of Burma, was elected on November 3, 1961 by the unanimous vote of the General Assembly to fill out the unexpired term of the late Secretary-General Dag Hammarskjöld, ending April 10, 1963. His election represents a compromise between the United States and the Soviet Union, following a long controversy between the two great powers over the nature of the United Nations Secretariat.

Although he has tried to adhere to a policy of genuine neutrality, U Thant believes that peace cannot be achieved by a mere passive neutralism, and has said that the Secretary-General "must be impartial, but not necessarily neutral." He feels that the U.N. Secretariat should be strong enough to cope with international crises as they arise.

As is the case with many of his compatriots, the United Nations official has only one name, Thant, which means "clean" or "pure." The word U, which customarily precedes it, is a term of respect, roughly akin to "Mr." He was born on January 22, 1909 at Pantanaw, in the Irrawaddy delta region of Burma, the eldest of the four sons of a prosperous landowner and miller of rice. His brothers are all prominent in Burmese government and business. U Thant received his secondary education at the National High School at Pantanaw, and he subsequently attended University College in Rangoon. His early ambition was to become a political news writer. At Rangoon he became acquainted with Thakin Nu, better known as U Nu, who later became Premier of Burma.

In 1928 U Thant was forced to leave college in his second year, because of the death of his father. He then went back to his old high school at Pantanaw, where Thakin Nu had become headmaster, and he took a position as senior master, teaching modern history and English. At the age of twenty, U Thant won the All Burma Translation Competition organized by the Burma Education Extension Association. In 1931, after having taken first place in the Anglo-Vernacular Secondary Teachership Examination, he was appointed headmaster of the Pantanaw National High School succeeding Thakin Nu, who returned to the University of Rangoon for the study of law. He also served on the executive committee of the Heads of Schools Association, and he was a member of

United Nations

U THANT

the Council of National Education and of the Text Book Committee.

U Thant continued his close friendship with Thakin Nu, who had joined the Burmese independence movement led by General U Aung San. Like Thakin Nu, he became a prolific free-lance journalist, contributing articles criticizing colonialism to newspapers and magazines. For several months in 1942, during the early period of the Japanese occupation of Burma, U Thant served as secretary to the government's education reorganization committee. In 1943 he returned to his position as headmaster of the Pantanaw National High School, where he remained until 1947.

The return of the British to Burma following the end of the war gave a strong impetus to the independence movement of General U Aung San and his nationalist coalition, the Burmese Anti-Fascist People's Freedom League. In April 1947 this bloc won a majority in the constituent assembly, and in June the assembly voted for the complete independence of Burma as a republic outside of the British Commonwealth of Nations. U Thant gave up teaching in 1947 to become press director for the interim government, headed first by U Aung San, and after his assassination, by Thakin Nu. The Anglo-Burmese treaty establishing the Union of Burma went into effect on January 4, 1948. In April 1948 Burma became the fifty-eighth member of the United Nations.

In 1948 U Thant was appointed director of broadcasting in the government of the newly established republic, and in 1949 he became secretary to the government in the Ministry of Information. In 1951 he participated in Burmese goodwill missions to Thailand and Indonesia, and in 1952 he was a member of the Burmese delegation to the seventh session of the United Nations General Assembly in New York. In 1953 U Thant was appointed

secretary for projects in the office of Prime Minister U Nu, and in 1955 he added the position of executive secretary of the Economic and Social Board to his other duties. As adviser to the Prime Minister, U Thant accompanied U Nu to the first two Colombo Plan Prime Ministers' Conferences at Colombo, Ceylon, and to the 1955 Asian-African Conference at Bandung in Indonesia. In 1956, while U Nu temporarily yielded the premiership to U Ba Swe, U Thant served as adviser to the latter at the third Colombo Plan Prime Ministers' Conference at New Delhi and at the Asian Socialist Conference at Bombay.

In 1957 U Thant was appointed permanent representative of Burma to the United Nations, and he has served as chairman of the Burmese delegation at the twelfth and subsequent regular sessions of the General Assembly. In 1959 he was vice-president of the General Assembly's fourteenth session. In 1961 he was chairman of the U.N. Congo Conciliation Commission and of the Committee on a United Nations Development Fund. In the U.N., U Thant has taken a position of independence with relation to the Communist and Western power blocs. In September 1957 he came out strongly against the Soviet Union for its suppression of the Hungarian revolt, but he declared his opposition to any tendency to convert the Hungarian issue into a weapon of the cold war. At the same time he urged that the General Assembly take action on the Algerian crisis, which he regarded as at least as important as the Hungarian question. In the debates on the dispute between Nationalist China and Communist China over control of the offshore islands Quemoy and Matsu, U Thant, in September 1958, criticized the Communist Chinese for their resort to force. On the other hand, he held the United States partly responsible for the crisis, because of its refusal to consider recognition of the People's Republic of China.

The question of disarmament has been of major concern to U Thant. In 1959 he supported a proposal by Premier Chou En-lai of Communist China that Asia and the Pacific area be cleared of all nuclear arms. Speaking before the General Assembly in November 1960, U Thant referred to both the United States and the Soviet Union as "prisoners of the past." He attributed the stalemate on disarmament to a "Pearl Harbor complex" in the United States on the one hand, and fear of "encirclement and aggression" on the part of the Soviet Union on the other. In 1960 he also favored United Nations intervention in the Congo and was active in the drafting of a resolution, supported by twenty-one African and Asian nations, calling for a referendum on Algerian independence, to be supervised by the U.N. In 1961 he criticized the United States for its role in the attempted invasion of Cuba, and the Soviet Union for its unilateral resumption of nuclear weapons testing. In September 1961 he attended the conferenceof nonaligned nations at Belgrade. He has, however, rejected proposals for the establishment of a neutralist bloc within the United Nations and has said that this "would result in the further splitting of an already divided world."

The death of Secretary-General Dag Hammarskjöld on September 18, 1961 was followed by seven weeks of dispute over the leadership of the United Nations. The Soviet Union had previously tried to replace the one-man office of the Secretary-General with a "troika," consisting of one member of the Communist bloc, one Westerner, and one representative of the neutral nations. The United States, on the other hand, has insisted upon a single Secretary-General unhampered by the veto, as specified in the U.N. Charter. Both the United States and the Soviet Union finally agreed on U Thant, the candidate of the uncommitted nations of Asia and Africa, with the stipulation that he would have several assistant secretaries-general, to act as principal advisers on important questions. U Thant has, however, refused to bind himself to the advice of these assistants.

In presenting the candidacy of U Thant to the General Assembly on November 3, 1961, Dr. G. P. Malalasekera of Ceylon said: "In an age when strength is often equated with the booming voice and the bouncing fist U Thant displays the strength of quiet dignity." Following approval by the Security Council without debate, U Thant was unanimously elected by the General Assembly by a vote of 103 to 0. In his acceptance speech he called attention to the policy of nonalignment and friendship for all nations that Burma had practised over the years, and he declared his intention to "continue to maintain this attitude of objectivity and to pursue the ideal of universal friendship." President John F. Kennedy, in a message to United States Ambassador to the U.N., Adlai E. Stevenson, hailed the election of U Thant as "a splendid achievement in which the whole world can rejoice."

On December 29, 1961 U Thant announced the establishment of an inner cabinet of eight undersecretaries, including Dr. Ralph J. Bunche of the United States and Georgi Petrovich Arkadyev of the Soviet Union. The most pressing problem facing the U.N. late in 1961 was the civil strife in the Republic of the Congo. Shortly after taking office, U Thant expressed his determination to use as much force as necessary to implement two Security Council resolutions aimed at expelling foreign mercenaries from the secessionist province of Katanga and restoring peace and unity to the Congo. In this policy U Thant has had the full backing of the United States State Department. A major step toward averting the financial bankruptcy of the U.N. was taken on December 19, 1961, when the General Assembly voted 45 to 11 with twenty-one abstentions to follow U Thant's suggestion and issue $200,000,000 in twenty-five-year bonds. The Soviet bloc opposed this measure. In January 1962 U Thant tried to obtain a solution of the controversy between the Netherlands and Indonesia over the latter's claims on West New Guinea, by means of peaceful negotiation.

In his own country U Thant belongs to a party dedicated to democratic principles and opposed to Communism, and he considers himself a democratic socialist. He is active in the Burma Research Society, the Burma Council of World Affairs, the Burma Translation Society, and the Burma Historical Commission. He has written several books, including one about cities and their stories (1930); another, about the League of Nations (1933); about the new education in Burma (1946); and a book about democracy in Burmese schools (1952). He is also the author of a three-volume history of post-war Burma, of which the first two volumes were published in 1961. The government of Burma has conferred several titles on U Thant, including Wunna Kyaw Htin (1949); Thiripyanchi (1953); Sithu (1957); and Maha Thray Sithu (1961).

U Thant is married to the daughter of a prominent Burmese lawyer. They have one son, Tin Maung, and a daughter, Aye Aye, the wife of Tyu Myintu. Both the son and the daughter are students of sociology at Hunter College in New York City. The United Nations official, who is five feet seven inches tall, wears impeccably tailored western suits in public, but at home he prefers his native *longyi*, or kilt. He chain-smokes expensive cigars and belongs to six different book clubs. He is described as tolerant, even-tempered, diligent and diplomatic, and although he has been known to unleash anger and impatience on occasion, he generally displays the detached and contemplative attitude of a Buddhist scholar.

References

N Y Times p7 N 2 '61 por
N Y World-Telegram p2 O 14 '61 por
Newsweek 58:47 N 13 '61 por
Time 78:33 N 10 '61 por
Asia Who's Who (1960)
International Who's Who, 1961-62

TILLINGHAST, CHARLES C(ARPENTER), JR. Jan. 30, 1911- Lawyer; corporation executive

Address: b. Trans World Airlines, Inc., 380 Madison Ave., New York 17; h. 101 Warwick Rd., Bronxville 8, N.Y.

During a period of fourteen years Trans World Airlines, Inc., has had five different presidents, a rate of turnover more common among baseball managers than in the top ranks of American industry. The sixth in this procession of TWA presidents, Charles C. Tillinghast, Jr., who assumed the title of president and chief executive officer on April 17, 1961, is expected to last considerably longer than any of his predecessors. The chief reason for his predicted executive longevity is that Tillinghast was hired not by Howard Hughes, the majority stockholder of TWA, but by Ernest R. Breech, one of three trustees named by the airline's creditors to vote Hughes' 78 per cent controlling interest in the company. Breech, who had known Tillinghast while both were associated with the Bendix Corporation, assured him a free hand in unraveling TWA's tangled financial affairs. A corporation lawyer of long experience and a successful manufacturing executive, Tillinghast has expressed confidence that he can do the job.

(Continued next page)

CHARLES C. TILLINGHAST, JR.

Charles Carpenter Tillinghast, Jr., was born on January 30, 1911 in Saxtons River, Vermont, the son of Charles C. and Adelaide B. (Shaw) Tillinghast. He has two brothers, John A., an engineer, and David R., a lawyer. His father was a teacher at the Vermont Academy in Saxtons River, who later became headmaster of the Horace Mann School in New York City. "Till," as he was nicknamed by his family, was raised by his grandmother in Shelburne Falls, Massachusetts. He attended the Horace Mann School, from which he graduated in 1928, and then entered Brown University in Providence, Rhode Island. "Brown at that time required a classical language for a B.A," Tillinghast recalled in an interview with Robert E. Bedingfield of the New York Times (April 2, 1961). "So I decided to major in philosophy, where it wasn't required." (Tillinghast has said elsewhere that he majored in English and political science while at Brown University). He was on the varsity football team, played basketball and lacrosse, and served as chapel monitor, waiter, and furnace tender. He graduated with the Ph.B. degree in 1932.

Tillinghast then entered the Columbia University School of Law, where he served as editor of the Columbia Law Review. After receiving the LL.B. degree in 1935 he entered the law office of Hughes, Schurman & Dwight, whose senior partner, Charles Evans Hughes, Jr., had been a college friend of the elder Tillinghast. In 1938 the young lawyer left the firm to serve as a deputy assistant to New York County District Attorney Thomas E. Dewey, and in this capacity he helped to secure the conviction of political boss Jimmy Hines. In 1940 he returned to the law firm as an associate, and two years later he became a partner in the successor firm of Hughes, Hubbard & Ewing (later Hughes, Hubbard, Blair & Reed).

In 1942 the Bendix Corporation retained the Hughes law firm as its counsel. The appointment came immediately after the appointment of Ernest Breech as president of Bendix. "Mr. Breech wanted an 'inside lawyer' working on the account," Tillinghast told Robert E. Bedingfield, "and I was nominated for the job. In 1947, when the partner in charge of the Bendix account followed Mr. Breech to Ford, I succeeded him on the Bendix account" (New York Times, April 2, 1961).

In the ten years that followed, Tillinghast spent much of his time with Bendix—so much so that in 1957 he accepted an offer to join Bendix as a director and vice-president in charge of international operations. Since this responsibility required considerable travel, Tillinghast was on the road about 50 per cent of his time, traveling about 75,000 miles a year.

In the meantime, Trans World Airlines was undergoing a series of changes. On July 28, 1960 Charles S. Thomas resigned as President. By December of that year, the company had borrowed $165,000,000 to acquire ownership of its fleet of jet planes. The banks and insurance companies that provided the funds for this program insisted that Howard Hughes relinquish his 78 per cent voting control of TWA to a three-man committee of trustees. One of the trustees named to supervise the company's affairs was Ernest R. Breech.

The presidency of TWA had been vacant for about seven months when Breech approached Tillinghast on February 21, 1961 with the offer to head the company. Although he was at first reluctant to accept, Tillinghast later said: "I guess the real reason for my decision was that, like all lawyers, I relish the new, bigger, more complicated cases that come along. It was a challenge and I just couldn't say no." On March 20, 1961 the directors of TWA elected Tillinghast as president, chief executive officer, and a director. He assumed his new office on April 17, 1961. His contract is reported to provide for an annual salary of $75,000 and a guarantee of $50,000 a year if his employment is terminated before he is sixty-five.

"Although I am new to the air transport business," Tillinghast said after his election, "I have had an opportunity to observe TWA closely through Bendix connections and regard it as one of the technically most sound airlines in the country. TWA did one of the best jobs in the industry in integrating jet service. I have a very high regard for the organization and look forward to serving with it." Tillinghast added that he would do nothing to disturb the company's air and ground operations, indicating rather that he would concentrate on the management tasks for which the president's office is responsible.

The company Tillinghast heads ranks as one of the biggest domestic airlines in the United States and one of the largest of the international carriers. Its routes cover 50,000 miles, including seventy cities in the United States and twenty-three cities abroad. A fleet of 168 planes flew 5,818,000 passengers in 1960. One indication of the financial troubles besetting the line, however, was reflected in the 1960 annual report, which showed a drop in net profits from $9,402,000 in 1959 to $6,473,000, despite a new all-time high in gross revenues.

Tillinghast's elevation to the presidency was the signal for an extensive company reorganization program, including the naming of Breech as board chairman. On May 1, 1961 Tillinghast announced that TWA was acquiring thirty new jetliners through a $187,000,000 lease-purchase arrangement with the Boeing Airplane Company, giving TWA more four-engine jets on hand and on order than any other airline in the United States. Subsequently the company filed a $111,235,900 financing plan through the issuance of subordinated bonds.

Not all of these moves were satisfactory to Howard Hughes, however. On May 19, 1961 Hughes wrote to the Securities and Exchange Commission that he was planning to take legal action against the voting trustees, the banks and insurance companies they represent, and the TWA directors. The TWA management in August 1961 filed a $115,000,000 damage suit against Howard Hughes and the Hughes Tool Company, in an effort to obtain a court order obliging Hughes to relinquish his stock and to end his efforts to control the company. One of the largest of its kind in the history of aviation, the suit charged Hughes with violation of the Sherman and Clayton antitrust acts.

To expedite the transition from piston to jet aircraft, TWA in September 1961 placed an order for twenty French Caravelle jet airliners, due in 1963, at a total cost of about $100,000,000. An innovation launched by the company in June 1961 was the exhibition of first-run, full-length movies in the air to first-class passengers on long-range jet flights.

TWA's reported net loss of $12,733,000 for the first nine months of 1961 was attributed by Tillinghast to "the industry-wide position of having provided greater seat capacity than required for the slack business experienced." Replying to proposals by Civil Aeronautics Board chairman Alan S. Boyd that mergers of airlines might solve their economic problems, Tillinghast maintained that mergers were an "oversold commodity" and noted that "two sick men don't make one well man." He suggested that the solution to the problems of the airline industry might lie in the "middle ground of part monopoly and part competition" (New York *Times*, November 7, 1961). He has also expressed doubts that reduced air fares would benefit the economic conditions of the airlines.

Tillinghast is a director of the Seaboard Surety Company and a trustee of the Yonkers Savings Bank. He has served as director and president of the Community Welfare Board of Bronxville, New York and as governor of Lawrence Hospital in Bronxville. A Republican and a Baptist, he serves on the board of managers of the New York Baptist City Society, and has been executive committee chairman of the ministers and missionaries benefit board of the American Baptist Convention. He is a trustee of Brown University and of New York City's Riverside Church.

His memberships include the American, Michigan, and New York City bar associations; the Consilium; Theta Delta Chi; the Rockefeller Center Luncheon Club; Brown University Club; St. Andrews Golf Club of Hastings, New York; Bronxville Field Club; and Shenorock Shore Club. In 1959 the South Dakota School of Mines

awarded him the honorary degree of Doctor of Humane Letters.

Charles C. Tillinghast, Jr., was married on November 16, 1935 to Elizabeth (Lisette) Judd Micoleau. They have four children—Charles C. 3d, Elizabeth (Mrs. Robert E. Nadeau), Jane (Mrs. Wallace I. Roberts), and Ann Shaw Tillinghast—and two grandchildren. Tillinghast is a tall and husky man, with blue eyes and brown hair. He speaks precisely and dresses conservatively. He often works twelve hours a day, six days a week. His hobbies are golf, gardening, and carpentry, and he enjoys traveling on vacations. Although he heads an international airline, Tillinghast expects to do less traveling as the president of TWA than he did as an official with Bendix.

References

N Y Herald Tribune p26 Mr 21 '61 por
N Y Times III p3 Ap 2 '61 por
Newswek 57:70 Ap 3 '61 por
Time 77:72 Mr 31 '61 por

Who's Who in America, 1960-61
Who's Who in Commerce and Industry (1961)

UNITAS, JOHN   (ū-nīt′ŭs)   May 7, 1933-
Football player

Address: b. Baltimore Colts, 2023 N. Charles St., Baltimore 18, Md.; h. Towson, Md.

For some years John Unitas, now of the Baltimore Colts, was the quarterback nobody wanted. Today many sportswriters acknowledge him to be the best quarterback in the National Football League. Unitas has led the once lowly Baltimore team to two world championships (1958 and 1959) and has chalked up a number of passing records, including one for the largest number of touchdown passes completed in a single season and another for consecutive games in which he passed for at least one score. He has been named quarterback of the All-Pro team a number of times.

Unitas' success story is well-known in professional football. Just after his graduation from the University of Louisville in Kentucky in 1955, he was drafted by the Pittsburgh Steelers of the National Football League. Released, however, at the end of the Steelers' training sessions, he turned to playing sandlot football in Pittsburgh for $6 a game. In 1956 he was signed to a contract with the Colts as a stand-in for George Shaw, the team's regular quarterback and one of the best in pro football. When Shaw suffered an injury early in the season, Unitas stepped into the breach to begin a meteoric rise to the top of his profession.

John Unitas was born on May 7, 1933, in Pittsburgh, Pennsylvania, the third of four children of Leonard and Helen Unitas. He is of Lithuanian ancestry. Johnny has a brother, Leonard, Jr., and two sisters, Millicent and Shirley. In October 1938 Johnny's father, who owned a small coal delivery business in Pittsburgh, died of pneumonia, leaving Mrs. Unitas with four young children to bring up. She worked hard to make a home for them, first at menial jobs and later, after taking a night

Wide World

JOHN UNITAS

school course, as a bookkeeper. Unitas has said that by her example of courage and persistence his mother taught him more than any coach about what it takes to win in football.

Mrs. Unitas was able to provide her children with at least a high school education. (She later remarried and is now Mrs. Helen Gibbs.) Johnny attended St. Justin's High School in Pittsburgh, where he played football. Although he was named quarterback on the city's All Catholic High School team in his senior year, his slender build (six feet, 145 pounds) dissuaded many universities, including Notre Dame, from offering him an athletic scholarship. Without a scholarship, college was out of the question, because of the family's financial condition. The University of Louisville, however, made Unitas a scholarship offer, and he eagerly accepted.

Louisville did not play a major football schedule and consistently fielded a far-from-adequate team. In the four years that Unitas played, the Cardinals won only 12 games and lost 23. Unitas, however, chalked up an eye-catching record. During the four seasons he completed 245 of 502 passes and tossed for 27 touchdowns. More important, he had filled out to a weight of 190 pounds to go with his six-foot-one-inch frame.

While at Louisville, Unitas had married his high school sweetheart, Dorothy Jean Hoelle. Now with family responsibilities, Unitas welcomed the chance to play with the Pittsburgh Steelers, who had picked him in the ninth round of the 1955 N.F.L. draft. He reported to the Pittsburgh training camp in July of that year, ranked behind three other quarterbacks, who were already on the team. Before the season started, Unitas was released.

In his high school years Unitas had worked during vacations on construction jobs in order to build up body toughness. When he was dropped from the Steelers, he returned to construction work with a pile-driving gang. Meanwhile, he kept active in football by playing, at $6 a game, with the semiprofessional Bloomfield Rams in the Greater Pittsburgh League. Reports about his sandlot playing eventually reached Don Kellett, general manager of the Baltimore Colts, who signed him in February 1956 to become an understudy for star quarterback George Shaw.

During the fourth game of the 1956 season, against the Chicago Bears, Shaw suffered a leg injury. Given a chance to play, Unitas erred time and again. The first pass he threw was intercepted by a Bear defender and returned for a touchdown. He fumbled three times in the Colt backfield and all three times the Bears recovered. The final score was Chicago 58, Baltimore 27. "Johnny wasn't the least bit shaken," one Colt player remembers. " 'If you just give me a chance,' he kept saying, 'I'll show you what I can do' " (Parade, September 20, 1959). Two games later Unitas led the Colts to a 56-21 win over the Los Angeles Rams.

Aided by a team that was improving steadily in all-around play, Unitas steered the Colts to a 7-5 record in 1957. That year Baltimore finished third in the six-team Western Division, just one game out of first place. For his play in the most critical of professional football positions, Unitas was voted the league's Most Valuable Player for 1957. The following season the Colts won their first six games before losing to the New York Giants, 24-21 at Yankee Stadium in New York. They bounced back, however, to win their next three games and they clinched the Western Division title with a 35-27 win over the San Francisco 49ers. For the Colts, who had entered the National Football League in 1950, it was their first divisional championship.

The Colts then met the giants for the N.F.L. title. The Giants, winners in the Eastern Division, were the favorites, but Baltimore won 23-17 in sudden-death overtime. The game has been described as one of the most thrilling ever played in the N.F.L. With some 90 seconds to play, Baltimore had the ball on its own 14-yard line, trailing 17-14. Unruffled by charging linemen, Unitas calmly threw four complete passes, which took Baltimore to the Giant 20-yard line. From there, with nine seconds to play, Steve Myrha kicked a field goal to tie the score. In the overtime period Unitas engineered an 80-yard drive for the winning touchdown.

Matching this record in 1959, the Colts again captured the Western Division title and again beat the Giants in the play-off game in December. The score that time was 31-16, and Unitas was never better. He ran for one touchdown and passed for two others. In all he completed 18 of 29 tosses, good for 264 yards. His play-off performance capped a season in which he set a new N.F.L. record by throwing 32 touchdown passes. At the conclusion of the year he was named winner of the Bert Bell Memorial Award as the league's outstanding player.

The 1960 season, however, was less successful. The Colts never did get their potent offense untracked, and as the season progressed it became increasingly apparent that Baltimore was not to repeat as Western Division champions. The Colts reached the end of the road in the eleventh game of the season, against the Los Angeles Rams. They lost to the Rams, paving the way for the Green Bay Packers to win the divisional title. The Los Angeles game also marked the end of a winning streak for Unitas. After throwing at least one touchdown pass in 47 consecutive games, he failed to connect that day. In January 1961, however, he was voted the Most Valuable Player of the annual National Football League's Pro Bowl event, for the second straight year.

Again, the 1961 season was on the whole an undistinguished one for the Colts, and during the early games Unitas suffered from a bruise on the middle finger of his throwing hand. His brilliant playing, however, brought his team a 45-21 victory over the Green Bay Packers in November, and for the seventh time in his six-year National Football League career he tossed four touchdown passes in one game.

John Unitas and his wife have a daughter, Janice Ann, and three sons, John, Jr., Robert, and Christopher Michael. They live in a modern split-level house in suburban Towson, Maryland. Unitas stays in condition all year and allows himself no more than an occasional glass of beer. Among his distinguishing characteristics are close-cropped blond hair, a gleaming smile, calmness on the field, and a serious approach to his bruising profession. During off-seasons he has done promotion work for a sporting goods company, and he owns a number of bowling alleys in Baltimore. Success in professional football, he once said, "was too long in coming, and it might end tomorrow."

References

> Look 23:110+ D 8 '59 por
> Newsweek 53:66 Ja 5 '59 por
> Parade p8+ S 20 '59 por
> Sat Eve Post 231:36+ N 1 '58 por
>
> Fitzgerald, Edward E. Heroes of Sport (1960)
> New York Times. Men in the News— 1958

VOLPE, JOHN A(NTHONY) (vōl'pā) Dec. 8, 1908- Governor of Massachusetts; contractor; engineer

Address: b. State House, Boston, Mass.; h. 10 Everett Ave., Winchester, Mass.

Voters of Massachusetts, who frequently upset the plans of party leaders by ticket splitting, responded in November 1960 to the slogan "Vote the Man. Vote Volpe" to elect a Governor who was the only successful Republican candidate for statewide office in the Commonwealth government. John A. Volpe, a building contractor and former state and federal highway official, had fought his campaign on the principal issue of maladministration and scandal in the highway building program and various state agencies. He succeeded Democrat Foster

Lenscraft Photos, Inc.

JOHN A. VOLPE

Furcolo for a two-year gubernatorial term beginning on January 5, 1961.

Like his predecessor, Governor Furcolo, whose father was a native of Italy, John Anthony Volpe is of Italian descent. He was born in Wakefield, Massachusetts on December 8, 1908, the eldest son of Vito and Filomeno (Benedetto) Volpe, both immigrants of a village near Teramo in Italy. He has three brothers, S. Peter, Patrick, and Richard J., and one sister, Mrs. Grace Gonella, all of Wakefield. Brought up in the northern suburbs of Boston, Volpe attended the Malden High School, where his extracurricular activities included track and the orchestra. He had hoped on graduation in 1926 to enter the Massachusetts Institute of Technology to study engineering, but his father's plastering business failed and he himself went to work as a hod carrier.

For two years beginning in July 1926 Volpe was employed in the Greater Boston area as a journeyman plasterer. Enrolling in the Wentworth Institute at Boston in September 1928, he majored in architectural construction. To meet expenses he continued as a plasterer in the summers and also worked as a salesman of clothing and coal.

In the summer of 1930 Volpe graduated from the Wentworth Institute and began working as a $25-a-week timekeeper for a Greater Boston residential and commercial construction firm. A year later he advanced to assistant superintendent of construction, but in February 1932 the Depression ended his job. He was back selling shirts and dresses when, later in the year, he and a friend scraped together enough money to bid on a church alteration in Everett, Massachusetts. They just failed to make the lowest bid, but early in the following year a contract for a $1,285 boiler-room addition in nearby Lynn gave Volpe his start in the construction field. In March 1933 he formed the John A.

VOLPE, JOHN A.—*Continued*
Volpe Construction Company, with himself as president.

During the next ten years the Volpe Construction Company enjoyed a steady growth; then in February 1943 Volpe closed down the business entirely and volunteered for World War II duty with the Civil Engineer Corps of the United States Navy. He was commissioned a lieutenant (j.g.) and subsequently assigned to the training of Seabees, an assignment that brought him the Navy's Civilian Service Award for outstanding performance.

Discharged in March 1946 in the rank of lieutenant commander, he immediately reactivated the John A. Volpe Construction Company, which in the next fifteen years built hospitals, schools, shopping centers, public buildings, and military installations along the Eastern seaboard and in other parts of the country. Volpe is a past president of the Association of General Contractors of Massachusetts and a past national president of the Society of American Military Engineers. He served for many years on labor legislation and other committees of Associated General Contractors, a national contractors' organization; was elected to its executive committee in 1958; and in 1960, after a year as vice-president, was elected president.

The multimillion dollar John A. Volpe Construction Company was never engaged in highway work and has accepted no state contracts of any kind since 1948, when its founder became active in Massachusetts politics. Volpe was elected deputy chairman of the Republican State Committee in 1950 and was an alternate delegate to the Republican National Convention two years later. He resigned as deputy chairman in 1953 when Governor Christian A. Herter appointed him commissioner of Public Works for Massachusetts. In later 1956 President Dwight D. Eisenhower named him interim Federal Highway Administrator, and he served in that office until February 1957, when the permanent appointee, Bertram D. Tallamy, was free to take over.

In September 1958, after the death of Attorney General George Fingold, the Republican nominee for Governor of Massachusetts, Volpe was the choice of the majority of the Republican State Committee's executive committee to fill the vacancy on the ticket. The full committee, however, nominated Charles Gibbons, a former speaker of the state House of Representatives, who decisively lost in November to the incumbent Democratic Governor, Foster Furcolo. At the Republican National Convention in 1960, Volpe was one of eight delegates who seconded the nomination of Ambassador Henry Cabot Lodge for the Vice-Presidency.

At the Republican State Convention in Worcester on June 11, 1960, Volpe won the nomination for Governor on the third ballot, and at the primary in September he was unchallenged for the Republican candidacy. A bitter preprimary fight, on the other hand, preceded the choice in September of the Commonwealth Secretary of State, Joseph D. Ward, as his Democratic opponent and left much interparty ill feeling.

Disclosures of irregularities in the highway building program during the administration of the incumbent Democratic Governor were a principal issue in the campaign. With his "Vote the Man" slogan Volpe, while stressing that he was no less a Republican, frankly bid for the support of independent voters and disgruntled Democrats. He defeated Ward by 1,233,855 votes to 1,101,186 in November, but was the only Republican elected to a Commonwealth constitutional office on a statewide basis.

On taking office on January 5, 1961 as Governor of Massachusetts, therefore, Volpe was entirely surrounded by a Democratic cabinet. His appointments had to be approved by a Democratic executive council, and the General Court, to which his legislative program had to be submitted, consisted of a Senate composed of twenty-six Democrats to fourteen Republicans and a House of Representatives with 156 Democrats to only eighty-four Republicans.

In his inaugural address on January 5, 1961, Governor Volpe promised a reform program to ease the tax burdens of cities and towns without recourse to new taxes; the purging of unnecessary political offices; reorganization of the Department of Public Works and the Metropolitan (Boston area) District Commission; a code of ethics for public officials; and revision of the Massachusetts constitution to provide four-year terms for the Governor and other elective officers. Although he preferred that the revision be achieved by legislative amendments, he said early in March that he would "get behind the movement for a popular constitutional convention" if nothing was accomplished in the 1961 session of the General Court. Volpe also proposed that the Governor be given the right to name his own department heads for terms coextensive with his own.

On March 7, 1961, following conferences with the governors of New York, Connecticut, and Rhode Island, states serviced by the New York, New Haven & Hartford Railroad, Volpe sent to the Massachusetts legislature a plan to give that system $1,200,000 in tax relief annually over a four-year period, as an alternative to bankruptcy. Also in the field of transportation, he announced a few days later that he would shortly propose to the legislature a reorganization of the politics-ridden and deficit-burdened Metropolitan Transit Authority, which operates subway, trolley, and bus services in Greater Boston. A bill to permit the city of Cambridge to sell a part of its historic Common for erection of an office building was the subject, on March 13, of Governor Volpe's first veto.

On several occasions during Volpe's first year in office, Massachusetts attracted nationwide attention because of disclosures of alleged corruption in public office. Considerable unfavorable publicity resulted from a national television program that exposed bookmaking in Boston. Since the Democrats controlled every phase of state government except the Governor's office, Volpe was not implicated in the scandals. In his annual message to the legislature in January 1962, he stressed as his principal objective the reaffirmation of "the moral fiber and moral consciousness" of the state.

Volpe is a past chairman of the Greater Boston Community Fund and was president of the Greater Boston Chamber of Commerce in 1958-59. He is an officer of five banks and the publisher of two suburban newspapers, the Malden *News* and the Medford *Daily Mercury.* He serves as a trustee of the Wentworth Institute and was awarded the honorary degree of Doctor of Humane Letters by St. Michael's College in 1954 and the Doctor of Engineering degree by Northeastern University in 1956.

Prominent in Italian-American activities, Volpe led a $340,000 fund-raising drive for the Don Orione Home for Aged Italians in East Boston and in 1959 served as chairman of the $400,000 drive of the supreme council of the Order of the Sons of Italy in America for the building of a national home in Washington. He was made a Grand Officer of the Order of Merit of the Republic of Italy in 1957 and a Knight of Malta in 1960.

Volpe, a Roman Catholic, includes the Knights of Columbus among his fraternal organizations. He is also a member of the Loyal Order of Moose and of the American Legion in Winchester. He belongs to the Malden Rotary Club, the Army and Navy Club, the Winchester Country Club, and the Ancient and Honorable Artillery Company.

Brown-haired, brown-eyed Governor John A. Volpe stands at five feet six and a half inches, and weighs 148 pounds. He lists golf, football, and baseball as favorite sports. His wife, Jennie (Benedetto) Volpe, was a nurse before their marriage on June 18, 1934. They have one daughter, Loretta Jean (Mrs. Roger Rotondi), and one son, John, Jr., a student at Boston College.

References

Boston Globe A p3 O 17 '60 por
Eng N 164:57+ Mr 31 '60 pors
N Y Times p39 N 10 '60 por

Italian-American Who's Who (1959-60)

WALSH, CHAD May 10, 1914- Writer; educator; clergyman

Address: b. Beloit College, Beloit, Wis.; h. 745 Church St., Beloit, Wis.

With his conversion to Christianity in the mid-1940's, the writing of Chad Walsh, professor and chairman of the department of English at Beloit College in Wisconsin, was quickened and given a compelling course. A teacher of English at Beloit since 1945, Walsh entered the Episcopal Church in that same year and was ordained an Episcopalian priest four years later. His first book, *Stop Looking and Listen,* which he has said, "is candidly designed as a recruiting pamphlet for Christianity," was published in 1947. Since then the flow of books from his typewriter has averaged nearly one a year. The variety of this flow has included poetry, which he had been writing since childhood.

Chad Walsh was born on May 10, 1914, in South Boston, Virginia, the youngest of three sons of William Ernest and Katie Lillian (Wrenn) Walsh. Both of his parents are deceased. His father had been a carpenter as a

Bennett, London

CHAD WALSH

young man and later became an insurance agent. One of his brothers, Edward Walsh, now deceased, had been an insurance superintendent in Atlanta, Georgia. The other brother, Ulysses Walsh of Vinton, Virginia, works on television productions and is a nationally known authority on the early days of the phonograph. Reared in Marion, Virginia, Chad was interested in writing from the time that he was in fourth grade. On one occasion he received praise from a teacher for a poem he had written. He attended Marion High School, where he acted in amateur plays, edited the high school newspaper during his senior year, and graduated in 1934. Before finishing high school Walsh began working part time in a variety of jobs, including linotypist, reporter, and writer of advertisements for two local newspapers owned by Sherwood Anderson. He continued this part-time work through two years at Marion Junior College.

Having become interested in foreign languages through listening to his brother Ulysses' phonograph records of operatic arias, Walsh majored in Romance languages at the University of Virginia. His extracurricular work was chiefly literary and dramatic. He was active on the college newspaper and did some writing for the college magazine. With a friend he founded a monthly magazine, *Virginia Verse.* Active backstage in college dramatic productions, he held an assistantship in drama in his senior year and received a prize for the best play written by a student. For outstanding contribution to the cultural life of the campus he received the "Jabberwock" award.

After receiving his B. A. degree from the University of Virginia in 1938, Walsh took up graduate work at the University of Michigan. In 1939 he received his M.A. degree in French. That same year he won the major playwriting award in the Hopwood contests. His interest having turned back from French to his native

WALSH, CHAD—*Continued*

language, Walsh pursued a doctorate in English. For two and one-half years he held the Rackman Predoctoral Fellowship. He was awarded the Ph.D. degree in February 1943. His dissertation was entitled "Preposition at the End of a Sentence in Early Middle English." From 1943 to 1945 Walsh worked in Washington, D.C., as a research analyst for the United States Army Signal Corps.

In 1945 Walsh went to Beloit, a liberal arts college in southern Wisconsin, as assistant professor of English. Although founded—in 1846—by Congregationalists and Presbyterians, Beloit is not a theological school. According to its Declaration of Principles, the college seeks to inspire Christianity uncontrolled by sectarianism and nationalism; integrity of purpose and performance; a tolerance of spirit that will perpetuate freedom; and constitutional government by the consent of the governed. Its founders specified that no student or faculty member would ever be accepted or rejected on the basis of his beliefs. Walsh subsequently became a full professor and chairman of the department of English. Besides carrying on his academic work at Beloit, he has lectured at other colleges and universities in the United States and abroad. In 1957-58 he was a Fulbright lecturer in American literature at Turku, Finland, and in 1958-59 he was a visiting professor of English at Wellesley College.

During his first year at Beloit, Walsh became a convert to Christianity. The "constricting" and "ferocious" Christianity that filled his youthful environment had repelled him and made him resolve, when he was only a boy, to avoid churches. He arrived at manhood an agnostic. The reaction against his early environment began to fade enough during his university years for him to be led to a fresh approach to Christianity through the writings of Reinhold Niebuhr and T. S. Eliot. "It is enough to say," Walsh sums up in his contribution to *Modern Canterbury Pilgrims*, edited by James A. Pike (Morehouse, 1956), "that by my late twenties I had about reached the point where I believed in God and in Christ as the incarnate Son of God." He was baptized by Father Johnson, rector of St. Paul's Episcopal Church in Beloit, in 1945, and confirmed the following spring.

Made a deacon in the Episcopal Church on October 1948, Walsh was ordained a priest in December 1949 after reading for his canonicals. The Right Reverend Benjamin Franklin Price Ivins, then Episcopal Bishop of Milwaukee, officiated at the ordination. Since his ordination he has been an associate rector of St. Paul's Church in Beloit, where his work is chiefly that of a weekend assistant. In the summer he sometimes fills vacant pulpits in Vermont. He has been a guest preacher in many other churches throughout the United States.

Walsh's acceptance of Christianity gave a new orientation to his writing talents, and inspired him to greater literary efforts. His *Stop Looking and Listen; An Invitation to the Christian Life* (Harper, 1947) is an introduction to basic Christian theology. When on the threshold of Christianity, he had become acquainted with the writings of C. S. Lewis, who "has never stopped ringing bells" in him. His *C. S. Lewis: Apostle to the Skeptics* (Macmillan, 1949) deals with the life and thought of the noted Oxford don. *Early Christians of the 21st Century* (Harper, 1950) relates Christianity to civilization and considers particularly the future of humanity. *Knock and Enter* (Morehouse, 1953), a confirmation manual in novel form, grew out of a series of letters Walsh wrote to his oldest daughter.

Finding that young people were entering college with their knowledge of Christianity inadequate for the defense of that faith, Walsh wrote *Campus Gods on Trial* (Macmillan, 1953). The book probes the problems of doubts of college students and the ideas that are offered them as substitutes for faith. Among these substitutes, as seen by Walsh, are progress, relativism, scientism, humanitarianism, and materialism. The latest aspect of materialism, according to Walsh, is the worship of security.

Walsh is the co-author, with Eric Montizambert, of *Faith and Behavior; Christian Answers to Moral Problems* (Morehouse, 1954), a question-and-answer book on Christian ethics. *Behold the Glory* (Harper, 1956) was his first purely devotional book. *Nellie and Her Flying Crocodile* (Harper, 1956) is a novel for children. *The Rough Years* (Morehouse, 1960), a novel dramatizing the problems of adolescents, was written for adolescents and for adults concerned with establishing communication with adolescents. Walsh's articles have appeared in several periodicals, including *Atlantic Monthly*, *Harper's Magazine*, *Saturday Review*, *American Speech*, *College English*, and the *Journal of Bible and Religion*. He frequently writes reviews for the New York *Times Book Review* and the New York *Herald Tribune Book Review*. A collection of Walsh's poetry, *The Factual Dark*, was published by Decker Press in 1949. Another volume of his poetry, *Eden Two-Way*, was published by Harper & Brothers in 1954. Walsh recognizes in his own poetry the influence of T. S. Eliot and Robert Frost, the two modern poets he reads with the greatest pleasure. He has published poems in *Poetry: A Magazine of Verse*, the *Sewanee Review*, *Saturday Review*, *Ladies' Home Journal*, *Experiment*, *Epoch*, the *New Republic*, and other periodicals. He was a founder, and remains on the editorial board, of the *Beloit Poetry Journal*. Walsh is currently working on a college text, *Doors into Poetry*, to be published by Prentice-Hall, Inc., and an anthology of modern British and American poetry to be published by Charles Scribner's Sons. He also has under way a study of the anti-Utopian novel, dealing with such books as Aldous Huxley's *Brave New World* and George Orwell's *1984*. In addition, Walsh hopes to complete work on a book of original devotional poetry based on the Twenty-second Psalm, as well as a cycle of poems on the Sacco-Vanzetti case.

Chad Walsh and Eva May Tuttle met when they both were graduate students at the University of Michigan. They were married on September 18, 1938 and have four daughters: Damaris Wrenn (Mrs. Donald McGuire), Made-

line Irvine, Sarah-Lindsay Tuttle, and Alison
Elise. The Walshes live in a large white frame
house near the Beloit campus. They spend their
summers at a cottage on Lake Iroquois in Vermont, about twelve miles south of Burlington.
There Chad Walsh does his most concentrated
writing, in a shack one hundred yards from the
cottage. He writes his poems in longhand and
types his prose.

Walsh is six feet tall, weighs 170 pounds,
and has brown hair and gray eyes. He is of
slender build and has been described as having
a quiet manner and a pleasant and expressive
voice. A liberal Democrat, he was a part-time,
unofficial assistant to Adlai E. Stevenson's staff
during the 1956 Presidential primary campaign
and credits this experience with saving him from
"the complete skepticism about political standards which seems to afflict so many academics."
His recreations are landscape painting, color
photography, playing the recorder, and playing
ping-pong with his daughters. During summers in Vermont he likes to swim, hike, and
climb mountains. He is a member of Phi Beta
Kappa, the American Association of University
Professors, the University of Virginia Raven
Society, and the National Association for the
Advancement of Colored People.

References

Milwaukee Journal V p4 Mr 6 '60 por
Directory of American Scholars (1957)
Pike, James A. ed. Modern Canterbury
  Pilgrims (1956)
Soper, David Wesley ed. These Found a
  Way (1951)
Walsh, Chad. Behold the Glory (1956)

WESKER, ARNOLD May 24, 1932- Play-
wright
Address: h. 39 Gloucester Dr., London N. 4,
England

A former pastry cook from London's East
End, Arnold Wesker became an overnight sensation in 1960, when his trilogy about proletarian life was presented at the Royal Court
Theatre in London. Since the success of his
Chicken Soup with Barley, Roots, and *I'm
Talking About Jerusalem,* Wesker has been
looked upon as one of the leaders of the new
movement in the British theater—a movement
that Noel Coward has attacked as "the dust-
bin school of drama." Because he treats the
working-class people in his plays with warmth,
realism, and compassion, Wesker has often been
compared with the American playwright Clifford Odets. However, Kenneth Tynan of the
London *Observer* detects more resemblances in
Wesker's dramas to the early work of Eugene
O'Neill than to the more romantic and insurgent proletarian dramas of Odets.

Wesker is much exercised over the fact that
the theater—whether in London, Paris, or New
York—has become the exclusive preserve of
the solvent middle class. So that the theater
may make a more direct bid to the interests of
workers, he has inaugurated "Centre 42," a
project under the auspices of Britain's Trade
Union Congress—as part of a cultural revolu-

Roger Mayne, London
ARNOLD WESKER

tion to expose workers to the arts. A "committed" or "engaged" writer, he has taken part
in ban-the-bomb demonstrations with other
young playwrights of his generation.

London's East End, an unlikely incubator of
British playwrights, was the birthplace of Arnold
Wesker on May 24, 1932. He is the son of
Joseph Wesker, a Russian-Jewish tailor's machinist who was often unemployed, and of
Hungarian-born Leah (Perlmutter) Wesker,
who often supported the family by working
in kitchens. When World War II broke
out in 1939, Arnold Wesker was sent out
of London as an evacuee, and he lived for the
next six years with foster parents in various
sections of England and Wales. "I never stopped
longing to get back to London, bombs or no
bombs," Wesker has recalled. "My childhood
was poor but happy. I come from pretty
earthy folks. We are a close family."

For a time Arnold Wesker attended Upton
House School in Hackney in London's East End,
where he studied bookkeeping, typing, and shorthand. He started to write when he was twelve,
but even before that had wanted to become an
actor. Wesker left school at the age of fourteen. If his formal education was scanty, he
more than made up for it with his wide-
ranging reading, especially of Arthur Miller,
Sean O'Casey, Clifford Odets, D. H. Lawrence,
and Dylan Thomas. Later major influences
were John Osborne and Bertolt Brecht. Wesker
has said that if he had not seen *Look Back
in Anger* he would probably never have become a playwright. He was "overwhelmed" by
his first reading of Brecht, whose work he
first came upon after he had written his first
four plays.

After leaving school, Wesker worked at a
succession of odd jobs. He was employed as a
furniture maker's apprentice, a carpenter's mate,
and a bookseller's assistant before he entered
the Royal Air Force in 1950, where his main

WESKER, ARNOLD—*Continued*

chore was emptying dustbins ("two hours work, a bath, then off duty for the rest of the day"). Discharged in 1952, he worked as a plumber's mate, farm laborer's seed porter, kitchen porter, and pastry cook for a large London restaurant. He spent some periods on the dole. The notes he took "behind his own back" as a kitchen porter eventuated in three long short stories that were never published. By this time Wesker was convinced that writing was his true vocation, but he had in the meanwhile kept up his interest in dramatics. He joined an amateur acting group when he was sixteen, ran a drama group for airmen while he was in the Royal Air Force, and passed the entrance examination for the Royal Academy of Dramatic Art two times. However, he failed the extra test for a London County Council grant that he needed to support himself as a student.

By working eight months as a pastry cook in Paris, Wesker managed to save up enough money to enter the London School of Film Technique, where Lindsay Anderson was his mentor. The school brought Wesker into contact with the Free Cinema group of younger makers of documentary films, a coterie that numbered Anderson among its members. When Anderson gave the script of *Chicken Soup with Barley* to Tony Richardson of the Royal Court Theatre, Richardson was enough impressed with Wesker's promise as a playwright to try out the play at the Belgrade Theatre in Coventry on July 7, 1958. Like the remaining two parts of the trilogy that followed, the play was later performed at the Royal Court Theatre in London.

An Arts Council grant of £300 and one half of an *Encyclopaedia Britannica* play prize provided Wesker with the leisure to learn more about the art of playwriting. He began to pick up money by writing or adapting scripts, and adapted the film script for *Hot Summer Night*. In 1959, after Wesker had enhanced his reputation with the opening of *Roots* at the Belgrade Theatre in Coventry on May 25, he won a London *Evening Standard* award as the most promising British dramatist of that year. *I'm Talking About Jerusalem*, the third play in the Wesker trilogy, opened at the Belgrade Theatre in Coventry on April 4, 1960. (*The Wesker Trilogy* was published in book form by Jonathan Cape, Ltd., in London in 1960 and by Random House in New York in 1961.) During the summer of 1960 the trilogy was produced in its entirety at the Royal Court Theatre in London. *Chicken Soup with Barley* opened on June 7, *Roots* on June 28, and *I'm Talking About Jerusalem* on July 27. *Roots* was performed in an off-Broadway production at the Mayfair Theatre in New York on March 6, 1961.

Chicken Soup with Barley deals with the reactions of the members of a London East End Jewish family to Communism during the mid-1930's and their subsequent disillusionment. *Roots* is about the apathetic response that a loutish family of farm laborers in Norfolk makes to the voyage of self-discovery undertaken by Beatie Bryant, the daughter, who has been exposed to art and music in London. *I'm Talking About Jerusalem* concerns Dave Simmonds' failure to live his life according to the precepts of the Socialism of William Morris.

Based on Wesker's own experiences as a pastry cook, *The Kitchen* was produced at the Royal Court Theatre in London on September 13, 1959 by the English Stage Society under the direction of John Dexter, and was revived on June 27, 1961. (A film version of *The Kitchen* was released in the United States by Kingsley in 1961.) In the kitchen of a huge London restaurant—a frenzied microcosm of the world outside—the employees mime the preparation of food for the lunch hour, a preparation that reaches its frenetic climax when a German employee runs amok. *The Kitchen* represents Wesker's own outlook upon the world. For a published version of the play (Penguin, 1961) he wrote: "The world might have been a stage for Shakespeare, but to me it is a kitchen: where people come and go and cannot stay long enough to understand each other, and friendships, love, and emmities are forgotten as quickly as they are made."

The note that Wesker provided for the actors and producers of *Roots* might apply equally well to the rest of his plays. "My people are not caricatures," Wesker wrote, "they are real (though fiction) and though the picture I have drawn of them is a harsh one, yet still my tone is not of disgust—nor should it be in the presentation of this play—it is only that I am annoyed with them and with myself."

Critics in Great Britain and the United States disagree about the importance of Wesker's contribution to British drama and his potential development as a playwright. They agree, by and large, that Wesker has a cinematic talent for creating images, that he can communicate emotionally, that he successfully carries into practice his belief that "the theatre is a place where one wants to see things happening." They readily concede his sympathy, his honesty, and his warmth, and approve of his tendency to dispense with the star system and let the spirit of the company working together carry the play.

On the other hand, most critics, with the exception of those who look upon him as a prodigy who can do no wrong, are not blind to the weaknesses of Wesker's plays, although they recognize that some are the weaknesses natural to a very young playwright. They point to his tendentiousness, his didacticism, his flimsy plots, his over-explicit and sometimes priggish moralizing, his lack of education, especially of political education. Some reviewers have charged him with confusing documentation and illustration with drama, with relying too heavily upon the inspirations of the actor and the director, and have wished that he had applied himself more ruthlessly to the art of editing. Several have gone so far as to suggest that the plays of the Wesker trilogy might be telescoped into one excellent play.

Arnold Wesker married Doreen Cecile Becker, whom he met when she was a waitress at a Norwich hotel, on November 14, 1958. They have two children: Lindsay Joe and Tanya Jo. Wesker is a slight, dark, and lively man with bright brown eyes. Modest about himself and about his achievement, he lives with his family in a home beside Clapton Common, not too far from the section in which he grew up. His Socialism is perhaps less an articulated program than a vaguely formulated aspiration. An active protestant against the manufacture of nuclear bombs, Wesker was sentenced to one month in prison for participating in a demonstration against nuclear weapons in September 1961. When he asked for pencils, paper, and a partly finished manuscript to while away his period of incarceration, his request was granted, but he was denied the services of a secretary and a typewriter. His latest play, *Chips with Everything*, has been accepted for production by Peter Hall of the Aldwych Theatre in London, and he has been working on his first musical, *Stand Up, Stand Up.*

Although he fashions his plays as vehicles for his Socialist opinions, Wesker insists that he wants no dictatorship in the theater from the British Labour party or the trade unions. Instead of looking forward to the abolition of aristocracy, he anticipates a society in which all men have the opportunity to become aristocrats. "Somewhere in my vision of the world," Wesker once said, "I see families living in large Elizabethan-type houses, where there are balconies for groups to play music and act, and where there is room to entertain friends. . . . Surely it is true that the aristocracy knew and know how to live with grace and dignity and enthusiasm."

References

> Manchester Guardian p7 Ja 18 '60
> N Y Herald Tribune IV p10 Ja 29 '61
> N Y Times II p1 F 26 '61
> Punch Ag 9 '61
> Theatre Arts 45;17 O '61
> International Who's Who, 1961-62
> Who's Who, 1961

WILLS, ROYAL BARRY Aug. 21, 1895-Jan. 10, 1962 Architect; designed over 2,500 houses during his thirty-five-year career; best-known for his designs of small homes in the Early American tradition; wrote several popular books on houses, including *Houses for Homemakers* (1945). See *Current Biography* (December) 1954.

Obituary

> N Y Times p33 Ja 11 '62

WINIARSKI, BOHDAN (STEFAN) Apr. 27, 1884- President of the International Court of Justice; jurist; author

Address: b. International Court of Justice, Palace of Peace, The Hague, the Netherlands; h. Grodziska 18, Poznan, Poland

Elected president of the International Court of Justice by his fourteen fellow judges on April 5, 1961, Bohdan Winiarski of Poland will continue to preside over the judicial arm of the United Nations until 1964. Winiarski has been a judge of the court since it became operative in 1946, succeeding the Permanent Court of International Justice of the League of Nations.

N. V. Ziegler, The Hague
JUDGE BOHDAN WINIARSKI

Winiarski was president of the Bank of Poland with the Polish government-in-exile during World War II. Before the war he had done legal work with the League of Nations and had taught law at Poznan University.

Bohdan Stefan Winiarski was born on April 27, 1884 at Bohdanowo in the province of Lomza, now the palatinate of Bialystok, Poland, into a family of landed gentry and officials. His parents were Stanislaw K. A. Winiarski, a forestry official, and Jadwiga (Mystkowska) Winiarski. After completing his secondary schooling in Lomza, he studied at the universities of Warsaw, Kraków, Paris, and Heidelberg. He received his doctorate in law in 1910.

After lecturing for three years (1911-14) at the Polish School of Political Science in Kraków, Winiarski was called up by the Russian army, in which he served for two years (1915-17). Secretary of the legal section of the Polish National Committee in Paris from 1917, he was legal adviser to the Polish delegation at the Paris Peace Conference (1919-20).

A member of the Polish delegations to many international conferences after World War I, Winiarski became particularly involved in the work of the League of Nations, which emerged from the Paris Peace Conference. He was in the delegations to the first three assemblies of the League (1920, 1921, 1922). Winiarski was a member of the League's permanent commission on communications and transit from 1921 to 1927, and he was vice-president of the commission from 1924 to 1926. He was also assessor of the Permanent Court of International Justice, set up under the League, for communications and transit questions. A member of the international Oder River commission, he was Polish agent at the court when the Oder dispute came before the Permanent Court of International Justice in 1929. He was a professor at the Academy of International Law in

WINIARSKI, BOHDAN—*Continued*

The Hague in 1933 and became a member of the permanent Conference of Higher Studies there in 1936. Beginning in 1925, he was president of the League's committee on inland navigation law.

Meanwhile Winiarski was active in both political and academic life in Poland. From 1924 to 1927 he was a member of the government commissary for the liquidation of German property. As a deputy in the Polish Diet (1928-35), he opposed the Pilsudski regime. Beginning in 1921, he taught at Poznan University (Uniwersytet Im Adama Mickiewicza). He was professor of public international law in the university's faculty of law beginning in 1922 and dean of the faculty of law from 1936 to 1939.

Arrested by the Germans in September 1939, Winiarski was held as a hostage until November. Shortly thereafter he was interned with his family and his property was confiscated. Early in 1940 he escaped from Poland and offered his services to General Sikorski, Prime Minister of the Polish government-in-exile. Winiarski was president of the London-based Bank of Poland from 1941 to 1946, and he taught international law in the Polish faculty of law at Oxford University from 1944 to 1946.

In 1944 and 1945 Winiarski was a member of the interallied committee that, under the chairmanship of Sir William Malkin, considered the future of the Permanent Court of International Justice. The charter of the United Nations, signed at the United Nations Conference on International Organization, held in San Francisco on June 26, 1945, stated that "the International Court of Justice shall be the principal judicial organ of the United Nations." Integral with the charter was a statute, based upon the statute of the old court, specifying the functions of the new one.

Winiarski was one of the fifteen judges elected to the International Court in February 1946. Election, as always, was by the Security Council and the General Assembly of the United Nations, voting separately. The Security Council and the General Assembly were then in the midst of their first meetings, held in London. Since his original term was only three years, Winiarski was re-elected to a nine-year term on October 22, 1948. In the 1948 election, when there were forty-one candidates, Winiarski was elected in the General Assembly (where the required absolute majority was thirty votes) on the fourth ballot and in the Security Council (where six votes were required) on the first ballot. He was again elected to a nine-year term in 1957.

His fellow judges elected Winiarski president of the court on April 5, 1961, succeeding Green H. Hackworth of the United States. At the same time Ricardo J. Alfaro of Panama was elected vice-president. Their terms are for three years. As president, Winiarski takes precedence over the other court members but has no more power than they in voting on cases and expressing opinions.

The International Court of Justice hears only cases in which the parties are states. Although the effectiveness of the court has been seriously limited by the optional nature of its jurisdiction, by 1958 thirty-eight states had agreed to submit to the judgment of the court all disputes about the interpretation of treaties, the application of international law, breaches of obligation, and damages payable for such breaches. The prestige of the court has been somewhat reduced by the fact that it does not exercise jurisdiction over any case that the United States chooses to consider a "domestic" matter.

Since Winiarski took his seat on it in 1946, the court has heard over forty-five cases. In 1950 it handed down several decisions to settle a dispute between the United States and France over rights of United States citizens in Morocco. In the dispute between Great Britain (on behalf of the Anglo-Iranian Oil Company) and Iran in 1952, the court ruled that Iran was not violating any rights coming under the court's jurisdiction, and the parties eventually came to an agreement between themselves. In April 1960 the court handed down three decisions on a right-of-passage dispute between India and Portugal: Portugal had the right to transport civil officials, private persons, and ordinary goods across Indian territory to two Portuguese villages within India; it did not have the right to so transport military forces and supplies; and an Indian blockade had not violated the rights of passage legitimately belonging to Portugal. In 1960 the court also settled an old border dispute between Honduras and Nicaragua with a decision favorable to Honduras and accepted by Nicaragua. In 1957, after seizing the Suez Canal, the Egyptian government pledged itself to keep the international character of the canal according to the Convention of 1888, and formally accepted as compulsory the jurisdiction of the court in all conflicting legal interpretations of the Convention and other treaties involving the canal. Besides settling disputes between nations, the court advises the General Assembly, the Security Council, or agencies of the United Nations on matters of international law or treaty interpretations.

A prolific writer on constitutional law, particularly in its historical aspects in Poland and France, Winiarski has written even more extensively on international law, particularly as related to aviation, legitimate defense, communications, arbitration, disarmament, and inland navigation. Among his numerous books are *Principes generaux du droit fluvial international*, lectures on international river law given by Winiarski at the Academy of International Law in The Hague in 1933 and published in Paris in 1934 as part three of volume forty-five of the academy's *Recueil des cours;* and *Wybór źródeł do nauki prawa międzynarodowego*, published in Warsaw in 1938.

Bohdan Winiarski married Wanda Markowska on April 5, 1913. They have one son, Maciej, and two daughters, Krystyna and Magdalena.

References

N Y Times p14 Ap 6 '61 por
Time 77:34 Ap 14 '61 por
U N Bulletin 5:936+ N 15 '48 por
International Year Book and Statesmen's Who's Who, 1961
Who's Who in the United Nations (1951)

CURRENT BIOGRAPHY—VOL. 23. NOS. 1-2

This is the index to the January-February 1962 issues. For the index to 1961 biographies, see December 1961 issue; for the index to 1940-1950 biographies, see 1950 Yearbook. For 1951-1960 index see CURRENT BIOGRAPHY Yearbook 1960.

CURRENT BIOGRAPHY

MARCH 1962
VOL. 23   NO. 3

Editor: Charles Moritz

PUBLISHED BY THE H. W. WILSON COMPANY, 950 UNIVERSITY AVE., NEW YORK

CONTENTS

ABOUT THIS PUBLICATION

Current Biography (published every month except August) presents articles on people who are prominent in the news—in national and international affairs, the sciences, the arts, labor, and industry. Sources of information are newspapers, magazines, books, and, in some cases, the biographees themselves. It should be pointed out, however, that these are objective rather than authorized biographies. At the end of the year the articles in the monthly issues are cumulated in one alphabet, revised, and printed in a single volume known as *Current Biography Yearbook.*

Authorities for biographees' full names, with some exceptions, are the bibliographical publications of The Wilson Company. When a biographee prefers a certain name form, that is indicated in the heading of the article: for example, MACMILLAN, (MAURICE) HAROLD means that he is usually referred to as HAROLD MACMILLAN. When a professional name is used in the heading, as, for example, GLENN FORD, the real name, in this case GWYLLYN SAMUEL NEWTON FORD, appears in the article itself.

The heading of each article includes the pronunciation of the name if it is unusual, date of birth (if obtainable), and occupation. The article is supplemented by a list of references to sources of *biographical* information, in two alphabets: (1) newspapers and periodicals and (2) books.

References to newspapers and periodicals are listed in abbreviated form; for example, "Sat Eve Post 217:14+ S 30 '44 por" means *Saturday Evening Post,* volume 217, pages 14 ff, September 30, 1944, with portrait. For full names, see the section "Periodical and Newspaper Designations," which is included in all *Current Biography* Yearbooks and in the January issue each year. Obituary notices appear for persons whose biographies have been published in *Current Biography.*

An index to names that have appeared this year is to be found at the back of this issue.

NOTE: Authors whose biographies do not appear in *Current Biography* may usually be found in *Twentieth Century Authors,* Kunitz & Haycraft, 1942, H. W. Wilson Company, or in the FIRST SUPPLEMENT (1955). Authors of books for young people are included in *The Junior Book of Authors* (Second Edition, Revised) edited by Kunitz & Haycraft, 1951, H. W. Wilson Company. Musicians whose biographies do not appear in *Current Biography* may usually be found in *Living Musicians,* compiled and edited by David Ewen, 1940, H. W. Wilson Company, or in its FIRST SUPPLEMENT (1957).

KEY TO PRONUNCIATION

ā	āle	N	Not pronounced, but indicates the nasal tone of the preceding vowel, as in the French *bon* (bôN).	û	ûrn; French eu, as in *jeu* (zhû); German ö, oe, as in *schön* (shûn), *Goethe* (gû'tĕ)
â	câre				
ă	ădd				
ă	ăccount				
ä	ärm				
à	àsk				
a̱	sofa̱			ŭ	tŭb
		ō	ōld	u̵	circŭs
ē	ēve	ô	ôrb	ü	Pronounced approximately as ē, with rounded lips: French u, as in *menu* (mē-nü); German ü, as in *grün*
ĕ	ĕnd	ŏ	ŏdd		
ē	makēr	oi	oil		
		o͞o	o͞oze		
g	go	o͞o	fo͝ot		
		ou	out		
ī	īce				
ĭ	ĭll	th	then	zh	azure
		th	thin	′ =	main accent
K	German ch as in *ich* (ĭK)	ū	cūbe	″ =	secondary accent

CURRENT BIOGRAPHY

MARCH 1962

ADOULA, CYRILLE Sept. 1921- Premier of
the Republic of the Congo
Address: Office of the Premier, Leopoldville, Republic of the Congo

The third Premier of the Republic of the
Congo, Cyrille Adoula, who was elected by the
Congolese Parliament on August 2, 1961 to succeed Joseph Ileo, is widely regarded as the man
who will probably conciliate the divergent factions in that strife-torn country. A former bank
clerk and trade union official, Adoula has served
in the cabinet of the Republic, and has been a
member of its Senate. Although he opposes
Communism, he is a convinced Socialist and
nationalist. He has staunchly supported Congolese President Joseph Kasavubu and United
Nations efforts to restore peace and unity to the
Congo. Among the achievements of his first six
months as Premier are the conclusion of a tentative agreement to end the secession of Katanga
province under Moise Tshombe and the dissolution of the Soviet-backed regime of Vice-Premier
Antoine Gizenga in Oriental province. He thus
removed two major obstacles to Congolese unity.

Descended, on his father's side, from Ban-
gala tribesmen of Equator province and, on
his mother's side, from the Baluba of Kasai,
in what was then the Belgian Congo, Cyrille
Adoula was born at Leopoldville, the colonial
capital, in September 1921 (one source gives
1924). His father, a dock worker, was aware
that the boy had a high intelligence and encouraged him to get an education. At first the
father did not believe that his son could ever
learn to read and write like the Europeans, and
he regarded it as a miracle when the boy
demonstrated these skills. In 1941 Adoula
completed his formal education at the St. Joseph
Institute, a Catholic missionary school in
Leopoldville, from which he graduated with
distinction. He was the first native African
employee of the Congo Central Bank and worked
as a bank clerk until he was thirty-five years old.
He also became an expert photographer. In
contrast to the tribal and village background of
other Congolese leaders, Adoula's is modern and
Westernized.

In 1956 Adoula left his position with the bank
to enter politics as a Socialist. He became secretary of the General Federation of Congolese
Workers, a subsidiary of the General Federation
of Labor sponsored by the Socialist party of
Belgium. In October 1958 Adoula, as a dedicated
nationalist, joined Patrice Lumumba and Joseph
Ileo in launching the Mouvement National
Congolais (M.N.C.), the first organized political
party in what since 1908 has been governed as a
Belgian colony with very limited native advisory

Wide World

CYRILLE ADOULA

participation. In the late spring of 1959 Adoula
took part with Lumumba in meetings of the independence movement in Nigeria, but in July of
that year, when moderate leaders moved to expel
the fiery-tongued and extremist Lumumba from
the M.N.C., Adoula aligned himself with the
moderate wing headed by Albert Kalonji of
South Kasai province. The Kalonji wing later
formed a loose coalition with Abako (Association
des Bakongo), led by Joseph Kasavubu.

On June 30, 1960 the independent Republic of
the Congo was proclaimed by King Baudouin of
Belgium. Lumumba, whose M.N.C. party obtained control of a plurality of the seats in the
lower house of Parliament, was appointed
Premier of a coalition cabinet, while Kasavubu
accepted what was expected to be the largely
ceremonial office of President. Shortly after independence had been proclaimed, the Congo
erupted into violence, marked by tribal conflicts
and mutiny in the Congolese army. On July 11,
1960 Moise Tshombe, the Premier of Katanga,
proclaimed the secession and independence of
that wealthy province from the Congo. Intervention by the United Nations, requested by
Lumumba, was authorized by Security Council
resolution on July 14, 1960.

Meanwhile, Lumumba, who was strongly supported by the Soviet Union, came increasingly
into conflict with President Kasavubu and United

ADOULA, CYRILLE—*Continued*

Nations Secretary-General Dag Hammarskjöld. On September 5, 1960 Kasavubu announced the dismissal of Lumumba as Premier and his replacement by Joseph Ileo. Adoula, who was at this time serving as a Senator from Equator Province, his ancestral home, sat in silence and abstained from voting when Lumumba called upon Parliament to oppose Kasavubu's efforts to depose him. In the new Ileo cabinet Adoula accepted the post of Minister of the Interior. Although Lumumba had the backing of a majority in Parliament, Colonel Joseph Mobutu, the chief staff of the Congolese army, seized power through a military coup and threw his support to Kasavubu. Lumumba was killed in February 1961, reportedly while trying to escape from imprisonment in Katanga.

Following admission of the Republic of the Congo to the United Nations in November 1960, Interior Minister Adoula was seated in the General Assembly as a member of the Kasavubu delegation. Backed by the United States, this delegation was given recognition over a Soviet-supported Lumumba delegation by a vote of 53 to 24. In the Congo, meetings of Parliament were resumed on February 11, 1961, when Kasavubu proclaimed the end of the military regime. At the Coquilhatville conference of 280 Congolese leaders, in April and May 1961, Adoula presented a plan for the creation of a federal republic of the Congo. This plan was subsequently adopted. At the conference Adoula, as Minister of the Interior, filed an act of internment against Moise Tshombe, to legalize the latter's arrest by the central government on charges of high treason.

In the elections for a new Parliament, held in late July 1961, followers of Premier Antoine Gizenga of Oriental province—the Soviet-backed self-styled heir of Lumumba—slightly outnumbered those who supported President Kasavubu. When the new Parliament convened, the U.N. Emergency Force kept the 201 members virtually imprisoned behind an electrified fence until on August 2, 1961, after seven days, they almost unanimously confirmed Cyrille Adoula, Kasavubu's choice, as Premier to succeed Joseph Ileo. Having no strong tribal or sectional ties, Adoula was able to transcend party differences and gained widespread confidence, including that of followers of the late Lumumba. The new "government of national unity," headed by Adoula, consisted of forty-two members representing virtually all factions except that of Tshombe, who boycotted the new central government. Gizenga was named one of the three Deputy Premiers, while Gizengists were appointed to the Ministries of the Interior, Justice, and Economic Affairs. Adoula himself retained the Ministry of Defense, previously refused by Tshombe.

Following his confirmation by Parliament, Adoula declared that "the Congo must not become a battlefield for the cold war." Addressing Parliament on August 3, 1961, he declared that neither Tshombe and the Belgian mining company in Katanga, the *Union Minière,* nor the Belgians behind the Katanga secession "can prevent the Congolese people from recovering their rightful heritage." He also pledged to take steps

to bring about financial stability, to alleviate unemployment, to reorganize the army and police under a more disciplined and unified administration, to settle tribal differences, to improve the educational system, and to release political prisoners. On August 15, 1961 Secretary-General Dag Hammarskjöld announced that the United Nations recognized Adoula's government as the only legitimate government in the Congo.

When Hammarskjöld was killed in an airplane accident in September 1961, while on a mission in the Congo, Adoula angrily charged the capitalist powers with responsibility for the Secretary-General's death. Noting that Katanga was "in the hands of capitalist imperialism," he said that Hammarskjöld was "the victim of certain financial circles for whom a human life is not equal to a gram of copper or uranium." Following a ceasefire—which was highly unsatisfactory to the Congolese government—Adoula, in late October 1961, sent a contingent of Congolese troops to end the Katanga secession. On December 19, 1961 Adoula and Tshombe reached an agreement in which the latter agreed to end the Katanga secession and to comply with United Nations resolutions.

Following the massacre, by mutinous Congolese soldiers, of thirteen Italian airmen attached to the U.N. mission, in November 1961, Adoula issued an agonized plea for help to the Congolese people. He expressed great anger and disgust over the crime, and pledged that its perpetrators would be punished. Although some supporters of Gizenga accused Adoula of "high treason" for his attack on the army, he had the overwhelming confidence of Parliament on this issue.

To gain the support of the followers of Gizenga, Adoula visited the Lumumbist stronghold of Stanleyville shortly after he took office as Premier, and he received an enthusiastic reception. Placing flowers upon the monument of Lumumba, he declared with emotion: "We have achieved what Lumumba wanted: 'one Congo, one Congo, one Congo.'" Although Gizenga had previously declared the dissolution of his Stanleyville regime, and had pledged support to the central government at Leopoldville, in late August 1961 he established a new political group, the National Party of Patrice Lumumba, and was installed as Provisional President. At the Belgrade conference of nonaligned nations in September 1961, the Congo was represented by both Adoula and Gizenga. The two men agreed on the necessity of a policy of nonalignment for the Congo, but their speeches disclosed acute differences. With the continued failure of Gizenga to co-operate with the central government, Adoula, supported by Acting Secretary-General U Thant of the United Nations, ordered General Victor Lundula, the new head of the Congolese army, to take all necessary measures to restore order to Stanleyville. In January 1962 Gizenga was arrested and stripped of his powers, while Adoula enjoyed the confidence of Parliament.

Relations between the Congo and Belgium, which had been broken off shortly after independence was achieved, were restored in November 1961, and Adoula has consulted with Belgian financial leaders on Katanga's problems. The Congo has also restored relations with the Soviet

Union, suspended since September 1960, but Adoula has insisted that all Soviet aid must be channeled through the U.N.—something the Soviet Union had previously refused to do. Adoula is known as a Pan-Africanist and has expressed sympathy for Africans in revolt against Portuguese rule in neighboring Angola. "Our nation will serve as a base for African nationalism," he said in August 1961. "My government will help all brother countries and will give total support, material and moral, to all African movements which fight for freedom." On the home front, Adoula has taken steps to ease the unstable financial situation. He has instituted an austerity program for his cabinet members, involving a 10 percent decrease in pay, and he has brought about the devaluation of the weak Congolese franc. He has also begun to organize an elite army of 2,000 men, to be trained by the U.N., and he plans to reduce the size of his cabinet and to ensure its greater loyalty.

Cyrille Adoula lives in Leopoldville with his second wife, Julienne, and five children. He is a Catholic. Seymour Freidin of the New York *Post* (August 31, 1961) has described him as "a rather cheerful man with a hairline mustache," who is "always accessible to curious foreigners," and has "a lively intelligence and a dry wit." The writer of a New York *Times* biographical sketch describes Adoula as somewhat shy and taciturn, and adds that he "is noted, in a land of impassioned political orators, for his crisp, logical, and soft-spoken bluntness" (August 3, 1961). According to a correspondent for the Manchester *Guardian* (August 10, 1961), he is "a tough, hot-tempered unionist with few of the social graces, but with a fund of the common sense which has stood him in place of tact."

References

N Y Herald Tribune p6 Ag 3 '61
N Y Post p44 F 6 '62 por
N Y Times p6 Ag 3 '61 por; IV p3 Ja 21 '62
Washington (D.C.) Post A p10 Ag 2 '61
International Who's Who, 1961-62

AMIES, (EDWIN) HARDY (ā'mēz) July 17, 1909- Fashion designer; businessman
Address: b. 14 Savile Row, London, W. 1, England; h. 22 Eldon Rd., London, W. 8, England

Like Norman Hartnell, couturier Hardy Amies holds a royal warrant of appointment as dressmaker to Queen Elizabeth II of England. His establishment at 14 Savile Row, London—traditionally a male sartorial stronghold since the heyday of Beau Brummel—bears the Royal Coat of Arms, the ultimate seal of success, prestige, and prosperity among tradesmen of Great Britain. Amies, who once headed the Incorporated Society of London Fashion Designers, has done a great deal towards making British women more fashion-conscious by popularizing sculptured suits, dramatic evening gowns, and light and colorful fabrics. His collections, unlike those of Norman Hartnell, are noted for their restrained and discreet look.

Michael Boys, Ltd., London
HARDY AMIES

In addition to creating four wholesale collections for women each year, Amies serves as design consultant for men's clothes at Hepworths, the London tailors and outfitters, and he runs a boutique that does a profitable business, especially when the summer onrush of American tourists begins. He recently added to his enterprises the making of ready-to-wear clothes, men's wear and perfumery, and maternity clothes. A witty and engaging lecturer, he toured the lecture circuit in the United States during the autumn of 1960, deftly parrying questions about Her Majesty's wardrobe.

Descended from an old Kentish family, Edwin Hardy Amies was born on July 17, 1909 in the Maida Vale section of London, England to Herbert William and Mary (Hardy) Amies. His father was an architect-surveyor and his mother was a saleswoman in the Court dressmaking establishment of Miss Gray of Bond Street. Amies has a sister, Rosemary Peggy. He has said that he was practically "born on the doorstep of a Court dressmaking establishment," where he spent much of his time as a child.

After several years at Upper Latimer School in Hammersmith, Hardy transferred to Brentwood School in Essex, an English public school. When Herbert Amies received an appointment to head a housing scheme in Essex for the London County Council, he moved his family there. Recalling his school days in his autobiography, *Just So Far* (Collins, 1954), Amies wrote: "I was bad at both football and cricket, but I quickly won a certain renown on the stage of the school theatricals . . . making a successful debut as Jessica in *The Merchant of Venice*. I was a great success as Mrs. Malaprop in *The Rivals*." He also read voraciously and rather indiscriminately in the novels of Ethel M. Dell, Sir Henry Rider Haggard, and Hugh Walpole. Of the finer books he read, the one that made the most lasting impression upon him was H. J. C. Grierson's

AMIES, HARDY—*Continued*

Classical and Romantic. Not surprisingly, he did his best work in English composition and in English literature.

Amies tried for an open scholarship to Cambridge University, but failed. Thinking that his son might have the makings of a journalist, Herbert Amies took Hardy to R. D. Blumenthal, editor of the London *Daily Express*, who recommended that Hardy travel abroad and learn French and German. Amies left for Antibes, France in 1927 and lived at the home of Mlle. Louise (Aunt Louie) Probet-Piolat, who had worked with his mother at a dressmaking establishment. He soon found work as a tutor in English to the sons of a Madame Vernet-Barbarroux at Nice, eleven miles away from Antibes. By the time that Christmas came around he had learned so much French that he easily obtained a job in Paris at a pound a week for carriers and customs agents, filling out forms and declarations for parcels going from the big French silk houses to London dressmakers. Although he worked a twelve-hour day, he somehow found time to see plays at the Comédie Française and the Théâtre de l'Atelier.

In Germany, the next stopping place in his travels, he acquired a taste for grand opera. He boarded at a vicarage at Bendorf on the Rhine, supporting himself by working in a tile factory. He was given more responsibility as he perfected his knowledge of German, and the firm began to send him on business trips to Berlin and Coblentz. After two and a half years in Germany, Amies returned to England as a representative of W. & T. Avery, Ltd., an English weighing machine concern with a factory in Karlsruhe, Germany. In 1930, after special training at the Birmingham factory, he became a salesman of weighing machines. Four years later a vacancy occurred in the London couturier establishment of Lachasse when Digby Morton, a young Irish designer, left to open his own business. Thanks to his mother's connections in the dressmaking world, Hardy Amies was given the opportunity to step into the vacancy.

Starting work at Lachasse on Farm Street in London on February 1, 1934, Amies began by making a thorough analysis of the establishment, which specialized in tweed suits for "the gay, rich racing set." In 1935 his employer, Fred Shingleton, promoted him to managing designer. "I literally learned the business by talking to customers," he has written in his autobiography, *Just So Far*. "The general machinery of the house, the functioning of the stockroom, the way materials were sent to the workrooms . . . all seemed to me as simple and as natural as if I had known them all my life." According to Amies, many of his designs were extravagant and hideous, but he kept on experimenting. In 1937, the year of the Coronation of George VI, when many American tourists and buyers were in London, he scored his first big success with a tweed suit that he called "Panic."

When World War II broke out in 1939, Amies volunteered for duty with the field security police. Later in the year he entered the British Intelligence Corps as a private. After having been intensively trained in organizing sabotage and resistance in occupied countries, he became liaison officer between the training school and intelligence headquarters in Baker Street, London. Meanwhile he continued to design for the House of Worth in London, and photographs of the clothes he created appeared in *Harper's Bazaar* and *Vogue*.

Hoping to accomplish something that would "expiate the sins of too easy living," Amies volunteered for parachute training in the spring of 1943. Although he made the required number of jumps, he never put his training as a parachutist to use. Instead, in 1944, he became head of the Special Forces Mission to Belgium. (For this service Belgium made him an Officier de l'Ordre de la Couronne in 1946.) In 1945 Amies was demobilized with the rank of lieutenant-colonel.

Soon after his demobilization Amies opened his own establishment at 14 Savile Row, in a beautifully paneled Georgian home, built in 1725, that had once been owned by Richard Brinsley Sheridan, the playwright. Although it had been badly bombed by the Germans during the war, its dark paneling remained intact, and Amies renovated the mansion throughout. He obtained financial backing from several Americans as well as from his stepmother and Mrs. Montague Meyer and Miss Agnes Linton of the Linton Tweed Mills in Cumberland, England. His associates were Dick Hinds-Howell, his accountant; Flora Campbell, who had worked with him at Lachasse; his father; and his solicitor, Fay Blacket-Gill.

In 1950 Hardy Amies introduced a line of ready-to-wear clothes, now on sale all over the world. Since then his business has greatly expanded, including the designing of men's clothes for Hepworths, the well-known multiple tailors; the making of men's scents; the Maxton Blouse Company; and Maternally Yours, a maternity line. As design consultant for Hepworths, Amies introduced fifty garments for men in September 1961.

With Norman Hartnell, Amies shares the title of Dressmaker to the Queen, for whom he first created daytime clothes in 1951. He had earlier designed fashions for some of her closest friends, including Lady Alice Egerton, her lady-in-waiting. In designing for the Queen, Amies has to keep in mind certain requirements: her hats have to cling close to her head; her skirts must not ride up; her colors must keep her conspicuous in a crowd; and her clothes must enable her to get in and out of a car gracefully. Guarded from interruptions by two Italian maids who act as watch-dogs, Amies works on his designs for the Queen at home. He then sends them off in a green morocco folder, and in a short time they come back with the Queen's choices clearly indicated. Amies' employees report that the Queen is "considerate, businesslike, and unvacillating." Amies sometimes takes the new models for the Queen off to Buckingham Palace in his own car, stowing them away in a trunk specially lined in spotless white rubber.

From 1954 to 1956 Hardy Amies served as vice-chairman of the Incorporated Society of London Fashion Designers. Since 1957 he has been vice-president of the Clothing Institute. As president in 1959-60 of the Incorporated Society of London Fashion Designers (comprising the "big twelve" of the British couturiers), Amies directed the fashion show presented at the Hotel Crillon in Paris and, later, at the Hotel Astor in New York, under the auspices of the Fashion Group. The latter occasion, preceding the British Fair at the Coliseum, was the first time that an exclusively British fashion show was given on a grand scale in the United States.

Hardy Amies stands six feet one inch in height, weighs 168 pounds, and has brown hair and brown eyes. One effusive female fashion writer called him "possibly the world's most handsome royal dressmaker"; other, more restrained, columnists have praised him for being "clearheaded," "vocal," "dapper," "witty," and "articulate." His debonair manner has charmed many a susceptible matron in his lecture audiences. A cosmopolite, he is fluent in French, German, and Italian, and feels very much at home in New York City. He once said, "You can't understand modern art or modern living until you've been to New York." He enjoys ice skating, tennis, music, and painting. As a loyal Englishman, he has defended the dowdiness of his countrywomen. "As a human being, I admire a certain British attitude toward dress, even though it defeats me as a dressmaker," Amies has remarked. "It is that clothes aren't really as important as all that."

References

N Y Herald Tribune p16 S 28 '60 por
N Y Times p35 O 13 '59 por
Amies, Hardy. Just So Far (1954)
Who's Who, 1961

BORING, EDWIN G(ARRIGUES) (gâr-ĭ-gōoz) Oct. 23, 1886- Psychologist; editor; author; former university professor
Address: b. Memorial Hall, Harvard University, Cambridge 38, Mass.; h. 21 Bowdoin St., Cambridge 38, Mass.

In the fall of 1959 the members of the American Psychological Association, meeting in Cincinnati, Ohio, presented Dr. Edward G. Boring with their gold medal. Dr. Boring, one of the few existing truly general psychologists and one of the most literate and dedicated members of his profession, was cited for his sevenfold usefulness as experimentalist, teacher, critic, theorist, administrator and statesman, popular expositor, and editor. He now holds the rank of Edgar Pierce Professor of Psychology Emeritus at Harvard University, where he was a member of the faculty for thirty-five years before he retired in 1957. In the fall of 1961 he retired as editor of *Contemporary Psychology,* a review journal that he helped to found for the American Psychological Association in 1955. Before that he served as a co-editor of the *American Journal of Psychology* for twenty-one years.

On the professional scene Boring has participated widely, serving at international con-

Fabian Bachrach

EDWIN G. BORING

gresses, on committees, and in war work. He has earned the respect of his colleagues for uniting psychologists of all schools under the banner of the American Psychological Association. In a career spanning fifty years Boring has influenced the teaching of psychology in the universities and has made a lasting contribution as an historian of psychology as a science.

Born in Philadelphia, Pennsylvania on October 23, 1886, Edwin Garrigues Boring is the only son and the youngest of four children of Edwin McCurdy Boring and Elizabeth (Garrigues Truman) Boring. His father, a Moravian, was a pharmacist who later became a trustee of the Philadelphia College of Pharmacy. The women of the family were Orthodox and Hicksite Quakers. The members of the family, who could trace their ancestry in America back to seventeenth-century settlers, prided themselves on their French Huguenot and Philadelphia Quaker Main Line antecedents. He had three sisters: Lydia T. Boring, a high school teacher; Katharine B. Rondthaler, the wife of a college president; and Alice M. Boring, a Ph.D. in biology, who taught at Yenching University in Peiping, China from 1920 to 1950.

Reared as one of two males in a matriarchal household with a mother, grandmother, maiden great-aunt, and three sisters, "Garry" Boring had a lonely childhood. Because he was considered a delicate child, he was forbidden to make friends with the boys in the neighborhood and he was kept at home and tutored by one of his sisters until he was nine years old. His only childhood playmate was an imaginary one—a girl he called "Mamie." In 1895 he entered the Friends' Select School, an Orthodox Quaker institution providing elementary and secondary education. He maintained an excellent scholastic average, although he was "utterly incompetent" in athletics, and

BORING, EDWIN G.—*Continued*

he joined the debating team and the editorial staff of the school magazine. He graduated in 1904.

Boring entered Cornell University in 1904 as a student of electrical engineering, a subject in which he had been interested since childhood, when he played with magnetism and electricity. When he graduated in 1908 with a degree in mechanical engineering he was hired by Eugene Grace of the Bethlehem Steel Company as an apprentice electrician in a program to teach college men the workings of the industry from the bottom up. Although he was offered a promotion to foreman after his first year of working for eighteen cents an hour on an eighty-four week, Boring turned down the opportunity. Explaining his shift from engineering to psychology, Boring said recently: "I did not like engineering, especially the practical aspects of it and I was poor at it. The great magnetism and charm of the Cornell psychologist, E. B. Titchener, captured me, and I did well in psychology, and also had a job in it given me after my first four months of graduate work."

As an escape from engineering, Boring taught science and physical geography for one year (1909-10) at the Moravian Parochial School in Bethlehem, Pennsylvania, but when the students shellacked the seat of his chair and painted his derby hat white, he decided that he was not suited for a teaching career. During the summer of 1909 he returned to Cornell to study physical geography and he also elected the laboratory course in experimental psychology under Madison Bentley.

There appeared to be no alternative for Boring but to pursue graduate study, and in the fall of 1910 he returned to the campus of Cornell University. An elementary laboratory course in psychology with E. B. Titchener that he had taken as an elective subject four years earlier had aroused his interest in that subject, and he decided to become a psychologist in spite of his parents' objections. A $500 assistantship, awarded him in February 1911 because of his proficiency in Bentley's course in comparative physiology, enabled him to be financially independent of his father and to continue his work with Titchener.

Often called the founder of the new experimental psychology, Edward Bradford Titchener (1867-1927) upheld the German tradition of introspection of consciousness as the proper psychological method and opposed the study of the behavior of men and animals as a concern of the psychologist. Boring has written: "Titchener had far more influence upon me than any other person in my professional life, the brilliant, erudite, magnetic, charming Titchener." Unlike some of the other graduate students in psychology, Boring did not leave the little band of those faithful to Titchener at Cornell. He did not resent the older man's interference in his private life, his unsolicited advice, or his claims to loyalty and deference.

During his graduate years at Cornell, Boring took his minor subjects in educational psychology and in the medical school. He was promoted to the rank of instructor at Cornell in 1913, and in

1914 he received his doctorate after submitting a thesis on the sensation of the alimentary canal. (Visceral sensibility was one of his paramount interests at the time.) At Cornell Boring began to develop a coterie of graduate students around him and he continued his research in both the psychological and physiological laboratories. His most important paper of the period was "Cutaneous Sensation After Nerve Division" (1916).

When the United States entered World War II, Boring volunteered for service. He was commissioned a captain in the newly created Psychological Service and assigned to do intelligence testing. After the Armistice Boring was sent to the office of the Surgeon-General in Washington, D.C., to work as associate editor of the gigantic report *Psychological Examining in the U.S. Army,* published as volume 15 of the *Memoirs* of the National Academy of Science in 1921. Working under Robert M. Yerkes, the famous American psychobiologist, Boring edited the report from November 1918 to July 1919.

In the summer of 1919 Boring accepted an appointment as lecturer in psychology at Harvard University, but revoked his decision before the fall term began when G. Stanley Hall, the psychologist who was then president of Clark University in Worcester, Massachusetts, offered him a chair there as professor of experimental psychology. Boring's work at Clark earned him the reputation of being an outstanding experimental psychologist.

As a result of a controversy with the university administration over freedom of speech, Boring left Clark in 1922 and accepted an appointment as an associate professor at Harvard. In 1924 he was made director of the psychological laboratory at Harvard and four years later he was promoted to a full professorship. He spent the 1920's in teaching, administration, writing, and directing research. He supervised the experiments of his graduate students and taught a basic course to undergraduates.

In 1925 Boring became a co-editor of the *American Journal of Psychology.* In 1928 he initiated the publication of a series of autobiographies under the title *A History of Psychology in Autobiography,* modeled upon the German series *Die Philosophie der Gegenwart in Selbstdarstellungen.* Four volumes have been published by the Clark University Press: the first appeared in 1930, the fourth, in 1952. Boring served on the author selection committee. His *A Experimental Psychology,* a classic in its field, was published by the Century Company in 1929. Boring had given a course in the subject at the University of California at Berkeley five years before. In the *American Psychologist* (April 1961) *A History of Experimental Psychology* was listed among the half dozen important books in psychology.

Temperamentally not an experimentalist, Boring allowed professional activities to lure him from the laboratory, and he spent little time in research. Nevertheless his books advanced both his reputation and the cause of psychology in the United States. *The Physical Dimensions of Consciousness* (Century, 1933) recorded his views on physicalism, a concept advanced by the majority of American psychologists. In 1935 he joined

H. P. Weld and H. S. Langfeld in editing *Psychology: A Factual Textbook* (Wiley, 1935; 1939; 1948), in which each chapter was written by an expert. The editors were responsible for eliminating controversy and presenting an authoritative volume on the college level. With the publication of *Sensation and Perception in the History of Experimental Psychology* (Appleton-Century, 1942), Boring's reputation was secure.

During World War II Boring was asked to prepare a manual on military psychology for the average GI. The result was *Psychology for the Fighting Man* (Penguin, 1943), prepared with the help of Marjorie Van de Water. *Psychology for the Returned Serviceman* (Penguin, 1944) and *Psychology for the Armed Forces* (Penguin, 1945) were issued by Boring and Van de Water after the first book had sold 360,000 copies.

As part of his never-ending quest for maturity, Boring underwent a year of psychoanalysis in 1934 and 1935 with Hanns Sachs, one of Freud's early associates. Boring believes that he never achieved the kind of transference that would have made a success of the analysis. In his autobiography, *Psychologist at Large* (Basic Books, 1961), he sums up the benefits of the analysis as: "a knowledge of the technique, the reassurance of knowing that I had not left a reputed remedy for my trouble untried, the realization that even what is called successful analysis does not create maturity, and an appreciation of the fact that we have here a procedure which claims validity but which lacks scientific control and the means of validation."

In 1949 Boring retired as chairman of Harvard's psychology department and director of the psychological laboratory, and he began to revise and expand his *History of Experimental Psychology*, the second edition of which was published by Appleton-Century-Crofts, Inc., in 1950. He was appointed Lowell television lecturer in 1956, delivering his Harvard Psychology 1 course on the Boston educational channel, WGBH-TV. Boring was the first to hold the chair of Edgar Pierce Professor of Psychology at Harvard (1956-57). He retired from his duties in 1957 with the rank of Edgar Pierce Emeritus Professor at Harvard University.

His retirement from Harvard did not bring stagnation. He wrote brief biographies of such great names in American psychology as R. M. Yerkes, Lewis M. Terman, and E. B. Titchener. In 1958-59 he was Phi Beta Kappa visiting scholar. From 1956 until 1961 he continued as editor of *Contemporary Psychology*, a journal of book reviews published by the American Psychological Association.

In addition to his books Boring has published articles in professional and scientific journals. He is a member of the American Psychological Association, serving on the council (1920-25), as secretary (1920-22) and as president (1928). In 1943 he served on the committee to reorganize the APA to include all smaller psychological societies in one united organization and he was the first chairman of the new policy and planning board. He is also a member of the British, French and Spanish psychological societies, Society of Experimental Psychologists. American

Academy of Arts and Sciences, National Academy of Sciences, and American Association for the Advancement of Science. Boring was awarded the gold medal of the American Psychological Foundation in 1959 and he is the recipient of honorary degrees from Harvard (1942), University of Pennsylvania (1946), and Clark (1956).

Boring, who is known to his intimates as Garry, is five feet seven inches tall and weighs 175 pounds. He has hazel eyes, receding brown-gray hair, and a prominent mustache. On June 18, 1914 he married the former Lucy Day, a fellow student who took her Ph.D. in 1912. Mrs. Boring taught at Vassar College before her marriage and at Wells College for one year before she started to raise her children, Barbara, Edwin, Jr., Frank, and Mollie. The youngest daughter, Barbara, died in 1950. Boring dispensed with any sports or hobbies and worked an eighty-hour week before he retired. At the age of sixty-five, having decided that vacations were in order, he bought a farm (which he is endlessly improving) at Harborside on Penobscot Bay in Maine. He has no church affiliation and in politics he considers himself "liberal, leaning toward democratic." He dislikes to travel.

Sometimes called "Mr. Psychologist," Boring has left an imprint on his profession as writer and editor as well as administrator and teacher. He has, by his own estimate, written about 40,000 letters in the last forty years and his tandem postcards are famous among his colleagues. Although he is held in affectionate regard for his warmth, his sense of humor, and his faith in people, he can become impatient with human derelictions and miscarriages of justice. When he was recently asked if there were any misstatements published about himself that he would like to correct, he replied, "No, all misstatements seem to me to have been in my favor."

References

American Men of Science vol 3 (1955)
Boring, Edwin G. Psychologist At Large (1961)
International Who's Who, 1961-62
Who's Who, 1961
Who's Who in America, 1960-61
World Biography, 1954

BUDD, RALPH Aug. 20, 1879-Feb. 2, 1962 Builder and operator of railroads; president of the Great Northern Railway (1919-32) and of the Chicago, Burlington and Quincy Railroad (1932-49); chairman of the Chicago Transit Authority (1949-55). See *Current Biography* (July) 1940.

Obituary

N Y Times p21 F 3 '62

BUNDY, McGEORGE Mar. 30, 1919- United States government official; author; educator
Address: b. The White House, Washington 25, D.C.; h. 5225 Partridge Lane, N.W., Washington, D.C.

When President John F. Kennedy named McGeorge Bundy his special assistant for na-

MCGEORGE BUNDY

tional security affairs he brought to Washington a man whose administrative and intellectual abilities qualified him to become the dean of the faculty of arts and sciences of Harvard University at thirty-four years of age. A Republican, Bundy occupies a post held during the Eisenhower administration by Gordon Gray, a North Carolina Democrat. Trained as a mathematician, but long a student of foreign affairs, the former educator now finds himself helping to make history, instead of writing it, as military and political planner for the National Security Council, a policy-making group presided over by the President.

Of distinguished New England ancestry on both sides of his family, McGeorge Bundy was born on March 30, 1919 in Boston, Massachusetts to Harvey Hollister Bundy, a lawyer, and Katharine Lawrence (Putnam) Bundy. His father, a Yale graduate, as a young man served as secretary to Justice Oliver Wendell Holmes. McGeorge Bundy has two brothers, Harvey H. Bundy, Jr., and William P. Bundy, now deputy assistant to the Secretary of Defense for International Security, and two sisters, Harriet L. Belin (Mrs. G. D'Andelot) and Katharine L., now Mrs. Hugh Auchincloss, Jr., who is related by marriage to Jacqueline Kennedy.

At the age of eight McGeorge Bundy enrolled at the Dexter School in Brookline, Massachusetts, where one of his classmates was John F. Kennedy. In 1931—the year that McGeorge Bundy entered Groton School—Harvey H. Bundy became Assistant Secretary of State in the Hoover administration under Henry L. Stimson —a post that he held until 1933. During World War II Harvey H. Bundy served under Henry L. Stimson again, this time as special assistant to the Secretary of War.

While a student at Groton, Bundy played the title role in Shakespeare's *Henry V*. He also perfected his tennis. After graduating from Groton in 1936 with a brilliant performance on his college board examinations, Bundy entered Yale College, where he majored in mathematics and engaged in politics and journalism as extracurricular activities. He belonged to the Liberal party in the Yale Political Union and wrote for the Yale *Daily News*. One of his contributions to the *Daily News* was a controversial column that advocated the abolition of football at Yale. This bold stand did not prevent him from being tapped for the secret society of Skull and Bones, however. Elected to membership in Phi Beta Kappa, Bundy graduated from Yale with a B.A. degree in 1940. After graduation he made a trip to South America with a friend, and in 1941 he became a junior fellow at Harvard University. That year he ran for the Boston City Council as a Republican, but lost.

In 1942, after signing waivers for his extreme nearsightedness, Bundy was admitted into the United States Army as a private. Trained as an intelligence officer, he participated in the planning of Operation Overlord, the invasion of France, and in the planning of Operation Husky, the invasion of Sicily. In London he attended Harold Laski's cerebral Tuesday evenings; during the weekends he relaxed at Lady Astor's. Discharged in 1946 with the rank of captain, Bundy returned to Boston. For the next year and a half he lived in a cottage on the Stimson estate, serving as the daily companion and research assistant of Henry L. Stimson, who was readying his manuscript of *On Active Service in Peace and War* for publication by Harper & Brothers in 1948. Bundy was co-author of the book, an autobiography based on Stimson's diaries, speeches, correspondence, and other papers. Half of the book dealt with World War II.

In April 1948 Bundy came to Washington as a consultant to the programs division of the Economic Cooperation Administration, which administered the Marshall Plan. He worked under Richard Bissell, under whom he had studied at Yale. In September 1948 he served as research analyst of foreign policy on a committee recruited by the Presidential candidate, Thomas E. Dewey. Other members of the special committee included John Foster Dulles, and Christian A. Herter.

Bundy then went to the Council on Foreign Relations in New York City as a political analyst in a study of the Marshall Plan conducted by a panel of which Dwight D. Eisenhower, then president of Columbia University, served as chairman. Returning to Harvard, Bundy became a lecturer in government in 1949. Two years later he was promoted to the rank of associate professor of government and in 1954 he became professor of government.

In his *God and Man at Yale* (Regnery, 1951) William Buckley, Jr., a young Yale alumnus, had charged his Alma Mater with teaching "collectivism" and "atheism." Bundy defended Yale against these charges in two heated articles entitled "Attack on Yale" that appeared in the *Atlantic Monthly* in November and December of 1951. The next year he engaged in another defense when he edited *Patterns of Responsi-*

bility (Houghton, 1952), a favorable presentation of the record of Secretary of State Dean Acheson in terms of his public papers: speeches, press conferences, and testimony before legislative committees. Supplying the connecting links between papers, Bundy candidly informed readers that his brother William had married Acheson's daughter and explained that he had assembled the material independently of Acheson. He also made it clear that he did not agree with Acheson on United States policy towards China in the years from 1945 to 1950.

In May 1952 Bundy was initiated into the security aspects of defense planning when he became secretary of the so-called Oppenheimer panel, of which Dr. J. Robert Oppenheimer was chairman. Other members of the committee, assigned the task of making a fresh appraisal of the problems of disarmament and atomic energy control, were Dr. Vannevar Bush, John Sloan Dickey, the president of Dartmouth College, and Allen W. Dulles.

When Bundy was appointed dean of the faculty of arts and sciences and of the Graduate School of Arts and Sciences at Harvard University in the summer of 1953, he was thirty-four years of age. He headed a staff of more than 1,000, including 288 full professors, responsible for the instruction of 5,000 undergraduates and some 1,800 graduate students. He conducted a popular undergraduate course on "The United States in World Politics." With Archibald MacLeish and John Mason Brown he helped to secure the construction of the Loeb Drama Center for Harvard and Radcliffe, and he brought Lillian Hellman to Harvard to teach a course in playwriting for a semester in 1961. In 1960 he served as a member of the advisory committee for the Survey of Federal Programs in Higher Education.

While at Harvard, Bundy castigated the loyalty and security programs of the federal and state governments. In 1953 he said that "the national security is not served when the security program becomes an instrument of insecurity and mistrust." In 1955 he contended that the security program has a tendency to "discourage that confident and eager sense of partisanship which has so often distinguished the relationship between American scholars and their government."

After John F. Kennedy became an overseer of Harvard University, he saw Bundy, as dean of Harvard College, several times a year, and at commencement exercises in June 1960 the two men sat together and chatted. Approving of what he heard, Bundy helped to organize a scientific and professional committee in support of Kennedy, although he had supported Eisenhower in 1952 and 1956. After Kennedy was elected, he considered Bundy for several posts in the State Department and as Assistant Secretary of Defense for International Security and as head of the United States disarmament team.

Named special assistant for national security affairs by President Kennedy on December 31, 1960, McGeorge Bundy became a daily overseer of foreign and defense policy and the factotum of the National Security Council and

its subsidiaries. One of the most secret of agencies, the Council was established in 1947 to co-ordinate domestic, foreign, and military policies of all government agencies charged with the nation's security, and to advise the President. The members of the National Security Council are the President, Vice-President, Secretary of State, Secretary of Defense, and the director of the Office of Civil and Defense Mobilization. As co-ordinator of military and political planning, Bundy presides over the planning staff of the Security Council—a small permanent group augmented from time to time by officials of the Central Intelligence Agency, State Department, Defense Department, and other departments. Members of the staff draft plans in the fields of foreign relations and defense and submit them to the National Security Council.

With a small coterie of insiders, including such special assistants and advisers as Theodore C. Sorensen, Arthur M. Schlesinger, Jr., and Jerome B. Wiesner, Bundy belongs to the unofficial cabinet of President John F. Kennedy. By means of their intimate relationship with the President, they serve as his eyes, ears, and sometimes his voice in his dealings with the government. The group has become known as the Kitchen Cabinet, a term that dates back to the administration of Andrew Jackson. Its members were subjected to varying degrees of criticism following the failure of the Cuban invasion in April 1961.

In a major policy speech on December 6, 1961 Bundy predicted the growth of a new Europe based on the countries comprising the European Common Market. Bundy cited this future great power, equal with both the United States and the Soviet Union, as one of the forces shaping the course of American foreign policy. He believes that the United States should negotiate with the Soviet Union from a position of strength.

Harvard University, Brown University, Oberlin College, and Hofstra College have conferred honorary degrees on McGeorge Bundy. Among the organizations to which he belongs are the American Political Science Association, the Council on Foreign Relations, the Academy of Political Science, the American Academy of Arts and Sciences, and the American Academy of Political and Social Science. He is an Episcopalian.

McGeorge Bundy married Mary Buckminster Lothrop, who used to be associate director of admissions at Radcliffe College, on June 10, 1950. They have four boys: Stephen, Andrew, William, and James. Bundy is a sandy-haired, bespectacled man with green eyes and brown hair, who stands five feet ten inches in height and weighs around 160 pounds. "Aggressive" and "brilliant" are adjectives that journalists have overworked in describing him. Businesslike and self-assured, he works at a breakneck pace, then relaxes with a game of tennis. Bundy used to travel to his destinations in Cambridge on a bicycle. He is fluent in French and Spanish, reads German, and commands an elementary knowledge of Russian. Some day he would like to write a book about the conflict between Wilsonian idealism and the exigencies

BUNDY, McGEORGE—*Continued*
of power politics. The late Learned Hand, who
was not given to hyperbole, once called Mc-
George Bundy "the brightest man in America."

References

Democratic Digest p41 Ja-F '61 por
N Y Post p42 Ja 5 '61 por
N Y Times p30 Ja 1 '61
N Y Times Mag p27+ Mr 5 '61 por
Sat Eve Post 234:19+ Je 10 '61 por
Tanzer, L. ed.   The Kennedy Circle
(1961)

COWARD, NOEL (PIERCE) Dec. 16, 1899-
Author; actor; producer; composer
Address: h. "Les Avants," sur Montreux, Switzer-
land

NOTE: This biography supersedes
the article that appeared in
Current Biography in 1941.

The century and Noel Coward were both in
their twenties when his glib and witty comedies
about British upper-class foibles rocketed his
popularity to a height that seemed unsustainable.
Now in the 1960's, the author of more than fifty
produced plays and revues, Coward may still be
difficult to assess as a force in the theater, but
he is no longer considered ephemeral. He is a
consummate artist of entertainment—a skilled
and versatile actor, composer of almost 100 songs
with lyrics, director, producer, film maker, night
club and TV performer, and short story writer
and novelist.

A fascination with "the human situation" runs
through much of Coward's work—in the duality
of his satire and romance, his scoffing and sentiment, his merriment and concern. Impudence,
irony, and gaiety are likely to remain his trademarks, but his favorites among his own plays
characterize him much more broadly: *Blithe
Spirit* as the best technically, *Bitter-Sweet* as the
best musically, and *Brief Encounter* as the best
story for motion-picture use.

Among Coward's protean talents, only his
musical aptitude seems clearly an inherited tendency, for the Coward family was "fiercely musical" and his mother was "also musical." He was
born on December 16, 1899 in Teddington, a
London suburb on the Thames, to Arthur Sabin
and Violet (Veitch) Coward. His brother, Eric,
was born five years later. His father, a traveling
representative for a piano firm, had some difficulty in maintaining even a modest home; so his
mother, who had been reared in the tradition of
a gentlewoman, took in paying guests.

It was not long before Noel could contribute as
a child actor to the family's income. For a time
he had attended the Chapel Royal School in
Clapham, and he later took dancing lessons.
Reading and early experience in the theater compensated for the sketchiness of his formal schooling. In January 1911 he made his first professional appearance, in London, as Prince Mussel
in *The Goldfish*, a children's fairy play.

Before the year was over, Noel Coward was
engaged to play in Charles Hawtrey's production
of *Where the Rainbow Ends,* and in 1913 Dion
Boucicault signed him for a tour in the part of
Slightly in *Peter Pan.* Having moved on to more
adult roles, he was acting in *The Saving Grace*
when the British Army called him for medical
examinations in 1918. He spent most of what he
has called his "brief and inglorious" army career
in hospitals recovering from coma and headache
spells, as he has related in his autobiographical
Present Indicative (Doubleday, 1937).

Coward's return to the theater after his discharge from the army meant not only finding
engagements as an actor but selling his work as
a lyricist and playwright. *The Rat Trap,* which
he regards as his first serious attempt at psychological conflict, was written in 1918, but was not
produced until 1926. Meanwhile, in 1920 Gilbert
Miller presented Coward's comedy *I'll Leave It to
You,* in which the author had written a part for
himself. Besides acting in this and other productions, he was busily pouring out a spate of plays,
songs, and sketches. When he made his first trip
to the United States in 1921, he had many manuscripts to sell but few dollars to spend.

For his first success in New York, Coward had
to wait until 1925, when he duplicated on Broadway his London triumph of the preceding season
as Nicky Lancaster in his sophisticated satire *The
Vortex.* During 1925, also, five of his plays or
revues were running simultaneously on the London stage, including the brilliant and gay *Hay
Fever* and *On With the Dance.* His drawing
room drama *Easy Virtue* had its world première
in the United States in late 1925.

Now the darling of the international set and
a pet of New York and London audiences, Noel
Coward could do little wrong. *Sirocco,* written in
1921 and revised and produced in London in
1927, was an exception. But the catcalls that
made a chaos of *Sirocco* were soon forgotten in
the applause that greeted his revue *This Year of
Grace* (1928) and his nostalgic and romantic
operetta *Bitter-Sweet* (1929), for which Coward
composed "I'll See You Again" and other memorable songs.

Travel for Coward has often been a means of
rest and a source of creative refreshment. In
Shanghai, on a trip to the Far East in 1929, he
wrote one of his wittiest and most entertaining
comedies, *Private Lives,* in which he starred with
Gertrude Lawrence when the play was produced
in England the following year. As Terence Rattigan points out in his Appreciation in *Theatrical
Companion to Coward* (Macmillan, 1957), "*Private Lives* deals with a theme of timeless and
universal significance—the equation of love and
hatred—and . . . it deals with it not only with
grace and wisdom and hilarity, but with an objective truth that endows it with that touching
quality that it so often the concomitant of great
comedy."

Looking for a subject that would allow him to
test his producing capabilities on a spectacular
scale, Coward wrote an episodic play depicting
thirty years of English life. *Calvacade,* in twenty-
two scenes, opened to an ovation in October 1931,
ran for 405 performances, and was made into a
successful motion picture by the Fox Film Com-

pany in 1932. Coward brushed aside some criticism of his play: "True, there had been a few
uneasy highbrows who had deplored my fall from
sophisticated wit into the bathos of jingoism"
(*Play Parade,* volume 1, Heinemann, 1934).

In *Words and Music,* a revue that Coward
wrote and produced in 1932, he included the
song "Mad Dogs and Englishmen," which he had
earlier contributed to *The Third Little Show* to
be sung by Beatrice Lillie in New York in 1931.
The song has remained a favorite of many of
Coward's admirers, and he sang it for both Winston Churchill and President Franklin D. Roosevelt upon request.

During another of his trips, this time on a
boat from Panama to Los Angeles, Coward
worked out his ideas for *Design for Living,* which
he had been thinking about for eleven years—a
vehicle for Alfred Lunt and Lynn Fontanne and
himself. It had its première in New York in 1933
and, with another cast, enjoyed a excellent run
in London in 1939.

Another Lunt-Fontanne play that Coward
wrote and produced, *Point Valaine,* opened in
New York in January 1935 and was described in
Brooks Atkinson's New York *Times* review as
"the drama of a lurid episode of lust in the semi-
tropics." The more familiar Noel Coward toured
England with Gertrude Lawrence during 1935
and 1936 in *Tonight at 8:30,* a collection of his
one-act plays. Some of them were later presented
as motion pictures, including *Brief Encounter*
(Cineguild, 1945) and *The Astonished Heart*
(Gainsborough Pictures, 1950), for which he prepared the film scripts.

In the spring of 1939, when England was on
the verge of war, Coward wrote an appreciation
of his English heritage, *This Happy Breed,* a
chronicle of middle-class family life since World
War I. During 1942 he toured in *This Happy
Breed* and two of his comedies, *Present Laughter*
and *Blithe Spirit,* under the title of *Play Parade,*
presenting the plays alternately. *Blithe Spirit,* a
farce about spiritualism, had opened in London
in 1941 for a run of 1,997 performances, the
longest on record for a nonmusical production in
England.

Coward's second autobiographical volume, *Future Indefinite* (Doubleday, 1954), tells the story
of his struggle to serve his government during
World War II in a capacity that would fully
utilize his celebrity value. He visited on special
assignments and gave performances in the United
States and many parts of the British Empire on
behalf of the war effort. A daily diary that he
kept of his tour of North Africa and the Middle
East in 1943 provided the material for his *Middle
East Diary* (Doubleday, 1944), which offended
some readers for "tactless lightheartedness" and
appealed to others as amusing and revealing.

One of Coward's achievements of the war years
was the motion picture *In Which We Serve*
(Denham Studios, 1942), an account of the sinking of a British destroyer in the Battle of Crete.
He wrote and produced the film, co-directed it
with David Lean, composed the incidental music,
and played the leading role of Captain "D."
Coward's only previous experience as a film

Peter Marshall, Toronto

NOEL COWARD

actor had been in the extraordinary American
picture *The Scoundrel* (Astoria Studios, 1935).

By the end of the war Coward was ready with
the revue *Sigh No More* (1945), which he followed with the musical romance *Pacific 1860*
(1946) and the more serious *Peace in Our Time*
(1947). Again for the talents of Alfred Lunt and
Lynn Fontanne he provided the romantic comedy
Quadrille (1952). While his *Nude with Violin,*
a comedy about an artist who did not paint his
own pictures, was in the middle of a long run in
London, Coward directed and starred in the New
York presentation of the play in late 1957.

An adaptation that Coward made of Georges
Feydeau's classic farce *Occupe-toi d'Amélie,* entitled *Look After Lulu,* had a disappointingly
brief New York run in March and April 1959.
His fiftieth produced play, *Waiting in the Wings,*
whose setting was a home for retired actresses,
fared better in London, where it opened in September 1960. He returned to Broadway in the
fall of 1961 in the triple role of author, composer,
and director with a jaunty cruise-ship musical,
Sail Away, a $400,000 show that won only mixed
reviews.

From time to time Coward turned his attention
from the theater—to perform in a $30,000-a-week
night club act in Las Vegas in 1955; to appear in
three American television shows in 1955 and 1956
(a song fest with Mary Martin and adaptations
of his *Blithe Spirit* and *This Happy Breed*); and
to compose his first original score for a ballet,
London Morning, which was produced by Anton
Dolin's Festival Ballet in London in 1959. Some
critics thought that his acting was the standout
of the brilliant cast of Carol Reed's screen version
of Graham Greene's thriller *Our Man in Havana*
(1960).

Besides his plays and revues, from which he
has recorded many songs and sketches, Coward

COWARD, NOEL—*Continued*
published two volumes of short stories: *To Step Aside* (Doubleday, 1939) and *Star Quality* (Doubleday, 1951). He had occasionally tried his hand at writing novels, but it was not until 1960 that he published his first novel. In *Pomp and Circumstance* (Doubleday), a story of havoc in high-society circles in a British South Sea Island possession, Coward combines the waspish satire of *Private Lives* with the tenderness of *Brief Encounter,* and most of the reviewers were delighted.

Noel Coward on occasion, in *Future Indefinite* and in press interviews, has objected to his public image as a decadent playboy, only witty and brittle, like the Nicky Lancaster of *The Vortex.* Although he works on a routine during morning hours and must be undisputably one of the world's most industrious playwrights, once he strikes the right note of a play that he has been thinking over for some time, he is able to complete his writing in a few days—in a seeming effortlessness that becomes a characteristic of the play itself.

At sixty-three Noel Coward remains an urbane and imperturable bachelor, tall, slim, brown-haired, and blue-eyed. Since 1956, in order to avoid what he considers excessive taxes, he has made his home away from England—in Bermuda, Jamaica, and Switzerland—and pays frequent visits to the United States. Creative even in his hobby, he passes his spare time drawing and painting. He is known for his cordiality and good manners, as well as his impishness; and to set one awed interviewer at ease he admitted to being himself impressed by his own versatility. At a Book and Author luncheon in New York in 1961 he replied to charges that his frivolous *Pomp and Circumstance* was out of touch with the times: ". . . now more than ever, when the present is overshadowed and the future is less assured than ever, the gift to amuse is not to be dismissed too contemptuously. . . . Who can truly say there is more truth in tears than in laughter?"

References

Hi Fi 11:62+ O '61 por
Theatre Arts 45:8+ S '61 por
Mander, Raymond and Mitchenson, Joe. The Theatrical Companion to Coward (1957)
Twentieth Century Authors (1942; First Supplement, 1955)
Who's Who, 1961
Who's Who in America, 1960-61
Who's Who in the Theatre (1957)

DARLING, JAY NORWOOD Oct. 21, 1876-Feb. 12, 1962 Cartoonist; conservationist; known professionally as Ding Darling; won the Pulitzer Prize twice while on the staff of the Des Moines *Register*; strongly opposed the New Deal. See *Current Biography* (July) 1942.

Obituary

N Y Times p27 F 13 '62

FERRISS, HUGH July 12, 1889-Jan. 29, 1962 Architect; artist; design artist for the New York World's Fair (1939); special consultant in designing the United Nations Building and Idlewild Airport; author of *The Metropolis of Tomorrow* (1929) and *Power in Building* (1953). See *Current Biography* (July) 1945.

Obituary

N Y Times p29 Ja 30 '62

GARDINER, JAMES GARFIELD Nov. 30, 1883-Jan. 12, 1962 Canadian government official; member of the Liberal party; elected Premier of Saskatchewan (1926 and 1934); Minister of Agriculture in the federal cabinet (1935-57). See *Current Biography* (June) 1956.

Obituary

N Y Times p21 Ja 13 '62

GOODSPEED, EDGAR J(OHNSON) Oct. 23, 1871-Jan. 13, 1962 Biblical scholar; taught Biblical and patristic Greek at the University of Chicago (1902-20); chairman of the university's New Testament department (1923-37); published *The New Testament: An American Translation* (1923), one of the first translations of the New Testament in present-day English. See *Current Biography* (November) 1946.

Obituary

N Y Times p84 Ja 14 '62

HOCKING, WILLIAM ERNEST Aug. 10, 1873- Philosopher; author; educator
Address: h. Eaton Rd., Madison, N.H.

Alone of the great representatives of the golden age of American philosophy—including James, Royce, Palmer, Santayana, and others with whom he was associated at Harvard University—William Ernest Hocking has had the opportunity to bring knowledge, logic, and speculative boldness and insight to the crucial issues that threaten civilization in the nuclear age. He is the author of a score of books and of hundreds of articles and published addresses and lectures; an idealist in metaphysical theory who says, "My central thesis: the world has a meaning immediately felt, and therewith a reason." Never an ivory tower philosopher, Hocking lives, not only sees, life steadily and as a whole—with particular enjoyment in reflecting, loving, teaching, writing, engineering, and farming. In a recent recognition of his high achievement he was elected in December 1961 as a member of the American Academy of Arts and Letters.

William Ernest Hocking, the eldest of the five children of William Francis and Julia Carpenter (Pratt) Hocking, was born in Cleveland, Ohio on August 10, 1873. His father, a Canadian-born physician of Cornish ancestry, was at that time practising medicine and teaching diagnosis in Cleveland. On his mother's side of the family, Hocking is a descendant of

Degory Priest, a Mayflower passenger. Her family's fondness for music, her own fine soprano voice, and the four-part singing festivals that enlivened the home during visits from relatives greatly delighted her son, who felt the rigorous restrictions of a Methodist upbringing of the nineteenth century.

With his four sisters—Grace Louise, Alantha, Julia, and Gertrude—Hocking was reared for the most part in Joliet, Illinois, to which the family had moved from homes in Maryland and Michigan. (Feeling never really settled in the United States, Dr. Hocking frequently changed residence.) "We enjoyed and occasionally suffered," Hocking recalls, "the firm discipline of a father who maintained the standards of his British concern for language, spelling, grammar (I was reading at three); while both parents adhered to a regular quarter-hour of family prayer before Father went to his office, and we were held to learning each day one verse from the Bible, to be repeated at that occasion. Being liberally endowed with original sin I used to single out the short verses—'And the Lord spake unto Moses, saying' (period)."

Very important among the many braids or strands of Hocking's life, as he sees it, are the educational and "the practical handiwork." During his high school years in Joliet he took care of his father's horse and buggy and worked for the Joliet *Daily News* as printer's devil and compositor. Graduating from high school at the age of fifteen, he followed his father's advice that he was too young for college and took a job as a surveyor that led, since he enjoyed drawing, to specializing in map making. The panic of 1893 consumed his savings and his hopes of entering the newly established University of Chicago.

Hocking's interest in engineering, architecture, and farming therefore had a chance to take roots because he moved, partly for economic reasons, to Iowa, where his father was then practising. He studied for two years at the State College of Agriculture and the Mechanic Arts in Ames, (now Iowa State College), specializing in engineering. This, however, was a period of spiritual distress for Hocking, who had read Herbert Spencer's *First Principles* in high school and had thereby lost his religion.

"Trying to find a way out," as Hocking describes his state of mind at that time, he encountered William James' *Principles of Psychology* one day in 1895 and became determined to go to Harvard University, where James was teaching. During another four years out of school, he earned tuition by teaching in Davenport, Iowa. For recreation he rowed on the Mississippi—thinking, "Preparation for work in a shell in days to come, on the Charles?"

Eventually Hocking did row a shell on the Charles River. He also boxed at Harvard and played the organ in Appleton Chapel and sang in the choir, while taking courses for his B.A. degree, which was granted in 1901. Then after he had earned his M.A. degree at Harvard in 1902, he studied at the universities of Göttingen, Berlin, and Heidelberg for a year as a Walker Fellow in philosophy before receiving his Ph.D. degree from Harvard in 1904.

WILLIAM ERNEST HOCKING

His thesis, "The Elementary Experience of Other Conscious Being in Its Relation to the Elementary Experience of Physical and Reflexive Objects," has been restated as "How We Know Other Minds" and is a subject to which he returned in later writings.

During the next two years Hocking divided his time between Harvard, where he taught a course in the history of modern philosophy, and Andover (Massachusetts) Theological Seminary, where he was an instructor in the history and philosophy of religion. He moved to the University of California at Berkeley in 1906 to teach philosophy, but returned to the East two years later to become assistant professor and then professor at Yale University. In 1914 Harvard offered him a professorship in philosophy, and he has been associated with Harvard ever since, from 1920 to 1943 as Alford Professor of Natural Religion, Moral Philosophy and Civil Polity and subsequently as professor emeritus.

While still at Yale, Hocking wrote his first major work, *The Meaning of God in Human Experience: A Philosophic Study of Religion* (Yale Univ. Press, 1912). In working out his own philosophical system he was influenced by both the idealism of Josiah Royce and the pragmatism of William James, and he sought a union of the two points of view in which absolutism would be modified by empiricism.

"Philosophy is the common man's business, and until it reaches the common man and answers his questions it is not doing its duty," Hocking said in an interview for *Wisdom For Our Time* (edited by James Nelson; Norton, 1961). In keeping with this conviction he early applied his metaphysics to problems of human action—to ethics, religion, and education in *Human Nature and Its Remaking* (Yale Univ. Press, 1918) and to political life in *Man and the State* (Yale Univ. Press, 1926).

(Continued next page)

HOCKING, WILLIAM ERNEST—*Continued*

Fairly recently in an approach to autobiography Hocking typed out a few slim volumes entitled "Varieties of Educational Experience"— a subject that covers many events of his life besides his university teaching. Soon after he moved to Cambridge, Massachusetts, he and his wife founded an experimental school to supplement the public school education of their children, the Shady Hill School. He started the school partly in protest against the progressive education idea that a teacher must cater to a student's interests, because he believed that interest was not a pre-existing quantity, but was rather *caught* from a teacher in love with his subject. (Hocking's connection with the school ended in 1926, but it continues to flourish.)

World War I provided a series of educational experiences for Hocking. After attending a Plattsburg, New York civilian training camp in 1916, he taught military engineering in the ROTC at Harvard in 1916-17. At the request of the British government, he spent the summer of 1917 at the British and French fronts in France studying the psychology of morale. He recorded his findings in *Morale and Its Enemies* (Yale Univ. Press, 1918), which included material that he had presented in lectures at Williams College in 1917 and at Yale in 1918. During 1918 he was also an inspector of war issues courses under the United States War Department's bureau of education.

In 1928 Hocking traveled to the Near East —Egypt, Palestine, Syria, and Turkey—and to Geneva to study mandates. He has pointed out that the trip belongs to the educational strand of his life because the purpose of a mandate was to educate peoples toward independence. "It was also on the strand of one's loves— the most important of all," he wrote in autobiographical notes for *Twentieth Century Authors* (H. W. Wilson Company, First Supplement, 1955), "because I fell in love with the Arabs and out of love with the Zionists. . . ." One product of his study was *The Spirit of World Politics: With Special Studies of the Near East* (Macmillan, 1932).

Another journey that Hocking considered significant for his writing was one that he made to the Far East in 1931-32 when he headed a fifteen-member Laymen's Foreign Missions Inquiry Commission to study and appraise missions in India, China, and Japan. The commission published the report *Re-Thinking Missions: A Layman's Inquiry after One Hundred Years* (Harper, 1932). On the same strand of education as his work on the undertakings of world propagation of religions is his investigation into the United States educational program in post-Nazi Germany during the occupation. Interested especially in what that effort could teach America about its own educational ideas, he wrote *Experiment in Education: What We Can Learn from Teaching Germany* (Regnery, 1954).

Some of Hocking's most valuable contributions in clarifying man's understanding of his problems have come through lectureships, at many universities over many years. His Mahlon Powell Lectures at the University of Indiana,

published as *Lasting Elements of Individualism* (Yale Univ. Press, 1937), examined the weaknesses of both traditional individualism and such contemporary substitutes as Communism and fascism. In certain aspects of the subject of human rights, the Powell lectures are related to *Freedom of the Press* (Univ. of Chicago Press, 1947), Hocking's personal statement as a member of the Commission on the Freedom of the Press, in which he insisted upon a moral responsibility that precludes the right to publish indiscriminately.

After examining the flaws and strengths of the principal outlooks that dominate the character of present day civilization—in political life, science, and religion—Hocking was able in *The Coming World Civilization* (Harper, 1956) to find grounds for hope for the civilization that is developing. His book won the 1957 Lecomte du Noüy Award. A future civilization, however, depends upon man's survival. Hocking made what he calls his contribution to settlement of the cold war in *Strength of Men and Nations: A Message to the USA vis-à-vis the USSR* (Harper, 1958), which attempts an impartial survey of the international issues involved in the crises that might precipitate nuclear war.

Man's purpose and destiny, his immediate awareness of God, and the ultimate nature of the world are the foremost concerns of Hocking's work. "The main drive of my life," he explains, "is toward 'a patch of ground to stand on' in our thoughts of the universe, another name for metaphysics." This concern, he says, has animated the two most ambitious efforts of his life, his yet unpublished Gifford lectures at Glasgow University in 1938-39 and the James lectures on law at Harvard in 1947.

Hocking's *The Meaning of Immortality in Human Experience* (Harper, 1957) is a companion to his early *The Meaning of God in Human Experience*. It includes his *Thoughts on Death and Life* (Harper, 1957) and focuses all man's scientific and philosophic knowledge on the meaning of life and death. "Anyone, believer or unbeliever," P. H. Phenix wrote in his review for *Christian Century* (December 18, 1957), "can hardly fail to be impressed by the intellectual vigor, deep sincerity, and beauty of Hocking's rational-mystical analysis of what is at once the most profound of human concerns and the deepest of mysteries."

A lifelong interest in art is evident in much of Hocking's writing, and his fondness for architecture has led to his building several houses. One of them is his present home— his stone house with a separate stone library —on a mountain top in Madison, New Hampshire. His wife, the former Agnes (Smiley) Boyle O'Reilly, a schoolteacher whom he married on June 28, 1905, died on May 15, 1955. They had a son, Richard Boyle O'Reilly, and two daughters, Hester and Joan. Hocking's church is the Congregational, and he says, with characteristic humor, that his political affiliation is Mugwump.

Now eighty-eight, Hocking, who has hazel eyes and gray hair, weighs 164 pounds and is five feet ten and a half inches tall. His exercise is restricted: "I used to play tennis, and do a certain amount of rowing on our pond, and swimming; now I walk a bit, chop wood, shovel snow within strict limits, do a little gardening." He prefers living in the country because it gives him time to think.

References

International Who's Who, 1961-62
National Cyclopaedia of American Biography current vol D (1934)
Nelson, James ed. Wisdom For Our Time (1961)
Twentieth Century Authors (First Supplement, 1955)
Who's Who in America, 1960-61
World Biography (1954)

HOWE, GORDIE Mar. 31, 1928- Hockey player
Address: h. Lathrup Village, Mich.; b. Detroit Red Wings, Olympia Stadium, Detroit 8, Mich.

During the 1950's an argument raged among fans as to who was the better ice hockey player —Maurice (Rocket) Richard of the Montreal Canadiens or Gordie Howe of the Detroit Red Wings. Maurice Richard has retired after a brilliant career in the National Hockey League, but Howe remains—somewhat slowed down in his sixteenth season—but still the type of offensive player who strikes fear into enemy defensemen and goal tenders. On defense he equals any forward in the league. The oldest player in point of service in the thirty-five-year history of the Detroit Red Wings, Howe played his 1,000th National Hockey League game in Chicago on November 26, 1961, breaking the record established by Ted Lindsey, a former linemate.

Howe has been awarded the Hart trophy, given to the league's Most Valuable Player, five times —a record number. When he entered the 1961-62 hockey season he had achieved a total of 1,049 points during his career, the greatest number ever scored by one man in the history of the National Hockey League. He has led the league five times in scoring and has been named to its All-Star teams twelve times. In 1957 he became the first currently active athlete to be voted into Michigan's Sports Hall of Fame.

The fifth of nine children of Ab Howe, a farmer, Gordon Howe was born on March 31, 1928 in Floral, Saskatchewan on the outskirts of Saskatoon in the heart of Canada's wheat-farming prairie country. Having failed at farming, his father moved to Saskatoon, where he ran a garage, and he is now a maintenance superintendent for the city of Saskatoon. Like many other families of the 1930's, the Howes were hit hard by the Depression, and even Gordie Howe's first pair of skates came to him secondhand.

"I was about five, and we were on relief at the time," Howe told W. C. Heinz in an interview for the *Saturday Evening Post* (January 10, 1959). "A woman came to the door one night with a whole potato sack of things, and my mother paid her a dollar and a quarter

James D. McCarthy
GORDIE HOWE

for it. I remember diving into that old bag, and there were four or five old pairs of skates in there and I grabbed a pair. They were so big I had to wear a couple of pairs of extra socks."

He soon learned to play hockey. Fortified by a breakfast of oatmeal, he used to put on his skates at home and skate down the ruts in the road to the rink. When he came home for lunch, his mother scattered newspapers on the kitchen floor so that her children could keep their skates on. Occasionally Gordie brought along his friends to share the stews or thick soups that his mother prepared for lunch or supper.

Like many Canadian families, the Howes built a hockey rink in their own backyard. In Saskatoon, where the temperature sometimes dips to fifty below zero, every school and playground has a skating rink. When the chinook, the warm wind, came to town, the water ran into the low areas and the Howe children could skate for long distances—sometimes for seven miles.

By the time that he was fifteen Howe was much sought after by scouts for hockey teams, who were desperate for players to replace men gone to war. Russ McCrorry of the New York Rangers was the first scout to visit the two-story shingled Howe house on Avenue L North in Saskatoon, in 1943. Howe was sent to New York City for a tryout, but he declined a contract with the Rangers and stayed only five days. Lonely in the big city, he went back home. In 1944 Fred Pinckney of the Detroit Red Wings paid a call to the Howes in Saskatoon and, as a result, Gordie Howe went to the Red Wings camp in Windsor, Ontario. There he proved to be so impressive in workouts that he was assigned to an amateur team in Galt, Ontario. Since, at sixteen, he was too young to play professionally, he practised until he came of age.

(Continued next page)

HOWE, GORDIE—*Continued*

In 1945 Gordie Howe signed a professional contract with Omaha in the now defunct United States Hockey League. He played for one year in Omaha, scoring 22 goals and registering 26 assists for 48 points. In 1946 he was promoted to the Detroit Red Wings. Playing in fifty-eight games during his unspectacular first year, he scored 7 goals and added 15 assists. He was better the following year, scoring 16 goals and registering 25 assists, but in 1948 he dropped to 12 goals and 25 assists. During the 1949-50 season Gordie Howe came into his own. Stationed at right wing, in seventy games he scored 35 goals and added 33 assists for 68 points, enough to rank him with the leaders in the National Hockey League.

Howe's emergence as a star was postponed by an almost fatal injury that he sustained in the Stanley Cup play-offs (the so-called World Series of ice hockey) at Detroit's Olympia Stadium in 1950. Skating at top speed, Howe collided with Ted Kennedy of the Toronto Maple Leafs and suffered a severe brain concussion. Surgeons at Harper Hospital were forced to drill into his head to relieve pressure on the brain. It looked for a time as if Gordie Howe would never play hockey again.

The following season, Howe was back on the rink with a flourish. Scoring 43 goals and 43 assists, he ended up the season as the leading scorer in the National Hockey League with 86 points. It was the first of four seasons in succession that he emerged as top scorer. In 1952 he won the first of his Hart trophies and again captured the coveted award in 1953, 1957, 1958, and 1960. Eddie Shore of the Boston Bruins had held the previous record for the number of Hart trophies won: four.

Overwhelmingly popular with hockey fans, in the course of a year Gordie Howe will receive approximately one thousand fan letters, and he answers each one in person. He never turns down a request for an autograph. For reasons that are not difficult to discover he is equally popular with his teammates. Some years ago, when the Detroit Red Wings checked into a hotel before a game, Howe learned from the hotel clerk that he had been assigned a suite of rooms in recognition of his distinction. He turned down the suite and insisted that he share a double room with one of his teammates, the same accommodation afforded the other players.

Gordie Howe married Colleen Joffa at Calvary Presbyterian Church overlooking the Grand River in Detroit on April 15, 1953. With their four children—Marty, Mark, Cathleen, and Murray—they live in Lathrup Village, a residential suburb fourteen miles from downtown Detroit. Howe's wife first heard of Gordie Howe after his almost fatal accident in the Stanley Cup game. "I didn't know anything about hockey then," she once said, "and I'd never heard of Gordie Howe. . . . The morning after he was hurt, when I came down to breakfast, my dad was storming around. He was a Red Wings fan and he was mad." She met Howe the following year when they were introduced by a mutual friend at a bowling alley. Mrs. Howe seldom misses an ice hockey game.

Standing six feet tall and weighing about two hundred pounds, Gordie Howe has a boyish appearance that is enhanced by his engaging grin. His face, crisscrossed with stitches, has suffered many cuts; he has a small crescent scar on his left cheekbone. His hair is beginning to recede. The strain of many seasons in one of the world's most dangerous sports shows up in a facial twitch that afflicts him while he is playing. "It's tiredness or nervousness," Howe explains. "My wife thinks it's the glare of the ice." He has had a fractured collarbone, two broken ribs, and his nose had been broken twice. Yet when the time to sign contracts with the Detroit Red Wings comes around, Gordie Howe is always one of the first to agree to terms and he misses very few games. He is a partner with Al Kaline, a Tiger star, and Frank Carlin in a tool and die firm, Howe-Kaline-Carlin, Inc., in Detroit, which they run in the off season. With his earnings—which, for a professional hockey player, run very high—he bought a new home for his parents in Saskatoon.

At thirty-three years of age, in his sixteenth season in the National Hockey League Gordie Howe is beginning to feel the approach of age and to take it into account. "I get tired more easily," he says. "I used to do a lot of needless skating, but now I try to cut it down." When he really starts to slow down, officials will probably move him to center and finally to defense. In that way he will be able to keep on playing for another four or five years, thus realizing his ambition to play twenty seasons in the National Hockey League. Sid Abel, the coach of the Detroit Red Wings, once said of their star player: "Howe is the best player in hockey, great on defense, and scores goals when we need them the most. He knows instinctively what to do and does it without too much effort. We'd be in a heck of a fix without him."

References

Life 46:71+ F 16 '59 por
Look 24:43+ Mr 1 '60 por
Sat Eve Post 231:30+ Ja 10 '59 pors
Time 75:78 Ja 25 '60
Washington (D.C.) Post D pl D 12 '58

HOWE, GORDON *See* Howe, Gordie

KATSH, ABRAHAM I(SAAC) Aug. 10, 1908-
Jewish scholar; educator
Address: b. New York University, Washington Square, New York 3; h. 901 Walton Ave., New York 52

Initiating enterprises that advance the causes of Jewish language, culture, and learning is a familiar experience to Dr. Abraham I. Katsh, who has achieved a number of important "firsts" since he began to teach the first American university course in modern Hebrew at New York University more than twenty-five years ago. Katsh, professor of Hebrew language and literature and chairman of the department of Hebrew culture and education at New York University, established the Jewish Culture Foundation there in 1937 to promote interfaith understanding and appreciation of the Jewish contribution to American life. He is founder (1942) and curator of the university's Library of Judaica and Hebraica, a repository of invaluable research materials, to which he himself added thousands of microfilmed documents that were culled from Eastern European libraries and had long been unavailable to Western scholars.

In 1949 Katsh organized the first academic workshop in the Middle East in the form of a summer institute for study in Israel, and in 1952 he supplemented this with a specialized "Land of the Bible" workshop for clergymen. He is the author of several books and hundreds of articles in Hebrew, English, and Arabic. New York University honored him by naming for him an endowed chair of Hebrew Culture and Education in 1957.

The family background of Abraham Isaac Katsh, one of eight children of Reuven and Raychell (Maskell-Eytan) Katsh, is securely rooted in the Jewish scholarly and religious tradition. He was born in Poland on August 10, 1908. His mother's forebears included distinguished rabbis and literary men; his father is at present the chief rabbi of Petah Tiqva, Israel. Two of his brothers (Shymon and Leon) are rabbis and two are scholars (Aaron, dean of a Talmudic college, and Michael, a professor at Yeshiva University). Nathan, another brother, is a businessman. His sister Dinah Harkavi is married to a librarian at Hechal Shlomo (the Chief Religious Center in Jerusalem) and his sister Hassidah Sorockin is the wife of a judge.

Katsh received his secondary schooling at a Gymnasium in Vilno, Poland, a Talmudic academy in Lomza, Poland, and in Petah Tiqva, graduating in 1924. The following year he came to the United States and enrolled at New York University, from which he took a B.S. degree in mathematics in 1931. While attending college, he was the head teacher of a yeshiva (Jewish parochial school) in Brooklyn.

In 1932, the year that Katsh became a naturalized United States citizen, he received his M.A. degree in education from New York University, having studied on a tuition scholarship. His thesis was entitled "The Nature of Measurement." To his degrees Katsh added, in 1936, a J.D. (N.Y.U.) and, in 1944, a Ph.D. (Dropsie College in Philadelphia), for which he had written a dissertation entitled "The Talmudic Backgrounds of the Koran." Also on a scholarship, Katsh attended the Princeton University graduate seminar on Islamic studies in 1941.

Katsh has taught at New York University since 1934, when he became an instructor in Arabic and Hebrew in the Division of General Education. After teaching in the School of Education as an instructor in Hebrew for seven years (1937-44), he became an assistant professor (1944), associate professor (1945), and finally professor (1947) of Hebrew language and literature. In 1953-54 he was chairman of the School of Edu-

New York University—
Irwin Gooen

ABRAHAM I. KATSH

cation's department of foreign languages and literature, and since 1953 he has been chairman of the department of Hebrew culture and education and director of the Washington Square College section in Hebrew language and literature. He was the first person to occupy a chair of Hebrew culture and education that was established at New York University in 1944. Thirteen years later, in 1957, he himself was honored in the naming of an endowed chair of Hebrew culture and education for him. During World War II, from 1942 to 1944, Katsh was civilian chaplain to soldiers in training at New York University.

The course in modern Hebrew that Katsh initiated at New York University in 1934 was the first of its kind to be taught at any American university or college. Interest in this language has since mounted, spurred in part by the creation of the state of Israel in 1948, and today modern Hebrew is taught in some fifty American institutions of higher learning as well as in many high schools. Katsh has helped several universities to establish programs in Hebrew. He prepared the first syllabus of Hebrew for the New York State Board of Regents. He has served as an examiner for Hebrew with the New York City Board of Education and as chairman of the Board of Licenses for Teachers and Colleges in the Field of Hebrew Studies. In 1950 Katsh founded and became the first president of the National Association of Professors of Hebrew in American Institutions of Higher Learning, of which he has been honorary president since 1952. After granting a private audience to Katsh in 1954, Pope Pius XII issued a statement favoring the teaching of modern Hebrew; Katsh also secured from the Soviet Deputy Minister of Education in 1956 a pledge that Hebrew would be taught in Russian schools, should there be sufficient demand.

(Continued next page)

KATSH, ABRAHAM I.—*Continued*

"The development of Hebrew courses in language and civilization in American institutions of higher learning affords an appreciation of the great contributions of the Jewish people to world civilization," Katsh recently pointed out. "These courses will give the Jewish student a better understanding of himself as a member of a creative people. They will enable non-Jews to gain an insight into the Hebraic origins and foundations of their faith and an acquaintance with their Jewish neighbors' culture and mode of living."

The Jewish Culture Foundation, established by Katsh at N.Y.U. in 1937, seeks to foster understanding by Jews and non-Jews of Jewish history and culture and the contributions Jews have made to American life. Katsh was executive director of the foundation from 1937 to 1944. In 1949, one year after Israel had achieved statehood, Katsh initiated the first American academic program in the Middle East—a six-week summer workshop through which students, teachers, social workers, community leaders, and private citizens could study the new country and its history *in situ*, meanwhile earning academic credits at New York University. Studies each summer since then have touched on all phases of Israeli life—government, geography, language, archaeology, Biblical history, labor movement, agriculture, integration of immigrants, with many details given in lectures by well-known personalities of the country. In 1952 Katsh formed a more specialized seminar on the Land of the Bible intended primarily for Christian professors of Hebrew and clergymen who are interested in the Middle East as the locale of Biblical events.

The Library of Judaica and Hebraica, which Katsh founded at New York University in 1942 and of which he is now curator, houses more than 25,000 rare books and manuscripts estimated to be worth over $1,000,000. To this collection he himself has added thousands of microfilms of old Jewish and Hebrew documents from Russia and Hungary that have been unavailable to Western scholars for the past half century. He is the first Western scholar in recent years to gain access to these materials, which, he has contended, could provide the basis for thousands of Ph.D. theses.

On trips to Eastern Europe that he undertook in 1956, 1958, 1959, and 1960 (the latter three on grants from the American Council of Learned Societies and the Rockefeller Foundation), Katsh found long-forgotten documents that had been assembled by scholars and wealthy collectors in the nineteenth century and deposited in various institutions and libraries in Russia and Hungary. Under a cultural exchange of Judaica that he established with these repositories, he has amassed and catalogued films of materials from the famous Antonin, Firkovich, Guensberg, Friedlander, and David Kaufmann collections. These comprise important historical records pertaining to the sacred and secular life and thought of early Jewish communities. Among the papers were a previously unpublished poem by the famous Hebrew poet of the Middle Ages, Judah ha-Levi; many Genizah items (worn-out or defective sacred books that may not be destroyed; apocryphal and secular documents) and Biblical texts of the ninth, tenth, and eleventh centuries; and ancient Jewish papers (written in Hebrew, Aramaic, and Judeo-Arabic) concerning theology, mathematics, language, science, medicine, and literature.

Katsh has been editor in chief of *Hebrew Abstracts* since 1954, assistant editor of the *Journal of Educational Sociology* since 1952, and managing editor of the *Modern Language Journal* since 1950. Among the books he has written are a study in Hebrew of Einstein's theory of relativity (1937), *Hebrew in American Higher Education* (N.Y. Univ. Press, 1941), *Hebraic Foundations of American Democracy* (New York Philosophical Library, 1951), and *Judaism in Islam* (N.Y. Univ. Press, 1954), the Hebrew edition of which won an award from the Hebrew Academy of America in 1956. Katsh has contributed to the *Hebrew Encyclopedia* and the *Encyclopaedia Britannica*. He has written hundreds of articles on all aspects of Jewish learning and education in technical and popular journals, in Hebrew, English, and Arabic, and has read papers at the International Oriental Congresses (Munich, 1958 and Moscow, 1960) and at the World Congress of Jewish Studies in 1947 and 1958. Katsh has served in advisory and executive capacities with numerous organizations dedicated to the teaching of Hebrew and to Jewish education; he was national education chairman of the Zionist Organization of America from 1949 to 1951 and delegate to a UNESCO conference in 1952.

Abraham I. Katsh and Estelle Wachtell, a teacher, were married on February 20, 1943. Their three children are Maskell Ethan, Salem Michael, and Rochelle. Katsh has brown eyes and dark hair, is five feet seven inches tall and weighs 160 pounds. His favorite recreations are fishing and playing chess. He is chairman of the Interfaith Council at N.Y.U., and his synagogue is the Hope of Israel in the Bronx.

References

Leaders In Education (1948)
Who's Who In America, 1960-61
Who's Who in New York, 1960
Who's Who in World Jewry (1955)

KAY, HERSHY   Nov. 17, 1919- Composer; arranger
Address: h. 4 E. 74 St., New York 21

Although his music has been heard by millions, the name of Hershy Kay is known only to those who read the credit line "arranged by" in small type on theatrical and dance programs. A leading orchestrator for the Broadway musical stage, Kay did the arrangements for *On the Town*, *Candide*, *Milk and Honey*, and *The Happiest Girl in the World*. He is, in addition, an important composer and arranger of contemporary ballet music whose achievements include the scores for *Stars and Stripes* and *Western Symphony*, both in the repertory of the New York City Ballet Company.

Hershy Kay was born in Philadelphia, on November 17, 1919, the son of Louis H. Kay, a printer, and Ida (Aisen) Kay. He has two sisters, Irma and Eleanor. After receiving his early education in the public schools of Philadelphia, Kay won a scholarship, at the age of sixteen to study the cello at the Curtis Institute of Music. Despite the scholarship Kay did not practise enough and was twice asked to leave the school because he was considered untalented.

Although he was not making much progress with the cello, Kay was making great strides in learning orchestration. "No one can teach you orchestration," he says. "The way I learned was to take short pieces—an early Beethoven Sonata or a Shostakovitch Prelude—and work them out in the composer's style. They were then played by the Curtis orchestra. You have to hear the final result to find out whether or not you have succeeded." Explaining why he always chose short pieces, Kay says: "I copied all my own parts . . . If I had the dough I could have had someone else do that for me" (*Musical America*, October 1961).

At the age of twenty Kay left the Curtis Institute and came to New York. He played the cello well enough to obtain jobs in orchestra pits, and while thus supporting himself, spent his spare time working out arrangements and distributing them to friends and classmates. In 1940 one of his arrangements came to the attention of the famous Brazilian soprano Elsie Houston who was then appearing at the Rainbow Room, and she gave him his first job as an arranger. More night club assignments followed and in 1944 Kay got his start on Broadway when Leonard Bernstein asked him to do the orchestration for the musical comedy *On the Town*. Based on the Jerome Robbins ballet *Fancy Free*, *On the Town* was a brash and exuberant show about some young sailors footloose in New York. It ran 463 performances and established Bernstein's reputation as a serious composer who could also write popular music.

Kay again worked with Bernstein in 1950 when he orchestrated his score for *Peter Pan* and in 1956 when he scored *Candide*. Although the latter ran only seventy-three performances, it was a critical success, and is considered by many to point the path that the future musical theater must follow. Meanwhile, in 1954, Kay did the arrangements for the Phoenix Theatre productions of John Latouche's *The Golden Apple*, a musical version of the Helen of Troy story, and the unsuccessful production of Earl Robinson's *Sandhog*. He orchestrated another Phoenix Theatre production, Jack Urbont's *Livin' the Life*, in 1957.

In 1958 Kay did the orchestration for *Once Upon a Mattress*, the first full-length musical venture by Mary Rodgers, the daughter of Richard Rodgers. That year he also did the arrangements for *Juno*, Marc Blitzstein's musical version of Sean O'Casey's *Juno and the Paycock*, and in 1961 he worked on two Broadway musicals: *The Happiest Girl in the World*, a musical version of Aristophanes' *Lysistrata* set to the music of Jacques Offenbach; and *Milk and Honey*, Jerry Herman's musical about modern Israel.

In scoring a musical, Kay usually has less than a month's time at his disposal. He does not really get started until about the second week of rehearsal, when dance routines are set, and even

HERSHY KAY

then he must sometimes change a waltz to a rhumba or a soft solo to a jazzy chorus on a day's notice. Kay sees his job as an orchestrator as "crawling into a composer's mind," and he can work with anything from a whistled melody to a piano sketch of the principal tunes of a show. He sees the modern orchestrator as "more of a dramatist than a thirty-two-bar song arranger," and believes in introducing freshness in scoring through the use of modern harmonies and new instrumental ideas.

Although the orchestrator of today is earning more and more freedom, the fact remains that the director, composer, lyricist, or producer can order a change in style or in an arrangement at any time. Perhaps for this reason, Kay has done his most important and most creative work not in the lucrative field of musical comedy, but in the highbrow field of ballet. Many of his ballet scores have achieved independent popularity on records and in concert halls.

Kay began to compose for dance groups in 1947 when he prepared some arrangements for Martha Graham's dance company. His first classical ballet score was *The Thief Who Loved a Ghost*, based on the music of Carl Maria von Weber, which he prepared for Ballet Theater in 1950. Billed as an "entertainment" rather than as a ballet, *The Thief Who Loved a Ghost* had an elaborate, tricky plot and did not last long in the repertory.

The first important ballet on which Kay worked was *Cakewalk*, which Walter Terry described as "a spritely example of Americana . . . based on the form and spirit of the minstrel show." Kay based his score on the music of Louis Moreau Gottschalk, a New Orleans-born composer whose music was popular among nineteenth-century minstrel show artists. Commenting on the score, James Lyons wrote in *Dance Magazine* (November 1955): "Hershy Kay waded through Gottschalk's piano pieces and re-tailored

KAY, HERSHY—*Continued*

the best of them into this whistleable medley, throwing in a handful of contemporaneous minstrel tunes for good measure." The ballet was choreographed by Ruthanna Boris for the New York City Ballet Company and first presented in June 1951.

In 1954 Kay was commissioned by George Balanchine to create an original score for a Western ballet. What Balanchine wanted was a formal symphonic work that would inspire him to "use the universal classic language of the academic ballet in a fresh way." That Kay succeeded in fulfilling his desires is attested by Balanchine's comment: "It was exactly as if I had ordered a beautifully tailored set of riding-clothes, admirably cut, free in the seat, smart at the hips and unobtrusively if personally elegant."

The score that Kay created for *Western Symphony* has the formal structure of a classical symphony, but its thematic material is based on folk songs of the American West. In addition to *Red River Valley*, which is used throughout the work as a unifying theme, the folk material quoted includes *Old Taylor, The Gal I Left Behind Me, Rye Whiskey, Golden Slippers, Candy Girl, Jim Along Josie, New London, Lolly-Too-Dum*, and others.

Western Symphony was first presented by the New York City Ballet Company on September 7, 1954. At the time the company could not afford costumes or scenery, so the ballet was performed on a bare stage with the girls dressed in tights and sweaters and the men dressed in dungarees. Despite these obstacles, *Western Symphony* was an immediate success with the audiences, if not with all the critics. John Martin thought the ballet looked like "an undress rehearsal for *Oklahoma!*" and found the score "a fairly literal arrangement of folk tunes . . . [that] really gets going only in its final movement" (New York *Times,* October 3, 1954). However, the favorable opinion of the audiences, and of other dance critics, such as Walter Terry and Edwin Denby, has won out. The year after *Western Symphony* was first performed, James Lyons wrote in *Dance Magazine* (December 1955): "Hershy Kay's infectious score . . . already seems to have attained to the proportions of a classic," and the ballet, subsequently costumed by Karinska, has remained continuously in the repertory of the New York City Ballet Company since its first season.

Kay's next ballet score was *The Concert,* based on the music of Chopin. Choreographed by Jerome Robbins, the ballet is a humorous examination of the images that float across the audience's mind as it listens to Chopin's romantic melodies. Michael Sonino wrote in *Musical America* (October 1961): "This score is so funny in its restraint that it is a perfect foil for the tomfoolery on stage. The combination leaves the audience weak with laughter." *The Concert* was first presented by the New York City Ballet Company in March 1956, and was revived, with extensive revisions, for inclusion in Jerome Robbins' *Ballets: U.S.A.* presented at The Festival of Two Worlds in Spoleto, Italy, in June 1958. It was later presented in New York City.

Following *The Concert,* Kay again collaborated with Balanchine on an American ballet. *Stars and Stripes* is based on the march music of John Philip Sousa, although Kay has said that he does not like march music. It was first performed by the New York City Ballet Company in January 1958, and was characterized by Walter Terry as "gorgeous, corny, affectionate, ebullient, humorous and tastefully vulgar" (New York *Herald Tribune,* January 26, 1958).

In addition to his work for the theater and ballet, Kay has orchestrated a number of movie scores, including *Man with the Gun* (United Artists, 1955), *The King and Four Queens* (United Artists, 1956), and a Cinerama production about the South Seas (1958), all based on the music of Alex North; and *Girl of the Night* (Warner, 1960), based on the music of Sol Kaplan. He has also worked on documentary films for the United States Department of State. He composed the original background music for Cyril Ritchard's recording of *Mother Goose,* and completed the opera *The Good Soldier Schweik* after the death of its young composer, Robert Kurka. For Eugene List, Kay has arranged Louis Moreau Gottschalk's *Grande Tarantella,* a piano score for performance by piano and orchestra. He has also done extensive work in radio and television, and has appeared successfully in New York as a conductor of symphony concerts.

Stockily built, Hershy Kay is only four feet eleven inches tall and weighs 135 pounds. His hobbies include hunting, fishing, photography, and sports cars. Kay's work is marked by wit and elegance and his humor has, on occasion, gone beyond the purely musical. He listed two dogs among his musical source materials in the printed score of *Western Symphony,* for example. He is not a frustrated "serious" composer, but finds his present work perfectly satisfactory in fulfilling his artistic goals.

References

Mus Am 81:10+ O '61 por
Time 78:41 Ag 18 '61 por

KOVACS, ERNIE Jan. 23, 1919-Jan. 13, 1962 Comedian of stage, screen, radio, and television; wrote many of his own stories and comedy routines in regular TV series and guest appearances; known for zany type of humor and for visual gags. See *Current Biography* (February) 1958.

Obituary

N Y Times p1+ Ja 14 '62

KREISLER, FRITZ Feb. 2, 1875-Jan. 29, 1962 Austrian-American violinist; one of the most popular virtuosos of the twentieth century; made his American debut in 1888 and thereafter appeared in concerts throughout the world; composer of some 200 works, including operettas and, chiefly, light violin pieces. See *Current Biography* (July) 1944.

Obituary

N Y Times p1+ Ja 30 '62

LOUW, ERIC H(ENDRIK) (lō) Nov. 21, 1890- South African diplomat
Address: b. Dept. of External Affairs, Union Bldg., Pretoria, Republic of South Africa; h. 20 Bryntirion, Pretoria, Republic of South Africa

One of the most ardent defenders before the world of the apartheid (racial segregation) policy in the Republic of South Africa is Eric H. Louw, Minister of External Affairs, who in October 1961 was censured by the United Nations General Assembly for the views he expressed in a speech before that body. Much of Louw's life has been spent explaining the policies of his country—in the 1920's and 1930's as a diplomatic representative to the United States and to various European countries, and after World War II as a cabinet member. He has served as Minister of External Affairs since 1955.

Louw is a member of the National party, which represents most of the Afrikaners (descendants of the Dutch settlers) and which favors apartheid, the policy by which about 3,000,000 whites are trying to hold the more than 12,000,000 natives, halfcastes, and Asians in a position of inferiority. Its refusal to negotiate or give way on this policy has increasingly isolated South Africa politically from other countries and from the United Nations, and led to its withdrawal from the Commonwealth of Nations in 1961. Louw maintains that people are misinformed about South Africa and has consistently upheld the position of the National party on these matters.

Eric Hendrik Louw, the son of Johannes A. and M. M. (de Villiers) Louw, was born on November 21, 1890, in Jacobsdal in the area that later became the Orange Free State of South Africa. His father was a merchant in Beaufort West. Eric Louw received his early education at Beaufort West and then studied at Victoria College, Stellenbosch University, graduating with the B.A. degree. He went on to study law at Rhodes University College in Grahamstown, where he received the LL.B. degree. From 1912 to 1916 he was private secretary to justices Sheil and Hutton. Admitted to the bar in 1917, he practised as a barrister before the Supreme Court in Grahamstown for a year.

After the death of his father, Louw went into business by himself from 1918 to 1925. During these years he also became prominent in his town's public life and was elected in 1924 to represent Beaufort West as a member of the National party in the House of Assembly, the lower house of Parliament of the Union of South Africa.

After one year in Parliament, Louw left South Africa to take up the first of several overseas appointments that were to keep him abroad for the next twelve years. In 1925 he was appointed the first trade commissioner of the Union of South Africa in the United States and Canada, and was stationed in New York City. For a brief period in 1929 he served as South Africa's High Commissioner in London.

In late 1929 Louw was appointed as the first envoy extraordinary and minister plenipotentiary to the United States. During these years he

State Inf. Office, Pretoria
ERIC H. LOUW

worked toward the international recognition of South Africa's sovereignty. The status of the Union of South Africa as an independent self-governing dominion was established by the Statute of Westminster in 1931. In 1933 Louw became minister plenipotentiary to Italy and in 1934 he was transferred to Paris for a three-year term as the first South African minister to France; he was also accredited to Portugal. He has represented South Africa at international conferences, including the International Immigration Conference in Havana (1928) and the International Red Cross Conference in Geneva (1929). He also attended the meetings of the Assembly of the League of Nations in 1929, 1934, and 1935.

In 1938 Louw was re-elected to the House of Assembly from Beaufort West, a seat he still holds as a member of the National party. In the late 1930's he openly supported Nazi Germany's colonial claims, and he was frequently a guest in Berlin. During World War II he attacked the pro-British United party government headed by Prime Minister Jan Christiaan Smuts, and made anti-Semitic speeches in Parliament. In 1948, when Daniel François Malan, a Nationalist, became Prime Minister, Louw was appointed Minister of Mines and Minister of Economic Affairs. In the cabinet of Malan's successor, Johannes G. Strijdom, Louw served as Minister of Finance from 1954 to 1956. In 1955 he also became Minister of External Affairs, and he continued to hold this position after Dr. H. F. Verwoerd became Prime Minister in 1958.

As a cabinet minister dealing with economic affairs from 1948 to 1956, he assumed major responsibility for the heavy import controls put into force in late 1948 and later strengthened. He also tried to change the unfavorable publicity about South Africa's racial policies, because it affected foreign investments and caused boycotts or

LOUW, ERIC H.—*Continued*

bans on trade with South Africa by other countries.

Upon becoming Minister of External Affairs under Strijdom in 1955, Louw ordered a reorganization of the African division of his department to provide for greater contact with nonwhite states and noted the need for good relations with them. He also proposed a guest house for diplomats and other distinguished nonwhite visitors to prevent embarrassment for them in segregated cities. South Africa's interest in an African defensive alliance led to assurances that apartheid was solely a domestic affair and not for export. Louw is believed to be more sympathetic toward South African representation abroad to new African nations than some of his colleagues. In 1959 he said that South Africa would invite international conferences that include nonwhite delegates.

As Minister of External Affairs, Louw has been particularly concerned with adverse publicity. He has set up an extensive propaganda agency operating through the State Information Office, a subdepartment of the Ministry of External Affairs, with the aim of presenting a more favorable picture of South Africa to other countries. He has consistently assailed foreign news correspondents whom he charged with presenting a distorted view of South African racial policies based upon bias and misinformation, holding them partly responsible for native resistance to government policies. He has contended that Communists were largely responsible for the antigovernment demonstrations of March 21, 1960, which led to the Sharpeville massacre resulting in the killing of fifty-six natives by South African police.

In April 1960, after Prime Minister Verwoerd was wounded in an assassination attempt, the acting head of state, Minister of Lands Paul O. Sauer, sought to institute milder racial policies in order to ease world animosity toward South Africa. Sauer was, however, sharply rebuked by Louw, who declared that only the Prime Minister himself could make any basic changes in governmental policies.

Louw represented the South African Prime Minister at the Commonwealth meetings in 1948, 1957, and 1960. The Nationalist party has not been anxious to maintain its ties with the Commonwealth of Nations, although the trading preferences and access to British capital available to members had to be considered. At the 1948 meeting, despite fears that Malan's new government would leave the Commonwealth, Louw gave assurances that he looked forward to the mutual discussions and settlement of matters of common concern.

As the Nationalists consolidated their power and as more African and Asian states became independent members of the Commonwealth, the South African view changed, and at the 1957 meeting Louw spoke of the prospect of South Africa's leaving the Commonwealth and becoming a republic. At the May 1960 meeting, which Louw attended in place of Prime Minister Verwoerd, difficulties over the apartheid question, although never discussed officially,

became more and more acute. An October 1960 referendum among South African white voters approved the decision for the country to become a republic on May 31, 1961, and South Africa withdrew its application on March 15, 1961 for readmission to the Commonwealth in light of the views expressed by the other prime ministers on the racial policies of the South African government.

Louw has had much responsibility for coping with the complex problems of South Africa's relationship with the United Nations. He has represented his country at many meetings of the U.N. General Assembly since 1948. Louw has consistently maintained that United Nations consideration of the apartheid question and the question of the treatment of Indians in South Africa constitutes interference in the domestic affairs of his nation, and thus is contrary to the charter of the United Nations. South Africa also maintains that the United Nations has no right of supervision over its administration of South-West Africa, a former mandate under the League of Nations.

Since 1948 South Africa has on various occasions staged walkouts and boycotted meetings, and has refused to co-operate with U.N. committees investigating the race question. In April 1955 Louw announced the withdrawal of South Africa from UNESCO. He has said that South Africa cannot accept the Universal Declaration of Human Rights because it would destroy the nation's multiracial structure. In his opinion the solution to the race problem lies in a policy of peaceful co-existence of separate Bantu communities, which can eventually attain self-government, and in a separate European community.

In October 1961 Louw delivered a strong speech before the U.N. General Assembly, pointing out abuses existing in other countries and criticizing those who opposed South Africa's policies. The African and Asian delegates assailed Louw, and the Liberian ambassador made the unprecedented demand that the speech be stricken from the record. A censure vote against the South African delegate was carried with sixty-seven voting in favor, twenty abstaining, nine (including the United States) not participating, and with only South Africa voting against the resolution.

On July 6, 1918 Eric H. Louw married Anna Snyman of East London, South Africa. His wife is an accomplished violinist. They have two sons, Jan and Martin. Louw, who is of slight build, has been described as a "shrewd and wily debater." He is an amateur artist and sketches portraits for Christmas cards and for gifts to his friends.

References

N Y Times p4 O 13 '61
Time 75:33 Ap 11 '60
International Who's Who, 1961-2
International Year Book and Statesmen's
     Who's Who, 1961
Who's Who, 1961
Who's Who in America, 1960-61
Who's Who of Southern Africa. 1961

LOVE, J(AMES) SPENCER July 6, 1896-Jan. 20, 1962 Business executive; founder in 1923 and subsequently chief executive officer of the Burlington Mills Company (since 1955, the Burlington Industries) in North Carolina. See *Current Biography* (November) 1957.

Obituary

N Y Times p89 Ja 21 '62

MEŠTROVIĆ, IVAN Aug. 15, 1883-Jan. 16, 1962 Yugoslav-American sculptor; made statues in wood, stone, and bronze, often of Biblical and legendary subjects; the first living artist to have a one-man show at the Metropolitan Museum of Art in New York (1947); served on the faculty of Notre Dame University (since 1955). See *Current Biography* (October) 1940.

Obituary

N Y Times p33 Ja 17 '62

MILLER, HARRY W(ILLIS) July 1, 1879-
Surgeon; missionary
Address: b. 11503 Pierce Place, Arlington, Calif.; h. 11384 Norwood Ave., Arlington, Calif.

HARRY W. MILLER

At a time when such books as *The Ugly American* paint an appalling picture of the American in the Far East, the life story of Harry W. Miller, told in *China Doctor* (Harper, 1961) by Raymond S. Moore, offers an inspiring contrast. Dr. Miller has friends on both sides of the so-called Bamboo Curtain after more than half a century of devoted work in China as a Seventh-day Adventist missionary and surgeon. He is credited with many advances in the area of thyroid surgery, and his research and development of soybean milk has resulted in great nutritional gain for people in underdeveloped and underfed countries.

Harry Willis Miller was born on July 1, 1879, in a log cabin at Ludlow Falls, Ohio, the first son of John Oliver Miller, a minister of the Seventh-day Adventist Church, and Amanda (Ehlers) Miller. One of two other sons in the family and one of two daughters also became missionaries to China. After attending elementary school at Pattytown, Ohio, Harry Miller studied at Mount Vernon Academy, a Seventh-day Adventist school in Ohio, and in 1898 he received the B.A. degree from Mount Vernon College.

The Seventh-day Adventists had recently opened a medical school, the American Medical Missionary College, in Battle Creek, Michigan, and Miller decided that the training he could get there would help him greatly in fulfilling his desire to work as a missionary. During the summer after his graduation from college, he sold books to earn money for medical school, and later, as a student at American Medical Missionary College, he took odd jobs at the Battle Creek Sanitarium. He graduated with the M.D. degree in 1902.

Miller served his internship at South Chicago Hospital in 1902-03, and during this period he was an instructor in dermatology at Rush Medi-

cal College as well as an instructor in ear, nose, and throat and anatomy and assistant professor of surgery at American Medical Missionary College. In addition he conducted skin-disease clinics at Chicago's Hebrew Hospital. Medical research that he undertook as an intern included a study of black blastomycetes fungus. In his first medical experiment he operated on a man with a saddlenose and evolved a technique for the injection of paraffin wax under the skin to build up the nose structure.

At the end of his internship Dr. Miller and his wife, the former Maude Thompson, a fellow graduate of American Medical Missionary College whom he had married in 1902, decided to go to China under the auspices of the Foreign Mission Board of the Seventh-day Adventist Church. Together with a former room-mate and his wife, the Millers left for China on October 3, 1903, traveling steerage on the *Empress of India.* Their possessions at this time included such donated gifts as surgical supplies, a typewriter, and a printing press, and they had an allowance of $14 per week donated by the Ohio and Iowa Conferences of the Seventh-day Adventist Church.

The group arrived at Hsintsai, where they set about establishing the mission station and adopting the Chinese dress and language. In the early years of the twentieth century, China lay heavily under the shadow of the Boxer Rebellion, and travel was difficult and restricted for all foreigners. In addition the missionaries had to win the Chinese away from their animosity toward "foreign devils."

After a year in Hsintsai, the Millers moved to Shangtsai, and here they set up a small print shop and medical dispensary. Acquiring a font of Chinese type, Dr. Miller built racks for the three-thousand-odd characters and began to print single-page tracts and famous Christian hymns. In 1905 Maude Miller was stricken with an unidentified disease, later known as sprue, and she

MILLER, HARRY W.—*Continued*

died at the age of twenty-five. A few years later the mission was moved to larger quarters at Sinyang. By this time Miller had the help of several other missionaries, including his brother, Esta.

On Christmas day in 1908, while on a visit to the United States, Dr. Miller married Marie E. Iverson, a trained nurse. When he returned to China, he found that he would be stationed in Shanghai. He had his printing equipment moved there and set up his shop in space he rented from Charles Jones Soong (whose daughter became the wife of Generalissimo Chiang Kai-shek). By 1910 Dr. Miller had established his first fully equipped medical unit, at Mokanshan Mountain near Hangchow, and as leader of the Seventh-day Adventist Church's general mission in China, he established the church's first school, at Chouchiakou.

Ill health forced Miller to return to the United States in 1911, suffering from the same disease that had killed his first wife. By 1912 he was enough recovered to become medical secretary to his church's General Conference in Washington and medical director of its Washington-Sanitarium in Takoma Park, Maryland, then running with a deficit of $168,000. He set about rehabilitating the sanitarium's finances and succeeded so well that by the end of World War I, a new unit for surgical cases had been added to the hospital. Taking advantage of his residence nearby, Miller enrolled in 1913 in Johns Hopkins University in Baltimore for a postgraduate course in surgery.

Returning to China in 1925, Dr. Miller supervised the building of Shanghai Sanitarium, which was opened on January 1, 1928. In a country seething with political unrest, he managed to keep himself apart from politics. "My business is medicine, not politics," he told the Chinese. "You know I wouldn't last five minutes as a politician, and I wouldn't be here to treat you now" (*China Doctor*).

When the Japanese occupied Shanghai on November 9, 1937, Dr. Miller moved up the Yangtze River to Hankow, where he established a clinic, and he continued to operate this clinic and the hospital at Wuchang after the Japanese occupation of Hankow on October 25, 1938. He also became unofficial "mayor" of a village that formed inside the hospital bounds composed of refugee civilians and soldiers. Forced to leave China in 1939, he spent the World War II years in the United States, concentrating on his soybean project. He returned to the Shanghai Sanitarium in 1949 for a short period before the Communist occupation. He organized a hospital on Formosa in 1953 and a hospital at Hong Kong in 1959, taking spells of relief work at hospitals in Libya, Malaya, and other places in the intervening six years.

As a surgeon, Dr. Miller attended Presidents Taft and Wilson and Mrs. Warren Harding, in the capacity of a consultant, and such Chinese notables as General and Madame Chiang Kai-shek and Madame Sun Yat-sen. One of his most colorful patients was Chang Hsueh-liang, the ruler of Manchuria known as the "Young Mar-

shal" of the Chinese Republic. Dr. Miller cured the Young Marshal and his two wives of opium addiction in 1933. Like many of Dr. Miller's wealthy Chinese patients, the Young Marshal donated large sums for hospital construction, in northern Manchuria, Lanchow, and Wuchang.

Dr. Miller's most significant achievements have been in thyroid surgery. While at Washington Sanitarium he studied the function of thyroxine in the heat centers of the body and accordingly limited the use of digitalis in these operations. As a result of this, and the particular stress he laid on aftercare, his ultimate record was less than one half of 1 percent fatalities in over six thousand thyroidectomies.

In China, with its great problem of malnutrition, Dr. Miller's work in the field of nutrition has had special importance. Believing firmly in preventive medicine, he pointed out, "If we can prevent illness, we don't have to cure." He was introduced to the soybean at Kobe on his first trip to China, where he tasted tofu loaf, a cheese made from the soybean. In the late 1920's at Shanghai Sanitarium he began experiments with this food.

His first task was to study soy liquid in comparison with cow, goat, and human milk, and he discovered that soy was richer in protein, lower in fat, and contained fewer carbohydrates. The main disadvantages of soy liquid were its bitterness and indigestibility, but by combining ideas gleaned from such diverse sources as Chinese cooks, a ship's galley, and a copra company, Dr. Miller developed a milk plant that consisted of a Japanese bean grinder, a Chinese stove, an American extractor for straining, and an American homogenizer.

By 1936 he had a milk plant working at Shanghai Sanitarium, and a report of his work appeared in the *Chinese Medical Journal*. On his return to the United States following the Japanese invasion, Dr. Miller continued with his research and formed, in association with his son, the International Nutrition Laboratory at Mount Vernon, Ohio. He built a research plant and from 1939 to 1941 supplied powdered dairy milk, Soyalac, to China and the Philippines.

Forced to stop production for Asia after the Japanese attack on Pearl Harbor, Dr. Miller developed a formula for domestic consumption for use with babies allergic to animal and human milk. He also developed Soyagen, a postoperative food for abdominal-surgery patients. His products were approved by the Council on Food and Nutrition of the American Medical Association, and a United States patent covers his products.

Early in the 1940's he sold his Mount Vernon plant to the Loma Linda Food Company, and with the proceeds of this sale he established the International Nutrition Research Foundation at Arlington, California. He became emeritus director of this foundation in 1960. Another organization established by Dr. Miller is the Harry W. Miller Foundation of New York, devoted to extending medical and nutritional help throughout the world. In addition to licensing milk plants in many countries, at the age of eighty-one he assisted the Japanese Ministry of Health in establishing soy-milk plants in the thirty thousand village tofu factories in the country. For some years he has been a consultant to the United Nations Children's Fund.

A Fellow of the American College of Surgeons and a licentiate of the Medical Council of Canada, Dr. Miller is also a member of the American and Ohio state medical associations and the Chinese, Philippine, and Japanese medical societies. He was decorated by Nationalist China with the Brilliant Blue Star in 1954. He is the author of medical manuals in several languages: *Health and Longevity* (1928), *Way to Health* (1920), and a tuberculosis manual. From 1920 to 1924 he was the editor of *Life and Health Magazine.*

By his second marriage, Dr. Miller has four children—Maude, Ethel, Harry Willis, and Clarence. His second wife died on October 9, 1950, and he married Mary Elizabeth Greer, a teacher, on July 13, 1954. The gray-haired, blue-eyed doctor is five feet eight and a half inches tall and weighs 175 pounds. He is a quiet, compassionate man who has spent a fortune of some $2,500,000 (from royalties and fees) on his medical and religious mission.

Although Dr. Miller talks more readily about health than politics, he says frankly that he considers it unrealistic for the United States to withhold recognition from Communist China. He also has decided opinions about the behavior of Americans in the Far East, asserting that both Christianity and democracy would gain more ground if missionaries and government emissaries would show respect and feeling for the people instead of treating them like second-class citizens and imposing an outsider's way of life.

References

N Y Mirror p46 My 21 '61 por
N Y Times p5 My 9 '61 por
N Y World-Telegram p10 N 1 '61

Moore, Raymond S. China Doctor (1961)
Who's Important in Medicine (1952)

NESTINGEN, IVAN A(RNOLD) Sept. 23, 1921- United States government official; lawyer
Address: b. Department of Health, Education, and Welfare, 330 Independence Ave., S.W., Washington, D.C. h. 4813 Potomac Ave., N.W., Washington 7, D.C.

The Under Secretary of Health, Education, and Welfare in the administration of President John F. Kennedy is Ivan A. Nestingen, who was sworn into office on February 17, 1961, succeeding Bertha S. Adkins. Nestingen, who began his career as a lawyer, has been active in local and state government in Wisconsin since 1951 and was mayor of Madison from 1956 to 1961. In his position as Under Secretary, Nestingen is an articulate spokesman for a greater role on the part of the federal government in providing for the health and welfare of the nation.

Ivan Arnold Nestingen was born in Sparta, Wisconsin on September 23, 1921, the son of Eddie Arthur Nestingen, a grocer, and Lena Gertrude (Espeseth) Nestingen. He has four brothers: Edward L., an ordained minister and associate director of the University of Illinois

Dept. of Health, Education & Welfare—S. Stanton Singer

IVAN A. NESTINGEN

YMCA; Stanley R., an engineer; John G., a lawyer; and Lyle E., an engineer. He attended Sparta High School, where he served as a class officer for four years, and graduated in 1939. His early interest in the fields of law, history, and politics influenced his choice of a career. From 1940 to 1942 he attended Wisconsin State College at La Crosse; he entered the University of Wisconsin in 1942. While attending school he took part in debating and supported himself by holding a variety of jobs. At the University of Wisconsin he served as a house Fellow, counseling residents of the university dormitories.

In 1943 Nestingen entered the United States Army as a private and served with the Corps of Engineers in the South Pacific. Discharged with the rank of first lieutenant in 1946, he returned to the University of Wisconsin, where he received both the Ph.B. degree in history and the LL.B. degree in 1949. After being admitted to the bar, Nestingen practised law in Madison from 1949 to 1956 and became a partner in the law firm of Arthur, Dewa, Nestingen & Tomlinson.

While engaged in the practice of law, Nestingen became active in politics and was elected to the Madison city council as alderman of the eighth ward in 1951. From 1954 to 1956 he was a member of the State Legislature, serving as Assemblyman from Madison's second assembly district. In April 1956 he was elected mayor of Madison, filling out the unexpired one-year term of his predecessor. He was re-elected in 1957 and 1959. During this period Nestingen wrote various articles for municipal government publications on traffic, off-street parking, and municipal employer-employee relationships.

Since 1949 Nestingen has been active in the Democratic party in Wisconsin. For a time he was secretary of the "Joe Must Go Club," which tried to have the late Senator Joseph R. McCarthy of Wisconsin ousted from office. In 1959-60 he

NESTINGEN, IVAN A.—*Continued*

was chairman of the Kennedy for President Club of Wisconsin, and in 1960 he was state chairman of the Citizens for Kennedy-Johnson. At the 1960 Democratic National Convention he was chairman of the Wisconsin delegation pledged to John F. Kennedy.

On January 26, 1961 President Kennedy announced the appointment of Nestingen as Under Secretary of Health, Education, and Welfare, and the Senate confirmed the appointment on February 6. Nestingen serves as Acting Secretary in the absence of the Secretary and performs such functions and duties as the Secretary may designate.

The Department of Health, Education, and Welfare was established when Congress adopted the President's Reorganization Plan 1 of 1953, giving departmental status to the Federal Security Agency, which had been established in 1939 to administer major programs in the fields of health, education, and economic security. The five major units included within the department are the Public Health Service, Social Security Administration, Office of Education, Food and Drug Administration, and Office of Vocational Rehabilitation. In his budget message of January 18, 1962 President Kennedy requested $5,100,000,000 for the budget of the Department of Health, Education, and Welfare for the fiscal year 1963, including substantial increases in appropriations for medical research and public assistance.

A few days after he took office as Under Secretary, Nestingen addressed a session of the National Industrial Conference Board in Washington, D.C. Referring to his experience as a municipal official, Nestingen stressed the need for the federal government to take a more positive role in matters of health, education, and welfare. He noted that states and local units of government frequently lack the financial resources and the taxing authority to meet these needs, and that in many areas, such as the pollution of natural elements, there is no political jurisdiction on a local level that can act on a broad base. Columnist David Lawrence, writing in the New York *Herald Tribune* (February 22, 1961) cited Nestingen's statements as prophecy of the new trend toward big, centralized government. He noted that Nestingen's speech went much further than President Kennedy's previously stated policy in advocating a strong role for the federal government. To Lawrence it was a further indication of "the gradual erosion of the constitutional powers of the states" by the taxing power of the Treasury Department.

Nestingen champions the Kennedy administration's plan for medical care for the aged, financed by Social Security. In reply to its critics, he has maintained that such a program would preserve the dignity of the individual, that it would not disturb the doctor-patient relationship, and that it is the only fair way of according equal treatment to all aged citizens. In October 1961 Nestingen and Secretary of Labor Arthur J. Goldberg signed a $135,000 agreement for a limited training program for unemployed workers in the depressed mining area of Huntington, West Virginia. Administered under the Area Redevelopment Act of 1961, the program provides for the retraining of 325 workers in new skills. Similar projects are also planned for other areas.

Speaking before the Air Pollution Control Association in New York City on June 14, 1961, Nestingen contended that existing allocations to combat air pollution were greatly inadequate. "I see no reason to wait until every scientist in the country is absolutely certain that air pollution is or may be one of the causes of rising rates of lung cancer before moving to minimize the danger," he said. In a speech before the American Municipal Association at Seattle, Washington on August 29, 1961, he said that the nation could go a long way in solving the problems of air and water pollution, if "geographic and jurisdictional" factors could be reconciled. "We have shining skyscrapers and slums," he said. "We have glorious expressways and smog. We have millions of pleasure boats and polluted water."

On June 28, 1952 Ivan A. Nestingen married Geraldine A. Krawczak, who was a director of the Junior Red Cross. They have three children, Laurel, Leslie, and Marcia. Nestingen is six feet two inches tall, weighs 188 pounds, and has brown hair and hazel eyes. He is a member of the Sons of Norway, Idum, Lodge 74, and he has served as a chairman of the American Veterans Committee. He is affiliated with the First Congregational Church of Madison. His favorite recreations are baseball and football (as spectator sports), playing cards, and reading.

Reference

New Frontiersmen (1961)

NEWHART, BOB Sept. 5, 1929-   Comedian

Address: b. c/o Frank J. Hogan Agency, 203 N. Wabash Ave., Chicago 1, Ill.

The first comedian in the history of the entertainment business to break into fame through long-playing records, Bob Newhart, a monologist, belongs to the new wave of comics that includes Mort Sahl, Shelley Berman, Lenny Bruce, and Nichols and May. His underplayed and merciful satire removes him from the school of "sick" comics, although he shares its rebellion against the bureaucratic bigness of modern life and the flood of paper work that threatens to drown the individual. In 1962 Bob Newhart was one of the few genuine satirists still operating in television—a medium noted for its high casualty rate among comedians. Ironically, the rapid rise of Bob Newhart was engineered by the advertising and public relations men who have been the targets of some of his most biting gibes.

Bob Newhart was born in Chicago, Illinois on September 5, 1929, the second of four children of George David and Pauline Newhart. The boy had been christened George Robert Newhart, but to avoid confusion at the Newhart home on Chicago's far West Side, he was called Bob. His father, a heating engineer, is part owner of a plumbing and heating supply business. Bob Newhart has three sisters: Mary Joan, a nun who teaches chemistry at Immaculate High School in Chicago; Mrs. Pauline Quan, a housewife; and Virginia, a student at Siena High School in Chicago.

"Sometimes I wonder how I ever got to be a comic," Newhart told Pete Martin in an interview for the *Saturday Evening Post* (October 14, 1961). "I didn't come from a broken home, so I'm not trying to get away from my drab and unhappy home life by retreating within myself and only coming out to poke fun at other people to turn their scorn from me. I wasn't an odd-looking kid that everybody made fun of, so I'm not batting ridicule directed at me back at others in self-defense— which is usually the way a comic gets wound up."

At St. Ignatius High School in Chicago Bob Newhart played the role of Banjo in a production of *The Man Who Came to Dinner* and gained a reputation among his classmates for his imitations of John Barrymore, James Cagney, Humphrey Bogart, and Jimmy Durante. He once ended up in second place in an elocution contest. He continued his education at Loyola University in Chicago, where he majored in accounting, and graduated in 1952 with the degree of Bachelor of Science in commerce. In August 1952 he entered the United States Army. In military service he kept personnel records and was discharged in August 1954. That fall he entered law school at Loyola University, but he flunked out in February 1956. He began a succession of jobs: as a copywriter, as a cigar store clerk, as a clerk with the Illinois State Unemployment Service, and—finally—as a maladjusted accountant who used to make the petty cash accounts come out all right by digging down into his own pocket.

As an escape from the petty cash box, Newhart acted in off hours with a theatrical stock company in Oak Park, a suburb of Chicago. He and a friend, Ed Gallagher, an advertising copywriter, would amuse themselves by making long and antic telephone calls to each other. Out of their crazy conversations came their idea of taping these comedy routines and selling them to radio stations as one way of breaking into show business. The plan fell through and the two men lost hundreds of dollars on the venture, but some of Newhart's monologues, recorded by Gallagher on a home tape machine, came to the attention of Dan Sorkin, a Chicago disk jockey. Finding them hilarious, Sorkin got Newhart a job on a local morning man-in-the-street show over television. It lasted five weeks.

In a more important move Dan Sorkin introduced Newhart to James Conkling, the president of Warner Brothers Records, and George Avakian, the company's director of artists and repertory. After hearing three of Newhart's monologues, the executives signed him to a contract and booked him into the Tidelands, a night club in Houston, Texas. There, during a two-week engagement that marked the first time that Newhart had ever faced a night club audience, six of his routines were recorded "live" in February 1960. *The Button-Down Mind of Bob Newhart* was released on April Fool's Day and soared to the best-seller list at once. Two more successful records followed: *The Button-Down Mind Strikes Back* and *Behind the Button-Down Mind*. Newhart has said that his albums are "based

NBC
BOB NEWHART

on circumstances and conversations which might have happened if you carry things a little further than they go in real life."

The Button-Down Mind of Bob Newhart led to guest appearances on *The Jack Paar Show* and on the "Emmy" awards television show in April 1960 and to his big-time television debut with *The Garry Moore Show* in June. Overnight, Bob Newhart became the country's most discussed new comedian. His casual, subtle, and low-keyed satire evoked an immediate response from everyone who has ever tried to catch a bus (Newhart has a routine in which bus drivers are taught to pull away from the curb as little old ladies rush up); has taught a woman to drive a car (he subtitles his driving-instructor routine "the world's most daring profession"); or has watched a Presidential press conference. His satire of this latter specimen of Americana takes the form of a telephone call to President John F. Kennedy from the advertising account executive representing the company sponsoring the telecasts of the press conference. To boost the Nielsen ratings, the account executive suggests that Ginger Rogers share the platform with the President. After all, she could volunteer her opinion on the situation in Laos.

After his Tidelands engagement, Newhart played one night club after the other, but he was unhappy in cabarets. He soon tired of staying in motels, where the pictures on the walls all looked alike from the East Coast to the West Coast, and he sometimes stuck his head out the window and watched the flashing electric signs to find out which town he was playing in at the moment. Above all, he disliked trying to purvey his subtleties to sodden customers.

"It's the drunks," Newhart once told a reporter from *Variety* (October 5, 1960). "My act depends on illusion—I create scenes in the

SPOTTSWOOD W. ROBINSON 3d

ated in 1957 and was originally intended to function for only two years, but its life has been extended twice by Congressional action. The function of the commission is to study and collect facts on claims of deprivations of rights of citizens of the United States on the grounds of race, color, religion, or national origin. Its members, whose work is on a part-time basis, receive no pay except for $50 a day when the commission is in session.

Kennedy's nomination of Robinson was seriously questioned by Senator Sam J. Ervin, Jr., of North Carolina, chairman of the Senate Judiciary Committee's subcommittee on constitutional rights at a hearing held on June 16, 1961. "I have some misgivings concerning your nomination for this post," Senator Ervin told Robinson, "because in the eyes of many people the occupancy of a post on the Civil Rights Commission by one who has been an advocate of the cause is somewhat like having counsel appointed a judge." To this Dean Robinson replied: "I certainly do not expect to play the role of lawyer for anyone or advocate for anyone as a member on the Commission."

The confirmation of Robinson, strongly endorsed by Senator Kenneth B. Keating of New York, was recommended. But in the full Senate on July 27 further Southern opposition developed, particularly from Senator Spessard L. Holland of Florida, who said that confirmation of Robinson would be as unfair as that of a "known member of the Ku Klux Klan." On a roll-call vote, however, Robinson was confirmed by 73 to 17.

Among the recommendations of the commission's 1959 report to the President and Congress were that the Census Bureau make a nationwide count of registered voters by race, color, and national origin and that Congress require that all state registration and voting records be preserved for five years and be open to the public. Another report, made public in October 1961, urged an amendment to the Landrum-Griffin Labor Relations Act barring any union from segregating, expelling, or refusing membership to any person because of race, color, creed, or national origin. The President was asked to issue executive orders forbidding segregation in National Guard and Reserve units, as well as in the regular armed forces, and making clear that employment supported by federal grant funds was subject to antidiscrimination rules.

In the fifth and final volume of its report, submitted in November 1961, the commission urged action by the Justice Department and Congress to correct the problem of police lawlessness and brutality, the brunt of which is borne by Negroes, proportionately, more than by any other group in the country. The commission also appealed directly to the President to use the influence and prestige of his office to help the cause of civil rights.

As early as 1946 Professor Robinson was inscribed on the honor roll of the Richmond *Afro-American,* and in the same year he was awarded the testimonial of merit in jurisprudence of Psi Phi chapter of Omega Psi Phi fraternity. Two years later he received a testimonial of merit from the National Bar Association and in 1951 received both the annual nonmember Citizenship Award of Beta Gamma Lambda chapter of Alpha Phi Alpha and the Howard University Annual Alumni Award for distinguished postgraduate achievement in law. His other honors include a citation by the Richmond chapter of Frontiers of America (1954) and an LL.D. degree from Virginia Union University (1955). He is a member of the National, American, and Old Dominion bar associations and of the Virginia State Bar.

Dean Spottswood W. Robinson 3d is married to the former Marian B. Wilkerson of Richmond. The Robinsons have one son, Spottswood William 4th, who in mid-1961 had just completed five years in the Air Force, and one daughter, Nina C., a graduate student at Howard University. Robinson has been a vestryman of St. Philip's Episcopal Church in Richmond since 1955 and a trustee since 1957. Fishing is among his favorite recreations. According to a New York *Times* biographical sketch (July 28, 1961), "Mr. Robinson's manner is mild. 'He is the precise opposite of a firebrand,' said one man who knows him. 'He is not the type you tell anecdotes about,' said another."

References

N Y Times p9 Jl 28 '61 por
Washington (D.C.) Post B p3 S 2 '60 por

SCHOEPPEL, ANDREW F. Nov. 23, 1894-Jan. 21, 1962 Republican Governor of Kansas (1943-47); United States Senator (since 1949); member of the Appropriations Committee and Interstate and Foreign Commerce Committee. See *Current Biography* (March) 1952.

Obituary

N Y Times p23 Ja 22 '62

SCOFIELD, PAUL Jan. 21, 1922- Actor
Address: The Gables, Balcombe, Sussex, England

When Paul Scofield came to Broadway in November 1961 as Sir Thomas More in *A Man for All Seasons*, his American audience suddenly realized something of which Englishmen had long been aware: there is an heir-apparent to the throne shared by Sir Laurence Olivier and Sir John Gielgud. As a matter of fact, Richard Burton sees Scofield no longer as heir, but as successor. "Of the ten greatest moments in the theater, eight are Scofield's," Burton has said.

A professional actor since the early 1940's, Scofield first attracted wide notice in England during the 1946 Stratford-on-Avon Shakespeare Festival. "No actor within memory had so captured the town and the festival," J. C. Terwin wrote in *Paul Scofield* (Rockcliff, 1956). His first starring role in the London commercial theater was that of Alexander the Great in *Adventure Story* in 1949. His subsequent successes included one of the longest running Hamlets in the history of the British stage and impressive performances as Coriolanus and Don Adriano de Armado at the 1961 Stratford (Ontario) Shakespearean Festival.

Paul Scofield was born David Scofield in Hurstpierpoint, Sussex, England, on January 21, 1922. His father, Edward H. Scofield, was master of the village school where Scofield received his primary education. He received his secondary education at the Varndean School for Boys in nearby Bristol. Participating in dramatics, he made his first appearance on the school stage at thirteen as Juliet in *Romeo and Juliet*. In early adolescence he also appeared on the stage of Brighton's Theatre Royal as one of a crowd in a production of *The Only Way*.

Leaving Varndean School before graduation, Scofield studied dramatics at the Croydon Repertory Theatre School. This school closed when war came, and Scofield entered London's Mask Theatre School. As a student, he was permitted minor participation in Mask Theatre productions. He spoke his first lines ("Yes, sir") on the professional stage in a Mask production of Drinkwater's *Abraham Lincoln* that opened on April 16, 1940 at the Westminster Theatre.

Evacuated to North Devonshire during the blitz of late 1940, Scofield soon was playing leading roles under the direction of Eileen Thorndike and Herbert Scott at the new all-student Bideford Repertory Theatre—roles that ranged from King Lear to Danny in Emlyn Williams' *Night Must Fall*. In the summer of 1941 the Thorndike-Scott company moved to Houghton Hall, Cambridge, where Scofield played the title role in Arthur Milmurt's translation of André Obey's *Noah*.

When the student company disbanded after the *Noah* production, in July 1941, Scofield (barred from military service for medical reasons) entered the cast of an E.N.S.A. (Entertainments National Service Association—British equivalent of the American USO) tour of *The Taming of the Shrew*. During the spring of 1942 he toured as the hotel clerk in *Jeannie*, and during the summer as Ainger in *Young Woodley*.

Wide World

PAUL SCOFIELD

Later in 1942 he joined Basil C. Langton's Traveling Repertory Theatre, which had leased the Birmingham Repertory Theatre. At Birmingham Scofield played Horatio in *Hamlet* and Stephen Undershaft in *Major Barbara*, among other roles. During late 1942 and early 1943 Langton's company made a C.E.M.A. (Council for the Encouragement of Music and the Arts) tour of factory towns with *Arms and the Man*, in which Scofield played Major Sergius Saranoff. When John Steinbeck's *The Moon Is Down*, under the direction of Langton, opened at the Whitehall Theatre, London, in June 1943, Scofield appeared in the role of Alex Morden. In the fall the Traveling Repertory Theatre went on another C.E.M.A. tour with *Three-Cornered Moon*, in which he played Donald. The tour lasted until the fall of 1944, other plays meanwhile being added to the repertory.

From the fall of 1944 through 1945 Scofield was a member of the Birmingham Repertory Company. His score of roles at Birmingham included young Marlow in *She Stoops To Conquer* and John Tanner in *Man and Superman*. From April 20 to September 28, 1946 he was a member of the Festival Company at the Shakespeare Memorial Theatre, Stratford-on-Avon. His festival roles included King Henry V, Cloten in *Cymbeline*, and Don Adriano de Armado in *Love's Labour's Lost*. In November 1946 he appeared as Tegeus-Chromis in Christopher Fry's *A Phoenix Too Frequent* at the Arts Theatre Club, London. He returned to Stratford-on-Avon for the 1947 and 1948 festivals as Don Adriano again, among other roles. Meanwhile he appeared with the Stratford-on-Avon company at His Majesty's Theatre, London, in the fall of 1947, as Mercutio in *Romeo and Juliet* and Sir Andrew in *Twelfth Night*. In December 1947 he was Young Fashion in Sir John Vanbrugh's *The Relapse; or, Virtue in Danger*,

SCOFIELD, PAUL—*Continued*

at the Lyric Theatre, Hammersmith. *The Relapse* moved in January 1948 to the Phoenix Theatre, London.

By 1949 Scofield was as well known in London as at Stratford. His first starring role was Alexander the Great in Terence Rattigan's *Adventure Story*, directed by Peter Glenville, which opened at St. James's Theatre, London, in March 1949. In October 1949 he appeared as Constantin Gavrilovitch in George Calderon's version of Anton Chekhov's *The Seagull*, first at the Lyric Theatre, Hammersmith, then at the St. James's Theatre, London. In January 1950 *Ring Around the Moon*, Christopher Fry's translation of Jean Anouilh's charade with music, *L'Invitation au Château*, opened at the Globe Theatre, London, with Scofield playing the twins. The production ran for about two years.

At the Phoenix Theatre, London, in January 1952, he took on the role of Don Pedro in *Much Ado About Nothing*, directed by John Gielgud. In August 1952, when Charles Morgan's *The River Line* opened at the Edinburgh Festival (Lyceum Theatre), Scofield played the soul-tortured American fleeing occupied France. He continued in the role when the play moved to the Lyric Theatre, Hammersmith, and to the Strand Theatre, London. In December 1952 he left the cast of *The River Line* to appear in the part of King Richard II in *Richard II* at the Lyric Theatre, Hammersmith. The following February, still at the Lyric, he was Witwoud in *The Way of the World*. In May at the Lyric he was Pierre in Thomas Otway's *Venice Preserv'd*. In December at the Piccadilly Theatre, London, he was Paul Gardiner in *A Question of Fact*, which ran well into 1954. In December 1955, when *Time Remembered*, Patricia Moyes' translation of Jean Anouilh's *Leocadia*, opened at the Lyric, Hammersmith, Scofield appeared as Prince Albert Troubiscoi. The production was later transferred to the New Theatre, London.

Scofield toured England as Hamlet, under Peter Brook's direction, in the fall of 1955, before an appearance in Moscow's Art Theatre in November. (It was the first time an English-speaking theatre company had played in Moscow since 1917.) In December the company took the play into the Phoenix Theatre, London. "I have known many touching Hamlets," J. C. Terwin said. "Only Scofield has gone at once to the heart." Productions of *The Power and the Glory* and *The Family Reunion* rounded out the 1955-56 Scofield-Brook season at the Phoenix. Scofield's subsequent London appearances were in *A Dead Secret* (Piccadilly Theatre, 1957), the musical *Expresso Bongo* (Saville Theatre, 1958), and *The Complaisant Lover* (Globe Theatre, 1959).

A Man for All Seasons, Robert Bolt's character study of Sir Thomas More, ran at London's Globe Theatre for nine months beginning July 1, 1960. Scofield played More, the Lord Chancellor to Henry VIII who chose, unto death, conscience over king. After the run,

Scofield traveled to Canada to participate in the Stratford (Ontario) Shakespearean Festival (summer 1961) and to release what Herbert Whittaker called "perhaps the most remarkable personal talent these festival plays have known' (Toronto *Globe and Mail*, June 21, 1961).

A Man for All Seasons opened at the ANTA Theatre, New York City, on November 22, 1961. The extraordinary ovation given Scofield after the première performance was prophetic of the subsequent unanimous praise from American critics. The critical consensus was that a remarkable talent and a subtle, difficult role had illumined each other. "With a kind of weary magnificence," a writer said in *Time*, "Scofield sinks himself into the part, studiously underplays it, and somehow displays the inner mind of a man destined for sainthood" (December 15, 1961).

Scofield has also played classical roles on British radio and television. Although he has been besieged by film makers since 1946, he has rejected most screen offers. For his film debut as Philip II of Spain in *That Lady* the British Film Academy chose him "the most promising newcomer to films" in 1955. More recently he appeared in *Carve Her Name With Pride*.

Paul Scofield married Joy Parker, an actress who has often appeared on stage with him, in 1943. With their two children, Martin and Sarah, they live quietly, shunning publicity, in the village of Balcombe, Sussex. Success has not spoiled Scofield's remarkable modesty and gentleness. At work he is dedicated but calm, quietly aloof by preference but warm in response when approached by others. He likes to leave for home as soon as work is done.

Scofield postpones learning his lines and his role until he attends the first rehearsal. Believing that spontaneous emotion offers nothing with which to fill the vacuum of an off-night, he relies on technique rather than "method." He finds that once he disciplines himself within the fundamental structure of a role, he is freer to flesh out the character emotionally. He does not identify rigidly with a character, but remains detached enough to recreate the role nightly. Kenneth Tynan has singled out as the most extraordinary aspect of Scofield's genius "his power to enlarge a role until it fits him" (*Time*, December 15, 1961). Scofield is lean, robust, and tall (six feet). His thick waves of hair are a graying brown, and his eyes are brown. His face is furrowed and mobile, with high cheekbones. The Scofield profile has often been described in sculptural metaphor. A mixture of diffidence and courtliness marks his manner. Early in his career, a native idiosyncrasy of speech, aggravated by fast delivery of lines was mistaken by a few critics for affectation. J. C. Terwin in 1956 reported that the Scofield voice "has strengthened to odd splendour; to a mountain voice, rifted, chasmed, that can glitter on the peak and fall, sombre, in the sudden." Scofield was awarded the C.B.E. (Commander,

Order of the British Empire) in 1956. He smokes a pipe. His recreations include walking, reading, riding, and gardening.

References

Christian Sci Mon Mag p15 Jl 8 '50 por
Maclean's 74:56 Ag 12 '61 por
N Y Post p46 D 13 '61
N Y Times II p1+ D 10 '61
Newsweek 58:78 D 4 '61 por
Show 1:70 N '61 por
Theatre Arts 33:4+ Je '49
Terwin, J. C. Paul Scofield (1956)
Theatre World Annual, 1955-56
Who's Who, 1960
Who's Who in the Theatre (1957)

SENGHOR, LÉOPOLD SÉDAR Oct. 9, 1906-
President of the Republic of Senegal; political leader; educator; poet

Address: b. Office of the President, Dakar, Republic of Senegal

One of the central figures in the enormous political changes that have taken place in French Africa since World War II is Léopold Sédar Senghor, a poet, professor, and statesman who is regarded as Africa's leading intellectual. He was elected on September 5, 1960 as the first president of the Republic of Senegal, formerly a part of French West Africa, where he heads the governing Union Progressiste Sénégalaise (Senegalese Progressive Union). Senghor's major goal has been the transformation of the French Community to allow former territories the same independence that the dominions have in the British Commonwealth. "We are paving the way, calmly and methodically," he has said, "for a future of peace and prosperity for my country and France, fraternally united in an order that is new because it is more human."

A member of the Mandingo tribe of the Serer ethnic group, Léopold Sédar Senghor was born on October 9, 1906 in Joal, Senegal, on the Atlantic coast south of Dakar. His father, a well-to-do planter and exporter of peanuts, supported a family of some twenty children. His mother was a Roman Catholic, and the boy, baptized in her faith, began his education at a missionary school in Joal. He then went to Dakar, where he graduated from the *lycée* with top honors. A scholarship enabled him to study at the Lycée Louis le Grand in Paris, and later he majored in literature and languages at the École Normale Supérieure of the University of Paris and received the degree of *agrégé de grammaire.*

Recognized at the university as one of the most brilliant contemporary students of any race, Senghor had the distinction, shortly after graduation in 1935, of being the first African appointed to the faculty of the *lycée* at Tours. "Here in addition to his teaching," observed Thomas Patrick Melady in *Profiles of African Leaders* (Macmillan, 1961), "he soon became the spokesman for his continent among the intelligentsia of France and Europe. In poems and essays he gave expression to the longing

Wide World
LÉOPOLD SÉDAR SENGHOR

of the African people for their own cultural identification. He was the first, really, to give written expression to the unique aspects of the African way of life."

During World War II Senghor served first in a French infantry battalion composed of natives of the colonies. After the surrender of France in 1940 he was interned by the Germans in a succession of prison camps. He helped to organize resistance groups and was sent to a punishment camp. Nevertheless, in 1943 he was permitted to resume teaching and in the following year joined the faculty of the Lycée Marcelin Berthelot in Paris, where he taught literature and African culture until 1948.

Like most of Senghor's subsequent verse, his collection of early poems entitled *Chantes d'Ombre* reflected the concept of *négritude,* which Melady interprets in English as "a mystic union with nature and its supernatural forces." *Chantes d'Ombre,* published in 1945, caused a furor in Parisian literary circles and made the author perhaps the most widely known Senegalese.

As a Deputy for Senegal to the French Constituent Assemblies of 1945 and 1946, Senghor did important work as a linguistic expert. In the latter year, when a new constitution conferred French citizenship on all territorial natives, along with limited-franchise representation in the French National Assembly, he was elected, as a Socialist, to both the Assembly in Paris and the General Council of Senegal. Senghor continued as a member of the National Assembly until the end of the Fourth Republic, though from 1948 onwards he was regarded as an Independent.

Also in 1948 Senghor left the faculty of the Lycée Marcelin Berthelot to become a professor for the École Nationale de la France d'Outre Mer (National College of France Overseas) in Paris. Four years later (1952) he saw one of

SENGHOR, LÉOPOLD SÉDAR—Continued

his dreams realized when an institute of higher studies was established at Dakar. This became the University of Dakar in 1957.

Senghor's differences with the established Senegalese Socialist party developed through his insistence on an "African road to socialism" on which the winning of independence by peaceful means would be followed by continued co-operation with France. His own party at home, the Bloc Démocratique Sénégalais, which he formed in 1948, brought him an important victory in 1951 when he was overwhelmingly re-elected to the French Chamber of Deputies.

Two years later as leader of a group of colonial Independents, Senghor proposed revision of the constitution to make the French Union a federal entity with equal status for the overseas territories. From February 1955 to January 1956 he served as Secretary of State for Scientific Research in the government of Premier Edgar Faure and as such attended the general conferences of UNESCO. Earlier he had been a delegate of France to the fifth session of the U.N. General Assembly, in 1950-51.

By provision of the loi cadre (framework law) for a new French Community enacted in Paris in June 1956, each French territory in Africa would elect, under universal suffrage, a Territorial Assembly, which would then elect an Executive Council. The election for assemblies in West Africa took place in March 1957. Senghor, who had become mayor of Thiès, near Dakar, in November 1956, headed the Convention Africaine, which sought consolidation of all parties. It won the Territorial Assembly in Senegal, but the election showed that the strongest group in French West Africa was Rassamblement Démocratique Africain, under Félix Houphouet-Boigny of the Ivory Coast.

In March 1958 Senghor helped to form in Dakar the Parti du Régroupment Africain (P.R.A.), and later as a party leader he was summoned to the Consultative Assembly for the new constitution of General Charles de Gaulle, who returned to power in France as Premier in June 1958. As spokesman for the P.R.A., Senghor called for the granting of immediate independence for the African territories and the formation of a Black African Federation, which would negotiate new ties with France on the basis of equality; but, as finally drafted, the de Gaulle constitution provided that the "autonomous republics" forming a new French Community should be autonomous only in most domestic matters, with foreign and defense policy and control of the courts and of higher education being reserved to the French Community. Although much dissatisfied, Senghor supported the de Gaulle constitution at the referendum on September 28, 1958, when it was ratified by 97 percent of the Senegal electorate.

In keeping with the de Gaulle constitution, a Republic of Senegal was proclaimed by the Territorial Assembly on November 25, 1958, with the adoption of its own constitution following on January 24, 1959. Meanwhile, on January 17, Senegal had joined with the adjacent Sudanese Republic (formerly French Sudan) to form the Mali Federation. At the election in Senegal on March 22, 1959 the profederation party led by Senghor captured all of the eighty seats in the new Federal Assembly. Although Senghor failed to draw any of the other former West African colonies of France into the federation, in June 1959 a customs union was formed by Mali and the republics of Mauretania, the Ivory Coast, Dahomey, the Niger, and the Upper Volta.

After a constitutional amendment had made possible the inclusion of a fully sovereign state in the French Community, the Mali Federation proclaimed its independence on June 20, 1960, with Senghor as leader of the Federal Assembly. But serious friction developed between what one newspaper report summed up as "left-leaning Sudan and cautious, commerce-minded Senegal." Only two months later, on August 20, Senegal withdrew from the federation and again proclaimed its independence.

The new constitution adopted by Senegal's Assembly on August 25, 1960 provided for the election of a President every seven years, and on September 5 Senghor was elected the first President of the new republic. He also serves as an advisory minister to the French government for the Community and during a state visit to Paris in October 1961 undertook to attempt unofficial mediation between France and Tunisia.

Under French sponsorship the republics of Senegal and Mauretania were admitted to the United Nations on September 28, 1960, and in October-November 1961 President Senghor visited the United States to address the U.N. General Assembly and to confer with President John F. Kennedy on aid to Senegal and other matters. Addressing the U.N. Assembly on October 31, he attacked not only the colonial policies of Portugal and South Africa, but also the tendency of some nations "to weight their neutralism" consistently to one side. "We have denounced," he said, "the imperialism of the great powers only to secrete a miniature imperialism toward our neighbors in the nonaligned group. We have demanded disarmament from the great powers only to transform our countries into arsenals. We proclaim our neutralism, but we do not always base it upon a policy of neutrality."

President Léopold Sédar Senghor also visited England in the fall of 1961 and lectured at Oxford University on modern Europe and Africa. Later in the year Fordham University in New York awarded him an honorary LL.D. degree, citing him as "as accomplished poet, an erudite professor and ardent patriot." Collections of Senghor's poetry, other than the celebrated Chants d'Ombre, include Hosties Noires (1948), Chants pour Näett (1949), Éthiopiques (1956), and, most recently, Nocturnes. Senghor is also the editor of Anthologie de la Nouvelle Poésie Noire et Malgache de Langue Française (1948), an important collection of contemporary Negro poetry.

Senghor's first wife, Mlle. Eboué, was a native African. He is now married to the former Colette Hubert, a Frenchwoman. "I'm color blind," he once told Rolf Italiaander. "I looked for a wife not on the basis of her skin color, but on whether or not I could love her and she could return my love. This is the woman of my heart, and it's only an accident that she is white." They have three sons, Francis, Guy, and Philippe.

References

N Y Post p44 O 31 '61 por
N Y Times p16 S 6 '60 por
Time 73:27 F 16 '59 por
Washington (D.C.) Post A p13 Je 28 '61 por
Dictionnaire Biographique Français Contemporain (1954)
International Who's Who, 1961-62
Italiaander, Rolf. New Leaders of Africa (1961)
Melady, Thomas Patrick. Profiles of African Leaders (1961)
Segal, Ronald. Political Africa (1961)
Who's Who in France, 1961-62

SMITH, MARGARET (MADELINE) CHASE
Dec. 14, 1897- United States Senator from Maine

Address: b. Senate Office Bldg., Washington 25, D.C.; h. Showhegan, Me.; 807 Milestone Dr., Silver Spring, Md.

> NOTE: This biography supersedes the article that appeared in *Current Biography* in 1945.

Republican Senator Margaret Chase Smith of Maine is the only woman ever to have been elected to the United States Senate for three terms. Beginning her career as a teacher, she later worked as an executive of a telephone company and of a newspaper. She was first elected to the United States House of Representatives in 1940, to fill a vacancy created by the death of her husband, and has served in the Senate since 1949, having been elected for her third consecutive term in November 1960.

As a Congresswoman and Senator, Mrs. Smith has maintained a highly independent position. She has frequently supported liberal legislation sponsored by the Democratic administrations, and she was one of the foremost adversaries of the late Senator Joseph R. McCarthy. She is an outspoken advocate of a strong policy of national defense and of a firm foreign policy.

Eldest in a family of six children, Margaret Madeline Chase was born on December 14, 1897 in Skowhegan, Maine, a mill town on the Kennebec River. Her father, George Emery Chase, who ran a one-chair barber shop, was the grandson of a Methodist minister and was of English-Irish stock. Her mother, Carrie Matilda (Murray) Chase, was of Scottish and French-Canadian background and a Daughter of the American Revolution.

Although the family was far from prosperous, Maggie Chase had a pleasant childhood. As a little girl she learned her father's barbering trade, and at thirteen she began working Saturday evenings in a local five-and-ten cent store. Later she worked occasionally as a substitute operator at the Skowhegan telephone exchange.

Shoaf

MARGARET CHASE SMITH

At the Skowhegan High School, where she was a leader among her classmates, she took commercial courses and received average-to-good marks. She excelled at basketball and managed the girls' basketball team.

After graduating from high school in 1916, Margaret Chase taught for seven months in a one-room primary school in Skowhegan, at a salary of $8.50 a week. Subsequently she worked with the local telephone company, first as an operator and later as an executive with the commercial department. Although she had hoped to go to a college or professional school, she was financially unable to do so. In 1919 she became circulation manager of a weekly newspaper, the Skowhegan *Independent Reporter,* and also worked in the advertising and editorial departments. In 1926 she was elected to a two-year term as president of the Maine Federation of Business and Professional Women's Clubs. From 1928 to 1930 she was office manager of the Daniel E. Cummings Company woolen mills in Skowhegan and treasurer of the New England Waste Process Company in Fairfield, Maine.

On May 14, 1930 Margaret Chase was married to Clyde Harold Smith, her senior by twenty-one years. A Skowhegan businessman and co-owner of the *Independent Reporter,* Smith was prominent in local and state politics. Mrs. Smith served as a member of the Republican state committee from 1930 to 1936. Clyde H. Smith was elected in 1936 to represent the Second Maine District in the Seventy-fifth Congress, and he was re-elected in 1938, winning his forty-eighth contest for political office without ever having encountered defeat. During his tenure as a Congressman, Mrs. Smith served as his secretary, often working fifteen hours a day.

When Representative Smith suffered a heart attack shortly before the filing date for the 1940 primary, Mrs. Smith, upon the urging of her

SMITH, MARGARET CHASE—*Continued*
husband filed for the candidacy. Smith died on April 8, 1940, and in a special election on June 3, 1940 Mrs. Smith was chosen to occupy his seat for the remainder of the Seventy-sixth Congress. She cast her first important vote in September, when she supported the Selective Service Act, in opposition to the majority of her Republican colleagues. In the regular Maine election in September 1940, Mrs. Smith was elected to the Seventy-seventh Congress with a plurality nearly three times that received by her husband in 1938. She was re-elected by a decisive majority in 1942 and again in 1944 and 1946.

After serving on several minor committee assignments, Mrs. Smith was assigned in January 1943, at her own request, to the House Naval Affairs Committee. For her work in protecting and furthering the status of women in the Navy she earned the affectionate title "Mother of the Waves." She also participated in a probe of World War II destroyer production and was the first woman to sail on a destroyer in wartime. As a member of the Naval Affairs subcommittee on congested areas, Mrs. Smith made a 25,000-mile tour of bases in the South Pacific during the winter of 1944-45. Her name was mentioned in 1945 for possible appointment as Under Secretary of the Navy. As a consistent supporter of the foreign policies of both Roosevelt and Truman, she was also suggested, in 1947, for appointment as Assistant Secretary of State.

After the enactment of the National Security Act, setting up a new National Military Establishment in 1947, Mrs. Smith became a member of the House Armed Services Committee and chairman of its medical subcommittee. One of her major concerns as a member of this committee was the improvement and regularization of the status of women in the armed forces, and she was largely instrumental in obtaining passage of the Women's Armed Services Integration Act, signed by President Truman on June 12, 1948.

During her eight years in the House of Representatives the decidedly independent Congresswoman from Maine supported much New Deal legislation, including extended Social Security, and amassed a record of one vote in three against the majority of her party. In February 1947 she was the only Republican in the House to oppose a cut in the Truman administration's budget. Although she had originally supported the Dies Committee to Investigate Un-American Activities, in 1945 she voted against the establishment of a permanent House Un-American Activities Committee. Having received the support of organized labor in 1944, she voted against the Case strike-control bill in 1946, but, on the other hand, she voted to override the Presidential veto on the Taft-Hartley labor-management relations bill in 1947. In 1944 she served as chairman of the Maine Republican convention and also as a technical adviser to the United States delegation at the International Labor Organization convention in Philadelphia.

In August 1947, after Maine's veteran United States Senator Wallace H. White had decided not to seek re-election, Mrs. Smith announced her candidacy for his seat. Virtually without campaign funds, she conducted a grass-roots campaign, visiting approximately 600 Maine communities. Although on one occasion she broke her arm in a fall on an icy pavement, she appeared as a speaker at a scheduled political meeting a few hours later. Campaigning with the slogan "Don't change a record for a promise," she won the Republican Senatorial nomination in the June 1948 primaries, receiving more than the combined number of votes of her three opponents, who included Governor Horace A. Hildreth and former Governor Sumner Sewall. In the national elections that September she won with 159,182 votes against 64,074 received by her Democratic opponent, Dr. Adrian Scolten, thus scoring the highest percentage majority and the greatest total vote majority in the history of Maine politics.

In 1949 Senator Smith began a United Features syndicated column, distributed to thirty newspapers in sixteen states, which she continued to write for over five years. In her first major address to the Senate on June 1, 1950 she assailed Senator Joseph R. McCarthy with a "declaration of conscience," formulated by herself and six other Republican senators. "The greatest deliberative body in the world," she asserted, had been "debased to the level of a forum of hate and character assassination sheltered by the shield of congressional immunity." She added: "I don't want to see the Republican Party ride to political victory on the four horsemen of calumny—fear, ignorance, bigotry, and smear."

In 1952 Senator Smith was widely mentioned as a possible Vice-Presidential candidate. A radio commentator once asked her what she would do if she woke up one morning and found herself in the White House. "I'd go straight to Mrs. Truman and apologize. Then I'd go home," she replied. In the Senate, Mrs. Smith has served on the Republican Policy Committee, the Appropriations Committee, the Armed Services Committee, the Space Committee, the Government Operations Committee, the Rules Committee, and the District of Columbia Committee. In the Maine Republican primary in 1954 she defeated a protégé of Senator Joseph R. McCarthy by a margin of five to one, setting a new record for the total number of votes in a contested primary.

In voting on key issues in the Senate, Senator Smith has taken a generally independent position. In 1949 she supported the anti-filibuster ruling, federal aid to education, and the North Atlantic security pact. In 1950 she supported the loan to Spain; in 1951 she voted for draft extension and universal military training, and for the loan to India; in 1952 she voted for the offshore oil bill and for reduction of TVA funds. She voted for the Bricker treaty amendment and for censure of Senator Joseph R. McCarthy in 1954. Early in 1956 she introduced to the Senate a bill for a five-year program of medical research. In 1957 she supported the civil rights bill and the Eisenhower doctrine of aid to the Middle East.

In June 1959 Senator Smith was one of the only two Republicans in the Senate to vote against confirmation of Lewis L. Strauss as

Secretary of Commerce. In that year she also voted for the Democratic depressed areas bill opposed by the President. She supported the Democratic housing bill of 1959, but did not vote for its passage over the President's veto. In 1960 she opposed the Anderson amendment providing medical care for the aged under Social Security. She voted for pay increases for federal employees and for overriding the President's veto on the Area Redevelopment Act. In December 1960 Senator Smith proposed a constitutional amendment for the direct nomination and election of Presidents and Vice-Presidents, and the elimination of the Electoral College.

Seeking election to a third Senate term in 1960, Mrs. Smith defeated her Democratic opponent, Minority Leader Lucia Cormier of the Maine House of Representatives, by 256,890 votes to 159,809, setting a new all-time record for Maine. Her percentage of the total was the highest received by any Republican Senatorial candidate.

In the Eighty-seventh Congress Senator Smith is a member of the Senate Armed Services, Appropriations, and Space committees and of the preparedness investigation subcommittee. In 1961 she voted for the area redevelopment bill, the Kennedy minimum wage bill, the school assistance bill, and the bill for extended foreign aid. She opposed confirmation of Charles M. Meriwether as director of the Export-Import Bank. In January 1962 she was one of the two Republicans voting against confirmation of John A. McCone as director of the Central Intelligence Agency.

Addressing the Senate on September 21, 1961, Senator Smith charged the Kennedy administration with apparent lack of will to use nuclear weapons, which, she claimed, weakened the nation's ability to deal with the Soviet Union. In a message to the British Labor party a few weeks later, Soviet Premier Nikita S. Khrushchev referred to Senator Smith as "the devil in a disguise of a woman" and accused her of beating "all records of savagery." Upon hearing of Khrushchev's denunciation, Mrs. Smith remarked: "Mr. Khrushchev isn't really mad at me. I am not that important. He is angry because American officials have grown more firm since my speech. . . ."

Although she has never attended college, Senator Smith holds thirty-six honorary degrees, conferred upon her by various universities, colleges, and institutes. She is a member of the American Academy of Arts and Sciences, and an honorary member of Pi Sigma Alpha, the political science honor society; Delta Kappa Gamma, the education sorority; Sigma Kappa, a social sorority; and Beta Sigma Phi, an international sorority. She has served as a lieutenant colonel in the Air Force Reserve.

Numerous honors and awards have been bestowed upon Senator Smith, including the Freedom Award from the Freedoms Foundation (1950); the Veterans of Foreign Wars medal for Americanism (1954); the Distinguished Service Award on National Defense from the Reserve Officers Association (1955). She has been cited as Woman of the Year several times and has been rated by the Gallup Poll three times as one of the ten most admired women in the world. *Newsweek* magazine's press gallery poll gave her the Most Valuable Senator rating in 1960. In 1952 she was designated the Most Charming Woman in Government by the Charm Institute. Senator Smith, who has traveled extensively throughout the world and conferred with the leaders of many nations, is considered one of America's most effective ambassadors of good will.

Senator Margaret Chase Smith is five feet four inches tall and has well-groomed gray hair. She speaks precisely and dresses smartly but conservatively. She has a modest apartment in Silver Spring, Maryland, an eight-room house in Skowhegan, and a summer home at Cundys Harbor, Maine. Her favorite recreations are badminton, gardening, swimming, and cooking. She is a Methodist.

References

Ladies Home J 78:66+ Ja '61 por
Nat Bsns Woman 39:2 O '60 por
Sat Eve Post 221:36+ S 11 '48 pors
Time 76:13+ S 5 '60 por

Clymer, Eleanor and Erlich, Lillian. Modern American Career Women (1959)
National Cyclopædia of American Biography current vol I (1960)
Who's Who in America, 1960-61

SWANN, W(ILLIAM) F(RANCIS) G(RAY) Aug. 29, 1884-Jan. 29, 1962 Physicist; authority on cosmic radiation, terrestrial magnetism, and atomic structure; director of the Bartol Research Foundation of the Franklin Institute in Swarthmore, Pennsylvania (1927-59). See *Current Biography* (December) 1960.

Obituary

N Y Times p29 Ja 30 '62

WARD, PAUL L(ANGDON) Feb. 4, 1911-College president; historian

Address: b. Sarah Lawrence College, Bronxville 8, N.Y.; h. 935 Kimball Ave., Bronxville 8, N.Y.

The fifth president of Sarah Lawrence College in Bronxville, New York, is Dr. Paul L. Ward, a scholar equally at home in the fields of medieval European history and modern educational theory. He succeeded interim president Harrison Tweed in July 1960 and was formally installed in May 1961. Approving the college's traditional policy of encouraging independent study for its students, the new president is dedicated to teaching methods that would implement this policy. In his inaugural address Ward noted that a good education today required a student "to live with confidence and discrimination in an intellectual world of clamorous diversity" and discussed a number of paths for improvement in education.

From 1953 until his appointment to Sarah Lawrence College, Ward was professor of history and head of the history department at Carnegie Institute of Technology in Pittsburgh, Pennsylvania. While there, he won recognition for his efforts to establish the Advanced Placement

Gary Gladstone

PAUL L. WARD

Program in Pittsburgh high schools and at Carnegie Tech. Ward is the author of several articles in history and in educational theory and has edited a book on Tudor constitutional law. He served with the Office of Strategic Services in Washington, D.C. during World War II and has also taught at Harvard, Radcliffe, Russell Sage, Colby, and Huachung University in Wuchang, China.

Paul Langdon Ward was born on February 4, 1911 in Diarbekr, Turkey to Edwin St. John and Charlotte Edwards (Allen) Ward, who were medical missionaries. His paternal grandfather, Langdon S. Ward, was for thirty years treasurer of the American Board of Commissioners for Foreign Missions of the Congregational Church; all of his seven children served as missionaries abroad. Paul Ward has two brothers, Philip H. Ward (a Congregational minister) and Richard S. Ward (a professor of psychiatry at Emory University), and two sisters, Mrs. William B. Easton, Jr., and Mrs. J. Richard Haynes.

One of Ward's earliest memories is of his being evacuated with his mother from Turkey by an American battleship in 1915, during World War I, when his father was working with the Red Cross. Later the family lived in Lebanon, where Dr. Ward was a professor of medicine and dean of the medical faculty at the American University at Beirut from 1924 to 1931. A seasoned traveler, Paul Ward had been around the world before his seventh birthday. His enthusiasm for travel has continued through the years, and he has made many trips to Europe, Asia, and the Middle East. His childhood travels, especially an automobile trip through France, Switzerland, and England in the autumn of 1924, greatly stimulated his interest in history.

After studying at the American Community School in Beirut, Ward attended Deerfield Academy in Massachusetts, where he wrote for the school newspaper and played on the soccer team. In 1929 he entered Amherst College, also in Massachusetts, winning the Porter Admission Prize, which is awarded to the freshman who achieves the best general record on college board tests taken for admission to Amherst. He captained the freshman soccer team, sang in the choir and glee club, and worked on the college newspaper. As the senior who had attained the highest scholastic standing in his freshman, sophomore, and junior years, he received the Addison Brown Scholarship in 1932. He graduated *summa cum laude* in 1933 with a B.A. degree in history.

In his graduating year Ward won an Amherst Memorial Fellowship, which he held from 1933 to 1935 and under which he began his graduate work at Harvard University. From 1935 to 1938 he was a Junior Fellow in the Society of Fellows at Harvard, and he was awarded his M.A. degree in 1934 and the Ph.D. degree in 1940. Meanwhile, in 1938, he had begun his career in teaching as an instructor and tutor at Harvard University and Radcliffe College. His research, in medieval history, centered on the English coronation and led to two publications: "The Coronation in Mediaeval England" (*Speculum,* April 1939) and "An Early Version of the Anglo-Saxon Coronation Ceremony; the Ratold Coronation Text" (*English Historical Review,* July 1942).

During the late 1930's Paul Ward participated in the Student Christian Movement of New England, and he attended the 1937 Oxford Conference of Churches as a delegate from the Congregational Church's youth group. While a graduate student at Harvard, he spent part of several summers on cycling tours through Europe. Years later, when his older children were planning a similar tour, he was able to refer them to his old *Guide Michelin.*

Dr. Ward left his teaching positions at Harvard and Radcliffe in 1941 to become assistant professor of history at Russell Sage College in Troy, New York. During his first year there the United States entered World War II, and in 1942 he temporarily gave up teaching and took a position in Washington, D.C. as an assistant section chief in the Office of Strategic Services, the United States wartime intelligence agency. Later as a liaison officer, he served with the OSS until 1945 when he moved to the State Department as a research technician.

In 1946 the Protestant Episcopal Church, of which Ward had become a member in 1941, appointed him to teach Western history at Huachung University in Wuchang, China. It was there that his wife, the child of medical missionaries, had been reared. Dr. Ward taught at the university for five semesters before having to leave China. He was in the first group of foreigners given exit permits by the Communists, in 1950, and rejoined his wife and children in Hong Kong, where they had gone the year before.

Upon his return to the United States, Ward accepted an appointment in 1951 as assistant professor of history at Colby College in Waterville, Maine. He left there in 1953 to become professor of history and chairman of the history department at Carnegie Institute of Technology in Pittsburgh. Much of the work load of the fourteen teachers in his department—a liberal arts department on an engineering campus—involved teaching at the introductory level and was concerned with the training of both students and teachers of history.

While at Carnegie Tech, Ward was a key figure in Pittsburgh's operation of the Advanced Placement Program, a national education project that permits students to take certain college-level courses in high school. If they can pass the Advanced Placement Examinations given by the College Entrance Examination Board, the students become eligible for advanced standing, or credit, when they enter college. The Pittsburgh program attracted wide attention because of its provisions for co-operation between the schools and the college in the study of the organization and teaching of the courses given. Along with intensive training institutes for the teachers, there was an exchange arrangement permitting members of the Carnegie staff to teach courses in the high schools and high school teachers to teach some of the freshmen sections at Carnegie Tech. The results achieved were of great interest to Dr. Ward, whose basic concern is with methods to improve the quality of education.

Soon after he had assumed the presidency of Sarah Lawrence College in mid-1960, Ward said in an interview for the New York *Post* (September 6, 1960), "Since I am deeply interested in exploring the ways of improving the quality of education, coming to Sarah Lawrence seemed a magnificent opportunity." He pointed out that a small, progressive college could offer him experience considerably different from his training at larger institutions following a more conventional system. He went on to say that because he could best judge and understand through participation, he intended to continue to do some teaching.

In his inaugural address at Sarah Lawrence on May 8, 1961, Ward advocated the conversion of more high school and college freshmen courses into "vigorous examinations of central concepts and issues directly related to advanced studies. Much that is unperceptive and sterile in advanced and graduate instruction around the country," he said, "simply reflects the slack and routinized handling of lower-level work in the recent past."

Since its founding in 1928, Sarah Lawrence College for women has been developing an experimental curriculum emphasizing in its liberal arts courses the particular talents and interests of individual students. It currently has an enrollment of 500 students. The faculty, which has always played a decisive role in the educational phase of the college's growth, welcomed Ward as president, according to the New York *Times* (May 9, 1961), because he is regarded as "a strong leader, but not a driver" and because he makes it clear where he stands on an issue.

Besides his articles on medieval history, Ward has written articles on English constitutional history during the sixteenth century. He and

Charles H. McIlwain edited William Lambarde's *Archeion; or a Discourse Upon the High Courts of Justice in England* (Harvard Univ. Press, 1957). This contemporary account of the English secular court system, which was first published in 1591, had last been printed in 1635. Dr. Paul L. Ward has said that as a scholar he enjoys "arguing for the importance of giving more explicit attention to the character of [the] historian's explanations." One of his publications that reflect his interest in improved teaching methods is *A Style of History for Beginners* (1959), written for the Service Center for Teachers of History of the American Historical Association.

Paul L. Ward married Catharine Frazee Wakefield on August 26, 1940. They have one daughter, Elisabeth, and three sons, John, Stephen, and Thomas. His wife was the state director of the records survey in Maine before her marriage, and she takes an active role in parent-teacher and civic organizations. Ward is nearly six feet tall and weighs 150 pounds; he has blue eyes and white hair.

In June 1961 Ward was awarded the honorary LL.D. degree from Amherst College. He is a Fellow of the National Council on Religion in Higher Education and a member of Phi Beta Kappa, the American Historical Association, and the Medieval Academy of America. He is a Democrat and belongs to Americans for Democratic Action. Langdon's manner is quiet but firm. With his family he shares an enjoyment in music, sailing, swimming, travel, and baseball. His own favorite recreation is returning through books to the sixteenth century.

References

N Y Times p27 My 9 '61 por

Directory of American Scholars (1957)
Who's Who in America, 1960-61

WATTS, ALAN (WILSON) Jan. 6, 1915-
Writer and lecturer on philosophy
Address: The Gate Five Gallery, P.O. Box 857, Sausalito, Calif.

Widely recognized as the most lucid interpreter of Zen Buddhism to the West, Alan Watts might more accurately be described as a philosopher who knows Eastern thought and explores the ways in which it can work as a catalyst in the West. Watts has been carrying on the exploration since 1936, when he published *The Spirit of Zen*. His latest published work is *Psychotherapy East and West*. In addition to writing, Watts lectures frequently at universities and before medical groups and other audiences, and he has conducted radio and television programs. "Alan Watts," Philip Wheelwright wrote in the *Sewanee Review* (summer 1953), "is one of those contemporary philosophers, far fewer than they seem, who start in . . . contemplation."

Alan Wilson Watts was born in Chislehurst, England, on January 6, 1915, to Laurence Wilson Watts and Emily Mary (Buchan) Watts. He was reared in the county of Kent. Watts' introduction to Eastern culture reportedly came when he was twelve, through the novels of Sax

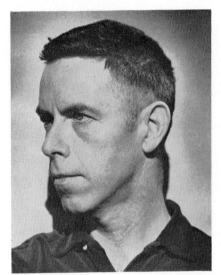

Louis Yates

ALAN WATTS

Rohmer. Watts himself has said that his fascination for Far Eastern art began when he was thirteen and developed within two years into a major interest in Indian and Chinese philosophy.

At King's School, Canterbury, England, Watts received his secondary education and participated in rowing, fencing, and debating. He also did some creative writing during those years. After graduation in December 1932 Watts worked in his father's office, raising funds for hospitals. During the 1930's he was also active in the organization in London of the World Congress of Faiths, in which he was a council member as well as member of the executive committee from 1937 to 1939.

Meanwhile he had begun to write, and at twenty, with a number of articles already published in periodicals, he wrote his first book, *The Spirit of Zen* (Dutton; J. Murray, 1936). John Murray published his *The Legacy of Asia and Western Man* in 1937. From 1934 to 1938 he was editor of *The Middle Way* in London. From 1937 to 1941 he was co-editor with L. Cranmer-Byng of the *Wisdom of the East* series published by John Murray and E. P. Dutton & Company.

Immigrating to the United States in 1939, Watts studied at Seabury-Western Theological Seminary in Evanston, Illinois. He was in residence at the seminary from 1941 to 1944 and earned his Master of Sacred Theology degree in June 1948. Ordained a priest of the Episcopal Church, he served as Episcopal chaplain at Northwestern University from 1944 to 1950. In 1950 he left the Episcopal Church. A writer in *Life* (April 21, 1961) quoted Watts as saying that he left the Church "not because it doesn't practice what it preaches but because it preaches." Later Watts summed up his religious position by saying, "I do not label

myself a Zen Buddhist, nor belong to any religious sect, on the ground that partisanship in religion closes the mind." At the American Academy of Asian Studies in San Francisco, a graduate school of the College of the Pacific, Watts taught comparative philosophy and psychology from 1951 to 1957 and was dean from 1953 to 1956. Since 1957 he has devoted himself to independent writing and lecturing.

In *The Meaning of Happiness* (Harper, 1940) Watts applies the wisdom of the East to the quest for freedom of spirit in modern psychology. *Behold the Spirit* was published by Pantheon Books, Inc., in 1947. Writing in the *Sewanee Review* (summer 1953), Philip Wheelwright said, "His earlier more special studies of Zen Buddhism and the mystical theology of St. Dionysius were preparations. *Behold the Spirit* . . . was his first full utterance *in propria persona*."

Studying the contemplative literature of various human societies in *The Supreme Identity* (Pantheon, 1950), Watts finds, beneath diverse symbols, an impressive unanimity of meaning. In *The Wisdom of Insecurity* (Pantheon, 1951) Watts indicates that rational argument is alien to the way of mystical faith, that the way lies through our daily confrontation of insecurity and paradox. *Easter: Its Story and Meaning* was published by Schuman in 1950.

In *Myth and Ritual in Christianity* (Vanguard, 1954) Watts treats his subject, as he says in his preface, as "a living symbolism which lies at the roots of our present civilization." Although Watts' suggestion that Christians have been misunderstanding the Christian mythos irritated some of them, it was a rare critic who did not recognize the book as significant. "Few readers will go all the way with Mr. Watts in his interpretations," Nash K. Burger wrote in the New York *Times Book Review* (April 18, 1954), "but his learning is considerable, and he has much to say that will interest anyone interested in cultural and religious history." In *Nature, Man, and Woman* (Pantheon, 1958) Watts begins by contrasting Eastern and Western approaches to nature and ends by applying the Western split between spirit and nature to the sexual realm.

The Way of Zen was published by Pantheon in 1957, when Zen Buddhism was rising rapidly in popularity in the United States, particularly among the so-called "beat generation." Watts, with his long background in the study of Zen, came to be looked upon as a leader in the imported Zen wave and somewhat reluctantly accepted the role. His essay "Beat Zen, Square Zen, and Zen," first published in the *Chicago Review* (summer 1958), was published in revised form as a pamphlet by City Lights Books in 1959. In it he points out that Zen Buddhism as applied by the beat generation is still ego-conscious, and is frequently used by inhibited persons to justify "sheer caprice in art, literature, and life." The "square" Zen of the traditional schools of Japan, with its ritualism and stern discipline is, according to Watts, also not free from self-justification.

In contrast to these two manifestations of Zen Buddhism, Watts describes the original Zen of the old Chinese masters of the T'ang dynasty. He depicts the Buddha or awakened man of Chinese Zen as "ordinary and nothing special"—a "holy man and sage who is not impossibly remote, not superhuman but fully human, and, above all, not a solemn and sexless ascetic." Such persons are "just like us, and yet much more at home in the world, floating much more easily upon the ocean of transience and insecurity." Watts points out that the Westerner who is attracted to Zen "must understand his own culture so thoroughly that he is no longer swayed by its premises unconsciously. He must really have come to terms with the Lord God Jehovah and with his Hebrew-Christian conscience so that he can take it or leave it without fear or rebellion. . . . For Zen is above all the liberation of the mind from conventional thought, and that is something utterly different from rebellion against convention, on the one hand, or adapting foreign conventions, on the other."

"Beat Zen, Square Zen, and Zen" was included in the collection of his essays published by Pantheon in 1960 under the title *This Is It*. In the title essay Watts explores his own experiences in search of *satori* or what he calls "cosmic consciousness," including his experiences with pharmacological means to that end. Reviewing *This Is It* in the New York *Times Book Review* (December 18, 1960), William Barrett wrote: "Alan Watts has come up with the simplest formula yet for the meaning of Zen: 'No fuss.' This would certainly be a tranquilizing doctrine if one could master it. Mr. Watts seems to have done it, for this book . . . rolls effortlessly and evenly." As Barrett found Watts the writer, so did Stephen Mahoney find Watts the lecturer: "Words flowed in an unending, shiningly lucid stream. He never looked at a note" (*Nation,* November 1, 1958).

Among the numerous universities at which Watts has been a guest lecturer since 1956 are Harvard, Cambridge (England), Columbia, Cornell, Chicago, Michigan State, Brandeis, Pennsylvania, Wesleyan, and California. He has also lectured at the Carl G. Jung Institute (Zurich), Massachusetts Institute of Technology, the New School for Social Research, Washington School of Psychiatry, various medical schools, and to the medical staffs of various state mental hospitals.

Since 1952 Watts has broadcast weekly half-hour talks for the Pacifica Foundation's station KPFA-FM in Berkeley, California. One series is entitled "Philosophy East and West." The programs, on tape, have subsequently been extended to KPFK-FM, Los Angeles, WBAI-FM, New York, and WGBH-FM, Boston. In 1959 and 1960 he did a series of twenty-six programs under the title "Eastern Wisdom and Modern Life" for the National Educational Television network. The series originated at station KQED in San Francisco. An additional thirteen programs under the same title were made at KQED and began to be presented on NBC-TV in New York City in November 1961.

Although identified popularly with Zen Buddhism, Watts has an equivalent interest in Buddhism more generally, Taoism, and Ve-danta. He said in late 1961: "More and more the center of my interest is shifting to the areas in which insights from these sources run parallel to certain Western sciences, and to the philosophy of science as a whole. Thus I am specially interested in the parallel between Taoist and Buddhist views of man and the 'field theory' of man as an organism-environment which is emerging ever more clearly in biology, ecology, social psychology, and biophysics." He regards the work of British biologist Joseph Needham as of major importance in the exploration of this parallel.

"I believe that the main assistance we can derive from Eastern man's experience," Watts has said, "is in methods for changing human consciousness so that the individual can actually *feel* his identity as an organism-environment (or man-universe), instead of a lonely ego sealed in a bag of skin." He sees many current developments in psychotherapy apparently moving in this direction. These include the work of Erich Fromm, Rollo May, the Gestalt therapists, A. H. Maslow at Brandeis University, Gregory Bateson at Stanford University, and the studies of Freud by L. L. Whyte and Norman O. Brown, as well as the work on constructive change of consciousness by pharmacological means. Watts' *Psychotherapy East and West* was published in 1961 by Pantheon.

Alan Watts is five feet seven inches tall, weighs 150 pounds, has blue eyes and brown, crew-cropped hair. He speaks with a British accent. Stephen Mahoney described his smile as "'shy, boyish." He has no political or religious affiliations. "In matters of this kind," he has said, "I am temperamentally not a joiner." He does, however, have membership in the American Oriental Society. His recreations are dancing, beachcombing, graphic arts, and cooking. Watts' marriage to Eleanor Everett on April 3, 1938 ended with divorce in April 1950. He has two children by that marriage, Joan and Ann. Since June 29, 1950, he has been married to the former Dorothy Marie DeWitt, a mathematician. They have five children: Tia, Mark, Richard, Lila, and Diane. "They ask the usual children's questions like 'Who made the world and who made me?'" a writer in *Life* (April 21, 1961) quoted Watts. "I ask them, 'Why use the word *made*, like a machine—why not use another word: *grew?*'"

Philip Wheelwright wrote of Watts in the *Sewanee Review* (summer 1953): "He is not advising that we shut off our looms and retire to a monastery or the banks of the Ganges. The wisdom of insecurity is not a way of evasion, but of carrying on wherever we happen to be stationed, without imagining that the burden of the world, or even of the next moment, is ours. It is a philosophy not of nihilism but of the reality of the present—always remembering that to be of the present is to be, and candidly know ourselves to be, on the crest of a breaking wave."

References

Life 50:88A+ Ap 21 '61 pors
Nation 187:311+ N 1 '58

Who's Who in the West (1960)

YAMASAKI, MINORU Dec. 1, 1912- American architect
Address: b. 1025 E. Maple Rd., Birmingham, Mich.; h. 3077 Livernois Rd., Troy, Mich.

Putting precast concrete to subtle and varied use, the American architect Minoru Yamasaki represents a trend away from the serried glass and steel boxes of the functional school toward buildings that give the people who use them

Joe Clark

MINORU YAMASAKI

"the delight of change and surprise." Yamasaki believes that in an age of technological chaos and monotony architecture should use technology to create habitations that put human lives in balance. "When people go into good buildings," Yamasaki says, "there should be serenity and delight."

Yamasaki manages his own firm of Minoru Yamasaki and Associates, which grew out of his partnership with Leinweber, Yamasaki & Hellmuth. Among the buildings he has designed are the American Concrete Institute building and the Reynolds Metals Company building, both in the Detroit metropolitan area, the United States Consulate General's office and headquarters at Kobe, Japan, and the American pavilion at the World Agricultural Fair, which opened in New Delhi, India in December 1959. Before he established his own enterprise, Yamasaki worked for Smith, Hinchman & Grylls, Raymond Loewy Associates, and other firms.

Minoru Yamasaki was born on December 1, 1912 in Seattle, Washington to John Tsunejiro Yamasaki, a purchasing agent, and Hana (Ito) Yamasaki, a pianist. He has a brother, Ken, who is a physician. Minoru attended Seattle's Garfield High School, graduating in 1929. He entered the University of Washington in Seattle and spent his summers working in Alaskan salmon canneries, where he earned $50 a month and lived on a diet of salmon and rice.

When his uncle, the architect Koken Ito, stopped in Seattle on his way back to Japan from Washington, D.C., and showed his teen-aged nephew the drawings for his project for the United States Embassy building in Tokyo, Minoru decided to become an architect. After receiving his Bachelor of Architecture degree from the University of Washington in 1934, he left Seattle, where his prospects, as a nisei, did not look bright, to seek his architectural career in New York City.

His first job in New York City was that of chinaware wrapper in the stock department of Morimura Brothers, importers. In 1935, during a week's vacation from the job, he volunteered his services to the New York architectural firm of Githens and Keally in drawing up competitive designs for the projected new Oregon State Capitol. When Githens and Keally won the competition, Yamasaki was given his first professional job as a designer for the firm, with which he remained from 1935 to 1937. Meanwhile (1935-36), he was doing graduate work and instructing in water color at New York University.

From 1937 to 1943 Yamasaki was designer, draftsman, and job captain with the New York firm of Shreve, Lamb & Harmon. While working as a designer for Harrison and Fouilhoix (1943-44) and for Raymond Loewy Associates (1944-45), he instructed in architectural design at Columbia University from 1943 to 1945. Yamasaki moved from New York to Michigan in 1945, when he accepted the position of chief architectural designer for the large Detroit office of Smith, Hinchman & Grylls. He remained with Smith, Hinchman & Grylls until 1949, when he entered into the partnership of Leinweber, Yamasaki & Hellmuth, which later became Yamasaki, Leinweber & Associates, and is now Minoru Yamasaki and Associates.

Yamasaki's principal achievements after he organized the partnership were the Urban Redevelopment Plan, St. Louis (1952), the Gratiot Urban Redevelopment Project, Detroit (1954), the University School, Grosse Point, Michigan (1954), and the Lambert Field-St. Louis Municipal Airport Terminal building (1955). His design for the airport terminal building, which utilized barrel-vaulted, poured concrete shell forms, was widely praised in architectural journals and won him the American Institute of Architects' first honor award in 1956.

His nearly fatal attack of ulcers in 1954 constituted a watershed in Yamasaki's career. He attributed his illness to the pressure of his work and to inferiority feelings implanted deeply in him as a nisei child on the West Coast and as a young man during World War II. (The nisei were identified with the stereotyped Japanese of American war propaganda and treated accordingly.) "After the airport and my ulcer," he reflected in an article for the *Architectural Forum* (August 1958), "I realized there's a danger of an architect getting involved in too many things for the sake of society. He's tempted to forget his real job is beauty." As he recovered from his illness he turned away more and more from big projects like airports and urban redevelopments and more toward smaller projects like the Filburg House, designed as a private bachelor's residence, at Comox on Vancouver Island in Canada, or groups of single projects like the layout of the new Wayne State University campus. In 1959 he told an interviewer for the *Architectural Forum* (July 1959): "As I grow older in life I find that it is really best to concentrate on a smaller area."

Convalescence provided Yamasaki with the leisure for a visit to Japan, where the use of light and shadow and the relating of building to garden in architecture impressed him and turned him more than ever against the architecture of glass or steel boxes. The Japanese impact brought to full flower his ideas about delight and serenity in architecture and about the need, as he has described it, to consider "what happens to a human being as he goes from space to space, and to provide the delight of change and surprise for him."

"Delight," Yamasaki told a meeting of architects in June 1959, "would include the play of sun and shadow, a use of texture in materials to give pleasure, and the silhouetting of a building against the sky." The distinctive material that he uses to compass these ends is precast concrete, which, he feels, gives the architect more freedom in controlling the building, just as the conventional wall system forces him to depend on the manufacturer's stock.

Several structures demonstrate the trend of Yamasaki's work in the latter half of the 1950's. One of them is the Reynolds Metals Company building on the outskirts of Detroit, which has been described by its owners as "a jewel on stilts." Another is the United States Consulate General's office and headquarters at Kobe, Japan, rimmed with glass-fiber shades and set in a garden, which won the Japan Architectural Institute's highest design award in 1957. Yet another is the American Concrete Institute office building in Detroit, roofed with folded concrete and walled with grilled concrete, which won *Progressive Architecture*'s highest award in the commerce division in 1957. Others include the American pavilion at the World Agricultural Fair in New Delhi, India, composed of multiple gold domes perched each on a column amid pools of water, and the Macgregor Memorial Community Conference Center at Wayne University, using angular folded concrete forms, which won the first honor award of the Ameri-

can Institute of Architects in 1959. The Macgregor Conference Center's pool of water, integral to the design, and its podium, environment-controlling wall, and skylighted central hall are features that are common to many buildings designed by Yamasaki.

The Michigan Consolidated Gas Company building, designed by Yamasaki at the close of the 1950's, has walls of precast concrete and narrow vertical windows and rises thirty stories on one side of Detroit's new Civic Center. Other buildings designed by Minoru Yamasaki include the Lincoln Elementary School in Livonia, Michigan, the Franklin Junior High School in Wayne, Michigan, and the Feld Clinic in Detroit.

Frequently called upon to lecture, Yamasaki has addressed the Royal Architectural Institute of Canada and the Royal Institute of British Architects, among other groups. He has contributed articles to such journals as the *Architectural Record*, the *Architectural Forum*, and *Progressive Architecture*.

Minoru Yamasaki married Teruko Hirashiki on November 5, 1941. They have three children: Carol, Taro, and Kim. The Yamasaki home at Troy, Michigan, is a remodeled, 130-year-old farmhouse. Yamasaki, called "Yama" by his friends, is five feet five inches tall, weighs 130 pounds, has brown hair, and has been described as looking "as deceptively serene as a sunning panther" (*Architectural Forum*, August 1958). Once a very active liberal Democrat and participant in Japanese-American affairs, he now restricts his participation in these areas for fear of scattering his energies. He received the Gold Medal award of the Detroit chapter of the American Institute of Architects in 1959. In 1960 he was given a certificate of fellowship from the American Institute of Architects, an honorary degree by Wayne University, the Alumnus Summa Laude Dignatus award by the University of Washington, and a fellowship in fine arts and literature by the American Academy of Arts and Sciences in Boston.

References

Arch Forum 109:84+ Ag '58
Time 74:81+ S 14 '59 por

American Architects' Directory (1958)
Who's Who in America, 1960-61

CURRENT BIOGRAPHY—VOL. 23. NOS. 1-3

This is the index to the January-March 1962 issues. For the index to the 1961 biographies, see December 1961 issue or 1961 Yearbook. For the index to 1940-1950 biographies, see 1950 Yearbook. For 1951-1960 index, see 1960 Yearbook.

CURRENT BIOGRAPHY

APRIL 1962
VOL. 23   NO. 4

Editor: Charles Moritz

PUBLISHED BY THE H. W. WILSON COMPANY, 950 UNIVERSITY AVE., NEW YORK

CONTENTS

ABOUT THIS PUBLICATION

Current Biography (published every month except August) presents articles on people who are prominent in the news—in national and international affairs, the sciences, the arts, labor, and industry. Sources of information are newspapers, magazines, books, and, in some cases, the biographees themselves. It should be pointed out, however, that these are objective rather than authorized biographies. At the end of the year the articles in the monthly issues are cumulated in one alphabet, revised, and printed in a single volume known as *Current Biography Yearbook.*

Authorities for biographees' full names, with some exceptions, are the bibliographical publications of The Wilson Company. When a biographee prefers a certain name form, that is indicated in the heading of the article: for example, MACMILLAN, (MAURICE) HAROLD means that he is usually referred to as HAROLD MACMILLAN. When a professional name is used in the heading, as, for example, GLENN FORD, the real name, in this case GWYLLYN SAMUEL NEWTON FORD, appears in the article itself.

The heading of each article includes the pronunciation of the name if it is unusual, date of birth (if obtainable), and occupation. The article is supplemented by a list of references to sources of *biographical* information, in two alphabets: (1) newspapers and periodicals and (2) books.

References to newspapers and periodicals are listed in abbreviated form; for example, "Sat Eve Post 217:14+ S 30 '44 por" means *Saturday Evening Post,* volume 217, pages 14 ff, September 30, 1944, with portrait. For full names, see the section "Periodical and Newspaper Designations," which is included in all *Current Biography* Yearbooks and in the January issue each year. Obituary notices appear for persons whose biographies have been published in *Current Biography.*

An index to names that have appeared this year is to be found at the back of this issue.

NOTE: Authors whose biographies do not appear in *Current Biography* may usually be found in *Twentieth Century Authors*, Kunitz & Haycraft, 1942, H. W. Wilson Company, or in the FIRST SUPPLEMENT (1955). Authors of books for young people are included in *The Junior Book of Authors* (Second Edition, Revised) edited by Kunitz & Haycraft, 1951, H. W. Wilson Company. Musicians whose biographies do not appear in *Current Biography* may usually be found in *Living Musicians,* compiled and edited by David Ewen, 1940, H. W. Wilson Company, or in its FIRST SUPPLEMENT (1957).

KEY TO PRONUNCIATION

ā	āle	N	Not pronounced, but indicates the nasal tone of the preceding vowel, as in the French *bon* (bôN).	û	ûrn; French eu, as in *jeu* (zhû); German ö, oe, as in *schön* (shûn), *Goethe* (gû′tĕ)
â	câre				
ă	ădd				
ȧ	ȧccount				
ä	ärm				
à	àsk				
ȧ	sofȧ	ō	ōld	ŭ	tŭb
		ô	ôrb	ŭ	circŭs
ē	ēve	ŏ	ŏdd	ü	Pronounced approximately as ē, with rounded lips: French u, as in *menu* (mē-nü); German ü, as in *grün*
ĕ	ĕnd	oi	oil		
ē	makēr	o͞o	o͞oze		
		o͝o	fo͝ot		
g	go	ou	out		
ī	īce				
ĭ	ĭll	*th*	*then*	zh	azure
		th	thin	′ =	main accent
κ	German ch as in *ich* (ĭκ)	ū	cūbe	″ =	secondary accent

CURRENT BIOGRAPHY

APRIL 1962

BARBER, CARL JEROME *See* Barber, Jerry

BARBER, JERRY Apr. 25, 1916- Golfer

Address: b. Wilshire Country Club, 301 N. Rossmore Ave., Los Angeles 4, Calif; h. 4748 Vineta Ave., La Canada, Calif.

The winner of the 1961 Professional Golfers Association championship—one of golf's most coveted titles—is diminutive Jerry Barber, who, in his mid-forties, became the oldest golfer ever to win this title. Success has come late in life to Barber. Although he has played golf since childhood, he did not begin playing full-time professional tournament golf until 1954. Dedicated to a scientific approach to golfing, Barber frequently uses a tape measure on the course. A believer in physical culture, he has developed a tremendous drive through vigorous exercise. His finish in the 1961 Professional Golfers Association tournament has been described as one of the greatest performances in putting in the history of professional golf.

Carl Jerome Barber was born on April 25, 1916 in Woodson, Illinois, one of nine children of Alfred J. Barber, a farmer, and Hettie Ellen (Ledferd) Barber. He has two brothers and six sisters. The Barber home was close to the Nichols Park public golf course in nearby Jacksonville, where Jerry began to caddy at the age of six, along with his two older brothers. The Barber boys constructed a four-hole golf course in the family orchard, using buried tomato cans as cups. Barber recalls that he liked the game, and that at this early age he dreamed of becoming a professional golfer. He went to the South Jacksonville Primary School, and then attended Jacksonville High School, where he was active in public speaking. He graduated in 1934.

After he graduated from high school, Barber played golf during the day and worked ten hours a night as a printer. In 1940 he began to play professional golf. In 1942 he went to work in a war plant and remained there until April 1945, when he was drafted into the United States Army. He was discharged with the rank of corporal in July 1946. Back in civilian life Barber opened a driving range in Los Angeles and continued to play practice rounds on local courses, using old golf balls so that his shots would feel livelier in tournaments.

Until 1947 Barber, with a wife and children to support, had been unable to set aside enough money for a try at playing golf in major tournaments. That year, however, Don McCallister, an amateur golfer from Los Angeles, developed a full-fingered and skin-tight golf glove.

JERRY BARBER

He took Barber in as a partner and the business soon proved a success. Buoyed by that comparatively small but steady income, Barber went on tour. "My friends told me I was a knothead," Barber recalled in an interview with Ray Cave. "They all said good luck, but not a one said he thought I would make good" (*Sports Illustrated,* July 25, 1960).

For the next six years Barber played part-time tournament golf without much success. In 1954, however, he won the All American Open tournament in Chicago, and was named to the Ryder Cup team. His winnings for that year totaled about $18,000. Also in 1954 he joined the Spalding golf consultant staff and became the full-time professional at the Wilshire Country Club in Los Angeles, a position he still holds.

Although Barber has maintained that it is "almost impossible to be a club pro and play the circuit too," he divides his time between the Wilshire Country Club and his professional tours, and he spends only about five to seven months of the year on the road. Working a sixty-hour week when he is on his home course, Barber teaches his students that the position of the hands and the strength of the grip are the most important factors in the swing. He also stresses the importance of strengthening the left hand.

(Continued next page)

BARBER, JERRY—*Continued*

In the mid-1950's Barber embarked on a program of physical conditioning. Each morning and evening he would complete between fifty and sixty pushups. He also used a ten-pound weight tied to a broom handle by a three-pound rope that he rolled up and down to develop his forearms. "If I had known how important conditioning is," Barber explains, "I would have started exercising years ago." Barber credits these exercises with developing him into a powerful golfer who can drive a ball as far as professional golfers of larger physical stature. In 1955 Barber started another scientific approach to the game. He began making notations of his shots in tournament practice rounds, going so far as to pace off the distance to landmarks on each hole, then sketching the course to see how it could best be played.

As a full-time professional player, Barber occasionally showed flashes of winning form. But for the most part he was nothing more than a journeyman golfer, ranked far below the top of his profession. In 1959 at the Professional Golfers Association tournament in Minneapolis it looked as if Barber were about to win his first major title. But after leading most of the way he dropped into a tie for second place behind Bob Rosburg. Some persons attributed his defeat to middle age, but Barber denied it. "When I failed to win, after leading until the last few holes, it was not because I was tired but because of errors of commission," Barber explained after the tournament.

Barber had gone without a tournament victory of major proportions since 1954, when in January 1960 he won the Yorba Linda Open by sinking a twelve-foot putt on the final hole. This triumph earned him an invitation to the lucrative Tournament of Champions at Las Vegas. He won the first prize of $10,000 by shooting consecutive rounds of 69-66-66-67 for a total of 268, four strokes better than runner-up Jay Hebert. Also in 1960 Barber lost the De Soto Lakes Open to Sam Snead by one stroke, finished second at the 500 Festival Open at Indianapolis, and had the opportunity to win the National Open until he fell behind at the twelfth hole. His total winnings for 1960 were slightly more than $34,000.

At the Professional Golfers Association championship tournament at Olympia Fields, Illinois in July 1961, Barber was regarded as an outsider for the title. During the first half of the year he had won only the Azalea Open, and his total earnings stood just above $8,000. In his first round at Olympia Fields Barber shot a 69 and followed it up with an even more spectacular 67 for a two-stroke lead over Don January at the halfway point. Barber and January were in the same foursome as they started out to play the final 36 holes in morning and afternoon rounds. January shot a 67 over the first 18 holes while Barber slipped to a 71. Going into the final round January held a two-stroke lead.

"The golf that followed," reported Alfred Wright in *Sports Illustrated* (August 7, 1961), "between two such opposite personalities as Barber and January won't be soon forgotten by the thousands who slipped and slithered through the mud in pursuit." With only four holes to play January maintained a four-stroke lead. On the 16th hole, he shot a five while Barber curled in a 20-foot putt for a birdie three. Both had pars on the 17th, but Barber had to sink a 40-foot putt to stay in contention. On the 18th and final hole January took a five. Barber dropped in a 60-foot putt for a three to tie January at 277. In the playoff round for the $11,000 first prize on the following day—something of an anticlimax—Barber shot a 67 and January a 68. Barber, talking of his three great putts on the final three holes of regulation play, commented: "I made up my mind I would never give up. Golf is a funny game. Even when I was so far behind at the end, I kept reminding myself that something would happen—maybe the sky would fall in."

Winning the Professional Golfers Association tournament earned Barber a place on the Ryder Cup team. He was elected captain by his fellow professionals and was instrumental in leading the Americans to victory over the British in October 1961. To cap a momentous year, Barber was voted player of the year for 1961 in a national poll of Professional Golfers Association membership and sportswriters. On January 23, 1962 he was one of several golfers honored at a dinner given by the Metropolitan Golf Writers Association.

On Christmas Eve in 1939 Jerry Barber married Lucile Evelyn Gorman. They have five children: Tom, Nancy, the twins Sally and Sandra, and Roger. The family home is in La Canada, California, a suburb of Los Angeles. Jerry Barber is five feet five inches tall, weighs 137 pounds, and has brown eyes and thinning brown hair. His face is deeply lined and he wears glasses. While playing, he generally wears a cap to conceal his baldness. He resents being referred to as "small," and he is noted for his sharp and dry wit.

Barber is a Methodist and a Republican. He belongs to the National Professional Golfers Association and he writes articles from time to time for golfing magazines. He has appeared in golfing exhibitions over television. Football and baseball are his favorite spectator sports. A nonsmoker and nondrinker, he once smashed a bottle of whiskey that he had won in a minor tournament. He tries to fire his children with his own determination. Once, while watching his oldest son, Tom, hit some practice balls, Barber advised him to get his hands higher on the backswing. "I can't, Dad," the boy answered. Barber replied: "Tell me you *haven't,* son, or tell me you *don't,* but never, never tell me that you *can't.*"

References

N Y World-Telegram Mag p3 Ag 19 '61
   pors
Sports Illus 13:40+ Jl 25 '60 pors

BISHOP, JOEY Feb. 3, 1919- Comedian

Address: b. Bellmar Enterprises, Desilu-Cahuenga Studios, 846 N. Cahuenga Blvd., Hollywood 39, Calif.

Comedian Joey Bishop spent more than twenty years on the way up from the obscurity of a comic in burlesque to master of ceremonies at the Democratic party's gala $100-a-plate celebration in Washington, D.C. on the eve of President John F. Kennedy's inauguration in January 1961. During his long climb to stardom in night clubs, television, and motion pictures, Bishop never tried to "fracture" his listeners with the sharpness of his wit; he tells no "sick" jokes and makes no comments on the foibles of human society. He has neither capitalized on his Jewishness by portraying Jewish characters nor avoided references to it in seeking broader acceptance. He has been described by a writer for *Time* (February 22, 1960) as a "sad-faced funnyman whose effortless humor seems spontaneous but is the product of endless preparation."

Joey Bishop was born Joseph Abraham Gottlieb on February 3, 1919, in the Bronx in New York City. He is the youngest of five children of Jacob and Anna (Siegel) Gottlieb, who had immigrated to the United States from Central Europe. At birth he weighed only three pounds, and was, as he has later said, the smallest baby ever born in Fordham Hospital. When Joey was three months old he moved with his parents, his brothers Morris and Freddie, and his sisters Claire and Betty to South Philadelphia, a section that also gave Mario Lanza, Eddie Fisher, and Fabian to the entertainment world. His father, helped out by other members of the family, ran a bicycle shop and also worked as a machinist. "My mother would ask the people who rented bikes, 'What's your name?' and scribble in the book," Joey Bishop has recalled. "Who knew she couldn't write English?" Although the times were bad the family atmosphere at home was warm and encouraging to a youngster who never wanted to be anything but an entertainer. Joey's father played the ocarina and taught his son Yiddish songs. The boy learned to do imitations, to tap-dance, and to play the banjo and mandolin. The first thing he ever remembers buying for himself was a false nose.

Although he was a bright pupil, and was elected head of the student council and vice-president of his graduation class at Furness Junior High School, Joey Bishop did not distinguish himself as a scholar. "In kindergarten I flunked sandpile," he has said. More interested in show business than in academic studies, he frequented the stage door entrance of the Earle Theatre in Philadelphia, waiting for vaudeville celebrities such as Benny Davis or Ted Lewis. In 1936 he won the first prize of three dollars in an amateur show for his imitations of Joe Penner, George Arliss, and Jimmy Durante. In the same year he ended his formal education, dropping out of South Philadelphia High School after two and a half years. Occasionally Joey helped out in

Frank Liberman

JOEY BISHOP

his parents' bicycle shop. He was employed for a time at Gimbel's department store, carried ice, and worked in a restaurant and in a candle factory.

In 1938 Joey Bishop teamed up with two other boys—Reisman and Spector—in a comedy act that they had once rehearsed in a Jewish neighborhood house in Philadelphia. The trio was booked into night clubs in New Jersey and Pennsylvania and its members, taking on the surname of Glenn Bishop, a Negro boy who drove them to their engagements, called themselves the Bishop Brothers. They toured the Eastern burlesque circuit, played vaudeville, and performed in night clubs and at summer resorts in the Catskill mountains. When Reisman and Spector were drafted into the Army, Joey Bishop was on his own. He received his start as a single entertainer in a club called El Dumpo in Cleveland. "I was nervous at first," he recalled in an interview with Arthur Steuer for *Esquire* (September 1961). "Rummy [Spector] had always supplied the punch lines, but as soon as I walked out there I knew it was going to be all right. I felt free, relaxed."

According to Robert De Roos, writing in *TV Guide* (December 2, 1961), Bishop "developed his offhand approach and became master of the throwaway line" in the noise of night clubs like El Dumpo. He also came to realize that a comedian's attitude is more important than his lines. "Taste is the big thing," he told Florence Fletcher in an interview for *Cue* (August 12, 1961), "taste and honesty. Then acceptance of your style and material will come." Bishop remained at El Dumpo for eight months until he too was drafted into the Army in April 1942. During his three and a half years with Special Services he rose to

BISHOP, JOEY—*Continued*

the rank of sergeant, and he ended his military service as recreation director at Fort Sam Houston, Texas.

Upon his discharge from the Army in September 1945 Bishop temporarily settled in San Antonio, Texas with his wife, and resumed his career as a night club comedian. Through the William Morris Agency, Inc., he obtained his first New York booking at the Greenwich Village Inn, where he began to acquire a reputation as a promising comic. Five years later, in 1952, when he was earning $1,000 a week at the Latin Quarter in New York, Frank Sinatra saw his performance and asked him to join his act at Bill Miller's Riviera in Fort Lee, New Jersey.

The encounter with Sinatra marked a turning point in Joey Bishop's career. He often accompanied Sinatra on his tours, and became a full-fledged member of the Sinatra "Clan," along with Dean Martin, Peter Lawford, Sammy Davis, Jr., and others. Bishop appeared in two of Sinatra's films, *Ocean's 11* (Warner Brothers, 1960) and *Sergeants 3* (United Artists, 1961). Earlier he had played several motion picture roles. In 1958 he appeared in the Warner Brothers productions *The Deep Six, Onionhead,* and *The Naked and the Dead* ("I played both parts," he has remarked), and in 1960 he briefly turned up in the Columbia production *Pepe,* starring Cantinflas.

Another major break for Bishop was his first appearance on the Jack Paar show on NBC-TV, where his wit as an ad libber made him a frequent guest and occasional pinch hitter for Paar. He became a familiar figure to millions of TV viewers. On TV he has also appeared with Perry Como, Ed Sullivan, Dinah Shore, and on the panel of *What's My Line* on CBS-TV. When Bennett Cerf, a regular panelist on the show, took only one guess to identify an eighty-four-year-old lady as a store detective, Joey ad libbed: "That doesn't say much for Bennett that he can spot a detective so quickly."

A significant development in Bishop's career was his decision in 1958 to give up forty weeks of night club bookings at nearly $5,000 per week and take a chance on an untried TV show, *Keep Talking,* on CBS-TV, that paid only one-fifth of that sum but offered him the chance to widen his range as a performer and to emerge as a comic personality. This personality has been described by Arthur Steuer in *Esquire* (September 1961) as that of "an eager, naïve, slightly awestruck yokel with whom the mass-communicated audience can sympathize." Bishop projects it in his own TV series, the *Joey Bishop Show,* which made its debut over NBC-TV on September 20, 1961. Although Harriet Van Horne characterized the first program of the series as "the familiar situation comedy, Hollywood style," she added: "None of this is of great consequence—because Joey Bishop is wonderful. He's wonderful when he has a funny line . . . and oddly endearing when he has a bad one. When silent he manages to look as if he were *thinking* something funny" (New York *World-Telegram and Sun,*

September 21, 1961). *Variety* reported on February 21, 1962 that the future status of the *Joey Bishop Show* was uncertain.

Bishop is highly esteemed by his fellow comedians. One of them—Jack Benny—has called him "the brightest young comedian today." In late 1960 the Friars Club gave Bishop a testimonial dinner. Both major political parties have recognized his talents. In July 1960 the office of Vice-President Richard M. Nixon invited Bishop to take part in the festivities accompanying the Republican National Convention, but Bishop politely turned down the bid because, as he told Marie Torre of the New York *Herald Tribune* (July 19, 1960), he was "a Kennedy man." Reportedly President John F. Kennedy first met Bishop in February 1960 and told him that for years he had been a Bishop fan. According to Jay Lewis (*Variety,* March 1, 1961), the President seemed genuinely amused when Bishop served as substitute master of ceremonies for Danny Thomas at the White House correspondents' dinner in Washington on February 25, 1961.

On January 14, 1941 Joey Bishop married Sylvia Ruzga. With their one son, Larry, the Bishops live in a comfortable brick home in Englewood, New Jersey. Bishop is a member of Temple Emanu-El in New York City. He served as fund-raising chairman of the National Cystic Fibrosis Research Foundation for 1961 and he has received a citation from Pope John XXIII for his work in behalf of Boys Towns of Italy. Standing at five feet nine and one half inches and weighing 160 pounds, Bishop has brown hair and brown eyes, and has been described by Bob Lardine as "a little, skinny, sallow guy with the closest crew-cut this side of Yul Brynner" (New York *Sunday News Magazine,* July 23, 1961). "I enjoy swimming and riding. But basically I'm a lazy bum," Bishop told Florence Fletcher of *Cue* (August 12, 1961). An excellent golfer, he plays regularly with fellow comedians Buddy Hackett, Dick Shawn, and Phil Foster at a golf club near his Englewood home. Each of the four comedians owns one-twentieth of the golf club.

To Kay Gardella of the New York *Sunday News,* (May 14, 1961), Joey Bishop explained his philosophy of comedy. "It's a lot more important to be known as a great human being and a so-so comic than be known as a great comic and not be accepted by the audiences as a human being," he told her. "If you depend solely on humor, you're in trouble, for the simple truth is that no one can be that funny every week. On the other hand, if you've built up public acceptance for yourself as a human being and for the character you're portraying, you don't have the need to be successfully funny every week and you'll last a lot longer."

References

Am W p10 S 17 '61 pors
Cue 30:10+ Ag 12 '61 por
Esquire 56:111+ S '61 por
N Y Times Mag p12+ Ja 1 '61 pors
N Y World-Telegram Mag p3 Je 4 '60 por

CALVIN, MELVIN Apr. 8, 1911- Chemist; university professor

Address: b. Dept. of Chemistry, University of California, Berkeley, Calif.; h. 2683 Buena Vista Way, Berkeley 8, Calif.

For his research into carbon-dioxide assimilation in plants and for establishing the sequence of chemical reactions involved in plant photosynthesis, Dr. Melvin Calvin received the 1961 Nobel Prize in Chemistry. Dr. Calvin, a professor at the University of California in Berkeley, directs the bio-organic chemistry group at the Lawrence Radiation Laboratory. Using radioactive carbon, he traced the complete path of carbon dioxide through the complex series of intermediate compounds to the end product: carbohydrates, fats and proteins, the basic foods for man and animals.

Although Dr. Calvin has made his major contribution to advanced science in the field of photosynthesis, he also has a distinguished record of accomplishment in the fields of physical chemistry, physical organic theory, and bio-organic chemistry. His most recent discovery suggests that nucleic-acid particles, precursor components of living molecules, are present in meteors from space, indicating that conditions are favorable for the development and existence of life on other planets.

Born on April 8, 1911 in St. Paul, Minnesota, Melvin Calvin is the son of Elias Calvin and the former Rose I. Hervitz. He was educated in the public schools and received a Bachelor of Science degree in 1931 from the Michigan College of Mining and Technology. As a graduate student at the University of Minnesota, Calvin showed an interest in a wide range of subjects and he worked in several fields of physical and organic chemistry research. For his doctoral dissertation he investigated the electron affinity of iodine and bromine.

After receiving the Ph.D. degree in 1935, Calvin was appointed a Rockefeller Foundation Fellow. He spent two years at the University of Manchester in England, doing postgraduate work on hydrogen paramagnetic-conversion and catalysis with Professor Michael Polanyi. Upon his return to the United States in 1937, Calvin was named an instructor in the chemistry department of the University of California at Berkeley. During these early years he also served as assistant to Professor G. N. Lewis, then dean of the college of chemistry. They conducted experiments on the relationship of electronic structure to the color of organic compounds. Calvin next worked in physical organic chemistry and his text on this subject has been credited with exercising a significant influence on modern theory.

Appointed an assistant professor in 1941, just before the outbreak of World War II, Dr. Calvin maintained a schedule of teaching combined with military research. Until the end of the war he was a member of a scientific team working on a National Defense Research Council contract (1941-44) and a Manhattan District project (1944-45). Calvin's research on oxygen-carrying chelate compounds, organic substances

Univ. of California

MELVIN CALVIN

having atoms of metal attached to them, was an important contribution to the war effort. The chemist provided a simple method of obtaining oxygen from the air for industrial purposes in much the same way as the human body takes oxygen into the blood. This process was used in welding and other industrial operations in the South Pacific during the war when regular supplies of oxygen were not available.

Dr. Calvin was named an associate professor in 1945 and two years later he was advanced to the rank of full professor. Since 1946 he has directed the bio-organic chemistry group at the Lawrence Radiation Laboratory at Berkeley. Immediately after World War II he began to apply his knowledge of radioactive tracers to unravel the highly complicated chemical steps in photosynthesis. This is the process in which chlorophyll, the green pigment in plants, uses light energy from the sun, carbon dioxide, and water to form the energy substances basic to life-sugars, proteins, fats, and carbohydrates. Photosynthesis is one of the fundamental processes of nature without which no life could exist, yet its intermediate chemical steps were a complete mystery. There had been no way to learn what happened between the intake of the simple materials and the formation of the finished energy compounds.

Using the green alga Chlorella in a suspension of water under a constant light, Dr. Calvin introduced carbon dioxide containing a known quantity of radioactive carbon 14. He traced the tagged carbon atoms from the moment carbon dioxide entered the plant through its conversion into various substances. Calvin spotted the chemical steps by making extracts of the plant at different stages of its growth, measuring the radioactivity and examining its contents. He was able to identify eleven intermediate compounds created in the plant, step

CALVIN, MELVIN—*Continued*

by step, between the intake of the simple ingredients and the formation of energy compounds. The only problem remaining is the question of how the sun's energy is converted to the form required to operate the intermediate chemical cycle.

Further research by Dr. Calvin revealed that chlorophyll has a phosphorescent quality enabling it to hold on to energy in the form of sunlight long enough for the energy to be transformed into sugars and other substances. The phosphorescence lasts about a tenth of a second, allowing enough time for the conversion process and the buildup of a reservoir of chemical energy so that photosynthesis can be carried on in the dark.

During the late 1950's Dr. Calvin devised ways of tracing the path of oxygen in the photosynthetic process. He and his staff bombarded the heavy isotopes of oxygen with protons and neutrons, making the oxygen radioactive and detectable. More recently, experiments conducted in Dr. Calvin's laboratory proved that chlorophyll, arranged in flat disc-like plates, captures light energy by the layer to layer method, operating very much like electronic solar batteries. Dr. Calvin has suggested that it may be possible to improve on the natural processes by which solar energy is turned into chemical energy and to duplicate photosynthesis in the laboratory.

When the 1961 Nobel Prize in Chemistry was bestowed on Dr. Calvin, the United States approached a monopoly of laureates in science. Dr. Calvin was the eleventh member of the University of California faculty to attain this distinction and the fourteenth American to win the prize in chemistry. His award carried a cash value of $48,300.

A recognized authority in theoretical organic chemistry, photochemistry, and biochemistry as well as photosynthesis, Dr. Calvin has published several hundred papers in scientific journals. In collaboration with his staff he wrote *The Theory of Organic Chemistry* (Prentice-Hall, 1941), *Isotopic Carbon* (Wiley, 1949) and *Chemistry of the Chelate Compounds* (Prentice-Hall, 1949). His most important contribution is perhaps his *Path of Carbon in Photosynthesis* (Prentice-Hall, 1957).

Widely honored for his achievements, Professor Calvin has received the Sugar Research Foundation Prize, the American Chemical Society Award for Nuclear Application in Chemistry, and the Research Corporation Award. He is a medalist of the British Chemical Society and the Northeastern and New York sections of the American Chemical Society. Honorary degrees have been conferred on Dr. Calvin by his alma mater, the University of Nottingham, Oxford University, and Northwestern. The University of Minnesota gave him its Outstanding Achievement Award. He is a member of Sigma Xi, Phi Lambda Upsilon, and Tau Beta Pi honoraries. He has been invited to lecture at principal colleges and universities throughout the United States and before scientific bodies.

The organizations with which Dr. Calvin is affiliated include the National Academy of Sciences, the American Academy of Arts and Sciences, American Philosophical Society, New York Academy of Sciences, Faraday Society, and American Society of Plant Physiologists. He is a Fellow of the American Physical Society and has served as an officer of the American Association for the Advancement of Science and the American Chemical Society. He is a foreign member of scientific societies in Great Britain, Scandinavia, and the Netherlands.

Dr. Calvin served as a member of the United States delegation to the International Conference on Peaceful Uses of Atomic Energy in Geneva in 1955 and supervised the design of a photosynthesis exhibit for the second conference in 1958. He is a member of the committee on bio-astronautics of the National Research Council and of the United States national committee for international union of biochemistry. Since 1960 Dr. Calvin has been an adviser to the National Aeronautics and Space Administration.

A spontaneous and amiable manner masks Dr. Calvin's seriousness of purpose and intense dedication to his work. He is balding and slightly built and has alert brown eyes. Dr. Calvin talks about politics, sports, and science in a spate of words that he usually punctuates with peals of laughter. He enjoys lunching with friends on the faculty, but his heavy schedule leaves little time for other recreations. He teaches, makes the rounds of his laboratories on campus, and reads extensively in his field and in the related areas of bacteriology, general systems theory, biophysics, and space science. He and his wife, the former Marie Genevieve Jemtegaard, whom he married in 1942, are devoting much of their leisure time to converting an old chicken ranch into a summer home for themselves and their three children.

References

N Y Herald Tribune p23 N 3 '61
N Y Times p24 N 3 '61
American Men of Science 10th ed (1960)
International Who's Who, 1961
Who's Who in America, 1960-61

CARROLL, JOSEPH F(RANCIS) Mar. 19. 1910- United States Air Force Officer; United States government official

Address: b. The Pentagon, Washington 25, D.C.

The first director of the Defense Intelligence Agency is Lieutenant General Joseph F. Carroll of the United States Air Force. The agency was organized to perform intelligence functions previously discharged separately by the Army, Navy, and Air Force. Its establishment is part of a overhaul of intelligence operations ordered by President John F. Kennedy following the ill-fated Cuban invasion attempt of April 1961.

Carroll has served the United States government since 1940, when he became a special agent of the Federal Bureau of Investigation. He entered the United States Air Force late in 1947 to head its Office of Special Investigations, and later became deputy inspector general for security. In 1958, 1959, and 1960 he served with the

United States Air Forces in Europe, first as a deputy commander and then as Chief of Staff. He was Inspector General of the Air Force from February 1960 until he was installed as head of the Defense Intelligence Agency on September 12, 1961.

Joseph Francis Carroll was born in Chicago on March 19, 1910 to James Michael and Sara (Kane) Carroll. In 1929 he entered St. Mary's College in Mundelein, Illinois, where he received his B.A. degree in 1933. He then went to work for the meat-packing firm of Swift & Company in Chicago and remained there until 1940, rising to the position of assistant sales manager. In the meantime, in 1936, he entered the law school of Loyola University in Chicago, where he won the Chief Justice White scholarship award and received the J.D. degree in 1940. He was admitted to the Illinois bar in the same year.

In October 1940 Carroll joined the staff of the Federal Bureau of Investigation, and for the next four years he worked as a special agent with its offices in Memphis and Knoxville, Tennessee, and in Chicago. In May 1944 he was transferred to the Washington, D.C. headquarters of the FBI, where he served, successively, as supervisor of bank robbery and kidnapping investigations, chief of the criminal section, and first assistant to the assistant director in charge of the general investigations and accounting division.

At the end of World War II the government was faced with the problem of disposing of war surplus property that had been distributed all over the world. In September 1945, upon special request of the surplus property administrator, Carroll was lent by the Department of Justice to the Surplus Property Administration (which became the War Assets Administration in March 1946). In this assignment he organized, and served as director of, the compliance enforcement division, and directed all investigative activity associated with the disposal of surplus property. In May 1947 Carroll returned to the FBI as an administrative assistant to the director, J. Edgar Hoover, and served as inspector in charge of fraud and accounting matters.

When the Air Force was established in September 1947 as a separate department under the provisions of the National Security Act, Carroll was lent to the services by FBI director J. Edgar Hoover, at the request of Air Force Secretary W. Stuart Symington, to organize and direct an Air Force security and inquiry division. Since this function was defined as a military operation, Carroll was commissioned, in January 1948, with the temporary rank of colonel in the Air Force Reserve. Called to active duty in May 1948, he was advanced to the temporary rank of brigadier general. He subsequently established and organized the Office of Special Investigations, and served as the first director of this centrally directed investigative agency, establishing district offices to service the various air commands in the United States, and furnishing trained specialists for the conduct of special investigations on a world-wide scale. He was promoted to the temporary rank of major general on August 11, 1950.

LIEUT. GEN. JOSEPH F. CARROLL

On September 6, 1950 Carroll was appointed deputy inspector general for security. In this capacity he was responsible for the safeguarding and physical protection of Air Force installations and activities against sabotage, espionage, and other dangers, and for the administering of all security plans and policies for the Air Force. He also directed the office of the provost marshal, and continued to head the Office of Special Investigations. Following the dismissal by the Air Force in 1953 of part of its civilian and military personnel as security risks, Carroll expressed the view that Communists should not be allowed to serve as officers or airmen. He added, however, that precautions should be taken to prevent "a loophole whereby anyone by merely asserting Communist affiliations may escape performance of military service."

Special legislation was introduced in Congress in the spring of 1950 to authorize the appointment of Carroll and the aviator-explorer Bernt Balchen to the permanent rank of colonel in the regular Air Force. At the hearing by a House Armed Services subcommittee in July 1951 Secretary of the Air Force Thomas K. Finletter referred to Carroll as "the Mr. Hoover of the Air Force," and voiced high praise for an improved anti-sabotage protection program that had been put into effect largely through the efforts of Carroll. On January 29, 1952 Carroll received the permanent rank of colonel in the regular Air Force and on April 7, 1954 he was advanced to the permanent rank of brigadier general.

Carroll realized a long-standing ambition to take a combat command when he was appointed, on April 1, 1958, as deputy commander (rear) of the United States Air Forces in Europe. His duty station was Wiesbaden, Germany. In September 1959 he was again doing investigative work, having been assigned by NATO commander General Lauris Norstad to look into complaints of mistreatment by the Turkish

CARROLL, JOSEPH F.—*Continued*

police of four United States sergeants arrested in Izmir, Turkey on currency violation charges. The complaints of mistreatment appeared to have been unjustified, but in the investigation General Carroll's agents found evidence of what has been characterized as a million dollar black market currency operation in the Middle East, involving both Americans and Turks.

In November 1959 General Carroll was advanced to Chief of Staff, United Air Forces in Europe, a position he held until he returned to the United States to assume, on February 1, 1960, the duties of the Inspector General, USAF, with headquarters at Bolling Air Force Base, Washington, D.C. The Inspector General, USAF, acts as an adviser to the Chief of Staff and as a professional assistant to the Secretary of the Air Force. He evaluates and reports upon the state of combat readiness, efficiency, and discipline of the Air Force, investigates violations of public trust and related activities, directs the counterintelligence program, and establishes safety and security policies. The promotion of Carroll to the temporary rank of lieutenant general was announced by President Dwight D. Eisenhower on December 15, 1959 and, on confirmation by the Senate, became effective on February 1, 1960.

In September 1960 Carroll was assigned by the Defense Department to investigate the defection to the Soviet Union of two employees of the National Security Agency, Bernon F. Mitchell and William H. Martin. On May 10, 1961 Secretary of Defense Robert S. McNamara revealed that he had assigned General Carroll to deal with the problem of preventing leaks of information "of benefit to our potential enemies."

Defense Secretary McNamara designated Carroll on August 12, 1961 as director of the newly established Defense Intelligence Agency from a list of several candidates submitted by the Joint Chiefs of Staff of the three services. Carroll assumed office on September 12, 1961. The agency, which is expected eventually to have a staff of about 1,500, has a director who must be a military officer of at least three-star rank, a deputy director, and a chief of staff, as well as such subordinate units and facilities as may be assigned. The director is responsible to the Joint Chiefs of Staff; they in turn are responsible to the Secretary of Defense. A primary purpose of the agency, according to an official announcement, is "to bring about greater unity of effort in the intelligence activities of the separate services . . . to eliminate duplication and improve the over-all capacity of the Defense Department in gathering, assessing, and distributing intelligence of military value."

General Carroll received the Legion of Merit decoration on July 5, 1949, the Distinguished Service Medal on November 3, 1955, and an Oak Leaf Cluster to the Legion of Merit on March 28, 1958. He is a Roman Catholic, and is honorary president of the European chapter of the Military Council of Catholic Men. Joseph F. Carroll and Mary Ann Morrissey of Chicago were married on August 21, 1937 and have five sons, Joseph Francis, Jr., James Michael, Brian Patrick, Dennis Thomas, and Kevin Martin.

References

Gen Army 3:4 Ag '55 por
Air Force Register, 1961
American Catholic Who's Who, 1962 and 1963
Who's Who in America, 1960-61

CHAVCHAVADZE, GEORGE Apr. 30, 1904-Feb. 5, 1962 Concert pianist; composer; expatriate Russian prince; toured England and the Continent in prewar years and gave concerts in England during World War II for the British Red Cross; made his debut in the United States in 1941. See *Current Biography* (March) 1943.

Obituary

N Y Times p6 F 15 '62

COBHAM, CHARLES JOHN LYTTELTON, 10TH VISCOUNT Aug. 8, 1909- Governor-General of New Zealand

Address: b. Government House, Wellington, New Zealand; h. Hagley Hall, Stourbridge, Worcestershire, England

In New Zealand, as in other member countries of the British Commonwealth, the Crown is represented by a Governor-General appointed by the monarch upon the recommendation of the state's Prime Minister. The present Governor-General, Charles John Lyttelton, 10th Viscount Cobham of Hagley Hall, Worcestershire, England, was named by Queen Elizabeth II in January 1957 to succeed Lieutenant-General Sir Willoughby Norrie, and he assumed his important, if mostly ceremonial, duties the following September. Viscount Cobham, a self-proclaimed traditionalist, also has the titles of Baron Lyttelton of Frankley in Worcestershire, Baron Westcote of Ballymore in Ireland, and Baronet of England. His family's association with New Zealand dates back over a century.

The only son and the eldest in a family of five children, Charles John Lyttelton was born on August 8, 1909 to John Cavendish Lyttelton, 9th Viscount Cobham, and his wife, the former Violet Yolande Leonard, daughter of Charles Leonard of Gloria, Cape Province, South Africa. His sisters are Viola Maud, Audrey Lavinia, and Lavinia Mary Yolande; another sister, Meriel Catharine, is not living. Hagley Hall in Worcestershire was established as the family seat of the Lyttelton family in 1760, four years after Sir George Lyttelton was elevated to the peerage. The title of Viscount Cobham is even older, dating from 1718.

One of Charles John Lyttelton's ancestors, his great-grandfather, the 4th Baron Lyttelton, was interested in the British settlement of New Zealand and in 1849-50 served as chairman of the Canterbury Association, which was concerned with carrying out an efficient and humane system of immigration to Canterbury Province. The town and harbor of Lyttelton were named after him, and the 500-acre Hagley Park in nearby Christchurch takes its name from Hagley Hall.

Charles John Lyttelton was educated at Eton and Trinity College, Cambridge, where he received his B.A. degree with honors in law in 1932. Like other members of his family he excelled in cricket at both school and the university. He became a member of the Worcester County Cricket Club and in 1935 was chosen its captain. Also in 1935 he was named vice-captain of an All-England team that toured New Zealand in the antipodean summer of 1935-36 under the auspices of the home team of Lord's Cricket Ground in London, the Marylebone Cricket Club, of which his father was then the president. (Lyttelton himself became president of the Marylebone Cricket Club in 1954.) On his return from the New Zealand tour, during which he had made the impressive scores of 80 against Canterbury and 60 against Auckland, he continued as captain of the Worcester County Cricket Club until the outbreak of World War II in 1939.

Since 1933 Lyttelton had been an officer of the 100th (Worcester Yeomanry) Field Brigade of the Royal Artillery, Territorial Army. His first wartime assignment was as a gunnery officer with the 53d (Worcester Yeomanry) Anti-Tank Regiment, Royal Artillery. He fought in France during 1940, was seconded the following year in the rank of major to the 3d Maritime Regiment of the Royal Artillery, and in 1943 took command of the 5th Maritime Regiment. At the end of the war he held the rank of colonel.

His father, before becoming 9th Viscount Cobham, had served for a number of years as a Conservative member of Parliament for a Worcester constituency. Later, in 1939-40, he had been Parliamentary Under Secretary of War. Looking forward to a similar political career after the war, Colonel Lyttelton became president of the Worcester City Conservative Association in 1947. The following year the Dudley and Stourbridge division of Worcestershire chose him as prospective Conservative candidate for the House of Commons. He resigned the appointment upon the death of his father on July 31, 1949, when he succeeded to the title.

Viscount Cobham's withdrawal from politics gave him the time and energy needed to control the family affairs and manage the 3,000-acre Hagley estate. The death duties imposed after his father's death were so heavy that in 1950 he visited New Zealand to arrange for the sale of property on South Island that the Lyttelton family had held since the settlement of the Canterbury Plains a century earlier. The property was sold for £70,000.

In January 1957 Viscount Cobham was chosen to be Governor-General of New Zealand, becoming the twenty-third representative of the sovereign to that country. At the time of his appointment, besides directing the agricultural work on his Worcestershire estate, he was serving as a justice of the peace, as deputy lieutenant of Worcestershire, and as a director of Lloyds Bank, Ltd. He arrived in New Zealand's capital, Wellington, from England on September

National Publicity Studios,
Wellington, New Zealand

VISCOUNT COBHAM

5, 1957 and in a colorful ceremony was immediately sworn into office as Governor-General and Commander in Chief. Prime Minister Sidney Holland had a prominent part in the public welcome for the Viscount.

On the day of his arrival Viscount Cobham endeared himself to New Zealanders by announcing that he and Lady Cobham were determined to see the country "from top to bottom." In between the constitutional duties that he has carried out, such as the opening of Parliament and approving of the legislature, he has since paid official visits to many parts of the Dominion, as well as to Fiji in August 1959. When the Queen Mother Elizabeth visited New Zealand in February 1958, Queen Salote Tupou of the Tonga Islands, a British protectorate, was honored along with the Queen Mother at a dinner given by the Governor-General. Viscount Cobham presided at the opening of the Council of Ministers of the South East Asia Treaty Organization in April 1959, and as representative of the Crown in the same year he officially opened the new Auckland Bridge and Wellington Airport.

Although his predecessors had included Lord Jellico of Battle of Jutland fame and Lord Freyberg, leader of the New Zealand Expeditionary Force in World War II, within two years after his appointment Viscount Cobham was being spoken of as the most successful Governor-General that New Zealand had known. Despite the vague and largely ceremonial nature of his duties, New Zealanders are said to be "convinced that a man like Viscount Cobham fills a role of the greatest value in their community. He has shown ability to draw attention, without giving offense, to shortcomings in the local outlook, to bestow praise and encouragement where it is due, to widen the horizons of an isolated community that

COBHAM, 10TH VISCOUNT—*Continued*

does not normally pay much attention to cultural matters" (New York *Times,* June 7, 1959).

As a public speaker, Viscount Cobham is noted for forthrightness and wit and for his ability to appeal to diverse audiences. He is a good mixer whose background of considerably wide interests, including art collecting, sports, and farming, enables him to talk to various groups in their own language.

Lady Cobham is the former Elizabeth Alison Makeig-Jones, younger daughter of John Reeder Makeig-Jones of Southerton House near Ottery St. Mary in Devonshire. The couple were married in London on April 30, 1942 and are the parents of a family that Viscount Cobham has described as being "of Biblical proportions." There are four sons, John William Leonard (the heir to the title), Christopher Cavendish, Richard Cavendish, and Nicholas Makeig, and four daughters, Juliet Muriel, the twins Lucy and Sarah, and Elizabeth Catherine. All attend schools in New Zealand. Physically a big man, Viscount Cobham enjoys a variety of outdoor recreations, including shooting and golf. He is still active in cricket matches and goes trout fishing in New Zealand lakes and rivers. The Governor-General and his family customarily live at Government House in Wellington during most of the year and spend part of the summer at New Zealand's other official residence in Auckland.

> *References*
>
> N Y Times p27 Je 7 '59 por
> Toronto Globe and Mail p22 Ag 3 '59
> Burke's Peerage, Baronetage and Knightage, 1959
> Debrett's Peerage, Baronetage, Knightage and Companionage, 1961
> International Who's Who, 1961-62
> Kelly's Handbook to the Titled, Landed and Official Classes, 1961
> Who's Who, 1962

COCKRELL, EWING May 28, 1874-Jan. 21, 1962 Former judge of the Circuit Court of Missouri (1917-29); founder in 1929 and subsequently president of the United States Federation of Justice in Washington, D.C.; one of nine Americans nominated for the Nobel Peace Prize in 1951. See *Current Biography* (May) 1951.

> *Obituary*
>
> N Y Times p25 Ja 29 '62

DALTON, (EDWARD) HUGH (JOHN NEALE) DALTON, BARON 1887-Feb. 13, 1962 Former British government official; economist; Minister of Economic Warfare and President of the Board of Trade in coalition government during World War II; held several cabinet positions in postwar Labour government, including Chancellor of the Exchequer (1945-47); was made a life peer in 1960. See *Current Biography* (August) 1945.

> *Obituary*
>
> N Y Times p35 F 14 '62

DELANEY, SHELAGH (dĕ-lā'nĭ shē'lȧ) 1939- British playwright

Address: b. c/o Hope, Leresche and Steele, 11 Jubilee Place, Chelsea, London S.W. 3, England

Many theater critics found "Angry Young Woman" a handy phrase to apply to Lancashire playwright Shelagh Delaney when her *A Taste of Honey* fascinated audiences in a long run in London before the author was twenty years old. Not a crusader, however, she has objected to the glib label, and the program note for the première of *A Taste of Honey,* on May 27, 1958, maintained that "she is the antithesis of London's 'Angry Young Men.' She knows what she is angry about." She entertains strong views on the theater, on matters currently troubling Great Britain, and on attitudes toward "Youth."

Just before *A Taste of Honey* opened on Broadway in the fall of 1960, in a production that won the New York Drama Critics' 1961 award as the best foreign play, Shelagh Delaney's second play, *The Lion in Love,* was presented in London. Both plays deal authentically, but with warmth and humor, with the seamy side of life of northern England's working class.

Shelagh Delaney was born in Salford, near neighbor of Manchester, in Lancashire, one of the heavily industrial counties in the North of England, in 1939. Her grandparents were Irish, and her father, who died in 1958, was a transport worker. He was also a great reader and storyteller. She attended three schools in Salford, one being Broughton Secondary School. At the age of fifteen, she took her General Certificate of Education and gained passing marks in five subjects. At the age of seventeen she left school and worked successively as a salesgirl, milk depot clerk, usherette, and as an assistant in the research photography department of Metro-Vickers, a large industrial firm with over 23,000 employees.

While at Broughton Secondary School Shelagh had been much influenced by a Miss Leek, the school's headmistress, who encouraged her to write and "didn't harp too much on rigid English." Another factor that convinced her she could write was the comparison of her essays with those of her schoolmates. It was through Miss Leek that she saw her first play, at the age of twelve—a school production of *Othello.*

The industrial North provided Shelagh Delaney with background material for her writing. She is not a product of the slums; she and her family have always lived in government-subsidized Council homes—a middle-income type of house. However, her native Salford and neighboring Manchester have many areas of back-to-back houses with outside toilets and no bathrooms, the kind of slum described in the 1930's by George Orwell in his book *The Road to Wigan Pier.* More recently, Salford and Manchester have been called places "devastated not by war, but by industry and by years of pre-war unemployment." She began a novel with a slum background, but after she saw Terence Rattigan's play *Variations on a Theme,* which she disliked intensely, she rewrote her novel as a play.

About the time that she finished the script, Shelagh Delaney read a newspaper report of a dispute between a London theater group named Theatre Workshop and the Lord Chamberlain's office, Britain's official censor. This encouraged her to send her play to Joan Littlewood, the director of Theatre Workshop, for criticism. Within two weeks Joan Littlewood had the play in rehearsal, and it was first performed on May 27, 1958, at the Theatre Royal, Stratford East, where it ran until June 28, 1958. Directed by Joan Littlewood, the cast included Frances Cuka and Murray Melvin. The play was restaged at the Theatre Royal in January 1959 and moved to Wyndhams Theatre in London's West End on February 10, 1959.

Theatre Workshop is dedicated to the production of what its director describes as "grand, vulgar, simple, pathetic" plays. The characters in *A Taste of Honey,* which proved so suitable for Workshop production, are products of a Salford slum. They include a mother of loose morals, a lovelorn schoolgirl daughter and her colored sailor lover, and a homosexual who looks after the daughter when she is pregnant and deserted by both mother and sailor. The play is punctuated by a jazz score written by Bobby Scott.

A Taste of Honey raised cries of protest in the North of England and Lancastrians were quick to defend their home county. However, some comments were on the favorable side, as the author realized: "One half of the population says, 'How disgusting to degrade your home town.' The other half says, 'Don't mind ignorant criticism, they simply don't understand.'"

London reaction to Salford "life-in-the-raw" was somewhat different. Alan Brian, writing in *Theatre Arts* (May 1959) described the audience as split into two camps: "On one side the posh Sundays and the literary weeklies frothed and lathered with excitement. On the other, the mass-circulated dailies reacted with baffled, suspicious shrugs."

In one of the mass-circulated dailies, *News Chronicle,* critic Alan Dent labeled the life-in-the-raw plays as "The Kitchen Sink school of playwriting," and letters from John Osborne and Shelagh Delaney appeared in the resulting controversy. Ivor Brown, deploring this argument, thought that some young authors were being "properly praised up to a point but stupidly praised beyond that." W. A. Darlington, another London critic, commented on the "vitality, humor and an understanding far beyond the author's years" that had been shown in the play.

On Broadway, *A Taste of Honey* was produced by Tony Richardson and George Devine and starred Angela Lansbury, Andrew Ray and Joan Plowright. It opened at the Lyceum Theatre on October 4, 1960 and on February 20, 1961 moved to the Booth Theatre and ran for a total of 391 performances. Most New York critics wrote enthusiastic notices. Describing Shelagh Delaney's work as "an expression of unusual gifts," Howard Taubman pointed out in the New York *Times* (November 6, 1960) that it was not "clamorous with wildly aimed, re-

SHELAGH DELANEY

bellious rage." The *Catholic World* reviewer (May 1961) said that it asserted "human dignity in a life of inhuman degradation," and Henry Hewes in the *Saturday Review* (October 22, 1960) thought it "the most exciting piece of theater the new Broadway season has so far offered."

The play was awarded the New York Drama Critics' citation as the best foreign play of the season in April 1961. Other awards it received were the 1958 Charles Henry Foyle New Play Award and a £100 ($300) Arts Council Bursary. At the conclusion of its Broadway run, the play went on tour to St. Louis, Detroit, Milwaukee, and Chicago. In addition, it has been produced in Denmark, Hungary, France, and Sweden. *A Taste of Honey* has also been presented on the British Broadcasting Corporation's radio programs.

The film rights of *A Taste of Honey* were sold for $50,000. Shelagh Delaney wrote the script, and it was shot on location in Manchester and London, starring British comedienne Dora Bryan and Rita Tashington, a newcomer from Lancashire. The aim of its director, Tony Richardson, was to "attempt a neo-realism more complete and far-reaching than has yet been attempted in a major British film." *Sight and Sound* (Autumn, 1961) which reviewed the picture after its London première in September 1961, called it Richardson's best work since *Look Back in Anger.*

Aesop's *Fables* gave Shelagh Delaney the theme of her second play, *The Lion in Love,* but the background was still "the large, drab yet picturesque hurly-burly of a northern industrial town." The play, directed by Clive Baker, had its first performance at the Belgrade Theatre in Coventry on September 5, 1960 and its London première at the Royal Court Theatre on December 29, 1960.

(Continued next page)

DELANEY, SHELAGH—*Continued*

Drama critics complained that the new play was verbose, lacking in dramatic unity, and missing in the focus of *A Taste of Honey*, though the author protested that it was intended to be a "loose and sprawling" play. Praise for Miss Delaney's "authenticity, honesty, restraint and a prevailing sense of humor" came from Kenneth Tynan; and Ann Giudici, who was scheduled to produce *The Lion in Love* off-Broadway in the spring of 1962, described it as a "warm and funny" play.

Shelagh Delaney, a self-styled "apprentice playwright," is working on her third play. She is also employed as a director with Granada T.V. Network, Ltd., one of Great Britain's independent television companies. On March 30, 1961 she appeared on the American *C.B.S. Reports* television program in a discussion of the changing society of England, and together with playwright Arnold Wesker she talked about the obstacles to gaining a higher education in Great Britain.

In articles in the New York *Times Magazine* (May 28, 1961) and the Toronto *Globe and Mail* (October 7, 1961), Miss Delaney has argued for youth's ability to produce genuine creative work. She is also deeply concerned with young people's interest in the theater, and although *The Lion in Love* received only mixed notices, she was pleased by the large number of young people who went to see it. She is a champion of a Salford Civic Centre, which has not yet been approved by the civic authority. Active in British movements advocating nuclear disarmament, on September 17, 1961 she took part in the sit-down demonstration staged in London's Trafalgar Square by the Committee of 100, and she and John Osborne were among the demonstrators arrested.

The six-foot tall playwright has been described by a London *Times* writer as having "the poised, rangy figure of a dancer or Californian tennis player, . . . hazel eyes and dark hair, worn in a style she cannot classify, though it could be Italian." She shares an apartment in Salford with her widowed mother, Mrs. Elsie Delaney, and has a younger brother, who is a scientific instruments engineer. She also has an apartment in the Tottenham Court Road area of London. Her favorite authors include Chaucer, Brecht, O'Neill, Chekhov, and Beckett, as well as the Elizabethan and Greek Classical authors. One of her most frequently mentioned characteristics is her integrity—she has a "fierce independence of mind and an integrity which is part of the classic Lancashire tradition; she is typical of many of today's young people in the North of England."

References

London Times p12 F 2 '59 por
Manchester Guardian p9 S 20 '60 por
N Y Herald Tribune p17 Mr 16 '61 por
Theatre Arts 43:16+ My '59 por

FITCH, ROBERT ELLIOT   Jan. 25, 1902-
Clergyman; author; educator

Address: b. Pacific School of Religion, 1798 Scenic Ave., Berkeley 9, Calif.; h. 2223 Marin Ave., Berkeley 7, Calif.

Largely because of his polemic wit the Reverend Dr. Robert Elliot Fitch, dean of the Pacific School of Religion in Berkeley, California, is able to use literary criticism as effective social satire in behalf of moral theology. In *The Decline and Fall of Sex* (1957) and *Odyssey of the Self-Centered Self* (1961) he turns his enormous arsenal of illustrations from past and present cultures on some of the more vicious weaknesses of contemporary American life. Dr. Fitch, a Congregational minister, has written several other books, one of them a study on Voltaire, and has taught philosophy and theology at several colleges and universities, including Columbia University, College of the City of New York, Pacific University, and Occidental College. Since 1949 he has been professor of Christian ethics and since 1951 dean at the Pacific School of Religion.

Robert Elliot Fitch was born on January 25, 1902 in Ningpo, China, the son and grandson of American Presbyterian missionaries. His parents, Robert Ferris and Isadore (Kloss) Fitch, were United States citizens. He attended elementary schools in Shanghai and Chefoo, China and, for one year, in Lausanne, Switzerland. From 1915 to 1919 he studied at St. Luke's School, Wayne, Pennsylvania and then entered Yale University.

Following his graduation from Yale in 1923, Fitch enrolled at Union Theological Seminary in New York City, where he earned the B.D. degree in 1926. He spent the next year studying at the University of Paris and then returned to New York, where he received the M.A. degree from Columbia University in 1929. He taught philosophy at the University of Virginia, summer session in 1929; at the College of the City of New York in 1929-30; at Columbia University, fall term in 1930; at the University of Texas from February 1931 to July 1932; and at Pacific University, Forest Grove, Oregon from 1932 to 1938. Meanwhile, in 1935, Columbia University had conferred on him the Ph.D. degree. His dissertation was entitled *Voltaire's Philosophic Procedure* (News-Times Publishing Company).

After he was ordained into the ministry of the Congregational Church on June 1, 1936, Dr. Fitch preached in various West Coast college chapels, including Occidental and Claremont, and Stanford University. He became professor of philosophy at Occidental College in Los Angeles in 1938, a post he held until 1949. From 1946 to 1949 he was also dean of the faculty. His war service was as a chaplain in the United States Naval Reserve from August 1944 to February 1946, at first in Washington, D.C. and then on active duty with a Navy attack transport in the Pacific.

Between 1944 and 1946 Fitch was a member of the Commission on the Relation of the Church to the War in the Light of the Christian Faith, under the Federal Council of Churches of Christ in America. Some of his sermons and essays on America in wartime and other subjects were published in 1944 by Charles Scribner's Sons under the title *A Certain Blind Man.* A reviewer for the *Journal of Philosophy* (July 6, 1944) commended the book as "exceptionally enjoyable reading . . . for it combines wittiness, earnestness, and analysis in an eloquent style." E. E. Aubrey observed in the *Christian Century* (March 1, 1944) that the author's treatment of the American mood and tradition "is not free from the conventional scolding of America for its addiction to sanitary plumbing and safety razors as an evidence of indifference to the things of the spirit. But on the whole, his criticisms are keen rather than querulous and his suggestions are constructive."

Since 1949 Dr. Fitch has been professor of Christian ethics at the Pacific School of Religion and also, since 1951, dean of the faculty. The Pacific School of Religion, the oldest theological seminary west of the Mississippi River, was founded in 1866 by the Congregational Churches of California and became interdenominational in 1912. It occupied sites in San Francisco and Oakland before moving in 1901 to Berkeley, which is a center for theological and allied studies. During a recent academic year students representing twenty-four denominations were enrolled from seventy-four colleges in twenty-seven states and from ten foreign countries. The school, noted for its high academic standards, grants the degrees of Master of Religious Education, Bachelor of Divinity, Master of Sacred Theology, and Doctor of Theology.

Maintaining wide academic contacts outside the Pacific School of Religion, Fitch was visiting professor at the Perkins School of Theology of Southern Methodist University in Dallas, Texas in the summer of 1952; Union Theological Seminary in New York City from February to August 1953; University of British Columbia in Vancouver in the summer of 1957; and at the University of Hawaii for the 1959 spring semester. He has also filled a number of special lectureships, including those of Tully Cleon Knoles Lecturer in Philosophy at the College of the Pacific in Stockton, California in 1952 and Remsen Bird Lecturer at Occidental College in 1957. His Tully Cleon Knoles Lectures were published by the College of the Pacific under the title of *The Limits of Liberty* in 1955.

In his philosophic and religious *Preface to Ethical Living* (Association Press, 1947) and *Kingdom Without End; A Prophetic Interpretation of History and Civilization* (Scribner, 1950), Fitch deplores man's failure to live according to the moral and spiritual values that Christianity offers. The books foreshadow in clarity of expression and freshness of insight his better-known volume of social criticism, *The Decline and Fall of Sex; with Some Curious Digressions on the Subject of True Love* (Harcourt, 1957).

Many reviewers were impressed by Fitch's erudition in his use of contemporary fiction and scientific writing to show the extent of sexual unwholesomeness in America. Anthopologist Ashley Montagu described *The Decline and Fall of Sex* in the New York *Times* (May 19, 1957) as a "brilliantly blistering attack on today's sexual morality" and characterized Fitch as "a wit in the Voltairean manner, who with

REV. ROBERT ELLIOT FITCH

zest and verve writes most delightfully." Although theologian Reinhold Niebuhr thought that the book had "an essentially right approach to the whole vexing problem of sex, a right response to both modern and ancient heresies about sex," Philip Wylie found considerable fault with Fitch in the *Saturday Review* (August 3, 1957): "His solution of a problem (which Freud and other scientists, along with writers and theologians agree to be real) is Cotton Mather's solution, Anthony Comstock's, Jonathan Edwards's, and John S. Sumner's."

One target of Fitch's satire is a cult of contemporary literature that he calls "the *mystique de la merde*" or "the deification of dirt." He objects to the reduction of sex to tedium in the works of Ernest Hemingway, Norman Mailer, Tennessee Williams, and other authors. "When sex is separated from love and honor, it sinks into the slime," he writes. "Hence the contemporary obsession with obscenity." In an address in 1957 before the Religious Education Association of the United States and Canada, he said that the increased popularity of westerns and of Shakespeare indicated a quest for a "deeper sanity." Both westerns and Shakespeare, he believes, "hold fast to the distinction between the clean and the unclean."

Comment on Dean Fitch's *Odyssey of the Self-Centered Self; or Rake's Progress in Religion* (Harcourt, 1961) ranged from high praise ("prickly entertainment. I shout hurrah for it"—Edmund Fuller, New York *Times Book Review,* June 25, 1961) to faint praise ("his essential targets have long since been peppered by profounder critics. . . [but] between the wailing and the railing, some valid points get made"—*Time,* March 31, 1961).

In *Odyssey,* Fitch attacks the cult of the ego, whether he finds it in the self-pitying poetry of the beatnik, the self-indulgence of the affluent, or the solipsism of the positivist and the existen-

FITCH, ROBERT ELLIOT—*Continued*

tialist. One of his chapters is entitled "Mighty Me! The Self in Love with Itself" and another, "Empty Me! The Self as Sick of Itself." As a solution, he suggests commitment of the self in service outside itself and rediscovery of the true self in glorifying God.

Dean Fitch often contributes articles and book reviews to such magazines as *Christian Century, Christian Scholar,* and *International Journal of Religious Education.* He also writes occasional pieces for *Mademoiselle, New Republic,* and other secular journals. In *This Week* (October 23, 1960) he criticized the over-permissive parents who give their child an "everything" that turns out to be nothing. "More than once," he wrote, "I have wondered how my parents managed to give me so much when they had so little. As missionaries in China, their income was negligible. . . . But I know Father and Mother gave me two things—their continuous love and concern, and their own sense of high standards. . . . To be given these things is to be given 'everything.' "

Discussing "The Scientist as Priest and Savior" in *Christian Century* (March 26, 1958), Dean Fitch warns scientists, "who constitute a new sort of religious order that sets itself apart from the world by a discipline, a language, and an attitude," that in a free society a scientist must play his role as a citizen, must put his truth and power in the service of a democracy instead of a tyranny, and he commends those scientist-statesmen like Conant or Killian who are valuable public servants.

Robert Elliot Fitch and Marion W. De Witt were married on March 26, 1931. They have three children—John Elliot, Robert De Witt and Shelley Annette. Dr. Fitch is over six feet tall and has blond hair and blue eyes. He is a member of Phi Beta Kappa, American Philosophical Association, and the Pacific Coast Theological Group, and was a member of the advisory council for the Pacific Southwest region of the National Student Y.M.C.A. Association from 1946 to 1951. In 1949 Lewis and Clark College conferred on him an honorary D.D. degree.

References

Directory of American Scholars (1957)
Who's Who in America, 1960-61
Who's Who in American Education, 1957-58

FORD, EDWARD CHARLES See Ford, Whitey

FORD, WHITEY Oct. 21, 1928- Baseball player

Address: b. New York Yankees, Yankee Stadium, New York; h. Lake Success, N.Y.

Although Whitey Ford, the southpaw groundball pitcher of the New York Yankees, has had some exceptional seasons during his ten years in the big leagues, his finest season was 1961, when he was chosen as winner of the Cy Young Award as the outstanding pitcher in the major leagues. The Baseball Writers Association of America selected Ford on the basis of his 25

victories against 4 losses—a performance that helped to assure the Yankees of the American League pennant. Until 1961 Ford had never gained twenty victories in one season, although he sometimes came close. In the World Series of 1961 Ford chalked up two victories over the Cincinnati Redlegs, increasing to 32 his number of consecutive shutout innings in World Series competition. (In the 1960 World Series Ford had blanked the Pittsburgh Pirates twice.) Ford was voted the Most Valuable Player of the 1961 World Series by *Sport* magazine and he was also awarded the Babe Ruth trophy as the Most Valuable Player of the 1961 World Series by the baseball writers of New York City.

At the end of the 1961 season Ford had registered 158 major league victories against 63 losses, thus achieving the highest-winning percentage of any pitcher in the history of baseball. His earned run average of 2.76 is the lowest of any pitcher now active and only once has he lost as many as ten games in a season. Most sportswriters agree that Whitey Ford is a candidate for baseball's Hall of Fame.

Of Irish and Swedish descent, Whitey Ford was born Edward Charles Ford on October 21, 1928 in a tenement district in midtown Manhattan to James Ford, a bartender, and Edith Ford. As a child, Whitey moved with his family to the Astoria section of Queens, one of the five boroughs of New York City. Although he was an undersized southpaw whose height was only five feet four inches when he entered his teens, he began to play first base with the Thirty-fourth Avenue Boys Club of Astoria, the most successful of the neighborhood's many sandlot teams. Since William Cullen Bryant High School in Long Island City near his home had no baseball team, Whitey traveled two hours a day on the subway to attend Manhattan High School of Aviation Trades, which did field a team. From 1944 through 1946 he alternated between first base and the pitcher's mound.

Two months after he graduated from high school in June 1946 Ford was invited by the New York Yankees to work out with forty other amateurs. He received little notice at that time, but in September of the same year he pitched the Thirty-fourth Avenue Boys to a victory over the Bay Ridge Cubs. He then attracted major league scouts, who made him some modest offers. After weighing bids from the New York Yankees, the Brooklyn Dodgers, and the Boston Red Sox, Ford signed with the New York Yankees for $7,000.

Fresco Thompson, the director of the Dodger farm system, has admitted his mistake. "By the middle of the next season I knew I'd pulled a bad boner," he said in the *Saturday Evening Post* (May 12, 1956). "Ford would have been a bargain at a bonus of fifty thousand. Everybody in the business is so hipped on getting big rookies who can throw the ball through a brick wall that we overlook kids with qualifications that are a helluva lot harder to find. Ford has the guts of a burglar and the curve ball of a mature pro who had been pitching for ten years."

Ford was broken into the New York Yankees farm system in 1947 and during the next four years he achieved a brilliant record in the minor leagues. In the middle of the 1950 season, when the Yankees were locked in a struggle with the Detroit Tigers for the American League pennant, Ford was called up to the parent club from Kansas City, then a New York Yankees farm team in the Class AA American Association. His was an arduous introduction to major league competition. Relieving against the Red Sox, he gave up seven hits, six walks, and five runs in five innings. "I'm not worried," Ford remarked after the game. He then ran off six straight wins, mainly against teams in the second division.

When the pennant race was in its final weeks, with Detroit holding a half-game lead, Casey Stengel, then the manager of the New York Yankees, picked Ford to pitch a crucial game against the Tigers. Ford won it, 8 to 1. Later he was besieged by baseball writers who asked him if that was the biggest game he had ever won. "I remember pitching the Maspeth Ramblers to a 17 to 11 victory over the Astoria Indians," Ford answered. "That was a good one, too." Ford may have been brash, but he backed up his brashness with a superior performance. The Yankees went on to win the pennant and Ford won the fourth game of the World Series against the Philadelphia Phillies.

Inducted into the United States Army in 1951, Ford spent the next two years at Fort Monmouth, New Jersey as a member of the Signal Corps. At one point in his military career Ford fell fifteen feet from a telephone pole, after which he was transferred to a desk job as a radar operator. He played baseball on his own time, at night and on Sundays. Weighing 190 pounds and acting somewhat subdued, Ford returned to the New York Yankees in 1953 "too scared to talk." "I knew I didn't have half my stuff before I went into the service," Ford has explained. "The trouble was I didn't pitch enough in the Army to get into condition." Winning his first seven games in an 18 to 6 season, he went on triumphantly for the next three seasons: 16 to 8 in 1954; 18 to 7 in 1955; 19 to 6 in 1956.

In 1957, however, Ford suffered a series of reverses. Plagued by arm and shoulder trouble, he won only 11 games and lost 5. He had strained his muscles by throwing sliders in jerky fashion and by resting too long between starts and for a while he thought that he was through in baseball. By delivering sliders smoothly with a long motion and by pitching at least every fourth day, he greatly improved the condition.

It was also the year in which Ford became involved in the much publicized Copacabana incident. On May 16, 1957 Ford and five other New York Yankees—Mickey Mantle, Yogi Berra, Hank Bauer, Johnny Kucks, and Billy Martin—attended the Manhattan night club to celebrate Martin's birthday. Another Copacabana patron charged that in the course of the evening he was beaten by Hank Bauer. The six merrymakers were each fined $1,000 by the management of the New York Yankees for having broken training rules. Billy Martin was later

WHITEY FORD

traded away; the others remained. During the next three seasons Ford won only 42 games and lost 26, probably because his arm and shoulder continued to bother him and because Casey Stengel, instead of using Ford on a regular rotation basis, held Ford out for starts against first-division teams.

When Ford won only 12 games and lost 9 in 1960, some observers muttered that he had reached the end of the road as an effective starting pitcher. But he silenced his critics by firing back-to-back shutouts against the Pittsburgh Pirates in the World Series. In 1961 the New York Yankees had a new manager, Ralph Houk, who announced in spring training that Ford would start every fourth day during the regular season—a departure from Stengel's routine. By late July Ford had chalked up 18 victories and only 2 defeats. During that period he won 14 consecutive games, tying the club record of the New York Yankees. In reaching his final mark of 25 to 4, Ford received a great deal of relief help from Luis Arroyo, the left-handed Puerto Rican pitcher. Ford would start a game, pitch seven or eight innings, then retire while Arroyo came in to clinch the victory. At one point Ford joked: "I'm going to hold out for $100,000 and split it with Luis."

In the first game of the World Series against Cincinnati Ford pitched a masterly two-hit shutout, beating the Redlegs 2 to 0. In the fourth game he blanked Cincinnati for five innings to establish his consecutive scoreless innings mark, then left the game because his foot had become swollen as the result of being struck by a batted ball. Other World Series records that Ford holds includes the most starts (sixteen), the most strikeouts (seventy), and most games won (nine). Ford has always performed at his best during the World Series, a fact of which he is well aware. Before the sixth game of the 1955 World Series between the New York Yankees and the Brooklyn Dodgers,

FORD, WHITEY—*Continued*

when the Yankees were trailing 3 games to 2, Ford appeared on a television show. Asked who was to pitch in the sixth game, he replied, "I am, and it will be Tommy Byrne in the seventh game on Tuesday," leaving no doubt in anybody's mind that he fully expected to beat the Brooklyn Dodgers—and he did.

In St. Patrick's Church in Astoria, on April 14, 1951, while he was still in military service, Whitey Ford married the attractive brunette Joan Foran, whom he had first met in a neighborhood ice cream parlor when he was sixteen and she was thirteen. Their three children, Sally Ann, Eddie, and Tommy have won trophies and medals for swimming, racing, and ice skating. A family man, Ford spends as much time with his children as possible and behaves more like an older brother than a father in their company.

Small in stature for a baseball player, Ford stands five feet ten inches tall and weighs about 184 pounds. He is rosy-faced and blue-eyed and has cropped blond hair, blond eyelashes, and blond eyebrows. (Even the stubble of his beard is blond.) Although he prefers Italian dishes, Ford has to guard against recurrence of the gout by taking pills and living on a low-purine diet. He may drink a beer or two or just lounge in the clubhouse to get rid of the tension that he bottles up during a game. He likes to watch sports shows on television and he indulges in an occasional game of golf, playing usually in the low 80's. He prefers sports clothes. In the off-season he works as a customer's man for the brokerage firm of Fahnestock & Company.

Away from his pitcher's mound Ford lives up to his nickname of Yankee Quipper by enacting the role of the clubhouse comedian; he is light-hearted, relaxed, and easygoing. But once he has made his way to the pitcher's mound he is transformed into another person—cocksure, intense, even arrogant. Ford uses three basic pitches: the slider, the curve, and the fast ball. He is already nervous when he enters the clubhouse, but by going over the names of the hitters in his mind he calms himself down, and once he is on the mound he loses himself so thoroughly in his pitching that he doesn't even hear the yelling of the fans. Even so, he has been known to sweat away as much as six to eight pounds during a game. He fumes and grows restless on the bench if he is kept there too often or for too long a period.

Whitey Ford once said that three constituents go into the making of a good pitcher: "Arm, heart, and head. Arm and heart are assets, head a necessity." That Ford possesses this triad seems evident from the testimony of his colleagues. Casey Stengel used to call Ford "my professional." One of his former competitors, Enos Slaughter, has said, "Of all the lefty pitchers I've seen, Whitey is the one I'd like to have going for me in one *must* game." The Yankee catcher Elston Howard has addressed Ford as "chairman of the board" and Ralph Houk has said of him: "He's game. He has all the pitches and can control them on any count. Confidence,

natural ability, courage, and ideal temperament make him great. . . . He's all pro."

References

N Y Post p60 Ag 28 '61; p5 Je 3 '57
N Y Times p44 O 13 '60
Sat Eve Post 228:32+ My 12 '56 por
Sports Illus 14:36+ Jl 24 '61 por

HARGRAVE, THOMAS J(EAN) Dec. 5, 1891-Feb. 21, 1962 Manufacturing executive; lawyer; president (1941-52) and chairman (since 1952) of the Eastman Kodak Company; guided company's expansion in chemicals, plastics, and synthetic fibers; chairman of the National Munitions Board (1947-48). See *Current Biography* (April) 1949.

Obituary

N Y Times p25 F 22 '62

HODES, HENRY I(RVING) Mar. 19, 1899-Feb. 14, 1962 Former United States Army officer; fought in Europe as a field commander in World War II; served as assistant commander of the 7th Infantry Division during the Korean conflict and figured in the truce negotiations in 1951; commanded the United States Army in Europe (1956-59) in the rank of four-star general. See *Current Biography* (February) 1959.

Obituary

N Y Times p29 F 15 '62

HU SHIH Dec. 17, 1891-Feb. 24, 1962 Chinese scholar; philosopher; statesman; served at times as adviser to Chiang Kai-shek; but also criticized the Kuomintang for suppression of civil liberties; Ambassador to the United States (1938-42); president of the Academia Sinica, a research institute on Formosa (since 1958). See *Current Biography* (February) 1942.

Obituary

N Y Times p89 F 25 '62

IVES, IRVING M(CNEIL) Jan. 24, 1896-Feb. 24, 1962 New York Republican legislator; member of the New York State Assembly (1930-47); United States Senator (1947-59); specialist in labor and civil rights legislation. See *Current Biography* (February) 1948.

Obituary

N Y Times p88 F 25 '62

JOHNSON, HAROLD OGDEN Mar. 5, 1895-Feb. 26, 1962 Comedian; formed a vaudeville team with John Sigvard Olsen in 1914; won success on Broadway with the zany revues *Hellzapoppin'* (1938-41) and *Sons O' Fun* (1941); appeared with Olsen also in several motion pictures and on radio and television. See *Current Biography* (September) 1940.

Obituary

N Y Times p33 F 28 '62

LIPCHITZ, JACQUES Aug. 22, 1891- Sculptor

Address: 168 Warburton Rd., Hastings-on-Hudson, N.Y.

> NOTE: This biography supersedes the article that appeared in *Current Biography* in 1948.

Among Jacques Lipchitz' qualifications to rank with the great masters of contemporary sculpture is his remarkable capacity to renew his genius, to keep turning his enriched creative powers in another direction through experiment and exploration in fulfillment of his continuing growth as an artist. Since making his home in the United States in 1941, the Lithuanian-born sculptor has been as much an innovator as he had been in Paris when he became a founder of the Cubist school of sculpture in 1916 and when he introduced transparent sculpturing to modern artists in the 1920's. His range of style, theme, and mood over a period of fifty years has been enormous—from monumental to delicate, from somberly religious to sensual, from anguish and moral fervor to whimsey.

Jacques Lipchitz owes the present form of his name to a French police official who issued him an identification card when he went to Paris at the age of eighteen. He was born Chaim Jacob Lipschitz on August 22, 1891 to Abraham and Rachael Leah (Krinsky) Lipschitz in the small Lithuanian village of Druskieniki, in Tsarist Russia, where the Jewish folkways of his ancestors had to struggle to survive. There were five younger children in the family: Paul, Rubin, Fanya, Jennie, and Dina. Only two are now living, Rubin in Paris and Dina in Russia.

In childhood Lipchitz stuffed his pockets with stones, fascinated by their texture and shape. He was an indifferent pupil at school in Bialystok, preferring to spend his time modeling little figures in red clay, which he painted white because all the sculptured figures that he had ever seen had been in plaster. However, Abraham Lipschitz, a prosperous building contractor, wanted his son to become a mechanical engineer and sent him to study at the *Realschule* in Vilna, the capital of Lithuania.

Despite family opposition, Lipchitz was determined to be a sculptor. Encouraged by Ilya Yakovlevich Günzberg, protégé of the renowned Russian sculptor Mark Matveyevich Antokolski, he decided to go to Paris. His mother gave him the money for his trip without his father's knowledge, and, since he could not leave Russia without his father's permission, arranged for him to be smuggled across the border.

Arriving in Paris in October 1909, Lipchitz took a small suite of rooms at the Hôtel des Mines on the boulevard St. Michel and enrolled as an *élève libre* (free pupil) at the École des Beaux-Arts to study under Professor Jean-Antoine Injalbert. As soon as his father gave up opposition to his ambition and agreed to send him an allowance, Lipchitz enrolled at the Académie Julian, where one of his teachers in sculpture during his four years of attendance was Raoul Verlet. For a time he also went to classes at the École des Beaux-Arts, studying anatomy and learning to carve directly in stone.

Wide World

JACQUES LIPCHITZ

As valuable to Lipchitz as his formal instruction was living in Paris itself—visiting its museums and galleries, searching through the Flea Market, and meeting other artists. During Lipchitz's second year in Paris, his father suffered financial ruin and Lipchitz had to move to cheaper lodgings on the rue du Dragon. He supported himself by pushing carts at night and hoisting sacks of vegetables at railroad stations. In 1911 he contracted tuberculosis and went to Belgium to convalesce, but his recovery was incomplete, and when he returned to Russia in 1912 for military service, he was exempted on medical grounds.

Within the year Lipchitz was back in Paris, now in a studio at 54 rue de Montparnasse. Devoted to archaic Greek and Gothic art, during his apprentice years in Paris he produced work of an imitative and naturalistic character. A bronze portrait *Head of Mlle. S.* (1911) was chosen to represent his early period in a 1961 retrospective exhibit in New York. His *Woman and Gazelles,* exhibited in a group show in Paris in 1912, and his rhythmic *The Encounter* (1913) are notable examples of his pre-Cubism. African wood carvings, just then beginning their vogue in Paris, appealed to him greatly, and he began a magnificent collection of Negro African art, although he has said that his work was not influenced by the African primitive.

Critical of his own work and ready to turn away from traditionalism, Lipchitz gradually allied himself with the Cubist coterie. Through his friend Max Jacob he met Modigliani, Picasso, Diego Rivera, and Juan Gris, establishing close associations that made him recognized as one of the experimenters of the so-called Parisian School. With Rivera and other artists he took a trip in 1914 to Majorca and then to Barcelona and Madrid, where he discovered the painters El Greco, Tintoretto, and Goya. When he saw

LIPCHITZ, JACQUES—Continued

Raphael's *Portrait of a Cardinal,* his experience of "entering into" a painting for the first time inspired him to find a way through a contemporary language to speak to his own generation.

While still in Spain, Lipchitz began work on his first Cubist pieces, including *Girl with Braid* (1914) and *Sailor with Guitar* (1914). For about a decade after his return to Paris, he vigorously explored the possibilities of Cubism in sculpture, exhibiting a large number of his early rectilinear, flat geometric figures in his first one-man show, at Léonce Rosenberg's Galerie de l'Effort Moderne in 1920. Michel Seuphor in *The Sculpture of this Century* (Braziller, 1959) pointed out that Lipchitz "built his figures out of purely plastic elements that subsequently are somehow tied up with the human motif." Using *Head* (1915-16) and *The Guitarist* (1918), among other pieces, as illustrations, Seuphor went on to say, "Were it not for some very brief signs which recall a hand here, there an eye . . . these stones or these bronzes of Lipchitz's would be authentic abstract sculpture." But for Lipchitz, being nonobjective meant ending up with nothing.

From the austerity or imprisonment of Cubism, Lipchitz escaped in 1925 to the freer, lyrical expression of his "transparents." His liberation came about through a process that he developed in defiance of Leonardo da Vinci's indictment of sculpture—that it could not represent the transparent or luminous. By piercing the solid form with grids and ribbons of metal, using an old melted-wax technique (the *cire-perdue* process), he displaced mass with space and was able to produce his open-spaced *Pierrot Escapes* (1926) and his aerial *Joy of Living* (1927), *The Harpist* (1930), and *The Song of the Vowels* (1930).

Lipchitz wrote to Roger Vitrac, the French dramatist, in 1927, "Providence inspired in me these things: aerial transparencies which can be seen, and can move us, from all sides at once. I soar with this thing heavier than air!" In 1930 he gave a retrospective exhibit of 100 sculptures at the Galerie de la Renaissance. His first one-man show in the United States was held at the Brummer Gallery in New York in 1935.

With a development that seemed, at least, a rejection of Cubism, Lipchitz' work took on a baroque quality, and his change in direction involved emotional content as well as style. Disturbed by political events in Europe, he turned to Biblical and mythological themes in monumental sculpture that conveyed his fear and hope for mankind. Moreover, as Irene Patai observed in *Encounters: The Life of Jacques Lipchitz* (Funk, 1961), his *The Return of the Prodigal Son* (1931) "was his own return to Mother Earth, to the source of life. It was the spring at which he restored his energy, the sculptor at last going back to romantic feeling." Other pieces that characterize his work of the 1930's are *Jacob Wrestling with the Angel* (1931), *Bull and Condor* (1932), *Prometheus Strangling the Vulture* (1936)—one of several pieces based on the Prometheus theme—and *Rape of Europa* (1938), all of which reflected his feelings toward Hitler and Mussolini.

Just before the Nazi occupation of Paris, Lipchitz fled to the south of France, and in 1941 he sailed for the United States aboard the Portuguese ship *Nyassa,* carrying among his few possessions his sculpture *Flight* (1940), which symbolized the tragedy of the war. Almost penniless when he arrived in New York, he accepted commissions for portraits. One famed portrait, of Marsden Hartley, required twenty-seven sittings. But he refused an offer of a teaching position. "Teaching is death," he explained to Selden Rodman many years later (*Conversations with Artists,* Devin, 1957). "If he teaches, the sculptor has to open up and reveal things that should be closed and sacred." A number of one-man shows at Curt Valentin's Buchholz Gallery, the first in 1942, helped Lipchitz to establish himself in the new country.

In the United States, according to Seuphor, Lipchitz' sculpture assumed a more sensual quality, as in *Mother and Child* (1941-45) and *Dancing Girl with Braids* (1948), as well as a more elaborate baroque, as in *Spring* (1942) and *Prayer* (1943). Another baroque piece, *Notre Dame de Liesse* or *Our Lady of Joy* (1947-54), was commissioned by Père Couturier for his Church of Assy in the French Alps. Lipchitz agreed to accept the commission provided that his sculpture would carry the inscription "Jacob Lipchitz, Jew, faithful to the religion of his ancestors, has made this Virgin to foster understanding between men on earth, that the life of the spirit may prevail."

Our Lady of Joy was lost in the fire that destroyed his Manhattan studio in January 1952. Lipchitz set to work at once to remake it and also re-created *The Spirit of Enterprise,* which then grew in grandeur and size to a figure twelve feet high and sixteen feet wide before it was mounted in October 1960 in Fairmount Park in Philadelphia. Working at the Modern Art Foundry in Astoria, New York after the fire had taken his studio, he recalled a technique that he had tried a year before of applying wax at random to chisels to form spontaneous pieces of sculpture. He made twenty-six of them in as many days, calling them *Variations on a Chisel.* Then he submitted to the discipline of working on his Madonna and his sculpture for Fairmount Park before he "exploded," as he has said, into his "semi-automatics."

Lipchitz' semi-automatics developed from his plunging a handful of hot waxy material into cold water and then elaborating the suggested form according to his state of mind. Within a year or so he had produced more than thirty semi-automatics—including *Only Inspiration, Head of an Old Man,* and *Gypsy Dancer*—that were exhibited at the Otto Gerson Gallery in New York in March 1957. For another year he let his imagination play upon a chance mingling of disparate objects, such as flowers, leaves, strings, sticks, pieces of clothing, and used the difficult lost-wax process to cast his metaphorical relationships. Among the bronze sculptures that belong to what he calls his *À la limite du possible* are *The Artichokes* (1958) and *The Bone* (1959).

Although he has worked hard at the foundry to perfect his language as a sculptor and to develop the methods that have contributed to his reputation as an innovator, Lipchitz has said in discussing his work that techniques were secondary. For him even Cubism was "a search for a syntax." He has explained his sculpture as an expression of himself, observing that he has a tendency to go in cycles from a period of tenseness and discipline to expansive lyricism, according to his emotions or the "encounters" between himself and objects in his environment. In *Jacques Lipchitz; His Sculpture* (Abrams, 1961) A. M. Hammacher shows how each of Lipchitz' periods or directions grew out of the preceding one to connect all his work organically.

To celebrate his seventieth birthday Lipchitz announced in 1961 his gift of 300 original plaster models of his sculpture to the American-Israel Cultural Foundation for the Jerusalem museum of art. His birthday was also celebrated with a retrospective exhibit at the Otto Gerson Gallery, "Fifty Years of Lipchitz Sculpture," ranging from his pre-Cubism pieces to the menacing religious composition, *Sacrifice*, of 1961. It was the first full-scale exhibit of his work in New York since the retrospective at the Museum of Modern Art in 1954. Among the many honors paid to Lipchitz are the Gold Medal of the International Paris Exposition (1937-38) for his *Prometheus* and a Doctor of Arts and Letters degree from Brandeis University, awarded in 1958. He was made a chevalier of the French Legion of Honor in 1947 and a member of the National Institute of Arts and Letters in 1961.

In France in 1915 Lipchitz married Berta Kitrosser, who accompanied him on his escape to the United States during the war. She did not, however, return with him from a visit to Paris in 1946, and they were divorced in 1947. Lipchitz later married Yulla Halberstadt, a Berlin refugee from Nazism, whom he had met in New York. Their daughter, Lolya Rachael, was born in October 1948, and soon afterward Lipchitz moved with his family to his present home in Hastings-on-Hudson, New York, where he also has his studio.

Jacques Lipchitz became an American citizen in 1958, giving up the French citizenship that he had held since 1925. He is six feet tall and has blue eyes and light-brown hair that has turned gray. His lifelong hobby had been collecting primitive art of all kinds, principally sculpture, from all regions and all eras.

References
> Patai, Irene. Encounters (1961)
> Rodman, Selden. Conversations with Artists (1957)
> Seuphor, Michel. The Sculpture of this Century (1959)
> Who's Who in America, 1960-61
> Who's Who in World Jewry (1955)

McCORMACK, JOHN W(ILLIAM) Dec. 21, 1891- Speaker of the United States House of Representatives
Address: b. House Office Bldg., Washington, D.C.; h. Hotel Washington, Washington, D.C.

> NOTE: This biography supersedes the article that appeared in *Current Biography* in 1943.

The forty-fifth speaker of the United States House of Representatives, succeeding Sam Ray-

Wide World
JOHN W. McCORMACK

burn of Texas, is John W. McCormack, a Boston Irishman who served an apprenticeship of thirty-three years as a member of the House, seventeen of them as Democratic floor leader. The first Roman Catholic to be elected Speaker, he is noted for his diligence as a legislator, his barbed wit in floor debate, and his influence among liberal and conservative Democrats alike. McCormack was elected Speaker at the opening of the second session of the Eighty-seventh Congress, on January 10, 1962.

John William McCormack was born in South Boston, Massachusetts on December 21, 1891 to Joseph H. McCormack, a bricklayer, and Ellen (O'Brien) McCormack. His grandparents on both sides came to the United States at the time of the Irish potato famines in the late 1840's. There were twelve children in the family, nine of whom died in infancy or youth. Two younger brothers survive: Edward ("Knocko") McCormack, who is assistant commissioner of markets in Boston, and Daniel McCormack, who lives in Texas. The neighborhood where the McCormacks lived was shabby but respectable, and it is said that it has produced more priests and nuns than any other community in the United States.

Just before John McCormack graduated from John Andrew Grammar School, his father died. The thirteen-year-old boy left school and went to work as the family breadwinner. His earnings as a newsboy were often supplemented by a "pauper's basket." "We're not proud of it," McCormack's brother Edward has remarked, "but we don't shun the fact that we were the poorest family in South Boston" (*Time*, January 19, 1962). John quit his newspaper route to take a $3.50 a week job as an errand boy with a brokerage firm, then switched to the law office of William T. Way, working as an office boy for $4 a week, a step that McCormack has called the turning point of his life. Encouraged

McCORMACK, JOHN W.—*Continued*

by his employer to read for the law, McCormack studied at night and between errands in the law office. When he was twenty-one he passed his bar examinations, three months after the death of his mother.

While practising law in Boston, McCormack began his political career. He took part in the Massachusetts Constitutional Convention in 1917-18. Subsequently he saw stateside World War I service in the United States Army and was discharged with the rank of sergeant major. In 1920 he was elected to the Massachusetts House of Representatives, serving for two years, and was a member of the state Senate from 1923 to 1926. In the 1926 Democratic primary McCormack ran against incumbent Congressman James A. Gallivan in the Twelfth Congressional District in South Boston, but lost. Meanwhile he had developed a reputation as a trial lawyer, and by 1928 the law firm of McCormack & Hardy, in which he was a partner, was grossing $30,000 a year. In the same year he was elected to the Congressional seat vacated by Gallivan's death, and he has been re-elected ever since.

As a freshman Congressman in Washington, McCormack worked diligently at his committee assignments and established close relations with John Nance Garner, then Democratic minority leader, and with Congressman Sam Rayburn, McCormack was an undeviating Democrat and an able poker player, qualities that appealed to Garner. When the Democrats won control of the House, McCormack was appointed to the powerful House Ways and Means Committee, the first Democratic Representative to win the influential and sought-after committee assignment after less than two terms in office. Loyalty to his political cronies and constituents became a McCormack trademark. In 1936 he helped to swing support in favor of Sam Rayburn's candidacy for the post of Democratic majority leader. When Rayburn succeeded to the Speakership in 1940, McCormack became the natural choice for majority leader. He served as Rayburn's political confidant and deputy for twenty-one years. In the Republican-controlled Eightieth Congress (1946-47) and again in the Eighty-third Congress (1953-54) when Rayburn was minority leader, McCormack served as Democratic whip.

In the House Congressman McCormack became known as a workhorse who taught himself to be an expert on tax matters. He revered Franklin D. Roosevelt and consistently supported the New Deal program. Although his name was not attached to any major piece of legislation, he was a major force in winning passage of such key New Deal measures as the Tennessee Valley Authority, (1933), the National Housing Act (1934), and the Securities and Exchange Act (1934). Other major legislation for which he voted was the Social Security Act (1935), the Wages and Hours Act (1938), and the revised Neutrality Act (1939). A foe of Communism, McCormack proposed several anti-Communist measures during the 1930's. In 1934 he was appointed as chairman of the first House Committee Investigating Un-American Activities, which probed Nazi and Communist activities in the United States. In 1939 he urged the State Department to recognize the government of Generalissimo Francisco Franco in Spain.

Although in 1940 he voted to delay peacetime selective service legislation until a voluntary enlistment program had been tried out, McCormack played a key role in winning extension of the draft act late in 1941. After the war, he was among the first members of Congress to recognize the importance of the scientific race against Soviet Russia. He served as first chairman of the House Science and Astronautics Committee and sponsored the bill creating the National Aeronautics and Space Administration in 1958. He was also active in curbing unnecessary military spending.

In the voting on key measures affecting foreign affairs since World War II McCormack voted for the Greek-Turkish aid bill (1947); Marshall Plan extension (1949); economic aid to Korea and Formosa (1950); President Eisenhower's Mideast doctrine (1957); the Mutual Security Act (1958); and President Kennedy's Peace Corps Act (1961). On domestic issues he supported the anti-poll tax bill and the employment-production bill (1945); the subversive activities control bill (1948); rent control extension (1950); draft extension (1951); increased unemployment benefits (1954); school construction aid (1956); civil rights legislation (1957; 1960); the Area Redevelopment Act (1961); and the Housing Act (1961). He opposed the two-term limitation on the Presidency (1947), the Tidelands oil bill (1948; 1951), and flexible farm price supports (1954). Although McCormack supported the Smith-Connally anti-strike bill early during World War II, he opposed the Case strike control bill (1946), and voted against overriding President Truman's veto of the Taft-Hartley bill (1947). He also voted against the Labor-Management Reporting and Disclosure Act (1959).

Illness necessitating the absence of Speaker Sam Rayburn, McCormack was elected, on August 31, 1961, as Speaker pro tempore for the remaining twenty-seven days of the session. When the second session of the Eighty-seventh Congress opened on January 10, 1962 McCormack was elected to the Speakership vacated by the death of Rayburn by a straight party vote of 248 to 166 over his Republican opponent, Charles A. Halleck of Indiana.

His position makes McCormack second in line of succession to the President, after the Vice-President, if death causes a Presidential vacancy. His annual salary is $35,000 a year plus $10,000 for expenses. The Speaker wields enormous influence in determining the course of government policy, both as presiding officer over the 437 members of the House of Representatives and as the President's chief advocate in Congress. He can entertain or refuse to entertain any motion at his own discretion, and he can refuse recognition to members trying to speak on the floor of the House. All legislative enactments must bear his signature.

During his long House career, McCormack has earned a reputation as a feared debater on the floor, where he is known as "the fighting Irishman." As Speaker, however, he follows the tradition of leaving the speechmaking to others.

McCormack is also known as "the great compromiser"; an ability to compromise is considered vital for the presiding officer of the House. His ability to bridge the gap between Northern liberals and Southern conservatives of the Democratic party was proved during the Democratic national conventions of 1944, 1952, and 1956, when he served as chairman of the Democratic platform committee and managed to keep the explosive civil rights issue from splitting the party in two.

Speaker McCormack's relations with President Kennedy, whose legislative program it is his task to push through in the House, have been closely scrutinized by political observers. Although both men are Democrats, both are from Boston and both are Roman Catholics, strained relations between the two are reported to date back to 1947, when Kennedy, then a member of the House, refused to sign a petition circulated by majority leader McCormack seeking a Presidential pardon for former Boston Mayor James M. Curley, who had been convicted of mail fraud. Political observers have also noted the contest between McCormack and Kennedy forces for control of the Massachusetts State Democratic Committee, and the charge that in 1961 McCormack helped to scuttle President Kennedy's aid-to-education bill on the ground that it did not provide for federal aid to parochial schools.

Another possible difference between McCormack and Kennedy has been the alleged rivalry between the Speaker's nephew, Massachusetts Attorney-General Edward J. McCormack Jr., whom the childless Speaker has raised as a son, and Edward Kennedy, younger brother of the President, both of whom were reported early in 1962 as seeking the Democratic nomination for the Senate. Speaker McCormack has denied that any of these differences are important, either as they affect his personal relationship with the President or his responsibility toward the President's legislative program. "The President and I are close friends," the Speaker is quoted in *Newsweek* as saying. "There are probably a few persons who for selfish reasons are trying to create the impression of a feud" (January 15, 1962). At the 1960 Democratic National Convention McCormack was chairman of the Massachusetts delegation for Kennedy, and he helped to bring about the nomination, by acclamation, of Lyndon Johnson as vice-presidential candidate.

In 1920 John W. McCormack married M. Harriet Joyce, a singer. The McCormacks have no children, and they make their permanent home in Dorchester, an old section of Boston, where they occupy half of an old two-family house. While Congress is in session they live in the Washington Hotel in Washington, D.C. According to Washington legend, the devoted McCormacks have never spent a night apart in forty-one years of married life. Tall, gaunt, and white-haired, McCormack stands at six feet two inches, and wears rimless glasses and dark suits. He is a heavy cigar smoker and a teetotaler. His one hobby, other than politics, is reading.

An active Roman Catholic—opponents call him "The Archbishop"—McCormack is a close friend of many clerical leaders of his church and holds the highest Papal decoration awarded to laymen, that of Knight Commander of the Order of St. Gregory the Great, with star. Several other honors and awards have been conferred upon him. He has received honorary LL.D. degrees from eleven colleges. McCormack is an Elk and a Moose, and he is a member of the South Boston Citizens' Association, the American Legion, the Knights of Columbus, the Catholic Order of Foresters, and the Ancient Order of Hibernians. He wears the rosette of the Knights of Malta (first class) in his lapel.

McCormack's close ties with the Catholic Church have not alienated him from other religious groups among his constituency. Many Jewish voters in his district refer to him as "Rabbi John." A consistent defender of minorities, he once told the late racist Representative John Rankin of Mississippi: "A man's racial origin means nothing to me, a person's name means nothing to me. A person's religion I respect. But what does mean everything to me is a person's mind. And when I meet a person with a bigoted mind, I am meeting a person I do not like, a person I have nothing but contempt for" (*Time,* January 19, 1962).

References

N Y Post Mag p4 F 18 '62 por
N Y Times p16 Ja 11 '62 por
Newsweek 59:15+ Ja 15 '62 pors
Time 78:16 Ja 19 '62 pors
American Catholic Who's Who, 1962 and 1963
Congressional Directory (1961)
Who's Who in America, 1960-61

MARAIS, JEAN (mä-rā') Dec. 11, 1913-
French actor

Address: b. 49 bis ave. Hoche, Paris 8ᵉ, France; h. Marnes la Coquette, Seine et Oise, France

One of the most durable of France's screen heroes, Jean Marais has been known to the moviegoers of his native land since *Le Pavillon Brûle* (*The Pavilion Burns,* 1941). He was introduced to American motion-picture audiences in 1947 as the triple hero of Jean Cocteau's *La Belle et la Bête* (*Beauty and the Beast*), a film that received the Grand Prix Louis Delluc. His more recent film appearances include the title role in *Pontius Pilate,* filmed in 1961. A stage career, dating to the late 1930's has paralleled his career on the screen. "Jeannot," Jean Cocteau has said, "brings forth from the most sophisticated Parisian theatregoer . . . gales of laughter . . . tears."

Jean Marais was born Jean Villain-Marais on December 11, 1913, in Cherbourg, France. His father, Alfred Villain-Marais, a veterinarian, had already begun to drop the first half of the name when Jean was born. Jean did not see much of his father, who left for the war in 1914. Almost immediately upon her husband's return four years later, Madame Villain-Marais left him, taking her sons Jean and Henri (now deceased) to Paris with her.

They soon settled a short distance from Paris, at Le Vésinet. With them lived the maternal grandmother, from whose Alsatian accent Jean acquired an inadequately rolled *r* and a reckless aspirate *h*. After a couple of years in a small

Yves Robertet, Paris

JEAN MARAIS

private school he became, at eight, a part-time boarder at the Collège de Saint Germain. He remembers himself between eight and twelve as an unbearably conceited brat. He was moved from school to school—from Saint Germain to Condorcet to Janson de Sailly and back to Saint Germain. He always stood at the bottom of his class in everything except gymnastics, art, and recitation. Finally he was consigned to Saint Nicolas, a school at Buzenval noted for its handling of difficult students. There he suddenly began to shine scholastically. His favorite childhood recreation was going to movies, and he was particularly impressed with the acting of "la belle Pearl White."

In 1930, just as he was developing a love of study, he was taken from school and apprenticed to a Le Vésinet photographer. In his spare time, for extra money, he caddied at local golf courses. Not interested in anything but acting as a life work, he was as bad an apprentice as he was a caddy. Nevertheless, he later found work with a succession of Paris photographers, principally retouching and working in the darkroom.

As adolescence receded, Marais felt that he would never become an actor without pursuing the goal more fully. He quit his job, telling his mother he had been fired. For a time his only work was painting. He exhibited few canvases, and sold even fewer, but his painting did serve as barter for dramatic lessons from a certain Monsieur Paupélix and as an excuse for financial help from film writer Marcel Lherbier. Lherbier obtained for Marais an unsuccessful screen test.

His dramatic lessons did not become obviously fruitful until Marais came under the tutelage of Charles Dullin. While studying under Dullin, Marais paid his way with walk-on-roles in Dullin's productions. His other money—never quite enough for living expenses—came from minor roles in films. He played several walk-on

roles in Dullin's production of *Jules César* (Julius Caesar) at the Théâtre de l'Atelier, Paris, in late 1936.

At the Antoine, Paris, in May 1937, in connection with the Paris Exposition, Marais appeared as the chorus in Jean Cocteau's *Oedipe Roi* and as Malcolm in *Macbeth*. Marais' relationship to Cocteau soon grew into a great and enduring friendship. Marais appeared as Galahad in Cocteau's *Les Chevaliers de la Table Ronde* at the Oeuvre, Paris, in the fall of 1937. Cocteau wrote *Les Parents Terribles* for Marais and Yvonne de Bray. The play opened at the Théâtre des Ambassadeurs, Paris, in October 1938, and soon moved to the Bouffes-Parisiens.

Conscripted in 1939, Marais served in the French army of the air until the fall of France the following year. In 1944 he joined the Leclerc division of the American Third Army. For his part in driving the Germans out of Alsace he received the Croix de Guerre. Meanwhile, during the occupation, Marais had appeared in Racine's *Brittanicus* at the Bouffes-Parisiens and the Hébertot theaters in February 1941; he had created the lead in Jean Cocteau's *La Machine à Écrire* at the Hébertot in April 1941; he had played major roles in Molière's *L'Avare*, directed by Charles Dullin, at the Théâtre Sarah Bernhardt in February 1942, and in Racine's *Andromaque* at the Théâtre Edouard VII in April 1944. After false starts in other projected films he had made his debut as a featured cinema actor in *Le Pavillon Brûle*, directed by Jacques de Baroncelli, in 1941. This was followed by leading roles in other films: *Le Lit à Colonnes* (1942); *L'Éternel Retour* (1943), written by Jean Cocteau and directed by Jean Delannoy; and Christian Jaque's *Le Voyage sans Espoir* (1944).

L'Éternel Retour, a modern version of the Tristan and Isolde legend, in which Marais played the young man who fell in love with the bride he brought home for his uncle, reached the United States in 1948 as *The Eternal Return.* It aroused less enthusiasm among American critics than had *La Belle et la Bête (Beauty and the Beast)*, a surrealistic treatment of the fairy tale, written and directed by Jean Cocteau, released in France in 1945 and in the United States in 1947. According to Bosley Crowther, Marais played the Beast-Prince with "the grace of a dancer, the voice of a muffled baritone" (New York *Times*, December 24, 1947). Other films in which Marais appeared in the immediate postwar years included *Les Chouans* (1946); *Ruy Blas* (1947), Cocteau's adaptation of Victor Hugo's story; and two films directed and written by Cocteau: *L'Aigle à Deux Têtes* (1947) and *Les Parents Terribles* (1948).

Les Parents Terribles, with Marais again in the male lead, had meanwhile been revived on the stage of the Théâtre Gymnase in October 1946. In Brussels Marais had appeared in *Renaud et Armide* in April 1946. Again in Brussels in October 1947 he appeared in *L'Aigle à Deux Têtes.* The latter play moved to the Théâtre Hébertot, Paris, in December. In March and April 1949 Marais toured Cairo, Alexandria, Istanbul, and Ankara with productions of *Les Parents Terribles, Britannicus, Léocadia, Huis*

Clos, and *La Machine Infernale*. At the Madeleine, Paris, he appeared in *Chéri* in November 1949. Other of his theater credits include *Pygmalion*, *Deux sur une Balançoire (Two for the Seesaw)*, and *César et Cléopâtre*. Since the early 1950's his stage appearances have included roles at the Comédie Française. He has also performed at the Cirque d'Hiver (Winter Circus), Paris.

His next cinema role after *Aux Yeux du Souvenir* (1948) was Crown Prince Rudolph of Austria in *Le Secret de Mayerling, (The Secret of Mayerling)* a fictional version of the prince's tragic love affair directed by Jean Delannoy. The film was released in France in November 1948 and in the United States in the spring of 1951. The response of American critics was lukewarm. *Orphée (Orpheus*, 1949), written and directed by Cocteau, fared somewhat better in the United States. "Jean Marais gives a handsome and tortured portrayal of Orpheus, modulating his characterization to suit the varying moods of the film," Howard Barnes observed in the New York *Herald Tribune* (November 30, 1950).

Marais appeared in the 1950 film releases *Le Château de Verre* (The Glass Castle), directed by René Clément, and *Les Miracles ne se Produisent qu'une Fois* (Miracles Only Happen Once), directed by Yves Allégret. The frothy *Julietta*, Françoise Giroud's adaptation of the novel by Louise de Vilmorin, directed by Marc Allégret, was released in the United States in 1957. Marais played the affianced lawyer embarrassed by the unsolicited presence in his household of a young woman not his fiancée. "At the end. . . ," William K. Zinsser wrote in the New York *Herald Tribune* (June 8, 1957), "he brings something quite touching to this unsubstantial tale." Made several years before, in Italy, *White Nights*, based on a story by Dostoevski and directed by Luchino Visconti, was pronounced dull by many critics when it was released in the United States in 1961. Marais' role, that of an idealized lover in the heroine's background who appears in flashbacks and in mists, was not auspicious, and more than one critic used the adjective "wooden." Marais played the title role in *Pontius Pilate*, a costume spectacle with an international cast filmed in Italy in 1961 by Lux Films, under the American director Irving Rapper. His other film credits include *Inside a Girls' Dormitory, Carmen, Deux sur une Balançoire*, and *Testament of Orpheus*.

Jean Marais is just under six feet in height, weighs 172 pounds, and has blue eyes and blond hair. He is a bachelor and a Roman Catholic. In his spare time he continues to paint. Some sources report swimming, horseback riding, and skiing as his recreations, and there is an implication of the athlete in his popular image. "Strange thing," Jean Cocteau wrote in *Jean Marais* (Calmann-Lévy, 1950), "but Jean Marais engages in no athletic exercise unless it is required by one of his roles. Then he imitates the bodily movements of professionals." Cocteau quotes Marais as having said: "It is odd that everyone tries to be physically beautiful when anyone can be morally beautiful and no one does the exercise for it." A pet dog, called Moulouk, became well known to Marais' fans in the 1940's and 1950's. He is known to his fans as well as to his intimates as Jeannot.

References

Cocteau, Jean. Jean Marais (1950)
Dictionnaire Biographique Français Contemporain (1954)
International Who's Who, 1961-62
Marais, Jean. Mes Quatres Verités (1957)
Who's Who in France, 1960-61

MARVEL, MRS. ARCHIE D. June 1, 1904-
Organization official

Address: b. Young Women's Christian Association, 600 Lexington Ave., New York 22; h. 50 Morningside Dr., New York 25; 919 N. Lincoln Ave., Hastings, Neb.

Growing in pace with the importance of woman's role in society, the Young Women's Christian Association of the United States of America now has some 2,250,000 members who take part in YWCA activities in several thousands of places throughout the country. Mrs. Archie D. Marvel, who was elected YWCA's national president for a three-year term in May 1961, has contributed to the goals and development of the association over a period of almost forty years. In other volunteer service, at the same time, she was prominent in groups concerned with health, education, recreation, and social welfare, in her hometown of Hastings, Nebraska. By providing residences, club and recreation rooms, lectures and classes, and vocational guidance, the YWCA gives girls and women opportunities to develop a sense of purpose in life and capacity for leadership so that they may play a more constructive part in the world today.

Elizabeth Newell Marvel was born in Alexandria, Nebraska on June 1, 1904, the only child of Harry J. and Charlotte (Douglas) Newell. Her father was a physician who started practice as a horse-and-buggy doctor in Alexandria, and her mother was a teacher. Elizabeth attended Alexandria High School, where her chief recreational interest was in dramatics, and graduated as valedictorian in 1921.

Then as a student at Hastings College in Hastings, Nebraska, Elizabeth Newell majored in home economics. The glee club and the yearbook, as well as dramatics, occupied a large part of her free time, and she was awarded the Student of the Year citation. She received the B.S. degree in 1926 and a few months after graduation, on September 12, 1925, married Archie D. Marvel.

Ever since her marriage, Mrs. Marvel has made her home in Hastings, where she has devoted herself to social service activities. In the 1930's she was a member of Nebraska's Governor's Coordinating Committee for Youth, and during World War II she served as Adams County chairman for Red Cross surgical dressings and as a member of the Red Cross board for Adams County. She is a past president of the Mental Health Association in Hastings and has belonged to the Hastings School board, the Hospital Auxiliary, Woman's Club, and to the

MRS. ARCHIE D. MARVEL

Faculty Woman's Club of Hastings College. From 1950 to 1956 she was chairman of social education and action for the Presbyterian Woman's Association.

While at Hastings College, she had been president of the College YWCA, and because of her experiences at that time she decided to choose the Young Woman's Christian Association as the organization through which she would do her major volunteer service. Mrs. Marvel's connection with the YWCA has covered nearly forty years, mostly on the regional level, where she is a member and past president of the Hastings group. She has worked with nearly every major national YWCA committee and has been a member of the national board of the YWCA since 1952, serving on the committee to review the structure of the national board at the time of her election to the presidency. Her past positions include Nebraska's representative on the national public affairs committee, a national YWCA recruiter of personnel, and vice-president and chairman of the central region of the YWCA.

Mrs. Marvel was elected president at the twenty-second triennial national convention of the YWCA, which was held in Denver, Colorado from May 8 to May 13, 1961. She succeeded Miss Lilace Reid Barnes of Illinois, who had served for two terms as president of the national YWCA and had earlier been president for eight years of the World YWCA at its headquarters in Geneva.

As president of the national YWCA, Mrs. Marvel is the presiding official of the 120-member national board and works closely with the general secretary and other national staff members and volunteers in creating policies and programs to aid local YWCAs. She finds her responsibilities awe-inspiring and challenging. There are more than 4,600 places throughout the United States where YWCA activities are being carried

on, including over 440 community organizations, 200 branches and centers, 310 resident and day camps, and 480 student associations.

Mrs. Marvel stepped into the top volunteer post in the YWCA at a challenging time in the history of the organization. The outgoing president, Miss Lilace Reid Barnes, expressed her conviction in the 1960-61 annual report that "never since the YWCA began over one hundred years ago in a period of vast social and economic upheaval have the winds of change, conflict, hope blown open so many doors of opportunity, responsibility for women." As the position of women in society grows increasingly vital and demanding, the YWCA seeks to equip its members physically, socially, intellectually, and spiritually to meet the demands placed upon them.

In keeping with its New Testament credo "I am come that they might have life and that they might have it more abundantly," the YWCA is a voluntary membership organization with a Christian purpose. It makes a conscious effort to include among its members women and girls from different economic, racial, occupational, religious, cultural, and age groups. In an interview with Mary Kelly of the *Christian Science Monitor* (June 20, 1961) Mrs. Marvel said, "Our organization cuts across the lines. It is a service to the minority group of a community, and to the majority group. It extends friendliness to those of differing nationality and race. It has something for the teen-ager and for the middle-aged. And while it's meeting the individual need, it builds a fellowship in which we seek to remember that Jesus loved all mankind."

In its effort to reach as many persons as possible the YWCA endorses community co-operation in social services and social action and co-operation with other organizations such as churches, religious groups, agencies working with youth, schools, organizations concerned with women's interests, civic groups, and community funds and health and welfare councils. The YWCA also continues its participation as one of the six member agencies, and the only woman's organization, in the USO (United Service Organizations). On September 1, 1961 the YWCA joined with the National Council of Jewish Women and the United Church Women to urge President John F. Kennedy to seek an inspected ban on the testing of nuclear weapons through the United Nations.

Mrs. Marvel pointed out in the *Christian Science Monitor* interview that two recent developments have called for new training and a new approach in YWCA work. In her words, "One of these is the population trend, the mushroom growths in suburbs, frequently around an industrial plant. The other is the problem of early marriage. Even 11th-graders sometimes need help about wedding gowns." To deal with the first problem some of the 132,000 volunteers and the 21,450 professional staff members of the YWCA in the United States experimented with new ways of bringing their services to the suburbs and other outlying areas. Neighboring YWCAs sometimes joined forces; small groups of experienced staff members and volunteers were sent out to explore needs and available resources;

and new YWCAs adapted themselves to whatever physical facilities they found in a new community.

The YWCA has also been placing great emphasis on its Y-Teen programs and on its college student groups. There are more than 500,000 teen-age girls (and boy associates) in the YWCA's 5,500 Y-Teen groups, and student associations on university and college campuses in the United States number almost 480. By constantly extending the availability of its membership and facilities, the association hopes to serve the needs of youth in today's world. In speaking of work with young people, Mrs. Marvel has said, "I believe the best attitude is to help them keep an open mind, to find the meaning of life without relating that faith to a particular theology" (*Christian Science Monitor*).

An around-the-world traveler, Mrs. Marvel is interested in the global development of the association. Today's nearly 2,250,000 registered members of the YWCA in the United States are also affiliated with the World YWCA, in which seventy countries are represented. As part of its international fellowship program, in January 1961 the YWCA initiated a Latin American-United States exchange between selected women leaders from the two continents concerned with the need for sharing inter-American problems and resources. From December 29, 1960 to January 9, 1961 in Salisbury, Southern Rhodesia, the first World YWCA Conference was held in recognition of the growing stature of African women.

Following through on its world fellowship policies and programs to work consciously to bring closer peoples of different nationalities, the delegates to the 1961 national convention of the YWCA reaffirmed the 1946 interracial charter in which the members of the association pledged themselves "to continue to pioneer in an interracial experience that shall be increasingly democratic and Christian." This action was taken in response to a report by the chairman of the committee on racial inclusiveness that "progress toward including Negro women and girls in the mainstream of association life is very uneven in depth, breadth and speed."

Mrs. Archie D. Marvel is the mother of a daughter, Marilyn (Mrs. Alexander M. Shafernich), and a son, John N. Marvel (an attorney in Hastings), and of two stepsons, Richard D. Marvel (a Nebraska legislator) and Robert J. Marvel (a doctor in Indianapolis). Her eyes are gray-blue and her hair is light-brown; she weighs 135 pounds and is five feet seven and a half inches tall. Her church affiliation is Presbyterian and she is a Republican. In 1960, while serving as vice-president for the YWCA in the central region, she was awarded the Hastings College alumnae citation.

Reference

Christian Sci Mon p7 Je 20 '61 por

MARVEL, ELIZABETH NEWELL *See* Marvel, Mrs. A. D.

MUENCH, ALOISIUS (JOSEPH), CARDINAL Feb. 18, 1889-Feb. 15, 1962 Roman Catholic prelate; was consecrated bishop of Fargo, North Dakota in 1935 and given the title of Archbishop in 1950; Papal Nuncio to West Germany (1951-59); became a Cardinal in 1959 and the only United States member of the Roman Curia in 1960. See *Current Biography* (April) 1960.

Obituary

N Y Times p29 F 16 '62

MURPHY, (ELEANOR) PATRICIA 1911(?)- Restaurateur; horticulturist
Address: b. c/o Westchester Candlelight Restaurant, 1703 Central Park Ave., Yonkers, N.Y.

As famous for her flowers as for her food, Patricia Murphy is the restaurateur who owns the popular Candlelight Restaurant in Westchester County, New York, and Bahia Mar, a smaller establishment in Fort Lauderdale, Florida. Miss Murphy came to New York City from her native Newfoundland at the age of seventeen and opened her first restaurant during the Depression. The many material rewards of her enterprises mean less to her than the satisfaction she has derived from her work in horticulture. Her restaurants, her estate in Florida, and her penthouse over-looking Central Park in New York City are beautified by magnificent gardens. Miss Murphy owns seven greenhouses, has over 100,000 orchid plants in cultivation, and has won many prizes and citations for her horticultural displays.

Eleanor Patricia Murphy was born around 1911 in Placentia, a small fishing village in Newfoundland, where her family had lived for four generations. Her great-grandfather left Dublin, Ireland under an assumed name to escape persecution by the English. Her father, Captain Frank Murphy, owned the general store in Placentia, which lived up to its motto of selling "everything from a needle to an anchor." As the elder daughter (she has a younger sister, Sheila), Patricia was occasionally allowed to help out in the store. She also worked on her father's four-page newspaper, *Murphy's Good Things,* for which she wrote obituaries. She attended school and studied music at St. Michael's Convent in nearby St. George.

With a sheaf of classical piano music and a small roll of bills Miss Murphy arrived in New York City in 1929 to continue her musical studies. She never realized this ambition, however, because she disliked the prospect of living in her great-uncle's house on Staten Island to reduce her expenses. The day after she arrived she moved to Manhattan and soon supported herself by playing the piano at a student cafeteria-restaurant near Columbia University. She made her debut in the restaurant business in the same establishment when she discovered that she could earn extra money by taking over behind the counter for workers who failed to show up.

Dishing up blue plate specials did not, however, guarantee Miss Murphy her job. Although jazz was sweeping the United States, she could

PATRICIA MURPHY

only play the classical repertoire and she was soon out of work. For a time she earned a precarious livelihood by handcoloring postcards at $3 per hundred. Having learned that when one works at a restaurant one is at least assured of regular meals, Miss Murphy next took a job as cashier in one of a chain of small tearooms run by a Mr. and Mrs. Foster. This time she was fired for her zeal in urging departing customers to buy chocolates, chewing gum, and cigarettes. Mr. and Mrs. Foster considered her enthusiasm bad form.

In the meantime the stock market had crashed. Although there seemed to be an endless supply of postcards to be handcolored at $3 per hundred, Miss Murphy was aware that there was a limit to the amount of money that she could earn in this fashion. Determined not to return to the fishing village in Newfoundland, she invested $60 of savings in her first Candlelight Restaurant—in half of a basement that had previously housed a run-down tearoom in Brooklyn Heights, New York.

From the beginning, Patricia Murphy established two of the features that were to be associated with her later enterprises. She introduced candlelight because naked electric light bulbs hung from the basement ceiling, and hot popovers because they were tasty, somewhat exotic, and not too difficult to make. She offered a 65 or 85-cent dinner, a 45-cent luncheon, and netted an even dime in profits on each meal.

Her equipment for opening night consisted of thirty-six seats and twenty cups and saucers that required some fast juggling. No wonder her expectations were modest. In *Glow of Candlelight,* her autobiography, Miss Murphy wrote: "All I wished for was to break a little better than even, so that there could be a second night." By the end of the month, when she counted the money in the till, the $60 had grown to $500.

Throughout the 1930's the Brooklyn Candlelight restaurant continued to prosper, and Miss Murphy took over the basement and backyard of the adjoining brownstone. After repeal she obtained a liquor license. In 1932 the Brooklyn Candlelight Restaurant became one of the first restaurants in the United States to install air conditioning, although some of Miss Murphy's elderly customers feared that it would bring on rheumatism.

Looking for new fields to conquer, Patricia Murphy expanded her business interests to include the importing and exporting of cotton and the marketing of lobsters. (She undertook the latter enterprise to help the fishermen of Newfoundland, whose cod fishing had been wrecked by an underwater earthquake.) When she was refused permission to market the lobsters at the Fulton Fish Market she obtained a concession running a cafeteria for the Brooklyn Union Gas Company, where she offered fresh lobsters on the 25-cent table d'hote luncheon. She also operated a lobster stand at Jones Beach, but it proved too much for her; the importing of lobster became the only business at which Patricia Murphy ever failed.

By 1939 the Brooklyn Candlelight restaurant was netting $50 a day and Patricia Murphy was running a profitable catering business on the side. She was eager to invade Manhattan, but she failed to obtain a restaurant site when the landlord discovered that Pat Murphy was a woman. She soon found an appropriate location on 60th Street just east of Madison Avenue. Although the new restaurant started with nearly six times the number of seats with which she had opened in Brooklyn, Miss Murphy brought with her to Manhattan not only candlelight and popovers but also the "extras" in food and service that had helped to make her first venture a success. Long after the time when she was serving over 500 meals a day, she was still serving only peeled tomatoes and making all her coffee in individual pots. She encouraged the patronage of white-collar girls, even though some of her East Side dowagers objected to the "riff-raff," and during World War II the restaurant became a favorite with servicemen, who seldom had to stand in line.

The 60th Street Candlelight Restaurant was twice enlarged during Miss Murphy's proprietorship. Meanwhile the Brooklyn Candlelight continued to prosper and she commuted between the two boroughs in a secondhand roadster. Recalling the establishment of her second restaurant, Patricia Murphy has written: "I see that this is when I really crashed the big city. I had made a go of it in Brooklyn, against heavy odds, but Sixtieth Street gave a different glow of candlelight, brighter and more exciting."

Her first suburban restaurant was situated in Manhasset, Long Island, where she introduced parking lots in front (cars had always been inconveniently parked behind rural restaurants) and brightly costumed waiters and waitresses whose uniforms changed with the seasons. To keep potential customers from going away when the restaurant was crowded, she set out attractive plantings on the grounds and opened a gift shop on the premises. One short-lived experiment was an outdoor spring painting show. Patricia Murphy's Manhasset Candlelight restaurant was an immediate success; it grossed almost $1,500,000 during its first year.

By 1954 Miss Murphy had discovered that running three flourishing restaurants was too much of a merry-go-round and she disposed of them so that she could have "one perfect candlelight." The site that she chose was a bleak and unpromising hillside near the New York Thruway, but before she had finished, after having spent more than $1,000,000, she had transformed "Patricia Murphy's Folly" into one of the garden spots of Westchester County. In 1956 she received a citation award from the Federated Garden Clubs of New York State for accomplishing the greatest improvement in a piece of property within a year.

One of the largest restaurants in the East, the Westchester Candlelight restaurant serves more than a million meals a year. Its grounds are so spacious that a Mercedes-Benz lounge car is used to whisk customers from the parking lot to the restaurant. While waiting for a table—and sometimes hundreds may be waiting at one time—customers can sample free shrimp and canapés at the bar, visit a greenhouse full of exotic orchids, or browse in a gift shop. Sixty thousand tulip plants bloom in the spring, 10,000 chrysanthemums in the fall, and in other seasons there are lilies, azaleas, roses, and daffodils. Much is made of holidays. At Christmas there is a Snow Queen, an outdoor carrousel, and a crèche with live animals; other holidays bring forth appropriate decorations.

In 1959 Miss Murphy bought the Bahia Mar restaurant in Fort Lauderdale, Florida. When she first saw the restaurant, built at the end of a pier, she dubbed it the "SS Concrete"; however her investment of nearly $75,000 in landscaping transformed Bahia Mar into another beauty spot. Smaller than the Westchester Candlelight restaurant, Bahia Mar serves 2,000 daily.

Patricia Murphy's mode of transportation has changed with her fortunes. Instead of driving the old roadster in which she used to commute between Brooklyn and Manhattan, she now travels between New York and Florida in a private twin-engined plane that she often flies herself. In addition to her American establishments, Miss Murphy owns and operates a supper club in London, England.

Although her financial success has been great, it is her horticultural activity that has been most gratifying to Patricia Murphy. In addition to the floral displays at her restaurants, she has created exquisite gardens at both her homes: Kinsale, her Florida estate where she has more than forty-eight acres under cultivation, and Sky High, her upper Fifth Avenue penthouse apartment in New York City, where the flowers on the terrace match the color scheme of each room. Among her many horticultural awards are the 1961 trophy of the Horticultural Society of New York for her arrangement of begonias and first prize at the 1961 International Flower Show in New York for her arrangement of orchids. Her orchid carrousel, which cost $25,000 to prepare, was the hit of the International Flower Show in 1959 and she has had both an orchid and a dahlia named after her.

In 1961 Miss Murphy added authorship to her manifold activities when her autobiography, *Glow of Candlelight,* was published by Prentice-Hall, Inc. The book contains a special section on gardening; another section, on food, presents the recipe for her famous popovers, of which something like 30,000,000 are now served annually. Patricia Murphy has also developed a line of floral perfumes, including Green Orchid, Gold Orchid, and Regina Rose.

In the 1930's Patricia Murphy was married briefly to a Wall Street broker, but the marriage was annulled. In 1948 she married Captain James Kiernan, a retired naval architect, who became a partner and important aid in all her business enterprises. He died in 1954. Miss Murphy, who has brown eyes and blond hair, darts about like a hummingbird. In addition to gardening, her hobbies include entertaining, horseback riding, and travel.

References

N Y Post Mag p15 N 26 '61 por
N Y World-Telegram p33 Mr 17 '59 por
Murphy, Patricia. Glow of Candlelight (1961)

OGBURN, CHARLTON Aug. 19, 1882-Feb. 25, 1962 Lawyer; author; general counsel for the American Federation of Labor (1933-38); counsel of the Reconstruction Finance Corporation (1936-43); wrote several books on law and on Shakespearean authorship, including *This Star of England* (1952), in collaboration with his wife. See *Current Biography* (February) 1955.

Obituary

N Y Times p27 F 26 '62

OSGOOD, CHARLES E(GERTON) Nov. 20, 1916- Psychologist; educator.

Address: b. Institute of Communications Research, University of Illinois, Urbana, Ill.; h. 304 E. Mumford Dr., Urbana, Ill.

The practical application of psychological research to international relations is a major concern of Dr. Charles E. Osgood, professor of psychology and director of the Institute of Communications Research at the University of Illinois, and president-elect of the American Psychological Association for 1962-63. He has devised a plan to reduce the tensions produced by the current nuclear testing stalemate and to hasten disarmament, and is at present the chairman of the A.P.A.'s committee on psychology in national and international affairs. Osgood has taught at Yale University and at the University of Connecticut. In 1945-46 he did research for the United States Army Air Force and the United States Navy. A regular contributor to scholarly journals and the author or co-author of several books, he is a recognized authority on human communication, cognitive processes, and the theory of learning. The American Psychological Association honored him for his work by giving him a Distinguished Scientific Contribution

CHARLES E. OSGOOD

Award in 1960. The American Psychological Association on September 2, 1961 announced that Osgood had been elected to succeed Dr. Neal E. Miller of Yale University as its president effective in September 1962.

Charles Egerton Osgood was born on November 20, 1916 in Somerville, Massachusetts, to Merrill White Osgood, then general manager of the Jordan Marsh Company department store in Boston, and Ruth Madeline (Egerton) Osgood. He was reared in Brookline, Massachusetts. At Brookline High School he edited both the high school newspaper and the literary magazine; he graduated in 1935. He entered Dartmouth University with an ambition to become a journalist, but a psychology course that he took in his sophomore year caused him to change his mind. He graduated in 1939 with a B.A. degree in psychology and anthropology. After spending an additional year at Dartmouth as a laboratory assistant he enrolled at the graduate school of Yale University where he received his Ph.D. degree in 1945. While at Yale, he was a research associate and taught the introductory course in psychology.

In 1945 Osgood became a research associate in the Office of Scientific Research and Development at the Smoky Hill Army Air Force Base in Salina, Kansas, where he aided in the training of B-29 gunners. During 1945-46 he did research at the United States submarine base in New London, Connecticut, and served as an instructor at Yale. He became Assistant Professor of Psychology at the University of Connecticut in 1946 and remained there for three years. In 1949 he joined the faculty of the University of Illinois in Urbana, Illinois as an associate professor. Four years later he became a full professor and in 1957 was appointed director of the Institute for Communications Research at the university's College of Journalism and Communication.

Dr. Osgood's special areas of interest in psychology have been human communications, cognitive processes, and learning theory. In 1950 he received a three-year faculty Fellowship, sponsored by the Social Science Research Council, which enabled him to undertake extensive research into the language and learning processes. In 1952 he helped to organize the council's committee on linguistics and psychology. He remained an active committee member until 1959, and took part in a number of conferences and summer seminars.

The results of Osgood's research on meaning and learning theory have been published in the *Journal of Applied Psychology*, the *Psychological Review*, the *American Journal of Psychology*, and other professional journals. His first book, *Method and Theory in Experimental Psychology* (Oxford, 1953) is an evaluation of the existing literature on sensory processes, perception, learning, and symbolic processes with suggestions of areas needing further research. Among these areas is what Osgood terms the "infant science" of language behavior. He maintains that further research is possible because the data of language behavior can be quantified and subjected to statistical analysis. One development in the field may be a fusion of learning theories with the techniques of mathematical statistics. "In terms of its central relevance to general psychological theory and its potential applicability to complex social problems," he says, "no other area of psychology so greatly demands attention as language behavior—and in the past has received so little."

Osgood's next work was *The Measurement of Meaning*, which was published in 1957 by the University of Illinois Press. Professors George J. Suci and Percy H. Tannenbaum, who were at that time members of the Institute for Communications Research, collaborated with him on the research and compilation of the book. Adopting a fresh approach to the measurement of meaning—an approach that Osgood calls the semantic differential—the authors used a technique that combined controlled association and scaling procedures. They intend the semantic differential to be used as a technique in devising tests for specific purposes. Studies in the book suggest how the semantic differential can be applied to the study of attitudes, assessment of personality, effects of psychotherapy, and the effects of messages in advertising and other forms of mass communication.

Osgood and his collaborators view their book as a progress report that allows much more room for study in the field of measurement of meaning. They admit that the major gap in the work is the lack of an "explicit statement of the relation between the theoretical conception of meaning as a representational mediation process, and the operations of measurements which constitute the semantic differential technique." Although he entertained some reservations, R. J. Hill, writing in the *American Sociological Review* (April 1958), called the book "stimulating and sophisticated." Charles Morris, who reviewed the book for the *American Journal of Sociology* (March 1958), felt that it was a significant contribution to the field of psychology that should inspire further research.

In 1958 Osgood was invited to spend a year at the Center for Advanced Study in the Behavioral Sciences at Stanford University. He accepted, intending to spend his time writing another book on the psychology of language, but his concern over the mounting tensions of the cold war led him to abandon the book in order to draft a disarmament plan based on a psychological approach. The first step of the plan calls for a reduction of international tensions through action rather than through meaningless and ineffective words.

Osgood calls the plan Graduated Reciprocation in Tension-reduction (GRIT). It envisions the United States as taking the initial steps towards disarmament by dismantling one of its nuclear striking bases near the Soviet Union. As the sincerity of the United States becomes evident, public opinion will force the Russians to reciprocate by cutting down their nuclear power "for reasons of good sense—even if not of goodwill."

The University of Illinois has circulated Dr. Osgood's plan to policy makers and to diplomatic correspondents as well as to psychologists. Speaking at a session of the 1960 annual convention of the American Psychological Association in Chicago, Osgood called the problems faced in the nuclear age "those of human nature and human relationships," and he concluded that they belong in the lap of the social sciences, including psychology. "We do want to preserve our own way of life," Osgood has said, "and to accomplish this we must stay alive" (New York *Times,* July 17, 1961).

At the sixty-eighth annual convention of the American Psychological Association, held in New York City in September 1961, Dr. Charles E. Osgood was elected to succeed Dr. Neal E. Miller of Yale University as president. He will take office in September 1962. Osgood, who joined the American Psychological Association in 1942, is a member of the division of experimental psychology and the division of personality and social psychology. He has served on the committee on academic freedom and tenure, and is a member of the board of scientific affairs, representative to the National Academy of Sciences, and chairman of the committee on psychology in national and international affairs. At the 1961 convention Osgood delivered a paper on the topic "Studies of the Generality of Affective Meaning Systems." He has been conducting a twelve-nation experiment on how people organize language meanings, and he feels that despite linguistic and cultural differences there is a unity of mental processes.

The American Psychological Association was founded in 1892 and had a membership of about 19,000 in late 1961. Its aim is the "advancement of psychology as a science, as a profession, and as a means of promoting human welfare." The association encompasses seventeen divisions and several committees, and it publishes twelve scholarly periodicals. The president is elected annually by a mail ballot during the summer and the results are announced at the annual fall conventions. Presidents are elected a year in advance.

Osgood was awarded a Guggenheim Fellowship for the year 1954-55, and in 1958-59 he was a Fellow at the Center for Advanced Study in the Behavioral Sciences at Stanford University. He was one of three psychologists chosen to receive the American Psychological Association's Distinguished Scientific Contribution Award for 1960, which included a $1,000 stipend. The citation praised his research on meaning within the context of learning theory as "a major factor in stimulating the current growing interest in higher mental processes" (*American Psychologist,* December 1960).

In addition to his membership in the American Psychological Association, Osgood belongs to the American Academy of Arts and Sciences, the Association of American University Professors, and the Linguistic Society of America. He is a member of Sigma Xi (the honorary society in science research) and of Phi Beta Kappa. He has served on the Air Force Scientific Advisory Board, and with the behavioral sciences study section of the National Institute of Mental Health. He is a consultant to the United States Disarmament Administration.

On June 27, 1939 Charles Egerton Osgood married Cynthia Luella Thornton. They have one son, Philip Thornton, a college student, and a daughter, Gail Ruth, who is studying art. Osgood is six feet tall, weighs 175 pounds, and has brown eyes and brown hair. He is an independent in politics and has no church affiliation. He enjoys swimming and tennis and collects jazz records. For relaxation he plays in a University of Illinois jazz combination. Although he has been a devotee of science-fiction, he once said to Alan Levin of the New York *Post* (September 27, 1961): "The world is getting so fantastic, I can get along just reading the newspapers."

References

N Y Post p50 S 27 '61 por

American Men of Science vol 3 (1956)

SPOTTSWOOD, STEPHEN GILL July 18, 1897- Clergyman; organization official

Address: b. National Association for the Advancement of Colored People, 20 W. 40th St., New York 18; h. 1931 16th St., N.W., Washington 9, D.C.

Over a period of nearly forty years Bishop Stephen Gill Spottswood has preached the gospel of freedom in the pulpits of the African Methodist Episcopal Zion Church, while as a member of the National Association for the Advancement of Colored People he has fought for freedom in the many battles of that organization to secure full democracy for all Americans. He believes in a moderate approach to the problem of civil rights and has found that protests involving economic considerations are the most persuasive. In April 1961 he was elected chairman of the national board of directors of the NAACP to fill out the unexpired term of Robert C. Weaver, who resigned from the chairmanship to take a federal appointment.

Stephen Gill Spottswood was born in Boston, Massachusetts on July 18, 1897, the only child of Abraham Lincoln Spottswood, a porter, and Mary Elizabeth (Gray) Spottswood. The devoutness of his parents, the religious atmos-

Scurlock

BISHOP STEPHEN GILL SPOTTSWOOD

phere of his home, and the evangelical church that he attended in boyhood instilled in him an early recognition of a sense of mission. He was reared in New England, and since his father had little confidence in Negro institutions, he was educated in integrated schools: the Cambridge Latin School in Massachusetts and the Freeport High School in Maine.

As a student majoring in history at Albright College in Reading, Pennsylvania, which was founded and is maintained by the Evangelical United Brethren Church, Spottswood began his training for the ministry. He also worked as a waiter, coal stoker, and grass cutter but still had time to become a letterman in football and baseball. After he had graduated with the B.A. degree in 1917, he enrolled at the Gordon College of Theology in Boston, where he received the Th.B. degree in 1919. Some years later, in 1923-24, he took graduate courses at Yale Divinity School.

Meanwhile, on his return to Massachusetts in 1917, he had become an assistant pastor at the First Evangelical United Brethren Church in Cambridge, and in 1918 he accepted an appointment as assistant pastor at the African Methodist Episcopal Zion Church in Boston. In 1919, after being ordained, he was made pastor of the African Methodist Episcopal Zion Church in both West Newton and Lowell, Massachusetts. Early in his career Protestant sects had offered him churches with white congregations, but he preferred the A.M.E. Zion Church. "The attitude of the soul-winner is much like the attitude of a lover," he explained to Beverly Gary in an interview for the New York *Post Magazine* (September 3, 1961), "and it would never do for a Negro man to win the soul of a white woman. I knew what the score was."

The African Methodist Episcopal Zion Church was formed in 1796 when nine parishioners left the main Methodist body because, as Negroes, they were not permitted to sit to receive communion with the white parishioners. Spottswood admires the courageous spirit of the nine men, citing them as examples of Negro dignity and belief in freedom that he feels existed even in times of slavery and oppression.

In 1919 Spottswood had also joined the National Association for the Advancement of Colored People and began working more diligently for the extension of Negro rights. On one early assignment for the NAACP he went to Washington to denounce a Senator from Maine for voting against the antilynch bill. During 1922 he was involved in sit-ins organized to attempt to force integration at a New Haven motion-picture theater, and several years later he participated in sit-ins at a dime store in Buffalo, New York. His record shows that he has taken part in sit-in, boycotting, and picketing demonstrations up and down the East Coast. He believes that the most effective form of protest is withholding patronage.

For several years after his ordination Spottswood continued to preach in New England, becoming pastor of the A.M.E. Zion Church in Portland, Maine in 1920 and in New Haven in 1922. He left Connecticut in 1925 to serve as pastor for the Croler Memorial A.M.E. Zion Church in Winston-Salem, North Carolina. He moved to churches in Indianapolis in 1928 and in Buffalo four years later. In 1936 he began sixteen years as pastor of the John Wesley National African Methodist Episcopal Zion Church in Washington, D.C.

On May 17, 1952, Spottswood was elected fifty-eighth bishop of the African Methodist Episcopal Zion Church. As one of fifteen bishops in the church, he has served as superintendent of the west Tennessee and Mississippi, south Mississippi, north Arkansas, Arkansas, Oklahoma, Texas, Michigan, Indiana, Ohio, Colorado, and Allegheny conferences. Since his election he has sponsored the construction of new churches, has organized an annual conference, and has made possible the building of a modern school in the Mississippi Delta. He continues to preach regularly at his Washington church.

Wherever his work in the ministry had taken him, Spottswood had served on the executive committee of local branches of the NAACP. From 1947 to 1952 he was president of the Washington branch and since 1954 has been a member of the organization's national board of directors. He was elected vice-chairman of the board in 1959, and on April 10, 1961 he was chosen to fill the unexpired term as chairman of Robert C. Weaver, who had begun his term in January 1961, but had resigned shortly afterward to accept an appointment as administrator of the Federal Housing and Home Finance Agency.

Founded in 1909 to insure the full political, civil, and legal rights of colored people and to obtain for them equality of opportunity, the NAACP now has more than 388,000 members in its 1,300 branches, youth councils, and college chapters, and an annual income exceeding $1,000,000. The organization supports the principles of sit-ins, Freedom Rides, and selective purchasing, but has formally condemned groups that advocate racial separatist policies, such as the Black Muslim or Negro nationalist organizations.

The highlight of the NAACP's annual convention in Philadelphia in July 1961 was a trip to Washington of some 1,000 delegates aboard the twenty-two car "Freedom Train." Spottswood and NAACP's executive secretary, Roy Wilkins, led a smaller group of the delegates at a meeting with President John F. Kennedy in which they urged him to encourage the enactment of more civil rights legislation.

Spottswood is a member of the board of trustees of Livingstone College, which in 1939 conferred upon him the honorary degree of Doctor of Divinity. He is also a member of the General Commission on Chaplains and Armed Services Personnel, a member of the National Council of Churches of Christ in the United States of America, and a member of the World Methodist Council of the International Frontiers Club. For over three decades he has been a member of the Masons, Odd Fellows, and the Elks. In addition, he has participated for years in all kinds of social work, having served in the YMCA, the Urban League, and various settlement houses.

For forty-five years Spottswood has been a contributor to such periodicals as *Zion's Herald*, Pittsburgh *Courier*, and African Methodist Episcopal Zion publications. He is frequently in demand as a preacher and lecturer at colleges and universities and is often called upon to speak in the field of civil rights. Sections of his keynote address at the 1961 NAACP annual convention reveal a fervor that probably contributes much to his effectiveness as a preacher. "We have led the people across the mountains in a trek that outlawed the White Primary, struck down the restrictive real estate covenants and brought forth the epoch-making Supreme Court school decisions of 1938 through 1954. And, by God's help, we will lead all Americans into the *green-pastures* of equal rights under the Constitution and to the *still waters* of the democracy encrouched in the American dream."

On June 10, 1919 Spottswood married Viola Estelle Booker, a milliner, who died on October 24, 1953. The Spottswoods had five children: Virginia Ruth Spottswood Simon, Stephen Paul Spottswood, Constance Booker Spottswood Miller, Viola Stephanie Spottswood Cabaniss, and Alleyne Hankerson Spottswood Nixon. Erect and distinguished-looking, with graying black hair and mustache, Spottswood stands six feet tall and weighs 205 pounds. His political affiliation is Democratic. His recreational activities until 1932 included tennis, basketball, and volleyball and, until 1953, reading, travel, table tennis, sunbathing, and family picnics. At present he most enjoys visiting his children, and his thirteen grandchildren.

Reference

N Y Post Mag p2 S 3 '61 por

SUNDERLAND, THOMAS E(LBERT) Apr. 28, 1907- Business executive; lawyer

Address: b. c/o United Fruit Company, 30 St. James Ave., Boston 16, Mass.; h. 88 Clyde St., Brookline, Mass.

When Thomas E. Sunderland succeeded Kenneth H. Redmond as president of the United Fruit Company, the world's largest purveyor of bananas, he mounted "one of the hottest seats in industry," according to *Forbes* magazine (November 1, 1959). In the decade preceding his accession on November 1, 1959, profits of the giant concern had dwindled drastically; its stock value had fallen from $7.54 a share in 1950 to $1.39 a share in 1959.

Familiarizing himself with the United Fruit complex, Sunderland effected a number of reforms that have spurred the company's recovery. Among them are new marketing procedures and a diversification program. Before directing United Fruit, Sunderland, an antitrust expert, had been general counsel, director, and vice-president of Standard Oil Company (Indiana).

Thomas Elbert Sunderland was born in Ann Arbor, Michigan on April 28, 1907 to Edson R. and Hannah Dell (Read) Sunderland. His father, a professor at the University of Michigan Law School, was a nationally known lecturer and writer on legal subjects. After attending schools in England and France (1924-25), Thomas returned to Ann Arbor to enroll at the University of Michigan. He was graduated *summa cum laude* with a B.A. degree in 1928.

Beginning his graduate studies at the University of Michigan Law School (1927-29), Sunderland transferred to the University of California (1929-30), where he took his LL.B. degree in 1930. He was admitted to the Michigan bar in 1930, and practised law in Detroit for one year. Admitted to the New York bar in 1933, Sunderland practised corporation law in New York City from 1931 to 1940 with the firms of Cadwalader, Wickersham, & Taft (1931-33), Milbank, Tweed, Hope, & Webb (1933-35), and Townley, Updike, & Carter (1935-40).

Between 1940 and 1948 Sunderland worked as general counsel for the American Oil Company, and for Pan American Petroleum & Transport Company, a subsidiary of Standard Oil Company (Indiana) with corporate headquarters in New York City. He became a director of the latter company in 1948. Sunderland took leave of absence from his posts when called to active duty in 1942 as a first lieutenant in the United States Army Air Force. Following a tour of duty at Wright Field in Dayton, Ohio, Sunderland served in the European and Mediterranean theaters of war, and with the United States Strategic Bombing Survey. Awarded a Bronze Star, he was discharged with the rank of lieutenant colonel in 1946.

After studying in the advanced management program at the Harvard University Graduate School of Business Administration in 1948, he moved to Chicago to become general counsel for Standard Oil Company (Indiana). Admitted to the Illinois bar in 1948, he became a director

Moffett Studio

THOMAS E. SUNDERLAND

of Standard Oil (Indiana) in 1949, and vice-president and member of the executive committee in 1954.

Over the years Sunderland became known as an expert in antitrust matters and international negotiation. At Standard Oil he bore major responsibility for unsnarling the legal and political tangles resulting from operations in such trouble spots as the Persian Gulf, Iran, Italy, and Argentina. In the United States Sunderland pushed through to victory a case in which the Supreme Court decision established the right of American companies to cut prices competitively "in good faith." Also he planned the reorganization of the Indiana corporation, transforming it from nine loosely run subsidiaries to four functional departments.

In an article entitled "Changing Legal Concepts in the Antitrust Field" (*Syracuse Law Review*, Fall 1951), Sunderland scored the current "disposition to attack big business blindly, . . . the tendency to protect the individual competitor against the hazards of competition without regard to his efficiency, . . . and a tendency to condemn various types of competitive conduct automatically as a matter of law." The article was based on a lecture that Sunderland gave at the University of Chicago, as one in a series on big business and public policy.

On November 1, 1959 Sunderland was elected president, chief executive officer, and director of United Fruit Company. In addition to being the largest banana concern in the world, selling about 60 percent of the American market, United Fruit deals in palm oil, cacao, livestock, and sugar. (Its sugar business has been drastically reduced since the 1960 confiscation of plantations by the Castro regime in Cuba.) It operates railroads and ships, and employs some 60,000 people.

By the time Sunderland became its president, however, this once flourishing giant that cautious Bostonians had long regarded as a safe investment had gone through a time of troubles. Crop diseases, falling prices, increased competition, antagonistic foreign régimes, and domestic trust-busting drove the net earnings from about $50,800,000 in 1950 to $2,171,094 in 1960.

No one was more surprised than Sunderland when he was invited to assume leadership of the United Fruit Company. But although he had had no experience in the banana business or in the transportation field, he did have an invaluable legal background. In an antitrust action in 1958 the company had been ordered to create a competitor to itself and to dispose of 35 percent of its import business. As one United Fruit executive put it, "Our problems right now are primarily legal ones, not production or distribution. Just the difficulties of implementing the consent decree, of setting up our own competitor, are utterly fantastic. We needed a man who knew the law, knew Washington, and knew what it is to deal abroad. Sunderland's all of that."

After spending a year in analyzing the company's difficulties, Sunderland implemented several measures designed to bring United Fruit out of its slump. A move to new offices and a simplified executive structure increased efficiency. Disease-resistant Lacatan bananas were developed to replace vulnerable varieties. In a shift of emphasis from a producing to a purchasing and marketing role, banana cultivations in Central America were sold or leased to independent operators on an "associate producer" basis. New methods of boxing the fruit before shipment and the revival of the Chiquita Banana trademark promised improved marketability.

Taking the first step in a diversification program, the company entered the new field of freeze-dry foods by buying Liana, Inc., a Texas concern. (The freeze-dry preservation technique involves removing water from frozen food, allowing it to be stored indefinitely without refrigeration. Soaking in water restores its edibility.) Other diversification measures include development of new beef cattle, petroleum, and mining operations in Central America. In 1961 the company's net income rose to $8,920,911, or $1.03 per share, as compared with twenty-five cents per share in 1960.

Thomas E. Sunderland and Mary Louise Allyn were married on December 21, 1946. They have three daughters, Louise Allyn, Anne Read, and Mary Compton. A son, Thomas Edson, is deceased. Sunderland, a founder of the American Bar Association section on antitrust law, was its chairman in 1956-57. He is a director of the First National Bank of Boston and of the National Cash Register Company; a trustee of Lake Forest College; and a member of the visiting committee of the University of Chicago Law School. Sunderland belongs to the American Law Institute, Phi Beta Kappa, Phi Delta Phi, Phi Gamma Delta, and Phi Kappa Phi. His clubs are the Country Club in Brookline, Massachusetts, the Chicago Club, the Glenview Club, and the Association Squadron A Club in New York. He was a director of the American Petroleum Institute from 1954 to 1959. Golf and fishing are his favorite recreations.

References

> Forbes 84:27 N 1 '59 por
> Fortune 60:77 N '59 por
> Newsweek 58:84 S 18 '61 por
> N Y Times p52 S 22 '59 por
> Who's Who in America, 1960-61

VILAR, JEAN (LOUIS CÔME) Mar. 25, 1912- French actor and director
Address: b. Palais de Chaillot, Place de Trocadéro, Paris 16ᵉ, France; h. 25 bis rue Franklin, Paris 16ᵉ, France.

Under Jean Vilar, France's Théâtre National Populaire has finally lived up to its name and its purpose. When Vilar became its director in 1951 the state-subsidized theatrical company, by keeping quality as low as the ticket prices, had confirmed the impression of the general public that the theater was a boring pastime. Vilar retained the low prices but changed everything else. When the T.N.P. now plays at the Palais de Chaillot in Paris, in the open air at Avignon, or elsewhere in the provinces, its audiences are swelled by the workmen, the students, the farmers, the shopgirls whom Vilar has wooed and won to good drama. The theater itself has been influenced by Vilar's boldness in removing curtain, footlights, scenery, and all props that limit the participation of the audience and the freedom of the actor to create his role. Vilar frequently appears in the cast of his productions. He has been acting as well as directing since the 1930's.

Jean Vilar was born in the French Mediterranean port city of Sète on March 25, 1912 to Étienne Vilar, a merchant, and Catherine (Biron) Vilar. From the age of twelve, he earned a living as a jazz violinist. After completing his *baccalauréat* at a secondary school in Sète, he began work for his *licence de lettres* at the University of Montpellier. In Paris, where he had gone after six months at Montpellier, he studied literature under Alain and submitted a thesis on the Cornellian tradition in the French theater. He failed to obtain his *certificat*, however. After a few months of precarious day-to-day subsistence in Paris, he took a job as tutor and proctor at the Collège Sainte Barbe, and, while keeping an eye on his charges, he annotated the works of Shakespeare.

In 1932, at the age of twenty, Vilar became a devoted student of Charles Dullin at the Théâtre de l'Atelier, Paris. His first stage appearances were at the Atelier in minor roles in Balzac's *Le Faiseur,* Shakespeare's *Jules César (Julius Caesar),* and Vitrac's *Camelot.* He remained at the Atelier for three years, studying, co-managing the theater with Pierre Valde, literally making it his home.

Following a period of service in the French army (1937-1940), Vilar toured Anjou and Brittany for two years as co-director of André Clavé's Compagnie des Comédiens de la Roulotte.

"After Dullin," Vilar has said, "this was my greatest lesson." In 1943 he played his first principal role in Synge's *La Fontaine aux Saints (The Well of the Saints),* at the Lancry, a small experimental Parisian theater. This was followed by his own low budget production, in a hall on the rue Vaneau, of Strindberg's *La Danse de Mort (The Dance of Death).* Although it was forced to close prematurely by the Société des Auteurs because Vilar had failed to obtain the rights to the play, the production brought Vilar's talent as a director to the attention of many influential people in the Paris theater world.

In September 1943, with his own troupe and borrowed money, Vilar presented Strindberg's *L'Orage (The Storm)* and Jean Schlumberger's *Césaire* to packed houses at the tiny Théâtre de Poche in Paris. The ten-day engagement was held over for seventy performances. He next founded a theatrical subscription society, La Compagnie des Sept, and produced for it Molière's *Don Juan* and Christiansen's *Un Voyage dans la Nuit.* In 1945 he again directed *La Danse de Mort,* which ran for 150 performances at Les Noctambules, and followed it with T. S. Eliot's *Meurtre dans la Cathédrale (Murder in the Cathedral),* which ran for 230 performances at the Vieux Colombier. These two productions firmly established his reputation among an élite of theatergoers and critics, and he was unanimously awarded the Prix du Théâtre (1945), a prize established by drama critics.

Wide public recognition, however, did not come to Vilar until 1947, with his establishment of the first French outdoor summer dramatic festival, the Festival d'Art Dramatique at Avignon. It was on the large platform set before the formidable Palais des Papes at Avignon that Vilar was able to work out the actor-liberating, uncluttered, and spacious *mise en scène* that would later typify the Théâtre National Populaire and have world-wide influence.

His first productions at Avignon were Shakespeare's *Richard II,* Paul Claudel's *L'Histoire de Tobie et de Sara,* and Maurice Clavel's *La Terrasse de Midi.* In 1948 he presented *La Mort de Danton* of Georg Büchner and *Shéhérazade* of Jules Supervielle; in 1949, Corneille's *Le Cid,* Montherlant's *Pasiphaé,* and Gide's *Oedipe;* in 1950, Shakespeare's *Henry IV* and Thierry Maulnier's *Le Profanateur;* and in 1951, Heinrich von Kleist's *Le Prince de Hombourg,* and Cardinal Dovizzi da Bibbiena's *La Calandria.*

Meanwhile, between 1946 and 1951, he directed as well as acted in Paris productions of Arthur Koestler's *Le Bar du Crépuscule (Darkness at Noon),* Anouilh's *Roméo et Jeannette,* Shakespeare's *Richard II,* Clavel's *La Terrasse de Midi,* Adamov's *L'Invasion,* Supervielle's *Shéhérazade,* and Gide's *Oedipe.* He also played Frère Dominique in Claudel and Honneger's opera *Jeanne au Bûcher;* Henry in Luigi Pirandello's *Henry IV;* and Heinrich in Sartre's *Le Diable et le Bon Dieu.*

In September 1951 Vilar succeeded Pierre Aldebert as director of the Théâtre National Populaire. The T.N.P. had been created by the French government in 1920 to make good the-

JEAN VILAR

ater available to a large audience at a moderate price. Over the years it had settled into a dull repertory of innocuous operettas and overworked classics, shoddily done. Vilar's appointment was part of a French Ministry of Education program to decentralize French theater effectively and put good drama within the means of everyone.

The first public appearance of the revitalized T.N.P. comprised a weekend of attractions in the Paris workers' suburb of Suresnes, including a musical matinée, *Le Cid* with Gérard Philipe, Bertolt Brecht's *Mère Courage (Mother Courage)*, an open debate between audience and actors, and meals for audience as well as actors in the basement of the theater.

At the Palais de Chaillot, the T.N.P.'s Paris home, an inexpensive restaurant and early evening performances make it easier for working people to attend a play. The program, costing less than fifty cents, contains a complete text of the play. Summaries of the play are free. In addition to plays, "cultural weekends" offer dances, jazz, films, and discussions—all for a single admission price under $4.

Between 1951 and 1960 the T.N.P. built up a varied and adventurous repertory of forty-eight French and foreign plays. The classics included not only well known works like Molière's *L'Avare,* Racine's *Phèdre,* and Shakespeare's *Macbeth,* but forgotten ones like Pierre de Marivaux' *L'Heureux Stratagème.* The 1951 production of Brecht's *Mère Courage* was followed in 1952 by the première of Henry Pichette's highly experimental *Nucléa,* with direction by Gérard Philipe and abstract décor by Alexander Calder, and of Vauthier's *La Nouvelle Mandragore.* Later productions included Pirandello's *Henri IV,* Claudel's *La Ville,* Alfred Jarry's controversial *Ubu-Roi,* and the première

of Samuel Beckett's *La Dernière Bande (Krapp's Last Tape).* In 1961 the T.N.P. added to its repertory Queneau and Pillaudin's *Loin de Rueil* and Sean O'Casey's *Roses Rouges Pour Moi (Red Roses for Me).*

The T.N.P.'s annual subsidy is less than one-third that of the Comédie Française. Vilar chooses his own plays and assembles his own permanent company of twenty to thirty players. His contract calls only for 150 performances a year in Paris. In addition to the 2,800-seat Palais de Chaillot, the small Théâtre Récamier in Paris is also used by the T.N.P., chiefly for experimental work. Performances are also given in the Paris suburbs. Once the Paris requirements of his contract are fulfilled, Vilar is free to take his troupe on tours of provinces. Since he has become its director, the T.N.P. troupe has accompanied him to Avignon for the summer festivals. At the 1961 festival the T.N.P. presented Pedro Calderon's *L'Alcade de Zalamea,* Carlo Goldoni's *Les Rustres,* and Sophocle's *Antigone.* In its first nine years under Vilar the T.N.P. gave 2,456 performances before a total audience of 3,779,944.

T.N.P. tours have extended beyond France to at least twenty-eight foreign countries. A United States tour in the fall of 1958 opened at the Broadway Theatre, New York, with Alfred de Musset's *Lorenzaccio,* staged by Gérard Philipe. Vilar directed Hugo's *Marie Tudor,* and staged and appeared in Corneille's *Le Cid,* Marivaux' *Le Triomphe de l'Amour,* and Molière's *Don Juan.* Judith Crist wrote of Vilar's delineation of Don Juan (New York *Herald Tribune,* October 29, 1958): "Jean Vilar brings to this too-easily-stereotyped portrait a depth and vitality that lends it the heroic stature and sense of humanity that distinguishes Molière's Don Juan. . . . It is Mr. Vilar's immaculate performance—a grin, a cynical lift of the eyebrow, a bored glance—that gives Don Juan life."

Other Vilar roles in T.N.P. productions have included the Gladiator in *Nucléa,* Harpagon in *L'Avare,* Thomas Beckett in *Meurtre dans la Cathédrale,* Robespierre in *La Mort de Danton,* Thibault in *Le Médicin Malgré Lui,* Auguste in *Cinna,* Macbeth, and, in 1960, Arturo Ui in the French première of Brecht's *La Résistible Ascension d'Arturo Ui.* Vilar has also appeared in films such as *Les Portes de la Nuit, Les Frères Bouquinquant, Les Eaux Troublés, Casabianca,* and *Till l'Espiègle.*

Jean Vilar married Andrée Schlegel on June 30, 1942. They have three children: Dominique, Christophe, and Stéphane. Vilar is five feet nine inches tall, weighs 141 pounds. He has a sharp nose, piercing eyes, and a resonant, somewhat gravelly, compelling voice. He finds it hard adjusting to other than French cuisine. His favorite wine is Bordeaux-Mouton. He collects clay pipes and smokes them when he isn't smoking cigarettes. He was awarded New York University's medal of honor in 1958. "The Théâtre National Populaire is a public service,"

Vilar has explained. "We saw it so from the beginning. It has become so, it seems to me. Our whole task in the future is to keep it so."

References

Dictionnaire Biographique Français Contemporain (1954)
Dictionnaire des Hommes de Théâtre Français Contemporains (1957)
International Who's Who, 1961-62
Who's Who in France, 1961-62
Who's Who in the Theatre (1961)

WADDINGTON, C(ONRAD) H(AL) Nov. 8, 1905- British biologist
Address: b. Institute of Animal Genetics, West Mains Rd., Edinburgh 9, Scotland; h. 15 Blacket Place, Edinburgh, Scotland

In its quest for understanding the chemistry of life and the basic mechanism of heredity, whereby all living things reproduce themselves in their own image, the science of biology stands on the threshold of a revolution far greater in its potential significance than the atomic or hydrogen bomb. C. H. Waddington, the Buchanan Professor of Animal Genetics at the University of Edinburgh, Scotland, is a man dedicated to pushing back the frontiers of knowledge to hasten this revolution. As an embryologist and geneticist, he has long been associated with the Agricultural Research Council's Unit of Animal Genetics, one of the leading animal breeding groups in the world. As a human being living in the twentieth century, interested in the present and the future of his fellow men and knowing it to be imperative that mankind decide its own fate, he asks, "Is any other stable configuration for our present world imaginable, except one in which the wealth which is at present dissipated in the conspicuous waste of the nuclear arms race has been turned to the constructive task of the human biological revolution?"

Conrad Hal Waddington, whose surname may have derived from the Saxon God Wotan, was born in Evesham, England on November 8, 1905. He has one sister, Doris (Mrs. James Christie). His parents, Hal and Mary Ellen (Warner) Waddington, were of long-established Quaker families, and, like both sets of his grandparents, they were first cousins. The Waddington family originated in the Lancashire village of Waddington, where the direct male ancestry can be traced back to the fourteenth century. Some members of the family became noted explorers, and one of them had a Canadian mountain, the highest in British Columbia, named Mount Waddington after him.

Because his father was a tea planter, Conrad Waddington spent his early childhood in Coimbatore in southern India. When he was five years old the family returned to England, to a farm in the southwestern part of the country. He attended Clifton College, Bristol, where he played cricket and Rugby. At Cambridge University, which he entered after graduating in 1923, his only athletic activity was track. A scholar of Sidney Sussex College, he took his

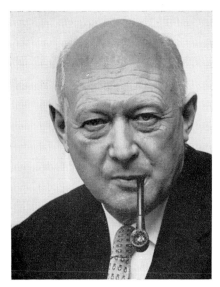

C. H. WADDINGTON

degree in 1926, with a first class in tripos part II. More interested in poetry than in science as an undergraduate, he edited and printed a magazine of poetry that had the distinction of being the first vehicle in which Christopher Isherwood, the English novelist, appeared in print.

Academically, Waddington's interest was geology, which he studied for the reason that becoming an oil geologist seemed a good way of earning a living. However, he reckoned without the influence exerted by an excellent tutor in the biological sciences. Soon his interest was captured by the theory and processes of evolution. He turned to genetics largely through his friendship with Gregory Bateson, son of William Bateson, who is credited with having introduced the study of genetics to Great Britain.

For two years at Cambridge, Waddington engaged in graduate research in systematics of fossil ammonites. In 1927 he was awarded the Arnold Gerstenberg Studentship for a thesis entitled "Vitalist-Mechanist Controversy." The award is made for the encouragement of philosophy among natural scientists. He came to the conclusion that he wanted to study biology rather than paleontology. Accordingly, while holding a government studentship in paleontology, he began by working on plant genetics and experimental embryology of birds at the Strangeways Laboratory, Cambridge.

Waddington's first major work in biology was the experimental embryology of birds and mammals in which he undertook a complete investigation of the formation of the embryo. In 1930, six years after the discovery in Germany of the phenomenon of embryonic induction in amphibian embryos, Waddington developed a method whereby bird embryos could be kept alive outside of the shell. Later, he did the same with mammalian embryos (rabbit), keeping them alive and developing in an artificial environment. In so doing, he enabled scientists to perform on the

WADDINGTON, C. H.—*Continued*

avian and mammalian embryos research of a nature similar to that which had previously been done only on amphibian embryos.

Waddington was appointed lecturer in zoology at Cambridge University in 1933, a position he held until 1945. He served also as research fellow at Christ's College, Cambridge from 1934 through 1945. He continued with his work in experimental embryology and more especially with the many different aspects of the causal embryology of birds. His *Epigenetics of Birds* (Cambridge University Press, 1952) summarizes much of his work in this field.

Then in collaboration with J. Needham, a biochemist, Waddington investigated the chemical nature of the active inducing substance, which later came to be identified as DNA (deoxyribonucleic acid). For this work he received from the Royal Academy of Belgium in 1936 the first Albert Brachet Prize, an award given annually for the best published work on embryology. He was a Rockefeller Traveling Fellow in Germany in 1932 and again in 1938 in the United States. He took the degree of D.Sc. in 1938 at Cambridge.

His work with Needham led Waddington to the question of how the embryonic cells are able to react with the inducer and, in particular, how their hereditary genes condition their ability to react. One result of his investigations was a study of the normal metamorphosis of the fruit fly Drosophila and the effects on development of many mutant genes. He determined in this way, and in considerable detail, the part played by normal genes in controlling development.

Another result was Waddington's *Introduction to Modern Genetics* (Allen, 1939), covering the whole subject of genetics. In one of the earliest statements on the subject in print Waddington propounded the general principle that has continued to serve as the basis of all the fundamental genetics which has gone on since: the hereditary material (genes) consist of a linear aggregate of elements as small as medium-sized molecules. Subsequent discoveries have revised an earlier theory that held these molecules, the master builders of life, to have been probably a set of amino acids making up a protein. Today, as biological science draws closer to cracking the genetic code, the key to the reproduction of all things living, it is held to be reasonably certain that instead they consist of a set of nucleotides making up a nucleic acid.

Biological research for Waddington was interrupted by World War II. From 1942 until 1945 he served with the operational research section, Coastal Command, Royal Air Force. The success of the operational research section, which raised the "killing rate" of attacks by aircraft on enemy submarines from less than 1 percent to over 40 percent without changing weapons or aircraft, but simply by determining how the attack should be carried out, profoundly influenced Waddington's outlook in the years to come. In the last year of the war he acted as scientific adviser to the commander in chief, operational research section.

At the end of the war Waddington accepted the task of setting up a research organization for genetics and animal breeding for the British Agricultural Research Council. One of the main objectives was the application of operational research ideas to peacetime activity. In January 1947 Waddington was appointed professor of animal genetics at Edinburgh University, Scotland, retaining his position as chief geneticist for the national animal breeding research organization.

An extremely economically important breeding activity, the artificial insemination of dairy cattle, is now being carried out in Great Britain according to a method developed by Alan Robertson. Robertson was formerly a member of Waddington's operational research section and more recently of his animal breeding and genetics staff at Edinburgh. The animal breeding group is considered to be one of the leading groups in the world on the fundamental science underlying practical animal breeding for economic characteristics.

Waddington's postwar scientific research interests lie in the direction of developing ideas touched upon but not fully elucidated in past experimental work, the ramifications of which, he believes, will open new avenues of advance in practical breeding. In addition, he has continued with his work in the field of experimental embryology. He has introduced several modern techniques into the field, including the use of isotopic tracers in induction work and the use of ultrasonics. At present, he is particularly interested in electron microscopy of early embryonic cells. One of his most recent books is *New Patterns in Genetics and Development* (Columbia Univ. Press, 1962).

A scientist concerned with the philosophical and social implications of his work, Professor Waddington does not confine his thinking to the laboratory. When the war temporarily halted his research, he turned his attention to explaining the meaning of science. In *The Scientific Attitude* (Penguin, 1940) he argued that science was not just a set of facts in a textbook but was much like art in being a way of looking at the world that involves the whole man, passions and all.

More recently Waddington has come to believe that the circumstances that place the scientist in the role simply of a technologist rather than in his proper position as a humanizing force in the world have their roots largely in the educative processes. He holds that those university courses that merely provide early training should be made ancillary to those that educate. At least room should be made in the curriculum for those liberalizing experiences that would serve to acquaint the scientist with the impact of his science on human affairs. He pointed out in *Science and Ethics* (Allen, 1942) and *The Ethical Animal* (Allen, 1960) that man's recognition of ethical authority is part of the mental make-up that enables him to transmit information from one generation to another not only by genes but by teaching through conceptual language.

In addition to frequently contributing papers to scientific journals, Waddington serves as editor of *Genetical Research*, a technical periodical published by the Cambridge University Press, and is on the editorial board of *Journal of Embryology and Experimental Morphology* and *Journal of Theoretical Biology*. He is a member of the

Minister for Science's Advisory Council on Scientific Policy and a member of the Agricultural Research Council's committee on animal research.

Waddington was made a Fellow of the Royal Society of London in 1947 and of the Royal Society of Edinburgh in 1948. He is also a Fellow of the International Institute of Embryology and a member of the International Committee for Genetics. He received an honorary D.Sc. degree from Montreal University in 1958 and the Commander of the British Empire, awarded by the Queen, in the same year. He was elected president of the International Union of Biological Sciences in 1961 and a member of the American Academy of Arts and Sciences in 1960 and the New York Academy of Sciences in 1961.

Answering invitations to lecture in most of the countries of Europe, as well as Africa, Australia, India, Japan, the Caribbean, Canada, and the United States, has made Waddington a world traveler. He delivered the Jesup Lectures at Columbia University in 1961, while serving as a Fellow of the Center for Advanced Studies at Wesleyan University, Connecticut. When visiting in the United States he enjoys listening to jazz, something he believes is "not worth doing elsewhere." His favorites are Miles Davis, the Modern Jazz Quartet, and Thelonious Monk.

C. H. Waddington married Cecil Elizabeth Lascelles in 1926. They had one son, Cecil Jacob, now a cosmic-ray physicist and lecturer at Bristol University. The marriage ended in a divorce in 1932. He married Margaret Justin Blanco White, an architect, in 1934, and they have two children, Caroline and Margaret Dusa. Waddington, who is usually addressed as Wad, has blue eyes and fair hair, is six feet tall, and weighs 200 pounds. He belongs to no political party, but says he is leftish. Abstract painting is his hobby and he is a member of the Institute of Contemporary Arts in London. His clubs are the Athenæum and The Establishment, a recently opened satirical night club.

References

London Times p10 Jl 20 '53; p9 Jl 2 '57; p11 Mr 11 '58; p11 Mr 12 '60
Nature 159:157 F 1 '47
Who's Who, 1962

WAGNER, RICHARD June 15, 1896- Business executive; organization official
Address: b. Champlin Oil & Refining Co., 135 S. La Salle St., Chicago 3, Ill.; h. Barrington, Ill.

The thirty-fourth president of the Chamber of Commerce of the United States is Richard Wagner, who succeeded the magazine publisher Arthur H. Motley on May 2, 1961 for a one-year term. A self-made man who rose from a job as a bank messenger to his present prominence as executive committee chairman of the Champlin Oil & Refining Company, Wagner is noted as a skillful entrepreneur and a supporter of tax reforms designed to stimulate the accumulation of venture capital and economic growth. The national chamber is the world's largest voluntary association of busi-

RICHARD WAGNER

nessmen and speaks for its thousands of individual and association members on economic and social issues.

Born in the Yorkville section of New York City on June 15, 1896, Richard Wagner is the son of Richard N. and Emma Elizabeth (Rinker) Wagner, both of whom immigrated to the United States from Germany while in their teens. The father was a singer who was obliged to take intermittent jobs as waiter or salesman in order to support his family; his wife was the daughter of a Lutheran minister. Although the Wagners were poor, there was a good deal of fun and happiness in his childhood. He and his younger brother, Albert, were raised in Chicago and attended public schools there. They had a sister, Estella, who is no longer living.

Leaving school at the age of fourteen, Wagner became a messenger for the bank that was the forerunner of the present Continental Illinois National Bank and Trust Company of Chicago. Although he worked fourteen hours a day at first, he studied shorthand on his own, and soon became a stenographer (1911-14) and then secretary to the bank's president (1914-26). Shorter working hours enabled him to attend night high school classes and, later, evening classes in business and banking at Northwestern University and the American Institute of Banking. "People give too much credit to the poor boy who succeeds," Wagner has said. "If you start with nothing, you have a powerful incentive to work hard and achieve something."

As a boy, Wagner worked during summers on an uncle's Wisconsin farm, and as a young man, he kept in good physical condition by exercising at a YMCA. Track and debating were two of his extracurricular activities while at school. At the age of nineteen he was

WAGNER, RICHARD—*Continued*

writing speeches for the bank's executives. From 1926 to 1930 he served as second vice-president of the bank.

Following the 1929 stock market crash, Wagner was asked to look after the bank's interests in the Chicago Corporation, an investment trust that had been badly shaken by the debacle. At that time the company had an annual gross income of less than $1,000,000 and the claims of its preferred stockholders exceeded the market value of its assets. Wagner became vice-president of the corporation in December 1930 and its president in March 1938.

Under Wagner's guidance the business was changed into a venture capital company that financed new enterprises or revived old ones in a wide variety of fields, including shipping, salmon packing, food processing, and real estate. It entered the oil business in 1938 by financing a new process for extracting light hydrocarbons from natural gas, and subsequently acquired a number of gas processing plants in Texas. After the start of World War II, the Chicago Corporation, with the help of the Reconstruction Finance Corporation, financed and constructed the Tennessee Gas Transmission pipeline, which extended some 1,200 miles from southern Texas to West Virginia. The line, first proposed by the company in 1940, proved strategic in compensating for the oil lost through destruction of tankers during the war.

With the construction of the pipeline the company could increase gas sales. It continued to expand into petroleum activities, leasing oil lands and buying a number of subsidiaries, including Baldridge and King, a small Gulf Coast oil firm. In 1954 the Chicago Corporation, by then concentrating mostly on oil ventures, bought a family-owned Oklahoma business, the Champlin Oil & Refining Company. After expanding and modernizing the plants, it emerged as a fully integrated producing, refining, and marketing oil company.

Wagner became executive committee chairman and chief executive officer of the Chicago Corporation in April 1954. The parent company assumed the name of its subsidiary in 1957, becoming the Champlin Oil & Refining Company. Champlin Oil has grown steadily to become one of the larger independent oil ventures. It holds leases on more than 200,000 net acres of oil producing lands in the United States and Canada; in 1960 it earned over $9,000,000 net, and its net assets totaled more than $160,000,000.

Wagner's own experience as an entrepreneur has made him an articulate advocate of measures like tax reform that will allow the accumulation of venture capital. "Risk capital is the seed corn of economic growth," Wagner has said. "The economy relies heavily on the use of retained corporate profits to finance necessary business expansion. But such profits as a whole have been diminishing in relation to our total economy because all of our growth in the past ten years has been diverted to wages and salaries, or to taxes. To pay for new plants and equipment, business has been forced to borrow money or sell equities. Corporate debt is now the highest it has ever been. This trend has serious implications for our future economic health, and it is imperative that all Americans, including organized labor, be made aware of its importance to them."

Wagner succeeded Arthur H. Motley as president of the Chamber of Commerce of the United States on May 2, 1961. He had previously served for one year as vice-president and for three years (1957-60) as a director with a special interest in taxation and finance. The membership of the national Chamber, which is the world's largest voluntary association of businessmen, comprises about 3,600 trade and professional organizations and state and local chambers of commerce as well as about 25,000 business firms and individuals. Its board of directors, elected by the affiliated associations, in turn elects the president for a one-year term. The Chamber, acting as a voice for the congregate business community, delivers its members' majority opinion on economic and social issues to the public and the government.

Conservative in his political and economic views, Wagner, as Chamber of Commerce president, has criticized President John F. Kennedy's liberal domestic spending policies, while praising his "remarkable poise" and forthright stand on international issues. The Chamber of Commerce supported the President's proposal for broad authority to negotiate tariff cuts. It also created a special committee for voluntary unionism to work for passage of state "right to work" laws, and affirmed its intention to continue participation in the International Labor Organization (a United Nations agency dealing with labor-management problems), in contradistinction to the National Association of Manufacturers, which had announced its withdrawal.

Wagner was adviser to the United States employer delegate at the International Labor Organization Conference in 1960, and the American employer delegate in 1961 and 1962. He served as business adviser to the United States delegation at the General Agreement on Tariff and Trade (GATT) in 1958. Wagner is a trustee of the United States council, International Chamber of Commerce. He is a member of the Illinois State Chamber of Commerce and the Chicago Association of Commerce and Industry. Presently a member of the budget and executive committees of the national Chamber of Commerce, Wagner has served as chairman of its policy committee and as member of its committees on finance, natural resources, nominations, and taxation.

At present a director of the Central Illinois Public Service Company and of the American Petroleum Institute, Wagner belongs to the Independent Natural Gas Association, the Independent Petroleum Association, the Mid-Continent Oil and Gas Association, and the Tax Institute. He is a past chairman of the business division, Community & War Fund (Chicago) and a former member of Northwestern University Associates and the citizens committee of the University of Chicago. His clubs are the Congressional Country Club, the Barrington Hills Country Club, the Chicago Club, the Economic Club of Chicago (past president), the

Park Ridge Country Club, the Executive's Club of Chicago, and the Mid-America Club. He has served as vice-president of the Barrington Countryside Association.

Wagner has been described by Louis Cassels (*Nation's Business*, May 1961) as a genuinely modest, amiable, and relaxed person, easygoing even in his hobbies, one of which is gem and rock collecting. Others are golf, fishing, hiking, canoeing, skiing, mountain climbing, and listening to music. He has a good baritone voice and can play several instruments fairly well. According to Cassels, he is "an articulate speaker . . . [with] an enormous vocabulary, which he uses with great precision, and a gift for vivid phrases which is doubtless a carry-over from his love of poetry."

Richard Wagner and Grace Lillian Sommer were married on March 28, 1917. They have a daughter, Grace Margaret (Mrs. Raymond G. Hanson), three sons, John Donald, Richard, and James Arthur, and many grandchildren. He is a Republican and a Lutheran. A man who never lapses into profanity, he staunchly believes in the old-fashioned virtues like honesty and he deplores the deterioration of ethical standards in modern American life. As Chamber of Commerce president he has urged businessmen and his fellow citizens to maintain a high degree of public and private morality essential to the survival of a free society. "If there are laws we think are wrong, we should work to get them changed," he says. "But we must never evade them."

References

Nations Bsns 49:40+ My '61 por
Time 45:79+ My 14 '45 por
Poor's Register of Directors and Executives, 1961
Who's Who in America, 1960-61
Who's Who in Commerce and Industry (1961)

WALTER, BRUNO Sept. 15, 1876-Feb. 17, 1962 Symphonic and operatic conductor; conducted in many European cities before World War II; came to the United States in 1939 as a refugee from Nazism; conducted the Metropolitan Opera orchestra and symphony orchestras in New York, Boston, Minneapolis, and other American cities, sometimes appearing also as piano soloist. See *Current Biography* (November) 1942.

Obituary

N Y Times p1+ F 18 '62

WILCOX, FRANCIS O(RLANDO) Apr. 9, 1908- Educator; specialist in international relations
Address: b. School of Advanced International Studies, 1906 Florida Ave., N.W., Washington 9, D.C.; h. 4323 Albemarle St., N.W., Washington 16, D.C.

Every facet of the career of Francis O. Wilcox—in scholarship, teaching, government service, and educational administration—reflects the

Dept. of State
—Herbert J. Meyle

FRANCIS O. WILCOX

same engrossment in international relations. In the most important of the government positions that he held over a period of almost twenty years, he was primarily concerned with the United Nations. Before going to Washington in 1942, he had taught political science at the University of Louisville, and he returned to the field of education in January 1961 when he resigned as Assistant Secretary of State for international organization affairs to become dean of Johns Hopkins University's School of Advanced International Studies in Washington.

Francis Orlando Wilcox was born to Francis Oliver Wilcox, a druggist, and Verna (Gray) Wilcox on April 9, 1908 in Columbus Junction, Iowa. There were three other children in the family: a boy, Rex, and two girls, Irene and Roduska. Francis Wilcox was reared in Montrose, Iowa, graduating in 1925 from Montrose High School, where he had been on the basketball and track teams and had taken part in dramatics.

Athletics continued to be one of Wilcox's chief extracurricular interests when he attended the State University of Iowa in Iowa City. He belonged to the track team and in his senior year won a cup given for excellence in scholarship and athletics. At the university he was also business manager of the 1930 *Hawkeye*, the yearbook; circulation manager of Student Publications, Inc.; and held a number of odd jobs, such as waiting on tables and selling programs at football games. He was elected to Phi Beta Kappa and was selected by a faculty committee as the representative male senior of his class. After receiving his B.A. degree in political science in 1930, he remained at the State University of Iowa to earn his M.A. degree in 1931 and his Ph.D. degree in 1933. His thesis, *Some Aspects of the Financial Administration of John-*

WILCOX, FRANCIS O.—*Continued*

son County, Iowa, was published the following year in the Iowa State Historical Society's Iowa Monograph Series.

In his university work Wilcox had found the study of international relations especially congenial, and when he was awarded a Carnegie Fellowship in 1934, he decided to attend the Universitly of Geneva in Switzerland. He received the Docteur ès Sciences Politiques degree in 1935, and in the same year his book *The Ratification of International Conventions: A Study of the Relationship of the Ratification Process to the Development of International Legislation* was published in London by George Allen & Unwin. Wilcox has also studied at the University of Chicago and The Hague Academy of International Law (1937).

While working for his doctorate at the State University of Iowa, Wilcox had taught a course in American government there as a teaching assistant from 1931 to 1933. He became an assistant professor of political science at the University of Louisville in Kentucky in 1935, advanced to associate professor in 1937, and was chairman of the division of social science from 1939 to 1942. In the summer of 1941 he was a visiting professor at the University of Michigan and from 1941 to 1943 he was a consultant for the American Council on Education.

During his seven years at Louisville, Wilcox published a number of articles on problems in international relations, including "Treaty Making in Post-War Germany," in collaboration with Walter Schiffer (*American Journal of International Law,* April 1936); "Geneva's Future" (*Current History,* April 1937); and "Localization of the Spanish War" (*American Political Science Review,* April 1938). In the field of education, he contributed the papers "Faculty Reading" (*Journal of Higher Education,* November 1938) and "Teaching Political Science in a World at War" (*American Political Science Review,* April 1941), among others.

Wilcox entered government service during 1942 as associate chief of the division of inter-American activities in the Office of the Coordinator of Inter-American Affairs, Nelson A. Rockefeller. In 1943 he became chief of the program services section of the Office of Civilian Defense and later in the same year joined the Bureau of the Budget as international relations analyst. A second lieutenant in the Organized Reserve Corps during his University of Iowa years (1930-1935), Wilcox saw World War II service in 1944-45 as a lieutenant (j.g.) in the United States Navy.

As chief international relations analyst for the Library of Congress, a position to which he was appointed in 1945, Wilcox was a member of the United States delegation to the United Nations Conference on International Organization in San Francisco in April 1945 and attended the first session of the U.N. General Assembly in London in 1946. At the request of Senator Tom Connally of Texas, then chairman of the Senate Foreign Relations Committee, Wilcox directed a survey and report on Soviet foreign policy that led in 1947 to his appointment as chief of staff of the Senate Foreign Relations Committee. "The summit of Communist hopes and aspirations," a key paragraph in the report declared, "is, in the last analysis, today as in Lenin's time, a complete change of the world's political, economic and cultural set-up." The report further maintained that Soviet leaders had adopted a "zigzagging" opportunist policy first outlined by Lenin, and were "prepared to play any card available at any time."

From 1947 to 1955, as part of his work as chief of staff of the Senate committee, Wilcox attended most of the meetings of the U.N. General Assembly, and in 1951 he was also a delegate to the Japanese Peace Conference. In collaboration with T. V. Kalijarvi, he wrote "Organizational Framework of the North Atlantic Treaty" (*American Journal of International Law,* January 1950) and co-edited the book *Recent American Foreign Policy; Basic Documents, 1941-1951* (Appleton, 1952). With C. M. Marcy, who was to succeed him as chief of staff, he conducted in 1954-55 the study published by the Brookings Institution in November 1955 under the title *Proposals for Changes in the United Nations.*

President Dwight D. Eisenhower appointed Wilcox in July 1955 as Assistant Secretary of State for international organization affairs, and after he was sworn into office in early September he became a delegate to the tenth session of the U.N. General Assembly. In his first address in his new position, to the American Association for the United Nations, he dealt again with the subject of changes in the U.N. On the question of a U.N. charter review, he discussed the stand of the United States that a preparatory commission should precede a review conference. He also made clear his country's view that the relationship of the proposed International Atomic Energy Agency to the U.N. should be similar to that of the specialized agencies.

Wilcox was a delegate to the World Health Assembly in Geneva in 1956 and Minneapolis in 1958 and to International Labor Organization Conferences in Geneva in 1957 and 1958. In a television interview in December 1959 Wilcox expressed the opinion that an international police force might ease the Berlin situation and pointed out that the United Nations' presence in Gaza, Jordan, Lebanon, and Laos had at that time brought an element of tranquility to those areas. A visit to some eight African countries in early 1960 left him deeply impressed by the changes involved in the transfer of power to African leadership, and in an address at the University of Kentucky in March, he discussed the relationship between the United Nations and the emerging African states.

Again as an Eisenhower appointee, Wilcox was a member of the United States delegation to the 1960 fall session of the U.N. General Assembly—a session memorable for the shoe-thumping antics of U.S.S.R. Premier Nikita S. Khrushchev. One of Khrushchev's outbursts protested Wilcox's attempt on October 12 to state that colonialism existed not only in Asia and Africa, but also behind the Iron Curtain, in Eastern European countries.

Shortly before the General Assembly opened on September 20, 1960, however, Johns Hopkins University in Baltimore had announced that Wilcox would become dean of its School of Advanced International Studies in Washington when he completed his U.N. assignment. Like a number of other important government officials concerned with foreign policy—including Paul H. Nitze, now Assistant Secretary of Defense—Wilcox had close ties with the School of Advanced International Studies, where from 1946 to 1952 he had been a lecturer on international organization and American foreign relations. He began his duties as dean on January 23, 1961, succeeding Philip W. Thayer.

Since its founding in 1943 the School of Advanced International Studies has been a graduate school offering specialized training to selected men and women of unusual promise (currently about 100) seeking careers of international service in the government, private business, and nongovernmental organizations. In 1950 it became a part of Johns Hopkins University, which has substantially helped in its recent expansion, including establishment of study centers abroad. When he took over as dean, Wilcox announced that as part of its $4,247,000 development program, the school was about to begin construction of a $1,500,000 building on Massachusetts Avenue in Washington. The move, from its present location on Florida Avenue, would bring the school nearer to the Brookings Institution and advance co-operative efforts.

Professional organizations of which Wilcox is a member have included the American Society of International Law, the American Political Science Association, the American Academy of Political and Social Sciences, and the American Association of University Professors. He was an executive committeeman of the American Society of International Law in 1948-49, and for the American Political Science Association he served as chairman of the committee on undergraduate instruction from 1946 to 1948 and president of the Washington branch in 1948-49. He has honorary LL.D. degrees from the University of Louisville and Hamline University.

Francis O. Wilcox and Genevieve C. Byrnes, an Iowan schoolteacher, were married on July 23, 1933; they had a daughter, Carol Lenore. Mrs. Wilcox died on August 19, 1946. Wilcox has hazel eyes and dark hair, is five feet eight and a half inches tall, and weighs 162 pounds. He belongs to the Kenwood Golf and Country Club and enjoys golf, dancing, swimming, and tennis. His church is the Methodist.

References

Department of State Biographic Register, 1960
Directory of the American Political Science Association (1953)
Who's Who in America, 1960-61
Who's Who in American Education, 1959-60

WILKINSON, BUD *See* Wilkinson, Charles (Burnham)

WILKINSON, CHARLES (BURNHAM) Apr. 23, 1916- Physical fitness consultant; college football coach
Address: b. University of Oklahoma, Norman, Okla.; h. 1408 Brookside Drive, Norman, Okla.

When, early in 1961, President John F. Kennedy saw the need for remedying the deteriorating physical condition of American youth, he appointed Charles (Bud) Wilkinson, head football coach and athletic director at the University of Oklahoma, to be his special consultant on youth fitness. Known by his friends as "the golden man of the gridiron," Wilkinson has coached Oklahoma's teams since

CHARLES WILKINSON

1947, and has one of the most successful coaching records in big-time college football. He continues his coaching duties at Oklahoma while donating his services to the government in formulating and applying a nationwide youth fitness program.

Charles Burnham Wilkinson was born on April 23, 1916, in Minneapolis, Minnesota. His father, Charles P. Wilkinson, had a mortgage and banking business in Minneapolis and at the time of his death in 1960 was president of Wilkinson's, Inc. Bud received his preparatory education at the Shattuck School in Faribault, Minnesota, where he was active in football, basketball, baseball, track, and hockey. He also found time for dramatics.

Graduating from Shattuck in 1933, Wilkinson went on to the University of Minnesota, which in the 1930's ranked as one of the country's leading football powers under coach Bernie Bierman. Wilkinson played guard on the Minnesota team in 1934 and again in 1935, then switched to quarterback in 1936. Minnesota won the national collegiate football championship in Wilkinson's sophomore and senior seasons. He climaxed his collegiate football career

WILKINSON, CHARLES—*Continued*

in the summer of 1937 by quarterbacking the
College All Stars to a victory over the Green
Bay Packers, who in 1936 had won the National Football League championship. At the
University of Minnesota Wilkinson paid his
own way, and never received any financial aid
from the university. During his senior year he
won the Conference Medal for all-around proficiency in athletics and scholarship.

After receiving his B.A. degree in 1937 Wilkinson worked briefly in his father's concern,
but soon returned to football, this time as a
coach. His first post was at the University of
Syracuse, where he served as assistant football coach from 1937 through 1941. In his
spare time he did graduate work in English
and education, and received an M.A. degree.
In 1941 he left Syracuse to return to his alma
mater as assistant coach. He remained there
until 1943 when he entered the United States
Navy and achieved the rank of ensign. He
served for a time as assistant coach at Iowa
Preflight School, and as a member of the
naval air training staff at Pensacola, Florida.
In 1944 and 1945 he saw extensive action in
the Pacific as hangar deck officer on the aircraft carrier *Enterprise*. He was discharged in
1945 with the rank of lieutenant commander.

After the war Wilkinson returned to Minnesota to try his hand again at banking. According to Wilkinson, the move was aimed
at simplifying his life and enjoying his family.
But before he was really settled, coach Jim
Tatum asked him to become his assistant at
the University of Oklahoma. "I thought it
would be fun," Wilkinson once remarked, "a
tapering off process while continuing to learn
Father's business throughout the rest of the
year; but after a month at Oklahoma I stopped
kidding myself and signed a full-time contract." The Sooner squad in 1946 enjoyed great
success, winning eight games and losing three
—such success, in fact, that the University of
Maryland lured Tatum away from the Norman
campus. Oklahoma officials promptly offered
Wilkinson the posts of athletic director and
head football coach and he accepted.

In his first season Wilkinson's team lost
two and tied one of its first five games. Rumblings of discontent were heard from the Oklahoma alumni, who had been somewhat spoiled
by the rich winnings of the previous season.
After the fifth game Wilkinson benched his
first team, made up mostly of ex-servicemen,
and turned to his youngsters, to whom winning
a football game was then the most important
thing in life. Oklahoma went on to win six
of its last seven games.

Eventually Wilkinson created a football
empire. His Oklahoma team dominated the
Big Seven conference, finishing first from 1948
through 1959. Five of his Sooner teams were
undefeated and untied during that time. For
eleven consecutive years (1948-1958) Oklahoma
finished in the top ten of the Associated Press
poll of the nation's leading football teams.

By late 1960 Wilkinson's Oklahoma teams
had won 118 games, lost eighteen, and tied four,
for a winning percentage of .867 over a period

of fourteen seasons. In seven seasons Wilkinson's teams were invited to play in post-season
bowl games, six of which they won. From 1953
through 1957 Oklahoma football teams won
forty-seven consecutive games, before losing 7-0
to Notre Dame. Between 1948 and 1950 Wilkinson's elevens captured thirty-one straight
games before they were defeated by the University of Kentucky, 13-7. Much of Oklahoma's
success is attributed to Wilkinson's application
of the Split-T formation, originated by Don
Faurot, a former coach at the University of
Missouri. Wilkinson was an assistant to Faurot
at the Iowa Preflight School during the war.
"Don Faurot . . . taught me everything I
know about football," Wilkinson once told
Arthur Daley of the New York *Times* (January
29, 1957).

Not until 1959 did a Wilkinson team lose
more than two games in a season. The Sooner
record for that year was seven won and three
lost. In 1960 Oklahoma suffered even sharper
reversals. The Sooners won only three games,
lost six, and tied one. Asked by Red Smith
to account for the sudden turnabout, Wilkinson
replied: "There are . . . more high school kids
playing football, getting better coaching, more
fine athletes coming up than ever. At the same
time fewer and fewer colleges are trying to
play on top level. . . . With more top material concentrated in fewer colleges under the
best coaching, the competition is just too tough"
(New York *Herald Tribune*, August 4, 1961).
In the 1961 season Oklahoma lost its first five
games and won three subsequent ones, defeating
Army 14-8 in November.

Although Wilkinson has been described as a
hard-driving perfectionist, his team members regard him as a fraternity brother, and he never
raises his voice to a player. "It takes hard
work for a boy to become and remain a football
player, but a coach cannot drive him to it," he
told Tim Cohane, the sports editor for *Look*
(November 13, 1956). "There must be a fun
angle—not frivolity, but fun through awareness
of the relationship between the end he knows
can be achieved and enjoyed in Saturday's game
and the sacrifice necessary to that end." He
does not regard the winning of games as the
most important aim of football, believing that
the role of a football coach is essentially that
of a teacher.

Shortly after his inauguration, President Kennedy invited Wilkinson to the White House for
a consultation, in the course of which the President expressed concern over the lack of physical
fitness of American youth. On March 23, 1961
Kennedy designated Wilkinson as special consultant on the fitness of youth. He serves in
this capacity without pay, while continuing as
athletic director and head football coach at the
University of Oklahoma. It is Wilkinson's task
to help formulate and put into effect the President's youth fitness program, working through
the nation's schools, and in co-operation with
government agencies and with such private organizations as the Boy Scouts of America and the
YMCA. The program involves extensive testing of school children for physical fitness, and
a minimum of fifteen minutes of physical exercise a day for each pupil, as well as progressive

developmental exercises for those regarded as physically unfit. According to a series of tests conducted under this program in late 1961 in various communities throughout the United States, about half of the children tested failed to meet minimum standards of physical fitness.

Wilkinson is the author of *Oklahoma Split T Football* (Prentice-Hall, 1952). In co-operation with Gomer Thomas Jones he also wrote *Modern Defensive Football* (Prentice-Hall, 1957). In 1949 he was named Coach of the Year by the National Football Coaches Association and in 1950 he was named Coach of the Year in a poll conducted by the Associated Press. The United States Junior Chamber of Commerce included him in its annual selection of the ten outstanding young men for 1949. In 1956 he was chairman of the Oklahoma Heart Fund drive and in 1959 he headed his home county's Cancer Crusade. He was honored for his civic work in 1957 by B'nai B'rith and in 1959 he received a national brotherhood citation from the National Conference of Christians and Jews.

On August 27, 1938 Bud Wilkinson married Mary Shifflett, his college sweetheart. They have two sons, Pat and Jay. Wilkinson and family live in a comfortable home in Norman, Oklahoma. Wilkinson is a member of Rotary International and of the American Football Coaches Association. He belongs to the vestry board of St. John's Episcopal Church in Norman.

Standing at six feet two inches and weighing 190 pounds, Wilkinson is almost as trim today as he was twenty-five years ago. He is a handsome man with blond hair touched with gray. He laughs easily and displays a winning candor and informality. He is a popular public speaker, an avid reader, and an amateur musician. Wilkinson relaxes by playing golf and he now shoots in the mid- or low eighties.

References

Collier's 126:36+ O 14 '50 por
Look 20:86+ N 13 '56 pors
N Y Times Mag p26+ N 9 '58 pors

WOOD, NATALIE July 20, 1938- Actress
Address: b. c/o Warner Brothers Pictures, Inc., Burbank, Calif.

One of the youngest "oldtimers" in Hollywood,, Natalie Wood has been continuously engaged in the making of movies since 1943 when she made her screen debut at the age of four. Since then she has appeared in more than thirty films, most of them undistinguished. With her 1961 portrayal of starring roles in the United Artists release *West Side Story* and in Warner Brothers' *Splendor in the Grass* she has emerged as a full-fledged adult star and as one of Hollywood's most promising and highest paid motion picture personalities. Not only experience and ability, but also a considerable amount of plain hard work has gone into the making of Miss Wood's success. She has said that she would "go to any lengths to give a good performance."

Natalie Wood was born Natasha Gurdin in San Francisco, on July 20, 1938. Her parents

NATALIE WOOD

had immigrated to the United States from Russia. Her father, Nicholas Gurdin, is a set decorator for motion-picture studios and specializes in miniatures. Her mother, Maria (Kuleff) Gurdin, is a former ballerina. Natalie has an older sister, Teddy, who is married and the mother of two children, and a younger sister, Lena, who has begun her own career as an actress and recording artist.

When Natasha was four years old the family moved to Santa Rosa, California, where director Irving Pichel was then filming the Twentieth Century-Fox production *Happy Land* (1943). Both she and her mother got bit parts in the movie, and Natasha so impressed Pichel that, two years later, when he was directing *Tomorrow Is Forever* (RKO 1946), he sent for her. After a "perfect" screen test, she was given a leading part in this film which starred Orson Welles and Claudette Colbert. She proved to be something of a scene-stealer in the role of an orphan waif adopted by Welles, and her screenland father found her "terrifying." A critic for the New York *Herald Tribune* thought she showed "promise of child stardom," and she received a Box Office Blue Ribbon Award for her performance. Before the picture was released, Natasha's last name was changed to Wood by production executives William Goetz and Leo Spitz, in honor of their friendship with the late director, Sam Wood. Her first name was Anglicized to Natalie.

Tomorrow Is Forever established Natalie Wood as a $1000-a-week child actress. Her next movie, which was also directed by Pichel, was the Paramount release, *The Bride Wore Boots* (1946). In the following year she turned in one of the top performances of her juvenile career in *Miracle on 34th Street* (Twentieth Century-Fox, 1947) which co-starred Maureen O'Hara, John Payne and Edmund Gwenn. As a progressively-educated child who was finally won over to belief in Santa Claus, she re-

WOOD, NATALIE—*Continued*

ceived general critical acclaim as well as a second Box Office Blue Ribbon Award. She also appeared in *The Ghost and Mrs. Muir* (Twentieth Century-Fox) and *Driftwood* (Republic) in 1947, and was named "the most talented juvenile motion picture star of the year" by *Parents' Magazine*.

In the next few years Natalie Wood developed into a reliable supporting juvenile. She made her appearance in *Scudda-Hoo! Scudda-Hay!* (Twentieth Century-Fox, 1948); *Chicken Every Sunday* (Twentieth Century-Fox, 1949); *Father was a Fullback* (Twentieth Century-Fox, 1949); and *The Green Promise* (RKO, 1949). The Children's Day National Council of New York chose her as child star of the year in 1949. "I was never a child *star* like Elizabeth Taylor," Miss Wood recalls, "but I've never known any other life. If I missed the fun of growing up, I didn't know about it. I worked steadily, had a ball and can't ever remember being miserable." She received her early education in studio lot schools. At the age of twelve she entered public school, where she was a good student but did not make many friends.

In contrast with most child stars, Miss Wood came through the so-called "awkward age" without any interruption in her screen career. In 1950 she made *No Sad Songs For Me* (Columbia); *The Jackpot* (Twentieth-Century Fox); *Never A Dull Moment* (RKO); and *Our Very Own* (RKO). In the following year she appeared in *The Blue Veil* (RKO); and in 1952 she was featured in *Just For You* (Paramount) and *The Rose Bowl Story* (Monogram). In 1953 she played as Bette Davis' daughter in *The Star* (Twentieth-Century Fox) and in 1954 she made her first appearance on the Warner Brothers lot in *The Silver Chalice*. She also appeared in the Universal-International release *One Desire* in 1955.

Natalie Wood's first breakthrough into young adult roles came in 1955 when Warner Brothers cast her, at the age of sixteen, opposite James Dean in *Rebel Without a Cause*. The movie dealt with juvenile delinquency as practised by teen-agers economically well-off but emotionally impoverished. Miss Wood turned in a fine performance, for which she received a nomination for the Oscar award of the Academy of Motion Picture Arts and Sciences as best supporting actress.

Almost as important as what happened on the screen, however, was what happened away from it. James Dean, the movie's star, was killed in an automobile accident shortly before the film was released. As one executive at Warner Brothers put it: "When Jimmy Dean died, the teen-agers made him a martyr and latched on to Wood and [Sal] Mineo [the movie's other star]. . . Anyway, the fan mail began coming in. So we signed Natalie."

Under contract with Warner Brothers Miss Wood appeared in *The Searchers* (1956), a Western, starring John Wayne, and in *A Cry in the Night* (1956), starring Edmond O'Brien, Brian Donlevy, and Raymond Burr. In the same year she was also co-starred with Tab Hunter in *The Burning Hills,* a Western, and

in *The Girl He Left Behind,* the Marion Hargrove story of a peacetime draftee. In 1957 she played the daughter of Karl Malden and Marsha Hunt in *Bombers B-52*. During this period her popularity grew steadily, particularly among teen-agers. Actor Gene Kelly referred to her as "the teen-agers' teen-ager, the one girl they all identify with."

In 1957 Miss Wood won the much-coveted title role opposite Gene Kelly in the screen adaptation of Herman Wouk's best-selling novel *Marjorie Morningstar,* released by Warner Brothers in 1958. She was chosen for this role from over 100 aspirants, including such leading actresses as Elizabeth Taylor and Audrey Hepburn. To some observers, including the film's director, Irving Rapper, *Marjorie Morningstar* marked Miss Wood's screen transition to an adult actress. "Natalie started this film as a teen-ager," he said, "but she completes it as an important star." Most reviews, while favorable, were somewhat less enthusiastic. A. H. Weiler wrote in the New York *Times*: "Natalie Wood, who only yesterday was playing with dolls in films, has blossomed into a vivacious, pretty brunette who very likely is as close to a personification of Marjorie as one could wish. But the character is hardly complex, and while Miss Wood is competent in the role, it is rarely a glowing performance" (April 25, 1958).

After *Marjorie Morningstar* Miss Wood's services were much in demand by rival studios. Frank Sinatra was able to obtain her for a role in *Kings Go Forth* (United Artists, 1958) by paying $100,000 to Warner Brothers and by agreeing to star in one Warner Brothers picture, a commitment worth about $350,000. Miss Wood was, however, not pleased with this arrangement, for her earnings, notwithstanding her success, had then declined to $750 a week under her existing contract with Warner Brothers. After completing *Cash McCall* for Warner Brothers in 1959 she was loaned to Metro-Goldwyn-Mayer for *All the Fine Young Cannibals* (1960) in which she co-starred with Robert Wagner, whom she had married in 1957.

With the release of *West Side Story* (United Artists) and *Splendor in the Grass* (Warner) in 1961, Miss Wood won general acceptance by the critics as an important actress. A writer for *Newsweek* noted: "After years of vacuous popularity, she suddenly finds herself being taken seriously" (October 23, 1961). In an interview published in *Time* (September 22, 1961) Miss Wood said: "I've done lots of lousy films, but I hoped they would be good. Now I've done two pictures I know are good, and it's affected my whole life. For the first time I come home after work tired but exhilarated, instead of tired and depressed." The two films also marked Miss Wood's transition into the higher financial brackets. Her new contract calls for as much as $250,000 per movie.

In *Splendor in the Grass*, a Warner Brothers production based on an original screenplay by William Inge, Miss Wood plays a small-town Kansas girl who loves and loses the town's rich boy (played by Warren Beatty), loses her sanity, and then slowly emerges from emotional bewilderment to a new maturity. The role was an emotionally demanding one, but she more than met its demands. According to the film's director, Elia Kazan, she "worked like she was saving her life." Bosley Crowther, reviewing the film in the New York *Times* wrote: "Miss Wood has a beauty and radiance that carry her through a role of violent passions and depressions with unsullied purity and strength. There is poetry in her performance" (October 11, 1961). Paul V. Beckley wrote in the New York *Herald Tribune*: "Miss Wood . . . has talents which to me were hitherto unsuspected" (October 11, 1961).

West Side Story, the United Artists screen version of the Arthur Laurents-Leonard Bernstein-Stephen Sondheim Broadway musical, was released shortly after *Splendor in the Grass.* Miss Wood played the role of Maria, a Puerto Rican girl, in this modern version of the Romeo and Juliet story set against a background of juvenile gang warfare in New York City. *West Side Story* marked her first appearance in a musical, and although her singing voice was dubbed by Marni Nixon, she performed every bit of the exacting choreography, often working fourteen hours a day as well as weekends, to keep up with the professional dancers in the cast. She also worked intensely with Rita Moreno, one of her co-stars in the film, to perfect her Puerto Rican accent. Her efforts paid off and the reviews were universally glowing. "Natalie Wood . . . is heart-breaking in her exquisite projection of the role," wrote Archer Winsten (New York *Post,* October 19, 1961). Bosley Crowther found her "full of luster and charm" (New York *Times,* October 19, 1961), while Paul V. Beckley described her performance as "splendid" (New York *Herald Tribune,* October 19, 1961).

A screen personality since the age of four, Miss Wood has lived most of her "private" life in public. While in her teens she made headlines by dating the late James Dean, Elvis Presley, Nicky Hilton, and other Hollywood celebrities. Her romance with Robert Wagner was one of the most publicized in Hollywood, as was their subsequent marriage on December 28, 1957. The couple announced their separation and prospective divorce in 1961.

Natalie Wood is five feet two inches tall, and weighs about 100 pounds. She has brown hair and large brown eyes. Such words as "wisp," "mosquito," "filly," and "pixie," have been invoked to describe her. She includes among her hobbies swimming, horseback riding, and golf. She also collects paintings and phonograph records. She admits to extravagance. After their marriage she and Robert Wagner acquired a large colonial mansion in Beverly Hills, which they remodeled in Greek Revival style. The house included separate "his" and "hers" swimming pools. In December 1961 Natalie Wood became the 138th film personality to have her footprints and handprints preserved in cement in the forecourt of Grauman's Chinese Theater in Hollywood.

References

Look 25:105+ Ap 11 '61 pors
Newsweek 58:102 O 23 '61 por; 59:54+ F 26 '62 pors
Parade p4 D 29 '57 por
Show 2:50+ Mr '62 pors
Time 78:60 S 22 '61 pors
International Motion Picture Almanac, 1960

CURRENT BIOGRAPHY—VOL. 23. NOS. 1-4

This is the index to the January-April 1962 issues. For the index to the 1961 biographies, see December 1961 issue or 1961 Yearbook. For the index to 1940-1950 biographies, see 1950 Yearbook. For 1951-1960 index, see 1960 Yearbook.

Gardiner, James Garfield obit Mar 62

Gilmore, Voit Feb 62

Goodspeed, Edgar J(ohnson) obit Mar 62

Gordon, Lincoln Feb 62

Greenebaum, Leon C(harles) Jan 62

Guinzburg, Harold K(leinert) obit Jan 62

Guion, Connie M(yers) Feb 62

Hall, Peter (Reginald Frederick) Feb 62

Hargrave, Thomas J(ean) obit Apr 62

Harris, Harwell Hamilton Jan 62

Hart, Moss obit Feb 62

Hartle, Russell P(eter) obit Jan 62

Heineman, Ben W(alter) Jan 62

Hillyer, Robert Silliman obit Feb 62

Hocking, William Ernest Mar 62

Hodes, Henry I(rving) obit Apr 62

Howe, Gordie Mar 62

Howe, Gordon See Howe, Gordie Mar 62

Hu Shih obit Apr 62

Ives, Irving M(cNeil) obit Apr 62

John, Augustus (Edwin) obit Jan 62

Johnson, Harold Ogden obit Apr 62

Katsh, Abraham I(saac) Mar 62

Kay, Hershy Mar 62

Keldysh, Mstislav (Vsevolodovich) Feb 62

Kennelly, Martin H(enry) obit Jan 62

Khouri, Faris el- obit Feb 62

Kiplinger, W(illard) M(onroe) Jan 62

Koestler, Arthur Jan 62

Kovacs, Ernie obit Mar 62

Kreisler, Fritz obit Mar 62

Lewis, John (Aaron) Jan 62

Lipchitz, Jacques Apr 62

Lober, Georg (John) obit Feb 62

Loeb, James (Isaac), Jr. Jan 62

Louw, Eric H(endrik) Mar 62

Love, J(ames) Spencer obit Mar 62

Luthuli, Albert John Feb 62

McClintic, Guthrie obit Jan 62

McConnell, F(owler) B(eery) obit Feb 62

McCormack, John W(illiam) Apr 62

McCracken, Joan obit Jan 62

Macy, John W(illiams), Jr. Jan 62

Marais, Jean Apr 62

Margai, Sir Milton (Augustus Strieby) Feb 62

Martin, Edmund F(ible) Jan 62

Marvel, Mrs. Archie D. Apr 62

Marvel, Elizabeth Newell See Marvel, Mrs. A. D. Apr 62

Meerloo, Joost A(braham) M(aurits) Jan 62

Mellers, Wilfrid (Howard) Feb 62

Meštrović, Ivan obit Mar 62

Miller, Harry W(illis) Mar 62

Miller, William E(dward) Feb 62

Moore, Charlotte Emma See Sitterly, C. M. Jan 62

Moses, Anna Mary Robertson obit Feb 62

Muench, Aloisius (Joseph), Cardinal obit Apr 62

Murphy, (Eleanor) Patricia Apr 62

Nestingen, Ivan A(rnold) Mar 62

Newhart, Bob Mar 62

Nitze, Paul H(enry) Feb 62

Ogburn, Charlton obit Apr 62

Olav V, King of Norway Jan 62

Osgood, Charles E(gerton) Apr 62

Ozbirn, Catharine (Freeman) See Ozbirn, Mrs. E. L. Jan 62

Ozbirn, Mrs. E. Lee Jan 62

Portinari, Candido obit Mar 62

Rabaut, Louis Charles obit Jan 62

Randolph, Jennings Jan 62

Rayburn, Sam(uel Taliaferro) obit Jan 62

Read, Sir Herbert (Edward) Mar 62

Reybold, Eugene obit Jan 62

Robinson, Spottswood W(illiam), 3d Mar 62

Russell, James S(argent) Jan 62

Schoeppel, Andrew F. obit Mar 62

Scofield, Paul Mar 62

Senghor, Léopold Sédar Mar 62

Shurlock, Geoffrey M. Jan 62

Sitterly, Mrs. Bancroft Walker See Sitterly, C. M. Jan 62

Sitterly, Charlotte Moore Jan 62

Slocum, (Manly) Harvey obit Jan 62

Smith, Margaret (Madeline) Chase Mar 62

Spottswood, Stephen Gill Apr 62

Stikker, Dirk U(ipko) Feb 62

Suggs, Louise Jan 62

Sunderland, Thomas E(lbert) Apr 62

Swann, W(illiam) F(rancis) G(ray) obit Mar 62

Switzer, Mary E(lizabeth) Jan 62

Taylor, A(lbert) Hoyt obit Jan 62

Teagle, Walter C(lark) obit Feb 62

Thant, U Feb 62

Thurber, James obit Jan 62

Tillinghast, Charles C(arpenter), Jr. Feb 62

Tobias, Channing H(eggie) obit Jan 62

Unitas, John Feb 62

Vertès, Marcel obit Jan 62

Vilar, Jean (Louis Côme) Apr 62

Volpe, John A(nthony) Feb 62

Waddington, C(onrad) H(al) Apr 62

Wagner, Richard Apr 62

Walsh, Chad Feb 62

Walter, Bruno obit Apr 62

Ward, Paul L(angdon) Mar 62

Watts, Alan (Wilson) Mar 62

Wenner-Gren, Axel (Leonard) obit Jan 62

Wesker, Arnold Feb 62

Wilcox, Francis O(rlando) Apr 62

Wilkinson, Bud See Wilkinson, C. Apr 62

Wilkinson, Charles (Burnham) Apr 62

Wills, Royal Barry obit Feb 62

Winiarski, Bohdan (Stefan) Feb 62

Wood, Natalie Apr 62

Yamasaki, Minoru Mar 62

CURRENT BIOGRAPHY

MAY 1962
VOL. 23 NO. 5

Editor: Charles Moritz

PUBLISHED BY THE H. W. WILSON COMPANY, 950 UNIVERSITY AVE., NEW YORK

CONTENTS

ABOUT THIS PUBLICATION

Current Biography (published every month except August) presents articles on people who are prominent in the news—in national and international affairs, the sciences, the arts, labor, and industry. Sources of information are newspapers, magazines, books, and, in some cases, the biographees themselves. It should be pointed out, however, that these are objective rather than authorized biographies. At the end of the year the articles in the monthly issues are cumulated in one alphabet, revised, and printed in a single volume known as *Current Biography Yearbook.*

Authorities for biographees' full names, with some exceptions, are the bibliographical publications of The Wilson Company. When a biographee prefers a certain name form, that is indicated in the heading of the article: for example, MACMILLAN, (MAURICE) HAROLD means that he is usually referred to as HAROLD MACMILLAN. When a professional name is used in the heading, as, for example, GLENN FORD, the real name, in this case GWYLLYN SAMUEL NEWTON FORD, appears in the article itself.

The heading of each article includes the pronunciation of the name if it is unusual, date of birth (if obtainable), and occupation. The article is supplemented by a list of references to sources of *biographical* information, in two alphabets: (1) newspapers and periodicals and (2) books.

References to newspapers and periodicals are listed in abbreviated form; for example, "Sat Eve Post 217:14+ S 30 '44 por" means *Saturday Evening Post,* volume 217, pages 14 ff, September 30, 1944, with portrait. For full names, see the section "Periodical and Newspaper Designations," which is included in all *Current Biography* Yearbooks and in the January issue each year. Obituary notices appear for persons whose biographies have been published in *Current Biography.*

An index to names that have appeared this year is to be found at the back of this issue.

NOTE: Authors whose biographies do not appear in *Current Biography* may usually be found in *Twentieth Century Authors,* Kunitz & Haycraft, 1942, H. W. Wilson Company, or in the FIRST SUPPLEMENT (1955). Authors of books for young people are included in *The Junior Book of Authors* (Second Edition, Revised) edited by Kunitz & Haycraft, 1951, H. W. Wilson Company. Musicians whose biographies do not appear in *Current Biography* may usually be found in *Living Musicians,* compiled and edited by David Ewen, 1940, H. W. Wilson Company, or in its FIRST SUPPLEMENT (1957).

KEY TO PRONUNCIATION

ā	āle	N	Not pronounced, but indicates the nasal tone of the preceding vowel, as in the French *bon* (bôN).	û	ûrn; French eu, as in *jeu* (zhû); German ö, oe, as in *schön* (shûn), *Goethe* (gû′tě)
â	câre				
ä	ădd				
ă	ăccount				
ä	ärm				
à	àsk				
a	sofá			ŭ	tŭb
		ō	ōld	ŭ	circŭs
c̄	ēve	ô	ôrb	ü	Pronounced approximately as ē, with rounded lips: French u, as in *menu* (mē-nü); German ü, as in *grün*
ĕ	ĕnd	ŏ	ŏdd		
ē	makēr	oi	oil		
		o͞o	o͞oze		
g	go	o͝o	fo͝ot		
		ou	out		
ī	īce				
ĭ	ĭll	th	then	zh	azure
		th	thin	′ =	main accent
ĸ	German ch as in *ich* (ĭĸ)	ū	cūbe	″ =	secondary accent

CURRENT BIOGRAPHY

MAY 1962

BACON, CHARLES L(ANGSTON) Oct. 14, 1909- Organization official; lawyer
Address: b. 915 Grand Ave., Kansas City, Mo.; h. 1263 W. 67th Terrace, Kansas City, Mo.

At its forty-third national convention, held in Denver, Colorado in September 1961, the American Legion chose Charles L. Bacon, a lawyer from Kansas City, Missouri, as national commander for the year 1961-62. A naval communications and legal officer during World War II, Bacon was the first World War II veteran to become, in 1950-51, the state commander of the Missouri American Legion, and he is the first Missourian to head the national organization since its founding, in Paris, in March 1919. The American Legion, the largest veterans' organization in the United States, had a membership of 2,681,035 in about 17,000 posts in late 1961. Approximately one-third of its members had served in World War I; the rest are veterans of World War II or of the Korean War.

Charles Langston Bacon was born on October 14, 1909 in Marshall, Saline County, Missouri to Charles Benjamin and Nettie (Fry) Bacon. His father, who had a real estate and insurance business, also was a deputy sheriff, and served as postmaster during the eight years of the Woodrow Wilson administration. An excellent student, Bacon graduated from Marshall High School at the age of sixteen. During his summer vacations he delivered ice. After finishing high school he attended Missouri Valley College at Marshall, where he was the honor graduate of his class when he received his B.A. degree in 1930. At the college he was one of the founders of the Tharsus club, which later became the Missouri Valley chapter of Sigma Nu fraternity. His activities in basketball and track were cut short when he suffered a broken leg during his sophomore year. Bacon played the drums in both his high school and college bands, and as a source of income he worked in an orchestra for several years. He also was a soloist in the Missouri Valley College glee club, and sang in a Presbyterian church choir.

Short of money following the death of his father in 1930, Bacon worked for a time in a clothing store and as a laborer on Missouri Valley flood control projects, before he entered the University of Missouri law school at Columbia in 1931. He was president of the student body and was elected to the editorial board of the *Missouri Law Review* in 1932. He received the LL.B degree in 1934 with honors, and was awarded the Shepard Barclay prize for the graduate who had "exerted the highest and best moral influence in the school" in addition to making the best scholastic record.

CHARLES L. BACON

Chase

Having passed the Missouri bar examinations in the year that preceded his graduation from law school, Bacon began to practise law in the Columbia office of R. M. Hulen, who later became a federal judge. After graduation he engaged for seven years in general and trial practice, in partnership with Robert D. Johnson. During these years he was active in Marshall civic affairs. He became the youngest local Chamber of Commerce president in Missouri, and was one of the organizers of Ban Johnson baseball league activities in the state. He has been vice-president of the Missouri Valley College board of trustees since 1938.

When Robert Johnson was elected a judge in 1941, Bacon formed with A. L. James the new Marshall law firm of James & Bacon. In the same year he joined the Missouri State Guard that was formed to replace the 138th Infantry of the Missouri National Guard, which had been called in federal service, and he became the commanding officer of its Marshall unit. In June 1942 he entered active World War II duty as a lieutenant junior grade in the United States Naval Reserve. Because of a shortage of communications officers, he was assigned to the Navy's communications school at Los Angeles. He remained there as an amphibious communications instructor until April 1944, when he was reclassified as a legal officer at the Seabee base at Camp Peary, Virginia, where he later also

BACON, CHARLES L.—*Continued*

served as provost marshal. In addition he did
some legal and personnel work on detachment
to the Fifth Naval District headquarters at Norfolk, Virginia, before his discharge in the permanent rank of lieutenant commander in April
1946.

When he returned to civilian status Bacon resumed the practice of law as a partner in James
& Bacon. He was admitted to the bar of the
United States Supreme Court in 1949. From
1949 to 1952 he was a member of the board of
governors of the Missouri Bar Association, and
from 1951 to 1953 he served on the Missouri
Citizens Commission for the Study of the Public
Schools. The firm of James & Bacon dissolved
in 1952 when Bacon moved to Kansas City to
become chief counsel for the marketing division
of the Skelly Oil Company. He made many
trips to Washington and to various states on
behalf of the company within the next few years.

In 1956 Bacon left the oil company to become
a member of the large Kansas City law firm of
Sebree, Shook, Hardy & Ottman, in which he is
still a partner. The firm engages in general civil
and trial practice, with particular emphasis on
corporation, reorganization, insurance, probate,
taxation, and administration law. Bacon is a
member of the Kansas City Lawyers' Association
and the Kansas City Bar Association as well as
of the American and Missouri bar associations.
He has served as secretary of the Jackson County
board of park commissioners.

Shortly after he left the service in 1946 Bacon
joined American Legion Post 191 in Marshall.
Becoming second vice-commander and program
leader of the post in the same year, he promoted
youth programs, including the oratorical contest,
Boy Scout activities, and Boys' State. In 1947 he
was made first vice-commander of the post and
oratorical chairman of the Missouri department
of the Legion. He became department judge
advocate in 1948 and in 1949 he was elected
senior vice-commander and membership chairman for the Missouri department. In 1950 Bacon
became the first World War II veteran to be
elected commander of the Missouri department.
When the doubling of the state Legion's membership since the end of World War II necessitated a readjustment program, he appointed
a five-man committee, which made recommendations for reorganization and budgetary reform
that were subsequently adopted by the Missouri
Legionnaires.

A year as adjutant for Post 191 in Marshall
followed Bacon's term as state commander. Also
in 1951 he was named to the national Legion's
merchant marine and national security commissions. In 1956 he moved on to the national housing committee, and in 1957 was named to the
Legion's national aeronautics committee. At the
American Legion's forty-third national convention in Denver, Colorado, Burke was the unopposed candidate to succeed the California public
relations counselor William R. Burke as national
commander for the year 1961-62. He was elected
by acclamation of the 2,997 delegates on September 14, 1961.

Resolutions adopted at the Legion's Denver
convention called for immediate resumption of
nuclear weapons tests by the United States and
demanded an active strength of at least 1,000,000
for the Army, 300,000 reservists on paid drill
status, and a National Guard complement of
400,000. The American Legion, which claims to
represent a cross-section of the nation's citizenry,
has become increasingly public-spirited and serious-minded in recent years. In late 1960 the
Legion's fun-making section, the 40 and 8, was
disaffiliated because of racial discrimination policies. While continuing to represent the interests
of the nation's veterans, the Legion is active in
many phases of national life, and has undertaken
an extensive youth-guidance program.

In the month after he took office Bacon
traveled some 30,000 miles and held twenty-two
regional conferences to become acquainted with
local leaders of the American Legion, whom he
wished to unite into a "leadership team." Early
in February 1962 he was the spokesman for the
commanders of the American Legion, the Veterans of World War I, the Veterans of Foreign
Wars, and the Disabled American Veterans in
announcing an agreement to promote "sound
public opinion in support of the President's efforts to stop advance of the Communist conspiracy." In a radio address on Lincoln's birthday, February 12, 1962 Bacon expressed the
Legion's view that "war is both justifiable and
preferable to the prisoner's peace which the
Kremlin offers the world." He added that "there
is no permanent, peaceful coexistence with a
power whose avowed objective is world conquest."
On March 1, 1962 Bacon presented the Legion's
Distinguished Service Medal to President John
F. Kennedy, who is a member of the Legion.

On December 28, 1941 Charles L. Bacon married Helen Elizabeth Selvidge of Nashville, Tennessee, the daughter of Robert W. Selvidge, a
former professor of engineering at the University
of Missouri. They have one daughter, Sharon
Ruth (Mrs. Charles Rule), living in New York
City; and one son, Charles L., Jr., a high school
student in Kansas City. Bacon is a deacon of
the Presbyterian church, a Freemason, and a
member of the Sigma Nu (social), Omicron
Delta Kappa (leadership), and Phi Delta Phi
(law) fraternities. Missouri Valley College conferred upon him an honorary LL.D. degree in
January 1962.

In a biographical sketch in the *American Legion Magazine* (December 1961) Robert B. Pit-
kin wrote that Bacon "is endowed with a good
and warm sense of humor, an infectious smile
which he does not use sparingly, a companion-
able habit of speech, an ear for listening. He is
fond of the outdoors, of hunting, of dogs." Pit-
kin also notes that Bacon is "sincerely dedicated
to the fundamental principles of the American
Legion and American citizenship . . . endowed
with a high order of organizational ability and
basic good sense, and . . . possessed of a personal
manner that is frank, friendly and reassuring."

References

American Legion Mag 71:12+ D '61 por
American Bar, 1962
Martindale-Hubbell Law Directory, 1962
Who's Who in the Midwest (1956)

BEATTY, WARREN (bā'tē) Mar. 30, 1937-
Actor
Address: b. c/o MGM Studios, Culver City, Calif.

A serious shortage of Hollywood leading men
and the praise of theater and film critics have
helped to bring Warren Beatty to quick stardom
after his appearances in only three motion pictures by the end of 1961. Beatty was turning
down film script after film script by the middle
of 1962, although he was being offered as much
as $150,000 for each picture. In each of his three
films—*Splendor in the Grass, The Roman Spring
of Mrs. Stone*, and *All Fall Down*—Beatty had
the advantage of superior co-stars and outstanding directors. But it was his mannerisms, reminiscent of the late James Dean or of Marlon
Brando, his smoldering good looks, and his controversial personality as disclosed in stormy interviews that more than any other factors explained
the rise of Warren Beatty. About him the outlines of a myth were already beginning to form.

Warren Beatty was born in Richmond, Virginia on March 30, 1937 to Ira O. Beaty and
Kathlyn (MacLean) Beaty. (The actor added
the extra "t" when he entered the theater.) His
father is a realtor who formerly was superintendent of Richmond High School; his mother, a
drama coach, directed amateur theatricals; his
grandmother taught elocution. Soon after Warren Beatty was born his family moved to Arlington, Virginia. His father taught him to read at
the age of five and his mother coached him in
acting along with his sister, Shirley MacLaine.
Uninterested in the activities of other children,
he had a lonely childhood.

At Washington and Lee High School in Arlington, Virginia Beatty became a star center on the
football team and president of his high school
class. Recalling these formative years in an interview with Joe Hyams for *Show Business Illustrated* (March 1962), Beatty said: "My earliest
childhood ambition was to be President of the
United States. That was until I was six years
old. At seven I decided to be Governor of Georgia. At eight I decided to become an actor.
People become actors because of a need within
themselves. I got most of my acting ambitions
temporarily pounded out of me in high school
football." At about the same time, in the spring
of 1962, he told Hedda Hopper: "I never really
decided to become an actor, just drifted along."

Although Beatty had appeared in amateur
plays under his mother's direction, it was not
until 1954 that he had his first brush with professional theater, when he was hired as a rat
watcher at the National Theatre in Washington,
D.C. (He was supposed to stand in the alley and
keep the rats from going in the stage door.) During the summer of 1955, after he graduated from
high school, he worked again at the National
Theatre, keeping the aisles clear for the entrances
and exits of Helen Hayes and George Abbott in
Thornton Wilder's *The Skin of Our Teeth*.

When Beatty graduated from high school he
received ten offers of football scholarships, but
he turned them all down. "I developed into a
fair player for a period of about a year," he once
explained to Hedda Hopper, "but I never could
have been as successful in college football as they

WARREN BEATTY

seem to think I would. I didn't enjoy it that
much. The important thing is doing what you
enjoy, not because you get a reaction from
others." Beatty also worried that football might
permanently damage his good looks.

In the fall of 1955 Beatty enrolled at the School
of Speech and Drama of Northwestern University
in Evanston, Illinois. After a year of study he
became bored with college and moved on to New
York City, where he enrolled as a student at the
Stella Adler Theatre Studio, once attended by the
late James Dean who, like Beatty, later came
under the tutelage of Elia Kazan. In the course
of his year with Miss Adler, Beatty followed the
pattern of many other aspirants to acting in New
York City who try to make ends meet. He lived
for a while in a furnished room on West 68th
Street, where he came down with hepatitis. He
played cocktail-hour piano in a bar on 58th Street
and in the Blue Room on Long Island. He
also worked as a bricklayer's helper and as a
sandhog on the new third tube of the Lincoln
Tunnel.

In the meantime, Beatty had broken into television, appearing on *Studio One* and *Playhouse
90* over CBS-TV among other shows, and he
played the lead in the *Kraft Theatre* production
of *The Curly Headed Kid* over NBC-TV. At
Gateway Theatre on Long Island Beatty appeared
in summer stock and at the North Jersey Playhouse in Fort Lee, New Jersey he played in winter stock. During his period with the stock companies Beatty had roles in *A Hatful of Rain, The
Happiest Millionaire, Visit to a Small Planet,
The Boy Friend*, and *Compulsion*.

It was while he was playing in winter stock
at the North Jersey Playhouse in the shadow of
the New Jersey Palisades that Warren Beatty
met the two men who would help to shape his
career. William Inge, the playwright, and Joshua
Logan, the director, appeared at the North Jersey Playhouse one night and both men were impressed with Beatty. The meeting led to a screen

BEATTY, WARREN—*Continued*

test arranged by Joshua Logan, in which Beatty's partner was Jane Fonda. Inge was contemplating writing a script for a film with Elia Kazan as director in which Beatty would appear. Forced to postpone the film, they first made use of Beatty's talents in Inge's play, *A Loss of Roses*.

Directed by Daniel Mann, *A Loss of Roses* had its tryout at the National Theatre in Washington, D.C., where Beatty had made his debut a few years before in humbler employment. Shirley Booth, its star, withdrew from the play in Washington and was replaced by Betty Field as the widow whose bewildered son, played by Warren Beatty, falls in love with a carnival actress. Like several of Inge's plays and motion pictures, the action of *Loss of Roses* took place in Kansas during the 1930's.

When *A Loss of Roses* opened at the Eugene O'Neill Theatre in New York City on November 29, 1959 it was coolly received by the critics. Beatty fared much better at their hands. Walter Kerr of the New York *Herald Tribune* (November 30, 1959) wrote: "Mr. Beatty's performance is mercurial, sensitive, excellent," and Kenneth Tynan, entering his verdict in the *New Yorker* (December 12, 1959), observed: "Mr. Beatty, sensual around the lips and pensive around the brow, is excellent as the boy." Despite the superior performances of Betty Field, Carol Haney, and Warren Beatty, *A Loss of Roses* retired from Broadway after only twenty-five performances. The play had, however, provided Beatty with the showcase that he needed, and after the reviews had been turned in, he received many offers. He later signed a nonexclusive contract with Metro-Goldwyn-Mayer.

Filmed on location on Staten Island in New York City and with a strong supporting cast that included Pat Hingle and Audrey Christie, *Splendor in the Grass* was released by Warner Brothers Pictures, Inc., late in 1961. Both the critics and the public acclaimed Warren Beatty as Bud Stamper and his co-star Natalie Wood as Deanie Loomis in the film written by William Inge and directed by Elia Kazan. An enthusiastic writer for *Life* magazine (November 3, 1961) hailed Beatty as "a new and major movie star, combining the little-boy-lost charms of the late James Dean and the smoldering good looks of Marlon Brando." Archer Winsten of the New York *Post* noted: "Ten years of intensive work put in by a notable talent could not improve upon this particular characterization. Even if he has been typecast, the way in which he projects his personality and emotions in front of the camera is an amazing achievement for a young man so lacking in experience."

Immediately after he completed work on *Splendor in the Grass* Beatty went off to Europe to work with Vivien Leigh on the film version of Tennessee Williams' novella *The Roman Spring of Mrs. Stone*, for which Gavin Lambert provided the script. The film was directed by José Quintero, in his first movie assignment, produced by Louis de Rochmont, and released through Warner Brothers. Although Beatty had been early nominated for the role of the Italian gigolo who preys on wealthy women in Rome, Tennessee Williams objected to the casting on the grounds that Beatty

was too young and too Anglo-Saxon in appearance for the part. Beatty flew down to Puerto Rico where Williams was staying at the time, demonstrated the Italian accent that he had acquired after hours of practice, and talked the playwright into giving him the role.

When *The Roman Spring of Mrs. Stone* was released late in December 1961, it appeared that some critics shared Tennessee Williams' misgivings. Ben Kubasik of *Newsday* (December 29, 1961), for example, dismissed Beatty's painfully acquired Italian accent as "a hopeless Italian dialect, which is nowhere near as authentic as comedian Pat Harrington Jr.'s Guido Panzini characterization." "As for Miss Leigh's young co-star, Warren Beatty," Kubasik commented, "he's lucky, with so little talent, to be cast in anything. Maybe that, after all, was the reason for making the film: to give Beatty a job." Bosley Crowther of the New York *Times* (December 29, 1961) wrote: "Mr. Beatty, who does very nicely as a middle-western youth in "Splendor in the Grass," is hopelessly out of his element as a patent-leather ladies' man in Rome. His manners remind one of a freshman trying airs at a college prom, his accent recalls Don Ameche's all-purpose Italian-Spanish one." On the other hand, Paul V. Beckley of the New York *Herald Tribune* (December 29, 1961) felt that Beatty played the gigolo with appetite and conviction, and Alton Cook of the New York *World-Telegram and Sun* (December 29, 1961) called Beatty "a dynamic and convincingly despicable purveyor of his youthful charms."

While awaiting the 1962 release of his new film *All Fall Down*, the Metro-Goldwyn-Mayer production based on James Leo Herlihy's novel of the same name, in which he co-stars with Eva Marie Saint, Warren Beatty took a short-term lease on a pink stucco house high above the lights of Hollywood's Sunset Strip. Six feet one inch in height and weighing about 175 pounds, Beatty has tousled brown hair and myopic blue-green eyes. Like the late James Dean, he squints and wears heavy-rimmed glasses away from the set. He dresses casually and neatly. Known to be rude or bored or both during interviews, Beatty peppers his speech with four-letter words and often breaks off in the middle of sentences in a search for precision. His laughter is loud, his sense of humor offbeat. Acting, he believes, is a matter of intuition. Before he reaches a decision to accept a role he reads through the submitted script at least three times. Resenting the comparisons to Dean and Brando, he would like to remain his nonconformist self and to keep his private life as a bachelor private, although he has been publicly in love, first with Joan Collins, then with Natalie Wood.

At no point in his career has Warren Beatty relied on his famous sister, Shirley MacLaine, to break into the theater or motion pictures. Three years younger than Miss MacLaine, he is much more subdued than she and lacks her elvish sense of humor. Beatty has said of their relationship: "Our lives have been absolutely separate, but there's not a big hostile thing," and Miss MacLaine has been quoted as saying of her brother: "I'm crazy about him, but he doesn't seem to want to communicate with me." At this early stage of Beatty's career at least two observers appear to be certain of the direction that it will take. Eva Marie Saint has asserted: "People say Warren is going to going to be a big star. I say they're right." Jill St. John, who appeared with him in *The Roman Spring of Mrs. Stone*, has predicted: "He's going to be a big star because he has the talent and the tenacity. He's very ambitious."

References

NY Herald Tribune p19 D 16 '59
New Yorker D 12 '59
Show Business Illus 2:61+ Mr '62 pors
NY Sunday News p100+ O 15 '61 pors
Time 78:53+ S 1 '61 por

BENNETT, ROBERT RUSSELL June 15, 1894- Composer; arranger; conductor

Address: b. 30 Rockefeller Plaza, New York 20; h. 140 E. 56th St., New York 22

NOTE: This biography supersedes the article that appeared in *Current Biography* in 1942.

Now the musical director of the National Broadcasting Company, Robert Russell Bennett is a dual personality in the American world of music: a productive composer of serious music who is also Broadway's leading arranger of musical comedy scores. His serious compositions include one full-length opera, two one-act operas, six symphonies, and other orchestral works. He has orchestrated more than 300 Broadway shows, including *Oklahoma, South Pacific, Kiss Me, Kate,* and *My Fair Lady,* and he has scored more than thirty films and many important television programs, among them the series entitled *Victory at Sea*.

Robert Russell Bennett was born in Kansas City, Missouri on June 15, 1894, the only son of George Robert and May (Bradford) Bennett. He has a sister, Beatrice (Mrs. C. E. Lawhon). Both of his parents were of Yankee stock, his mother tracing her ancestry back to William Bradford, an early governor of the Plymouth Colony. Robert Russell Bennett's father played the trumpet and violin in the Kansas City Philharmonic symphony orchestra and his mother taught piano. The boy exhibited the first fruits of this musical inheritance at the age of three, when he picked out the melody of a Beethoven sonata that he had heard his mother play on the piano.

At the age of four Bennett contracted polio, and to speed his recovery, the family moved to a farm forty miles south of Kansas City. There, beginning with the next year, his mother taught him to play the piano and his father taught him band instruments well enough so that he was able to sit in for any absent member of a local band that the senior Bennett had organized. By the age of ten Robert Russell Bennett was also giving piano recitals.

In 1909 Robert Russell Bennett's family moved back to Kansas City and there, at the age of fifteen, he began to study harmony, counterpoint, and composition with the Danish musician, Carl Busch. Bennett's musical personality, however,

had already started to halve. To support his classical studies, he played in dance halls, movie houses, and pit orchestras about town, sometimes holding down as many as four jobs at once.

In 1916 Bennett took his savings of $200 and set out for New York City. At first he pounded the piano in dance halls and cheap restaurants; from that he graduated to a job as a copyist at George Schirmer, Inc., the music publishers. This career was interrupted in 1917 when the United States entered World War I and Bennett enlisted in the Infantry. Because of a crippled foot he was transferred to a headquarters unit, where he organized and conducted Army bands and scored dance arrangements.

As a result of his army experience, Bennett applied for a job as an orchestrator at T. B. Harms and Company when he returned to civilian life. As a trial he was given Cole Porter's "An Old Fashioned Garden" to orchestrate; it became the biggest hit of the year and Bennett was hired. By 1922 he was orchestrating full-length musicals and had started on a career that was to make him the acknowledged master of his craft and to earn him such titles as "the Beethoven of modern orchestration" and "the DiMag of his particular dodge."

Bennett has been credited as the man who is the reason why the orchestrator gets his name on theater programs today. He has done arrangements for nearly every important composer to appear on Broadway over the past thirty years. Among the scores he has orchestrated are those for Rudolph Friml's *Rose Marie,* Jerome Kern's *Show Boat, Roberta,* and *Very Warm for May* and Arthur Schwartz's *The Bandwagon.* He did the arrangements for *Of Thee I Sing* and *Porgy and Bess* for George Gershwin and for Cole Porter, who once called Bennett "the finest orchestrator in America," he scored *Kiss Me, Kate.* He did the arrangements for Burton Lane's *Finian's Rainbow* and for Kurt Weill's *Lady in the Dark;* he reorchestrated Bizet's *Carmen* for the Negro production of *Carmen Jones.* His most fruitful association has probably been with Richard Rodgers, who considers Bennett's musical taste "just about impeccable." Bennett, Rodgers once said, ". . . wouldn't know how to put down a vulgar bar of music." He was Rodgers' orchestrator for *Oklahoma!, Carousel, South Pacific, The King and I, Pipe Dream, Flower Drum Song* and *The Sound of Music.* He also scored Fritz Loewe's musicals, *My Fair Lady* and *Camelot.*

During his long career as a Broadway arranger Bennett has seldom scored fewer than four or five musicals in a season and he has sometimes had as many as twenty-two shows on the boards at one time. Known as a "speed merchant," he can turn out as much as eighty pages of orchestration a day. He accomplishes this partly through his work method: he watches a number two or three times in rehearsal, then scores it from memory. During the last week or two before a show opens he often puts in as much as eighteen to twenty hours a day. Oscar Hammerstein once said: "Russell can work twenty hours at a stretch, then take a shower and come out looking as though he just had a vacation."

Bennett is convinced that the quality of the tune, rather than any combination of instruments, determines the success of a song. "The

ROBERT RUSSELL BENNETT

orchestrator's value," he says, "is his sensitiveness to melody. If the melody has something to say, he can put colors into the outlines—if the melody has nothing to say, he is powerless." Although he has successfully scored more than 5,000 melodies, the one song he wrote himself—*Sue Ann,* in 1942—sold only fifty copies.

Despite his success as an arranger, Bennett considers his work on Broadway the worst kind of potboiling and believes that something must be happening to his soul in the process. In 1926 he gave up a lucrative career (he had, by then, orchestrated sixty musicals) to study classical composition in Paris with Nadia Boulanger. Under her instruction he composed his *Symphony,* which received honorable mention in a contest sponsored by *Musical America,* and *Endymion,* an "Operetta Ballet a l'Antique." In 1927 and 1928 Bennett received Guggenheim Fellowships that enabled him to continue his studies in London, Paris, and Berlin. During that period he wrote his second symphony, the *Abraham Lincoln Symphony,* and a one-act opera, *An Hour of Delusion.*

Despite these achievements, Bennett was still uncertain about his future as a serious composer. In 1931 the Radio Corporation of America sponsored a contest offering $25,000 for the best musical work by an American. Bennett submitted two compositions (the *Abraham Lincoln Symphony* and *Sights and Sounds,* an orchestral piece), and struck a bargain with himself. "If either of these wins even a mention," he said, "I'll go on composing." When the judges were unable to agree upon a single winner the prize was divided into five equal parts. One share each went to Aaron Copland, Ernest Bloch, and Louis Gruenberg; the remaining $10,000 was awarded to Bennett.

Committed to continued composition, in 1932 Bennett collaborated with Robert A. Simon, then music critic of the *New Yorker,* on a full-length

opera entitled *Maria Malibran.* It had its première at the Juilliard School of Music in New York City in 1935 and it received mixed reviews. Appraising it for *Musical America* (April 25, 1935), Oscar Thompson registered his opinion that *Maria Malibran* did not even qualify as an opera because "so much of the text is spoken rather than sung and so much of the music assumes an incidental character in accompanying rather than projecting the dialogue." But Lawrence Gilman of the New York *Herald Tribune* (April 9, 1935) heard in *Maria Malibran* "music of rare delicacy and subtlety . . . music of a composer who has worked out for himself a very personal sort of poetic comedy."

The RCA award led to so many demands upon Bennett as an arranger that he had little time for his own composition during the latter part of the 1930's. He spent four years in Hollywood, contributing original music as well as orchestrations to more than thirty films, most notably *Show Boat* (1936), *Hunchback of Notre Dame* (1939), *Brigham Young—Frontiersman* (1940) and *Rebecca* (1940). Bennett's major original composition during this period was *Eight Études for Symphonic Orchestra* (1938). He also wrote the music for the Lagoon of Nations at the New York World's Fair of 1939-1940.

Bennett returned to New York City in 1940 and in November of that year introduced his own program, *Russell Bennett's Notebook,* on radio station WOR. Virtually a one-man show, since Bennett did the arranging, conducting, composing and commenting, the *Notebook* dealt with various aspects of musical Americana. One of its features was Bennett's *Music Box Operas,* which were operas in miniature based on American themes. Among them were witty treatments of such songs as *O, My Darling Clementine* and *The Man on the Flying Trapeze.*

It was radio that led Bennett back to orchestral composition. In 1941 WOR commissioned him to write a symphony on baseball which, as a former semi-pro player, he undertook with enthusiasm. Called *Symphony in D—for Dodgers,* its last movement featured a play-by-play description of a game in progress. At its première at New York City's Lewisohn Stadium, the sportscaster Red Barber was "soloist."

Bennett's fourth symphony, *On College Themes,* was also commissioned by a radio station, for performance on Football Day. His most popular orchestral work is his fifth symphony, *The Four Freedoms,* which was comissioned by the *Saturday Evening Post* in 1943 and is based on Norman Rockwell's famous painting of the Four Freedoms. The symphony has four movements, each one interpreting a freedom illustrated by Rockwell. The work greatly impressed Eugene Ormandy, who played it dozens of times with the Philadelphia Orchestra, and it was often performed throughout the United States during World War II.

In 1946 Bennett composed his second one-act opera, *The Enchanted Symphony,* and in 1948 he wrote his *Sixth Symphony,* which he was tempted to call his "first," because it was the first one written as he wanted it. "There is nothing back of it," he said. "No commission, no special reason for writing it. . . . And no one needs to like it but me." In addition to his symphonies and operas, Bennett has written many orchestral works, including a march for two pianos and orchestra, a concerto for violin and orchestra, a suite of old American dances, and an *Overture to the Mississippi*.

His chamber music includes *Toy Symphony* and a dance scherzo, both for woodwind quartet, and *Water Music* for string quartet. In addition he has written many solo pieces for violin and flute. Bennett has also created a number of "symphonic pictures" based on his musical comedy scores. Widely played by leading symphony orchestras, these include *Porgy and Bess, Carousel, Finian's Rainbow, Lady in the Dark* and *Kiss Me, Kate*.

In 1952 Bennett undertook his first important television assignment when he orchestrated Richard Rodgers' music for *Victory at Sea*, a Naval history of World War II originally presented in twenty-six half-hour episodes. A series of RCA Victor recordings based on this score have been steady best sellers. *Victory at Sea* has also been abridged into a feature film lasting 100 minutes. Since 1954 Bennett has been associated with NBC-TV's *Project 20*. He has also returned to Hollywood from time to time to work on films. On one of these occasions he scored the movie version of *Oklahoma* (1955), for which he won an Oscar from the Academy of Motion Picture Arts and Sciences.

Robert Russell Bennett married Louise Edgerton Merrill on December 26, 1919. They have a daughter, Beatrice Jean. He is tall, graying, and distinguished in appearance. His hobbies are tennis, baseball, and pool, and every morning he consults a racing form to place his paper bets. Bennett is a member, among other organizations, of the American National Theatre and Academy, the National Association of Authors, Composers, and Conductors, and of the American Federation of Musicians. His clubs are the Bohemians, the Los Angeles Tennis Club, and the West Side Tennis Club.

References

New Yorker 27:46+ N 17 '61

Baker, T., ed. Biographical Dictionary of Musicians (1958)

Goss, Madeleine. Modern Music Makers (1952)

Who's Who in America, 1960-61

Who's Who in Music (1951)

BOULANGER, NADIA (bōō-äN-zhā′) Sept. 16, 1887- French music teacher and conductor
Address: 36 rue Ballu, Paris 9°, France

One of the many prominent protégés of Nadia Boulanger, Virgil Thomson, the composer, has called her "the greatest music teacher in the world." Miss Boulanger, the director of the American Conservatory of Fontainebleau, France, and a teacher for more than a half century, has been accorded similar titles by other observers of the international musical scene. Jay S. Harrison of the New York *Herald Tribune* has called her "the greatest music teacher of the twentieth cen-

tury," adding: "apart from that, she is a woman of profound and enlightened spirit whose dedication to art, and the explication of it, is unmatched in our time." Nadia Boulanger's international reputation as a teacher is enhanced by her own performances on the podium and at the keyboard. She was the first woman to conduct the Boston Symphony, the Royal Philharmonic, and the Philadelphia Orchestra, among other orchestras.

Nadia Boulanger was born in Paris, France on September 16, 1887 to Ernest Boulanger and Russian-born Raissa (Princess Mytchetsky) Boulanger. Her father, like his father before him, taught singing at the Conservatoire National Supérieur de Musique in Paris, and her mother had been one of the father's students. The paternal grandmother had been a well known singer. Although the infant Nadia hid herself and howled when music was played, she did not represent a break in the flow of musical talent. As a student at the Conservatoire National from 1897 to 1904, where Gabriel Fauré was one of her teachers and Maurice Ravel and Georges Enesco were among her classmates, she won first prizes in solfège, counterpoint, fugue, organ, and keyboard harmony.

In the years immediately following the completion of her studies, Miss Boulanger composed as well as taught. She published a few short orchestral, instrumental, and vocal pieces, collaborated with Raoul Pugno in the orchestration of the opera *La Ville Morte*, and won second place in the 1908 Grand Prix de Rome competition with her cantata *La Sirène*. Her younger sister Lili, one of her first pupils, won the first Grand Prix de Rome five years later—the first woman ever to do so.

After death cut short her sister Lili's career in 1918, Miss Boulanger stopped composing. Some observers have seen a direct relation between the two facts. Miss Boulanger herself has said, however: "I had to give it up because I wrote music that was not even bad—just useless. And I love music too much to do that. I am very happy that I reached the decision I did. My calling is to teach."

She settled down to teaching in the Paris apartment where she lived with her mother after the death of her father. Although she continued her private teaching, she gradually taught more and more in institutions. Since 1909 she had been an assistant at the Conservatoire National, and in 1920 she began teaching at the École Normale de Musique de Paris. When the Conservatoire Américain de Fontainebleau was established through the initiative of Walter Damrosch in a wing of the palace of Fontainebleau in 1921 as a summer music school for American students, she became a teacher of harmony there. Her class load at Fontainebleau soon embraced other subjects as well, including piano accompaniment, composition, and the history of music. At the École Normale she taught harmony, counterpoint, organ, and fugue. (In addition to her teaching she was second organist at the Church of the Madeleine in Paris and worked on score-reading committees for the Société Musicale Indépendente and the Concerts Colonne.) Appointed head of the École Normale's composition department in

Wide World
NADIA BOULANGER

1935, she remained in that position until she left for a prolonged visit to the United States during World War II.

America, in the person of composition students Melville Smith, Aaron Copland, and Virgil Thomson, discovered Nadia Boulanger in 1921. "All three found her so perfect a purveyor to their musical needs that they spread the news of her quickly throughout America," Thomson recalled in the New York Times Magazine (February 4, 1962). Copland wrote in Copland on Music (Doubleday, 1960): "Nadia Boulanger knew everything there was to know about music; she knew the oldest and the latest music, pre-Bach and post-Stravinsky, and knew it cold. All technical know-how was at her fingertips: harmonic transposition, the figured bass, score reading, organ registration, instrumental techniques, structural analyses, the school fugue and the free fugue, the Greek modes and the Gregorian chant. . . . More important to the budding composer . . . was her way of surrounding him with an air of confidence."

Among those who subsequently flocked to Miss Boulanger were Roger Sessions, Roy Harris, Marc Blitzstein, and Walter Piston. "It is really difficult to name an American composer of the post-World War I generation who has not at one time or another benefited from Miss Boulanger's instruction," Harold C. Schonberg wrote in the New York Times (April 27, 1958). Her American protégés are but part of an international student body that has included such men as Jean Françaix and Igor Markevitch. In recent years an increasing proportion of her students have come from the newly developing nations.

In 1925 Nadia Boulanger visited the United States for the first time. Her lecture-recital tour included an appearance as organist in a New York Symphony Society concert featuring her sister Lili's Pour les funérailles d'un soldat and lectures on modern French music, Debussy, and Stravinsky, at Rice Institute. (The Rice lectures have been preserved as the Rice Institute Pamphlet for April 1926.) She made her second visit in 1938, when Serge Koussevitzky invited her to be guest conductor of the Boston Symphony Orchestra. Asked by a Boston reporter how it felt to be the first woman conductor of the Boston Symphony, she replied, "I've been a woman for a little more than fifty years, and I've gotten over my initial astonishment." On February 11, 1939 she became the first woman to conduct the New York Philharmonic Symphony Orchestra, and shortly thereafter the first to conduct the Philadelphia Orchestra.

During 1939 she took teaching positions at Wellesley College and Radcliffe College and lecturing assignments at the Juilliard School of Music in New York City and the Longy School of Music in Cambridge, Massachusetts. On April 4, 1941 she conducted forty-five members of the New York Philharmonic Symphony, the Potsdam State Crane Choir, and soloists, in a program of religious music by Heinrich Schuetz, Gabriel Fauré, and others, at Carnegie Hall, New York City, in honor of Jan Paderewski and for the benefit of Polish exiles in Great Britain and Switzerland. " Few events of the season can be looked back upon with livelier feelings of pleasure and satisfaction than this one . . . ," Oscar Thompson wrote in the New York Sun (April 5, 1941). "Miss Boulanger's conducting was as sure as it was free from fussiness. . . . There was no baton." After Nadia Boulanger conducted a program of French vocal ensemble music in New York City on May 7, 1942, under the sponsorship of the Co-ordinating Council of French Relief Societies, Virgil Thomson wrote in the New York Herald Tribune (May 8, 1942): "Miss Boulanger's performances have a kind of professional swank that is impressive for its complete and systematic avoidance of everything that might in any way suggest the theater. Even in our biggest halls she establishes a relation with her audience that is at once friendly, informal, and serious. . . . We are not used to musicianship that is at the same time so gentle and so firm. . . ." In the fall of 1945 she conducted an orchestra composed of members of the Boston Symphony, the Harvard Glee Club, and the Radcliffe Choral Society, in a festival of concerts at Harvard University devoted to the music of Gabriel Fauré. During the war she was also on the faculty of the Washington [D.C.] College of Music and was an instructor of music at the Peabody Conservatory in Baltimore.

After the end of World War II Nadia Boulanger returned to France as titular professor of accompaniment at the Conservatoire National and as professor at the Conservatoire Américain. Four years later she became director of the Conservatoire Américain, and has continued in that position to the present time.

Under the auspices of the Visiting Artists and Professors Program of the Institute of Contemporary Arts (Washington, D.C.), Miss Boulanger lectured and conducted for a month in the United States in the spring of 1958, at New York University's Maison Française, Harvard, Southern Illinois University, State University Teachers College, Potsdam, New York, and other institutions throughout the country. In the middle of February 1962 Miss Boulanger, on another visit to the United States, conducted the New York Philharmonic and the Choral Arts Society in a program, thrice repeated at Carnegie Hall, composed of Gabriel Fauré's *Requiem Mass, Opus 48,* Virgil Thomson's *A Solemn Music,* and three Psalms set to music by Lili Boulanger. "Mme. Boulanger's program was highly personalized, almost too much so," Harriett Johnson commented in the New York *Post* (February 18, 1962), "and she presided over it like a high priestess. . . . She was simultaneously realistic and businesslike. . . . Her beat . . . had a pert flourish at terminal points, like a punctuation mark." "She conducted with poise," Paul Henry Lang wrote in the New York *Herald Tribune* (February 17, 1962). "By no means a professional conductor, she neverthless has thorough control . . . ." Harold C. Schonberg wrote in the New York *Times* (February 17, 1962). "She proved that she could hold up her end of the baton with most of her male colleagues." Also in Miss Boulanger's itinerary before her scheduled return to France in early May 1962 were participation in a memorial concert for Theodore Chanler (a former pupil) at the Museum of Modern Art, New York City, on April 5, and lecturing, conducting, and giving of recitals at major university and other music institutions throughout the country.

In England Nadia Boulanger was the first woman to conduct the Royal Philharmonic in a whole program (November 4, 1937). Previously she had conducted the Royal Philharmonic in a performance of Fauré's *Requiem* (November 1936). Among several other concerts she has conducted in England have been those in series broadcast over the BBC. She has often conducted concerts on the Continent. In recent years she has traveled to Poland, Hungary, and Rumania. She has conducted in the recording studio as well as in the concert hall and over the air, and some of her work may be heard on RCA Victor records. She is *maître de chapelle* to the Prince of Monaco. Other activities in her busy schedule besides teaching and conducting have included the translation into French of works on musical theory.

Although her brunette hair has turned to gray, Nadia Boulanger has kept her stately bearing and firm stride. "Those who meet her or hear her talk are unlikely to forget her physical presence," her former student Aaron Copland wrote in 1960. "Of medium height and pleasant features, she gave off, even as a young woman, a kind of objective warmth. . . . She possessed an almost old-fashioned womanliness . . . that seemed quite unaware of its own charm. Her low-heeled shoes and long black skirts and pince-nez glasses contrasted strangely with her bright intelligence and lively temperament. In more recent years she has become smaller and thinner, quasi nun-like in appearance. But her low pitched voice is as resonant as ever and her manner has lost none of its decisiveness."

A woman of extraordinary vitality, she has always slept but little; she works from dawn to midnight. She reads music quickly, even when she is surrounded by great distractions, memoriz-

ing and hearing it as she reads. From the students who ascend to the same fourth-floor Paris apartment where she lived in the 1920's she demands strict discipline, although her relationship to them is warm. No student arrives late more than once. Her approach to music is open and free of preconceptions. Whether chromatic innovation is good or bad depends, so far as she is concerned, upon whether or not it makes the composer's music move. She imposes only the grammar of music on her students, viewing technique as the only aspect of music that can be controlled. She exhorts them to constant and rigorous work—to work with integrity, as the only means by which genius will be revealed, if it exists at all. When conducting, she dispenses with a baton, and makes more than usual use of her left arm.

Her religious affiliation is Roman Catholic, her political sentiment Royalist. Among her honorary distinctions are several university degrees, including one from Harvard, the Legion of Honor, membership in Phi Beta Kappa and Phi Kappa Lambda. She is an officer of Polonia Restitua and of Saint Charles of Monaco.

References

Life 45:95+ Jl 21 '58 pors
Music Teacher and Piano Student 26:301 Ag '47
N Y Times II p9 Ap 27 '58; II p9 F 25 '62
N Y Times Mag p24+ F 4 '62 pors
Newsweek 59:81 F 26 '62 por
Time 70:83 S 30 '57 por

Blom, Eric ed. Grove's Dictionary of Music and Musicians (1955)
Copland, Aaron. Copland on Music (1960)
Larousse de la Musique (1957)
Ewen, David ed. Living Musicians (1940)
Who's Who in France, 1961-62

CANADAY, JOHN (EDWIN) Feb. 1, 1907- Art critic; author

Address: b. New York Times, 229 W. 43d St., New York 36; h. 25 Sutton Place S. New York 22

By firing critical barrages against abstract expressionism, the prevailing style in contemporary painting, John Canaday, art news editor of the New York *Times* since September 1959, has incurred the wrath of many prominent abstract artists and their admirers. The title of his anthology of New York *Times* pieces, *Embattled Critic,* which Farrar, Straus & Cudahy has scheduled for publication in 1962, befits the controversy that his frank and sometimes severe criticism has aroused. Before joining the staff of the New York *Times,* he had taught art in universities and had been chief of the division of education at the Philadelphia Museum of Art. Under the pseudonym of Matthew Head, he also writes mystery novels.

John Edwin Canaday was born in Fort Scott, Kansas on February 1, 1907 to William Franklin and Agnes Florence (Musson) Canaday. He was reared in Kansas and in Texas, and he received the B.A. degree from the University of Texas at Austin in 1929. He then attended Yale University and earned the M.A. degree in art

JOHN CANADAY

history in 1933. At Yale he also took a four-year course in professional painting. Following several years of study in Paris, at the École du Louvre and elsewhere, Canaday returned to the United States to become a college teacher. From 1938 to 1941 he was an associate professor of art history in the department of architecture of the University of Virginia in Charlottesville, Virginia.

When the United States entered World War II, Canaday spent a year, 1942, in the Belgian Congo with the Bureau of Economic Warfare. He then enlisted in the United States Marine Corps and served during 1944 and 1945 as a first lieutenant in an air warning squadron in the South Pacific. After the war he resumed teaching at the University of Virginia; then he taught at Newcomb College of Tulane University, in New Orleans, Louisiana, where he directed the school of art from 1950 to 1952.

Turning to another form of art education, Canaday directed the educational activities of the Philadelphia Museum of Art from 1953 to September 1959. One of the articles that he wrote for the *Philadelphia Museum Bulletin* was "The Realism of Thomas Eakins" (Spring 1958). While he was still in Philadelphia, the Metropolitan Museum of Art in New York City engaged him to write the text for its *Metropolitan Seminars in Art,* which it described as "assisted self-education" in the appreciation and history of art. The seminars, comprising twenty-four "portfolios," were published from 1958 to 1960 in cooperation with the Book-of-the-Month Club.

On September 1, 1959 Canaday was appointed to succeed Howard Devree as art news editor of the New York *Times.* His articles in the New York *Times Magazine* and in the art section of the Sunday *Times* have ranged widely in subject, including pieces on individual painters such as Miró and Degas, on more general topics like Flemish art and American taste in art, and on many exhibitions, among them an exhibit of technical designing and art by Soviet children.

One of Canaday's articles, "Lesson for the Clinic-Museums" (New York *Times Magazine,* September 4, 1960), is devoted to praise of the Louvre, which he has greatly admired since he first visited it in 1929 and which he believes is a perfect place to show pictures, unlike some modern museums. In another article, "What Should a Museum Be?" (*Art in America,* number 2, 1961), he again deplored the clinical efficiency of several new museums in which a painting is displayed as a specimen. He enjoys museums where "pictures seem to have taken up a residence of their own accord." In his opinion, the Louvre and the Duncan Phillips' converted home in Washington, D.C. "are the most fitting habitations . . . ; the Guggenheim's spiral ramp, the least." Stressing the importance of quality of art as well as the atmosphere in which it is shown, he advises officials of museums that do not have large amounts of money for buying good paintings to arrange for circulating exhibits of masterpieces.

In his *Times* articles Canaday has often found fault with the work of abstract expressionists, whose style has been predominant in American art since the 1940's. His frequent prophecies of the impending death of the nonobjective movement, sometimes called the action-painting school, have antagonized avant-gardists. He has ridiculed the techniques of abstract expressionism as "splash-and-splatter-and-drip," and although he has acknowledged the talent of a handful of action painters, he has made clear his general view that "the nature of abstract expressionism allows exceptional tolerance for incompetence and deception."

In the New York *Times* (April 3, 1960) Canaday reported on a panel discussion held at the Philadelphia Museum of Art in which four abstract painters (Jack Tworkov, Philip Guston, Robert Motherwell, and Ad Reinhardt) defended their style of painting. Canaday concluded: "If contemporary painting fails, it is not because good men aren't trying. The trouble, by the evidence of this panel, is that the contemporary painter paints for himself, walled off by his 'fantastic self-consciousness' in an isolation peculiar to the individual in history's most crowded world." Despite the earnest discussion, he felt that the audience was left puzzled.

An editorial that Thomas B. Hess wrote in *Art News* (October 1960) maintained that Canaday had demonstrated his own incompetence as a critic of modern art because he lacked "interested sympathy" and because he did not take the trouble to inform himself about work that he disliked. Canaday struck back at the magazine, a champion of abstract expressionism, asking, "At what level does interested sympathy become partisanship?" He insisted that he had been misunderstood, that he had once been a "missionary" for abstract art and had gone through the "fire" but had not wanted to stay, and that his pointing out the weaknesses of a movement did not mean that he condemned it entirely.

Forty-nine artists, historians, critics, dealers, collectors, and professors joined in March 1961 in writing a letter to the *Times* deploring Canaday's frequent impugning of motives of artists. They cited quotations from his columns containing such words as "fraud" and "charlatan." The *Times* opened its pages for two Sundays to letters both pro and con its critic's position and announced on March 12 that so far 367 letters had been received, 311 in defense of Canaday's position and fifty-six in support of his critics.

Another aspect of Canaday's controversy with the avant-garde concerned a memorandum that he sent in September 1960 to Dore Ashton, a New York *Times* art critic and the wife of abstract expressionist Adja Yunkers. The memorandum allegedly directed Miss Ashton to change her point of view as well as the language of her writing. The American section of the International Association of Art Critics voted for a resolution in January 1961 recognizing Canaday's freedom to exercise critical judgment but censuring him for not allowing the same freedom to Miss Ashton, who had left the staff of the *Times* in November 1960. Turner Catledge, managing editor of the *Times*, said that his paper considered the matter an internal one and not the proper concern of the International Association of Art Critics.

Canaday's *Mainstreams of Modern Art* (Holt, 1959) surveys the major trends in European art from the French revolution to the present, from realism to nonobjectivism. Several reviewers observed that Canaday dealt with the nineteenth century artists with remarkable skill and wealth of knowledge, but that his treatment of contemporary art was not so satisfactory. One enthusiastic critic, Edith Weigle, wrote in the Chicago *Sunday Tribune* (November 29, 1959), "Here is one book in a thousand to read, enjoy, and treasure. The author is not didactic and is never the pedagog, but he engages the mind, and often the heart, in his character studies of painters and in his fascinating account of the great European art movements."

Detective story readers know John Canaday as Matthew Head, the author of seven mystery novels published by Simon & Schuster. His first, *The Smell of Money*, has been called the detective-literary find of 1943. His stories with a Belgian Congo background—*The Devil in the Bush* (1945), *The Cabinda Affair* (1949), and *The Congo Venus* (1950)—are notable for their exotic and sometimes eerie atmosphere and for their colorful and authentic setting.

Some of Canaday's crime books—*The Accomplice* (1947), *Another Man's Life* (1953), and *Murder at the Flea Club* (1955)—have been recommended as novels of character perception as well as stories of intrigue and suspense. The plot of *Another Man's Life* concerns a philanthropist and three people whom he is aiding with fellowships in creative art. Reviewing it in the New York *Times Book Review* (November 22, 1953), Anthony Boucher wrote, "Canaday is one of the subtlest, at once the most artistic and most artful of American murder writers."

John Canaday and Katherine S. Hoover were married on September 19, 1935; his wife was an editor before her marriage. They have two sons, Rudd Hoover and John Harrington Canaday. Rudd is on the teaching staff of Massachusetts Institute of Technology. Canaday received the

Athenaeum Award for the most outstanding book written in Philadelphia in 1959, his *Mainstreams of Modern Art*.

References

N Y Times p38 Je 28 '59 por
Newsweek 56:82 O 31 '60 por
Time 77:78 Mr 10 '61 por
Who's Who in the South and Southwest (1952)
Who's Who in America, 1960-61

COMPTON, ARTHUR H(OLLY) Sept. 10, 1892-Mar. 15, 1962 Physicist; winner of the Nobel Prize in Physics in 1927 for research on X rays; a key figure in the development of the atomic bomb; chancellor of Washington University (1945-53) and professor of natural philosophy (1953-61). See *Current Biography* (September) 1958.

Obituary

N Y Times p1+ Mr 16 '62

DAVIES, CLEMENT (EDWARD) Feb. 19, 1884-Mar. 23, 1962 British political leader; lawyer; Liberal member of Parliament for Montgomeryshire, Wales (since 1929); leader of the Liberal party (1945-56). See *Current Biography* (October) 1950.

Obituary

N Y Times p25 Mr 24 '62

DAY, DOROTHY Nov. 8, 1897- Roman Catholic journalist; social worker
Address: b. 175 Chrystie St., New York 2; h. Peter Maurin Farm, Pleasant Plains, Staten Island 9, N.Y.

"Here is a woman who has placed her stamp on American Catholicism," Father Dennis Geaney, the Roman Catholic educator, has said of Dorothy Day, head of the personalist-pacifist Catholic Worker movement, which she founded with the late Peter Maurin in 1933. "By their mission-field approach to reform," historian Aaron I. Abell wrote in *American Catholicism and Social Action* (Hanover House, 1960), "the Catholic Workers furnished a sense of direction to the enlarging corps of Catholics anxious to crusade for social justice."

A writer for Communist and Socialist publications before her conversion to Roman Catholicism, Miss Day has been described as "a radical who never got tired." A catalyst in the 1930's of what has since become the Catholic labor movement, she continues to march a little in advance of the popular and acceptable. She has appeared in the news most prominently over the past few years as a perennially jailed protestant against preparation for nuclear war. The Catholic Worker, which approaches social problems from the ground up, has as its headquarters a house of hospitality for the needy near New York's Bowery. There the *Catholic*

DOROTHY DAY

Worker, a penny monthly tabloid wherein the social philosophy of the movement is expressed, is published. Miss Day divides her time between St. Joseph's House of Hospitality in the city, a farm that the Catholic Workers run on Staten Island, and visits to adherents and loose affiliates of the movement around the country.

Dorothy Day was born in Brooklyn Heights, New York City on November 8, 1897. She was the third of five children—three boys and two girls—of John I. Day and Grace (Satterlee) Day. Although the mother had been born Episcopalian, and the father Congregationalist, the family religious atmosphere was largely agnostic. The father, of Tennessee stock and very conservative, insisted on a quiet household, free of visitors, newspapers, and light literature. Family life was happy, but affection was restrained. "We were like most Anglo-Saxons," Miss Day remarked in her autobiography, *The Long Loneliness* (Harper, 1952).

Family fortunes and residence shifted with changes in her father's employment as a sports journalist and editor. The Days lived in Bath Beach, Brooklyn, until Dorothy was six, when they moved to California—first to Berkeley, later to Oakland. In 1906, immediately after the great earthquake, they moved to Chicago, where Dorothy spent her adolescence. In Berkeley Dorothy had become acquainted with the Bible through a copy she had found in an attic. In Oakland she had been impressed with the Methodist piety of a neighboring family. In Chicago she began attending Episcopal services, became deeply impressed with "the formal prayer of the Church in her Psalms," and was baptized and confirmed in the Episcopal Church. Much of her attention was occupied, she wrote in her autobiography, with "the conflict of flesh and spirit. . . . This conflict was to go on for years."

At Robert Waller High School in Chicago Dorothy found history dull but liked languages, and under a Mr. Matheson studied Greek and Latin well beyond the curriculum. Finishing high school at sixteen, she won a three-hundred-dollar scholarship sponsored by a Chicago newspaper that enabled her to enter the University of Illinois in 1914. At Urbana she supplemented the scholarship by writing for the local newspaper, baby-sitting, and doing housework. She formed a close friendship with fellow student Rayna (Simons) Prohme, whose extraordinary personality Vincent Sheean has managed to capture in *Personal History.* She pursued courses in Latin, English, history, and science, without the intention of obtaining a degree. Fed by the reading of Peter Kropotkin, Upton Sinclair, Jack London, and others, and by the sight of poverty in Chicago, her consuming interest had become social justice. This interest became less and less reconcilable with a religion that seemed to her to ignore the misery of the world. "The ugliness of life in a world which professed itself to be Christian appalled me . . ." she wrote in *The Long Loneliness.* "Both Dostoevski and Tolstoi made me cling to a faith in God, and yet . . . I felt my faith had nothing in common with that of Christians around me . . . that I must turn from it as from a drug. . . . So I hardened my heart." She joined the Socialist party in Urbana.

After two years at the university Miss Day moved with her family to New York City in the summer of 1916, when her father became racing editor of the *Morning Telegraph.* Because her father objected to women in journalism she soon left home permanently, to take a job as reporter and columnist with the Socialist *Call.* She joined the International Workers of the World because she preferred the direct action and Americanism of the I.W.W. to the state-centeredness and foreign flavor of some of the other radical groups. In 1917 she left the *Call* and, after a brief time working for the Anti-Conscription League, joined the staff of the radical *The Masses,* edited by Max Eastman, Floyd Dell, and Merrill Rogers. Following the suppression of *The Masses* six months later, she picketed the White House with the suffragists and was arrested and jailed.

Waiting for a successor to *The Masses* after her return to New York, she frequented the Provincetown Playhouse on MacDougal Street in Greenwich Village, where Eugene O'Neill, Mike Gold, and others of her friends newly have plays produced. One of Miss Day's most vivid memories of the period is Eugene O'Neill intoning from memory Francis Thompson's poem, "The Hound of Heaven," in a nearby tavern. Misinterpretation of the mention of Dorothy Day in published reminiscences of literary acquaintances of this period has occasionally brought into print the false assumption that for a long time she abandoned East Side radicalism for Village bohemianism.

When Crystal Eastman began the *Liberator* as successor to *The Masses,* Miss Day went to work for it. She was not as satisfied with the *Liberator* as she had been with *The Masses,* however, and left after a short time. In 1918, when the war had created a shortage of nurses, she became a probationary nurse at Kings County Hospital in Brooklyn and remained for a year, until the influenza epidemic was over. After the war, personal problems occasioned a vacation in Europe, where she remained for a year, writing a novel that critics and public quickly consigned to oblivion, where she is happy to leave it.

After returning from Europe Miss Day worked in Chicago as secretary to Robert Minor, editor of the *Liberator,* which had been resumed as a Communist monthly, and in New Orleans as a feature writer for the New Orleans *Item.* From New Orleans she moved to a cottage she had purchased on Raritan Bay, at Huguenot, Staten Island, at the suggestion of her friend Peggy Baird.

In 1925 Miss Day entered into a common-law marriage with Forster Batterham. A child, Tamar Teresa, was born in March 1927. The event fanned into flame a fire that various influences, from living with a Roman Catholic family in Chicago to the reading of Huysmans, had kept smoldering over the years. She wanted the child to be a Roman Catholic, and Tamar Teresa was baptized in July 1927. Keeping Miss Day from the Church was her relationship to Batterham, a sincere and uncompromising atheist. "To become a Catholic meant for me to give up a mate with whom I was much in love. It got to the point where it was the simple question of whether I chose God or man. . . . It was not because I was tired of sex, satiated, disillusioned, that I turned to God," she wrote in *The Long Loneliness.* She entered the Roman Catholic Church on December 28, 1927.

Her first years in the Roman Catholic Church were dark ones. All of the friends who shared her radicalism were outside the Church. She supported her daughter and herself by writing. For three months she was employed as a script writer by Pathé Films in Hollywood. The only outlet for her old radicalism within the bounds of her new faith was in her reports on life in Mexico, on the 1932 "hunger march" of unemployed on Washington, and the like, for the *Commonweal,* a weekly journal of opinion published by Roman Catholic laymen. After three years of Catholicism she did not know one Catholic layman personally.

Then, on December 10, 1932, Dorothy Day met French-born Roman Catholic layman Peter Maurin. From the thought of the English distributists and of Father Vincent McNabb, St. Thomas Aquinas, Peter Kropotkin and others Maurin had synthesized a philosophy and a program for a "green revolution" that would unite scholars and workers in houses of hospitality for the needy, farming communes, and round table discussions. He expressed his ideas in carefully constructed "easy essays," that he would deliver in Union Square and across the United States to anybody who would listen. (The latest appearance of the essays between covers is *The Green Revolution,* published by Academy Guild Press in 1961.)

Dorothy Day and Peter Maurin published the first issue of the *Catholic Worker* from Miss Day's tenement apartment in lower Manhattan in time for distribution (and heckling by old Communist acquaintances) in Union Square during the May Day celebration of 1933. By 1934 the circulation had risen from 2,500 to 100,000, by 1936 to 150,000. The paper addressed itself to many problems, from race to labor, but the staff soon had a more immediate problem—housing and feeding the unemployed who began knocking at the paper's door. Thus began St. Joseph's House of Hospitality.

Thirty such houses of hospitality sprang up in cities across the United States during the 1930's. The number declined with the waning of the depression and the coming of World War II, when the Catholic Worker's pacifism did not budge to accommodate the shift to pro-war sentiment of some of its supporters. Previously the movement's refusal to join in wide Roman Catholic support of Spain's Franco had cost it some support. During World War II the circulation of the paper fell well below 60,000. It has increased since the war to a present figure of approximately 70,000, while continuing to take unpopular stands. In 1949 the Catholic Worker took sides with the gravediggers against the Roman Catholic Archdiocese of New York in a local Catholic cemetery strike. (The event was untypical. Miss Day is no clergy-baiter. The points on which some individual members of the hierarchy withhold agreement with her are in an area where ecclesiastical concern and jurisdiction are not *de rigeur,* or where church theology is still ambiguous and the layman with initiative and courage may contribute to clarification of thought by speaking out. It was generally assumed, for example, that Catholics could not be conscientious objectors, until the Catholic Worker became the rallying place for the Association of Catholic Conscientious Objectors during World War II. Miss Day has frequently said that if the choice of silence or leaving the church were ever forced upon her, she would without hesitation choose the silence.)

The Catholic Worker has opposed preparation for nuclear war in any of its manifestations. It was Miss Day and Ammon Hennacy and a handful of followers who initiated in 1955 the demonstration of noncooperation with New York's compulsory civil defense drill that now fills City Hall Park annually with hundreds who refuse to take shelter. Miss Day has spent several short terms in New York's Women's House of Detention for this annual breach of the law. The most recent unpopular Catholic Worker stand recalls its attitude toward the Spanish Civil War: a refusal to add its editorial voice to the otherwise almost unanimous Roman Catholic condemnation of Fidel Castro.

Forced by an urban development project out of a large building it owned at 223 Chrystie Street, New York City, where it was able to house as well as feed a large "family," the Catholic Worker now makes do with a smaller building it rents at 175 Chrystie Street. Three hundred meals are served there daily, and the facilities are adequate for editorial offices, a free used clothes dispensary, and Friday night discussions of social philosophy, but not for lodging. Over one thousand dollars a month

DAY, DOROTHY—*Continued*

is paid out in rents for tenement apartments, Bowery hotel rooms, and the Catholic Worker building itself. The Catholic Worker also has a twenty-three acre farm at Pleasant Plains, Staten Island, where a score of people are housed, and two beach houses on Staten Island, where families in need are often housed. Although the number of houses of hospitality and farms throughout the country that are vaguely related to the Catholic Worker is difficult to arrive at, nine autonomous houses and farms with definite connection can be counted. Miss Day's New York staff, which, like her, lives in voluntary poverty, is in more or less constant flux. It now numbers twelve.

Besides *The Long Loneliness*, Miss Day has written *From Union Square to Rome* (Preservation of the Faith Press, 1938), an apologia for her conversion addressed to her relatives and Communist friends; *House of Hospitality* (Sheed and Ward, 1939) and *On Pilgrimage* (Catholic Worker Books, 1948), journals of life in the Catholic Worker movement; and *Thérèse* (Fides, 1960), a life of St. Theresa of Lisieux. In 1962 she was finishing another book, dealing with the history of the Catholic Worker and the personalities involved in a less subjective manner than in previous books.

Dorothy Day is five feet nine inches tall and weighs 185 pounds. She has lively, slightly slanting, blue eyes, set above high cheekbones. Her mouth breaks into a gentle smile as she speaks. Although she has been traveling the length and breadth of the United States on speaking trips for years, she has none of the manner of a professional speaker, a fact that somehow enhances the effectiveness of her softly spoken words. She wears her white hair in a single plait wound around her head. Her clothes look neat but never new, tasteful but simple and sensible. Miss Day has nine grandchildren. She loves the sea and usually has around her study shells, gnarled pieces of seawashed wood, or seaweed.

She regularly retreats to prayer to replenish her interior strength. She laughs at occasional statements that she is a saint. "When they say you are a saint," she once told an interviewer, "what they mean is that you are not to be taken seriously." Like Gandhi in much of her private as well as her public life, she finds relaxation in carding, spinning, and looming wool.

References

N Y Times p31 Mr 22 '56 por
New Yorker 28:37+ O 4 '52; 28:37+ O 11 '52
American Catholic Who's Who (1962 and 1963)
Day, Dorothy. The Long Loneliness (1952)
Hoehn, Matthew. Catholic Authors (1947)
McDonald, Donald. Catholics in Conversation (1960)

DAY, J(AMES) EDWARD Oct. 11, 1914-
Postmaster General of the United States
Address: b. Post Office Department, Washington 25, D.C.

In August 1961, seven months after the New Frontier moved into Washington, columnist Doris Fleeson reported that "it is the belief of astute Senators that no Kennedy Cabinet member has yet dug deeply enough into the entrenched bureaucracy he found in his department except one. Postmaster General J. Edward Day's performance at the Post Office is much admired. . . ." Before joining the Kennedy administration, Day had been a vice-president of the Prudential Insurance Company of America. Although he had been active on the political sidelines, he had never been a professional politician. From 1950 to 1953 Day was insurance commissioner of Illinois. His administration of the Post Office Department has been marked by quiet but aggressive pursuit of economy and efficiency. Among the innovations of his administration is the Flying Forty-Niner, a jet providing nonstop air mail service overnight between the East Coast and the San Francisco area.

James Edward Day was born on October 11, 1914, in Jacksonville, near Springfield, Illinois to Dr. James Almond Day and Frances (Wilmot) Day. His first name became an initial because of the numerous Jameses in the Day family. He was educated in the public schools of Springfield. An elementary school teacher has recalled him as a boy who liked to talk and who had a solution to offer for every problem. In high school he distinguished himself in all subjects except mathematics, which did not interest him. Even in math he won a prize on one occasion after determining to do so. A boyhood hobby was stamp collecting. Family travel made him what he has called "a fanatical sightseer."

As early as high school Day had decided to break with the family tradition of medicine and enter law. He studied political science at the University of Chicago for three years, taking his B.A. degree in 1935, before entering Harvard Law School. While at Harvard he edited the *Harvard Law Review* (1936-37). During a vacation from Harvard he worked in the law office of Stuart & Lincoln in Springfield. He received his LL.B. degree *cum laude* in 1938 and then worked as a law clerk in the Chicago law office of Sidley, Austin, Burgess, & Harper (later Smith) from 1939 to 1941. During the war he served as a naval officer (ensign to lieutenant). For his performance as commanding officer of a convoy vessel in the South Pacific he received the Navy Commendation ribbon.

In his spare time in the Navy, Day had written a romantic novel, *Bartholf Street*. After the novel had been rejected by numerous publishers, he subsidized its publication by Dorrance & Company in 1947. (In 1961 he was reported to be writing another novel.) Meanwhile, he had returned to the law practice in Chicago that the war had interrupted. Adlai E. Stevenson had been a partner in Sidley, Austin, Burgess, & Harper when Day had worked there before the war. When Stevenson became governor of Illinois, he made Day his legal legislative assistant in Springfield (1949-50). From 1950 to 1953 Day served as insurace commissioner of Illinois, distinguishing himself by the forthright manner in which he dealt with a major insurance scandal.

In 1953 Day accepted the position of associate general solicitor with the Prudential Insurance Company of America. Much of his early work with the company was in explaining a new plan for investing policyholders' money to state insurance commissions. In 1956 he became associate general counsel with Prudential and in 1957, vice-president in charge of the company's Western operations. From his base in Los Angeles he directed more than 7,500 employees in thirteen states.

In California, Day gave influential support to Edmund G. Brown during Brown's successful 1958 gubernatorial campaign. He served Governor Brown on various committees and commissions concerned with urban, water, and other problems. He was the leader in southern California of Governor Brown's successful drive for voter affirmation of the $1,750,000,000 Feather River bond issue (to finance diversion of some northern water to parched southern California). He also led a successful drive for school bonds. He helped form, and became chairman of, Democratic Associates, a politically orientated group of Los Angeles businessmen. He was a member of the finance committee of the California Democratic State Central Committee. In 1959 he urged Governor Brown to seek the 1960 Democratic Presidential nomination, but in the primary showdown he threw his weight behind John F. Kennedy, and he was prominent in Kennedy's California campaign.

President-elect Kennedy completed the selection of his Cabinet with the announcement, on December 17, 1960, that Day was his choice for Postmaster General. Day was formally nominated for the post by Kennedy on January 16, 1961, and the Senate confirmed the nomination on January 21, 1961. Day entered the job eager to face what he considered its two principal challenges: increased efficiency and diminution of the annual deficit. He told postal workers in Washington on January 31, 1961 that he aimed to improve postal service while cutting down on "waste and frills." "There will be some changes in policy and emphasis," he told them, "but in a huge and complex organization such as this, continuity and steady progress are far more important than drastic and unsettling change. . . . We will experiment with new equipment but we are not interested in gadgets and gimmicks for their own sake."

The opinion of much of the press during Day's first year as Postmaster General was that he pursued policies similar to those of his predecessor, Arthur J. Summerfield, but with less draining of energy and money into press agentry. He continued the campaign against obscenity in the mail, for example, dispensing, on the one hand, with employing people to make cross-country speaking tours and increasing, on the other, actual arrests and convictions for violation of postal obscenity statutes. He cut down drastically on fees to outside management firms, consultants, and artists by utilizing available talent within the Post Office or other government agen-

Wide World
J. EDWARD DAY

cies. He reduced by more than half the number of expensive commemorative issues, stopped the making of Post Office publicity movies, and dropped the costly experimentation with speed facsimile mail. He cut the price of official signs at sites of new post offices under erection from $800 to $39 apiece.

In addition to reducing expenditures, Day raised what prices he could. Rate increases on foreign mail—amounting to an expected annual increase in revenue of $16,000,000—went into effect on July 1, 1961. Certain money order and special delivery fees were also raised at the same time. On August 15, 1961, an increased fee for registering mail valued to ten dollars went into effect. For other increases he needed the permission of Congress, which was not forthcoming in 1961. On January 24, 1962 a bill which would permit the Post Office to boost postal rates generally passed the House of Representatives. The bill would increase Post Office revenue by an estimated $691,000,000 annually and would raise second and third class rates as well as first class and air. Some Senators were reported to be in favor of scaling down the second and third class increases. Day himself, in testifying before a Senate committee on March 6, 1962, emphasized the importance of first class and air mail increases. "First class is a premium service," he said. "Rates for first class mail should be fixed to cover not only measurable costs but also the intangible values of preferred handling." If the bill became law, he told the Senators, the Post Office would have its first balanced peacetime budget since 1916.

Generally public criticism of large users of non-first class mail was directed not so much against magazine and newspaper publishers as against what the critics called the "junk" mailers. From the time of his appointment Day had said he would not ban junk mail, because many good businesses depended on it. One controver-

LARSON, LEONARD W(INFIELD) May 22, 1898- Physician; organization official

Address: b. 221 5th St., Bismarck, N.D.; h. 200 Tower Ave., Bismarck, N.D.

The selection of Dr. Leonard W. Larson as president of the American Medical Association for 1961-62 reflects in part the organization's growing recognition of its need to cope with the problem of providing more and better medical coverage through prepayment plans if it wants to prevent government interference in medicine. Larson, a pathologist and one of five partners operating the Quain and Ramstad Clinic in Bismarck, North Dakota, became a specialist in medical care plans as chairman of AMA study groups on the subject. "Basically," he has said, "I am a conservative. But I believe all of us have to . . . recognize that we're in an age of social change. My concern is to preserve freedom in the practice of medicine." He opposes any legislation tying hospitalization to Social Security, but would support an actuarially sound system of voluntary prepayment.

Both John and Ida (Anderson) Larson, the parents of Leonard Winfield Larson, were emigrants from Norway who had moved to Wisconsin, where John Larson worked as a hardware merchant and a tinsmith. They later settled in Clarksfield in southwestern Minnesota. Leonard Larson was born in Clarksfield on May 22, 1898 and attended grade school and high school there. His father had become the proprietor of a pharmacy and had also built up a flour-milling business. Through working in his father's drug store, Larson was introduced to medicine and he used to tag along with a country doctor on professional calls.

To complete his preparation for college, Larson studied at St. Olaf Academy in Northfield, Minnesota; he then attended the University of Minnesota in Minneapolis, where he was graduated with the B.S. degree in 1918. After giving some thought to dentistry as a profession, he decided to enter the University of Minnesota Medical School. He did particularly good work in bacteriology and was awarded his M.D. degree *magna cum laude* in 1922.

From medical school Dr. Larson went into general practice at Northwood, Iowa. But since that community had no hospital, he had to spend much of his time traveling from one patient to another. After six months in Iowa, he returned to the University of Minnesota for postgraduate work in clinical pathology. In March 1924 he joined the Quain and Ramstad Clinic in Bismarck, North Dakota, and from that time on he has also worked as pathologist with the Bismarck Evangelical Hospital. Among the early papers that Dr. Larson contributed to medical periodicals were "Normal and Pathological Physiology of the Liver" and "Pathology of the Thyroid Gland," which appeared in the Minneapolis *Journal-Lancet* in March 1926 and June 1928 respectively. Many of his numerous articles since 1930 have dealt with laboratory medicine and in particular with tumor diagnosis and treatment.

Since a specialist in pathology has the task of diagnosing morbid changes in tissues removed in operations, many pathologists seldom see a patient. "Larson is too social-minded for that sort of remoteness," *Time* (July 7, 1961) noted. He was the only private-practice pathologist in North Dakota because he felt that pathologists should examine patients when necessary and act as consultants. In 1935 he became pathologist at St. Alexius Hospital in Bismarck, while continuing his work at the Evangelical Hospital, and since 1939 he has been one of five partners operating the Quain and Ramstad clinic. The clinic, which is modeled on the Mayo Clinic in Rochester, Minnesota, has thirty-seven doctors and 110 employees serving an area with a population of about 250,000.

Soon after settling in North Dakota, Dr. Larson was made secretary of the Bismarck local medical society and before long became secretary of the North Dakota Medical Association, for which he served also as legislative watchdog at the state capitol. He is said to have attended all but one of the annual sessions of the American Medical Association since 1926, and in 1940 he was elected to the AMA house of delegates as a representative for the section on pathology and physiology. Continuing as a delegate until 1950, Dr. Larson was elected to the council of scientific assembly, which is responsible for arrangement of scientific programs and exhibits at annual and interim sessions of the association.

During his tenure in the house of delegates Larson was named chairman of the AMA's correlating committee on lay-sponsored health plans. He took part in formulating the so-called "twenty principles" that covered the relationship between the medical profession and the health plans. The study, conducted in co-operation with a committee from the Group Health Association, resulted in a report that the house of delegates endorsed with slight modification.

In 1950 Larson was elected to the AMA's nine-member board of trustees, the executive body that conducts the association's business between conventions, and in 1958 he was named chairman of the board. Meanwhile, he had been appointed chairman of the commission on medical care plans, an outgrowth of the correlating committee. The report of Larson's fifteen-member commission took four years to prepare and was subjected to six months' study by the house of delegates before being unanimously approved in June 1959. It included a comprehensive statistical analysis of all types of medical care plans and also covered such important subjects as free choice of physician. Barbara Yuncker (New York *Post Magazine* (July 2, 1961) called the Larson report a "major policy breakthrough" because for the first time in the history of the association it "put organized medicine on record as recognizing that good and effective medicine could be—and was being—practiced in prepaid group clinics, even in closed-panel plans like that serving the United Mine Workers."

Other AMA committees of which Larson served as chairman were the trustees' committee and the committee on blood. He helped organize, and was for four years president of, the

Joint Blood Council, which is sponsored by the AMA, American Hospital Association, American Society of Clinical Pathologists, American Association of Blood Banks, and the American Red Cross. He was named president-elect of the AMA in June 1960.

Dr. Larson was installed as AMA's 115th president on June 27, 1961, succeeding Dr. E. Vincent Askey, and in a keynote speech at the annual convention he urged that the medical profession police itself in regard to incompetence and unethical conduct. He said that the doctor "must bear in mind that the medical profession does not exist to provide social status, community prestige or high incomes for its members." Delegates at the convention supported the country's drug industry in opposing extension of government control over drugs, approved the Sabin live-virus polio vaccine as more effective than the Salk vaccine, and assailed the administration-backed King-Anderson bill for medical care for the aged.

The association does, however, support the Kerr-Mills law, which provides matching funds to states desiring to broaden the scope of medical aid for the aged. In January 1952 officials of the AMA and Blue Shield jointly announced a program of medical and surgical benefits at a monthly cost of about $3 a person for elderly people with annual incomes of $2,500 or less.

Another professional organization in which Larson has been prominent is the American Society of Clinical Pathologists, of which he was president in 1939-40 and chairman of the executive committee from 1940 to 1950. He has been a Fellow of the College of American Pathologists since 1922. He is a director and past vice-president of the American Cancer Society, which in 1953 awarded him its Gold Medal for his contributions to cancer control. In January 1961 he was a member of the national advisory council for the White House Conference on Aging, held in Washington, and served as chairman of its committee on health and medical care.

In 1952, 1953, and again in 1959 Dr. Larson was a member of the United States delegation to the United Nations World Health Organization assemblies in Geneva, Switzerland, and in 1961 he attended a fourth assembly, in New Delhi, India. For four years, also, Dr. Larson was a delegate to the World Medical Association, attending meetings in West Berlin, Istanbul, Copenhagen, and Havana. He was elected to its council in September 1960.

At home, in Bismarck, Larson was for nine years a member of the school board and helped to organize Bismarck Junior College. He is currently a trustee of Jamestown College, which conferred on him an honorary Doctor of Science degree in 1961. He has also received the University of Minnesota's Outstanding Achievement Award. He is a past president of Bismarck Rotary and a director of the local Provident Life Insurance Company. His fraternities are the Sigma Xi, Alpha Omega Alpha, and Phi Beta Pi. He is a Presbyterian and a Scottish Rite Freemason.

Leonard W. Larson and Ordelia Miller were married on October 23, 1923. They have two daughters, Margery Doris (Mrs. George Mitchell

Fabian Bachrach
DR. LEONARD W. LARSON

of Bismarck) and Dorothy Lenore (Mrs. John Collett of Lenoir, North Dakota) and eight grandchildren. Larson owns a small farm outside Bismarck and used to hunt and ride horseback for recreation. Now he makes attending conventions his hobby. He has blue eyes and graying blond hair and is quiet, deliberate, and somewhat formal in manner.

References

N Y Post Mag p2 Jl 2 '61 por
N Y Times p19 Je 26 '61 por
Time 78:56+ Jl 7 '61 por

American Medical Directory, 1961
Directory of Medical Specialists, 1961
Who's Who in America, 1960-61

MAO TSE-TUNG (mä'ō dzŭ' dŏong') Dec. 26, 1893- Chinese Communist party official; political writer

Address: Peiping, People's Republic of China

> NOTE: This biography supersedes the article that appeared in *Current Biography* in 1943.

The leader of some 700,000,000 Chinese is Chairman Mao Tse-tung of the Communist party of the People's Republic of China. A soldier, politician, poet, and scholar, he is considered by many as the leading interpreter of Marxist-Leninist doctrine. Himself of peasant origin, Mao has deviated from orthodox Marxism by placing the peasantry rather than the urban proletariat in the vanguard of the revolutionary struggle, in accordance with existing realities in China.

Like many of the Chinese Communist leaders, Mao Tse-tung came from an area of Central China where militarism had made itself most harshly felt, where relations between landlords and peasants were at their worst, and where Western ideas were looked upon with disfavor.

(Continued next page)

Wide World

MAO TSE-TUNG

He was born on December 26, 1893 in the village of Shao Shan in Hsiang T'an county of Hunan province, the eldest of four children of Mao Jensheng. His mother's family name was Wen. He had two brothers: Tse-min (who died in a Nationalist prison in 1941) and Tse-t'an (who was killed in the early 1930's); and one sister. His father, once a poor peasant, paid off his debts after serving in the army, and gradually acquired three and a half acres of land and a rice-trading business. He treated his family and his servants harshly, providing them with only the barest means of sustenance. Mao's mother, a devout Buddhist, gave charity to the poor behind her husband's back, and hoped that her son might eventually enter the priesthood.

Mao, a frail child, began to work in his father's fields at seven and sympathized with his father's farm laborers and with the poverty-ridden but rebellious peasants of Hunan. In his youth he engaged in a "dialectical struggle" against the authority of his father, forming a "united front" with the other members of his family. On at least two occasions he ran away from home.

Entering the local private elementary school at the age of eight, Mao studied the Confucian classics, but grew to dislike Confucius, whom he identified with the authoritarianism of his father and his teachers. He much preferred the romantic novels of ancient China. After completing elementary school at thirteen he returned to the farm, where he helped his father with accounts.

In September 1907 Mao entered middle school at Hsianghsiang, fifteen miles from home, with the reluctant approval of his father, who wanted to apprentice him to a rice merchant. At the school he studied science and other modern subjects and came into contact with the ideas of the reform movement of K'ang Yu-wei and Liang Ch'i-ch'ao, who sought to modernize the Manchu dynasty. During vacations, Mao and a schoolmate became wandering scholars, exposing their bodies to the elements and earning their way by writing scrolls.

In 1911 Mao entered secondary school at Changsha, where he wrote anti-Manchu political essays. Although he had not yet fully accepted the policies of Sun Yat-sen's revolutionary Kuomintang movement, he decided in late 1911 to join the Nationalist regular army, where he served as an orderly to the younger officers. He was discharged in the summer of 1912.

In late 1912 Mao, who no longer received an allowance from home, entered the tuition-free teachers' training college at Changsha, and remained for six years. There he first became influenced by Socialist writings, although his understanding of Socialism was superficial. He also founded the New People's Study Organization, many of whose members later joined the Communist movement.

Graduating in 1918, shortly after his mother's death, Mao did not return home but went to Peiping, where he helped to organize a "work and learn" program for students who wished to study in France. Subsequently he took a menial position as an assistant at the Peiping University library, while studying in his spare time. During this period he had no great ambition and would have been satisfied with eventually taking a minor government post. In 1919 he returned to Hunan province, where he edited the *Hsiang River Monthly Review,* and organized Hunanese students in an effort to overthrow a corrupt military governor. In 1920 he became a teacher in the first normal school at Changsha.

Having in the meantime become a convinced Marxist, Mao was caught up in the May Fourth movement, which originated in student demonstrations in Peiping on May 4, 1919, protesting against the provisions of the Treaty of Versailles that granted Japan the former German concessions in China. This movement formed the core of the Chinese Communist party, which held its founding congress in Shanghai in the summer of 1921. Mao, representing a small group of Communists in Hunan, was one of the twelve founding members of the party. The congress rejected affiliation with the Communist International in Moscow, and it was not until 1922 that the party established formal relations with the Comintern. After the founding congress Mao returned to Hunan, where he set up the provincial branch of the Communist party and organized a number of trade unions.

After the Communist party decided, in 1923, to collaborate closely with the Kuomintang in a united front against the northern militarists, Mao became a member of the Kuomintang, while continuing to serve as a member of the central committee of the Communist party. He was regarded at this time as representing the extreme right wing of the Communist party. He continued to be active in both the Communist party and the Kuomintang until 1927, when Chiang Kai-shek's massacre of the Shanghai workers brought about the break between the two parties.

In the spring of 1925 Mao had come to recognize the potential revolutionary role of the peasants, and began to organize peasant unions in Hunan. In 1927, under party instructions, he wrote *Report of an Investigation into the Peasant Movement in Hunan*, ascribing a central role to the peasantry in the revolutionary class struggle. At first the report was tabled by the central committee of the party, but later in the year it was published in the central party organ.

In September 1927 Mao led some 2,000 Hunan peasants in the abortive Autumn Harvest Uprising, and he was removed from his Politburo position and from the Hunan provincial committee. He then retreated with the remnants of his forces to Chingkanshan mountain in Kiangsi province, where he was joined in April 1928 by Chu Teh, a former warlord who had gone over to the Communists. Together they established the Fourth Workers' and Peasants' Red Army, with Mao as political commissar and Chu Teh as military commander. During his years in the mountains Mao continued to develop the tactics of guerilla warfare.

In November 1931 the first national congress of soviets was held at Juichin in Kiangsi province, marking the formal establishment of the China Soviet Republic, and Mao was elected chairman of the provisional soviet government. Meanwhile, in late 1930, Chiang Kai-shek had begun his "extermination campaigns" against the Communists. Four of these campaigns were successfully repulsed by the Red armies, but in the fifth campaign, which took up the greater part of 1934, the Communist forces were severely defeated.

In October 1934 the Communists, pressed by Kuomintang forces, began their long march some 6,000 miles northward from Kiangsi to Shensi province. This legendary march was marked by heroism on the part of the Red forces, only a fraction of whom survived. In its course, Mao greatly increased his stature, and at the party conference held at Tsunyi in Kweichow province from December 1934 to January 1935 his authority was virtually unchallenged.

Arriving at northern Shensi province in October 1935, Mao re-established the Soviet Republic of China, with headquarters first at Pao An and later at Yenan. Meanwhile the pressure of the Japanese, who had invaded Manchuria in 1931, was mounting, and in March 1936 Mao called for an anti-Japanese united front with the Kuomintang. As a result of Mao's efforts an agreement was reached in the spring of 1937 after the Communists had pledged to abandon the agrarian revolution.

During the Japanese war Mao lived in a cave in Yenan, where he raised his own tobacco and spent his nights studying and writing political essays. By 1938 he was universally recognized as the authoritative leader and theoretician of the Communist movement. His primer on guerilla warfare was published in 1937. In *The New Democracy* (1940) Mao justified the compromise between the Kuomintang and the Communists and depicted democracy as an interim stage between feudalism and Socialism. In *Coalition Government* (1945) he called for a government reflecting the will of the people.

Although Mao had acquired a reputation of being merely an agrarian reformer, in practice he tended to be increasingly influenced by the policies of Stalin. From 1942 to 1944 he instituted a far-reaching "rectification" program aimed at tightening party discipline and purging undesirable elements. At the seventh party congress, in April 1945, Mao was elected chairman of the central committee and of the revolutionary military council.

When the war with Japan ended in August 1945 the Communists were in a strong position. For a time they made attempts to reach an agreement with the Kuomintang. Following a conference between Mao and Chiang Kai-shek shortly after the Japanese surrender, Mao complained with some bitterness that Chiang had treated him "like a peasant." Mao was said to have been strongly criticized, in late 1945, by some of the more radical elements of his party for his willingness to grant too many concessions to the Kuomintang in the effort to form a coalition government. During this period he was still looked upon by many Western observers as an agrarian reformer with strong democratic tendencies.

After the failure of efforts by General George C. Marshall, representing the United States government, to bring about a coalition government, the civil war resumed in the summer of 1946. The Communists constantly increased the number of their peasant adherents by promising them land redistribution. When the Red armies crossed the Yangtse River on April 21, 1949, the end of Kuomintang rule on the Chinese mainland was in sight. A few months later Mao Tse-tung was virtually the supreme ruler of China. On October 1, 1949, a week and a half after the republic had been proclaimed by the Chinese people's political consultative conference, Mao Tse-tung was elected chairman of the new central people's government, and an organic law and common program were adopted.

In December 1949 Mao left China for the first time to visit Moscow for Soviet Premier Joseph Stalin's seventieth birthday. The visit resulted in the negotiation, in February 1950, of a thirty-year treaty of "friendship, alliance, and mutual assistance" between China and the Soviet Union. On the domestic scene, Mao proceeded with great vigor to transform the face of his war-torn nation. During the early 1950's he instituted a series of rectification campaigns against waste, bureaucracy, and corruption. Against the landlords he began a reign of terror that lasted until 1954. Mao himself admitted later, in 1957, that during these early years some 800,000 persons were liquidated. (Other estimates of the number of persons killed by the Communists run much higher.) The first five-year plan, providing for large-scale industrialization and collectivization of agriculture was launched in November 1952. By 1956 about 83 percent of all Chinese peasants were on collective farms.

Under the constitution of September 1954, emphasizing a unified state and setting up the basic organs of government, Mao was installed as Chairman of the People's Republic of China and of the National Defense Council. He was also made honorary chairman of the national committee of the Chinese people's consultative conference and was elected a deputy to the National People's Congress. At the same time he retained

MAO TSE-TUNG—*Continued*

his Communist party positions as chairman of the central committee, chairman of the Polit-buro, and member of the Politburo standing committee. He was re-elected to these positions in the party in September 1956.

On February 27, 1957, fearing the possibility of revolts such as occurred in Hungary in 1956, and noting the adverse economic conditions prevailing in China at the time, Mao gave a major speech on "the correct handling of contradictions among the people." He conceded that contradictions could and did exist within a Socialist society and said that these could best be resolved, not by the terror that had marked the early years of Communist rule, but by means of free discussion and criticism. "Let a hundred flowers blossom! Let a hundred schools of thought contend!" he declared. Although the new policy was received with great enthusiasm, criticism of the government far exceeded the expectations of Mao Tse-tung. By June 1957 the government again instituted police rule and suppressed its critics by force.

Under an economic program designated as the "big leap forward" Mao, in April 1958, launched a model commune, which he named "Sputnik." A few months later people's communes were established on a nationwide scale. Unlike the earlier collective farms, which were economic institutions under county administration, the communes were political units under party rule and controlled virtually every phase of an individual's life. However, the communes failed to alleviate the adverse economic situation and by mid-1961 the government was forced to grant farmers a greater degree of freedom and some measure of free enterprise.

In late 1958 Mao requested that he not be re-elected as head of state in the elections of January 1959 in order to concentrate more fully on questions of Marxist-Leninist theory and on policy matters. He was replaced as Chairman of the People's Republic of China by Liu Shao-chi on April 27, 1959. Most observers agree that Mao's position of leadership remains undiminished, in view of the fact that he retains his chairmanship of the Communist party, where the real power in China resides.

Unlike Premier Nikita S. Khrushchev of the Soviet Union, Mao Tse-tung has expressed little fear of the possible consequences of a nuclear war and has maintained that China could absorb hundreds of millions of casualties and emerge victoriously. He believes that the threat of global conflict could be removed only by the victory of the Communist revolution over "the United States reactionaries and their lackeys." On the other hand, he has conceded that compromises between "imperialist" and Socialist countries could occur under certain circumstances.

Within the Communist bloc Mao's stature has steadily grown, especially since the death of Stalin in 1953, and he is regarded by many as overshadowing Khrushchev as the ideological leader of the Communist world. His prestige was greatly enhanced when, at a meeting of world Communist leaders in November 1957, he was instrumental in bringing about the adoption of

an "anti-revisionist" manifesto aimed at Marshal Tito of Yugoslavia. In recent years relations between Communist China and the Soviet Union have become increasingly strained. In private correspondence and at international conferences Chinese Communist spokesmen have accused the Soviet Union of having abandoned orthodox Marxist-Leninist doctrine and of having adopted a revisionist policy. Khrushchev, on the other hand, has accused Mao of seeking to incite a global conflict.

Although Mao Tse-tung has renounced the ideas of Confucius, he is considered a scholar in the classical tradition of China. A four-volume English translation of his writings has been published by Lawrence and Wishart Ltd. and by International Publishers under the title *Selected Works of Mao Tse-tung* (1954-56). As a poet Mao relies heavily on ancient classical forms, although he maintains that all art and literature must serve the revolution. In 1957 he reluctantly permitted the publication of some of his poems, in spite of his fears that they might have an adverse influence on Chinese youth.

Mao Tse-tung was first married at the age of fourteen to a twenty-year-old peasant girl, in a traditional ceremony arranged by his parents. This marriage was never consummated. In 1920 he married Yang K'ai-hui, the daughter of a professor at Peking University who bore him two sons. She was executed by the Nationalists during the early part of Chiang Kai-shek's anti-Communist campaigns. Mao's third wife, Ho Tsu-cheng (or Ho Tse-nien), a former school-teacher, was reportedly divorced by him and is said to be living in the Soviet Union. She bore him five children, some of whom had to be abandoned to peasants during the long march of the 1930's. His eldest son, Mao An-ying, was reportedly killed in the Korean War in November 1950. Mao is now married to Nan P'ing (or Lan Ping), a former motion picture actress, by whom he has two daughters.

Among the people of Communist China Mao Tse-tung is regarded as a "living Buddha" hailed in song and story as "the people's great savior." His portrait is displayed everywhere and his theories are considered infallible. On the other hand, it has been said that he is a poor administrator. Although he has acquired some wealth through royalties on his writings, he avoids worldly vanities except for good food, wine, and cigarettes. He often travels among the peasants, wearing a simple uniform without insignia of rank. In 1956 he swam the Yangtse River from Wuchang to Hankow three times.

References

Atlan 204:56+ D '59

Asia Who's Who (1960)

Dean, Vera Micheles. Builders of Emerging Nations (1961)

Elegant, Robert S. China's Red Masters (1951)

Payne, Robert. Portrait of a Revolutionary: Mao Tse-tung (1961)

Tang, Peter S.H. Communist China Today vol I (1961)

Who's Who in Modern China (1954)

MÖSSBAUER, RUDOLF L(UDWIG) (mŭs'-
bou-ĕr) Jan. 31, 1929- Physicist
Address: b. California Institute of Technology,
Pasadena, Calif.; h. 1041 E. Beverly Way,
Altadena, Calif.

A co-recipient of the 1961 Nobel Prize in
Physics is Rudolf L. Mössbauer, a thirty-three
year old German scientist who is on leave from
his teaching post at the Technische Hochschule
München (Munich Technical University) and is
doing research at the California Institute of
Technology. He shared the $48,300 prize with
another California scientist, Professor Robert
Hofstadter of Stanford University. Mössbauer
was honored for developing a way to produce
and utilize gamma rays of remarkably constant
wavelengths and frequencies as extremely precise
measuring tools for gauging the effect of natural
forces such as gravity, electricity, and magnetism on infinitesimal particles. Using the
Mössbauer effect, as it has come to be known,
physicists have been able to confirm for the
first time one of the basic hypotheses of Einstein's general theory of relativity—that gravity
can change the frequency of a light beam.

Born on January 31, 1929 in Munich, Germany,
Rudolf Ludwig Mössbauer is the only son of
Ludwig Mössbauer, a photo-technician, and his
wife, the former Erna Ernst. He has a sister,
Mrs. Eva-Maria (Mössbauer) Rheinfelder.
Rudolf was reared in Munich and attended the
local schools. He completed his secondary education at the *Oberschule* of Munich-Pasing in
1948 and then worked for several months as a
laboratory assistant in an optical firm. In 1949
he enrolled as a student at the Technische
Hochschule München, from which he received a
preliminary diploma in 1952. During 1953 and
1954, while completing graduate work for the
diploma at the technical physics laboratory of
the Technische Hochschule, Mössbauer was an
instructor in the mathematics section of the
same school. During this period he began the
investigations of the absorption of gamma rays
in matter that led in time to his prize-winning
discoveries.

After receiving his diploma in 1955, Mössbauer
undertook doctoral research at the Institute for
Physics of the Max Planck Institute for Medical
Research in Heidelberg. During the course of his
work, he made the first experimental observations
of the phenomenon of recoil-free nuclear
resonance absorption. Having completed his
doctoral work under Professor Heinz Maier-
Leibnitz of the Technische Hochschule München,
he received his degree from that school in
January 1958. Following additional work at the
Max Planck Institute in 1958, Mössbauer taught
at the Technische Hochschule as a scientific
assistant in 1959.

The essence of Mössbauer's work lies in his
discovery that gamma rays emitted from highly
charged nuclei of certain radioactive isotopes
maintain a sharp, unvarying wavelength and
frequency if the emitting nuclei are tightly bound
in the lattice of a crystal. Normally, the energy
of such rays would be altered by the recoil of
the radiating nucleus, much as the energy of a
bullet is reduced by the kick of a firing rifle.

Harvey

RUDOLF L. MÖSSBAUER

If the rays resulting from a recoil-free emission
strike an atom of the same type as their emitter,
and if this receiving atom is also bound in a
solid and thus capable of recoil-free absorption,
the receiving nucleus will send out a gamma ray
at random. This "resonance" effect takes place
only if both the emitting and absorbing atoms
are held fast in crystals. Moreover, the absorbing
atom will receive only those rays of a wavelength
identical to its own radiation. Mössbauer found
that gamma rays resulting from recoil-free emission have wavelengths invariable to one part in a
trillion, while other scientists have improved the
precision to one part in a quadrillion. Even very
small effects of external forces upon the rays
can thus be detected through slight variations
in their frequency and wavelength.

Mössbauer reported his findings in the German
physics journal *Zeitschrift für Physik* early in
1958. The scientific world showed no immediate
interest in his discovery and he later complained
that "no one reads German scientific literature
anymore." In the latter part of 1959, however,
two Harvard University scientists proposed to
use the Mössbauer effect for testing Einstein's
prediction that gravity distorts light or other
electromagnetic radiation by shifting its wavelength (commonly known as the gravitational
red shift). Until this time these shifts were
much too small to be registered by existing
measuring methods.

Using the radioactive isotope Iron 57, Dr.
Robert V. Pound and Glen A. Rebka, Jr., of
Harvard University confirmed Einstein's hypothesis by beaming gamma rays up and down a
seventy-foot tower. Supposedly, if any distortion
of their frequency occurred due to the force of
gravity, this could be detected when the altered
rays were rejected by the nuclei of radioactive
atoms that would normally absorb unchanged
rays. Scientists in England performed similar

MÖSSBAUER, RUDOLF L.—Continued

experiments and stated that they had observed a frequency shift that corresponded to .96 of the value predicted by Einstein.

Other experimental uses for the effect have been and are still being devised. It has been used to measure the powerful magnetic fields that surround the nuclei of atoms in magnetic materials and to test Einstein's premise that time moves more slowly as the speed of light is approached, i.e. when the device measuring time is moving at extremely high speed. While Mössbauer originally worked with iridium, a platinum-like metal, more than fifteen radioactive isotopes, among them Iron 57 and zinc 67, have been found to exhibit the scientifically valuable Mössbauer effect. Its past and future utilization in experiments was discussed by about eighty scientists at a conference in Illinois in June 1960.

Mössbauer, on leave from the Technische Hochschule München, has been with the California Institute of Technology since March 1960, first as a Research Fellow, then as a Senior Research Fellow, finally as a guest professor of physics. He and his colleagues are studying little-known internal electric and magnetic fields in isotopes of the rare earth elements. The group, supported by the Atomic Energy Commission, has gathered data on the complex electrical interactions in the crystalline structure of these compounds and on the magnetic and electric properties of excited nuclear states. Papers by Mössbauer that describe his work with gamma radiation and recoil-free nuclear absorption have appeared in German and Russian scientific journals. His research on rare earths was reviewed before the second International Congress on the Mössbauer Effect held in Paris in 1961.

For his outstanding contribution to the development of new insight into the physical world of gamma radiation, Mössbauer was named by the Royal Swedish Academy of Science as a co-winner, with Dr. Robert Hofstadter, of the 1961 Nobel Prize in Physics. The prizes were presented to the Nobel laureates by King Gustav of Sweden on December 10, 1961 at ceremonies held in Stockholm. Soon after Mössbauer was named as a Nobel Prize winner, the Technische Hochschule München announced his promotion to the rank of full professor of physics at that school. In addition to the Nobel Prize Mössbauer has received a $5,000 award from the Research Corporation (1960), the Elliott Cresson Medal of the Franklin Institute in Philadelphia (1961), and the Röntgen Prize of the University of Giessen, Germany (1961). He belongs to the American Physical Society.

On the campus of the California Institute of Technology Mössbauer looks more the student than the professor. He is slight-framed, standing five feet eight inches tall and weighing only 132 pounds. He has brown eyes, a thick shock of dark hair, and a very serious manner. He and his wife, a former fashion designer née Elizabeth Pritz, have two children, Peter and Regine. An exact explanation of the mechanics of his discovery "is always a little tricky to say," Mössbauer finds. "We still have fights among the scientists to describe it." "My husband can make his work very plain and exciting," Frau Mössbauer adds, "but sometimes even physicists don't understand."

References

Christian Sci Mon p3 N 3 '61 por
N Y Herald Tribune p23 N 3 '61 por
N Y Times p24 N 3 '61
N Y World-Telegram p8 N 2 '61

PEDEN, KATHERINE (GRAHAM) Jan. 2, 1926- Business executive; organization official

Address: b. Radio Station WHOP, Hopkinsville, Ky.; h. 2118 S. Virginia St., Hopkinsville, Ky.

The youngest president in the forty-three-year history of the National Federation of Business and Professional Women's Clubs is Miss Katherine Peden, vice-president and station director of radio station WHOP in Hopkinsville, Kentucky. Active in the work of Business and Professional Women's Clubs since 1944, Miss Peden has served as president of the Hopkinsville club and of the Kentucky federation, and as vice-president of the national federation. Since her installation as the twentieth president of the national federation on July 27, 1961, succeeding Miss Fannie Hardy, she has conducted an extensive educational campaign to make members more aware of international problems.

Katherine Graham Peden was born on January 2, 1926 in Hopkinsville, Kentucky to William Edward Peden, a construction superintendent, and Mary (Gorin) Peden, a former schoolteacher. She has three brothers: Major Maxie Burton Peden, on active duty with the United States Army at Fort Chaffee, Arkansas; T. Renfro Peden of Seneca, South Carolina; and James E. Peden of Hopkinsville, Kentucky. She attended public schools in her native city and graduated in 1944 from Hopkinsville High School, where she was class president and a member of the honor society, and was voted the "most likely to succeed" by her classmates. She was also editor of the school annual and newspaper, and was a member of the school band and of the debating team.

Planning to study pharmacy, Miss Peden took a summer office job in 1944 at radio station WHOP (an affiliate of the Columbia Broadcasting System) in Hopkinsville, in order to earn funds for college. Her work proved so interesting that she relinquished the idea of becoming a pharmacist. "I'd rather solve problems than mend headaches," Miss Peden later told Elizabeth Ford of the Washington Post and Times Herald (August 20, 1961). She worked in the traffic department of the station from 1944 to 1949, serving as control room operator and announcer, and later as program director. She was made sales manager in 1949. Having in the meantime acquired an engineer's license from the Federal Communications Commission, Miss Peden became vice-president and station director in 1957, and she continues to serve in these two posts. She has visited almost every state in the union, and in May and June 1961 she made a 35,000-mile trip to twelve countries in Africa and the Middle East. There she made tape recordings of interviews with persons from all walks of life, for a series of public service broadcasts on station WHOP.

Miss Peden first became associated with the Business and Professional Women's Clubs in 1944, when she joined the Hopkinsville organization. Serving successively as president of the Hopkinsville club and as second and first vice-president of the Kentucky Federation of Business and Professional Women's Clubs, she was elected president of the Kentucky federation for the year 1955-56. During her presidency the Kentucky federation experienced its largest growth, and its membership increased at a greater rate than that of any other state. An editorial in *National Business Woman* said of Miss Peden in March 1958: "Her magnetic personality, poise, diplomacy, and sense of fairness, as well as her convincing and dynamic manner of public speaking, qualify her for capable leadership on a national scope. She presides with justice, ease and dispatch. Her sound judgment, outstanding leadership are exemplified by the unexcelled manner in which she has executed each assignment." After serving as second vice-president of the National Federation of Business and Professional Women's Clubs she became first vice-president for 1960-61.

The National Federation of Business and Professional Women's Clubs is the largest all-inclusive group of business and professional women in the world. A nonpartisan, nonsectarian, nonprofit organization, it was founded in St. Louis, Missouri in 1919 by a group of 212 working women whose aims were to elevate the standards for women in business and the professions, to promote their interests, and to extend opportunities along lines of industrial, scientific, and vocational activities.

The federated clubs have accomplished these aims through activities at the club, state, and national levels in four major areas: individual development, community concern, national awareness, and hemispheric co-operation. The federation seeks to help solve the problems confronting the world, and to create international understanding by actively supporting the United Nations and its specialized agencies. The membership of the National Federation of Business and Professional Women's Clubs included, in late 1961, some 175,000 working women in over 3,500 clubs in the fifty states, the District of Columbia, Puerto Rico, and the Virgin Islands. It is affiliated with the International Federation of Business and Professional Women's Clubs, which has members in twenty-four countries.

At the twenty-seventh convention of the National Federation of Business and Professional Women's Clubs, held in Chicago in July 1961, Katherine Peden was installed as the twentieth president of the organization by past national president Helen G. Irwin. On accepting the position Miss Peden promised: "You will receive all I have to offer in leadership, in planning, in carrying out these directives." She then outlined three projects to be undertaken by the federation during her 1961-62 term: a program to train women in executive or managerial positions, in co-operation with leading universities; a conference of business and professional women from all parts of the Western Hemisphere; and a joint

KATHERINE PEDEN

effort to raise $100,000 to build the Dr. Minnie L. Maffett Chinese Nurses' Home on Formosa. The convention was addressed by F. Ernest Lackey, the mayor of Hopkinsville and owner of station WHOP, who said of Miss Peden: "Though she never got to college, this girl has acquired the knack of separating the worthwhile from the trivia and her store of knowledge transcends much that she might have missed through failure to attend a school of higher learning. . . . Brace yourselves for an active year. Katherine Peden not only will not accept the status quo— she won't let you."

In November 1961 Miss Peden represented the United States delegation to the Conference of Business and Professional Women of the Americas, held at San Juan, Puerto Rico. The goals of the conference were "to establish ways to promote Hemispheric friendship, co-operation, and understanding between women of the Americas, and to determine ways in which women can contribute to the social, cultural and economic progress of the Western Hemisphere."

Miss Peden believes that "as a citizen, wherever you are, you're responsible for sharing your time and your talents with your community." Acting on this conviction, she was chairman of the March of Dimes campaign in Hopkinsville from 1951 to 1955; a director of the Community Chest in 1955-57; and a director of the Mental Health Association since 1956. Since 1958 she has been co-chairman of the Western State Hospital Chapel Fund and a trustee of the Business and Professional Women's Foundation. In 1960 she was appointed by the Governor of Kentucky to a four-year term as the only woman member of a five-member personnel board whose function is to establish and administer Kentucky's first merit system for state employees. She was the first woman to be elected to the board of directors of the Hopkinsville Chamber of Commerce,

PEDEN, KATHERINE—*Continued*

on which she served from 1957 to 1959. The Kentucky Broadcasters' Association elected her in 1956 as the first woman member of its executive committee. She served on this committee until 1960, and was secretary-treasurer of the association from 1956 to 1959.

In 1951 Miss Peden's services to her community were recognized when she was the recipient of the Hopkinsville Woman of the Year award. Her home town again honored her on September 14, 1961 when that day was set aside as "Katherine Peden Day" by the mayor of Hopkinsville. She was saluted in the press and on the radio in recognition of her outstanding achievements as a career woman and a community leader. Although she has traveled widely, she indicated in her acceptance speech her fondness for her own town: "The end of my rainbow is where it started—in Hopkinsville."

Miss Peden is five feet ten inches tall, weighs 160 pounds, and has brown hair and brown eyes. An employee at station WHOP has observed: "Katie has only one head, but it's just crammed full of brains. There's no job here that she can't do—and probably better than anyone else." Tom Duncan, writing in the Louisville *Courier-Journal* (July 25, 1961) noted that she has "a genuine liking for people, a warm personality, and what one employee calls 'a fiendish sense of humor'." Miss Peden is an expert golfer, playing in the middle eighties. She belongs to the First Christian Church and has been a deaconess since 1956. She is a Democrat.

As a businesswoman who has come a long way, Miss Peden feels that women in business have "a tendency to level off on a plateau" and that they "don't push hard enough for the job at the top." She also believes that the American people should become better informed on their country's foreign policy before they criticize it, and that in giving foreign aid the United States "should help people to help themselves." Writing a Thanksgiving meditation in the November 1958 issue of *National Business Woman,* Miss Peden exhorted clubwomen to be "grateful for time—to give, time to serve," and to "be aware of the value of each moment, be always grateful for it, and spend it well."

References

Christian Sci Mon p4 Ag 7 '61
Washington Post Cp19 Jl 27 '61 por; Fp6 Ag 20 '61 por
Who's Who of American Women (1961-62)

PICCARD, AUGUSTE Jan. 28, 1884-Mar. 24, 1962 Swiss physicist; educator; an explorer during the 1930's of the stratosphere, for which he invented an airtight gondola, and then of the ocean depths, for which he developed a bathyscaphe in 1946. See *Current Biography* (September) 1947.

Obituary

N Y Times p1+ Mr 26 '62

REISCHAUER, EDWIN O(LDFATHER) (rī' shou-ēr) Oct. 15, 1910- United States Ambassador to Japan; historian; university professor *Address*: United States Embassy, Tokyo, Japan

Edwin O. Reischauer, who succeeded Douglas MacArthur II as United States Ambassador to Japan on April 6, 1961, is a diplomat whose abilities and background are well suited to his assignment. A leading expert on eastern Asia and an historian, he is on leave from Harvard University, where he has been professor of Japanese history since 1950. Reischauer was born in Japan of American missionary parents and can speak, read, and write Japanese. His appointment to a post that has usually been filled by a career diplomat was viewed by some observers as a bid by United States officials to strengthen faltering relations between Japan and the United States.

Edwin Oldfather Reischauer was born in Tokyo on October 15, 1910 to August Karl and Helen Sidwell (Oldfather) Reischauer, who were American educational missionaries. August Reischauer taught philosophy at Meiji University in Tokyo and, with his wife, established Japan's first school for deaf-mutes. Reischauer has a sister, Felicia. His brother, Robert Karl, died in 1937.

Brought up in Japan, Reischauer attended the American School in Tokyo, from which he graduated in 1927. In addition to being editor of his school yearbook and class president, he played baseball, tennis, soccer, and basketball. An item in a school publication, commenting on his proficiency in basketball, stated: "Playing center, Ed is indispensable both on offense and defense. It will be hard to find a replacement for next year."

At seventeen Reischauer enrolled at Oberlin College in Ohio, where he majored in history and was captain of the tennis team. He held a part-time job as a dishwasher. Graduated as a Phi Beta Kappa with a B.A. degree in 1931, he then went to Harvard University, from which he received an M.A. degree in history in 1932. From 1931 to 1938 Reischauer was a Traveling Fellow of the Harvard-Yenching Institute, which supports exchange fellowships and other academic programs in Asia.

He did postgraduate work at the University of Paris (1933-35), at the universities of Tokyo (1935-36) and Kyoto (1937-38) and in China, receiving his Ph.D. degree in Far Eastern languages from Harvard University in 1938. His dissertation, entitled "Ennin's Travels in T'ang China," was published as a book by the Ronald Press in 1955. Reischauer has also translated from the Chinese Ennin's *Diary: A Record of a Pilgrimage to China in Search of the Law* (Ronald, 1955) and issued, with Joseph K. Yamagiwa, *Translations from Early Japanese Literature,* published in 1951 by the Harvard University Press.

After having been an instructor at Harvard University from 1938 to 1942, Reischauer took leave from its faculty to work as a senior research analyst for the Department of State during the summer of 1941 and for the War Department from 1942 to 1943. In 1943 he entered the United States Army with the rank of major and served for the next two years with the military intelligence service. He was awarded the Legion of Merit and discharged in 1945, with the rank of lieutenant colonel.

Reischauer's first civilian post after the war was with the Department of State as chairman of the Japan-Korea secretariat and special assistant to the director of the Office of Far Eastern Affairs. In 1946 he rejoined the Harvard faculty as an associate professor of Far Eastern languages. In 1950 he was promoted to his present position as professor of Japanese history. Since 1956 he has been the director of the Harvard-Yenching Institute. He is also associate director of the Center for East Asian Studies.

With his colleague John K. Fairbank, an authority on China, Reischauer taught, beginning in 1939, a popular survey course in Asian history known informally around the Harvard Yard as "rice paddies." One result of their long collaboration is the book *East Asia: The Great Tradition* (Houghton, 1960), a history of China, Japan, and Korea from pre-Christian times to the middle of the nineteenth century. The authors trace political, social, economic, intellectual, and cultural developments and the modifications imposed by each country upon the institutions and traditions it borrowed from the others. Reischauer has also devised a comprehensive chart showing the epochs and stages of Asian history, country by country, that has become a valuable scholar's tool.

Compiler of a number of basic texts for students of the Japanese language, Reischauer is also the author of *Japan, Past and Present* (Knopf, 1946; 1952), *The United States and Japan* (Harvard Univ. Press, 1950; 1957), and *Wanted: An Asian Policy* (Knopf, 1955). The latter examines the changes wrought in Asia by industrialism and nationalism in the past century and the lack of understanding of that continent often shown by Western policymakers. On various occasions Reischauer has criticized certain aspects of United States policy in Asia, including the administration of Okinawa, trade policies, the "misestimate" of the situation that led to riots against the United States-Japan Mutual Security Treaty in 1960 and the cancellation of President Dwight D. Eisenhower's visit to Japan, and the failure of the United States to invest concepts of democracy with meaning for Asians.

When he became United States Ambassador to Japan on April 6, 1961, Reischauer acquired a privilege rarely accorded a critic—the opportunity to test his theories in the field. His opportunity, however, is restricted by the limitations inherent in the ambassadorial role: that of conveyor, but not initiator, of policy decisions. He agrees that there are whole areas about which he can no longer speak frankly in public as he did as a detached commentator on the political scene. His authoritative opinions are respected and still given careful attention by key people in the government, however. He has done his best—perhaps more successfully than most envoys—to interpret the people and interests of his host country to Washington, and to cultivate an understanding of American motives in Japan.

The latter task is often difficult, particularly in the presence of a vocal opposition that agi-

Dept. of State—
Robert H. McNeill

EDWIN O. REISCHAUER

tates for neutralism (rather than strong Western ties advocated by the ruling Liberal-Democratic party) and that keeps fresh in the Nipponese mind general dissatisfactions like the American occupation of Okinawa (formerly held by Japan) and looming United States protectionist trade moves on textiles, which account for 30 percent of Japanese exports and bring in more than $1,000,000,000 yearly. Another area in which Reischauer has worked assiduously to achieve concord is the relationship between South Korea and Japan. He believes it to be to the interest of both countries to exchange their long-standing enmity for economic co-operation.

Disagreeing with those who maintain that democracy was imposed on Japan after World War II, Reischauer contends that democratic institutions accompanying an industrial revolution arose naturally in that country in 1868 after the shogunate had fallen, and that these were only temporarily suspended during the rule of the militaristic and dictatorial régime that fell in 1945. Moreover, disputing a pet belief of Japanese intellectuals that the way to progress is socialism, he maintains that Japan's rapid rise from feudalism to modern democracy was effected largely because a balanced relationship existed historically between government and private enterprise. "The real contrast in the modern world," Reischauer has said, "is not that between capitalism and socialism, neither of which exists in a pure form anywhere, but between free, humanistic democracies and . . . totalitarian régimes, whether they be called Fascist or Communist, in which the few . . . dictate the lives of the common people."

Reischauer's major diplomatic mission has been to seek resumption of the "broken dialogue" between America and Japan, to contact Japanese

REISCHAUER, EDWIN O.—*Continued*

outside "the establishment," many of whom subscribe to Marxist ideology. Seeking out opposition politicians, labor leaders, and the alienated and vastly discontented intellectuals and students, whom he has called "the would-be ideological pathfinders and the generation to which the future Japan belongs," he has tried, by objective discussion, to correct stereotyped views of the West and to assure these groups of American interest in their opinions and problems.

His efforts have profited greatly from his tremendous personal popularity (A. M. Rosenthal in the New York *Times,* March 25, 1962, has called him "far and away the best known and most talked-about American in . . . [Japan]") and the respect traditionally accorded scholars in that country. His fluency in Japanese has encouraged relaxed meetings with many influential people who, because of their poor English, would otherwise feel uncomfortable or stay away entirely. "How wonderful it is," a Tokyo editorial writer once remarked, "to write an editorial and know that the American Ambassador will actually be able to read it." Following the announcement of his appointment, a Japanese newspaper printed a cartoon showing Premier Hayato Ikeda brushing up on his Japanese, with the caption "Reischauer-san is coming."

Reischauer has made a point of becoming acquainted with his own staff at the Embassy, and he has opened its swimming pool to most of the 2,469 employees, five-sixths of whom are Japanese (his predecessor had reserved the pool for personal use). Following a recent baseball victory over the Japanese Foreign Office team, the Embassy staff gave Reischauer its "most valuable player" award. Blue-eyed, with dark brown hair, he is five feet eleven inches tall and weighs 160 pounds. On occasion he dons traditional native dress—a kimono and geta (raised clogs).

Reischauer received an honorary Litt.D. degree from Oberlin College in 1957. He is a member of the Japan-United States Committee on Cultural and Educational Exchange and belongs to the American Historical Society, the American Oriental Society, the Japan Society, and the Association for Asian Studies (formerly the Far Eastern Association), of which he was president in 1955-56.

Reischauer married Haru Matsukata, a foreign correspondent, on February 4, 1956. Born of a nisei mother, she is the granddaughter on her father's side of Prince Masayoshi Matsukata, who was Japanese Prime Minister. By a previous marriage to Adrienne Danton, which lasted from July 6, 1935 until her death on January 17, 1955, Reischauer has three children: Ann, Robert Danton, and Joan.

The Japanese welcome of Ambassador Reischauer might be summed up by this editorial comment, which appeared shortly after the news of his appointment reached Japan: "There has rarely been such a right-man-in-the-right-place appointment as that of Reischauer," the writer of the editorial observed. "The professor was born here in Japan and is well-versed in Japanese. Moreover, he is well informed about Japan,

probably having no equal among foreigners on that point."

References

Christian Sci Mon p7 Mr 16 '61 por
N Y Times p45 D 3 '61
N Y Times Mag p30+ Mr 25 '62 pors
Reporter 25:40+ D 7 '61
Time 79:20+ Ja 12 '62 por
Directory of American Scholars (1957)
International Who's Who, 1961-62
Who's Who in America, 1960-61

RUSSELL, DONALD J(OSEPH) Jan. 3, 1900- Railroad executive

Address: b. Southern Pacific Co., 65 Market St., San Francisco 5, Calif.; h. 2298 Pacific Ave., San Francisco 15, Calif.

During a vigorous railroading career spent entirely in the service of the Southern Pacific Company, Donald J. Russell rose from a timekeeper for a maintenance gang in 1920 to president and chief executive officer in January 1952. The Southern Pacific Railroad, running from San Francisco to Ogden, Utah and from Portland, Oregon southward to the Mexican border and eastward to New Orleans, not including its subsidiaries, is second in mileage only to the Atchison, Topeka, & Santa Fe. Largely because of Russell's insistence upon streamlining, cutting costs, and eliminating waste, the Southern Pacific, which has an annual net income of more than $65,000,000, is one of the few major railroads in the country currently reporting an increase in both gross revenues and net earnings.

Donald Joseph Russell, the son of Donald McKay and Josephine (Nunan) Russell, was born on January 3, 1900 in Denver, Colorado. His father, a native of Scotland, worked as a furniture salesman. He died when his son was still an infant, and the boy was brought up by his mother and an aunt in Oakland, California, where he attended a Roman Catholic high school. In 1917 he entered Stanford University with the intention of earning a degree in engineering.

At eighteen, however, Russell left college in the middle of his freshman year to join the Royal Air Force in Canada for World War I service. Later in 1918 he crashed while piloting a repairs-testing flight and suffered multiple bone breaks and facial injuries that required extensive plastic surgery. On recovery, he returned to Stanford to continue his engineering course. In the summer of 1920 he took a vacation job as a timekeeper for a maintenance-of-way gang on the Sacramento division of the Southern Pacific Railroad, and at the beginning of October, instead of returning to the university, he joined the Southern Pacific's engineering department at a $193-a-month salary.

Realizing that track experience would help him to advance as an engineer, he applied, at a reduction in salary, for a foreman trainee's job with a track gang. From this he went ahead quickly to extra gang and section gang foreman. He had married shortly after becoming a full-time Southern Pacific employee, and during the first year and a half of marriage he and his wife lived in a railroad work car. In June 1923 he was promoted to assistant engineer and given the assignment, which he carried out for almost three years, of supervising tunnel, bridge, snow-shed, and grading work in the double-tracking of the old Central Pacific line across the Sierra Nevadas between Emigrant Gap, California and Truckee, Nevada.

From March 1926 to June 1927 Russell was in charge of rehabilitation of the line between Grass Lake in northern California and Kirk, Oregon, and the construction of new terminal facilities at Klamath Falls and Crescent Lake, Oregon. When that assignment was completed, he was transferred from the Sacramento to the Portland, Oregon division, becoming roadmaster at Oakridge, Oregon in June 1927. In September 1928 he was promoted to assistant trainmaster at Eugene, Oregon and in June 1929, to train-master. He moved to Portland in September 1934 as assistant superintendent and from there to San Francisco in 1937 as general manager at Southern Pacific headquarters.

As superintendent of the Southern Pacific's Los Angeles division, beginning in 1939, Russell attracted the attention of President Angus D. McDonald, who made him his assistant in July 1941. "He . . . proceeded," according to *Time* (August 11, 1961), "to ram through, against the judgment of his superiors, decisions on equipment allocation that enabled the S.P. to haul more freight for the Pacific war than any other railroad." In December 1941, when Armand T. Mercier succeeded McDonald as president, Russell was made a vice-president. He was elected a director of the Southern Pacific Company in August 1943 and executive vice-president in February 1951.

On January 1, 1952 in succession to Mercier, who had reached the mandatory retirement age, Donald Russell took over the chief executive position, becoming at fifty-one the Southern Pacific's youngest president since the days of its founders. He also serves as president of the subsidiary Texas & New Orleans Railroad Company and chairman of the board of the St. Louis Southwestern Railway Company (Cotton Belt Route), of which the Southern Pacific controls 88 percent of the stock. In 1953 Russell introduced piggyback freight cars to the Southern Pacific, and by the end of 1954 the railroad's profits had risen to $58,000,000, making it the third most prosperous railroad in the United States. Much of the profit was plowed back into roadbed and rolling stock improvements and into expansion and modernization of railroad yards.

Very early in his presidency, Russell engaged the Stanford Research Institute to study the outlook for a railroad-owned pipeline to carry refined petroleum from Los Angeles and El Paso to points in Arizona. The report was favorable, and in March 1953 construction began on the first pipeline of its kind to be owned and operated by a railroad company. It began servicing ten oil companies and the United States Air Force on January 3, 1956 and almost at once showed a profit. Plans for an additional pipeline from Oakland, California to Reno and Fallon, Nevada were announced in

Fabian Bachrach
DONALD J. RUSSELL

April 1956, and by December 1957 this pipeline, too, was in operation.

Also in 1956 Russell concluded agreements between the Southern Pacific's highway subsidiary, the Pacific Motor Trucking Company, and three airlines for provision of an integrated truck-air freight service. In somewhat more recent moves, Russell is said to have saved his company more than $1,000,000 a year by placing inventories under an electronic brain and to have speeded freight movement at the Houston yards through a radar-electronic shunting control system.

If the tracking of its controlled affiliates, among them the St. Louis Southwestern, is included, the Southern Pacific may be considered the nation's largest rail transportation system, according to the New York *Times* (October 13, 1960), with a trackage of 14,437 miles. Not content with an already vast mileage, the Southern Pacific, through a subsidiary, began in April 1960 to buy up shares of the Western Pacific, whose main line from Salt Lake City to San Francisco roughly parallels the Southern Pacific in this area. When Russell announced in October 1960 that his company was petitioning the Interstate Commerce Commission for authority to acquire control of the Western Pacific, the Atchison, Topeka & Santa Fe countered by buying 20 percent of the Western Pacific stock and winning the support of Western Pacific's president.

In July 1961 an Interstate Commerce Commission examiner, Paul C. Albus, began hearings on the rival merger propositions. In his testimony President Russell argued that Southern Pacific acquisition of the Western Pacific would lead to "the elimination of waste which now exists in the duplications of many of the facilities" of the two railroads. "If costs are brought down," he said, "rates may be reduced or held reasonably under control in the face of gen-

SHIRER, WILLIAM L.—*Continued*

reconstructs the development of post-World War I Germany. He sketches the major personalities, traces ideological origins, and details political and military events that contributed to the ascendance and demise of Hitler's régime.

The book has aroused much adverse reaction in West Germany, where critics feel that Shirer equates the Germans with Nazis in such a way as to imply that the German character made Hitler's success inevitable, and that consequently Germans cannot be trusted. They believe that the book has markedly encouraged Americans in new anti-German feeling. They have also attacked it as embodying "oversimplifications" and "half-truths" in its historical presentation.

Most American critics, however, adjudged it an accurate, balanced, and comprehensive survey, of value especially to those unfamiliar with the period. It became a Book-of-the-Month Club choice and the first $10 book ever to top the best-seller list, and was chosen as one of the notable books of the year by the American Library Association. Simon & Schuster received the 1960 Carey-Thomas Award for their publication of *The Rise and Fall of the Third Reich*, while Shirer won a 1960 National Book Award of $1,000 as well as a special award from the Sidney Hillman Foundation in 1961. Metro-Goldwyn-Mayer bought the movie rights, and Fawcett World Library bought the paperback rights. Shirer's *The Rise and Fall of Adolf Hitler*, a paperback, was published as a World Landmark Book by Random House in 1961.

Because of the length of his project, Shirer experienced some financial difficulties while writing the *Third Reich*; he supplemented his income by writing magazine articles and lecturing during this period. At a press conference preceding the presentation of the National Book Awards (March 1961), he reiterated his belief that some sort of interim financial aid should be available to free-lance writers.

Shirer holds an honorary Litt.D. degree from Coe College (1941), and the Wendell Willkie One World Award (1948). He is a chevalier of the French Legion of Honor and a member of Tau Kappa Epsilon. Shirer belongs to the Authors' Guild, of which he was president in the year 1956-57, and to P.E.N., the Council on Foreign Relations, the Foreign Policy Association, and the Century Club in New York.

William Lawrence Shirer married Theresa Stiberitz, a Viennese painter, on January 30, 1931. They have two daughters, Eileen Inga and Linda Elizabeth. He is a Presbyterian. For recreation he plays the accordion and the piano, and enjoys walking, skiing, playing golf, going to the theater or the ballet, listening to symphonic and chamber music, and reading novels and history. In New York City he writes in his study overlooking the East River; during the summer he works in an old barn on his farm in Connecticut.

References

N Y Herald Tribune Bk R p20 O 8 '50
Sat R 30:9 S 27 '47; 37:10 My 29 '54
International Who's Who, 1961-62
Murrow, Edward R. This I Believe (1952)

National Cyclopædia of American Biography current vol H (1952)
Shirer, William L. Berlin Diary (1941); End of a Berlin Diary (1947)
Twentieth Century Authors (First Supplement, 1955)
Who's Who, 1962
Who's Who in America, 1960-1961

SPAHN, WARREN (EDWARD)   Apr. 23, 1921   Baseball player

Address: b. Milwaukee Braves, County Stadium, Milwaukee, Wis.; h. Hartshorne, Okla.

Considered one of the greatest left-handed pitchers in the history of baseball, Warren Spahn of the Milwaukee Braves recorded the 300th win of a long baseball career on the night of August 11, 1961. He was the first baseball player in twenty years to accomplish this feat, which has been achieved by only six other major league pitchers since the turn of the century.

A baseball player for most of his life, Spahn has been a paragon of pitching consistency since he entered the big leagues with the Boston Braves. The 1961 season marked the twelfth time that the seemingly ageless and peerless left-hander won twenty or more games. (Only the legendary Cy Young and Christy Mathewson ever exceeded this record.) Spahn's lifetime total of fifty-five shutouts is a National League record for lefthanders. It is not difficult to understand why the Braves once rejected an offer of $500,000 for his services.

Warren Edward Spahn was born on April 23, 1921 in Buffalo, New York, the eldest son in a family of six children. He inherited his enthusiasm for baseball from his father, Edward Spahn, a wallpaper salesman. When Warren was a small boy his father began to teach him the rudiments of playing first base and of pitching, and father and son played catch in the back yard during every spare moment. On weekends they watched the Buffalo Bisons of the International League. "Mind the first baseman," Edward Spahn would tell his son. "Look how the pitcher stretches with men on base. Try that in the sandlot games." At nine Warren was first baseman on the midget team of the Lake City Athletic Club and his father played third base on the senior team; a few years later father and son were playing on the same team. Spahn recalls that he was forced to dig his spikes into the turf to hold on to some of the rifle-like throws that his father fired across the diamond. "But most of the time," he says, "I managed to hold on to the ball."

At South Park High School in Buffalo, however, Spahn gave up all ideas of playing first base when he discovered that he was no match for the incumbent first baseman, and he decided to concentrate on pitching. He won only a few ball games in his freshman and sophomore years, but when he reached physical maturity he became virtually unbeatable. He attracted the attention of Red Sox scout Billy Myers (later the manager of the Pittsburgh Pirates), but Myers did not succeed in his attempt to interest Red Sox officials in the young southpaw. Eventually

Myers offered Spahn to the Boston Braves and in 1940 the National League club signed Spahn to a contract. His first stop was the Bradford, Pennsylvania farm team in the Pony League, achieving a 5-4 record and a 2.73 earned run average and scoring 62 strikeouts in 66 innings.

In 1941 Spahn—who had been christened "Spahnie" by his teammates—was advanced to Evansville, Indiana in the Three I League. He won 19 games, lost 6, and acquired a 1.83 earned run average. His next stop in the minor leagues was Hartford, Connecticut in the Eastern League. After winning 17 games and losing 12, Spahn was called up to the Boston Braves late in the 1942 season. He appeared in 4 games but was not involved in any decision.

In the winter of 1942 Spahn was drafted into the United States Army. As a member of the 276th Combat Engineers he saw action in the battle for the Remagen bridge on the Rhine, was wounded by shrapnel, and received a Purple Heart and a Bronze Star. He was the only major league baseball player to win a World War II battle field commission. Characteristically, he has said, "I got it only because all our officers were killed," and has called his wound "only a scratch in the foot." He was discharged from the Army on April 23, 1946.

Returning to civilian life, Spahn became a regular member of the Boston Braves' pitching staff. In 1946 he was the winner of 8 games, and lost 5, but his earned run average was excellent—2.93. In the 1947 season his wins exceeded 20 for the first time. He won 21 games for the Braves, and lost 10. In the following year Spahn teamed up with Johnny Sain to help Boston win the National League pennant. In the World Series against the Cleveland Indians, Spahn won 1 game and lost 1, as the Braves lost 4 games to 2.

For the next three seasons Spahn was a twenty-game winner. During the 1951 pennant race he chalked up the 100th major league win of his career. The sole season in which he lost more games than he won was 1952 when he won 14 games and lost 19, although he managed to obtain an earned run average of 2.98. His pitching slump was caused in part by the weakness of the Boston team; there were rumors abroad that the club was to be moved out of Boston and most of the players were on edge. In 1953 the Braves moved to Milwaukee.

Around 1952 Spahn began to lose his chief pitching weapon—his fast ball. "The batters told me," he has said. "They began hitting it." If Spahn had not been so competitive and if he had not been such a close student of the game, he might not have lasted much longer as a pitcher. Instead he developed a variety of pitches to go with pinpoint control. Today he uses the fast ball to keep the hitters off balance, but relies mainly on the curve, the screwball, the slider, and change-ups. Spahn throws each of these with precisely the same arm speed and motion, and he can place the ball with a fantastic degree of accuracy. "The plate is seventeen inches wide," he says, "but I ignore the middle twelve inches. . . . I pitch to the two and a half inches on each side."

"I'm smarter now than when I had the big fastball," Spahn said to a sportswriter for *Time* (October 3, 1960). "I do a lot of things now

WARREN SPAHN

besides just knowing the batters and being able to hit the spots. Sometimes I get behind hitters on purpose. That makes them hungry hitters. They started looking for fat pitches. I make my living off hungry hitters." He adds: "I don't lose easily and I pitch that way. You can't be content with half-way measures. I start every game intent on a no-hitter. When they get a hit I try for a one-hit shutout." Convinced that self-confidence is the greatest asset a pitcher can have, Spahn has said: "When I'm out there on the mound I make up my mind I'm the best damned pitcher in the league. And that I am as good, if not better than any of the hitters I face. The more I pitch to a hitter, the less I'm impressed by him. All a pitcher has to do is remember he's one human being pitted against another."

The power of Spahn's positive thinking has been proved by his record since 1952. Only once since then has he failed to win at least 20 games in a season—in 1955 when he posted a mark of 17-14. He pitched the Braves to National League pennants in 1957 and 1958, winning 21 games and 22 games respectively. In the 1957 World Series against the New York Yankees he won one game and lost one as the Braves won the championship in seven games. In 1958 he won two games over New York as the Yankees regained the crown in a seven-game series. Other high points of his career include his first no-hitter against the Philadelphia Phillies on September 16, 1960 and his second no-hitter against the San Francisco Giants on April 28, 1961. But no single triumph will ever match his 300th win, on August 11, 1961, when he defeated the Chicago Cubs 2-1 in a six-hitter.

"It really was a big thrill—the thrill of my life," Spahn recalled a few months later. "Winning the pennant and the World Series a few years back was a big thing from a team basis. But this had to be the biggest personally. . . . The game was the kind I always wanted it to be.

(Continued next page)

SPAHN, WARREN—*Continued*

No fluke. No big scoring game where I would be sitting in the clubhouse at the end. It was low scoring and hard fought. . . . I was glad when it was over" (New York *Sunday News*, March 11, 1962). To appreciate Spahn's feat, one must remember that the six others to win 300 games or more since 1900 were Cy Young, Walter Johnson, Christy Mathewson, Grover Cleveland Alexander, Eddie Plank and Lefty Grove, all of whom are established in baseball's Hall of Fame. In true humility, Spahn said after his 300th win: "Walter Johnson . . . Christy Mathewson. Now me. It seems almost immoral"

During the 1961 season Spahn won 21 games, giving him a life-time total of 309 victories and 195 defeats, and his 1961 earned run average was the best in the National League. Spahn's next ambition is to become the top winning left-hander in the history of baseball. Eddie Plank holds the current mark of 325 lifetime victories. Spahn is the highest-paid pitcher in the history of baseball, and his 1962 contract with the Milwaukee Braves is said to provide for a salary exceeding the $75,000 he received in 1961.

In 1953, 1957, and 1958 Spahn was chosen the best pitcher in the National League by the *Sporting News*. The Milwaukee baseball writers picked him as the club's Most Valuable Player in 1956 and 1958. In 1957 he was voted the Cy Young Award as the season's outstanding pitcher in both the American and National leagues.

In August 1946 Warren E. Spahn married Lorene Southard of Tulsa, Oklahoma. They have one son, Gregory. Spahn spends the off-season on his 800-acre cattle ranch in Hartshorne, Oklahoma. His favorite recreations are fishing and swimming. A rawboned six-footer, he weighs 175 pounds and has a hawklike nose, a receding hairline, hazel eyes, and a long, narrow jaw. He is quick to smile, quick with a quip, and is one of the best liked and most respected players in the game.

References

Am W p12 Jl 10 '55 por
Christian Sci Mon p9 O 1 '57
Life 51:13 S 1 '61 pors
N Y Post p40 Ag 13 '61 por
Time 76:47 O 3 '60 por
Danzig, Allison and Reichler, Joe. The History of Baseball (1959)
Shoemaker, Robert H. The Best in Baseball (1959)

TURNER, EWALD (WALTER)   Oct. 27, 1922- Educator; organization official

Address: b. Helen McCune Junior High School, Pendleton, Ore.; h. 310 N. Main St., Pendleton, Ore.

Ewald Turner, the hundredth president of the National Education Association, has brought to the office a Western informality. A native Missourian, he moved to the Pacific Northwest in 1949. Since that time he has worked on the staff of the Helen McCune Junior High School in Pendleton, Oregon, first as an industrial arts teacher, now as its director of vocational guid-

ance. Turner is on leave from the school for the academic year of 1961-62.

Succeeding Clarice Kline, Turner assumed the presidency of the world's largest professional organization for teachers in June 1961, for a one-year term. He had previously been vice-president and president-elect of the National Education Association (1960-61) and president (1958-59) of its largest division, the department of classroom teachers. As the NEA theme for 1961-62, Turner selected "Teach for Tomorrow."

Ewald Walter Turner was born in Urich, Missouri on October 27, 1922 to Aaron O. Turner, a farmer, and Bertha (Getz) Turner. His parents, now retired, still live on the family farm in Creighton, Missouri, where Ewald Turner and his brother, Floyd W. Turner, were raised. The small town of Creighton is located in the rolling countryside of west central Missouri, a section of livestock, poultry, and grain farms. Turner began his education in a one-room country school, graduating in 1940 from Creighton High School in a class of eleven.

While still in high school, Turner spent a summer hitchhiking through the West, an experience that left him enthusiastic about all things Western, especially the landscape. After graduating from Central Missouri State College, Warrensburg, with a B.S. degree in education in 1944, he taught for five years in schools in Warrensburg and Joplin, Missouri.

Taking the advice of one of his teachers at Central Missouri State College, Turner decided to attend the Colorado State College in Greeley to obtain a Master's degree in education. During the summer session, when he was working as a waiter in the school cafeteria, he met the assistant superintendent of schools from Pendleton, Oregon, who encouraged him to seek a position with the Pendleton school system. Since his summer in the western states had already stimulated his interest in this area, the young teacher was not hard to convince.

Turner started as a teacher in the industrial arts department at Helen McCune Junior High School in Pendleton in 1949 and has been there ever since. More recently he became the school's director of vocational guidance, although he retains a strong interest in the industrial arts program. He has done additional graduate work at the University of Wisconsin.

Soon after he arrived in Pendleton, Turner joined the NEA and began to take an active role in the local and state educational organizations. He served one year as president of the Pendleton Association of Teachers and for three years was the membership chairman of the Umatilla County unit of the Oregon Education Association. He was regional director of the OEA department of classroom teachers for two years and president of the department, also for two years. At the same time, he represented Oregon on the advisory council of the NEA department of classroom teachers.

Turner served as president of the Eastern Oregon Education Conference during the year 1955-56. The following year he was elected vice-president of the NEA department of classroom teachers. He had previously served (1953-54) on the department's credentials committee; participated in a study conference on professional salary schedules for classroom teachers; and directed a national study conference on utilization of the teacher's time. During the school year 1958-59 he took a leave of absence from the Pendleton school system to serve as president of the NEA department of classroom teachers. His tour of duty included visiting thirty-six states and representing classroom teachers at many national meetings.

As an NEA delegate, Turner attended the 1959, 1960, and 1961 meetings of the World Confederation of Organizations of the Teaching Profession. The August 1961 meeting of WCOTP, held in New Delhi, India, and concerned with the theme, "Educating for Responsibility," was attended by over 400 delegates from seventy countries.

The NEA, which was founded in 1857, is an organization of elementary and secondary school teachers, college and university professors, administrators, principals, counselors, and others interested in American education. Its many departments and committees encompass every facet of educational activity, and it is affiliated with other groups in the field. In addition to its regular publications—the *NEA Journal*, the *Research Bulletin*, and the annual *Proceedings*—the association publishes many books and pamphlets about teaching.

After serving as vice-president and president-elect of the NEA during the year 1960-61, Turner succeeded Clarice Kline as president at the Atlantic City convention in June 1961 that was attended by 10,000 persons. At this session a proposal was passed to strengthen professional requirements for NEA membership. Also the association went on record for the first time as pledging its support of the 1954 Supreme Court decision on public school desegregation. The resolution, the strongest yet adopted by the NEA on this subject, was passed despite opposition from Southern state teachers organizations.

On leave from Helen McCune Junior High School during the year 1961-62, Turner has addressed many conferences and meetings throughout the United States on the role that education must play in the future. He has also criticized some current practices, notably those of parents who push their youngsters into premature socializing as a means of acquiring status, and those of junior high schools that promote "the big production . . . tournaments . . . hoopla and bands" at the expense of regular academic programs. Addressing the Northwest Regional Instructional Conference in November 1961, Turner cautioned his audience against approving the tactics of "the hysterical 'far right' wing of the superpatriots," represented by such organizations as the John Birch Society. "This is not the sort of patriotism we need to inculcate into the youth in our schools," he said.

Educational areas to which Turner has given particular attention during 1961-62 are the improvement of reading skills in elementary school children; expanding the use of new instruction methods like television, language laboratories, and teaching machines; stimulating teacher exchanges with foreign countries; and probing further into the serious and vexing problem of school dropouts. In 1961 the NEA received a $190,000 grant from the Ford Foundation, which

Fabian Bachrach

EWALD TURNER

it will use to set up a national clearing house for co-ordination of programs designed to alleviate the school dropout problem.

The NEA is trying to acquaint the public with new educational aims and teaching methods by means of a series of television programs on subjects like teaching machines, school dropouts, automation and education, college admissions, and education, initiated on major networks in the fall of 1961. Turner has also sought to "focus the attention of the public on an image of the teacher and the association of teachers not as a grasping, divisive lobby, but as a group of people devoted to the education of the youth of America."

Ewald Turner, who was voted "most likely to succeed" in his high school graduating class, combines sincerity and dedication to his profession with an air of informality and western geniality. A bachelor, he is tall and has reddish hair and a pleasant smile. He is an elder of the Presbyterian Church and has been a Sunday school teacher of junior high school students for over fifteen years. In 1957 he was vice-president of the Oregon Synod of Presbyterian Men. He has served on the board of the Pendleton Junior Chamber of Commerce and in 1956 was named the Outstanding Young Citizen of Pendleton. He belongs to the Pendleton Toastmasters Club, of which he is a past president.

For leadership in education and for service to his community, Turner was made an honorary lifetime member of the Pendleton Chamber of Commerce. He is also an honorary member of the "Main Street Cowboys," an organization formed to publicize the world-famous Pendleton Round-Up. Held annually since 1912, the Round-Up attracts thousands of visitors to its mid-September rodeo and re-creation of a typical cow town of the Old West. Profits from the enterprises are spent for civic improvements—projects in which Turner is always interested.

VIERECK, GEORGE SYLVESTER Dec. 3, 1884-Mar. 18, 1962 Poet; novelist; journalist; pro-German propagandist during World War I and World War II; wrote the poetic autobiography *My Flesh and Blood* (1931), *All Things Human* (1949), and other books. See *Current Biography* (November) 1940.

Obituary

N Y Times p37 Mr 20 '62

WALSH, WILLIAM B(ERTALAN) Apr. 26, 1920- Foundation president, physician

Address: b. The People to People Health Foundation, Inc., 1818 M St. N.W., Washington, D.C.; 1835 I St. N.W., Washington, D.C.; h. 5101 Westpath Way, Washington, D.C.

Within the framework of the people-to-people program initiated by President Dwight D. Eisenhower in 1956, many Americans have taken advantage of opportunities to extend concrete and personal assistance to people of developing nations. A dramatic example of the kind of project that has fostered goodwill abroad is the SS *Hope,* a hospital ship that passed a year in the waters of Southeast Asia while its medical personnel went ashore to exchange professional knowledge with native doctors and nurses.

The founder of Project HOPE and one of its most tireless supporters is Dr. William B. Walsh, president of the People to People Health Foundation, Inc. Dr. Walsh, a noted internist and heart specialist, was invited by President Eisenhower in the fall of 1958 to assume co-chairmanship of the Committee on Medicine and the Health Professions of the people-to-people program. Shortly thereafter his proposal for a peacetime hospital ship to be lent by the government and financed by private contributions was approved, and the foundation and its main endeavor, Project HOPE, were born. Since that time Dr. Walsh has devoted much of his time to arousing public support for the project. In recognition of his work, he has received several awards, including the Distinguished Service Award of the United States Information Agency in 1960.

William Bertalan Walsh, the son of Dr. Joseph W. and Irene (Viola) Walsh, was born in Brooklyn, New York City on April 26, 1920. He has a brother, John, also a physician, who is Jacqueline Kennedy's obstetrician, and two sisters, Mrs. Bennett and Gladys. After graduating from Brooklyn Preparatory School, Walsh attended St. John's College, where he received the Hamilton Scholarship and majored in biology. In 1940 he received his B.S. degree from St. John's College. He studied at the Georgetown University School of Medicine in Washington, D.C., taking his post-graduate training as an intern in the Long Island College Hospital and at the Georgetown University Hospital, where he was chief resident in internal medicine in 1948.

From 1943 to 1946 Walsh served in the Pacific as a United States Navy medical officer aboard a destroyer, advancing from lieutenant junior grade to lieutenant senior grade. He was licensed in 1946 and received his M.D. degree from Georgetown University School of Medicine in January 1948. Since then, he has had a private practice, which he has much curtailed in recent years so that he can devote more time to Project HOPE. He also teaches, as an assistant professor of internal medicine, at Georgetown University.

"My interest [in Project HOPE—Health Opportunities for People Everywhere] stemmed from my service . . . in the Pacific during World War II," Walsh has explained. "Anyone who has been in that part of the world knows how badly better health care is needed. Health is a real weapon in the struggle for world peace." Walsh feels that in a land where the proportion of doctors to population approaches one to several hundred thousand and basic medicines and sanitation are in short supply, it would be futile to attempt treatment alone. He set as the primary goal of the project the conveying of modern medical knowledge to local doctors, nurses, midwives, technicians, and sanitary personnel, thus diffusing better health care to the maximum number of people.

The SS *Hope,* a fully outfitted, reconditioned navy hospital ship, was lent by the United States government to Project HOPE. The three and a half million dollars needed to operate the ship for one year was gathered solely through contributions by the general public and corporations. ("This isn't a do-gooder project," Dr. Walsh emphasizes.) The ship visited only those places to which it had been invited by local physicians.

The eleven ports-of-call in South Vietnam and the islands of Indonesia at which the SS *Hope* touched between September 1960 and September 1961, include Djakarta, Surabaya, Bali, Makassar, and Saigon. Both aboard the ship and on shore (with field teams moving into the interior), local personnel were instructed in latest medical techniques through lectures, films, and observation of actual operations and treatment of patients. The permanent staff of fifteen physicians, two dentists, twenty-five nurses, and other personnel worked individually with their counterparts in Indonesia and Vietnam. Every few months additional volunteer physicians were flown to the SS *Hope* to participate for a short time in the program.

Dr. Walsh spent time on the ship but he also shouldered the burden of publicizing the ship's activities in the host countries and of raising funds and gaining public support in the United States. He feels that since the *Hope* is privately outfitted and carries on without government sponsorship, she dramatically demonstrates to her Asian hosts the goodwill of the American people. "The symbol of this white ship coming in with no propaganda leaflets to distribute, with nothing but American volunteers on board to render a service," he says, "is something which is seen by thousands and thousands of people in each of these countries, and for the first time it brings home to them what the American people are really like."

The tally of the *Hope* team's accomplishments in Indonesia and Vietnam is impressive. Some 1,200 major operations were performed; some 36,000 patients were examined and treated; hundreds of lectures were given; and some 8,000 books and medical journals and more than 86,000 pounds of medical supplies were distributed in

Southeast Asia. In Indonesia *Hope* personnel were asked to staff a hospital built by the Ministry of Health as a teaching and training institute. In Vietnam the first mass inoculation program for children was instituted and oral surgery was introduced. An orthopedic rehabilitation center was established and equipped, and American doctors will continue to staff it as a treatment and training center.

Encouraged by the enthusiastic reception the project received, Walsh envisages the return of the SS *Hope* to Asia and the outfitting of another ship for a similar mission in South America and, perhaps, Africa. According to Walsh, not the least of the benefits arising from the project is its impact on behalf of the free world in the cold war. "It is a weapon for democracy the Russians find difficult to understand," he says. "It is propaganda without pamphlets, without ideology. It is simply one people helping another. . . ."

By early 1962 the SS *Hope* had run into foul weather. Dr. Walsh had expected the Navy to permit the ship to dock free in a United States harbor; instead it presented a docking bill of $34,000 and, by evaluating the twenty-year-old ship at over $3,000,000, increased its insurance bill to $84,000. The SS *Hope* also faced a re-wiring job at an estimated cost of $70,000—an amount it could not afford—before it could sail for Peru in April 1962. Its outlook brightened when Attorney General Robert Kennedy and his wife Ethel, who had become interested in Project HOPE during their round-the-world trip in early 1962, agreed to be co-chairmen of a fund-raising Passport to HOPE ball to be held on May 11, 1962. The SS *Hope* also benefited from a $100-a-plate fund-raising dinner held on March 27, 1962.

Walsh is a past president of the National Medical Veterans Society, a consultant to the Surgeons General of the Public Health Service on Medical Practice Relations and of the Air Force, and an Associate Fellow of the American College of Physicians. He belongs to the American Medical Association and the District of Columbia Medical Society, and is a member of the President's Advisory Committee on the Physical Fitness of Youth and of the AMA Council on National Defense.

William Bertalan Walsh and Helen Rundvold, a nurse, were married on December 19, 1943. They have three sons: William Bertalan Jr., John Thomas, and Thomas Stephen. Dr. Walsh, a Republican and a Roman Catholic, has hazel eyes and black hair. He stands five feet ten and a half inches tall and weighs 180 pounds. Walsh belongs to the University Club in Washington, the Columbia Country Club in Chevy Chase, Maryland, and the Circumnavigators Club in New York. His favorite recreation is playing golf.

Named "Voluntary Leader of the Year" by the American Society of Association Executives in September 1961, Walsh has also received the Distinguished Service Award from the United States Information Agency (1960); the Health U.S.A. Award (1961), the Detroit International Freedom Festival Award (1961), and the Georgetown University Alumni Award (1961). Perhaps he cherishes more than any awards the appre-

DR. WILLIAM B. WALSH

ciation expressed by those whom the SS *Hope* has helped. One example is this editorial from the Indonesian *Observer*, hailing the arrival of the *Hope:* "In this world where goodwill is usually entwined in a never-ending length of string and red tape, the simplicity and goodness, the impact and the quality that the visit of this hospital ship offers, places this goodwill visit tops on the list of mankind's hopes."

References

National Business Woman 40:12 Je '61
American Medical Directory (1956)

WEBB, JAMES E(DWIN) Oct. 7, 1906-
United States government official
Address: b. National Aeronautics and Space Administration, 1520 H St. N.W., Washington 25, D.C.; h. 3200 Idaho Ave. N.W., Washington 6, D.C.

NOTE: This biography supersedes the article that appeared in *Current Biography* in 1946.

A man with much experience as an administrator in private industry and public service, James E. Webb was appointed by President John F. Kennedy in February 1961 to serve as administrator of the National Aeronautics and Space Administration. Established in 1958, the agency is a governmental, civilian body responsible for programs of research and development on peaceful uses of outer space. Before succeeding T. Keith Glennan as head of NASA, Webb had been director of the Bureau of the Budget and Under Secretary of State in the Truman era, and had headed many organizations as president or director.

Born on October 7, 1906 at Tally Ho, a village in Granville County, North Carolina, James Edwin Webb is one of five children of Sarah

National Aeronautics and
Space Administration

JAMES E. WEBB

(Gorham) Webb and John Frederick Webb, who for twenty-six years was superintendent of Granville County schools. James attended high school at Oxford, the county seat, working after school and on Saturdays in local groceries and dime stores. In 1923 he enrolled at the University of North Carolina but, unable to meet his expenses despite part-time work, dropped out at the end of his freshman year.

From 1924 to 1925 Webb worked for a Raleigh construction firm, the R. G. Rossiter Company, first in the accounting department and, after learning typing and shorthand at Kings Business College, as secretary to the president. Returning to the University of North Carolina in 1925, he majored in education and worked part-time as secretary of the Bureau of Educational Research at the School of Education. A Phi Beta Kappa, he received his B.A. degree in 1928.

For a year after his graduation Webb stayed on at the Bureau of Educational Research. He then entered the offices of Parham and Lassiter, attorneys in Oxford, as a law clerk and stenographer. In 1930 he became a United States Marine Corps reservist and, as a private first class, learned to fly at the Naval Air Station in Pensacola, Florida.

Commissioned a second lieutenant in the Fleet Marine Corps Reserve in 1931, Webb served a tour of active flying duty as a naval aviator with the aircraft squadron of the East Coast Expeditionary Force in Quantico, Virginia until his discharge in 1932. While serving as secretary (1932-34) to Democratic Congressman Edward W. Pou of North Carolina, who was chairman of the House Rules Committee, Webb continued his association with the Marine Corps as operations officer and, later, commanding officer of a reserve unit in Anacostia, District of Columbia. From 1934 to 1936, when he was admitted to the District of Columbia bar, Webb studied law in

evening classes at the George Washington University Law School. During this period he served as an assistant to O. Max Gardner, ex-Governor of North Carolina, who was then general counsel to the Aeronautical Chamber of Commerce of America. Webb thus became familiar with the problems of the aeronautical industry.

From 1936 to 1943 Webb worked with the Sperry Gyroscope Corporation on Long Island, first as personnel director and assistant to the president, then as secretary-treasurer. In 1943 he became its vice-president and in the same year he also became assistant secretary-treasurer of the Sperry Corporation, the parent company that owns a number of subsidiaries. The company fulfilled a vital function in wartime: working under some 1,800 contracts, it manufactured a wide variety of complex scientific equipment for military use.

At this time Webb also remained active in aviation. He served as an operations officer for the Marine Reserve Aviation Squadron at Floyd Bennett Field in Brooklyn, held a commercial pilot's license, and belonged to several aeronautical organizations, including the National Aeronautic Association, and the Institute of Aeronautical Sciences. He was also a member of the airways operations board of the Department of Commerce, which in 1938 evolved the first clearly delineated federal airways plan. In 1944, after attending the Naval Radar Training School at St. Simons Island, Georgia, he resumed active service, as a major with the 9th Marine Aircraft Wing, and served as operations officer and commanding officer of the 1st Marine Air Warning Group at Cherry Point, North Carolina. He has retained his commission in the Marine Reserve and has been a lieutenant colonel since 1950.

Joining the law firm of Gardner, Morrison & Rogers after the war, Webb was again associated with O. Max Gardner, who was appointed Under Secretary of the Treasury by President Truman in 1946. Webb was named Gardner's executive assistant, and a few months later he succeeded Harold D. Smith as director of the Bureau of the Budget.

Known as an advocate of the balanced budget, Webb ordered reductions in the number of federal civil service employees soon after he took office. He did, however, support federal aid to education and a permanent universal military training program. Under his direction the Bureau of the Budget prepared the first complete report, listing all federal research and development activities, for inclusion in the United States Budget. Resulting from this were a study and report by Dr. John R. Steelman that led to the establishment of the National Science Foundation.

For three years, from 1949 to 1952, Webb served as Under Secretary of State in the Truman administration. He was also a member of the President's advisory committee on management and of the President's committee to study the United States military assistance program. Meanwhile he also held posts as a deputy governor of both the International Bank for Reconstruction and Development and the International Monetary Fund. Webb supervised the reorganization of the Department of State in accordance with recommendations of the first Hoover commission.

These recommendations urged expansion of scientific activity and Webb was instrumental in establishing several science attachés in United States embassies abroad.

Having resigned from the Department of State early in 1952, Webb devoted the next ten years to his private business activities and to public service. At the time that he was named administrator of the National Aeronautics and Space Administration, he was a director and assistant to the president of Kerr-McGee Oil Industries, Oklahoma City and a director of McDonnell Aircraft Corporation, St. Louis. He has also been a director of Simmonds Aerocessories, Inc., Tarrytown, New York; a director of the Oak Ridge Institute of Nuclear Studies, Inc. in Tennessee (1959-60); president (1953-58) and chairman of the board of directors (1958) of the Republic Supply Company, Oklahoma City; director (1953-58) of the Petroleum Equipment Suppliers Association, Houston; director (1954-59) of the Oklahoma City Chamber of Commerce; director (1956-59) of the Better Business Bureau of Oklahoma City; and director of Topeka, Kansas and Oklahoma City banks.

Webb has been president of Educational Services, Inc., a nonprofit organization financed by the National Science, Ford, and Alfred Sloan foundations to improve the teaching of physics in secondary schools. He is a trustee and member of the executive committee of George Washington University, a member of the advisory council of the School of Industrial Management, Massachusetts Institute of Technology, and has served in a number of capacities for Oklahoma State University and the University of Oklahoma. Webb was the first president (1956-57) of the Frontiers of Science Foundation of Oklahoma, Inc. He is a member of the United States Committee for the United Nations.

As chairman of the Municipal Manpower Commission, Washington, D.C., Webb has been concerned with the problem of attracting talented people to government service at the local level. He himself has served the United States government in a number of ways. From 1955 to 1957 he belonged to the advisory council on study of civil service of the Senate Committee on Post Office and Civil Service. During the year 1957-58 he was a member of the Bayne-Jones committee, which advised the Secretary of Health, Education, and Welfare on medical research and education. He has served on the President's committee to study the United States military assistance program (Draper committee), on the special stockpile advisory committee to the Director of Defense Mobilization, Washington, D.C., and on the National Advisory Cancer Council of the Public Health Service.

Webb succeeded Dr. T. Keith Glennan as administrator of the National Aeronautics and Space Administration in February 1961. His appointment was supported by Vice President Lyndon Johnson, chairman of the National Aeronautics and Space Council, and by Jerome B. Wiesner, the White House advisor on science. When he accepted the position, Webb severed his connection with the McDonnell Aircraft Corporation, manufacturers of the Mercury man-in-space capsule, and with other businesses and organizations that might result in conflict of interest.

Admittedly Webb has no expertise on space science or technology; he was named to the post for his outstanding administrative ability. His predecessor had built up the space program and a crew of experienced men to implement it. "The next phase here is administration and reorganization," Webb said soon after his nomination. "I have simply been told that there is a real job here to do." The NASA is an independent civilian governmental agency that is charged with the exploration and utilization of space for peaceful purposes. It conducts research in aeronautics and space flight, and supervised the development of Project Mercury under which John H. Glenn became the first American astronaut to orbit the earth.

Honorary LL.D. degrees were conferred on Webb by the University of North Carolina in 1949, by Syracuse University in 1950, and by Colorado College in 1957. He is a member of Phi Delta Phi, the Masons, the American Bar Association, the Marine Corps Reserve Officers Association, the American Management Association, the American Academy of Political and Social Sciences, the National Planning Association, the Oklahoma Historical Society, and many other groups. His clubs are the University and the Brook in New York; the University, Metropolitan, Army and Navy, Country, and Chevy Chase of Washington, D.C., and the Beacon of Oklahoma City.

Blue-eyed and brown-haired, James Webb stands at five feet nine and a half inches and weighs about 178 pounds. He likes to work with tools, and does a lot of serious reading (he does not care for television). Webb has been married since May 14, 1938 to the former Patsy Aiken Douglas. They have one daughter, Sarah Gorham (Sally), and a son, James Edwin, Jr. Webb is a Democrat and a director of Presbyterian Homes, Inc. of Norman, Oklahoma.

References

    Aviation W 74:29 F 6 '61 por
    Christian Sci Mon p8 Ja 31 '61 por
    Data 6:22+ Mr 31 pors
    Newsday p18 Ja 31 '61 por
    Space World 1:22+ Ag '61 pors
    Time 77:15 F 10 '61

    National Cyclopaedia of American Biography current vol H (1952)
    New Frontiersmen (1961)
    United States Congress. Senate. Hearing before the Committee on Aeronautical and Space Sciences, F 2 '61 (1961)
    Who's Who in America, 1961-62

WHITTON, REX M(ARION) Aug. 7, 1898- United States government official; civil engineer
Address: b. Bureau of Public Roads, Matomic Bldg., 1717 H St., N.W., Washington, D.C.; h. 4201 Cathedral Ave., N.W., Washington, D.C.

In directing the Bureau of Public Roads, Federal Highway Administrator Rex M. Whitton has the responsibility of carrying out a federal-aid highway program that includes the 41,000-mile

REX M. WHITTON

National System of Interstate and Defense Highways. This vast road-building project, now in the sixth year of its sixteen-year schedule, has been called man's largest single construction undertaking. Whitton, an engineer who succeeded Bertram D. Tallamy in the federal post on February 10, 1961, had worked for forty years with the Missouri State Highway Department. He has received the highest awards in his profession.

The only child of a Midwestern farmer, Rex Marion Whitton was born on August 7, 1898 to Shelley and Susan Catharine (Rucker) Whitton in Jackson County, Missouri, where he attended grade and high schools. While a student at Ruskin High School in Hickman Mills, Missouri, not far from Kansas City, he played on the basketball team. He entered the University of Missouri in Columbia in 1916, served briefly there in 1918 as a private in the Student Army Training Corps during the last months of World War I, and received his B.S. degree in civil engineering in April 1920.

Just eleven days after graduation Whitton began working for the Missouri State Highway Department as a member of a survey group on a fifteen-mile stretch of proposed highway in Johnson County. From his first job as a levelman, or instrument man, he had advanced to plans designer by 1922. He became assistant project engineer in 1923 and a year later, having been promoted to project engineer, he was put in charge of grading and paving twenty miles of road in Johnson County.

As he continued to advance in the department, Whitton was employed in many capacities—as assistant resident engineer, resident engineer, chief of survey party, assistant engineer in charge of construction, construction engineer, engineer on special assignments in surveys and plans, assistant engineer of surveys and plans, and district engineer in Springfield from 1933 to 1936. He

was engineer of maintenance in Jefferson City from 1936 to 1951 and chief engineer from 1951 to 1961.

During Whitton's forty years with the Missouri Highway Department, the number of employees of that agency grew from fewer than 200 to over 6,000 and in mileage the system grew from 400 to 32,000. By 1961 Missouri had invested an estimated $1,119,398,000 in highways. It is generally acknowledged that Whitton is the major reason for Missouri's leadership in the development of the interstate highway system. It was during his administration as chief engineer that Missouri let the first contract for an interstate highway project. During the nine years he served as chief engineer, before becoming Federal Highway Administrator, 12,000 miles of road were put under state supervision.

In 1958 Whitton received the George S. Bartlett Award for outstanding service in highway progress to the nation. The American Public Works Association and Kiwanis International selected him as one of the "Top Ten Public Works Men of the Year" in 1960. Also in 1960 he received the Thomas H. MacDonald Award for continuous outstanding service in the highway engineering field. These national honors reflect the widespread recognition of the efficiency of Missouri's highway administration that perhaps brought Whitton to the attention of John F. Kennedy. In late December 1960 Kennedy, then President-elect, appointed Whitton Federal Highway Administrator, and he took office on February 10, 1961. The Federal Highway Administrator, who receives a salary of $20,000 a year, directs the Bureau of Public Roads, the government's principal road-building agency, which since 1949 has been part of the Department of Commerce.

Praised by his associates and by newsmen and editorial writers as a responsible and honest administrator as well as a capable planner and builder of roads, Whitton told Congress about six weeks after he was sworn into his new office that Bureau of Public Roads examiners are dedicated to eliminating opportunities for fraud, collusion, and corruption in the roads program. In testimony before the House roads subcommittee, he said that scandals uncovered by a special House subcommittee pointed to a need for tightening his bureau's procedures and practices.

As Federal Highway Administrator, Whitton is responsible for directing the spending of $2.2 billion a year, the construction of as many as possible of the 41,000 miles of superhighway planned by 1972, and the supervision of approximately 32,000 miles of road annually. In addition, he administers the federal-state fifty-fifty matching program involving $925,000,000 in federal funds for primary, secondary, and urban roads. Since the Bureau of Public Roads has to approve all phases of every plan and program that the states initiate, including design and construction, Whitton's problems in his Washington office are multiplied many times over those that he handled in Missouri, especially in regard to route locations. His goal as a federal official, however, is the same as it had been when he was a state official: "To approve the location that will do the best job for the most people at the least cost."

During 1961 Whitton reported that a record 73,895,274 motor vehicles had been registered in the United States in 1960. One of the Bureau of Public Roads' first activities under his leadership was concentrated work on its national driver register service, which will make available to cooperating states information on motorists who have lost their licenses for drunken driving or involvement in a fatal accident.

Rex M. Whitton is co-author of a highway engineering handbook published by McGraw-Hill Book Company. He has served on important technical committees for the American Road Builders Association and is a member of the executive committee (chairman in 1957) of the Highway Research Board, which is concerned with improving design, construction, and maintenance of highways. Also prominent in the American Association of State Highway Officials, he was elected a member of its executive committee in 1954 and 1957 and its president in 1956. Other professional organizations of which he is a member are the American Society of Civil Engineers and the Missouri Society of Professional Engineers.

Among the civic associations to which Whitton belongs are the Rotary clubs of Jefferson City and Fulton, Missouri (honorary member). He is a York-Rite Mason (a Knight Templar, Shriner, and Jester) and a past president of the Ozarks Council of Boy Scouts of America. He

serves on the board of trustees of William Jewell College, is a member of the National Academy of Sciences, and holds an honorary D.Sc. degree from the University of Missouri. A Baptist, he is a past chairman of the board of deacons of the First Baptist Church in Jefferson City. His political party is the Democratic.

On one of his early jobs in road building Rex M. Whitton was stationed at Blue Springs, Missouri, where he met Callie Maude Lowe. They were married on April 22, 1925 and have a son, Rex M. Whitton, Jr., and three grandchildren. Whitton is a dapper, distinguished-looking man with graying hair and blue eyes; he stands five feet ten inches tall and weighs 170 pounds.

When driving around Missouri, Whitton prefers to take the back roads, which he finds more relaxing than the highways. They also afford an opportunity to see Missouri and to discover out-of-the-way antique shops. One of his hobbies, which he shares with his wife, is collecting antique glass. He specializes in butter dishes and has collected over forty of them, some with matching bottoms and lids found in different places.

References

Am Road Builder 38:18+ F '61 por
Eng N 167:50+ Jl 27 '61 pors
Jefferson City Sunday News and Tribune p12 Ja 15 '61 por
Washington (D.C.) Post A p2 D 28 '60
Who's Who in America, 1960-61
Who's Who in Engineering, 1959

KEY TO ABBREVIATIONS

AAAA	Amateur Athletic Association of America
A.A.U.	Amateur Athletic Union
ABC	American Broadcasting Company
A.C.L.U.	American Civil Liberties Union
ADA	Americans for Democratic Action
AEC	Atomic Energy Commission
AEF	American Expeditionary Force
AFL	American Federation of Labor
AFL-CIO	American Federation of Labor and Congress of Industrial Organizations
ALA	American Library Association
AMA	American Medical Association
A.P.	Associated Press
ASCAP	American Society of Composers, Authors and Publishers
ASNE	American Society of Newspaper Editors
B.A.	Bachelor of Arts
BBC	British Broadcasting Corporation
B.D.	Bachelor of Divinity
B.L.S.	Bachelor of Library Science
B.S.	Bachelor of Science
CAA	Civil Aeronautics Administration
CAB	Civil Aeronautics Board
C.B.	Companion of the Bath
C.B.E.	Commander of (the Order of) the British Empire
CBS	Columbia Broadcasting System
C.E.	Civil Engineer
CEA	Council of Economic Advisers
C.E.D.	Committee for Economic Development
CENTO	Central Treaty Organization
CIO	Congress of Industrial Organizations
C.M.G.	Companion of (the Order of) St. Michael and St. George
Com.	Commodore
D.A.R.	Daughters of the American Revolution
D.C.L.	Doctor of Civil Law
D.D.	Doctor of Divinity
D.Eng.	Doctor of Engineering
DEW	Distant Early Warning Line
D.F.C.	Distinguished Flying Cross
D.J.	Doctor of Jurisprudence
D.Lit.	Doctor of Literature
D.Mus.	Doctor of Music
DP	Displaced Person
D.Pol.Sc.	Doctor of Political Science
D.Sc.	Doctor of Science
D.S.C.	Distinguished Service Cross
D.S.M.	Distinguished Service Medal
D.S.O.	Distinguished Service Order
ECA	Economic Cooperation Administration
ECOSOC	Economic and Social Council
EDC	European Defense Community
ERP	European Recovery Program
ESA	Economic Stabilization Administration
FAO	Food and Agriculture Organization
FBI	Federal Bureau of Investigation
FCA	Farm Credit Administration
FCC	Federal Communications Commission
FEPC	Fair Employment Practice Committee
FHA	Federal Housing Administration
FOA	Foreign Operations Administration
FPC	Federal Power Commission
FSA	Federal Security Agency
FTC	Federal Trade Commission
GATT	General Agreement on Tariffs and Trade
G.B.E.	Knight or Dame, Grand Cross Order of the British Empire
G.C.B.	Knight Grand Cross of the Bath
G.O.P.	Grand Old Party
H.M.	His Majesty; Her Majesty
ICA	International Cooperation Administration
ICBM	Intercontinental Ballistic Missile
ICC	Interstate Commerce Commission
I.C.F.T.U.	International Confederation of Free Trade Unions
IGY	International Geophysical Year
I.L.A.	International Longshoremen's Association
I.L.G.W.U.	International Ladies' Garment Workers' Union
I.L.O.	International Labor Organization
INS	International News Service
IRO	International Refugee Organization
J.D.	Doctor of Jurisprudence
K.B.E.	Knight of (the Order of) the British Empire
K.C.	King's Counsel
K.C.B.	Knight Commander of the Bath
L.H.D.	Doctor of Humanities
Litt.D.	Doctor of Letters

LL.B.	Bachelor of Laws
LL.D.	Doctor of Laws
M.A.	Master of Arts
M.B.A.	Master of Business Administration
MBS	Mutual Broadcasting System
M.C.E.	Master of Civil Engineering
M.D.	Doctor of Medicine
M.E.	Master of Engineering
METO	Middle East Treaty Organization
MGM	Metro-Goldwyn-Mayer
M.Lit.	Master of Literature
M.P.	Member of Parliament
M.P.P.D.A.	Motion Picture Producers and Distributors of America
MRP	Mouvement Républicain Populaire
MSA	Mutual Security Agency
M.Sc.	Master of Science
Msgr.	Monsignor, Monseigneur
NAACP	National Association for the Advancement of Colored People
NAB	National Association of Broadcasters
NAM	National Association of Manufacturers
NASA	National Aeronautics and Space Administration
NATO	North Atlantic Treaty Organization
NBC	National Broadcasting Company
N.E.A.	National Education Association
NLRB	National Labor Relations Board
N.M.U.	National Maritime Union
NRA	National Recovery Administration
NRPB	National Resources Planning Board
NYA	National Youth Administration
O.A.S.	Organization of American States
O.B.E.	Officer of (the Order of) the British Empire
OCD	Office of Civilian Defense
OEEC	Organization for European Economic Cooperation
OPA	Office of Price Administration
OPM	Office of Production Management
OWI	Office of War Information
P.E.N.	Poets, Playwrights, Editors, Essayists and Novelists (International Association)
Ph.B.	Bachelor of Philosophy
Ph.D.	Doctor of Philosophy
PWA	Public Works Administration
Q.C.	Queen's Counsel
RAF	Royal Air Force
RCA	Radio Corporation of America
REA	Rural Electrification Administration
RFC	Reconstruction Finance Corporation
RKO	Radio-Keith-Orpheum
ROTC	Reserve Officers' Training Corps
SAC	Strategic Air Command
SCAP	Supreme Command for the Allied Powers
SEATO	Southeast Asia Treaty Organization
SEC	Securities and Exchange Commission
SHAEF	Supreme Headquarters, Allied Expeditionary Force
SHAPE	Supreme Headquarters, Allied Powers Europe
S.J.D.	Doctor of Juridical Science
SLA	Special Libraries Association
S.T.B.	Bachelor of Sacred Theology
S.T.D.	Doctor of Sacred Theology
TVA	Tennessee Valley Authority
T.W.U.A.	Textile Workers Union of America
UAR	United Arab Republic
U.A.W.	United Automobile, Aircraft, and Agricultural Implement Workers of America
UMT	Universal Military Training
U.M.W.A.	United Mine Workers of America
U.N.	United Nations
UNESCO	United Nations Educational, Scientific, and Cultural Organization
UNICEF	United Nations Children's Fund
UNRRA	United Nations Relief and Rehabilitation Administration
U.P.I.	United Press and International News Service
USO	United Service Organizations
U.S.S.R.	Union of Soviet Socialist Republics
U.S.W.A.	United Steel Workers of America
VA	Veterans Administration
V.F.W.	Veterans of Foreign Wars
W.E.U.	Western European Union
W.F.T.U.	World Federation of Trade Unions
WHO	World Health Organization
WMC	War Manpower Commission
WPA	Work Projects Administration
WPB	War Production Board
YMCA	Young Men's Christian Association
YWCA	Young Women's Christian Association

CURRENT BIOGRAPHY—VOL. 23. NOS. 1-5

This is the index to the January-May 1962 issues. For the index to the 1961 biographies, see December 1961 issue or 1961 Yearbook. For the index to 1940-1950 biographies, see 1950 Yearbook. For 1951-1960 index, see 1960 Yearbook.

Mössbauer, Rudolf L(udwig) May 62

Muench, Aloisius (Joseph), Cardinal obit Apr 62

Murphy, (Eleanor) Patricia Apr 62

Nestingen, Ivan A(rnold) Mar 62
Newhart, Bob Mar 62
Nitze, Paul H(enry) Feb 62

Ogburn, Charlton obit Apr 62
Olav V, King of Norway Jan 62
Osgood, Charles E(gerton) Apr 62
Ozbirn, Catharine (Freeman) See Ozbirn, Mrs. E. L. Jan 62
Ozbirn, Mrs. E. Lee Jan 62

Peden, Katherine (Graham) May 62
Piccard, Auguste obit May 62
Portinari, Candido obit Mar 62

Rabaut, Louis Charles obit Jan 62
Randolph, Jennings Jan 62
Rayburn, Sam(uel Taliaferro) obit Jan 62
Read, Sir Herbert (Edward) Mar 62
Reischauer, Edwin O(ldfather) May 62
Reybold, Eugene obit Jan 62

Robinson, Spottswood W(illiam), 3d Mar 62
Russell, Donald J(oseph) May 62
Russell, James S(argent) Jan 62

Savage, Augusta (Christine) obit May 62
Schoeppel, Andrew F. obit Mar 62
Scofield, Paul Mar 62
Senghor, Léopold Sédar Mar 62
Shirer, William L(awrence) May 62
Shurlock, Geoffrey M. Jan 62
Sitterly, Mrs. Bancroft Walker See Sitterly, C. M. Jan 62
Sitterly, Charlotte Moore Jan 62
Slocum, (Manly) Harvey obit Jan 62
Smith, Margaret (Madeline) Chase Mar 62
Spahn, Warren (Edward) May 62
Spottswood, Stephen Gill Apr 62
Stikker, Dirk U(ipko) Feb 62
Suggs, Louise Jan 62
Sunderland, Thomas E(lbert) Apr 62
Swann, W(illiam) F(rancis) G(ray) obit Mar 62
Switzer, Mary E(lizabeth) Jan 62

Taylor, A(lbert) Hoyt obit Jan 62
Teagle, Walter C(lark) obit Feb 62
Thant, U Feb 62
Thurber, James obit Jan 62
Tillinghast, Charles C(arpenter), Jr. Feb 62

Tobias, Channing H(eggie) obit Jan 62
Turner, Ewald (Walter) May 62

Unitas, John Feb 62

Vertès, Marcel obit Jan 62
Viereck, George Sylvester obit May 62
Vilar, Jean (Louis Côme) Apr 62
Volpe, John A(nthony) Feb 62

Waddington, C(onrad) H(al) Apr 62
Wagner, Richard Apr 62
Walsh, Chad Feb 62
Walsh, William B(ertalan) May 62
Walter, Bruno obit Apr 62
Ward, Paul L(angdon) Mar 62
Watts, Alan (Wilson) Mar 62
Webb, James E(dwin) May 62
Wenner-Gren, Axel (Leonard) obit Jan 62
Wesker, Arnold Feb 62
Whitton, Rex M(arion) May 62
Wilcox, Francis O(rlando) Apr 62
Wilkinson, Bud See Wilkinson, C. Apr 62
Wilkinson, Charles (Burnham) Apr 62
Wills, Royal Barry obit Feb 62
Winiarski, Bohdan (Stefan) Feb 62
Wood, Natalie Apr 62

Yamasaki, Minoru Mar 62

CURRENT BIOGRAPHY

JUNE 1962
VOL. 23 NO. 6

Editor: Charles Moritz

PUBLISHED BY THE H. W. WILSON COMPANY, 950 UNIVERSITY AVE., NEW YORK

CONTENTS

ABOUT THIS PUBLICATION

Current Biography (published every month except August) presents articles on people who are prominent in the news—in national and international affairs, the sciences, the arts, labor, and industry. Sources of information are newspapers, magazines, books, and, in some cases, the biographees themselves. It should be pointed out, however, that these are objective rather than authorized biographies. At the end of the year the articles in the monthly issues are cumulated in one alphabet, revised, and printed in a single volume known as *Current Biography Yearbook*.

Authorities for biographees' full names, with some exceptions, are the bibliographical publications of The Wilson Company. When a biographee prefers a certain name form, that is indicated in the heading of the article: for example, MACMILLAN, (MAURICE) HAROLD means that he is usually referred to as HAROLD MACMILLAN. When a professional name is used in the heading, as, for example, GLENN FORD, the real name, in this case GWYLLYN SAMUEL NEWTON FORD, appears in the article itself.

The heading of each article includes the pronunciation of the name if it is unusual, date of birth (if obtainable), and occupation. The article is supplemented by a list of references to sources of *biographical* information, in two alphabets: (1) newspapers and periodicals and (2) books.

References to newspapers and periodicals are listed in abbreviated form; for example, "Sat Eve Post 217:14+ S 30 '44 por" means *Saturday Evening Post,* volume 217, pages 14 ff, September 30, 1944, with portrait. For full names, see the section "Periodical and Newspaper Designations," which is included in all *Current Biography* Yearbooks and in the January issue each year. Obituary notices appear for persons whose biographies have been published in *Current Biography.*

An index to names that have appeared this year is to be found at the back of this issue.

NOTE: Authors whose biographies do not appear in *Current Biography* may usually be found in *Twentieth Century Authors,* Kunitz & Haycraft, 1942, H. W. Wilson Company, or in the FIRST SUPPLEMENT (1955). Authors of books for young people are included in *The Junior Book of Authors* (Second Edition, Revised) edited by Kunitz & Haycraft, 1951, H. W. Wilson Company. Musicians whose biographies do not appear in *Current Biography* may usually be found in *Living Musicians,* compiled and edited by David Ewen, 1940, H. W. Wilson Company, or in its FIRST SUPPLEMENT (1957).

KEY TO PRONUNCIATION

ā	āle	N	Not pronounced, but indicates the nasal tone of the preceding vowel, as in the French *bon* (bôN).	û	ûrn; French eu, as in *jeu* (zhû); German ö, oe, as in *schön* (shûn), *Goethe* (gû'tĕ)
â	câre				
ă	ădd				
ȧ	ȧccount				
ä	ärm				
à	àsk				
ȧ	sofȧ				
		ō	ōld	ŭ	tŭb
		ô	ôrb	ŭ	circŭs
ē	ēve	ŏ	ŏdd	ü	Pronounced approximately as ē, with rounded lips: French u, as in *menu* (mē-nü); German ü, as in *grün*
ĕ	ĕnd	oi	oil		
ē	makēr	ōō	ōoze		
		ŏŏ	fŏŏt		
g	go	ou	out		
ī	īce				
ĭ	ĭll	*th*	*then*	zh	azure
		th	thin	′ =	main accent
ᴋ	German ch as in *ich* (ĭᴋ)	ū	cūbe	″ =	secondary accent

CURRENT BIOGRAPHY

JUNE 1962

ALBERS, JOSEF Mar. 19, 1888- Artist

Address: 8 North Forest Circle, New Haven 15, Conn.

Abstract art is not necessarily bound up with improvisation. Josef Albers, the celebrated German-born American painter and teacher, has devoted almost his entire life, both in theory and in practice, to the proposition that a painting can be carefully calculated and designed. An inveterate experimenter and lover of paradoxes, Albers works exclusively within the medium of geometric abstraction and, more especially, with rectilinear forms. Dedicated to widening the discrepancy between physical fact and psychic effect, his work proves that order is not anathema to freedom. His paintings play on the distinctions between appearance and reality with precise subtlety, and in his art geometry acquires dramatic undertones. The result is a luminous and lyrical expressiveness, achieved by means of purity and tranquility.

Josef Albers was born in the industrial Ruhr district of Battrop, Germany, on March 19, 1888, the only child of Lorenz Albers, a housepainter, and Magdalena (Schumacher) Albers. He attended the *Präparanden-Schule* in Langenhorst from 1902 to 1905 and then the teachers college in Büren, graduating in 1908. Albers began what was to be his long teaching career by becoming an instructor in several Westphalian primary schools. (He has noted that another nonobjective painter who taught elementary school in the early years of his career was the Dutch artist Piet Mondriaan, perhaps the foremost exponent of geometric abstraction.)

Then, in 1913, the artistic inclinations in his father's family manifested themselves in Albers. He enrolled at the Royal Art School in Berlin, studying there until 1915. From 1916 to 1919 he studied at the School of Applied Art at Essen and, in the succeeding year, at the Art Academy in Munich. Albers' enthusiasm for the traditional and representational in art waned, however. His own concept of the making of a painting seemed more related to his Westphalian family tradition of craftsmen—blacksmiths on his mother's side, carpenters and tinkers on his father's.

It was not surprising, then, that in 1920 Albers was attracted to the Bauhaus. The Bauhaus, which has been described as "a kind of university of pure construction and applied art," was founded in Weimar in 1919 by Walter Gropius, who later headed the department of architecture in the Graduate School of Design at Harvard University. Albers studied at the famous laboratory-workshop until 1923, preparing himself slowly and carefully.

JOSEF ALBERS

When Albers had completed his studies, he remained at the Bauhaus, teaching a new concept of basic design that he had developed and constantly experimenting in a wide range of materials, until the school was closed by the Nazis in 1933. Albers' teaching associates included Paul Klee, Wassily Kandinsky, and László Moholy-Nagy. These artists, and the study, teaching, and research carried on at the Bauhaus, not only prepared the way for the acceptance and understanding of abstract art, but helped break down the barriers between fine and applied art. The principles of artistic creation that Albers taught were as enlightening to the industrial designer as to the painter or sculptor.

In the same year that the Bauhaus was closed, Albers moved to the United States to teach at Black Mountain College in North Carolina. For the next sixteen years he gave the unorthodox and far-reaching courses in design that formed the avant-garde art policy of Black Mountain. During these years he also taught at the Harvard University Graduate School of Design (in 1936, 1937, and 1941) and lectured in Cuba in 1934 and Mexico in 1936. He had his first one-man show at the New York galleries of J. B. Neumann in 1936.

In 1950, when Yale University established a department of design, Albers was named to head it. In preparing art students for professional opportunities in graphic arts and product design.

ALBERS, JOSEF—*Continued*

he urged "less expression and more visualization." While at Yale he taught and lectured at leading universities, art schools, and museums throughout the United States and abroad, including the School of Architecture in Lima, Peru in 1953, Ulm Hochschule in Germany in 1953-54 and 1955, Honolulu University in Hawaii in 1954, Carnegie Institute in Pittsburgh in 1957 and 1958, and Princeton University in 1960. Professor Albers retired as chairman of the art department at Yale in 1958, but remained at the university as visiting critic in advanced painting for the next two years.

Unlike many other artists, Albers managed his twofold career of teacher and painter without sacrificing either. On the contrary, each seems to have formed an integral part of the whole man. His paintings demonstrate his theories, while his theories constantly draw upon his discoveries in design and color.

With their precise control of both color and design, Albers' paintings dramatize the conflict between order and freedom, between identity and change and show his faith in their reconcilability. Holding that the artist's concern is with the discrepancy between physical fact and psychic effect, or between reality and appearance, Albers consistently isolates and illuminates this discrepancy. He does so working exclusively within the medium of geometric abstraction, with special emphasis on rectilinear forms. His *Homage to the Square* is actually a generic title applied to a series of experiments begun more than a decade ago. It consists of a group of progressively smaller squares, asymmetrically set on the horizontal axis, but symmetrically on the vertical one. Of the thirty-eight pictures in his exhibition at the Sidney Janis Gallery in New York in the fall of 1961, thirty-three came under the *Homage to the Square* classification.

Calculating relationships of color and shape with rigorous care, Albers uses color, most often clear and flat, as an instrument. Because colors influence and change each other, the eye sees color almost never unrelated and, therefore, almost never unchanged. Color, according to Albers, is changing continually, with changing light, with changing shape and placement. The particular expressions he achieves in a picture are conditioned by the juxtapositions of line and color. His *Gray Turns Violet* is an example of how Albers makes colors change each other. In her review of Albers' exhibition at the Janis Gallery in 1959, Emily Genauer wrote in the New York *Herald Tribune* (December 6, 1959), "Am I looking, in the work called 'Homage to the Square—Floating,' at a series of interlocking yellow and gray boxes or am I looking into the sun?"

To those who object that his works are without emotion, Albers replies that clear thinking does not stand in the way of feeling. "Why," he asks, "are we afraid that thinking and planning—necessary in all human activities—will spoil the painting of a picture?" Alike and yet different from Piet Mondriaan, with whom he is often associated, Albers does not arrive at his strict, geometric forms through sensibility. Rather, his is a completely intellectual attack. Measuring and surveying with almost obsessional precision, Albers manages, paradoxically enough, to achieve more and more freedom through more and more discipline.

Because of the staggering variety of experiences and visual performances that Albers finds within his finely colored geometric configurations, he is never lured away from his straight lines and symmetrical designs. He is also acutely aware of the role of the observer collaborating with the picture to produce illusion. The combined results often make it appear that the modifications engendered in his strictly controlled pictures are really magical transformations. Although Albers limits himself to the straight line in his graphic constructions, he is at home in more than one medium. In 1961 he designed a glass and metal mural for the Time & Life Building in New York City, using the square motif.

Josef Albers has had more than 100 one-man shows and has been represented in hundreds of exhibitions. A major one-man show, which opened at the Museum of Modern Art in New York in 1949, circulated for three and a half years. His many awards include the Ada S. Garret Prize of the Chicago Art Institute (1954) for his *Homage to the Square: White Monument,* an honorary Doctor of Fine Arts degree from the University of Hartford (1957), and a Ford Foundation Fellowship (1959). Albers, who has been a citizen of the United States since 1939, was decorated by his native Germany (German Federal Republic) with the Officers Cross of the Order of Merit in 1957.

There is said to be little about Albers outwardly that suggests the magical and lyrical quality of his art. He has been described as a man of infinite patience, quiet, unassuming, perhaps somewhat somber. At the same time he has a flashing wit. Articulate, both in the classroom and out, Albers contributes articles to art journals and is the author of *Poems and Drawings* (Readymade Press, 1958). His epigrammatic, gnomic poems, like his paintings, play on the distinctions between reality and appearance.

On May 9, 1925 Josef Albers married Anni Fleischmann, a student of one of his fellow professors at the Bauhaus. She traveled with her husband to Black Mountain College in 1933, where, as an assistant professor of art, she taught weaving. Anni Albers is especially celebrated for her elegant tapestries and fabric designs. She has continued to lecture, contribute to art magazines, and exhibit her work both at home and abroad. The Albers have no children. A slightly built man, Albers is five feet seven inches tall and weighs 155 pounds; he has blue eyes and what he describes as "blonde, grey, white" hair. He is a member of American Abstract Artists. A man who has uncompromisingly devoted himself over the years to his art, he stands as one of the old masters of precise abstraction.

References

Art N 49:40+ N '50
Time 67:80+ Je 18 '56
Bucher, François. *Josef Albers, Despite Straight Lines* (1961)
International Who's Who, 1961-62
Who's Who in America, 1962-63
Who's Who in American Art, 1959

BAILEY, JOHN M(ORAN) Nov. 23, 1904-
Political party official; lawyer

Address: b. 1730 K St., N.W., Washington, D.C.;
h. 150 Scarborough St., Hartford, Conn.

Regarded as one of the most effective professional politicians in the United States, John M.
Bailey, chairman of the Democratic National
Committee and the Connecticut State Democratic
Committee, was a major architect of the organization and campaign that helped win John F.
Kennedy's election to the Presidency in 1960.
Yet after thirty years of full-time political activity, Bailey has kept what David S. Broder in
the New York *Times Magazine* described as "the
amateur's wide-eyed enthusiasm for politics as a
game." Professional or amateur, Bailey has demonstrated the kind of skill as a picker of candidates and issues, distributor of patronage, en-
forcer of party discipline, and legislative "trader"
and lobbyist that has won him the respect of
political experts in both camps.

John Moran Bailey learned politics at the dinner table while growing up in Hartford, Connecticut. His father, Dr. Michael A. Bailey, a physician, was active in politics as a member of the
Hartford Board of Education, Common Council,
and Board of Aldermen. His mother, the former
Louise A. Moran, was the first woman to serve
as vice-chairman of Hartford's Second Ward and
the first woman in the city to be appointed to
a city commission (the Hartford Juvenile Commission) after women had won the right to vote.
John Bailey, the only child in the family, was
born on November 23, 1904 in Hartford. A Catholic, he attended St. Peter's Parochial School before entering Hartford Public High School in
1918. Later, at Catholic University in Washington, D.C., he was captain of the university baseball team, quarterback of the football team, and
a member of the basketball team. After receiving
a B.A. degree in science in 1926, Bailey enrolled
in Harvard Law School, where he won his LL.B.
degree in 1929.

Before the year was over, he had opened a law
office in Hartford and had launched his political
career, eventually becoming a protégé of Thomas
J. Spellacy, a power in Democratic state politics.
In 1931 he was appointed to his first paid political post, that of secretary to Mayor William
Rankin, and a year later he became a member
of the Democratic State Central Committee. He
was appointed judge of the Hartford Police Court
in 1933, clerk in 1935, and judge again in 1939.
Around this time Bailey persuaded another young
Hartford lawyer named Abraham A. Ribicoff to
enter public life. Ribicoff became Bailey's successor as police judge in 1941.

During his climb to political power and prestige, Bailey served as a member of the Connecticut Statute Revision Commission (1941-46), as
treasurer of the National Young Democrats (1937-
41), and as executive secretary to Governor Wil-
bert Snow (1946). He ran for public office only
once—in 1940—and was soundly defeated for the
post of probate court judge. But as a practical
politician, Bailey proved himself to be an effective and tireless operator. In 1946 he gained control of the Democratic State Convention and won

George Maniatis
Continental Photo Service
JOHN M. BAILEY

for himself the post of chairman of the Democratic State Commission, a post he has held ever
since.

In 1954 Bailey backed Abraham A. Ribicoff
for the gubernatorial nomination. In a political
upset, Ribicoff defeated the Republican incumbent, John Davis Lodge, by 3,115 votes. Four
years later Ribicoff won re-election by 242,000
votes. Bailey recalled the gain in votes when he
assumed office as National Democratic chairman
on January 21, 1961. Noting President Kennedy's
narrow margin of victory, he declared: "In 1964
we want to give President Kennedy the biggest
majority ever given a President."

Bailey had first served the Kennedy cause in
1956, at the Democratic National Convention,
when he and Governor Ribicoff proposed Senator
Kennedy for the Vice-Presidency. With Kennedy
adviser Theodore Sorensen, Bailey prepared a
state-by-state table of the United States Catholic
population, indicating fourteen vitally important
states in which the proportion of Catholics was
large enough to help—rather than hurt—Kennedy's chances. The total came to 261 electoral
votes, only eight less than the amount needed to
win. This effective political argument, combined
with John Bailey's adroit maneuvering on the
convention floor—he had been coming to Democratic conventions since 1932—came within
twenty and a half votes of capturing the nomination for Kennedy.

Early in 1960 Bailey was pressed into full-time
service in the Kennedy drive for the Democratic
nomination. *Time* magazine pointed out that he
was the "trouble shooter on difficult local situations as well as adviser to the candidate in overall strategy." One of his first tasks in the pre-
convention phase was to win upstate New York
for the Kennedy forces. Theodore H. White described Bailey's operation, in *The Making of the
President 1960* (Atheneum, 1961), as "an over-

BAILEY, JOHN M.—*Continued*
the-border political raid unmatched in domestic politics since Huey Long raided Arkansas from Louisiana." After sewing up New York, Bailey moved on, "dealing with the brokers of politics in every state of the Union, raiding, wheedling, persuading the support that Kennedy must have." At the 1960 convention Bailey played a strategic behind-the-scenes role and during the election campaign itself he served as personal liaison man between Senator Kennedy and state and county political leaders.

On January 21, 1961, the day after President Kennedy's inauguration, Bailey was unanimously elected by some 100 party leaders in Washington to succeed Senator Henry M. Jackson of Washington as chairman of the Democratic National Committee. Bailey immediately began to build a strong organization in an effort to push Kennedy programs through Congress and elect Democrats in 1962 and 1964. At the same time he was given a major voice in handling political patronage. Yet it was typical of John Bailey's political "style" that he informed state Democratic organizations that he had no interest in "taking care of" mediocrities but would insist on men of character and ability whose appointments would strengthen the Democratic party for future election campaigns.

At his new post in Washington, Bailey remains the cool political technician but apparently no longer holds the view that a party organization chief's primary duty is to operate, not talk. One remark the national chairman made in November 1961 about New York Governor Nelson A. Rockefeller, accusing him of "political larceny in the robber baron tradition," drew a strong rebuke from Representative William E. Miller, Republican National Committee chairman, and a disclaimer by White House Press Secretary Pierre Salinger of Presidential endorsement of the statement. On December 31, 1961 Bailey made headlines again in describing what he called the "curious union of Republicans and right-wing fanatics," whom he dubbed the "Fanatican party."

As Democratic National Committee chairman, Bailey receives no salary, although his expenses are paid. Reported to be independently wealthy, he is the senior partner in the Hartford law firm of Bailey & Wechsler, which he formed on his graduation from Harvard Law School. Among the business organizations with which he is affiliated as a director are the New Amsterdam Casualty Company and the South End Bank. He serves on the Connecticut Economic Planning and Development Committee, on several other state committees including one on fiscal study, and on the Greater Hartford Flood Commission. He is also a member of the board of directors of St. Francis Hospital in Hartford, of the founders' committee of the University of Hartford, and of the board of governors of the Catholic University Alumni Association, which in 1961 presented him with its achievement award in the field of politics. He is a fourth degree member of the Knights of Columbus and a communicant of St. Joseph's Cathedral in Hartford.

On August 1, 1933 John M. Bailey married Barbara Leary, a teacher. They have four children—Louise (now Mrs. Conrad Kronholm), Barbara (now Mrs. James Kennelly) and twins Judith and John—and two grandchildren. Bailey is just under six feet tall, weighs 185 pounds, and has hazel eyes and brown hair. An ardent golfer, he shoots in the low 70's and belongs to the Burning Tree Club in Washington and the Wethersfield Country Club in Hartford, among others.

In *The Making of the President 1960,* Theodore H. White described Bailey as "a tall, cigar-smoking, baldheaded man . . . who affects an exterior of hardness of manner, talks in a high, rusty, confidential tone of voice, and effectively conceals the fact that he is a Harvard Law School graduate." While operating "the tightest New England political machine . . . with merciless efficiency," White wrote, Bailey is nevertheless "a transitional political type. Able to talk politics in the toughest parochial terms with his fellow bosses across the Northeast, he is nonetheless able to go beyond that to an understanding of modern government too."

References

Democratic Digest p47 Ja-F '61 por
N Y Times p46 Ja 22 '61 por
N Y Times Mag p26+ O 16 '61 por
Washington (D.C.) Post A p2 Ja 22 '61 por
White, Theodore H. The Making of the President 1960 (1961)
Who's Who in America, 1962-63
Who's Who in United States Politics (1952)

BAINTON, ROLAND H(ERBERT) Mar. 30, 1894- Theologian; educator; writer
Address: h. 191 King's Highway, Woodmont, Conn.

One of the leading specialists in Reformation history and the life of Martin Luther, the Reverend Dr. Roland H. Bainton was Titus Street Professor of Ecclesiastical History at the Yale Divinity School from 1936 until his retirement in June 1962. The author of nineteen books and scores of articles, Bainton won the $7,500 Abingdon-Cokesbury award in 1950 for his biography *Here I Stand; A Life of Martin Luther.* In addition to his scholarly work on the Reformation are his several church histories written especially for students and laymen. A personal interest in the extension of Christian principles into everyday life is reflected in his articles as well as in his book *Christian Attitudes Toward War and Peace.* Bainton, who began his career as an instructor at Yale Divinity School in 1920, has been an ordained Congregational minister since 1927.

Roland Herbert Bainton was born in Ilkeston, England on March 30, 1894, the only son of the Reverend James Herbert and Charlotte Eliza (Blackham) Bainton. He has one sister, Hilda, married in 1919 to Charles Glen King, the chemist who isolated vitamin C in 1932. After eight years as pastor of the Ilkeston Congregational Church, the Reverend James Bainton received a call from a church in Vancouver, British Columbia. In his warm and revealing biography of his father, *Pilgrim Parson* (Nelson, 1958), Roland Bainton describes the life of a minister's family in the early 1900's. In addition to carrying out his many pastoral and civic duties, the elder Bainton became an enthusiastic gardener and truck farmer to supply the parsonage table. Bainton recalls his own particular family responsibility in Vancouver with some humor: "I weeded the lawn, often sulkily, until I realized that Grandma in Heaven had her eye on me."

The Bainton family moved to the state of Washington in 1902, where the Reverend James Bainton became pastor of the Congregational Church in the pleasant community of Colfax. Formerly a cattle town, Colfax had by then become the center of a prosperous area of wheat-producing farms. The Palouse River, which parallels the town, periodically overflows; on one occasion in Bainton's youth it almost washed away his father's church. The Baintons lived in Colfax for eighteen years. In the summers, when church duties permitted, they took camping trips to Lake Chatcolet, Idaho or to the family farm in Westlake, Idaho.

Roland Bainton received the equivalent of an English youth's education in the classics; he began the study of Latin at twelve and added German a year later. His father always encouraged an inquiring mind, with extensive reading as a prerequisite for discussion. "His library was my library," Bainton relates in *Pilgrim Parson*, "and one of the privileges of being sick was to have my bed placed beside the shelves." The Reverend James Bainton never tired of discussing ideas with his son. When Roland Bainton went off to college these discussions were continued by correspondence.

In 1910 Bainton graduated from Colfax High School. He entered Whitman College, in Walla Walla, Washington, where he received a B.A. degree in the classics in 1914. Inspired by his father, who was himself one of six Congregational ministers in two generations, Roland Bainton entered Yale Divinity School to prepare for the ministry. He was awarded a B.D. degree in 1917.

During World War I Bainton, a pacifist like his father, chose to serve without military rank in a unit of the American Friends Service Committee under the American Red Cross in France. After the war, he returned to Yale University, where he earned a Ph.D. degree in Semitics and Hellenistic Greek in 1921. Some years later, in 1926, he studied under a Guggenheim Fellowship. He had been appointed instructor in church history and the New Testament at Yale Divinity School in January 1920. In his comprehensive history of the school, *Yale and the Ministry* (Harper, 1957), Bainton points out, "In 1920, Dumas Malone was being tested in Church History; Roland Bainton in the New Testament; and Robert Calhoun in the history of Religious Education. . . . No one of the three is now working in the area of his apprenticeship."

Within three years Bainton was promoted to assistant professor and nine years later, in 1932, became an associate professor. In 1936 he was appointed Titus Street Professor of Ecclesiastical History, a position he held until his retirement in June 1962. He was the third incumbent of the chair since it was endowed in 1867 by Au-

Yale News Bureau
REV. DR. ROLAND H. BAINTON

gustus Street in memory of his father. Like George P. Fisher and Williston Walker before him, he played an important role in the development of the department of church history within the Yale Divinity School.

In addition to teaching, Bainton has often been invited to participate in lecture series at colleges and seminaries. Many of these lectures served as nuclei for his books. His speaking ability is summed up by A. C. Outler in his review of *Yale and the Ministry* for *Christian Century* (November 6, 1957): "Alumni of Yale Divinity School will have their own sufficient reasons for reading this book. They need only be told that it reads like Roland Bainton lectures."

Bainton has been a prolific author. His writings range from scholarly and erudite articles on the Reformation to biographies and general church histories for the layman. Many of his earlier books and articles are chiefly products of historical research on the Reformation. Some of them appear only in foreign publications. Bainton recognizes, however, the need for authoritative church histories that also have wide popular appeal. "Unfortunately," he says, "scholars frequently lack the capacity to make their work understandable and appealing to the non-specialist, and the popularizers do not have a mastery of the facts."

The Church of Our Fathers (Scribner, 1941) avoids both of these pitfalls. Written for young people from nine to nineteen and attractively illustrated by woodcuts from Bainton's own collection, this book was well received and has become almost a classic. Over three-quarters of a million copies have been sold, and it has been translated into Spanish, Japanese, Siamese, Hebrew, Chinese, and French. Two other books written for students or laymen are *The Reformation of the Sixteenth Century* (Beacon, 1952), which later was published in paperback edition and translated into Italian and Hebrew; and

BAINTON, ROLAND H.—*Continued*

Early Christianity, an Anvil Book published by D. Van Nostrand Company in 1960.

In 1950 Roland Bainton received the $7,500 Abingdon-Cokesbury Award for *Here I Stand; A Life of Martin Luther*. The book, based on the author's intimate acquaintance with Luther's writings, and with the events of the sixteenth-century Reformation, is illustrated with contemporary woodcuts and engravings. It proved to be popular both with readers and with reviewers. In *Christian Century* (October 4, 1950) D. J. Campbell called it "an exciting biography of one of history's greatest men," and went on to say, "I use the adjective purposely. The book is written in such an easy, readable style and with such a vivid portrayal of one of the most dramatic lives in history that it makes exciting reading." H. E. Fey commented in the *Saturday Review of Literature* (February 10, 1951) that it was "a great biography because it deals sensitively and presciently with the most important of all conflicts—the inward war between faith and doubt, between fear and courage, between God and the devil—in one of the great souls of Christian history."

A major concern of Bainton's books is for the rights and duties of conscience. He is the author of individual biographies of Sebastianus Castellio, David Joris, Bernardino Ochino, and Michael Servetus—men persecuted for their beliefs—and a collective biography, *The Travail of Religious Liberty* (Westminister, 1951). These books examine the problem of civil and religious liberty in relation to the state. *Hunted Heretic* (Beacon, 1953), the life of Servetus, won this praise from W. E. Garrison in *Christian Century* (November 18, 1953): "No professional student of history can put down a book by Bainton without sincere admiration for the thoroughness of the research underlying it and the clarity with which the findings are expressed." G. C. Boyce remarked in his review for the *Annals of the American Academy of Political and Social Science* (May 1954): "Although he writes of the sixteenth century, his pages offer a constant challenge as we face modern problems and should make us ponder long his concluding admonition that 'the story of . . . Servetus should demonstrate for us that our slogans of liberty need continually to be thought through afresh.'"

Dr. Bainton demonstrates the application of Christian principles to daily life in *What Christianity says about Sex, Love and Marriage* (Association Press, 1957) and *Christian Attitudes toward War and Peace* (Abingdon, 1960). The latter, expressing his own philosophy for preserving peace, is the culmination of over thirty years of research. It surveys the historical Christian view of war, beginning with the crusading war of the Old Testament, moving on to the pacifism practiced by the early Christian Church and to the theory of the "just war" waged in the Middle Ages. He reviews the failure of all these approaches and the relative failure of the peaceful protests of modern churches, or the outlawing of war by nations. The ominous threat of the atomic era prompts Bainton to offer a suggested Christian solution. Allen Hackett, writing in *Christian Century* (January 25, 1961), explains:

"The dream of peace is built on the bedrock of enlightened self-interest. Its walls rise with the building blocks of Christian humanism. . . . Impressively and incisively, Prof. Bainton leads us to his concluding plea, based on the sweep of 4,000 years of history which could end overnight."

Of the faculty of Yale Divinity School, Bainton once wrote: "They cannot be accused of taking their ease in the tranquil retirement of a blissful hilltop" (*Yale and the Ministry*). All indications are that this will continue to be eminently true of Dr. Bainton himself. Despite his retirement in June 1962 after forty-two years as a teacher, he remains at work as an author. Another Luther anthology, *Luther's Meditation on the Gospels*, and the first volume of his Collected Papers in Church History, entitled *Early and Medieval Christianity* (Beacon), were scheduled for publication in 1962.

Bainton holds honorary D.D. degrees from Meadville Theological Seminary, Oberlin College, and Whitman College and the Litt.D. degree from Gettysburg College. In 1948 he was awarded the honorary D. Theol. degree at the University of Marburg, the oldest Protestant seminary in Germany. He is a member of the American Historical Association, the Medieval Academy, the American Society of Church Historians, the American Society for Reformation Research, and the American Association of University Professors. He is an honorary member of the American Academy of Arts and Sciences, the International Academy of Arts and Letters, and the Heidelberger Akademie der Wissenschaften. He has been an ordained minister of the Congregational Church since 1927 and is also an affiliated member of the Society of Friends. In the summer of 1948 Bainton and his wife, who is a full member of the Society of Friends, traveled to Germany as religious visitors for the American Friends Service Committee. Politically, he is independent.

Roland H. Bainton married Ruth Mae Woodruff, a teacher, on June 8, 1921. They have five children: Olive Mae (Mrs. Roger Robison), Joyce (Mrs. William Peck), Herbert, Cedric, and Ruth (Mrs. Richard Lunt). They also have twelve grandchildren. Dr. Bainton is five feet eight inches tall, weighs 150 pounds, and has gray-green eyes and white hair. He enjoys riding a bicycle and painting in water colors. For many years he has collected medieval and Renaissance woodcuts, drawings, and engravings, and has used his hobby as a source of illustrated material for his Reformation texts. His own clever line sketches add pictorial interest to some of his other books.

References

Bainton, Roland H. Pilgrim Parson (1958)
Who's Who in America, 1962-63

BOUCHER, ANTHONY (bou'chēr) Aug. 21, 1911- Writer; editor; reviewer; radio commentator

Address: h. 2643 Dana St., Berkeley, Calif.

By his own admission, Anthony Boucher has done "just about everything . . . possible in the field of murder." Boucher has written seven full-length mystery novels, edited three crime anthologies and a monthly detective magazine, and supplied introductions to some thirty other books. He has also written several hundred radio shows and countless short stories and novelettes, done translations from French, Spanish, and Portuguese, served as book reviewer, and even composed light verse—all dealing with assorted forms of homicide. Fascinated also by science fiction and fantasy, Boucher compiled an annual anthology of best science fiction stories for eight years and edited a monthly magazine of fantasy and science fiction for a decade. As a reviewer of science fiction he uses the pseudonym of H. H. Holmes.

Neither "Anthony Boucher" nor "H. H. Holmes" is, however, the writer's real name, although he now lives almost entirely under the name of Boucher. He was born William Anthony Parker White on August 21, 1911 in Oakland, California, the son of James Taylor White and Mary Ellen (Parker) White. Both of his parents were physicians, his father serving chiefly as a doctor in the United States Revenue Cutter Service. On both sides Boucher's ancestry goes back to the pioneers of California and Oregon. His maternal grandfather and his uncle were both lawyers, district attorneys, and superior court judges. His father's father was a captain in the United States Navy.

An only child, Boucher was brought up in Oakland, San Rafael, and Pasadena, California and in Reno, Nevada. Although he was an invalid during most of his high school career, he managed to graduate from Pasadena High School in 1928. He attended Pasadena Junior College for two years and then entered the University of Southern California, where he majored in German and spent much of his extracurricular time in little theater work—acting, directing, and writing. Elected to Phi Beta Kappa, he graduated from the University of Southern California with a B.A. degree in 1932. He was awarded a scholarship to the University of California at Berkeley, from which he graduated with an M.A. degree in 1934 after he had submitted a thesis entitled "The Duality of Impressionism in Recent German Drama."

Originally Boucher had planned to become a teacher of languages, but, having become tired of academic life, he decided to be a playwright. After a few unsuccessful years of trying to market his plays he tried writing a mystery novel. In 1936 he sold his first mystery novel to Simon & Schuster: *The Case of the Seven of Calvary*, published in 1937. All published by Simon & Schuster, there followed in rapid succession, *The Case of the Crumpled Knave* (1939); *The Case of the Baker Street Irregulars* (1940); *The Case of the Solid Key* (1941); and *The Case of the Seven Sneezes* (1942). In 1955 Ballantine Books, Inc., published a collection of Boucher's short stories called *Far and Away*. Under the name of H. H. Holmes he wrote *Nine Times Nine* (1940) and *Rocket to the Morgue* (1942), both published by Duell, Sloan, & Pearce.

Among the books that Anthony Boucher has edited are *The Pocket Book of True Crime Stories* (Pocket Books, 1941); *Great American Detective Stories* (World, 1945); *Four-and-Twenty*

ANTHONY BOUCHER

Bloodhounds (Simon & Schuster, 1950); *The Best from Fantasy and Science Fiction*, an annual anthology published by Little, Brown & Co. in 1952 and 1953 and by Doubleday & Co., Inc., from 1954 through 1959; and *A Treasury of Great Science Fiction* (Doubleday, 1959). Boucher says that he has no idea how many short stories, novelettes, and articles he has had published. The periodicals in which they have appeared include *Esquire, Playboy, Astounding Science Fiction*, the *Baker Street Journal, American Cookery, Ed McBain's Mystery Book*, and many others. His work has been published in some forty anthologies. From 1945 to 1948 he wrote for the Sherlock Holmes and Gregory Hood radio mystery programs, often plotting as many as three half-hour shows a week. In 1952 and 1953 he edited *True Crime Detective*.

As a critic, Boucher covered theater and music for the *United Progressive News* of Los Angeles (1935-37), reviewed mysteries for the San Francisco *Chronicle* (1942-47), and wrote science fiction and fantasy reviews for the Chicago *Sun-Times* (1949-50). Since 1949 he has conducted the "Criminals at Large" column for the New York *Times Book Review*, and, since 1957, he served as critic for *Ellery Queen's Mystery Magazine* (with which he had earlier been associated, from 1948 to 1950). He won the annual Edgar award given by the Mystery Writers of America for the best mystery criticism in the United States in 1946, 1950, and 1953. As H. H. Holmes, he has reviewed science fiction and fantasy for the New York *Herald Tribune Book Review* since 1951.

One of the earliest enthusiasts of science fiction as a literary genre, Boucher helped to found the *Magazine of Fantasy and Science Fiction*, which he also edited from 1949 to 1958. "We wanted to retain the standards of the genre, while at the same time imposing the standards of general literature," Boucher told Robert McCary of the San Francisco *Chronicle* (February 9, 1958). He de-

BOUCHER, ANTHONY—*Continued*

plores what he calls the "ghettoizing" of murder mysteries and science fiction and those readers who insist on differentiating between entertainment and literature. Boucher is particularly annoyed by "people who say they never read science fiction but who think *1984* and *Brave New World* are wonderful." Boucher also told McCary: "In any special field you will find as many levels as you will find in the field of literature as a whole. In science fiction, as in other fields, the very best writers are creating literature." More recently, however, he has expressed the view that "mysteries are good; science fiction is dull; opera is entering on one of its greatest eras."

Boucher has long been interested in music and opera. All his life he has been a passionate devotee of opera, and since fourteen he has been a collector of historic vocal records. His collection now numbers approximately 6,000 records. In 1949 he started the *Golden Voices* program of historic vocal recordings over station KPFA-FM in Berkeley. The program is now also heard over KPFK-FM in Los Angeles and over WBAI-FM in New York City. In 1960 he conducted the program *Introduction to Opera* over station KQED-TV in San Francisco. He contributes articles to *Opera News* and reviews operas for station KPFA-FM, the Canadian Broadcasting Corporation, and *Opera News. Escape,* his most recent weekly radio program over KPFA-FM, is a biweekly survey of books on crime, murder, fantasy, and science fiction.

In an article for the New York *Times* (November 12, 1961) Boucher described the monomania of collecting old vocal records. He explained why men who are otherwise rational turn into record collectors—"creatures who will spend hours in a salvage shop poring one by one over hundreds or even thousands of ancient and forgotten records . . . to emerge plastered with sweat and grime, with cramped limbs and weary eyes and strained muscles. . . ." In what was apparently an autobiographical note he added: "The walls of his [the collector's] house are entirely given over to record shelves and what he needs is more walls or possibly a new house and even probably a new housewife, since the old one has had enough of living with an incomprehensible monomaniac. . . ."

Boucher disclaims any special talent for singing or for music. "I have no musical skills," he once wrote, "and look upon myself as (in the truest sense) an amateur—an articulate enthusiast trying to infect others with my enthusiasm." According to Boucher, his other enthusiasms include "spectator sports (especially football, basketball, track, Rugby, and gymnastics); food and wine; British crossword puzzles; silent films; poker (or is this a hobby? It's more profitable than some of my professional activities); and women (in a reasonably monogamous way)."

On May 19, 1938 Anthony Boucher married Phyllis Mary Price, a librarian. They have two children: Lawrence Taylor White, and James Marsden White. Brown-eyed and brown-haired, Boucher stands five feet ten inches in height, and weighs 165 pounds. He is a Roman Catholic. A member of the Democratic party, he served as a member of the party's state central committee from 1948 to 1952. He belongs to the Mystery Writers of America, of which he served as president in 1951; the Baker Street Irregulars, an organization of Sherlock Holmes buffs; the Scowrers and Molly Maguires of San Francisco; the Elves', Gnomes' and Little Men's Science Fiction Chowder and Marching Society; and the San Francisco Opera Guild. Recently asked if there were any misstatements published about himself that he would like to correct, he replied, "I am *not* soft-spoken."

References:

> Twentieth Century Authors (First Supplement, 1955)
> Who's Who in America, 1962-63

BRAND, OSCAR Feb. 7, 1920- Folk singer; folklorist; author; producer

Address: b. 147 Sullivan St., New York 12; c/o Hollis Music, Inc., 10 Columbus Circle, New York 19; h. 79 W. 12th St., New York 11

One of the most versatile and colorful interpreters of the rich heritage of folk music is Oscar Brand—balladeer, humorist, scholar, and writer—who since 1945 has conducted his weekly *Folksong Festival* over New York City's municipal radio station, WNYC. The multitude of folksongs that he has presented over radio and television, in concert appearances, and on his many recordings, represent virtually every aspect of life, including the seamy side. Through his free and easy style of singing he conveys the down-to-earth quality of folk music to his audiences. His many and varied activities, including the writing of books, articles, and songs, and the production of films, musical comedies, and children's programs, have brought him numerous awards and honors.

Oscar Brand was born on February 7, 1920 on a wheat farm near Winnipeg, Manitoba, Canada, the son of I. Z. and Beatrice (Schulman) Brand. He has one sister, Edythe, who works for the publishing house Simon & Schuster, and a brother, Harry, who is a milk-driver. His father was an interpreter to the Indians for the Hudson's Bay Company at Portage La Prairie, Manitoba and later ran a theatrical supply store and a pawnshop.

The creative impulse dawned early in Oscar Brand, and he has recalled: "Since I first learned that words had meaning and that they could be communicated via the printed page, I have wanted to be a writer. I've also had a love affair with the stage—since the day in 1924 when I was admitted free into the Pantages Theatre in Winnipeg." His love of folk music stems from the early influence of his parents and grandparents, who were singers, and from the occasions during his childhood when he had the opportunity to listen to the radio and the player piano. It also arose from his subsequent travels through the United States and Canada.

When he was seven years old Oscar Brand's family moved to the United States, settling first in Minneapolis, then in Chicago, and finally in Brooklyn, New York, where his father was employed as a salesman. At Erasmus Hall High

School in Brooklyn Brand played on the baseball team, was active in the service club and on the school newspaper, and won the Pan-American Medal. After graduating in 1937 he spent some time roaming about the country with his banjo, working on farms along the way. He then entered Brooklyn College, where he was chairman of the varsity dramatics group, wrote and directed productions for senior class events, and was awarded the Student Council Silver Medal. After graduating with the B.A. degree in abnormal psychology in 1942 he worked for a short time as a research assistant at Bellevue Hospital in New York City.

Entering the United States Army in late 1942, Brand served as section chief of the psychological section of the Army induction station in New York City, and later became editor-in-chief of a newspaper for psychiatric patients in the Army's Mason General Hospital. He also conducted therapeutic folk-song sessions for hospital patients, and received an Army citation for his work. He has said that his musical activities helped him to dodge kitchen-police duty. After his discharge, with the rank of sergeant, in 1945, Brand decided to turn to professional folk singing, which, he maintained, was "easier than working for a living."

In December 1945 New York City's municipal radio station, WNYC, engaged Brand as co-ordinator of folk music. In this capacity he has presented each week his half-hour Sunday evening broadcast, *Folksong Festival,* which has attained immense popularity. Among his guests on the program Brand has included almost every well known folk singer, and many persons from all walks of life and from various parts of the world, who have visited his studio. Carrying the flavor of informal "song-swapping sessions," the programs are often tape-recorded to enable Brand to go on his concert tours. Although Brand derives no income from his WNYC program, he regards it as his favorite broadcasting venture. *Folksong Festival* is transcribed by the United States Information Service of the Department of State, and by the Armed Forces Radio Network, for rebroadcast overseas.

Over the years Brand has appeared on many radio and television programs, including *Today, Omnibus,* Firestone's *Americana,* Norman Corwin's documentary series, the *Kate Smith Show,* the *Ted Steele Show,* and the *Dr. Christian* series. For a while he had a daily radio program over WCBS, *The World of Music,* which has been discontinued. In March 1962 he began a weekly Saturday morning children's show, *American Treasure Chest,* presented over NBC-TV. He is also producing a series of weekly broadcasts, entitled *The World of Folk Music,* for the United States Department of Health, Education, and Welfare. These broadcasts are presented over some 1,300 radio stations, including WBAI-FM in New York City.

Brand has provided scenarios, scores, and narrations for many documentary films for such organizations as the Anti-Defamation League of B'nai B'rith, the National Lutheran Council, Encyclopædia Britannica, Ford Motor Company, Allied Chemical Company, Remington Arms, and Evinrude Motors. He has written and sung

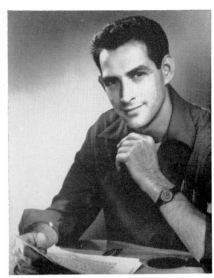

Herman Leonard

OSCAR BRAND

television commercials for Cheerios, Ipana, Oldsmobile, Bardahl Oil, and others. Agnes De Mille commissioned Brand to write the script and act as technical adviser for her musical *The Gold Rush,* which has been presented over CBS-TV. In collaboration with Paul Nassau, Brand is writing a musical comedy based on Marguerite Cullman's book *Ninety Dozen Glasses* (Norton, 1960), which is scheduled for presentation on Broadway in late 1962.

On his concert tours Brand has sung to enthusiastic audiences throughout the United States and Canada. Early in his career he went on an extended singing tour with Herb Shriner. In his own city he has appeared, among other places, in Town Hall, Carnegie Hall, the Brooklyn Academy of Music, and in Cooper Union. He has given concerts and lectures for the Colston-Leigh Lecture Bureau, and he has conducted seminars at Rutgers University and at the Bayonne, New Jersey Community Center.

Among the hundreds of songs that he has recorded Brand has included election songs, children's songs, vaudeville songs, college songs, sports car songs, boating songs, courting songs, drinking songs, nonsense songs, topical-political songs, and outlaw songs. An area of special interest to him has been the songs of American servicemen, of which he has recorded several albums, including *G.I.: American Army Songs* (Riverside), *Every Inch a Sailor* (Elektra), *Tell it to the Marines* (Elektra), and *The Wild Blue Yonder* (Elektra).

His *Bawdy Songs and Backroom Ballads* (Audio-Fidelity), of which seven albums have been recorded to date, have elevated the eyebrows of some strait-laced critics. The collection includes such indelicate classics as "The Chandler's Wife," "Christopher Colombo," and "One-eyed Reilly." His latest recordings are *Morality* (ABC Paramount), *Sea Shanties* (Audio-Fidelity), and *Folk Songs for Fun* (Decca), which he made

BRAND, OSCAR—*Continued*

with the Tarriers. His own composition, "A Guy is a Guy" (a laundered version of an old bawdy song), topped the *Hit Parade* in 1952 and sold over a million Columbia records. Another hit that he has written is "Anymore," based on the off-color song "Ball o' Yarn." In early 1962 Brand, in collaboration with Paul Nassau, wrote English lyrics to the Russian song "Moscow Nights" for Hollis Music Publishing Company, under the title "You Can't Keep Me from Loving You."

Brand has contributed considerably to the literature of folk music, and he is the author of a number of magazine articles in the field. From 1953 to 1955 he wrote reviews and feature articles for the *Saturday Review*. His book *Singing Holidays: The Calendar in Folk Song* (Knopf, 1957) contains some ninety songs dealing with thirty special dates in the American calendar. His *Western Guitar* (Alfred Publishers, 1958) is an instruction book for students of the guitar. He has also published *Bawdy Songs and Backroom Ballads* (Grove Press, 1959) and *Folk Songs for Fun* (Hollis Music, 1961). *The Balladmongers*, a survey of the music world that he is currently writing, is scheduled for publication by Funk and Wagnalls in 1962.

For his film productions Brand has received the Valley Forge Memorial Award, the Golden Reel Award, the Scholastic Award, and the awards of the Edinburgh and Venice film festivals. For his recordings he has won the New York Critics Award and for his books he has received an award from the National Council of Christians and Jews. He also has been awarded the Peabody citation for an anti-bias jingle that he sang for the Advertising Council. Brooklyn College conferred upon him its Community Service Award in 1958. In 1961 he received the Thomas Alva Edison Award for the best children's program.

In selecting his songs Brand seeks out the "simple, traditional sound" that is generally associated in people's minds with folk music. He notes that this sound is frequently found in songs of relatively recent vintage (for example, the ballads of Woody Guthrie), whereas many of the so-called "authentic" folksongs that have been handed down through generations by the traditional oral process seem to lack this quality. Brand insists on a high degree of artistic freedom for the folk singer, and rejects the notion that a song must always be sung in its "authentic version." He says that folk songs "live and breathe" by change, and he often rewrites the lyrics of songs to suit specific audiences. In his performances he usually explains the background of each song to his listeners. He accompanies himself with a twelve-string guitar, made in Sweden to his own design.

After an early unsuccessful marriage Oscar Brand married Antonia Rubyan Saber on May 10, 1955. They have two children, Jeannie (named after folk singer Jean Ritchie, her godmother) and Eric. Mrs. Brand, a former ballet dancer and a talented artist, operates an art gallery in Greenwich Village and helps her husband in his various activities. Tall, gaunt, and perpetually youthful, Brand is six feet two inches tall, weighs 175 pounds, and has brown hair and brown eyes. Despite his busy schedule he frequently takes time out for friendly conversation with the many visitors, including children, who drop into his studio. He is a Democrat and a member of the Dissenters, a private debating club under the chairmanship of Roger Baldwin. His favorite recreations are sailboating and carpentry. He serves as president of Heritage Music and of Harlequin Productions. Thoroughly at home in the medium of folk music, Brand says: "If you're carrying a guitar, you can feel safe anywhere in the world."

References

N Y Times II p13 F 1 '59
Toronto Globe and Mail p26 Ja 19 '62
Lawless, Ray M. Folksingers and Folksongs in America (1960)

BRYAN, JAMES E(DMUND) July 11, 1909-
Librarian

Address: b. Newark Public Library, Newark 1, N.J.; h. 666 Highland Ave., Newark 4, N.J.

At the eightieth annual conference of the American Library Association, held in Cleveland in July 1961, it was announced that James E. Bryan had been elected first vice-president of the ALA and would succeed Mrs. Florrinell F. Morton as president in 1962. In professional library work since 1932, Bryan has been with the Newark Public Library, New Jersey's largest public library, since 1943. He has been its director since 1958.

As the director of a large metropolitan library serving a wide area, Bryan has been articulate on the problems facing such libraries. Interest, experience, and aptitude in library architecture have made him a much-consulted expert in that field, also. "The public library building is the practical expression in brick, stone, wood and metal of one of the greatest American ideals ever dreamed, and ever put into use . . ." Bryan wrote in 1955. He is scheduled to take office as president of the American Library Association at its eighty-first annual conference, to be held in Miami, Florida in June 1962.

The second of three children, James Edmund Bryan was born in Easton, Pennsylvania on July 11, 1909 to William Whiteley Bryan, who was in the real estate and insurance business, and Florence Catherine (Shimer) Bryan. His older sister is Josephine (Bryan) Seibert. His younger brother, William W. Bryan, is librarian of the Peoria (Illinois) Public Library. Bryan received his secondary education at Easton High School and at Mount Hermon School in Mount Hermon, Massachusetts, where he managed the tennis team and contributed to the school newspaper. He graduated from Easton High School in 1926.

At Lafayette College, in Easton, Bryan majored in economics, and among his other extracurricular activities he served as captain of the fencing team. When he became a student assistant in the library of Lafayette College he began to consider librarianship as a possible profession. The interest and encouragement of Theodore E. Norton, the college librarian, and of Henry F. Marx, librarian of the Easton Public Library, also influenced Bryan's eventual choice of his career. In 1931 he received his B.S. degree from Lafayette College.

In 1932 Bryan took his B.S. in L.S. degree from the Drexel Institute of Technology in Philadelphia. That same year he became an assistant at the Washington (D.C.) Public Library, a post in which he remained for four years, working in main library circulation, branches, science and technology, and acquisitions departments. While working at the Washington Public Library he studied political science at American University, and obtained his M.A. degree in 1937.

In 1936 Bryan became librarian of the Easton Public Library, directing the libraries in the Easton system until 1938, when he moved to Pittsburgh to head the adult lending department of the Carnegie Library. He remained in charge of adult circulation at the Carnegie main library and its branches in Pittsburgh for five years. The building improvements that took place in the main library and its branches at that time stimulated his interest in library architecture—an interest that has endured.

Bryan has been called in as a consultant on library site and building studies that have been conducted in eight eastern states. In a talk that he gave before the 1954 annual meeting of the Massachusetts Library Association (abridged as an article in the Massachusetts Library Association *Bulletin*, April 1955) he detailed the application in functional buildings of the basic purposes of the library. After articulating the philosophy behind the American public library, and before going into the details of the building program, he sketched the bridge between the two: "The building is for use by . . . literally everyone in the community. It must be friendly and inviting. . . . More people would use libraries if they could 'see-in'. . . . Libraries should be amenable to the general needs and habits of people." He also noted the consideration that must be given to the economizing of time and effort of library workers and the flexibility that the building permits both in regard to public use and staff operations.

In 1943 Bryan went to the Newark (New Jersey) Public Library as its assistant director. Except for an interruption of six months in 1945, when he was employed as an engineer in the specialty products of the Western Electric Company at Kearny, New Jersey, he has been there ever since. He succeeded John B. Kaiser as director of the Newark Public Library in July 1958.

The Newark Public Library has more than 820,000 volumes, an annual circulation figure of more than 2,000,000, and an average of some 3,800 visitors a day to its main building and branches. The library is an important reference center for the whole northern New Jersey area. As director of such a core metropolitan area library, Bryan has been concerned with a problem that confronts such libraries throughout the country: the increasing load being put upon them by nonresidents and by students.

Commenting on this problem in a speech before the forty-seventh annual conference of Eastern College Librarians, Bryan proposed several steps to ease the burden on core city libraries.

Augusta Berns
Bamberger Studios

JAMES E. BRYAN

A broadened basis for public library support was among them. "Most of all," he said, "is the need for a sense of mutual helpfulness and co-operation; a willingness to talk over problems of who is to supply what, who is to develop this special collection or that one."

Bryan has taken advantage of the opportunities for leadership that the directorship of the Newark Public Library brings with it. He organized the Essex County Conference of Library Directors shortly after he became director of the Newark Public Library, and he meets once a month with the directors of the county's twenty-two other public libraries to discuss common problems and to chart patterns of co-operation.

At the opening of the eightieth annual conference of the American Library Association in Cleveland on July 9, 1961, it was announced that James E. Bryan had been chosen vice-president and president-elect of the American Library Association. He had been elected by mail balloting of the American Library Association's more than 26,000 members. His installation as president is scheduled to take place at the eighty-first conference of the American Library Association, to be held in Miami, Florida from June 17 to June 23, 1962.

A devoted worker for the advancement of professional objectives through state and national associations, Bryan had served as chairman of several committees of the American Library Association before he was elected as its president. He was the president of the New Jersey Library Association from 1952 to 1954 and figured prominently in its successful efforts toward legislation establishing a graduate library school at Rutgers, the State University, and toward legislation granting state financial aid to libraries. In 1959-60 he was president of the Public Library Association, a division of the ALA. He was program chairman of the Middle Atlantic States Regional Li-

BRYAN, JAMES E.—*Continued*

brary Conference in 1947 and general chairman in 1949. His other professional activities include membership on the advisory committee of the Graduate School of Library Science at the Drexel Institute of Technology and chairmanship of the advisory board of the Graduate School of Library Service at Rutgers, the State University.

Active in civic affairs, Bryan is president of the Intercultural Council of Newark, a board member of the New Jersey Citizens Council, and a board member of the Visiting Nurse Association. He is also a member of the New Jersey Association for Adult Education, the Adult Education Association of the U.S.A., and the cultural subcommittee of the Greater Newark Economic Development Committee. He was commissioner of the Robert Treat Council, Boy Scouts of America, from 1956 to 1958 and he is chairman of the Historic Sites and Building Committee of Newark.

The *NPL News*, once published by the Newark Public Library, often contained articles by Bryan. He also contributes to other professional journals, including the *ALA Bulletin*, the *MLA Bulletin* (published by the Massachusetts Library Association), and the *Library Journal*. He is the author of building and site studies and of library surveys.

On July 2, 1938 James E. Bryan married Elizabeth Lamb. They have two sons, James, Jr., and Arthur. Bryan, known to his intimates as Ned, has brown hair and brown eyes, is five feet ten and one-half inches tall, and weighs about 180 pounds. He is a Presbyterian and a Democrat. He is a Kiwanian and a member of the Beta Phi Mu and Delta Upsilon fraternities. Although he finds less and less time for it, he likes to go fishing. As an administrator, Bryan encourages members of his staff to contribute their opinions to the formulation of decisions. (The several staff committees at the Newark Public Library represent a cross section of employees.) Once asked to characterize Bryan, Bernard Schein, deputy director of the Newark Public Library, wrote: "I think readily of such qualities as seriousness of purpose, integrity, perseverance, complete devotion, genuine interest in people, and humility (not to be confused with meekness)" (*ALA Bulletin,* July-August 1961). Bryan was awarded the Drexel Institute of Technology alumni citation in 1961.

References

ALA Bul 55:630+ Jl-Ag '61 por
NPL News 14:17+ O '58 por
Who's Who in America, 1962-3
Who's Who in Library Service (1955)

BUCKLEY, WILLIAM F(RANK), JR. Nov. 24, 1925- Editor; author; lecturer

Address: b. National Review, 150 E. 35th St., New York 16; h. Wallack's Point, Stamford, Conn.

The paradox in William F. Buckley, Jr.'s, description of himself as a "radical conservative" is sustained, and may seem compounded, by his dedication to revolution against the past social revisions brought on largely by Franklin D. Roosevelt that have created the present liberal order. But Buckley uses a capital letter, "L," in writing *liberalism* in order to distinguish between what the word once meant and what he feels it has come to mean in American politics because he believes that the prevailing liberalism diminishes freedom. One of conservatism's most stimulating and articulate spokesmen, Buckley works to define and refine the beliefs of his political faith, in many lectures, many magazine articles, several hotly controversial books, and in the weekly journal *National Review,* which he founded in 1955.

Unlike most native New Yorkers of Irish descent, William Frank Buckley, Jr., who was born on November 24, 1925, came somewhat circuitously to have Manhattan as his birthplace. His grandfather, a Canadian son of an Irish emigrant, had moved to Texas in 1879 to become a rancher and a sheriff. Buckley's father, a lawyer who had begun investing in Latin-American oil companies, married Aloise Steiner of New Orleans in 1917. They had ten children: Aloise (Mrs. Benjamin Wilde Heath), John William, Priscilla Langford, James Lane, Jane (Mrs. William Smith 2d), William Frank, Jr., Patricia (Mrs. Leo Brent Bozell), Fergus Reid, Maureen (Mrs. Gerald O'Reilly) and Carol (Mrs. Thomas Charlton, Jr.).

According to Dan Wakefield's article in *Esquire* (January 1961), at the time of his death in 1958 William F. Buckley, Sr., headed an oil empire worth an estimated $110,000,000, with holdings in seven countries, and he passed along to his children not only his considerable fortune, but also "a rigid ideology based on free enterprise and the survival of the fittest." William F. Buckley, Jr., was reared in France, England, and the United States. Claiming protest as his right even in childhood, he wrote a letter at the age of six to the King of England to urge that England pay its war debts. Besides being privately tutored, he attended the St. Thomas More School in London and St. John's, Beaumont, in Old Windsor, England. He received his college preparatory training at the Millbrook School in Millbrook, New York, where his extracurricular interests were music, the yearbook, and the school newspaper.

For a year after his graduation from the Millbrook School in 1943, Buckley studied at the University of Mexico. He began World War II service in the Army as a private in 1944 and was discharged in 1946 in the rank of second lieutenant. Then at Yale University he concentrated academically on history, political science, and economics, while he distinguished himself as a member of the debating team that defeated Oxford University and as class day orator. He belonged to the Torch Honor Society, Fence Club, and Skull and Bones; and as chairman of the *Yale Daily News* he cut his teeth in polemic journalism through antiliberal attacks that furthered circulation along with controversy.

Buckley received his B.A. degree with honors in 1950, but he remained at Yale until 1951 as a teacher of Spanish, a position that he had held on the university faculty since 1947. About a year after his graduation he completed his *God and Man at Yale; The Superstitions of Academic*

Freedom (Regnery, 1951), in which he, a Roman Catholic and a conservative, pointed out what he had found to be the faults in Yale's curriculum, basing his criticism on his own experience and on such other sources as examination of textbooks in basic courses.

More than an assault upon what he saw as antireligious and procollectivist teachings at Yale, and as its façade of academic freedom, Buckley's book was generally viewed as an indictment of all liberal education. It became one of the most widely reviewed books of the year. Some critics approved of its forcefulness as a counterbalance to "the complacent left," of its sincerity and its thoughtfulness. Many Yale graduates, however, disagreed with Buckley, and one of them, McGeorge Bundy, wrote in the *Atlantic Monthly* (November 1951), "As a believer in God, a Republican, and a Yale graduate, I find that the book is dishonest in its use of facts, false in its theory, and a discredit to its author."

In 1952 Buckley joined the staff of the *American Mercury* as associate editor, but soon resigned to do free-lance work in writing and lecturing. While *God and Man at Yale* was enjoying a number of reprintings, he collaborated with his brother-in-law, L. Brent Bozell, to write the equally controversial *McCarthy and His Enemies* (Regnery, 1954), which has been called an apologia and an intellectual justification of Senator Joseph R. McCarthy, Republican of Wisconsin, and of McCarthyism.

Although Buckley and Bozell acknowledged that on occasion McCarthy had made serious mistakes, had dealt in tactics of exaggeration and smearing and in "gratuitous sensationalism," they argued that his attack on the Communist conspiracy was a public benefit. They maintained that "as long as McCarthyism fixes its goal with its present precision, it is a movement around which men of good will and stern morality can close ranks." William S. White, not the harshest reviewer of the book, contended in the New York *Times Book Review* (April 4, 1954), "What is urged is not only that the end justifies the means, but that a moral end justifies immoral means."

In his third book, *Up from Liberalism* (McDowell, 1959), Buckley considers many aspects of American intellectual, economic, and political life in examining the ideas and actions shared by prominent liberals such as Mrs. Eleanor Roosevelt and Edward R. Murrow and by the *New Republic,* the St. Louis *Post-Dispatch,* and certain other publications. His purpose and conclusions are summarized in one of his introductory statements: "There are those of us who are greedy to externalize the conditions of freedom and grace and faith that have sustained [Boris] Pasternak in Hell. To do that we must bring down the thing called Liberalism, which is powerful but decadent; and salvage a thing called conservatism, which is weak but viable."

Convinced that the mistaken predictions and faulty analyses (as they seemed to him) of the liberals were dangerous to the United States, Buckley had founded a weekly journal of conservative opinion, the *National Review.* In the first issue, which appeared on November 14, 1955, he explained in a publisher's statement that

WILLIAM F. BUCKLEY, JR.

his magazine "stands athwart history, yelling 'Stop!' at a time when no one is inclined to do so, or to have much patience with those who urge it." Among the editors of the *National Review* are L. Brent Bozell and James Burnham; its managing editor is Priscilla L. Buckley, and five of Buckley's brothers and sisters have contributed articles to it.

Other contributors to the *National Review* have included William F. Knowland and Russell Kirk, as well as repentant left-wingers Whittaker Chambers ("Confessions of a Middle-Class Radical") and Max Eastman ("I Acknowledge My Mistakes"). Protesting a New York *Times* description of the *National Review* as a publication "far off to the Right," Buckley wrote a letter to the editor of the *Times* (October 28, 1961) in which he pointed out that one of his magazine's editors was a former daily book reviewer of the *Times* and one of its regular contributors had been a *Times* editorial writer.

By late 1960 the five-year-old *National Review* had built up a circulation of 65,000—almost equal to the combined circulation of its liberal counterparts, the *New Republic* and the *Nation.* Buckley's magazine flourishes in part on lively controversy sometimes arising from unexpected quarters. The July 29, 1961 issue criticized as "a venture in triviality" the encyclical *Mater et Magistra* of Pope John XXIII, which advocated state welfare programs that do not interfere with individual freedom. In reply to a rebuke from the Catholic *America,* Buckley said that the position taken by his magazine was determined by the Catholic, Protestant, and Jewish members of its editorial board. Similarly, although Buckley is a Republican, he and the *National Review* occasionally find fault with the Republican party.

Some conservatives have also been surprised at the *National Review*'s denunciation of Robert Welch, the founder of the John Birch Society, who Buckley feels is damaging the cause of the right-wing movement by distorting reality in such

BUCKLEY, WILLIAM F., JR.—*Continued*
assertions as that former President Dwight D. Eisenhower was "an agent of the Communist conspiracy." In another area of controversy, Buckley helped organize in December 1961 the American Committee for Aid to Katanga Freedom Fighters, which supported Katangan efforts for self-determination against United Nations military action in the Republic of the Congo.

Buckley and other editors of the *National Review*, along with several of its associates and contributors, collaborated on *The Committee and Its Critics: A Calm Review of the House Committee on Un-American Activities* (Putnam, 1962). The purpose of the book, which is perhaps less dispassionate than its subtitle suggests, is to dispel ignorance and misunderstanding about the committee and, as Buckley explained in the opening chapter, "to crystallize the arguments against the Committee and to analyze them in the light of our dual commitment to our national defense and to our free society." *The Committee and Its Critics* brings in a verdict generally favorable to the committee.

Among the periodicals to which Buckley has contributed are *Esquire, Atlantic Monthly, Commonweal, Catholic World,* and *Yale Review.* In one fairly recent article, for the *Saturday Review* (November 11, 1961), he argued "No" on the question "Desegregation: Will it Work?" He has also discussed his religious, economic, and political views in many interviews for newspapers, magazines, and radio and television programs. As brilliant a controversialist on the platform as he is in print, he has become a leading champion of campus conservatism. Unabashed in standing up for unpopular views and unwilling to approach his audience with anything less than he considers "straight thought and straight talk," he readily debates with adversaries like Norman Thomas, Arthur Schlesinger, Jr., and James A. Wechsler. College students are often his audience, and he has been called the spiritual leader of the right-wing Young Americans for Freedom.

When he became a syndicated newspaper columnist in the spring of 1962, Buckley suddenly enlarged his audience to some 7,000,000 readers. Entitled "A Conservative Voice," his weekly column appears every Sunday in thirty-eight newspapers, ranging from the Los Angeles *Times* to the Crown Point, Indiana *Lake County Star.* All of the newspapers are published outside New York City, and all of them are of a conservative persuasion.

Buckley has some business affiliations, including the Canso National Gas Company, of which he is a director, but most of his interests aside from politics and writing are recreational. He races a forty-two-foot cutter called *The Panic* and has contributed to the book *Ocean Racing* (Van Nostrand, 1959) and to the magazines *Motor Boating* and the *Skipper.* Gliding, skiing, swimming, and horseback riding are his other sports; indoors, he plays the piano and a seventeenth-century clavichord that his father gave him at graduation. His clubs include the New York Yacht, Stamford Yacht, National Press, and Overseas Press.

Shortly after his graduation from Yale, William F. Buckley, Jr., married Patricia Austin Taylor, on July 6, 1950. They have a son, Christopher Taylor Buckley. Tall, trim, and debonair, Buckley is six feet one inch in height and weighs 170 pounds; he has blue eyes and brown hair. Every year he makes between fifty and sixty speeches. Dan Wakefield, who heard him lecture at Harvard, described him in the *Esquire* article: "He is a totally engaging platform performer, and he delivered his message, as usual, with eloquence, wit, class, and charm. His manner is that of the sharp professor, rather than the politician, and he stealthily stalked the platform as he spoke, rose on his toes and molded the air for emphasis, reflectively touched a finger to his nose, paced a while with hands on hips, returned to grasp the podium and drive home points with deep-voiced persuasion."

References

Esquire 55:49+ Ja '61 por
Mlle 53:79+ Je '61 por
Time 76:54 O 31 '60 por
American Catholic Who's Who, 1962-63
Tanner, Louise Here Today (1959)
Who's Who in America, 1962-63

BUITONI, GIOVANNI (bū-tō'nē) Nov. 6, 1891- Businessman
Address: b. 450 Huyler St., S. Hackensack, N.J.; h. 122 Fairway Terrace, Paramus, N.J.

The present head of the culinary empire comprising Buitoni pasta products and Perugina chocolates and confections is Giovanni Buitoni, the great-grandson of Giulia Buitoni, who started a small macaroni business in San Sepolcro, Italy in 1827. Although the company expanded steadily over the years under the direction of each generation of Buitonis, it is Giovanni Buitoni who is credited with building it into an international complex with pasta plants in Rome, San Sepolcro, Paris, and South Hackensack, New Jersey; a candy installation and a lithography plant in Perugia, Italy; several American subsidiary corporations; and many retail stores. Connected with the business for fifty-three years, he is chairman of the board of directors of the International Buitoni Perugia Organization in Rome. In recent years he has devoted much attention to his avocational interest in opera: he has studied operatic roles and sung as an amateur basso profundo in Carnegie Hall.

Born on November 6, 1891 in Perugia, Italy to Francesco and Maria Egiziaca (Marchettoni) Buitoni, Giovanni Buitoni represents the fourth generation of his line to have a hand in developing the family business. His great-grandmother, Giulia Buitoni, had established it in 1827 in San Sepolcro to provide a livelihood for herself and her sons in the face of her husband's illness. She pawned her wedding jewels and started to produce macaroni with a few simple implements. Her son, Giovanni (1822-1901), expanded the business and concocted Pastina Glutinata, which eventually became a very popular food. His sons, Antonio and Francesco, opened new macaroni plants in Città di Castello and Perugia, and Francesco formed S.p.a. Perugina Cioccolato & Confetture, a chocolate and confection manufacturing company, in Perugia. The present Giovanni Buitoni's brothers, Marco, Bruno, Luigi, and Giuseppe, head the San Sepolcro, Perugina, Rome, and Paris operations, respectively.

Giovanni received excellent marks at the secondary school he attended in Perugia. His extracurricular activities included fencing, swimming, horseback riding, and presiding over the Dante Alighieri Society. After his graduation in 1909 his father made him a present of a trip to Germany, where Giovanni studied the German language and observed industrial operations. While in Germany he received news of the impending failure of the Perugina chocolate company. Eighteen years old at the time, he asked his father for permission to become its general manager and try to build it up again.

The permission was granted, and with the help of the candy-manufacturing Spagnoli family, Giovanni Buitoni enlarged a staff of fifteen workers in a basement to hundreds of workers in a large factory. Meanwhile he attended the University of Perugia, which granted him a doctor of laws degree. He continued as general manager of Perugina until 1938 and was its president from 1938 to 1959. From 1927 to 1959 he also was president of the pasta concern in San Sepolcro. Under his guidance additional Buitoni pasta factories were established in Rome and Paris, as well as Stabilimento Polografico Buitoni, a lithography plant, in Perugia. Perugina chocolate retail stores, the first in Italy, were set up in major Italian cities. Buitoni was president of the Rome and Paris pasta factories and of the lithography plant from 1938 to 1959.

Buitoni became intrigued with advertising before other Italian businessmen had given it much thought. In the early 1930's he hatched an advertising stunt, the first of its kind in Italy, which caught the public imagination and continues to be popular to this day. The contest of the figurines, as it was called, required consumers to collect colorful numbered picture cards, one of which was found in each package of Buitoni and Perugina products. Those who held the most cards and those who amassed a complete set of figurines in numerical order won autos, motorcycles, phonographs, refrigerators, stoves, sewing machines, and other prizes that were desirable, particularly during the Depression. Some figurines were rarer than others and wide bartering ensued; eventually figurines were quoted like stocks and bonds on the business pages of newspapers.

In 1939 Buitoni and his wife attended the thirtieth anniversary celebration of the Hershey Chocolate Company in Pennsylvania as representatives of the Italian candy industry. While in the United States they opened a Buitoni restaurant in the Italian building at the New York World's Fair and a Perugina store on Fifth Avenue. They had already given some thought to staying in America when the entry of Italy into World War II cut them off from their native country without funds or merchandise to start afresh. Mrs. Buitoni pawned her jewels as Giulia Buitoni had once done, and she and her husband established a modest branch of the Buitoni business in Jersey City, New Jersey, followed by two

J. Abresch

GIOVANNI BUITONI

popular Buitoni restaurants on Broadway. Customers, entering the restaurant through a turnstile, got all the spaghetti they could eat for twenty-five cents from a conveyor belt counter that rolled out straight from the kitchen.

Business prospered over the years and in 1952 a modern $2,000,000 plant was built in South Hackensack, New Jersey. A plaque in its entrance hall reads: "In fond memory of my beloved and unforgettable parents who taught me the religion of God and the religion of work, I dedicate this Buitoni enterprise in the New World. Giovanni Buitoni." The South Hackensack installation manufactures the exclusive Buitoni line of enriched 20% protein spaghetti and macaroni whose starch content has been reduced; sauces, ravioli, spaghetti and meatballs, and other Italian specialties; and frozen macaroni products and grated cheeses. In 1956 Buitoni introduced frozen Italian foods to the Italian market. "It may seem like taking coals to Newcastle," he said, "but the modern housewife in Italy is as ready to find short cuts to food preparation as her American counterpart." Another innovation was the establishment of a dish-a-minute restaurant on Broadway near Times Square in 1962. Cooked frozen Italian delicacies like ravioli, egg plant parmigiana, and bavette with lobster and shrimp are sent directly from the South Hackensack plant to the restaurant. Special ray ovens then defrost them in about one minute.

The San Sepolcro factory produces macaroni, dietetic foods, biscuits, and baby foods, while the Rome plant makes macaroni products in bulk and the Paris plant supplies the French market. Perugina chocolates and confections are sold in many countries, including Italy, where there are some sixty Perugina retail stores. The lithography plant in Perugia prints all literature and packaging material for the Perugina-Buitoni complex.

(Continued next page)

BUITONI, GIOVANNI—Continued

In 1953 Buitoni founded the International Buitoni Perugina Organization to co-ordinate all operations. He is the chairman of its board of directors, and the board chairman of the Rome, San Sepolcro, and Paris plants, the printing and Perugina factories, and Buitoni Foods New England, Inc., (Boston). As president and chairman of the board of directors he heads Buitoni Foods Corporation in South Hackensack, Buitoni Delaware Valley, Inc., (Gloucester, New Jersey), Buitoni Foods West Coast, Inc., (Los Angeles), Buitoni Foods Northwest, Inc., (Oakland, California), Buitoni Foods of Florida, Inc., (Miami), Perugina Chocolates and Confections, Inc., (Mahwah, New Jersey), and Buitoni Perugina, Inc., (New York).

A man with a flair for administration, Buitoni served as mayor of Perugia from 1930 to 1935. There he is remembered for his insistence on using cement pipes in aqueducts where iron pipes, subject to rapid disintegration, had been used before. This reform is now required as standard practice by Italian law. Endowed with a fine basso voice, he has for years been interested in music, and in 1948 he began to study singing. In November 1961 he realized a dream of long standing when he hired Carnegie Hall and the services of Anselmo Colzani and Licia Albanese for an evening. With them he sang arias from *Rigoletto, Ernani,* and *Don Giovanni.* "As Don Juan," a New York *Times* (November 28, 1961) critic commented, "Mr. Buitoni made up for the lack of power in his singing with the ardor necessary in the role." A *Life* magazine (December 8, 1961) reporter wrote, "As a tribute to Verdi, pasta, and Walter Mittyism, it couldn't have been better."

Buitoni speaks English, French, and German fluently and has a sound knowledge of classical Greek and of Latin. He has often contributed to charitable organizations and has been awarded the Italian Star of Solidarity for his efforts in promoting understanding between the United States and Italy. He also holds the Unico national award and the Columbia University Casa Italiana award. He belongs to the New York Athletic Club and Tiro a Segno and is a cavaliere of Sts. Maurizio and Lazzaro and a cavaliere del Lavoro.

Giovanni Buitoni married Letizia Cairone, an opera singer, on October 22, 1936. A distinguished looking man with white hair and blue eyes, he stands six feet one inch tall and weighs 180 pounds. Besides singing, his hobbies are playing the organ, swimming, and horseback riding. In 1960 he bought twenty-nine acres of land in Paramus, New Jersey that, together with previously acquired land, gave him a forty-acre area in which to indulge in horseback riding.

References

N Y Times III p3 N 4 '51

Who's Who in Commerce and Industry (1961)

Who's Who in Italy (1958)

BURNETT, CAROL Apr. 26, 1934(?)- Comedienne; singer

Address: h. 36 Central Park South, New York 19

While still in her twenties, Carol Burnett has emerged as one of the freshest and funniest talents in show business. Miss Burnett is an exuberant redhead whose mobile face, distinctive voice, and faultless timing have brought her acclaim as a comedienne and singer. She is perhaps best known for her clowning on the *Garry Moore Show* and for her performance as a tomboy princess in a leading role in *Once Upon a Mattress,* a musical with a score composed by Mary Rodgers. Miss Burnett first attracted attention in 1957 when she sang the comic love song, "I Made a Fool of Myself Over John Foster Dulles."

Carol Burnett was born on April 26, 1934 (one source says 1935) in San Antonio, Texas, the elder daughter of Jody Burnett, a movie theater manager, and Louise (Creighton) Burnett. Her parents were constantly separating and reuniting and, in 1935, left her in Texas with her grandmother, Mrs. Mae (Nanny) White, while they moved to California. She joined them in Los Angeles in 1940. Jody Burnett died in 1954, and his wife worked as a publicity writer for a Hollywood movie studio until her death in 1958. Since 1956 Carol has taken care of her sister, Christine, who was born in 1944.

Miss Burnett attended Hollywood High School, where she was a good athlete, had many friends, and edited the school newspaper. She graduated in 1952 and received a scholarship to the University of California at Los Angeles, where she intended to major in journalism. But a course in playwriting that required the students to get acting experience changed her plans. "The night I stepped on that stage and got my first laugh," she says, "that was it. I was in heaven." She switched to the university's theater arts department, participated in several campus theater groups, and won an award for acting.

One of the groups in which Miss Burnett took part was the opera workshop. During her junior year, Dr. Jan Popper, head of the music department, asked members of the opera workshop to entertain at a party in San Diego. Carol and a young man named Don Saroyan did a scene from *Annie Get Your Gun.* Their performance so impressed one of the guests, a building contractor, that he staked them each to $1,000 to get started in show business. The conditions attached to this fairy-godfather loan stipulated that it be repaid within five years, that they use it to try to launch their careers in New York City, and that, when they became successful, they help other young people to get their first breaks in show business. They also agreed that they would never reveal their benefactor's name. (They never have, and the loan has since been repaid.)

Miss Burnett came to New York City in August 1954, soon after she completed her junior year at college. She moved into the famed Rehearsal Club, the hotel for aspiring actresses that served as the scene for the Broadway play, *Stage Door,* and she got a job checking hats three days a week at a restaurant in the Rockefeller Center area. Her tips averaged $30 a week, and since room and board at the Rehearsal Club cost only $18 a week, she had an ample $12 to spend on incidentals. Recalling her own experience, she has remarked, "The one thing I can tell them [aspiring actors] is 'Get a part-time job.' So when you go to see a producer you don't have that desperate, starved, I'm-going-to-kill-myself look." The job also left her with enough time to make the rounds of theatrical agents, who told her time and time again that they couldn't give her a job until someone else had done so first, enabling them to see her work.

This problem was not an uncommon one at the Rehearsal Club where, by now, Carol had been elected president. Under her leadership the girls solved it by chipping in money to hire a rehearsal hall, badgering writers into preparing material for them, inviting all the agents and theatrical notables they could cajole into coming, and putting on a highly successful audition show. Miss Burnett's big number was a spoof of Eartha Kitt's sexy rendition of *Monotonous*, which she did wearing an old bathrobe and curlers in her hair. As a result she acquired a leading Broadway agent, Martin Goodman, as well as her first professional jobs in summer stock and at a Chicago industrial show, where she sang the praises of aluminum foil.

Her first break into television came on Paul Winchell's children's show over NBC-TV where, for thirteen weeks, she was the girl friend of Winchell's dummies. Although she did only straight singing and no comedy, Winchell predicted at the time that she would "hit it real big one day." A stint as Buddy Hackett's girl friend on the television series *Stanley* followed, but neither she nor Hackett could rise above their mediocre material, and the program was short-lived. On November 9, 1956 Miss Burnett first appeared on Garry Moore's morning show over CBS-TV and was an immediate success. During the next three years she was often seen on Garry Moore's daytime program and was a guest performer on many other television shows, among them the *Ed Sullivan Show* over CBS-TV, the *Dinah Shore Show* over NBC-TV, and *Pantomime Quiz* over ABC-TV.

In July 1957 Miss Burnett made her first night club appearance at the Blue Angel in New York City. Her opening number, written by Ken Welch, was a spoof of teen-age adoration of rock 'n' roll singers entitled "I Made a Fool Of Myself Over John Foster Dulles." The Secretary of State's name was chosen because he was a most unlikely (and therefore potentially hilarious) object of teen-age devotion. Jack Paar asked her to perform it on the *Tonight* show over NBC-TV, and she also sang it on Ed Sullivan's program. Dulles himself was much amused by it. The song won a lot of attention for Carol Burnett, but she soon realized that she had to be careful not to become identified in the public mind as "that girl who sings that song about. . . ." In June 1959 she played a four-week return engagement at the Blue Angel.

On November 19, 1959, three years after she first appeared on his morning program, Miss Burnett became a regular performer on the

CAROL BURNETT

evening *Garry Moore Show*. In the course of a single hour she usually played five or six different comic characters, and, as Pete Martin wrote in the *Saturday Evening Post* (March 10, 1962), she was "equally convincing as a slob or a slinky glamour puss." Critics have been unanimous in praising her, and she has been called "the new first lady of television" and a performer on a par with Carole Lombard, Kay Kendall, and Bea Lillie. Miss Lillie is one of Carol Burnett's favorite comediennes, whom she has uncannily impersonated along with her other favorites: Carol Channing, Fanny Brice, Lucille Ball, and Charlie Chaplin.

In May 1959 Miss Burnett achieved one of her greatest ambitions when she opened in a leading role in *Once Upon A Mattress*, a musical comedy based on the fairy tale *The Princess and the Pea*. Playing a rowdy princess named Winnifred who preferred to be called Fred, Miss Burnett scored both a critical and a popular success and was hailed as a funny new clown of the musical theater. The musical, which opened modestly at the Phoenix Theatre off-Broadway, was still going strong when it was forced to evacuate the theater for a previously scheduled replacement. Showing the same vitality offstage as she displays in her performances, Miss Burnett led the cast in picketing for the right to continue the show's run elsewhere. Public response was so enthusiastic that *Once Upon A Mattress* was transferred first to the Alvin Theatre, then to the Winter Garden and the St. James Theatre before it closed, after 460 performances, on July 2, 1960.

During the entire run of *Once Upon a Mattress* Miss Burnett continued to appear on the *Garry Moore Show*. Although her television performances were taped, her work load was tremendous, and she reached the point of collapse. The stage remains her first love, and she has said, "I'd love to do musical comedies for the rest of my life." On February 13, 1962

BURNETT, CAROL—*Continued*

Miss Burnett announced that she would not appear on the *Garry Moore Show* as a regular performer after the close of the 1961-62 season. Her parting with Mr. Moore, whom she likes as a boss and a friend, was amicable. She expects to make many guest appearances on his program, and Moore, who thinks highly of her abilities, has said that the change was made "so she can try her wings in other fields—particularly Broadway and motion pictures."

In June 1961 Miss Burnett was chosen by *TV Guide* as the favorite female performer on television. She performed on a radio show over WCBS with Richard Hayes in September 1961, and she appeared with Harpo Marx in *The Wonderful World of Toys*, a DuPont Show of the Week, over NBC-TV, in November 1961. She has also starred in one of Rod Serling's *Twilight Zone* plays over CBS-TV. In March 1962 she and Julie Andrews taped a television special entitled *Julie and Carol at Carnegie Hall*. Although she has appeared as a guest on several television shows, she rejects the idea of a series of her own. ("Yich!" was her comment when such a series was proposed.) She has been booked to appear for six weeks at the elegant Persian Room of New York's Plaza Hotel starting in October 1962.

Although she has been called a clown and a comic, Miss Burnett considers herself a comedienne—that is, an actress who takes on funny roles. She always keeps in mind a remark that Ed Wynn once made to her: "Some people say funny things—but a true comedian says things funny." She does, however, say funny things too, such as her characteristic explanation of why she left California: "To succeed in the movies, you have to look like Marilyn Monroe or Tony Curtis. Unfortunately, I look more like Tony Curtis."

A slim, willowy redhead with hazel eyes, Miss Burnett is five feet seven inches tall and weighs 120 pounds. She was married in 1955 to Don Saroyan, the man who performed opposite her in the sketch from *Annie Get Your Gun*. They separated in 1959. Miss Burnett is an Episcopalian. She enjoys water-skiing, cartooning, and going to the theater, and she has two pet Yorkshire terriers, Bruce, a female, and Fang, a male.

Asked by Pete Martin why topflight comediennes are so scarce, Carol Burnett replied: "Most women are obsessed with an outmoded sense of modesty. They labor under the necessity of being ladylike. They are afraid that being funny is unfeminine. Most men seem to have the same idea about comediennes. They laugh at us, but they're wary of us as women. . . . In my own case, however, I'm never onstage in my private life. Actually I freeze when I go to a party and strangers say, 'Make us laugh!' My idea is to be funny when I'm supposed to be and shut up when I'm supposed to shut up."

References

N Y Post p90 Ap 25 '61 por
N Y Times II p15 Mr 6 '60
N Y World Telegram p6 Ap 2 '60
Sat Eve Post 235:36+ Mr 10 '62

COOKE, LESLIE E(DWARD) May 22, 1908-
World religious organization leader; clergyman

Address b. World Council of Churches, 17 route de Malagnou, Geneva, Switzerland; h. 29 route de Malagnou, Geneva, Switzerland

By holding its third assembly in New Delhi, India in December 1961, the World Council of Churches took an important step toward its ecumenical goal. The failure of the contemporary Christian church to achieve universality, the Reverend Dr. Leslie E. Cooke, the council's associate general secretary, believes, is due to its predominantly Western character and to its racial and social segregation. Cooke, a minister of the Congregational Union of England and Wales, which he formerly headed as general secretary, has been both associate general secretary of the World Council of Churches and director of its division of interchurch aid and service to refugees since 1955. The council, established in 1938, a year before the outbreak of World War II, has since had the Reverend Dr. Willem A. Visser 'T Hooft as its chief executive officer.

Leslie Edward Cooke was born in Brighton, England on May 22, 1908, one of two sons of Robert James Cooke, a factory foreman, and Emily Daisy (Allfrey) Cooke. His brother, Robert Henry Lewis Cooke, is a director of a London company. Leslie Cooke received his preparatory education at Varndean Secondary School in Brighton, graduating in 1927. For his theological training he attended a Congregational college, the Lancashire Independent College of Victoria University of Manchester, and was awarded the B.A. degree in 1930 and the B.D. degree in 1933. Following his graduation he was ordained to the Congregational ministry on July 10, 1933, and for the next five years he was pastor of Gatley Congregational Church in Cheshire, England. He moved to Coventry in 1938 to become pastor of Warwick Road Congregational Church, and he remained at this church until 1948.

The period of his ministry in Coventry included what could be described as that city's "darkest days," for it was one of the main targets of the heavy bombing raids on England during World War II. From 1939 to 1943 Dr. Cooke served as a volunteer member of the Coventry unit of the Royal Observer Corps. After the war he was associated with the planning of the new cathedral and Christian center, which replaced bomb-damaged buildings.

Cooke's service to his denomination on the national level began in 1948 when he became general secretary of the Congregational Union of England and Wales. In this position he was chief executive officer of an organization responsible for the administration of 3,250 churches. He represented the union on the Chaplaincy Advisory Boards to the British Forces and in 1951 toured troops stationed in Europe, traveling from Trieste to Hamburg. He took an important part, too, in the work of the British Council of Churches.

Also in 1948 Cooke began his work in behalf of the ecumenical movement as a delegate to the first assembly of the World Council of Churches, in Amsterdam, a meeting that was attended by church leaders representing 147 churches in forty-four countries. The World Council of Churches was established at a meeting in Utrecht, the Netherlands in 1938 as a "fellowship of Churches." During World War II it did its utmost to maintain contact between church leaders in friendly and enemy countries. At the present time the council, which has headquarters in Geneva, Switzerland, is composed of 198 Anglican, Orthodox, and Protestant denominational bodies. Over thirty major United States churches with a total membership of more than 30,000,000 members participate in the work of the council.

The first assembly of the World Council dealt with the theme "Man's Disorder and God's Design." The theme of the second meeting, at Evanston, Illinois in 1954, was "Christ, the Hope of the World." In the period between these two assemblies, Cooke, who attended both, served on several of the World Council's committees, notably the executive, finance, and central committees. He was also a member of the building committee that supervised the remodeling of the council's Ecumenical Institute at Bossey, Switzerland, established in 1946.

For about seven years Cooke had been helping to forward the development and purposes of the World Council of Churches while filling also the position of general secretary of the Congregational Union of England and Wales. In the summer of 1955 he resigned from his executive post in the Congregational Union to become associate general secretary of the World Council of Churches. He was also appointed director of the council's division of interchurch aid and service to refugees, one of the three divisions through which the council carries out its work. The other divisions are those for studies and for ecumenical action. The present structure of the council was set up at the 1954 assembly as a result of the recommendations of the committee on structure and functions, of which Cooke was chairman.

As director of the interchurch aid and service to refugees division of the World Council of Churches, Dr. Cooke heads a relief and resettlement program that operates in forty-five countries. This division is the successor to the department of reconstruction and interchurch aid, which was established during World War II to bring help to an estimated 15,000,000 displaced persons in Central Europe. In 1958 the division had a temporary field staff of 500 working with 150,000 refugees, providing food, clothing, medical care, and other assistance. The division also played a leading role in World Refugee Year (1959-60) and has been credited with the resettlement of over 200,000 refugees since 1945.

The third assembly of the World Council, held in 1961 in New Delhi, had the theme of "Jesus Christ, the Light of the World." There were three significant achievements at the New Delhi assembly. The first of these was the merging of the International Missionary Council with the World Council of Churches. The second was the enrollment of new member churches from African countries, Chile, Poland, Rumania, Bulgaria, and the Soviet Union. The final important innovation of the New Delhi assembly was

LESLIE E. COOKE

the attendance of Roman Catholic observers for the first time at a council assembly. This development was followed by an announcement in December 1961 that Pope John XXIII had invited denominations other than Roman Catholic to attend the Ecumenical Conference to be held in 1962, only the fifth such conference since 1500.

In great demand as a speaker, Dr. Cooke preached the Cambridge University sermon in 1953, the following year spoke at the General Council of the United Church of Canada in Sackville, Brunswick, and in 1959 gave the Fondren Lectures at Southern Methodist University, Dallas, Texas. He is a member of the central religious advisory committee of the British Broadcasting Corporation and has given many talks over that network. In 1955 he conducted the BBC's Easter religious broadcasts.

After the Interchurch Center in New York was dedicated on May 29, 1960, Dr. Cooke was invited to speak at the dedication dinner held on June 1 to mark the opening of the first national headquarters building for Protestant and Orthodox churches in the United States. Speaking on the role of national councils of churches he proved to be a realistic as well as inspiring speaker, for he told those present "Personally, I do not see Christian unity of whatever form coming on a world scale in the first place. I do not see it coming through the drawing together even of world confessional bodies. The actual practical steps must be taken among the churches of a nation."

In addition to being a gifted speaker, Dr. Cooke is known as a writer, and his books have included *Upon This Rock* (Independent Press, 1937), *Token of Our Inheritance* (Independent Press, 1943), *Faith Stakes a Claim* (Independent Press, 1943), and *The Church is There* (Seabury Press, 1957). From 1946 to 1948 he was associate editor of the *Congregational Quarterly*, and articles by him appeared in that magazine as well

COOKE, LESLIE E.—*Continued*

as in such others as *Ecumenical Review* and *Holborn Review*.

A world traveler, Dr. Cooke first visited the United States in 1944 when he made a sixteen-week tour of the country under the sponsorship of the British Ministry of Information. He has also traveled in Asia, Australia, and New Zealand. He attended the first assembly of the East Asia Christian Conference, which was held in Kuala Lumpur, Malaya in 1959.

Leslie E. Cooke married Gladys Evelyn Burrows on July 4, 1936; they have no children. Six feet tall, he weighs 220 pounds, and he has brown eyes and gray-black hair. His hobbies are the theater, motoring, and golf. He belongs to the Athenæum Club in London. In 1949 an honorary D.D. degree was conferred on him by Chicago Theological Seminary, and the following year he received the same degree from Emmanuel College of Victoria University, Toronto. He was awarded an honorary LL.D. degree from Mount Allison University, New Brunswick in 1954.

In his many pleas for Christian unity, Dr. Cooke has appealed many times to his hearers to listen to the voice of the Gospel. He regards the failure of the Christian church to attain true unity as its "great tragedy." "The voice of enlightened Christianity, the Galilean accent," he has said, "is the only one in which the Christian gospel may be truly proclaimed and it is the only one to which men at last will listen."

References

Who's Who, 1962
Who's Who in America, 1962-63

DAVIS, MILES (DEWEY, JR.) May 25, 1926- Trumpet and fluegelhorn player; jazz composer and conductor

Address: h. 881 10th Ave., New York 19

Like all creative fields, American jazz has evolved through the years, from the field hollers that led into blues, through the New Orleans, Kansas City, and Chicago schools into swing and bebop and from these, into the sophisticated and cerebral "cool" or "progressive" jazz that dominates the jazz world today. At the forefront of this world stands Miles Davis, trumpet and fluegelhorn player, jazz composer, and band leader. The melancholy, introspective, and somewhat soulful cast of Miles Davis' music making has given a new dimension to jazz, captured a large audience among younger intellectuals, and has influenced the youngest generation of jazz musicians.

Unlike many American jazz musicians, Miles Dewey Davis, Jr., was born in prosperous circumstances in Alton, Illinois on May 25, 1926. His father was a prominent dentist, dental surgeon, animal breeder, and real estate owner; his grandfather had owned 1,000 acres of land in Arkansas. Miles Davis' grandmother used to teach organ and his mother plays the violin and piano. In 1927 the Davis family moved to East St. Louis, Illinois, across the river from St. Louis. Miles's father gave the boy his first trumpet on his thirteenth birthday (although his mother had

wanted to give him a violin) and Miles Davis was soon playing in his high school band. By 1941 he was studying in East St. Louis with Eddie Randall, who once worked with Bobby Hackett and with Hal Baker. Davis soon discovered that, unlike Dizzy Gillespie, he could not play in the very high range and that he was much more at home in the middle register. About this time Dizzy Gillespie himself and Charlie (Yardbird) Parker passed through town with Billy Eckstine's band, and for three weeks Miles Davis substituted for Eckstine's third trumpet man, who was sick. At sixteen he was playing with Randolph's Blue Devils, a local combo. Davis' first idol was Roy Eldridge, who was later supplanted by such heroes as Gillespie, Parker, and Clark Terry, a trumpet and fluegelhorn player who lived in the St. Louis area.

When Miles Davis graduated from high school his mother wanted to send him on to Fisk University because she had heard of its strong music department and its famed Jubilee Singers, but Miles, who was tempted by the jazz opportunities in New York City, obtained his father's permission to go to the Juilliard School of Music. He moved in with Charlie Parker and studied harmony and theory at Juilliard. Taking the advice of Dizzy Gillespie, he also studied piano so that he could master variations in chording. Soon Davis was sitting in on jazz sessions in the night clubs on West 52d Street—a thoroughfare not yet given over to the ecdysiasts—where he learned how to play by listening to Charlie Parker, absorbing the influences of Parker, Gillespie, and Coleman Hawkins into his own style: fast, light, with no vibrato. Realizing that a symphony orchestra was obviously not to be his ultimate destination, he left Juilliard for West 52d Street.

A tour with the Benny Carter band led Miles Davis to a job with Billy Eckstine that lasted for five months on the road during 1946-47. Returning to New York City in 1948, he organized his own group, the Capitol band, so called because of the series of recordings that it made for Capitol Records. It was a nine-man combination that played arrangements by Gil Evans, the former arranger for Claude Thornhill, although Davis himself wrote much of his own material. Gerry Mulligan was on baritone saxophone, Kai Winding on trombone, Lee Konitz on alto saxophone, Johnny Carisi on trumpet, John Lewis on piano, and Max Roach on drums. Although listeners conceded that the Capitol band had a new and exciting sound, including a French horn and a tuba, the group was able to get only one two-week engagement at the Royal Roost in Times Square and a one-week booking at the Clique Club. If Davis had little commercial success, with this combination he had, however, achieved what he had long been looking for: a lighter sound in jazz.

But the group could not continue without bookings or live on the appreciation they received from a few connoisseurs of jazz. Continuing to play with small combos, Davis appeared at the Paris Jazz Festival in May 1949 and then returned to New York City, where he made eight records with his group of nine musicians for the Capitol label. Now available on a

Capitol long-playing album called *Birth of the Cool*, these records of 1949 and 1950 vintage made jazz history and, by ushering in the age of "cool" jazz, set the stage for the "chamber" jazz of small ensembles that was to follow.

In the early 1950's Davis worked only irregularly. In 1950 and 1951 he appeared in the small jazz clubs of New York; in 1952 he toured with a group that included Zoot Sims, the saxophonist, and Milt Jackson, the vibraharpist, pianist, and guitarist. According to Nat Hentoff in *The Jazz Life* (Doubleday, 1961), the early 1950's was a trying period for Davis, when he scrutinized himself closely, tried to find new bearings, and to lay the foundations for a new career. Out of that period of self doubt, self hatred, and self confrontation came the crystallization of the Miles Davis style. After hovering in the background of the New York jazz scene for several years, he finally came into his own at the Newport Jazz Festival of 1955.

In Gil Evans, Miles Davis had found the arranger to provide him with the right framework for his distinctive sound. "Every artist has to have the right setting," Evans has said. "Miles knew before I did that I could supply it for him." Evans had admired Davis' work for over ten years, having heard it first in a night club on West 52d Street. Using Evans' arrangements, Davis began to record for Columbia Records. By 1957 he had turned out both *Porgy and Bess* and *Miles Ahead*, which Ralph Gleason in the San Francisco *Chronicle* (November 17, 1957) called "one of the most fascinating big band LPs to come along in quite some time." Gleason noted that Davis had drawn a warm and full sound from the usually blatant fluegelhorn (a brass wind instrument with a cupped mouthpiece, somewhat like the saxhorn). John S. Wilson of the New York *Herald Tribune*, who by no means had been an idolater of Davis, wrote of his Columbia record *Music for Brass* (June 2, 1957): "Mr. Davis' playing is especially noteworthy—well-formed, clean-edged and deeply imbued with jazz feeling in contrast to the fuzzy tone and hesitant presentation he normally affects."

After undergoing an operation during the summer of 1957, Davis reorganized his quintet—which he at times expanded into a sextet. He divided his time between the jazz festivals of the East Coast and the comparative calm of the Café Bohemia in New York, a room that he much preferred to the riotous festivals. On November 22, 1957 the Miles Davis Quintet appeared in its first concert at Carnegie Hall as part of a program that included the Gerry Mulligan Quartet, Chico Hamilton and his group, Helen Merrill, and Lionel Hampton. Reviewers noticed that the tricks and the oddities with which Miles Davis had experimented in his search for his own jazz idiom had vanished, leaving behind the pure, new sound.

In 1958 Miles Davis was in Paris, writing background music for a film called *L'Ascenseur Pour l'Échafaud* (*Elevator to the Gallows*), the sound track of which was later released in the United States, as an LP called *Jazz Track*. In the late summer of 1959 he played a concert on Randall's Island in New York, using Cannonball Adderley on the saxophone, John Coltrane on the

MILES DAVIS

tenor saxophone, Jimmy Cobb on drums, and Paul Chambers on bass. They played their jazzed up ballads with the teamwork and intimacy of a chamber group.

In Europe in 1960, Davis appeared in movie houses in London and went on tour in France and Sweden. Wherever he performed he befuddled audiences by his detachment and his refusal to acknowledge applause. Returning to the United States, he appeared over CBS-TV in a filmed half-hour show, *The Sound of Miles Davis*, for which he received enthusiastic reviews. On May 19, 1961 he reappeared at Carnegie Hall with the Miles Davis Quintet in a program conducted by Gil Evans. After hearing a rehearsal of the program, George T. Simon of the New York *Herald Tribune* (May 14, 1961) predicted that a "round sound" would emanate from the Miles Davis Quintet at Carnegie Hall—a sound that he described as "the warm tone and the soft attack Miles gets on trumpet and flugel horn." The critics liked what they heard and Davis became even more deeply entrenched in the affections of the young intellectuals who constitute a large part of his audience. Since the spring of 1961 Davis and his group have appeared at the Village Vanguard in New York and have continued a series of recording sessions.

Among the outstanding albums that Davis has produced for Columbia Records are *Milestones; Round About Midnight; Sarah Vaughan; Sketches of Spain; Miles Davis in Person;* and *Someday My Prince Will Come.* For Prestige Records he has recorded, among other items, *Musings of Miles; Miles; Blue Haze; Cookin'; Walkin'; Relaxin'; Workin'; Miles and Horns; Miles and Milt;* and *Conception.* In addition to his historic *Birth of the Cool* for Capitol Records, Davis has recorded volume 4 of Capitol's *History of Jazz,* with the Metronome All Stars. In conjunction with Charlie Parker he recorded for Savoy, Dial, and Verve.

(Continued next page)

DAVIS, MILES—*Continued*

Miles Davis received the New Star Award of *Esquire* magazine in 1947. In the *Metronome* polls of 1951-53 he was tied with Dizzy Gillespie. In 1958 he took first place in *Down Beat's* Readers' and Critics' Poll and was adjudged the Outstanding Jazz Personality of the Year. In 1959, at the Newport Jazz Festival, he won first place in trumpet, second in combo in *Down Beat's* International Jazz Critics' Poll. His recording of *Miles Ahead* was awarded France's L'Oscar du Disque de l'Académie du Jazz.

In spite of his international fame, Davis remains something of an enigma—a musician who seldom grants interviews and who almost never appears as a guest on radio or television programs. He is married to a former dancer, and has a girl and two boys by an earlier marriage. Reserved, intense, and moody, he makes no concessions to his audiences. He neither speaks to them, nor looks at them, and most of the time he seems unaware of their existence—a fact of which they are painfully reminded when he turns his back or walks off the stand between choruses. As he plays he keeps his short, slightly hunched, and thin body motionless, pointing the bell of his horn straight at the floor. For slow numbers he uses a mute on his trumpet, removing it for pieces with moderate and fast tempos. Davis makes a policy of never listening to his own recordings.

The delicate facial features of Miles Davis are somewhat misleading. According to Nat Hentoff, he is a skilled boxer and devotee of physical culture who works out regularly in gyms both at home and on the road. A musician who plays more for his own pleasure than for profit, he turns down bookings when it pleases him to do so—a predilection increasingly encouraged by his solvency. He invests in the stock market and in real estate and owns a brownstone building in New York's West Seventies. Davis is a connoisseur of costly sports cars and drives a Ferrari. "That's all there is to life," he once told Stanley Goldstein in an interview for *Playboy* magazine (August 1960). "You work at what you do best and if the time comes when people don't like it, you do something else." In 1962 that time appeared remote indeed.

References

Playboy Ag '60

Charters, Samuel B. and Kunstadt, Leonard. Jazz; A History of the New York Scene (1962)

Feather, Leonard. Encyclopedia of Jazz (1960)

Hentoff, Nat. The Jazz Life (1961)

EDDY, MANTON S(PRAGUE) May 16, 1892-Apr. 10, 1962 United States Army officer; headed the Ninth Infantry Division in North Africa and Europe during World War II; commanded the reactivated Seventh Army in Germany after the war; retired in the rank of lieutenant general in 1953. See *Current Biography* (February) 1951.

Obituary

N Y Times p43 Ap 11 '62

FLEMING, SAM(UEL) M. Apr. 29, 1908- Banker; organization official

Address: b. Third National Bank, Nashville, Tenn.; h. Chickering Rd., Nashville, Tenn.

Sam M. Fleming, the president of the American Bankers Association for 1961-62, is an outspoken proponent of tax equality for commercial banks, which, he feels, are at a distinct disadvantage in their competition with savings and loan associations and other tax-favored institutions. President of the Third National Bank at Nashville, Tennessee, since 1950, and vice-president of the American Bankers Association in 1960-61, Fleming was elected to succeed Carl A. Bimson of Arizona as president of the A.B.A. at the Association's eighty-seventh annual convention in San Francisco on October 17, 1961. Representing more than 96 percent of the banks in the United States, the association had in 1961 a total membership of 17,536 banks and branches including 131 in foreign countries.

Samuel M. Fleming was born in Franklin, Tennessee on April 29, 1908, to Samuel M. and Cynthia Graham (Cannon) Fleming. His great-great-grandfather on his mother's side was Newton Cannon, who twice served as Governor of Tennessee. His father was a director of the Harpeth National Bank at Franklin, and Sam Fleming likes to recall that he began his banking career as an eight-year-old runner for the Harpeth National Bank. Fleming attended Battle Ground Academy, a boys' preparatory school at Franklin, from 1919 to 1924, and received his B.A. degree from Vanderbilt University at Nashville in 1928. At Vanderbilt Fleming joined Sigma Alpha Epsilon fraternity. He also managed the track team and served on his dormitory's board of managers.

For three years after graduation from college Fleming was employed by the New York Trust Company in New York City as assistant credit manager. Returning to Tennessee in 1931 he was made manager of the credit department of the Third National Bank at Nashville. In 1936 he was appointed assistant vice-president, and in 1941 he became vice-president. In 1942 he joined the United States Naval Reserve for World War II service. Three years later he was discharged with the rank of lieutenant-commander. In 1947 he became executive vice-president of the Third National Bank in Nashville, a director in 1949, and its president in 1950.

The efforts of the Third National Bank to stimulate business in Nashville received a new impetus when Fleming became its president. Under his guidance a trust solicitation program was begun and a business development department was established, which now calls on about 6,000 businessmen a year. The consumer finance department of the Third National Bank operates in thirty Tennessee counties, and its small-business investment company, the first to be licensed in the state under the Small Business Investment Act, has granted sixteen loans totaling more than $400,000. The 360 correspondents in the bank's trading area are said to account for approximately 20 percent of its deposits. The Third National Bank of Nashville now ranks among the 120 leading banks in the United States.

Founded in 1875 at Saratoga Springs, New York, the American Bankers Association is an organization to promote the usefulness of banks. Over the years it has kept pace in meeting the ever-changing needs of banking. The working groups of the A.B.A. include a national bank division, a state bank division, a savings division, and a trust division, as well as twenty-three standing committees dealing with various phases of banking, a state association section, and the American Institute of Banking section. The American Institute of Banking, the educational section of the A.B.A., is the largest institution of its type in the world. It offers courses in 545 communities throughout the United States, and had a membership of 173,253 in 1960-61, including 91,706 enrollments in its classes. Other educational projects of the A.B.A. are the Stonier Graduate School of Banking and the National Trust School.

Fleming served the national bank division of the American Bankers Association as vice-president, executive committee chairman, chairman of the research and operations committee, and as a member of the real estate loans committee. In 1956-57 he was president of the national bank division and in this capacity he appeared as a witness before the United States Senate banking subcommittee early in 1957, at which time he urged that bank supervisory agencies be given sole control over bank mergers. Fleming also served, for three years, as a director of the Nashville branch of the Federal Reserve Bank of Atlanta. He was a director of the Association of Reserve City Bankers from 1957 to 1960 and chairman of its federal relationships committee in 1959-60. He is active in the Tennessee Bankers Association and is a life member of Robert Morris Associates. His other business associations include membership on the boards of directors of the Louisville and Nashville Railroad, the Bucyrus-Erie Company, the Flagg-Utica Corporation, the American Pencil Company, the Venus Pen and Pencil Company, and other corporations.

After his election to the vice-presidency of the American Bankers Association at its eighty-sixth annual convention in New York City on September 20, 1960, Fleming worked closely with association president Carl A. Bimson. Fleming traveled some 70,000 miles in preparation for his presidential responsibilities, addressing fifteen state associations and national bank associations and local groups. In September 1961 he represented the A.B.A. at the annual meeting of the International Monetary Fund in Vienna. He has also served on the association's centennial commission, which is planning to observe the 100th anniversary of the national banking system in 1963.

In his speeches Fleming has called for teamwork between government, labor, and industry, for a stable economy, and for a high standard of ethics in banking. He has demanded federal legislation that would ease tax restrictions on commercial banks, thus enabling them to compete with rival institutions on more even terms. Addressing the Tennessee Bankers Association in May 1961 Fleming suggested that the problem of

SAM M. FLEMING

technological unemployment might be mitigated if banks financed new programs of education and training for unskilled marginal workers. He also observed that if the United States is to compete on the world market "inflationary policies such as budget deficits, wage advances beyond the increase of productivity, and imprudent fiscal policies can no longer be countenanced."

At the eighty-seventh annual convention of the American Bankers Association in San Francisco on October 17, 1961 Sam Fleming was elected president of the association for a one-year term ending October 1962. In his acceptance speech he touched upon the problems and opportunities that face banking and concluded: "I am resolved to do my utmost to furnish the type of leadership which you have every right to expect of me; and with your help, I am confident that many of our problems can be resolved and that our industry will go forward with assurance to new and higher plateaus."

Addressing a panel of the White House regional conference at Nashville on November 10, 1961, Fleming asserted that economic growth was being slowed down by the widely held belief that the Kennedy administration had an anti-business attitude. He noted that this was indicated by the administration's failure to restrain organized labor and to limit wage increases to the level of increased productivity. He also called for a revision of the tax structure to shift the tax burden from personal income and to tie taxes more closely to the consumption of goods, and he criticized the increase of "tax sheltered organizations" that compete with private enterprise. In a speech before the national savings conference of the American Bankers Association in New York City on March 5, 1962 Fleming called for a reappraisal on the part of commercial banks to see what they could do to regain leadership in the savings field. He maintained that "commercial banks are the safest depository for savings because of their diversified loan and invest-

FLEMING, SAM M.—*Continued*

ment portfolio, their capital and reserves and . . . their deposit insurance program." His statements were subsequently challenged by spokesmen for savings banks who contend that a claim of safety must rest solely on deposit insurance.

Long active in civic and community affairs in Tennessee, Fleming is a trustee of Battle Ground Academy, Vanderbilt University, Meharry Medical College, Ensworth School, and Harpeth Hall School. He is a past president of the Vanderbilt Alumni Association and of the Navy League of Tennessee. His interests include the Boy Scout movement, Youth, Inc., and Junior achievement programs. He is treasurer of the Tennessee Historical Society and a member of the Tennessee Civil War Centennial Commission, the Sons of the American Revolution, and the Newcomen Society. He serves as a director of the Nathan Crockett Foundation, as a chairman of the Junior League advisory board, and as an elder of the First Presbyterian Church of Nashville. His club memberships include the Belle Meade Country Club (Nashville), the Augusta (Georgia) National Golf Club, and the Links and University clubs of New York City.

On December 30, 1930 Sam M. Fleming married Josephine Cliffe of Franklin, a descendant of veterans of the Revolutionary War and the Civil War. The Flemings have two children, Joanne Cliffe and Daniel Milton, and they spend their leisure time on their large farm near Franklin, where they raise tobacco, grain, and cattle. Fleming plays golf and bridge with his wife and likes to go fishing with his son. He is an ardent collector of books on the Civil War and on the history of Tennessee.

References

Banking 54:38+ N '61 pors
N Y Times p63 O 18 '61 por
Who's Who in America, 1962-63
Who's Who in Commerce and Industry (1961)
Who's Who in the South and Southwest (1959)

GLENN, JOHN H(ERSCHEL), JR. July 18, 1921- Astronaut

Address: b. National Aeronautics and Space Administration, Washington 25, D.C.; h. 3683 N. Harrison St., Arlington, Va.

The pilot of America's first earth-girdling spacecraft is Lieutenant Colonel John H. Glenn, Jr., who rode the capsule *Friendship* 7 through three orbits (about 81,000 miles) on February 20, 1962. His flight represented the consummation of tremendous financial and emotional investments; it elevated the low spirits of Americans who had been questioning their nation's lead in world affairs ever since Russians Yuri Gagarin and Gherman Titov made the world's first orbital flights in 1961.

The Glenn shot was part of the Project Mercury program of the National Aeronautics and Space Administration. The oldest of the seven American astronauts at the age of forty, Glenn is the only United States Marine among them.

An aviator for twenty years, he flew missions in World War II and the Korean conflict, and has been a test pilot since 1954. In July 1957 he broke previous speed records for transcontinental jet travel by making the first supersonic (at 35,000 feet) crossing from Los Angeles to New York City.

John Herschel Glenn, Jr., was born in Cambridge, Ohio on July 18, 1921 to Clara Glenn and John Herschel Glenn, a railroad conductor and owner of plumbing and auto businesses before his retirement. The boy and his sister, Jean (now Mrs. Jean Pinkston), were raised in New Concord, Ohio, a predominantly Presbyterian town of some 2,000 people. John, Jr., led a busy life during his teens. An honor student in high school, he won letters in football, basketball, and tennis, was junior class president, and took the lead in the senior class play, *Fanny and the Servant Problem.* In his spare time he played the trumpet, sang in the church choir, cleaned cars for pocket money, and worked as a lifeguard at a summer camp.

Deeply but not ostentatiously religious as an adult, Glenn took ethical dicta seriously even as a boy. A childhood acquaintance, now the Reverend C. Edwin Houk, recalls that he and Glenn, as members of a group called the Ohio Rangers, had vowed never to use profanity. "One evening," Houk remembers, as related in *Time* (March 2, 1962), "the group started singing *Hail, Hail, the Gang's All Here.* I continued with the phrase, 'What the hell do we care.' Well, I can tell you, it didn't sit well with Johnny. He came up to me, white-faced and righteous, and told me to stop. I think he was ready to knock my block off."

Graduating from high school in 1939, Glenn enrolled at Muskingum College in New Concord, where he maintained a "B" average and played on the football team. After learning to fly in a Navy program for civilians at New Philadelphia, Ohio, he joined the Naval Aviation Cadet Program in March 1942 and received preflight training at the University of Iowa. On completing flight school at the Naval Air Training Center in Corpus Christi, Texas, he took an option to join the Marine Corps and became a second lieutenant in the Marine Corps Reserve and a naval aviator on March 31, 1943. Glenn was promoted to the rank of first lieutenant in October 1943.

In February 1944 he was shipped to the Pacific theater of war, where he joined Marine Fighter Squadron 155, 4th Marine Aircraft Wing. Flying fifty-nine missions with F4U fighters in the Marshall Islands campaign, he earned two Distinguished Flying Crosses and ten Air Medals. From February 1945 to March 1946, when he was integrated in the regular Marine Corps, Glenn served with the 9th Marine Aircraft Wing at the Marine Corps Air Station in Cherry Point, North Carolina and the Naval Air Station at Patuxent River, Maryland. He became a captain in July 1945. For nine months, until December 1946, he was based at the Marine Corps Air Station in El Toro, California.

Sent overseas again in 1947, Glenn spent two years on North China patrol and in Guam as a pilot with Marine Fighter Squadron 218, 1st

Marine Aircraft Wing. From January 1949 to June 1951 he was a flight instructor at Corpus Christi. Transferred to Quantico, Virginia in July 1951, he attended the Amphibious Warfare School and served as an assistant G-2/G-3. In July 1952 he was promoted to major. After completing the jet refresher course at Cherry Point, he was assigned to duty in Korea. Attached to Marine Fighter Squadron 311 and, as an exchange pilot, to the 25th Fighter Squadron of the Fifth United States Air Force, Glenn flew ninety missions between February and September 1953. During the last nine days of the fighting, he flew F-86 Sabrejets along the Yalu River and managed to destroy three enemy MIGs. While in Korea, Glenn won his third and fourth Distinguished Flying Crosses and eight more Air Medals.

Glenn completed a course at the Navy Test Pilot Training School in Patuxent River in July 1954. Subsequently he was project officer on a number of aircraft at the Naval Air Test Center, Patuxent River and, beginning in November 1956, a project officer with the Fighter Design Branch, Bureau of Aeronautics, Navy Department in Washington, D.C. On July 16, 1957 Glenn made the first nonstop supersonic transcontinental flight in an F8U-1 Crusader, setting a speed record with a flying time from Los Angeles to Floyd Bennett Field in New York City of 3 hours, 23 minutes, 8.4 seconds. He did not exceed the speed of the earth's rotation and the speed of sound at sea level (760 miles an hour) as he had hoped, because he averaged only about 726 miles an hour. His flight was considered supersonic, however, because at his average altitude of 35,000 feet the speed of sound is only about 660 miles an hour. For this feat Glenn received his fifth Distinguished Flying Cross.

On April 1, 1959 Glenn became a lieutenant colonel. Eight days later he was one of seven volunteers, chosen from a group of 110 Air Force, Navy, and Marine test pilots, to be named an astronaut with the National Aeronautic and Space Administration's Project Mercury man-in-space program. The others are Malcolm S. Carpenter, Walter M. Schirra, Jr., and Alan B. Shepard, Jr., of the Navy and Leroy G. Cooper, Jr., Virgil I. Grissom, and Donald K. Slayton of the Air Force.

Starting in May 1959 the seven underwent extensive training, designed to prepare them for every conceivable aspect of space flight, at Langley Research Center, Hampton, Virginia and at the Missile Test Center, Cape Canaveral, Florida. They were given exhaustive physical and psychological tests. They studied astronomy, astronautics, astrophysics, meteorology, geography, and aviation biology, and they practised desert and water survival. In simulation machines, they were exposed to high heat, strong forces of gravity, and the sensation of weightlessness—conditions they would experience in actual space flight. Moreover, each astronaut specialized in a particular aspect of the program. Glenn was responsible for the layout of the cockpit, controls, and instrumentation, and he contributed substantially to their design, suggesting (among other things) an auxiliary power system that

Wide World

JOHN H. GLENN, JR.

was adopted by the manufacturers of the space capsule.

Under a rigorous personal schedule, Glenn ran two miles every day and dieted to bring his weight down from 195 to 168 pounds. He gave over his evenings to the study of books, charts, and maps. To concentrate on his work, he lived in bachelor quarters during the week and visited his family in Arlington, Virginia only on weekends. (He kept a diary on tape, however, and played it back at home to share his daily experiences with them.)

Although he was disappointed when Alan B. Shepard, Jr., and Virgil I. Grissom were chosen to make the first American suborbital flights on May 5, 1961 and July 21, 1961, respectively, Glenn patiently awaited his turn. On November 29, 1961 he was named as the astronaut who would make the first United States orbital space flight. His patience was even more tried when this flight, originally scheduled for December 20, 1961, was postponed ten times over a period of two months because of technical difficulties or unsuitable weather conditions. Once, on January 27, 1962, Glenn lay in his capsule atop the Atlas missile for more than five hours, waiting for the lift-off.

Meanwhile the atmosphere around the country and at Cocoa Beach, Florida, where television crews jostled one another for the best shooting positions, alternated between tense expectancy and gloom. The tension became so palpable that many observers wondered whether Glenn would not be adversely affected by his wait. The astronaut filled in the time by studying, practising in the simulation trainers, and improving his ability to hand-control the capsule, a skill that later proved useful. He urged his fellow-Americans to stay as calm as himself. "This mission has been in preparation for a long time," Glenn said. "I'm so happy to have been chosen to be the pilot for this mission that I'm not

GLENN, JOHN H., JR.—*Continued*

about to get panicky over these delays. I learned early in the flight-test business that you have to control your emotions—you don't let these things throw you or affect your ability to perform the mission."

Glenn's capsule, *Friendship 7*, was boosted aloft by the Atlas-D rocket at 9:47 A.M. (Eastern Standard Time) on February 20, 1962. (He chose the ship's name, the 7 denoting the number of astronauts, as on Shepard's *Freedom 7* and Grissom's *Liberty Bell* 7.) Glenn had arisen at 2:20 A.M. that morning and had been closed into the spacecraft at 6:59 A.M. His three-orbit trip, during which he passed over Africa, Australia, and Hawaii, lasted four hours and fifty-six minutes and covered about 81,000 miles at altitudes between ninety-nine and 162 miles. It ended at 2:43 P.M. when the capsule splashed into the Atlantic just north of Puerto Rico. *Friendship 7* was recovered by the destroyer *Noa*, and Glenn was helped out of the craft at about 3:24 P.M.

He had encountered two difficulties during the flight: improper functioning of the hydrogen peroxide jets that govern the balance of the capsule in space and a faulty mechanism that erroneously signaled detachment of the heat shield that protects the capsule during re-entry. Glenn himself took over manual control of the hydrogen jets, a move that made it possible for the *Friendship 7* to complete its scheduled three orbits instead of two and that indicated the possibility of replacing several automatic controls by human direction in the future. The apparent heat shield problem was countered by ground control officials, who ordered retention of the retro-rocket pack (strapped to the bottom of the capsule under the heat shield) in order to minimize the possibility of premature detachment of the shield.

Glenn reported his condition during and after the flight as being "go," (or fine). For about four hours and forty minutes he experienced the sensation of weightlessness (zero-G) and became so accustomed to it that at one point he unthinkingly let go of his camera in mid-air to reach for something and then casually picked the hovering object out of the air again. He ate special food, which he squeezed from tubes.

Through the window of *Friendship 7* Glenn saw irrigated areas on earth and different-colored water patterns in the ocean. By day and by night he saw stars, which "seemed to jump out" at him and which resembled those of a clear night in the desert, except that they were unblinking. Glenn saw three sunsets; the light, at first a brilliant white, changed from orange to blue, darker blue, and black as the sun sank beneath the horizon. He also noted a peculiar phenomenon that puzzled scientists: luminous bright yellowish-green specks that looked like fireflies and floated slowly past his capsule.

Glenn's flight was longer than that of Yuri Gagarin, who made one orbit around the world on April 12, 1961, but shorter than that of Gherman Titov, who circled the earth seventeen and a half times on August 6, 1961. The Russians' capsules were heavier and their rockets were capable of more thrust. Yet Glenn's successful ride did much to restore the confidence of Americans in their nation's prowess and dispel the self-searching doubt that had plagued them since the U.S.S.R. launched the first earth-orbiting satellite in 1957. Glenn has punctiliously directed the major share of credit for the success of the project to the thousands of persons involved in design, manufacture, maintenance, and recovery of the space capsule.

After a two-day period of examination and rest at Grand Turk Island, Bahamas, Glenn was reunited with his family at Patrick Air Force base in Florida. He then traveled by motorcade to Cape Canaveral, where he was greeted by President John F. Kennedy. He was welcomed by parades in Washington, D.C., New York City, and his home town, New Concord, Ohio, and personally received congratulations from delegates at the United Nations. On February 26th, 27th, and 28th he addressed a joint session of Congress and meetings of the House Committee on Science and Astronautics and the Senate Committee on Aeronautical and Space Sciences. A New York *Times* (February 28, 1962) writer called him "the Administration's star witness on Capitol Hill" in support of its long-range $20,000,000,000 man-to-the-moon program. Project Mercury itself has already cost NASA about $400,000,000. A new space center is being built at Houston, Texas, and the astronauts will spend much of their time there.

In recognition of his space flight achievement, Glenn received the Navy's Astronaut Wings (1962) and the Marine Corps' new insignia, an Astronaut Medal (1962). New York City awarded him its Medal of Honor and Muskingum College gave him an honorary D.Sc. degree and a Distinguished Merit Award in 1961. Glenn signed the globe of the American Geographic Society that carries the signatures of famous fliers and explorers. In addition to his Distinguished Flying Crosses and Air Medals, Glenn holds the Navy Unit Commendation for service in Korea during 1952 and 1953, the Asiatic-Pacific Campaign Medal, the American Campaign Medal, the World War II Victory Medal, the China Service Medal, the National Defense Service Medal, the Korean Service Medal, the United Nations Service Medal, and the Korean Presidential Unit Citation.

Shortly after the news of Glenn's safe landing became known, the United States Post Office issued a blue and yellow four-cent stamp captioned "U.S. Man in Space." The seven astronauts had previously sold *Life* magazine exclusive rights to their first-person stories and those of their families for $500,000. They have used part of this money to invest in a luxury motel at Cape Canaveral, a middle-income apartment house project in Washington, D.C., and a motel on Grand Bahamas Island. Glenn makes over $10,000 a year; his five-hour trip through space entitled him to extra flight pay of $245 for the month.

Glenn has been described as a modest though self-possessed man who "talks easily and enthusiastically, pacing his remarks even on official occasions with light touches and an impish sense of humor" (*Newsday*, January 22, 1962). He is five feet ten and a half inches tall and has thinning red hair, green eyes, and a freckled, deeply tanned face. He enjoys listening to music (one favorite is Puccini's *Madama Butterfly*); in 1957 his knowledge of popular songs won him $12,500 on the television program *Name That Tune.*

John H. Glenn, Jr., married his high school sweetheart, Anna Castor, in April 1943. They have two children: Carolyn (Lyn) and David. Glenn was formerly a Sunday school teacher and lay leader in the Presbyterian church, and the family is still active in church affairs. At home, they often read the Bible together and sing hymns while Mrs. Glenn plays the electric organ. Before Glenn entered the Project Mercury program, he and his wife discussed with their minister the right of man to probe space.

"A lot of people ask why a man is willing to risk hat, tail, and gas mask on something like this space flight. . . . I've got a theory about this," Glenn once remarked. "People are afraid of the future, of the unknown. If a man faces up to it and takes the dare of the future, he can have some control over his destiny. That's an exciting idea to me, better than waiting with everybody else to see what's going to happen."

References

Life 43:15+ Jl 29 '57; 50:24+ Mr 3 '61; 52:22+ F 2 '62; 52:25+ Mr 9 '62
N Y Times p1+, 20, 23+ F 21 '62
Time 79:11+ Mr 2 '62
U S News 52:22+ Mr 5 '62

GREGORY, DICK 1932- Comedian

Address: b. c/o American Guild of Variety Artists, 110 W. 57th St., New York 19

When he first appeared at the Blue Angel, a fashionable supper club on New York's East Side, on March 17, 1961, Dick Gregory, the Negro comedian, was introduced by the master of ceremonies as "the Negro Mort Sahl." Stepping into the spotlight, Gregory waved his cigarette and replied, "Yes, but in the Congo they call Sahl the white Dick Gregory." Whether Gregory is the Negro Mort Sahl, Shelley Berman, Lenny Bruce, or Will Rogers, it is safe to say that this satirist of segregation is the first Negro to join the new wave of avant-garde, literate, and topical standup night club comedians of today.

Other Negro standup comedians like Timmie Rogers, Nipsey Russell, Dewey (Pigmeat) Markham, and Moms Mabley, aware of their all colored audiences, have slanted their material toward their own race. Not so Dick Gregory, who tells his predominantly white listeners, "When I get drunk, I think I'm Polish. One night I got so drunk I moved out of my own neighborhood." Gregory's offhand approach to racial tensions, a far remove from the rubber-stamped Amos 'n' Andy Negro humor, has brought him from appearances at $5 a night to $6,500 a week in a little more than two years.

Born in St. Louis, Missouri in 1932, at the depth of the Depression, Dick Gregory knew the meaning of abrasive poverty through all his years of growing. The second of six children,

DICK GREGORY

he is the son of a father who disappeared for a time at the birth of each new baby and who finally deserted the family permanently when Gregory was a small boy, leaving his wife and children destitute. "I was on relief from 1932 to 1950," Gregory has told his affluent audiences. "No matter how rich I get I can always kid the poor. Rockefeller can't." He has also informed them that "When you came into my house, you didn't have to knock the snow off your shoes. It wasn't going to melt anyway." His mother, from whom he seems to have inherited his sense of humor, was the one bright center of security and warmth in his childhood. "We're not poor," she used to tell her children, "we're just broke," and she taught her children the difference. When the relief truck drew up before the door she would ask, "Aren't we lucky to get such service?" and when their electricity was turned off she lit candles in the dark. While his mother took in washing, Dick Gregory scurried through the streets and alleys of St. Louis for food and fuel, carried packages, lugged groceries, and at the age of seven shined shoes in a billiard parlor where the white customers used to rub his head for good luck.

In his first year at Sumner High School in St. Louis Gregory continued to help with the family finances. He sandbagged levees on the Mississippi River at flood time, heaving hundred-pound sacks that weighed only thirteen pounds less than he did. He worked in a steel plant, loading shells. In the meantime, he had become a bass drummer in the school band, and, although his grades were poor to middling, he rapidly became a track star. "I knew getting ninety on my tests wouldn't get me what winning the mile in the city meet would," Gregory has explained. In 1951 he won the Missouri State mile championship with the time of 4.28. He became president of his senior class, wrote, staged, and acted in his class revue, won the Sumner High School citizenship award, and

HESTER, JAMES M.—*Continued*

with a military government team working in the Fukuoka district of Japan. He was concerned with the democratization of Japanese schools in an area that served some 3,000,000 people.

After his release from active military service in 1947 Hester resumed his interrupted education. He obtained a Rhodes scholarship and attended Pembroke College of Oxford University in England where he received the B.A. degree in 1950. He then returned to the United States to become an assistant to the American secretary to the Rhodes trustees, Dr. Frank Aydelotte. However, the Korean conflict caused his recall to the Marines in 1951 and he served at Quantico, Virginia, as a battalion adjutant. His duties included scheduling classes, organizing the program, and housing trainees. In 1952 he was separated from the Marines with the rank of first lieutenant, and was later promoted to captain.

Returning to civilian life Hester spent several months working at the National Archives in Washington, collecting material for his doctoral thesis. In 1953 Oxford University conferred upon him the M.A. degree with second class honors in philosophy, politics, and economics. Later that year he became assistant to the president of Handy Associates, Inc., a firm of management consultants in New York City. (He had his first contact with New York University when he enrolled in the university's division of general education and took the course "Accounting for Non-Accountants," taught by John N. Myer.) In 1954 he left Handy Associates to take a position with the advertising research firm Gallup and Robinson of Gallup poll fame, located in Princeton, New Jersey. During his first year there he took a leave of absence for a few months in order to complete his doctoral thesis. He received the D.Phil. degree in international affairs from Oxford in 1955, after submitting the thesis "America and the Weimar Republic: A Study of the Causes and Effects of American Policy and Action in Respect to Germany, 1918-1925." During his three years with Gallup and Robinson, Hester was an account supervisor, analyzing the effectiveness of television commercials.

In 1957 Hester entered the field of education when he became provost of Long Island University's Brooklyn Center. The following year he was appointed a vice-president of Long Island University, and in 1959-60 he served as a member of the board of trustees. He also became a member of the Princeton University chapel advisory council in 1959 and a trustee of the Brooklyn Institute of Arts and Science in 1960. In 1957 he became a member of the board of trustees of the Brooklyn Academy of Music, and he was made a vice-chairman in 1960.

Hester's connection with New York University as a faculty member began in 1960 when he became dean of the Graduate School of Arts and Science, at the same time assuming the newly created position of executive dean of arts and science of the university, as well as that of a professor of history. In these posts he was responsible for the supervision of the university's instructional and research programs in academic fields, and was in charge of both graduate and undergraduate programs.

In November 1961, when he was named to succeed Dr. Carroll V. Newsom as president of the university, effective January 1, 1962, Dr. Hester had already been offered the presidency of a Midwestern institution, which he turned down in favor of N.Y.U. In welcoming his successor, Dr. Newsom commended him for having "great talent for searching out the significant, for making decisions, and for obtaining co-operation on matters of common concern." Dr. Newsom went on to say that Dr. Hester is highly regarded "not only as an able administrator but also as a scholar and educator."

It did not take the new president long to pinpoint the most important needs of New York University. He envisioned the need for new and improved laboratories, better faculty offices, additional classrooms and athletic facilities, and the improvement of the university's library service. He views the library as "the measure of our seriousness as a university" and is aware that N.Y.U., as a "commuter" university located in a major city, lacks the dormitory facilities of a campus college. He believes that this lack should be filled by additional study and reading rooms.

Dr. Hester inherited from Dr. Newsom what the latter had described as his "worst headache": the problem of fund-raising for the university. He took over the $75,000,000 program for Leadership and Service in the Sixties, which had been initiated during 1961 when N.Y.U. celebrated its 130th anniversary. Toward the end of January 1962, he announced a tuition increase of $5 a point to take effect in September. This increase means that the student taking a four-year degree course will be paying tuition fees of $1,440 a year, a figure that is almost triple the 1952 fees. Dr. Hester also announced faculty raises, including a minimum salary of $12,000 a year for full professors.

Dr. Hester is aware that the creation of an academic atmosphere is one of the main problems faced by a vast "commuter" university such as N.Y.U., consisting of fifteen schools with a faculty of about 4,000 and a total of some 43,000 students. "The primary function of a university president is his academic program," he has said. "And if you have a good one, this in itself can prove the greatest aid to fund-raising." He added: "It is my aim that New York University shall offer the finest academic program possible in every area in which it functions." He intends to involve the deans of the various schools and colleges in the making of policy decisions, so that they are aware of problems facing the university as a whole. He believes that this will strengthen the institution and prevent it from being merely a "loose assortment of schools and colleges."

Looking upon his experience as a businessman as an invaluable preparation for his present role of educational administrator, Dr. Hester contends that there is no great difference between the administration of a business and an educational institution. He feels that when dealing with the latter there are additional rewards arising from the contact with academic life and helping young people in their formative years.

On May 23, 1953 James M. Hester married Janet Rodes of Louisville, Kentucky, whom he had met while he was a student at Oxford.

Mrs. Hester is the daughter of Brigadier General Peter Rodes, at one time chief of intelligence to General Lucius Clay. The Hesters have three daughters, Janet, Margaret, and Martha. Dr. Hester is five feet eleven and a half inches tall, weighs 170 pounds, and has dark brown hair. He plays what he calls a "conversational" game of squash. Dr. and Mrs. Hester are amateur painters and they enjoy dancing.

Since his appointment as N.Y.U. president, Dr. Hester considers himself committed to the field of higher learning. Believing that the ultimate weapon is "not the hydrogen bomb, but education," he is well aware of the problems that face educators in an era of population explosion and increased educational needs. He has said: "One of the biggest problems before us is how to educate the number of people we have today without turning it into a mass communications game in which the student acquires knowledge but no individuality of thought. Far too many youngsters are going to college for what it will do *for* them, rather than *to* them. They are graduating, having completed subjects, but with little informed curiosity, which is, after all, the mark of an educated person" (New York *Post,* November 29, 1961).

References

> N Y Herald Tribune p1 + N 29 '61 por
> N Y Post p46 N 29 '61 por
> N Y Times p34 N 29 '61 por
> Who's Who in America, 1962-63

LEFÈVRE, THÉO(DORE JOSEPH AL-BÉRIC MARIE) (lĕ-fâ′vr′) Jan. 17, 1914- Premier of Belgium; lawyer

Address: b. Wetstraat 16, Brussels, Belgium; h. Savaanstraat 43, Ghent, Belgium

To meet the grave political and financial problems of Belgium, heightened by the loss of the Congo, Théo Lefèvre has provided an energetic and statesmanlike government since he became Premier in April 1961. Lefèvre, who has been a member of the Belgian Parliament since 1946 and was president of the Social Christian party from 1950 to 1961, formed a coalition cabinet with his party's long-time opponents, the Socialists. The international criticism of Belgium over the Congo, the critical financial situation, and the crisis in morale, led him to try to unify all elements in the country, divided by linguistic, religious, and economic interests, most notably between the French-speaking Walloons in the south and the Dutch-speaking Flemish in the north of Belgium.

Théodore Joseph Albéric Marie Lefèvre was born in Ghent, in the Flemish part of Belgium, on January 17, 1914, the son of Étienne and Marie (Rogman) Lefèvre. His father, a barrister at the Court of Appeal in Ghent, was concerned with the conditions of the Flemish workers and was one of the founders of the Social Christian union movement. Théo Lefèvre was only six years old when his father died in 1920 from wartime gas poisoning. He received a classical education at the colleges of St. Joseph and St. Liévin in Ghent, and then entered the

Robert Kayaert & Co., Brussels
THÉO LEFÈVRE

University of Ghent, where he studied law and was known as a "mediocre and ambitious" student. After receiving his doctor of laws degree in 1937 he embarked upon his legal career and was admitted to the bar at the Court of Appeal in Ghent in 1940. Later he also became a professor at the Centre de Formation d'Assistantes Sociales in Ghent, where he taught civil law.

When the Germans attacked Belgium in May 1940 Lefèvre served as a sergeant in the Belgian army during the eighteen-day campaign of resistance, and he received the badge of the campaign. During the Nazi occupation of Belgium following the unconditional surrender he fought against the Germans as a member of the underground movement, the *Mouvement Royaliste Belge,* and he also edited the underground Flemish newspaper, *Vrij.* After the liberation of Belgium at the end of World War II, he was awarded the badge of the resistance and the Grand Cross of the Legion of Honor.

Lefèvre was one of the postwar founders of the Social Christian party (formerly the Catholic party) in East Flanders, and he soon became influential in its inner circles. The party, which draws its main strength from the Flemish areas of Belgium, has a strong center group, but also includes members of conservative and leftist orientations. The left wing favors social reforms similar to those advocated by the Socialists, and generally supports the interests of the Catholic trade unions. The adherents of the party include Catholic labor groups, Flemish peasants, nobility, and industrialists.

In the first postwar elections, held in February 1946, Lefèvre was elected to represent the district of Ghent-Eekloo in the lower house of the Belgian Parliament, the Chamber of Representatives. He was re-elected in subsequent campaigns and continues to hold this seat. Within Parliament Lefèvre has served as rapporteur of the budget and as a member of the national defense

LEFÈVRE, THÉO—*Continued*

commission, and he has also worked on temporary commissions for the study of problems of public law.

A major conflict between the Social Christians and the Socialists occurred in 1950, when King Leopold III, who had been accused of pro-Nazi activities during World War II, tried to return to the throne of Belgium after six years in exile. The Social Christian party favored the King's return while the Socialist party, led by Paul-Henri Spaak, formed the center of the opposition. When the older members of the Social Christian party acquiesced in the Socialist demand for the King's abdication, Lefèvre led a "young Turk" revolt and was subsequently chosen to succeed to the presidency of the party. (Although in a referendum in March 1950 57.6 percent of the Belgian voters favored Leopold's return, the ensuing civil strife caused him to transfer his powers to Prince Baudouin, and on July 16, 1951 he formally abdicated.) Upon assuming leadership of the party in 1950 Lefèvre strengthened its propaganda apparatus, tightened its discipline, worked toward integrating its disparate conservative and progressive elements, and led the party in its many political battles with the Socialists.

The Social Christian party under Lefèvre's leadership, has given unqualified approval to Belgium's membership in the North Atlantic Treaty Organization and in the organizations promoting European co-operation in the economic, political, cultural, and military spheres. Lefèvre has participated in the consultative assembly of the Council of Europe (1950), the European constitutional assembly (1952), and the Western European Union assembly (1954). From 1952 to 1959 he was a member of the common assembly of the European Coal and Steel Community (ECSC) and in 1959-61, of the European Parliamentary Assembly, a deliberative body for the three institutions of "Little Europe": the Common Market, the European Community of Atomic Energy (Euratom), and the ECSC. In 1960 Lefèvre was the international president of the Nouvelles Équipes Internationales (N.E.I.), a nongovernmental organization promoting co-operation among various Christian Democratic groups in Europe.

In 1958, the year he was appointed Minister of State, Lefèvre embarrassed the government of Social Christian Premier Gaston Eyskens over an issue involving education, by urging party members to withdraw their money from the national savings banks and to boycott public loans. For more than a decade the schools problem had been a source of major disagreement between the Social Christians, who favored subsidies to the "free" (mainly Roman Catholic) schools and the Socialists and Liberals, who insisted on priority for the development of official schools. After interparty negotiations, a compromise formula, valid for twelve years, was reached in 1958. For this, major credit was given to Lefèvre, who emerged from the dispute once again as the undisputed leader of the Social Christian party.

In a speech in 1960 Lefèvre advanced ideas of social reform and of bonds between the Catholics and Socialist laborers. Despite the opposition of the conservative members of his party, he continued in this course, to promote unity in his country as it faced the international and financial problems resulting from the granting of independence to the Congo in mid-1960.

The Eyskens government's measures of increased taxation and decreased welfare benefits to meet the financial difficulties led to a general strike in December 1960 and January 1961 in the French-speaking areas of Belgium. In a spirit of bitterness, some Walloon and Flemish elements demanded a loose federation and separate institutions for the two areas. After new general elections on March 26, 1961, Lefèvre was asked by King Baudouin on April 6, 1961 to form a new coalition government and he decided to end the feud with the Socialists. "Belgium must end its violent quarreling, its partisan rivalry, its sterile rancors," he declared. "A new generation demands a more farseeing attitude." On April 19, 1961 Lefèvre formed a new cabinet, composed of eleven Social Christians and nine Socialists, with Paul-Henri Spaak as Vice-Premier and Foreign Minister. Lefèvre was sworn in as Premier by King Baudouin on April 25, 1961. The coalition government won its initial test of confidence on May 5, 1961 when the Chamber of Representatives voted in its favor 147 to 38, with 15 abstentions.

As a major objective of the new government Lefèvre pledged that concrete measures would be taken toward the resolution of the Flemish-Walloon conflict. In the economic sphere he promised governmental steps to expand industry, absorb unemployment, and increase the benefits of the social welfare program. In foreign policy he stated that Belgium would support the policy of the United Nations in the Congo and collaborate with the organization. Lefèvre also promised that Belgium would co-operate in the efforts to create a united Europe through Benelux, the Western European Union and the European communities. On July 18, 1961 Lefèvre met at Bonn with the leaders of the five other member states of the European Common Market—West Germany, Italy, France, the Netherlands, and Luxembourg. They agreed on a system of regular political consultation and co-operation, aimed at giving "form and body to the will of political unity."

Théo Lefèvre is married to the former Marie-Josée Billiaert. They have three children: Marie-Caroline, Étienne, and Pascal. Lefèvre's large and aquiline nose, which has earned him the nickname "des-Neus" (Dutch for "the nose"), has made him a favorite among cartoonists and caricaturists. He speaks Dutch and French equally well and has written articles on politics for Belgian newspapers, including *Die Nieuwe Gids* and *La Nation Belge*. He has made a political survey that was published in the monthly *Streven*. In the summer of 1954 Lefèvre visited the United States on a study tour, as a guest of the Department of State. A Roman Catholic, he counts the study of the Bible among his favorite avocations, and he reads widely, including philosophy, novels, and detective stories. His favorite authors are said to be Pascal, Bergson, and Camus. Lefèvre also enjoys the theater and music (including Bach, Beethoven, and jazz), and he collects modern paintings.

References

N Y Times p12 Ap 7 '61 por
London Times p10 Ap 27 '61
Time 77:24 My 5 '61 por
International Who's Who, 1961-62
Le Livre Bleu (1950)
Who's Who in Belgium, 1957-58

OCHOA, SEVERO (ō-chō'ä) Sept. 24, 1905-
Biochemist; university professor
Address: b. New York University College of Medicine, 550 1st Ave., New York, 16; h. 110 East End Ave., New York 28

Scientific investigations directed by Dr. Severo Ochoa, chairman of the biochemistry department at the New York University College of Medicine, have resulted in significant progress toward breaking the genetic code of life. The work is of major importance in understanding the basic chemical instructions used by nature to control heredity and the manufacture of proteins and represents the key to the reproduction of all living matter.

Crucial to the interpretation of the code was Dr. Ochoa's original research relating to the synthesis of ribonucleic acid (RNA). For his achievement Dr. Ochoa was named a co-winner of the 1959 Nobel Prize in Medicine. He shared the award with Dr. Arthur Kornberg, professor of biochemistry at Stanford University, who was honored for similar research on the creation of an artificial molecule of deoxyribonucleic acid (DNA). Both men used a bacterial enzyme as a catalyst to obtain the nucleic acids synthetically.

A native of Spain, Severo Ochoa was born in the town of Luarca, on the Bay of Biscay, on September 24, 1905 to Severo and Carmen (Albornoz) Ochoa. He received the greater part of his education in Malaga, Spain and was graduated in 1921 from the college in that city with a Bachelor of Arts degree. Severo Ochoa completed his university training and medical work at the University of Madrid, which awarded him the M.D. degree with honors in 1929.

For several years during his early career, Dr. Ochoa traveled and studied abroad. During the summer of 1927 he worked with physiologists at the University of Glasgow. After he received his medical degree he spent two years in Germany as a postgraduate student. He worked at the Kaiser Wilhelm Institute for Biology in Berlin (1929-30) and the Kaiser Wilhelm Institute for Medical Research in Heidelberg (1930-31) with Otto Meyerhof, 1922 Nobel laureate in physiology and medicine. When he returned to Spain in 1931 Ochoa was appointed a lecturer in physiology and biochemistry at the University of Madrid Medical School. In 1935 he was named head of the physiology division of the university's Institute for Medical Research, but one year later Ochoa returned to the institute in Heidelberg as a guest research assistant in physiology. Dr. Ochoa went to England in 1937, where he served for six months at the Marine Biological Laboratory at Plymouth before he joined the

Wide World
DR. SEVERO OCHOA

staff of the Oxford University Medical School as a Nuffield research assistant in biochemistry for 1938-40.

As the outlook for scientific endeavor in Spain narrowed, Dr. Ochoa immigrated to the United States "as a better place for science." He had begun his research on enzymes while still in Europe, and he continued his work at the medical school of Washington University in St. Louis, where he was an instructor and research assistant in pharmacology in 1941. Since 1942, when he was appointed a research associate in medicine, Dr. Ochoa has been on the staff of the College of Medicine of New York University, a unit of the New York University-Bellevue Medical Center. He was advanced to assistant professor of biochemistry in 1945 and one year later was named a professor of pharmacology and invited to chair the department.

Much of Dr. Ochoa's original work with enzymes involved studies of the chemical processes in plants and animals. In the early 1950's he discovered and isolated a key chemical compound, triphosphopyridine nucleotide (TPN), long known to be a component of both plant and animal tissue. Dr. Ochoa recognized TPN as one of the vital agents in the process of photosynthesis, in which light is used to convert water and carbon dioxide into complex sugars and other foods. TPN was found to work as a "hydrogen acceptor"; that is, the highly reactive hydrogen was held temporarily after the water molecule was split into hydrogen and oxygen preparatory to the food-building steps. Dr. Ochoa suggested that in animals TPN assisted in the reverse chemical process of changing ingested food to gaseous carbon dioxide and water, with the release of chemical energy essential later to conducting body functions.

In 1954 Dr. Ochoa was named professor and chairman of the department of biochemistry at the College of Medicine. One year later he an-

OCHOA, SEVERO—*Continued*

nounced his momentous discovery, which was to change the course of all future biochemical research and shed new light on the chemistry of life. His studies of the reactions between inorganic and high energy phosphate led to the creation of the enzymatic synthesis of ribonucleic acid. He made the discovery in a "casual" way. RNA, as this chemical is called, is the basic material for all living tissue and an essential ingredient in the production of protein. It is found in the cytoplasm, the protoplasmic envelope surrounding the nucleus. As seen under the microscope, RNA is a long double-coil-shaped chain of four small basic nucleotides—adenine, guanine, uracil, and cytosine (A, G, U, & C)—which are all different, but are related. RNA differs from deoxyribonucleic acid, or DNA, the genetic substance in the nucleus (core of the cell) that controls heredity.

To obtain RNA artificially in the test tube, Dr. Ochoa used the enzyme polynucleotide phosphorylase, obtained from the sewage bacteria Acetobacter vinelandii, with some primer material. Under most test-tube conditions enzymes are used to break down or digest large molecules, but Dr. Ochoa found that his enzyme welded simple constituents together to form the RNA-like molecule. He created molecules consisting of various combinations of the four basic nucleotides, as well as unnatural chains of RNA-like material, composed of just a single nucleotide. This research marked the first time in history that man put molecules together in a chain outside the living organism.

The first practical application of Dr. Ochoa's discovery was the creation of an artificial virus in a test tube with RNA material. This research was conducted early in 1956 with Dr. Wendell M. Stanley, a Nobel Prize winner and virus specialist at the University of California. The RNA compound was slipped inside the noninfective protein "overcoat" that protects the active infective part of the virus and serves to pick the host in which the virus will proliferate. Delicate chemical examinations with an electron microscope proved that the combination had the characteristics of a real virus. The research could not be considered conclusive, however, until a susceptible animal or plant could be found to serve as a host. If the artificial virus could reproduce in its host, it would be the first instance where science could create life out of lifeless parts.

Dr. Ochoa's research has brought man further along the road to creating life in a test tube. The synthesis of RNA and DNA has opened the possibility of transplanting into animals and men genetic material containing more desirable characteristics. His work has clarified questions concerning the nature of viruses, cell reproduction, protein synthesis, and the continuity of life. The positive influence of Ochoa's work on the cancer problem was acclaimed by the American Cancer Society as "a major step in the study of such abnormal growth as involved in the cancer process." Professor Ochoa's research has also proved crucial in advances toward deciphering the genetic code, a system of messages between the RNA and the DNA in the nuclei of all living cells.

Dr. Severo Ochoa shared the 1959 Nobel Prize for Medicine with his "best student," Dr. Arthur Kornberg, head of the biochemistry department at Stanford University. Although their combined efforts have provided a new understanding of the life process, the scientists had worked on their projects independently since Arthur Kornberg studied under Professor Ochoa in 1946. The men, recognized as "two of the best biochemists of the present time," shared the citation and a money prize of $42,606.

In addition to holding honorary memberships in scientific societies in Great Britain, Argentina, Uruguay and Chile, Dr. Ochoa is a Fellow of the American Association for the Advancement of Science, American Academy of Arts and Sciences, New York Academy of Medicine, and New York Academy of Sciences. Other organizations to which he belongs are the American Chemical Society, Society for Experimental Biology and Medicine, National Academy of Sciences, and the Harvey Society, of which he was elected a vice-president (1952-3) and president (1953-4). Dr. Ochoa has served on the nominating committee and the editorial board of the *Journal of the Society of Biological Chemists* and was president-elect (1957) and president (1958) of the national committee for biochemistry of the National Research Council. He has also served on scientific advisory boards of Brookhaven National Laboratory, Massachusetts General Hospital, and the Office of Naval Research. He has participated in biochemistry study groups for the United States Public Health Service and was the United States representative to the International Union of Biochemistry (1955-61).

Other honors bestowed on Dr. Ochoa include the Newberg Medal Award in Biochemistry (1951), the award of the Societé de Chimie Biologique (1955), and the Borden Award in the Medical Sciences of the Association of American Medical Colleges (1958). He has held honorary lectureships and professorships at universities in the United States and South America, and he has received honorary degrees from Washington University in St. Louis (1957) and Oxford University (1961).

The tall, white-haired doctor has the manners and habits of a Continental gentleman. His wife is the former Carmen G. Cobian, whom he married in Spain on July 8, 1931. They have no children. In his spare time Dr. Ochoa indulges in color photography; he also listens to music and has a preference for Mozart and Bach. He has been a United States citizen since 1956. At the university, the professor is known as "an exacting but fair teacher," and one of his colleagues, as reported in *Newsweek* (October 26, 1959), has described him as "a kind, quietly humorous, stimulating friend."

References

N Y Herald Tribune p 1+ O 16 '59 por
N Y World-Telegram p4 O 15 '59 por

American Men of Science 10th ed (1961)
Collier's Encyclopedia Year Book (1960)
International Who's Who, 1961-62
World Biography (1954)
Who's Who in America, 1962-63

PAGE, RUTH 1903(?)- Dancer; choreographer
Address: b. c/o Columbia Artists Management,
Inc., 165 W. 57th St., New York 19; h. 1100
Lake Shore Dr., Chicago, Ill.

Few figures in the dance world can match the
international success of Ruth Page, who is director and choreographer of the Chicago Opera
Ballet and of the Lyric Opera Company of Chicago. Her forte—opera-into-ballet—is a bold
new art form that she pioneered and developed
in the United States and in Europe. Her repertoire includes such diverse creations as ballets
based on *Die Fledermaus, La Traviata, Il Trovatore, Carmen,* and *The Barber of Seville.* She
has choreographed and danced in such well-
known ballets as *Frankie and Johnny, Billy
Sunday, An American in Paris,* and *The Bells.*
Throughout her career, as a dancer and choreographer, Miss Page has been associated with
the world's best known dancers and ballet
producers.

Ruth Page was born about 1903 in Indianapolis, Indiana to Dr. Lafayette and Marian
(Heinly) Page. Her father, a distinguished brain
surgeon, helped to establish the crippled children's wing of the James Whitcomb Riley Hospital. Her mother, a professional pianist, was
one of the founders of the Indianapolis Symphony Orchestra. Miss Page had two brothers:
Lafayette, Jr., who is deceased, and Dr. Irving
Page, who is head of the research department
of the Cleveland Clinic. She received her early
education at the Tudor Hall School, a private
school in Indianapolis. As a child she often entertained the artists, writers, and composers who
visited the Page household by what was then
called "fancy dancing" (moving to rhythm while
waving a scarf).

One day the great ballerina Anna Pavlova
came to tea and was greatly impressed by the
talents of the fifteen-year-old girl. She urged
Mrs. Page to allow her daughter to take summer
ballet classes in Chicago with the Pavlova com-
pany. Subsequently Ruth, accompanied by her
mother, joined the company on a tour of Latin
America. After the tour she attended the French
School, a girls' boarding school in New York
City, at the same time studying ballet with
Adolph Bolm, who had come to the United
States with the Diaghilev company.

Returning to Chicago in 1919, Ruth Page made
her Chicago debut in the leading role in the
ballet *The Birthday of the Infanta,* based on the
story by Oscar Wilde, with music by John Alden
Carpenter and choreography by Adolph Bolm.
While appearing in the same ballet in London,
a year later, Miss Page studied with Enrico Cecchetti, the teacher of Pavlova. Upon her return
to the United States she went on several tours
as the partner of Bolm in his Ballet Intime, one
of the first American ballet companies. Engaged
in 1921 as *première danseuse* for Irving Berlin's
second *Music Box Revue,* Miss Page played in
the Broadway show for two years, including a
long tour. In 1924 she became the prima ballerina of the Chicago Allied Arts, an experimental group, which gave her her first opportunity to work at choreography in the jazz *pas de
deux The Flapper and the Quarterback,* in which

RUTH PAGE

she also had a leading role. Next she worked on
Oak Street Beach, inspired by the local color of
the famous Chicago beach.

Following her marriage, in 1925, Miss Page
resumed her classes with Cecchetti in Monte
Carlo, and then she appeared with Adolph Bolm
in *Coq d'Or* with the Municipal Opera Company
in Buenos Aires. From 1926 to 1928 she was
guest soloist with the Metropolitan Opera Company in New York City, and for seven summer
seasons, beginning 1926, she was *première danseuse,* ballet mistress, and choreographer for the
Ravinia Opera Company, at an outdoor theater
near Chicago. On April 27, 1928 she starred
in the world première of Stravinsky's *Apollon
Musagète* (with choreography by Bolm) at a new
theater in the Library of Congress in Washington, D.C.

In the fall of 1928 Miss Page set out on her
own, with a partner and two female dancers,
and toured the Orient for three months. Her
performances included an appearance in Tokyo
at the enthronement ceremonies of Emperor
Hirohito. In 1930, at the invitation of the Soviet
government, she presented a series of American
dances in Moscow, before the Sophil Society.
At the time of the Century of Progress Exposition in Chicago, in 1933, Miss Page created new
ballets that were performed to the accompaniment of the Chicago Symphony Orchestra.
Among the dances she staged was *Guiablesse,*
which featured the noted Negro dancer Katherine
Dunham.

Beginning in 1934 Miss Page went on a number of tours with Harald Kreutzberg, presenting
many original dances for the next three years
in the Orient, Europe, and the United States.
Also from 1934 to 1937 she was *première danseuse* and ballet director of the Chicago Opera
Company, for which she arranged a number of
all-ballet evenings, the first to be presented by
a major American opera company. Among the
original ballets she choreographed for these pro-

PAGE, RUTH—*Continued*

grams were *Hear Ye! Hear Ye!*, with music by Aaron Copland, and *An American Pattern*, with music by Jerome Moross. She also repeated her earlier creation of a ballet to Ravel's *Bolero*, which she later performed eighty times on Midwestern tours.

In 1938-39 Miss Page was director of the Federal Theatre Project in Chicago. In 1938 she and Bentley Stone established the Page-Stone Ballet, which toured the United States and Latin America for a number of years. Their production of *Frankie and Johnny*, created in 1938 under the auspices of the Federal Theatre Project, ran longer than any other ballet in the history of Chicago. In 1942-43 and in 1945 she again was ballet director and *première danseuse* with the Chicago Opera Company. Her partnership with Stone continued until 1946 when Stone entered military service.

In 1939 Miss Page choreographed her first opera-into-ballet, converting Bizet's *Carmen* into *Guns and Castanets,* set in contemporary civil war Spain. A lover of opera since childhood, Miss Page believes that operatic music lends itself easily to the dance and that opera stories can be choreographed. "I felt that the dancing body could successfully express the drama and emotion conveyed by the voice of the singer," she told Saul Goodman in an interview for *Dance Magazine* (February 1961), "and that the dramatic ideas of the composer and the librettist could be expressed in dance as well as in song." Her opera-into-ballet repertoire includes *Die Fledermaus*, a frolicsome comedy based on the opera by Johann Strauss, Jr.; *Camille*, a dance version of Verdi's *La Traviata; Revenge,* based on Verdi's *Il Trovatore*; and a new version of *Carmen*, corresponding more closely to Bizet's opera than her 1939 production. Alfred Frankenstein wrote in the San Francisco *Chronicle* that Miss Page had made "a brilliant translation of Bizet's libretto into the language of choreography."

From 1946 to 1950 Miss Page was guest dancer and choreographer for the Ballet Russe de Monte Carlo. She added *Love Song, The Bells,* and *Billy Sunday* to the company's repertoire, and restaged the earlier production of *Frankie and Johnny.* For several years she experimented with reciting poems while dancing. A critic for *Dance Magazine* (May 1943) wrote that "her voice is full and expressive, her diction clear and unaffected," and that "she doesn't even get out of breath combining pirouettes with Carl Sandburg." In 1950 she brought her Chicago group, Les Ballets Américains, to Paris, where she startled audiences with her unorthodox presentations. Subsequent Paris appearances were highly successful, and she has choreographed *Minnie Moustache*, a French musical based on gold-rush days in the American West, for the French stage. Always an innovator, Miss Page has commissioned new scores for her own dances. Her *Triumph of Chastity* was especially composed by Jacques Ibert, as was *Concertino pour Trois,* a jazz work by Marius Constant. In recent years she has created works for the Ballets des Champs Élysées, the Lyons Festival, and London's Festival Ballet. In 1954 Miss Page was invited to

become the ballet director of the newly established Chicago Lyric Opera. In December 1955 she brought her company to Broadway, with Alicia Markova dancing the leading role in Miss Page's version of Franz Lehár's operetta *The Merry Widow.*

Since 1956 Miss Page has been ballet director and choreographer with the Chicago Opera Ballet, which she was instrumental in organizing in connection with the Chicago Lyric Opera. The group performs before sold-out houses with the opera company during its regular seasons and goes on tour throughout the United States. The principal dancers in the Chicago Opera Ballet (numbering about fifty members) are Sonia Arova and Kenneth Johnson, accompanied by an orchestra directed by Neal Kayan. Guest soloists have included a galaxy of international stars including Josette Amiel and Flemming Flindt of the Paris Opera Company. Such famous artists as Alicia Markova, Maria and Marjorie Tallchief, Oleg Briansky, and Mia Slavenska have also appeared with the company.

On February 8, 1925 Ruth Page married Thomas Hart Fisher, a Chicago lawyer, who was executive secretary of Chicago Allied Arts at the time of their marriage. Their comfortable and cheerful apartment in Chicago is a port of call for visiting ballet stars, musicians, designers, and other artists. She also has a studio in Paris and a villa at St. Tropez on the French Riviera called the "Villa l'Herbe Folle." Her studio there is an old stone *grenier*, where great artists have rehearsed their roles in Ruth Page's ballets.

Although Miss Page has appeared in ballets as recently as 1959, when she danced the role of Susannah in *Susannah and the Barber* (her version of Rossini's *The Barber of Seville*), she devotes most of her time to choreography and direction. She expects, however, to continue to take a daily ballet class for the rest of her life. Chic, animated, magnetic, and vibrant, the diminutive, dark-haired, dark-eyed choreographer has no time for hobbies; she feels "the world of ballet is so rich in resources and so fascinating" that she has no time for anything beyond its scope. Some day, she hopes, there will be a community-supported resident ballet, and symphony and opera organizations in every large city in the United States.

References

Dance Mag 35:24+ F '61 por; 35:40+ D '61 pors
Mus Am 79:13+ Ja 15 '59 por
Chujoy, Anatole. Dance Encyclopedia (1949)
Maynard, Olga. The American Ballet (1959)
Who's Who in America, 1962-63
Who's Who of American Women, 1961-62

PEVSNER, ANTOINE Jan. 18, 1886-Apr. 12 1962 Russian-born French sculptor and painter with his brother, Naum Gabo, founded the constructivist school, which applied cubism to sculpture. See *Current Biography* (March) 1959.

Obituary

N Y Times p25 Ap 14 '62

ROGERS, FRANK B(RADWAY) Dec. 31,
1914- Medical librarian
Address: b. National Library of Medicine,
Bethesda, Md.; h. 10316 Freeman Pl., Kensington, Md.

Director of the nation's largest medical library
and custodian of one of the world's most valuable collections of medical literature, Dr. Frank
B. Rogers of the National Library of Medicine
in Bethesda, Maryland, has been called the man
who helped put the word "National" in the title
of the vast library he directs. A major bureau
of the Public Health Service, the library has a
collection of more than 1,000,000 important
items in the field of medicine. Rogers has been
associated with the library since 1949, when it
was under the auspices of the Army as the Army
Medical Library, and he was in large measure
responsible for the library's achieving national
status in 1956. From its founding in 1818, as
the Library of the Surgeon General's Office, to
the present, all of its directors have been physicians. None except Dr. Rogers, however, has
received formal training in library science in
addition to his medical education.

Frank Bradway Rogers is a scion of another
medical doctor far back on the family tree,
Dr. J. George Rogers, whose obstetric skill was,
in some measure, responsible for the outcome of
the Civil War. It was Rogers' great-great-grandfather who, 140 years ago in Point Pleasant,
Ohio, delivered a baby boy who grew up to be
General Ulysses S. Grant. Frank Rogers was
born on New Year's Eve of 1914 in Norwood,
Ohio, the son of Frank Shane Rogers, a postoffice clerk, and Nettie (Bradway) Rogers. He
was reared mainly in Cincinnati, where he attended the local schools, graduating in 1932 from
the Walnut Hills High School. In the fall of
the same year Rogers enrolled as premedical
student at Yale University. During his four
years at New Haven, he wrote movie reviews for
the campus newspaper, participated in amateur
dramatics and the student council, and was employed as a waiter. He received his B.A. degree
in 1936 and began his career that year as an
office boy for *Newsweek* magazine with his eye
on a future in medicine.

After brief experience in the business world,
he left to continue his studies and matriculated
at the Ohio State University Medical School. He
graduated with an M.D. degree in 1942. Immediately upon completing his medical training,
Dr. Rogers entered the Army as a first lieutenant
and served as an intern at the Letterman Army
Hospital in San Francisco. A year later he was
assigned to the post of instructor at the Medical
Field Service School in Carlisle Barracks, Pennsylvania, where he remained for about a year.
In 1945 Rogers joined the 3d Battalion of the
35th Infantry Regiment in Luzon, the Philippines as battalion surgeon. Also in that year
he was decorated with the Bronze Star for
meritorious service to the armed forces.

Transferred at the end of World War II to
the 25th Infantry Division in Japan, again as
battalion surgeon, Rogers remained in the Far
East until 1947. From first lieutenant, Medical
Corps, he advanced through the grades to his

National Library of Medicine
DR. FRANK B. ROGERS

present rank of colonel. When he returned to
the United States, Rogers accepted an appointment as resident in surgery at the Walter Reed
Army Hospital in Washington, D.C. After a
year's residency he saw an announcement on a
bulletin board that the position of director of
the Army Medical Library, was open to qualified
military personnel. He trained for the position
at the Army Medical Library for six months, and
then, sponsored by the Army, he entered the
School of Library Service at Columbia University in 1948. He took his M.S. in L.S. degree
a year later.

The transition from surgeon to librarian was
apparently a very natural and uncomplicated
process for Dr. Rogers. "I discovered after my
first few weeks with the Library," he recalls,
"that it offered the work to which I wanted to
devote my energies. I found it fascinating and
challenging then and do now" (*Scope Weekly*,
June 8, 1960). Largely because of his dual professional specialties, Dr. Rogers has contributed
invaluably to the progress and recognition attained by the library under his directorship.
Serving first as director of the Army's medical
library, he effected numerous changes in the
regular operating procedures enabling his staff
members to make better use of their creative
abilities and established a serious set of standards and goals for the library's future.

Part of the library's daily function is the preparation of the index to medical literature *Index
Medicus*, which indexes nearly 1,500 medical
journals. Rogers revises and edits the monthly
publication. In connection with the indexing of
medical literature, he has devoted his energies
to studying the field of automatic data processing and has replaced some of the "very primitive" operations in the library with new mechanized systems to help codify and index scientific
information. Dr. Rogers' ultimate aim is to so
advance in the field of information storage and

ROGERS, FRANK B.—*Continued*

retrieval "that machines may do the dirty work . . . and our people can devote their energies to more interesting and creative efforts." He hopes that existing systems for automatic access to scientific information can be refined so that current literature in a given field can be automatically assembled for publication. At the present time partial automation has been developed by the library and is in effect now, enabling each monthly issue of *Index Medicus*, approximately 500 pages, to be put together in two days.

The most memorable accomplishment of Dr. Rogers' career and admittedly the most important change evidenced in the past twelve years of Dr. Rogers' association with the Library of Medicine was the establishment of a legal basis for the institution. In 1956 Congress acted on a bill submitted by Senator Lister Hill and Senator John F. Kennedy to create a national medical library "to promote the progress of medicine and to advance the national health and welfare," combining in one system the Army Medical Library and the medical libraries of the Navy, the Air Force, and the Public Health Service. As the last director of the Army Medical Library and the only director of the Armed Forces Medical Library (the title of the library from May 1952 to 1956), Dr. Rogers assumed the directorship of the newly created National Medical Library on October 1, 1956. New quarters were approved and built. A $7,-300,000 building was constructed on a ten-acre site in Bethesda, Maryland to replace the crowded building in Washington that had housed the Medical Library for the past seventy-four years. It was ready to receive the staff and the collection in time to celebrate the 125th anniversary of the founding of the library, marked by the years 1961-63. After the celebration was over, Dr. Rogers' only comment was that he didn't believe he had stamina enough "to live through a year like 1956 again."

In commemoration of the 125th anniversary, Rogers is compiling a book of the selected writings of Dr. John Shaw Billings, director of the library during the last years of the nineteenth century and, according to Rogers, one of the great men of medicine of the nineteenth century. Billings was a brilliant innovator and a prolific writer, dedicated to the advancement of the Medical Library as an indispensable instrument of the medical profession. Rogers' study of his predecessor coincides with his deep interest in medical Americana of the nineteenth century. In connection with the library's history, Rogers has also co-authored, with Dorothy M. Schullian, an article that appeared in the *Library Quarterly* (January and April 1958) entitled "The National Library of Medicine." He has also contributed to a number of other professional organs, among them *Bulletin of the Medical Library Association, Libri, Journal of Cataloging and Classification, Military Surgeon, Library Journal, Texas Reports on Biology and Medicine, Medical Arts and Sciences,* and *Journal of Medical Education.* Along with many reviews of books, he has written a chapter "Application and Limitations of Subject Headings: the Pure and Applied Sciences" in *Institute on the Sub-*

ject Analysis of Library Materials, edited by Maurice Tauber (Columbia Univ. Bkstore, 1953).

Several organizations to which Rogers belongs reflect his interest in the sciences: History of Science Society, American Association for the Advancement of Science, American Medical Association, and Association of Military Surgeons. He is ex officio member of the science information council of the National Science Foundation; belongs to the Medical Library Association, American Library Association, American Documentation Institute; and served as honorary vice-president at the International Congress of Medical Librarianship in London in 1953. Rogers has also served as trustee of the Osler Library of McGill University in Montreal, Canada. In 1961 the Marcia C. Noyes award was presented to him by the Medical Library Association for his outstanding contributions to medical librarianship.

Frank B. Rogers married Barbara Pitt, a schoolteacher, on June 5, 1942. They have three children, Ellen, Peter, and Shane. Rogers stands five feet ten and a half inches tall, weighs 190 pounds, and has brown eyes and brown hair. He is regarded by his colleagues as an indefatigable worker and is rarely seen leaving his office after a day's work, according to his associates, "without his customary accessory, the bulging briefcase." As his principal recreations, Rogers lists golf, the preparation of his forthcoming book, and "tinkering with home repairs."

References

Scope Weekly p9 Je 8 '60 por

American Men of Science 10th ed (1961)
Who's Who in America, 1962-63
Who's Who in Library Service (1955)
World Biography (1954)

ROGERS, RUTHERFORD DAVID June 22, 1915- Librarian

Address: b. Library of Congress, Washington 25, D.C.; h. 5124 Westpath Way, Washington 16, D.C.

The largest library in the United States has as its chief assistant librarian Rutherford David Rogers. Rogers went to the Library of Congress in Washington, D.C. in December 1957 from the largest *public* library in the United States, the New York Public Library, where he had been chief of the reference department and, before that, chief of the personnel office. During earlier periods he had been director of the Rochester (New York) Public Library and the Grosvenor Library, Buffalo, New York, and librarian of the Columbia College Library, New York City.

The Library of Congress, whose function far exceeds its original purpose of providing books for the use of Congress, serves governmental departments generally and opens its research resources to scholars among the general public. As deputy head of the library, Rogers shares the administration of the library's multifarious operations, which range from copyrighting to recording of music.

Rutherford David Rogers was born on June 22, 1915 in Jesup, Iowa to David Earl Rogers, a creamery manager, and Carrie Zoe (Beckel) Rogers. He has one brother, Ronald B. Rogers, and two sisters, Mrs. Rosalie V. Arnold, and Mrs. Romayne I. Brown. At the Jesup Consolidated School, where he received his secondary education, he participated in dramatics, sang in the chorus, and won two letters in baseball and three in basketball. He was graduated from high school in 1932. Two factors provided a youthful impetus toward a library career: a great interest in reading and no local public library in which to satisfy it. Rogers thus came to realize what a library could mean to a young person.

At Iowa State Teachers College (now Iowa State College), Cedar Falls, Rogers majored in English and was a reader in the English department. He directed the all-college variety show and also played in the college band. Graduating with the highest scholastic average in his class, he received the B.A. degree in 1936. A Lydia Roberts Fellow at Columbia University from 1936 to 1938, he took his M.A. degree in English and comparative literature in 1937 and his B.S. degree (with honors) in library science in 1938. His master's thesis was entitled "Byron's Attitude Toward the Oppressed."

Meanwhile, in 1937-38, Rogers had held his first professional position, as assistant in the circulation and reference departments of the New York Public Library. From 1938 to 1941 he was a reference assistant at Columbia College Library. In 1941 he became acting librarian of the Columbia College Library and in 1942, librarian. He retained his position at the Columbia College Library while on leave with the Army Air Force Air Transport Command from July 1942 to June 1946. He entered the command with the rank of private and left with that of captain. While at the Columbia College Library he had written the *Columbia College Library Handbook* (1941).

After Rogers was discharged from the Army, the Wall Street firm of Smith, Barney & Company employed him as a financial research analyst from 1946 to 1948. In the latter year he took the post of director of the Grosvenor Library, a reference library of half a million volumes in Buffalo, retaining it until 1952. In 1952 and 1953 Rogers was director of the Rochester Public Library, a central city library with twelve city branches. During his administration in Rochester he established the Monroe County Library System (thirteen libraries and a bookmobile) and co-ordinated the work of the system.

Returning to the New York Public Library as chief of the personnel office in 1954, he directed the 2,000-employee personnel program of the main New York library and its eighty branches until February 1955. On February 9, 1955 the trustees of the New York Public Library appointed him chief of the library's reference department. The reference department of the New York Public Library, housed in the library's central building at Fifth Avenue and Forty-second Street in mid-town Manhattan, has a research collection of 4,000,000 volumes and differs from the circulation department in that it is supported by private gifts rather than city taxes.

Fabian Bachrach

RUTHERFORD DAVID ROGERS

In 1957 Rogers resigned his post at the New York Public Library to become chief assistant librarian of Congress. As deputy to L. Quincy Mumford, librarian of Congress, Rogers shares the overall administration of the Library of Congress on Capitol Hill in Washington. The Library of Congress, which was set up in 1800, now has more than 12,329,600 books and pamphlets. Its total inventory, including maps, recordings, and manuscripts, comprises more than 41,282,900 items. Intended originally for the use of Congress, its services extend also to other governmental departments, and accommodation is made for the research needs of nongovernmental scholars. A legislative reference service is maintained. Publications of the library include catalog cards bought by other libraries throughout America. Numerous exhibits include the annual White House News Photographers' Association exhibit. Concerts, readings by poets and authors, and lectures on literature are presented in the Library's Coolidge Auditorium. Records of poets reading their poetry are issued in the library's Twentieth Century Poetry in English series. The library's Archive of Folk Song releases long-playing records of American folk music. In 1961 the money available for the use of the Library of Congress from appropriations, gifts, and other sources was $24,131,102. The Copyright Office is one of the library's functions.

The third annual Mary C. Richardson lecture at the New York State University College of Education, Geneseo, New York, was delivered by Rogers and published by the college in 1960 as *No Room at the Top: Observations on Selected European National Libraries.* His "A County Library Program" appeared in the *Wilson Library Bulletin* for December 1949. In *Library Trends* he has published "Measurement and Evaluation" (October 1954) and "Library Administration in its Current Development" (January 1959). For the *ALA Bulletin* he has written

ROGERS, RUTHERFORD DAVID—*Cont.*

"Yes, Ivan Reads: A First Report of the American Library Mission to Russia" (July-August 1961) and "Shelving Books by Size" (June 1957). His articles for *College and Research Libraries* include "Appraising a Research Collection" (January 1952), "Regional Depository Libraries and the Problem of Optimum Size of College and University Libraries" (April 1950), "Subject Bibliography Versus Subject Catalog and Periodical Index" (July 1950), "Administrative Problems of Reference and Research Libraries" (July 1949), and "Undergraduate Reference Work" (June 1942). He published "Inter-Library Cooperation" in *New York State Library Bookmark* for January 1952 and "The Charging Pocket Solution for Overdues" in *Library Journal* for December 15, 1951.

At the 1951 ALA midwinter meeting in Chicago Rogers reported on the situation in Scarsdale, New York, where attempts had been made "to purge school libraries of 'subversive' literature" (*ALA Bulletin*, March 1951). The report on labeling of the ALA committee on intellectual freedom was presented to the ALA council by Rogers on July 13, 1951. The policy recommended by the committee and adopted by the council was that "librarians should not use the technique of labeling as a means of predisposing readers against library materials" (*ALA Bulletin,* July-August 1951). The committee pointed out the totalitarian aspect of labeling, and called it a "censor's tool." "We are . . . anti-communist," the committee concluded, "but we are also opposed to any other group which aims at closing any path to knowledge."

Among Rogers' professional organizations are the American Library Association, the Association of College and Reference Librarians, and the District of Columbia Library Association. He was chairman of the ALA's committee on intellectual freedom in 1951-52. He was a member of the New York state examination committee for public librarians' certificates from 1951 to 1954 and vice-chairman of the committee in 1953-54. Other governmental advisory bodies on which he served were the federal advisory committee on scientific information (1959-60) and the United States government interagency committee for the United States-Japan centennial in 1960. He is a member of the Grolier Club, the Cosmos Club, the Archons of Colophon, the Bibliographical Society of America, Blue Key, Kappa Delta Pi, Sigma Tau Delta, and Theta Alpha Phi. Iowa State Teachers College bestowed its alumni achievement award on Rogers in 1958.

Rutherford David Rogers married E. Margaret Stoddard on June 4, 1937. They have a daughter, Jane Shelley Rogers. Rogers is five feet six inches tall and weighs 150 pounds. His eyes are brown and his hair is black. He describes himself politically as "independent," and his religion is Protestant. He finds recreation in woodworking, refinishing antiques, gardening, and tennis.

Edward G. Freehafer, a former colleague of Rogers, has called him "one of the country's ablest librarians, who combines experience with intelligence, success with modesty. As an administrator he guides with a gentle rein, and under his direction things seem to fall naturally into their proper places. . . . He has won respect and loyalty, one reason being that, in addition to his more obvious qualities, he is . . . a most loyal colleague" (*College and Research Libraries,* November 1957).

References

N Y Times p23 F 10 '55 por
Who's Who in America, 1962-63
Who's Who in Library Service (1955)

ROSE, (IAIN) MURRAY Jan. 6, 1939-
Swimmer

Address: University of Southern California, Los Angeles, Calif.

The youngest triple gold medal winner in the history of the Olympic Games is the Australian swimmer Murray Rose, who won these prizes at the 1956 Games in Melbourne, Australia when he was seventeen for excelling in the 400-meter and 1,500-meter freestyle events and the 800-meter relay race. He set a record for the marathon 1,500-meter distance of 17 minutes, 58.9 seconds. Four years later, at the 1960 Games in Rome, he became the first man in the history of the Olympics to retain his 400-meter title. Rose, a vegetarian, is majoring in telecommunications at the University of Southern California, from which he expects to graduate in June 1962.

A native of Birmingham, England, Iain Murray Rose was born on January 6, 1939 to Ian Falconer Rose, an advertising executive, and Eileen (Folwell) Rose. The Rose family is descended from Hugh de Ros, an early Scottish baron. Murray's first name, Iain, which he does not normally use, is spelled with an extra "i" in honor of his Gaelic ancestor who fought for Prince Charlie at the battle of Culloden Moor in 1746.

With the advent of World War II the Roses moved from Birmingham to Sydney, Australia when Murray was one year old. Their home in the resort area of Double Bay was but a minute's distance from a beach, and Mrs. Rose, a fine swimmer herself, took Murray there every day from the time he was one and a half. Hesitant at first about entering the water, Murray soon learned to like it. His mother taught him to swim, and by the age of three he could dogpaddle fifty yards without trouble. A healthy and attractive boy, he was photographed for a World War II defense poster that was distributed in Australia.

At about this time he underwent an experience that for years perpetuated in him, his mother says, "a quiet terror of the water." As she was watching him swim about one day, she saw an older boy push him under the water several times. Rushing to the scene, she pulled Murray out by his hair and, holding him heels up, shook the water out of him. For several months after nearly drowning in this way Murray would not swim at all, but gradually he regained his confidence in the water. "Sometimes I think the need to overcome that nightmare and fear played the determining part in my discipline in the water," Rose has said. "The chain of events and circumstances leading from that day . . . to the day when I won my first medal have been valuable experiences, I know. Philosophically, I sometimes wonder how my life's path might have differed if Mother hadn't taught me to face that challenge."

By the time he was five, Murray was ready for more advanced teaching than his mother could give him, and she turned him over to Sam Herford, his first coach, whom Rose credits with much of his success. At Cranbrook School, a private school in Sydney, which he entered at the age of six, Murray began to swim competitively while still in kindergarten. At nine he entered the new South Wales championship in the 55-yard race for children under twelve. The following year he won this event and with it the first of his many state titles. Before he was sixteen Rose won the Australian National Senior championship at 220, 440, and 880 yards, setting new Australian records in the last two distances. "Swimming was never just something to do for me," he has said. "It is a way of life made possible by the fact that, even as a child, I found it exciting to do things for a purpose, to work toward a big reward."

Murray Rose made his biggest splash at the 1956 Olympic Games in Melbourne, Australia, where he captured the 400-meter freestyle, the marathon 1,500-meter freestyle (in a record time of 17 minutes, 58.9 seconds), and was a member of Australia's victorious 800-meter relay team. Not since Johnny Weissmuller did so in 1924 had any swimmer won three gold medals in Olympic competition. Moreover, Rose, then seventeen, was the youngest triple gold medalist in any sport in the history of the Games.

Two facets of Rose's style that have helped him become a winner are his smoothness in turning at the end of a lap and his "old-fashioned" form, reminiscent of Weissmuller's. Instead of employing a streamlined straight-arm style now used by most American competitive swimmers, Rose pulls against the water with his hands and forearms. A special characteristic of his is a split-second pause that occurs as he leans on his extended right arm and breathes on his left side. Like other swimmers, he knows the value of psychological factors in gaining precious seconds. Through such techniques as a sudden change of his own swimming pace, he tries to instill doubt or confusion in his opponent's mind. "The big thing," he explains, "is to make him feel you are controlling the race."

Another factor to which Rose ascribes his success in sports is his diet. He has been a vegetarian all his life, both his parents having become so before his birth. Rose does not eat meat, fish, or poultry (meats produce acids that produce fatigue, he has noted), nor does he drink coffee, tea, or alcoholic beverages. He eats organically grown vegetables and avoids foods that have been sprayed with chemicals or made with processed flour or sugar. Items in his diet are cheese, eggs, soya beans, nuts, halvah, sunflower seeds, millet, sesame products, unpolished rice, seaweed jelly, cookies and cakes made of honey and brown sugar, goat's milk, and apple, tomato, grape, pineapple, and carrot juices. "But I don't

Yoshikatsu Sugano, Tokyo
MURRAY ROSE

see how anyone can take celery or beet juice," he says. Far from being a food faddist, he does not discuss his diet unless pressed, nor does he try to impose his views on others.

Following his Olympics triumph, several American colleges asked him to enroll in their undergraduate programs. After visiting Yale University, Harvard University, Michigan State University, Stanford University, and the University of California, Rose chose to attend the University of Southern California. The West Coast appealed to him because of its congenial climate and because he found people there more conscious of nutrition and health practices. Also the university had promised to supply him with the vegetarian diet he required. His parents accompanied him to the United States, where his father became an executive with the J. Walter Thompson advertising agency in New York City.

In the 1958 Amateur Athletic Union (A.A.U.) meets Rose won the 220, 440, and 1,500-meter freestyle events, and he and his fellow Trojans won the A.A.U. team title for the University of Southern California. He was named Mr. Trojanality during his freshman year. At the A.A.U. contests in New Haven, Connecticut in April 1959, Rose retained his three freestyle titles, setting one American and three meet records and in each case improving on his 1958 time, despite the fact that he had a bad cold and a temperature of over 100 degrees at the time.

In the summer of 1959 Rose was invited by the Japanese Chamber of Commerce to accompany American swimmers to a series of meets in Japan. Competing as a guest, he surpassed two world marks recorded at that time, one of them the official time of 9 minutes, 14.5 seconds in the 800-meter individual freestyle, which Rose improved to 9 minutes, 8.6 seconds. During the Japanese contests he was outdistanced for the

ROSE, MURRAY—*Continued*

first time by Tsuyoshi Yamanaka, with whom he had long carried on an informal rivalry. Rose traveled in the Japanese mountains with an American missionary and Japanese friends; he also met young people of the country, one of whom, Asae, later painted his portrait from memory and sent it to him in America in a hand-carved frame. Rose was much impressed with Japan and its people, particularly its women, who, Rose says, "have a very sensitive and unassuming quality."

Rose began his junior year at the University of Southern California in September 1959, but he withdrew the following February and returned to Australia to train for the 1960 Olympics in Rome. Reunited with Sam Herford, he began his program with a weight-lifting and calisthenics course in Sydney and then went to the northern Australian city Townsville with the Olympic swimming squad. There he received more thorough training than he had been able to get in four years. At the university he had averaged only about an hour and a half of swimming practice a day. During the Australian Olympic trials Rose improved the world record scores of Jon Konrads, the Australian swimmer who attended the University of Southern California with him, in the 200, 400, and 1,500-meter races.

Rose does not do his own cooking, nor can he always rely on restaurants to supply his dietary needs. His mother, therefore, has always managed to ensure his food supply; during the summers of 1958 and 1959 she cooked for him while the university cafeteria was closed, and when he was training in Australia, she stayed with him for four months, arranging for his meals. During the 1960 Olympic Games his parents took an apartment in Rome for a month, and his mother prepared his meals there.

Rose is the first swimmer ever to have successfully defended his distance title at the Olympics; he retained the 400-meter title with a time of 4 minutes, 18.3 seconds at the 1960 Games. Also he placed second in the 1,500-meter distance event and was a member of the 800-meter relay team that placed third. For these feats he won another gold medal and a silver medal and a bronze medal. His achievement, at the age of twenty-one, was considered remarkable since swimmers are normally at their peak in their teen-age years, and each year a new crop of potential champions rises to displace "old men" like Rose. "Champion swimmers in these days of freely frangible records go out of style almost as rapidly as last year's automobiles," Arlie W. Schardt wrote in *Sports Illustrated* (August 14, 1961). "In meet after meet they are washed aside by sleeker, swifter, more powerful models. . . . Murray Rose . . . stands out among the newer swimmers like a Rolls-Royce in a traffic jam."

At the A.A.U. indoor meet at New Haven in 1961 Rose regained the 1,500-meter freestyle title he had held in 1958 and 1959 by swimming the distance in a meet record time of 17 minutes, 43.7 seconds. In addition to competing with the University of Southern California team he has represented the Los Angeles Athletic Club. Rose

was named captain of the USC swimming team for his senior year, 1961-62.

Having appeared on radio and television as a sports celebrity since his youth, Rose became interested in telecommunications and dramatics; at USC he majored in these areas. He played many leading roles in university productions, including Jules Feiffer's first play, *Crawling Arnold,* in January 1962. In addition to courses in acting and directing, he enjoys classes in psychology, philosophy, and oriental religions. In December 1961 he was named to the national men's honorary society Blue Key, whose members have outstanding academic and service records. He is a member of Beta Theta Pi. Rose has appeared on such television shows as Art Linkletter's *House Party* and *To Tell the Truth* on CBS-TV, *Today* on NBC-TV, and a Groucho Marx show. His 1956 Olympics 400-meter and 1,500-meter freestyle victories were commemorated in a postage stamp bearing his name, issued by the Dominican Republic.

Rose won the nickname "Golden Boy" at the 1956 Olympics because of his blond hair, bronze suntan, and fine physical condition. He has blue-gray eyes, is six feet one inch tall, and weighs 180-odd pounds. Rose enjoys water skiing and playing handball and Rugby. He likes to read, to listen to music (especially opera and ballet music and jazz), and to play chess and cards. After his graduation in June 1962 he expects to enter television or, perhaps, the motion pictures, for which he has already had several offers.

References

Christian Sci Mon p15 Jl 26 '57 por
Sports Illus 14:30+ Ag 14 '61 por

WELSH, MATTHEW E(MPSON) Sept. 15, 1912- Governor of Indiana; lawyer
Address: b. State House, Indianapolis 4, Ind.; h. 719 Busseron St., Vincennes, Ind.

The forty-first Governor of Indiana, Matthew E. Welsh, achieved a signal victory by defeating his opponent in an election year when Republican Presidential candidate Richard M. Nixon carried the Hoosier State by a decisive majority. With one exception, Welsh was the only Democrat elected to state executive office. His Lieutenant Governor is Republican, and he has had to work with a General Assembly in which his party has only 34 seats in a 100-member House and a scant majority of 2 in the Senate. He was installed on January 9, 1961.

Stressing the value of the bipartisan approach, Welsh has gained legislative approval for important measures like the reform of the scandal-ridden highway commission and the establishment of a Department of Administration to curb bureaucratic waste. At his induction ceremonies he pledged to rid the administration of any persons who failed to "discharge their responsibilities as citizens in a free society according to the highest standards of personal honesty and integrity."

Born in Detroit, Michigan, on September 15, 1912, Matthew Empson Welsh was named for his father, Matthew William Welsh, and his mother, Inez (Empson) Welsh. Both parents came from Jackson County in southern Indiana; their son attended grade school at Brownstown, the county seat. He received his high school diploma in 1930 from the Lincoln High School in Vincennes, Indiana, where his father had established a business, M. W. Welsh and Company, Inc. Welsh is presently secretary-treasurer of this enterprise.

Preparing for a business career, Welsh entered the Wharton School of Commerce at the University of Pennsylvania, where he majored in economics, served as managing editor of the *Daily Pennsylvanian,* and became a member of the Friars (senior society) and of Delta Kappa Epsilon. He had undergone change in vocational interest by the time he received his B.S. degree in 1934. He studied law for two years (1934-36) at Indiana University in Bloomington and in 1936 served on the board of editors of the Indiana University *Law Review.* Welsh graduated from the University of Chicago Law School with a J.D. degree in 1937, the year he was admitted to the Indiana bar. He is also a member of the American and Knox County (Indiana) bar associations.

In November 1940, three years after he had started to practise law in Vincennes, Welsh was elected on the Democratic ticket as state representative from Knox County to the Indiana General Assembly. Since the Indiana legislature meets every two years, in January, Welsh took part in two sessions, in 1941 and 1943. During the 1943 convention he served as Democratic caucus chairman in the House and as the Democratic House member of the state Budget Committee.

Welsh resigned his state post in 1943 to accept an appointment as a lieutenant junior grade in the United States Navy. His active service began in March 1944 and ended with his release from duty in May 1946. One month later, in June, Welsh was nominated by his party for the post of judge of the state appellate court, but he suffered his first political defeat in the November elections.

In May 1948 Welsh was elected chairman of the Seventh District Democratic Committee, and in February 1950 he was appointed United States Attorney for the Southern District of Indiana. He resigned from that position in April 1952 to resume private law practice in Vincennes in partnership with Curtis G. Shake, a former chief justice of the state supreme court. The firm of Shake and Welsh engaged in general practice in all courts and represented the Vincennes public school board and many Vincennes business enterprises.

Welsh again ran for a seat in the Indiana General Assembly in November 1954, and he was elected state Senator from Knox and Daviess counties for the 1955 and 1957 sessions. During the 1957 session he served as Democratic floor leader in the state Senate. He retained both posts by election for the 1959 session.

In his first bid for his party's gubernatorial nomination, Welsh was backed by former Democratic national chairman Frank E. McKinney. At the state convention in June 1956, however,

MATTHEW E. WELSH

he was defeated on the ninth ballot by Mayor Ralph Tucker of Terre Haute. (Tucker, in turn, lost in the November elections.) In 1960 Welsh was more successful. After gaining the Democratic nomination, he went on to defeat the Republican candidate, Crawford F. Parker, by some 23,000 votes. Parker had been Lieutenant Governor in the outgoing administration of Harold W. Handley. (Under Indiana law a Governor may not succeed himself.)

Although Handley dissociated himself in 1956 from the corrupt régime of his Republican predecessor, his own administration was not strong enough to withstand the barrage of criticism that Welsh fired against it. Describing Welsh's campaign, a writer for the *Christian Science Monitor* (November 4, 1960) observed that Welsh's "appearances on television were effective and he campaigned vigorously. He attacked the Republican administrations on the issue of highway scandals, accused Governor Handley's régime of 'gross inefficiency,' asserted that there had been misuse of state-owned cars, and stressed again and again the need for a change and a cleanup of the state government. Unlike other Democratic candidates in the past, Mr. Welsh . . . stated that he wants federal aid for Indiana, and is quite prepared to take it."

Elected Governor of Indiana on November 8, 1960, Welsh prevailed by 1,072,717 votes to Parker's 1,049,540. Parker suffered his first political defeat because he was repudiated by many normally Republican voters who wanted to show their protest against the governments of Handley and his predecessor, George N. Craig. Accompanying Welsh to the statehouse was a Republican Lieutenant Governor, Richard O. Ristine. The Democrats scored a small lead of 26 to 24 in the state Senate, while the Republicans carried a 32-man lead in the House.

Inaugurated on January 9, 1961 for a four-year term, Governor Welsh shortly afterward proposed

WELSH, MATTHEW E.—*Continued*

the creation of a Department of Administration as a key measure in a streamlining program designed to abolish the maze of overlapping governmental agencies. This proposal was put into effect, along with his demand for replacement of Indiana's traditionally partisan highway commission by a four-member, bipartisan, professional board. "This professionalized group," Welsh explained, "will make its selection of highways based upon engineering needs, traffic counts, etc. —and not upon the basis of political favors. This was not a popular measure with some of the more partisan members of both parties. But we got the legislation through. . . . Out of bipartisanship, Indiana will build integrity and professionalism."

Other gubernatorial proposals included the establishment of a Port of Indiana Authority, reestablishment of an independent Department of Mental Health, creation of new divisions on mental retardation and emotionally disturbed children, and provisions for the continuity of government in the event of a devastating enemy attack.

Throughout the first few months of his tenure, Welsh expressed grave concern that incoming monies collected by the state were not enough to meet expenditures. In his opinion, unless taxes were increased or services cut, Indiana could "go broke" within a year. Several tax increase proposals were defeated in the Assembly, and in June 1961 Welsh announced economy measures. He halted new construction projects valued at $14,000,000 and an impending $1,300,000 salary raise for state employees. He ordered reduction of state staffs and called for a cut in local school aid. "Indiana cannot spend money it doesn't have. . . ." Welsh said. "We cannot operate government on wishful thinking nor well intentioned hopes that revenue will increase."

Welsh is a director of the Security Bank and Trust Company and secretary of the Universal Scientific Company, both at Vincennes. He is a trustee of Vincennes University and the Vincennes Young Men's Christian Association, and a director of the Kennedy Memorial Christian Home in Martinsville, Indiana. The Governor is a member of the Vincennes Kiwanis Club, the Elks, the American Legion, the Indianapolis Athletic Club, and Phi Delta Phi, the law fraternity.

Matthew Empson Welsh and Virginia Homann of Washington, Indiana were married on September 25, 1937. They have twin daughters, Kathryn Louise and Janet Marie. The Governor is described as having a wiry build and graying hair. He is a trustee and elder of the First Christian Church of Vincennes. Welsh resigned his private law practice when he took office as Governor, hoping thereby to set a good example in the area of government ethics. "As in my own case," he says, "I have insisted that all of our principal heads of government here be full-time department heads."

References

American Bar, 1961
Martindale-Hubbell Law Directory, 1960
Who's Who in America, 1962-63
Who's Who in the Midwest (1958)
Who's Who in United States Politics (1952)

WHALEN, GROVER A(LOYSIUS) June 2, 1886-Apr. 20, 1962 Businessman; New York City's official greeter of famous people; established the ticker-tape parade as a symbol of welcome; held numerous city positions, including police commissioner (1928-30) and president of the New York World's Fair (1939-40). See *Current Biography* (September) 1944.

Obituary

N Y Times p1+ Ap 21 '62

CURRENT BIOGRAPHY—VOL. 23. NOS. 1-6

This is the index to the January-June 1962 issues. For the index to the 1961 biographies, see December 1961 issue or 1961 Yearbook. For the index to 1940-1950 biographies, see 1950 Yearbook. For 1951-1960 index, see 1960 Yearbook.

Martin, Edmund F(ible) Jan 62
Marvel, Mrs. Archie D. Apr 62
Marvel, Elizabeth Newell See Marvel, Mrs. A. D. Apr 62
Meerloo, Joost A(braham) M(aurits) Jan 62
Mellers, Wilfrid (Howard) Feb 62
Meštrović, Ivan obit Mar 62
Miller, Harry W(illis) Mar 62
Miller, William E(dward) Feb 62
Moore, Charlotte Emma See Sitterly, C. M. Jan 62
Moses, Anna Mary Robertson obit Feb 62
Mössbauer, Rudolf L(udwig) May 62
Muench, Aloisius (Joseph), Cardinal obit Apr 62
Murphy, (Eleanor) Patricia Apr 62

Nestingen, Ivan A(rnold) Mar 62
Newhart, Bob Mar 62
Nitze, Paul H(enry) Feb 62

Ochoa, Severo Jun 62
Ogburn, Charlton obit Apr 62
Olav V, King of Norway Jan 62
Osgood, Charles E(gerton) Apr 62
Ozbirn, Catharine (Freeman) See Ozbirn, Mrs. E. L. Jan 62
Ozbirn, Mrs. E. Lee Jan 62

Page, Ruth Jun 62
Peden, Katherine (Graham) May 62
Pevsner, Antoine obit Jun 62
Piccard, Auguste obit May 62
Portinari, Candido obit Mar 62

Rabaut, Louis Charles obit Jan 62
Randolph, Jennings Jan 62
Rayburn, Sam(uel Taliaferro) obit Jan 62
Read, Sir Herbert (Edward) Mar 62
Reischauer, Edwin O(ldfather) May 62
Reybold, Eugene obit Jan 62
Robinson, Spottswood W(illiam), 3d Mar 62
Rogers, Frank B(radway) Jun 62
Rogers, Rutherford David Jun 62
Rose, (Iain) Murray Jun 62
Russell, Donald J(oseph) May 62
Russell, James S(argent) Jan 62

Savage, Augusta (Christine) obit May 62
Schoeppel, Andrew F. obit Mar 62
Scofield, Paul Mar 62
Senghor, Léopold Sédar Mar 62
Shirer, William L(awrence) May 62
Shurlock, Geoffrey M. Jan 62
Sitterly, Mrs. Bancroft Walker See Sitterly, C. M. Jan 62
Sitterly, Charlotte Moore Jan 62
Slocum, (Manly) Harvey obit Jan 62
Smith, Margaret (Madeline) Chase Mar 62
Spahn, Warren (Edward) May 62
Spottswood, Stephen Gill Apr 62
Stikker, Dirk U(ipko) Feb 62
Suggs, Louise Jan 62
Sunderland, Thomas E(lbert) Apr 62
Swann, W(illiam) F(rancis) G(ray) obit Mar 62
Switzer, Mary E(lizabeth) Jan 62

Taylor, A(lbert) Hoyt obit Jan 62
Teagle, Walter C(lark) obit Feb 62

Thant, U Feb 62
Thurber, James obit Jan 62
Tillinghast, Charles C(arpenter), Jr. Feb 62
Tobias, Channing H(eggie) obit Jan 62
Turner, Ewald (Walter) May 62

Unitas, John Feb 62

Vertès, Marcel obit Jan 62
Viereck, George Sylvester obit May 62
Vilar, Jean (Louis Côme) Apr 62
Volpe, John A(nthony) Feb 62

Waddington, C(onrad) H(al) Apr 62
Wagner, Richard Apr 62
Walsh, Chad Feb 62
Walsh, William B(ertalan) May 62
Walter, Bruno obit Apr 62
Ward, Paul L(angdon) Mar 62
Watts, Alan (Wilson) Mar 62
Webb, James E(dwin) May 62
Welsh, Matthew E(mpson) Jun 62
Wenner-Gren, Axel (Leonard) obit Jan 62
Wesker, Arnold Feb 62
Whalen, Grover A(loysius) obit Jun 62
Whitton, Rex M(arion) May 62
Wilcox, Francis O(rlando) Apr 62
Wilkinson, Bud See Wilkinson, C. Apr 62
Wilkinson, Charles (Burnham) Apr 62
Wills, Royal Barry obit Feb 62
Winiarski, Bohdan (Stefan) Feb 62
Wood, Natalie Apr 62

Yamasaki, Minoru Mar 62

CURRENT BIOGRAPHY

JULY 1962
VOL. 23 NO. 7

Editor: Charles Moritz

PUBLISHED BY THE H. W. WILSON COMPANY, 950 UNIVERSITY AVE., NEW YORK

CONTENTS

ABOUT THIS PUBLICATION

Current Biography (published every month except August) presents articles on people who are prominent in the news—in national and international affairs, the sciences, the arts, labor, and industry. Sources of information are newspapers, magazines, books, and, in some cases, the biographees themselves. It should be pointed out, however, that these are objective rather than authorized biographies. At the end of the year the articles in the monthly issues are cumulated in one alphabet, revised, and printed in a single volume known as *Current Biography Yearbook*.

Authorities for biographees' full names, with some exceptions, are the bibliographical publications of The Wilson Company. When a biographee prefers a certain name form, that is indicated in the heading of the article: for example, MACMILLAN, (MAURICE) HAROLD means that he is usually referred to as HAROLD MACMILLAN. When a professional name is used in the heading, as, for example, GLENN FORD, the real name, in this case GWYLLYN SAMUEL NEWTON FORD, appears in the article itself.

The heading of each article includes the pronunciation of the name if it is unusual, date of birth (if obtainable), and occupation. The article is supplemented by a list of references to sources of *biographical* information, in two alphabets: (1) newspapers and periodicals and (2) books.

References to newspapers and periodicals are listed in abbreviated form; for example, "Sat Eve Post 217:14+ S 30 '44 por" means *Saturday Evening Post,* volume 217, pages 14 ff, September 30, 1944, with portrait. For full names, see the section "Periodical and Newspaper Designations," which is included in all *Current Biography* Yearbooks and in the January issue each year. Obituary notices appear for persons whose biographies have been published in *Current Biography*.

An index to names that have appeared this year is to be found at the back of this issue.

NOTE: Authors whose biographies do not appear in *Current Biography* may usually be found in *Twentieth Century Authors,* Kunitz & Haycraft, 1942, H. W. Wilson Company, or in the FIRST SUPPLEMENT (1955). Authors of books for young people are included in *The Junior Book of Authors* (Second Edition, Revised) edited by Kunitz & Haycraft, 1951, H. W. Wilson Company. Musicians whose biographies do not appear in *Current Biography* may usually be found in *Living Musicians,* compiled and edited by David Ewen, 1940, H. W. Wilson Company, or in its FIRST SUPPLEMENT (1957).

KEY TO PRONUNCIATION

ā	āle	N	Not pronounced, but indicates the nasal tone of the preceding vowel, as in the French *bon* (bôN).	û	ûrn; French eu, as in *jeu* (zhû); German ö, oe, as in *schön* (shûn), *Goethe* (gû'tě)
â	câre				
ă	ădd				
ȧ	ȧccount				
ä	ärm				
à	àsk				
ȧ	sofȧ	ō	ōld	ŭ	tŭb
		ô	ôrb	ŭ	circŭs
ē	ēve	ŏ	ŏdd	ü	Pronounced approximately as ē, with rounded lips: French u, as in *menu* (mē-nü); German ü, as in *grün*
ĕ	ĕnd	oi	oil		
ē	makēr	o͞o	o͞oze		
		o͝o	fo͝ot		
g	go	ou	out		
ī	īce				
ĭ	ĭll	th	then	zh	azure
		th	thin	′ =	main accent
ᴋ	German ch as in *ich* (ĭᴋ)	ū	cūbe	″ =	secondary accent

CURRENT BIOGRAPHY

JULY 1962

BARRETT, FRANK A. Nov. 10, 1892-May 30, 1962 Former Republican Senator (1953-58), Governor (1951-52), and Representative (1943-50) from Wyoming; rancher. See *Current Biography* (July) 1956.

Obituary

N Y Times p27 My 31 '62

BEATON, CECIL (WALTER HARDY) (bē't'n sĭs'l) Jan. 14, 1904- Photographer; designer; writer; artist
Address: b. c/o Little Brown and Co., 34 Beacon St., Boston 6, Mass.; h. 8 Pelham Place, London S.W. 7, England; "Reddish House," Broadchalke, near Salisbury, England

NOTE: This biography supersedes the article that appeared in *Current Biography* in 1944.

Except for his World War II photographic assignments with the British Ministry of Information, Cecil Beaton's work has been largely focused on the world of celebrated men, women, and places—the sophisticated, fashionable, distinguished, exotic, and beautiful in society and the arts. He is the "unassailable" arbiter of taste, the connoisseur of elegance, the portraitist of the Royal Family, who took pictures of Prince Andrew when he was five weeks old. If the range of Beaton's interests seems a little too limited, the facets of his talent are not. In photography, painting, drawing, stage and costume designing, and in his writing his deftness is equal to the demands of his exalted subjects. Visually and verbally, he is capable of much charm and grace; he can also be tart, and he knows how to use a trifling detail to expose falseness.

The eldest of four children in what he has called "a nice, ordinary, middle-class family," Cecil Walter Hardy Beaton was born in London on January 14, 1904 to Ernest Walter Hardy and Etty (Sisson) Beaton. His sisters are Nancy (Lady Smiley) and "Baba" (Mrs. Alec Hambro); his brother, "Reggie," died in a train accident in 1933. His father was a timber merchant and a cricket enthusiast who also took some delight in the amateur theater, but otherwise neither of his parents cared particularly about the arts. Beaton writes in his autobiographical *The Wandering Years: Diaries: 1922-1939* (Little, 1961) that in his ambition to break away from the "anonymity" of his background, he developed "ridiculous aspects of aestheticism" in adolescence such as growing his hair "like a piano-tuner."

At his first boarding school, St. Cyprian's in Eastbourne, Cecil Beaton's greatest enjoyment

CECIL BEATON

was in student theatrical productions. Then during "three escapist years," as he has called them, at Harrow School, he showed a flair for watercolor sketches and theater design, but when he entered St. John's College, Cambridge University, in 1922, he was not aware of any special aptitude. He lacked the confidence to make a career of his hobbies, but while reading *Macbeth*, he spontaneously chose colors for designs of its scenes, and during his Christmas vacation in 1922 he bought photographic equipment to develop his own negatives.

Having spent his university years enjoying plays and art exhibits in London, traveling around the countryside to visit churches and antique shops, and devoting much of the rest of his time to the Amateur Dramatic Clubs, Beaton left Cambridge in 1925 without a degree. He had come to realize that what he wanted was to set up a studio to create theatrical designs, paint, and take photographs, but since he had no money he went to work as a clerk in his father's office in London. In his free time, meanwhile, he designed stage settings in hopes of obtaining a contract with a theatrical company. Unsuccessful in that effort, he went to work as a typist in the firm of a Mr. Schmiegelow, a Danish friend of his father. Often idle and bored in the office, he thought about designs that he would work on in the evening. Weekends he used his sisters as models in photographic experiments, and when

BEATON, CECIL—Continued

he attracted other sitters, he sometimes spent all night processing his films with rather makeshift equipment at home.

Edith Sitwell was among the first of the notables who submitted to exotic poses for Beaton's unconventional photographs. She and her brothers, Osbert and Sacheverell, helped speed his way in London circles of people who appealed to him as glorious and glamorous—the world of the "illuminati," who held weekend parties at country manor houses. In 1928 he held an exhibition of his somewhat startling photographs, caricatures, and stage designs at a Bond Street gallery.

When Beaton left England for the first of his many visits to the United States in the fall of 1929, he was a photographer much in demand in London. He has said that only Queen Mary and Virginia Woolf rejected his summons to watch the birdie. One result of his trip to America was a contract with Condé Nast, publisher of Vogue magazine. Aboard ship on his way home in April 1930 he met one of the most dazzling figures of the world he so much admired—Noel Coward, who advised him, "It's important not to let the public have a loophole to lampoon you on. . . . You should appraise yourself. Your sleeves are too tight, your voice is too high and too precise. You mustn't do it. It closes so many doors" (The Wandering Years).

Attracted to a glittering social life, Beaton made friends with key figures among both the British and American elite. Their introductions and his own charm enabled him to photograph such elusive celebrities as Greta Garbo in Hollywood in 1932 and Mrs. Wallis Warfield Simpson (soon to become the Duchess of Windsor) in London in 1935. His photographs of Mrs. Simpson and other fashionable sitters impressed the New York art world at a show at the Carroll Carstairs Gallery in 1936.

Beaton's first published collection of portraits, The Book of Beauty (Duckworth), appeared in 1930. Now prosperous, he leased an eighteenth-century country house, "Ashcombe," on the edge of the Wiltshire Downs; he later described his improvements on the house and his life there in Ashcombe; The Story of a Fifteen-Year Lease (Batsford, 1949). He could also afford to indulge his enthusiasm for travel. During the 1930's he visited North Africa, revisited America on several occasions, and spent considerable time on the Continent. Always alert with pen, brush, and camera to catch the telling detail, he often captured the authentic character of the people and places that he saw, although his factual information might remain superficial.

Cecil Beaton's Scrapbook (Scribner, 1937) contained a selection of sketches, articles, and photographs that, at the suggestion of the artist Christian Bérard, Beaton had compiled from some fifty scrapbooks covering his career. In Cecil Beaton's New York (Lippincott, 1938) he offered his impressions of the city in another combination of words, photographs, and drawings. As the title indicates, My Royal Past, by Baroness von Bülop, née Princess Theodora Louise Alexina Ludmilla Sophie von Eckermann-Waldstein, as Told to Cecil Beaton (Batsford, 1939) is a spoof of royal diarists of the Edwardian Era.

Meanwhile, Beaton had fulfilled a long-standing ambition in theater design when Charles B. Cochran engaged him to do the scenery and costumes for the ballets in Follow the Sun, presented at the Adelphi Theatre in London in 1935, and in Apparitions, which opened at the Sadler's Wells Theatre in 1936. Later in 1936 he designed the scenery and costumes for the ballet Le Pavillon, produced by Colonel de Basil's Ballets Russes de Monte Carlo at Covent Garden. He has recorded his memories of his work in the ballet and his association with famous dancers in Ballet (Doubleday, 1951).

In midsummer 1939 Beaton reached the apex thus far of his career in photography when Queen Elizabeth, the Queen Mother, asked him to photograph her in Buckingham Palace. "In choosing me to take her photographs," Beaton wrote in The Wandering Years, "the Queen made a daring innovation. It is inconceivable that her predecessor would have summoned me—my work was still considered revolutionary and unconventional." He owes much of his fame to his photographs of the Royal Family, but before he photographed Princess Elizabeth, Heir Presumptive to the British throne, just before she came of age in the spring of 1944, World War II diverted his talents to less glamorous subjects.

From 1940 to the end of the war Beaton worked for the Ministry of Information, taking documentary photographs on special government assignments. He produced several books on wartime England, including Air of Glory, published by H.M. Stationery Office in 1941. In collaboration with Peter Quennell, who wrote the commentary, he brought out a collection of his photographs of the between-war period from 1923 to 1940, Time Exposure (Scribner, 1941). Loaned to the Air Ministry in 1942, he became the official photographer for the Royal Air Force in the Middle East, and his Winged Squadrons (Hutchinson, 1942) was followed by The Near East (Batsford, 1943), a publication of his diary excerpts and photographs. His nine-month assignment in China and India during 1944 gave him material for The Far East (Batsford, 1945). Under different circumstances many years later, in 1958, he also visited Japan, and in his handsome and expensive Japanese (Day, 1959) he recorded his experiences through his usual graceful photographs, drawings, and impressionistic notes.

At the end of the war Beaton turned eagerly to the theater. For a revival of Oscar Wilde's Lady Windermere's Fan in San Francisco in August 1946, he not only designed the scenery and costumes, but also made his first appearance as an actor, in the role of Cecil Graham. Later in the year he played the same part in a production at the Cort Theatre in New York. In London he did the stage designs for the Return of the Prodigal (1948), Charley's Aunt (1949), and Aren't We All (1953), among other plays.

On Broadway, Beaton's set of an extravagantly furnished baroque château and his flamboyant costumes of 1912 France enhanced the lush production of Cry of the Peacock, but did not prevent its closing after two performances in April 1950. He also designed period costumes for Noel Coward's *Quadrille* (1954) and a stage adaptation of Henry James's *Portrait of a Lady* (1954). His costumes for *My Fair Lady* won him an Antoinette Perry Award in April 1957. Among his designs for the Metropolitan Opera were the boldly colorful sets and costumes of oriental splendor for a new production of Puccini's *Turandot*, presented in February 1961. In motion pictures his resplendent scenery and costumes glorified Paris in 1900 for *Gigi* (MGM, 1958) and Victorian England for the British-made *The Doctor's Dilemma* (Comet: MGM, 1958). The Academy of Motion Picture Arts and Sciences awarded him an Oscar for his *Gigi* costumes.

Because Beaton's work is highly personal, always a reflection of his own taste, it is scarcely surprising that some of his books since the war have been noticeably autobiographical in tone. In *Photobiography* (Doubleday, 1951), which traces the progress of his work in photography, he accompanies pictures of his family and famous people with prose accounts of his experiences with them. His *Glass of Fashion* (Doubleday, 1953) presents a pageant of fashion over the past fifty years through 146 line drawings and lively verbal characterizations. Cleveland Amory described it in the New York *Times* (January 10, 1954) as "one part history of fashion to two parts history of himself, with a heaping teaspoonfull of his friends and relatives, and a dash of bitters (by leaving them out) of his enemies."

I Take Great Pleasure (Day, 1956) is a record of Beaton's first lecture tour of the United States in sprightly, not-always-flattering word and line sketches of caricature and factual observation. He changed his focus in *The Face of the World; An International Scrapbook of People and Places* (Day, 1957) to a more varied coverage in photographs, pen sketches, and text—including among his dozens of subjects Bernard Berenson, Gertrude Stein, Somerset Maugham, Picasso, and E. M. Forster. "His is inevitably the close-up view seen through worldly, tasteful eyes," Leo Lerman wrote in the New York *Times* (December 1, 1957). "He sees theatrically, dramatically, nostalgically."

In centering attention on himself in *The Wandering Years* (1961), however, Cecil Beaton ranged far beyond himself in the excerpts from the diaries that he kept between the ages of eighteen and thirty-six. He spared himself, as he has pointed out, no more than he spared others. George Cloyne commented in the New York *Herald Tribune Book Review* (January 14, 1962), "The interest in his journal . . . lies in his ability to convey, beyond the glitter of a legendary career, the flavor of a genuine personality. . . . He noticed everything. That is what made him dangerous. Not a smut on the nose, not a crumb on the waistcoat escaped him. And if his photographs seem often charmingly romantic, his prose portraits are regularly needle-sharp."

Cecil Beaton was made a Commander, Order of the British Empire in 1957, and he holds the decoration of the Legion of Honor. He belongs to the Church of England and in politics prefers the Conservatives. In his portraiture, especially, he reveals himself as an artist of wisdom and wit with an acute sensitivity not only in understanding people but also in dealing with them tactfully. Despite the self-criticism of his diaries, he cuts a figure that he himself might be well expected to admire; he is slim and tall (six feet two inches) and has blue eyes and gray hair. Portraits of him over the years are likely to catch expressions of thoughtfulness, aesthetic preoccupation, or amusement. In choosing his own clothes he shows the same fastidious care that he takes with his costume designs. He freely admits to the pursuit of many enjoyments in life; and his recreations, again, reflect the oneness of the man and his work—interior decoration, travel, gardening, art collecting, and keeping diaries and scrapbooks.

References

> Beaton, Cecil. The Wandering Years (1961)
> Who's Who, 1962
> Who's Who in America, 1962-63
> Who's Who in the Theatre (1957)

BOK, WILLIAM CURTIS Sept. 7, 1897-May 22, 1962 Justice of Pennsylvania Supreme Court (1958-62); president judge, Philadelphia Court of Common Pleas No. 6 (1937-58); in 1949 handed down often cited decision absolving nine novels of charges of obscenity; author of two semi-fictional books stressing humane side of law. See *Current Biography* (May) 1954.

Obituary

> N Y Times p45 My 23 '62

BRECKINRIDGE, AIDA DE ACOSTA July 28, 1884-May 27, 1962 Founder and former executive director (1945-55) of the Eye-Bank for Sight Restoration, Inc.; promoter of many other welfare causes. See *Current Biography* (June) 1954.

Obituary

> N Y Times p31 My 29 '62

BUCK, SOLON J(USTUS) Aug. 16, 1884-May 25, 1962 Former Archivist of the United States (1941-48); chief of manuscript division (1948-51) and assistant librarian (1951-54), Library of Congress; taught history at several midwestern universities; author of historical books. See *Current Biography* (May) 1947.

Obituary

> N Y Times p29 My 28 '62

CARROLL, THOMAS H(ENRY 2D) May 12, 1914- University president; educator

Address: b. George Washington University, Washington, D.C.; h. 2330 Tracy Pl., Washington, D.C.

The thirteenth president of George Washington University is Dr. Thomas H. Carroll, who

Harris & Ewing

THOMAS H. CARROLL

took office in February 1961. After a career of twenty-five years as an educator and administrator, he regards his present position as the most challenging in his experience, and he has great plans for the university during his presidency. Taking Harvard University as his American model, Carroll aims at making the capital's university into an institution that serves the community, the nation, and the world. He would like George Washington University to have as great an impact on Washington, D.C. as European universities have on their capital cities.

Thomas Henry Carroll 2d was born in San Francisco, California on May 12, 1914, the son of William Edward and Charlotte (Castle) Carroll. His father, whose ancestors had come from Maryland and settled in California as pioneers, was a mechanical engineer. Carroll and his three sisters, Edith M., Jessie D., and Marie E., were reared in San Francisco, where he attended Lowell High School. He was active in journalism and was a member of the student honor society. When he graduated in 1930 he received an award for the greatest service rendered by a member of the graduating class. He then attended the University of California in Berkeley, where he majored in economics and business. During summers he worked on freighters going through the Panama Canal, and one summer he worked for Standard Oil Company of California. In his junior year he was elected to Beta Gamma Sigma and to the national business administration scholastic society. He received the B.S. degree with honors in 1934.

Having won the San Francisco-Harvard Alumni scholarship, Carroll entered the Harvard University Graduate School of Business Administration, where he received the M.B.A. degree with distinction in 1936. His choice of a career in higher education was greatly influenced by a "scholarly, practical, and humane" senior pro-

fessor, under whom he worked as a research assistant at the graduate school in 1936. While working on his doctorate, Carroll served as an instructor at the Graduate School of Business Administration from 1937 to 1939. He received the degree of Doctor of Commercial Science in the latter year, after submitting the thesis "Some Financial and Regulatory Problems of Retirement Accounting in Public Utilities." From 1939 to 1942 he was assistant dean and assistant professor at the Harvard Graduate School of Business Administration.

Entering the United States Naval Reserve in the rank of lieutenant junior grade in 1942, Carroll served with the Bureau of Naval Personnel from August 1942 to December 1945. His last assignment before his separation with the rank of commander in 1946 was as director of officer candidate procurement. He was awarded the Secretary of the Navy commendation ribbon and received the Chief of Naval Personnel commendation letter. Returning to academic life in 1946, Carroll became dean and professor at Syracuse University College of Business Administration and did much to improve conditions there. In 1950 he was appointed dean and professor at the University of North Carolina School of Business Administration.

Meanwhile, in 1948-49, Carroll had been a member of the study commission that set up the policy and program of the Ford Foundation. In November 1953 the trustees of the Ford Foundation announced that the foundation's panel of five associate directors had been enlarged to include Carroll as sixth associate director. In this capacity he worked with Dr. Robert Maynard Hutchins, Milton Katz, Dyke Brown, William McPeak, and Don K. Price, Jr., in administering the foundation and investigating the merits of requests for grants. He continued to serve the University of North Carolina on a part-time basis until June 1954, when he resigned from the university to devote his full time to the Ford Foundation. He served as director of the foundation's program in economic development and administration from 1953 to 1955. In 1954 he was named a vice-president of the foundation, and in this capacity he participated in seminars on management and economic development in Africa and Latin America.

The unanimous choice of Dr. Carroll as the thirteenth president of George Washington University, to take office on February 1, 1961, was announced by the university's board of trustees on August 6, 1960. He succeeded Cloyd Heck Marvin, who retired in 1959 after two years as president. In the interim Oswald S. Colclough, provost and dean of the faculties, had served as acting president. The red brick campus of the 141-year-old George Washington University is located in the Foggy Bottom area of Washington, D.C., three blocks from the White House. In 1961 the university had about 9,400 students and 1,000 faculty members, of whom about two-thirds served on a part-time basis. George Washington University has an outstanding medical school and law school, and a number of its graduates have become prominent in government.

Following his appointment as president Carroll outlined his plans for George Washington University, declaring that the university had "lifted itself by its bootstraps," but that it had "not lived up to its potential." One of his first aims is to raise the admission requirements, so that the university's degrees will carry increased weight as professional qualifications. He would also like to have more scholarships available to attract top students. He feels that the university has missed some opportunities for research, and he plans improvements in this area, thereby attracting to Washington highly qualified professors to increase faculty strength. He envisages the establishment of a national law center at George Washington University, and he would like to see additional laboratories, classrooms, and dormitories built during his presidency. As president he will be responsible for raising funds to fulfill all these ambitions.

As one of his major goals President Carroll is seeking to make George Washington University play an important role in the national life, comparable to that of universities located in the capitals of other countries. Citing the University of London as one example, Carroll believes that a university located in a national capital can exercise a great impact upon the life of the community, the nation, and the world. He also feels that such a university could help to build "greater mutual understanding among business, the professions, and government."

In addition to being president, Dr. Carroll holds the academic rank of professor of economic development and administration, and he hopes to find time for teaching and research in addition to his other duties. He believes that the president should provide intellectual leadership and feels he will be in a better position to do so as a "colleague of the faculty" and as an active teacher and researcher. Carroll's specialty is management training, which he describes as "preparation for an uncertain future." He was pleased by the recent change when George Washington University's School of Government was renamed the School of Government, Business and International Affairs, for he sees these as interrelated subjects that should be studied together.

Carroll has observed that higher education in the field of business has been growing so rapidly in recent decades that one out of five male students is majoring in business at the present time. He notes with satisfaction that serious attention is belatedly being given to the upgrading of business schools in colleges and universities throughout the United States and that the work of the Ford Foundation has been "singularly impressive" in this field.

The author of a number of articles for such publications as *Advanced Management, Business Horizons,* and *California Management Review,* Carroll also edited and contributed to the publication *Business Education for Competence and Responsibility* (Univ. of N.C. Press, 1954). A participant in civic affairs, he served as a member of the board of education of Darien, Connecticut from 1958 to 1961 and helped to prepare an incentive pay report, submitted in 1961, which examined teachers' demands for salary increases. From 1957 to 1961 he was a member of the board of directors of the Community Council of Darien, and he has served as vice-president of the Darien Mental Health Association. Previously he had been a member of the board of directors of the Community Council of Chapel Hill, North Carolina; a director of the John E. Mason Foundation, Inc.; and a member of the board of Stamford (Connecticut) Hospital. He has been a member of the national advisory committee of the White House Conference on Aging, and he serves as a consultant to the United States Navy on procurement policy.

A Fellow of the American Association for the Advancement of Science, Dr. Carroll is also an honorary member of the North Carolina Association of Certified Public Accountants. He has been elected to membership in Beta Alpha Psi, Delta Sigma Pi, Tau Theta Upsilon, Beta Gamma Sigma, Sigma Iota Epsilon, and Lambda Chi Alpha. He is a member of the American Economic Association and of the Controllers Institute of America. From 1948 to 1953 he was on the executive committee of the American Association of Collegiate Schools of Business, and he has served on the executive committee of the National Commission on Education and Experience of Certified Public Accountants. He was president of the Harvard Business School Association in 1955-56 and director of the Harvard Alumni Association in 1956-58. He is a member of the New England Society of New York City, and of the University clubs of New York City and Washington, D.C.

On December 13, 1941 Dr. Thomas H. Carroll married Polly Holcomb Burgess, a member of a New England pioneer family that had moved westward. They have two sons, Thomas Henry 3d (known as Terry) and Bruce Burgess. The family lives in a new Washington town house, purchased by George Washington University for its president. Carroll is six feet three inches tall and has hazel eyes and brown hair. His religious affiliation is with the Congregational Church and he is an independent in politics. His favorite recreations are hiking and reading. Music, books, and good conversation are part of the family life of the Carrolls.

References

Washington (D.C.) Post Fp25+ S 24 '61 por
Who's Who in America, 1962-63

DEAN, H(ENRY) TRENDLEY Aug. 25, 1893-May 13, 1962 Dental surgeon; pioneer in determining effects of fluoridated water on tooth decay; secretary of council on dental research, American Dental Association (1953-59); director of National Institute of Dental Research (1948-53). See *Current Biography* (June) 1957.

Obituary

N Y Times p39 My 15 '62

DROZNIAK, EDWARD (drŏzh' nĕ-ăk) Aug. 21, 1902- Polish Ambassador to the United States

Address: b. Embassy of the Polish People's Republic, 2640 16th St., N.W., Washington 9, D.C.; h. 4242 Mathewson Dr., N.W., Washington 11, D.C.

The Ambassador from the Polish People's Republic to the United States is Edward Drozniak, a banker and economist who is seeking to promote friendly relations between the two countries and to exert a favorable influence on possible projects of economic co-operation. A member of the dominant Polish United Workers' party, Drozniak was associated from 1925 to 1945 with the Central Bank of Farmers' Co-operatives. Since 1945 he has served in various government posts—as president of the National Bank of Poland, deputy minister of finance, member of the Polish parliament (Sejm), and head of the state commission for governmental appointments. On June 20, 1961 he was appointed to succeed Romuald Spasowski as Ambassador to the United States.

The Polish people have long been held in high esteem by the United States. Following the three partitions in 1772, 1793, and 1795, Poland was divided between Russia, Prussia, and Austria, and ceased to exist as a national entity. After World War I it was restored as a nation, only to be divided again in 1939 between Nazi Germany and the Soviet Union. Since World War II Poland has been a member of the Communist bloc, with close ties to the Soviet Union.

Edward Drozniak was born on August 21, 1902 (August 8, according to the Julian calendar) in Czestochowa, a major industrial center located in an iron-mining district, in the southwestern part of what was then Russian Poland. He was one of six children of Jakub and Stanislawa (Idzik) Drozniak. He received his secondary education at the *Gymnasium* in Czestochowa, graduating in 1921, at a time when Poland was resuming its national independence under the peace settlement following World War I. He then entered the Higher School of Trade in Warsaw for his university education and received his diploma in 1925. During his second year at the school he began working in the foreign trade department of the Polish United Land Bank, a private commercial bank. In 1923 he began teaching at the university level in the Higher School of Trade, and he remained there as an assistant professor until 1932.

After receiving his diploma in 1925, Drozniak became active in the Polish co-operative movement, and for the next twenty years he was associated with the Central Bank of Farmers' Co-operatives. In 1925 he was appointed executive secretary of the bank, and two years later he became deputy director. Drozniak also served as secretary, and later as president, of the Co-operative Association. In 1927 he completed his thesis for the Higher School of Trade, on the history and development of the financial management of co-operatives. The thesis was later published by the Central Organization of Co-operatives.

In 1935 Drozniak became the director of the Cracow branch of the Central Bank of Farmers' Co-operatives, and in 1939 he was chosen a member of the bank's national board of directors in Warsaw. Meanwhile, following the Nazi-Soviet pact of August 1939, Poland was divided between Nazi Germany and the Soviet Union. Two years later, after conquering and occupying much of Europe, Nazi Germany turned to attack the Soviet Union and swept toward Moscow. During World War II Drozniak belonged to the political underground in Poland, at the same time retaining his position with the bank until the end of the war.

In January 1945, while the liberation of Poland by Soviet and free Polish forces was under way, Drozniak was given the task of organizing the National Bank of Poland, and in the following month he was made a governor of the bank. He also became vice-chairman of the economic committee of the Polish cabinet. As a result of an agreement reached at the Yalta conference in February 1945 a Polish Provisional Government of National Unity was established, based upon the Soviet-backed Polish Committee of National Liberation, which had been set up in Lublin in the preceding year. With the addition of several Polish democratic leaders from the Polish government-in-exile in London, the new government was recognized by the United States and Great Britain on July 5, 1945.

Following recognition by the Western powers the new Polish government appointed a commission to secure all Polish property in Great Britain. Appointed to preside over this commission, Drozniak went to London in July for negotiations. One of his tasks was to gain control of Poland's gold reserve, estimated at about $60,000,000, which had been brought to London for safekeeping during the war. At this time the representatives of the Polish government-in-exile in London were determined not to give up their assets or their authority except to a government formed on free Polish soil. Meanwhile, the National Bank of Poland was issuing notes secured by Poland's industrial production. In a press conference held shortly after he arrived in London, Drozniak described his country as physically, mentally, and economically exhausted and declared that help from Great Britain, the United States, and the Soviet Union was imperative. He noted that Poland, with between 6,000,000 and 7,000,000 persons (including 3,000,000 Polish Jews) killed during the war, was in dire need of manpower, as well as machinery, food, and medicine.

Negotiations over the Polish assets continued for a year, and in June 1946 Drozniak signed the Anglo-Polish financial agreement, which settled most Polish war debts to Great Britain and transferred the assets of the former Polish government-in-exile to the Provisional Government of National Unity. This agreement was concluded despite British concern over the Warsaw government's treatment of the Polish Peasants' party in the pre-election political maneuvers. Poland agreed to pay for the maintenance, welfare, and education of all Poles in the British Commonwealth up to June 1, 1946, while Great

Britain eliminated the Polish debt for military supplies furnished under the lend-lease arrangements to Polish forces during the war. After these settlements, the gold was transferred to the Polish government.

In April 1946 Drozniak became president of the National Bank of Poland and held the position for the next five years. The bank has exclusive authority to issue currency, is charged with the control of money and credit, and has the responsibility for the financial implementation of governmental economic plans. As the Polish economy became more and more government-controlled, the bank in 1947 was given control of the financial side of all planned transactions and the right of detailed supervision of each enterprise's financial plan. By subsequent acts in 1948 and 1951 its hold on state enterprises was strengthened and it functioned in much the same way as the Soviet National Bank.

In 1946 Drozniak headed the Polish delegation to the inaugural meeting of the combined boards of governors of the International Monetary Fund (IMF) and the International Bank for Reconstruction and Development (IBRD), held in Savannah, Georgia. Until 1950 he was a member of the Polish delegation to the annual IMF meetings and of the board of governors of the IBRD. From 1947 to 1951 he also served as deputy minister of finance in the Polish government.

Drozniak became president of the Polish state commission for governmental appointments in 1951 and remained in this position for five years. In 1956, the year when the uprisings in Poland led to increased liberalization of the regime, he was reappointed president of the National Bank of Poland and deputy minister of finance. He continued to hold these positions until 1961. From 1957 to 1958 he was also a member of the State Planning Commission. In the January 20, 1957 elections to the Polish parliament (Sejm) he was elected for a four-year term as a delegate of the Polish United Workers party.

Within the co-operative movement Drozniak has continued to be active and has held several important posts. From 1953 to 1961 he was chairman of the supervising council of the Consumers' Co-operative Union, and from 1953 to 1958 he was president of the Supreme Co-operative Council. He has also been a member of a number of other economic and social organizations.

On June 20, 1961 Drozniak was appointed Ambassador of the Polish People's Republic to the United States. His primary mission is to improve economic relations between the two countries and to increase Poland's dollar income by finding a larger market for its products in the United States. Since 1957 the United States has sold Poland a large amount of grain and other commodities for zlotys. The resulting saving of her foreign currency is credited with having spared Poland the choice of accepting a major food crisis or of sharply curtailing her industrial development.

Drozniak has written many articles on finance and the management of co-operatives, primarily for Polish journals on economic affairs. In 1947 the Polish government conferred upon Drozniak

Adams Studio

EDWARD DROZNIAK

the Commander's Cross of "Polonia Restituta," and in the same year he was decorated by the Czechoslovakian government with the Order of the White Lion, Second Class. In 1954 he received the Order of "Sztandar Pracy," First Class, from the Polish government.

On August 4, 1928 Edward Drozniak married Halina Konkowska. They have one daughter, Elzbieta, and a son, Andrzej. Drozniak is five feet six inches tall, weighs 132 pounds, and has blue eyes and gray hair. He enjoys reading classical and modern literature and listening to music, and his favorite outdoor recreations are skiing and mountain climbing. He is a member of the Polish Climbing and Touring Society.

References

International Who's Who, 1961-62
World Biography (1948)

DUBUFFET, JEAN (dōō-bōō-fā') July 31, 1901- French painter
Address: 114 bis rue de Vaugirard, Paris 6ᵉ, France

Probably no artist is more honored by American art critics, collectors, and curators today than Jean Dubuffet, the French painter who has sworn in his heart to destroy their canons. "Too highly honored," Dubuffet has said, "art is rarely nowadays a free celebration. . . . It should . . . be stripped of all the tinsel, laurels, and buskins . . . and be seen naked with all the creases of its belly. Once disencumbered, it will doubtless begin again to . . . dance and yell like a madman, which is its function, and stop putting on preposterous airs from its professor's chair."

Believing that the untrained vision is the unhampered vision, Dubuffet, a sophisticated primitive, has taken his inspiration from the *art brut* of the child, the madman, and the savage. His

Alexander Liberman

JEAN DUBUFFET

paintings look like slabs of sidewalk scrawled upon by children or pieces of earth in which a savage has doodled with a stick. A wholesale wine merchant who painted on and off for years, Dubuffet did not settle down singleheartedly to his vocation until 1942, when he was forty-one. Since then he has worked zealously and ceaselessly, always experimenting, always changing. His early paintings were thin oils. In the mid 1940's he was using oils in thick relief. He experimented with house paints and other material. By the early 1950's his paintings were thick impastos that included sand, tar, pebbles, or other matter. They had also become quite abstract. His work in 1961 showed a tendency away from the abstract, toward subjects like bright Paris street scenes.

Jean Dubuffet was born in Le Havre, France on July 31, 1901. He was the first child of George S. Dubuffet and Jeanne (Paillette) Dubuffet. (The second child, a girl, was born thirteen years later.) His father was a wine and liquor merchant. "My parents were bourgeois. . . ," Dubuffet told a writer for the *New Yorker* (March 17, 1962). "They had a house, and a chauffeur and other servants. . . . I hated my *famille de commerçants* and their constant talk of money."

Completing his secondary studies at seventeen, Dubuffet, bored with Le Havre and unhappy with his family, went to Paris to live alone and paint. He lived in miserable quarters in the Montparnasse section of Paris, exulting in poverty, spending the small allowance from his family as soon as it arrived and living on nothing the rest of the month. For a brief period he studied art at the Académie Julian. He read widely in ancient and modern literature, paleography, and ethnology, and, also on his own, studied music and languages (Spanish, Latin, English, Russian, Arabic, German, and Italian).

When he was in his early twenties, Dubuffet became persuaded that his work was imitating that of his friends Raoul Dufy, Suzanne Valadon, and Fernand Léger, and he stopped painting. He traveled to Italy and Brazil. In 1925 he returned to Le Havre and began studying commerce. He married Paulette Bret on February 25, 1927 and by her had a daughter. In 1930 he started a wholesale wine business in the Bercy section of Paris.

About 1933 Dubuffet put an associate in charge of his wine business and turned to a bohemian life. Living with his second wife in cheap lodgings on the Left Bank, he entertained his friends by playing the piano and accordion and by giving puppet shows. Some of his friends were artists and musicians (but not established or serious artists and musicians, a group that Dubuffet has always avoided). They in turn hardly thought of him as a painter, much less one headed for success, although he was doing some *peinturlage* and making marionettes and theatrical masks.

Since his wine business was failing in the hands of his associate, Dubuffet reassumed direct control of it in 1937. The business ended with the coming of war and Dubuffet's mobilization in 1939. Discharged in 1940 because of his inability to submit to army discipline, Dubuffet started a new wine business with a new associate. The new associate proved more capable than the previous one, and Dubuffet left the running of the business to him in 1942. (The venture continued to profit under the associate until 1946, when Dubuffet sold it.)

The year 1942 is commonly considered to mark the real beginning of Dubuffet's career. It was then that he not only began to devote himself completely to his art, but began afresh, renouncing much of his previous work, some of which Thomas B. Hess has described as "reminiscent of *art populaire*" (*Art News*, May 1952). He experimented widely with oil and gouache, trying, in the judgment of Clement Greenberg, "to find an equivalent in color for the 'primitivist' reduction to which he subjects his drawings."

His first exhibition, at the Galerie René Drouin in Paris in the fall of 1944, was a *succès de scandale*. His celebrity as a primitive "*plus fauve que les fauves*" was only augmented by the envious protests of more academic artists. "It is true," Dubuffet replied to the latter, "that the method of design employed in these paintings is totally aloof from the kind of expertism generally found in pictures by professionals and it is also true that no one would need to undergo special studies or to have inborn gifts in order to do things like them. To that I reply that I find such studies and gifts exceedingly tiresome, their effects tending to suppress all spontaneity, to cut all communion, and to swamp the work with ineffectiveness. . . . To walk beautifully is it necessary to have longer legs than other people, or to walk on one's hands?"

From October 1944 to March 1945 Dubuffet did only lithographs. Resuming his painting in March 1945, he completed within a few days three mural-size canvases of jazz musicians, including *Jazz Nouvelle Orléans*. Later in 1945 he made walls the subjects of several paintings. His work in 1946 included *Vue de Paris* and *Grand Paysage*. This 1945-1946 work was included, with paintings from the earlier 1940's, in his first American exhibition, at the Pierre Matisse Gallery in New York City in early 1947. Clement Greenberg, one of the first American art critics to give respectful attention to Dubuffet, writing in the *Nation* (February 1, 1947), found the earlier work "impoverished, giving us to suspect frustrated talent at the most," but the 1945-1946 work he thought "on the whole . . . original and profound. . . . 'Vue de Paris' . . . is proof . . . of how completely Dubuffet has assimilated all that the School of Paris has had to teach since 1908. . . . 'Grand Paysage' . . . bears resemblance at points to a sort of thing many painters over here have been trying to do with Klee's heritage. . . . But where Americans mean mysticism, Dubuffet means matter. . . . Three or four more pictures on the level of 'Promeneuse [au Parapluie]' would suffice to make Dubuffet one of the major painters of the twentieth century. This, even though his art still suffers under the limitation of being too essentially personal."

In the late 1940's Dubuffet traveled in North Africa, particularly in the Sahara, and the influence of the journeys later became evident in some of his pictures. He spent a few months in the United States in late 1951 and early 1952, living in Greenwich Village, New York City, and working in a loft just off the Bowery. Thomas B. Hess, who visited the loft, described Dubuffet's working methods at that time in *Art News* (May 1952). Dubuffet covered a masonite panel with spot putty and drew on the drying putty with a corner of the putty knife. Then he beat and manipulated the surface until, in Dubuffet's words, it looked like "the hide of a hippopotamus." The wrinkled surface was left to dry overnight before paint was applied. The application of the paint depended partly on the effect desired. Sometimes it was thrown hard at the surface, making a thin splatter. Sometimes it was dripped gently, making a blob. Sometimes it was applied with a housepainter's brush, sometimes with a rag. Dubuffet's earlier relief paintings, the *hautes pâtes* of the mid-1940's, had been done in oil, and much of the reason for his experimentation with putties and other materials (house paint mixed with sand, chalk and zinc oxide compounds, various oil and water emulsions) derived from an impatience with long-drying oil and a desire for rapid realization.

There were two notable exhibitions of Dubuffet's work in Paris in 1954. One was a retrospective exhibition at the Cercle Volney; the other was an exhibition at the Galerie Rive Gauche of about forty little statues he had devised from slag, clinkers, and other refuse. Michael Seuphor compared it to the similar work done by Kurt Schwitters "with less success and a more real naïveté." "These statuettes," Seuphor wrote, "have a flavor of belated expressionism, as in fact does all of Dubuffet's work."

Since his first appearance at the Pierre Matisse Gallery, Dubuffet has had several New York exhibitions—at the Pierre Matisse, the Cordier-Warren Gallery, and the Museum of Modern Art. By the time that the Museum of Modern

Art held a retrospective exhibition of some 200 of his works from February 1 to April 8, 1962, a majority of American critics had reached the consensus that Dubuffet was indeed what Clement Greenberg had called him in the 1940's: "the most original painter to have come out of the School of Paris since Miró." After leaving the Museum of Modern Art the 1962 retrospective exhibition traveled to Chicago and Los Angeles. Reviewing the exhibition, John Canaday of the New York *Times* (February 21, 1962) wrote, "One measure of Dubuffet's achievement is that he beautifies without idealizing, while in the hands of this expert technician the power of technically innocent work is retained. . . . The element that unites Dubuffet's disparate qualities . . . [is] tremendous gusto for life."

Jean Dubuffet is short, bald, and blue-eyed. After photographing Dubuffet, Alexander Liberman wrote, "He looks like a being who could have lived untold years ago." He usually gets up at seven and works in his Left Bank studio from eight in the morning until seven at night. His usual recreation is sitting at home in the evenings with his wife, Lili, listening to music or reading. When he does go out for recreation he prefers the local bistro to the ballet or theater, rejecting as he does all pretensions to culture. He drinks little but is a connoisseur of French *petits vins* and (when in the United States) of coffee and Scotch whisky. To maintain the stance of the amateur, the ordinary man, he shuts himself off as much as possible from the art world and the press. He collects *art brut,* the work of children, criminals, and psychotics, and in early 1962 he said that he had just bought a large house in Paris in which to keep and display it. At the same time he announced that he was building a retreat at Etaples, a fishing town in Picardy. Until he became disgusted with the hordes of tourists and the excess of sunlight, he used previously to spend more than half of each year at Vence, in the south of France. No longer interested in European music, he has lately taken to playing Arabian flutes, Chinese chimes, and other exotic instruments.

Alexander Liberman has written of Dubuffet: "He has broken more violently with the conventions of traditional easel painting than any painter I have photographed. I watched him throw sand, or gravel into amorphous mixtures smeared over a plaster board. With a knife, trowel, rag, or his hand, he shaped the lavalike flows of earth color until he finally brought them to a stop. I marveled at the amount of stored-up skill he summoned to fix the fleeting images that seemed to well up like volcanic eruptions."

References

Art News 51:30+ My '52 pors
New Yorker 38:36+ Mr 17 '62
Newsweek 59:84 F 26 '62 por
Time 76:100+ N 7 '60 pors

International Who's Who, 1961-62
Langui, Emile. Fifty Years of Modern Art (1959)
Liberman, Alexander. The Artist in His Studio (1960)
Parrot, Louis. Jean Dubuffet (1944)
Ragon, Michel. Dubuffet (1959)

EKLUND, (ARNE) SIGVARD June 19, 1911-
International agency official; physicist

Address: b. International Atomic Energy Agency,
Kaernterring, Vienna 1, Austria

As director-general of the International Atomic
Energy Agency, under the auspices of the United
Nations, Dr. Sigvard Eklund has put to good use
his expert knowledge of the peaceful uses of
atomic energy and his administrative experience
with the Swedish Atomic Energy Company, a
joint private and government enterprise. An
eminent Swedish nuclear physicist and nuclear
reactor expert, Dr. Eklund was elected for a four-
year term beginning on December 1, 1961 by the
general conference of the International Atomic
Energy Agency, consisting of seventy-seven participating nations, in October 1961. Dr. Eklund
succeeded Sterling Cole, an American, in the
post.

Before he took office with the International
Atomic Energy Agency, Dr. Eklund had been
technical director of the Swedish Atomic Energy
Company, beginning in 1957, and headed the
department responsible for the development of
reactors. The last purely scientific project in
which he was involved before he became primarily an administrator was the construction of
the first Swedish nuclear reactor, which began
operation in 1954. Dr. Eklund has contributed
his services to several international organizations
and acted as secretary-general to the 1958 United
Nations International Conference on the Peaceful Use of Atomic Energy, held in Geneva,
Switzerland.

Arne Sigvard Eklund was born in Kiruna in
Norrbotten province, the northernmost city in
Swedish Lapland and a rich iron mining center,
on June 19, 1911 to Severin E. Eklund, a locomotive engineer, and Vilhelmina (Pettersson)
Eklund. Since boyhood he had dreamed of becoming a physicist. After graduating from the
secondary school in nearby Luleå, he attended
the University of Uppsala and received his Master's degree in physics in 1936. He began his
career by working at the Nobel Institute for
Physics in Stockholm under the direction of
Professor Karl Manne Georg Siegbahn, who won
the Nobel Prize in Physics in 1925. In 1945
Eklund joined the staff of the Research Institute
of National Defense, where he was placed in
charge of the section responsible for research in
nuclear physics. There he studied methods of
detecting and measuring amounts of radiation.

Continuing his education, Eklund earned a
Ph.D. degree from the University of Uppsala in
1946. In the same year his doctoral thesis in
nuclear physics so impressed local scientists and
administrators that he was appointed an associate
professor of physics at the Royal Institute of
Technology in Stockholm. In 1950 the Swedish
Atomic Energy Company (AB Atomenergi) invited Dr. Eklund to join the staff as director of
research, and in 1957 he was promoted to technical director. (The government owns fifty-seven
percent of the Swedish Atomic Energy Company
and seventy private industries hold the remaining shares.) While working for the Swedish
Atomic Energy Company, Dr. Eklund was engaged in the construction of the first nuclear re-

actor in Sweden—a 300-kilowatt research model
—that was completed in 1954. He wrote a
description of the reactor for the *Chemical
Engineering Progress Symposium,* published in
1954. As technical director, Dr. Eklund functioned mainly as an administrator whose responsibility was to stimulate and organize the
work and research performed by others.

At the suggestion of President Dwight D.
Eisenhower, the United Nations sponsored the
first International Conference on the Peaceful
Use of Atomic Energy at the Palais de Nations
in Geneva, Switzerland in July 1955. The conference proved so successful in the free exchange
of information previously considered secret between the East and the West that another conference was planned for the future. Another
outgrowth of the conference was the establishment, two years later, of the International
Atomic Energy Agency. Dag Hammarskjöld appointed Dr. Eklund secretary-general of the second United Nations International Conference on
the Peaceful Use of Atomic Energy, held in
Geneva from September 1 to 13 in 1958. Its
purpose was to survey the progress that had been
made during the three years that had elapsed
since the previous conference in the fields of
physics (including fusion), chemistry, isotopes,
radiological protection, metallurgy, and reactor
technology.

Dr. Eklund prepared the program for the conference and supervised the publication of the
thirty-three volume encyclopedia containing the
information disseminated there. Over 2,500 abstracts of scientific papers had been submitted to
the United Nations for presentation, and it was
his task, aided by an international group of
scientific secretaries, to choose the 714 technical
reports to be read at the conference. He was also
responsible for supervising the translation of
2,135 papers submitted by forty-six nations and
six international organizations into the four official languages of the conference: English, French,
Russian, and Spanish. He arranged and appor-
tioned the floor space for the exhibits of the
twenty governments that participated.

When, in June 1961, Dr. Eklund was nominated by the twenty-three directors of the International Atomic Energy Agency to be the second
director-general, he became the center of a controversy. The United States had proposed Dr.
Eklund because he is a nuclear scientist experienced in the peaceful application of atomic
energy, an able administrator, and a citizen of
a neutral country. However, the Russian delegation and the African-Asian bloc, led by India,
opposed his nomination on the grounds that the
next director-general should come from one of
the underdeveloped nations.

Accordingly, Professor Vasily S. Yemelyanov,
the head of the Russian delegation, tried by various tactics to block Dr. Eklund's election at the
general conference of the International Atomic
Energy Agency, held in Vienna in October 1961. He
objected to Dr. Eklund on the grounds that since
he was not the official candidate of the Swedish
government, he was merely a tool in the hands
of the West. He also charged that Dr. Eklund
had passed on Swedish atomic secrets to the
British—an allegation that had been investigated

and proved false—and tried to cast doubts on his ability as a scientist. When the members of the conference ignored these charges and confirmed Dr. Eklund's appointment by almost two-thirds of the votes, Yemelyanov threatened the withdrawal of the Soviet Union from the international agency. He himself walked out of the conference before Dr. Eklund was inaugurated on October 6, 1961, but the other members of the Russian delegation remained. When the board of directors met again in February 1962, the Soviet Union indicated that it was ready to co-operate. In the meantime, Dr. Eklund had pledged himself to "abide by the statutes of the agency and not submit to pressures from any government or group." He succeeded Sterling Cole, former Republican member of Congress from New York, who had completed a four-year term.

As director-general, Dr. Eklund is faced with problems that have plagued the agency since its establishment in 1957 with headquarters in Vienna. Its purpose is to increase the peaceful use of atomic energy by serving as an intermediary between nations that produce nuclear fuel and governments that desire it, and by providing, under a system of safeguards, any information, material, equipment, and service needed for the development and use of atomic energy. Although the agency exerts no control over the military use of atomic energy, it has the power to inspect facilities built with its aid and to withdraw its support from any country that violates its rules. But such questions as what kind of supervision and how much supervision should be given to prevent radioactive material from being diverted to military use and the disposal of radioactive waste have not yet been answered. The Russians have always contended that the agency is dominated by the West and that not enough attention has been given to the underdeveloped countries.

On March 30, 1962 Harlan Cleveland, Assistant Secretary of State for International Organizations Affairs, and Dr. Eklund signed an agreement (that became effective on June 1, 1962) to allow experts from the agency to inspect four atomic reactors in the United States. Officials hoped that the Soviet Union would make a similar agreement. The inspections will demonstrate the effectivenesss of the International Atomic Energy Agency's safeguards system.

After World War II ended, people believed that atomic energy would solve Europe's power shortage, but the dream of cheap and abundant nuclear power has not materialized. According to Dr. Eklund, one reason for this failure is the fact that conventional fuels such as coal and oil have dropped in price as the result of discoveries of new deposits of these resources.

Dr. Eklund has devoted much of his time and talents to such international organizations as the European Atomic Energy Society. He was chairman of the International Board of Management of the high-temperature reactor in Britain known as the Dragon Project and served on a committee administering the Halden boiling-water nuclear reactor in Norway. He has written

United Nations

SIGVARD EKLUND

papers on nuclear physics and has been a member of the Swedish Academy of Engineering Sciences since 1953.

Arne Sigvard Eklund married Anna-Greta Johansson, an assistant principal in a secondary school, in 1941. They live with Kerstin and Gudrun, their daughters, and Anders, their son, in a suburb north of Stockholm. During the short Swedish summer, when time permits, the family retreats to a small cottage on the north shore of the Gulf of Bothnia in Dr. Eklund's native province of Lapland.

Described in a New York *Times* sketch (October 7, 1961) as a "quiet, orderly and popular but exacting taskmaster who looks the man of action even in his walk," Dr. Eklund has won the respect of his subordinates. His work is his hobby. He goes occasionally to a gymnasium to keep his five-feet, nine-inch and 156-pound frame in shape, and when he has an opportunity to do so, enjoys reading modern literature, especially the works of John Steinbeck and Carl Sandburg.

References

N Y Times p4 O 7 '61 por
International Who's Who, 1961-62

ELLIS, ELMER July 27, 1901- University president
Address: University of Missouri, Columbia, Mo.

When the board of curators of the University of Missouri named Elmer Ellis president of the university to succeed Frederick A. Middlebush on April 16, 1955, they appointed a man who had already won the respect and admiration of colleagues and students for his accomplishments as a scholar, teacher, and administrator. Ellis had first come to the university in 1930 as an assist-

ELMER ELLIS

ant professor of history. He was subsequently promoted to professor and to the posts of dean of the faculty of the College of Arts and Science (1946-55) and acting president of the university (1954-55). Under his leadership the university has acquired an able teaching staff and has expanded its physical plant. Ellis believes that the state universities of America represent the "highest expression of democratic educational philosophy."

Elmer Ellis, the sixth of eleven children, was born on July 27, 1901 on a farm near the village of Anamoose in McHenry County, North Dakota. His paternal grandparents had moved from New England to Minnesota in the 1850's and had later joined homesteaders who beat a trail to the Dakotas in the closing decades of the nineteenth century. Ellis' mother, Lillie Jane (Butterfield) Ellis, was a teacher. His father, Thomas Clarkson Ellis, gave up farming in 1902 to become a storekeeper in Anamoose and, later, in the county seat, Towner, where he kept a hardware store. During the last years of his life, from 1914 to 1920 and again from 1922 to 1927, he served as a judge of McHenry County. After his death his wife was selected by the county commissioners to complete his term of office.

Elmer Ellis grew up in Towner and attended its elementary and secondary schools. After school and on weekends he helped out in a grocery store, and during one summer vacation he worked as a harvest hand. He also found time to belong to the Boy Scouts and to play high-school baseball and basketball. Imbued by his parents with a desire for education, he entered Fargo (North Dakota) College, which two of his brothers had attended, in 1920. No longer solvent, Fargo College was forced to close the following year. Ellis, too, experienced financial difficulties, and he left school after his freshman year to earn funds to continue his education.

For nine months, from September 1921 to May 1922, he was the principal and one of three teachers at the Sherman District School near Antler, North Dakota. Receiving a monthly salary of $175, Ellis taught algebra, grammar, history, and science, and stoked the coal stove during the winter. He lived rent-free in a four-room teacher's residence adjacent to the school. During the evenings he worked on correspondence courses that he was taking from the University of North Dakota.

He became a full-time student at the University of North Dakota at Grand Forks in the fall of 1922. His studies and his work at the university library left him little time for extracurricular activities. Ellis majored in history and education as an undergraduate. He received the B.A. degree in 1924 and was elected to Phi Beta Kappa. While studying for the M.A. degree in history and political science, Ellis taught ninth-grade civics and algebra at a high school in nearby East Grand Forks, Minnesota. He received his M.A. degree in 1925, after submitting a thesis on the topic, "Minor Parties from the Civil War to 1900." During the summer of 1925 he served as an instructor in history at the University of North Dakota.

That fall he joined the department of social science at the State Teachers College in Mayville, North Dakota, and for the next three years, until 1928, he taught history and government there. He also belonged to the curriculum committee and the convocation committee of the college, spoke before community groups and teachers' conventions, and wrote magazine articles and (as co-author) a geography workbook. "Dr. Ellis was well liked by the staff, the student body, and the town's people," Erich Selke, a former colleague of Ellis, is quoted as saying in Elmer Ellis: Teacher, Scholar and Administrator (1961). "Elmer was a serious-minded, studious young man who devoted much of his time to the preparation of his work. This helped to make him an inspired teacher. . . . He had a good sense of humor. . . . He was stable and energetic. . . . He was interested in all school activities as well as community affairs. . . ."

In 1928 Ellis entered the University of Iowa to study for the doctorate. Working part-time as a lecturer and as a teacher at the university high school, he completed his studies in American history and received the Ph.D. degree in 1930. The subject of his dissertation was the public career of Henry Moore Teller, a Colorado senator and a leading exponent of free coinage of silver. The dissertation was subsequently used as the source of several articles and expanded into a book, Henry Moore Teller: Defender of the West (Caxton, 1941).

In 1930 Ellis became an assistant professor of history in the College of Arts and Science of the University of Missouri. He was popular as an adviser of graduate students, and his courses were well attended, particularly "Recent United States History," "Social Forces in American History," and "Foundations of Twentieth Century America." Also he supervised the training of potential social studies teachers enrolled in the university's School of Education, and he taught methods courses in education at both the undergraduate and the graduate levels.

Ellis' interest in teaching extended beyond the classroom. He attended teachers' conventions in the state and was an active member of the Mississippi Valley Historical Association and of the National Council for the Social Studies, of which he was president in 1937. Since the early 1930's he had stressed the importance of maintaining objectivity in social studies teaching. He delivered his presidential address to the National Council for the Social Studies in 1937, when Hitler's propaganda machine was working at full blast. Discussing the predicament of the social studies teacher who tries to reconcile his ideal of objective teaching with his desire to indoctrinate students with the value of democratic ideals, Ellis declared that the best protection against propaganda is the ability to think independently. In 1937 he edited the council's seventh yearbook, *Education Against Propaganda.*

Speaking before the council in 1938 on "American History in the Junior and Senior High School," Ellis criticized social studies curricula that rehashed the same material in four different sequences during a student's academic career. In 1939 he and W. Francis English outlined a social studies curriculum that would avoid repetition and yet cover history, geography, and current events. Their article appeared in the bulletin *The Future of the Social Studies*, edited by James A. Michener and published by the National Council for the Social Studies in 1939. The Ellis-English course of study was adopted by the Missouri public school system in 1940.

During the summers of 1936, 1939, and 1941 Ellis served as acting dean of the University of Missouri graduate school, and in the summer of 1937 he was a visiting professor of history at Ohio State University. For the year 1939-40 Ellis received a Guggenheim Fellowship that enabled him to finish *Mr. Dooley's America; A Life of Finley Peter Dunne* (Knopf, 1941). Dunne (1867-1936) was a Chicago journalist who created the character Mr. Dooley, an Irish-American saloonkeeper given to humorous philosophizing, especially about politicians. Ellis had previously collected and edited some of Dunne's writings in *Mr. Dooley at His Best* (Knopf, 1938).

Commissioned a captain in the United States Army in 1943, Ellis served in the historical branch of the War Department general staff. Stationed first at Schofield Barracks in Hawaii and then at the Pentagon, he served as a military government officer and compiled histories of campaigns in the Pacific. He was discharged with the rank of major in 1945. After the war his responsibilities at the University of Missouri became increasingly administrative, but he continued to teach a seminar and an occasional course and to advise graduate students on their dissertations.

In 1945-46 Ellis was vice-president in charge of extra-divisional educational activities, responsible for the library, student health, and physical education. He had previously (in 1943) obtained a grant from the Rockefeller Foundation to establish the Western Historical Manuscripts Collection in the University of Missouri library. Ellis became dean of the faculty of the College of Arts and Science in February 1946. One of

his major tasks over the next nine years was to recruit new teachers and to ensure the overall capability of the faculty. Largely through his efforts the university in 1949 received a $50,000 grant from the Carnegie Foundation for the Advancement of Teaching for a five-year study of ways to improve teaching in Missouri colleges and universities.

During the year 1951-52 Ellis took a leave from his administrative duties and, supported by a Fulbright grant, served as a visiting lecturer in American history at the University of Amsterdam. He also taught on the faculty of the Salzburg Seminar of American studies in 1952. When President Frederick A. Middlebush retired on September 10, 1954, Ellis became acting president of the University of Missouri. Less than one year later, on April 16, 1955, he was appointed president.

Soon after he took office, Ellis recommended that a bond issue be authorized to expand educational facilities throughout Missouri. Governor Phil M. Donnelly appointed him as head of the executive committee that directed the successful state-wide campaign for the passage of a $75,000,000 state bond issue bill. Along with other state institutions, the University of Missouri benefited from these funds. New buildings for business and public administration and for fine arts, a theater, dormitories, and classroom buildings went up on the campus. Additional facilities were provided for the departments of agriculture, electrical engineering, home economics, veterinary medicine, journalism, and industrial education, and for the library.

In 1956 and 1961 Ellis went to England to to represent the Association of American Universities at meetings of the Association of Universities of the British Commonwealth. In December 1959 he made a six-week inspection of the University of Missouri's agricultural education advisory unit in India. The unit is helping the Indian government to develop an agricultural program for improvement of food and livestock production.

Ellis was president of the Mississippi Valley Historical Association from 1950 to 1951 and a member of the editorial board of the *Mississippi Valley Historical Review* from 1947 to 1950. He is on the executive committee of the Missouri State Historical Society and on the board of trustees of the Midwest Research Institute in Kansas City, Missouri. From 1947 to 1951 he served on the board of directors of the Social Science Research Council. He holds an award for distinguished service to higher education from Rockhurst College in Kansas City, Missouri and five honorary doctorates.

Ellis was on the commission on instruction and evaluation of the American Council on Education in 1953, and he was its chairman from 1957 to 1959. Since 1958 he has been a member of the board of foreign scholarships of the United States Department of State. He has been president of the board of directors of the Harry S. Truman Library Institute for National and International Affairs at Independence, Missouri since 1957. He is also a member of the governor's council on public higher education and chairman of a special committee that is

ELLIS, ELMER—*Continued*
studying tuition policies, fees, scholarships, and admission standards in state institutions.

On August 14, 1925 Elmer Ellis married Ruth Edna Clapper, whom he met in high school. They have no children. Ellis is five feet eight inches tall, weighs 160 pounds, and has brown hair and blue eyes. He is a Democrat and a Presbyterian. Ellis collects records, of which his favorites are Gilbert and Sullivan operettas, and old textbooks and books of American humor. Except for these two hobbies, his chief recreation is his work, which he performs with vigor and relish.

References

> Directory of American Scholars (1957)
> Fite, Gilbert ed. Elmer Ellis: Teacher, Scholar, and Administrator (1961)
> International Who's Who, 1961-62
> Who's Who in America, 1962-63
> Who's Who in American Education, 1961-62

FOERSTER, FRIEDRICH WILHELM June 2, 1869- Educator; philosopher; author

Address: h. 1781 Riverside Dr., New York 34

A lifelong opponent of Prusso-German nationalism and militarism is the German-born educator, philosopher, author, and diplomat, Professor Friedrich Wilhelm Foerster, who defines a patriot as one "who trembles that his nation might stray from the path of justice and truth." Because he has remained true to the high ethical principles, which, he insists, must underlie every aspect of life, including politics, Foerster has spent much of his life in exile and isolation. He has conveyed his ethical Christian viewpoint in numerous books and articles in the fields of education, ethics, religion, politics, economics, sociology, and history, which he has written over a period covering almost seventy years. Now in his nineties, Professor Foerster, who has lived in the United States since 1940, continues to be actively interested in the fate of humanity.

Friedrich Wilhelm Foerster was born in Berlin on June 2, 1869, the eldest of five children of Dr. Wilhelm Julius and Karoline (Paschen) Foerster. His father, who was born in Silesia, was a noted astronomer, university professor, and author, and served as director of the Berlin observatory. His mother, a native of Mecklenburg, was a grand-niece of the Prussian field-marshal Helmuth von Moltke. Foerster, who has described his childhood as a very happy one, recalls that his home environment was imbued with the cosmopolitan humanism of Humboldt and Goethe and that the Prussian militarism of Bismarck had always seemed to him like a foreign occupying power that did not represent the true Germany. Occasionally he accompanied his father to scientific conferences in Paris.

After having received his early education in a private school, Foerster entered the Friedrich-Wilhelm Gymnasium in Berlin in 1879. The strong emphasis on Prussian patriotism, as well as the absence of loftier goals in the educational program of the Gymnasium, sharply contrasted with his home environment. Consequently he frequently occupied the last place in his class. In 1889 he entered the University of Freiburg im Breisgau, where he studied philosophy, economics, and physiology. He received his doctorate in philosophy in 1893 after submitting the dissertation *Der Entwicklungsgang der Kantschen Ethik bis zur "Kritik der Reinen Vernunft."* In 1894 Foerster became editor of *Ethische Kultur*, the organ of the German Society of Ethical Culture, which his father had founded.

Having become interested in the problems of the working classes, Foerster visited England in the fall of 1893 to study the labor movement there. For a time he did social work among the poor of Berlin through a private organization. He frequently attended and lectured at meetings of the Social Democratic party and the trade union movement, although he criticized the purely mechanistic nature of Marxist ideology, which predominated within the German working class movement at the time. In 1895 Foerster defended the Social Democrats in an article in *Ethische Kultur* against a severe attack that Emperor William II had made upon them in a speech commemorating the twenty-fifth anniversary of the Battle of Sedan. As a result Foerster was arrested on charges of libeling the Emperor and sentenced to three months' imprisonment early in 1896.

Unable to obtain a teaching position in Prussia because of his imprisonment Foerster moved to Switzerland in 1897 and became a *Privatdozent* at the University of Zurich. In the same year he was elected general secretary of the International Union for Ethical Culture. In Switzerland Foerster organized, on his own initiative, seminars for groups of young people, at which basic problems of life were informally discussed. In 1901 he became professor at the Polytechnic Institute of Zurich, while continuing to teach at the University of Zurich. His first book in the field of education, *Jugendlehre,* was published in 1904.

Although his home environment and early training had been largely devoid of religious influence, Foerster became more and more aware of the need for religion, and in 1899, during a visit to the United States, he became converted to Christianity. Convinced that the Christian faith conformed far more to the realities of human life and human nature than the abstract intellectualism of Kant and of the Ethical Culture movement, Foerster drifted away from that movement. At the University of Zurich he became involved in controversies between the religiously-oriented and the free-thinking elements of the faculty. In 1911 he resigned his teaching positions in Zurich to concentrate on his writing. He accepted a teaching position at the University of Vienna in 1913, and in the following year, a few months before the outbreak of World War I, he returned to Germany to take a chair as professor of education at the University of Munich.

As a result of his undaunted criticism of Germany's war policies Foerster found himself more and more isolated, and many of his former friends and colleagues turned against him. In an article published in *Friedenswarte* in 1916 he criticized the legacy of Bismarck and advocated a supernational confederation of Central Europe in the tradition of the old Holy Roman Empire. This had been proposed by Bismarck's opponent, Constantin Frantz, in the preceding century. Foerster's preoccupation with Central European problems prompted the Austrian Emperor Charles to invite him to Vienna in 1917 to ask his advice on the federal reorganization of the rapidly disintegrating Austro-Hungarian Empire.

In an effort to bring an end to the war Foerster conferred with Allied statesmen and diplomats during 1917-18, but his attempts to convince the German authorities to accept a peace based on Woodrow Wilson's Fourteen Points fell on deaf ears, and he was widely denounced by his countrymen. In November 1918, following the armistice, Foerster went to Switzerland as Ambassador of the newly established Bavarian government, headed by his friend, the Independent Social Democratic leader Kurt Eisner. Following Eisner's assassination by a nationalist extremist in early 1919, Foerster returned to Munich, where he sought to make the German intellectuals aware of their share of responsibility for the war. He described his conflict with German militarism in his book *Mein Kampf gegen das militaristische und nationalistische Deutschland* (Stuttgart, 1920).

Seeing the same forces that had dominated Germany before the war again in the ascendancy under the Weimar Republic, Foerster returned to Switzerland in the summer of 1922, after being warned by a friendly Bavarian colonel that he was in danger of being assassinated. From 1923 to 1929 Foerster edited the journal *Menschheit*, and in his weekly columns he pointed out the danger of a resurgent German militarism. In 1926 he published revelations of secret German rearmament efforts and was accused of treason by the German foreign minister, Gustav Stresemann. In an article in *Menschheit* (July 8, 1927) Foerster predicted that a rearmed Germany would launch a new world war between 1933 and 1938.

Having established residence in Paris in 1926, Foerster, with his former student Hans Schwann, edited the semi-monthly journal *Die Zeit: Organ für grundsätzliche Orientierung*, which was published in Berlin from 1929 until Hitler came to power in 1933. Foerster's books were among the first to be burned by the Nazis, along with those of his friends, Martin Buber and Albert Einstein. During the 1930's Foerster continued to warn the world of the imminent German danger, and he criticized the pacifism and complacency that prevailed in England and France at the time. In his book *Europe and the German Question* (Sheed, 1940) he analyzed the history of Germany and concluded that the German problem could be solved only within the context of a European federation.

From 1937 until the fall of France in 1940 Foerster lived in Haute-Savoie in the French Alps. He then fled to Portugal, having received a personal invitation from Portuguese Premier António de Oliveira Salazar. Sponsored by the Carnegie Endowment for International Peace, Foerster came to the United States in December 1940 and continued his work of education and

Wide World

FRIEDRICH WILHELM FOERSTER

enlightenment. In the spring of 1941 he was invited to Washington, D.C., where he testified before the Army General Staff about German war plans. Over the next few years he lectured widely at universities, before government bodies, and to private organizations, on German world policies.

In the spring of 1943 Foerster, in co-operation with T. H. Tetens, published an *Open Letter to the "Loyal Americans of German Descent,"* in which he criticized the contention of some German-Americans that the German people were not really responsible for Nazism. Hitler's system, he declared, was the "terrible fulfillment of a century of German nationalistic lawlessness." His charges that Victor F. Ridder, the publisher of the *New Yorker Staats-Zeitung und Herold,* and other prominent German-Americans harbored pro-Nazi sympathies resulted in a lawsuit, from which Foerster, represented by the attorney Louis Nizer, emerged victorious.

As World War II drew to a close, Foerster urged a rigid Allied military control over a defeated Germany and proposed dismemberment of Germany based on regional self-determination. He emphasized the importance of removing Nazis from all areas of public life. Speaking at a dinner given in his honor by Senator James E. Murray of Montana in Washington, D.C. in July 1944, Foerster reiterated his view that everything must be done to prevent a resurgence of German nationalism and militarism.

Although his eyesight has been failing in recent years, the flow of books from the pen of Professor Foerster remains undiminished. In *Erlebte Weltgeschichte 1869-1953* (Nürnberg, 1953) he presents his personal memoirs against a background of world history. In his book *Christ and the Human Life* (Philosophical Library, 1953) Foerster shows the relationship between religion and reality. Among his earlier works that he has recently revised are *Lebenskunde* (Mainz, 1953)

FOERSTER, FRIEDRICH WILHELM—Cont.

and *Lebensführung* (Mainz, 1954), which are guidebooks on the conduct of life, written for young people; *Politische Erziehung* (Freiburg i.B., 1959), in which he calls for education for political awareness and responsibility as an essential part of the basic training of every citizen; *Sexualethik und Sexualpädagogik* (Recklinghausen, 1952), in which he argues for a truly moral relationship between the sexes; and *Schuld und Sühne* (Trier, 1961), in which he calls for a more enlightened treatment of criminals and delinquents, while stressing the importance of the acceptance of moral responsibility on the part of the offender.

Foerster's view that all political action must have a strong ethical foundation is presented in his *Politische Ethik* (Recklinghausen, 1956), in which he seeks a moral and religious answer to the vital problems of the atomic age. In *The Jews: A Christian View* (Farrar, Straus, 1961) he pays tribute to the Jewish contributions to Western civilization and stresses the inseparability of the Old and New Testaments. He brought his observations on the German question up to date in *Deutsche Geschichte und Politische Ethik* (Nürnberg, 1961), an analysis of German history, in which he expresses the hope that the German people would someday rise above narrow nationalism and return to their old universal traditions. Foerster is currently planning a book on the relation between religion and natural science.

A democrat in the deepest sense, Foerster believes that democracy is a universal possession of humanity—"the political expression of 2000 years of Christian civilization." He rejects the deterministic and dehumanizing influence of Marxism and believes in the freedom of the human will and the full responsibility of each individual at every moment. Although he has criticized the excesses of capitalism, he feels that the problems of mankind can best be met in a free economy. He attributes the insecurity of Western man to his lack of moral preparation for the immense technological and economic developments of the modern era. In the present world crisis Foerster believes that permanent peace can be established only through a total spiritual and moral regeneration of the peoples of the world, and he rejects such partial solutions as isolated disarmament efforts. Once a genuine understanding between nations were to take place, he believes, international disarmament would come about automatically.

Foerster's influence is world-wide, and his works have been translated into many languages. Although he has never become a member of the Roman Catholic Church, his ideas on education and ethics have received high praise from its hierarchy. In 1948 the University of Leipzig conferred upon him an honorary doctor of theology degree. A group of Foerster's friends and former students established the Friedrich-Wilhelm-Foerster-Gesellschaft in Cologne in 1951 to disseminate his writings and keep his ideas alive. A similar organization has been established in Vienna. At the present time an archive of Foerster's letters and manuscripts is being organized. In 1957 a public school in West Ber-

lin was named the Friedrich-Wilhelm-Foerster-Schule in his honor. On his ninetieth birthday, in 1959, Foerster was honored at a luncheon held at the Carnegie Endowment International Center in New York City.

Professor Friedrich Wilhelm Foerster, now a citizen of the United States, lives quietly with his wife, the former Marie Werber, to whom he has been married for more than sixty-five years, in their apartment on New York's Riverside Drive. Tall and stately in appearance, Foerster conveys the dignity and wisdom of a scholar, the sincerity of a genuine humanitarian, and the integrity of a man who has remained constant to his ideals throughout his life. He speaks English fluently and displays an amazing vitality and presence of mind. A lover of horses, Foerster was fond of riding during his younger years. At present he confines his outdoor recreation to occasional walks in a nearby park. Louis Nizer has written in his book *My Life in Court* (Doubleday, 1961): "One cannot control the length of one's life, but one can control its depth and width. Foerster had succeeded in these latter dimensions, and nature had bestowed the first upon him."

References

Foerster, Friedrich Wilhelm. Erlebte Weltgeschichte 1869-1953 (1953)
Foerster, Friedrich Wilhelm, Schwann, Hans, and Pöggeler, Franz. Programm einer Lebensarbeit (1961)
Nizer, Louis. My Life in Court (1961)

FORRESTER, MAUREEN (KATHLEEN STEWART) 1931- Singer

Address: b. c/o Columbia Artists Management Inc., 165 W. 57th St., New York 19; h. 338 Roslyn, Westmount, Montreal, P.Q., Canada

The rich and velvety voice of the Canadian contralto Maureen Forrester, who has often been compared to the late Kathleen Ferrier, within the last few years has delighted music lovers all over the world. A recital artist known for her interpretation of lieder, art songs, and the works of Gustav Mahler, she is one of the few singers to achieve international fame in concert and oratorio rather than in opera. Miss Forrester made her Canadian debut in Montreal in 1953 and her American debut at New York's Town Hall in 1956. She has given recitals and has appeared with symphony orchestras in the United States, Canada, and Europe and has recorded for RCA Victor.

Born in the French East End section of Montreal in 1931 to a Scottish cabinetmaker and his Irish wife, Maureen Kathleen Stewart Forrester is the youngest of their four children. She has been bilingual in French and English since she began to talk. When her mother sat down at the piano to lead family song sessions, Maureen took part, and she started to take piano lessons at the age of five. Leaving school at the age of thirteen, she held various jobs for the next eight years, including one as a receptionist for the Canada Dry Ginger Ale Company.

When she was seventeen Miss Forrester took her first singing lessons from a Mrs. Sally Mar-

tin. (The lessons were paid for by her brother
Arnold.) Shortly thereafter she joined the choir
of the Fairmount-Taylor Presbyterian Church in
Montreal—her parents' church—and sang solos
at that church and in local concerts. When
Mrs. Martin retired, Frank Rowe became her
teacher. At this time Miss Forrester was more
interested in singing with a dance band than in
appearing on the concert stage.

When Miss Forrester was twenty-one, she attended a recital by Bernard Diamant, a Dutch-
born lieder singer living in Montreal. His performance so impressed her that she asked him
to accept her as a pupil. Deciding that her
massive voice was completely uncontrolled, Diamant advised her to give up singing in public
for six months, to take two or three lessons a
week, and to spend six or eight hours a day
practising. Despite the high cost of the lessons
and her fears that the public might forget her in
the meantime, she embarked upon Diamant's
rigorous program. She left her full-time job
with an advertising agency, became a part-time
switchboard operator on an early morning shift
at a construction company, and devoted the rest
of her day to lessons and practice.

Diamant has since called Maureen Forrester
"a pupil such as you get once in a lifetime." In
his opinion she has qualities indispensable to a
concert singer: a beautiful, versatile, and powerful voice; a good memory; a quick ear; musicianship; health; drive; and a calm temperament.
Miss Forrester made her formal Canadian debut
at the Montreal YWCA in March 1953. Shortly
afterward she took a solo part in a performance
of Mendelssohn's oratorio *Elijah* at the St. James
United Church in Montreal. Her artistry attracted the attention of the conductor Otto
Klemperer, who engaged her as a soloist in
Beethoven's Symphony No. 9 ("Choral") with a
Canadian orchestra under his direction.

Engagements at the Erskine and American
United Church and at Temple Emanu-El followed. The Ladies Morning Music Club awarded
her a $50 scholarship and the Montreal Social
Club gave her $500. She was a finalist on the
Canadian Broadcasting Company's program *Opportunity Knocks*. Miss Forrester used her prize
money and her $30-a-month salary to continue
her training under Diamant. Eventually she attracted the attention of a Montreal publisher,
who financed her debut in Paris at the Salle
Gaveau in 1955. "Talent isn't enough," Miss
Forrester has explained. "It costs about $20,000
between the education and the profession. I
couldn't have made it without my angel—or at
least, it would have taken me five years longer."

Sponsored by the concert organization Les
Jeunesses Musicales du Canada, Miss Forrester
gave about sixty recitals in Quebec and Ontario.
In 1955 the organization booked her for a three-
month tour of Europe, and she was so well
received in the countries she visited that the tour
was extended to a year's sojourn abroad. Each
year since then, Miss Forrester has made some
European appearances. She has sung in England,
Scotland, Ireland, France, Spain, Portugal, Italy,
Belgium, the Netherlands, Luxembourg, Switzerland, Germany, Denmark, Norway, Sweden, and
Austria. The orchestras with which she has performed include the Berlin Philharmonic, the

MAUREEN FORRESTER

Royal Philharmonic of London, the BBC Or-
chestra, the Amsterdam Concertgebouw, the
Lamoureux of Paris, the Oslo Philharmonic, and
the Tivoli of Copenhagen. She has appeared at
European music festivals at Stockholm, Berlin,
Montreux, Switzerland, and Bournemouth, Eng-
land. In 1957 she was a soloist at the Edinburgh
International Festival. In the fall of 1960 Miss
Forrester made her first tour of Israel, and dur-
ing the 1961-62 season she visited the Soviet
Union and Australia for the first time.

Miss Forrester has, of course, given numerous
recitals in her native Canada. She has appeared
with several Canadian orchestras including the
Toronto and Montreal symphonies, and she has
performed at the Stratford Festival of Drama
and Music, at the Vancouver Festival, and at the
Montreal Music Festival. The National Film
Board of Canada made a film of her life story
on location at a Casals Festival in Puerto Rico.

At her New York debut in Town Hall on
November 12, 1956 Miss Forrester's program included Schubert lieder, Brahms's *Zigeuner-
lieder*, Wagner's Wesendonck songs, Francis Poulenc's *La Fraicheur et le Feu*, Benjamin Britten's
A Charm of Lullabies, and music by C.P.E. Bach
and Johann Wolfgang Franck. Critics welcomed
the program as refreshingly unconventional and
the singer as unusually gifted. "Miss Forrester
has a superb voice of generous compass and
volume," Edward Downes wrote in the New
York *Times* (November 13, 1956). "Its color
ranges from a darkly resonant chest register to a
brilliantly focused top with a middle register
that she makes velvet soft or reedy according to
her expressive intent."

Meanwhile Maureen Forrester had attracted
the attention of the conductor Bruno Walter,
who invited her to audition privately in New
York. Walter himself played the piano accompaniment, and she sang, among other things, the
entire contralto part of the Brahms *Alto Rhapsody*. In February 1957 she made her American

FORRESTER, MAUREEN—*Continued*

orchestral debut with the New York Philharmonic under Walter's direction, singing in Mahler's Symphony No. 2 in C Minor ("Resurrection"). Since then she has become something of a specialist in Mahler. She sang his Symphony No. 3 in D Minor with the Concertgebouw under Eduard van Beinum at the Holland Music Festival. With his *Song of the Earth (Das Lied von der Erde)* she helped to open the 1958 season of the Berlin Philharmonic. She also sang its contralto part with the Toronto Symphony Orchestra in 1958, with the Cleveland Orchestra in 1960, and with the New York Philharmonic during the Mahler centennial in April 1960. With the tenor Richard Lewis and the Chicago Symphony Orchestra under Fritz Reiner, Miss Forrester has recorded *Das Lied von der Erde* for RCA Victor Records. For the same label she has also recorded Mahler's *Songs of a Wayfarer* (*Lieder eines fahrenden Gesellen*) and *Kindertotenlieder* with the Boston Symphony Orchestra under Charles Munch.

"I love singing Mahler," she has said. "It is so different from being a prominent soloist. Mahler treats the voice almost like an instrument, and you're part of the whole. . . . And, of course, he is sentimental, and so am I. But when you're singing, you can't let sentiment get in your way. You have to remain analytical, because if you become involved emotionally it affects your breathing. . . ."

Reviewing Miss Forrester's return appearance at Town Hall on December 1, 1957, a *Musical America* critic (December 15, 1957) said, "The sound of her voice . . . is remarkable, for it is a real contralto, still youthfully fresh, at once velvety and shining. Technically secure, the singer was able to do anything she wanted to with her voice, and she put it at the service of a musically exacting program, which she interpreted with an intelligence and emotional penetration of great distinction." The program on this occasion included compositions by Crüger, C. P. E. Bach, Beethoven, Schumann (the cycle *Frauenliebe und Leben*), and Dvořák (*Gypsy Songs*). Miss Forrester likes to perform little-known music and pieces by contemporary composers; the program also included songs especially composed for her by Samuel Barber, Kelsey Jones, Patrick Ewing, and Violet Archer. Miss Forrester's recital at Town Hall in February 1961, during which she sang old Spanish songs and compositions of Schumann, Brahms, Poulenc, Paul Nordoff, and Ned Rorem, received excellent notices from music critics. She has also appeared as guest artist with the Bach Aria Group in New York City.

Miss Forrester has performed several times as a soloist at the Empire State Music Festival at Bear Mountain, New York with the Symphony of the Air. During the 1959-60 season she sang a part in Prokofiev's cantata *Alexander Nevsky* under the direction of Leopold Stokowski. She has also participated in the Caramoor Festival at Katonah, New York, the Ipswich (Massachusetts) Music Festival, and the Lewisohn Stadium concerts in New York City. In July 1959 she sang in Verdi's *Requiem* at Lewisohn Stadium and in July 1961 she contributed to the stadium's

Brahms evening, singing the *Alto Rhapsody* and *Four Serious Songs*.

With the Orchestra of America under Richard Korn, Miss Forrester gave the first New York performance of *Five Songs for Dark Voice*, a song cycle by the Canadian composer Harry Somers, in March 1962. She also sang the première of Marvin David Levy's *One Person*, based on an Elinor Wylie sonnet, which the composer had dedicated to her. "Maureen Forrester sang both works magnificently," Alan Rich wrote in the New York *Times* (March 15, 1962), "with splendid vocal resource and an understanding of the style that few concert singers of her caliber care to acquire." She has been a soloist with many American orchestras, including the New York Philharmonic (over twenty times) and the Buffalo, Chicago, Pittsburgh, Detroit, Boston, San Francisco, New Orleans, Minneapolis, Philadelphia, and Cleveland orchestras. In the 1959-60 season she appeared with the New York Philharmonic under the direction of the Brazilian conductor Eleazor de Carvalho in a special U.N. Day concert at the United Nations.

In addition to singing in Beethoven's Ninth Symphony on stage many times, Miss Forrester recorded it for RCA Victor Records with the soprano Leontyne Price, the tenor David Poleri, the bass Giorgio Tozzi, and the Boston Symphony Orchestra under the direction of Charles Munch. Miss Forrester has also recorded for RCA Victor *A Brahms-Schumann Recital*. Reviewing this record in the New York *Herald Tribune* (March 1, 1959), John D. Molleson praised "the clarity of her singing, the deep and golden tones of her expressive voice, the understanding of words and music, and an unfailing sense of phrasing and of pitch."

When approaching a new work, Miss Forrester concentrates on learning the words, for she believes that an understanding of the text is basic to a full interpretation of the composer's music. Often praised for the clarity of her diction, Miss Forrester sings in seven languages, including Russian.

Although she has little desire to be an opera star ("I'm just not the Delilah or Carmen type, and I wouldn't want to be a Wagnerian mother-in-law forever"), she has appeared in concert versions of several operas. On November 18, 1958, she sang the role of Cornelia in *Giulio Cesare*, which was performed by the American Opera Society as part of a Handel bicentennial celebration. She made her operatic stage debut as Orfeo in Gluck's *Orfeo ed Euridice* at Toronto's O'Keefe Centre on May 28, 1962.

Maureen Forrester is married to the Canadian violinist and conductor Eugene Kash. They have four children: Paula, Gina Deborah, Daniel Joshua, and Linda Valerie. Although she is often away on tour, she tries to arrange her tours in blocks of two or three weeks and is at home with her family between engagements. When both parents are away, the children are cared for by a housekeeper-nurse. Statuesque Maureen Forrester is five feet nine inches tall and has golden blonde hair and deep set brown eyes. She has been characterized as lighthearted, spontaneous, exuberant, informal, enthusiastic, and wholesome. She sings not for career reasons, but because she loves it. Her sumptuous contralto voice has pealed forth since she was twenty. "God helped me to mature early," she has said, "because he knows I want to retire young."

References
Christian Sci Mon p4 My 22 '57 por
Globe Mag p11+ D 12 '59 por
High Fidelity Mag 10:12+ Jl '60 por
N Y Times II p13 D 7 '58
Who's Who in Music and Musicians' International Directory, 1962

FRANCIS, CONNIE Dec. 12, 1938- Singer; actress
Address: b. 161 W. 54th St., New York 19; h. Dalebrook Rd., Bloomfield, N.J.

One of the top recording artists in the world of popular music is Connie Francis, whose driving rendition of new hits and old favorites has won her "best singer" awards and thousands of fans (many of them teen-agers) in the United States and Europe. Eight of her single records—including "Who's Sorry Now?," her first hit, in 1957, and "Where the Boys Are," the title song of a film in which she played—have sold over 1,000,000 copies each.

Miss Francis, who sings in French, German, Spanish, Italian, Yiddish, and Japanese, has directed some of her albums, such as *Italian Favorites, Spanish and Latin American Favorites,* and *Jewish Favorites,* at specific ethnic groups. She is equally adept at rock 'n' roll, swing, motion-picture songs, and popular love ballads. Connie Francis has appeared as a guest on several television variety shows, has had her own television special, and has entertained in night clubs from coast to coast. She owns four music publishing companies.

Born Concetta Franconero on December 12, 1938 in the Down Neck section of Newark, New Jersey, Connie Francis is the daughter of George Franconero, a former dockworker and roofing contractor, and Ida (Ferrara) Franconero. Her grandparents came to the United States from Italy. She has a younger brother, George, Jr., a pre-law student at Seton Hall University. Connie's father, who liked to play the concertina, sent his daughter to Miss Masciola's Music School in Newark to take lessons on a miniature accordion when she was three and a half years old. "My father is an absolutely wonderful, unselfish, warm-hearted, very affectionate person," Miss Francis avers. "He possesses a very mild temper. He is greatly responsible for my success."

After making her debut by singing *O Sole Mio* at a school recital, Connie sang and played the accordion at benefits, lodge celebrations, church socials, and other community gatherings for several years. In 1950 her father took her to audition for George Scheck's *Startime,* a juvenile variety television show. Although Scheck was unwilling to listen to any more "kid singers," he was interested in Connie's accordion talent, and she first appeared on the show with that instrument. She later discarded it from her act, however. Meanwhile she had also won first place

CONNIE FRANCIS

on Arthur Godfrey's *Talent Scouts* show (CBS-TV) on which she used the name Connie Francis for the first time.

Connie Francis appeared on the *Startime* show weekly for four years and toured the borscht circuit in the Catskills during the summer. After a while she began working backstage as well, contributing production ideas, typing scripts, and learning lighting, makeup, and camera techniques. About this time she began to overeat because she felt lonely and alienated among her co-workers. "They wore spike heels and a lot of makeup and had their hair in long pony-tails, and I felt inferior, . . ." she recalls. "Every girl has to have some kind of release, someone to tell problems to, and I had no one. . . . When we were doing the summer . . . circuit . . . these kids had wild parties and used strong language. I had never seen anything like that at home. But I didn't dare tell my mother because she would have taken me off the program, and I felt that the show was important and I needed it. I never mixed socially with these other kids. I just sat around by myself and ate. . . ." For a while her four-feet-ten-inch frame weighed 140 pounds.

In the meantime Connie attended the Bergen Street school and the Arts High School in Newark and the Belleville (New Jersey) High School, from which she graduated in June 1955. She was a member of the National Honor Society, editor of the school newspaper, and a member of the glee, dramatic, debating, and international relations clubs. She organized student assemblies, wrote and produced musical comedies, and won the New Jersey state typing championship at the age of fifteen.

When the *Startime* show closed, Scheck became Connie Francis' personal manager. Before she was eighteen, she began to sing in night clubs and cocktail lounges around the country with the help of an identity card that falsified her age. (Until about two years ago, her mother

FRANCIS, CONNIE—*Continued*

always traveled with her.) During her last year in high school, Scheck negotiated a contract with MGM Records; between June 1955 and September 1957 Connie Francis recorded ten single discs for this company, none of which made a hit. She also sang on the soundtracks of the movies *Jamboree* and *Rock, Rock, Rock.* Although she auditioned for some 200 large night clubs, radio and television shows, and Broadway musicals, she passed only three of the tryouts.

Discouraged by her lack of success, Connie Francis decided to leave the entertainment field. She received a four-year scholastic scholarship to New York University and began attending classes in radio and television production. Since she had one more record to make under the MGM contract, her father suggested she make an old favorite, "Who's Sorry Now?," with a new rock 'n' roll beat in the background. Released in November 1957, this disc climbed above the million mark in sales within six months. Connie was jubilant and, ending her five-month attendance at the university, cast her lot once and for all with show business.

Since her first success, Miss Francis has recorded over eighteen singles and seventeen albums. Her other best-selling records are "My Happiness," "Everybody's Somebody's Fool," "My Heart Has a Mind of Its Own," "Lipstick on Your Collar," "Frankie," "Mama," and "Where the Boys Are." Her album releases are *Connie Francis Country and Western Golden Hits; Connie Francis Rock 'N' Roll Million Sellers; Connie's Greatest Hits; More Greatest Hits; Christmas in My Heart; Connie Francis Sings Fun Songs for Children; Connie Francis Sings Italian Favorites; Connie Francis—More Italian Favorites; Connie Francis Sings Spanish and Latin American Favorites; Connie Francis Sings Irish Favorites; Connie Francis Sings Jewish Favorites; Songs to a Swingin' Band; Connie Francis Sings Folk Song Favorites; Connie Francis, Do the Twist; Who's Sorry Now?; The Exciting Connie Francis; My Thanks To You;* and *Connie Francis Sings Never on Sunday and Other Title Songs From Motion Pictures.*

After 1958 Miss Francis made personal appearance tours through the United States, Australia, New Zealand, and Europe. She has performed in England, Scandinavia, Germany, Italy, Belgium, Luxembourg, Scotland, and Ireland and in countries in South America and the Far East. During 1961 she appeared in such night clubs as the Town Casino in Buffalo, Sciolla's in Philadelphia, Blinstrub's in Boston, the Gatineau Club in Ottawa, Canada, the Three Rivers in Syracuse, and Holiday House in Pittsburgh. She has also entertained at the Sahara Hotel in Las Vegas, the Cloister in Hollywood, and the Copacabana in New York City. "This vivacious young . . . lady belts out a tune with a vigor, a voice, and a vitality and all of the know-how she has learned in half a lifetime in show business, . . ." Dale Wright of the New York *World-Telegram and Sun* (December 2, 1960) wrote of her Copa debut. "She uses her very expressive face—and in fact, all of the rest of her body—in selling a song."

Television celebrities like Jimmie Rodgers, Dick Clark, Perry Como, Jack Benny, and Ed Sullivan have hired her as a guest star. She appeared as "mystery guest" on *What's My Line* (CBS-TV) and was the subject of *This is Your Life* (NBC-TV) and *Person to Person* (CBS-TV) programs. On September 13, 1961 she starred in her own hour-long television special on ABC-TV, singing and doing a comedy routine, with Art Carney, Eddie Foy, Jr., and Tab Hunter as her guests. Both her voice and her ability as a comedienne won praise from reviewers who saw her first film, *Where the Boys Are* (MGM, 1960).

Miss Francis, who earns between $5,000 and $12,000 a week for night club and hotel engagements, made about $1,000,000 during the past year. She owns four music publishing companies (her father manages them), and she has granted licenses to manufacturers of Connie Francis charm bracelets, socks, sweaters, diaries, and other products that carry her name. Through 1966 she is committed to sing two months a year at the Las Vegas Sahara, to record five albums and eight single discs a year for MGM, and to make at least one movie a year. Her days are crowded with performances, interviews, rehearsals, travel, and business. She is kept abreast of her commitments by her manager, George Scheck, and her secretary, Sandra Constantinople. In 1958 Miss Francis developed skin trouble, which she feels was the result of overwork and nervous tension. The condition has for the most part disappeared, however.

During comparatively free moments Connie Francis listens to records and signs photographs of herself that are requested by thousands of fans the world over; she receives about 5,000 letters a week. Miss Francis was named four times as the "best female singer of the year" by *American Bandstand* (ABC-TV) television viewers, and she was designated "most programmed vocalist of the year" by *Billboard*, "best female singer of the year" by *Cashbox*, and "best female vocalist of the year" by *Photoplay Magazine*. Radio Luxembourg gave her the Golden Lion Award as the most programmed singing artist in Europe. She has also received the Laurel Award from *Exhibitor Magazine* as the best newcomer in films.

Connie Francis lives with her family and their dog, Mambo, in a split level house in Bloomfield, New Jersey. Their back yard covers a bomb shelter. For recreation she enjoys roller skating, ballroom dancing, and writing letters. For the past nine years she has kept a diary, much of it in shorthand, and she collects stuffed toy animals. Brown-eyed with dark brown hair, she is five feet one and a half inches tall and weighs about 105 pounds. Although Miss Francis has developed a protective shell toward most of the gossip and speculation that inevitably surround a public figure, she denies for the time being any rumors of romance the columnists foist upon her. Despite her rapid rise she still identifies herself with young people, and she is writing, with Barbara Perlman and Sandra Constantinople, a book especially for teen-agers.

Having since childhood squeezed more into her life than most people twice her age, Connie

Francis sometimes regrets that her time is hardly her own. She recently told a *Newsweek* (February 5, 1962) reporter: "When I signed my new contract with MGM a few weeks ago, they said, 'You've got the best contract in the record business. Aren't you thrilled?' I said 'sure'. I didn't know why I didn't feel so great. It hit me later. I had signed away another five years of my life." For the most part, however, she is content with popularity. "If you love your work, like I do," she says, "it isn't too big a sacrifice."

References

Newsweek 59:56 F 5 '62
Sat Eve Post 234:38+ S 23 '61

GRANT, GORDON (HOPE) June 7, 1875-May 7, 1962 American painter of ships and seamen; his picture of the frigate *Constitution* hangs in the White House; author and illustrator of books on ships. See *Current Biography* (June) 1953.

Obituary

N Y Times p39 My 8 '62

Wide World

TAMMY GRIMES

GRIMES, TAMMY (LEE) Jan. 30, 1934-Actress; singer; dancer; comedienne

Address: b. c/o Actors Equity Assn., 226 W. 47th St., New York 36; h. 24 Bank St., New York 14

Gravel-voiced and hoydenish Tammy Grimes is one of the few comediennes in American show business who manages to be an attractive woman of the world and a clown at the same time. Comedy, she believes, is not incompatible with sex appeal. Equally at home in Shakespeare, musical comedy, or French farce, Miss Grimes achieved her first important recognition on television, after having made several wrong starts in her career. Meredith Willson's musical comedy *The Unsinkable Molly Brown* solidly established her as a star and certified her future as an off-beat entertainer talented enough to carry a whole show on her shoulders.

Tammy Lee Grimes was born in Lynn, Massachusetts on January 30, 1934 to Luther Nichols Grimes, a hotel and club manager, and Eola Willard (Niles) Grimes. ("Tammy" is not a nickname, but a Scottish feminine first name.) She has a married sister, Nancy Lou, and a younger brother, Luther Nichols Grimes, Jr., who recently graduated from Harvard. During her childhood her family moved to Chestnut Hill, a fashionable suburb of Boston, and her father became manager of the Brookline Country Club. In Chestnut Hill Tammy Lee Grimes was known as "the most picturesque young lady ever to enroll at Beaver Country Day School." Her childhood idols were her father, Napoleon, Andrew Jackson, Marlon Brando, and Manolete, the bullfighter. She spent most of her childhood (and adolescence) in going to the movies, and when she was about thirteen she decided to become an actress.

At Beaver Country Day School she played a lady-in-waiting to Queen Victoria in *Victoria Regina,* and the audience burst into laughter at her first entrance. At sixteen she attempted the role of Sabina, the maid, in *The Skin of Our Teeth* by Thornton Wilder. Her performance was witnessed by the playwright, who came backstage after it was all over and informed her, "Young lady, even Tallulah Bankhead didn't do the things you did to the role." She soon discovered that she would never look like an ingenue and, since she liked to make people laugh, she decided to become a comedienne. In 1951 she graduated from Beaver Country Day School.

After making her social debut in the Brookline Country Club in 1951, Tammy Grimes enrolled at Stephens Junior College in Columbia, Missouri because it had a two-year curriculum, a flourishing drama department, and a "jewel box of a theater" in which to produce plays. She was fiercely determined not to follow the route of the girls in her social set whom she envisioned as "knitting their way through Wellesley, and then getting married to men with nine-to-five jobs, and living happily ever after with their wall-to-wall carpeting." At Stephens Junior College she majored in English, read voraciously, and acted in a new play about every three weeks, undertaking such roles as that of Billie Dawn in *Born Yesterday* and Lady Bracknell in *The Importance of Being Earnest.* Continuing her compulsive habit of movie-going, she saw *The Foxes of Harrow* ten times.

She began the summer of 1952 as an apprentice actress at the Falmouth Playhouse in Massachusetts, but was transferred to duty backstage as property mistress after her performance in *Three Men On a Horse.* In 1953 she graduated from Stephens Junior College with honors in English and in 1954 joined the staff of the Westport Playhouse in Connecticut. When she gave away $500 worth of tickets at the box office, she was relieved from her job as ticket taker. On Apprentice Night—the chance of the season to exhibit her acting ability—she was caught

GRIMES, TAMMY—*Continued*

short in a costume change and appeared on stage in nothing but an old raccoon coat.

After working in the New York suburb, Tammy Grimes migrated to the metropolis itself, where she enrolled at the Neighborhood Playhouse under the direction of Sanford Meisner, who futilely tried to assign her roles in Ibsen plays. When she made her New York debut at the Neighborhood Playhouse in May 1955, she made her bow not as Hedda Gabler or Rebecca West but as Eshtemoa, "a leading citizen," in *Jonah and the Whale.* In the spring of 1955 she served as a standby for Kim Stanley as Chérie in William Inge's *Bus Stop* and replaced the star for a period of two weeks.

Having sampled Miss Grimes's talents in *Bus Stop,* Anita Loos, the author of *Gentlemen Prefer Blondes,* assigned her the title role in *The Amazing Adele,* a farce that Miss Loos had adapted from the French, with music and lyrics by Albert Selden. Directed by Herb Ross and Jack Landau, *The Amazing Adele* collapsed during its Philadelphia tryout in December 1955 and never reached New York, to the amazement of nobody. A sharpsighted critic for *Variety* (December 28, 1955), however, speculated: "It's not unlikely that [Tammy Grimes] can be built into a more emphatic personality."

In the late spring of 1956 Tammy Grimes was one of the ten bright young people who sang and acted out sketches in *The Littlest Revue* at the off-Broadway Phoenix Theatre. Although most critics were only mildly interested in the production, one of them, Walter Kerr of the New York *Herald Tribune* (May 23, 1956) called attention to Tammy Grimes as "a firm-jawed girl who cannot keep her blonde hair out of her eyes." When the revue ended its run she went on a cross-country tour with Julie Harris in *The Lark,* playing the mistress of the Dauphin. But it was not until she appeared in *Clérambard,* which opened at the off-Broadway Rooftop Theatre on November 7, 1957, that Tammy Grimes received her first important notices from the critics. Reviewing Norman Denny's and Alvin Sapinsley's adaptation of Marcel Aymé's satirical comedy, Walter Kerr of the New York *Herald Tribune* (November 8, 1957) noted that "Tammy Grimes comes closer than anyone to capturing a suitably impudent mood" and Brooks Atkinson of the New York *Times* (November 8, 1957) informed his readers that "Tammy Grimes' good-humored, awkward, sensible prostitute is also amusing." Critics gave *Clérambard* mixed reviews, but acclaimed its star, Claude Dauphin. The show extended its run beyond its originally scheduled twelve weeks and closed in the late spring of 1958. The summer of 1958 found Tammy Grimes at the Stratford (Ontario) Shakespeare Festival, where she acted Mistress Quickly in *King Henry IV, Part One,* and Mopsa in *The Winter's Tale.*

One member of the audience who endorsed Tammy Grimes's work in *Clérambard* was Julius Monk, the night club impresario and professional discoverer of talent. Disappointed in her attempt to get an important understudy role in Budd Schulberg's *The Disenchanted,* Miss Grimes accepted Monk's offer to hire her as a chanteuse in his New York supper club, Downstairs at the Upstairs. A writer for *Life* (January 5, 1959) reported that "Tammy makes the torrid songs seem tame, the sophisticated simple, the sweet saucy. She does all this so winningly, with so little voice and so much expression, that she has kept Julius Monk's Downstairs at the Upstairs filled."

Her fogbound voice provided her with the way back to acting. Noel Coward, who happened to be in the audience one night at Downstairs at the Upstairs, urged Miss Grimes to read a script that he was about to produce on Broadway. After giving her a ten-minute audition, he cast her in the title role of *Look After Lulu,* his adaptation of George Feydeau's farce, *Occupe-toi d'Amélie.* The combined talents of Noel Coward, Cecil Beaton, its designer, and Cyril Ritchard, Roddy McDowall, and Tammy Grimes, its featured players, could not salvage *Look After Lulu* after the battering it sustained from the critics when it opened in March 1959. It closed at the Henry Miller Theatre in April after thirty-eight performances. Miss Grimes appeared at the Cambridge (Massachusetts) Drama Festival in Shakespeare's *Twelfth Night* in the summer of 1959. When Marc Blitzstein's opera, *The Cradle Will Rock,* was revived at the New York City Center in February 1960, she played the role of Moll.

Tammy Grimes contends that she won the title role in *The Unsinkable Molly Brown* by singing "Melancholy Baby" when she auditioned for the producers. The most expensive musical comedy that has ever reached Broadway, *The Unsinkable Molly Brown* was produced by Dore Schary (who also directed it) in association with the Theater Guild. Meredith Willson wrote the music and lyrics and Richard Morris furnished the book for the musical based on the true story of the indomitable Molly Tobin Brown, an illiterate rustic from Hannibal, Missouri, who struck it rich by marrying a lucky miner and later survived the sinking of the *Titanic.* Only two of the seven New York critics liked the production as a whole, but all of them agreed that unsinkable Tammy Grimes kept the show afloat. Within a little more than a year after it opened at the Winter Garden Theater it paid back to its angels their original investment of $520,000, and on April 24, 1961 Tammy Grimes was elevated to star status. The musical ended its New York run on February 10, 1962, and went on the road with its original star.

A frequent performer on television, Tammy Grimes appeared as Mary in a revival of George M. Cohan's *Forty-Five Minutes from Broadway* on *Omnibus* over NBC-TV on March 15, 1959. With Tony Randall, Beatrice Lillie, and Cyril Ritchard, she appeared in *Four for Tonight,* a special over NBC-TV, on February 24, 1960. On *Hollywood Sings,* another special over NBC-TV, on April 3, 1960, she teamed up with Eddie Albert in a program for which Boris Karloff served as guest host. In May 1960 on *The Play of the Week* she co-starred with Eddie Bracken in *archie and mehitabel,* an adaptation of the 1957 Broadway musical *Shinbone Alley,* on WNTA-TV. Rex Harrison was her co-star on *The Datchet Diamonds* in the series *The Hour* of *Great Mysteries* over NBC-TV on September 20, 1960. In David Susskind's production of Jan de Hartog's *The Four Poster* over CBS-TV on January 13, 1962 she co-starred with Jackie Cooper.

Among the honors that Tammy Grimes has received are the 1961 Comoedia Matinee Club Award and a 1961 Tony Award (Antoinette Perry Award) for "best musical featured or supporting actress." On June 21, 1961 she won the twenty-third annual *Variety* poll of drama critics for the "best musical woman performer."

On August 16, 1956 Tammy Grimes married Christopher Plummer, the actor, whom she once eulogized as "a thin, keen sword edge that catches the light" and as a "really great actor." They were divorced in April 1960. Miss Grimes is five feet five inches tall, weighs 123 pounds, and wears her reddish-blonde hair in a wild mop. Her hoarse, childlike, occasionally cracked, yet piercing voice with its finishing-school accent has led her to be called "the Back Bay Beatrice Kaye." In 1961 she sat for René Bouché, the famous portrait painter. She is a Republican who voted for John F. Kennedy. No gourmet, she dotes on hamburgers and hot dogs, washed down from time to time by Bloody Marys. She likes to drive sports cars, play baseball, dance, paint, and read. With her daughter, Amanda Michael, she lives in a Greenwich Village duplex apartment that is often filled with roses. Someday she would like to play Ophelia because she too lived in a world of her own. When once asked to comment on a current issue, she replied, "Don't muck about with the moon."

References

Holiday 31:99 F '62 por
Life 46:43 Ja 5 '59 pors; 49:141+ D 5 '60 pors; 50:89 My 19 '61 pors
N Y Times Mag p101+ Mr 20 '60 pors
Vogue 133:94+ Ap 1 '59 por

HAMMOND, JOHN HAYS, JR. Apr. 13, 1888- Inventor

Address: b. Hammond Research Corp., Gloucester, Mass.; h. Abbadia Mare, Hesperus Ave., Gloucester, Mass.

An "inventor's inventor," whose hundreds of patents underlie much of our modern technology, John Hays Hammond, Jr., lives and works in a medieval-style castle, which he built on the rocky New England coast near Gloucester, Massachusetts. He has made many contributions to the development of radio, television, and radar, and his pioneering work in the field of remote control radio, begun more than a half century ago, is basic to the guided missile program. His early developments in frequency modulation broadcasting were the precursors of many modern radio-electronic techniques. He heads his own organization, the Hammond Research Corporation, and has served as a consultant to a number of firms and government agencies.

John Hays Hammond, Jr., was born in San Francisco on April 13, 1888 to John Hays and Natalie (Harris) Hammond. He has two brothers, Richard P. and Harris Hammond, and a sister, Natalie Harris Hammond. His father, an American geologist and mining engineer, was closely associated with Cecil Rhodes in the exploration of the South African gold and diamond fields. Upon returning to the United States, the senior Hammond worked as chief mining engineer for the Guggenheim family at a salary reputed to be one million dollars a year. In 1911 he served as special ambassador representing the United States at the coronation of King George V of England.

As if an illustrious father were not enough, John Hays Hammond, Jr.'s, uncle, John Hays, was one of the founders of the Texas Rangers. "As an engineer, I would always be second best to my father, and as a man of action, I could never hope to compete with my uncle," Hammond told Richard H. Miller in an interview for *True* magazine (November 1960). "But I had a compulsion to compete with both of them. I wasn't going to waste my life clipping stock coupons." Living wherever his father's fortunes took him, Hammond grew up in England, Washington, D.C., and Gloucester, Massachusetts, and he began to demonstrate his inventiveness at an early age. His father numbered among his friends such noted scientists and inventors as the Wright brothers, Thomas Alva Edison, Alexander Graham Bell, Guglielmo Marconi, and the Yugoslav inventor Nikola Tesla. Tesla's early studies in electric power transmission formed the basis of much of Hammond's later work in this field.

For his preparatory education Hammond attended the Lawrenceville School in New Jersey. There he developed his first invention, a circuit-breaker connected to the door of his room, enabling him to circumvent the school's eight P.M. lights-out rule. After graduating from Lawrenceville he attended his father's alma mater, the Sheffield Scientific School of Yale University, from which he received the B.S. degree in 1910. Even before his graduation, Hammond was intrigued by the prospect of remote control by radio, but he was afraid that some other inventor might have staked out a prior claim to the field. To familiarize himself with the latest developments in this area, he took a job as file clerk in the Patent Office in Washington, D.C. In the course of the next two years, he became an authority on patents in radio and telephony. He also became convinced that the field of remote radio control was wide open and was ready to begin his own work.

Aided by his father, Hammond established the Hammond Radio Research Laboratory in 1911. His initial outlay for equipment came close to a quarter of a million dollars, but as he later said: "I had an eminently successful father who was both willing and able to support my costly experiments." When for the first time he succeeded in controlling a boat by radio his excitement was so great that he forgot to turn off the controls, and the boat was wrecked on the rocks. It was soon replaced, however, and before long his crewless "ghost ship" was frightening the fishermen in Gloucester Bay. When, on the eve of World War I, Hammond successfully incorporated a gyroscope into the boat's receiving system, he established the basis of all radio control. Using this Gyrad principle (the blending of

JOHN HAYS HAMMOND, JR.

gyroscope and radio), he was able, in March 1914, to send an experimental yacht from Gloucester to Boston and back, a distance of 120 miles, without any human control on board.

After perfecting Gyrad, Hammond went on to develop a system to prevent enemy jamming of radio orders and to work on a radio-guided torpedo. He also designed many other devices for military and civilian radio communication. By 1916 he held over 100 patents of military value and the War Department asked Congress to appropriate $750,000 to pay him for their use. Although the House approved the appropriation the Senate failed to do so, and it was not until 1932 that Hammond finally was reimbursed.

Earlier Hammond had been in some difficulty with the government over a light incendiary bomb that he had invented in 1914. Neither the American government nor the British government was interested in buying the bomb, but when incendiary bombs started showering London during World War I, Hammond was accused of selling out to the Germans. It was only when one of his former employees was caught spying and confessed to having stolen the plans for the bomb that he was fully cleared. Another of Hammond's early inventions—an "electric dog" with selenium cell "eyes" that enabled it to follow a moving beam of light—was a step toward the development of radar. The "dog" proved a sensation when it was sent on a vaudeville tour, and it later served as a model for the artificial animals now used for psychological study.

In the field of radio Hammond conducted some of the earliest experiments in frequency modulation broadcasting, invented single-dial tuning for radio, filed a patent for telephone amplification (purchased by the Bell Telephone Company for use on its long distance lines), and made substantial contributions to the development of the modern radio tube. In 1923 the Radio Corporation of America bought his patents in this field for $500,000.

During the 1920's Hammond began to perfect a private communications system that operated by means of radio telephony. After having first offered such a system to the Vatican, he was approached, in 1926, by Italian dictator Benito Mussolini, who was anxious to obtain a secret communications system. Hammond was greatly impressed by the speed and efficiency with which the dictator was able to make all the needed equipment available to him. He was soon disillusioned, however, when he found that his system was being used to trap surviving anti-Fascists, among them a number of Hammond's personal friends.

During World War II Hammond was active in the development of various national defense projects, and he worked for a time with the Office of Scientific Research and Development in Washington, D.C. In 1943 he developed a variable pitch propeller that ensures the most effective use of a ship's power according to operating conditions of the moment. His more recent inventions include a high-speed method of transmitting civilian defense intelligence, known as "Telespot," and an electronic teaching machine that he developed with a colleague. In 1961 he worked on a project, sponsored by the United States Navy, for broadcasting from a single station to any part of the world and into outer space. His pioneering work on radiodynamic torpedoes used by the Allies in World War I and World War II forms the basis of the present-day development of intercontinental ballistic missiles.

One of Hammond's main interests is music, and it has served as a stimulus for additional projects, which he developed with the help of such friends as Serge Koussevitsky, Igor Stravinsky, and Leopold Stokowski. His inventions in this field include a "dynamic amplifier" for the compression, expansion, and reduction of noise in audio systems; a new type of reflecting modulator for pianos; an "accentor" for improving the tonal quality of pipe organs; and the "Oirafon," a combination piano, radio, and phonograph. Among Hammond's lesser inventions are a naval war game for adults, a toy locomotive for children, a panless stove (its aluminium foil surface is thrown away after each use), a mobile apartment unit, a device for injecting sauces into roasts, and a magnetized tray that prevents food from spilling into the laps of air travelers. He also invented a luxury shaving cream that proved too expensive to market and a hair restorer that failed to improve his own balding condition.

Hammond's home and laboratory are located in "Abbadia Mare," a medieval-style castle near Gloucester, Massachusetts, which he began to build in the 1920's to house his collection of medieval art and artifacts. It overlooks the Reef of Norman's Woe, the site of Henry Wadsworth Longfellow's The Wreck of the Hesperus. Complete with a moat and drawbridge, towers, battlements, and narrow stone staircases, it incorporates in its structure portions of various European buildings. One bedroom had been an inquisition chamber; other rooms are composed of what were once a beer hall, an inn, a catacomb, and the adjunct to a cathedral. An inner court-yard with a Roman pool is surrounded by tropical foliage, which is kept lush by artificial rain-storms.

The outstanding feature of the castle is its Great Hall with an eighty-five-foot tower, designed to house a gigantic pipe organ, which Hammond began to assemble in the 1920's. This instrument, which has 10,000 pipes, four manuals, and 144 stops, many of which were taken from old churches, is one of the most magnificent in the world. Occasionally organ recitals are given in the Great Hall, which seats about 200 persons. Such noted organists as Virgil Fox and Richard Ellsasser have used the organ to make recordings. Hammond, who serves as director and curator of the castle museum, opens the castle to the public during July and August, charging $1.00 for admission.

In 1912 Hammond served as United States delegate to the International Radio-Telegraphic Conference in London, and in 1927 he was appointed by President Calvin Coolidge to represent the United States at the International Radio Conference in Washington, D.C. He has served on advisory boards concerned with national defense and has acted as a consulting engineer for several firms, including the General Electric Company and the Westinghouse Electric Corporation. He is president of the Hammond Research Corporation and also serves as a research consultant and a director of the Radio Corporation of America.

Hammond was awarded an honorary Sc.D. degree by George Washington University in 1919. He received the Elliott Cresson Award of the Franklin Institute in Philadelphia in 1959, and in the same year the Institute of Radio Engineers conferred upon him its Fellow award. He is a Grand Officer of the Crown of Italy. An early member of the Institute of Radio Engineers, Hammond is a former treasurer and director of that organization and has served as chairman of its special committees on membership and finance. He is a governor of the Aero Club, vice-president of the American Society of Aeronautical Engineers, and a Fellow of the American Geographic Society. He holds honorary memberships in the American Society of Mechanical Engineers, the National Institute of Inventors, and the Harvard Aeronautic Club. Other organizations to which he belongs include the Royal Society of Arts (London), the American Society of Aeronautical Engineers, and the University and Explorers clubs.

John Hays Hammond, Jr., was married to the former Irene Fenton, an artist, who died in December 1959. They had no children. Hammond is five feet eight inches tall, weighs 170 pounds, and has brown eyes, thinning brown hair, and what has been described as a "Byronic profile." He lives in his castle with a staff of servants, his English butler, and several generations of Siamese cats. He generally dresses informally, dislikes crowds, and chooses as his companions artists, musicians, actors, and play-wrights. He is a connoisseur of fine wines, and his interests include astrology and sailing. A seasoned world traveler, he has taken part in expeditions to Venezuela and Labrador. Taking

the advice of Alexander Graham Bell, he does most of his work late at night. According to Richard H. Miller, Hammond is "a man who has done exactly what he wanted to do, exactly as he planned to do it, and has relished every moment of it."

References
Coronet 50:168+ Jl '61 por
Esquire 41:119+ Je '54 por
True p24+ N '60 pors
American Men of Science 10th ed (1960)
Who's Who in America, 1962-63
World Biography (1954)

HARDENBROOK, DONALD J(OHNSON)

Feb. 10, 1896- Business executive; organization official
Address: b. c/o Union Bag-Camp Paper Corp., 233 Broadway, New York 7; h. 200 E. 66th St., New York 21

The president of the National Association of Manufacturers for 1962 is Donald J. Hardenbrook, chairman of the board of the American Creosoting Corporation and a vice-president and director of the Union Bag-Camp Paper Corporation. He was elected to succeed John W. McGovern for a one-year term at the association's sixty-sixth congress of American industry, held in New York City from December 6 to 8, 1961. Hardenbrook started his business career in 1915 as an office boy. He worked in the investment banking field for twenty years and was an independent member of the New York Stock Exchange from 1933 to 1943.

Donald Johnson Hardenbrook was born in Jamaica, Long Island, New York on February 10, 1896 to David Langdon and Laurestine (Johnson) Hardenbrook. His ancestors were among the Dutch colonists of Manhattan; their name was originally spelled Hardenbroek. One ancestor, John A. Hardenbrook, was a founder of the New York Stock Exchange in 1792; another, Sara Jansen de Rapelje, was reputedly the first white child born in New York.

Donald Hardenbrook attended Jamaica Normal School from 1902 to 1911 and then enrolled at the Polytechnic Preparatory School in Brooklyn, where he won letters in football, baseball, basketball, and track. After graduating in 1915 he became an office boy with the Atlas Portland Cement Company in New York City, but he rose to the position of assistant advertising manager within a year and a half. In 1917 he enlisted as a seaman in the New York Naval Militia, which preceded the Naval Reserve. At the end of his World War I service in 1919 he had attained the rank of ensign and had become executive officer of a squadron of thirteen submarine chasers.

After the war Hardenbrook became president of his own ship brokerage firm, the American International Shipping Company, which specialized in ocean freight forwarding. In 1920 he joined the staff of the First National Bank of New York. After two years at the bank, he entered the investment banking line by becoming the manager of Taylor Ewart & Company.

(Continued next page)

DONALD J. HARDENBROOK

From 1921 to 1929 he was a partner in the investment trust company Harrison, Smith & Company.

Hardenbrook continued to rise in the banking world, holding the post of president of the American International Securities Corporation from 1929 through 1932 and attending the New York Stock Exchange as an independent member from 1933 to 1943. In 1942 he was a master of ceremonies at the celebration of the 150th anniversary of the founding of the Exchange. Hardenbrook became assistant to the president of the Union Bag and Paper Corporation in 1943. The concern became the Union Bag-Camp Paper Corporation in 1956. He has been vice-president of this company since 1945 and one of its directors since 1946. In 1958 Hardenbrook became chairman of the board of the American Creosoting Corporation, a wholly-owned subsidiary of Union Bag-Camp Paper Corporation. He has been vice-president in charge of finance, woodlands, industrial and public relations, and the service departments of American Creosoting Corporation at various times.

In 1961 the Union Bag-Camp Paper Corporation employed 11,296 people, made net sales of $228,431,568, and had a net income of $16,972,622. Its principal raw material is wood, and it owns nearly 1,500,000 acres of woodland. Its products include corrugated boxes, retail store bags and sacks, printing and office papers, treated paper, consumer display packages, school stationery supplies, and finished lumber. The company owns three paper converting subsidiaries, Allied Container Corporation (Boston), Eastern Box Company (Baltimore), and Miller & Miller, Inc. (Atlanta, Georgia).

With Dr. Charles F. Roos, a mathematician and an economist, Hardenbrook helped to establish the Institute of Applied Economics. For several years he served as chairman of its board. He has been a member of the economics principles commission, established in the early 1940's to prepare monographs on the American individual enterprise system under the sponsorship of the National Association of Manufacturers. Hardenbrook has been active in the NAM since 1944 and since 1957 has served on its board of directors.

Hardenbrook was elected president for 1962 of the National Association of Manufacturers at the sixty-sixth annual congress of American industry, held at the Waldorf-Astoria Hotel in New York City from December 6 to 8, 1961. A major portion of the conference was taken up with discussing the Communist threat to the American way of life. Representing about 75 per cent of the total manufacturing in the United States, the NAM numbers some 17,500 corporations and partnerships as members. Although it is often viewed as a spokesman of big business, 83 percent of its members are small businesses with less than 500 employees. During the past four years, according to Hardenbrook, the NAM has lost about 2,525 members because of mergers, liquidations, increase of dues, and recessions.

When President John F. Kennedy addressed the NAM on December 6, 1961, he was the first President to do so since President William McKinley spoke before the annual meeting in 1898. In his forty-seven minute speech Kennedy asked for "new and bold" powers to negotiate tariff reductions on a broad basis rather than item by item as is required under the long-standing Reciprocal Trade Agreements Act that expires in June 1962. He pointed out that broad tariff cuts would increase American exports and improve America's international balance of payments. Assuring his audience that his administration is not "anti-business," he stressed the fact that the well-being of the government depends on the health of the business community, and he invited businessmen to submit economic plans to assure the American position in world competition.

The first official NAM reaction to Kennedy's speech was given by Hardenbrook at a meeting of the Economic Club of New York on January 10, 1962. Increased exports and successful American competition with the Common Market countries, he said, would not be possible unless supported by a reduction of taxes on personal and corporate incomes. Specifically he favored a tax bill that would lower the maximum personal income tax rate from 91 percent to 47 percent and the maximum corporate income tax rate from 52 percent to 47 percent.

In March 1962 the NAM made public a detailed report that called for a reduction of $5,662,500,000 in the projected federal budget of $92,500,000,000 for the fiscal year 1963. Nondefense cuts would total $4,184,500,000 and defense reductions $1,478,000,000. Reducible or dispensable items, according to the NAM study, include foreign aid, civil service pay raises, and government training and youth opportunity programs. The report also urged dropping all new program proposals and reducing expenditures on existing programs such as conservation, medical treatment of veterans' disabilities not sustained during tour of duty, and civil public works programs.

Hardenbrook has served on the executive committee of the New York Chamber of Commerce. He is the chairman of Keep America Beautiful, Inc., which is conducting an anti-litter campaign, and he was the president of the New York Osteopathic Hospital and Clinic for twenty years. Hardenbrook belongs to the Merchants Club (New York City), the Oglethorpe Club (Savannah, Georgia), the Sankaty Head Golf Club (Nantucket, Massachusetts), and the Royal and Ancient Golf Club (St. Andrews, Scotland). Playing golf and reading are his chief relaxations.

Donald J. Hardenbrook married Helen Vinson, an actress, on December 20, 1946. He has two daughters by a previous marriage: Hope (Mrs. Whitley Y. Dresser) and Marilyn A. (Mrs. Curtis Bacon). Murray Kempton in the New York *Post* (December 6, 1961) has described Hardenbrook as having "a thin nose and glasses, and the very good manners we find only in the shy." He is six feet tall with thinning gray hair. He is a member of the Dutch Reformed Church. A New York *Times* biographical sketch (December 8, 1961) pictured him as having "the stern, straight-backed mien of one of his solid Calvinist ancestors posing for a Dutch master's portrait."

References

N Y Times p28 D 8 '61 por

Who's Who in America, 1962-63

HERBSTER, BEN M(OHR) Aug. 26, 1904-
Clergyman; church official
Address: b. United Church of Christ, 297 Park Ave. S., New York 10; h. 82 Soundview Ave., White Plains, N.Y.

The United Church of Christ was formed through the merger of the Congregational Christian Churches with the Evangelical and Reformed Church. The union—which had been in the planning stage for twenty years—was formally sealed by the adoption of a constitution in July 1961. The first president of the United Church of Christ is the Reverend Dr. Ben M. Herbster, who was elected to a four-year term beginning October 1, 1961. The seventh largest Protestant church in the United States, the United Church of Christ comprises 6,391 member churches that serve approximately 2,000,000 people.

Ben Mohr Herbster was born in Prospect, Ohio on August 26, 1904 to Richard W. Herbster, a bank manager and hardware dealer, and Mary (Mohr) Herbster. He has one sister, Mrs. Annetta Schmid. At Prospect High School, Ben Herbster took part in debating and edited the school paper. After school he sometimes worked in his father's hardware store; at one time he also ran a local gas station. After graduating in 1922, he enrolled at Heidelberg College in Tiffin, Ohio, where he majored in sociology and continued to debate. By the time he finished his sophomore year he had determined to become a minister. In 1926 he graduated *magna cum laude* with a B.A. degree. He then attended Central (now Eden) Seminary at Webster Groves, Missouri, which granted him the B.D. degree in

REV. DR. BEN M. HERBSTER

1929. Herbster has done postgraduate work at Ohio State University, McCormick Theological Seminary, and Chicago Theological Seminary.

Following his ordination at Dayton, Ohio on June 2, 1929, Herbster became pastor of the Corinth Boulevard Reformed Church. He held this position until 1931 when he became pastor of the Zion Evangelical and Reformed Church in Norwood, Ohio, a suburb of Cincinnati. During his thirty years (1931-61) with Zion Evangelical and Reformed Church its membership increased from 281 members to over 900 and an old stone mansion used for church activities in the early 1930's was supplanted by a new sanctuary building that provided modern facilities for worship, instruction, and social gatherings.

From 1947 to 1958 Herbster served on the General Council of the Evangelical and Reformed Church. As a member of this group he became involved in 1947 in the discussions on possible union between his denomination and the Congregational Church that had begun in 1942. He is credited with having kept these parleys going in 1957 when they were on the verge of collapsing over church technicalities. When the United Church of Christ was established later that year, he was elected to its executive council; since 1958 he has been its co-chairman. He was also a member of the commission that drafted the constitution of the United Church of Christ, which was adopted at a meeting in Philadelphia on July 4, 1961.

At this meeting Dr. Herbster was elected president of the United Church for a four-year period under the terms of the new constitution. His name was put forward at the election by the nominating committee as the only candidate. However, at the meeting, Dr. James E. Wagner was nominated from the floor. Dr. Herbster was elected by 513 votes against 165 votes for Dr. Wagner, who pledged his support to the new president and described him as "one of the finest

HERBSTER, BEN M.—*Continued*

pastors and best administrators we have in the Evangelical and Reformed Church."

At the present time the United Church of Christ is made up of 6,391 member churches from every state in the Union and Puerto Rico. Of this total, 3,665 are Congregational Christian churches and 2,726 are Evangelical and Reformed churches. Total membership is estimated at 2,000,000. The United Church of Christ budget for 1962 and 1963 is set at $14,300,000 for each year. One of the stated aims of the United Church is that it should be a uniting as well as a united church.

The United Church of Christ has discussed possible merger with several Protestant denominations. In April 1962 Herbster met with representatives of the United Presbyterian Church, the World Methodist Council, and the Episcopalian church to consider a union between the four churches, a union that would join over 20,000,000 Protestants in what Herbster has described as a "united church—truly catholic, truly reformed and truly evangelical." When the talks ended the leaders of the four religious bodies invited three more Protestant denominations to future consultations: the International Council of Christian Churches (Disciples of Christ), the Evangelical United Brethren, and the Polish National Catholic Church.

Through its General Synod and its Council for Christian Social Action, the United Church of Christ makes known its views on current issues. It has urged the diplomatic recognition of Red China and its admission to the United Nations; deplored as "ill-advised" the Cuban invasion of 1961; and called for multilateral cessation of nuclear testing. The United Church of Christ supports the abolition of segregation; it has endorsed the policy of planned parenthood.

Herbster has spoken out against ultra-conservative groups that have attacked the National Council of Churches for alleged "softness to communism." He opposes federal aid to parochial schools on the grounds that this would violate the principle of the separation of church and state. Herbster agrees with his church's stand in favor of medical care for the aged that is linked to the social security system.

In December 1961 the United Church of Christ outlined its plans to build retirement centers in ten states for persons over the age of 62 and with an income as low as $1,800 a year. The first of these projects is to be the Firelands Retirement Centers, Inc., of Lorain County, Ohio, which will be ready to accept tenants by January 1964. In addition to thirty to seventy unfurnished living units, the center will offer core dwellings for persons unable to maintain individual living units, as well as cafeteria and medical services.

Dr. Herbster has urged members of his Church to experiment with new ways of disseminating Christian teaching. Speaking to the New York City Congregational Association at Riverside Church on November 2, 1961, he pointed out that "religion has not yet even begun to use television programs for confronting people" nor has it even "touched the surface" in migrant work or in the Christian training of youth.

From 1947 to 1948 Herbster was president of the Cincinnati Council of Churches. He has been a member of the United Church of Christ's Board of National Missions and an exchange preacher for the National Council of Churches and the British Council of Churches. In 1944 he was awarded an honorary D.D. degree by Heidelberg College, of which he is a trustee. Hazel-eyed with graying hair, he is five feet seven inches tall and weighs 160 pounds. On June 25, 1929 he married Elizabeth Beam, the daughter of medical missionaries. The Herbsters have two daughters, Annetta Jane (Mrs. Marcus S. Buehrer) and Anne Kathryn (Mrs. Roger Liston). Although he has no other hobbies, Herbster likes to relax at the 275-acre farm in Marion County, Ohio that he owns jointly with his sister. The farm produces wheat, oats, hay, and corn and supports a herd of seventy-five Aberdeen Angus cattle.

At a time when the goal of Christian unity is eagerly being pursued by the Protestant denominations, the observation that Herbster made shortly after he was elected to the presidency of the United Church of Christ seems apt. "It seems to me that the United Church of Christ has a unique opportunity . . . not only to demonstrate the need for unity among Christian churches," he said, "but also has the responsibility to witness to the world that the ties that bind us together, as Christians, are much stronger than anything that separates us."

References

N Y Times p16 Jl 6 '61
United Church Herald p7 Jl 20 '61

HOUK, RALPH (GEORGE) Aug. 9, 1919-
Baseball club manager

Address: b. c/o New York Yankees, 745 5th Ave., New York 22; h. "Crossroads," Saddle River, N.J.

When Ralph Houk was named to succeed Casey Stengel as manager of the New York Yankees on October 20, 1960, it was generally agreed that he had been chosen for a difficult assignment. In the twelve seasons that he directed the team the colorful Stengel led the Bronx Bombers to ten American League pennant victories and seven World Series championships. He brought home his last pennant winner in September 1960, just a few weeks before he was retired from the Yankees because of his age (he was seventy years old). Houk was accordingly under great pressure to produce a winner when the New York Yankees opened defense of their American League title in 1961.

"Major" Houk's previous managerial experience had been limited to three years (1955-57) with a Yankee farm team—Denver, of the American Association. He had played on Yankee organization teams since 1939, when he spent a season with the Neosho (Missouri) club of the Arkansas-Missouri League. Between 1947 and 1954 he played major league ball with the New York Yankees, but he was mainly a reserve catcher until he became a coach under Stengel in 1958.

Ralph George Houk, the fourth of five children of George Houk, was born on August 9, 1919 on his father's 160-acre farm near Lawrence, Kansas. Four of Ralph's uncles, who lived nearby, played weekend baseball on a semi-professional team, the Belvoirs, which was managed by his uncle Charlie Houk, and Ralph absorbed a knowledge of the sport even before he could write. At the age of eleven he tried out for the Eagles' team in the Twilight League, for players aged eleven to seventeen. After playing left field in his first year with the Lawrence team, he settled down behind home plate as catcher, a position he held during most of his later career. "I liked catching," Houk recalls. "I had the whole game in front of me. I was in on every pitch. At fifteen I was as solid as a rock, 170 pounds of hard-muscled flesh. I could block onrushing base-runners at home plate. In fact blocking was easy for me."

When Houk entered Lawrence High School, the school had no baseball team, and he consequently became an offensive quarterback and a defensive fullback on the football squad. In his senior year he made the all-state team. Several colleges offered him athletic scholarships, but he turned them down so that he could continue to play baseball. Houk had begun playing with the Belvoirs at the age of sixteen, and he also played with the Lawrence team of the Ban Johnson League. During a national tournament game in which the Lawrence team competed, Yankee scouts spotted the catcher Houk and signed him up, giving him a $200 bonus. "My $200 bonus bought me one suit of clothes, one fall overcoat, and a few dates," Houk says. "More important was that I'd made it, that baseball was to be my career. For I was grimly determined to be a success on the diamond. Nothing could stop me, I thought."

He began his baseball career in the minor leagues in 1939 as a $75-a-month rookie with the Neosho (Missouri) club of the class D Arkansas-Missouri League. A catcher in 119 games, he batted .286. The following year he moved up to the Joplin (Missouri) club of the class C Western Association and batted an impressive .313 in 110 games. In 1941 Houk played five games with the Binghamton (New York) team of the class A Eastern League and finished the year with the Augusta (Georgia) club of the class A South Atlantic (Sally) League, hitting .271 in ninety-seven games. His progress toward the major leagues was interrupted by the outbreak of World War II.

At the beginning of 1942 Houk and his brother Harold joined the United States Army. Private Ralph Houk's first assignment at Fort Leavenworth, Kansas was to whip the camp's baseball team into shape. Accepted for Officers Candidate School, he was sent to Fort Knox, Kentucky to train at the armored forces school. As a second lieutenant, Houk was shipped to England with the 89th Cavalry Reconnaissance Squadron of the Ninth Armored Division.

Moving in advance of the armored division eastward through France from Normandy to Ardennes, Houk's outfit scouted out the land ahead for signs of the enemy. In the Ardennes forest Houk's group was cut off from the rest of the battalion, and the men fell back to a small

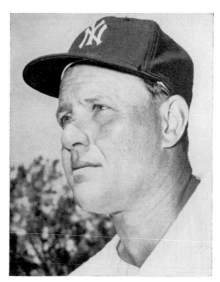

RALPH HOUK

Luxembourg town, Waldbillig, where they found themselves menaced by six German tanks. Placed in command after two superior officers had been killed, Houk slipped away through the woods, retrieved a tank destroyer, drove it to Waldbillig, and smashed the enemy tanks. On another occasion he had a narrow escape when a sniper's bullet passed through his helmet, leaving his head untouched. For gallantry at Waldbillig he received a Silver Star. He was also decorated with a Bronze Star and the Purple Heart, and he left the Army at the end of 1945 with the rank of major.

Houk returned to civilian life in 1946 as a player with the Kansas City club of the triple-A American Association and the Beaumont club of the double-A Texas League, where he batted .294 in eighty-seven games. In 1947—the year he made the major leagues—he played as third-string catcher with the New York Yankees in forty-one games and batted .272. In 1948 Houk was sent back to Kansas City and played with its team until the end of 1949, except for a few games that he played with the Yankees. He remained with the New York Yankees from 1950 through 1954, but he served mainly as a reserve catcher and appeared as a batter only thirty-one times during those years. All in all, Houk played ninety-one major league games with a batting average of .272.

During his years as a bullpen catcher, Houk absorbed a knowledge of baseball that later served him well as a manager. "A bullpen inmate gets a wide perspective of the game and, by the way, a much better view than from the bench," Houk has explained. "If he keeps his eyes open he learns why winners win and losers get cuffed around. The picture from out there is clear and informative. He constantly comes into personal contact with pitchers. . . . He catches relievers regularly and starters while they're limbering up. If he has a card-index mind he files

HOUK, RALPH—Continued

away each experience and knows what makes some ballplayers tick and others run down."

To supplement his card-index mind, Houk kept written records over the years that analyzed each play, each player, and each game in detail. Recognizing his flair for leadership and his thorough knowledge of baseball, New York Yankee officials appointed Houk as manager of their Denver team in the triple-A American Association in 1955. The team finished third in that year's pennant race, finished second in 1956, and second again in 1957. In 1957, moreover, they won the intra-association playoffs and the Little World Series, which pits the winner of the American Association playoffs against the winner of the International League playoffs.

The victory enhanced Houk's reputation and earned him a berth as first-base coach with the Yankees. Even then the management apparently had him in mind as Stengel's successor. During the three years, from 1958 to 1960, that he coached the team he is said to have turned down several offers to manage other major league teams. During June 1961 he managed the New York Yankees while Stengel was ill.

When he became the sixteenth manager in the history of the New York Yankees on October 20, 1960, Houk made it clear from the start that he had no intention of imitating Stengel, although he respected his ability as a manager. "I realize," he said at his first press conference, "that there will be great pressure on me in following behind a great manager like Casey Stengel. I know I'll be a prime target for second-guessers. But I don't fear it because this is the goal I've been shooting for all my life. I've been around Casey a long time and I feel I've learned a great deal from him. After all, there's only one Casey Stengel; I'm Ralph Houk." At the same time, Houk let it be known that he would not tolerate any infringement on his duties by the Yankee front office. "In no shape or form am I going to be a yes-man," Houk remarked. "I don't think I have been hired for the purpose of being a yes-man."

To show what he could do before the New York Yankees committed themselves for a longer period, Houk initially signed a one-year contract as manager on his own request. After leading his team to victory in the American League over the second-place Detroit Tigers, Houk sent them on to win the 1961 World Series (played between October 4 and October 9) with the Cincinnati Redlegs. The New York Yankees won four out of five games, with scores of 2 to 0, 3 to 2, 7 to 0, and 13 to 5. After the season ended Houk signed another contract—this time for two years.

Houk has won the respect and affection of his ballplayers by abandoning Stengel's system of "platooning" (alternating players at the same position, instead of allowing each to appear at one position regularly), by keeping his criticism of their mistakes private, and by showing sympathy with their personal problems. He has tried to curb the fiery temper, directed mainly at umpires, that several times in his career cost him fines and suspensions.

Winning or losing, Houk can always be sure of at least four loyal rooters—his wife, the former Bette Porter, and their three children, Donna (Mrs. Walter Sloboden), Dick, and Robert. The Houk family lives in a 200-year-old, refurbished farm house, called Crossroads, in Saddle River, New Jersey. Houk is five feet eleven inches tall and weighs about 193 pounds. He has blue eyes and blond hair. On the field he chews tobacco; at other times he smokes cigars. His favorite off-season recreations are fishing and hunting.

References

N Y Herald Tribune p24 O 21 '60
N Y Times p38 O 21 '60 por
N Y Times Mag p10+ Jl 2 '61 por
Time 78:76+ O 6 '61 por
Houk, Ralph and Dexter, Charles. Ballplayers are Human, Too (1962)

HUBBARD, BERNARD (ROSENCRANS)

Nov. 24, 1888-May 28, 1962 Jesuit, known as the "Glacier Priest"; Alaskan explorer; geologist; oceanographer; paleontologist; lecturer and author. See *Current Biography* (July) 1943.

Obituary

N Y Times p31 My 29 '62

HUGHES, RICHARD J(OSEPH) Aug. 10, 1909- Governor of New Jersey

Address: b. State House, Trenton, N.J.; h. "Morven," Princeton, N.J.

The 1961 gubernatorial election in the state of New Jersey put into the governor's mansion a relatively unknown Democrat, Richard J. Hughes, the first Roman Catholic to hold that office. His election was an upset not only because he was unknown, but because his opponent, former United States Secretary of Labor James P. Mitchell, was a national figure with the personal endorsement of former President Dwight D. Eisenhower. Hughes campaigned for increased educational aid and urban and suburban redevelopment with a record budget and has already taken steps to follow through on his proposals. He is a lawyer who has served in several state judicial positions.

Richard Joseph Hughes was born on August 10, 1909 in Florence, New Jersey, the son of Richard Paul and Veronica (Gallagher) Hughes. He has one brother, now the Reverend Joseph Hughes, and two sisters, now Mrs. Edward Hulse and Mrs. Kathryn Cope. His boyhood home was in Burlington County, where his father had an insurance business; he served at various times as mayor and postmaster in Burlington, as State Civil Service Commissioner, and as warden of the State Prison in Trenton. For thirty-seven years Richard Hughes was also Democratic state committeeman from Burlington County.

A graduate of Cathedral High School in Trenton in 1926, Hughes received his prelaw training at St. Charles College in Catonsville, Maryland from 1926 to 1928 and at St. Joseph's College in Philadelphia in 1928. He graduated from New Jersey Law School, now part of Rutgers University, in 1931 and the following year was admitted to the bar and established his first practice in Trenton.

Almost immediately Hughes began working for the Democratic party in Mercer County, which at that time was solidly Republican. He was elected statewide president of the Young Democrats and in 1937 was elected a Democratic State Committee member from Mercer County. In 1938 he accepted the nomination to the House of Representatives from the Fourth Congressional District, a Republican stronghold, and campaigned as "a Roosevelt Democrat." He lost the election, but he gained the attention of political leaders.

At the age of thirty, in 1939, Hughes was named assistant United States attorney for New Jersey. During the war years he administered such measures as the Enemy Alien Act and had a high percentage of convictions in prosecuting members of the German-American Vocational League, the Bund, and similar groups. He resigned his position in 1945 to form a law partnership in Trenton with his chief, United States Attorney Thorn Lord, the present State Democratic Committee chairman. The two men set to work to revitalize the Mercer County Democratic party. As chairman of the county Democrats, he campaigned vigorously and, despite party factionalism within the state, succeeded in wresting his county from its traditional Republican control by 1948. This success brought him an appointment to the Mercer County Court bench that same year, one of the youngest men in the state's history to hold that office.

In 1952 Governor Alfred E. Driscoll, a Republican, elevated Hughes to the State Superior Court, and in October 1953 he was assigned to Union County. He was named chairman of the State Supreme Court's committee on juvenile and domestic relations courts, which after a two-year study presented a report that served as a foundation for New Jersey's present handling of youthful offenders. Hughes gained prominence as an authority on probation systems and was a member from 1952 to 1960 of the advisory council of judges of the National Probation and Parole Association.

During the four years that he worked in Union County, Hughes maintained his offices in Elizabeth. He moved to offices in Trenton, of which he was a resident, in 1957 when he was appointed to the appellate division of New Jersey's Superior Court. Some observers expected him to go on to the State Supreme Court, but financial and family responsibilities outweighed other considerations, and he resigned the same year to resume his law practice after almost a decade on the bench. In his new practice his clients included some of the nation's biggest drug firms and the Association of New Jersey Railroads, which he served as legislative representative.

In February 1961 state Democratic leaders named Hughes to succeed Governor Robert B. Meyner, who was prohibited by state law from seeking a third term. Hughes was chosen by leaders from twenty of the twenty-one counties, an endorsement interpreted as a clear victory for party leaders over Governor Meyner, who had urged the selection of two other candidates. However, Meyner said of the candidate at a press conference after the meeting, "He is intelligent, articulate and very well informed. He has all the qualifications necessary to make him a fine candidate and a fine Governor."

The GOP gubernatorial candidate was former Secretary of Labor James P. Mitchell, who had the personal endorsement of former President Eisenhower. Religion was no factor in the contest since both men were Roman Catholics. Mitchell campaigned primarily on the charge that Hughes was under obligation to the Democratic party bosses and was a "paid lobbyist of the New Jersey railroads." Hughes campaigned on a platform of expanded civil defense facilities and increased state aid for education. To Mitchell's charges of his lobbying he countered by offering to open his financial records if Mitchell would do likewise. He proposed a series of debates with his opponent, but Mitchell turned him down.

Both candidates had influential people stumping for them. Secretary of Labor Arthur J. Goldberg, Edward Kennedy, and even President John F. Kennedy, though noncommittal at first, came out for Hughes. Meanwhile, Governor Nelson A. Rockefeller and Senator Jacob K. Javits, both of New York, spoke out for Mitchell, and Eisenhower toured the state on his behalf.

Hughes was elected governor on November 7, 1961 by such a narrow margin that Mitchell went to bed on election night without conceding defeat. The totals were certified at 1,084,194 votes for Hughes to 1,049,274 votes for Mitchell, a margin of only 34,920 votes for the Democratic candidate. His victory was attributed by Earl Mazo of the New York *Herald Tribune* (November 9, 1961) to the fact that the party got out the vote: "Hughes won by virtue of an extraordinarily heavy turnout in populous counties and communities where Democratic organizations are strongest. . . . Mitchell lost largely because of a relatively light turnout in centers of normal Republican strength."

In his inaugural address on January 16, 1962 Hughes pledged that the state would shoulder the burden of adequate aid to education and would work on the problems of slum decay and haphazard suburban growth through a new Department of Urban and Suburban Affairs that he hoped to create. He asked for a bipartisan review of New Jersey's finances to determine whether a broad-based tax such as a state sales or income tax would be considered. New Jersey and Nebraska are the only two states without such taxes, and though New Jersey is the country's seventh wealthiest, it has the lowest revenue of all the states. He appointed the State Tax Policy Commission to review the matter and to recommend a method for underwriting the state's additional costs.

The governor submitted a record budget just short of $500,000,000 to the Legislature on February 19, 1962 and assured the legislators that it could be balanced as required by state law, but strongly hinted that he would have to ask for a personal income or general sales tax no later than 1963 to finance a substantial expansion of state school aid, a mental health program, and highway building. He has introduced legislation to permit the establishment of junior colleges at

Van Dyke Studio
RICHARD J. HUGHES

the county level, increase teachers' salaries, tighten the state law against discrimination in the rental of housing units, and prohibit discrimination against the aged in employment. Other bills pending would establish conflict-of-interest rules for legislators and other state employees, revamp the state's child welfare laws, and permit the counties to redevelop any section of the Meadowlands within their borders.

As governor, Hughes has helped to negotiate a settlement of a devastating statewide bus strike, signed a "tough" waterfront bill granting wider powers to the New York–New Jersey Waterfront Commission in dealing with ex-convicts employed by waterfront unions, and urged New York to raise its legal minimum drinking age to twenty-one to conform with New Jersey's. He successfully pushed through legislation on a Port Authority program and was credited with a major victory as he ended a twelve-month impasse between New Jersey and New York over rail and trade projects.

A leader in numerous civic affairs, Hughes was chairman of the Delaware Valley United Fund, a fund-raising campaign for St. Francis Hospital in Trenton, and the Citizens' Advisory Committee to investigate welfare practices in Trenton. He has been Past Exalted Ruler in the Elks and Past Grand Knight of the Knights of Columbus. He is former president of the Mercer County Bar Association and a member of the New Jersey and American bar associations. He also belongs to the American Judicature Society and is a Fellow of the American Bar Foundation.

Energetic and youthful-looking, Governor Richard J. Hughes has black hair and blue eyes, stands six feet tall, and weighs 200 pounds. He enjoys occasional games of golf and bridge, but spends most of his leisure time with his family. He was a Cub Scout den father, and the governor's mansion in Princeton rings with the voices of the ten Hughes children. Hughes's first wife, Miriam (McGrory) Hughes, whom he married in 1934, died in 1950, leaving him with four children: Richard, Robert, John, and Mary. On May 7, 1954 he married Mrs. Elizabeth (Sullivan) Murphy, whose husband had died in an airplane crash. Her three sons by that marriage are William Michael, Patrick, and Timothy. The governor and his wife have added three more to the family, Brian, Helen, and Thomas More.

References

> Newsday p38 Ja 16 '62 por
> N Y Post Mag p2 Ap 23 '61 por
> N Y Times p18 F 2 '61 por; p1 N 8 '61
> N Y World-Telegram Mag p1 Ja 13 '62 por
> Time 78:18 N 17 '61 por
> Martindale-Hubbell Law Directory, 1962
> Who's Who in America, 1962-63

KOBAK, EDGAR   Apr. 18, 1895-June 3, 1962 Former president of the Mutual Broadcasting System radio complex (1944-49); executive of the National Broadcasting Company and the Blue Network Company (now the American Broadcasting Company), 1934-36 and 1940-44; associated with McGraw-Hill Publishing Company from 1916 to 1934 as salesman, editor, executive. See *Current Biography* (April) 1947.

Obituary

> N Y Times p41 Je 5 '62

KORTH, FRED (H.)   Sept. 9, 1909- United States Secretary of the Navy; banker; lawyer
Address: b. Department of the Navy, Washington 25, D.C.; h. The Westchester, Washington 16, D.C.; Azleway Ranch, 5100 Azle Ave., Fort Worth 14, Tex.

Succeeding John B. Connally, Jr., Fred Korth, a Texas banker and lawyer, became the fifty-ninth Secretary of the United States Navy on January 4, 1962. As civilian head of the nuclear-powered American Navy, Korth is subordinate to Secretary of Defense Robert S. McNamara. Korth was president of the Continental National Bank of Fort Worth from 1959 to 1961, an assistant secretary of the Army in 1952, and a civilian aide to the Secretary of the Army during 1961.

Fred H. Korth was born at Yorktown, Texas on September 9, 1909 to Eleanor Maria (Stark) Korth and Fritz R. J. Korth, a banker and rancher. His brother, R. J. Korth, is a rancher in Ecleto, Texas. The boy grew up on a cattle ranch near San Antonio and attended public schools and Brackenridge High School in that city. His secondary education completed, Korth enrolled at the University of Texas in Austin, where he took a prelaw course. After having worked his way through college, he received the B.A. degree in 1932 and then entered the law school of George Washington University, which granted him the LL.B. degree in 1935. He did some postgraduate work at the Southwestern Louisiana Institute and at Columbia University.

Admitted to the District of Columbia and Texas bars in 1935, Korth joined the law firm of Thompson & Barwise in Fort Worth, Texas the same year. In August 1942 he was commissioned a second lieutenant in the Air Transport Command of the United States Army and received officer training at Miami Beach, Florida. Korth served at Hensley and Love Fields in Texas and at Fairfax Field in Kansas. His last assignment during World War II was with the ferrying division of the Air Transport Command at Cincinnati, Ohio, where he was chief of staff for personnel until his release from active duty, with the rank of lieutenant colonel, in January 1946.

Returning to Fort Worth, Korth formed his own law firm in partnership with Fred L. Wallace, with whom he was associated until 1951. He was a delegate to the national convention of Young Democrats in 1947 and to the state Democratic convention in 1948. He has been president of the Fort Worth Junior Bar Association and of the Young Democratic Club of Texas, and he has represented Texas on the national committee of Young Democratic Clubs of America. Korth belongs to the American Bar Association, the Texas Bar Association (he once was its president), the American Law Institute, and the American Judicature Society.

In March 1951 Secretary of the Army Frank Pace, Jr., with whom he had served in the Air Transport Command, asked Korth to go to Washington, D.C. as a deputy department counselor to the Department of the Army. On May 22, 1952 Korth was sworn into office as an assistant secretary of the Army, in charge of manpower and reserve forces. For distinguished service in this post during the next year he was awarded the Exceptional Civilian Service Award by the Department of the Army.

Although he returned to Fort Worth after the change of administration in January 1953, Korth was retained as a consultant by the new Secretary of the Army, Robert T. Stevens. In 1959, shortly before he gave up this post in 1960, he received the Army's Outstanding Civilian Service Award. In 1953 Korth gave up the practice of law to become executive vice president of the Continental National Bank of Fort Worth. In 1959 he became president of the bank, which by the end of 1960 employed 682 people and had total assets of $88,572,000, including deposits of $79,195,000.

Korth has been a director of the Panama Canal Company, of the Professional Businessmen's Life Insurance Company, of the All States Life Insurance Company, of the Bell Aerospace Corporation, and of the Texas and Pacific Railway Company. He is a member of the Fort Worth Chamber of Commerce, of the American and Texas Bankers Associations, and of the National Planning Association. He has been part-owner of several Texas ranches and a stockholder in a number of banks.

Following President Kennedy's election victory in November 1960, Korth was considered for appointment as Secretary of the Army in the incoming Democratic administration. He declined the post, however, after the Texas lawyer John B. Connally, Jr., had been made Secretary of the Navy, because he considered it unwise

FRED KORTH

for two men from the same city to hold key defense posts at the same time. From June 2, 1961 until December 11, 1961, when he was named Secretary of the Navy, Korth served as a civilian aide to Secretary of the Army Elvis J. Stahr, Jr. As one of three aides-at-large, he was responsible for interpreting Army policy to civilians and for advising the Secretary of civilian views of the Army.

Sworn into office on January 4, 1962, Korth succeeded John B. Connally, Jr., who had resigned to run in the Texas gubernatorial race. At hearings of the Senate Committee on Armed Services, Korth testified that he had resigned all posts and disposed of all stocks that might give rise to a conflict of interest. Asked whether he had given any thought to the length of time he would serve, Korth replied, "I certainly intend to serve as long as the president desires me to serve, barring any unforeseen circumstances, and as long as I think I can be effective in my position." However, he does not want to follow a career in government and plans to return to Fort Worth and perhaps to his bank post within a few years.

Active in many civic enterprises, Korth received an award in 1954 for helping to raise funds for Radio Free Europe. He also headed the Texas Crusade for Freedom campaign, which bought a radio transmitter to send "truth messages" to the Russian people. Korth was president of the Fort Worth and Tarrant County United Fund in 1957-58. He has been Red Cross chairman for Tarrant County, a co-chairman of the St. Joseph's Hospital Expansion Fund, and chairman of the Tarrant County Committee for the 1960 White House Conference on Children and Youth. A past member of the investment advisory board of the Teachers Retirement System of Texas, Korth has been a trustee of Texas Christian University, a member of the advisory board of Dallas University, and a trustee of the

KORTH, FRED—*Continued*

Hockaday School for Girls at Dallas, Texas. He is a member of the Texas Atomic Energy Commission and of the Navy League. He has been treasurer of the Texas and Southwestern Cattle Ranchers Association and director of the Texas and Southwestern Exposition and Fat Stock Show.

Fred Korth married Vera Connell on September 12, 1934. Their children are Nina Maria (Mrs. T. Gary Cole), Fritz-Alan, and Vera (Verita) Sansom. Korth is six feet two inches tall, weighs about 195 pounds, and has blue eyes and gray hair. A New York *Times* (January 5, 1962) writer called him exuberant and gregarious and mentioned his "booming 'fo'c'sle' voice." He enjoys hunting small game like doves and quail. Korth holds an honorary LL.D. degree from George Washington University and a Civic Achievement Award from the B'nai B'rith. He is a special Texas Ranger. His clubs are the Fort Worth, the River Crest Country, the Ridglea Country, the Shady Oaks Country, the Army and Navy (Washington, D.C.), and the Confrerie des Chevaliers du Tastevin. A member of the Phi Delta Phi and Sigma Phi Epsilon fraternities and of the Newcomen Society, Korth belongs to the St. Andrew's Episcopal Church in Fort Worth and to the Fort Worth Area Council of Churches.

References

N Y Times p10 Ja 5 '62 por
Newsday p50 D 12 '61 por
United States Congress. Senate. Hearing before the Committee on Armed Services, Ja 18 '62 (1962)
Who's Who in America, 1962-63
Who's Who in Commerce and Industry (1961)
Who's Who in United States Politics (1952)

McCARTHY, CLEM Sept. 9, 1882-June 4, 1962 Radio sports announcer; covered horse races, including the Kentucky Derby (1928-50), and boxing. See *Current Biography* (October) 1941.

Obituary

N Y Times p41 Je 5 '62

MOWRER, EDGAR ANSEL Mar. 8, 1892-
Author; journalist

Address: b. c/o McClure Newspaper Syndicate, 229 W. 43rd St., New York, 36; h. 3301 Garfield St., Washington 8, D.C.

NOTE: This biography supersedes the article that appeared in *Current Biography* in 1941.

Regarded by many as the dean of American foreign correspondents, Edgar Ansel Mowrer as author, journalist, and lecturer is an outspoken proponent of a vigorous foreign policy on the part of the United States and its allies. Mowrer began his career in journalism as a war correspondent for the Chicago *Daily News* in 1914

and was its chief foreign correspondent for more than twenty years. Having occupied a ringside seat at many of the major events of recent history, Mowrer came to know a number of its leaders personally; he was one of the first to recognize the bellicose intentions of Mussolini, Hitler, and the Japanese. In 1933 he received a Pulitzer Prize as the best foreign correspondent. Mowrer has written ten books dealing with political affairs and many articles for national magazines. Currently he presents his political analyses in a widely read column for the McClure Newspaper Syndicate.

Edgar Ansel Mowrer was born in Bloomington, Illinois on March 8, 1892, the younger of two sons of Rufus Mowrer, a businessman, and Nell (Scott) Mowrer, who won the Pulitzer Prize as the best foreign correspondent in 1929, served as editor of the Chicago *Daily News* from 1935 to 1944. He has written six volumes of poetry. Edgar Ansel Mowrer attended Hyde Park High School in Chicago, where he was active in tennis, basketball, and golf and edited the school annual. After graduating from high school in 1909 he entered the University of Chicago but interrupted his studies there to attend the University of Paris for a year. Returning to the United States, he studied philosophy and literature at the University of Michigan, edited the university's monthly magazine *The Painted Window*, and shared the poetry prize. Mowrer received the B.A. degree in 1913.

Following his graduation from the University of Michigan Mowrer returned to Paris, where his brother was a correspondent for the Chicago *Daily News*. At the time he had no intention of becoming a journalist, but considered entering the legal profession, teaching philosophy, or becoming a literary critic. In Paris he lived for a time on the Left Bank and wrote essays and critical studies on philosophy and literature, which were published in "the more emancipated English reviews." With the outbreak of World War I Mowrer was pressed into service at the Paris office of the Chicago *Daily News* when his brother was sent to cover the Battle of the Marne. During his brother's absence he filed dispatches, which his brother subsequently approved, and he thus stumbled into a career as a journalist.

Assigned by his brother to bicycle to the battlefields around Meaux, Mowrer later covered the war in western Flanders. He was arrested in Ypres on charges of espionage, deported to England, and again arrested upon his return to Belgium. After his release he continued as a war correspondent, reporting on the desolation, starvation, and cruelty he saw around him. In May 1915 he was assigned to the Rome office of the Chicago *Daily News*, and there he interviewed Benito Mussolini, then a Socialist, who was urging Italy to enter the war on the side of the Allies. After his marriage in London in February 1916 Mowrer returned with his wife to Italy, where he covered the battlefronts and witnessed the Italian defeat at Caporetto in 1917. For a time he was seriously ill with Spanish influenza. His first book, *Immortal Italy* (Appleton, 1922), was praised by C. E. Merriam in the *Political*

Science Quarterly (December 1922) as "a very readable and useful contribution to the understanding of the Italy that is in the making."

Transferred to Berlin in 1923, Mowrer spent the next decade in Germany. His second book, *This American World* (Sears, 1928), in which he predicted that the United States would ultimately attain world empire, was designated by Leon Whipple in *Survey* (June 1, 1928) as "the best book of the year, in philosophical depth, in range of synthesis, and in pure excellence of language." During this period he also wrote *The Future of Politics* (Routledge, 1930). Mowrer predicted the downfall of the Weimar Republic in his book *Germany Puts the Clock Back* (Morrow, 1932; revised edition, 1939), which was first published shortly before Adolf Hitler came to power and was subsequently banned in Germany. Joseph Shaplen described the book in the New York *Times* (January 8, 1933) as "a genuine contribution to modern history, a keen, incisive, authoritative and extremely well-written account of what has happened in Germany since the war and why."

As president of the Foreign Press Association in Germany Mowrer defied the Nazis when they threatened to expel reporters who filed dispatches unfriendly to the new regime, and he refused to accede to Nazi demands that he resign his post. After the Nazis imprisoned Goldmann, a Jewish correspondent for the Vienna *Neue Freie Presse* who was a friend of his, Mowrer offered to resign the presidency of the Foreign Press Association in exchange for Goldmann's freedom. This was arranged, and when Mowrer reluctantly left Germany on orders from the Chicago *Daily News*, his colleagues gave him a silver bowl inscribed to a "gallant fighter for the liberty of the press." Upon his return to the United States Mowrer lectured for a time to American audiences, warning them of the burgeoning power of Fascism.

Although he had expected to be sent to Tokyo, Mowrer was assigned in January 1934 to replace his brother as chief of the Paris bureau of the Chicago *Daily News*. From this vantage point he covered the events that led to the outbreak of World War II, and he acquired a growing distrust of plebiscites and treaties. In 1936 he covered the beginning of the civil war in Spain and visited the Soviet Union to report on the adoption of the new Soviet constitution. Upon his return to France he witnessed the fall of the Popular Front government headed by his friend Léon Blum. He visited China for a few months in 1938 to gather material for his book *The Dragon Wakes: A Report From China* (Morrow, 1939) and then returned to Paris, where he remained until the fall of France in June 1940.

Assigned in August 1940 to Washington, D.C. as correspondent for the Chicago *Daily News*, Mowrer collaborated with William J. Donovan on a series of articles on fifth-column activities in Europe. Several trips to the Far East in the next two years resulted in the book *Global War: An Atlas of World Strategy* (McClelland, 1942), which he wrote in co-operation with Marthe Rajchman. From 1941 to 1943 he served as deputy director of the Office of Facts and Figures in the Office of War Information and broadcast

EDGAR ANSEL MOWRER

news analyses from his post in Washington.

In his postwar book *The Nightmare of American Foreign Policy* (Knopf, 1948) Mowrer criticized the foreign policy of the United States since 1918. He expressed pessimism about the American love of the status quo and warned that the United States must choose between "world leadership and rapid decline." He advocated a voluntary federation, strong enough to keep world order by the enforcement of world law, and he maintained that the United Nations, which he described as "an unfinished bridge leading nowhere," was inadequate to undertake this task. E. W. Fox, writing in the New York *Times* (October 31, 1948), called the book "incomparably the best study of American foreign policy for this period that has yet been written." Pursuing his ideas on international organization further in *Challenge and Decision: A Program for the Times of Crisis Ahead* (McGraw, 1950), Mowrer urged the United States to take the lead in forming a "peace coalition" and the ultimate federation of non-Communist countries, with the aim of weakening the "expansionist bloc." M. S. Watson noted in the *Saturday Review of Literature* (December 9, 1950) that Mowrer's program resembled that of the United World Federalists.

In his *A Good Time to be Alive* (Duell, 1959), a collection of articles he wrote for the *Saturday Review*, *Zionist Quarterly*, *Western World*, and the *New Leader*, Mowrer surveyed the impact of world affairs upon the United States. He suggested that Soviet successes were compelling Western peoples to "pull themselves together in a real effort to survive as free men," and concluded that America's pioneer spirit was "still warm beneath the ashes of self-indulgence." Mowrer's most recent book, *An End to Make-Believe* (Duell, 1961), analyzes the history of the cold war and its meaning to Americans. In it he contrasts what he calls the "fanatical ambition of international Communism with the un-

MOWRER, EDGAR ANSEL—*Continued*

shakeable complacency of most Americans," and maintains that in "the sinister game of international poker forced on us by Moscow and Peiping" the West still "holds the aces" but needs "bolder, better players."

Discussing the hazards of overpopulation in the *Saturday Review* (December 8, 1956) Mowrer expressed his view that the soaring birth-rate leads to increasing constraint, conformity, and loss of freedom, and the destruction of natural beauty. A champion of what he calls the "Open Universe" theory, Mowrer wrote in the *Saturday Review* (April 19, 1958) that from an early age he "craved wildness . . . the quality of unpredictability that defies control." He maintains that the modern scientists' unified field theory constitutes "a painful shrinkage of the area of surprised anticipation."

From 1957 to 1960 Mowrer was editor-in-chief for North America of *Western World*, an independent, international monthly, published in English and French editions and "dedicated to the preserving and strengthening of the Atlantic community of nations." Three times a week Mowrer analyzes world affairs in a column for the McClure Newspaper Syndicate. His columns appear in newspapers in the United States, Latin America, France, Belgium, and the Philippines. Mowrer has served as a consultant to Radio Free Europe, and he is a trustee of Freedom House. He was awarded the 1933 Pulitzer Prize for his reporting from Germany, and he has received the ribbon of the Legion of Honor from the French government.

Edgar Ansel Mowrer and Lilian May Thomson were married on February 10, 1916. Mrs. Mowrer, a native of England, is the author of several books, including *Journalist's Wife* (Morrow, 1937; Grosset, 1940). They have one daughter, Diana Jane. Mowrer is five feet nine inches tall, weighs 150 pounds, and has gray hair and brown eyes. He belongs to the Century Club in New York and to the Adventurers Club in Chicago, as well as to professional organizations. He has no religious or political affiliations. Formerly fond of skiing and canoeing, Mowrer now lists his favorite recreations as walking, mountain climbing, and chess.

References

Mowrer, Lilian T. Journalist's Wife (1940)
Twentieth Century Authors (1942; First Supplement, 1955)
Who's Who in America, 1962-63

PETRI, EGON Mar. 23, 1881-May 27, 1962 Internationally renowned German-born pianist and piano teacher; lived since 1940 in the United States. See *Current Biography* (November) 1942.

Obituary

N Y Times p29 My 28 '62

RIVERS, THOMAS M(ILTON) Sept. 3, 1888-May 12, 1962 Physician; authority on virus diseases and pioneer in recognition of viruses as separate disease-causing agents; vice-president for medical affairs of the National Foundation (formerly National Foundation for Infantile Paralysis), 1957-62; associated with Rockefeller Institute for Medical Research, 1922-55. See *Current Biography* (July) 1960.

Obituary

N Y Times p88 My 13 '62

SATTERFIELD, JOHN C(REIGHTON) July 25, 1904- Lawyer; organization official

Address: b. P.O. Box 466, Yazoo City, Miss.; h. Sunset Dr., Yazoo City, Miss.

The first Mississippian to head the American Bar Association, John C. Satterfield became its eighty-fifth president on August 11, 1961 for a one-year term, succeeding Whitney North Seymour. During the year 1960-61 he acted as president-elect of the 102,000-member organization, the national professional association for lawyers, judges, and others in the legal field. Satterfield, who has served on committees of the ABA for some thirty years, practises law in Jackson and Yazoo City, Mississippi and was once a representative in the state House of Representatives.

John Creighton Satterfield was born on July 25, 1904 in Port Gibson, Mississippi, the son of Milling Marion and Laura Stevenson (Drake) Satterfield. At the age of ten he began helping out in the office of his father, who was the county attorney of Claiborne County, Mississippi for fifty years. John Satterfield graduated from Port Gibson Junior College in 1924 and then enrolled at Millsaps College, a Methodist school in Jackson, Mississippi, from which he received the B.A. degree in 1926.

Having decided to become a lawyer like his father, he enrolled at the University of Mississippi, where he took an LL.B. degree in 1929. While he was a student, he worked as a correspondent for the Associated Press, the Memphis *Commercial Appeal,* and the New Orleans *Times-Picayune* to finance his legal education. "I was just an amateur newspaper man," he once explained, "but I paid my way. It cost my father exactly $100 to send me through college and law school."

He was in his early twenties when he was elected to the Mississippi House of Representatives, in which he served from 1928 to 1932. He helped to draft the law under which most of the modern highways in Mississippi have been built and prepared a workmen's compensation bill and a compulsory auto insurance bill. Admitted to the Mississippi bar in 1929, he began his career as an attorney with Alexander & Alexander, a law firm in Jackson. From 1935 to 1943 he practised law as a partner in the firm of Alexander & Satterfield and in 1943 he became a senior partner with Satterfield, Shell, Williams & Buford, with whom he is still associated. The firm maintains a general insurance, oil, and gas practice, a civil and trial practice, and a real estate, corporation law, and tax practice.

The work of the American Bar Association is carried on through its eighteen sections and about seventy special and permanent committees. Satterfield has served the ABA in a number of capacities over the past thirty years, having been a member of the committees on rules and calendar; jurisprudence and law reform; resolutions; individual rights as affected by national security; continuing legal education; and Gavel Awards to media of information. Satterfield served on the board of governors of the ABA from 1955 to 1958, and was a member of the house of delegates, the national policy-making body of the association, for about twelve years. From 1950 to 1956 he was Mississippi commissioner of the national conference of commissioners on uniform state laws, which is sponsored by the ABA.

Perhaps recalling his own early struggles as a young lawyer earning only $85 a month, Satterfield continues to try to raise the income of American lawyers. As chairman of the ABA's special committee on the economics of law practice from 1957 to 1960, he addressed the legal profession in forty states, maintaining that its income has not kept pace with other professions. He has written several articles on this topic. One, entitled "The Economic Dilemma of the American Lawyer" (*Oklahoma Bar Association Journal*, December 26, 1959), points out that although other professions like medicine and dentistry had shown an annual gain in income of about 131 percent between 1929 and 1951, the income of lawyers had risen only 58 percent in the same period. As the president of the Mississippi bar in the year 1955-56, he established a program to fix a minimum-fee schedule for lawyers in that state.

Satterfield was designated president-elect of the American Bar Association in 1960. He took office as the eighty-fifth president of the ABA on August 11, 1961 after having been formally elected to the post by the house of delegates at the ABA convention in St. Louis, Missouri. Sylvester C. Smith, Jr., was named president-elect for the year 1962-63. The American Bar Association, with headquarters at 1155 East 60th Street in Chicago, is the national organization of the legal profession. It is the principal spokesman on current national issues for its 102,000 members who include lawyers, judges, and law teachers, and its opinions are often sought on the qualifications of prospective appointees to public legal posts.

Shortly after taking office, in October 1961, Satterfield set up a committee to determine if lawyers should be allowed to proclaim themselves specialists in one aspect of legal work as many doctors do in medical practice. The question had previously been considered and then abandoned by the ABA. It is a controversial one for members, some of whom maintain that the job of constructing qualifying tests and of supervising a specialization program would be too difficult.

Also during Satterfield's term of office a committee was established to review Canon 35, which prohibits news photography and broadcasting in the courtroom during a trial. It was incorporated into the ABA's canon of judicial ethics in 1937 to prevent distraction of witnesses and interference with the dignity of trial proceedings. Many representatives of news media

Chicago Photographers
JOHN C. SATTERFIELD

have urged the repeal of this ban, maintaining that the freedom of the press calls for unrestricted coverage of trials and denying that such coverage would degrade or interrupt the proceedings.

In January 1962 the American Bar Association announced the establishment of a new fund for the promotion of public education programs. Among other sums, the fund received $25,000 from the Richardson Foundation of New York to assist the ABA's committee on Communist tactics, strategy, and objectives, which is conducting a series of regional seminars for the bar and the public on the nature and techniques of Communism. In February 1962 the special committee on education in contrast between liberty under law and Communism issued a booklet entitled *Instruction on Communism and Its Contrast With Liberty Under Law*. Distributed to educators and bar associations, it urged that "the subject of Communism . . . should be taught factually, thoroughly, and objectively" in the nation's high schools to prepare young people to understand the advantages of the free system and to combat Communism.

"As a Mississippian, Mr. Satterfield is generally felt to share the racial and other views of his area," the writer of a New York *Times* profile (August 31, 1960) observed. "But he has not been militant on the question, and it is doubtful that he could have been elected to head the ABA if he were considered an extremist on the race question." The same reporter noted that Satterfield's tour of the United States, made as chairman of the ABA special committee on the economics of law practice between 1957 and 1960, has broadened his outlook from that of a "regional-minded to a national-minded person."

Satterfield is a Fellow of the American Bar Foundation, which sponsors education and research in the field of law. He belongs to the American Judicature Society, the International

SATTERFIELD, JOHN C.—*Continued*

Association of Insurance Counsel, and the Mid-Continent Oil & Gas Association. He has been a director of the Hinds County (Mississippi) chapter of the American Red Cross and a state director of the YMCA. His fraternities are Phi Delta Phi, Beta Theta Pi, Omicron Delta Kappa, and Sigma Upsilon; his clubs are the Scribes, the Jackson Country, the Petroleum, and the Kiwanis (Jackson). Satterfield is a Mason and a Democrat.

Known for his folksy humor, John C. Satterfield is a slight, balding, and exuberant man. He married Mary Virginia Fly on September 5, 1943. They have one daughter, Mary Laura, whom Satterfield described in 1960 as "age fourteen going on eighteen, if you know what I mean." By a previous marriage on November 13, 1923 to Ruth Quin, who is no longer living, he has two children, John Creighton, Jr., and Ellen Drake. Satterfield attended Methodist general conferences in 1952 and 1960 and southeastern jurisdictional conferences in 1952, 1956, and 1960. He was formerly on the general board of social and economic relations of his church and is now a member of its national commission on inter-jurisdictional relations.

References

N Y Times p14 Ag 31 '60 por

Martindale-Hubbell Law Directory, 1962
Who's Who in America, 1962-63
Who's Who in the South and Southwest (1961)

SPEICHER, EUGENE (EDWARD) Apr. 5, 1883-May 11, 1962 American portraitist and landscape painter; won many prizes including a National Academy of Design award in 1947 for his canvas *Consuela*. See *Current Biography* (October) 1947.

Obituary

N Y Times p23 My 12 '62

STOKES, ANSON PHELPS, JR. Jan. 11, 1905- Protestant Episcopal bishop
Address: b. 1 Joy St., Boston 8, Mass.; h. 182 Walnut St., Brookline 46, Mass.

The Right Reverend Anson Phelps Stokes, Jr., the eleventh bishop of the Protestant Episcopal diocese of Massachusetts, is considered to be a middle-of-the-road Episcopalian, inclining toward the evangelical wing but acceptable to high churchmen. Dr. Stokes, a member of a prominent New England family, was previously rector of churches in Columbus, Ohio, Honolulu, and New York City and served for two years as bishop coadjutor before being installed as bishop on November 1, 1956. Organized in 1784, the diocese of Massachusetts numbered, at the time of Bishop Stokes's consecration, approximately 123,000 baptized Episcopalians with some 78,000 communicants served by 260 clergymen in about 200 communities.

Anson Phelps Stokes, Jr., was born in New Haven, Connecticut on January 11, 1905, the eldest of three children of the Reverend Dr. Anson Phelps Stokes and Caroline Green (Mitchell) Stokes. His brother, Isaac Newton Phelps Stokes, is a member of the New York City law firm Webster, Sheffield, Fleischmann, Hitchcock & Chrystie. His sister, the former Olivia Egleston Phelps Stokes, is Mrs. John Davis Hatch, Jr. of Lenox, Massachusetts. Thomas Stokes, his great-great-grandfather, helped to found the London Missionary Society in 1793 and came to the United States a few years later. The elder Dr. Anson Phelps Stokes, who died in 1958, had served as canon of Washington Cathedral, secretary of Yale University, and president of the Phelps Stokes Fund for educational work among Negroes. He is also remembered for his authorship of the monumental history *Church and State in the United States* (Harper, 1950).

After spending his childhood and early youth in New Haven, Anson Phelps Stokes, Jr., received his secondary education at St. Paul's School in Concord, New Hampshire, from which he graduated in 1922. Following a year at Corpus Christi College, Cambridge University, England, he entered Yale University, where he majored in history and English, served on the junior promenade committee and the student council, and was active in rowing. He also was a member of Skull and Bones and of Alpha Delta Phi fraternity and was elected president of the Yale University Christian Association. He graduated with the B.A. degree in 1927.

Influenced by his parents and by several clergymen whom he admired to make the Protestant Episcopal priesthood his career, Stokes remained at Yale for an additional year as secretary of the University Christian Association, doing religious work among students. At the same time he attended the Yale Divinity School as a part-time student. In 1928 he entered the Episcopal Theological School at Cambridge, Massachusetts, but interrupted his work there in the following year to make an extended tour of Russia, China, Japan, the Philippines, India, and Palestine. He returned to the theological school in 1930 to work on his thesis, "The Contribution of Baron Friedrich von Hügel," dealing with the noted Roman Catholic philosopher, and he received the B.D. degree in 1932.

Ordained a deacon of the Protestant Episcopal Church in 1932, Stokes was invited to become assistant rector of St. Mark's Church in Shreveport, Louisiana. He was also offered the post of assistant to the dean of St. Paul's Cathedral Church in Boston.

While recovering from an illness at the Harvard infirmary, he talked the matter over with his mother, who was convinced of the great need at Shreveport and persuaded him to take the position there. After a year as assistant rector, Stokes became associate rector of St. Mark's Church upon his ordination as a priest in 1933. During his five years at Shreveport he worked among the Negro population and was active in the Council of Social Agencies, the City Planning Commission, the Y.M.C.A., and the American Red Cross.

From 1937 to 1945 the Reverend Anson Phelps Stokes, Jr., was rector of Trinity Church in Columbus, Ohio. During this period he served as a deputy to the triennial general convention of the Protestant Episcopal Church, in 1940 and in 1943. He was also active on behalf of the Columbus Community Chest. Moving to Hawaii in 1945, he became canon of the cathedral and rector of the cathedral parish at St. Andrew's Cathedral in Honolulu. While in Hawaii he served on the territorial Governor's Committee on Public Welfare.

After five years in Hawaii Stokes was called to New York City to become the eighth rector of St. Bartholomew's Church on Park Avenue, succeeding the Reverend Dr. George Paull T. Sargent. He was consecrated there on November 12, 1950 with Bishop Horace W. B. Donegan officiating and his father assisting in the ceremony. In late September 1951 Stokes participated in a three-day pilgrimage of leading churchmen from twenty-five states to Washington, D.C. There he accepted on behalf of his now retired father the Clergy Churchman of the Year award in recognition of a "long life of unselfish service as a Christian clergyman, economist, historian, and author." In July 1954 Stokes was elected one of eleven directors of the Citizens Housing and Planning Commission of New York City.

On June 29, 1954 a special diocesan convention was held at St. Paul's Cathedral in Boston to elect a bishop coadjutor for the diocese of Massachusetts in view of the fact that Bishop Norman Burdett Nash, who had served since 1947, would reach retirement age in 1956. (A bishop coadjutor automatically succeeds his bishop.) Although he had been approached a few weeks earlier by friends who wished to make him a candidate, Stokes declined the bid because he was contented with his position as rector of one of New York City's largest parishes. He was nevertheless nominated from the floor and, after taking third place on the first ballot, was elected on the fifth, receiving 85 of 139 lay votes and 102 of 172 clergy votes. Although he belongs to the evangelical or non-Anglo-Catholic persuasion he was elected as a "middle-of-the-road Episcopalian" with the aid of high churchmen, after an Anglo-Catholic candidate had withdrawn.

Although he felt greatly honored by his election, Dr. Stokes was reluctant to leave his New York parish and delayed acceptance until he had talked with Bishop Nash, who had been his teacher of New Testament and Christian Social Ethics at the Episcopal Theological School. He announced his acceptance on July 17, 1954, but because the election of a bishop must be confirmed by a majority of the bishops and standing committees of all the dioceses in the United States, he did not become installed as bishop coadjutor until five months later. On November 21, 1954 Dr. Stokes delivered his farewell sermon at St. Bartholomew's Church, taking as his theme the feeding of the multitude with five loaves and two fishes. "These meager resources in the hands of Jesus were more than adequate," he declared. "So it is with us. Our resource of time is very small, but if we take each day and give it to God we use it much more effectively."

In a two-hour ceremony at Trinity Church in Boston on December 4, 1954, Dr. Stokes was consecrated as bishop coadjutor of the diocese of Massachusetts by the Right Reverend Henry Knox Sherrill, presiding bishop of the Protestant

Wide World

BISHOP ANSON PHELPS STOKES, JR.

Episcopal Church, with the elder Dr. Anson Phelps Stokes as one of the attending presbyters. In addition to sharing in all the normal tasks of the diocese, Dr. Stokes as bishop coadjutor was responsible for the mission churches and the Episcopal lay organization, and he worked in co-operation with the Massachusetts Council of Churches. He also bore some responsibility with regard to the problem of remarriage of individuals under the canon of divorce. On November 1, 1956, following the retirement of Dr. Nash, Dr. Stokes was consecrated as the eleventh bishop of the Protestant Episcopal diocese of Massachusetts.

Speaking from his former pulpit at St. Bartholomew's Church in March 1957, Bishop Stokes listed as the three essentials for a strong Christian life a public commitment to Christianity, a personal fellowship with God, and the development of bonds of brotherhood with other human beings. In October 1960, during the Presidential campaign, 165 Roman Catholic laymen issued a statement deploring the "bigotry abroad in the land" and were criticized by some Protestant spokesmen for evading the "real religious issue," i.e., the "use of public funds for church institutions." Bishop Stokes called for an enlightened attitude on the part of the American people. In a statement to the members of his diocese he said: "We shall not be helping the development of Roman Catholic life along ways that contribute most helpfully to America if we deny Catholics opportunity of sharing fully in our American experience—including that of elections to the Presidency." In January 1962 he participated with other Protestant leaders in Massachusetts in a week-long program of prayer for Christian unity at the Cathedral Church of St. Paul in Boston. During this week all clergymen united in a special litany prepared by the Commission of Faith and Order of the World Council of Churches. Bishop Stokes personally

STOKES, ANSON PHELPS, JR.—*Continued*
opened and closed the week with a service of holy communion.

An honorary D.D. degree was conferred upon the Reverend Anson Phelps Stokes, Jr. by Kenyon College at Gambier, Ohio in 1953. Columbia University awarded him an honorary S.T.D. degree in 1954. Dr. Stokes is the author of a booklet on Bishop Kinsolving of Brazil, published by Seabury Press in 1954. He is a trustee of the Groton School in Groton, Massachusetts and of St. Mark's School in Southborough, Massachusetts, and he is on the board of St. Timothy's School in Stevenson, Maryland. He also serves on the Committee on Friendly Relations Among Foreign Students.

On July 10, 1943 Anson Phelps Stokes, Jr., married Hope Procter of Stockbridge, Massachusetts, whose grandfather was an Episcopalian missionary to the Zulu tribes in South Africa. They have two daughters, Hope Carol and Mary Elizabeth. Described in the Boston *Herald* (December 5, 1954) as a "simple, straightforward man, unpretentious and untouched by his advantages," Bishop Stokes is six feet tall, weighs about 180 pounds, and has blue eyes and brown hair. An independent in politics, he is a member of the Century Association and the Yale Club in New York City and of the Country Club in Brookline, Massachusetts. Walking is his favorite outdoor relaxation.

References

    Boston Globe Mag p1+ D 5 '54 pors
    N Y Herald Tribune p17 Jl 18 '54 por
    Newsweek 44:55 Jl 26 '54 pors
    Clerical Directory of the Protestant Episcopal Church of the United States (1959)
    Who's Who in America, 1962-63

THOMAS, NORMAN (MATTOON) Nov. 20, 1884- Socialist leader; author; lecturer; former clergyman
Address: b. 112 E. 19th St., New York 3; h. 77 Huntington Rd., Huntington, N.Y.

> NOTE: This biography supersedes the article that appeared in *Current Biography* in 1944.

The elder statesman of American Socialism, Norman Thomas, has used his formidable talents as a speaker and writer for over forty years to criticize shortcomings in American society and to champion unpopular causes. Regarded by many as the conscience of America, this social philosopher has been accepted by society because he lives within, rather than outside, the present social order, and his Socialism is of a Christian liberal rather than Marxist type. Many of the old Socialist causes that he has championed over the years have since become part of the social code and the law of the land.

Thomas, who was trained for the ministry, has run as the Socialist candidate for President of the United States six times and for many other offices in New York state. Since he has never held public office, his idealism and energy could be focused, not as a politician, but as an educator, on social, political, and economic problems. As the leading public advocate of the Socialist party-Social Democratic Federation, he is still fighting for democratic Socialism, for civil rights, and for a positive policy of peace.

Of middle class and Protestant fundamentalist background, Norman Mattoon Thomas was born in Marion, Ohio on November 20, 1884, into what he has described as a "very happy home." He is the oldest of six children of Welling Evan and Emma (Mattoon) Thomas. His three brothers, Ralph L., Evan W., and Arthur R., and his two sisters, Agnes E. and Emma E., are all still living. (An older sister died in infancy.) Both of his grandfathers, as well as his father, were Presbyterian ministers. Thomas attended the public schools in Marion, earning extra money by delivering the Marion *Star* (published by Warren G. Harding). After his graduation from Marion High School in 1901 his father moved to a parish in Lewisburg, Pennsylvania, where Norman Thomas entered Bucknell University.

Through the financial help of an uncle Thomas was able to transfer in 1902 to Princeton University in New Jersey. There he majored in history and politics and attended classes taught by Woodrow Wilson. He was a member of the debating team, played in the orchestra, sang in the glee club and was elected to Phi Beta Kappa. During this period he was still basically conservative in his political views. To earn extra money he tutored other students, and during summers he worked as a salesman and as a helper in a chair factory. He graduated with the B.A. degree in 1905 and was valedictorian of his class.

After his graduation Thomas became a social worker at the Spring Street Presbyterian Church and Settlement House in a blighted neighborhood in New York City. During a trip around the world in 1907, he spent considerable time in Asia and became an opponent of colonialism. Upon his return later in the year he continued his social service work as assistant to the pastor of Christ Church in a tenement district of New York City. From 1910 to 1911 he served as associate minister of the fashionable Brick Presbyterian Church in New York City, while attending Union Theological Seminary. At the seminary he was greatly influenced by the writings of Walter Rauschenbush, a Protestant theologian who taught and preached the social gospel. Upon receiving the B.D. degree in 1911, Thomas was ordained in the Presbyterian Church. He became pastor of the East Harlem Presbyterian Church and chairman of the American Parish, a federation of Presbyterian churches and social agencies located in immigrant neighborhoods in New York City.

The outbreak of World War I turned Thomas toward Christian pacifism and Socialism. In early 1917 he joined the Fellowship of Reconciliation, an organization of religious pacifists with strong social-reform tendencies. In the fall of 1917 he supported the New York City mayoralty candidacy of Morris Hillquit, the Socialist who campaigned on the antiwar issue. Thomas joined the American Union against Militarism, and, with Roger N. Baldwin, founded its new division, the Civil Liberties Bureau (which subsequently became the American Civil Liberties Union). In 1918 he founded *The World Tomorrow,* the official magazine of the Fellowship of Reconciliation. He served as its editor until 1921.

Thomas resigned from his church responsibilities in 1918, since he felt that his views were endangering financial contributions to these institutions. (He left the ministry in 1931.) The forces that drove him to the decision to join the Socialist party later in 1918 were, he has said, the "grotesque inequalities, conspicuous waste, gross exploitation, and unnecessary poverty all about me." As a Socialist, Thomas favored public ownership and democratic management of the means of production and distribution, while rejecting the Marxist emphasis upon changing the social order by force. As a pacifist, he defended the position of conscientious objectors during and after World War I. He participated in many free speech fights, walked in picket lines, and addressed workers' rallies, and he was a star witness in one of the trials resulting from the "Red scare" of 1919 and 1920.

In 1921-22 Thomas served as an associate editor of the *Nation.* In the latter year he became codirector, with Harry W. Laidler, of the League for Industrial Democracy, an educational institution that promoted ideas for a new social order based on production for use rather than for profit. He remained in this position until 1937. During 1923 he was editor of the New York *Leader,* and from 1924 to 1935 he was a regular contributor to the *New Leader.*

The "Socialist clergyman," as the newspapers called him, ran for the office of governor of New York in 1924 on the Socialist and Progressive tickets. In subsequent years he ran again for the governorship, campaigned twice for the office of mayor of New York City, and was nominated for such offices as state senator and alderman. In 1926 he addressed the striking wool workers in Passaic, New Jersey and protested the "unconstitutional" police measures used to end the strike. He was arrested, but a grand jury refused to indict him.

After the death of Eugene V. Debs in 1926 Thomas gradually came to assume leadership of the Socialist party. In 1928, in his first campaign as the Socialist candidate for the United States Presidency, he received 267,420 votes. The Depression period helped to revitalize the Socialist party, and Thomas advocated such measures as public works, unemployment insurance, minimum wage laws, a shorter work week, and abolition of child labor. In the 1932 Presidential election he received 884,781 votes.

In his campaigns during the 1930's Thomas publicized the hardships of the sharecroppers and played a leading role in organizing the Southern Tenant Farmers' Union (subsequently the Agricultural Workers' Union). In Terre Haute, Indiana he spoke in 1935 in favor of the rights of free speech, freedom of assembly, and picketing. In the same year he was a leader in the action against the Ku Klux Klan and the Tampa (Florida) police in the death of Joseph Shoemaker. Throughout this period he strongly criticized the New Deal, which, he felt, was neglecting moral issues in its efforts to meet economic emergencies.

In the factional dispute that developed within the Socialist party during the 1930's Thomas, who represented the "progressive" faction, was closer to the young "militant" group than to the old-line Marxist ideologists of the "old guard." In 1935 he severed his ties with the *New Leader,* which had come to be dominated by the old guard, and he became associated with the newly founded militant newspaper, the *Socialist Call.* The factionalism, as well as the success of the New Deal, contributed to the decline of the number of votes received by Thomas in the 1936 Presidential election. This factionalism continued in the late 1930's on issues involving Communism, fascism, the New Deal, the growing strength of organized labor, and the coming of World War II.

Thomas continued his work for freedom of speech by going to Jersey City in 1938 to speak at a Socialist meeting and defying the dictatorial rule of Mayor Frank Hague. His trip to Moscow in 1937, during the purge trials, weakened his faith in the Soviet experiment; his complete disenchantment came with the signing of the Nazi-Soviet pact in August 1939. His sympathy with the Loyalist cause during the Spanish Civil War led him to abandon absolute pacifism, but he became a leading member of the Keep America Out of War Congress. He felt that entry into World War II would bring fascism to America without curing it abroad. This noninterventionist policy led to the further disintegration of the Socialist party, and Thomas received even fewer votes in the 1940 Presidential campaign than in that of 1936.

During the war, the Socialist party adopted a policy of "critical support" toward the war effort. Thomas sought to preserve the democratic values that the war threatened and to prevent the fascism he had predicted. He acted strongly against the internment of the Japanese-Americans on the West Coast. He criticized American foreign policy during the war and denounced Soviet totalitarianism at a time when the United States felt that the Soviet Union was a great ally. He urged democratic and concrete peace terms rather than unconditional surrender. In the 1944 presidential campaign, he received about 80,000 votes.

Thomas stood almost alone among prominent Americans in his immediate reaction of horror at the dropping of the atom bombs on Hiroshima and Nagasaki, which led to his quest for universal disarmament after the war. He felt that war as a method of settling disputes had become obsolete in an age of atomic weapons. In his final Presidential campaign in 1948, in which he received 95,908 votes, he attributed the main war danger to the actions and policies of the Soviet Union and particularly criticized Henry A. Wallace's Progressive party, which, he maintained, was Communist-dominated. After 1948 Thomas favored the reconstitution of the Socialist party as an educational and research body rather than as a vote-seeking political party. In 1952 and 1956 the Socialist Presidential candidate, Darlington Hoopes, received only

Wide World

NORMAN THOMAS

a handful of votes, and in 1960 the party abandoned the idea of selecting a Presidential candidate.

Thomas continued, after 1948, to be a critic of, and a commentator upon, the American scene. In 1955 he resigned from all official posts in the Socialist party, while remaining its official spokesman. In 1960, after the *Socialist Call* ceased publication, he began contributing to *New America,* which had been established as the official newspaper of the Socialist party-Social Democratic Federation. During the 1960 Presidential campaign, he felt that neither the Democrats nor the Republicans provided a program adequate to maintain peace in the nuclear age. He said that American resources could alleviate world poverty and that steps should be taken to institute a planned economy of disarmament. Thomas called for world disarmament under international inspection, but opposed unilateral disarmament. Thomas has been particularly critical of the extreme right-wing groups that have emerged on the American scene in the early 1960's, and he regards their influence as more dangerous than the McCarthyism of the preceding decade.

In addition to his previously mentioned memberships, Thomas belongs to the Workers Defense League, the Post War World Council, the Institute for International Labor Research, the National Committee for a Sane Nuclear Policy, the American Committee for Cultural Freedom, the American Committee on Africa, and Spanish Refugee Aid, Inc. He has written many pamphlets and articles for labor, Socialist, and general newspapers and periodicals. He is a member of the American Newspaper Guild. In 1932 Princeton University conferred an honorary Litt.D. degree on him.

Thomas is the author of many books, including *The Conscientious Objector in America* (Viking Press, 1923); *America's Way Out: A*

Program for Democracy (Macmillan, 1931); *As I See It* (Macmillan, 1932); *The Choice before Us; Mankind at the Crossroads* (Macmillan, 1934); and *Human Exploitation in the United States* (Stokes, 1934). He also wrote *War: No Glory, No Profit, No Need* (Stokes, 1935); *After the New Deal, What?* (Macmillan, 1936); *Socialism on the Defensive* (Harper, 1938); *We Have a Future* (Princeton Univ. Press, 1941); and *What is Our Destiny?* (Doubleday, 1944).

His more recent books include *Appeal to the Nations* (Holt, 1947); *A Socialist's Faith* (Norton, 1951); *The Test of Freedom* (Norton, 1954); *Mr. Chairman, Ladies and Gentlemen . . . Reflections on Public Speaking* (Hermitage, 1955); *The Prerequisites for Peace* (Norton, 1959); and *Great Dissenters* (Norton, 1961). With Paul Blanshard he wrote *What's the Matter with New York; A National Problem* (Macmillan, 1932) and with Bertram D. Wolfe he collaborated on *Keep America out of War; A Program* (Stokes, 1939). With Harry W. Laidler he edited three books published by the Vanguard Press: *New Tactics in Social Conflict* (1926), *Prosperity?* (1927), and *The Socialism of our Times* (1929).

On September 1, 1910 Norman Thomas married Frances Violet Stewart, who died in 1947. Mrs. Thomas was a volunteer social worker who had independent means. They had six children: Norman Mattoon, Jr. (deceased), William Stewart, Mary Cecil, Frances Beatrice, Rebekah Lovett, and Evan Welling 2d. Thomas has fifteen grandchildren. He is six feet two inches tall, weighs 185 pounds, and has white hair and blue eyes. For recreation he used to like gardening and working outdoors, and he still enjoys swimming and "loafing in the country." He has said that he regrets not having cultivated his liking for music. Endowed with a good sense of humor and an inborn sense of dignity, Thomas is strongly affected by the condition of humanity. His physical well-being actually seems to vary with the changing world scene.

In an interview published in James Nelson, ed., *Wisdom for our Time* (Norton, 1961), Thomas was asked by Steven Siteman what he believed his achievements had been over the years. He replied: "I suppose it is an achievement to live to my age and feel that one has kept the faith, or tried to . . . to be able to sleep at night with reasonable satisfaction . . . to have had a part . . . in some of the things that have been accomplished in the field of civil liberties, in the field of better race relations, and the rest of it. It is something of an achievement, I think, to keep the idea of socialism before a rather indifferent or even hostile American public. That's the kind of achievement that I have to my credit. As the world counts achievement, I have not got much."

References

Ed & Pub 86:55 Ja 17 '53
Sat Eve Post 224:104 F 2 '52
Britannica Book of the Year, 1957
Seidler, Murray B. Norman Thomas; Respectable Rebel (1961)
Who's Who in America, 1962-63

VANDIVER, S(AMUEL) ERNEST (văn'dĭ-
vûr) July 3, 1918- Governor of Georgia; lawyer
Address: b. State Capitol, Atlanta, Ga.; h. Lavonia, Ga.

A political protégé of Senator Richard B. Russell and Senator Herman E. Talmadge, Governor
S. Ernest Vandiver of Georgia was elected to
his four-year term in 1958 by an overwhelming
majority. He is a lawyer and a former lieutenant
governor who is regarded as a man of high
personal integrity, and his administration has
been marked by a continuous fight against corruption. Although he is an avowed segregation-
ist, in early 1961 he became the center of
national attention when he yielded peaceably to
a federal order not to interfere with the admission of two Negro students to the University of
Georgia.

Samuel Ernest Vandiver was born on July 3,
1918 at Canon, Franklin County, Georgia and
is named after his father, a well-to-do farmer,
businessman, and social leader who was also
active in politics. His mother's maiden name
was Vanna Bowers. The story is told that the
elder Vandiver, on the day after his son's arrival,
told friends at Lavonia, the county seat, that "a
future Governor of Georgia was born yesterday."
The boy, who was brought up in Lavonia, went
on to the University of Georgia, the recognized
academy for the state's political leaders, after he
had graduated from the Darlington Preparatory
School at Rome, Georgia in 1936. He received
his B.A. degree from the University of Georgia
in 1940 and his LL.B. degree from its law school
in 1942. Before passing his bar examinations,
however, he volunteered for World War II
service and from 1942 to the end of the war
was engaged as an Army Air Forces fighter pilot.

Returning to civilian life and to his home
town in 1945, Vandiver was elected mayor of
Lavonia for the year 1946 and at the age of
twenty-seven was the state's youngest mayor.
After he had been admitted to the Georgia bar
in December 1946, he moved to Winder in
Barrow County, where he formed with Joseph
D. Quillian the law partnership of Quillian &
Vandiver. In the summer of 1948 he managed
the campaign for election to the governorship of
Herman E. Talmadge, son of former Governor
Eugene Talmadge.

When Talmadge won the election in November
1948, he appointed Vandiver adjutant general of
Georgia, a post that he held for the next six
years. He was first given the rank of brigadier
general in the National Guard and then, in
November 1949, was advanced to major general.
In April 1953 he was federally recognized as a
major general in the Air National Guard of the
United States, the youngest person to be accorded
this distinction. He served at the same time as
a member of the influential legislative committee
of the National Guard Association of the United
States and was one of seven members elected to
the executive council of the Adjutant General
Association of the United States.

Throughout his tenure as adjutant general of
his state, Vandiver was in addition the director
of selective service for Georgia, and for three
years beginning in 1951 he undertook also the

Jack Kanel, Atlanta
S. ERNEST VANDIVER

duties of state director of civil defense. "This
job," as Sylvan Meyer of the Gainesville (Georgia) *Times* pointed out in September 1958,
"placed his name before the people: on highway
signs marking escape routes 'in case of enemy
attack.'" He was elected president of the National Association of State Civil Defense Directors in October 1953.

Under the Georgia constitution of 1945, Herman E. Talmadge was ineligible for another consecutive term as governor, and the primary in
September of 1954 found nine different candidates vying for the Democratic nomination,
which was won by Lieutenant Governor Marvin
Griffin, a newspaper publisher, after a last-
minute endorsement by Talmadge. Vandiver,
who had resigned as adjutant general in June in
order to seek nomination as lieutenant governor,
easily won his contest, carrying 121 counties and
318 unit votes. With Griffin, he went on to November victory in a state where the Democratic
nomination assures election. It was not long,
however, before friction developed between the
new governor and lieutenant governor. As president of the state Senate, according to Sylvan
Meyer, Vandiver "declared himself for 'legislative independence' from the Governor's extraordinary control over the budget." Early in 1958
matters came to a head when the governor
asked the General Assembly to increase the
Rural Road Authority's bonding power from
$100,000,000 to $150,000,000. This proposal was
assailed by Vandiver as "a political slush fund"
and was voted down by the Legislature, which
tended to follow the lead of the lieutenant
governor rather than the governor.

Vandiver has always adhered sincerely to the
principle of racial segregation. According to
New York *Post* special correspondent Reese Cleg-
horn, he could probably have been elected governor in 1958 without giving any assurance on
the race issue. In the primary campaign, how-

Kennelly, Martin H(enry) obit Jan 62
Khouri, Faris el- obit Feb 62
Kiplinger, W(illard) M(onroe) Jan 62
Klahre, Ethel S(usan) May 62
Kobak, Edgar obit Jul 62
Koestler, Arthur Jan 62
Korth, Fred (H.) Jul 62
Kovacs, Ernie obit Mar 62
Kreisler, Fritz obit Mar 62

Larson, Leonard W(infield) May 62
Lefèvre, Théo(dore Joseph Albéric Marie) Jun 62
Lewis, John (Aaron) Jan 62
Lipchitz, Jacques Apr 62
Lober, Georg (John) obit Feb 62
Loeb, James (Isaac), Jr. Jan 62
Louw, Eric H(endrik) Mar 62
Love, J(ames) Spencer obit Mar 62
Luthuli, Albert John Feb 62

McCarthy, Clem obit Jul 62
McClintic, Guthrie obit Jan 62
McConnell, F(owler) B(eery) obit Feb 62
McCormack, John W(illiam) Apr 62
McCracken, Joan obit Jan 62
Macy, John W(illiams), Jr. Jan 62
Mao Tse-tung May 62
Marais, Jean Apr 62
Margai, Sir Milton (Augustus Strieby) Feb 62
Martin, Edmund F(ible) Jan 62
Marvel, Mrs. Archie D. Apr 62
Marvel, Elizabeth Newell See Marvel, Mrs. A. D. Apr 62
Meerloo, Joost A(braham) M(aurits) Jan 62
Mellers, Wilfrid (Howard) Feb 62
Meštrović, Ivan obit Mar 62
Miller, Harry W(illis) Mar 62
Miller, William E(dward) Feb 62
Moore, Charlotte Emma See Sitterly, C. M. Jan 62
Moses, Anna Mary Robertson obit Feb 62
Mössbauer, Rudolf L(udwig) May 62
Mowrer, Edgar Ansel Jul 62
Muench, Aloisius (Joseph), Cardinal obit Apr 62
Murphy, (Eleanor) Patricia Apr 62

Nestingen, Ivan A(rnold) Mar 62
Newhart, Bob Mar 62
Nitze, Paul H(enry) Feb 62

Ochoa, Severo Jun 62
Ogburn, Charlton obit Apr 62
Olav V, King of Norway Jan 62
Osgood, Charles E(gerton) Apr 62
Ozbirn, Catharine (Freeman) See Ozbirn, Mrs. E. L. Jan 62
Ozbirn, Mrs. E. Lee Jan 62

Page, Ruth Jun 62
Peden, Katherine (Graham) May 62
Petri, Egon obit Jul 62
Pevsner, Antoine obit Jun 62
Piccard, Auguste obit May 62
Portinari, Candido obit Mar 62

Rabaut, Louis Charles obit Jan 62
Randolph, Jennings Jan 62
Rayburn, Sam(uel Taliaferro) obit Jan 62
Read, Sir Herbert (Edward) Mar 62
Reischauer, Edwin O(ldfather) May 62
Reybold, Eugene obit Jan 62
Rivers, Thomas M(ilton) obit Jul 62
Robinson, Spottswood W(illiam), 3d Mar 62
Rogers, Frank B(radway) Jun 62
Rogers, Rutherford David Jun 62
Rose, (Iain) Murray Jun 62
Russell, Donald J(oseph) May 62
Russell, James S(argent) Jan 62

Satterfield, John C(reighton) Jul 62
Savage, Augusta (Christine) obit May 62
Schoeppel, Andrew F. obit Mar 62
Scofield, Paul Mar 62
Senghor, Léopold Sédar Mar 62
Shirer, William L(awrence) May 62
Shurlock, Geoffrey M. Jan 62
Sitterly, Mrs. Bancroft Walker See Sitterly, C. M. Jan 62
Sitterly, Charlotte Moore Jan 62
Slocum, (Manly) Harvey obit Jan 62
Smith, Margaret (Madeline) Chase Mar 62
Spahn, Warren (Edward) May 62
Speicher, Eugene (Edward) obit Jul 62

Spottswood, Stephen Gill Apr 62
Stikker, Dirk U(ipko) Feb 62
Stokes, Anson Phelps, Jr. Jul 62
Suggs, Louise Jan 62
Sunderland, Thomas E(lbert) Apr 62
Swann, W(illiam) F(rancis) G(ray) obit Mar 62
Switzer, Mary E(lizabeth) Jan 62

Taylor, A(lbert) Hoyt obit Jan 62
Teagle, Walter C(lark) obit Feb 62
Thant, U Feb 62
Thomas, Norman (Mattoon) Jul 62
Thurber, James obit Jan 62
Tillinghast, Charles C(arpenter), Jr. Feb 62
Tobias, Channing H(eggie) obit Jan 62
Turner, Ewald (Walter) May 62

Unitas, John Feb 62

Vandiver, S(amuel) Ernest Jul 62
Vertès, Marcel obit Jan 62
Viereck, George Sylvester obit May 62
Vilar, Jean (Louis Côme) Apr 62
Volpe, John A(nthony) Feb 62

Waddington, C(onrad) H(al) Apr 62
Wagner, Richard Apr 62
Walsh, Chad Feb 62
Walsh, William B(ertalan) May 62
Walter, Bruno obit Apr 62
Ward, Paul L(angdon) Mar 62
Watts, Alan (Wilson) Mar 62
Webb, James E(dwin) May 62
Welsh, Matthew E(mpson) Jun 62
Wenner-Gren, Axel (Leonard) obit Jan 62
Wesker, Arnold Feb 62
Whalen, Grover A(loysius) obit Jun 62
Whitton, Rex M(arion) May 62
Wilcox, Francis O(rlando) Apr 62
Wilkinson, Bud See Wilkinson, C. Apr 62
Wilkinson, Charles (Burnham) Apr 62
Wills, Royal Barry obit Feb 62
Winiarski, Bohdan (Stefan) Feb 62
Wood, Natalie Apr 62

Yamasaki, Minoru Mar 62

CURRENT BIOGRAPHY

SEPTEMBER 1962
VOL. 23 NO. 8

Editor: Charles Moritz

PUBLISHED BY THE H. W. WILSON COMPANY, 950 UNIVERSITY AVE., NEW YORK

CONTENTS

ABOUT THIS PUBLICATION

Current Biography (published every month except August) presents articles on people who are prominent in the news—in national and international affairs, the sciences, the arts, labor, and industry. Sources of information are newspapers, magazines, books, and, in some cases, the biographees themselves. It should be pointed out, however, that these are objective rather than authorized biographies. At the end of the year the articles in the monthly issues are cumulated in one alphabet, revised, and printed in a single volume known as *Current Biography Yearbook*.

Authorities for biographees' full names, with some exceptions, are the bibliographical publications of The Wilson Company. When a biographee prefers a certain name form, that is indicated in the heading of the article: for example, MACMILLAN, (MAURICE) HAROLD means that he is usually referred to as HAROLD MACMILLAN. When a professional name is used in the heading, as, for example, GLENN FORD, the real name, in this case GWYLLYN SAMUEL NEWTON FORD, appears in the article itself.

The heading of each article includes the pronunciation of the name if it is unusual, date of birth (if obtainable), and occupation. The article is supplemented by a list of references to sources of *biographical* information, in two alphabets: (1) newspapers and periodicals and (2) books.

References to newspapers and periodicals are listed in abbreviated form; for example, "Sat Eve Post 217:14+ S 30 '44 por" means *Saturday Evening Post*, volume 217, pages 14 ff, September 30, 1944, with portrait. For full names, see the section "Periodical and Newspaper Designations," which is included in all *Current Biography* Yearbooks and in the January issue each year. Obituary notices appear for persons whose biographies have been published in *Current Biography.*

An index to names that have appeared this year is to be found at the back of this issue.

NOTE: Authors whose biographies do not appear in *Current Biography* may usually be found in *Twentieth Century Authors*, Kunitz & Haycraft, 1942, H. W. Wilson Company, or in the FIRST SUPPLEMENT (1955). Authors of books for young people are included in *The Junior Book of Authors* (Second Edition, Revised) edited by Kunitz & Haycraft, 1951, H. W. Wilson Company. Musicians whose biographies do not appear in *Current Biography* may usually be found in *Living Musicians*, compiled and edited by David Ewen, 1940, H. W. Wilson Company, or in its FIRST SUPPLEMENT (1957).

KEY TO PRONUNCIATION

ā	āle	N	Not pronounced, but indicates the nasal tone of the preceding vowel, as in the French *bon* (bôN).	û	ûrn; French eu, as in *jeu* (zhû); German ö, oe, as in *schön* (shûn), *Goethe* (gû'tĕ)
â	câre				
ă	ădd				
ă	ăccount				
ä	ärm				
à	àsk				
ȧ	sofȧ				
		ō	ōld	ŭ	tŭb
		ô	ôrb	ŭ	circŭs
ē	ēve	ŏ	ŏdd	ü	Pronounced approximately as ē, with rounded lips: French u, as in *menu* (mē-nü); German ü, as in *grün*
ĕ	ĕnd	oi	oil		
ê	makêr	o͞o	o͞oze		
		o͝o	fo͝ot		
g	go	ou	out		
ī	īce				
ĭ	ĭll	*th*	*then*	zh	azure
		th	thin	′ =	main accent
K	German ch as in i*ch* (ĭK)	ū	cūbe	″ =	secondary accent

CURRENT BIOGRAPHY

SEPTEMBER 1962

ADAMS, EVA B(ERTRAND) Sept. 10, 1908-
United States government official; lawyer
Address: b. Room 3464, Main Treasury Building,
Washington, D.C.; h. 1 Skyline Blvd., Reno,
Nev.

Miss Eva B. Adams, who was born and reared
in the heart of the gold and silver mining country of Nevada, became the director of the United
States Mint on October 30, 1961. In this position
she oversees the use of gold and silver and other
metals in the manufacture of almost three and a
half billion coins and medals a year for the
United States and other countries. Miss Adams
came to the post after more than ten years as a
teacher and twenty-one years as administrative
aide to three Nevada Senators.

Eva Bertrand Adams was born in Wonder,
Nevada, on September 10, 1908 to Verner Lauer
and Cora E. (Varble) Adams. She has one
sister, Alice (Mrs. David Herstine). Miss Adams
spent her early childhood in small mining towns
in Churchill County, Nevada and in Colorado,
where her father was a miner and ran a chain
of hotels for miners and prospectors. Until the
age of nine, she attended a small one-room
school in Fairview, south of Fallon, Nevada, and
she fondly remembers the atmosphere of the
rural school, where the older children helped the
younger ones and set strict examples of learning.

In 1924 Miss Adams graduated from Reno
High School, where she had taken part in athletics, dramatics, and journalism. She went on
to major in English, history, and physical education at the University of Nevada, in Reno,
which granted her a B.A. degree in 1928. Active
in many extracurricular activities at the university, she served as women's editor on the college
paper, *Sagebrush*, as president of the YWCA,
and as vice-president of her senior class. She
was a member of the women's athletic association and the campus dramatic group and was
elected to the athletic honorary society Gothic N,
to the social fraternity Kappa Alpha Theta, and
to the women's honorary society Cap and Scroll.
In addition to her other honors she received a
chemistry prize. After graduation Miss Adams
taught at Las Vegas High School. In 1936 she
returned to the University of Nevada as an
English instructor and assistant dean of women.
In 1937, after having submitted a thesis on
Mark Twain, she received an M.A. degree in
English from Columbia University.

In 1940, while teaching at the University of
Nevada, Miss Adams was asked by Senator Pat
McCarran, Democrat of Nevada, an old friend
of the family, to come to Washington to head
his office staff. She accepted and stayed on as
administrative assistant to McCarran and his

EVA B. ADAMS

successors for twenty-one years. During that time
she earned an LL.B. degree in 1950 from the
Washington College of Law of American University and an LL.M. degree in 1952 from George
Washington University. Miss Adams was admitted to the Nevada bar in 1950 and to practise before the Supreme Court of the United
States in 1954.

Senator McCarran, who served Nevada from
1933 until his death in 1954, was chairman of
the Senate Judiciary Committee and a leading
Congressional spokesman for the silver bloc,
which repeatedly tried to achieve remonetization
of silver. He was a member of the Senate Special Silver Committee, which advocated raising
the price of silver to stimulate the production
of its by-products. He favored limiting the use
of the Treasury's supply of silver as reserves for
the issuance of silver certificates rather than for
non-monetary purposes. He advocated the recognition of silver as a world monetary metal.
McCarran was also known as a co-author of the
McCarran-Walter Immigration and Nationality
Act of 1952.

When Senator McCarran died in 1954, Miss
Adams was asked by his temporary successor,
the Republican Senator Ernest Brown, to stay on
as his assistant. Late in 1954 the Democratic
Senator Alan Bible won the Senate seat by election and was re-elected for the full six-year term
in 1956. Miss Adams continued as administrative

ADAMS, EVA B.—*Continued*

assistant and remained with Senator Bible's staff until she was appointed to her present position in 1961.

As administrative assistant to Senator Bible, Miss Adams brought an assured continuity of administrative responsibility to the new Senator's office. Senator Bible adhered to the McCarran tradition with regard to the mining industry. He presented a bill to establish a National Minerals Advisory Council and to amend the Domestic Minerals Program Extension Act of 1953, expanding the program and encouraging the discovery and production of domestic minerals.

After John F. Kennedy was elected President, Miss Adams was mentioned as a likely candidate for the $16,530-a-year job of director of the Mint. The President planned to follow the Democratic precedent of naming a woman to the job, which President Franklin D. Roosevelt had established with Mrs. Nellie Tayloe Ross, who directed the mint for two decades under Roosevelt and Harry S. Truman. Under President Dwight D. Eisenhower, William H. Brett, an Ohio businessman was director, and after his resignation the bureau was run by the assistant director, Dr. F. Leland Howard, a civil service expert in coinage problems. On September 21, 1961, President Kennedy nominated Miss Adams for the post, and two days later she was approved for a five-year term by the Senate. She was sworn into office on October 31, 1961 by Associate Justice of the United States Supreme Court Tom Clark, one of her old friends.

As director of the Mint, Miss Adams oversees one of the oldest bureaus of the government. Created by Act of Congress on April 2, 1792, to provide for the coinage of gold, silver, and copper, the first United States Mint was established at the seat of government in Philadelphia. Subsequent legislation set up branch mints in various parts of the country, and the Bureau of the Mint was established in 1873, consisting of the Office of the Director in Washington and six field institutions: in Philadelphia and Denver, where coins are manufactured; in San Francisco, which is an assay office and bullion depository; in Fort Knox, which is a gold bullion depository; in New York, an assay office; and in West Point, a silver bullion depository.

Eva B. Adams is responsible for all the gold and silver assets of the government in the custody of the Mint. She establishes the general policies and directs the activities of all the Mint field offices in the production of coin, both domestic and foreign. The United States manufactures coins at present for Costa Rica, the Dominican Republic, Korea, Liberia, the Philippines, and Venezuela. Miss Adams has charge of the custody, processing, and movement of gold and silver bullion, and she administers the issuance and denial of licenses for the purchase of gold and the sale of gold for industrial use. In addition she supervises the manufacture and sale to the public of historic and special government medals and commemorative coins.

When Secretary of the Treasury C. Douglas Dillon welcomed Miss Adams to her new post, he said, "You are taking charge of the Mint at a time when the largest number of United States coins in our history is being made—about three and a quarter billion this fiscal year. . . I can confidently predict that your business will continue on the upgrade."

In fiscal year 1963 Miss Adams will administer the manufacture of 3,470,000,000 coins, almost a million more than were produced in fiscal year 1960. However, her new post has been stripped of some of its former responsibility for policy-making decisions affecting the domestic gold and silver market. In a directive on October 9, 1961, Secretary Dillon transferred these policy decisions to the Undersecretary of the Treasury and to a new Office of Domestic Gold and Silver Operations, presently headed by Dr. F. Leland Howard. This move effectively forestalled charges that the administration was giving silver interests in Nevada control over domestic silver policy in appointing Miss Adams as the Mint director.

Eva B. Adams belongs to the Baptist Church and is a member of Soroptimists International. She was the president of the Senate Administrative Assistants' Association in 1943-44, and she is an honorary member of the National Executive Secretaries Association of Las Vegas. Law groups to which she belongs include the American Bar Association, the American Judicature Society, the Federal Bar Association, the Federal Communications Commission Bar Association, and the Women's Bar Association.

When she can take time off from her busy schedule, Miss Adams enjoys horseback riding, swimming, reading, listening to music, and hunting sage hens back home in Nevada, where she returns regularly. An administrator who takes her job as Mint director very seriously, Miss Adams says, "I dread the day when the housewife can't get a dime or a quarter for her laundromat. It's my responsibility to be sure that the people of the United States have enough coins to meet their needs. With the increasing use of the vending machine, demand is constantly growing."

A petite (five feet two inches tall and 125 pounds) woman with light brown hair and gray eyes, Eva B. Adams has the habit of walking around her office with her shoes off. Possessing an interest and knowledge from childhood of mining and processing of silver, she is not above climbing onto the machinery for a closer look at coinage operations in a Mint tour. She is much in demand as a speaker before various groups, and whenever she gives a speech, she wears an unusual charm bracelet filled with gold coins of different denominations, many of them rare, given to her by friends over the years. Soon after her appointment, she returned to Reno for a visit and attended a dinner in her honor. She was touched and surprised when a tremendous cake surrounded by coins and topped by lettering was set before her. It read: "In God We Trust; In Eva Too."

References

Christian Sci Mon p6 Mr 21 '62 por
N Y Times p19 O 27 '61 por
N Y World-Telegram p21 N 15 '61 por
Who's Who of American Women (1961-62)

BABBITT, MILTON (BYRON) May 10,
1916- Composer; educator
Address: b. Princeton University, Princeton,
N.J.; h. 242 E. 19th St., New York 3

A mathematician as well as a musician, Milton
Babbitt is the first composer to apply the operations of the twelve-tone system to such non-
pitch elements as rhythm, register, dynamics, and
timbre. Since 1938 Babbitt has been a teacher
of music at Princeton University, and since 1959
he has been a director of the Electronic Music
Center of Columbia and Princeton Universities
in New York City. On the occasion of its 1959
award to Babbitt, the National Institute of Arts
and Letters cited his "imaginative compositions"
for revealing "an original and penetrating grasp
of musical order that has had a great influence
on many younger composers." Babbitt has said,
"The electronic production of music makes possible the conjunction of all my interests: my
scientific interests, my theoretical concerns, and
the realization of the needs and aspirations of
my non-electronic music."

Milton Byron Babbitt was born in Philadelphia, Pennsylvania on May 10, 1916 to Albert E.
Babbitt, an actuary, and Sara (Potamkin) Babbitt. A student of music from the age of four,
Babbitt also early became interested in mathematics, under the influence of his father—an
influence later augmented by his only brother,
Albert E. Babbitt, Jr., a mathematician now
employed by the International Business Machines
Corporation.

Reared in Jackson, Mississippi, Babbitt attended its Central High School, where he played
in the band. After graduating in 1931, he entered New York University with the intention of
working in mathematical logic, but in 1933 he
discovered the music of Arnold Schoenberg and
Anton von Webern. The discovery directed him
back to musical composition and theory, and
music became his major subject at New York
University. In 1935 he received his B.A. degree
from New York University, where he had been
elected to membership in Phi Beta Kappa.

Three teachers of music under whom Babbitt
studied were Marion Bauer and Philip James,
who were on the New York University faculty,
and Roger Sessions, who was on the faculty of
Princeton University. Gilbert Chase reports in
America's Music (McGraw-Hill, 1955) that Babbitt has acknowledged that his greatest debt is
to Sessions, who, according to Chase, "revealed
to him the path he should take." Babbitt did
his postgraduate study at Princeton, taking his
master of fine arts degree in music in 1942, and
he began to teach music at Princeton in 1938.
Moving up the academic ranks from instructor
to his present post of professor of music, Babbitt
has taught a range of subjects at Princeton, including composition, analytical theory, musical
acoustics, electronic musical media, and twelve-
tone theory. From 1943 to 1945 he was an instructor in mathematics at Princeton, teaching
undergraduate civilians as well as members of
Army, Navy, and Marine training programs.

Babbitt's non-electronic *Three Compositions
for Piano* (1946-47) and *Composition for Four
Instruments* (1947) were the first applications of
the operations of the twelve-tone system and

MILTON BABBITT

serial ideas of musical organization to such non-
pitch components as rhythm, register, instrumentation, dynamics, and timbre. These predated
European attempts at what is sometimes called
"totally organized" music by some four or five
years. A performance of Babbitt's *Composition
for Four Instruments* and of his *Composition for
Viola and Piano* (1950) comprised one side of a
long-playing record released by Composers Recordings, Inc., in 1961.

In reviewing the record for the New York
Times (June 11, 1961), Eric Salzman wrote, "one
trouble with totally-organized-music-European-
style was that it is (or was) too purely numero-
logical, too obviously based on arbitrary and
irrelevant application of numbers schemes. . . .
What Mr. Babbitt does is subtler, more organic,
richer and, in the end, infinitely more artistic."
Composition for Four Instruments won the citation of the New York Music Critics' Circle in
1949. For an earlier work, *Music for the Mass,*
Columbia University had awarded Babbitt the
Joseph Bearns Prize in 1941. Other works by
Babbitt include *Composition for Twelve Instruments* (1948); *Du,* a song cycle (1954); Woodwind Quartet (1953); String Quartet No. 2
(1954); *All Set,* for seven jazz instrumentalists
(1957); and *Composition for Tenor and Six Instruments* (1960).

As far back as 1939 Babbitt reportedly became
interested in the composition of electronic music,
which Eric Salzman defined in the New York
Times (February 9, 1962) as "a generic term for
music on electromagnetic tape, which is put together by a variety of electronic and tape techniques." Salzman went on to distinguish between the "purist" variety, in which the sound
and noises are produced by purely electronic
means, and "musique concrète," in which real
sounds that have been recorded are spliced in a
kind of collage technique. Occasionally both
methods are used. The Columbia-Princeton
Electronic Music Center, which developed out of
the Columbia University laboratory for electronic

BABBITT, MILTON—*Continued*

music with the help of a Rockefeller Foundation grant in 1959, is the first center associated with universities to be entirely devoted to composition and research in the field of electronically produced music.

Since 1959 Babbitt has been one of the four members of the Columbia-Princeton Electronic Music Center's committee of direction. The other directors are Otto Luening and Vladimir Ussachevsky of Columbia and Roger Sessions of Princeton. Located near the Columbia campus in Manhattan, the Center houses the massive RCA Electronic Sound Synthesizer that was designed and built at the David Sarnoff Research Center. Theoretically the RCA Electronic Sound Synthesizer, with its punched holes passing under a row of wire brushes and with music emanating from its speaker, can produce all possible sounds. Babbitt, whose electronic work has been exclusively with this artifact, has described it as providing "complete programming control of the specification, generation, and regulation of every component of the musical event, and the mode of progression of such an event to the following event."

Babbitt's *Composition for Synthesizer*, completed in April 1961, was the first extended musical composition produced entirely on the RCA Electronic Sound Synthesizer. Later in the same year he wrote *Vision and Prayer*, a setting of a poem by Dylan Thomas, for soprano and synthesized accompaniment. It was given its first public performance at the Grace Rainey Rogers Auditorium of the Metropolitan Museum of Art in a concert presented by the Fromm Foundation in conjunction with the eighth congress of the International Musicological Society. After hearing it, Eric Salzman wrote in the New York *Times* (September 7, 1961), "The electronic music is shaped around the central vocal part. . . . The rational quality of measured sound—electronic or no—spins itself out in the tension of inevitability and the drama of lucid thought." The soprano was Bethany Beardslee, who again sang the vocal part when *Vision and Prayer* was presented for a second time, at Town Hall in New York City on March 25, 1962.

Milton Babbitt was a faculty member of the Salzburg Seminar in American Studies in 1952, a member of the composition faculty of the Berkshire Music Center (Tanglewood) in 1957 and 1958, and a faculty member of the Princeton Seminar in Advanced Musical Studies in 1959 and 1960. He has lectured on electronically produced music at Harvard, Dartmouth, Syracuse, and other American universities. At a panel meeting of the eighth congress of the International Musicological Society at Columbia University on September 8, 1961 he delivered a paper entitled "Past and Present Concepts of the Nature and Limits of Music." He held that "the limits of music reside ultimately in the perceptual capacities of the human receptor, just as the scope of physical science is delimited by the perceptual and conceptual capacities of the human observer."

It is Babbitt's belief that the serious musician has to ignore lack of approval on the part of an uninitiated public. His article "Who Cares If You Listen?" was published in *High Fidelity* for February 1958. Other articles by Babbitt include "Twelve Tone Invariants as Compositional Determinants" in the *Musical Quarterly* for April 1960, "Set Structure as a Compositional Determinant" in *Journal of Music Theory* for April 1961, and "Electronic Music" in *University* for spring 1960. He is a member of the editorial board of *Perspectives of New Music*, a new semi-annual periodical sponsored by the Fromm Foundation and published by Princeton University Press. The first issue is scheduled to appear in the fall of 1962.

In an interview reported in *Musical America* (February 1951) Babbitt told Anthony Bruno, "I believe in cerebral music. I never choose a note unless I know why it is there." Reiterating his conviction that the twelve-tone set should determine *every* aspect of the composition, he said, "The structural idea is the idea from which I begin. . . . I have the end in mind as well as the beginning and middle, and the piece ends when the possibilities or the resources of the particular set are exhausted." He pointed out the rhythmical independence which is gained when tonality is sacrificed. "We can structuralize rhythm as we cannot in tonality," he said. Joseph Machlis in his *Introduction to Contemporary Music* (Norton, 1961) has summarized Babbitt's view thus: "Babbitt prizes the structural logic of the twelve-tone method. . . . He believes in maintaining the fixed order of the twelve tones in the vertical (harmonic) as well as horizontal (melodic) succession. . . . The result is a music concentrated in thought, complex in facture, and marked by the utmost degree of organic unity, which embodies the composer's ideal of 'a really autonomous music that does not depend upon analogies with tonal music.'"

Milton Babbitt married Sylvia Miller on December 27, 1939. They have a daughter, Betty Ann. Babbitt is five feet eight inches tall and weighs 135 pounds. His eyes are blue and his hair is brown-gray. He has said that he has no religious or political affiliation "unless logical empiricism is so classified." His principal recreations are mathematics (particularly group theory, combinatory theory, probability, and mathematical logic), mathematical linguistics, acoustics, psycho-acoustics, philosophy of science, electronics, computer theory, perception, and learning theory. He also relaxes by watching professional football, baseball, and old movies on television. He is a member of the International Society of Contemporary Music, the American Music Center, the American Institute of Physics, the Acoustical Society of America, the Audio Engineering Society, and the American Musicological Society. Since 1954 he has been a member of the board of directors of the League of Composers. In 1960 and 1961 he received a Guggenheim Fellowship for research in electronic music.

References

High Fidelity 10:40+ Ag '60 pors
N Y Times II p15 Je 11 '61 por
Baker's Biographical Dictionary of Musicians (1958)
Machlis, Joseph. Introduction to Contemporary Music (1961)
Who's Who in America, 1962-63

BANNOW, RUDOLPH F(REDERICK) Apr. 15, 1897-June 23, 1962   Former president of National Association of Manufacturers (1960); president of Bridgeport Machines, Inc.   See *Current Biography* (December) 1960.

Obituary

N Y Times p69 Je 24 '62

BATT, WILLIAM L(OREN), JR. Dec. 30, 1916- United States government official
Address: b. Department of Commerce, Washington 25, D.C.; h. 6425 31st St. N.W., Washington, D.C.

The administrator of a "domestic Marshall plan" to aid economically depressed areas of the United States, William L. Batt, Jr., has headed the Area Redevelopment Administration since its establishment on May 1, 1961. The program that he directs extends federal funds to communities suffering from chronic unemployment to help them revitalize their industries and create more jobs. An expert on unemployment problems, Batt served as Pennsylvania's Secretary of Labor and Industry from 1957 to 1961.

William Loren Batt, Jr., was born on December 30, 1916 in Cleveland, Ohio to Ruby (Burroughs) Batt and William Loren Batt. The senior Batt was chairman of the board of S.K.F. Industries, Inc., a Philadelphia subsidiary of a Swedish ball bearing company and, during World War II, vice-chairman of the War Production Board. William Loren Batt, Jr., has three sisters: Barbara (Mrs. Richard Bond) of Haverford, Pennsylvania; Martha (Mrs. Robert Abbott) of Alexandria, Virginia; and Jean (Mrs. Syoma Kagan) of Corvallis, Oregon; and one brother, Robert, of Philadelphia.

Raised in affluent circumstances in Philadelphia, William attended Montclair (New Jersey) High School and Phillips Exeter Academy in Massachusetts. After completing his secondary education in 1934, he attended Harvard University, from which he graduated *cum laude* with a B.A. degree in 1938. Batt played football at Harvard but was forced to give it up after he sustained an injury in his freshman year. Soon after he graduated he took his first job in Washington, D.C., as a staff member of the Temporary National Economic Committee. In 1941 he accompanied W. Averell Harriman, then the co-ordinator of the lend-lease program, to London. As a young man in pre-World War II society, Batt was known as a good dancer and entertaining conversationalist, and he was much sought after by hostesses for their dinner parties and social affairs.

When the United States entered World War II, Batt enlisted as a private in the United States Army. He received promotions up to the rank of major and held military government posts in North Africa, Sicily, Italy, and Germany. When the war ended, he was in charge of food and agriculture for the western military area of Europe. From 1946 to 1948 he was engaged in private business in Philadelphia.

The Depression of the 1930's and the welfare programs of Franklin D. Roosevelt made a strong impression on Batt and awakened his interest in

WILLIAM L. BATT, JR.

unemployment problems. "I remember sitting around at Army headquarters after the war was over," he relates. "There were three of us New Dealers—a social worker, a rabbi [and I]—and I remember us deciding there were two things the United States had to achieve—become involved in the world, where we had goofed after World War I, and achieve full employment in the United States. So I came back and worked on full employment in the United States."

Batt headed the Democratic National Committee research staff during President Harry S. Truman's election compaign in 1948, and in 1949 he was appointed special assistant to United States Secretary of Labor Maurice Tobin to develop programs for economically depressed areas. In 1950 he was the American representative at the UNESCO conference on full employment, and during 1953 he was senior economist on the President's Commission on Foreign Economic Policy.

From 1954 to 1957 Batt worked in his native state, Ohio, as the executive secretary of the Toledo Industrial Development Council. In an effort to attract new industries to Toledo, the council established America's first industrial park, an area outside the city that is especially designed for occupancy by businesses and industries. Batt recalls similarities between the situation in Toledo and the problems of depressed areas that are his present concern. "One of the problems we had was selling Toledo on itself," he has explained. "It's the problem we're facing with all of these communities now. Toledo was too closely wedded to the automobile industry. When Detroit sneezed, Toledo got pneumonia. This is the problem of all of these communities. They are too closely wedded to one industry."

One example of an area whose economy is insufficiently diversified is the state of Pennsylvania, of which Batt was Secretary of Labor and Industry from 1957 to 1961. Because of dwindling markets, mechanization, and other factors, the

BATT, WILLIAM L., JR.—*Continued*

principal industries—coal and steel—absorb a lower proportion of the eligible worker population than formerly. The lack of alternative job openings and, sometimes, of adequate training keep a large percentage of workers unemployed. Other examples cited by Batt of one-industry areas where the employment of workers has declined are Wichita, Kansas (airplane production); northern Michigan (copper and iron); West Virginia, parts of Ohio and Illinois, and Kentucky (coal); northern Minnesota (iron); southern Michigan (automobiles); and New England (textiles).

On May 1, 1961 President John F. Kennedy signed into law a bill providing federal assistance for communities characterized by "substantial and persistent" unemployment and authorizing the establishment of the Area Redevelopment Administration (ARA) with Batt as its administrator. An industrial area suffering from substantial unemployment is defined as having more than 6 percent of its workers idle and a level of joblessness from 50 to 100 percent above the national level for one to three years. In November 1961 the ARA issued a list of 823 depressed areas in 1,035 counties throughout the United States eligible for aid under the ARA law. One hundred and thirty-five of these were industrial labor market areas, 641 were primarily rural communities, and forty-seven were Indian reservations. The five states with the highest total number of such areas were Georgia with 63, Mississippi with 54, Texas with 49, Pennsylvania with 42, and Kentucky with 41.

In appointing Batt to the ARA post, President Kennedy called him the man "who has probably more experience in working in this matter than any other American." Pockets of high unemployment amidst general prosperity in the United States first became noticeable in the 1950's. Since 1955 Senator Paul H. Douglas of Illinois annually sponsored bills to alleviate this condition. Although he recognized that help was required, President Dwight D. Eisenhower twice vetoed bills providing for area redevelopment. During his campaign for the Presidency, John F. Kennedy called on labor experts and governors of economically depressed states to discuss the problem at a meeting in West Virginia in 1960. The law that established the ARA was born at this conference, at which Batt presided. Batt was instrumental in preparing the study on which the bill was based.

The program of federal aid to communities was authorized for a four-year period. The ARA was officially established within the Department of Commerce on May 10, 1962, and Batt was confirmed as its administrator on May 17, 1962. Of the $394,000,000 provided under the law, $300,000,000 in loans was earmarked for renovating and building plants, machinery, and equipment in industrial and rural areas and for constructing public facilities like sewers or water lines, which would attract new industries to an area. For communities unable to afford loans, $75,000,000 was provided in grants.

Attacking the problem of unemployment on two fronts, the program not only seeks to attract new industries to depressed areas but also provides for training workers in skills that they can use in new or existing enterprises in their communities. The law designated $4,500,000 for worker training programs and $10,000,000 for subsistence payments to workers enrolled in the programs. Working with the Department of Commerce in putting the program into effect are the Departments of Labor; Health, Education, and Welfare; Interior; and Agriculture; and the Small Business Administration and Housing and Home Finance Agency. Some of these have also allotted part of their own funds to the area redevelopment scheme.

In July 1962 Secretary of Commerce Luther H. Hodges announced that the ARA had already invested $32,500,000 in seventy-six industrial and commercial projects that will create 30,000 new jobs. Projects under way include the construction of a new sporting goods business in Missouri, a furniture plant in West Virginia, an industrial tape concern in Illinois, a seafood cannery in Florida, and sewerage and water systems in Arkansas, Georgia, and Tennessee. Also, the ARA is sponsoring sixty-eight worker retraining programs. By law the federal government is limited to 65 percent participation in all projects; the rest of the funds are to be raised by local communities. Referring to requests for aid under the ARA program, Batt remarked, "We get none of the simple ones. If there is any other source of funds they don't come to us. We just get the ones that can't be put together without our help." On another occasion, writing a letter about the program to the New York *Times* (November 6, 1961), Batt concluded: "This program is not a panacea for our economic ills. But it does attack the problem of persistent pockets of poverty for the first time. The joint efforts of business, the communities, the states, and the federal government can improve the economic climate of these areas."

From 1957 to 1961, while he was the Secretary of Labor and Industry in Pennsylvania, Batt was also the chairman of the governor's committee on employment of the handicapped; chairman of the governor's committee on migratory labor; and chairman of the East Coast states committee on migrant labor. At a Senate labor subcommittee hearing on May 17, 1961 Batt urged the adoption of legislation guaranteeing American migrant farm workers a minimum wage, workmen's compensation, and other benefits.

Described as "tall, tweedy, slightly bald," by a New York *Times* profile writer (May 2, 1961), Batt has brown eyes and brown hair, stands six feet six inches tall, and weighs 210 pounds. He is a Democrat and a Unitarian. William L. Batt, Jr., married Jane Read on June 1, 1946. They have two daughters, Karen and Jane. In his spare time he enjoys reading history and working around the house. "We're rebuilding some of the most beat-up parts of the world here," the ARA administrator has said. "We've got the most exciting job in Washington. The only one that can compete with us is the Peace Corps and they don't operate in the United States."

References

N Y Herald Tribune V p1+ Ap 8 '62 por
N Y Post p30 Je 12 '61 por
N Y Times p27 My 2 '61 por

BEEBE, (CHARLES) WILLIAM July 29, 1877-June 4, 1962 Naturalist and explorer; set world deep-sea diving record with Otis Barton in 1934 by descending 3,028 feet in a bathysphere; wrote books describing his adventures. See *Current Biography* (July) 1941.

Obituary

N Y Times p41 Je 6 '62

BESS, DEMAREE (CAUGHEY) (July 28, 1893-June 2, 1962 Journalist; foreign correspondent in Europe and Far East; on staff of *Saturday Evening Post* since 1938; wrote for *Christian Science Monitor* from 1931 to 1938. See *Current Biography* (January) 1943.

Obituary

N Y Times p88 Je 3 '62

BLAIR, JAMES T(HOMAS), JR. Mar. 15, 1902-July 12, 1961 Governor of Missouri, 1957-61. See *Current Biography* (April) 1958.

Obituary

N Y p24 Jl 13 '62

BORZAGE, FRANK Apr. 23, 1893-June 19, 1962 Motion picture director; won awards of the Academy of Motion Picture Arts and Sciences (Oscars) for his direction of *Seventh Heaven* (1927) and *Bad Girl* (1931). See *Current Biography* (December) 1946.

Obituary

N Y Times p32 Je 20 '62

BRISTOL, LEE H(ASTINGS) Nov. 11, 1892-Businessman

Address: b. Bristol-Myers Co., 630 5th Ave., New York 20; h. 700 East Ave., Bay Head, N.J.

Heading one of the largest pharmaceutical houses in the United States, Lee H. Bristol is chairman of the board of the Bristol-Myers Company, which was founded by his father in 1887. The company manufactures and markets ethical drugs, toiletries, and proprietary products, including such well-known items as Ipana toothpaste, Sal Hepatica, Vitalis hair tonic, Mum deodorant, and Clairol hair coloring. Bristol has been chairman of the company since 1958; he was president from 1949 to 1958.

Lee Hastings Bristol is the second of three sons of Mary Seymour (Lee) Bristol and William McLaren Bristol, who in 1887 founded a drug concern in Clinton, New York with John Ripley Myers. Known as the Clinton Pharmaceutical Company, the business was transferred in 1890 to Syracuse, New York, where Lee H. Bristol was born on November 11, 1892. When the boy was six years old, the company again moved, this time to Brooklyn, where it was incorporated in June 1900 as the Bristol-Myers Company.

After attending the Stone School at Cornwall-on-Hudson, New York, Lee H. Bristol entered

LEE H. BRISTOL

Hamilton College in Clinton, New York, where six generations of his family had been educated. He received the Ph.B. degree in 1914. Bristol began his business career with the Bishop Calculating Recorder Company and rose to the position of vice-president. During World War I he served as a naval aviator and acquired a distrust of aircraft. "So many of my friends crashed and died in those tin-lizzie planes of the '20's," he said in an interview with Jinx Falkenburg (New York *Herald Tribune,* April 17, 1959), "that I began to feel the law of averages breathing down my neck. That's why I said, no more planes for me."

In 1924 Bristol became secretary and advertising manager at the Bristol-Myers Company, where his two brothers, Henry Platt Bristol (now deceased) and William McLaren Bristol, 3d, were already working. Until that time little advertising had been done, since the company was an ethical drug house whose founder disapproved of publicizing its wares. His eldest son, Henry, encouraged national advertising, however, and between 1924 and 1928 Bristol-Myers spent $4,000,000 on advertising. During his first year as advertising manager Lee H. Bristol doubled the advertising outlay, spending $300,000 on ads for Ipana toothpaste alone.

Joining the Association of National Advertisers (then the National Advertising Association) in 1925, Lee H. Bristol became one of the best known advertising men in the United States. He served as president of the Association of National Advertisers during 1931 and 1932. During the 1930's he promoted better advertising, helped to organize the Advertising Research Foundation, and wrote a book dealing with advertising and marketing, *Profits in Advance* (Harper, 1932). In 1941 he attended meetings at which advertising men discussed measures to counter attacks then being made on their publicity methods. Out of these sessions emerged the Advertising Council,

BRISTOL, LEE H.—Continued

which Bristol has called "the public conscience of advertising at work." In 1960 Bristol was elected chairman of the board of the Advertising Council. He also serves on the advisory board of the Association of National Advertisers.

Beginning in 1925, Bristol-Myers was one of the first companies to use radio as a medium to publicize its products. It sponsored shows by performers like Fred Allen, Henry Morgan, Eddie Cantor, Ed Gardner, and Tex McCrary and Jinx Falkenburg. Lee H. Bristol, who sometimes appeared on these shows himself, was often the butt of a joke made by the master of ceremonies (such as the remark that Bristol's balding pate was a poor advertisement for Vitalis, a hair preparation). "Many of my friends wondered why I submitted to such kidding," Bristol has said. "There was a good reason. . . . I wanted to prove that there is no stuffiness about Bristol-Myers."

The Bristol-Myers Company had been, until 1920, a small pharmaceutical house that sold ethical drugs through dispensing physicians and drugstores. Beginning in that year it gradually narrowed its line and concentrated on selling proprietary products like Sal Hepatica, an effervescent antacid laxative, and Ipana toothpaste. Within the next decade Bristol-Myers became one of the biggest manufacturers of proprietary items in the United States. Henry Bristol attributed much of its growth to advertising.

In 1928 Lee H. Bristol was named a vice-president and a director of Bristol-Myers and his brother Henry became a director and president. In the same year Bristol-Myers acquired the Frederick F. Ingram Company, and in 1929 the company purchased the hair tonic Vitalis from Lewis Brothers, Inc. Other properties added were the Mum Manufacturing Company (deodorant) in 1933; the Rubber and Celluloid Products Company (later the Rubberset Company) in 1934; the Minit-Rub Company (liniment) in 1934; Harris Laboratories, manufacturers of vitamins, in 1942; the Cheplin Biological Laboratories (now the Bristol Laboratories) in 1943; the Sun Tube Company, producers of collapsible tubes, in 1945; and the Charles Ammen Company (antiseptic powder) in 1947.

After serving for four years, from 1945 to 1949, as executive vice-president of Bristol-Myers, Lee H. Bristol became president of the company in January 1949, when his brother Henry was made chairman of the board. During the ten years he served as president the company continued to expand. In 1952 it acquired the Angier Chemical Company in England, and in 1955 it added Luzier's, Inc., which distributed a line of cosmetics. An important expansion move was the purchase in 1958 of Grove Laboratories, Inc., of St. Louis, Missouri, the manufacturers of Bromo Quinine, 4-Way Cold Tablets, and Fitch hair preparations. During this period new products like Bufferin and Ban, a deodorant, were developed by Bristol-Myers. The publicizing of Bristol-Myers products was continued on a large scale, and much of the advertising budget was spent in sponsoring television programs like *Candid Camera, Naked City, Dr. Ben Casey,* the

documentary *CBS Reports,* and newscasts. Lee H. Bristol succeeded his brother as chairman of the board of Bristol-Myers on January 1, 1958.

The present Bristol-Myers complex includes five major divisions: Bristol-Myers Products Division and Grove Laboratories, Inc., which manufacture and market proprietary products like Vitalis, Ipana, Bufferin, Ban, Bromo Quinine, Minit-Rub, and Fitch; Bristol Laboratories Division, which produces antibiotics and other prescription drugs; Clairol, Inc., makers of hair colorings; and Luzier, Inc., which sells its own line of cosmetics on a door-to-door basis. These divisions have foreign subsidiaries in Canada, England, France, Germany, Australia, New Zealand, South Africa, Thailand, and South America. In 1961 the Bristol-Myers Company and its North American subsidiaries had a sales income of $164,420,656 and net earnings of $12,957,049 as compared with a sales income of $56,610,504 and net earnings of $2,589,499 in 1952.

Lee H. Bristol is a former director of the National Association of Manufacturers and a member of the board of the National Industrial Conference Board. He received an honorary LL.D. degree from Hamilton College in 1952 and an honorary D.Sc. degree from the New England College of Pharmacy in 1960. One of six American business executives to receive the first annual Eastman Achievement Award from the Eastman School of Business, Bristol also received the first Paul West award (1961) of the Association of National Advertisers.

A member of the New Jersey Tercentenary Commission, Bristol is a past chairman of the New Jersey State Safety Council Triennial Fund and of the highways and parkways committee of the New Jersey State Chamber of Commerce. He is national chairman for 1962 of United Community Campaigns for America and a director of the Deafness Research Foundation. Bristol has been a director of the National Conference of Christians and Jews and of the National Urban League, and he is a former chairman of the United Negro College Fund. In May 1962 he donated $400,000 to Hamilton College in memory of his father. Bristol's clubs are the University in New York City, the Manasquan River Golf, the Bay Head (New Jersey) Yacht, the Army-Navy in Washington, D.C., and the Fort Schuyler in Utica, New York.

A tall, affable man, Bristol is a widower who was married to the former Elizabeth Wigton. He has two sons, Frederick Wigton and Lee Hastings, Jr., a Bristol-Myers executive who is also a lay reader of the Episcopalian church and co-editor of *Hymns for Children and Grownups To Use Together* (1953).

References

N Y Herald Tribune p13 Ap 17 '50 por; p23 My 30 '51 por
Ptr Ink 270:24 Mr 25 '60 por

Poor's Register of Directors and Executives, 1961
Who's Who in America, 1962-63
Who's Who in Commerce and Industry (1961)
Who's Who in the East (1961)

BUCHANAN, SCOTT (MILROSS) Mar. 17, 1895- Educator; foundation consultant; author; philosopher

Address: b. 2056 Eucalyptus Hill Rd., Santa Barbara, Calif.; h. 2125 Piedras Dr., Santa Barbara, Calif.

During his long career as an educator, philosopher, author, and foundation consultant Dr. Scott Buchanan has been concerned with the fundamental problems facing mankind in a rapidly changing industrial era. In his philosophical work he has dealt with questions of mathematics, medicine, theology, and law, and he has written several books and a number of articles on these subjects. He has taught at the College of the City of New York, the University of Virginia, and Fisk University, and he has dealt with problems of adult education as assistant director of the People's Institute in New York City.

During his nine years as dean of St. John's College at Annapolis, Maryland, Buchanan helped to inaugurate and implement its "great books" curriculum, which has exercised a considerable influence upon American education. Since 1957 he has served as a consultant to the Fund for the Republic, an educational fund established by the Ford Foundation in 1953 to study the traditional American freedoms with a view to preserving them in the face of growing domestic and international tensions.

Scott Milross Buchanan was born in Sprague, Washington, on March 17, 1895, the only child of William Duncan Buchanan, a country doctor, and Lillian Elizabeth (Bagg) Buchanan. He was brought up in Jeffersonville, Vermont and attended high schools in Worcester and Pittsfield, Massachusetts. Upon his graduation from secondary school in 1912, he entered Amherst College in Amherst, Massachusetts, where he majored in Greek and mathematics and won the Walker prize in Greek. His reading of Plato in Greek helped to influence him in his choice of a career in philosophy and teaching. His extracurricular activities at college included long-distance running. To help earn his way he waited on tables and taught Greek at the Amherst high school for three years. He graduated with the B.A. degree from Amherst in 1916, and from 1917 to 1918 he was an instructor in Greek at the college.

In June 1918 Buchanan entered the United States Navy with the rank of second class seaman. He was discharged as an ensign in December of that year. Having been chosen a Rhodes Scholar from Massachusetts in 1917, he went to England from 1919 to 1921, to undertake special work in philosophy at Balliol College, Oxford University. Returning to the United States, he entered Harvard University as a graduate student in philosophy, with an emphasis upon logic and scientific method. From 1922 to 1924 he taught as an assistant in the university's philosophy department, and from 1924 to 1925 he held the position of instructor in philosophy at the College of the City of New York.

In 1925 Buchanan was awarded the Ph.D. degree from Harvard after submitting a doctoral thesis on the philosophical question of possibility. His book, *Possibility*, was published in 1927 as part of the International Library of Psychology,

The McAllisters

SCOTT BUCHANAN

Philosophy and Scientific Method by Kegan Paul, Trench, Trubner and Company Ltd. in London, and Harcourt, Brace and Company, Inc., in New York. The book dealt with the fundamental philosophic problem of the relationship between actuality and possibility. John Dewey, in a review for the *Nation* (April 18, 1928), wrote that the book was "a first-class piece of much needed intellectual work," and that it "offers seeds with which to sow many a flourishing intellectual garden."

From 1925 to 1929 Buchanan served as assistant director of the People's Institute in New York City. There he co-operated with the director Everett Dean Martin in dealing with the problems and satisfactions of adult education. During this period he was concerned in his philosophic work with breaking down the rigid man-made barriers separating such fields of human endeavor as mathematics and literature. In *Poetry and Mathematics* (Day, 1929), he includes an example of his thinking along these lines by showing the relationship of an episode in Lewis Carroll's *Alice in Wonderland* to the Pythagorean theorem as demonstrated by Euclid.

In 1929 Buchanan joined the faculty of the University of Virginia as assistant professor of philosophy. He became a full professor in 1930 and remained at the university until 1936. His book *Symbolic Distance in Relation to Analogy and Fiction* (Routledge, 1932), is a study in analysis, the genesis, and the reduction of fictions. In 1935 he wrote a pamphlet on adult education, which was printed by the extension division of the University of Virginia.

In 1936 Dr. Robert Maynard Hutchins, then president of the University of Chicago, invited Buchanan and Dr. Stringfellow Barr to help institute certain curriculum changes at Chicago. (Buchanan and Barr had been friends as Rhodes Scholars at Oxford University and as teachers at the University of Virginia.) As chairman of the

BUCHANAN, SCOTT—Continued

liberal arts committee of the University of Chicago in 1936-37 Buchanan helped to introduce Hutchins' plan for a "great books" course. He also helped Hutchins to establish a four-year liberal arts college program beginning with the usual junior year of high school, which went into effect in 1937. Buchanan's interest during these years in medicine and philosophy led to his writing *The Doctrine of Signatures: A Defence of Theory in Medicine* (Routledge, 1938). In this book he calls on the liberal arts and sciences to develop, clarify, and realize the potentialities of human observation. A reviewer for the London *Times Literary Supplement* (May 7, 1938) called the book "an important plea for the restoration of humanism in medical education and practice."

When Barr became president of St. John's College in Annapolis, Maryland in 1937, Buchanan was appointed dean and Hutchins was elected a trustee of the college. There, in one of the oldest American colleges, which by the mid-1930's was on the verge of closing its doors, they introduced a four-year program of reading and discussing only the great books of the past—about 120 classics. They revised the list that had been compiled by the late American educator, John Erskine, and they added books in the sciences to those of philosophy, history, politics, economics, and *belles lettres*. Remaining in his position as dean of St. John's until 1947, Buchanan was largely instrumental in inaugurating and refining this experiment in liberal education, which made St. John's College one of the institutions that became synonymous with the "great books" idea.

From 1947 to 1949 Buchanan was the director of Liberal Arts, Inc., in Pittsfield, Massachusetts. During 1948-58 he served as a consultant, trustee, and secretary of the Foundation for World Government, established in 1948 by Mrs. Anita McCormick Blaine for the pursuit of an educational campaign in the principles of world federal government. In 1953 the Philosophical Library published Buchanan's *Essay in Politics*, in which he maintained that under current conditions the consent of the governed to the traditional republican form of government is frustrated and changed by the appearance of many unrecognized governmental institutions, such as the corporation.

Buchanan served as professor of philosophy and chairman of the department of religion and philosophy at Fisk University in Nashville, Tennessee during 1956-57. In June 1957 Robert M. Hutchins, then president of the Fund for the Republic, announced the selection of ten distinguished Americans to serve as consultants to the Fund's project for determining the conditions under which a free society may best be maintained in the United States in the face of persistent international tension. Named one of the consultants, Buchanan moved to the Fund's headquarters in Santa Barbara, California.

The Fund for the Republic, established in 1952 by the Ford Foundation, promotes research and activities directed toward the elimination of restrictions on freedom of thought, inquiry, and expression in the United States, and toward the development of policies and procedures designed to protect those rights. It is concerned with the problems that emerge when the governmental principles of eighteenth-century America meet the ideas and practices of the present-day highly developed industrial society. In 1958 the Fund published Buchanan's pamphlet "The Corporation and the Republic," a study of the role of business, charitable, and public corporations and public utilities in a democratic society.

Buchanan has spoken on radio programs and was a visiting lecturer at the Christian Gauss Seminar at Princeton University in 1956. He wrote the introduction to, and edited, *The Portable Plato: Protagoras, Symposium, Phaedo, and the Republic* (Viking, 1948), about which a critic for the New York *Herald Tribune Weekly Book Review* (December 5, 1948) wrote: "Scott Buchanan has produced, in *The Portable Plato*, as sound an introduction to that master as I have ever seen." Buchanan's articles have appeared in the *Saturday Review, Nation, American Scholar, Survey Graphic, Virginia Quarterly Review, Forum, Psyche,* and other journals.

On February 5, 1921, Scott Buchanan married Miriam Damon Thomas, a teacher and social welfare worker. They have one son, Douglas. Buchanan is five feet nine inches tall, weighs 175 pounds, and has blue eyes and gray hair. He is a Democrat and his religious affiliation is with the Congregational Church. He is a member of the American Philosophical Society, the American Mathematical Association, and Delta Upsilon fraternity. Carpentry is his favorite recreational activity.

References

Harper 179:64+ Je '39
Directory of American Scholars (1957)
Leaders in Education (1957)
Register of Rhodes Scholars, 1903-45 (1950)
Who's Who in America, 1962-63
World Biography (1948)

CARPENTER, MALCOLM SCOTT May 1, 1925- Astronaut

Address: b. National Aeronautics and Space Administration, Washington 25, D.C.; h. Langley Air Force Base, Virginia

The space program of the United States took a suspenseful turn on May 24, 1962, when the astronaut Malcolm Scott Carpenter appeared to be lost for a period of about forty-five minutes after he had completed a three-orbit flight in his space capsule *Aurora 7*. The fact that Carpenter had overshot the landing point by some 250 miles demonstrated that, despite the success of Project Mercury, the factor of human fallibility must still be reckoned with.

A lieutenant commander in the United States Navy, Carpenter is a former naval test pilot. When, in 1959, he was chosen by the National Aeronautics and Space Administration to be a candidate for participation in Project Mercury, he was an air intelligence officer on the USS *Hornet.* His space flight, which largely duplicated the feat performed by the astronaut John

H. Glenn on February 20, 1962, demonstrated that the United States could hold its own in competition with the space efforts of the Soviet Union, whose astronauts Yuri Gagarin and Gherman Titov had made the first orbital flights in 1961. Carpenter's flight is regarded as a major step toward the goal of landing a man on the moon.

Malcolm Scott Carpenter was born in Boulder, Colorado on May 1, 1925, the only child of Dr. Marion Scott Carpenter, a chemist, and Florence (Noxon) Carpenter. "Bud" Carpenter's parents were divorced when he was a small boy, and he seldom saw his father. When his mother entered a sanatorium with tuberculosis he turned to his maternal grandfather, Victor Noxon, the editor of the Boulder County *Miner and Farmer*, with whom he formed a close relationship. Victor Noxon taught him many useful things, including woodcraft, and gave him his first job, delivering newspapers once a week at a salary of 35 cents. He died when Scott Carpenter was fourteen years old.

Carpenter has denied the contentions of local newspapers that he was "just a normal boy." He told Loudon Wainwright in an interview for *Life* (May 18, 1962): "I had a wonderful time, but I was a real rounder. I didn't study hard and I had to quit high school football because I couldn't devote myself to learning the plays. I stole things from stores and I was just drifting through, sort of a no-good." He roamed over the hills on his horse, Lady, and raced over them later in his "souped-up" 1934 Ford coupé. A good skier and dancer, Carpenter was the envy of his classmates because he was free from parental authority. For a time he wanted to become a horse rancher.

After graduating from high school in 1943 Carpenter entered the Navy's V-5 flight training program at Colorado College. (He had decided to become a naval pilot after seeing the movie *Wake Island.*) He received further training at St. Mary's Preflight School in Moraga, California, and at Ottumwa, Iowa, but the war ended before he was able to receive his wings. After the war he entered the University of Colorado to study aeronautical engineering, but failed on two occasions. While waiting to be reinstated he worked as a day laborer. He has recalled that although he generally excelled in physical activities he met with little success in his intellectual efforts. In 1946 he nearly lost his life in an automobile accident. He had apparently fallen asleep while driving home from a party along a mountain road, and his car plunged about 100 feet into a ditch. Upon his recovery from this experience he decided to apply himself more intensively to his college studies, while working in his spare time as a hod carrier.

In 1949 Carpenter saw an opportunity to return to the Navy as a pilot under a program that required a college degree. For his engineering degree he was lacking one course—heat transfer—that he had failed previously. He proceeded to take the course again, but dropped out in the middle of it when he failed to understand it. In the meantime the Navy, unaware that he had not received his degree, processed his application and accepted him.

Wide World

MALCOLM SCOTT CARPENTER

From November 1949 to April 1951 Carpenter took flight training at Pensacola, Florida and Corpus Christi, Texas. He then entered the Fleet Airborne Electronics Training School in San Diego California, and received additional instruction in a Lockheed P2V transitional training unit on Whidbey Island, Washington. In November 1951 he was assigned for Korean war duty to Patrol Squadron 6, based at Barbers Point, Hawaii. As a member of this squadron he flew antisubmarine patrols, conducted aerial mine-laying activities, and engaged in shipping surveillance missions in the Formosa Straits, the Yellow Sea, and the South China Sea.

Carpenter entered the Navy Test Pilot School at Patuxent River, Maryland in 1954, and upon completion of his training he was assigned to the electronics test division of the Naval Air Test Center there. His assignment as a test pilot gave him the sense of freedom and adventure that he had longed for, and he developed great skill in testing the latest naval jets. He undertook flight-test projects with the A3D, F11F, and F9F, and took part in other flight-test programs. He received additional training at the Navy's General Line School at Monterey, California and at the Naval Air Intelligence School in Washington, D.C. Carpenter has accumulated a total of approximately 2,900 hours of flying time, 400 of them in jet aircraft.

In accordance with a policy requiring all Navy men to spend some time at sea, Carpenter was assigned, in August 1958, to the non-flying position of air intelligence officer on board the antisubmarine aircraft carrier USS *Hornet.* Because sea duty kept him away from his family for long periods and because he failed to receive an expected promotion to lieutenant colonel, Carpenter became somewhat discouraged, and for a time he seriously considered returning to civilian life. However, his experience as a test pilot, his engineering training, and his Navy record quali-

CARPENTER, MALCOLM SCOTT—*Cont.*

fied him to become one of the 110 servicemen chosen as possible candidates for the National Aeronautics and Space Administration's Project Mercury for the development of manned space flights. The invitation came while Carpenter was away at sea, and his wife, knowing that he was anxious to take part in the program, volunteered his name for him.

On April 9, 1959 the National Aeronautics and Space Administration announced that of the 110 original candidates seven—including Carpenter—had been chosen to participate in Project Mercury. The other astronauts are Leroy G. Cooper, Jr., John H. Glenn, Jr., Virgil I. Grissom, Walter M. Schirra, Jr., Alan B. Shepard, Jr., and Donald K. Slayton. "I volunteered for this project for a lot of reasons," Carpenter said after he was chosen. "One of them, quite frankly, is that it is a chance for immortality. Most men never have a chance for immortality." He added: "This is something I would willingly give my life for, and I think a person is very fortunate to have something he can care that much about."

Under an exhaustive training program, begun in May 1959, the seven astronaut trainees acquired a mass of scientific knowledge on virtually every subject related to astronautics. They were given many physical and psychological tests, and their bodies underwent the stresses and strains to which they would be subjected in actual space flight. Carpenter, whose physical prowess was largely responsible for his being chosen as one of the seven astronauts, scored highly in the tests. He excelled in the airplane maneuvers that duplicated the condition of weightlessness involved in orbital flight. In the division of labor among the astronauts, Carpenter specialized in electronics and navigation. Dr. Robert Voas, the psychologist of Project Mercury, has said that Carpenter "developed a habit of intense concentration toward his duties," and that he had "changed quite a bit since his younger days."

America's first suborbital flight was made by astronaut Alan B. Shepard, Jr., on May 5, 1961, and duplicated, with minor variations, by Virgil I. Grissom on July 21, 1961. The Soviet astronauts Yuri Gagarin and Gherman Titov made the first manned orbital flights, on April 12, 1961 and August 6-7, 1961, respectively. On November 29, 1961 Lieutenant Colonel John H. Glenn was chosen to make the first United States manned orbital space flight, and Carpenter subsequently became his backup pilot. He worked closely with Glenn in preparation for the flight, which was successfully concluded on February 20, 1962, when Glenn orbited the earth three times in his capsule *Friendship 7.*

Originally Major Donald K. Slayton of the Air Force had been chosen to make the second manned orbital flight, but when it was discovered that Slayton had a minor heart ailment, Carpenter received the assignment. Unapprehensive about his forthcoming flight, Carpenter said in an interview for the New York *Herald Tribune* (April 22, 1962): "We know more about the systems involved than the people who sit back and watch television. And I think the more you know about anything, the less there is to fear."

Explaining the name of his space capsule—*Aurora 7*—Carpenter said: "I think of Project Mercury and the open manner in which we are conducting it for the benefit of all mankind as a light in the sky. Aurora also means dawn—in this case, dawn of a new age." Carpenter's flight, originally scheduled for May 19, 1962, was delayed for a few days to permit the rewiring of the capsule's parachute deployment system and to correct other minor technical difficulties.

On May 24, 1962 at 4:42 A.M. (Eastern Standard Time) Carpenter climbed into his space capsule at the launching pad at Cape Canaveral, Florida. At 7:45 A.M. the ninety-five-foot Atlas 107-D rocket boosted the capsule off the launching pad with a thrust of 362,000 pounds. Carpenter's three-orbit flight, which followed almost the same path as that of Glenn, lasted four hours and fifty-six minutes, covering a distance of about 81,200 miles at altitudes ranging between 99.2 and 167.4 miles and at a maximum speed of 17,532 per hour. During his flight Carpenter experienced weightlessness for four hours and twenty-nine minutes. Although he met with some difficulties during his first two orbits—notably the excessive heating of his space suit and the too-rapid depletion of the attitude-control fuel—the decision was made to go into a third orbit.

Re-entering the atmosphere at 12:32 P.M., *Aurora 7* overshot the impact area, apparently because its nose was pointed too high when the retro-rockets fired to bring it out of orbit. At 12:41 P.M. the capsule hit the Atlantic Ocean 138 miles northeast of Puerto Rico—some 250 miles beyond the point where it was to have landed. Since Carpenter was well beyond the range of radio communication with Cape Canaveral, his fate and location were unknown for about three-quarters of an hour, while millions of observers all over the world waited anxiously. At 1:22 P.M. the crewmen of a Navy plane spotted Carpenter in a life raft beside the capsule. He was hoisted aboard a helicopter from the aircraft carrier SS *Intrepid* at 3:38 P.M., in good physical condition. In a telephone conversation, President John F. Kennedy told Carpenter: "We are relieved and very proud of your trip," and Carpenter apologized for "not having aimed a little bit better on re-entry."

Returning to Cape Canaveral on May 27, 1962, Carpenter said that the space trip was the "supreme experience" of his life and that he was ready for two weeks in orbit. He expressed confidence that the space project would profit from the mistakes that he had made on his flight. During it Carpenter conducted a number of experiments and discovered facts that had not been known previously. By means of photography and through personal observation he was able to gather much more detailed information on the appearance of the earth and its atmosphere and of various celestial phenomena than had been obtained on the earlier space flights.

Through his efforts to control his capsule manually Carpenter learned much about the navigation of spacecraft, although his fuel supply was almost exhausted as a result of his maneuverings. He also studied the movements of liquids freed from gravity, and he learned by trailing a balloon that space offers practically no resistance. He became the first spaceman to drink large quantities of water for the purpose of restoring water balance after perspiration, and he proved that solid, high-protein foods could be digested during weightlessness. He observed that the luminous objects in space, which Glenn had described as "fireflies," were apparently particles from the skin of the capsule.

Observers all over the world hailed Carpenter's successful flight. Soviet Premier Nikita S. Khrushchev lauded Carpenter's "great courage" and conceded that the Soviet Union was "not alone in space." The Distinguished Service Award of the National Aeronautics and Space Administration was conferred upon Carpenter on May 27, 1962. His home town, Boulder, Colorado, celebrated his feat with the small-town version of a ticker-tape parade, and the University of Colorado awarded him the B.S. degree in aeronautical engineering that he failed to receive in 1949. On June 5, 1962 Carpenter visited New York City, where he received the city's Gold Medal of Honor and the Mayor's Scroll for Distinguished and Exceptional Service.

On September 9, 1948 Malcolm Scott Carpenter married Rene Louise Price, a former movie usherette. They have four children, Mark Scott, Robyn Jay, Kristine Elaine, and Candace Noxon. Another son, Tim, died in 1951. Carpenter is five feet ten and a half inches tall, weighs 155 pounds, and has green eyes and brown hair. The astronauts' personal physician, Dr. William S. Douglas, has said: "Carpenter's extreme simplicity sometimes gives the impression that he is bordering on immaturity. In fact, I would call him the least mature of the astronauts. I don't mean that he is callow or adolescent. . . . But his motivations are essentially simple and uncomplicated. He is interested chiefly in three things: his job, his family, and in keeping his body in top physical condition" (*Time,* June 1, 1962). Carpenter's hobbies include archery, skiing, skin diving, and strumming folk songs on the guitar. An Episcopalian, Carpenter says: "I have what I consider an abiding faith which sustains me at all times."

References

Life 52:33+ My 18 '62 pors
N Y Herald Tribune p11 My 25 '62
N Y Post p49 My 24 '62 pors
N Y Times p14 My 25 '62 por
Time 79:14+ Je 1 '62 pors

CARROLL, DIAHANN (dī-ăn') July 1935-
Singer; actress
Address: b. c/o General Artists Corp., 640 5th Ave., New York 19

When Richard Rodgers' musical comedy *No Strings* opened on Broadway in March 1962 its star, Diahann Carroll, was, in her own words, "at the bottom of the top." She had already won recognition as a nightclub and television entertainer, had appeared in four films, had played a featured role in the Broadway musical *House of Flowers,* and had been named entertainer of the year in 1961 by *Cue* magazine. Her performance in *No Strings* in the role of a fashion model who loves a writer in Paris was

DIAHANN CARROLL

unanimously praised by drama critics as a major asset of the show and placed her many rungs higher on the ladder of success.

Diahann Carroll was born Carol Diahann Johnson in the Bronx, New York City in July 1935, the elder daughter of John Johnson, a New York City subway conductor, and Mable Johnson, a nurse. She has a younger sister, Lydia. Diahann began performing at an early age, acting in school plays from the time she was six years old. At about the same time, she joined the Abyssinian Baptist Church choir, as a member of the Tiny Tots group.

When Diahann was ten years old she won a Metropolitan Opera scholarship, but the free lessons to which she was entitled lasted only a month. "I told my mother I wanted to be the roller-skating champion of the world," she says, "and those damned singing lessons interfered with my practice." After attending New York's Public School 46 and a junior high school that she has described as "my own blackboard jungle," Diahann Carroll entered the High School of Music and Art, "a wonderful, beautiful oasis" in her life. Beginning at the age of fifteen, she modeled suits and lingerie for advertisements that appeared in Negro publications.

Her parents wanted her to attend college, and mostly to please them she enrolled in New York University as a sociology major. But she had already been bitten by the show business bug, and during her freshman year she auditioned for a part in an all-Negro revue, *Jazz Train.* The revue never materialized, but the audition led to her appearance on *Chance of a Lifetime,* a television talent show, on which she won top honors and $1,000 for three consecutive weeks. Finally convinced that their daughter deserved to try a stage career, her parents gave her permission to leave school for the world of entertainment, but they imposed the condition that if she made no progress within two years she

CARROLL, DIAHANN—*Continued*

would return to college. Because she was successful during that period she never had to redeem her promise.

Following her appearance on *Chance of a Lifetime,* Lou Walters booked Diahann Carroll into New York's Latin Quarter for a week. Perhaps because of stage fright, which usually attacks her on opening nights, she reportedly sang all her numbers on the first night in a different key from the orchestra. Her affliction often takes the form of hives or partial loss of hearing. Despite her stage fright at the Latin Quarter, she was so popular there that her engagement was extended to four weeks. She has also entertained at the Persian Room of the Hotel Plaza and at the Waldorf-Astoria Hotel in New York City, at Ciro's, the Mocambo, and the Cloister in Hollywood, at the Fontainebleau and the Eden Roc in Miami, at the Olympia Theatre in Paris, at the Black Orchid in Chicago, and at the Latin Casino in Philadelphia.

In December 1954, when she was nineteen years old, Miss Carroll appeared in her first Broadway show, Harold Arlen's musical adaptation of Truman Capote's *House of Flowers.* Although the show was short-lived, she scored a personal triumph as Ottilie (alias Violet), an innocent young protégée of a bordello proprietess. Writing in the New York *World Telegram* (December 31, 1954), William Hawkins called her "a great find" with "a rich, lovely, easy voice, and rare freshness of personality." Walter Kerr (New York *Herald Tribune,* December 31, 1954) found her "a plaintive and extraordinarily appealing ingenue" and said that she delivered some of the best songs in the show ("A Sleepin' Bee" and "House of Flowers") with "serious eyes and the enthusiasm of a newly-hatched bird." Perhaps more important to her career than the praise of the critics was the favorable impression she made on the composer Richard Rodgers who, after seeing her for the first time in *House of Flowers,* decided that he would someday write a show for her.

Earlier in 1954 Miss Carroll had played her first movie role as Myrt in the Twentieth Century-Fox release of *Carmen Jones.* She made her professional television debut as a guest on the *Red Skelton Show* (WCBS-TV), and she has appeared on the *Steve Allen Show,* the *Garry Moore Show* (WCBS-TV), the *General Electric Theater* (WCBS-TV), *Peter Gunn* (WNEW-TV), a Westinghouse special, a Rex Harrison special, *One Night Stand* (WNTA-TV), and the *Jack Paar Show* (WNBC-TV) (over fifty times).

In 1958 Richard Rodgers tried to make good his promise to use her in a show by casting her as an Oriental in *Flower Drum Song.* "I was the tallest, brownest Oriental you've ever seen," Miss Carroll has explained. After many makeup tests it was necessary to give up the attempt. In 1959 she acted the role of Clara in Samuel Goldwyn's movie adaptation of *Porgy and Bess,* but her voice was considered too low to sing Clara's big number, *Summertime,* and she merely mouthed the lyrics. (The dubbed-in singing was done by Loulie Jean Norman.) Miss Carroll, however, made a United Artists record with the André Previn Trio on which she sings numbers from

Porgy and Bess. Other recordings she has made include *The Persian Presents Diahann Carroll* (United Artists), *Diahann Carroll Sings Harold Arlen* (RCA Victor), *Best Beat Forward* (RCA Victor), and *Showstopper!* (Camden).

In 1960 Miss Carroll played her first straight movie role in *Paris Blues* (released by United Artists in 1961), in which she acted an American tourist in love with a jazz musician, played by Sidney Poitier. While on location in Paris, she was tapped for a small part in *Goodbye Again* (United Artists, 1961), the screen adaptation of Françoise Sagan's *Aimez-Vous Brahms?*

When Richard Rodgers saw Miss Carroll performing on the *Jack Paar Show* one evening in 1961, he was reminded of his long-standing desire to create a vehicle for her. Over cocktails the next day he asked her what kind of show she would like to play in. "I wanted to do a play that dealt with . . . a Negro person in the everyday situations of ups and downs . . . without making the play special because of a Negro player," she recalls. "I was also interested in a light sophisticated comedy like *The Moon is Blue.* . . . I wanted to do a girl who fell in love, who had her heart broken, who came back together with the man she loved. It didn't matter whether it was a happy or unhappy ending. What I wanted most was the message to be given in an intelligent manner, rather than with a hammer. . . . I felt it was time for people to enter the theater, watch a Negro performer . . . as an actor and leave saying, 'I'll be doggoned. You know that girl stood there and was just like anyone else.' "

The musical *No Strings,* with music and lyrics by Rodgers and a book by Samuel Taylor, opened at the 54th Street Theatre in New York City on March 15, 1962. The book, dealing with a love affair in Paris between an American Negro high-fashion model and a weak-kneed white Pulitzer Prize novelist, makes no mention of the racial problem except for one fleeting reference. Staged with originality, the musical features instrumentalists who stroll about among the actors and lightweight settings that are moved by members of the cast. Although critics agreed that the book is inadequate, they praised the inventive staging, Rodgers' lyrics and tunes, and, above all, Diahann Carroll. "Miss Carroll is a stunning looking girl who sings enchantingly, has a charming stage manner and is generally a credible actress," a *Variety* reviewer (March 21, 1962) observed. Howard Taubman of the New York *Times* (March 16, 1962) wrote, "Miss Carroll brings glowing personal beauty to the role of the model, and her singing captures many moods." An original cast album of *No Strings* was released by Capitol Records in the spring of 1962.

Journalists have noted certain similarities between Miss Carroll and the fictional Barbara Woodruff, the character she portrays in *No Strings.* They cite both girls' love of clothes and determination to succeed, point to similar backgrounds (Barbara's father was pictured as a New York City bus conductor), and draw parallels between Barbara's white lover and Miss Carroll's husband, who is a Caucasian.

Much of Miss Carroll's success in *No Strings* can be attributed to her special interest in lyrics and her unusual flair for dealing with them. (This is so much a trademark of her singing career that she has been compared to Frank Sinatra.) "To do justice to a song," she says, "a singer should have a feeling for dramatic interpretation as well as an ear for musical sounds. You must be able to create a mood, to make the audience feel that the words have meaning to the singer, that you are not just repeating them, but that they come from your very being." Some of her skill in acting and communicating lyrics was undoubtedly gained during the three years she studied drama with Lee Strasberg.

Diahann Carroll has been characterized by Walter Kerr as "a girl with a sweet smile, brilliant dark eyes, and a profile regal enough to belong on a coin." She is just under five feet six inches tall and weighs about 120 pounds. In 1956 she married the concert impresario Monte Kay, who had been the casting director for *House of Flowers*, and who is now the manager of the Modern Jazz Quartet and other jazz musicians. Their daughter is Suzanne Patricia Ottilie. The Kays live in a spacious apartment on Manhattan's West End Avenue that is decorated with the antiques that Miss Carroll collects. Recently, when asked about her plans for the future, she replied, "I want to get better. I want to work." Summarizing her past, she told a *Look* interviewer (May 22, 1962), "It's all been great, but if it ends tomorrow, I'll still have had a marvelous time."

References

Look 26:110+ My 22 '62 pors
N Y Post p50 D 4 '61 por
N Y Times IIpl Ap 15 '62
N Y World-Telegram p5 Mr 19 '62
Newsweek 59:85 Mr 26 '62 por
Show Bsns Illus 2:44+ Ap '62 pors

CASE, FRANCIS (HIGBEE) Dec. 9, 1896-June 22, 1962 Republican United States Representative (1937-50) and United States Senator (1951-62) from South Dakota. See *Current Biography* (May) 1946.

Obituary

N Y Times p23 Je 23 '62

CASTILLO (DEL REY), ANTONIO (CÁNOVAS DEL) Dec. 13, 1908- Fashion designer

Address: c/o La Maison Jeanne Lanvin, 22 rue du Faubourg-St. Honoré, Paris 8ᵉ, France; h. 25 bis rue de Constantine, Paris 7ᵉ, France.

The beautiful ball gowns, elegant coats, and dramatic capes that are presented under the name Lanvin-Castillo by the Spanish-born, Paris-trained designer Antonio Castillo are worn by his internationally prominent customers through many seasons, for they never go out of style. An artistic designer with the top French fashion house La Maison Jeanne Lanvin since 1950, Castillo in his creations represents the best of *haute couture*. Also acclaimed for his theater and ballet designs, Castillo has costumed several

ANTONIO CASTILLO

shows on Broadway, including the design of Lynn Fontanne's gowns in Friedrich Duerrenmatt's *The Visit* (1958). He is also known in the United States for collections that he designed for Elizabeth Arden's salon in New York City between 1945 and 1950.

Antonio Cánovas del Castillo del Rey was born in Madrid, Spain on December 13, 1908, the son of Jesús Cánovas del Castillo, a lawyer, and Elvira (del Rey) del Castillo. His great-uncle, Antonio Cánovas del Castillo, was Prime Minister of Spain between 1875 and 1897 under King Alfonso XII. The boy studied at the Colegio del Pilar in Madrid, at the University of Madrid, and at El Sacro Monte in Granada, Spain. He at first studied architecture, but later decided on a diplomatic career.

In 1936, at the beginning of the Spanish civil war, Castillo went to Paris, where he met Mme. Missia Sert, the wife of José María Sert, a Spanish painter living in Paris. It was she who persuaded him to change his career plans and introduced him to the inner circle of Paris *haute couture*. He began to design dresses, hats, and jewelry for French couturiers like Paquin's (now defunct) and Piguet and for French motion pictures.

In 1944 Elizabeth Arden, the noted manufacturer of cosmetics, opened a fashion department at her salon on Fifth Avenue in New York City. She talked Castillo into coming to the United States to design for her, and between 1945 and 1950 he created about nine collections of custom and ready-made clothes for her salon. Prominent women flocked to buy his designs. Shortly after he arrived he presented a collection that featured a slim silhouette and small hats. According to a New York *Times* fashion writer (October 18, 1945), he was the first designer to abandon the fullness that had been in vogue during World War II and to design natural shoulder lines.

His second New York collection, presented in September 1946, was described by the fashion

CASTILLO, ANTONIO—*Continued*

reporter Virginia Pope in the New York *Times* (September 19, 1946) as having great strength and originality. She particularly praised his inventiveness with coats and his consistent good taste. "He dares to venture into new forms," she wrote, "and . . . yet he never loses sight of the fashion importance of the feminine figure."

Miss Pope also praised his third Arden collection, presented in February 1947, commenting that Castillo "has ideas that he knows how to translate into good clothes." She was favorably impressed with his modernized versions of Victorian capes and wraps and his ball gowns of chiffon over pyramided hoop skirts in a Goyesque manner. "While he maintains a fluidity of line," she said, "he confines it to a slender silhouette, save in formal evening gowns." Castillo also featured petal necklines and loose capelets and wraplets, with a discreet use of furs.

Commissions for theatrical and ballet designs also came his way, and the credit line "Costumes by Castillo" appeared in playbills during his five-year sojourn in America. In March 1947 his costumes were seen at the New York City Center in the Ballet Russe de Monte Carlo's première of the Spanish ballet *Madroños*. The New York *Times* dance reviewer found his designs "brilliant" and "piquantly satirical." During the 1947-48 season he designed costumes for Robinson Jeffers' *Medea*, which opened on Broadway on October 20, 1947, and for P. G. Wodehouse's adaptation of a Ferenc Molnar play, *The Play's the Thing*, which started its Broadway run on April 28, 1948.

The following season Castillo created evening gowns for Edna Ferber's and George S. Kaufman's play, *Bravo!*, which opened on November 11, 1948. With Valentina he did the gowns for a Theatre Guild production of *My Name is Aquilon*, a play by Jean-Pierre Aumont, which began its Broadway run on February 9, 1949. He again costumed a production of Jeffers' *Medea*, which opened on May 2, 1949. During the 1950-51 season he created costumes for Christopher Fry's adaptation of an Anouilh play, *Ring Around the Moon*, produced during November and December of 1950, and for an ANTA production of Robinson Jeffers' play *The Tower Beyond Tragedy*, which opened on November 26, 1950. Castillo outfitted Lynn Fontanne for her performance in Friedrich Duerrenmatt's *The Visit*, presented on Broadway starting in May 1958. He has also executed designs for Metropolitan Opera ballets.

In 1950 Castillo returned to Paris and joined the staff of the fashion firm La Maison Jeanne Lanvin, which he soon restored to its former prestige. The esteem in which it was held was reflected in a flood of new clients. The House of Lanvin was established as a modest enterprise in 1890 by Mme. Jeanne Lanvin. A former milliner, she produced original dress designs that eventually earned her the patronage of some of the most fashionable and select clients in France and abroad. She also founded a perfume industry and a men's clothing house. When she died in 1946, her daughter, Countess Jean de Polignac, took over the business. It was she who in 1950 persuaded Castillo to return to France to design

for Lanvin. Upon her death in 1958 Mme. Lanvin's nephew, Yves Lanvin, and his wife, Pierrette, became heads of the Lanvin enterprises.

For the past twelve years members of the world of fashion have looked forward to attending Castillo's fashion shows, which twice a year are presented in the grand manner. In 1951 his daytime clothes showed restraint and freedom from trimming, and his evening gowns made use of magnificent embroidery and rich fabrics. That year, in memory of Mme. Lanvin, he presented a group of white satin gowns, trimmed with white mink. Over the years he has carried on the Lanvin tradition of creating *robes de style* (close-fitting bodices with soft flowing skirts), for which Mme. Lanvin had become well-known. One of his 1952 collections featured the "trumpet ensemble"—unfitted coats that flared gracefully from shoulder to hem—and cowl-draped necklines on cocktail dresses.

Always intrigued by scarves, Castillo has become noted for creating them in brilliant colors and with delicate thread embroidery. In 1954 he evinced a light touch in presenting middies, pullovers, and necklines with scarf and loop arrangements. He also devised a print—a design of ermine tails on white satin—that evoked enthusiastic reviews. Castillo usually favors soft fabrics for dresses and coats, and hip drapery, soft bodices, and fluid side panels are also characteristic of his designs.

In 1956 Castillo introduced big hoods that fall softly away at the neck and capes that were fringed or triple-tiered. The following year he presented straight, short skirts, with aprons over contrasting sheaths, Castillane sleeves for "a new fluid look," "Madame Butterfly" boleros, and "Japanese Lantern" jackets. An outstanding feature of his summer 1959 collection was artistic fur collars on coats, including cape collars, shawl collars, and draped leis. A New York *Herald Tribune* reporter (July 31, 1959) complained, however, that his mid-calf-length skirts looked "somber and resigned" compared to short lengths of other designers.

Capes dominated Castillo's February 1960 show, styled in hip lengths for day and floor lengths for evening. In July 1960 he introduced the "tear-drop shape" for dresses, skirts, and coats, involving fullness of skirts ending in a pulled-in hemline. He also brought back the definite waistline and the fitted bodice. "What a show!" rhapsodized Phyllis Heathcote of the *Guardian* (July 29, 1960). "Line, colour, fabrics, mood, it was all there—just as you dream that a Paris fashion collection should be."

His entire February 1961 collection was based on a kimono cut, showing short, wide-open kimono sleeves and slits up the side of coats to make them swing. In 1962 he concentrated on back-flaring coats and suits; orange and apricot shades predominated. "When Castillo is good he is very good," remarked a New York *Herald Tribune* fashion reporter on January 27, 1962. "This year his new clothes have the right balance of elegance for customers and salability when reproduced." Described by a New York *Times* writer (August 26, 1958) as "a small, rather round man with an air of polished chic about him," Castillo has made a hobby of collecting cigarette boxes, old silver, and *objets d'art*.

References

N Y Times p19 O 18 '45; p32 Ag 26 '58
por
Who's Who in France, 1960-61

DEL CASTILLO (DEL REY), ANTONIO (CÁNOVAS) *See* Castillo (del Rey), Antonio (Cánovas del)

DICKERSON, NANCY HANSCHMAN *See* Hanschman, Nancy (Conners)

DICKSON, (HORATIO HENRY) LOVAT
June 30, 1902- British publisher and author
Address: b. Macmillan & Company Ltd., St. Martin's St., London W.C. 2, England; h. 23 Montagu Square, London W. 1, England

The senior director of the London publishing firm Macmillan & Co. Ltd., Lovat Dickson is also an author, whose book *The Ante-Room* (1960), an account of the first twenty-seven years of his life, has been described by C. P. Snow as "an outstanding autobiography, painfully honest and naked to life." After spending his childhood and early youth in Australia, Africa, and England, Dickson moved with his family to Canada, where he worked at a variety of jobs, from mining to teaching. He entered the London publishing world in 1929 and began his association with Macmillan in 1938, becoming a director of the firm in 1941. He has said that he "gravitated naturally" into the field of publishing and writing, and that he had "never thought of doing anything else."

Horatio Henry Lovat Dickson was born in Victoria, Australia on June 30, 1902 to Gordon Fraser Dickson, a consulting mining engineer, and Josephine Mary (Cunningham) Dickson. He has two older sisters, Mitta and Irene. His younger brother, Gordon Clive, is deceased. (By his father's second marriage Dickson has two half-brothers, one of whom is Gordon Dickson, the author.)

The family was deeply religious. The mother came from a Roman Catholic background. The paternal ancestors were Scotch-Irish Presbyterians who had emigrated from England to settle in New England and Nova Scotia. The father dominated the family and a Puritan strain prevailed, although the children were sent to convent boarding schools. Lovat Dickson early acquired a love of Dickens and Thackeray from his father, who did not believe in reading to his children "that trash written for simple hungry minds." Recitations in the home gave him, even at the age of five, an ear for the music and rhythm of great English poetry.

The father's work took the family to Salisbury, Southern Rhodesia in the spring of 1909 and Lovat Dickson attended the Alfred Beit School there. His closest friend during this period was Harry, a native boy. Dickson received his secondary education at the Berkhamstead School in Berkhamstead, England, where the family had

Portrait by Robin Guthrie
LOVAT DICKSON

moved in the summer of 1913. In the fall of 1917 the Dicksons took up residence in Canada because the mother's health required a change in climate.

When he was fifteen Lovat Dickson worked in Ottawa successively as a laborer on an experimental dairy farm, a bank messenger, and a clerk with the Imperial Munitions Board. During this period his mother died and the family began to break up. After a few months as a Royal Air Force cadet-officer and as a farmhand in Ontario in 1918 Dickson worked in Montreal briefly as a driller's helper in the Vickers shipyards and for nine months as an administrative clerk—more or less a case-worker, supervising pensioned war widows—with the Board of Pension Commissioners. In September 1919 he entered the Haileybury (Ontario) School of Mines but his antipathy for mathematics and scientific subjects hampered his studies and he dropped out in 1920. Heart trouble cut short a period of manual labor in the Temiskaming silver mine near Cobalt, Ontario, which his father was then managing.

During the last half of 1920 Dickson worked at an uncongenial job in the sales department of Paramount Pictures Corporation of Canada, promoting exhibition of Paramount films at Toronto movie houses. At the beginning of 1921, regarding himself as a chronic failure, he went again to live with his father, who was now managing the Blue Diamond coal mine at Brule in the Canadian Rockies. Subsidized by Jack P. Bickell, owner of the Blue Diamond mine, Dickson started a weekly newspaper in Brule, the *Blue Diamond Weekly*. The United Mine Workers of America were trying to organize the Blue Diamond miners at the time. Unable in conscience to defend the uncompromising company point of view in its entirety, Dickson abandoned the paper just as it was beginning to thrive.

(Continued next page)

DICKSON, LOVAT—*Continued*

In the fall of 1921 Dickson entered the University of Alberta. In his sophomore year at the university he came under the influence of Professor Edmund Broadus, who awoke in him the ability to concentrate and drove him to increase his reading and sharpen his writing style. During the summer of 1922 he worked as a chauffeur, driving tourists through Jasper National Park in Alberta. While an undergraduate Dickson contributed a column of political and humorous comment to the Edmonton *Journal* two or three times a week. He took his B.A. degree in English with first class honors in 1927, receiving also the Lieutenant-Governor's Gold Medal and the University Fellowship, and sharing the Shakespeare prize.

Returning to the university as an assistant lecturer in the fall of 1927, he gave a course in freshman English and an undergraduate Shakespeare course. Meanwhile he worked on his master's thesis, which dealt with the relationship between John Lyly's *Endimion* and Elizabethan political events. He spent the summer of 1928 as assistant to Professor Broadus at the University of California at Los Angeles, where the professor was giving a course in the summer school. The University of Alberta conferred the M.A. degree upon him in 1929. Meanwhile, in late 1928, Dickson had met Frederick Hammond, a wealthy mine owner, who, having just purchased the *English Review*, urged Dickson to give up teaching and come to England to help him reorganize the publication. Consequently, in December 1928, before the end of the term, Dickson resigned his position at the university, much to the dismay of his mentor, Professor Broadus.

As he sailed into the harbor of Dover, England in 1929 Dickson had a "moment of clarity" about himself, which he has described in *The Ante-Room.* "I saw the mistake I was making: People are more important than words; happiness is more satisfying than success. But the subtle drug had been an addiction too long. . . . When had it begun to fasten on me? Perhaps in those early days in Australia when my father read me books too exciting for a young mind to bear. . . . No, it was in those lonely months following my mother's death, when words were my only friends. . . . How much more horrible they would have been if I . . . had not been able to lose myself in a world created by others, or in the ones I tried to create for myself."

Dickson was associate editor of the *Fortnightly Review* in London from 1929 to 1932, and over much of the same period of time he was editor of the *Review of Reviews.* In 1932 he founded his own publishing house, Lovat Dickson Ltd. in London, and he was its managing director until 1938. Meanwhile, from 1930 to 1938, he was also editorial scout in London for the Macmillan Company of New York. In 1938 he joined Macmillan & Co. Ltd., London. He became a director of the company in 1941 and is now senior director of that firm.

Macmillan & Co. Ltd. (not to be confused with the London branch of the New York Macmillan Company), founded in 1843, has published the works of many authors illustrious in English literature. Its Canadian associate is the Macmillan Company of Canada Ltd.; its New York associate is St. Martin's Press, Inc. Dickson is vice-president of the latter. He is, in addition, a director of Pan Books Ltd., London paperback publishers specializing in reprints, and a director of the Reprint Society Ltd., London.

Dickson edited *Green Leaf; A Tribute to Grey Owl,* which was published in 1938 by Peter Davies Ltd. in London and by the Macmillan Company of Canada in Toronto. He wrote *Half-Breed; The Story of Grey Owl,* published in 1939 by Transatlantic Arts and in 1941 by Davies and by Macmillan (Toronto); and the novel *Out of the West Land* (Collins, 1944). His *Richard Hillary,* an intimate memorial biography of the young writer killed on an R.A.F. mission during World War II, was published by Macmillan (London) in 1950. The first volume of his autobiography, *The Ante-Room,* covering his life to the age of twenty-seven, was published in London by Macmillan in 1959 and in New York by Atheneum Publishers in 1960.

The Ante-Room drew varied responses from the critics. A reviewer for the *New Yorker* (September 10, 1960) praised it as "an absolutely first-rate book," while a critic for the London *Times Literary Supplement* (November 13, 1959) observed: "Mr. Dickson writes, for the most part, a plain, workmanlike prose which, if not very inspired, is always pleasant to read." Orville Prescott, reviewing *The Ante-Room* in the New York *Times* (December 5, 1960), wrote: "His book discloses that he is an exceedingly capable writer. . . . For two reasons it is more interesting than most such indulgences in fond recollection. The first is that Mr. Dickson's life was dramatic and colorful. . . . The second is that Mr. Dickson was not just young; he was an interesting and complex combination of many paradoxical qualities. On the one hand he was shy, sensitive, timid, innocent, tense and emotional. On the other he was tough, ambitious, energetic, self-confident and enterprising." Robertson Davies wrote in the New York *Times Book Review* (October 2, 1960): "Here is a book of uncommon literary distinction in which a man reveals himself in spare, elegant prose which carries us far below what can be achieved by undisciplined confession."

"The whole of my life has been devoted to books, as *The House of Words,* my forthcoming book, explains," Dickson wrote in late 1961. *The House of Words,* the second volume of his autobiography, is scheduled for publication in the United States by Atheneum in 1963. Dickson's other writing has included frequent articles on trade matters in *Publishers' Weekly* (New York) and *The Bookseller* (London). He has contributed a series of articles on "Publishing in the 1960's" to the London *Times.* Dickson often engages in public speaking and usually lectures on problems concerning the writing and publishing field.

Lovat Dickson married Marguerite Isabelle Brodie on December 26, 1934. They have one son, Jonathan Alexander Brodie Lovat Dickson. Blue-eyed and gray-haired, Dickson is six feet two inches tall and weighs 166 pounds. His religious affiliation is with the Anglican Church, and politically he considers himself a radical conservative. He is a member of the Garrick

Club in London and an executive of the London center of P.E.N., the international writers' association. As president of the Canadian Universities Society in London he works extensively with Canadian graduate students in the United Kingdom. When not closeted with his reading and writing he enjoys sailing. His work and social activities have brought him into contact with most of the leading figures of the English literary world and with a number of prominent American authors.

References

Dickson, Lovat. The Ante-Room (1960)
Who's Who, 1962

DOBRYNIN, ANATOLY F(EDOROVICH)

(dō-brē'nĕn ăn-ă-tō'lĭ)   Nov. 16, 1919-   Soviet Ambassador to the United States

Address: Embassy of the Union of Soviet Socialist Republics, 1706 18th St., N.W., Washington 9, D.C.

A leading Soviet expert on America, Anatoly F. Dobrynin succeeded Mikhail A. Menshikov as Soviet ambassador to the United States in March 1962, at a time when crises in Berlin and Southeast Asia threatened to create new problems in the cold war. Beginning his diplomatic career with the Soviet Ministry of Foreign Affairs in 1944, he served with the Soviet Embassy in Washington, D.C. from 1952 to 1955, and with the United Nations Secretariat in New York from 1957 to 1960. His friendliness with Western diplomats and his knowledge of American life led some observers to speculate whether his appointment might indicate a new era of good feeling between the United States and the Soviet Union.

Anatoly Fedorovich Dobrynin was born on November 16, 1919—the first Soviet ambassador to the United States to be born after the Bolshevik Revolution. Little is known about his early life or education. It is reported that he is a Ukrainian. He graduated from a technical college before the outbreak of World War II and he holds a master of science degree in history. During the war he served as an engineer at an aircraft plant. In 1944, as the war was coming to an end, Dobrynin entered the Soviet diplomatic service.

During the next five years Dobrynin gradually assumed more important positions in the Soviet foreign ministry. From 1949 to 1952 he served as assistant to the deputy minister of foreign affairs. In 1952 he was sent abroad to serve as counselor at the Soviet Embassy in Washington, D.C., and from 1954 to 1955 he was the second-ranking man at this embassy, holding the position of minister-counselor. During his three-year stay in the United States, Dobrynin was involved, among other things, in negotiations over the unsettled issue of World War II lend-lease obligations. In 1954 he delivered an official Soviet protest to the United States Department of State about a statement, attributed to an American Air Force general, that the United States was ready to launch rapid atomic retaliatory attacks from Great Britain against the Soviet Union.

Novosti Press Agency—
Yu. Abramochkin

ANATOLY F. DOBRYNIN

Returning to the Soviet Union in 1955, Dobrynin became a counselor in the Ministry of Foreign Affairs, with the rank of ambassador extraordinary and plenipotentiary. For a time he served as assistant to Soviet Foreign Minister Dmitri T. Shepilov. During this period he took part in a number of international conferences. In June 1955 he attended the tenth anniversary celebration of the United Nations, and in the following month he was present at the Geneva meeting of the heads of government of Great Britain, France, the United States, and the Soviet Union. In August 1956 he was a member of the Soviet delegation to the London conference on the Suez Canal, and later in the same year he returned briefly to the United States as adviser to the Soviet delegation to the United Nations General Assembly.

Dobrynin joined the Secretariat of the United Nations in July 1957 as undersecretary without portfolio, and in this position he undertook various special assignments. In a reorganization of the Secretariat in the summer of 1958, he was named undersecretary in charge of the Department of Political and Security Council Affairs. Under this arrangement, disarmament problems, which normally would have been under the jurisdiction of his department, were put under the personal charge of Secretary-General Dag Hammarskjöld.

As undersecretary, Dobrynin was the highest-ranking Soviet official on the U.N. Secretariat staff, and he is credited with revitalizing his department. He enjoyed the confidence and respect of Hammarskjöld and was reputed to be one of the few men who could talk with the Secretary-General on equal terms. His term of service with the U.N. marked a period of cooperation between the Soviet leaders and Hammarskjöld that lasted until the outbreak of the Congo crisis in 1960. In early 1959 Dobrynin accompanied the Secretary-General on a visit to

DOBRYNIN, ANATOLY F.—*Continued*

the Crimean residence of Soviet Premier Nikita S. Khrushchev, and in September of that year he accompanied Khrushchev on his visit to the United States.

Although his contract with the United Nations was not due to expire until June 30, 1963, Dobrynin was called back by his government in February 1960 to return to the Ministry of Foreign Affairs. Secretary-General Hammarskjöld noted his departure "with very great professional and personal regret." At the Ministry of Foreign Affairs Dobrynin became a member of the collegium and served as head of the American department, which was concerned with the problems of the entire Western Hemisphere. He returned briefly to New York in the summer of 1960 to assist Soviet Foreign Minister Andrei A. Gromyko at the U.N. Security Council meetings that considered Soviet complaints about the United States' U-2 flights. In the summer of 1961 Dobrynin attended the meeting of Khrushchev and United States President John F. Kennedy at Vienna, and he accompanied the secretary of the Presidium of the Supreme Soviet of the U.S.S.R. on a trip through Latin America.

When Mikhail A. Menshikov's term as Soviet ambassador to the United States expired early in 1961, the Presidium of the Supreme Soviet of the U.S.S.R. appointed Dobrynin to succeed him. The new ambassador presented his credentials to President Kennedy on March 30, 1962. At that time he declared that the Russians were convinced that "by joint effort, the difficulties existing between the two countries can be surmounted," and asserted that the Soviet Union was dedicated to securing "durable peace with justice" and to maintaining peaceful co-existence.

In the months before Dobrynin took office as ambassador the question of the status of Berlin had loomed large in the negotiations between Soviet and American officials. The Soviet position had been that the Western forces should evacuate West Berlin, and the Soviet Union has thus challenged the West's right to free access to the city and the stationing of garrisons there. The Western allies in turn have sought to show their determination to maintain their position in the city, by force if necessary, on the basis of post-World War II agreements.

On April 16, 1962 Dobrynin began exploratory talks with United States Secretary of State Dean Rusk on the Berlin issue. Dobrynin's practice of conferring with Rusk directly in English, without an interpreter, was a marked departure from the usual Soviet practice in negotiations. The talks opened in a relatively favorable atmosphere, and the Soviet Union suspended its harassment of air and ground access routes to West Berlin. In ensuing talks Rusk reportedly told Dobrynin that the presence of Western forces in West Berlin was not a negotiable topic. Criticizing what it called the rigid position of the United States, the Soviet Union insisted that American, French, and British forces in West Berlin be replaced by neutral or United Nations forces for a fixed period, and that West Berlin should eventually become a demilitarized free city.

United States proposals for a possible solution of the Berlin problem included an international authority to control access to and from West Berlin, a nonaggression pledge by the NATO and Warsaw Pact countries, a reciprocal pledge to refrain from giving nuclear weapons to other countries, and the creation of a system of all-German committees to improve technical relations on such matters as trade and travel. Dobrynin and Rusk met for their fourth round of talks on the Berlin question on May 30, 1962. Although neither side seemed willing to deviate from its established position, there were some indications that future talks might result in a compromise solution.

Another possible source of friction between the United States and the Soviet Union that developed in the weeks after Dobrynin assumed the ambassadorship was the crisis in Laos, where pro-Communist forces, violating a previously established cease-fire, were moving toward the Mekong River, thus presenting a possible threat to neighboring Thailand. President Kennedy responded by dispatching American troops to Thailand to bolster its defenses, while continuing in the effort to obtain a diplomatic settlement to the Laotian problem. In a conference with Rusk on May 15, 1962 Dobrynin declared that the Soviet government continued to adhere to the agreement on a Laotian settlement concluded between Kennedy and Khrushchev at Vienna in June 1961. This agreement called for an effective cease-fire and the creation of an independent Laos under a neutral coalition government.

Considered one of the outstanding specialists in the field of Russian-American affairs, Anatoly F. Dobrynin combines his diplomatic work with extensive research activities. For a number of years he gave a lecture course on Soviet-American relations at the State Institute of International Relations in Moscow. He speaks English and French fluently. Although he is a member of the Communist party, he has held no high party positions. His wife, Irina (or Irena) Nikolaevna, whom he met when both were engineering students, also speaks English, is interested in American literature and art, and is an accomplished pianist. They have one daughter, Yelena. While Dobrynin was with the United Nations, he and his wife traveled widely throughout the United States by bus and automobile.

Dobrynin is six feet one inch tall and has thinning gray-blond hair. His hobbies include skiing, playing chess, collecting records of modern music, and visiting the theater. He is also an amateur movie photographer. A fellow diplomat has said of Dobrynin: "He has a keen sense of humor and intellectual honesty. He even engages in small talk, and I have never known another Russian who does" (*Newsweek*, May 7, 1962). He has been described as "the sort of Russian who, while he remains an ardent Communist, realizes that it is necessary to come to terms with the West and live with it" (*Toronto Globe and Mail*, January 4, 1962).

References

N Y Post p32 D 29 '61 por
N Y Times p4 Ap 24 '62 por
N Y World-Telegram p14 Mr 15 '62 por
Newsday p24 D 29 '61 por
Time 79:16 Ja 5 '62 por
Washington (D.C.) Post Bp19 Mr 17 '62

DOBZHANSKY, THEODOSIUS (GRIGORI-
EVICH) (dŏb-zhăn'skĭ) Jan. 25, 1900- Geneti-
cist; university professor
Address: b. Department of Zoology, Columbia
University, New York 27; h. 39 Claremont Ave.,
New York 27

The need for a synthesis of the vast accumulation of knowledge in the sciences is regarded
by Theodosius Dobzhansky, Da Costa Professor
of Zoology at Columbia University, as one of the
major tasks of a scientist. An internationally
known authority on genetics and evolution,
Dobzhansky has spent over thirty years investigating the mechanics of heredity in the *Drosophila*, or fruit fly. But it is with mankind that
he is ultimately concerned. Exploring the philosophical and social implications of modern biology is, he feels, as incumbent upon the scientist
as specialized research. Dobzhansky has been a
professor of zoology at Columbia University
since 1940.

Theodosius Grigorievich Dobzhansky was born
on January 25, 1900, in Nemirov, Russia, the
only child of Gregory Dobzhansky, a teacher,
and Sophia Voinarsky. He was reared in the
city of Kiev and attended secondary school there,
graduating in 1917. At an early age he evinced
an interest in nature, and his interest in genetics
and evolution is said to date from his reading
of Charles Darwin's *On the Origin of Species*
when he was fifteen years old. Dobzhansky went
on to study at the University of Kiev, majoring
in biology. He received his diploma in 1921.

That same year Dobzhansky began his teaching
career as an instructor in zoology at the Institute
of Agriculture at Kiev. He remained in this
position until 1924. Then for the next three
years, until 1927, he served as a lecturer in
genetics at the University of Leningrad. During
the year 1926-27 he headed an expedition to
central Asia that engaged in the study of domestic animals. In 1927 Dobzhansky came to the
United States as a Fellow of the International
Education Board of the Rockefeller Foundation.
As a research Fellow he worked at Columbia
University in New York and at the California
Institute of Technology until 1929.

At the University of California, Dobzhansky
studied with the famous American zoologist
Thomas Hunt Morgan (1866-1945), who won
the 1933 Nobel Prize in Physiology and Medicine
for the theory that hereditary unit characters
depend upon certain genes in the chromosomes.
Morgan, who has been called "the twentieth-
century Mendel," was then director of the Kerck-
hoff Laboratories of Biological Science. He was
so impressed with the young Russian-born scientist that he invited Dobzhansky to stay on permanently after he completed the term of his
Fellowship. Dobzhansky accepted, and in 1929
he joined the faculty of the California Institute
of Technology as an assistant professor of genetics. Seven years later, in 1936, he was named
a full professor. In 1940 he returned to Columbia University to take up an appointment as
professor of zoology. At the same time he was
named to direct research in the University's recently established laboratory of genetics.

Dobzhansky's area of specialization within the
field of genetics has been the study of *Drosophila*

THEODOSIUS DOBZHANSKY

populations. The fruit or vinegar flies of the
genus *Drosophila* lend themselves well to the
study of inherited and mutant genes, since the
flies produce about fourteen generations of off-
spring a year. Dobzhansky has, however, ranged
beyond the confines of his subject specialization.
In the preface to his book *Mankind Evolving*
(Yale Univ. Press, 1962) he maintains that in
addition to accumulating knowledge it is the
biologist's task to make intelligible the intellectual revolution ushered in by Darwin whereby
all things were understood to evolve. Accordingly, Dobzhansky has explored and explained
the roles that genetic and environmental factors
play in the origin and structure of populations
and in the process of biological evolution.

He holds that man possesses both a nature
and a history. Human evolution, he explains,
comprises two components—the biological or organic and the cultural or superorganic. Neither
component mutually excludes the other, since
biological heredity and culture are interrelated.
Human evolution cannot be viewed as strictly a
biological process because man is more than
simply an animal. Dobzhansky believes that
dwelling on only one aspect can lead to distorted
theories of biological racism and to class
prejudice. At the 128th annual meeting of
the American Association for the Advancement of
Science in Denver, Colorado in January 1962 he
surprised many listeners by speaking on racial
equality. Addressing himself to the question of
the intellectual capacities of Negroes and whites,
Dobzhansky contended that heredity was but a
"predisposition," which can be molded by environment.

In answering those who describe human evolution exclusively in terms of a history of culture,
Dobzhansky has maintained that man's genetic
endowment cannot be ignored: culture itself is
conditioned by heredity. He assails Soviet agrono-
mist T. D. Lysenko's theory that environment is

(Continued next page)

DOBZHANSKY, THEODOSIUS—*Continued*

the sole force governing the formation of species. Dobzhansky acknowledges that *adaptation* to the environment is the main causative agent of organic evolution, but he also holds that environment does not impose changes on the organism. He sees the relationship in evolution between the organism and its environment as being best epitomized by the historian Arnold Toynbee's phrase, "challenge and response."

Dealing as he does with changes or mutations in genes, Dobzhansky is naturally concerned with the effects of atomic radiation on human populations. High energy radiation, whether resulting from medical X-rays or nuclear fallout, induces mutations in the hereditary materials. Scientists look upon most of these changes as being harmful. Dobzhansky contends that there is no minimum or safe amount of radiation below which mutations would not be induced. Exposure to radiation may damage the genetic endowment of mankind for generations to come. In his book *Radiation, Genes and Man* (Holt, 1959), written with Bruce Wallace, Dobzhansky proposes that the question of nuclear weapons testing rest not on genetic, but ultimately on ethical, standards.

In weighing the question of where evolution is taking man, Dobzhansky disagrees with the fashionable view that predicts the final extinction of mankind. Biological evolution, he believes, has transcended itself by producing the genetic basis of culture, the superorganic. Man alone alters his environment to meet his needs, and man is the only animal who, knowing that he has evolved, is aware that he continues to be part of the evolutionary process. Man therefore can help to shape his own destiny.

Man's ability to change his environment explosively, however, holds as much of a threat as a promise. Cultural evolution, in the form of technological and scientific knowledge, may have outdistanced biological evolution. Dobzhansky believes that the biological and cultural evolutions must eventually be brought under human control. Man must replace the blind force of nature, manifested in natural selection, by consciously directing improvement of his hereditary endowment. To undertake—let alone succeed in —such a momentous enterprise, man must increase his knowledge of his nature and its evolution. This Dobzhansky looks upon as both man's greatest challenge and his ultimate hope.

A prolific writer, Dobzhansky has contributed many articles to scientific journals. He has also tried to present some of the philosophical implications of modern biology in terms that an educated layman can understand. His classic text *Genetics and the Origin of Species*—for which he received the Daniel Giraud Elliot medal and prize from the National Academy of Sciences in 1941—has gone through three editions. Dobzhansky was the first biologist invited to deliver the Page-Barbour lectures at the University of Virginia in 1954 and his *Biological Basis of Human Freedom* (Columbia Univ. Press, 1956) grew out of these lectures. His more recent Silliman lecture series at Yale University resulted in *Mankind Evolving* (Yale Univ. Press, 1962). He has also written *Heredity, Race, and Society*, with L. C. Dunn, first published in the New American Library, as a paperback, in 1946; *Principles of Genetics*, written with E. W. Sinnott and L. C. Dunn and first published by McGraw-Hill in 1950; and *Evolution, Genetics, and Man*, published by John Wiley in 1955.

Dobzhansky has traveled extensively in central Asia, Siberia, Peru, Mexico, Guatemala, Alaska, and Egypt. He was an exchange professor at the University of São Paulo, Brazil in 1943 and again in 1948-49. As a Guggenheim Fellow in 1959 he spent a year of research on the evolutionary genetics of *Drosophila* populations at the University of Sydney in Australia. He received an honorary D.Sc. degree from the University of São Paulo in 1943, from the College of Wooster (Ohio) in 1945, from the University of Münster (Germany) in 1958, from the University of Montreal (Canada) in 1958, from the University of Chicago in 1959, and from the University of Sydney (Australia) in 1960.

The National Academy of Science, of which he is a member, presented Dobzhansky with the Kimber Genetics award in 1958. He also holds membership in the Royal Danish, Royal Swedish, and Brazilian academies of science. He served as president of the American Society of Genetics in 1941 and as president of the American Society for the Study of Evolution in 1951. In addition, Dobzhansky is a member of the American Philosophical Society, the American Society of Naturalists, and the American Society of Zoologists.

A vigorous man whose once blond hair is now graying, Dobzhansky likes to indulge in horseback riding and mountain climbing. He has blue eyes, stands five feet ten inches tall, and weighs 180 pounds. Dobzhansky became an American citizen in 1937. He is a member of the Russian Orthodox Church. On August 8, 1924 he married Nathalie Sivertzev. They have a daughter, Sophia, who is the wife of Michael Douglass Coe, an anthropologist at Yale University.

References

American Naturalist 80:27 Ja 1 '46
N Y Times p29 My 15 '40; p26 Ap 28 '58
Scientific American 190:14+ Ja '54; 203: 48+ S '60
American Men of Science 10th ed (1961)
Who's Who in America, 1962-63

DULLES, ELEANOR LANSING (dŭl'ĕs) June 1, 1895- Economist; former United States government employee
Address: h. Spring Hill Rd., McLean, Va.

In its record of public service the Dulles family stands among the most prominent in American history. The contribution that Eleanor Lansing Dulles has made to that record is probably best indicated in her achievement as an economic specialist for the State Department in the reconstruction of West Berlin from 1952 to 1960. Before her retirement in January 1962 she had worked for twenty-six years for the United States government, surpassing the length of service of both her well-known older brothers, the late Secretary of State John Foster Dulles and the former head of the Central Intelligence Agency,

Allen W. Dulles. Mrs. Dulles, the widow of David Simon Blondheim, combines her marriage title with her maiden name.

Among the distinguished diplomats and scholars who established the family's tradition in international interests were John Welsh, envoy to Great Britain during President Rutherford B. Hayes's administration, and John Watson Foster, Secretary of State under President Benjamin Harrison. Eleanor Lansing Dulles was born in Watertown, New York on June 1, 1895 to the Reverend Allen Macy and Edith (Foster) Dulles. Besides her two brothers, John and Allen, she has two sisters, now Mrs. Margaret (Dulles) Edwards and Mrs. Nataline (Dulles) Seymour.

During Eleanor Dulles' childhood the Reverend Allen Dulles gave up his pastorate at a Presbyterian church in Watertown to teach at the Auburn Theological Seminary in Auburn, New York. In preparation for college she attended the Auburn Academic High School and later Mount Vernon Seminary in Washington, D.C. and Wykeham Rise. In 1914 she entered Bryn Mawr College in Pennsylvania as a recipient of the first New England Entrance Scholarship and in 1917 was graduated with the B.A. degree. During her secondary school and college years she enjoyed vigorous sports like hockey, basketball, and water polo.

Like her mother, Eleanor Dulles had a particular interest in social work. In college she spent considerable time on the initial planning and early development of the Bryn Mawr Community Center and also worked in fresh-air camps and at the Philadelphia Social Settlement. Immediately after her graduation from Bryn Mawr she went to Paris, and later to the war-devastated areas of France, to work for the next two years on refugee rehabilitation and reconstruction, during part of the time in association with the American Society of Friends.

For almost a decade Eleanor Dulles continued to follow a pattern that combined study and research with practical experience. In 1919 she returned to Bryn Mawr under a fellowship in labor and industrial economics, and after receiving an M.A. degree in 1920 she went into industry to study management and employment problems. During 1920-21 she was employed as assistant manager of the American Tube & Stamping Company in Bridgeport, Connecticut, where she worked in the shop, running a punch press, as well as in the office. She later spent about a year as employment manager and payroll clerk in a hair net factory in Long Island City, New York.

As part of the research on which she later based her teaching of industrial management and labor problems, Eleanor Dulles also visited hundreds of factories in the United States, and in 1921-22, while studying at the London School of Economics, she investigated English industrial methods in seventy-five firms. She also took courses in economics at Radcliffe College and Harvard University, earning an M.A. degree in 1924 and a Ph.D. degree in 1926.

Appointed a research assistant of Harvard, Radcliffe, and the Bureau of International Research, Eleanor Dulles studied at the University of Paris (Faculté de Droit) from 1925 to 1927, and again with the Bureau of International Re-

Dept. of State—Whit Keith, Jr.
ELEANOR LANSING DULLES

search she studied in Basel and Geneva from 1930 to 1932. Her research in international financial problems led to her books *The French Franc, 1914-1928; The Facts and Their Interpretation* (Macmillan, 1929), *The Bank for International Settlements at Work* (Macmillan, 1932), and *The Dollar, the Franc, and Inflation* (Macmillan, 1933) and to a number of articles.

Eleanor Dulles had begun teaching as a lecturer in 1924-25 at Simmons College in Boston. From 1928 to 1930 she was assistant professor of economics at Bryn Mawr College, and from 1932 to 1936 she was a lecturer at Bryn Mawr and a lecturer and research associate at the Wharton School of the University of Pennsylvania. Her book *Depression and Reconstruction—A Study of Causes and Controls* was published in 1936 by the University of Pennsylvania Press.

In 1936 Mrs. Dulles entered government service in the position of director of financial research of the Social Security Board. She planned and supervised studies of the Social Security Act of 1936 and of the fiscal capacity of states. In 1938 she represented the United States at the Geneva Conference on Investment of Social Security Funds. Leaving the Social Security Board in 1942, she served briefly as a social science analyst with the Board of Economic Welfare before she joined the State Department in September 1942.

Eleanor Dulles' early work at the State Department concerned postwar planning in international finance, in part involving problems relating to the United Nations Relief and Rehabilitation Administration. She attended the Bretton Woods Conference on the International Monetary Fund in New Hampshire in 1944. Even before the end of the war she had become engaged in Austrian reconstruction work. For seven years she handled matters dealing with the reopening of the national bank and the restoration of key industries and utilities, particularly

DULLES, ELEANOR LANSING—*Continued*
power; in this way she helped the Austrians to launch their part of the Marshall Plan. She was serving as adviser on German-Austrian affairs in the division of financial affairs when in 1951, in the midst of the Korean conflict, she was detailed to the National Production Board to be a representative on the petroleum committee on defense.

Upon her return to work at the State Department in late 1952, Mrs. Dulles assumed the important role that she was to play for the next eight years in the reconstruction of West Berlin, one of the most crucial battlegrounds of the cold war. In April 1954 she was appointed special assistant to the director of the department's office of German affairs. She was responsible for the planning of aid programs costing some $300,000,000 annually and for negotiations with West German officials for financial contributions and co-operation in carrying out the programs.

Mrs. Dulles' major goal was to make West Berlin "a showcase for freedom," and in keeping the city before the American public and leaders throughout the world, she tried to present a contrast with Communist-controlled East Berlin that would speak for itself. Her achievements include the construction of a student village, a hospital, educational centers, and social housing. She was also instrumental in building the Berlin Congress Hall, an auditorium that Berliners nicknamed "the Dulleseum." In a general comment on her responsibilities in Berlin, Mrs. Dulles has said, "The work with industry, the universities, the refugee centers, the cultural and political officials, like my work for Austria . . . , required wide economic and political capacities. The impact on Berlin could thus represent my work there and elsewhere over several decades."

In October 1959 Mrs. Dulles was assigned to a special State Department project involving aid to underdeveloped countries. For about a year, in 1960-61, she traveled in more than forty countries in the Middle East, Asia, and Africa and made studies of sixty countries for the office of intelligence and research. In January 1962, while holding the title of special assistant to the director of intelligence and research, she resigned from the State Department.

During her nineteen years in the State Department, Eleanor Dulles had held positions of responsibility much greater than those usually assigned to a career woman in government service, and in 1960, just before she set out on special research missions abroad, President Dwight D. Eisenhower had granted her the personal rank of minister. In an interview, however, with Christine Hotchkiss for *This Week* (May 10, 1958) when she was asked whether there were any advantages in being a woman in the State Department, she replied, "This place is a real man's world—if there ever was one. It's riddled with prejudices! If you are a woman in government service you just have to work ten times as hard—and even then it takes much skill to paddle around the various taboos. But it is fun to see how far you *can* get *in spite of* being a woman."

Among the many honors that have been conferred on Mrs. Dulles are several in recognition of her accomplishments in Berlin: a doctorate in political and economic science of the Free University of Berlin (1957), the Carl Schurz-Steuben Plaque for Distinguished Service in furthering German-American cultural relations (1957), and the Ernst Reuter Medallion for Service to Berlin (1959). The University of Pennsylvania awarded her membership in Phi Beta Kappa (1934), and she holds honorary LL.D. degrees from Wilson College (1950) and Western College (1957). She is a member of the overseas education committee of the League of Women Voters in Washington, the German Language Society in Washington, the American Economic Association, and the Cosmopolitan Club in New York. Fond of sailing, swimming and other water sports, she also belongs to the Henderson Harbor Yacht Club. Her church is the Presbyterian, and she is independent in politics.

Eleanor Lansing Dulles and David Simon Blondheim a philologist, were married on December 2, 1932. Their children are David Dulles and Ann Welsh Dulles. After the death of her husband in 1934, Mrs. Dulles resumed the use of her maiden name. She has blue-gray eyes and curly gray hair, is five feet four and a half inches tall, and weighs 145 pounds. Her extraordinary energy and capacity for long hours of work can perhaps be explained in part by her strong conviction that "the world needs the efforts of every decent person to keep it free and secure from destruction."

References

    This Week p22+ My 10 '59 por
    Department of State Biographic Register, 1961
    Who's Who in America, 1962-63
    Who's Who of American Women (1958-59)

FAULKNER, WILLIAM Sept. 25, 1897-July 6, 1962 American writer; received 1949 Nobel Prize in literature for his novels about the fictional Southern county, Yoknapatawpha, and the Pulitzer Prize for his novel *The Fable* (1954); writer-in-residence at University of Virginia, 1957-62. See *Current Biography* (January) 1951.

Obituary

    N Y Times p1+ Jl 7 '62

GAVIN, JOHN Apr. 8, 1928- Actor
Address: b. c/o Universal-International Pictures, Universal City, Calif.

Within the last six years John Gavin has become one of the most popular young male romantic leads in motion pictures, despite the generally lukewarm reaction his acting has elicited from critics. Tall and darkly handsome, he has the same Hollywood agent, Henry Willson, and is employed by the same studio, Universal-International Pictures, as Rock Hudson, another young star with whom he is sometimes compared. Gavin appeared in twelve pictures between 1956 and 1961, but acting is not his only vocation. Fluent in Spanish and Portuguese and twice decorated for his efforts in behalf of Pan-Americanism, Gavin was appointed special advisor to Secretary-General José Mora of the Organization of American States in July 1961 and charged with helping to win popular support for President John F. Kennedy's Alliance for Progress program of aid to Latin America.

John Gavin was born John Anthony Golenor on April 8, 1928 in Los Angeles, California. (His name was changed to Gavin by Universal-International.) His father, H. Ray Golenor, had mining interests in Mexico; his Mexican-born mother, Delia Diana (Pablos) Golenor, was related to early Spanish settlers of California. The boy became familiar with Latin America and with the Spanish language at an early age. The family was in comfortable circumstances, and he attended St. John's Military Academy at Los Angeles, Beverly Hills High School, and Villanova Preparatory School at Ojai, California before he entered Stanford University.

At Stanford Gavin belonged to the Chi Psi fraternity and took a prelaw course, majoring in political science and economics. He was enrolled in the Holloway Plan, under which some 2,500 Naval ROTC men are financed each year, after qualifying examinations, at the colleges of their choice. During the summer he worked on construction jobs, mostly as a laborer, in order to earn extra money and to keep in good physical condition, and during the school year he held part-time jobs like those of gas station attendant and theater usher.

After graduating from Stanford in June 1951 Gavin served four years with the United States Navy, including a tour of duty in Korean waters as an officer aboard the USS *Princeton,* during which he took part in five battles. His knowledge of Spanish and Portuguese resulted in his assignment to Panama, where he was Pan-American affairs officer to Admiral Milton E. Miles, Commandant of the Fifteenth Naval District during 1953-54. During floods in Honduras in 1954 he was on special duty with American rescue teams.

Released from active duty in June 1955, Gavin approached a family friend, the motion picture producer Bryan Foy, and asked for a job as technical adviser on a Navy film about to be produced. Foy suggested instead that the young naval veteran take a screen test. He put him in touch with Henry Willson, the Hollywood agent, who took him to Universal-International, and a career was launched.

His first role was in *Behind the High Wall* (1956), a minor prison melodrama. A *Variety* reviewer (June 13, 1956) mentioned him briefly: "John Gavin, a new face, does well as the film's younger male lead." Next came two more grade B pictures—*Four Girls in Town* (1957) and a western, *Quantez* (1957). Of Gavin's performance in the latter film, William Peper in the New York *World-Telegram and Sun* (August 29, 1957) wrote, "He is a handsome, personable young man whose talents will have to await a more provocative test."

That test came in Gavin's next picture, *A Time to Love and a Time to Die* (1958), based

JOHN GAVIN

on the novel about World War II by Erich Maria Remarque, famous for his *All Quiet on the Western Front.* The film was a major production that gave Gavin his first starring role, as Ernst Graeber, a young German soldier who finds love amid the devastation of war. Gavin's performance was variously received. Paul V. Beckley of the New York *Herald Tribune* (July 10, 1958) found him "a very personable young actor, remarkably unpretentious and quite lacking in mannerisms" who had "done very well in a role that would have been tough for a very experienced actor." But Bosley Crowther of the New York *Times* (July 10, 1958) called Gavin "a good-looking, awkward young man whose speech, attitude and dull delivery betray the tyro from Hollywood."

In *Imitation of Life* (1959), a remake of a 1934 film based on a novel by Fannie Hurst, Gavin played opposite Lana Turner as a photographer and her loyal suitor. A *Variety* reporter (February 4, 1959) noted that "Gavin admirably underplays . . . and with this role is on his way to the ranks of full-blooded screen heroes." Gavin played the supporting role of Julius Caesar in *Spartacus* (1960), the story of a Roman slave rebellion, in which he appeared with world famous stars like Kirk Douglas, Sir Laurence Olivier, Jean Simmons, Charles Laughton, Tony Curtis, and Peter Ustinov. A *Time* writer (October 24, 1960) apparently felt Gavin had been miscast in the role, for he called him "a rose-lipped, sloe-eyed young man who looks as though he never got to the first conjugation, let alone the Gallic Wars."

Lent to Paramount Studios, Gavin again played romantic leads in Alfred Hitchcock's *Psycho* (1960) and in *A Breath of Scandal* (1960), which was based on Ferenc Molnar's *Olympia.* Reviewing the latter, Archer Winsten wrote in the New York *Post* (December 18, 1960), "The actors act, and those who cannot, like Gavin, look beautiful." In the thriller

GAVIN, JOHN—*Continued*

Midnight Lace (1960), starring Doris Day and Rex Harrison, Gavin was cast as a young construction foreman. He played Igor Romanoff, son of a Russian ambassador, to Sandra Dee's Juliet, daughter of an American envoy, in *Romanoff and Juliet* (1961), an updated version of the Montague-Capulet feud. In *Tammy Tell Me True* (1961) he was a young college professor, and he starred as a lover in a remake of another Fannie Hurst story, *Back Street* (1961). "The range of Gavin's expression is narrow," a *Variety* reviewer (October 11, 1961) said of his performance in *Back Street*, "but he needn't fret. This handsome young man is well on his way to becoming a number one romantic lead in motion pictures."

In July 1961, about two months before the première of *Back Street* took place in Chicago, Gavin was named special advisor to José Mora, Secretary-General of the Organization of American States, which fosters co-operation between the United States and Latin American countries. The following month Gavin attended the Inter-American Economic and Social Conference at Punta Del Este, Uruguay, and several weeks after that he went to Washington, D.C. to confer with Mora, with de Lesseps Morrison, American Ambassador to the OAS, and with Richard Goodwin, a special assistant to the President.

Assigned to help develop public support throughout the Americas for President Kennedy's Latin American aid program, Alliance for Progress, Gavin in May 1962 called on the United States film industry to co-operate with producers and distributors south of the border. "There is a desire and a need for coproduction that can bolster Latin American films in the United States and aid our own American image in their countries," Gavin said. "There is a tremendous pro-American feeling, but an exaggerated anti-Yankee area that gets notice because it's organized. With more American film influence, our communication would be greater on a people-to-people basis that could help detract this anti-Yankee organization."

Shortly thereafter Gavin went to Mexico to conduct discussions with Mexican film producers and to speak before student groups on the subject of informational values in the film medium. For his contributions to better Pan-American relations Gavin was awarded the Order of Balboa by the Government of Panama and the Order of the Eloy Alfaro Foundation, presented by Eloy Alfaro II, grandson of the Ecuadorian general and political leader for whom the foundation is named. These decorations are held by only a few North Americans. Gavin has often made pleasure and business trips to Latin America, where he has financial interests in a Mexican housing project, an egg business in Panama, and plantations in South America. He is a partner in Panama-Boston Industries, manufacturers of vegetable oil, soap, and detergent.

On August 2, 1957, after an eight-year courtship, John Gavin married Cicely Evans, whom he had met while in college. She owns a women's clothing shop, Act Three, in Manhattan. On the fourth anniversary of their marriage a daughter, Cristina Miles, was born to them. The Gavins live quietly in the Outpost Drive section of Hollywood Hills, California in a house they themselves redesigned and redecorated.

Brown-eyed with black hair, Gavin is six feet four inches tall and weighs 194 pounds. "He is handsome," Hedda Hopper wrote (Washington *Post and Times Herald*, July 20, 1958), "and has a silken sort of threat which gives women little chills up and down the spine." Gavin plays handball and touch football to keep in shape, and he owns a private pilot's license. He has a collection of rare pre-Columbian art objects, having become interested in primitive South American art while serving with the Navy in Panama. He likes to read Somerset Maugham, Ernest Hemingway, and William Faulkner.

Although he once thought of giving up his motion picture career, Gavin is now determined to pursue it and to improve his acting skill. "I wouldn't be an actor," he has said, "if I didn't feel I would be good at it some day." On another occasion he remarked, "I find the more I work and study, the better I get, and the more fascinating I find it."

References

    Look p65 Jl 22 '58 por
    N Y Mirror p46 Ag 3 '58 por
    N Y Post Mag p3 O 29 '61 por
    Washington (D.C.) Post Hp7 Jl 20 '58

GOOSSENS, SIR EUGENE May 26, 1893-June 13, 1962 British conductor and composer; knighted in 1955; conducted the Sydney (Australia) Symphony and the New South Wales Conservatory orchestra, 1947-56, and the Cincinnati Symphony, 1931-47; composed operas, an oratorio, symphonies, orchestral works, chamber music, songs and piano pieces. See *Current Biography* (May) 1945.

Obituary

    N Y Times p1+ Je 14 '62

GOULART, JOÃO (BELCHIOR MARQUES) goō-lar' joō-ou') Mar. 1, 1918- President of Brazil
Address: Palácio da Alvorada, Brasília, Brazil

When João Goulart assumed the Presidency of Brazil in September 1961, after a bitter power struggle that nearly plunged his country into civil war following the resignation of President Jânio Quadros, he inherited immense problems—and equally immense possibilities. Brazil is Latin America's largest and wealthiest country, a pivotal factor in President John F. Kennedy's Alliance for Progress; it is also a country beset by runaway inflation, social unrest, and political instability.

President Goulart (affectionately called "Jango" by millions of Brazilians) is a political enigma in an enigmatical land. A wealthy rancher, he has angered the propertied classes by his advocacy of extensive economic reform; an avowed believer in democracy, he has puzzled many observers with his friendliness to Communist nations. Goulart's trip to the United States in April 1962 won him the confidence of American government officials as well as the high praise of President Kennedy for his leadership of Brazil.

A native of the state of Rio Grande do Sul in southern Brazil, João Belchior Marques Goulart was born in São Borja on March 1, 1918 to Vicente Rodrigues and Vicentina Marques Goulart. He grew up on his father's cattle ranch, which was located next to the ranch of Dr. Getúlio Vargas, the "strongman of the gauchos," who later ruled Brazil for nearly twenty years. At the age of sixteen Goulart entered Pôrto Alegre University for the study of law, and he graduated in 1939 with a doctor of jurisprudence degree. Upon returning home, he concentrated on the management of his father's farm estates, which prospered under his direction. After a few years he established close contact with Getúlio Vargas, who had controlled Brazil's government since 1930 but who was ousted in 1945 and had returned to his São Borja ranch.

Goulart entered Brazilian politics in 1946, when he was elected to the state legislature of Rio Grande do Sul as a member of Getúlio Vargas' newly-formed Brazilian Labor party. When, in 1950, Vargas again became President of Brazil—this time by free elections in contrast to his 1930 seizure of power—Goulart, who had campaigned for him, rose to national prominence. After being elected to the federal Chamber of Deputies as a representative for Rio Grande do Sul, he was appointed that state's secretary of justice and of the interior. In 1952 he became chairman of the Brazilian Labor party, and a year later, in recognition of his role as champion of the underprivileged workers, he was appointed by President Vargas as federal Minister of Labor, Industry and Commerce, an office he held until August 1954. During this period Goulart was active in reforming labor legislation.

President Vargas, whose administration was marred by scandal, committed suicide in 1954— an event that presented Goulart with a great opportunity. On October 3, 1955 Goulart was elected Vice-President of the republic with Juscelino Kubitschek as President, and on January 31, 1956 he took office. In July 1956 he briefly served as interim President during a temporary absence of President Kubitschek. In 1960 Dr. Goulart was again a candidate for Vice-President, as the running mate of Field Marshal Henrique Teixeira Lott. As a result of a new constitutional amendment, Brazilians were permitted to vote separately for President and Vice-President. In the October election Goulart won the Vice-Presidency by a 200,000-vote plurality, but Marshal Lott lost the Presidency to Jânio Quadros.

The controversial régime of President Quadros ended abruptly when he resigned on August 25, 1961, as a result of his mounting conflict with the Congress. As Vice-President, João Goulart was constitutionally entitled to assume Brazil's highest office. The nation's military leaders, however, worried by Goulart's apparent leftist tendencies and friendliness to Communist countries, decided to oppose his taking office. During the power struggle that ensued in the following two weeks, Brazil appeared to be on the brink of civil war while the world watched apprehensively.

Wide World

JOÃO GOULART

Brazil's Ministers of War, Navy, and Air Force, led by War Minister Odilio Denys, issued a statement accusing Goulart of demagoguery and sympathy to Communism. The Vice-President, who was just completing a tour of the Far East, was scored for having praised the efforts of Mao Tse-tung's régime while visiting Communist China. The generals' manifesto warned that "as President, Goulart would become an incentive to all those who want to see the country fall into chaos, anarchy, and civil strife." Declaring that "the time has come to choose between democracy and communism in Brazil," Denys threatened to arrest Goulart "as soon as he sets foot on Brazilian soil." High-ranking pro-Goulart officers —including Marshal Lott—were arrested, Brazil's four armies were alerted, and partial press censorship was invoked.

Popular reaction to the moves of the military soon made itself felt. Students and labor unions demonstrated in Goulart's behalf to defend "constitutional order." Senators and Deputies, many of them politically opposed to Goulart, defended his right to assume the Presidency. One Deputy said: "I will fight for Jango until the day he is inaugurated. Then I will fight against him." Among Goulart's supporters was former President Juscelino Kubitschek. In Rio Grande do Sul, Governor Leonel Brizola, a brother-in-law of Goulart, blockaded Pôrto Alegre harbor, called the state militia, and mobilized for armed resistance to the forces of General Denys. Moreover, the support of General M. José Machado Lopes, commander of the Third Army, was obtained. The Second Army in São Paulo refused to obey an order of Denys to "attack and dominate" the Third Army in Rio Grande do Sul.

Goulart returned to Brazil on September 1, 1961 amid an enthusiastic welcome by his supporters. On the following day the Brazilian Congress approved Goulart for the Presidency,

GOULART, JOÃO—Continued

after passing a constitutional amendment curtailing the functions of the President and assigning most of the executive power to a Prime Minister. The amendment was opposed both by the military, who did not want Goulart in office under any conditions, and by leftist supporters of Goulart, who denounced it as a "masked coup d'état." On September 7, 1961, on the 140th anniversary of Brazilian independence, Goulart was inaugurated as President, and Dr. Tancredo de Almeida Neves was inaugurated as Prime Minister.

Although he accepted the Presidency on the terms set forth by Congress, Goulart proceeded to press for restoration of full executive powers for his office. Dismissing the three armed service heads who had temporarily prevented him from assuming office, he then proposed that the constitutional amendment weakening the Presidency be submitted to a national referendum. Exercising far more outspoken leadership than Premier Neves, Goulart continued the drastic economic and social reforms begun by his predecessor. He inaugurated a program to reduce inflation by stopping the issue of new currency, restricting credit, encouraging exports, and devising means of increasing revenue.

In April 1962 Goulart made a state visit to the United States, where he conferred with President Kennedy. In a joint communiqué the two Presidents "reaffirmed the dedication of their countries to the inter-American system," and "agreed on the need for rapid execution of the steps necessary to make the Alliance for Progress effective." Speaking before a joint session of the United States Congress on April 4, Goulart asserted that Brazil adhered to "the democratic principles which united the peoples of the West," but that it was "not part of any politico-military bloc." He called for peaceful coexistence between East and West and said that the result would "show that representative government is the more perfect form of government, and more compatible with the protection of man and the preservation of his liberty." The speech drew favorable reactions from members of Congress.

At a news conference in New York on April 6, 1962, following a visit to the United Nations, Goulart declared that Brazil would give "every freedom and every guarantee" of fair profits to foreign investors whose properties were being expropriated in Brazil. The occasion of Goulart's visit elicited widespread speculation in the American press as to the reliability of Brazil's new President. The New York *Times* (April 3, 1962) noted editorially that Goulart, "despite a previous record of radicalism, has proved a moderate and responsible executive." Writing in the New York *Herald Tribune* (April 8, 1962), Joseph Newman observed that Goulart actually belonged to the moderate or conservative wing of the Brazilian Labor Party, and that President Kennedy was apparently "satisfied that Goulart, contrary to widely spread press reports, was not a Communist nor a Communist sympathizer." A writer for *Time* (April 13, 1962), noting that in the past Goulart had been known as a "rabble-rousing labor leader" and opportunist, added that

"as President, he has proved surprisingly moderate in his approach," and that American businessmen in Brazil were "reassured by his apparently genuine desire for free enterprise and foreign investment."

On April 13, 1962 the United States and Brazil signed an agreement providing for the investment of $276,000,000 in Alliance for Progress funds in the poverty-stricken and politically unstable northeastern section of Brazil. Under the agreement the United States was to invest $131,000,000 while Brazil would provide the equivalent of $145,000,0000, to be used for such projects as irrigation, water purification, school construction, education, electric power development, rural electrification, and road improvement. The agreement has been described as one of the most ambitious thus far undertaken under the Alliance for Progress program.

Upon his return to Brazil President Goulart enjoyed increased support and was widely regarded as a symbol of national unity. A number of his former opponents, especially among conservative and business elements, praised him greatly and expressed considerable hope for Brazil's future under Goulart's leadership. The *Jornal do Brasil* commented: "The picture of President Goulart as a pro-Communist, a demagogue and agitator has given way to that of a moderate President Goulart, politically able and young, just like President Kennedy." On May 23, 1962 the Council of Ministers approved Goulart's plan to nationalize all major public utilities in Brazil with due reimbursement to their owners.

After Premier Tancredo de Almeida Neves resigned on June 26, 1962 to prepare for the coming congressional elections, a conflict erupted between President Goulart and the more conservatively oriented Chamber of Deputies over the choice of a successor for the Premiership. Goulart's first choice, the former foreign minister Dr. Francisco San Tiago Dantas, was rejected by the Chamber. Although the Chamber approved Senate president Dr. Auro Soare Moura Andrade for the Premiership on July 3, 1962, he resigned a day later after failing to agree with Goulart on cabinet appointments. Meanwhile, trade union leaders, supporting Goulart, called a general strike, accompanied by food shortages and riots.

João Goulart is a stocky five feet seven inches tall, weighs 175 pounds, and has a magnetic smile and handsome appearance. He is a Roman Catholic. In 1955 he married Maria Teresa Fontela, who had been a neighbor of his. They have a son, João Vicente, and a daughter, Denise. Mrs. Goulart, who is regarded as one of the most beautiful women in Latin America, is highly popular among the people of Brazil. Recently the *Jornal do Brasil* published an editorial strongly criticizing Goulart's administration, but added: "But say what you will about this government, in the matter of its First Lady it's a winner."

References

N Y Times p16 Ag 29 '61 por
Time 78:40+ S 8 '61 por
Toronto Globe and Mail p8 Ja 20 '62 por
International Who's Who, 1961-62

GOULET, ROBERT (GERARD) (gōō-lā')
Nov. 26, 1933- Singer; actor
Address: b. c/o Norman Rosemont, 120 E. 56th
St., New York 22; h. 25 Central Park West,
New York 23

ROBERT GOULET

Before he became famous in his first Broadway
role, as Lancelot in Lerner and Loewe's musical
Camelot, in December 1960, Robert Goulet had
attained great popularity with Canadian audiences through his appearance on stage and television. Goulet's rich baritone voice, good looks,
ambition, and determination to become a better
actor are assets that make him a candidate for
stardom. The late Jerry Wald, the motion picture
producer, predicted that when Goulet appears in
a motion picture "he'll take off as if headed for
outer space."

Of French extraction, with one-eighth Irish
ancestry, Robert Gerard Goulet was born on
November 26, 1933 in Lawrence, Massachusetts,
to Joseph and Jeanette (Gauthier) Goulet. A
sister, Claire, is now Mrs. Paul Dumont of
Girouxville, Alberta, Canada. Bob Goulet and
his family became aware early in his life that
he had an unusual singing voice. He has recalled: "When I was six years old I refused to
sing at a family party. My father scolded me
and said I must not waste God's gift. I have,
since then, tried not to." Under the watchful
supervision of his father, Robert Goulet sang in
church choirs and at community affairs. When
he was fourteen, his father died, and the family
moved to Edmonton, Alberta, Canada to be near
relatives. While attending St. Joseph's High
School in Edmonton, Goulet played varsity football and was president of the dramatic organization. He also sang with local orchestras and
appeared in local musical productions. In 1951
he graduated from high school.

Goulet's first job was that of disc jockey
and radio announcer with station CKCA in
Edmonton. His work in a production of Handel's
Messiah won him a scholarship to the opera
school of the Royal Conservatory of Music in
Toronto. There he studied acting and singing
with Josef Furst and Dr. Ernesto Vinci and
seized every opportunity to perform on television,
in the theater, and in revues. In the winter of
1954 Goulet came to New York to try his luck
on the Broadway stage. For four months he
lived in a dismal garret apartment with an actor
friend, while contacting Broadway producers. The
only work he was able to get, however, was selling stationery in Gimbel's department store.

Soon after he returned to Toronto, the outlook
for Goulet's career considerably brightened. He
was cast in a leading role in the Canadian
Broadcasting Corporation's television production
of *Little Women*, and he won an important part
in the annual Canadian topical stage revue
Spring Thaw. Subsequently he joined the cast of
Canada's leading television variety program
Showtime, in which he starred for three years.
Goulet's appearance on this program made him
a favorite with Canadian television audiences.
Fan clubs began to multiply and Goulet was
dubbed "Canada's first matinee idol," a title of
which he is not particularly fond. For three
consecutive years he won honors as the best
male singer on Canadian television.

When television schedules permitted, Goulet
appeared in stage productions of *Thunder Rock*
and *Visit to a Small Planet*. In the summer of
1958 he played the role of Captain MacHeath
in the Stratford, Ontario Shakespeare Festival
production of John Gay's *The Beggar's Opera*.
He also spent two summers at the Theatre Under
the Stars in Vancouver, British Columbia, where
he starred in *South Pacific, Gentlemen Prefer
Blondes,* and *Finian's Rainbow.* In the summer
of 1959 he appeared with Debra Paget in *Pajama
Game*, with Anne Jeffreys in *The Bells Are Ringing*, and with Dorothy Collins in *Dream Girl*,
at the Packard Music Theatre in Warren, Ohio.

Goulet's great opportunity came in 1959, when
a theatrical agent recommended him to librettist
Alan Jay Lerner and composer Frederick Loewe.
Lerner and Loewe were at the time planning a
musical based on Terence Hanbury White's
novel *The Once and Future King* (Putnam,
1958), dealing with the legendary King Arthur
and his Round Table, and they were having
difficulty in casting the role of Lancelot. Goulet's
audition for the role greatly impressed Lerner
and Loewe, and they promptly signed him to
co-star with Richard Burton, who played the role
of King Arthur, and Julie Andrews, who portrayed Queen Guenevere. They then proceeded
to write the words and music of the show, which
they named *Camelot*.

Camelot opened for a pre-Broadway tryout at
the O'Keefe Center for the Performing Arts in
Toronto on October 1, 1960. According to John
Kraglund of the *Toronto Globe and Mail* (October 12, 1960), Goulet, in the role of the brave
knight who loves Queen Guenevere, displayed a
"strong, pleasant baritone voice, and an apparent
acting ability, which seems to be strengthening."
A reviewer for *Variety* (October 5, 1960) wrote
that Goulet "has the looks and the speaking and
singing voice of the ideal Lancelot," and that
he was apparently "destined to scale the heights."
After playing in Toronto for twenty-six perform-

GOULET, ROBERT—*Continued*

ances *Camelot* moved to the Shubert Theater in Boston for four and a half weeks, before it opened at New York's Majestic Theatre on December 3, 1960. It was the most expensive musical that has ever been produced on the Broadway stage.

Although *Camelot* was not universally acclaimed in the reviews, Robert Goulet stopped the show on opening night and evoked applause from the critics. John Chapman of the New York *Daily News* (December 5, 1960) pronounced Goulet a "fine and handsome baritone," and Walter Kerr of the New York *Herald Tribune* (December 5, 1960) noted that he played and sang "magnificently." Howard Taubman of the New York *Times* (December 11, 1960) wrote that Goulet was a "fine performer who deserves a better fate." In *Newsday* (December 7, 1960) George Oppenheimer observed: "As Lancelot Robert Goulet is a fine figure of a man and the possessor of an excellent voice. He can also act, although he is given little chance to portray anything but a composite portrait of purity and puritanism couchant."

On January 8, 1961 Goulet made his first appearance on American television on the *Ed Sullivan Show*, over CBS-TV. He has also appeared on the *Garry Moore Show* over the same network. Although he had been signed for the relatively small salary of $900 weekly to appear in *Camelot*, he now reportedly receives $6,500 for a single television appearance. Goulet has appeared in the 1961 special Christmas program *The Enchanted Nutcracker*, over ABC-TV, and in *The Broadway of Lerner and Loewe*, presented over NBC-TV on February 11, 1962. He served as host of the NBC-TV salute to Rockefeller Center, *Rainbow of Stars*, on April 17, 1962. In November 1961 he briefly flew to Hollywood to make the cartoon film *Gay Purr-ee,* in which he and Judy Garland did the voice characterizations of cats. Goulet is eager to appear in motion pictures, but his manager, Norman Rosemont, is willing to release him from *Camelot* "only if just the right role comes along." After his *Camelot* contract expires, in September 1962, Goulet is scheduled to appear in supper clubs with his own act. He plans to make his debut at the Persian Room in New York's Plaza Hotel in November 1962.

Goulet's relationship with Rosemont is an unusual one in the world of Broadway. There is no contract between them. Rosemont pays Goulet's bills, gives him a personal allowance, and sets the fees for his appearances, which are booked through Goulet's talent agency, the Music Corporation of America. Rosemont, who has never handled a performer before, says it is a question of personal satisfaction. "He's the kid from Canada put up against the big metropolis," Rosemont has said. "But he's growing up fast." Rosemont, who is vice-president and business manager of the Lerner-Loewe Corporation, formed a separate corporation with Goulet in January 1962 to produce shows starring Goulet. In addition to his personal manager and his agency, Goulet also has a lawyer, a personal publicity man, and a male secretary to handle his fan mail.

Part of Goulet's maturing process includes a greater interest in world affairs, politics, and books and a determination to improve both his understanding of the world around him and his skills as an actor. On his own he began to study acting, enrolling in a class conducted by Nick Colasanto, himself a student at the Actors Studio. "The only thing that will save me from being just another performer is if I can learn to act," Goulet has said. Colasanto has been quoted as saying that his student shows outstanding promise.

Early in 1962 Goulet was earning about $100,000 a year, hardly a munificent sum for one of Broadway's hottest properties. At that stage of Goulet's career, however, the major effort of the persons who handle his affairs was not to make a lot of money for him quickly but to plan his career shrewdly and to merchandise it effectively. Goulet has expressed full confidence in their ability to do so. "I have faith in these people but I don't just take their word as law," he told Judith Krantz in an interview for *Maclean's Magazine* (January 27, 1962). "I have confidence in their good judgment but we discuss everything. Knowing that I'm a property has given me a little more confidence. I feel better about my future than if I were trying to do it all on my own."

Robert Goulet married Louise Longmore in 1956, and he is the father of a daughter, Nicolette Ginette. The couple are now legally separated. Goulet is six feet tall, weighs 170 pounds, and has blue eyes and dark brown hair. He dresses casually but neatly. Music is his hobby as well as his career. He is an enthusiastic golfer when his busy schedule permits, and he keeps himself in good physical condition with barbells and other gymnastic equipment.

As he readies himself for a career that promises to reach the heights of the entertainment world, Goulet recognizes his limitations. "I still don't think of myself as an actor," he told Judith Krantz. "First I'm a singer, second a performer—a guy who can do skits, variety, that sort of thing—third an actor and fourth . . . God knows!" But he is determined to improve himself. "I don't really know how good I can hope to be eventually," he says. "It's a question of reaching for the moon and then working like hell to make it to the top of the Empire State Building."

References

Macleans Mag 75:13+ Ja 27 '62 pors
N Y Sunday News Mag p6 My 21 '61 por
N Y World-Telegram Mag p6 Je 17 '61 por
Toronto Globe and Mail Globe Mag p28+ N 23 '57 pors; p51+ O 1 '60 pors

HANSCHMAN, NANCY (CONNERS)

(hänsh'măn) 1929(?)- News correspondent
Address: b. c/o CBS News, 485 Madison Ave., New York 22

"Newspapermen meet such interesting people" —so ran a topical song of the 1940's—and this is also true of newspaperwomen. At least Nancy Hanschman thinks so. The first woman correspondent on the news staff of the Columbia Broadcasting System network, she enjoys consorting with the Congressmen, government VIPs, journalists, and others who frequent the Washington scene. Miss Hanschman has had her own five-minute program, *One Woman's Washington,* on CBS radio since November 1960. Before being named a correspondent with CBS News in February 1960, she was producer of *The Leading Question* and associate producer of *Face the Nation,* news programs on the CBS radio and television networks.

Nancy Conners Hanschman, the daughter of F. R. Hanschman, was born about 1929 in Wauwatosa, Wisconsin, a residential suburb of Milwaukee. She attended the University of Wisconsin, where she majored in English, Spanish, and Portuguese. After receiving her B.A. degree in 1948, she taught in a Milwaukee public school for two or three years. One summer she took a course in Russian politics at Harvard University.

Having decided to move to the East, Miss Hanschman made New York City her first stop, in the summer of 1951, but the difficulty of finding a suitable job soon led her to Washington, D.C. There she worked first as a registrar at the Institute of Languages of Georgetown University. She then found a position as a staff assistant to the Senate Committee on Foreign Relations, in which she did research and editorial work.

In the course of her work with the Senate committee she kept abreast of major political issues and came to know Congressional figures and newsmen who worked around Capitol Hill. From some of her journalist friends she learned that the Columbia Broadcasting System was casting about for a newsman to produce the radio show *The Leading Question.* Although CBS wanted a man for the spot, Miss Hanschman applied. Her knowledge of the Washington political scene stood her in good stead, and she was appointed producer of *The Leading Question* in 1954. She also became associate producer of the weekly radio and television news-interview program *Face The Nation.*

To gather material for these shows Miss Hanschman visited Capitol Hill daily when Congress was in session. She obtained interviews with Representatives, Senators, and government officials, talked to assistants and aides, and spent time in the press gallery picking up news leads. Then she would discuss the information she had gathered with the head of the CBS news department, who would decide what to use on network programs emanating from Washington. On friendly terms with many Congressmen, Miss Hanschman has proved so adept in persuading them to give her personal interviews or to appear on her radio and television programs that she is sometimes called "CBS's secret weapon." Even while attending the cocktail parties and dinners that abound in Washington, D.C. she cannot resist picking up interesting news items. "My social life always seems to revolve around business," she has said.

Miss Hanschman maintains contacts with politicians of both major parties. The Republicans she has interviewed include Senator Kenneth B. Keating of New York, Senator Margaret

Harris & Ewing
NANCY HANSCHMAN

Chase Smith of Maine, Senator Everett M. Dirksen of Illinois, former Senator H. Alexander Smith of New Jersey, Representative Leslie C. Arends of Illinois, and Representative Joseph W. Martin, Jr., of Massachusetts, who made his first television appearance as a result of Miss Hanschman's arts of persuasion.

On the Democratic side of the fence she is acquainted with President John F. Kennedy (whom she first met when he was a Senator), Vice-President Lyndon B. Johnson (whom she first knew as Senate Majority Leader), Senator John J. Sparkman of Alabama, Senator Hubert H. Humphrey of Minnesota, Senator Stuart Symington of Missouri, and others. A *TV Guide* writer reported in June 1960 that Miss Hanschman often turned for the liberal point of view on current issues to Senator Humphrey, sounded out the middle-of-the-road position with Senator Symington, and listened to the conservative viewpoint from a favorite contact, the Republican Senator Carl T. Curtis of Nebraska. As a producer Miss Hanschman scheduled appearances on CBS news programs for every leading contender for the Presidential nomination in 1960.

Her producer's role permitted Miss Hanschman to emerge from behind the scenes occasionally to appear on programs, but this did not satisfy her. She admired veteran newsmen like Edward R. Murrow and Eric Sevareid, and she had long hoped to become a full-fledged news correspondent herself. But although the American Broadcasting Company and the National Broadcasting Company already employed women correspondents, the CBS news staff was exclusively male.

In the summer of 1959 Miss Hanschman visited Germany, largely on her own vacation time, to do a story on the peacetime activities of the Women's Army Corps. So well was the coverage done that John Day, vice-president for news at CBS, used the reports on Blair Clark's radio show, *The World Tonight.* Other reports that

HANSCHMAN, NANCY—*Continued*

she prepared were used on CBS broadcasts. Some months later, in January 1960, she obtained an exclusive filmed interview with Sam Rayburn, then Speaker of the House, which was used on Douglas Edwards' news program.

CBS News executives remembered Miss Hanschman's first-class reporting when they decided to expand their staff in preparation for the approaching Presidential conventions, campaigns, and election. On February 22, 1960 Nancy Hanschman became the first woman correspondent of CBS News. One of her first assignments was to cover the Democratic candidates' declarations for office; another was to report on the Senate civil rights filibuster, which began on February 29 and set a record for long nonstop sessions.

During the spring of 1960 Nancy Hanschman accompanied Senator Hubert H. Humphrey, a candidate for the Democratic Presidential nomination, on his campaign tour through West Virginia, often setting up his appointments or making arrangements for him. (The Senator lost the West Virginia primary election to John F. Kennedy in May 1960 and withdrew his candidacy.) She also followed Vice-President (then Senator) Lyndon B. Johnson on a campaign tour through eight states. With several other correspondents Miss Hanschman was assigned to cover the Democratic national convention held in July 1960 at Los Angeles. Armed with a walkie-talkie, she spent long hours on the convention floor, trailing her special assignment, Lyndon B. Johnson, and picking up spot interviews with other politicians.

Since November 28, 1960 Miss Hanschman has broadcast her own weekday five-minute show, *One Woman's Washington*, over CBS radio, on which she presents personalities and discusses events in the nation's capital of special interest to women. The program may cover a fashion show or an embassy reception or present an interview with a visiting diplomat, a government official, or the wife of a Congressman. In general it is an attempt "to put serious government issues in human perspective." By reading four daily newspapers and several magazines, Miss Hanschman keeps abreast of current events and opinion.

Long before she went on the air Miss Hanschman had groomed herself for the role of newscaster on radio and television by watching other women on television and taking speech and drama classes at the Catholic University of America in Washington, D.C. Since women's voices tend to rise, particularly under stress, she makes a special effort to keep her voice low and relaxed. "A small, high voice commenting on the news doesn't sound very important," she has explained. That she has succeeded in attaining on-the-air poise is evident from the invitations that she has received to lecture to Congressional wives and other Washington women on how to talk and comport themselves on television.

Although she does not try to disguise her attractive appearance and pleasant personality, Miss Hanschman would prefer to be admired for the quality of her journalism rather than for her looks or for the fact that she is a woman working in a predominantly masculine profession.

Insofar as she is a member of the working press, she rejects any move that would single out women journalists from their male counterparts. "Women have had a difficult time getting into the profession but they're in there now, in greater number and variety than ever," she has said. "The days of Nelly Bly and Dorothy Dix are over. Women work in journalism according to their general training and ability and not according to their knowledge of the relatively narrow area of women's interests."

Newswomen admittedly do encounter occasional obstacles in their work. For instance, when Premier Nikita S. Khrushchev of the Soviet Union addressed the all-male National Press Club in September 1959, the women had to insist on their rights as journalists to gain admittance. (Women have their own press association.) A stereotype that Miss Hanschman particularly dislikes is one that ridicules women for taking hours to dress. She can be completely ready to go out in about fifteen minutes, if necessary, and she keeps a bag packed in readiness for calls to urgent news breaks.

Clothes are Nancy Hanschman's hobby, and she is noted for her simple but stylish appearance. "If I have to choose between style and comfort," she once said, "style usually wins." Miss Hanschman has green eyes and brown hair. On February 24, 1962 she was married to C. Wyatt Dickerson, Jr., of Leesburg, Virginia. A second vice-president of the Women's National Press Club, she is a member of the American Newspaper Women's Club, the Radio-Television Correspondents Association, and the American Women in Radio and Television group. Her career in Washington, D.C. puts Nancy Hanschman in the thick of the political life of the nation, and she revels in it. "I've always been charmed by political maneuvering," she explains. "It amuses me—it delights me."

References

Cosmopolitan 144:56+ My '58 por
Good Housekeeping p31+ Ag '60 por
TV Guide p5+ Je 11 '60 por

HARTIGAN, GRACE Mar. 28, 1922- Artist
Address: 112 S. Calvert St., Baltimore 2, Md.

The most celebrated woman painter in the United States today, Grace Hartigan is a leading member of the New York School of abstract expressionists. She produces approximately one major painting a month and often sells a work before the oil is dry. A self-taught painter in the formal sense, Miss Hartigan has had more than ten one-man shows since her career began in 1949. Her work is represented in the permanent collections of the nation's outstanding galleries and museums and has been displayed in major exhibitions throughout the world.

Of Irish and English ancestry, Grace Hartigan was born in Newark, New Jersey on March 28, 1922 to Matthew A. and Grace (Orvis) Hartigan. Her father is a certified public accountant; her mother, a real estate agent, is a member of the Daughters of the American Revolution. She has two sisters, Barbara Sesee and Virginia von Spreckelsen, who are housewives, and one brother, Arthur M. Hartigan, an industrial engineer. She has said that she is the only member of her family involved in any kind of creative activity. For the first seven years of her life she lived in Bayonne, New Jersey, where she spent much of her time with her paternal grandmother, who told her stories and sang old English and Welsh ballads.

At the age of five Grace Hartigan contracted pneumonia and, confined to bed for more than a year, taught herself to read and draw. For the benefit of her health her family moved from industrial Bayonne to more rustic and elevated Millburn nearby in 1929. There she attended the local schools and was active in dramatics at the Millburn High School, from which she graduated in 1940. One of the strongest influences of her adolescent years was an understanding teacher of English, who recognized Miss Hartigan's imagination and sensitivity and helped to develop her curiosity and consciousness, although she was still unaware that this would eventually find an outlet in painting.

After graduating from high school Miss Hartigan worked for a time as a draftsman in an airplane engine factory in Newark, New Jersey, while attending evening drawing classes. She recalls that her early efforts at painting during this period showed "absolutely no talent." Moving to New York City, she held various jobs, including editing market research reports, running the night desk of a travel bureau, and fashion modeling. She drew her inspiration for her painting from New York's colorful East Side, working and living in a studio that formerly housed a sweatshop. She has said that her teacher, Isaac Lane Muse, "who valued creative imagination and feeling above skill," provided her with the courage to persist as an amateur.

"It was not until 1949 that any of my paintings began to give me hope of eventually reaching a full expression," Miss Hartigan recalls. After a year of painting in San Miguel de Allende, Mexico, she returned to the East and met a group of younger artists in New York's Greenwich Village, among them Albert Leslie and Robert Goodnough. With them she organized a show of works by new painters. Two artist-critics, Meyer Shapiro and Clement Greenberg, who were selecting for an exhibition called *Talent—1950*, chose one of the canvases painted by Miss Hartigan in Mexico. The exhibition attracted wide public attention in New York's Kootz Gallery.

In 1951 the newly established Tibor de Nagy Gallery in New York opened its first one-man show featuring Miss Hartigan's works. The show was well attended by art patrons and her success at the exhibition inaugurated her steady rise to prominence. She continued to exhibit in one-man shows at the gallery in the years to follow and was described by the art critic James Thrall Soby as one of the "most personal and talented artists of her generation" (*Saturday Review*, October 5, 1957). From 1950 to 1953 the name George Hartigan appeared on the artist's canvases. "I had a shyness and lack of confidence which made me hope I could dissociate the 'person' from the 'work,'" Miss Hartigan has revealed. "As my belief in myself and my painting grew it became unnecessary to continue with a mask."

Walter Silver

GRACE HARTIGAN

Feeling no particular affiliation with any groups or movements in art, Miss Hartigan speaks of having "learned from Jackson Pollock's passionately creative personality and also from . . . de Kooning's quieter and more coherent theories." She recalls that she wanted to paint out her own art history and that she eventually won her own freedom. Concentrating first on the Spanish masters and studying, in depth, such painters as Velásquez, Zurbarán, and Goya, she was, in some measure, reappraising the virtues of the art of the past. Subsequently she passed through several other periods of technical training including the "pure abstract." A writer for *Time* magazine, referring to her later creative efforts, noted that Miss Hartigan's colors are "pounded into every available space, her strokes seem committed out of rage; the effect is one of extraordinary power" (May 2, 1960). Another critic maintained that her painting appears to "venture frankly and deliberately into utter chaos."

In 1953 the Museum of Modern Art in New York City acquired *Persian Jacket* by Grace Hartigan for its permanent collection. With this acquisition, Miss Hartigan attained a reputation as one of the more important American artists of the "advanced tendency." In the same year the Artist's Theater in New York commissioned her to design the sets for a production of *Red Riding Hood* by Kenneth Koch. A one-man show in the Vassar College Art Gallery followed in 1954. A year later her work was exhibited in *Rising Talent*, an exhibition of contemporary American art at the University of Minnesota.

Unexpectedly, after having painted abstractly for years, Miss Hartigan relinquished the bond with her former colleagues in abstraction and began painting recognizable figures evolving "a more overtly emotional kind of art." Characteristic of this new painting was *Grand Street Bride*, depicting a New York store window "where wedding gowns are on display in a strange

HARTIGAN, GRACE—Continued

rivalry of ugliness and hope." Since 1956 Miss Hartigan's work has been widely represented in exhibitions in the United States and abroad. In the exhibition entitled Modern Art in the United States; Selections from the Collections of the Museum of Modern Art her paintings were viewed in New York and European cities in 1955-56. Twelve Americans, a collection including her works, shown at the Museum of Modern Art in New York in 1956, also attracted considerable attention. Other exhibitions in which Miss Hartigan's paintings have been displayed include Artists of the New York School, Second Generation, Jewish Museum (1957); Fourth International Art Exhibition, Japan (1957); Third International Contemporary Art Exhibition, India (1957); IV Bienal, São Paulo, Brazil (1957); The New American Painting, shown in eight European cities and New York (1958-59); and Contemporary American Art at the World's Fair in Brussels (1958). Her works were also featured in Art USA, New York Coliseum (1959); in an exhibition in Kassel, Germany (1959); Contemporary American Painting, Columbus Gallery of Fine Arts, Columbus, Ohio (1960); Sixty American Painters, Walker Art Center, Minneapolis (1960); The Face of the Fifties, University of Michigan Art Museum (1961); and Abstract Expressionists and Imagists, Guggenheim Museum, New York (1961). The United States Information Agency included her work in its exhibition American Vanguard, which was shown in Austria, Yugoslavia, and England in 1961-62.

Grace Hartigan's works are exhibited in the permanent collections of the Museum of Modern art, Miss Hartigan merits her reputation as a truly American painter. She has expressed a "pioneering faith that Americans will someday recognize what its most powerful artists are doing." Showing a compassion for what she described to and the William Rockhill Nelson Gallery of Art in Kansas City. Her paintings are also on display at the Carnegie Institute Museum in Pittsburgh, the Vassar College Art Gallery, the Washington Gallery of Modern Art, the Minneapolis Museum, and Washington University in St. Louis.

Deeply involved with America and American art, Miss Hartigan merits her reputation as a truly American painter. She has expressed a "pioneering faith that Americans will someday recognize what its most powerful artists are doing." Showing a compassion for what she described to Marvin D. Schwartz in Apollo (September 1959) as that which is "vulgar and vital in modern American life," Miss Hartigan has a deep attachment to America that stems from her feeling that "the United States is the only country that lives in the present." After a trip to Europe Miss Hartigan returned with an even stronger conviction that New York was for her "the center of modern painting," and said, "I couldn't work in Europe."

Working mainly in oils, Grace Hartigan is noted for her brilliantly bold pictorial expressions of the everyday American scene. She uses slashing strokes and strident color to depict the garish jumble and excitement of her subjects—billboards, signs, the busy market districts of New York, traffic lights, or the blazing sun of the American Midwest in August—executing her canvases to "capture the quivering moment that is now." The sense of immediacy with which she works is reflected in Montauk Highway, one of a group of works she painted one summer on Long Island. The canvas, suggestive of racing motion, captures, in a sense, the American landscape as viewed while passing in a speeding car.

The artist's imaginative talents have turned, from time to time, to collages, craypas (a mixture of crayon and pastel), and other media. Her other artistic activities include the illustration of "Salute" by James Schuyler in Silk Screen Paints for Four Volume Poetry (1961), and representation in a portfolio of lithographs, scheduled for publication in 1963. A chapter on her work, by Emily Dennis, is included in Bernard Harper Friedman's collection of essays, School of New York: Some Younger Artists (Grove, 1959). In 1957 Miss Hartigan received the Mademoiselle Magazine Merit Award for Art.

Grace Hartigan was first married, in 1941, to Robert L. Jachens, and she has one son, Jeffrey A. Jachens. The marriage ended in divorce in 1947. Her second marriage, to the artist Harry Jackson, lasted eighteen months. On December 24, 1960 she was married to Dr. Winston H. Price. Miss Hartigan is five feet eight inches tall, weighs 135 pounds, and has brown hair and blue eyes. Aside from painting, her favorite recreations are gardening and reading.

Intensely absorbed in her work, Grace Hartigan admits that when she is working on a painting she does not leave it until it is finished. When a painting stops haunting her, she has said, then she can finally lift her brush from the canvas knowing she is free of it and that she is finally finished. Having completed a work, she feels that for a few moments she has "captured life, held it in [her] hands for a little while." She adds: "Other people, those who don't create, must feel that life has all gone by."

References

Look 24:72 S 27 '60 por
Newsweek 53:113 My 11 '59 por
Sat R 40:26+ O 5 '57 por
Washington (D.C.) Post Ap3, Ja 18 '60 por; Ep7 Ja 24 '60
Who's Who of American Women (1961-62)

HAYAKAWA, SESSUE (hä-yǎ-kä'-wǎ) June 10, 1890- Actor

Address: c/o Actors Equity Assn., 226 W. 47th St., New York 36

The Japanese-born character actor Sessue Hayakawa has had a successful acting career that dates back to the early days of the silent movies, when he shared the glory of such bright lights of the silent screen as Douglas Fairbanks, Mary Pickford, and Francis X. Bushman. Since making his debut in the 1914 Hollywood production of Typhoon Hayakawa has appeared in more than 130 films in the United States, Japan, England, and France, and he has given numerous stage performances. An ordained Zen Buddhist priest, Hayakawa believes that the concentration and discipline of Zen have greatly aided him in his acting. In his autobiography Zen Showed

Me the Way (Bobbs, 1960) he wrote: "Through Zen I am able to empty my mind of all thoughts that may hinder my performance."

Kintaro Hayakawa (he later changed his first name to Sessue) was born on June 10, 1890 in the Nanaura township of Chiba province, on Honshu, the largest of the four main islands comprising Japan. He was the youngest of five children of an aristocratic family that has been traced back some 2,600 years, "into the mists of time." His mother's name was Kane. His father, Yoichiro Hayakawa, who was the governor of Chiba province, brought up his sons according to samurai ideals under the strict warrior code known as Bushido. Although he was born in comfortable circumstances, "Kimbo" Hayakawa was assigned to perform menial domestic tasks during his childhood. "I let you clean the lamps because I do not want you to grow up a soft man of a rich family," his father told him. "I let you wipe ceilings because I think you might grow taller, and your chest become broader."

Slated for a career as a naval officer, Hayakawa entered the Navy Preparatory School in Tokyo, where he was active in judo and *kendo* (the Japanese art of fencing). During the Russo-Japanese War of 1904-5 he shared with his schoolmates the enthusiasm for the Japanese victories. After graduating from the preparatory school in June 1908 he was accepted by the Naval Academy in Etajima. During that summer he ruptured an eardrum while diving; the untreated infection that followed caused him to become seriously ill and resulted in his dismissal from the academy a few months later. The shame of being disqualified from a naval career prompted Hayakawa to attempt to commit hara-kiri, but he fainted after stabbing himself at least thirty times and hovered near death for weeks.

Upon his recovery Hayakawa spent some time in solitude at an abandoned temple on a mountainside, where he practised meditation and sought to master the principles of Zen Buddhism under the tutelage of Eichi, a Zen priest. His period of solitude ended in May 1909, when he aided in the rescue of passengers from an American ship that had foundered on rocks in Tokyo bay. The contact with Americans inspired in him the ambition to visit the United States. Although his father at first opposed his plans, he subsequently permitted him to go to America to study political science at the University of Chicago. If, at the university, Hayakawa did not distinguish himself as a scholar, he did so as an athlete, and during his second year he became a member of the football team. His use of judo body techniques overcame the handicap of his small stature, until it led to his expulsion from the team for excessive foul penalties. To supplement the allowance he received from home he worked as an iceman in his free time and during summer vacations.

After his graduation in 1913, Hayakawa was on his way back to Japan for a career in politics when he stopped overnight in Los Angeles. Upon seeing a poor production at the Japanese Theatre in the Little Tokyo section of the city he boasted to the manager that he could do better. Given a chance to try, he changed his first name to Sessue and began to act and direct regularly in the Japanese Theatre. In 1914 Hayakawa's produc-

SESSUE HAYAKAWA

tion of an English adaptation of Melchior Lengyel's play *Typhoon* came to the attention of the motion picture producer and director Thomas H. Ince, who decided to film the play with Hayakawa in the lead, as a change from his usual repertory of Western thrillers. The successful *Typhoon* was followed by a second movie with Ince, *The Wrath of the Gods*.

In 1915 Hayakawa signed with the Jesse Lasky Feature Play Company, an affiliate of Paramount Pictures Corporation. After starring with Fannie Ward in the 1916 production of *The Cheat*, directed by Cecil B. De Mille, his motion picture career was firmly established. He appeared in *Alien Souls*, *The Victorian Cross*, and *The Clue* in 1916; in *The Bottle Imp*, *Each to His Kind*, *The Jaguar's Claws*, *Forbidden Paths*, *His Honorable Friend*, *Hashimura Togo*, *The City of Dim Faces*, and *The Soul of Kura san* in 1917; and in *The Secret Game*, *The Honor of His House*, *The Call of the East*, *Hidden Pearls*, and *The Bravest Way* in 1918. Hayakawa has said of his early film career: "Public acceptance of me in romantic roles was a blow of sorts against racial intolerance, even though I lost the girl in the last reel."

Aided by a $1,000,000 loan from the parents of a college friend, in March 1918 Hayakawa formed his own company, the Haworth Pictures Corporation, which produced twenty-three films in four years. By 1920, when the company merged with Roberts & Cole, Hayakawa had repaid the loan and netted over $2,000,000 of his own. In 1921, while working on the picture *The Swamp*, he became desperately ill as a result of a burst appendix; he attributes his recovery to the practice of Zen Buddhism. Shortly thereafter he went to the White House in Washington, D.C., where he was received by President Warren G. Harding.

During his period of prosperity, when he was making as much as $7,500 a week, Hayakawa and his wife lived in a three-story mansion on

HAYAKAWA, SESSUE—*Continued*

Argyle Avenue and Franklin Street in Hollywood. Their dinner parties and Prohibition "tea parties," attended by hundreds of guests and costing thousands of dollars, became a Hollywood legend and earned their home the nickname of Argyle Castle. Hayakawa later gave the home to Jewish friends who converted it into a synagogue, and it was ultimately torn down to make room for a Hollywood freeway. Hayakawa left Hollywood in March 1922 after a motion picture executive, who stood to gain in insurance money by his death, had allegedly made an attempt on Hayakawa's life during the filming of *The Vermilion Pencil.*

Following a visit to Japan, Hayakawa toured several cities with Fred de Gresac's play *Tiger Lily,* which never reached New York. In early 1923 he went to France to appear in *La Bataille,* a film about the Russo-Japanese War; it was later shown in the United States under the title *The Danger Line.* In December 1923 Hayakawa appeared in a command performance before the King and Queen of England, in Sir William Archer's play *The Samurai,* which he later took on a tour of England. In England he made two films. Returning to France he filmed *J'ai Tué* and appeared in vaudeville at the Casino de Paris. While on vacation in Europe he lost about $965,000 in one night at the gambling casino in Monte Carlo—a loss that left him unperturbed despite newspaper reports that he had committed suicide.

In January 1926 Hayakawa returned to the United States to appear in Lee Shubert's production of Hans Bachwitz's play *The Love City.* He also appeared in a vaudeville production of his own sketch based on his novel *The Bandit Prince* (Macaulay, 1926). In 1927 he founded a Zen study hall in New York and, with the aid of Sasaki, a Zen priest, established a serious study group that flourished for several years. Hayakawa's first talking picture, *Daughter of the Dragon,* was released by Paramount in 1931. In the same year he returned to Tokyo where he appeared in his own stage production of *The Honorable Mr. Wong,* which ran for six years. In 1932 he went on a lecture tour of the Far East, emphasizing the necessity for peace, and winning the enmity of the military party of Japan. Subsequently he made a few Japanese films, and in 1934 he appeared in the role of Claudius in a production of *Hamlet* at the Meiji Theater in Tokyo.

In 1937 Hayakawa went to Paris to appear in the film *Yoshiwara* for Pathé Studios. He remained in France to co-star with Erich Von Stroheim in *Macao,* released by the Demofilm company in 1939. After the outbreak of World War II Hayakawa's sympathy with the West and his family connections with the party opposed to the warlords made it impossible for him to return to Japan. Rejecting efforts of the German occupation forces to win him over to a policy of collaboration, he lived quietly in Paris during most of the war and later moved to the south of France, where he was friendly with the French underground. To make a living he sold watercolors that he painted on silk.

Although he was glad to see the war end, Hayakawa regarded the atom bombing of Hiroshima and Nagasaki as futile and inhuman. After the war he appeared in several more French films, and in 1947 he was a judge at the International Film Festival in Venice. Following clearance by the United States authorities he returned to Hollywood in January 1949, having received an invitation from Humphrey Bogart to take a role in *Tokyo Joe* (Columbia, 1949). He next appeared as the head of a prisoner-of-war camp in *Three Came Home* (Twentieth Century-Fox, 1950), starring Claudette Colbert.

Returning to Tokyo in late 1949, Hayakawa was reunited with his family after a separation of about twelve years, and he renewed his formal association with Zen masters. To restore, in some measure, the religiosity and morality lost during the war, he produced the play *The Life of the Buddha,* which he had written ten years earlier. It proved an artistic success but a financial failure. As a result of his work in behalf of Zen, Hayakawa was chosen as a candidate for the Zen Buddhist priesthood. Passing an examination by the *koan*—the Zen question, which can only be answered intuitively, rather than rationally—he was deemed worthy by a court of six priests and was ordained in the traditional Zen Buddhist ceremony.

Hayakawa's peaceful life in Japan was interrupted in 1956 by another invitation from Hollywood, this time to play the role of Colonel Saito in the screen version of Pierre Boulle's novel, *The Bridge Over the River Kwai* (Vanguard, 1954). At first he was reluctant to accept the role, but at his wife's insistence he read the script several times, each time becoming more aware of the film's possibilities. "From the conflict of two men—Nicholson, the English colonel, and Saito, the Japanese colonel—stems all the power and the compelling emotional impact, the irony, anguish and pathos, the symbolization of the futility of war and the ridiculousness of what men fight for—the whole tragic human comedy encompassed by the film," Hayakawa wrote in *Zen Showed Me the Way.* "With this image burning in my mind, I accepted the role of Colonel Saito."

Zen Buddhism enabled Hayakawa to achieve oneness with Colonel Saito. Filmed in Ceylon, the CinemaScope production of *The Bridge on the River Kwai* took fourteen months to complete, at a cost of about $3,000,000. When it was released by Columbia Pictures Corporation in December 1957 it was universally acclaimed by the critics. For his performance Hayakawa was presented the Golden Globe Award of the Hollywood Foreign Press Association, and he was nominated for the Oscar award of the Academy of Motion Picture Arts and Sciences, for the best supporting actor.

Of lesser significance were Hayakawa's performances in the Jerry Lewis comedy *Geisha Boy* (Paramount, 1958), and in the screen adaptation of W. H. Hudson's novel *Green Mansions* (MGM, 1959), in which he appeared as an Indian chief. In recent years Hayakawa has appeared in several stage and television productions in the United States. On March 12, 1958 he starred in the television version of Shimon Wincelberg's two-man play *Kataki,* presented on the *Kraft Television Theater* (NBC-TV) under the title *The Sea Is Boiling Hot.* The play deals with an American airman and a Japanese soldier stranded on a Pacific island. The stage production of *Kataki* opened at the Ambassador Theater in New York City on April 9, 1959 with Hayakawa and Ben Piazza in the two roles. Although Richard Watts, Jr., of the New York *Post* (April 19, 1959) described Hayakawa's performance as "nothing short of magnificent," the play closed after twenty performances.

On May 1, 1914 Sessue Hayakawa married the motion picture actress Tsuru Aoki at the Zen temple in the Little Tokyo section of Los Angeles. Mrs. Hayakawa died in Tokyo on October 18, 1961. Hayakawa has one son, Yukio, an industrial engineer, and two daughters, Yoshiko, a member of Japan's modern theater, and Fujiko, a ballet dancer. A meticulous dresser, Hayakawa looks like a man in his forties, and he still engages in athletics. He smokes cigars and likes lavish living, although his Zen Buddhism has made him largely indifferent to material success. He has taught himself to speak French, Spanish, German, Chinese, East Indian, and Malay, and he retains a slight Oriental accent when he speaks English. He owns a dramatic school in Tokyo, where students are first given intensive religious training before they are taught acting.

In an interview with Sidney Skolsky of the New York *Post* (October 19, 1958) Hayakawa said: "Today in maturity nothing annoys me. I pity the man who tries to hurt me. Never am I angered. I feel only pity." In his autobiographical *Zen Showed Me the Way* he wrote: "Destiny has brought me much. She has been kind. But it has been left to me to fashion the acumen of deeds in the pattern destiny has drawn, to solve the great *koan* of life for myself."

References

Coronet 50:146+ My '61 pors
Los Angeles Times V p1+ D 22 '57 por
N Y Herald Tribune IV p1+ Ap 5 '59 por
N Y Post Mag p3 O 19 '58 por
N Y Times II p13 Mr 9 '58 pors

Hayakawa, Sessue. Zen Showed Me the Way (1960)

KIRK, RUSSELL (AMOS) Oct. 19, 1918-
Author; lecturer; educator; philosopher
Address: h. Mecosta, Mich.

Since the publication of his *The Conservative Mind* in 1953, Russell Kirk has come to be widely regarded as the chief philosopher of the new American conservatism. The conservatives with whom Kirk identifies himself are those whom he has described as "resolved that all the intricate fabric of the civil social order, woven by the spirit of religion and the spirit of a gentleman, shall not be destroyed by the appetites of our present unruly generation." Secondary to writing as an instrument in Kirk's defense of "the moral and social heritage of the ages" has been teaching. He has taught at Michigan State College and at the New School for Social Research, and since 1956 he has been research professor of politics at C. W. Post College of Long Island University. He spends much of his

RUSSELL KIRK

time on lecture tours throughout the United States.

Descended from Scottish farmers on his father's side and from New England Puritans on his mother's, Russell Amos Kirk was born in Plymouth, Michigan on October 19, 1918. From his earliest years he shared the antipathy for technological civilization of his father, Russell Andrew Kirk, a railroad engineer, who looked back to the land with nostalgia. The greatest influences on his youth, however, were his mother, Marjorie Rachel (Pierce) Kirk, a tender, romantic woman who early fed his imagination with readings from Grimm, Lewis Carroll, Scott, Hawthorne, Stevenson, and the Round Table legends; and his maternal grandfather, Frank Pierce, a well-read man with whom young Kirk delighted to converse on long walks. Kirk has a sister, Carolyn, now Mrs. Richard Pierce, residing in Teheran, Iran.

Although Kirk begrudged the hours that elementary school in Plymouth took from his reading and family talk, he was later grateful to have at least suffered them before "the deluge of Deweyism." At Plymouth High School he participated in debate and oratory, and was class poet at his graduation, but shunned social activities, which bored him. His recreation was walking and his passion was reading—Prescott, Gibbon, Macaulay, H. G. Wells, "and all the novelists." Although he had been reared in the Christian tradition, he came to espouse a mechanistic atheism during his high school years. (The Christianity of his parents was non-institutional, but having, as Kirk has described it, no doubt "of an Omniscience governing this world, or of a morality ordained by that Power, or of an immortality that was His gift.")

Graduating from high school in 1936, Kirk entered Michigan State College at East Lansing on an alumni scholarship in the fall of that year. Devoted to the classical disciplines, which he saw as teaching a man to form his own opin-

KIRK, RUSSELL—Continued

ions and to respect those of past thinkers, Kirk felt hostile toward college aims that he considered conformist, utilitarian, and barely tolerant of humane learning. Nor did he share the rabid anti-unionism of his fellow students. "Unlike most students in the great city universities or the Eastern colleges during the thirties, then," he has written, "I found myself (though a Tory, or at least an Old Whig, by instinct) almost an advanced thinker in the midst of folk convinced that whatever is, is right." He was on the debating team at Michigan State and won prizes in oratory and extemporaneous speaking as well as in writing. He lived frugally, so that none of the time he lavished on wide-ranging extracurricular reading would be sacrificed to economic demands.

In his third year at Michigan State Kirk moved out of his solitude into a small circle of student-friends, and he came to know some of the professors of literature and history intimately. One of the professors encouraged him in his writing, and while still a student he published articles in *College English* and other scholarly journals. He took his B.A. degree in history in 1940. While in college he had changed his religious point of view to Stoicism.

At Duke University, Durham, North Carolina, Kirk worked for his M.A. on scholarship in 1940 and 1941, taking the degree in the latter year. His master's thesis was a study of the political thought of John Randolph of Roanoke, anti-egalitarian republican who served in Congress from 1799 to 1829. When the study was published as a book—*Randolph of Roanoke; A Study in Conservative Thought* (Univ. of Chicago Press, 1951)—it received more praise than Kirk himself thought it deserved—praise such as that accorded it by Samuel Flagg Bemis in the *Yale Review* (Winter 1952): "Never has an historian of politics done a better job of this kind." The writing of Randolph had an influence on Kirk's thought and style, but not as great an influence as that of Edmund Burke was to become.

For a few months after finishing his studies at Duke, Kirk worked in the River Rouge plant of the Ford Motor Company. Inducted into the United States Army in the summer of 1942, he became a technician, third grade, in the Chemical Warfare Service. Three of his four years in the army were spent in the Great Salt Lake Desert, in experiments with biological weapons and incendiary bombs. Desert meditations moved him from Stoicism to a reconsideration of his religious position. "If I was now scarcely better than a skeptic, still that was a far cry from the positivism of my teens," he has written. He became aware that his affinity was not, as he had thought, with the Enlightenment, but with the Middle Ages. "Mine . . . was a Gothic mind. . . . I was groping for faith, honor, and prescriptive loyalties. . . . The men of the Enlightenment had cold hearts and smug heads; now their successors were in the process of imposing a dreary uniformity upon all the world, with Efficiency and Progress and Equality for their watchwords—abstractions preferred to all those fascinating and lovable peculiarities of human nature and human society which are the products of prescription and tradition."

Shortly after his discharge from the army in 1946, Kirk accepted the post of assistant professor in the history of civilization at Michigan State College. In 1948, without relinquishing the Michigan State post, he went to St. Andrews, Scotland to write a book on the heritage of conservative thought in Britain and America. The completed book fulfilled the dissertation requirement for his doctor of letters degree, which St. Andrews University bestowed on him in 1952. His book was published in 1953 by the Henry Regnery Company under the title *The Conservative Mind; From Burke to Santayana.*

Kirk distilled the consensus of the various thinkers covered in the history into six principles: a divine intent rules society, and political problems are basically religious and moral problems; radical egalitarianism is a drab choice beside varied tradition; civilized society needs orders and classes; freedom and property are inseparably connected; social prescription is a salutary check on man's anarchic impulse; and constructive social change is largely the slow work of providence. August Heckscher found the book "carefully wrought and honestly made" and "a revealing guide to anyone who wants to read for himself in the original texts" (New York *Herald Tribune Book Review,* August 2, 1953). The assessment was fairly typical of the critical response generally. Even politically antipathetic reviewers treated *The Conservative Mind* as a book deserving serious attention.

In *A Program for Conservatives* (Regnery, 1954) Kirk focused on the contemporary scene and the place of conservatives in it. "It seemed to bewilder a good many people," Kirk wrote of the book later, "for the program I commended was not a neat system of positive law, but a change of heart, by which order and justice and freedom may live through these dark days, and the past may be blended with the present."

A Program for Conservatives bypassed individualistic capitalism as well as socialism in recommending Christian philosophy to the mind and the restoration of community (through family, church, profession, local government, and neighborhood) to the heart. "American Conservatives ought to talk a great deal less about the laws of economics and a great deal more about the laws of justice," Kirk wrote. Lawrence Fertig, professing shock at "this cavalier treatment of private capitalism as a basis for conservative philosophy," detected "a vague mystique about Dr. Kirk's philosophy which at times talks like the language of a new-day liberal" (New York *World-Telegram and Sun,* December 27, 1954). In the New York *Times Book Review* (November 21, 1954), Raymond English wrote, "One cannot help feeling that Mr. Kirk is a gloomy and learned diagnostician rather than a physician for our ills, but his diagnosis is one we cannot afford to neglect."

In 1953 Kirk left Michigan State College. He was not pleased with what he had found in "the Petrified Forest of Academe" and noted with some misgivings the majority of students who "resent the presence of the minority who read books," as well as the administrators "who have not read Newman, nor anyone else worth reading, and do not intend to." He observed that these administrators "pander to the silliest impulses in state legislatures and associations of alumni," and that they "would establish colleges of necromancy if they thought anyone would enroll." Kirk was also highly critical of the professors who "are bullied by educationists of John Dewey's school who verge on feeble-mindedness, . . . professors who decline to profess anything." "Professors and priests," he wrote in the same context, "are meant to be the conservators of mankind, . . . reminding us that we are not the flies of a summer. . . . I resolved to do what I could . . . to restore this sense of . . . conservative function."

In addition to many articles on the subject of higher education, Kirk published *Academic Freedom; An Essay in Definition* (Regnery, 1955), in which he attacked, among others, "the doctrinaire secularists and doctrinaire levelers in our colleges and universities" and set forth the truths to which he believes the Academy should be dedicated. Roswell G. Ham, president of Mount Holyoke College, called it "a brilliant and exciting study" (New York *Times Book Review*, March 20, 1955). Kirk's book *St. Andrews*, published in 1954 in Batsford's British Cities and Towns series, is a history and description of that Scottish university town.

Beyond the Dreams of Avarice (Regnery, 1956) is a varied collection of Kirk's essays in social criticism. His *The Death of Art* was published as a special supplement to a translation of Ilya Ehrenburg's novel *The Thaw* (Regnery, 1955). In 1957 Regnery published his *The American Cause* and the Devin-Adair Company published his *The Intelligent Woman's Guide to Conservatism*. Kirk's first novel, *Old House of Fear* (Fleet, 1961) is a Gothic romance with political overtones. A collection of his essays about education and a volume of his short stories are scheduled for publication in 1962. Kirk has contributed essays to anthologies and has written introductions to several books.

Kirk writes a monthly column on education, "From the Academy," for *National Review*. Founder of the critical quarterly *Modern Age: A Conservative Review*, he was its editor from 1957 to 1959. Since 1960 he has been editor of *The University Bookman*. In 1962 he began writing a syndicated column for General Features Corporation, appearing five days a week in some thirty newspapers in the United States. In this column, which is entitled *To the Point*, he comments informally on virtually all aspects of life. He frequently contributes articles to *Kenyon Review, Sewanee Review, Yale Review, Fortune,* New York *Times Magazine, The Critic, Southwest Review, America, Commonweal, Catholic World, Church Quarterly Review, Queens Quarterly,* and other publications.

Since 1956 Kirk has been research professor of politics at C.W. Post College of Long Island University. This is a part-time occupation, involving the conducting of one eight- to ten-week seminar a year. He was a member of the faculty of politics of the New School for Social Research in New York City from 1958 to 1960, and in 1954 he was Daly lecturer at the University of Detroit. He delivered some 200 lectures in various parts of the United States in 1961, and he has been the principal speaker at several university commencements.

Kirk's concern for educational standards has led him to participate in state and national educational group activities. Since 1960 he has been president of the Educational Reviewer, Inc., an educational foundation with headquarters in New York City. He is a member of the National Trust for Historic Preservation, the English Association (London), St. Andrews Preservation Trust, the Mississippi Valley Historical Association, the American Catholic Historical Association, the Samuel Johnson Society, and the Foundation for Religious Action. He has received honorary Litt.D. degrees, from Boston College in 1955, and from St. John's University, Jamaica, Long Island, in 1957. Park College, in Parkville, Missouri conferred upon him an honorary LL.D. degree in 1960. He was a senior Fellow of the American Council of Learned Societies in 1950-52 and a Guggenheim Fellow in 1954-55.

Russell Kirk is five feet six and one-half inches tall, weighs 170 pounds, and has brown hair and green eyes. Politically he considers himself an "eccentric" Republican, and he has participated in local and national Republican politics. He has no formal church affiliation and describes his religious position as that of a "pre-Reformation Christian." A bachelor, he shares with a maiden great-aunt a house in the village of Mecosta, Michigan that had been built by his great-grandfather, Amos Johnson. He is a justice of the peace in Mecosta County. He smokes cigars, favoring those imported from Southeast Asia. Walking is his favorite recreation: he has walked extensively in Michigan, Scotland, England, Ireland, and Austria. Preferring the serenity of the countryside to the turbulence of cities, Kirk once wrote: "I am best content when planting little trees at Mecosta."

Asked to comment upon current issues, Kirk listed what he regards as the primary needs of present-day society: "(1) Restoration of political theory, in what Leo Strauss calls 'The Great Tradition,' and its application to our age in practical politics; (2) reawakening of modern normative consciousness in morals and taste; (3) recovery of standards in education, including genuine principles of academic freedom; and (4) revival of humane learning, through criticism which relates letters to ethical and social principles."

References

Directory of American Scholars (1957)
Who's Who in America, 1962-63
Who's Who in American Education, 1959-60
Who's Who in the Midwest (1956)

McSWIGAN, MARIE May 22, 1907-July 16, 1962 Writer of children's books. See *Current Biography*, 1953.

Obituary

N Y Times p29 Jl 18 '62

MORISON, SAMUEL ELIOT July 9, 1887-
Historian
Address: b. c/o Little, Brown & Co., 34 Beacon
St., Boston, Mass.; h. 44 Brimmer St., Boston 8,
Mass.

> NOTE: This biography supersedes
> the article that appeared in
> *Current Biography* in 1951.

Like the Greek historian Thucydides and the
American historian Francis Parkman, Samuel
Eliot Morison writes his books as much as possible from firsthand experiences. In direct con-
tact with the events that he recorded in his
monumental *History of United States Naval
Operations in World War II* (1947-60), he
gathered his material under the actual stress of
battle as a commissioned officer in the Navy.
Morison's meticulous scholarship has not interfered with his desire to avoid pedantry and to
reach a large number of contemporary readers.
He is widely known for his biographies of
Christopher Columbus (1942) and John Paul
Jones (1959), both of which won Pulitzer Prizes.
Several of his other books have established him
as an authority on early American history and
on the history of Harvard University, where he
taught for almost forty years.

New England has been the earliest, the most
profound, and the most prolonged of the several
major influences on Samuel Eliot Morison's life
and writings. He was born on July 9, 1887 to
John Holmes and Emily Marshall (Eliot) Morison in Boston, Massachusetts at 44 Brimmer
Street in a house that his grandfather, Samuel
Eliot, an historian and educator, had built. His
other grandfather, Nathaniel H. Morison, originally from Peterborough, New Hampshire, had
been the first provost of the Peabody Institute
in Baltimore.

As Morison has related in his autobiographical notes for *Twentieth Century Authors* (H.W.
Wilson Company, First Supplement, 1955), he
was reared in "an atmosphere where scholarship,
religion and social graces were happily blended."
He attended Noble's School in Boston and St.
Paul's in Concord, New Hampshire in preparation for Harvard University, which he entered in
1904. Charles Homer Haskins and Edward
Channing were among the distinguished scholars
and professors at Harvard who aroused Morison's
interest in history. Receiving his B.A. degree
cum laude in June 1908, he went at once to
France for a year's study, at the University of
Grenoble during the summer and at the École
des Sciences Politiques in Paris during the
winter.

Throughout his career, Morison has returned
to Harvard repeatedly. In 1909 he took his M.A.
degree there, and he remained at the university
for the next three years (while assisting as a history instructor at Radcliffe College) to work for
his Ph.D. degree, which was conferred in 1913.
He had followed the suggestion of Professor Albert Bushnell Hart in choosing one of his own
ancestors as the subject of his dissertation: his
first book, *The Life and Letters of Harrison Gray
Otis, Federalist, 1765-1848*, was published by
Houghton Mifflin Company in 1913.

After another trip to Europe, in 1913, which
he spent partly in on-the-scene study of the

Balkan Wars, Morison taught history briefly at
the University of California. He joined the
Harvard faculty in 1915 as an instructor, but
three years later enlisted as a private in the
Army. Instead of returning to the classroom at
the end of World War I, he served as an attaché
to the Russian division of the American Commission to Negotiate Peace and was also a delegate on the Baltic commission of the Paris Peace
Conference. Unsympathetic towards the Treaty
of Versailles, he resigned in July 1919 and went
back to Harvard in the fall.

The courses that Morison taught at Harvard
included one on the history of Massachusetts.
His enthusiasm for the subject led to *The Maritime History of Massachusetts, 1783-1860*
(Houghton, 1921), which he ranks among his
most successful books. It is a result of both
scholarly research and the personal observations
that he made while enjoying his hobby of sailing
up and down the coast of New England. In its
fusion of the authentic and the interesting, it is
an early fulfillment and illustration of the aims
that he set forth in his pamphlet *History as a
Literary Art*, published in 1946 and reprinted in
his collection of essays *By Land and By Sea*
(Knopf, 1953).

In 1922 Oxford University invited Morison to
become the first incumbent of its new chair of
American history. During the next three years,
while teaching at Oxford as Harold Vyvyan
Harmsworth Professor of American History, he
worked on his *Oxford History of the United
States, 1793-1917*, a textbook that met the needs
of British readers of American history. Later, in
collaboration with Henry Steele Commager, he
enlarged his book into *The Growth of the
American Republic* (Oxford, 1930; fourth revised edition, 1950).

Home again at Harvard, where he accepted
a professorship in history in 1925, Morison
turned to more local subjects. He occupied himself in *Builders of the Bay Colony* (Houghton,
1930) with early New England and the culture
that the Puritans had brought to America. In
1926 Harvard had appointed him the official
historian for its 300th anniversary. By the time
the tercentenary was celebrated in 1936, the Harvard University Press had published a book that
he had edited called *The Development of Harvard University Since the Inauguration of President Eliot, 1869-1929* (1930); most of Morison's
multivolume *Tercentennial History of Harvard
College and University, 1636-1936;* and his more
popular survey *Three Centuries of Harvard,
1636-1936*. The *Tercentennial History* brought
him both the Jusserand Medal and Columbia
University's Loubat Prize.

Professor Morison deplores the lack of knowledge of foreign languages that he finds in many
young historical researchers. He told Earl W.
Foell of the *Christian Science Monitor* (September 29, 1960) that when he encouraged his students to work on the discovery of America in
celebration of the 450th anniversary of Christopher Columbus' discovery of America, they
shied away from the subject because of language
difficulties: "Nobody was left but poor me to do
anything on Columbus." Following the example
of Francis Parkman, who had prepared for his
Pioneers of France in the New World (1865) by

retracing the routes of the French explorers and living among the Indians, Morison tried to approximate the experiences of Columbus on his voyages to America. Between 1937 and 1940 he made four trips in sailing vessels in the waters that Columbus had explored, crossing and re-crossing the Atlantic in 1939-40 as commodore of the Harvard Columbus Expedition.

Several of Morison's major books grew out of these adventurous investigations: *The Second Voyage of Christopher Columbus from Cadiz to Hispaniola and the Discovery of the Lesser Antilles* (Oxford, 1939); *Portuguese Voyages to America in the Fifteenth Century* (Harvard, 1940); and *Admiral of the Ocean Sea; A Life of Christopher Columbus* (Little, 1942). His work on Columbus, for which he was awarded the Pulitzer Prize in biography in 1943, was hailed as a monument of scholarship. The comments of Lincoln Colcord in the New York *Herald Tribune Books* (March 1, 1942) reflected the opinion of many reviewers: "Combining extreme erudition and the art of good writing in almost equal quantities, the narrative flows like a superb novel, while all the facts and observations are buttressed and re-buttressed with four centuries of references until there is hardly anything left to say."

Admiral of the Ocean Sea proved to be an excellent recommendation for Morison when he set out in early 1942 to interest President Franklin D. Roosevelt in his proposal to prepare "a full, accurate and early record" of the part played by the United States Navy in World War II. Morison has said that the welcome that sailors everywhere gave him as the biographer of Columbus was an even greater advantage to him than his commission as lieutenant commander in the Naval Reserve, which he received in May 1942. Although he held the title of historian of naval operations and was given a staff of officers and access to naval documents, he was not an official historian for the Navy.

Beginning in July 1942 with a convoy trip across the Atlantic, during the next three years Morison covered almost all the battle areas and important naval operations of the war. He was an eyewitness to the North Africa landings in the fall of 1942, participated in the Central Solomons campaign in the summer of 1943 and later in the Gilbert Islands assault, visited the beachheads at Salerno and other areas of the European theater, and in 1945 saw the battle for Okinawa from the bridge of the flagship *Tennessee.* He served on some dozen ships during the war, earning seven Battle Stars and the Legion of Merit with combat clasp.

Much of Morison's naval history was based on the notes of facts and impressions that he jotted down with pencil on yellow paper during interviews and battles. He filed these away, with official reports and other documents, to await the end of the war. He did not begin to publish his *History of United States Naval Operations in World War II* (Little) until he could examine enemy records. Working for the most part at an office in Harvard's Widener Library, he produced about one volume every year between 1947, when *The Battle of the Atlantic: 1939-43* appeared, and 1960, when *Victory in the Pacific, 1945* closed the fourteen-volume series. (*Victory in the Pacific* is the last of the narrative vol-

Harvard University News
Office—Walter R. Fleischer

SAMUEL ELIOT MORISON

umes; a fifteenth volume contains a cumulative index and list of errata and various annexes.)

Because Morison's work is his own history, rather than the authorized or official record of the Navy, he has room for personal judgment in his treatment of Navy heroes and for his own conclusions in considering such questions as the justification of dropping the atom bomb on Japan. Hanson W. Baldwin, military editor of the New York *Times,* expressed the view in the *Times Book Review* (November 6, 1960) that among the minor defects of Morison's cycle was occasional indulgence in "sweeping generalizations impossible to prove or disprove." He found, however, that "The virtues are self-evident—a combination of painstaking research and clear dramatic writing . . . in a sweeping pageant of action."

During the fifteen postwar years that Morison worked on his naval history he wrote eight other books, including *The Story of the Old Colony of New Plymouth* (Knopf, 1956) and *Intellectual Life of Colonial New England* (N.Y. Univ. Press, 1956), as well as *John Paul Jones; A Sailor's Biography* (Little, 1959), for which he won his second Pulitzer Prize in biography. Columbia University awarded him its Bancroft Prize in 1949 for the third volume of his history of World War II naval operations, *The Rising Sun in the Pacific, 1931-42* (1948), and in 1962 he received the Gold Medal for History and Biography of the National Institute of Arts and Letters for the excellence of his work as a whole. His autobiographical *One Boy's Boston* has been scheduled for publication by Houghton Mifflin Company in the autumn of 1962.

Since August 1951 Morison has been on the Navy's honorary retirement list in the rank of rear admiral. Since 1955 he has also been retired from teaching at Harvard, having become Jonathan Trumbull Professor of American History, Emeritus, after holding that professorship

MORISON, SAMUEL ELIOT—*Continued*
in active service for almost fifteen years. Un-retired as an historian, however, he began work-ing on his *Oxford History of the American People* before the final volume of his World War II cycle was off the press.

Morison has also continued to add to the scores of articles that he has written for scholarly jour-nals and for more popular periodicals like the *Saturday Evening Post.* He has been a member of the editorial boards of the *New England Quarterly* and the *American Neptune;* president of the American Antiquarian Society, the Colo-nial Society of Massachusetts, and the American Historical Society; and a Fellow of the American Philosophical Society, the British Academy, and the Royal Academy of History in Madrid. His many other professional affiliations have in-cluded the chairmanship of the council of his-torians of the Institute of Early American His-tory at Williamsburg, Virginia, trusteeship of the Franklin D. Roosevelt Library, and vice-presidency of the Naval Records Society.

A large number of colleges and universities—Yale, Oxford, Notre Dame, and Columbia, among others—have awarded Morison honorary degrees. He is a member of the Charitable Irish Society and of several clubs, including the St. Botolph and Somerset in Boston and the Athenæum in London. His church is the Epis-copal. For some forty years he had been a mem-ber of the Democratic party, but in 1952 he voted Republican in support of Dwight D. Eisen-hower. Morison is six feet one inch tall and has the hale look of a seagoing man and the dig-nified, somewhat reserved manner generally associated with a Boston Brahmin.

Samuel Eliot Morison and Elizabeth Shaw Greene, a painter, were married on May 28, 1910 and had four children, Elizabeth Gray (Mrs. Edward Spingarn), Emily Marshall (Mrs. Brooks Beck), Peter Greene, and Catharine. His first wife died in 1945, and in December 1949 he mar-ried Priscilla Barton of Baltimore. She has ac-companied him on his travels to the Far East to revisit the scenes of World War II and on the trips he took to collect material for his biog-raphy of John Paul Jones. She also shares Mori-son's hobby of sailing his yawl out of Northeast Harbor on Maine's Mount Desert Island, his lifelong favorite vacation resort, which he cele-brated in *The Story of Mount Desert Island* (Atlantic-Little, 1960). His home otherwise is still Boston's Brimmer Street.

References

Christian Sci Mon p11 S 29 '60 por
N Y Times Bk R p6 Je 5 '60 por
Twentieth Century Authors (First Supple-
     ment, 1955)
Who's Who in America, 1962-63

PARKER, COLA G(ODDEN) July 1, 1890-June 27, 1962 Former president of the National Association of Manufacturers (1956); former chairman (1953-55) and president (1942-53) of Kimberley-Clark Corporation. See *Current Biog-raphy* (September) 1956.

Obituary

N Y Times p31 Je 28 '62

RAMÍREZ, PEDRO P(ABLO) Jan. 1884-June 11, 1962 Became president of Argentina (1943-44) after leading military coup; promulgated generally Fascistic program. See *Current Biog-raphy* (August) 1943.

Obituary

N Y Times p37 Je 12 '62

SANDSTRÖM, (ALFRED) EMIL (FRED-RIK) Oct. 11, 1886-July 6, 1962 Former chair-man of the board of governors of the Interna-tional League of Red Cross Societies (1950-59); chairman of United Nations Special Committee on Palestine, 1947; former justice of the Swedish Supreme Court. See *Current Biography* (Jan-uary) 1951.

Obituary

N Y Times p64 Jl 8 '62

STELLE, JOHN Aug. 10, 1891-July 5, 1962 A founder and national commander (1945-46) of the American Legion; governor of Illinois for ninety-nine days in 1940. See *Current Biography* (January) 1946.

Obituary

N Y Times p17 Jl 7 '62

SWIFT, HAROLD H(IGGINS) Jan. 24, 1885-June 8, 1962 Executive of the meat packing concern Swift & Company; youngest son of the company's founder. See *Current Biography* (Feb-ruary) 1950.

Obituary

N Y Times p25 Je 9 '62

VAN PELT, JOHN V(REDENBURGH) Feb. 24, 1874-May 30, 1962 Architect; designed churches and other buildings in Europe and the United States; taught architecture at several American universities. See *Current Biography* (December) 1946.

Obituary

N Y Times p19 Je 2 '62

WALD, JERRY Sept. 16, 1911-July 13, 1962 Motion picture producer; headed Jerry Wald Productions since 1956; produced films for Twen-tieth Century-Fox, Columbia Pictures, Warner Brothers; credits include *The Man Who Came to Dinner; Mildred Pierce; Johnny Belinda; The Glass Menagerie; The Inspector General; Sons and Lovers; Peyton Place; The Sound and the Fury; Kiss Them For Me.* See *Current Biography* (May) 1952.

Obituary

N Y Times p1+ Jl 14 '62

WATSON, LUCILE May 27, 1879-June 24, 1962 Character actress of the stage and screen, noted for her crisp, witty performance of dowager roles; credits include parts in *Watch on the Rhine* (1941) and *Ring Around the Moon* (1950). See *Current Biography* (December) 1953.

Obituary

N Y Times p29 Je 25 '62

WICKENS, ARYNESS JOY Jan. 5, 1901- United States government official; economist

Address: b. Department of Labor, Washington 25, D.C.; h. Box 212, Rt. 2, Vienna, Va.; Avon, S.D.

When the consumer price index skips upward a point, Aryness Joy Wickens is the person likely to know the reasons why. Supervising the gathering and analysis of the complex data upon which the index is based is only one of her duties as special assistant and economic advisor to the United States Secretary of Labor. A noted economist and statistician, Mrs. Wickens has been with the Department of Labor since 1938. From 1954 to 1955 she served as acting commissioner of the Bureau of Labor Statistics and from 1956 to 1959, when she assumed her present post, she was deputy assistant secretary of labor. Mrs. Wickens has received the Federal Woman's Award (1961) for her "outstanding skill in initiating, organizing, and directing wholly new and enormous statistical programs."

Aryness Joy was born in Bellingham, Washington on January 5, 1901, the daughter of Oliver Hodgdon and Elizabeth (Chapman) Joy. A Phi Beta Kappa, she graduated from the University of Washington with a B.A. degree in 1922. At the University of Chicago, where she took her M.A. degree in economics in 1924, she served as an assistant to Senator Paul Douglas, who was then teaching there. Miss Joy taught at Mount Holyoke College for four years (1924-28), first as an instructor, then as an assistant professor. In 1928 she took a leave of absence from the college in order to become a research assistant in the division of research and statistics of the Federal Reserve Board (1928-33). Liking government work, she decided to stay in Washington permanently.

Between 1934 and 1937 Mrs. Wickens was chief statistician in the office of the economic advisor (1934-35) and chief statistician and economist of the central statistical board (1935-37). In 1938 she joined the staff of the Bureau of Labor Statistics, serving as assistant to the commissioner of that bureau until 1940. Subsequently she was chief of the prices and cost of living branch (1940-45) and assistant commissioner for program operations (1945-49).

The Bureau of Labor Statistics, which has existed in its present form since 1913, is the government's chief fact-finding agency in the area of labor economics. It collects data and produces nation-wide statistics on such matters as employment and manpower, wages, wholesale prices, cost of living, housing construction, industrial relations, and industrial accidents. From 1949 to 1954 Mrs. Wickens was deputy commissioner of labor statistics. From August 1954

ARYNESS JOY WICKENS

through 1955, pending the appointment of a commissioner, she served as acting commissioner of labor statistics. On October 9, 1954 she received the 1954 achievement award of the District of Columbia State Federation of Business and Professional Women for outstanding professional work in the federal government.

Appointed deputy assistant secretary of labor in January 1956, Mrs. Wickens worked with the assistant secretary in charge of the Bureau of Employment Security (which governs public employment service and unemployment insurance programs) and the Bureau of Apprenticeship and Training. She was specially concerned with programs of manpower and employment and directed the Department of Labor's manpower development staff, which co-ordinates all Department of Labor programs on occupational outlook, counseling and placement services, and the employment of older workers.

In May 1959 Mrs. Wickens was appointed economic advisor to the Secretary of Labor. In this post she made significant contributions to the development of new techniques for gathering and analyzing social and economic statistics. These techniques provide data for policy-making officials within and outside the government, promptly, soundly, and at the lowest cost consistent with obtaining information that is generally accepted as impartial and reliable. She has worked closely with Secretary of Labor Arthur J. Goldberg on an area redevelopment plan aimed at preparing management and labor to meet the new demands of automation. She frequently attends international conferences and participates in panels on subjects related to her work.

In April 1961 Mrs. Wickens spoke at a seminar on economics that was sponsored by the Business and Professional Women's Foundation in Cincinnati. She called attention to the rapid change overtaking communities in the twentieth century and enumerated several factors that are

WICKENS, ARYNESS JOY—*Continued*

responsible, like the exhaustion of natural resources, the shift of industries, and the rise of new products. She also mentioned several attendant problems that arise in the areas of housing, transportation, loss of taxes, and blighted areas. Mrs. Wickens suggested that a community might profit from an economic survey of its resources and urged local Business and Professional Women's Clubs to become involved in community planning and development.

The first annual Federal Woman's Award was bestowed on Mrs. Wickens in February 1961. She was one of six women to receive this citation, the first government-wide prize designed to honor career women in the federal government. In accepting the award she thanked her fellow workers in the Department of Labor for their co-operation. "I have a large pool, mostly women, who do work for me," she explained, "like gathering food prices in 100 cities or making 3,500 rent surveys."

Published monthly by the Bureau of Labor Statistics, the national consumer price index measures changes in retail prices of goods and services bought by families with moderate incomes. It includes about 300 items like food, clothing, house furnishings, services, and rents, for which the bureau receives more than 100,000 quotations a month from some forty-six cities. The reports on prices are obtained by thousands of agents who visit stores, inspect merchandise, and examine price tags. Through 1961 the index was computed by using prices in the years 1947-49 as a base of 100 against which to compare current prices. Beginning with January 1962 the prices in the years 1957-59 serve as a base of 100.

The most common use of the index is as a reference for escalator clauses in wage bargaining agreements that provide for a wage rise of a cent an hour every time the index moves up a certain amount. More than four million contracts are explicitly linked to the index and many more rely informally upon it. The index is also used in personal income contracts between individuals like divorce settlements and alimony agreements and in adjusting maintenance payments in public institutions. Information on separate components of the index—such as retail food prices—is used by special groups in the community. The bureau also issues indices for individual cities. Mrs. Wickens has explained the consumer price index in detail in an interview published in *Nation's Business* (September 1959). In July 1962 President John F. Kennedy appointed a twelve-member Consumers Advisory Council to represent the interests of American consumers. Mrs. Wickens was appointed liaison officer to the council from the Department of Labor.

Mrs. Wickens has served as adviser to the United States government delegations that attended the International Labor Conference (1947 and 1948), the Conference of American States Members of the International Labor Organization (1949), and sessions of the Economic and Social Council of the United Nations (1951 and 1952). She was the American government delegate to the first general assembly of the Inter-American Statistical Association in 1947.

A member of the American Economics Association, Mrs. Wickens also belongs to the American Statistical Association (of which she was vice-president in 1935 and 1937 and president in 1952). Mrs. Wickens has received a number of citations in addition to the Federal Woman's Award (1961) and that of the District of Columbia State Federation of Business and Professional Women (1954). She holds the Department of Labor's Distinguished Service Award, an alumnae award from her social sorority, Kappa Kappa Gamma, and a Civil Service League merit citation. Her club is the Tower in Washington, D.C. On June 29, 1935 she married David Lawrence Wickens, who is an economist and cattle rancher in Avon, South Dakota. They have two sons, Donaldson Vickers and David Elder.

References

Washington (D.C.) Post Fp3 F 19 '61 por
Who's Who in America, 1962-63
Who's Who of American Women (1961-62)

YOUNG, OWEN D. Oct. 27, 1874-July 11, 1962 Industrialist and monetary expert; founder and first chairman (1919-33) of Radio Corporation of America; chairman of the board of General Electric (1922-39); following World War I was co-author of the Dawes Plan for German reparations and author of the Young Plan for fiscal rehabilitation of Germany. See *Current Biography* (August) 1945.

N Y Times pl+ Jl 12 '62

CURRENT BIOGRAPHY—VOL. 23. NOS. 1-8

This is the index to the January-September 1962 issues. For the index to the 1961 biographies, see December 1961 issue or 1961 Yearbook. For the index to 1940-1950 biographies, see 1950 Yearbook. For 1951-1960 index, see 1960 Yearbook.

Howe, Gordon See Howe, Gordie Mar 62

Hubbard, Bernard (Rosencrans) obit Jul 62

Hughes, Richard J(oseph) Jul 62

Hu Shih obit Apr 62

Ives, Irving M(cNeil) obit Apr 62

John, Augustus (Edwin) obit Jan 62

Johnson, Harold Ogden obit Apr 62

Katsh, Abraham I(saac) Mar 62

Kay, Hershy Mar 62

Keldysh, Mstislav (Vsevolodovich) Feb 62

Kennelly, Martin H(enry) obit Jan 62

Khouri, Faris el- obit Feb 62

Kiplinger, W(illard) M(onroe) Jan 62

Kirk, Russell (Amos) Sep 62

Klahre, Ethel S(usan) May 62

Kobak, Edgar obit Jul 62

Koestler, Arthur Jan 62

Korth, Fred (H.) Jul 62

Kovacs, Ernie obit Mar 62

Kreisler, Fritz obit Mar 62

Larson, Leonard W(infield) May 62

Lefèvre, Théo(dore Joseph Albéric Marie) Jun 62

Lewis, John (Aaron) Jan 62

Lipchitz, Jacques Apr 62

Lober, Georg (John) obit Feb 62

Loeb, James (Isaac), Jr. Jan 62

Louw, Eric H(endrik) Mar 62

Love, J(ames) Spencer obit Mar 62

Luthuli, Albert John Feb 62

McCarthy, Clem obit Jul 62

McClintic, Guthrie obit Jan 62

McConnell, F(owler) B(eery) obit Feb 62

McCormack, John W(illiam) Apr 62

McCracken, Joan obit Jan 62

McSwigan, Marie obit Sep 62

Macy, John W(illiams), Jr. Jan 62

Mao Tse-tung May 62

Marais, Jean Apr 62

Margai, Sir Milton (Augustus Strieby) Feb 62

Martin, Edmund F(ible) Jan 62

Marvel, Mrs. Archie D. Apr 62

Marvel, Elizabeth Newell See Marvel, Mrs. A. D. Apr 62

Meerloo, Joost A(braham) M(aurits) Jan 62

Mellers, Wilfrid (Howard) Feb 62

Meštrović, Ivan obit Mar 62

Miller, Harry W(illis) Mar 62

Miller, William E(dward) Feb 62

Moore, Charlotte Emma See Sitterly, C. M. Jan 62

Morison, Samuel Eliot Sep 62

Moses, Anna Mary Robertson obit Feb 62

Mössbauer, Rudolf L(udwig) May 62

Mowrer, Edgar Ansel Jul 62

Muench, Aloisius (Joseph), Cardinal obit Apr 62

Murphy, (Eleanor) Patricia Apr 62

Nestingen, Ivan A(rnold) Mar 62

Newhart, Bob Mar 62

Nitze, Paul H(enry) Feb 62

Ochoa, Severo Jun 62

Ogburn, Charlton obit Apr 62

Olav V, King of Norway Jan 62

Osgood, Charles E(gerton) Apr 62

Ozbirn, Catharine (Freeman) See Ozbirn, Mrs. E. L. Jan 62

Ozbirn, Mrs. E. Lee Jan 62

Page, Ruth Jun 62

Parker, Cola G(odden) obit Sep 62

Peden, Katherine (Graham) May 62

Petri, Egon obit Jul 62

Pevsner, Antoine obit Jun 62

Piccard, Auguste obit May 62

Portinari, Candido obit Mar 62

Rabaut, Louis Charles obit Jan 62

Ramírez, Pedro P(ablo) obit Sep 62

Randolph, Jennings Jan 62

Rayburn, Sam(uel Taliaferro) obit Jan 62

Read, Sir Herbert (Edward) Mar 62

Reischauer, Edwin O(ldfather) May 62

Reybold, Eugene obit Jan 62

Rivers, Thomas M(ilton) obit Jul 62

Robinson, Spottswood W(illiam), 3d Mar 62

Rogers, Frank B(radway) Jun 62

Rogers, Rutherford David Jun 62

Rose, (Iain) Murray Jun 62

Russell, Donald J(oseph) May 62

Russell, James S(argent) Jan 62

Sandström, (Alfred) Emil (Fredrik) obit Sep 62

Satterfield, John C(reighton) Jul 62

Savage, Augusta (Christine) obit May 62

Schoeppel, Andrew F. obit Mar 62

Scofield, Paul Mar 62

Senghor, Léopold Sédar Mar 62

Shirer, William L(awrence) May 62

Shurlock, Geoffrey M. Jan 62

Sitterly, Mrs. Bancroft Walker See Sitterly, C. M. Jan 62

Sitterly, Charlotte Moore Jan 62

Slocum, (Manly) Harvey obit Jan 62

Smith, Margaret (Madeline) Chase Mar 62

Spahn, Warren (Edward) May 62

Speicher, Eugene (Edward) obit Jul 62

Spottswood, Stephen Gill Apr 62

Stelle, John obit Sep 62

Stikker, Dirk U(ipko) Feb 62

Stokes, Anson Phelps, Jr. Jul 62

Suggs, Louise Jan 62

Sunderland, Thomas E(lbert) Apr 62

Swann, W(illiam) F(rancis) G(ray) obit Mar 62

Swift, Harold H(iggins) obit Sep 62

Switzer, Mary E(lizabeth) Jan 62

Taylor, A(lbert) Hoyt obit Jan 62

Teagle, Walter C(lark) obit Feb 62

Thant, U Feb 62

Thomas, Norman (Mattoon) Jul 62

Thurber, James obit Jan 62

Tillinghast, Charles C(arpenter), Jr. Feb 62

Tobias, Channing H(eggie) obit Jan 62

Turner, Ewald (Walter) May 62

Unitas, John Feb 62

Vandiver, S(amuel) Ernest Jul 62

Van Pelt, John V(redenburgh) obit Sep 62

Vertès, Marcel obit Jan 62

Viereck, George Sylvester obit May 62

Vilar, Jean (Louis Côme) Apr 62

Volpe, John A(nthony) Feb 62

Waddington, C(onrad) H(al) Apr 62

Wagner, Richard Apr 62

Wald, Jerry obit Sep 62

Walsh, Chad Feb 62

Walsh, William B(ertalan) May 62

Walter, Bruno obit Apr 62

Ward, Paul L(angdon) Mar 62

Watson, Lucile obit Sep 62

Watts, Alan (Wilson) Mar 62

Webb, James E(dwin) May 62

Welsh, Matthew E(mpson) Jun 62

Wenner-Gren, Axel (Leonard) obit Jan 62

Wesker, Arnold Feb 62

Whalen, Grover A(loysius) obit Jun 62

Whitton, Rex M(arion) May 62

Wickens, Aryness Joy Sep 62

Wilcox, Francis O(rlando) Apr 62

Wilkinson, Bud See Wilkinson, C. Apr 62

Wilkinson, Charles (Burnham) Apr 62

Wills, Royal Barry obit Feb 62

Winiarski, Bohdan (Stefan) Feb 62

Wood, Natalie Apr 62

Yamasaki, Minoru Mar 62

Young, Owen D. obit Sep 62

CURRENT BIOGRAPHY

OCTOBER 1962
VOL. 23 NO. 9

Editor: Charles Moritz

PUBLISHED BY THE H. W. WILSON COMPANY, 950 UNIVERSITY AVE., NEW YORK

CONTENTS

ABOUT THIS PUBLICATION

Current Biography (published every month except August) presents articles on people who are prominent in the news—in national and international affairs, the sciences, the arts, labor, and industry. Sources of information are newspapers, magazines, books, and, in some cases, the biographees themselves. It should be pointed out, however, that these are objective rather than authorized biographies. At the end of the year the articles in the monthly issues are cumulated in one alphabet, revised, and printed in a single volume known as *Current Biography Yearbook*.

Authorities for biographees' full names, with some exceptions, are the bibliographical publications of The Wilson Company. When a biographee prefers a certain name form, that is indicated in the heading of the article: for example, MACMILLAN, (MAURICE) HAROLD means that he is usually referred to as HAROLD MACMILLAN. When a professional name is used in the heading, as, for example, GLENN FORD, the real name, in this case GWYLLYN SAMUEL NEWTON FORD, appears in the article itself.

The heading of each article includes the pronunciation of the name if it is unusual, date of birth (if obtainable), and occupation. The article is supplemented by a list of references to sources of *biographical* information, in two alphabets: (1) newspapers and periodicals and (2) books.

References to newspapers and periodicals are listed in abbreviated form; for example, "Sat Eve Post 217:14+ S 30 '44 por" means *Saturday Evening Post,* volume 217, pages 14 ff, September 30, 1944, with portrait. For full names, see the section "Periodical and Newspaper Designations," which is included in all *Current Biography* Yearbooks and in the January issue each year. Obituary notices appear for persons whose biographies have been published in *Current Biography*.

An index to names that have appeared this year is to be found at the back of this issue.

NOTE: Authors whose biographies do not appear in *Current Biography* may usually be found in *Twentieth Century Authors,* Kunitz & Haycraft, 1942, H. W. Wilson Company, or in the FIRST SUPPLEMENT (1955). Authors of books for young people are included in *The Junior Book of Authors* (Second Edition, Revised) edited by Kunitz & Haycraft, 1951, H. W. Wilson Company. Musicians whose biographies do not appear in *Current Biography* may usually be found in *Living Musicians,* compiled and edited by David Ewen, 1940, H. W. Wilson Company, or in its FIRST SUPPLEMENT (1957).

KEY TO PRONUNCIATION

ā	āle	N	Not pronounced, but indicates the nasal tone of the preceding vowel, as in the French *bon* (bôn).	û	ûrn; French eu, as in *jeu* (zhû); German ö, oe, as in *schön* (shûn), *Goethe* (gû'tĕ)
â	câre				
ă	ădd				
ă	ăccount				
ä	ärm				
à	àsk				
à	sofà			ŭ	tŭb
		ō	ōld	ŭ	circŭs
ē	ēve	ô	ôrb	ü	Pronounced approximately as ē, with rounded lips: French u, as in *menu* (mē-nü); German ü, as in *grün*
ĕ	ĕnd	ŏ	ŏdd		
ê	makêr	oi	oil		
		ōō	ōōze		
g	go	ŏŏ	fŏŏt		
		ou	out		
ī	īce				
ĭ	ĭll	*th*	*then*	zh	azure
		th	thin	′ =	main accent
к	German ch as in *ich* (ĭк)	ū	cūbe	″ =	secondary accent

CURRENT BIOGRAPHY

OCTOBER 1962

ANDERSON, VICTOR E(MANUEL) Mar. 30, 1902-Aug. 15, 1962 Former governor of Nebraska, from 1955 to 1959. See *Current Biography* (September) 1956.

Obituary

N Y Times p27 Ag 16 '62

BENNETT, HENRY GORDON Apr. 15, 1887-Aug. 1, 1962 Former Australian army officer; lieutenant general (ret.); commanded Australia's Eighth Division in Malaya in World War II. See *Current Biography* (March) 1942.

Obituary

N Y Times p25 Ag 2 '62

BRITTON, EDGAR C(LAY) Oct. 25, 1891-July 31, 1962 Chemist; synthesized amino acids; held nearly 300 patents on insecticides and resins; president of American Chemical Society in 1952. See *Current Biography* (April) 1952.

Obituary

N Y Times p25 Ag 2 '62

DEARBORN, NED H(ARLAND) June 2, 1893-Aug. 1, 1962 Educator; dean of Division of General Education of New York University (1934-42); president of National Safety Council (1944-58); member of War Department's scientific committee during World War II. See *Current Biography* (January) 1947.

Obituary

N Y Times p25 Ag 2 '62

DWORSHAK, HENRY C(LARENCE) Aug. 29, 1894-July 23, 1962 Republican Senator (1946-48; 1949-62) and Representative (1938-46) from Idaho. See *Current Biography* (January) 1950.

Obituary

N Y Times p27 Jl 24 '62

EDWARDS, VINCENT July 7, 1928- Actor
Address: b. c/o Bing Crosby Productions, 9028 Sunset Blvd., Los Angeles 46, Calif.

The opera of the operating table seems to be rivaling soap and horse operas in the affections of the American viewing public. The most successful new show of the 1961-62 television season was an hour-long weekly melodrama that

VINCENT EDWARDS

chronicled the adventures of Dr. Ben Casey, an angry young neurosurgeon whose tough exterior masks the soul of Hippocrates. Much of the show's success depended on the skill of its leading actor, Vincent or (more commonly) Vince Edwards, who first became well known as Ben Casey, after playing secondary roles in films and television for about twelve years. During the 1961-62 season Edwards practised medicine before an estimated 32,000,000 American viewers each week; his program was scheduled to appear again over the television network of the American Broadcasting Company during the 1962-63 season.

Vincent Edwards, whose name was originally Vincent Edward Zoino, was born in a slum section of Brooklyn, New York City on July 7, 1928. He is a twin and the youngest of seven children born to Vincent Zoino, an Italian-American bricklayer and construction worker, and Julia Zoino. He has one surviving sister, Mrs. Nancy Albanese, and two surviving brothers, Anthony (his twin) and Joseph. His other brother and sisters—Marie, Helen, and Carl— are deceased. His mother, who has been described as "a hard-working, strong-willed woman who possessed the immigrant's classic zeal to make something of her children," was largely responsible for the fact that Edwards did not wind up in jail, as many of his boyhood friends did. "We rubbed elbows with hoods and gamblers," Edwards has recalled. "When my

EDWARDS, VINCENT—*Continued*

mother saw what a bum I was becoming when I was a kid, she pulled me off the streets every night at seven and made me study. There were a lot of fights about my continuing in school, but I finally decided I wanted to be an aviation mechanic and I took the vocational course at East New York High School."

A second influence that kept Edwards on the right side of the law was his interest in sports. A hulking teen-ager (he weighed 170 pounds) and a natural athlete, he became a lifeguard at Coney Island the summer he was fourteen. Seymour Schlanger, a fellow lifeguard and star swimmer for the Flatbush Boys Club team, encouraged Edwards to join the team, and for the next three years Edwards trained at the club every afternoon. During the evenings he took college preparatory courses to qualify for an athletic scholarship at Ohio State University, where Schlanger had gone.

Edwards received the scholarship to Ohio State in 1946 after winning the Metropolitan A.A.U. 100-meter backstroke championship. At college he was a member of the swimming team and first studied business administration, then English. He supplemented his income by waiting on tables at fraternity and sorority houses. During one summer vacation he got a job as a lifeguard at the Olympic Hotel in the Catskill Mountains in New York State. At night the young swimmer with the magnificent physique was pressed into service in entertaining the guests and helping out visiting stars such as Milton Berle and Myron Cohen. While serving as master of ceremonies, singer, dancer, and straight man for the comedians, Edwards was badly bitten by the acting bug.

In 1948 Edwards transferred to the University of Hawaii so that he could train all year for the Olympic games under the well-known coach, Soichi Sakamoto. He was the only non-Oriental on the team. Gradually, however, he became more interested in the Honolulu Community Theater and the University of Hawaii Players than in the swimming pool. In the middle of the term he left school and returned to New York. There he registered at the American Academy of Dramatic Arts, where his classmates included other young hopefuls named Grace Kelly, Anne Bancroft, and John Cassavetes.

Edwards' first job in the theater was as a chorus boy in the Broadway musical *High Button Shoes*. He toured with a road company of *Come Back, Little Sheba*, began getting roles in television dramas emanating out of New York, and then, in 1951, signed a $150-a-week movie contract with Paramount Pictures, only to be fired a few months later. A succession of jobs in Hollywood followed.

He appeared on television shows like *General Electric Theater, Studio One, Alfred Hitchcock Presents, The Untouchables,* and Henry Fonda's *Deputy* series; took theatrical stock company assignments and café singing dates; and eventually played secondary roles, mostly of villains, in about twenty-two movies. Among his film credits are *Mr. Universe, Sailor Beware, Hiawatha, Rogue Cop, Serenade, The Three Faces of Eve, Hit and Run, The Scavengers,* and four low-

budget crime movies that received good reviews: *The Night Holds Terror, City of Fear, Murder by Contract,* and *The Killing.* Edwards was praised for his performance in these Columbia films; the movie critic of the New York *World-Telegram and Sun* (May 21, 1956) wrote, for example, that Edwards played the role of a hoodlum in *The Killing* "with vigor and conviction."

A brief acting job took Edwards to Hong Kong in 1959, and he stayed there a year, returning to Hollywood only when his friend John Cassavetes offered him a role in the film *Too Late Blues.* By the spring of 1961 Edwards had turned to making rock 'n' roll records, but his vocalizing was not very successful. At about the same time James Moser, the television writer who had written the defunct series *Medic,* was casting about for an actor to play the leading role in *Ben Casey,* a new dramatic series about a young chief resident in the neurosurgical department of a large general hospital. The part demanded a talent for exhibiting a combination of surliness and dedication that was apparently hard to find. Some 100 actors were tested for the role before Edwards was chosen to play it.

The program, which had its première on the American Broadcasting Company network in October 1961, was popular from its outset, particularly with women of all ages. *Variety* called it the "most spectacular success of the 1961-62 television season"; the public, in the *TV Guide* poll, designated Edwards as "favorite male performer" and the show as "favorite new series"; and both the show and Edwards were nominated for the Television Academy's Emmy awards.

Such adjectives as "churlish," "ill-mannered," "boorish," and "testy" have been applied to the hero of the *Ben Casey* show, which has been described as being constituted of "skilfully implied violence." "Casey is an irate surgeon who has no qualms about tangling with the hospital board, patients' relations, other doctors and most of the human race," a *Look* writer (May 8, 1962) remarked. "As played by Edwards, he runs the gamut all the way from snapping to snarling." Yet the show makes clear that beneath the brash exterior of Ben Casey lies a dedication to his profession and to suffering humanity. *Ben Casey* has been shown in fourteen countries, and its vogue has spurred the concoction of some ten new clinical series for the 1962-63 television season in the United States. Some 11,000 women have shown their devotion to Casey by buying white blouses modeled upon his high-necked jacket, which he usually wears open in a casual, Byronic fashion. In the meantime the shows have been ridiculed by members of the medical profession on the grounds that they are remote from reality.

Edwards makes between $2,000 and $5,000 a week for doing the *Ben Casey* show. He commands $10,000 for a guest appearance on television and at fairs and expositions, where he is in great demand. After long years of relative obscurity Edwards has attained a measure of fame, but he appears unenthusiastic about his success. "I've won a kind of pyrrhic victory," he was quoted in the New York *Herald Tribune* (February 14, 1962) as saying. "The anticipation of success was far greater than the reality."

Bill Davidson wrote in the *Saturday Evening Post* (May 12, 1962) that "his principal emotion about his success . . . seems to be one of bitter annoyance that it was so long in coming, and one of his favorite expressions . . . is 'Big deal, I'm an eleven-year overnight sensation.'" Edwards has said that he hopes to play Casey for perhaps another two or three years and then move on to other things.

A bachelor, Vince Edwards keeps his six-foot-two-inch, 200-pound frame in shape by swimming, lifting weights, and working out in a gym. He has called himself—"a nut on one subject—the benefits of organically grown foods." He has dark hair and dark eyes and a broken nose. The intensive shooting schedule of Ben Casey leaves him little spare time for his hobbies, which include watching his two thoroughbred race horses run and working on the manuscripts of "a few plays" he is writing. A licensed pilot, Edwards has now given up flying. In heavy demand by movie-makers, he was scheduled to take a ten-week leave of absence from *Ben Casey* in August 1962 to make a film in England and Italy, *The Victors*, with Sophia Loren.

T. S. ELIOT

References

N Y Sunday News Mag p5 Je 24 '62 por
N Y Times II p11 Jl 22 '62
Sat Eve Post 235:62+ My 12 '62 por
International Motion Picture Almanac (1962)
International TV Almanac (1962)

ELIOT, T(HOMAS) S(TEARNS) Sept. 26, 1888- Poet and critic

Address: b. 24 Russell Square, London W.C. 1, England

Revolutionaries who win sometimes become a part of the Establishment. Reviled as much as cheered when he was revolutionizing English poetry in the 1920's, T. S. Eliot is by now so well established that the recently published second edition of the *Concise Cambridge History of English Literature* calls its final chapter "The Age of T. S. Eliot." Although pockets of resistance remain, the revolution is over and Eliot has won.

His poem "The Waste Land" spearheaded the revolt. Unhappy with an English poetic diction divorced from ordinary speech, Eliot went to the French symbolists and other foreign influences for his apprenticeship. Unhappy with a civilization cut off from its roots in myth and ritual, he placed that civilization and its origins into juxtaposition to represent, in poetry, the horror of the contemporary situation. When Eliot was able to make personal contact with religious ritual, his art made similar contact. In his verse plays connected with the liturgy—notably *Murder in the Cathedral*—he found the modern equivalent he had been seeking for the blank-verse drama of the Elizabethans, and with *The Cocktail Party* (1949) he mastered the idiom.

Eliot is a director of the London publishing firm of Faber and Faber, with which he has been associated since 1925. In 1948 he received

the Nobel Prize for Literature for his "work as a trail-blazing pioneer of modern poetry."

Thomas Stearns Eliot, the youngest of seven children, was born in St. Louis, Missouri on September 26, 1888 to Henry Ware Eliot and Charlotte Chauncy (Stearns) Eliot. The family faith was Unitarian and the ancestry, on both sides, was Massachusetts Puritan. Many of Eliot's direct ancestors were Boston merchants, some were ministers. The poet's father was a prosperous brick manufacturer; his mother was the author of a dramatic poem about Savonarola and a biography of her father-in-law, the Reverend William Greenleaf Eliot, a founder of Washington University in St. Louis.

Brought up in St. Louis, Eliot entered Smith Academy (attached to Washington University) there in 1898. During his adolescence he was much influenced by the *Rubaiyat*, Christina Rossetti, and Byron. His first published poem, "A Fable for Feasters," a comic narrative in *ottava rima*, appeared in the *Smith Academy Record* for February 1905. Eliot spent his final year of preparatory school at Milton Academy in Massachusetts (1905-06).

As a Harvard University undergraduate, from 1906 to 1909, Eliot was brilliant in his studies, proper and reserved in manner, and quiet and witty in conversation. He attended the lectures of George Santayana and studied under Irving Babbitt, whose antiromantic approach to literature had an acid effect upon Eliot's romanticism. Eliot was an editor of the Harvard undergraduate literary magazine, the *Harvard Advocate*, and contributed poetry to its pages. Introduced to Jules Laforgue's poetry through Arthur Symons' *The Symbolist Movement in Literature* in 1908, he began to write under the influence of Laforgue's irony and evasion, and of Elizabethan drama. He belonged to both Harvard literary clubs, the Stylus and the Signet, and was class odist.

Completing the requirements for his B.A. degree a year ahead of his class, Eliot worked for

ELIOT, T. S.——*Continued*

his M.A. in philosophy at Harvard during the year 1909-10 (the year in which he also began to write "The Love Song of J. Alfred Prufrock"). At the University of Paris during the school year 1910-11, Eliot had Alain-Fournier for a tutor and attended the lectures of Henri Bergson. During a visit to Germany he finished "Prufrock" in Munich in August 1911.

Returning to the Harvard graduate school for three years (1911-14), Eliot studied the epistemological systems of Alexius Meinong and Francis Herbert Bradley under Josiah Royce, Sanskrit under Charles R. Lanman, and Patanjali's metaphysics under James Wood. During 1913-14 he was an assistant in philosophy at Harvard. Although he never took his doctorate at Harvard, he completed his doctoral dissertation, "Experience and the Objects of Knowledge in the Philosophy of F. H. Bradley," in 1916. Bradley's monist view of personality greatly influenced Eliot's poetic sensibility, reinforcing the romantic theme of isolation in guilt.

In the summer of 1914 Eliot went to Marburg University in Germany on a Sheldon Traveling Fellowship, but the outbreak of World War I cut short his stay. It also prevented his return to the United States, and he spent the school year 1914-15 reading Aristotle's *Posterior Analytics* with Professor Joachim at Merton College, Oxford University. Meanwhile, in September 1914, Eliot had met Ezra Pound in London. Pound importuned the editor Harriet Monroe to publish "The Love Song of J. Alfred Prufrock" in *Poetry* magazine in June 1915—an event that marked the beginning of frequent publication of Eliot's work in *Poetry, Blast, Little Review,* and other little magazines in the United States and Europe. "Prufrock" and other poems that Eliot wrote between 1909 and 1915 were collected in *Prufrock and Other Observations* (The Egoist, Ltd., 1917). From 1917 to 1919 Eliot was assistant editor of the *Egoist.*

Meanwhile the involuntary expatriate was making a living by teaching grammar school at High Wycome and junior school near London (for a brief period beginning in 1915), and by giving extension lectures on French and English literature at Oxford and the University of London (1916-18). From 1917 to 1925 he worked in the foreign exchange department of Lloyd's bank, in London. To the *New Statesman, Athenaeum, Times Literary Supplement,* and other periodicals he was contributing between 1917 and 1921 the book reviews that Hugh Kenner has described as "the most arduous, the most concentrated critical labor of which detailed record exists; nothing less than a rethinking, in the specific terms exacted by conscientious book-reviewing, of the traditional heritage of English letters."

Many of these seminal critical essays appeared in *The Sacred Wood* (Methuen, 1920; Knopf, 1921), which contains Eliot's celebrated description of poetry as "not a turning loose of emotion, but an escape from emotion," and his equally famous statement of the "objective correlative": the only way to express an emotion in art is to find "a set of objects, a situation, a chain of events which shall be the formula for that emotion." A later succession of essays, including the

title essay in *Homage to John Dryden* (Hogarth Press, 1924), played a large part in rescuing Donne and Dryden from the shadow of Milton and called attention to the fusion of thought and feeling, of formal diction and living speech, which is found in the metaphysical poets and against which Milton prevailed.

The most obvious techniques that Eliot used in the poetry of his late twenties and early thirties involved exaggerative contrast. After a brief flirtation with Imagism, Eliot studied Théophile Gautier's technique, under the stimulus of Pound, and the Gautier influence is palpable in the poems that Eliot wrote between 1917 and 1919. These were published, with earlier poems, in *Ara Vos Prec* (Ovid Press, 1920) and the almost identical *Poems* (Knopf, 1920).

In 1922, while still working at Lloyd's bank, Eliot became founding editor of the quarterly review, *Criterion,* which under his editorship until its demise in 1939, enjoyed wide respect for its seriousness and high standards of content and style. In the *Criterion* for October 1922 Eliot's poem "The Waste Land" was first published. In the United States Boni and Liveright published it as a book in December of the same year. Using as a framework the symbolism of certain fertility myths that reputedly formed the pagan basis of the Christian Grail legend, and overlaying this with profuse literary and popular allusion and quotation (some in foreign languages), Eliot created a poetic representation of the horror of contemporary civilization dying of spiritual drought. ("I wrote 'The Waste Land,'" Eliot said years later, "simply to relieve my own feelings.") The poem caused a furor. Its elliptical style, esoteric use of allusion, and play with echo led some critics to denounce it as deliberate obscurantism, pure hoax, or perverse brilliance. The "lost generation" generally, however, embraced it as its scripture, and the key position of "The Waste Land" in twentieth century English poetry and its influence on world literature has since become patent.

The gray pessimism of "The Waste Land" deepened into black despair in "The Hollow Men" (1925), but in "Ash Wednesday" (1930) the color of Eliot's mood approximated the purple of Lent and the Christian "dark night of the soul"—much to the consternation of such secular admirers of the earlier poems as critic Edmund Wilson. In 1926 Eliot's spiritual development had led him into the Church of England, and he had become a British subject in the same year. In the following year, in the preface to his book *For Lancelot Andrewes; Essays on Style and Order* (Faber, 1928), he declared himself to be "Anglo-Catholic in religion, royalist in politics, and classicist in literature." The relationships in Eliot's thought between religion, politics, and culture, here crudely stroked, were drawn ever more finely in the political works that followed: *After Strange Gods* (Faber, 1934), *The Idea of a Christian Society* (Faber, 1939; Harcourt, 1940), and *Notes Toward the Definition of Culture* (Faber, 1948; Harcourt, 1949).

Since holding the Clark lectureship at Cambridge University in 1926, Eliot has lectured from time to time at American as well as British universities. He visited the United States after an absence of eighteen years when he accepted the Charles Eliot Norton visiting professorship at Harvard University in 1932-33. That first return to America constitutes a convenient watershed in Eliot's poetic career. Perhaps he had arrived at a firm footing in his spiritual quest. Perhaps he had arrived at that poetic point where the reunion of the written word and the everyday spoken word had been achieved and where, in Eliot's own words, "the poetic idiom can be stabilized . . . a period of musical elaboration can follow." Perhaps America struck him with its freshness after his period of long absence. Whatever the cause or admixture of causes, the "Landscapes," the place-name minor poems ("Cape Ann," "New Hampshire," "Usk," and "Virginia") that he began to write during the 1932-33 visit to the United States prefigured the philosophic calm and musical variation of *Four Quartets.* "East Coker," "Burnt Norton," "The Dry Salvages," and "Little Gidding"—issued separately between 1940 and 1942—were published under the title *Four Quartets* by Harcourt, Brace in 1943.

His meditation on time, history, eternity, and redemption in the *Four Quartets* harks back, within the same period, to Eliot's dialogue for *The Rock* (Faber, 1954), a pageant play written for performance at Sadler's Wells Theatre, London, in behalf of the Forty-five Churches Fund of the Diocese of London. The most enduring portions of Eliot's contribution to the pageant are the Choruses. The Rock speaks for the Church as eternal witness; the Chorus represents the Church in fields of action.

Eliot's next attempt at drama was wholly his own, and a much greater popular success. *Murder in the Cathedral* (Faber; Harcourt, 1935) was written for the Canterbury Festival of June 1935. A production of the play at the Mercury Theatre, London, later in the same year was the first of many productions throughout the world. The struggle of the drama takes place between St. Thomas à Becket, facing martyrdom at Canterbury in 1170, and a series of temptations that rise from the gross to the subtle. In the film version of *Murder in the Cathedral* (Venice première, 1951; London and New York, 1952) Eliot is heard on the sound track as the voice of the Fourth Tempter. (The well modulated, sepulchral voice of Eliot, now more British in accent than American, may also be heard in several recorded readings from his own work released by Harvard and by the Library of Congress.)

Much less a popular success than *Murder in the Cathedral* was *The Family Reunion* (Faber; Harcourt, 1939), a melodramatic tragicomedy in which the Greek Eumenides haunt a modern drawingroom. Hugh Kenner wrote of Eliot's earlier, unfinished play, *Sweeney Agonistes* (Faber, 1932): "It was ultimately finished after some fifteen years, rewritten from beginning to end and entitled *The Family Reunion.*" The *Family Reunion* opened at the Westminster Theatre, London, in March 1939.

The audience that had underwritten the success of *Murder in the Cathedral* was not the usual theater public. The first Eliot play to draw the commercial theater public of London and New York was *The Cocktail Party* (Faber; Harcourt, 1950), a comedy in verse first produced for the Edinburgh Festival of 1949, in which the serious themes of grace and salvation are carried beneath the satiric veneer of upper middle class banter. Eliot has said that in *The Cocktail Party* he succeeded for the first time in creating a poetry of "strict dramatic utility."

In *The Cocktail Party* Eliot did not bring the supernatural on stage as he had in *The Family Reunion,* but left it implicit in the inadequacy of human relationships. In *The Confidential Clerk* (Faber; Harcourt, 1954), a farce about the tangled identity of bastard progeny, originally produced for the 1953 Edinburgh Festival, there is a similar message about human relationships, but the supernatural implications are even more unobtrusive. *The Confidential Clerk* was not a popular success. *The Elder Statesman* (Faber; Farrar, Straus, 1959), about an aristocrat faced at the end of his life not only with the follies of his youth but also with the same follies carried on in his son, is the mellowest and most straightforward of Eliot's plays. It was first presented at the 1958 Edinburgh Festival. Walter Kerr wrote of the play: "Mr. Eliot showed us that verse was possible in our theater . . . possible in the sense that its inflections were contemporary. . . . Mr. Eliot has moved on to a second theatrical task. . . . The excuse that poetry was admissable so long as it confined itself to religious and/or historical subjects had to be exposed. . . . Mr. Eliot has . . . said that theatrical verse need not conceal itself behind protective draperies of any sort" (New York *Herald Tribune* Sunday book section, May 10, 1959).

The most recent collection of Eliot's poetry and plays is *The Complete Poems and Plays 1909-1950* (Harcourt, 1952). Among the collections of his essays are *Selected Essays 1917-1932* (Faber; Harcourt, 1932); *Elizabethan Essays* (Faber, 1934); *Essays Ancient and Modern* (Faber; Harcourt, 1936); and *On Poetry and Poets* (Faber; Farrar, Straus, 1957). His 1932-1933 Harvard lectures, *The Use of Poetry and the Use of Criticism,* were published by Faber in 1933. Eliot's works have been translated into at least twenty-two foreign languages, and Eliot in his turn has translated from the French St.-John Perse's *Anabasis* (Faber, 1930; Harcourt, 1938). The sum of his contributions to periodicals has been enormous (568 pieces through 1951). Many of his poems have appeared first in print in little known, fledgling reviews, to which, as to budding poets, he is sympathetic (and often helpful—despite his reputed aloofness).

T. S. Eliot married his secretary, Esmé Valerie Fletcher, in 1957. His first wife, Vivienne Haigh-Wood, whom he married in 1915 and from whom he separated in 1933, died in 1947. Eliot is six feet tall. His face is sharp and ascetic. Various reports described him during his sixties as carrying himself "with a haggard, hawklike elegance," stooping a little, wearing a handkerchief in his cuff, drinking sherry and burgundy, preferring the company of aristocrats, playing mediocre chess, afraid of high places, subtle, sensitive, and "always ironical." V. S. Pritchett described him, half symbolically, as "a trim anti-Bohemian with black bowler and umbrella . . . ushering us to our seats in hell." Whatever his political and cultural declarations, he maintains a certain detachment regarding both politics and culture. He

ELIOT, T. S.—*Continued*

is also detached from his own cult, poking fun at the dreary snobs among his coterie. The long list of honors bestowed upon him includes the Order of Merit, the Hanseatic Goethe Prize, and honorary doctorates from a score of universities. "It isn't that you get bigger to fit the world," he once said in reaction to the honors bestowed on him. "The world gets smaller to fit you."

References

Braybrooke, Neville ed. T. S. Eliot; A Symposium for His Seventieth Birthday (1958)
Gallup, Donald. T. S. Eliot; A Bibliography (1953)
Kenner, Hugh. The Invisible Poet; T. S. Eliot (1959)
Matthiessen, F. O. The Achievement of T. S. Eliot (1958)
Twentieth Century Authors (1942; First Supplement 1955)
Untermeyer, Louis. Lives of the Poets (1959)
Who's Who, 1962
Who's Who in America, 1962-63

ELVEHJEM, C(ONRAD) A(RNOLD) May 27, 1901-July 27, 1962 President of the University of Wisconsin (1958-62); biochemist; identified nicotinic acid (niacin) as an essential diet item and thus made possible the cure of human pellagra. See *Current Biography* (May) 1948.

Obituary

N Y Times p19 Jl 28 '62

FOLKERS, KARL (AUGUST) Sept. 1, 1906-Chemist

Address: b. Merck Sharp & Dohme Research Laboratories, Rahway, N.J.; h. 617 Belvidere Ave., Plainfield, N.J.

A noted biochemist who has contributed to medical science through his research on therapeutic agents, Dr. Karl Folkers took office as president of the American Chemical Society in January 1962, succeeding Dr. Arthur C. Cope. A member of the staff of Merck & Company at Rahway, New Jersey since 1934, Folkers became executive director of fundamental research at Merck Sharp & Dohme Research Laboratories in 1956. He is a strong advocate of teamwork in scientific research, and has won honors and awards for his work in the discovery, isolation, structural determination, synthesis, and evaluation of biochemicals.

Karl August Folkers was born on September 1, 1906 in Decatur, Illinois to August William and Laura Susan (Black) Folkers. At an early age Karl Folkers was determined to become a chemist, and upon graduating from high school he entered the University of Illinois, where he majored in chemistry. After earning the B.S. degree with honors in 1928 he undertook graduate studies in organic chemistry at the University of Wisconsin and received the Ph.D. degree in 1931.

During the summer of 1928 Folkers worked for the Sherwin-Williams Company in Chicago and

in the summer of 1930 he worked for the Commercial Solvents Corporation in Terre Haute, Indiana. From 1931 to 1934 he held a postdoctoral research Squibb & Lilly Fellowship in organic chemistry, working at the Sterling Chemical Laboratory of Yale University, in collaboration with Professor Treat B. Johnson. His research centered on the synthesis, mechanism of formation, and reactions of certain pyrimidine derivatives.

Having worked for Merck & Company, Inc. in Rahway, New Jersey during the summer of 1933, Folkers began his permanent association with that firm in June of 1934, when he joined the staff of its laboratories for pure research. Merck & Company, Inc., is a major producer of medicinal, industrial, and agricultural chemicals. Its activities include the development of products from the initial stages of fundamental research and the merchandising of these products for domestic and international markets. One of four major divisions of the parent corporation is Merck Sharp & Dohme Research Laboratories, established after the merger of Merck & Company with Sharp & Dohme in 1953. The laboratories conduct fundamental and applied research with emphasis on the discovery and development of chemicals and drugs to serve both industry and public health.

In 1938, following the establishment of the division of research and development of Merck and Company, Folkers was appointed assistant director of research. In 1945 he became director of the organic and biochemical research department. He was named an associate director of the research and development division in 1951, and director of the organic and biochemical research division of the Merck Chemical Division in 1953. Since 1956 he has served as executive director of fundamental research at Merck Sharp & Dohme Research Laboratories.

Folkers' research at the Merck laboratories has been concerned essentially with therapeutic agents, including morphine alkaloids, erythrina alkaloids, curare, biotin, pantothenic acid, penicillin, streptomycin, vitamin B_6, vitamin B_{12}, and corticotropin B. His recent studies have been concerned with inhibitors of virus multiplication, the isolation and structure of novobiocin, the discovery of mevalonic acid, and the chemistry of the co-enzyme Q group. In 1948 Folkers and four other Merck scientists, aided by two outside collaborators, succeeded in isolating crystalline vitamin B_{12}, the anti-pernicious anemia factor. This achievement was the result of long years of patient research, interrupted by World War II, during which Folkers was a member of the division of chemistry in the Office of Scientific Research and Development.

As executive director of fundamental research at Merck laboratories Folkers is particularly concerned with accelerating the pace of scientific discovery. He believes that this can best be achieved by placing increased stress on the concept of planned research, *i.e.*, basic research directed toward a specific end and aimed at helping man to deal with the problems of his more immediate environment. He feels that planned research would not conflict with the type of research carried out for the accumulation of new knowledge only; instead it would complement it. A supporter of teamwork in scientific research, Folkers believes that essential knowledge in contiguous fields, such as biology, chemistry, and nutrition, could be successfully integrated through close co-operation among scientists working in these fields.

As a member of the American Chemical Society since 1928, Folkers has acquired much experience in ACS affairs, and he has held a number of posts within the society on both the national and local levels. He served as councilor of the Northern New Jersey section in 1944-47, 1954-59, and 1960, and was its chairman in 1955. In 1949 and in 1951-52 he was councilor of the division of organic chemistry, and he served as chairman in 1958-59. In 1951 he was on the council committee on national meetings and division activities, and in 1956-58 he served on the council committee on nominations and elections. He was a member of the editorial board of the *Journal of Organic Chemistry* from 1953 to 1957. At present he is a member of the board committees on education and students (1961-63) and on grants and fellowships (1961-63).

In December 1960 Folkers was chosen president-elect of the American Chemical Society for 1961. He took office as president on January 1, 1962, succeeding Dr. Arthur C. Cope, chairman of the chemistry department of the Massachusetts Institute of Technology. The president-elect for 1962, who is to succeed Folkers in 1963, is Dr. Henry Eyring, dean of the University of Utah graduate school. As president of the American Chemical Society, Folkers heads the world's largest association devoted to a single science. The society has twenty-three scientific and technical divisions representing the various fields of chemistry, and 163 local sections serving some 93,000 member chemists and chemical engineers.

In addition to *Chemical and Engineering News* the American Chemical Society publishes several specialized periodicals, and it sponsors a national employment clearing house. In the field of higher education the society publishes the *ACS Directory of Graduate Research,* and it has established a graduate school clearing house, aimed at facilitating contact between graduating students and graduate schools. "No talented student should be allowed, through lack of motivation, information, or assistance, to set minimum educational goals," Folkers said upon taking office as president. "Every undergraduate science and engineering major should be encouraged to attain the highest level of academic training of which he or she is capable."

Folkers has received a number of honors and awards for his biochemical research work. In 1940, and again in 1949, he was co-recipient of the Mead Johnson & Company award for research on the vitamin B complex. The 1940 award was for work on the structure, isolation, and synthesis of vitamin B_6, and the award in 1949 was in particular for work on vitamin B_{12}. In recognition of his meritorious work in pure chemistry he was given the American Chemical Society award in 1941. In 1948 he was awarded a Presidential Certificate of Merit for his wartime work with the Office of Scientific Research and Development.

In 1949 Folkers was chosen Harrison-Howe award winner and lecturer by the Rochester

KARL FOLKERS

section of the American Chemical Society. The board of directors of Merck & Company conferred on Folkers their scientific award in 1951 for his research on antibiotics and the isolation and synthesis of vitamins. At the same time the sum of $25,000 was made available to the universities of Illinois and Wisconsin to establish an annual lecture series in Dr. Folkers's name. In 1957 he received the Julius Sturmer lecture award from the Rho Chi chapter at the Philadelphia College of Pharmacy and Science, and in 1959 he received the Charles F. Spencer award sponsored by the Kansas City section of the American Chemical Society. In general recognition of his achievements he was awarded the fifty-fourth annual Perkin medal by the Society of Chemical Industry in 1960.

In addition to his activities at Merck & Company Folkers has lectured at academic institutions in the United States and abroad. In 1953 he was the George Fisher Baker nonresident lecturer in chemistry at Cornell University, and in the following year he was a medical faculties lecturer at the universities of Lund, Stockholm, Uppsala, and Göteborg in Sweden. In 1956 he served as chairman of the conference on vitamins and metabolism at the Gordon Research Conferences. He was a Regents' lecturer at the University of California at Los Angeles in 1960. As a guest lecturer for the American-Swiss Foundation for Scientific Exchange in 1961, Folkers delivered a series of lectures in Zurich, Bern, Basel, and Geneva. At the present time he is chairman of the advisory council of the department of chemistry at Princeton University, and a member of the scientific advisory committee of the Institute of Microbiology at Rutgers University.

Folkers belongs to a number of professional associations, including the American Association for the Advancement of Science, the American Institute of Nutrition, the American Society of Biological Chemistry, the New York Academy

FOLKERS, KARL—*Continued*

of Sciences, and the Society for Experimental Biology and Medicine. He was elected to the National Academy of Sciences in 1948. He is a member of Alpha Chi Sigma (chemistry fraternity), Phi Lambda Upsilon (honor society in chemistry), and Sigma Xi (science research honor society). A contributor to scientific journals, Folkers is also on the Committee on Revision of the United States Pharmacopoeia.

On July 30, 1932 Karl Folkers married Selma Leona Johnson, whom he met while engaged in postdoctoral research at Yale University. They have two children, Cynthia Carol and Richard Karl. Folkers is of slender build, five feet eleven inches tall, with brown hair and blue eyes. His youthful look is said to belie his age. He relaxes by indulging in his favorite hobby, photography.

References

> Chem & Eng N 27:3183 O 31 '49 por; 40:74 Ja 1 '62 por
> American Men of Science 10th ed (1960-61)
> Chemical Who's Who, 1956
> Who's Who in America, 1962-63

FRISCHE, CARL A(LFRED) Aug. 13, 1906- Industrial executive; physicist; inventor

Address: b. c/o Sperry Gyroscope Co., Great Neck, L.I., N.Y.; h. 114 Wheatley Rd., Glen Head, L.I., N.Y.

Since January 1958 Dr. Carl A. Frische, a physicist, has been president of the Sperry Gyroscope Company. He joined the company's staff as a research engineer in 1933. Before and during World War II Frische was in charge of research on precision instrument developments for the armed forces, and he became the company's vice-president for engineering in 1945. He served as vice-president for operations from 1954 to 1957 and as executive vice-president during 1957-58. Frische is the holder of some twenty-three patents.

The Sperry Gyroscope Company is one of the largest divisions of the huge Sperry Rand Corporation, which was formed in 1955 through the merger of Remington Rand, Inc., with the Sperry Corporation. In addition to producing aircraft instruments, pilots' fire control systems, and radar, marine, and electronic apparatus, the company has played a major role in advancing the guided missile program of the United States.

A native of Freeport, a small town in south central Kansas, Carl Alfred Frische was born on August 13, 1906 to Ernst Frische, a farmer, and Julie (Kordarning) Frische. He was reared in Kansas and received his secondary education at Anthony, the seat of Harper county. His extracurricular activities at Anthony High School included football and track. After graduating from high school in 1923 he entered Park College at Parkville, Missouri, and two years later he transferred to Miami University at Oxford, Ohio. Guided in his choice of a career by a general interest in science and invention, Frische majored in physics at the university and was a member of the track team. After receiving his B.A. degree

in 1928 he entered the University of Iowa for postgraduate study in physics, and from 1928 to 1932 he served as an assistant in physics at the university. He received the M.S. degree in 1931 and the Ph.D. degree in 1932.

During the academic year 1932-33 Frische held a research fellowship in physics at Columbia University in New York City. His article "Ionization and Scattering Accompanying Positive Ion Impact in Gases" was published in the *Physical Review* in February 1933. Subsequent articles that he has written are "Soundproofing of the Martin 130 'China Clipper'" (*Aero Digest,* December 1935) and "Dynamic Balancing of Small Gyroscope Rotors" (*Electrical Engineering,* June 1937).

The Sperry Gyroscope Company, with which Frische has been continuously associated since the end of his fellowship year at Columbia, had been founded in 1911 to develop and market the gyrocompass, the marine gyrostabilizer, and other inventions of Elmer Sperry. In 1928 Sperry Gyroscope passed to the control of North American Aviation, Inc., a holding company. Five years later, when General Motors acquired a substantial interest in North American Aviation, the Sperry Gyroscope Company and the Ford Instrument Company (established by Hannibal Ford in 1915) were separated from it, and the Sperry Corporation, with Thomas A. Morgan as chairman of the board, was formed to nurture these two orphaned subsidiaries.

Frische joined the Sperry Gyroscope Company in 1933 as a research engineer in development engineering. He made considerable contributions to the soundproofing of Martin and Sikorsky flying boats for Pan American Airways and he worked on flight research projects. During his early years with Sperry, Frische, who is a licensed pilot, did much flying in bad weather while undertaking research on the testing of new instruments and controls.

In the years preceding the outbreak of World War II the Sperry Corporation greatly expanded its operations. In 1937 it added to its subsidiaries Vickers, Inc., of Detroit, manufacturers of hydraulic pumps and variable speed transmissions. By 1939 the corporation was mass-producing antiaircraft equipment, airplane instruments, searchlights, and deep-sea gyro equipment. Frische had begun to take charge of precision instrument developments for the armed forces before the war, and in 1940 he was appointed senior project engineer for the Sperry Gyroscope Company. He was advanced to the position of research director in 1941 and became chief research director in 1943. His contributions to aviation during this period included the development of bombsights, automatic pilots, and instrument landing systems. He also participated in developments in radar bombing that proved highly effective against Axis submarines.

In November 1945 Dr. Frische became vice-president for engineering with the Sperry Gyroscope Company, a position which he held for nine years. In the months following the end of the war the volume of business of the Sperry Corporation greatly declined, and its work force was reduced by about three-fourths. Part of the Sperry plant at Lake Success, New York was leased to the United Nations, and the early meetings of the Security Council were held there. Meanwhile the Sperry Gyroscope Company was gradually building up and consolidating a considerable business with commercial aviation. An automatic pilot device and a hydraulic flight control system, personally patented by Frische in 1946 and 1947, contributed materially to the success of this enterprise.

Unable to depend solely on government contracts, the Sperry Corporation continued to expand its facilities for more normal industrial production. In 1947 the corporation purchased the New Holland Machinery Company and proceeded to make it into a farm machinery division, which flourished within the next few years. The corporation also acquired packaging machinery companies, and Vickers, Inc., which provided the automobile industry with hydraulic power units for steering mechanisms. In June 1955 lengthy negotiations between Roy Franklin Vickers (who had succeeded Thomas A. Morgan as president of the Sperry Corporation in 1952) and James Rand culminated in the merging of the Sperry Corporation and Remington Rand, Inc., into the Sperry Rand Corporation, with General Douglas MacArthur as chairman of the board. By this time government contracts for precision instruments, electronics equipment, and guided missiles accounted for about 75 percent of the Sperry Corporation's volume of business.

In 1954 Frische became vice-president for operations of the Sperry Gyroscope Company. He succeeded to the senior post of executive vice-president in January 1957 and to the post of president in January 1958. In recent years the Sperry Gyroscope Company has become increasingly involved in the guided missile program of the United States. It became the prime contractor on the Army's Sergeant missile, and it has produced advanced inertial navigation and guidance systems for the Lockheed Aircraft Corporation, the prime contractor on the Navy's Polaris missile.

The activities of the Sperry Gyroscope Company continue to cover a wide variety of fields. In July and August of 1961 the company received contracts from the Air Force for the continued development, installation, and testing of specialized and long-range radar sets. In November 1961 Sperry Gyroscope obtained a Federal Aviation Agency contract for an extensive study of the ability of pilots to foresee and avoid collisions. A result of this study was the patenting, in April 1962, of a device for lighting cockpit dials uniformly, and an instrument for informing pilots if their crafts will reach take-off speed at a safe point on the runway. In September 1961 Sperry Gyroscope introduced a telephone-size magnetic digital computer for guidance and control systems in space vehicles. In the same month the company's microwave engineers announced that they had developed a plan to increase the number of charged particles in the ionosphere to aid the transmission of high-frequency radio and television signals.

In 1955 Miami University in Oxford, Ohio conferred upon Frische an honorary Doctor of Science degree in recognition of "his contributions to national defense and for his efforts to encourage brilliant young people to pursue the study of physics." In 1957 Frische was made a

Sperry Gyroscope Company
CARL A. FRISCHE

member of the Scientific Advisory Board to the Chief of Staff of the United States Air Force. He was named advisory board chairman of the Human Resources Corporation in June 1959; since September 1960 he has served on the New York State Legislative Committee for School Financing. He is a Fellow of the Institute of Radio Engineers, an Associate Fellow of the Institute of Aeronautical Sciences, and a member of the American Institute of Physics, the American Association for the Advancement of Science, and the American Ordnance Association. Frische belongs to the Phi Beta Kappa honor society and is also a member of the Sigma Xi science research honor fraternity, the Gamma Alpha graduate recognition society for science, and the Beta Theta Pi social fraternity.

On June 2, 1930 Carl A. Frische married Harriet Catherine Ross, a former schoolteacher. They have two sons, Richard Henry and Eric Ernst, and one daughter, Gretchen (Mrs. C. H. Gillespie, Jr.). Frische is six feet one-and-one-half inches tall, weighs 175 pounds, and has brown hair and blue eyes. He is an Episcopalian and a Republican. His favorite recreations are hunting ducks and pheasants, fishing, working at shop hobbies, golfing, and romping with his grandchild. He takes pride in a fine collection of fishing rods that he fashioned himself with great precision. He is a member of the University Club, the Deepdale Country Club, the Sands Point Golf Club, and the Manhasset Bay Yacht Club.

References

N Y Times III p3 O 16 '60 por

American Men of Science 10th ed (1960)
Who's Who in America, 1962-63
Who's Who in Commerce and Industry (1961)
Who's Who in World Aviation and Astronautics (1958)
World Biography (1954)

FUCHS, JOSEPH (PHILIP) Apr. 26, 1900-
Violinist
Address: b. c/o Herbert Barrett Management,
Inc., 250 W. 57th St., New York 19

The American violinist Joseph Fuchs has won
international renown as a concert artist, chamber
music performer, and soloist with symphony
orchestras. Fuchs, who made his official New
York debut in 1943, has gained a reputation for
presenting new works by contemporary composers. With Artur Balsam he gave thirty recitals
of violin and piano sonatas over a Boston television station between 1957 and 1960. His command of style and phrasing once elicited from
Louis Biancolli of the New York *World-Telegram
and · Sun* the comment: "Mr. Fuchs deservedly
rates high, with both musicians and music lovers,
in the hierarchy of world fiddlers."

Joseph Philip Fuchs was born in New York
City on April 26, 1900, the eldest of five children
of Philip and Kate (Weiss) Fuchs. His father
was an amateur violinist; his sister Lillian is a
concert violist and his brother Harry is a cellist.
Joseph and Lillian Fuchs have often appeared
together in recitals and duo-performances with
major symphony orchestras.

When he was three or four years old Joseph
Fuchs broke his left arm in a fall, and it
emerged from the cast wasted and thin. To help
strengthen his son's arm muscles Philip Fuchs
taught him to play the violin. The boy showed
an aptitude for playing the instrument, and he
attended the Institute of Musical Art (now Juilliard School of Music) on a full scholarship from
1906 to 1913. He studied with Louis Svecenski,
the violist with the famous Kneisel Quartet, and
then with Franz Kneisel, the first violinist and
founder of the quartet. After another year of
study (1917-18) on a scholarship at the institute,
Fuchs received a diploma in June 1918. He took
up postgraduate violin there from 1918 to 1920
and received an artist's diploma in June 1920.

JOSEPH FUCHS

Soon after graduating from the Institute of
Musical Art, Fuchs received the Morris Loeb
Memorial Prize of $1,000 and the Isaac Newton
Seligman Prize. The cash awards that accom-
panied these prizes enabled him to travel in
Europe following his New York debut at Aeolian
Hall in November 1920. In 1926 Fuchs accepted
the post of concertmaster (leader of the violins)
with the Cleveland Orchestra, which he held
through 1940. He also became the leader of the
Cleveland String Quartet.

In the late 1930's the arm that had been
broken in childhood began to pain Fuchs again,
and, although he persisted in carrying out his
duties on the violin for a while, he was eventually driven to seek help from medical specialists.
He successfully underwent an operation that
might have ended his career, and over the next
few years he painstakingly retrained his hand
to its former flexibility.

Fuchs appeared in the recital that marked his
official debut as a virtuoso at Town Hall in New
York City in November 1943, and in the following year he appeared as a soloist with the New
York Philharmonic at Carnegie Hall. These performances ushered in a highly successful career
of concert and orchestra engagements in the
United States and Europe. Fuchs has played
with most of the major American orchestras and
has been a soloist with the New York Philharmonic more than seven times.

When Fuchs played the D-Major Violin Concerto at the Brahms Night of Lewisohn Stadium
in 1958, Louis Biancolli wrote in the New York
World-Telegram and Sun (July 22, 1958), "That
extraordinary artist and technician, Joseph Fuchs
. . . communicated his superb command of style
and phrasing. . . . The control and workmanship
were of the first order, as was also . . . the
artistry that turned every note, phrase, and
melodic contour into a wondrous blend of poetry
and feeling." Reviewing a Fuchs recital at Town
Hall in 1960, Raymond Ericson of the New York
Times (December 7, 1960) called Fuchs "the
kind of violinist who makes you listen not to
himself but to the music." "Fuchs knows what
the music is about," wrote Ericson, "and he
projects his knowledge in specific terms, whether
he is using melody, rhythm or color. Although
he draws an attractive tone from his instrument,
it is not lush or sweet and does not blur the
image of the work."

Since 1954 Fuchs has made several tours of
Europe. In 1954 he appeared at the Rome International Festival, at the Casals Festival in
Prades, and in Italy, Switzerland, Luxembourg,
and Paris. Two years later, in 1956, he performed all of Beethoven's sonatas for violin and
piano in London and was so enthusiastically
received that he was asked to repeat the series the
following year. In the summer of 1957 he visited
South America for the first time under the
auspices of President Dwight D. Eisenhower's
Special International Program for Cultural Presentations, administered by the American National
Theatre and Academy (ANTA).

In March 1959 Fuchs was one of ten American
concert artists who received grants from the Ford
Foundation under a program designed to recognize and encourage proved talent in the hu-

manities and arts. The cash award enabled him to commission a work from the composer Walter Piston, and this work, Piston's Second Violin Concerto. was given its première by Fuchs and the Pittsburgh Symphony Orchestra under William Steinberg on October 28, 1960. Later it was also performed in Detroit, Buffalo, San Antonio, and New York.

Fuchs believes that the universities can play an important part in fostering music in America. In the 1955-56 season he and the pianist Artur Balsam were asked to play two recitals at Boston University, but because of inadequate facilities on the campus they played the second—a sonata recital—over television in Boston. The program drew so many favorable comments from the public that Boston University decided to engage Fuchs, Balsam, and a music commentator to prepare a three-year series of music programs for television. Co-financed by the Ford Foundation, ten one-hour shows a year, under the title *Sonata*, were heard throughout New England over the Lowell Institute station, WBGH-TV, and were taped for distribution to educational television stations throughout the world.

Presenting most of the sonata literature for violin, the programs included sonatas by Beethoven, Brahms, Mozart, Schubert, Handel, Bach, Grieg, Franck, Debussy, Fauré, and Richard Strauss. Fuchs and Balsam also played the sonatas of contemporary composers like Igor Stravinsky, Paul Hindemith, Arthur Honegger, Arthur Berger, Walter Piston, Peter Mennin, Virgil Thomson, Quincy Porter, Gardner Read, Ernest Bloch, Nicolai Lopatnikoff, and Bohuslav Martinu.

Fuchs makes a special effort to perform new works by contemporary composers: in addition to those mentioned above he has played works by Ben Weber, Peter Racine Fricker, Mario Pergallo, and William Schuman. (He gave the New York City première of Schuman's third revised version of his Violin Concerto on February 21, 1960.) He is a co-founder of the Musicians Guild, a group that gives new works their rare second or third performances. Fuchs feels that the contemporary composer depends upon the performer to win recognition for his compositions and that often the performer can make a work better by contributing his own insights. The player, on the other hand, finds new elements in untried works that challenge his technical and artistic ingenuity. It is essential, Fuchs believes, that the musician like and understand the work that he is introducing. "It is the duty of the performer to play and encourage the writing of new works by composers," he has said. "I can think of no greater satisfaction than performing a new work by a fine contemporary composer in whom one believes."

Another means by which Fuchs encourages the development of new talent is teaching; he feels that too few musicians do this. Although he gives no private instruction, he has taught at Juilliard, Yale University, and, during summers, at Blue Hill, Maine. He has recorded contemporary and traditional pieces for Decca, Everest, and Columbia Records. His virtuosity is enhanced by his use of a priceless Stradivarius, which he has owned since 1947. Known as "the

Cadiz," the dark red instrument was completed by the famous Italian violin maker Antonius Stradivarius in 1722.

A resident of New York City, Joseph Fuchs is married and has a daughter. On his travels he has amassed many recipes for one of his favorite dishes, the soup-meal, as well as a collection of serving tureens, ranging from eighteenth-century Meissen ware to a Peruvian clay bowl. A dedicated and accomplished violinist who continues to strive for more perfect mastery of his instrument, Fuchs has said, "High standards may be inspired from without, but the highest standard comes from a deep inner conviction, which is the prime requisite for true individuality in art."

References

Etude 69:15+ Ap '51
International Musician 57:34+ Jl '58 por
Musical America 75:12+ Ap '55 por; 80: 43+ N '60 por
Saleski, Gdal. Famous Musicians of Jewish Origin (1949)
Who's Who in American Jewry (1928)

GOODMAN, BENNY May 30, 1909- Clarinetist; orchestra leader
Address: 200 E. 66th St., New York 21

> NOTE: This biography supersedes the article that appeared in *Current Biography* in 1942.

On March 10, 1937, on the stage of New York's Paramount Theatre, a young clarinetist and bandleader from Chicago named Benny Goodman took the American jazz world by storm. Twenty-five years later the middle-aged King of Swing took his jazz to the Soviet Union on an official United States government mission. There, with Premier Nikita Khrushchev as a willing if unenthusiastic listener, the swing music that had once set the jitterbugs dancing in the Paramount aisles almost blew down the Iron Curtain. In the quarter of a century that spanned the two events, swing (with the Dixieland jazz that preceded it and the "progressive" jazz that succeeded it) had become respectable. It had developed into a major cultural weapon in the cold war, and Benny Goodman had won international acclaim not only as the pied piper of swing but also as a classical clarinet virtuoso with the leading symphony orchestras of the United States.

Benny Goodman was born Benjamin David Goodman in Chicago on May 30, 1909, the eighth of eleven children of David Goodman, an impoverished tailor, and Dora (Grisinsky) Goodman. Goodman's parents were Jewish immigrants from Eastern Europe; his father had come from Warsaw, Poland, his mother from Kovno, Lithuania. The family was poor and work was scarce. "I can remember a time when we lived in a basement without heat during the winter, and a couple of times when there wasn't anything to eat," Goodman wrote in his autobiography, written with Irving Kolodin, *The Kingdom of Swing* (Stackpole Sons, 1939). Goodman's mother, who had started to work in the old country when she was

Wide World

BENNY GOODMAN

eight years old, never learned to read or write; his father, who always envied educated people, discovered that the Kehelah Jacob Synagogue gave musical lessons and lent musical instruments to students for about twenty-five cents a week. One day in 1919 Benny went to the synagogue with two older brothers. Harry, the oldest and biggest, was given a tuba, Freddie got a trumpet, and Benny, the youngest and smallest, a clarinet.

Goodman received his early musical training in the synagogue orchestra and at Hull House, the noted Chicago settlement house founded by Jane Addams, where he began private lessons with Franz Schoepp of the Chicago Symphony Orchestra. By doing an imitation of Ted Lewis, he earned his first money as a musician when he was twelve. After attending Sheppherd elementary school, the boy entered Harrison High School, but music, not studies, was his main interest, and when he was only thirteen he got his first union card. Once, when he was playing on a Lake Michigan excursion boat, he was ordered off the bandstand by the famous trumpet player, Bix Beiderbecke, who wanted no truck with the kid in short pants. In the spring of 1923 Goodman entered Lewis Institute in Chicago, where classes did not begin until 11:30 in the morning, thus giving him the chance to get some sleep after playing a night engagement. That fall, having obtained his first steady job at Guyon's Paradise, a Chicago dance hall, Goodman left Lewis Institute and ended his formal education after a year in high school. He was fourteen years old.

"The kid in short pants" began to acquire a reputation in Chicago musical circles that belied his juvenile appearance. When he was sixteen Ben Pollack sent for him to join his band at the Venice ballroom in Los Angeles. When Goodman left Pollack in 1929, he had behind him some impressive achievements. He

had already cut recordings, some as a leader of a combo and some that included his only recorded solos on alto and baritone saxophones. His first recorded solo, made with Ben Pollack's band in Chicago on December 17, 1926, had betrayed the influences of Jimmie Noone, Leo Rappolo, and Frank Teschemacher on his early style. In 1929 he had played with the Pollack band in the pit of the Lew Fields' Theatre in New York City during the run of the musical comedy *Hello Daddy*. He had performed with the outstanding white and Negro musicians of the day. During the next five years he was much in demand as a free-lance sideman in the lucrative radio, pit, and recording fields. He led his own pick-up groups at college proms and similar dates and became the main support of his widowed mother and his younger brothers and sisters.

In September 1933 Goodman met John Henry Hammond, Jr., a socially prominent jazz fan, critic, and promoter, who has played a key role in the development of contemporary American jazz. Hammond helped Goodman to assemble a group of leading jazz men for a recording date to meet the growing interest in jazz in England. The sides were also released by Columbia Records in the United States, where they were wildly received by a small but growing coterie. Goodman also sat in on the last recording date of Bessie Smith, the great Negro blues singer, in which he played with Leon (Chu) Berry, Billy Taylor, and other Negro jazz stars. He credits John Hammond with arranging his recording dates with Negro musicians; Goodman later became the first white bandleader to put Negro musicians on his bandstand.

Goodman formed his first permanent band, with Hammond's help, in March 1934 and opened in Billy Rose's New York theater restaurant, the Music Hall. This led to the band's appearance on the coast-to-coast Saturday night radio showcase, *Let's Dance*, over NBC. After a dismal cross-country tour in the winter of 1934-35, the band almost broke up, but suddenly it caught on with dancers in the Palomar Ballroom in Los Angeles. They crowded around the bandstand, listening instead of dancing, applauding the improvised solos and the arrangements by Fletcher Henderson. The era of swing had been ushered in.

There followed a period of smash engagements, hit records, and jazz innovations. In December 1935 the first jazz concert was held in Chicago; on Easter Sunday in 1936 the first "chamber music" jazz was performed by a swing trio featuring Teddy Wilson, the first Negro musician to play side by side with white men before a paying audience. In March 1937 the band moved to New York City to perform on the *Camel Caravan* radio show. Goodman expected to do no more than fair business when he took his band to the Pennsylvania Hotel in New York City, doubling at the Paramount Theatre at the same time, but on the first day of his Paramount date 21,000 fans paid their way into the theater, jitterbugged in the aisles, and crowned him the King of Swing.

In 1938 Goodman brought jazz to Carnegie Hall in a now famous concert immortalized on records that have grossed more than $1,000,000 in sales. It featured virtuoso performances by such Goodman sidemen as Harry James, Gene Krupa, Ziggy Elman, Lionel Hampton, and Jess Stacy in a solid and swinging repertory of classics like "Sing Sing Sing," "Stompin' at the Savoy," and "Don't Be That Way." Into the concert had gone hours of long rehearsals and the musical discipline and no-nonsense atmosphere imposed by Goodman. The event was dominated by what a *Time* writer (January 5, 1953) once called Goodman's "quicksilver brilliance of improvisation backed by more jazz technique than any other clarinetist can approach."

But Goodman the perfectionist has never rested on his past or present achievements. Since 1938 he has maintained a career as a classical clarinetist that has co-existed with his career as a jazz musician. He recorded with the Budapest String Quartet and commissioned Bela Bartók to write an original work for him, *Contrasts*, which he recorded in 1940 for Columbia Records with Joseph Szigeti, the violinist. He also commissioned Paul Hindemith and Aaron Copland to compose clarinet concertos for him.

In the summer of 1941 he played Mozart's Concerto in A Major for Clarinet (K. 313) at New York's Lewisohn Stadium. He has taught at the Juilliard School of Music in New York. After World War II, when the enthusiasm for the big bands waned and then died out, Goodman suffered several bouts of illness. He broke up his band, but he has never been long away from the public eye.

In 1949, when he was forty, Goodman decided to study with Reginald Kell, one of the world's leading classical clarinetists. To do so, he had to change his entire technique: instead of holding the mouthpiece between his front teeth and lower lip, as he had done since he first took a clarinet in hand thirty years earlier, Goodman learned to adjust his embouchure to the use of both lips and even to use new fingering techniques. He had his old finger calluses removed and started to learn how to play his clarinet again—almost from scratch. That his jazz style remained intact was confirmed by a review in the *New Yorker* (March 19, 1955) when Goodman opened at Basin Street, a New York night club. "The exciting news is that the Master has never been more masterly," the magazine's jazz critic wrote.

In 1955 Universal-International produced *The Benny Goodman Story*, for which Benny Goodman and a specially assembled band recorded the sound track, and in which Steve Allen starred as the King of Swing. Although the cliché-ridden film failed to draw queues at the box office, it at least forced Goodman to re-assemble another band. In February 1956 he led it at New York's Waldorf-Astoria Hotel. Other motion pictures in which Goodman has appeared include *Sweet and Lowdown, The Big Broadcast of 1937, A Song is Born, Powers Girl, Hollywood Hotel,* and *Stage Door Canteen*.

A sellout tour of the Far East in the winter of 1956-57, under the joint auspices of the United States Department of State and the American National Theatre and Academy, demonstrated Goodman's far-reaching fame. In Bangkok he became fast friends with King Bhomibol Adulyadej of Thailand, a jazz afficionado, with whom he took part in a jam session. In the summer of 1958 the Goodman band played at the Brussels Fair and in 1959 toured Western Europe in a series of jazz concerts. For two successive spring seasons, in 1958 and 1959, Goodman had his own TV show, *Swing Into Spring*.

Goodman had long wanted to play in the Soviet Union, but the Russians had officially condemned jazz as a product of "decadent American culture" and had imposed a ban on jazz concerts. After months of delicate negotiations between the United States and the Soviet Union, a cultural exchange visit was organized for Benny Goodman and his band. On May 30, 1962, Goodman's fifty-third birthday, the Goodman band launched a swing concert tour of the Soviet Union, stopping at Sochi, Tiflis, Kiev, Leningrad, and Tashkent in addition to Moscow, playing thirty-two concerts that were attended by some 180,000 Russians, including Premier Khrushchev himself in the opening-night Moscow audience. The Soviet cultural newspaper, *Sovietskaya Kultura*, proclaimed Goodman a "true poet of the clarinet." The strain of the trip took its toll on the band members, however, some of whom complained that Goodman had performed too many standard swing arrangements when they wanted to play "modern stuff." Although a few Soviet jazz fans echoed their protests, most Russian listeners were wildly enthusiastic.

The music of Benny Goodman can be heard on many record labels, including Capitol, Brunswick, Columbia, Decca, RCA Victor, Harmony, Chess, Vanguard, Epic, and MGM. Goodman has won the *Playboy* poll as clarinetist every year since it began in 1957 and received the *Esquire* Gold Award every year that the poll was held, from 1944 to 1947. He has been voted a favorite soloist in polls conducted by *Down Beat* and *Metronome*.

In March 1942 Benny Goodman married Mrs. Alice Hammond Duckworth, a sister of John Hammond. The Goodmans have two daughters, Rachel, a concert pianist, and Benjie. His mother and most of his brothers and sisters still live in Chicago. His hobbies are golfing and fishing. In helping to transform a unique American musical form into an international language, Benny Goodman has expressed himself more successfully in music than in words. How articulate he can be in words he demonstrated when he wrote in *House and Garden* in April 1951: "Good results depend inevitably on the work one is willing to put into it, and in the work itself—whether practising or planting—you find your true enjoyment."

References

House & Gard 99:135+ Ap '51 por
N Y Times p2 Mr 9 '62 por
Show Bsns Illus 1:56+ N 28 '61 por
Time 61:43 Ja 5 '53 por

Feather, Leonard. The Encyclopedia of Jazz (1960)
Goodman, Benny and Kolodin, Irving. Kingdom of Swing (1939)
Who's Who in America, 1962-63

GOVE, PHILIP B(ABCOCK) (gōv) June 27, 1902- Lexicographer
Address: b. G. & C. Merriam Co., Federal St., Springfield 2, Mass.; h. Old Patrick Rd., Warren, Mass.

During the decade or more of intensive preparation of *Webster's Third New International Dictionary,* published by the G. & C. Merriam Company in 1961, Philip B. Gove supervised a substantial part of the 757 "editor-years" of work required to complete the world's largest current dictionary. After its publication he found himself faced with a need to explain and defend the principles of the newly emergent science of Structural or Descriptive Linguistics, which has radically affected the techniques of lexicography —an area of endeavor never entirely free from dispute. Dr. Gove believes that language changes constantly, that such change is normal, that spoken language is *the* language, that correctness rests upon usage, and that all usage is relative.

The nationwide controversy arising from the numerous and sometimes clamorous pro and con reviews of the new dictionary has centered largely on differing points of view regarding the purpose of a dictionary. On the one hand, purists and many writers, editors, students, and nonspecialist dictionary users want a dictionary to prescribe correct usage. A large number of linguists, on the other hand, favor a descriptive and permissive, rather than a prescriptive, approach in lexicography; they insist that a dictionary should only record usage, not sanction it. Gove, who stands firmly in the latter camp, is a former teacher of English. He has been associated with the Merriam company since 1946 and has been its editor in chief since 1961.

Philip Babcock Gove, the son of Dr. John McClure Gove, a physician, and Florence Amy (Babcock) Gove, was born on June 27, 1902 in Concord, New Hampshire. He has one sister, Jean (Mrs. W. Earle Royer). He attended Concord High School and then Dartmouth College, also in New Hampshire, where he was a member of the editorial staff of the daily *Dartmouth* and of the *Aegis* (1922).

English was Gove's major subject at Dartmouth, and after receiving his B.A. degree in 1922, he took graduate courses in English at Harvard University, which awarded him the M.A. degree in 1925. He taught English for seventeen years, as an instructor at Rice Institute in Houston, Texas from 1924 to 1927 and at New York University (University Heights) from 1927 to 1942. Meanwhile he had returned to graduate study, and as the William Bayard Cutting Traveling Fellow in Columbia University, he spent a year (1939-40) doing research at the British Museum in London and the Bodleian Library at Oxford University. The dissertation for his Ph.D. degree, awarded by Columbia in 1941, was *The Imaginary Voyage in Prose Fiction.*

During World War II Gove served in the air branch of the United States Naval Reserve, entering the service as a lieutenant in 1942 and advancing to the rank of lieutenant commander. He had long wanted to work on a Merriam-Webster dictionary, and when he was discharged from the Navy in 1946, he took a position as assistant editor with G. & C. Merriam Company in Springfield, Massachusetts, which has been publishing Webster dictionaries since 1847, four years after Noah Webster's death. As he moved up gradually to the top editorial post, Gove became associate editor in 1949, managing editor in 1951, general editor in 1952, and editor in chief in January 1961.

In the vast research and editorial dictionary-making project at Merriam, Gove directs the work of a permanent staff of more than 100 specialists and hundreds of outside consultants in the arts, sciences, and other areas of knowledge. The lifeblood of a Merriam-Webster dictionary is an enormous file that records how words are used in speaking and writing. The file, now containing over 10,000,000 citations, covers innumerable sources of almost infinite variety from the English-speaking world, including newspapers, books, timetables, mail-order catalogues, menus, and even theater stubs. A similarly wide range of sources provides information about contemporary pronunciation. According to the company's periodical publication, *Word Study* (October 1961), "Nothing approaching The Merriam-Webster files exists elsewhere." They are insured for $1,000,000, but Gove has said that insuring the files is like trying to insure the Louvre collection. They supply the evidence for determining the meaning of new words and changes in the meaning of old words.

Merriam's staff is continuously engaged in gathering material for revising its dictionaries. A reprinting of *Webster's New Collegiate Dictionary* may include several thousand revisions. As soon as *Webster's Second New International Dictionary* was off the press in 1934, the staff began to collect examples of usage on which to base definitions for the next edition. Intensive work on a new edition of the unabridged dictionary began in 1950, and in September 1961, at a cost of more than $3,500,000, Merriam published its *Webster's Third New International Dictionary.*

Reflecting the enormous changes in society over the last three decades, such as those brought about by World War II and by developments in science and technology, the new dictionary included among its 450,000 entries some 100,000 new words or new meanings. It also used a new defining technique and a simplified list of sound symbols to show pronunciation. In one of its radical departures from the second edition it dropped "colloquial" as a description of the standing of a word because, as Gove has explained, there is now less distinction between written and spoken English than there was in the earlier decades of the century.

The third edition suffered one of its earliest attacks in an editorial in the New York *Times* (October 12, 1961), which charged that Merriam had failed to live up to its responsibility as "a peerless authority on American English." (The *Times* editors still follow Webster's second edition for spelling and usage except for new—mainly scientific words—for which they consult the third.) Unfavorable criticism also came from Wilson Follett in the *Atlantic Monthly* (January 1962) and from Dwight Macdonald in the *New Yorker* (March 10, 1962). The *American Bar Association Journal* (January 1962) made its displeasure known in an editorial, and a flurry of disapproving reviews appeared in other periodicals. Many critics objected to the new dictionary because it accepted a large number of words that in other dictionaries had been regarded as substandard, such as "finalize" and "corny" and even, though with qualifications, of "ain't." Such acceptance, they felt, lowered the standard, debased the language, and accelerated its deterioration.

As if he had anticipated the controversy, Gove had discussed in an article in *Word Study* (October 1961) the effect that the fairly recent emergence of linguistics as a science has had on lexicography. "Lexicography," he wrote, "is not yet a science. It may never be. It is an intricate and subtle and sometimes overpowering art, requiring subjective analysis, arbitrary decisions, and intuitive reasoning. . . . But it should have no traffic with guesswork, prejudice, or bias or with artificial notions of correctness or superiority. It must be descriptive and not prescriptive."

Later, in defending the third edition's editorial principles, Gove repeated his arguments that language is changing; correctness rests upon current usage and usage is relative; the dictionary records usage, but does not approve or disapprove it; the citations that the dictionary uses show a standard, but do not set it. He also protested that some critics blamed the dictionary for the many inconsistencies of the English language. In a press interview at the annual Conference on College Composition and Communication (a division of the National Council of Teachers of English) in April 1962, he pointed out that the learned journals had not yet reviewed the third edition and predicted that attacks against it would be answered in time. Meanwhile the dictionary found champions in an increasing number of linguistic specialists, including Professor Sumner Ives of Syracuse University (*Atlantic Monthly*, March 1962) and Professor Bergen Evans of Northwestern University (*Atlantic Monthly*, May 1962).

As the author of some twenty articles in learned journals, Gove has shown that he is not a vulgarian, and his writing tends to bear out the contention that usage is relative. He has made a special study of Dr. Samuel Johnson, who in his own dictionary defined a lexicographer as "a harmless drudge." In 1939 Gove was elected to membership in the Johnson Society of London after giving a paper before the Oxford Bibliographical Society on Johnson's dictionary, "Notes on Serialization and Competitive Publishing: Johnson's and Bailey's Dictionaries, 1755." He belongs to many other professional groups, including the Linguistic Society of America, the American Dialect Society, the International Society for General Semantics, the National Society for Study of Communications, and the English Graduate Union of Columbia University. He also serves on the advisory board of the Center for Documentation and Communication Research at Western Reserve University. His fraternity is Phi Gamma Delta.

When Gove joined the Merriam editorial staff in 1946, he bought a 210-acre farm in the Naultaug Valley, just east of Warren, Massachusetts, where he raises Aberdeen Angus cattle. A soil and water conservation plan that he

Fabian Bachrach

PHILIP B. GOVE

developed in 1955 brought substantial improvements on his land and won him the Conservation Award for 1958 of the Southern Worcester Soil Conservation District. Farming is a part-time career to Gove, rather than a hobby. But much of the weekday work falls to his wife, Grace Edna (Potter) Gove, formerly of Worcester, whom he married on August 17, 1929. They live in a 250-year-old frame house on their farm, and they have two daughters, Doris and Susan (Mrs. Rosser A. Rudolph, Jr.), and a son, Norwood B., a physicist with the Atomic Energy Commission. Gove's religion is Protestant.

With his quiet manner, steel-rimmed glasses, and graying hair, Philip B. Gove easily meets the traditional image of a scholar. He stands five feet ten inches tall and weighs 170 pounds; his eyes are brown and he has a close-clipped mustache. An article in the Worcester *Sunday Telegram* (December 10, 1961) pictures him further, "He wears dark suits, drives a small foreign import, picks out his thoughts like beautiful beach stones and polishes them with words. 'I've never heard him repeat himself,' an associate said admiringly."

References

Dartmouth Alumni Mag 51:24+ My '59 por
N Y Times p28 Mr 1 '62 por
Springfield (Mass.) Union p18 Ja 3 '61 por
Who's Who in America, 1962-63

GRAHAM, JOHN May 8, 1908- Architect

Address: b. John Graham and Co., 1426 5th Ave., Seattle 1, Wash.; 444 5th Ave., New York 18; h. 1323 Willard Ave. W., Seattle 99, Wash.

Through its pioneering work in the development of the planned regional shopping center, John Graham's architectural and engineering firm

JOHN GRAHAM

has had an enormous influence on America's retailing business during the past fifteen years. John Graham is an architect and a businessman who has built on his own account and sometimes takes part in the management of his clients' commercial undertakings. He has given special consideration to the economic aspects of an impressive variety of commissions ranging from the Space Needle of the 1962 Seattle World's Fair to huge urban renewal projects and industrial parks in United States cities and to office buildings in the Far East. Maintaining offices in Seattle and New York, John Graham and Company operates on the principle that for economy in construction and efficiency in operation of its projects, an architectural firm must provide a team of designers, planners, engineers, and technological experts to integrate the handling of complicated problems that increase with scientific advances in building.

The son of an architect, John Graham was born to John and Hallie Corrine (Jackson) Graham in Seattle, Washington on May 8, 1908. There were also two daughters in the family, Helen and Elizabeth (who is no longer living). About eight years before the birth of his son, John Graham, Sr., a native of Liverpool, had moved from England to Seattle, where he set up a practice in architecture. His firm became one of the largest on the West Coast, and a branch of John Graham and Company in Detroit designed the expansion of more than thirty Ford Motor Company plants in the United States and Canada.

From his father, John Graham acquired both an interest in architecture and a love of the sea. In boyhood he owned and sailed small boats, and sailing was his favorite sport during the years that he attended the Moran School and later Queen Anne High School in Seattle. After his graduation from high school in 1927 he went to sea aboard a ship on a run between Seattle and Nome, Alaska. In 1927 he entered the

University of Washington in Seattle, intending to become a naval architect, and during his summer vacations he worked in his father's company as a draftsman.

When Graham was in his sophomore year he became the first student from the University of Washington to win an award of the Beaux Arts Institute of Design in New York in a national competition for architectural students. One of his projects, for a war memorial shaft, won a First Mention Placed award and another project received a First Mention. Graham then transferred to the Yale University School of Architecture, where he was awarded two Second Medals, one First Medal, and a Beaux Arts Silver Medal.

Leaving Yale in 1931 with the Bachelor of Fine Arts degree, Graham spent the following year as an assistant in his father's office. His approach to architecture required a knowledge of business operations, and in order to learn retail merchandising he took a job in the statistical merchandising division of Allied Stores. His work there convinced him that merchandising and architecture have a common base in economics. "Both deal with customer appeal, color, design, cost analysis and mathematics," he has pointed out. "Both require logical analysis of problems and situations."

At the end of about a year's employment in Allied Stores' New York office, Graham moved on to the company's Seattle store, the Bon Marché, which owes the design for its original building, in 1916, and its subsequent expansion to John Graham and Company. There he first held the position of assistant general merchandise manager for merchandise control systems. Later he also acquired experience as a buyer of sporting goods and luggage and eventually as divisional merchandising manager for the main-floor accessory departments.

Meanwhile, during some four years at the Bon Marché, Graham spent evenings and weekends designing office buildings and department stores for his father's company. In 1937 he began his own architectural practice as a partner in the firm of Graham and Painter in New York City, which specialized in the design of department stores. One of his commissions was for the Pomeroy store in Harrisburg, Pennsylvania.

America's involvement in World War II, however, soon changed Graham's plans. Finding that he was ineligible for service in the Navy because of an old injury to his elbow, he formed a company to help in the defense effort through the construction of war housing. He built three housing developments under the Federal Housing Administration: one in Maryland, one in Paterson, New Jersey for workers of the Curtiss-Wright aviation plant; and another, the Suburban Heights Development, in Washington, D.C.

Shortly after the war, in 1946, Graham took over the management of John Graham and Company in Seattle. He later opened offices in New York and Honolulu, and his company has a subsidiary in Toronto, John Graham Consultants, Ltd., which does not practise architecture but offers services in engineering and planning to Canadian clients and their architects. In 1947 he began to work out some of the ideas in industrial architecture for which he has become nationally known. The sketches that he prepared at this time for a large regional suburban shopping center were eventually developed into designs for Northgate, just outside Seattle. Northgate, which opened in 1950 and became a prototype for shopping centers throughout the country, has a straight-line pedestrian mall with stores on both sides close to parking areas and is serviced by an underground concourse for trucks.

Many of the more than seventy shopping centers that Graham's company has designed since 1947 are in the suburbs and have been planned with the expectation that they will inevitably become urban centers. Graham has also made important contributions to urban retail developments. One of his triumphs is Lloyd Center in downtown Portland, Oregon, a complex of over 100 stores, office buildings, hotels, and institutional buildings, with protected parking facilities for some 8,000 cars. His Wellington Square in London, Ontario encompasses a city block and is Canada's first shopping center with an enclosed, air-conditioned mall. The mall, which has clerestory lighting, is bordered by thirty-six shops and ends in a department store.

Among other major shopping centers of John Graham and Company are Ala Moana in Honolulu; Bergen Mall in Paramus, New Jersey; Westchester Plaza in New Rochelle, New York; River Roads in Jennings, Missouri; and Cottonwood Center in Salt Lake City, Utah. Besides the buildings in these centers, Graham has designed many individual department stores and specialty shops throughout the United States.

In another area of commercial architecture Graham's company has designed more than forty office buildings, many in foreign cities, including the American International Assurance Company's buildings in Singapore and Kuala Lumpur, Malaya, where he has introduced special sun-screening devices for tropical climates such as aluminum "egg-crate" facades. These devices, which lower the cost of air conditioning, typify Graham's efforts to reduce maintenance expenses. For some of its industrial buildings, like that of the Container Corporation of America in Seattle, John Graham and Company cut down maintenance expenses by using tilt-up concrete wall construction, among other recently developed techniques. One of Graham's largest and most complex projects in industrial architecture is the seventy-four-block, $100,000,000 industrial park planned for Newark, New Jersey.

The versatility of the company is also evident in the large number of apartments, hotels, motels, restaurants, and institutional buildings such as hospitals, schools, and churches it has designed. Perhaps Graham's most dramatic recent structure is the Space Needle, which keynoted the Seattle World's Fair of 1962. The 600-foot tower, rising on three pairs of slender steel legs, is crowned by a restaurant, mezzanine, observation deck, and other spectacular features. Its restaurant, which seats 260 diners, makes a complete revolution every hour and is modeled in part on a revolving restaurant atop a twenty-five story skyscraper that Graham had designed in Hawaii shortly before he received the World's Fair commission.

Whether planning a world's fair symbol or a candy store in a shopping center, Graham not only is concerned with engineering techniques and aesthetic values but also tries to assure his client a profitable return on his building investment by analyzing the economic soundness of a venture. During the development of any project he draws upon his organization's twelve departments to co-ordinate under one roof all the work of specialists in economic planning; architectural design; décor; civil, electrical, mechanical, and structural engineering; highway and traffic problems; cost control; and the other technological services that today's huge shopping centers and industrial parks demand.

John Graham is a member of the American Institute of Architects, and he belongs to the Union League and Yale clubs in New York and to the Rainier, University, Seattle Yacht, and Corinthian Yacht clubs in Seattle. He is an Episcopalian and a Republican. During World War II, when he was working on a housing project in Washington, D.C., he met Marjorie Belle Clark, a specialist in fashion and merchandising who was then employed in the Office of Price Administration. He married her on February 20, 1943 and they have three children, Jane Jackson, Barbara Ann, and John Thomas. Athletic and energetic, Graham is five feet eleven inches tall and weighs 175 pounds; he has hazel eyes and brown hair.

His frequent transcontinental flights to and from his offices on the East Coast and the West Coast, and his trips to the many parts of the world where his company has built, require Graham to spend almost as much time in travel as an airplane pilot. He prefers to be in Seattle over weekends so that he can enjoy his hobby of sailing. His sixty-seven-foot yawl, the *Maruffa*, competed in the 1959 Trans-Pacific Race from Los Angeles to Honolulu, arriving fourth and finishing second in class. His other recreations include hunting, fishing, water skiing, and playing bridge and chess. A music lover, he attends performances of the Symphony Orchestra in Seattle and of the Metropolitan Opera in New York.

GUGGENHEIM, PEGGY 1898- Art patron and collector; writer

Address: Palazzo Venier dei Leoni, Venice, Italy

In a celebrated vine-covered palazzo on the Grand Canal in Venice, Peggy Guggenheim preserves and presents for public enjoyment a multimillion-dollar collection of modern art that is unique in Europe, especially in its representation of American abstract expressionism. She gradually acquired her collection during some twenty years of openhanded encouragement of the modern art movement, when she personally patronized a number of influential pioneering efforts and subsidized at her own expense many artists in whom she detected signs of genius—notably Jackson Pollock.

Peggy Guggenheim is a niece of Solomon R. Guggenheim, whose museum in New York City has brought the name of Guggenheim international renown in modern art. Her own contribu-

Sidney Waintrob

PEGGY GUGGENHEIM

tions in a similar cause have been independent of her uncle's. Before moving to Venice in 1946, she had established and directed avant-garde galleries in London and New York that have proved to be decisive victories in the art revolution of the twentieth century. Always a colorful figure, she upheld her reputation for unconventional living in her provocative and scandalous memoirs, *Out of This Century* (1946) and *Confessions of an Art Addict* (1960).

As the daughter of Benjamin and Florette (Seligman) Guggenheim, Marguerite Guggenheim could claim by birth the advantages of wealth and social prestige on both sides of her family. Her grandfather James Seligman, who was born in a stable, had immigrated to the United States from Bavaria and had made a fortune in banking. One of seven sons of Meyer Guggenheim, the copper-mining magnate, her father prospered in the family's American Smelting and Refining Company. About two years before his death during the sinking of the *Titanic* in 1912, however, he had forfeited his rights to a huge fortune by discontinuing his partnership with his brothers and going into business for himself. The $450,000 that his daughter inherited in 1912 and a similar amount left her upon her mother's death in 1939 made her wealthy, but far less wealthy than she has been reputed to be.

Peggy Guggenheim was born in 1898 in New York City. Her "gilt-edged childhood," as she has described it in *Confessions of an Art Addict* (Macmillan, 1960), was excessively unhappy and lonely. One sister, Benita (now deceased), was three years older than she, and her other sister, Hazel, was five years younger. From her father, who took his family to Europe every summer and was concerned about his children's education, she acquired an early love of art. She had private tutors until the age of fifteen, when she was sent to the Jacobi School, a private school for Jewish girls on New York's West Side.

After her graduation in 1915 Peggy Guggenheim began to liberate herself bit by bit from what she considers to have been a stifling Jewish bourgeois background. She took courses in several subjects, including economics and Italian, and through the influence of one of her teachers, Lucile Kohn, who "had a passion for bettering the world," she eventually became a radical. (She still has the outlook of a left-wing liberal.) Not long after the end of World War I she went to Europe on a visit that was to last for twenty-one years.

In Paris she became an energetic convert to international Bohemianism, having been introduced to many American and French writers and artists through Laurence Vail. She married Vail in May 1922 and had two children, Sindbad and Pegeen. As she has related in her autobiographies, after her divorce from Vail in July 1930, she formed two successive liaisons in Paris. Through one of these associations she gained a stepdaughter, Debbie, whom she raised with Pegeen.

Somewhat out of boredom, while living in England in 1937, Peggy Guggenheim began to look around for something useful to do and decided to open a modern art gallery. In the 1920's she had read Bernard Berenson's books on Italian Renaissance art and had studied great paintings in many cities and small towns of Europe. She knew little about modern art, however, and has said that in 1937 she could not distinguish abstract art from surrealism and cubism. The Irish writer Samuel Beckett, with whom she was then in love, encouraged her to accept the living art of the day; and with the guidance of Marcel Duchamp, an experimentalist in modern art, she opened her gallery, the Guggenheim Jeune, in London on January 24, 1938.

The first show at the gallery honored France's Jean Cocteau. Later shows included the works of the English abstract painter John Tunnard, the French surrealist Yves Tanguy, the Russian abstract expressionist Vasily Kandinsky, and many other avant-garde artists, as well as special exhibits of sculptures, collages, and children's art. From each show Peggy Guggenheim bought at least one work of art so that the artists would not be disappointed if she failed to sell any of their paintings. In that way and for that reason she began her collection.

Guggenheim Jeune appeared to prosper, but actually in its first year it lost about $6,000. Peggy Guggenheim felt that she could get more for her money from a museum of modern art, even though her expenditures would have to be much greater. In March 1939 she turned for help to Herbert Read, one of England's most enthusiastic champions of modern art. He agreed to serve as the museum's director, and he drew up a list of painters whose representative work would cover a systematic survey of all the important art movements since 1910. The list, which she later revised, became the basis of her collection, guiding her in her many purchases. The outbreak of World War II in the summer of 1939, however, put an end to her museum project.

Deciding, despite the war, to try to acquire all the works of art that would have been displayed in her museum, Peggy Guggenheim set out in France to buy a picture a day. She also bought sculptures by Brancusi and Giacometti. "The day Hitler walked into Norway," she wrote in *Confessions of an Art Addict,* "I walked into Léger's studio and bought a wonderful 1919 painting from him for one thousand dollars." As the Germans approached Paris, she asked the Louvre to help her hide her collections; but, according to her memoirs, the Louvre did not consider her collection worth saving, although it included paintings by Klee, Braque, Gris, Mondriaan, Miró, and Max Ernst and sculptures by Lipchitz, Moore, and Arp—besides the works of artists already mentioned.

For several months, however, she was able to have her collection stored in Grenoble before arranging to ship it to the United States as "household objects." She herself sailed from Lisbon with her children, Laurence Vail, and Max Ernst in the summer of 1941 and arrived in New York on July 14. She married Ernst the following December, and with him and fellow surrealist André Breton she visited New York galleries to complete her purchase of pictures by the painters on Read's list. She and Breton also gave a good deal of time and effort to the preparation of a catalogue that became an important document of modern art. *Art of This Century,* as the catalogue was called, included statements by each of the artists represented in the collection (and photographs of their eyes), as well as manifestos of the various art movements and introductions by Breton, Mondriaan, and Arp.

Art of This Century was also the name Peggy Guggenheim gave the gallery that she opened in New York on West 57th Street on October 20, 1942. Frederik Kiesler's spectacular and fantastic décor for the gallery, which cost her some $7,000, was in itself an avant-garde attraction. From time to time she supplemented her permanent collection with special exhibitions and gave one-man shows to Jackson Pollock, Robert Motherwell, Mark Rothko, Hans Hoffmann, and other painters.

Convinced that Pollock was the most promising of the painters she discovered, Peggy Guggenheim made a contract with him that enabled him to work without financial pressure. She has said that he became "the central point" of her gallery, that she "dedicated" herself to him for four years (1943-47), and that she regards her success in furthering his career as her "most honorable achievement." Under the contract she acquired a large number of his paintings, but unable to foresee the enormous sums that his work would soon bring, especially after his death in 1956, she gave away eighteen of his pictures, thus making what she considers to be the most tragic mistake of her life as a collector.

In *The Proud Possessors* (Random, 1958) Aline B. Saarinen stressed the significance of the Art of This Century Gallery as "a center in New York for discovery and opportunity." Alfred H. Barr, Jr., director of the Museum of Modern Art, pointed out in his introduction to *Confessions of an Art Addict* that Peggy Guggenheim, "as patron, played an important, and in some cases,

a crucial role" in the development of an internationally respected group of artists that has helped make New York a pre-eminent city of the art world.

In 1946, divorced from Max Ernst and weary of being a slave to her gallery, she decided to close Art of This Century and seek freedom in Europe, this time in Venice. She was invited in 1948 to show her collection at the 24th Biennale of Venice, where she was given an entire pavilion. "I felt," she has said, "like a whole country all by myself." She was later invited to exhibit at museums in Brussels, Milan, Zurich, and other cities.

After about three years in Venice, Peggy Guggenheim found a suitable home for herself and her collection—the Palazzo Venier dei Leoni. She has sponsored a number of Italian painters, including Tancredi and Bacci. "Apart from this," she wrote in *Confessions of an Art Addict,* "and opening my house to the public three afternoons a week, I have not done much in Italy." Aline B. Saarinen gives a different evaluation of her work there: "Her collection has become not only one of the sights of Venice, but also one of the sights of Europe. Nowhere else in Europe is there a similar historic survey of modern art, nor one that exhibits the Americans—like Pollock and Rothko—who are major figures in the international world of art" *(The Proud Possessors).*

In recent years Peggy Guggenheim has turned to collecting pre-Columbian art, having found that the modern art movement has become a business venture in which some collectors buy merely for investment in an overrun and overpriced market. She feels, furthermore, that the quality of contemporary art has declined considerably in the past twenty years. In a review of *Confessions of an Art Addict* a critic for the London *Times Literary Supplement* (July 15, 1960) expressed the opinion that Peggy Guggenheim is "not a shrewd judge of quality or originality." He went on to remark, "However, she is shrewd enough to have detected the 'racket' which has sprung up."

The question of the soundness of Peggy Guggenheim's taste in art has been raised elsewhere from time to time and received particular consideration in the generally unfavorable reviews given her earlier autobiography, *Out of This Century* (Dial, 1946), an informal book of memoirs dealing in some detail with her flamboyant and frequently amorous adventures in Bohemian circles. Alfred H. Barr, Jr., however, credits her with "a strong sense of historic significance, as well as of aesthetic quality."

Both her autobiographies, in their matter-of-fact outspokenness, reveal a woman of tremendous curiosity and enthusiasm, warm-heartedness and generosity, whose ingenuousness is never entirely hidden behind butterfly eyeglasses, long cigarette holders, silver-painted toenails, and other sophisticated trimmings. For many years she dyed her hair raven black, but at present she prefers white. She has blue eyes, weighs 114 pounds, and is five feet three inches tall. In Venice, which awarded her honorary citizenship in 1962, she is known as "L'Ultima Dogaressa" (The Last Duchess). Her hobbies are cooking, reading, listening to music, and riding in a

GUGGENHEIM, PEGGY—*Continued*

gondola. In recent photographs she is usually surrounded by Lhasa terriers, one of them named Sir Herbert Read.

References

Newsweek 56:106+ N 14 '60
Time 70:76 D 16 '57 por
Guggenheim, Peggy. Out of This Century (1946); Confessions of an Art Addict (1960)
Saarinen, Aline B. The Proud Possessors (1958)

GUGGENHEIMER, MRS. CHARLES S.
See Guggenheimer, Minnie

GUGGENHEIMER, MINNIE Oct. 22, 1882-
Music patron and philanthropist
Address: h. 155 E. 72d St., New York 21

Since 1918 music lovers in New York City have been able to enjoy music under the stars every summer at the Lewisohn Stadium of the City College of New York. The chief fund-raiser for these concerts since their inception has been Mrs. Charles S. Guggenheimer, known as "Minnie" to the stadium audiences to whom she has endeared herself over the years. Her uninhibited personality has perhaps best been described by Jack Paar: "Minnie is one of the brightest gems in my collection of colorful and unexpected characters. She looks like a Norman Rockwell grandmother, but occasionally talks like one out of Erskine Caldwell."

Minnie Guggenheimer was born Minna Schafer in New York City on October 22, 1882, the seventh of eight children of Samuel and Sophie (Schwab) Schafer. Her mother was of French-Alsatian background. Her paternal grandfather, who had come to the United States from Bavaria in the early nineteenth century, had made a small fortune in the California gold rush, enabling his sons, Samuel and Simon, to establish a firm of stockbrokers. The birth of Minna Schafer, followed two years later by that of another daughter, fulfilled Samuel Schafer's boast that he could produce a second generation of children when his first six children had already reached maturity.

Minnie Schafer was educated at a succession of private schools in New York City—Madame de Silva's, St. Mary's School, Dr. Gardiner's School, and Dr. Sachs' School for Young Ladies. As each of these became the most fashionable educational establishment of the moment, she was entered as a pupil. The house in which she was born and reared, located on West 46th Street in Manhattan, was furnished with "monstrous and uncomfortable antiques and a dust-gathering clutter of bric-a-brac." She learned to play the piano at an early age, and her showpiece became Liszt's piano transcription of "Liebestod" from Wagner's *Tristan und Isolde*. In addition to the family home in the city, the Schafers also maintained a summer house in West End, New Jersey. It was there that Minnie Schafer met Charles S. Guggenheimer, a promising young lawyer who was a friend of her brother Edward.

On April 22, 1903 Minnie Schafer married Charles S. Guggenheimer at Temple Emanu-El in New York City. The young couple went to live with Eliza Katzenberg Guggenheimer, who grudgingly took "the little Schafer" as a daughter-in-law into her household. The Guggenheimer town house on Fifth Avenue often received distinguished visitors from the musical world, for Eliza Guggenheimer was a woman of considerable musical talent and a hostess who welcomed to her salon the foremost artists and musicians of the day.

The young bride's contribution to the artistic life of the Guggenheimer ménage was sharply curtailed by her mother-in-law and sister-in-law, who told her that the only thing she knew anything about was having babies. Although she was content to withdraw into the background of her new home, she was compensated for her dreary life by the afternoon entertainments at the Guggenheimer mansion, where she heard such notables as Rachmaninoff, Prokofieff, Fritz Kreisler, and many others. On one occasion she accompanied Enrico Caruso at the piano.

Mrs. Guggenheimer's first child, a boy, died in 1904, four months after he was born. Her second child, Elizabeth, who was born in 1905, died of a mastoid infection at the age of seven. Mrs. Guggenheimer spent the next few years trying to forget her sorrow. It was during this period of bereavement that the conductor Arnold Volpe and his wife Marie tried to enlist her support for a plan to present outdoor concerts at the newly built Lewisohn Stadium on the campus of New York's City College.

The first concerts had been held at the stadium during the summer of 1917, but the city's park department, which had sponsored them, was forced to withdraw its support because of the lack of funds. Impressed by the physical facilities of the stadium, the Volpes envisoned an ambitious program of symphony concerts in place of the usual blare of brass bands and were determined to rally the $10,000 needed to underwrite their project. They discussed their plan with Aaron Barron, the music critic for a series of Yiddish newspapers, who put them in touch with Minnie Guggenheimer.

Although she was at first reluctant, Mrs. Guggenheimer arranged a meeting between Barron, the Volpes, and Adolph Lewisohn. This led to a further meeting with the conductor and pianist Ossip Gabrilówitsch. Lewisohn eventually agreed to invest one thousand dollars in the undertaking if Minnie Guggenheimer and Marie Volpe could secure the balance. They succeeded in this initial fund-raising and on June 23, 1918 Arnold Volpe conducted Sir Edward Elgar's "Pomp and Circumstance March," opening the first City College Stadium open-air concert.

During her early years as chairman and chief fund-raiser for the stadium concerts Mrs. Guggenheimer worked largely behind the scenes and seldom came into contact with the public. It was not until the 1940's, when the stadium concerts had already become an established institution, that she began to address stadium audiences during intermissions in her inimitable style.

Reportedly the late Mayor Fiorello H. La-Guardia urged Mrs. Guggenheimer to play a more active public role.

The $10,000 needed for the first series of concerts proved a fair estimate, for the cost was approximately $41,000 and the box office receipts came to nearly $32,000. Over the years the original two-week season of stadium concerts has been tripled in length, and the cost of the season has reached over $300,000 for the total of some thirty concerts. Because some concerts are inevitably rained out each year, the deficit is rarely under $50,000; it is this deficit that Minnie Guggenheimer tries to cover with her fund-raising activities. The capricious effects of weather on the cost of the concert season have made Mrs. Guggenheimer a regular patron of New York City's weather bureau. She has a private line over which she expects weather predictions for June from the middle of March onward.

Relying on a select list of donors, carefully graded as to amount of subscription, Minnie Guggenheimer has also been known to approach complete strangers who look wealthy. She claims that she can tell the difference between Oriental, cultured, and imitation pearls at a distance of from six to eight paces. Wearers of the genuine article she approaches, generally with success, for, she observes, they're usually respectable as well as loaded, and they'll come across with something just to get rid of me."

In her role as chief fund-raiser and guiding spirit of the stadium concerts Minnie Guggenheimer has become known to the public as the "Mrs. Malaprop of twentieth-century America." During her intermission announcements to stadium audiences over the years she has been responsible for mispronounced names, *non sequiturs, faux pas* in front of celebrities, and candid observations that have evoked hearty laughter from her listeners. The confusion engendered by her particular brand of humor has been described as "pandeminnium" in the book *Mother is Minnie* (Doubleday, 1960). It was written by her daughter, Sophie Guggenheimer Untermeyer, in collaboration with Alix Williamson, the publicity director of the stadium concerts.

Perhaps almost as many people visit Lewisohn Stadium to hear the intermission announcements of Minnie Guggenheimer as to listen to the famous musical personalities whom she presents in her concerts. Typical of her announcements are her presentation of such notables as "Rodger Hammerstein" and her forecast of a performance of *H.M.S. Pinafore* by "Gilbert and Solomon." She once confided to a stadium audience that she had always wanted to be a ballet dancer, and then demonstrated her ability. On another occasion she asked an audience of 10,000 to say "one at a time" if they preferred jazz to Beethoven.

So firmly established is her reputation for malapropisms that Douglas Watts in the New York *Daily News* reported after one of her appearances that "Minnie Guggenheimer was a disappointment at last night's Stadium opening. She made sense. . . . The crowd was perfectly able to follow her comments and felt it just hadn't gotten its usual money's worth."

Dr. I. W. Schmidt

MINNIE GUGGENHEIMER

Aside from her role as "mistress of ceremonies" Mrs. Guggenheimer has played a major part in arranging the programs presented at the Lewisohn Stadium and has been instrumental in presenting many famous names to stadium audiences. A number of noted artists have made their first important appearances at stadium concerts. In 1925 a nervous young Marian Anderson made her debut with an aria from Donizetti's *La Favorita.* Nelson Eddy made his first major appearance when he sang a solo part in Verdi's *Requiem* at the stadium. In 1927 a young composer named George Gershwin appeared at the Lewisohn Stadium to play his piano concerto, *Rhapsody in Blue,* for the first time. Other musical celebrities who have made important debuts at stadium concerts include Eugene Ormandy, William Kapell, and Ethel Merman.

When the young piano virtuoso Van Cliburn appeared at the stadium in 1958 to repeat the performance that had won him the first prize in Moscow's International Tchaikovsky Competition, Minnie Guggenheimer, observed to the audience: "It's just too bad that the *Russians* had to discover him!" Mrs. Guggenheimer has formed many close friendships with musical celebrities, notably with the late composer Charles Martin Loeffler, whom she first met in 1919. Her own preference is for instrumental music and her favorite musician is Pierre Monteux, the only conductor whose concerts she sits through from beginning to end.

Minnie Guggenheimer has experienced minor failures from time to time over the years. Misunderstanding the advice of her staff, she once missed a chance to book Liberace for an appearance at the stadium. Her generosity to seemingly worthy but indigent musicians has occasionally led her to inflict a travesty of entertainment on audiences. But the overall history of the stadium concerts, despite failure of acoustics, noisy audiences, and the whims of weather, has been a

GUGGENHEIMER, MINNIE—Continued

brilliant one. Veteran visitors to the stadium recall such memorable occasions as the time that Jascha Heifetz played valiantly through a rainstorm on an improvised stage; Grace Moore's performance of the aria *Un Bel Dì* from Puccini's opera *Madama Butterfly*, a few days before the end of World War II; and Louis Armstrong's first appearance after a serious illness at the Fourth of July concert in 1959.

In addition to her official position as chairman of Stadium Concerts, Inc. Minnie Guggenheimer is also a member of the board of directors of the New York Philharmonic Symphony Orchestra. In recognition of her work she received the ribbon of the French *Legion d'Honneur* in 1951. The National Arts Club conferred its third annual award on Mrs. Guggenheimer in 1959. In 1960 she received the Annual Music Award of New York City from Mayor Robert F. Wagner, and in 1961 she was awarded the annual Gold Medal of the 100 Year Association.

Minnie Guggenheimer's husband, Charles S. Guggenheimer, died in 1953, five months before their golden wedding anniversary. During his last illness Mrs. Guggenheimer kept a day and night vigil at his bedside for weeks. She has a daughter, Mrs. Sophie Guggenheimer Untermeyer, and a son, Randolph Guggenheimer, a lawyer. She also has grandchildren and one great-grandchild. Minnie Guggenheimer's passion in life, apart from the stadium concerts, is mushrooming, which she pursues from the middle of August onward, with a fine disregard for Private Property and Keep Out signs. Another passion, which dates from her first appearance on the *Jack Paar Show* (NBC-TV), is television —as a performer, rather than as a viewer. In her younger days she played tennis, and she takes pride in the forty-three silver cups that she won at it. A chain smoker, she likes "those ones with the tissue paper inside that taste like peppermints," and always gives up smoking one week, only to start again in the next. Her recipe for health is characteristic: "I just take six pills a day recommended to me by six different friends, and a straight double scotch before lunch and dinner."

In *Mother is Minnie* Sophie Guggenheimer Untermeyer analyzes her mother's "compulsive dedication" to the stadium concerts and says: "I have often secretly suspected that she would not like to see the Stadium Concerts become completely self-supporting during her lifetime. For this would eliminate altogether her now dearly cherished role as the gallant little heroine who manages somehow, year after year, to save the situation all by herself at the eleventh hour."

References

N Y Herald Tribune IV p6 Je 19 '60 por
N Y Times Mag p8 Jl 16 '61 por
Newsweek 55:64 Je 27 '60 por
Read Digest 80:109+ Je '62 por

Untermeyer, Sophie Guggenheimer and Williamson Alix. Mother is Minnie (1960)

HANSEN, CARL F(RANCIS) Jan. 18, 1906-
Educational administrator

Address: b. Franklin Administration Bldg., 13th and K Sts., N.W., Washington 5, D.C.; h. 3510 Quesada St., N.W., Washington, D.C.

Dr. Carl F. Hansen, who has been superintendent of schools for the District of Columbia since 1958, is one of the leading advocates of "basic" education in the United States. Hansen began his career as a high school teacher of English and Latin in 1925, and subsequently served as an educator and administrator in the school system of Omaha, Nebraska. In 1954 he played an important role in the desegregation of the schools of Washington, D.C. Hansen's concepts of education (which have been criticized by supporters of progressive education) have been incorporated into the school system of the nation's capital—notably at the Amidon Elementary School, established in 1960. Hansen believes that modern teaching methods should be blended with a strongly academic curriculum to provide the best possible schooling for every child at every level.

Carl Francis Hansen was born in Wolbach, Nebraska on January 18, 1906 to Peder and Barbara (Cutler) Hansen. He attended the Wolbach Public High School, where he participated in debating. After graduating in 1923, he entered the University of Nebraska, where he majored in English, with political science and Latin as his minor fields. He was a member of the university's debating team and was elected to the honorary forensic society, Delta Sigma Rho. In 1925, while still at the university, he began to teach English, Latin, and speech at Wolbach Public High School.

Having graduated from the University of Nebraska with the B.A. degree in 1927, Hansen became a teacher of English and debating at the high school in Grand Island, Nebraska. He organized the Grand Island Teachers Association and was its first president. During the summers of 1931 and 1932 he attended the University of Wisconsin law school, where he studied such subjects as torts, contracts, and personal property law. He was granted a leave of absence from his teaching position at Grand Island during 1935-36, to work as personnel officer and supervisor of adult education for the District 4 office of the Works Progress Administration. In 1936 he moved to Omaha, where he taught English, journalism, and guidance at the Omaha Technical High School. In 1939-40 he held a teaching fellowship at the University of Southern California. The University of Nebraska granted him an M.A. degree in 1940, after he had completed a program of study and research in education and psychology, with English as a minor field.

From 1940 to 1945 Hansen was head of the language arts department at the Omaha Technical High School. He received his Ed.D. degree from the University of Southern California in 1944 after he completed an advanced program in education, administration and supervision, and psychology, with comparative literature as his minor subject. His dissertation was entitled "Utilization of Semantics in Instruction in English." During 1945-47 he served as principal of the Omaha Technical High School, at the same time lecturing at the Municipal University of Omaha on administration and supervision.

In Omaha, Hansen did much research on educational problems. He developed curriculum materials and teaching aids, and he established a high school reading improvement program with appropriate testing. During 1944-47 he directed a survey of spelling and language difficulties cn all school levels, and he headed textbook committees for the adoption of elementary school spellers and English texts. He also served on the president's advisory council of the Municipal University of Omaha and on the superintendent's curriculum council. He was a member of the Omaha Educational Association, the Nebraska Educational Association, and the National Educational Association.

In March 1947 Hansen became executive assistant to the superintendent of schools in Washington, D.C. From August 1947 until 1955 he served as associate superintendent in charge of elementary schools for white children and curriculum planning for all schools and levels in the nation's capital. In addition he taught part-time at George Washington University during 1954-55. He served as assistant superintendent in charge of senior high schools from 1955 until his appointment as superintendent of schools in 1958

By the time he became associated with the Washington school system Hansen had developed clearly defined concepts on the needs of education, and he has tried to incorporate these ideas into the curriculum. Described by James D. Koerner in the *Saturday Review* (December 16, 1961) as "a man with a strong academic bent and a low tolerance for permissive education," Hansen differs with the followers of John Dewey on many points. He rejects the notion that the school must reflect "life," maintaining that the school environment is created to provide organized instruction in basic subjects for all students at all levels. He also rejects the "postponement" or "readiness" theory, which contends that children should not be taught subjects that they are not "ready" to learn. He believes that content in teaching in the early grades should be broadened to provide a sound basis for the child's further schooling.

As an associate of school superintendent Hobart Corning, Hansen played a major role in the desegregation of Washington's schools in accordance with the May 1954 ruling of the United States Supreme Court. In effecting the integration of the city's schools, which at the time had an enrollment that was about 75 percent Negro, the administrators concentrated on providing the best educational program possible for every child and tried to ignore the explosive possibilities of desegregation. Although basic educational problems persisted as a result of the almost overnight integration of Washington's schools, Hansen found that Negro children could respond as well as children of any other ethnic group to the intellectual demands of a solid school program. He has written several articles on the progress of integration. The Anti-Defamation League of B'nai B'rith published his pamphlets *Miracle of Social Adjustment: Desegregation in the Washington, D.C. Schools* (1957) and *Addendum: A Five-Year Report* (1960).

CARL F. HANSEN

As one means of coping with the problems of the newly integrated schools, which included many pupils from culturally deprived backgrounds, Hansen established a "four-track" system in the city's high schools in 1955. Under this system the student enrolls in one of four tracks, depending on the level of his achievement. The four tracks are: (1) honors—for top students only; (2) regular—a basic college preparatory program; (3) general—a combination of academic and vocational courses; and (4) basic—a course for retarded students entering high school with an aptitude for reading and mathematics on a level of sixth grade or under. At these four levels Hansen established a strongly academic program of systematic instruction corresponding to the abilities of the individual student. Ideally he would like to see the enrollments in the third track decrease in favor of the honors and regular courses. He has criticized the contention of some educators that the education of less gifted students should be predominantly vocational, believing that the slow learner needs effective instruction in basic academic subjects. In 1959 the board of education of Washington extended the track system to all schools within the District of Columbia.

Hansen's other achievements include his direction of the changeover to annual grade promotion in the elementary schools, and the reorganization of the elementary school system on a city-wide basis. He also directed an extensive curriculum development program in reading, language arts, science, intergroup education, civic responsibility, and citizenship. He has established a high school for emotionally disturbed children, a special language arts program on an elementary school level in the poorer neighborhoods, and a "talent search" program for gifted students.

Interested in up-to-date educational techniques, Hansen undertook extensive research in educational television, and he reported the results in several articles and pamphlets. Using local

HANSEN, CARL F.—*Continued*

facilities and financing, he extended the educational television program of the District of Columbia to serve about 35,000 students, who were offered courses in languages, sciences, music, and other fields. However, the program was discontinued when it showed poor test results at the end of a five-year trial period.

His most significant achievement to date has been the establishment, in September 1960, of the Amidon Elementary School, which embodies many of his educational ideas. Incorporating the track system used in the other Washington schools, Amidon is "teacher-centered" rather than "child-centered." It provides systematic instruction in basic subjects, with experience units designed to supplement the direct teaching of fundamentals. Departing from the "look-say" method of teaching reading, which (according to its supporters) should not be taught to a child before he is six and a half, Amidon uses the phonovisual system of "sounding out words," and reading instruction in Amidon begins in kindergarten, along with instruction in other basic subjects, such as mathematics. This program has brought about a notable improvement in the reading ability of Amidon's students. Although the Amidon plan has been strongly criticized by some educators (one critic called it "a sop to all the reactionary forces afloat"), the response from parents, teachers, and pupils has been generally favorable.

The details of the Amidon program, together with test results, were reported by Hansen in his book *The Amidon Elementary School* (Prentice-Hall, 1962). Denying that the program returns to the "horse and buggy days" of education, Hansen says that it is "a new step toward the fusion of two main streams in American educational thought: the bringing together of the best that has been discovered about the learning process and selected logically organized subject matter."

As a result of its success the Amidon plan has been extended to other levels of the Washington school system. In the fall of 1962 the Jefferson Junior High School is operating on a strongly academic curriculum, which exposes students to the major ideas in seventy-five works of literature and scientific, political, and social thought. To widen educational opportunities for students with special talents, Hansen has announced a special program in art and music, to take effect in 1963 at the McKinley High School in Washington. Hansen hopes to establish a two-year junior college in the nation's capital, to accommodate students who are capable of college work but who cannot afford to go to college.

Hansen has ardently campaigned for the improvement of material conditions in the Washington schools, and he has succeded in obtaining government appropriations for the purchase of textbooks. In June 1962 he requested from the federal government a $120,000,000 interest-free loan to finance school construction over a period of six years. As one of nineteen authors who took part in a written symposium "Education for Survival in the Struggle Against Communism," published by the Senate International Security Subcommittee in 1962, Hansen advocated a strong educational program on the subject of Communism and added: "Any teaching about Russia must presuppose a thorough grounding in the essentials of the American way of life and must be a means of reconfirming these views." Hansen's articles have appeared in the *Atlantic Monthly*, the *Harvard Educational Review*, *Nation's Schools*, *School Executive*, *School and Society*, and other journals. He has written book reviews for the *New Republic* and *American Scholar*.

On June 11, 1929 Carl F. Hansen married Ruth Williams, a teacher. They have two children, Karen Barbara and Richard Williams Hansen. Dr. Hansen belongs to the American Association of School Administrators, the National Education Association, the National Association of Secondary School Principals, and the Washington Board of Trade. A member of the educational fraternity Phi Delta Kappa, he also belongs to the Cosmos Club and attends the Chevy Chase Presbyterian Church. In June 1962 Bucknell University in Lewisburg, Pennsylvania conferred an honorary LL.D. degree upon him. With an eye to the future, Hansen feels that "the skills and techniques needed in the modern school for today and tomorrow must be superior . . . to anything so far developed in education."

References

    Sat R 44:49+ D 16 '61 por

    Leaders in Education (1948)

HARRISON, JAMES L(ERLIE) June 3, 1906- United States government official

Address: b. Government Printing Office, Washington 25, D.C.; h. 4000 Massachusetts Ave. N.W., Washington 16, D.C.

The Public Printer of the United States, James L. Harrison, is the fifteenth person to hold the position since the Government Printing Office was created by Congressional joint resolution on June 23, 1860. Under his direction the office prints publications of the Congress, the federal departments, government agencies, and the judiciary. It is the largest general printing plant in the world and employs about 6,500 people. Before Harrison was named Public Printer by the President, he had been for twelve years the staff director of the Joint Congressional Committee on Printing, which controls certain activities of the Government Printing Office.

James Lerlie Harrison was born on June 3, 1906 in Greer, South Carolina, the son of John DeBert and Sallie (Pitts) Harrison. His father was in the textile business. When Harrison was ten years old, the family moved to Gastonia, North Carolina, and he was raised there and educated in the local public schools. He had three brothers, John A., Luther P., and Earl R. Harrison, and six sisters, of whom only two, Mrs. James E. Webb and Mrs. Warren Schiesser, are living.

At Gastonia High School, from which he graduated in 1927, Harrison was active in athletics, the school band and orchestra, the glee club, and the dramatic club. He also worked on the school newspaper and yearbook and had an after-school job in a printing plant—experiences he credits today with having influenced his choice of life work.

Harrison went to Washington, D.C. in 1928 and entered the wholesale and retail food business. After five years he joined the Bureau of the Census, where he worked first as a draftsman and later as field and area supervisor. In 1942 he was transferred to the field division of the Office of Price Administration. Six months later he was named OPA liaison officer at the Capitol, serving in that capacity until the OPA was dissolved in 1947. For the next two years he was the president of a wholesale appliance company, returning to Capitol Hill in May 1949 as staff director of the Joint Congressional Committee on Printing. He held this post for twelve years and acquired what has been described as "a wholesome regard for the magnitude of problems confronting the nation's largest printing establishment."

This committee, created by Act of Congress in the nineteenth century, consists of three members of the Senate and three members of the House of Representatives. It is charged with correcting any delay or waste in the public printing, binding, and distribution of government publications. It also fixes the standards of paper used in public printing, approves contracts for such paper and other materials, and passes on wage agreements that the Public Printer is authorized by law to conclude with the committees representing the various trades in the Government Printing Office. In sum, the Committee acts generally as the board of directors of the Governing Printing Office.

As staff director of the Joint Committee, Harrison was in daily and often hourly contact with the Government Printing Office. He acted as consultant on the use of color and illustrations in public printing and on the need for printing any particular government publication—both matters subject to the control of the Joint Committee. He also personally visited many printing plants operated by various governments around the world.

This long and varied experience with government printing operations led President John F. Kennedy to name Harrison Public Printer in March 1961, despite the fact that Harrison was not, as required by law, "a practical printer," versed in the art of bookbinding." The White House announcement that Harrison had been selected for the job, which pays $20,000 a year, was greeted with protests by the nation's master printers. "We have nothing against Mr. Harrison personally, and do not question his integrity," said a spokesman for the Printing Industry of America, Inc., which represents 8,000 master printers. "We just do not believe that he is qualified. Certainly he does not meet the requirement of the law." The Senate, however, confirmed the appointment, apparently satisfied that although Harrison changed his post in becoming the Public Printer, he would meet few problems with which he was not already familiar.

In its function as print shop for the government, the Government Printing Office prints 43,000 copies of the *Congressional Record* daily, ranging in volume from sixteen to 280 pages or more. All bills, hearings, resolutions, and other

JAMES L. HARRISON

publications required by Congress in the performance of its legislative functions are also printed by the office. Each year the Public Printer receives a direct appropriation of funds that form a working capital from which the cost of printing and binding for Congress is deducted. All other government establishments employing the service of the printing office pay the Public Printer from their own appropriations for the cost of printing and materials they order.

The range of printed materials published by the Government Printing Office is unusually wide. For the federal post office it prints postal cards—more than three billion annually. For the Department of Health, Education, and Welfare it produces booklets on child care; for the Treasury Department, income tax returns; for the State and Defense Departments, secret documents. The office also furnishes blank paper, inks, and similar supplies to all government offices; distributes government publications and maintains catalogs and a library of these publications; and prints, for sale to the public, documents that are not confidential.

Government publications offered to the public are sold by the Government Printing Office's division of public documents, which annually mails out approximately 150,000,000 copies of various publications, with sales totaling some $7,000,000. When the volume of work at the office exceeds its capacity, printing jobs are awarded to commercial facilities. About one-third of the government's total printing is done commercially.

Harrison is the compiler of *Biographical Directory of the American Congress—1774 to 1949*. He also served as editor and compiler of the *Congressional Directory* and compiled and edited, under the direction of the Joint Congressional Committee on Printing, the *Government Printing and Binding Regulations* and the *Government Paper Specification Standards*. Deeply interested in the graphic arts and in

HARRISON, JAMES L.—*Continued*

printing research, as well as in the training of printing craftsmen, Harrison is vice-president of the Washington Lithographic Council, which conducts courses in lithography and photography at Gallaudet College (for the deaf) in Washington, D.C.

James Harrison is a Democrat and a member of Washington's Minnesota Avenue Christian Church. His hobbies are golf and woodworking; he is a member of the Kenwood Golf and Country Club and the Litho Club, both in Washington D.C. He has been married since December 31, 1960 to the former Margaret Elizabeth Scott, a transportation expert. His first wife was the former Irene Martin, whom he married April 1, 1928. This union terminated in divorce on December 19, 1955. By this marriage Harrison had a daughter, Dorothy Joan, now Mrs. Albert Silbaugh. On June 20, 1956 he married Mary Jo Chadduck, who died on May 10, 1959.

The Public Printer has been particularly interested in winning the friendship of the printing office employees and in building plant morale. Shortly after he was appointed, he staged a banquet and celebration to mark the office's centennial, March 4, 1961. He also directed the preparation of a centennial history of the office, which won acclaim as an historical document, and he has tried to improve the physical conditions under which the printing office employees work. He became generally recognized, during his first year in office, as a talented organization leader who may prove to be one of the most active Public Printers in the history of the office.

References

New Frontiersmen (1961)
Who's Who in America, 1962-63

HEATH, EDWARD (RICHARD GEORGE)
July 9, 1916- British Cabinet member
Address: b. House of Commons, London S.W.1, England; h. Helmdon, King Edward Ave., Broadstairs, Kent, England

The Right Honorable Edward Heath, Lord Privy Seal in the cabinet of the United Kingdom, is so dedicated an advocate of Western European unity that he has sometimes been called Great Britain's "Minister for Europe." A member of the House of Commons since 1950, Heath served as government chief whip from 1955 to 1959, and as Minister of Labor in 1959-60.

The office of Lord Privy Seal, to which Heath was assigned in July 1960, is titular and carries no departmental duties. Its incumbent is generally someone whose views on policy-making are important, and who is available for special assignments. As Lord Privy Seal, Heath became responsible for Foreign Office affairs in the House of Commons, and particularly for European affairs. Since the summer of 1961 he has been engaged in negotiations for Great Britain's entrance into the European Economic Community or Common Market, a step that he regards as Great Britain's most important decision of the century.

Edward Richard George Heath was born on July 9, 1916 to William George and Edith Anne Heath. He is a native of Broadstairs, a seaside resort in the county of Kent, England, where his father was a master builder and businessman. He was educated at the Chatham House School, a private school in the adjacent town of Ramsgate. Developing an interest in music at an early age, Ted Heath preferred practising the piano and reading to playing on the beach. He sang in the choir of a church in Broadstairs, and he learned to play the organ.

His musical proficiency won Heath the organ scholarship at Balliol College, Oxford University, and he became organist in the college chapel. A student of the "Modern Greats"—philosophy, politics, and economics—he developed a keen interest in public affairs while at Oxford. In 1937 he was elected president of the University Conservative Association and in the following year he became chairman of the Federation of University Conservative Associations. Addressing a conference of the federation at Caxton Hall, London in January 1939, Heath appealed to Prime Minister Neville Chamberlain to abandon the policy of appeasement and adopt a firmer policy, which would unite the party and the country. During his final year at Oxford Heath was the president of the Oxford Union—the university's debating society. He graduated with a Second Class Honors degree in 1939.

In the summer of 1939 Heath hitchhiked across northwestern Europe and visited the trouble spots of Poland and Danzig. In October of that year he went to the United States as a member of a debating team touring American universities. On his return in 1940 Heath joined the Royal Artillery as a gunner, and during the next five years he saw active service in France, Belgium, the Netherlands and Germany. He was mentioned in dispatches and received an M.B.E. (Member of the Order of the British Empire) in the Military Division. Advanced to lieutenant colonel while second in command of an artillery regiment in 1945, he was discharged in that rank in 1946. After the war Heath retained his connection with the Honourable Artillery Company, and from April 1947 until August 1951 he commanded the company's 2d regiment in the Territorial Army. From 1951 to 1954 he served as master gunner in the Tower of London.

Upon his return to civilian life in 1946 Heath entered the civil service as an administrator in the Ministry of Civil Aviation. In 1947 he resigned to enter politics, having been chosen as the prospective Conservative candidate to represent Bexley, a suburb of London, in the House of Commons. At the same time he joined one of the oldest merchant banking firms in London and remained on its staff until 1951. In the general election of February 23, 1950, when the Labor government of Clement Attlee was returned to power with a scant majority, Heath won by a narrow margin in Bexley (which was formerly held by the Labor party), and he has represented that constituency continuously since that time.

As a newly elected member of the House of Commons Heath made French Foreign Minister Robert Schuman's proposal for the pooling of European coal and steel resources the subject of his maiden speech on June 26, 1950. (The

Schuman plan, which resulted in the establishment of the European Coal and Steel Community in August 1952, was rejected by the British Labor government at the time.) Heath was one of nine Conservative Members of Parliament who contributed to the symposium *One Nation: A Tory Approach to Social Problems,* published in 1950. In February 1951 he was named assistant whip for the Conservative minority. Following the election of October 25, 1951, which returned Winston Churchill and the Conservatives to power, Heath was appointed a Lord Commissioner of the Treasury, or government whip. In May 1952 he became joint deputy chief whip, and in June of the following year he was made deputy chief whip.

In 1953 Heath made another visit to the United States, this time on a Smith-Mundt Fellowship at the invitation of the Department of State. In 1954 he attended the Commonwealth Parliamentary Association conference at Nairobi, Kenya as a United Kingdom delegate. He was retained as deputy chief whip by Prime Minister Anthony Eden following the election of May 1955. In December 1955 Heath was named Parliamentary Secretary to the Treasury, a post that carries the duties of government chief whip, and at the same time he was made a Privy Councillor. As chief whip Heath was responsible for ensuring the attendance of all members of the government party on vital roll calls. Although his sole contribution to House of Commons debates consisted of the sentence "I beg to move that this House do now adjourn," he was regarded as one of the most important Conservative Members of Parliament.

During his service as government chief whip, Heath guided the Conservatives in the House of Commons through several crises, including the one induced by Egypt's seizure of the Suez Canal in 1956. The failure of the British intervention in the Suez affair was attributed by many Britons to the lack of United States support and aroused anti-American sentiments within Conservative ranks. However, by means of skillful diplomacy Heath restored a large measure of unity to the party. When in January 1957 Eden's illness necessitated his resignation, Heath was largely instrumental in the choice of Harold Macmillan to succeed as party leader and Prime Minister. Following the Conservative landslide victory in October 1959 Macmillan reorganized his cabinet, and Heath received the portfolio of Minister of Labor. During his nine months in this position he scored some notable successes in the arbitration of industrial disputes.

On July 27, 1960 Macmillan again revamped his cabinet and Heath was appointed to the office of Lord Privy Seal, a ministry without portfolio maintained for special assignments. ("I am neither a lord, nor a privy, nor a seal," Heath has quipped.) Assigned to the Ministry of Foreign Affairs, he became its spokesman in the House of Commons, since the new Secretary of State for Foreign Affairs, Lord Home, was a member of the House of Lords. At this time Great Britain was considering the possibility of joining the European Economic Community (EEC) or Common Market. The EEC was established by France, Italy, West Germany, Belgium, the Netherlands, and Luxembourg in ac-

British Inf. Services

EDWARD HEATH

cordance with the treaty signed in Rome in March 1957 with the purpose of removing tariff barriers between signatories and agreement on a common tariff in relation to outside countries. (In 1959 the United Kingdom had joined with Austria, Denmark, Norway, Portugal, Sweden, and Switzerland—nations not included in the EEC—in establishing the European Free Trade Association.)

Heath did most of the spadework in connection with Great Britain's application for membership in the Common Market under Article 237 of the Treaty of Rome. At a meeting of the Council of Europe at Strasbourg in September 1960 Heath expressed the view that the EEC, the EFTA, and British preferential treatment for Commonwealth nations were all compatible, and that Britain would be prepared to make concessions to bring about accommodation. Returning from additional talks in Paris in the following month, he told the annual conference of the Conservative party that the Macmillan government wanted "to see unity established in Europe and . . . to be a party of it."

Great Britain's decision to apply for membership in the Common Market was communicated to her partners in the EFTA in late July 1961. On October 10, 1961 Heath told the foreign ministers of the six EEC nations that Great Britain was ready to subscribe fully to the aims and objectives of the Common Market. "We desire to become full, wholehearted, and active members of the European Community in its widest sense, and to go forward with you in the building of a new Europe," he declared. "Europe must unite or perish. We are convinced that our destiny is intimately linked with yours."

In January 1962 Heath visited the United States to discuss with Secretary of State Dean Rusk the whole range of foreign economic issues. He then visited Ottawa to discuss with Canadian Premier John G. Diefenbaker the effects of British entrance into the Common Market upon

HEATH, EDWARD—*Continued*

the Imperial Preference system, which governs the economic relations between the thirteen members of the Commonwealth of Nations. Formal negotiations on the terms of Britain's admission to the Common Market were begun in Brussels on May 11, 1962, with Heath heading the British delegation.

Although the British decision to seek membership in the Common Market was approved by the House of Commons on August 3, 1961 by a vote of 313 to 5 (with many abstentions), there remained much opposition to it, notably from Labor party representatives led by Hugh Gaitskell, and from spokesmen for Commonwealth nations, who feared that the interests of the Commonwealth would suffer by British adherence to the European Economic Community. Some Conservative Members of Parliament also criticized the move, on the grounds that Britain would thereby lose her traditional independence in relation to Europe.

Speaking on a nationwide radio and television broadcast on June 20, 1962, Heath reassured the Labor party that membership in the EEC would not preclude continued social planning. He said that although membership might entail the surrender of some sovereignty, Britain would play a major role in all European institutions. Although he conceded that certain problems regarding Britain's relation to the Commonwealth remained to be solved, he concluded that entry into the Common Market would be "best for Britain, for our Commonwealth, for Europe and for the Western world."

As the government's official spokesman on foreign affairs in the House of Commons, Heath has had to explain and defend the government position on such issues as the crises in Berlin, the Congo, and Laos, and the question of nuclear weapons testing. In general, his position has hewed closely to that of the Kennedy administration. When on July 13, 1962 Prime Minister Macmillan dismissed and replaced seven members of his twenty-one member cabinet, in an effort to restore confidence in the Conservative government after a series of losses in recent by-elections, Heath was one of the ministers retained in his post. Many political observers regard Heath as standing in the front rank of possible contenders for the prime ministership in a future Conservative government.

Edward Heath was described in the Toronto *Globe and Mail* (November 2, 1959) as "a reticent man, not noted for his sense of humor, apparently friendless but undoubtedly strong and, above all, loyal to his chief who confides in him." On the other hand, a personality sketch in the New York *Times* (August 1, 1961) noted that he is "a persuasive and at times brilliant speaker whose calm, even-tempered manner and quiet courtesy discourage hot-blooded political exchanges and promote reasoned discussion." "Although reserved," the sketch continued, "he is a good companion with an easy laugh and an utter lack of pomposity." Heath has blue eyes and silvery hair. He does not smoke and drinks only in moderation. Although he has remained a bachelor, he occasionally squires a girl to dinner. His colleagues regard him as a "totally dedicated politician who has ruthlessly eliminated from his

personal life any pleasure that would interfere with his career" (*Time*, July 13, 1962). Nevertheless Heath is fond of horticulture, music, art, and travel and likes to listen to the stereophonic records he has collected. He takes an interest in the local affairs of his home district and often visits his favorite tavern, the King's Head, in Bexley. His clubs are Buck's and the Carlton.

References

N Y Times p21 N 13 '57 por; p2 Ag 1 '61 por
Time 80:29+ Jl 13 '62 pors
Toronto Globe and Mail p7 N 2 '59 por; p8 Mr 31 '62 por
International Who's Who, 1961-62
International Year Book and Statesmen's Who's Who, 1962
Kelly's Handbook to the Titled, Landed and Official Classes, 1961
Who's Who, 1962

HESSE, HERMANN (hěs'ě) July 2, 1877-
Novelist and poet
Address: h. Montagnola, Ticino, Switzerland

> BULLETIN: Hermann Hesse died on August 9, 1962. *Obituary*: N Y Times p19 Ag 10 '62

Long regarded as one of the greatest of contemporary European men of letters, the German-Swiss novelist and poet, Hermann Hesse, has only in recent years attained some measure of popularity in the United States. The contemplative, sometimes mystical, quality of his novels, stories, essays, and poems, which is basically foreign to the pragmatic American mind, seems to have an increasing appeal in the light of the insecurities of the mid-twentieth century. Although Hesse, as a citizen of the world and as a critic of modern technological civilization, is greatly concerned with the fate of humanity, he rejects utopian solutions and mass movements, and is primarily preoccupied with the individual in his search for self-realization.

The theme of the relationship between nature and spirit, between childish innocence and worldly sophistication, and between the lonely wanderer and the solid citizen, constantly recurs in Hesse's writings, many of which are partly autobiographical. Hesse resolves these seeming conflicts between opposites by his conception of the basic oneness of the universe and of all human experience. Works by Hesse that have been translated into English include *Demian*, *Siddhartha*, *Steppenwolf*, *Death and the Lover*, *Journey to the East*, and the monumental novel *Magister Ludi*, for which he won the Nobel Prize for literature in 1946.

In his writings Hermann Hesse fondly recalls his home town, the Swabian town of Calw in Wurttemberg, situated on the river Nagold at the edge of the Black Forest. He was born on July 2, 1877, the second of six children, two of whom died in infancy. (Hesse also had two elder half-brothers from his mother's first marriage.) His father, Johannes Hesse, a native of Estonia and the son of a physician, was a missionary, teacher, writer, and publisher, who had served in India before settling in Calw. Hesse's mother, the former Marie Gundert-Dubois, was born in India of French-Swiss parentage. Her father was the noted missionary and Indologist, Dr. Hermann Gundert.

The Christianity of Hesse's parents was of the Pietist variety, with a strong puritan strain and an emphasis on inner contemplation. The culture of the Orient also was a major influence on Hesse's early life. The Hesse home was filled with art objects from India and China and was frequently visited by missionaries and scholars from Asia. A headstrong, sensitive, and highly imaginative boy, Hesse was fond of nature and of folk songs and composed poems by the time he was five. He received his early education in Basel, Switzerland, where his father taught at a mission house and edited a missionary journal from 1881 to 1886. Although Hesse took little interest in his school work, he stood at the head of his class without much difficulty. He began his self-education early in life, making use of the extensive library of his maternal grandfather, and he liked in particular the works of the German Romantic poets.

Although Hesse had determined to become a writer by the time he was thirteen and had become a religious skeptic at fourteen, his parents wanted him to follow in the family tradition and study for the ministry. From February 1890 to May 1891 Hesse attended the preparatory Latin school of Rector Otto Bauer, in Göppingen.

After passing the *Landexamen* in July 1891 Hesse was admitted to the theological seminary at Maulbronn. The rigid, medieval atmosphere of Maulbronn caused Hesse to rebel, and in March 1892 he ran away. His parents, believing that he was possessed by the devil, took him to the noted theologian and faith healer, Christoph Blumhardt, who failed to quell his rebellious spirit. Following an attempt at suicide Hesse briefly attended the *Gymnasium* at Canstatt, but was expelled in 1893, in the middle of the school year. He was subsequently apprenticed to a bookseller in Esslingen, but ran away after three days and returned to Calw, where he worked for six months as an assistant to his father in the Calwer Verlagsverein.

In the spring of 1894 Hesse became an apprentice in the clock factory of Heinrich Perrot in Calw, where he learned to assemble steeple-clocks. He moved to the university town of Tübingen in October 1895 and became an apprentice to a bookseller and antique dealer. Upon completing his apprenticeship in September 1898 he worked as an assistant in the bookshop until July of the following year. At Tübingen he associated with professors and students and continued his self-education, devoting himself particularly to the study of Goethe. From 1899 to 1903 Hesse worked for the bookdealer Reich in Basel, where he was strongly influenced by the ideas of Friedrich Nietzsche and of the cultural historian Jakob Burckhardt. While visiting Florence in 1901 Hesse first became conscious of his antipathy to modern civilization and felt that he would forever remain an outsider in relation to his own society.

In his early writings Hesse reflects the Romantic tradition and paints idyllic scenes of nature and of rural and small-town life. His first two

Wide World

HERMANN HESSE

volumes of poetry were published in 1899 under the titles *Romantische Lieder* and *Eine Stunde hinter Mitternacht.* In 1901 he published his partly autobiographical *Hinterlassene Schriften und Gedichte von Hermann Lauscher,* followed by another volume of poems, *Gedichte* (1902). His first novel, *Peter Camenzind* (1904), about a young man who breaks away from his bourgeois environment to take up the simple life close to nature, won him the Bauernfeld prize of Vienna in 1905.

In 1904, the year of his first marriage, Hesse moved to Gaienhofen, on the German shore of the Lake of Constance. In addition to poems, short stories, and essays he wrote the novels *Unterm Rad* (1906), describing the sorrows and hardships of a schoolboy; and *Gertrud* (1910; English translation *Gertrude and I,* International Monthly, Inc., 1915). Although he was essentially nonpolitical in his outlook Hesse contributed articles and reviews to several German liberal periodicals. In 1907 he helped to found *März,* journal for German culture, and he edited its literary section until 1912. Feeling restless, Hesse left his family in 1911 to take a journey to India, but the experience failed to provide him with the inner liberation he had hoped for. In 1912 he moved with his family to Bern.

The outbreak of World War I came as a profound shock to Hesse. Although he was not an absolute pacifist, he formed a close friendship with the French pacifist writer Romain Rolland and joined him in condemning the war hysteria rampant everywhere. In the early months of the war he wrote several articles in which he called upon artists and intellectuals of all nations to rise above nationalist passions. From 1914 until the spring of 1919 Hesse worked as a volunteer through the German consulate in Bern on behalf of German prisoners of war. He edited the *Sonntagsbote für Deutsche Kriegsgefangene* and served as co-editor of the *Deutsche Internierten-*

HESSE, HERMANN—*Continued*

Zeitung. His writings during the early war period include *Rosshalde* (1914), a novel reflecting his own marital difficulties; and *Knulp* (1915), a series of three stories about a lovable vagabond.

Hesse's concern with the war, as well as the serious illness of his youngest son and the mental breakdown of his wife led him to preoccupy himself more and more with the problems of the human mind. He delved into the works of Sigmund Freud, Carl Gustav Jung, and Rudolf Steiner. For a time he underwent psychiatric treatment and was a patient at a sanatorium. In 1917-18 he wrote several essays condemning the continuing slaughter and calling for an end to the war.

In 1919 Hesse moved to the village of Montagnola on Lake Lugano, in the Swiss canton of Ticino, where he lived for the next few years in almost complete isolation. He acquired some measure of popularity among the bewildered German youth of the postwar generation. In his essay *Zarathustras Wiederkehr* (1919) he called upon the youth of Germany to reject doctrines and dogmas that claim to reform the world, and to listen only to the voice that comes from within. He became a citizen of Switzerland in 1923

Hesse's first postwar novel, *Demian; die Geschichte einer Jugend* (1919), reflecting his preoccupation with psychoanalysis and the workings of the subconscious mind, deals with an individual's quest for self-fulfillment under the guidance of a friend. The English translation (*Demian*, Boni & Liveright, 1923) drew mixed reactions from the critics. Although it was described in the Boston *Transcript* (April 14, 1923) as "a nightmare of abnormality, a crazed dream of a paranoiac," a reviewer for the New York *Times* (April 8, 1923) called it "an unusual piece of work . . . a book in a hundred. . . . written with an animation and warmth that can issue only from the deepest sincerity." Published under the pseudonym Emil Sinclair, the book won the Fontane prize, which Hesse returned, since this prize was intended only for new authors.

In *Klingsors letzter Sommer* (1920) Hesse symbolizes the decline of Europe in the death of the artist Klingsor. His lack of faith in the future of Europe made him turn to the Orient for the theme of *Siddhartha; eine indische Dichtung* (1922; English translation, *Siddhartha*, New Directions, 1951), which was described as "quite possibly one of the best short novels of this century" by Gisela Stein, who praised it for its "beautiful rhythmic, almost Biblical prose" (New York *Times Book Review*, July 1, 1962). Set in India, this story of a Brahmin, who undergoes various life experiences in his quest for ultimate reality, emphasizes the basic oneness of the universe and conveys the message that ultimate wisdom cannot be taught but can only be attained through inner experience. Hesse's other writings during this period include *Kurgast* (1925) and *Die Nürnberger Reise* (1927).

Der Steppenwolf (1927; English translation, *Steppenwolf*, Holt, 1929), perhaps his most powerful work, is a semi-autobiographical account of a man torn between animal instincts and bourgeois respectability, and depicts humanity as the bridge between nature and spirit. *Steppenwolf* proved to be strong medicine for the English-speaking world. A critic for the British journal *Nation and Athenæum* (May 11, 1929) called it "a peculiarly unappetizing conglomeration of fantasy, philosophy, and moist eroticism," and a reviewer for the Boston *Transcript* (September 4, 1929) commented: "It seems as if every madness of the post-war era, every devilish vice, every perversion, and every despair . . . is mingled here as in a witch's broth."

The theme of the relationship between nature and spirit is further developed in *Narziss und Goldmund* (1930; English translation, *Death and the Lover*, Dodd, 1932), which is regarded by some critics as Hesse's greatest novel. The book deals with the friendship between two medieval men, one a man of the spirit, the other a wanderer searching for the ultimate in life. In his short novel *Die Morgenlandfahrt* (1932; English translation, *The Journey to the East*, Noonday, 1957) Hesse describes a symbolic journey, beyond time and space, to an all-embracing realm of the spirit.

In 1931 Hesse remarried and moved to his own home near Montagnola. In the same year he resigned from the Prussian Academy of Poets of which he had been a member since 1926, because, as he wrote to Thomas Mann, he had little faith in the German nation. With the rise of Nazism in Germany his home became a favorite stopping place for refugee scholars and artists from Germany. Because he had remained largely silent on political matters, and because of the esteem in which he was still held in Germany, the Nazi authorities attempted for a time to win Hesse over to their fold, but they ultimately placed him on their blacklist when their efforts failed.

From 1931 to 1942 Hesse worked on his monumental novel, *Das Glasperlenspiel* (1943; English translation, *Magister Ludi*, Ungar, 1949), which won him the Nobel Prize for literature in 1946. The book was published in Zurich after an unsuccessful attempt to have it published in Germany. The novel is set in the remote future, in Castalia, a community of scholars charged with the task of preserving the cultural values of humanity. The story centers around the life of Josef Knecht, who, after having attained the highest position in the order, that of Magister Ludi or master of the "bead-game" (a universal intellectual language, symbolizing the sum total of human culture), ultimately leaves Castalia to go out into the world to serve his fellow man. The book, which recapitulates all of Hesse's earlier themes, reveals a high degree of philosophic insight and offers much lucid commentary on our times.

Since the end of World War II Hesse has again become one of the most popular authors in Germany, and his works have acquired an increasing appeal among readers throughout the world. (In Japan no modern German author is more highly honored or more widely read than Hesse.) Recent publications of works by Hesse include *Krieg und Frieden* (1946), *Späte Prosa* (1951), *Gesammelte Dichtungen*, 6 vols. (1952), *Gesammelte Schriften*, 7 vols. (1957), and *Bericht an die Freunde; Letzte Gedichte* (1960). Several volumes of his voluminous correspondence have been published in recent years. Over the years he has edited a number of volumes of world literature, including folk songs and works of German Romantic poets. Although Hesse has no basic quarrel with the film industry (he is a great admirer of Charles Chaplin), he has refused requests by motion picture producers for permission to film his novels.

In addition to the Nobel Prize Hesse has received a number of other awards and honors, including the Gottfried Keller prize of 1936. When in 1946 the city of Frankfurt conferred upon him the Goethe prize he accepted it with some reluctance, fearing that he might thereby appear to recognize the "official" Germany. The University of Bern conferred an honorary doctorate upon Hesse in 1947. In 1950 he was awarded the Wilhelm Raabe prize by the city of Brunswick, and in 1955 he received the peace prize of the German book trade in Frankfurt. He is a knight of the order Pour le Mérite (Friedensklasse).

Hermann Hesse was first married on August 2, 1904 to Maria Bernoulli. The marriage ended in divorce in 1923. Hesse has three sons by this marriage: Bruno, Heiner, and Martin. His second marriage, to Ruth Wegner, in January 1924, lasted only a few months. Hesse continues to live in seclusion near Montagnola, Switzerland with his third wife, the former Ninon (Ausländer) Dolbin, whom he married in November 1931, and who manages his business affairs. White-haired, blue-eyed, and of slender build and erect bearing, Hesse conveys the simplicity and sincerity of a Swabian peasant, and he combines a firmness of his convictions with a sense of humor, a love of life and of humanity, and an inner contentment. He is fond of gardening and painting, and he has produced many watercolors and drawings over the years. An accomplished violinist, Hesse has reflected his love for classical music in many of his writings. Despite his isolation from the mainstream of modern life he is well informed on world affairs.

In recent years Hesse has been increasingly disturbed by the cold war and by the danger of nuclear conflict, and he has little faith in either the United States or the Soviet Union. His belief that the artist should lead a contemplative rather than active life, and his rejection of "programs, leagues, and collectives," has not deterred him from speaking out on behalf of peace and human brotherhood.

References

Ball, Hugo. Hermann Hesse: Sein Leben und Werk (1947)

Columbia Dictionary of Modern European Literature (1947)

Gnefkow, Edmund. Hermann Hesse: Biographie 1952 (1952)

Hafner, Gotthilf. Hermann Hesse: Werk und Leben (1954)

Mileck, Joseph. Hermann Hesse and His Critics (1958)

Nadler, Käte. Hermann Hesse (1957)

Schmidt, Hans Rudolf. Hermann Hesse (1928)

Twentieth Century Authors (1942; First Supplement, 1955)

Who's Who in Switzerland, 1960-61

Zeller, Bernhard, ed. Hermann Hesse: Eine Chronik in Bildern (1960)

HESSELGREN, KERSTIN Apr. 1, 1872-Aug. 19, 1962 Swedish social worker and campaigner for women's rights; first woman member of Swedish Parliament (1921-34; 1936-44). See *Current Biography* (January) 1941.

Obituary

N Y Times p33 Ag 22 '62

HODGES, GIL(BERT RAY) Apr. 4, 1924- Baseball player
Address: b. c/o New York Mets, 680 5th Ave., New York 19

When players were chosen to fill the roster of the New York Mets, the new National League team, for the 1962 baseball season, there was no more popular selection, from the point of view of the fans, than that of the first baseman Gil Hodges. Regarded by his fellow players as one of the "nicest guys" in the game, Hodges was remembered with affection by New Yorkers as a slugging star of the outstanding teams assembled by the Brooklyn Dodgers in the decade 1947-57. Hodges had never really felt at home after he was transplanted, with the Dodgers, to Los Angeles in 1958, and although he was slowed by age and regretted leaving the Dodgers, he was glad to be playing again in New York. "I was glad because it meant I was coming home," he explained.

In signing Hodges, the Mets secured one of the finest first basemen in baseball history and, at his peak, an outstanding hitter. He placed among the top ten on a list of career home run hitters when he hit his 370th home run on July 6, 1962, and he is one of the few men who have hit four home runs in a single nine-inning game. Hodges had started the 1962 season with a flourish despite a knee injury, but in July he was required to undergo a kidney stone operation that took him off the field for an indeterminate period.

Although the borough of Brooklyn in New York City has been Gil Hodges' adopted home for the past fifteen years, he is by birth a Midwesterner. He was born on April 4, 1924 in Princeton, Indiana, a town of about 8,000 people in a farming and mining area in the southwestern part of the state. Gilbert Ray Hodges is the second son of Irene Hodges and Charles Hodges, a coal miner who had played semiprofessional baseball until he lost some toes and his right eye in a mining accident. Hodges has a younger sister, Mrs. Marjorie (Hodges) Sent, and an older brother, Bob, who pitched in the minor leagues until his pitching arm went "dead" and who now runs a sporting goods store.

Following a large mine explosion that occurred when Gil was eight years old his father decided to leave his job near Princeton and look for mining work near Petersburg, Indiana. There

GIL HODGES

the Hodges children grew up. Bob and Bud, as Gil was then called, attended Petersburg High School, where Bud participated in track, basketball, and six-man football. He played baseball with sandlot teams, too, and he was a fine hitter even then, but at that time he was much less enthusiastic about the sport than his brother, who was convinced that the Hodges boys had a future in professional baseball.

Gil and his brother joined the American Legion team in Petersburg in the spring of 1940, and Gil played with the team for two seasons. In the summer of 1941 he was spotted by a scout for the Detroit Tigers and offered a berth with a Class D minor league club. He refused it, however. Having graduated from Petersburg High School in February 1941 with seven sports letters, he had decided to follow his brother to St. Joseph's College in Rensselaer, Indiana (which had a good athletics department) with the tentative idea of preparing for a career as a college coach. He attended the college for two years, from 1941 to 1943. Some years later, between the 1947 and the 1948 baseball seasons, he took additional courses at Oakland City College in Indiana.

During the summer of 1942 Gil Hodges worked at Switzer Cummins, an Indianapolis concern, and played with their team in the industrial league. The following summer he was with the industrial league team of the P. R. Mallory Company, for whom he worked as a drill-press operator. He proved to be an outstanding hitter. Late in the 1943 season he was seen by a Brooklyn Dodger scout, and, after tryouts in Olean, New York and New York City, he was signed to a contract with the Dodger organization. He played one game at Ebbets Field that season, holding down the third base position.

Meanwhile Hodges had arranged to enlist in the United States Marine Corps, and he was called up in September 1943. He served with the Sixteenth Antiaircraft Artillery Battalion at Pearl Harbor, Tinian, and Okinawa and was discharged in February 1946 with the rank of sergeant. Upon his return to civilian life and to the Dodgers, he was assigned to a Brooklyn minor league team at Newport News, Virginia (Piedmont League) for the 1946 baseball season. The Dodgers hoped to train him as a catcher; he played that position with the Newport News team and compiled an average of .278 in 129 games. During his early years in professional baseball he had trouble hitting curve balls.

Recalled to Ebbets Field in 1947, one of the Dodgers' pennant-winning years, Hodges played in only twenty-eight games, as a catcher, and batted .156. He improved his average to .249 in 134 games in 1948; that season, also, he yielded the catcher's spot to Roy Campanella and began to play the first base position in which he achieved his baseball fame. In later years Hodges upheld his reputation as one of the most able and co-operative players in the sport by filling in at other positions as needed, but, after 1948, he always put in at least part of the season on the first base bag.

The 1949 season was a good one for Hodges as well as for the Dodgers, who won the pennant that year. Playing in 156 games, he batted .285, hit twenty-three home runs, and had 170 hits. One of his memorable moments at bat came in the 1950 season, during which he piled up thirty-two home runs; on August 31, 1950, in a game against the Boston (now Milwaukee) Braves, he became one of the few players in the history of baseball to hit four home runs in a single nine-inning game. Hodges hit so many home runs through the middle of the 1951 season that fans and commentators began to wonder whether he might not break Babe Ruth's 1927 record of sixty home runs in 154 games. But he went into his habitual end-of-the-season slump and finished the year with forty home runs and an average of .268.

The batter's bugbear, the prolonged hitting slump, became only too real for Hodges as his decline of 1951 extended through the 1952 and into the 1953 seasons. Although he hit thirty-two home runs in 1952, he was weak on singles and his batting average was only .254. Never was Hodges' popularity with baseball fans more apparent than during his 1953 nadir. Letters of encouragement, goodwill souvenirs, and even the prayers of a Brooklyn congregation were sent his way to help him out of the slump, and even during his worst performances in Ebbets Field he was not booed. Rallying about midway through the 1953 season, Hodges finished with a .302 average (the first time he had exceeded the .300 mark).

As excellent as his overall performance was in 1953, Hodges surpassed it in 1954. Appearing in 154 games, he compiled a batting average of .304, hit forty-two home runs, his career high for a single season, and batted in 130 runs, also a career high. Despite his feats the Dodgers only finished second to the New York (now San Francisco) Giants. In 1955 Hodges trailed off somewhat, hitting twenty-seven home runs and batting in 102 runs. But the Dodgers won the pennant and then their first world's championship, topping the New York Yankees in a seven-game world series.

The Dodgers again won the National League pennant in 1956; Hodges compiled an average of .265 and hit thirty-two home runs. In 1957, the last year the Dodgers played in Brooklyn, Hodges batted .299, hit twenty-seven home runs, and batted in ninety-eight runs. When the Dodgers became the Los Angeles National League team, beginning with the 1958 season, Hodges accompanied them; he and his family moved out to the West Coast.

Although some of the Dodger players welcomed the move to the West Coast, Hodges undoubtedly regretted having to leave Brooklyn, although he continued to give his best to the team. He had married a Brooklyn girl in 1948 and had come to look upon that borough as his home. His family was not happy in Los Angeles, and after the first season they moved back to Brooklyn, while Hodges played ball on the Coast. The unpredictable, sometimes zany, but never dull Brooklyn fans had entertained a special respect and affection for him, but in Los Angeles he was just another ballplayer. Then, too, many of the Dodgers had difficulty in adjusting to the great Coliseum, which was a converted football field, especially to its exceedingly shallow left field. During the four seasons that he spent in Los Angeles Hodges was often benched in favor of younger players. His batting averages for the years 1958 through 1961 were .259, .276, .198, and .242, respectively.

A second parting within five years—this time from his old team—was exacted from Hodges when he was bought for $75,000 from the Dodgers by the New York Mets in October 1961. Again he had regrets, but these were mixed with the pleasure he felt at coming home to New York. "My association with the Dodgers was long and pleasant," he explained, shortly after he was chosen by the Mets. "In a way I hated to leave but there's nothing like being home with my family. This change should give me the lift I've been needing. I felt better physically this season than I have since we left Ebbets Field but we had so many talented kids on the club that I didn't play as much as I would have liked. I welcome the chance to play regularly. . . ."

Unfortunately Hodges developed trouble with his left knee early in 1962. He was able to play some games with the Mets, however, and by the middle of June had appeared in thirty-one games and compiled an average of .317. On July 6, 1962 he hit the 370th home run of his career, which made him tenth on the list of career home run hitters and first among right-handed hitters in National League history. He also holds the National League record for the most grand-slam home runs (fourteen) in a lifetime. Some eight days later, while attending an old-timers' party at Toots Shor's, he was stricken with a painful kidney stone attack and required to undergo an operation. Doctors predicted a layoff of a month to six weeks, perhaps longer.

Already past his playing peak and old, as years are counted in baseball, Hodges had expected to play for only two or three more seasons before retiring from the field. At the top of his career he earned about $38,000 for the season. In the past he had been a salesman during the winter months; he now owns a bowling alley in Brook-

lyn. A king of the home run, Hodges is one of the best first basemen in the history of the sport. His huge hands, spanning nearly twelve inches, are perfect for the job. Although he stands six feet one inch tall and weighs about 205 pounds, he displays a grace in the field that has often been commented upon. A national magazine once photographed him in play and compared his movements to those of a ballet dancer.

Once described as the manager's ideal of what a player should be, Hodges is even-tempered, co-operative, genial, well-mannered, uncomplaining, and modest. He has sometimes taken on the role of peacemaker among his fellow players, and he has taught younger players how to field. In 1956, when the Dodgers were making an exhibition tour in Japan, he delighted Japanese audiences by clowning in the field and spoofing in pantomime the actions of other players. In January 1962 Hodges received the "Good Guy" award from the New York chapter of the Baseball Writers Association. Nine years before that, in 1951, he had been given a commander's citation from the Queens County chapter of the Catholic War Veterans in recognition of his "clean personal life" and his ability on the diamond. Proceeds donated on the occasion of "Gil Hodges Night," held at the Polo Grounds on August 24, 1962, are destined for a Gil Hodges Foundation for "worthy youngsters in this area who otherwise might not be able to attend college."

Gilbert Ray Hodges, a devout Roman Catholic, and Joan Lombardi were married on December 26, 1948 in St. Gregory's Roman Catholic Church in Brooklyn. They have four children, Gilbert Ray, Irene, Cynthia, and Barbara Lynn. In the winter Hodges enjoys visiting his family in Indiana and going hunting. Arthur Daley wrote in the New York *Times* (October 13, 1961), "It so happens that Gilbert Ray Hodges is one of the finest persons ever to wear a big league uniform. He is in a category with such extra-special personalities as Stan Musial, Pee Wee Reese, Alvin Dark, Herb Score, Tommy Henrich and so few others. They are a distinct cut above the rest as far as character goes and each at his peak was an extraordinary ballplayer."

References

Christian Sci Mon p6 Jl 19 '62 por
N Y Times p43 O 13 '61 por
Sat Eve Post 224:29+ S 8 '51 por
Daley, Arthur. Kings of the Home Run (1962)
Shapiro, Milton. The Gil Hodges Story (1960)

HOFSTADTER, ROBERT Feb. 5, 1915- Physicist; university professor
Address: b. Physics Department, Stanford University, Stanford, Calif.; h. 639 Mirada Ave., Stanford, Calif.

The head of the physics department at Stanford University, Dr. Robert Hofstadter was awarded the Nobel Prize in Physics in 1961 for his pioneering research into the heart of the nuclear particles that are the basic building

Stanford University
ROBERT HOFSTADTER

blocks of the material universe. He shared the prize and the cash award of $48,300 with Dr. Rudolf L. Mössbauer of the California Institute of Technology. With the aid of a new apparatus that he helped to design, Hofstadter and his team made the first precise measurements of the size and shape of protons and neutrons, particles that compose the atomic nucleus, and anatomized their internal structure. He has been at Stanford University since 1950.

The third of four children, Robert Hofstadter was born in New York City on February 5, 1915, the son of Louis Hofstadter, a salesman, and the former Henrietta Koenigsberg. He has two older brothers, George and Albert (who is a professor of philosophy at Columbia University), and a younger sister, Shirley. Robert Hofstadter was reared in New York City and educated at local secondary schools and the College of the City of New York.

At college he had at first the inclination to emulate his brother Albert and major in literature and philosophy. Influenced by an inspiring physics professor and convinced that "the laws of physics could be tested and those of philosophy could not," he decided to concentrate on the sciences instead. He won the Kenyon Prize for outstanding work in physics and mathematics, and he was elected to Phi Beta Kappa. He graduated from City College *magna cum laude* with a B.S. degree in 1935.

With the aid of a Coffin Fellowship from the General Electric Company and of a Procter Fellowship, Hofstadter became a graduate student in physics at Princeton University. After taking his M.A. and Ph.D. degrees from the university in 1938, he did research for an additional year as a Harrison Fellow at the University of Pennsylvania. Hofstadter was an instructor in physics at the University of Pennsylvania from 1940 to 1941 and an instructor in physics at his alma mater, the College of the City of New York, from 1941 to 1942.

During World War II, from 1942 to 1943, he worked as a physicist at the National Bureau of Standards in Washington, D.C. As a member of a research team he helped to develop the proximity fuse, an important anti-aircraft weapon that detonated a shell when it detected approaching objects by radar. From the end of 1943 to 1946 Hofstadter was the assistant chief physicist at Norden Laboratories Corporation in New York. He returned to teaching and research in 1946, when he was appointed assistant professor of physics at Princeton University. In 1950 he was invited to join the faculty of Stanford University as an associate professor, and four years later he was promoted to a full professorship. He is now the head of the department of physics at Stanford.

The question of how the material universe is composed has fascinated scientists for thousands of years, and Hofstadter is one of those who has sought the answer. Shortly after he arrived at Stanford he began to investigate the structure of the atomic nucleus. In 1953 the university announced that he and his co-workers had made a significant discovery: the particles composing the nucleus (protons and neutrons) were less closely and less uniformly packed than had formerly been supposed. Previously thought to be a solid, uniformly composed sphere, the nucleus was instead found to possess a densely packed core of component particles, which gradually thinned out toward the edges of the nucleus. The core was found to be 130 trillion times denser than water; a drop of water as dense would weigh about 2,000,000 tons.

These discoveries were made by using two machines, one the university's linear accelerator (atom smasher) and the other a scattering machine developed by Hofstadter and his team. The accelerator shot electrons at very high energies down a controlled path toward targets of atomic nuclei, which in this case were nuclei of the metal elements gold, lead, tantalum, and beryllium. The electrons penetrated the nuclei and, while not actually hitting the particles within the nucleus, but passing freely through them, they were deflected from their original paths by the particles' electrical fields. The scattering machine, the most powerful microscopic equipment then built, with a gigantic "eyepiece" or magnet, counted the number of electrons coming through and measured their angles of deflection. Hofstadter was thus able to distinguish the positions of nuclear particles only two one-hundredths of a trillionth of an inch apart and to obtain a good idea of the structure of the nucleus.

Probing further, with larger, more powerful accelerating and scattering machines, Hofstadter next examined individual protons and neutrons within the nucleus. These two particles, in different combinations, make up the nuclei of all atoms, except the hydrogen nucleus, which consists of one proton. The protons have a positive electrical charge; the neutrons have no charge. (The remaining component of atoms, the electrons, have a negative charge.)

In 1956 Hofstadter reported at a meeting of the American Physical Society that he and his co-workers had measured, for the first time, the size and shape of a proton, which they found to be .00000000000003 inches in diameter and which appeared to be "soft" on the outside and "hard" on the inside, like a peach with a pit. The following year, in December 1957, he announced that his team had measured the size and shape of the neutron, which they found to be very much like those of the proton.

Speaking before a meeting of the American Physical Society in April 1961, Hofstadter described his pioneering investigations into the details of the internal structure of protons and neutrons. Both particles, he said, consist of a dense, point-like core of mesons (even smaller nuclear particles, sometimes called the nuclear "glue") and two interpenetrating layers of meson clouds surrounding the core. The size of the core and clouds were the same in protons and neutrons. In the proton, however, the core and both cloud layers are positively charged; in the neutron, the core and the outer cloud layer are positively charged while the inner cloud layer carries a negative charge. Negative and positive charges in the neutron are so balanced as to make the neutron appear to have no charge at all. "This," Hofstadter has said, "is what I really believe, after working on this problem for seven years, that the neutron and the proton look like."

Hofstadter was awarded the Nobel Prize in Physics on December 10, 1961 at Stockholm, Sweden for his work in measuring precisely the size and shape of the proton and neutron and for presenting the first "reasonably consistent" picture of atomic nuclear structure. He shared the prize and the cash award of $48,300 with Dr. Rudolf L. Mössbauer, a German scientist working at the California Institute of Technology. Hofstadter was the fifth member of the present Stanford faculty to become a Nobel laureate.

The Nobel award is not Hofstadter's first honor. In 1959 he was named California Scientist of the Year, and in 1958 he was elected to membership in the National Academy of Sciences. During the year 1958-59 he worked at the European Organization for Nuclear Research in Geneva. A medal in honor of Hofstadter was struck by the College of the City of New York in 1962 and presented to him in June of that year. Hofstadter is a Fellow of the American Association for the Advancement of Science, the American Physical Society, and the Physical Society of London. He is a member of the Italian Physical Society, and he belongs to Sigma Xi, the honorary science research fraternity.

A prolific author, Hofstadter has written more than seventy-five papers on molecular structure, solid state physics, and nuclear physics and review articles on crystal counters, electron scattering, and nuclear and nucleon structure. In collaboration with Robert Herman he wrote *High-Energy Electron Scattering Tables* (Stanford Univ. Press, 1960). Hofstadter has been a co-editor of *Investigations in Physics* since 1951 and an associate editor of *Reviews of Modern Physics* since 1958. He also served as associate editor of the *Physical Review* from 1951 to 1953 and of the *Review of Scientific Instruments* from 1954 to 1956.

Robert Hofstadter married Nancy Givan on May 9, 1942. They have three children, Douglas Richard, Laura James, and Mary Hinda. Described as a modest, easy-going person, Hofstadter has brown hair and blue-gray eyes and stands five feet seven-and-a-half inches tall. The family enjoys skiing together on the California slopes; Hofstadter's other recreations are photography, reading, and listening to classical jazz.

References

N Y Herald Tribune p23 N 3 '61 por
N Y Times p24 N 3 '61
N Y World-Telegram p8 N 2 '61 por
American Men of Science 10th ed (1960-61)
Who's Who in America, 1962-63

HOLMAN, EUGENE May 2, 1895-Aug. 12, 1962 Former board chairman (1954-60) of Standard Oil Company (New Jersey). See *Current Biography* (May) 1948.

Obituary

N Y Times p31 Ag 14 '62

HUSING, TED Nov. 27, 1901-Aug. 10, 1962 Sports announcer; covered boxing, baseball, football, and racing events. See *Current Biography* (June) 1942.

Obituary

N Y Times p17 Ag 11 '62

JACOBSON, LEON ORRIS Dec. 16, 1911- Medical scientist; university professor
Address: b. Argonne Cancer Research Hospital, 950 E. 59th St., Chicago 37, Ill.; h. 1222 E. 56th St., Chicago 37, Ill.

The research on blood formation and disease and on the effects of radiation on living tissues that Dr. Leon Orris Jacobson has conducted during the course of his long career as a medical scientist has no doubt saved many lives. His work in radiobiology and hematology has significance not only for people suffering from cancer and other diseases treated with radiation, but also for astronauts venturing beyond the earth's atmosphere, which ordinarily protects men from the intense radiations of outer space. Dr. Jacobson has been at the University of Chicago for more than twenty years; he became chairman of its department of medicine in 1961. He has also been since 1951 the director of the Argonne Cancer Research Hospital, operated by the university on its campus for the United States Atomic Energy Commission.

Leon Orris Jacobson, the son of John and R. Patrine (Johnson) Jacobson, was born in Sims, North Dakota, on December 16, 1911. From 1929 to 1933, before he had his bachelor's degree, he taught in a country school. After earning a B.S. degree from North Dakota State College in 1935, he progressed rapidly and directly toward a career in medical research, in which he has become an outstanding figure.

(Continued next page)

DR. LEON ORRIS JACOBSON

His academic activities have centered largely around the University of Chicago.

Jacobson entered the university as a medical student and took his M.D. degree there in 1939. During the next three years he was progressively an intern, an assistant resident in medicine, and an assistant in medicine. He joined the university's faculty as an instructor in 1942, and he became an assistant professor in 1945, an associate professor in 1948, and a professor of medicine in 1951. From 1945 to 1951 Jacobson served as associate dean of the division of biological sciences, which includes the university's hospital, the School of Medicine, and graduate teaching and research programs in clinical and other sciences. In November 1961 he was appointed chairman of the department of medicine, the largest academic unit of the division of biological sciences.

Between 1943 and 1946 Jacobson was associate director of health and then director of health of the Plutonium Project of the Manhattan District, the project at the University of Chicago that developed the atomic bomb. Since 1951 he has been the director of the Argonne Cancer Research Hospital, which the university operates on its campus for the United States Atomic Energy Commission. The hospital was the first in the United States to be completely devoted to the study and use of radiation for fighting cancer.

Hematology and radiobiology are Jacobson's fields of specialization. In 1939 he pioneered the use of radioisotopes at the University of Chicago clinics, using radioactive phosphorus-32 in the treatment of certain types of leukemia, a disease characterized by the formation of too many white blood cells, and of polycythemia rubra vera, a disease in which red blood cells are produced in excessive amounts. He was also one of the first physicians to use nitrogen mustard in the treatment of Hodgkins' disease, a leukemia-like disorder of the white blood cells.

In 1947 he wrote, with A. M. Brues, a paper comparing the effects of chemical agents, such as nitrogen mustard, and radioactive agents on cancerous diseases of the blood-forming tissues. Jacobson's interest in the use of chemical agents persisted, but in the 1950's a major portion of his publications began to deal with the biological and medical aspects of radioactivity.

Jacobson has investigated, often with others, the mechanics of blood formation. For instance, he worked on perfecting measurements of erythropoietin, a hormone produced by the kidneys necessary for the production of red blood cells by the bone marrow. He examined the effects of kidney surgery and diseases on the output of the hormone and studied the role played by the element cobalt, which must be present for the hormone to appear in the body. In addition, Jacobson has made important studies of the body mechanism by which blood-forming tissues recover after they are subjected to radiation. For his work in this area he received the Robert Roesler de Villiers Prize of the Leukemia Society of New York in 1956.

Although radiation may be used to restore health, it can also be injurious when sustained in overly strong doses. Jacobson and his colleagues have sought methods for protecting living things from the deleterious effects of radiation. They recently discovered that death could be delayed or averted by injecting bone marrow cells from a healthy young animal into an animal that had been exposed to a dose of radiation that would ordinarily have been fatal.

Probably more important for the practical protection of human beings against lethal results of radiation (for example, during treatment of cancer or in space travel) is another approach intensively investigated by Jacobson. This method consists of protecting a part of the body—usually the spleen—during the time that the body as a whole is exposed to radiation. In a recent work, *Radiation Protection in Mammals* (Reinhold, 1962), J. F. Thompson calls some of the work of Jacobson and others "one of the most dramatic experiments carried out [in this field]."

The experiment referred to is one in which the spleens of mice were surgically isolated, with great care taken not to harm the blood vessels; the spleens were then protected with lead shields. When these mice were exposed to radiation, they were able to survive nearly twice as much radiation as control mice, whose spleens were not shielded from the penetrating rays. Jacobson also surgically transplanted spleens from unexposed animals into exposed ones and even tried injecting homogenated suspensions of spleen and liver cells of very young animals into exposed animals in an attempt to prevent radiation injury. The results were encouraging, although sometimes the experimental animals died after several weeks. Death resulted from delayed immunological reactions because of the presence of foreign cells. These reactions were similar to those commonly met whenever the tissues or organs of one animal (the donor) are transplanted into those of another animal not closely related to the donor. This type of complication was averted by transplanting cells from animals of the same strain or species.

Jacobson has done much speaking and consulting in his specialties. He gave the R. W. Stewart Memorial Lecture at the Pittsburgh Academy of Medicine in 1952, the Janeway Lecture at the American Radium Society in 1953, the Ralston Lecture at the University of Southern California in 1957, the Alice Messenger Band Memorial Lecture in Hematology at the University of Maryland in 1959, and the George Minot Memorial Lecture at the American Medical Association in 1960. He has also lectured at the International Congress of Radiology in 1950 and 1959, the Fifth International Cancer Congress in 1950, the Symposium on Radiobiology in 1954, meetings of the International Society of Hematology in 1952, 1954, 1956, 1958, and 1960, and the CIBA Foundation Conference on Experimental Leukemias in 1953 and Symposium on Hemopoiesis in 1960.

The advisory boards and committees on which Jacobson has served are the division of biological and medical research of the Argonne National Laboratory; the advisory committee on isotope distribution of the United States Atomic Energy Commission; the hematology study section of the United States Public Health Service's committee for radiation studies; the committee on cancer diagnosis and therapy of the National Research Council; the advisory committee on biophysics to the Surgeon General of the Army; and the medical and scientific committee of the American Cancer Society, Illinois Division. Jacobson was a member of an expert advisory panel on radiation of the World Health Organization in 1959 and was sent to Yugoslavia in 1960 with an advisory committee of the United States Atomic Energy Commission and Department of State. He was the United States representative at the first and second International Conference on Peaceful Uses of Atomic Energy in 1955 and 1958.

Jacobson is a Fellow of the American College of Physicians and a member of the Association of American Physicians, the American Society for Clinical Investigation, the American Association for Cancer Research, the American Medical Association, the International, American, and European societies of hematology, the Society for Experimental Biology and Medicine, the Central Society for Clinical Research, the Chicago Society of Internal Medicine, and the American Society for Experimental Pathology. He was the president of the Chicago Pathological Society in 1955-56. Jacobson belongs to several fraternities: Sigma Xi, Theta Chi, Nu Sigma Nu, Blue Key, and Alpha Omega Alpha.

Leon Orris Jacobson and Elizabeth Louise Benton were married on March 18, 1938. They have two children, Eric Paul and Judith Ann. The broad nature of the field in which Jacobson works has brought him to the borders of such diverse fields as bacteriology, endocrinology, embryology, immunology, and even to the consideration of social problems. His interests, however, are not confined to his professional activities. He has taught himself Scandinavian languages and reads Scandinavian books for relaxation. He recently remarked to an interviewer, "I just got through reading a Zane Grey book in Swedish. Imagine getting cow-poke expressions into that language!"

References

Chicago Sun-Times p24 F 5 '62 por
American Men of Science 10th ed (1960-61)
Who's Who in America, 1962-63

KAHN, HERMAN Feb. 15, 1922- Physicist; consultant on military strategy
Address: b. Hudson Institute, P.O. Box 551, White Plains, N.Y.; h. 19 Birch Lane, Chappaqua, N.Y.

Acknowledged as one of the most brilliant military strategists in the United States, Herman Kahn has been called the Karl von Clausewitz of the nuclear age. At present the director of the Hudson Institute, a nonprofit research organization concerned with problems of national security, Kahn was formerly a military analyst for the RAND Corporation, the idea center for the United States Air Force. Although a trained physicist and a civilian, Kahn is a specialist in the subject of deterrence of nuclear warfare between nations. In his two books, *On Thermonuclear War* and *Thinking About the Unthinkable,* and in many articles Kahn has considered the possible alternatives if deterrence strategy should fail. By inventing situations and incidents where the "balance of terror" has not been maintained, Kahn has tried to show why and how nuclear war becomes increasingly possible.

Unlike some of his critics—whom he considers intellectually timid—Kahn has explored such questions as how a nuclear war would start, how it would be fought, how long it would last, and how much damage would result from it. He maintains that although a nuclear war might differ in *degree* from all past wars, it may not necessarily differ in *kind.* Kahn does not believe that there would be total destruction, although the amount of damage would depend on whether the war started accidentally or intentionally, whether it was fought rationally or punitively, and whether civil-defense preparations had been undertaken. Kahn's critics have suggested that his logic and predictions are in error and that by minimizing the dangers of a nuclear war, he is destroying one of the important controls that has prevented a nuclear disaster from occurring.

One of the three children of Abraham and Yetta Kahn, Herman Kahn was born on February 15, 1922 in Bayonne, New Jersey. He and his two brothers, Morris and Irving (who is deceased), spent their early childhood in New York City before the family moved to California. Kahn graduated from the Fairfax High School in Los Angeles in 1940 and attended the University of Southern California before transferring to the University of California at Los Angeles. "Intense interest in economics, public affairs, and science all contrived to lead me into my current work," Kahn has recalled. To help pay for his tuition and expenses, he held jobs as a ship steward, checker in a supermarket, and machinist in a camera

HERMAN KAHN

shop. Before he could complete his undergraduate education, Kahn entered the Army, where he served from May 1943 to November 1945.

Kahn received a B.A. degree from the University of California at Los Angeles in 1945, and in December of that year he accepted his first professional position as a mathematician with the Douglas Aircraft Company. He was appointed a teaching assistant at the University of California at Los Angeles in May 1946, and joined the Northrop Aviation Company as a mathematician in June 1947. In October of that year he again took a position with the Douglas Aircraft Company working as a laboratory analyst on a project for the RAND Corporation. During these years Kahn attended classes at the California Institute of Technology in Pasadena and in 1948 he was awarded an M.S. degree. In the fall of 1948 he was appointed a senior physicist with the RAND Corporation, a nonprofit research organization working on contracts for the United States Air Force.

Kahn's years of association with the RAND Corporation gave him the background to qualify as a military strategist, since he was assigned to study the critical relations between weapons and tactics. One function of his job was to conduct lectures for military and civilian leaders. Some of America's chief policy-makers attended his briefings and were undoubtedly influenced, at one time or another, by Kahn's ideas. During the 1950's his field of concentration was applied mathematics, involving primarily the modification and application of the Monte Carlo method and its techniques. Kahn has been a proponent of the games theory as applied to strategic warfare. He also gained considerable experience in operations research and systems analysis and became an expert on the problems of weapons design. One of Kahn's chief fields of interest lies in preparing the United States to accept a strong civil defense

program for protection and as a deterrent to war.

A series of lectures that Kahn gave at the Princeton University Center of International Studies in 1959 resulted in the publication of his controversial book *On Thermonuclear War* (Princeton Univ. Press, 1960), which launched him as a national figure. The thesis of the book revolves around the possibility and even probability of another world war in the nuclear age. Kahn expressed his lack of faith in deterrence strategy that depended solely on disarmament talks, although he did not suggest a cessation of these meetings. He criticized those who have refused to take what he considers a realistic and long-range view of the nature and consequences of thermonuclear war and for whom a discussion of survival programs is tantamount to disaster.

Unlike many public figures, Kahn does not subscribe to the belief that a nuclear war would spell the annihilation of civilization. He maintains that there are "degrees of awfulness" and that an adequate defense program would alleviate the effects of nuclear war. In his opinion, it would also greatly decrease the number of victims so that "normal and hopeful lives would not be precluded for the survivors."

Max Lerner praised Kahn's book for dealing with thermonuclear war "not as a paralyzing abstraction but in all its sizes, shapes, degrees, possibilities, probabilities." "Kahn has instructed, absorbed, and shaken me," Lerner wrote, "far more than any writer in the field of military strategy today." On the other hand, James R. Newman, one of the editors of the *Scientific American* (March 1961) asked, "Is there really a Herman Kahn?" and denounced the book as "a moral tract on mass murder: how to plan it, how to commit it, how to get away with it, how to justify it." "This evil and tenebrous book," Newman wrote, "with its loose-lipped pieties and its hayfoot-strawfoot logic, is permeated with a bloodthirsty irrationality such as I have not seen in my years of reading."

In September 1961 Kahn left the RAND Corporation, because, he said, "it was bound too closely by government work." With the financial aid of an anonymous donor Kahn and several associates established the Hudson Institute in White Plains, New York. Referred to as "a high-class RAND" by Kahn, who serves as its director, the Hudson Institute was set up for the purpose of dealing with problems of national security and international order. It has received contracts from business and research organizations seeking information on military strategy, civil defense, and command and control operations.

The Hudson Institute also affords Kahn a quasi-official platform for his ideas. He has endorsed the request of the Kennedy administration for funds for a fallout shelter program, and believes that "a realistic civil defense program should be undertaken now to protect the nation ten years hence."

In January 1962 Kahn took part in a panel discussion at a meeting of the American Rocket Society in New York. He said that, within limits, Soviet superiority in space research might benefit the rest of the world, since it might prevent the Russians from harboring inferiority feelings that lead to aggression. In addressing the first national conference of the Congress of Scientists on Survival, in June of the same year, he noted that while there was still considerable danger of war, the major powers were less inclined than ever before to use nuclear weapons. He attributed this to a fear of retaliation and a moral and political revulsion at the thought of war.

With the publication of his second book, *Thinking About the Unthinkable* (Horizon Press, 1962), Herman Kahn achieved new literary prominence. The book restated his case for the need to speculate on the problems of a nuclear disaster. Kahn insisted that the facts of life under the thermonuclear threat should be faced, and he denounced those who would act like "ancient kings who punished messengers who brought them bad news." Reviewing the book in the New York *Post* (July 15, 1962), Fred J. Pannwitt maintained that by presenting a variety of alternatives to the grim possibilities of war Kahn "performs a most valuable service for the layman." On the other hand, Stuart Chase, in an article in the *Saturday Review* (June 30, 1962), called Kahn a wild romantic, who refuses to admit "the central problem of our age, that nuclear weapons have made war obsolete."

Despite the controversy that his ideas have engendered, Kahn is a recognized authority in his field, whose writings have been well received and widely read. He has contributed many articles to scientific journals and to such lay magazines as the *Saturday Evening Post, Fortune,* and *Commentary.* He is also the author of many classified documents, which are not available to the public. Kahn has lectured extensively before private groups and at colleges and universities, including the Air War College, the University of Chicago, and Harvard and Princeton universities. He served as a consultant to the Oak Ridge National Laboratory in 1950-52, to the Gaither Committee on Strategic Warfare in 1957, and to the Stanford Research Institute on Non-Military Defense in 1958.

Kahn has been a technical adviser to private firms including the Boeing Aircraft Company and the Radio Corporation of America. He was a consultant to the Librascope Corporation on the design of mechanical drum computers in 1954-55 and, in 1956, to the Pratt-Whitney Aircraft Corporation on reactor calculations. In 1950 he served with the technical advisory group of the Atomic Energy Commission, and in 1955-56 he was a member of the computing council of the National Bureau of Economic Research. He is a member of the American Physical Society. The Southern California section of the Society for Industrial and Applied Mathematics elected Kahn chairman for 1956-57.

On March 31, 1953 Herman Kahn married Rosalie Jane Heilner. They have two children, Deborah Yetta and David Joshua. Described by Laurence Barrett in the New York *Herald Tribune* (November 26, 1961) as "a lively sort with a Kris Kringle shape," Kahn is five feet eleven inches tall, weighs 265 pounds, and has black hair and brown eyes. He speaks rapidly and

"peers calmly from behind thick glasses." His favorite recreations are hiking, swimming, reading, and conversation. The Kahns' new home in Chappaqua, New York is equipped with a combination blast and fallout shelter.

References

N Y Herald Tribune II p1 N 26 '61 por
American Men of Science 10th ed. (1960-61)

KINDELBERGER, J(AMES) H(OWARD) May 8, 1895-July 27, 1962 Chairman of the board of North American Aviation, Inc., (1948-62). See *Current Biography* (March) 1951.

Obituary

N Y Times p19 Jl 28 '62

KINGMAN, DONG (MOY SHU) Mar. 31, 1911- Artist
Address: b. Wildenstein & Co., Inc., 19 E. 64th St., New York 21; h. 21 W. 58th St., New York 19

Charm and humor are trademarks of the carefully crafted watercolors by the Chinese-American artist Dong Kingman. An academist of the National Academy of Design, Kingman has won many awards for his paintings, and since 1953 he has been a guiding force in the Famous Artists School at Westport, Connecticut. Even in his commercial assignments, such as the water-color prelude to the film version of Rodgers and Hammerstein's *Flower Drum Song*, Kingman maintains an integrity of style that is consistent with his rare skill.

The second son in a family of eight children, Dong Moy Shu Kingman was born in Oakland, California on March 31, 1911. (According to one source, he was christened Tsang King-Man.) His father, Dong Kwon, was a farmer who came from Kwang-Tung in the hills of Hong Kong. In 1900 he migrated to the United States, where he became a laundryman and dry goods merchant. His mother, Lew Shee, painted in her spare time. At the age of five Dong Kingman briefly attended kindergarten at the Lincoln School in Oakland before the family returned to Hong Kong, where the father purchased another dry goods store. Kingman recalls making chalk drawings on the pavement in front of the store, in an effort to attract customers. His father instilled in him a love for the theater by taking him often to the Cantonese opera, which deeply impressed the boy. Through the study of Chinese writing Kingman became highly skilled in the use of paint brushes at an early age.

Until 1925 Kingman attended the Lingnan Grammar School in Hong Kong. After graduating he studied painting under Sze-to Wai, the headmaster of the school and Kingman's first and only art teacher, who taught him Oriental *hsieh-yi* (drawing a conception) and Occidental *hsieh-cheng* (drawing reality), along with the elements of distance painting. While growing up in Hong Kong Kingman held various jobs, including selling newspapers and working in a

Zoltan Hencze—
Famous Artists

DONG KINGMAN

pattern factory. He also was employed for
six months in an architectural drafting office,
and then worked for a short period with a
motion picture company, hoping at the time
that he might some day become a movie director.

At the age of eighteen Kingman left the
Orient for his native California and found work
in an overalls factory owned by his brother.
Some time later he acquired a restaurant for
$75, but the business failed because Kingman
neglected his customers for his painting. Subsequently he worked as a houseboy for a wealthy
San Francisco family, while painting and attending art school in Oakland in his free time.
In 1933 he gave his first exhibition when he
displayed twenty watercolors at the San Francisco Art Association Annual, held at the San
Francisco Museum. He was acclaimed by the
city's art reviewers. In the following year he
held his first one-man show at the Vallejo
Library in San Francisco. In 1935, when the
depression-born Works Progress Administration
organized an art project, Kingman had his first
chance to develop his talents professionally. He
worked on the WPA project for five years at a
salary of $90 per month. In 1938 he began to
lecture and teach at the Academy of Advertising
Art in San Francisco. He lectured in Sacramento
under WPA auspices in 1939 and in San Diego
during the summer of 1940.

In 1940 the Metropolitan Museum of Art in
New York City bought the first of its three
Kingman paintings. Two years later, his first
New York exhibition won wide public attention at the Midtown Galleries and launched his
reputation as one of America's inimitable stylists
in watercolor. As the recipient of a two-year
Guggenheim Fellowship Kingman traveled
throughout the United States in 1942 and 1943.
He continued in his efforts to learn every facet
of watercolor art, and he acquired a mastery of
his brushes and paints at once obvious to the

viewer of his later works. During the summer
of 1944 he lectured at the University of Wyoming, and in 1945 he gave a summer art
course at Mills College in Oakland. Kingman entered the United States Army in 1945,
serving first at Camp Beale, California and
later in Washington, D.C., where he prepared
charts and graphs for the Office of Strategic
Services. Discharged in 1946 with the rank of
technician, fifth grade, he re-entered civilian
life with a renewed ambition for success in the
art world.

Gradually developing his twofold art career
of painter and teacher, Kingman taught part-
time at Columbia University from 1946 to 1958.
In 1948 he moved his entire studio from the
West coast to the Brooklyn Heights section of
New York City, overlooking New York harbor.
From 1948 to 1953 he served as full-time instructor of painting at New York's Hunter College, and in the summer of 1952 he returned
to Oakland to teach at Mills College. Since
1953 Kingman has been teaching at the Famous
Artists School in Westport, Connecticut, and
since 1957 he has made painting tours to Mexico
during the summer months.

A ten-year retrospective show of Dong Kingman's works was held at New York City's Manhattan Gallery in 1951. The much praised
exhibition was described in *Life* (May 14, 1951):
"Trolley cars, signposts, pigeons and skyscrapers
tumbled into his paintings in bright profusion
—humdrum city streets were transformed into
colorful scenes as festive as firecracker celebrations on Chinese New Year's." Next to Hong
Kong, Kingman feels most drawn to New York.
His paintings, which include his vivid impressions of such scenes as the Brooklyn Bridge,
Central Park, Wall Street, Grand Central terminal and other famous city landmarks, usually
contain bright dabs and flashes of brilliant color.
His Oriental semi-stylization of people, water,
sky, buildings, birds, and trees has been called
by Eugene M. Ettenberg in *American Artist*
(September 1961) a "gentle satire, a satire with
no sting."

In 1954 the United States Department of
State invited Kingman to go on a lecture tour
around the world as part of its international
cultural exchange program, and he visited Japan,
Korea, Formosa, Hong Kong, Singapore, the
Philippines, Malaya, Thailand, India, Turkey,
Norway, Austria, England, and Iceland. *Life*
(February 14, 1955) featured the colorful illustrated report of his travels that he made on
a forty-foot scroll of rice paper, describing in
a luminous, light-hearted way his encounters
and observations while touring.

Kingman's earlier ambition to work with
motion pictures materialized when *Life* magazine
assigned him in 1960 to cover the filming of
the Paramount production *The World of Suzie
Wong* in Hong Kong. He also helped in the
production and promotion of the film. In 1961
he was asked to execute a series of background
paintings for the prologue of the Universal-
International film *Flower Drum Song*, an adaptation of the Rodgers and Hammerstein musical,
set in San Francisco's Chinatown. Kingman,
who had lived in San Francisco for a number
of years, was regarded as the artist most ideally

equipped by birth, familiarity with the subject, and artistic excellence for the assignment. His paintings required three months of work and were seen only for three minutes on the screen, but they evoked the proper mood for the film that followed.

Kingman has illustrated covers and articles for *Fortune, Holiday, McCall's, This Week, Time,* and other publications. He has done illustrations for several children's books, including *The Bamboo Gate* by Vanya Oakes (Macmillan, 1946); *China's Story* by Enid LaMonte Meadowcroft (Crowell, 1946); and *Johnny Hong of Chinatown* by Clyde Robert Bulla (Crowell, 1952). He has also executed two murals, one for the Lingnan Restaurant in midtown Manhattan in 1951 and the other for the ABC Transportation Company in New York City in 1953.

Since 1935 Kingman has painted approximately fifty pictures a year, and since he finds a ready market for each one, he does not own a single finished watercolor of his own, but only a dozen or so in various stages of completion. He told Hollywood columnist Joe Hyams that at one of the exhibitions of his Hong Kong pictures fifty had been sold before the show opened, although there were only forty available. Since he had just returned from a painting tour of Mexico, where the vegetation is similar to that of Hong Kong, he simply put Chinese lettering on the signs in his Mexican pictures, and changed the donkeys into cows. "This was like prostituting myself," he said, "but I was desperate to have enough pictures" (New York *Herald Tribune,* November 14, 1961).

The works of Dong Kingman are found in the permanent collections of over thirty major museums and galleries of art in the United States, including the Metropolitan Museum of Art, the Whitney Museum of American Art, the American Academy of Arts and Letters, the Museum of Modern Art, the Brooklyn Museum, the Boston Museum of Fine Arts, the Art Institute of Chicago, and the San Francisco Museum of Art. Since 1959 he has been represented by the Wildenstein Gallery in New York City. Alan D. Gruskin's book *The Water Colors of Dong Kingman; and How the Artist Works* (Studio, 1958) is an illustrated account of Kingman's unique watercolor methods with an introduction by William Saroyan. In 1954 Kingman's friend, the noted movie cameraman James Wong Howe, made a 16mm. motion picture of the artist while he was creating a painting in New York's Chinatown. Entitled *Dong Kingman,* it was subsequently shown around the world as an educational film. Two other film demonstrations of his work have been made by the Harmon Foundation.

Kingman has earned many awards and prizes in national and international exhibitions. In 1944 he received the award of the Chicago International Watercolor Exhibition and in 1946 he won the gold medal of honor of the Audubon Artists Exhibition. He has received five prizes of the American Watercolor Society, the Pennell Medal of the Pennsylvania Academy, the San Francisco Art Association Prize, and the Metropolitan Museum of Art Award. In 1951 the National Academy of Design elected Kingman to full rank.

Accustomed to taking a sketchbook with him wherever he goes, Kingman is said to be seen working "from half concealed positions behind garbage cans and in doorways so as not to attract attention." At times, Kingman has revealed, "a crowd would gather anyway, and I'd have to drive them away by singing Chinese songs—very hard on the ears" (*Time,* April 18, 1949). His sketchbooks, which he calls his diaries, contain his lively impressions of everything he sees and fill a closet stacked from floor to ceiling in his studio.

In oriental fashion Kingman holds his pen vertically at right angles to the paper, drawing rapidly without pause to catch the shifting light. His friend, William Saroyan, once commented "I don't know anyone who sees what Dong Kingman sees . . . he sees the world this instant and in a glance . . . in the instantaneous and miraculous reality of matter and color, of living vision, of memory captured in the painters of great skill, he sees the world gone—forever" (*American Artist,* September 1961).

Dong Kingman's first wife, Janice, whom he married in 1929, died in 1954. Two sons were born to this marriage: Eddie Kingman and Dong Kingman, Jr. In 1956 Kingman married the former Shanghai journalist and author Helena Kuo. Kingman is five feet one inch tall, weighs 120 pounds, and has brown eyes and black hair. He is an Episcopalian and a member of the American Watercolor Society, the Audubon Society, and the Dutch Treat Club. His favorite recreations are chess and contract bridge. He is described as a happy man whose humor and affection for all that surrounds him is reflected in the wistful interpretations of the world he sees.

References

Am Artist 25:24+ S '61 por
N Y Sunday News Mag p30 Ag 20 '61
N Y World-Telegram Mag p3 F 6 '60 por
Who's Who in America, 1962-63
Who's Who in American Art (1959)

KRAG, JENS OTTO (kräg yĕns) Sept. 15, 1914- Danish Cabinet member
Address: b. Christiansborg Slot, Copenhagen, Denmark; h. 61 Egernvej, Copenhagen 7, Denmark

The Danish Minister of Foreign Affairs, Jens Otto Krag, has won international recognition for his persistent efforts to bridge the gap between Europe's two rival trade organizations. Krag is convinced that if Western Europe is to continue to prosper economically, some measure of unity must be created between the European Free Trade Association (EFTA) or "Outer Seven," and the European Economic Community (EEC), otherwise known as the "Inner Six" or Common Market. Under his guidance, Denmark, a member of the EFTA, applied for admittance to the EEC on August 9, 1961.

Krag has had a leading role in shaping his country's economic policies since World War II. Before his appointment as Foreign Minister in 1958, he held four ministerships beginning with

JENS OTTO KRAG

the office of Minister of Commerce, Industry and Shipping to which he was named in 1947. He is one of the youngest members, but also the senior minister, in the Social Democratic government of Prime Minister Viggo Kampmann. After Kampmann suffered a heart attack in May 1962 Krag was appointed acting Prime Minister.

Jens Otto Krag was born in Randers, Denmark on September 15, 1914, the son of Anders Krag, a cigar merchant, and Astrid (Marcussen) Krag. After completing his lower schooling he attended the University of Copenhagen, from which he graduated with a degree in political science in 1940. An ardent Social Democrat, Krag was active in the Social Democratic youth movement from the age of sixteen. Following graduation he took a position with the Board of Supply, the central government body in charge of rationing during World War II. He served with the board until 1945, when he was named director of the economic council of the labor movement, a post he held until 1947. At the same time he continued to be active in the Social Democratic party, and he played a major role in formulating its postwar economic program.

In 1947 Krag was elected to the Danish Parliament (Folketing) as the Social Democratic representative of his native town of Randers. Shortly thereafter he was appointed Minister of Commerce, Industry, and Shipping in the cabinet of Prime Minister Hans Hedtoft, and in this capacity he dealt with economic problems resulting from the war. As a member of the government Krag participated in Denmark's decision, in 1949, to depart from her traditional policy of neutrality by joining the newly established North Atlantic Treaty Organization. In 1950, when Hedtoft's Social Democratic minority government resigned in favor of a non-Socialist coalition government, Krag was granted a leave of absence from the Folketing. He was subsequently appointed economic counselor to the

Danish Embassy in Washington, D.C., and in this capacity he performed special duties in relation to the European Recovery Program. Some spokesmen for the Danish press believed at the time that Krag was being groomed for the foreign ministership.

When Hedtoft formed his second government in 1953, Krag became a minister without portfolio in the new government, and a few months later he was appointed Minister of Economy and Labor. At the same time he edited the monthly journal *Verdenes Gang* in 1953-54, and in the latter year he became editor of *Tidehverv og Samfundsorden*. After the death of Hedtoft in 1955 Krag continued as Minister of Economy and Labor under the new government of Hans Christian Hansen. When in 1957 Hansen created the new post of Minister of Foreign Economic Relations to ease his work load, Krag was the logical choice for the position.

In October 1958 Hansen, who had previously served as both Prime Minister and Minister of Foreign Affairs, appointed Krag to the Foreign Ministry, in view of the growing problems relating to the North Atlantic Treaty Organization and to Denmark's impending choice of membership in one of the two European economic groupings. Krag was retained as Minister of Foreign Affairs by Viggo Kampmann, who became Prime Minister after Hansen's death in February 1960.

As Foreign Minister, Krag has been steadily working towards a solution to his country's trade problems. Denmark, which in 1959 became a member of the EFTA along with Great Britain, Norway, Sweden, Austria, Switzerland, and Portugal, is in the unique position of having her European trade almost evenly divided between the EFTA and the EEC. The EEC, composed of France, West Germany, Italy, Belgium, the Netherlands, and Luxembourg, takes almost all of Denmark's exports of beef, veal, dressed poultry, eggs and barley. Great Britain, a fellow EFTA member, buys nearly all the Danish bacon and butter exported. Danish agriculture began to experience the effects of the economic division of Western Europe in 1959, when exports of farm products to the Common Market began to decline.

At a meeting of NATO foreign ministers in Oslo on May 9, 1961 Krag announced that Denmark was ready to join the European Common Market if Great Britain decided to do so. Two months later, in an interview with correspondent Jan Hasbrouck for the New York *Herald Tribune* (July 10, 1961), he said: "Denmark's foreign trade situation will remain unsatisfactory as long as our main markets are in two separate groups. . . . Our paramount objective is to do away with the division." Denmark's application for membership in the European Economic Community on August 9, 1961 followed British Prime Minister Harold Macmillan's announcement that Great Britain would open negotiations to join the Common Market.

Speaking at a meeting of the Scandinavian Commercial Group in New York City in October 1961, Krag said that any other course than following Great Britain into the Common Market would have been economically disastrous. He pointed out that Denmark's position as a top supplier of farm products to Great Britain and West Germany would sink to that of a reserve supplier, if his country did not join the EEC. "Denmark wouldn't be allowed to sell on the Common Market until the last Dutch dairyman had disposed of his last pound of butter or the last French farmer had sold his last pound of cheese," he explained. Later in the same month, at a meeting of cabinet ministers of the six EEC nations in Brussels, Krag emphasized Denmark's interest in participating in the creation of European unity.

Under Krag's leadership, the primary objective of Danish foreign policy is to strengthen international co-operation through the United Nations, while adhering to NATO. A zealous proponent of disarmament, Krag proposed to the United Nations General Assembly in September 1960 that the Eastern and Western powers take a new step toward disarmament by opening corresponding sections of their territories to international inspection. He offered the Danish territory of Greenland as a possible proving ground for the feasibility of the plan. "We hope that this offer could be the first step toward the development of an international inspection arrangement and that other countries will approach this problem in the same spirit," he told the Assembly.

In the following year Krag repeated Denmark's offer to the General Assembly. He noted that disarmament talks had failed so far because of the fear that staged disarmament might carry "the risk of upsetting the balance of power which is the actual upholder of peace in the present-day world." He proposed that a disarmament program be devised whereby the existing balance of power would be maintained. Krag also urged the representation of Communist China in the United Nations, maintaining that this would be essential if any disarmament agreement were to be of value. As a possible means of alleviating the Berlin crisis Krag suggested that one of the permanent bodies of the U.N. be moved to Berlin. "It might have useful psychological effects if the world organization were present in Berlin, sharing the same atmosphere as its citizens, and if Berlin, instead of being a point of tension, could become a center of constructive international co-operation," he said.

Notwithstanding his advocacy of disarmament, Krag insists that under present conditions Denmark needs to maintain adequate national defenses in co-operation with NATO. In December 1961, he announced that the Danish Parliament had endorsed the organization of a joint Danish-West German NATO command in the Baltic in the event of war. He emphatically denied a Soviet accusation that by accepting a joint command with West Germany, Denmark was increasing tension in the Baltic area. On May 5, 1962 Krag was appointed acting Prime Minister by King Christian IX, during the illness of Prime Minister Kampmann, who had suffered a heart attack two days earlier.

On July 31, 1959 Jens Otto Krag married Helle Virkner, a popular Danish stage and screen actress. They have two children, Jens Christian and Stephan. Krag, who is described in the Washington *Post and Times Herald* (October 13, 1960) as "a disarming Dane with a ruddy face and a ready smile," has the reputation of being a lively and entertaining conversationalist. He is the author or co-author of several books and articles on politics and economics. The Foreign Minister has his offices in Christiansborg Castle in Copenhagen, which also houses the Parliament and King Frederik's reception rooms.

References
International Who's Who, 1961-62
International Year Book and Statesmen's Who's Who, 1962
Kraks Blå Bog, 1961
Who's Who in America, 1962-63

LUHAN, MABEL DODGE Feb. 26, 1879-Aug. 13, 1962 Patron of artists and writers; friend of D. H. Lawrence; befriended post-impressionist painters; author of memoirs. See *Current Biography* (January-February) 1940.

Obituary
N Y Times p31 Ag 14 '62

McCORMICK, MYRON Feb. 8, 1908-July 30, 1962 Stage, screen, and radio actor, best known as a comedian; appeared in *South Pacific* (1949-54) and in *No Time for Sergeants* (1955-57). See *Current Biography* (January) 1954.

Obituary
N Y Times p27 Jl 31 '62

MONROE, MARILYN June 1, 1926-Aug. 5, 1962 Motion picture actress, noted for her beauty and for her talents as a comedienne; credits include *The Misfits* (1961); *Some Like It Hot* (1959); and *Bus Stop* (1956). See *Current Biography* (July) 1959.

Obituary
N Y Times p1+ Ag 6 '62

SHOTTON, BURT(ON EDWIN) Oct. 18, 1884-July 29, 1962 Manager of the Brooklyn Dodgers baseball club in 1947 and 1949. See *Current Biography* (June) 1949.

Obituary
N Y Times p27 Jl 31 '62

CURRENT BIOGRAPHY—VOL. 23. NOS. 1-9

This is the index to the January-October 1962 issues. For the index to the 1961 biographies, see December 1961 issue or 1961 Yearbook. For the index to 1940-1950 biographies, see 1950 Yearbook. For 1951-1960 index, see 1960 Yearbook.

Graham, John Oct 62
Grant, Gordon (Hope) obit Jul 62
Greenebaum, Leon C(harles) Jan 62
Gregory, Dick Jun 62
Grimes, Tammy (Lee) Jul 62
Guggenheim, Peggy Oct 62
Guggenheimer, Mrs. Charles S. See Guggenheimer, M. Oct 62
Guggenheimer, Minnie Oct 62
Guinzburg, Harold K(leinert) obit Jan 62
Guion, Connie M(yers) Feb 62

Hall, Peter (Reginald Frederick) Feb 62
Hammond, John Hays, Jr. Jul 62
Hanschman, Nancy (Conners) Sep 62
Hansen, Carl F(rancis) Oct 62
Hardenbrook, Donald J(ohnson) Jul 62
Hargrave, Thomas J(ean) obit Apr 62
Harris, Harwell Hamilton Jan 62
Harrison, James L(erlie) Oct 62
Hart, Moss obit Feb 62
Hartigan, Grace Sep 62
Hartle, Russell P(eter) obit Jan 62
Hayakawa, Sessue Sep 62
Heath, Edward (Richard George) Oct 62
Head, Matthew See Canaday, J. May 62
Heineman, Ben W(alter) Jan 62
Herbster, Ben M(ohr) Jul 62
Hesse, Hermann biog Oct 62 obit Oct 62
Hesselgren, Kerstin obit Oct 62
Hester, James M(cNaughton) Jun 62
Hillyer, Robert Silliman obit Feb 62
Hocking, William Ernest Mar 62
Hodes, Henry I(rving) obit Apr 62
Hodges, Gil(bert Ray) Oct 62
Hofstadter, Robert Oct 62
Holman, Eugene obit Oct 62
Holt, Isabella obit May 62
Houk, Ralph (George) Jul 62
Houle, Cyril O(rvin) May 62
Howe, Gordie Mar 62
Howe, Gordon See Howe, Gordie Mar 62
Hubbard, Bernard (Rosencrans) obit Jul 62
Hughes, Richard J(oseph) Jul 62
Hu Shih obit Apr 62
Husing, Ted obit Oct 62

Ives, Irving M(cNeil) obit Apr 62

Jacobson, Leon Orris Oct 62

John, Augustus (Edwin) obit Jan 62
Johnson, Harold Ogden obit Apr 62

Katsh, Abraham I(saac) Mar 62
Kahn, Herman Oct 62
Kay, Hershy Mar 62
Keldysh, Mstislav (Vsevolodovich) Feb 62
Kennelly, Martin H(enry) obit Jan 62
Khouri, Faris el- obit Feb 62
Kindelberger, J(ames) H(oward) obit Oct 62
Kingman, Dong (Moy Shu) Oct 62
Kiplinger, W(illard) M(onroe) Jan 62
Kirk, Russell (Amos) Sep 62
Klahre, Ethel S(usan) May 62
Kobak, Edgar obit Jul 62
Koestler, Arthur Jan 62
Korth, Fred (H.) Jul 62
Kovacs, Ernie obit Mar 62
Krag, Jens Otto Oct 62
Kreisler, Fritz obit Mar 62

Larson, Leonard W(infield) May 62
Lefèvre, Théo(dore Joseph Albéric Marie) Jun 62
Lewis, John (Aaron) Jan 62
Lipchitz, Jacques Apr 62
Lober, Georg (John) obit Feb 62
Loeb, James (Isaac), Jr. Jan 62
Louw, Eric H(endrik) Mar 62
Love, J(ames) Spencer obit Mar 62
Luhan, Mabel Dodge obit Oct 62
Luthuli, Albert John Feb 62

McCarthy, Clem obit Jul 62
McClintic, Guthrie obit Jan 62
McConnell, F(owler) B(eery) obit Feb 62
McCormack, John W(illiam) Apr 62
McCormick, Myron obit Oct 62
McCracken, Joan obit Jan 62
McSwigan, Marie obit Sep 62
Macy, John W(illiams), Jr. Jan 62
Mao Tse-tung May 62
Marais, Jean Apr 62
Margai, Sir Milton (Augustus Strieby) Feb 62
Martin, Edmund F(ible) Jan 62
Marvel, Mrs. Archie D. Apr 62
Marvel, Elizabeth Newell See Marvel, Mrs. A. D. Apr 62
Meerloo, Joost A(braham) M(aurits) Jan 62
Mellers, Wilfrid (Howard) Feb 62
Meštrović, Ivan obit Mar 62
Miller, Harry W(illis) Mar 62
Miller, William E(dward) Feb 62
Monroe, Marilyn obit Oct 62

Moore, Charlotte Emma See Sitterly, C. M. Jan 62
Morison, Samuel Eliot Sep 62
Moses, Anna Mary Robertson obit Feb 62
Mössbauer, Rudolf L(udwig) May 62
Mowrer, Edgar Ansel Jul 62
Muench, Aloisius (Joseph), Cardinal obit Apr 62
Murphy, (Eleanor) Patricia Apr 62

Nestingen, Ivan A(rnold) Mar 62
Newhart, Bob Mar 62
Nitze, Paul H(enry) Feb 62

Ochoa, Severo Jun 62
Ogburn, Charlton obit Apr 62
Olav V, King of Norway Jan 62
Osgood, Charles E(gerton) Apr 62
Ozbirn, Catharine (Freeman) See Ozbirn, Mrs. E. L. Jan 62
Ozbirn, Mrs. E. Lee Jan 62

Page, Ruth Jun 62
Parker, Cola G(odden) obit Sep 62
Peden, Katherine (Graham) May 62
Petri, Egon obit Jul 62
Pevsner, Antoine obit Jun 62
Piccard, Auguste obit May 62
Portinari, Candido obit Mar 62

Rabaut, Louis Charles obit Jan 62
Ramírez, Pedro P(ablo) obit Sep 62
Randolph, Jennings Jan 62
Rayburn, Sam(uel Taliaferro) obit Jan 62
Read, Sir Herbert (Edward) Mar 62
Reischauer, Edwin O(ldfather) May 62
Reybold, Eugene obit Jan 62
Rivers, Thomas M(ilton) obit Jul 62
Robinson, Spottswood W(illiam), 3d Mar 62
Rogers, Frank B(radway) Jun 62
Rogers, Rutherford David Jun 62
Rose, (Iain) Murray Jun 62
Russell, Donald J(oseph) May 62
Russell, James S(argent) Jan 62

Sandström, (Alfred) Emil (Fredrik) obit Sep 62
Satterfield, John C(reighton) Jul 62

Savage, Augusta (Christine) obit May 62

Schoeppel, Andrew F. obit Mar 62

Scofield, Paul Mar 62

Senghor, Léopold Sédar Mar 62

Shirer, William L(awrence) May 62

Shotton, Burt(on Edwin) obit Oct 62

Shurlock, Geoffrey M. Jan 62

Sitterly, Mrs. Bancroft Walker See Sitterly, C. M. Jan 62

Sitterly, Charlotte Moore Jan 62

Slocum, (Manly) Harvey obit Jan 62

Smith, Margaret (Madeline) Chase Mar 62

Spahn, Warren (Edward) May 62

Speicher, Eugene (Edward) obit Jul 62

Spottswood, Stephen Gill Apr 62

Stelle, John obit Sep 62

Stikker, Dirk U(ipko) Feb 62

Stokes, Anson Phelps, Jr. Jul 62

Suggs, Louise Jan 62

Sunderland, Thomas E(lbert) Apr 62

Swann, W(illiam) F(rancis) G(ray) obit Mar 62

Swift, Harold H(iggins) obit Sep 62

Switzer, Mary E(lizabeth) Jan 62

Taylor, A(lbert) Hoyt obit Jan 62

Teagle, Walter C(lark) obit Feb 62

Thant, U Feb 62

Thomas, Norman (Mattoon) Jul 62

Thurber, James obit Jan 62

Tillinghast, Charles C(arpenter), Jr. Feb 62

Tobias, Channing H(eggie) obit Jan 62

Turner, Ewald (Walter) May 62

Unitas, John Feb 62

Vandiver, S(amuel) Ernest Jul 62

Van Pelt, John V(redenburgh) obit Sep 62

Vertès, Marcel obit Jan 62

Viereck, George Sylvester obit May 62

Vilar, Jean (Louis Côme) Apr 62

Volpe, John A(nthony) Feb 62

Waddington, C(onrad) H(al) Apr 62

Wagner, Richard Apr 62

Wald, Jerry obit Sep 62

Walsh, Chad Feb 62

Walsh, William B(ertalan) May 62

Walter, Bruno obit Apr 62

Ward, Paul L(angdon) Mar 62

Watson, Lucile obit Sep 62

Watts, Alan (Wilson) Mar 62

Webb, James E(dwin) May 62

Welsh, Matthew E(mpson) Jun 62

Wenner-Gren, Axel (Leonard) obit Jan 62

Wesker, Arnold Feb 62

Whalen, Grover A(loysius) obit Jun 62

Whitton, Rex M(arion) May 62

Wickens, Aryness Joy Sep 62

Wilcox, Francis O(rlando) Apr 62

Wilkinson, Bud See Wilkinson, C. Apr 62

Wilkinson, Charles (Burnham) Apr 62

Wills, Royal Barry obit Feb 62

Winiarski, Bohdan (Stefan) Feb 62

Wood, Natalie Apr 62

Yamasaki, Minoru Mar 62

Young, Owen D. obit Sep 62

CURRENT BIOGRAPHY

NOVEMBER 1962
VOL. 23   NO. 10

Editor: Charles Moritz

PUBLISHED BY THE H. W. WILSON COMPANY, 950 UNIVERSITY AVE., NEW YORK

CONTENTS   Page   Page

ABOUT THIS PUBLICATION

Current Biography (published every month except August) presents articles on people who are prominent in the news—in national and international affairs, the sciences, the arts, labor, and industry. Sources of information are newspapers, magazines, books, and, in some cases, the biographees themselves. It should be pointed out, however, that these are objective rather than authorized biographies. At the end of the year the articles in the monthly issues are cumulated in one alphabet, revised, and printed in a single volume known as *Current Biography Yearbook.*

Authorities for biographees' full names, with some exceptions, are the bibliographical publications of The Wilson Company. When a biographee prefers a certain name form, that is indicated in the heading of the article: for example, MACMILLAN, (MAURICE) HAROLD means that he is usually referred to as HAROLD MACMILLAN. When a professional name is used in the heading, as, for example, GLENN FORD, the real name, in this case GWYLLYN SAMUEL NEWTON FORD, appears in the article itself.

The heading of each article includes the pronunciation of the name if it is unusual, date of birth (if obtainable), and occupation. The article is supplemented by a list of references to sources of *biographical* information, in two alphabets: (1) newspapers and periodicals and (2) books.

References to newspapers and periodicals are listed in abbreviated form; for example, "Sat Eve Post 217:14+ S 30 '44 por" means *Saturday Evening Post,* volume 217, pages 14 ff, September 30, 1944, with portrait. For full names, see the section "Periodical and Newspaper Designations," which is included in all *Current Biography* Yearbooks and in the January issue each year. Obituary notices appear for persons whose biographies have been published in *Current Biography.*

An index to names that have appeared this year is to be found at the back of this issue.

NOTE: Authors whose biographies do not appear in *Current Biography* may usually be found in *Twentieth Century Authors,* Kunitz & Haycraft, 1942, H. W. Wilson Company, or in the FIRST SUPPLEMENT (1955). Authors of books for young people are included in *The Junior Book of Authors* (Second Edition, Revised) edited by Kunitz & Haycraft, 1951, H. W. Wilson Company. Musicians whose biographies do not appear in *Current Biography* may usually be found in *Living Musicians,* compiled and edited by David Ewen, 1940, H. W. Wilson Company, or in its FIRST SUPPLEMENT (1957).

KEY TO PRONUNCIATION

ā	āle	N	Not pronounced, but indicates the nasal tone of the preceding vowel, as in the French *bon* (bôN).	û	ûrn; French eu, as in *jeu* (zhû); German ö, oe, as in *schön* (shûn), *Goethe* (gû'tĕ)
â	câre				
ă	ădd				
ȧ	ȧccount				
ä	ärm				
à	àsk				
ȧ	sofȧ				
		ō	ōld	ŭ	tŭb
ē	ēve	ô	ôrb	ū̆	circŭs
ĕ	ĕnd	ŏ	ŏdd	ü	Pronounced approximately as ē, with rounded lips: French u, as in *menu* (mē-nü); German ü, as in *grün*
ê	makêr	oi	oil		
		o͞o	o͞oze		
g	go	o͝o	fo͝ot		
		ou	out		
i	ice				
ĭ	ĭll	th	then	zh	azure
		th	thin	′ =	main accent
ᴋ	German ch as in *ich* (ĭᴋ)	ū	cūbe	″ =	secondary accent

CURRENT BIOGRAPHY

NOVEMBER 1962

AHMAD, IMAM OF YEMEN 1891-Sept. 19(?), 1962 Conservative, despotic monarch of the theocratic Middle Eastern country Yemen, 1948-62; one of the last absolute monarchs in the world. See *Current Biography* (March) 1956.

Obituary

N Y Times p1+ S 20 '62

ANDERSON, GEORGE W(HELAN), JR.
Dec. 15, 1906- United States Navy officer

Address: b. Department of the Navy, The Pentagon, Washington, D.C.; h. 3634 Upton St., N.W., Washington, D.C.

The senior military officer of the United States Department of the Navy is Admiral George W. Anderson, Jr., who was appointed by President John F. Kennedy to a two-year term as Chief of Naval Operations on June 22, 1961. A specialist in naval aviation for much of his career, Anderson helped to formulate the American aircraft program for World War II. In 1953-55 he served as special assistant to the chairman of the Joint Chiefs of Staff, and in 1957-58 he was chief of staff and aide to the Commander in Chief of the Pacific Command. He conducted naval operations in the Near East at the time of the Lebanon crisis in 1958 and was appointed Commander of the Sixth Fleet in September 1959. Upon the retirement of Admiral Arleigh A. Burke, who had served as Chief of Naval Operations for six years, Anderson was installed in his place on August 1, 1961. An effective planner and organizer, Anderson has a reputation as "a perfectionist who runs a taut ship."

A native of Brooklyn, New York, where his father ran a real estate business, George Whelan Anderson, Jr., was born on December 15, 1906 to George W. and Clara (Green) Anderson. He was brought up in the Roman Catholic faith and received his secondary education at the Jesuits' Brooklyn Preparatory School, where he proved an exceptionally bright student. In 1923 he entered the United States Naval Academy at Annapolis, Maryland, and when he received his B.S. degree and ensign's commission in June 1927, he stood twenty-seventh in his class. He stayed on at the Naval Academy for a short course in naval aviation and in 1930, after having served as a junior officer aboard the USS *Cincinnati*, was ordered to the Naval Air Station at Pensacola, Florida for flight training. He was designated a naval aviator in October 1930.

On duty with the Atlantic Fleet, Anderson served in the aviation units of the USS *Concord* and USS *Raleigh* until 1933, when he was assigned to the flight test division of the Naval Air

ADM. GEORGE W. ANDERSON, JR.

Station at Norfolk, Virginia. In 1935 he returned to duty afloat with Fighting Squadron Two based on the USS *Lexington,* and for two years, beginning in September 30, 1937, he served aboard the newly commissioned USS *Yorktown.*

Briefly, from late 1939 until early 1940, Anderson was attached to Patrol Squadron 44, Patrol Wing Four, based at Seattle, Washington. In his next assignment, with the plans division, Bureau of Aeronautics, Navy Department, in Washington, D.C., he participated in the formulation of the American aircraft program for World War II. His responsibilities brought him into association with wartime agencies concerned with the production and allocation of all United States aircraft. For his liaison work with the Army Air Forces, he received a letter of commendation from the War Department, with authorization to wear the Army Commendation Ribbon.

When the new USS *Yorktown* (CV-10) was commissioned on April 15, 1943, Anderson became navigator and tactical officer. Commended for outstanding services during her early action in the Pacific, he also shares in the Presidential Unit Citation awarded the *Yorktown* for "extraordinary heroism in action against enemy Japanese forces in the air, at sea and on shore" from August 31, 1943 to August 15, 1945. As head of the plans division of the staff of Commander, Air Force, United States Pacific Fleet during the

ANDERSON, GEORGE W., JR.—*Continued*
period from November 1943 to March 1944,
Anderson earned the Legion of Merit for exceptionally meritorious conduct. In recognition
of his further expert planning as assistant to the
Deputy Commander in Chief, United States
Pacific Fleet and Pacific Ocean areas between
March 28, 1944 and April 16, 1945 he was
decorated with the Bronze Star Medal. His final
World War II duty, beginning in June 1945,
was as aviation officer in the strategic plans
section on the staff of the Commander in Chief,
United States Fleet, at Washington, and as
deputy Navy planner on the Joint Planning Staff.

Appointed to the Permanent Joint Board on
Defense (Canada-United States) in November
1946, Anderson also served as a Navy member
of the Brazilian-United States Defense Commission before returning to sea in July 1948 as
commanding officer of the antisubmarine carrier
Mindoro. From August 1949 to July 1950 he
attended the National War College at Washington, and on completion of his course he was
assigned as fleet operations officer for the Sixth
Fleet in the Mediterranean. A wartime mission
to Britain in connection with his aircraft allocation duties had brought Anderson to the attention
of General Dwight D. Eisenhower, and in December 1950, after the latter had been appointed
Supreme Allied Commander in Europe, Anderson
was called to Eisenhower's Paris headquarters
(SHAPE) to become senior United States officer
in plans and operations. For a year beginning in
July 1952, Anderson was in command of the
carrier *Franklin D. Roosevelt* in the Mediterranean. Insisting on high spiritual and moral
standards, "he would address the crew before
arriving at a port, telling them what the port
offered, mentioning arrangements for liberty and
other things and weaving in some counsel about
proper behavior," as John G. Norris has related
in the Washington *Post and Times Herald* (October 18, 1959).

Shortly after being recalled to Washington in
June 1953, Anderson was appointed special assistant to Admiral Arthur W. Radford, the chairman of the Joint Chiefs of Staff. Advanced to
rear admiral as of August 1, 1954, he was placed
one year later in command of the Formosa
Patrol Force with additional duty as commander,
Fleet Air Wing One. His title was changed late
in 1955 to commander of the Taiwan Patrol
Force.

In May 1957, after ten months as chief of staff,
Joint Staff, Commander in Chief, Pacific, Anderson reported as chief of staff and aide to Admiral
Felix B. Stump, Commander in Chief, Pacific.
He thus became second on the staff of the largest
military command in the world. Promoted at
the same time to vice-admiral, Anderson abruptly
asked to be reduced to two-star rank so that he
could head a carrier division and comply with
an old tradition that the flag of an admiral is
not genuinely earned unless it is flown at sea.
It was as a rear admiral, accordingly, that he took
command of Carrier Division Six, consisting of
the *Saratoga* and *Essex*, and of Task Force 60,
which supported the landing of Marines in
Lebanon on July 15, 1958. During the first seven
days of the operation Task Force 60 flew an
average of 250 sorties every twenty-four hours in
providing air cover over the Sixth Fleet and
Lebanon.

Resuming the rank of vice-admiral in August
1959, Anderson in the following month succeeded
Vice-Admiral Clarence Ekstrom as commander,
Sixth Fleet and commander, Naval Striking and
Support Forces, Southern Europe, which with its
fifty ships, 200 aircraft, and 25,000 men has been
regarded as one of the world's most powerful
air-sea striking forces. "The reason we are here,"
he said at a later fleet commander's conference,
"as part of Allied strength, is to deter any
potential aggressor. . . . That is our overriding
requirement—sophisticated readiness in our case,
which is to put the right weapons on the right
targets at the right time." As a reason for his
mission he also stressed "respect," which he defined as making new friends, keeping old friends
and impressing those who are not friends of the
United States. According to *Time* (June 30,
1961) Anderson has proved a gracious host to
leading political figures of the world aboard his
flagship.

On June 22, 1961 President Kennedy announced his choice of Vice-Admiral Anderson to
succeed retiring Admiral Arleigh A. Burke as
Chief of Naval Operations. The appointment
was made on recommendation of Navy Secretary
John B. Connally, who had interviewed 109
eligible admirals, about ten of whom were Anderson's seniors on the Navy list. He was installed
on August 1, 1961, following confirmation by the
Senate. The Chief of Naval Operations, who
holds the rank of full admiral, is the principal
naval adviser to the President and the Secretary
of the Navy on the conduct of war, and acts as
principal adviser and naval executive on the
conduct of the activities of the Navy Department.
He is responsible to the Secretary of the Navy
for the command, utilization, and administration
of the Navy's operating forces, and determines the
personnel and material needs of these forces. He
is the department's representative on the Joint
Chiefs of Staff.

Despite a career about evenly divided between
carrier and staff duty, Admiral Anderson is no
"air fanatic" but recognizes the value of all the
Navy's equipment from oilers to Polaris-equipped
submarines. Addressing the annual meeting of the
Naval Architects and Marine Engineers in
November 1961, he said that the Navy's research
and shipbuilding program was "geared to keeping
the sea lanes of the world open" and that "with
no apparent lessening of the Communist desire
to dominate the world . . . our requirements for
naval power will change but little in general
form." He went on to say: "Our Navy of five
years from now is already designed and is in
some cases in actual production." When testifying before the Senate Armed Services Committee on January 31, 1962, Anderson agreed with
the Secretary of the Navy in emphasizing the
increasing size of the Polaris-armed nuclear-
powered submarines and their improved performance. He warned, however, that although
Soviet submarine-launched missiles were "far
from being as advanced," they did "pose, without question, a positive threat." Commenting
late in the following month on the performance
of the world's largest ship and first nuclear-
powered aircraft carrier, the recently commis-

sioned USS *Enterprise,* he noted that it had already gone faster than any other carrier, and that there was "every indication . . . that the designers and builders have hit the jackpot."

By his marriage to Muriel Buttling on October 3, 1933, Admiral George W. Anderson has two sons, Ensign George Whelan 3d and Thomas Patrick, and one daughter, Mary Annette (Mrs. Daniel Coughlin, Jr.). His first wife died in 1947, and on May 15, 1948 he married Mary Lee Lamar Sample of Pensacola, Florida. Her daughter Carolyn is Mrs. David Abshire. Anderson is over six feet tall, weighs about 200 pounds, and has silvery hair. One interviewer has noticed that "his eyes are blue, twinkling when he is pleased, cold blue steel when angered" (*Christian Science Monitor,* June 23, 1961). A Roman Catholic, he urges men under his command to go to church, and he dislikes profanity. "I think we all need a lot of divine assistance," he has said. He has a number of foreign decorations, including the Order of Prince Henry the Navigator (Portugal) and the Order of the British Empire. His clubs are the Brook in New York City and the Chevy Chase in Washington. His recreations are swimming and playing golf.

References

Christian Sci Mon p14 Je 23 '61 por
N Y Herald Tribune p2 Je 23 '61
N Y Times p1 Je 23 '61 por
Time 77:14+ Je 30 '61 por
Washington (D.C.) Post E p1 O 18 '59 por
American Catholic Who's Who, 1962 and 1963
Who's Who in America, 1962-63

BARTH, KARL (bärt) May 10, 1886-   Swiss theologian
Address: Pilgerstrasse 25, Basel, Switzerland

For more than forty years the neo-orthodox theology of the Reverend Dr. Karl Barth has been an important influence in world Protestantism. Since 1919—the year in which the Swiss theologian initially set it forth—he has developed it in some 200 books and in lectures at the University of Basel, where he served as a professor of theology from 1935 to 1962. His major work, the multi-volume *Church Dogmatics,* is, in the words of a *Time* writer (April 20, 1962), "the most exhaustive compendium of what a Christian must believe, and why he believes it, that Protestantism has had in more than a century."

Karl Barth, the first of five children of Fritz and Anna (Sartorius) Barth, was born in Basel, Switzerland on May 10, 1886. His father was a New Testament scholar of the Swiss Reformed Church who gave up his pastorate to teach theology at a seminary in Basel. Barth attended a *Gymnasium* and the university in Bern. He then studied at the university in Tübingen and at the universities of Berlin and Marburg, where he came into contact with the liberal humanistic theology that dominated German Protestantism around the turn of the century.

Liberal Protestantism focused upon the subjective human religious experience rather than upon the objective attributes of God. It con-

Wide World

KARL BARTH

ceived of religion as only one of the means to achieve a better world, and it encompassed the "higher criticism," an evaluation and justification of Biblical events in scientific and historical terms. Barth studied under two of the outstanding exponents of liberal Protestant theology, Adolf von Harnack at Berlin and Wilhelm Herrmann at Marburg. Originally a liberal himself, he was considered a credit to his teachers.

Ordained by his father in 1908 in the Reformed church in Bern, Barth worked for a time under the direction of Martin Rade, a friend of Harnack, on the staff of *Die Christliche Welt,* the chief organ for the propagation of liberalism in Germany. From 1909 to 1911 he served as an assistant pastor in a small church in Geneva, and in 1911 he was given the pastorate of Safenwil, a small Swiss village, where he remained until 1921. An active socialist during his first few years at Safenwil, Barth earned the nickname "the Red pastor" for his action in organizing poorly paid Safenwil textile workers into a union and his refusal to recognize distinctions between rich and poor.

Dismayed by the co-existence of pious sentiment with economic exploitation, he also became disillusioned by the impotence of German Social Democracy and the inadequacy of Protestant social thought. (When the Church in Germany approved the Kaiser's war policy, not one of his former mentors protested.) World War I, with its destruction of optimistic faith in man's inevitable progress toward a better world, created in him, as in many other clergymen, a doubt as to the relevance of the liberal theology, a theology in which God as the principal actor had become largely obscured. He discussed his doubts with Edward Thurneysen, another disillusioned young preacher from a neighboring village; together they undertook a critical review of the theology they had learned.

(Continued next page)

BARTH, KARL—*Continued*

The result of Barth's search was published in his book *Römerbrief* (1919), a commentary on Paul's Epistle to the Romans that proved to be a manifesto of his rejection of the liberal theology. In it Barth restored to theology a view of God as supreme, transcendent, and divine. God's divinity, he said, is the antithesis, not the fulfillment, of humanity. Man cannot know God nor initiate communication with him; if there is to be a relationship between God and his creature, it is God who must establish it. "The Bible," Barth said, "tells us not how we should talk with God but what he says to us; not how we find the way to him, but how he has sought and found the way to us." Barth also revived attention to the sinfulness of humanity, which he felt liberals had neglected in overemphasizing the goodness and dignity of man.

The volume drew a storm of criticism from European theologians, especially from his former colleagues of the liberal school. Barth also had his advocates, however, and as his name became widely known, he attracted disciples and was asked to lecture in several European cities. In 1921 he was invited to assume a post as professor of reformed theology at the University of Göttingen, a chair maintained by gifts from the American Reformed Church. While teaching there he also helped to edit a new magazine that continued the attack upon liberalism. In 1925 he took the official chair of theology at the University of Münster.

Barth revised the *Römerbrief* in 1922, and the book eventually ran into some seven printings (with various new prefaces added). The English translation, entitled *The Epistle to the Romans,* was published in 1933 by Oxford University Press. Barth viewed his book as being essentially a correction and reorientation of theological systems that had gone too far in one direction. "I do not presume to put alongside . . . of the great and venerable creators of theological systems anything equal or of like measure," he said in 1922. "It is rather a kind of query in the margin, it is a 'pinch of spice' to flavor and correct others."

However, as he became more prominent and was called upon to give lectures and guidance, Barth found it necessary to define more precisely his position on theological questions. His book *Christian Dogmatics in Outline* was published in 1927, but when he came to revise it for a second edition he decided that, instead of a revision, a new work was needed. The first volume of his major work, *Church Dogmatics,* was entitled "The Doctrine of the Word of God" and came out in two parts in 1932 and 1938. "The Doctrine of God," Volume II in two parts, appeared in 1940 and 1942, and "The Doctrine of Creation," Volume III in four parts, appeared in 1945, 1948, 1950, and 1951. Parts 1 and 2 of Volume IV, "The Doctrine of Reconciliation," came out in 1953 and 1955, and two books of Volume IV, part 3, were published in 1959. *Church Dogmatics* thus consists to date of twelve large books. Volume V, "The Doctrine of Redemption," has not yet been completed.

"Dogmatics, in Barth's definition, is the critical examination of the Christian message in light of what the Scriptures say," a *Time* writer (April 20, 1962) has explained. "Barth's own examination of this message is garrulous, eye-wearying, and studded with trackless deserts of scholarly footnotes. . . . But *Dogmatics* is also wreathed with a knowledge of 1,900 years of Christian writing and stands as the century's only equivalent to the *summa* of the medieval scholastics."

In 1919, providing a counterbalance to the liberal theology, Barth had emphasized the distance between God and man. In *Church Dogmatics* he examines the ways in which contact between them has been established. Man, he says, cannot deduce God's existence. He must wait for God to reveal himself, and he can know God only through faith in this revelation. God has revealed himself in the person of Jesus Christ and speaks to man through the Bible, which bears witness to Christ. Since God's message comes to us in the Bible through human agents, it is distorted to some degree, and the continuing task of the Church and her theologians is to study the Bible in the light of faith and try to improve their understanding of the Word of God. The death and resurrection of Christ, Barth says, has made it possible for sinful humanity to be reconciled to God. *Church Dogmatics* is Christ-centered. A theologian has commented, "In 1920 the theology of Barth set itself up in a rather inhuman grandeur. Today it is clothed with indulgence and mercy."

Barth was one of the most vehement opponents of Nazism. He taught theology at the University of Bonn from 1930 to 1935, during the early days of Hitler's rise to power. He had always considered politics uninteresting, and at first he did not protest against the new regime; but when the Nazis tried to foist upon the German church the idea of deification of the state, Barth rebelled. He was one of 200 leaders of German churches who issued the Barmen declaration, a proclamation of the autonomy of the church from all temporal interference. As a professor, Barth was required to take the civil servants' oath of allegiance to Hitler; he would have done so with the qualification that his allegiance was limited by his higher loyalty to God. This did not satisfy the government, and in 1935 he was condemned by a Nazi court of "seducing the minds" of German students and dismissed from his post at Bonn.

He accepted a professorship of theology created especially for him at the University of Basel in 1935, and he remained in this position until his retirement in the spring of 1962. In 1936, when he tried once more to speak in Germany, he was deported by the Gestapo. At home in Switzerland Barth joined the auxiliary corps of the Swiss Army and did sentry duty on the Swiss border. As he learned of the anti-Semitic and racial policies of the Nazis he became outspoken in his condemnation of the Nazi state as a "basically anti-German counterchurch," and he addressed messages to Protestants in Czechoslovakia, France, Britain, and America, urging them to resist Hitler. He generally couched his vigorous opposition to the Third Reich in theological terms. After the war he spoke out against cherishing a feeling of hatred for the Germans. In the year 1946-47 he was a guest professor at the University of Bonn.

Although Barth believes that the church should resist any invasion of its domain by the state, his conviction that the church should not, on the other hand, interfere with the state nor align itself with any political cause has led him to maintain a neutrality with regard to the question of the cold war. He was not one of those theologians who spoke out in 1956 against the Soviet repression of the Hungarian rebellion. Indeed, he has counseled Protestants in Communist countries to try to get along with their governments. In books like *Against the Stream* (Philosophical Library, 1954) and *How to Serve God in a Marxist Land* (Association Press, 1959) he explains his refusal to become involved in what he sees as a strictly ideological, political, temporal struggle. Theologians like Reinhold Niebuhr have criticized his position as being irrelevant to those Christians who "take their moral responsibilities seriously."

In April 1962 Barth made his first visit to the United States. He gave a series of lectures, in which he explained his theology, at the University of Chicago and at Princeton Theological Seminary, on the occasion of the seminary's 150th anniversary celebration. Barth received a D.D. degree from the University of Chicago. The citation that accompanied the degree stated, "Barth's concern was to reassert the centrality of God over and against the centrality of man in the method and message of theology. He has devoted a lifetime of research, writing, and teaching to this concern." Barth also holds D.D. degrees from the universities of Münster, Utrecht, Glasgow, and Oxford, and an LL.D. degree from St. Andrews University. He is an honorary member of the British and Foreign Bible Society and a foreign honorary member of the American Academy of Arts and Sciences.

In his first lecture in Chicago on April 23, 1962, Barth pointed out that his "evangelical" theology centered on a God who is "just as lowly as He is exalted." "A God who confronted men simply as exalted, distant, and strange," he said, "would be a God men would have to avoid because they would not be able to meet his demands." Evangelical theology, he continued, speaks of "the God who reveals Himself in the Gospel, who Himself speaks to men and acts among and upon them." Thousands of people heard his lectures; many traveled considerable distances to hear them.

Barth delivered the lectures in English, which he first began to learn when he was about forty years old and which he practised by reading detective novels. After the lecture series he visited Washington, D.C. and, since he is a Civil War buff, the Civil War battlefields in the South. On his own request, he was also taken to see an American prison, and he expressed himself as being shocked at its condition compared to those in Swiss prisons, which he often visits to preach and to lead the services of the prisoners.

A short, blue-eyed, gray-haired man, Barth smokes a pipe and sometimes peers owlishly over the rims of his dark-rimmed glasses. He is genial, modest, sympathetic, and patient and has a pixyish sense of humor. Karl Barth married Nelly Hoffman, a violinist, in 1913 or 1914. They had four children: Markus, an associate professor

at the University of Chicago Divinity School; Christoph, a professor of the Old Testament at the University of Indonesia in Jakarta; Franziska; and Matthias, who died in a mountain climbing accident. Barth usually rises early and listens to phonograph recordings of the music of Mozart, his favorite composer, about whom he once wrote a book, *Wolfgang Amadeus Mozart, 1756-1956* (1956). He does not like modern literature or art. "What I object to is the disappearance of the object," he says. "In art, as in theology, it is the object that counts, not the subject."

References

N Y Post Mag p2 My 13 '62 por
N Y Times p21 Ap 30 '62 por
Time 79:59+ Ap 20 '62 pors
Allen, E. L. A Guide To the Thought of Karl Barth (1951)
Herberg, Will ed. Community, State and Church (1960)
Who's Who in America, 1962-63
Who's Who in Switzerland (1955)

BENSON, JOHN 1872-Aug. 23, 1962 Former president (1928-44) of the American Association of Advertising Agencies. See *Current Biography* (April) 1940.

Obituary

N Y Times p22 Ag 24 '62

BOWATER, SIR ERIC (VANSITTART) Jan. 16, 1895-Aug. 30, 1962 Chairman of the Bowater Paper Corporation. See *Current Biography* (September) 1956.

Obituary

N Y Times p21 Ag 31 '62

BRAMUGLIA, JUAN A(TILIO) Jan. 1, 1903-Sept. 4, 1962 Foreign Minister of Argentina from 1946 to 1949, under General Juan Perón; Argentinian representative on the U.N. Security Council during the late 1940's. See *Current Biography* (May) 1949.

Obituary

N Y Times p39 S 5 '62

BRISTOL, LEE H(ASTINGS) Nov. 11, 1892-Sept. 22, 1962 Board chairman (1958-62) and former president (1949-58) of Bristol-Myers Company. See *Current Biography* (September) 1962.

Obituary

N Y Times p29 S 24 '62

COBLENTZ, W(ILLIAM) W(EBER) Nov. 20, 1873-Sept. 15, 1962 Physicist; worked with the United States National Bureau of Standards from 1905 to 1945; pioneered in the measurement of heat and light; investigated the infrared and ultraviolet spectra. See *Current Biography* (March) 1954.

Obituary

N Y Times p39 S 19 '62

COREA, SIR (GEORGE) CLAUDE (STANLEY) Sept. 5, 1894-Sept. 3, 1962 Head of the Ceylonese delegation to the United Nations, 1958-61; Ceylonese Ambassador to the United States, 1948-54. See *Current Biography* (March) 1961.

Obituary

N Y Times p19 S 8 '62

DUFFY, EDMUND Mar. 1, 1899-Sept. 13, 1962 Political cartoonist; won the Pulitzer Prize in 1931, 1934, and 1940 for his cartoons; was editorial cartoonist with the Baltimore *Sun* from 1924 to 1948. See *Current Biography* (January-June) 1940.

Obituary

N Y Times p37 S 13 '62

EISLER, HANNS July 6, 1898-Sept. 6, 1962 Composer; wrote motion picture scores, operas, symphonies, chamber music; composed the East German national anthem; lived in the United States from 1940 to 1948, later in East Berlin. See *Current Biography* (May) 1942.

Obituary

N Y Times p29 S 7 '62

LEHMANN, INGE May 13, 1888- Seismologist; geodesist

Address: h. Kastelsvej 26, Copenhagen, Denmark

One of the most distinguished seismologists of the twentieth century is a shy and modest woman from Denmark, Inge Lehmann, who has devoted her career to the scientific study of the earth's interior. For a quarter of a century, as state geodesist and chief of the seismological department of the Danish Geodetic Institute, Miss Lehmann made some notable contributions to the recording and interpretation of seismic data, and she was the first to discover the earth's inner core. Now retired, she continues to study the interior of the earth. Her discoveries and singlemindedness over the years have done much to project the emerging science of seismology, the study of earthquakes and related phenomena, into its position of international importance.

Inge Lehmann was born in Copenhagen, Denmark on May 13, 1888 to Alfred Georg Ludvig Lehmann, an eminent professor of psychology at the University of Copenhagen, and Ida Sophie (Tørsleff) Lehmann. She has one sister, Mrs. Harriet Hofmann. In 1894 Inge Lehmann enrolled at a private school in Copenhagen run by a Mr. Adler; she graduated in 1906. That same year she entered the University of Copenhagen, where she studied mathematics from 1907 until 1910. The academic year of 1910-11 she spent in England, continuing her studies in mathematics at Newnham College of Cambridge University. Returning to Denmark, she served as an actuarial assistant in the offices of the Insurance Society of Denmark from 1912 until 1918. Two years later, in 1920, Inge Lehmann received her mas-

ter's degree in mathematics from the University of Copenhagen.

In the autumn of 1922 Miss Lehmann traveled to Germany to study mathematics under Professor Wilhelm Blaschke at the University of Hamburg. From 1923 to 1926 she was an assistant in actuarial science to Professor J. F. Steffensen at the University of Copenhagen. Meanwhile, beginning in 1925, she had also served as a staff member of the Danish Geodetic Institute, helping in the preparations for the establishment of seismological stations at Scoresbysund and Ivigtut, Greenland. In those days before extensive air travel, she had to travel by ship to get to those faraway outposts. Miss Lehmann also helped to set up the seismographs at the seismological station in Copenhagen.

To groom herself for a career in seismology, in 1927 Inge Lehmann took a leave of absence from her work for further study. In France, the Netherlands, Belgium, and Germany she studied under some of the leading seismologists of the day. She received her Master of Science degree in geodesy from the University of Copenhagen in 1928. In the same year she was appointed state geodesist and made chief of the recently established seismological department of the Danish Geodetic Institute. Holding those appointments until she retired in 1953, she supervised the seismological stations in Greenland and at Copenhagen and prepared their bulletins. Fortunately, Miss Lehmann was able to engage in scientific research while performing her administrative duties.

Inge Lehmann's outstanding achievement was her discovery of the inner core of the earth. Although the deep interior of the earth remains inaccessible to man's eye, he is able to "see" the interior by interpreting the shock waves generated by earthquakes, recorded on the seismograph as time-curves or travel-time curves. By studying these seismic curves, seismologists can define the layering within the earth and determine the physical properties within these layers.

As early as 1910 scientists believed that the presence of a shadow zone in the earth's interior indicated the existence of a core within the earth, but seismographs had not been refined to the point where they might substantiate this theory. It was not until the 1930's that new and more sensitive seismographs were developed, and the data recorded by these instruments soon rendered the older theories inadequate. Working with the greatest precision, Inge Lehmann, in 1936, interpreted the newly revealed data to confirm the existence of a small inner core in the interior of the earth. Subsequent research has supported her discovery.

Seismic studies have made the general configuration of the earth's interior known to man. The particular province of the seismologist, however, is the uppermost region of our planet, just beneath the earth's crust, known as the upper mantle. This is the region in which most earthquakes occur. Precise and detailed information about this area is of great importance to geophysicists in many fields.

Since her retirement in 1953 Inge Lehmann has continued to study the upper mantle in institutions in Denmark and abroad. In Canada she has worked at the Dominion Observatory in Ottawa; in the United States she has conducted research at the Seismological Laboratory, California Institute of Technology, the University of California at Berkeley, and the Lamont Geological Observatory of Columbia University in New York. Her work in this field has taken on special significance since the proposal made in 1960 at a meeting of the International Union of Geodesy and Geophysics to undertake a study of the upper mantle on an international basis.

Since World War II nuclear explosions have been used by the seismologist, when feasible, to explore the earth's interior further. Because scientists know the focus or source of the explosion exactly, they can formulate time-curves with greater precision than with earthquakes. If recording stations are properly located, scientists can obtain more useful data from these explosions than they can from natural tremors. Just as the seismologist is turning to artificial earthquakes to learn more about the earth, others are resorting to the seismologist and his instruments to learn more about man-made and natural earthquakes.

Now that scientists have learned how to simulate earthquakes with nuclear explosions the work of Inge Lehmann, with that of other seismologists, has doubled in importance. Before the seismologist can properly distinguish between natural and artificial rumblings within the earth, he has to learn more about the planetary mass through which the shock waves travel. Inge Lehmann's studies are contributing to the development of an international language of science that may dispel the mutual suspicions of men everywhere.

During her career as chief seismologist for Denmark Miss Lehmann was active in national, regional, and international scientific organizations. She was one of the founders of the Danish Geophysical Society in 1936, and she served as its president from 1941 until 1944. She was made an honorary member in 1961. Miss Lehmann helped to formulate the constitution of the European Seismological Federation and was elected its first president in 1950. (The federation has been superseded by the European Seismological Commission.) She found time to attend most of the meetings of the International Union of Geodesy and Geophysics and served as a member of the executive committee of the Seismological Association from 1936 to 1944, from 1951 to 1954, and from 1957 to 1960.

Instead of bringing relaxation from work or a flagging of professional interest, retirement for Miss Lehmann has simply meant a relief from the routines involved in station operation. She continues to hold membership in various organizations: the Danish Geological Society; the Danish Mathematical Society; the Society for the Advancement of Natural Science, in Copenhagen; the International Federation of University Women; the French Association of Experimental Seismology; the Seismological Society of America; and the American Geophysical Union.

In 1938 Inge Lehmann received a Tagea Brandt grant. In 1957 she was elected an Asso-

Elfelt, Copenhagen

INGE LEHMANN

ciate of the Royal Astronomical Society, in London. In 1959 she was elected an Honorary Fellow of the Royal Society of Edinburgh and in 1960 she received the Henry Oscar Wood Award in seismology. Her papers on geophysics have been published in many international scientific journals.

Far from being an austere scientist, Inge Lehmann is a warm and friendly woman who is genuinely concerned with social welfare. She is especially interested in the work being done for the poor by Kofoed's Skole in Copenhagen and in the program being carried on for European refugees by the Inomeuropeisk Mission in Lund, Sweden. Her profession has afforded her the opportunity to indulge in her two main hobbies: art appreciation and the outdoors. She knows the inside of most of the art galleries in Europe and of the leading galleries in the United States. She has no religious or political affiliation. In addition to being a tireless walker and mountain climber, she is an excellent skier who, although once adept at both Austrian and French skiing techniques, restricts herself these days to Norwegian trail skiing. Miss Lehmann is proficient in English and German, fluent in French, and has some knowledge of Italian. However far she may travel from her native Denmark she always returns to her small cottage in Copenhagen with its whitewashed walls and roof of red tiles, overlooking a plot of woodland and a small lake. There, surrounded by her favorite fruit trees, she works in her garden and relaxes from the busier pace of her visits to Western Europe and the United States.

References

Sat R 44:38+ Ag 5 '61 por

Kraks Blå Bog 1961

LEWIS, JERRY Mar. 16, 1926- Comedian; producer; director

Address: c/o Jerry Lewis Productions, Inc., Paramount Studios, 5451 Marathon St., Hollywood 38, Calif.

Without the encouragement of critics, sophisticates, or intellectuals Jerry Lewis has become one of the most financially successful clowns in the history of American show business. Children make up the majority of his movie audiences. None of his twenty-six films—with or without his former partner, Dean Martin—has grossed less than $5,000,000 at the box office and the first record that he cut sold over 1,000,000 copies.

Perhaps Lewis has been more appreciated in Europe than in the United States, where critics have berated him for his lapses of taste, primitive slapstick, and prehistoric jokes. He has repelled the discriminating viewer with his mannerisms, including spastic contortions, crossed eyes, distended mouth, and splay-legged walk. Yet, at his best, the unsubtle and raucous Lewis has impressed some critics with his pantomime, his sense of timing, his Chaplinesque aura of pathos, and his skilled ad-libbing. In the youthful comic they have discerned the potentialities of a great clown, and Harriet Van Horne of the New York *World-Telegram and Sun* has called Lewis a "sort of witless genius."

Jerry Lewis was born Joseph Levitch in Newark, New Jersey on March 16, 1926 to Danny and Mona Lewis ("Lewis" is a stage name), both of whom were in show business. His father was—and still is—a night club singer whose specialty is nostalgic songs of the 1920's; his mother played the piano at New York City's radio station WOR, made musical arrangements, and sometimes accompanied her husband's singing. At the age of five Jerry made his debut at a hotel in New York's borscht circuit on September 7, 1931, singing "Brother, Can You Spare a Dime?" His father was working in the hotel at the time as a master of ceremonies. Their bookings often took Danny and Mona Lewis away from home, and Jerry was placed in the care of friends or relatives or left alone. He used to dream of becoming a movie star.

At Irvington High School in Irvington, New Jersey Jerry is remembered as one of the craziest cheerleaders in the school's history. His classmates nicknamed him "Id"—not in the Freudian sense—but short for "Idiot." To make them like him and to make them laugh, he clowned for them, but he was not a favorite of the teachers, who tried to drive him to the textbooks. Never one for book learning, Lewis reportedly has read only one book all the way through in his life—an autographed copy of the best-selling *Courtroom* by Quentin Reynolds. After the tenth grade Lewis left high school, a move that he has since often regretted. Over the years his mercurial mind has enabled him to pick up a fund of information from listening to lawyers, doctors, press agents, producers, directors, cameramen, and assorted hangers-on.

By the time he was fifteen Jerry Lewis had perfected his own comedy "record" act (a "dumb" act in the lingo of show business), pantomiming

and silently mouthing the lyrics of operatic and popular songs played on a phonograph off stage. He had also run through a series of odd jobs, including that of counterman at a drugstore lunch counter, shipping clerk in a hat factory, and usher at Loew's State Theatre in New York City. Dressed in a drape jacket and pegged pants, his hair pomaded to a high gloss, he braved the offices of booking agents. He was booked into the Palace Theatre, a burlesque house in Buffalo, where he was at first hooted off the stage. Ready to give up in discouragement, he was advised to continue his career by a veteran burlesque comedian.

During the summer of 1942 Jerry Lewis tried out his record act at Brown's Hotel in Loch Sheldrake, New York, where he was working as a bellboy and his father was serving as master of ceremonies. The routine proved to be so funny that Irving Kaye, a comedian then working for Danny Lewis, helped the boy to get some bookings. Kaye was promptly fired by Danny Lewis, who wanted to keep his son out of show business, and just as promptly hired by Jerry Lewis as traveling companion and road manager. Kaye is still employed by Lewis.

In July 1946 Jerry Lewis was performing his record act at the 500 Club in Atlantic City when one of the entertainers on the bill suddenly quit. Lewis suggested that the owner hire a young singer named Dean Martin, whom Lewis had met when they both worked at the Glass Hat in New York City. For the first few nights Jerry Lewis did his usual record act while Martin delivered his own numbers separately. But on the night of July 25, 1946 Lewis and Martin discarded their usual routines and ad-libbed instead. They improvised insults and witticisms, squirted seltzer water, hurled bunches of celery, turned off the lights, tripped passing waiters, and broke into each other's act. The audience loved it, and the phenomenally successful team of Martin and Lewis was born. In less than eight months their salaries soared from $350 to $5,000 a week.

Hal Wallis, the motion picture producer, saw Martin and Lewis do their act at the Copacabana club in New York City and signed them to a motion picture contract for Paramount Pictures. During the next ten years Dean Martin and Jerry Lewis sandwiched in sixteen money-making films between night club engagements, personal appearances, and television bookings. When their first film *My Friend Irma* was released in 1949, Bosley Crowther wrote in the New York *Times* (September 29, 1949): "We could go along with the laughs which were fetched by a new mad comedian, Jerry Lewis by name. This freakishly built and acting young man, who has been seen in night clubs hereabouts with a collar-ad partner, Dean Martin, has a genuine comic quality. The swift eccentricity of his movements, the harrowing features of his face and the squeak of his vocal protestations . . . have flair. His idiocy constitutes the burlesque of an idiot, which is something else again. He's the funniest thing in it. Indeed, he's the only thing in it that we can expressly propose for seeing the picture."

There followed *My Friend Irma Goes West* (1950); *At War with the Army* (1951); *That's My Boy* (1951); *Jumping Jacks* (1952); *Sailor Beware* (1952); *The Caddy* (1953); *Scared Stiff* (1953); *The Stooge* (1953); *Living It Up* (1954); *Money From Home* (1954); *Three Ring Circus* (1954); *Artists and Models* (1955); *You're Never Too Young* (1955); and *Pardners* (1956). By 1956, however, the films were making fewer and fewer variations on the same theme, and Martin and Lewis decided to break up the team. Martin had reportedly grown tired of playing straight man to a knockabout comedian, and Lewis was eager to try a career on his own. Their last film together was *Hollywood or Bust,* and on July 24, 1956 Martin and Lewis did their last show together at the Copacabana night club in New York City. There seems to be little or no chance of a professional reunion, since each man has proved that he has the talent to go it alone— Lewis as a comedian, Martin as a straight dramatic actor and singer.

Left without Martin, Lewis wondered if he could gain audience acceptance by himself. His doubts were dispelled in July 1956 at Las Vegas, when Judy Garland was forced to cancel an engagement because of laryngitis, and Lewis volunteered to go on in her place, without any prepared material. The audience extended him an ovation for his improvisations and it was a long time before he could bow off the floor. By 1961 Lewis had developed into a new kind of comedian, a subtler and more topical pantomimist and satirist at far remove from his former low comedy routines. Although the breakup of the team had been accompanied by anguish on the part of fans and no little personal recrimination between the two stars, the decision to liquidate the partnership now seems justified. Today Lewis and Martin remain cool to each other.

With increased confidence, Lewis has become a singer, screen writer, producer, and director as well as actor. His movies drew from the Hollywood director Leo McCarey the comment: "He's the Pied Piper of the business, the heir to the mantle of Charlie Chaplin and Harold Lloyd. He can do no wrong." In spite of a voice that has been described as yapping and nasal, Lewis has also succeeded as a singer. His "Rock-a-Bye Your Baby," released by Decca Records, has sold over 1,000,000 copies, more than Al Jolson's original recording. For Decca Lewis has also recorded the albums *Jerry Lewis Just Sings* and *More Jerry Lewis.* His single records that have become hits include "The Lord Loves a Laughing Man" and "Dormi-Dormi-Dormi."

In the spring of 1959 Lewis signed a contract between Paramount-York Corporation and his own company, Jerry Lewis Productions. The contract represented the biggest single transaction in film history for the exclusive services of one star—a payment of $10,000,000 to star in fourteen films over a seven-year period: seven for Jerry Lewis Productions, seven for Paramount-York Corporation. In the first two, *The Ladies Man* (1961) and *The Errand Boy* (1962), Lewis served as writer, director, and producer as well as star. Other pictures he has made since the Martin and Lewis team broke up are: *The Deli-*

JERRY LEWIS

cate Delinquent (1957), his first film without Dean Martin; *Rock-a-Bye Baby* (1958), produced by Jerry Lewis; *The Sad Sack* (1958), based on the cartoon character with the same name; *The Geisha Boy* (1958); *Don't Give Up the Ship* (1959); *CinderFella* (1960), a modern spoof of the fairy tale; *The Bellboy* (1960), written, produced, and directed by Jerry Lewis; *Visit to a Small Planet* (1960), based on Gore Vidal's Broadway hit; and *It's Only Money,* reportedly in production in 1962.

Jerry Lewis has harnessed his restless energy to many charitable causes. As national chairman for more than ten years of the Muscular Dystrophy Associations of America, he personally raised the entire cost of a multimillion dollar building for the Institute for Muscle Disease in New York City. Lewis raised much of this in a twenty-hour New York telethon, which he did annually to benefit the fund drive. Earlier the Martin and Lewis team had raised $15,000,000 for the Associations. In 1957 Lewis was made chairman of the Permanent Charities annual funds drive in Los Angeles, and he has made many personal appearances for Bonds for Israel. He estimates that he has given away more than $5,000,000 over the years.

In April 1962 Jerry Lewis won the International Award from Boystown of Italy. He has served as toastmaster for the Screen Producers Guild, of which he is a member, and for the National Conference of Christians and Jews. In 1957 the Theater Owners of America selected him as Star of the Year. When the awards ceremony of the Academy of Motion Picture Arts and Sciences was televised nationally in April 1959, Jack Gould of the New York *Times* (April 8, 1959) felt that Lewis, as master of ceremonies for the event, had tried to turn the telecast into a Lewis TV comedy show and summed up his performance as a "tour de force of uncompromising ineptitude."

(Continued next page)

LEWIS, JERRY—*Continued*

Over television (which has never given him the satisfaction that movies have) Lewis has appeared on *Startime* over NBC-TV, on the *Ed Sullivan Show*, and on *Person to Person*, both over CBS-TV. He has performed on specials over ABC-TV and NBC-TV and on October 13, 1959 starred in *The Jazz Singer* over NBC-TV. Critical response to his appearance in the latter strengthened his conviction that television critics are "caustic, rude, unkind, and sinister." In July 1962 he surprised NBC-TV network officials, sponsors, and critics by making a hugely successful two-week stand as host of the *Tonight* show, with mail counts and ratings that exceeded those of Jack Paar himself.

On October 3, 1944, when he was only eighteen, Jerry Lewis married Patti Palmer (née Colonica), who used to sing with Jimmy Dorsey's orchestra. They have five boys: Gary; Ronnie, who is adopted; Scott Anthony; Christopher Joseph; and Anthony Joseph. Although Mrs. Lewis is a Roman Catholic, they were married in Jerry Lewis' Jewish faith, with the agreement that while any daughters would be baptized as Catholics, the sons would be exposed to both religions with the right to make up their own minds. Lewis dreams of giving each son a fine *bar mitzvah*, the traditional Jewish ceremony marking a boy's coming of age, perhaps because he remembers his own as having taken place in "a big bleak barn of a place, and at a little table, with a little bottle of wine and a little cake. There was the rabbi, and I, and my father and mother, who got there just in time for the ceremony and had to rush off when it was over."

Jerry Lewis and his family live in Bel Air, outside Los Angeles, in a house with thirty-one rooms and seventeen bathrooms that was formerly owned by the Hollywood tycoon Louis B. Mayer. Lewis is said to have paid $350,000 for the mansion, which he has staffed with a full complement of servants and equipped with thousands of dollars worth of film and recording equipment. His den, which is his office, retreat, and apartment within a home, is furnished with autographed baseballs, figures of clowns, and photographs of relatives, friends, and pet animals.

Six feet in height and weighing about 175 pounds, Lewis has brown eyes and crew-cut black hair. Unlike his stage and screen squeak, his usual voice is low. Something of a fashion plate, he spends a small fortune each year on his wardrobe. So hard does he drive himself that he collapses from time to time from exhaustion, and in the winter of 1958 he suffered from a perforated, bleeding ulcer. To make up for loss of sleep he takes double doses of vitamins. Lewis dislikes liquor and smokes only moderately. A family man, he takes all or part of his brood along with him when he is on the road, and when he appears on the stage he carries snapshots of his family in his pockets as talismans to ward off bad luck. He is hypersensitive to criticism. To people he likes he sometimes presents sentimentally engraved plaques.

Explaining why he is so popular with children, Lewis once told Lloyd Shearer of *Parade* magazine (November 27, 1960): "I get paid for doing what children are punished for. . . . In doing this, I help the audience to get rid of its hostility quotient." One fourteen-year-old fan has put it in another way: "Jerry Lewis is just a nice big kid who makes us laugh. He's also generous. Kids love him, because he's really one of us."

References

International Motion Picture Almanac, 1962
International Television Almanac, 1961
Who's Who in America, 1962-63

LILLY, JOHN C(UNNINGHAM) Jan. 6, 1915- Biophysicist; neurophysiologist
Address: b. Communication Research Institute, 3908 Main Highway, Coconut Grove, Miami 33, Fla.

The dolphins that delight ocean voyagers with their frolics may be as intelligent as the human beings who watch them play—perhaps more intelligent. Dr. John C. Lilly, who is studying these large-brained mammals at his Communication Research Institute in St. Thomas, Virgin Islands, feels that they may possess reasoning powers and a complex language and that human beings may one day learn to communicate with them. Dr. Lilly, who established the institute in 1959, describes his work with dolphins in his book, *Man and Dolphin*, published by Doubleday in 1961. A neurophysiologist, Dr. Lilly has done much investigation of animals' brains by electrical means. From 1953 to 1958 he was chief of the cortical integration section at the Laboratory of Neurophysiology, National Institute of Mental Health, and from 1952 to 1956 he was associate professor of experimental neurology at the University of Pennsylvania.

John Cunningham Lilly was born in St. Paul, Minnesota on January 6, 1915. He was educated at the California Institute of Technology, from which he received his B.S. degree in 1938, at Dartmouth Medical School, and at the University of Pennsylvania, where he took the M.D. degree in 1942. Lilly received the John Clark Research Prize in 1943 for his development of the electrical capacitance manometer (an instrument for measuring the pressure of gases). From 1942 to 1946 he was a Fellow in biophysics at the E. R. Johnson Foundation of Medical Physics at the University of Pennsylvania.

During the same period, 1942 to 1946, Lilly did war research, as a civilian, for the Committee on Medical Research of the Office of Scientific Research and Development and for the United States Air Force. He devised an electrical method for measuring and recording blood pressure and invented the nitrogen meter, an electronic instrument for recording the amount of nitrogen in air that is being inhaled and expired. He also did research on human respiration. During 1944 he was on the reserved list of scientific personnel of the War Manpower Commission. In 1945 he received the Effective Service Award from the Committee on Medical Research.

Lilly was an associate with the E. R. Johnson Foundation from 1946 to 1949, an assistant professor of biophysics from 1949 to 1952, and an associate professor of medical physics from 1952 to 1956. Also from 1952 to 1956 he was an associate professor of experimental neurology with the neurological department and with the graduate school of medicine at the University of Pennsylvania. During the 1940's and early 1950's he investigated methods of recording electrical impulses resulting from brain activity.

In December 1951 Lilly and two of his co-workers, Dr. Ruth Cherry and Dr. A. A. Lurie, reported at a meeting of the American Association for the Advancement of Science that they had developed a television-like apparatus for recording the electrical activity of the brain in terms of visible light and shade. Describing their experiments with cats, they explained that twenty-five electrodes had been placed in an area of an animal's brain, one-tenth square inch in size, where sounds are converted into electrical waves. When a buzzer was sounded into the animal's ear, small electrical impulses, generated in the brain, were picked up by the electrodes, amplified, and flashed through twenty-five light bulbs, which glowed according to the strength of the impulses reaching them. A high-speed movie camera photographed the bulbs, thus recording a pattern of light and shade that corresponded to the electrical patterns formed in the brain as it received sound.

Although he formally held teaching posts at the University of Pennsylvania until 1956, Lilly was actually on leave from the school starting in July 1953, when he became a surgeon, full grade (reserve) with the United States Public Health Service Commissioned Officers Corps. During his five years in the corps, from 1953 to 1958, he served as chief of the section on cortical integration in the research branch of the Laboratory of Neurophysiology, National Institute of Mental Health. He was promoted to senior surgeon (reserve) in 1955.

While in the Public Health Service Lilly did further research involving electrical stimulation of animals' brains. For it he devised a new technique: the use of a noninjurious diphasic current rather than a direct current damaging to brain cells. Reporting to the Senate appropriations subcommittee on health in April 1956, Dr. Robert Felix, director of the National Institute of Mental Health, called Lilly's new technique "the most exciting single discovery in the field of brain physiology." He said that the use of the technique and the research that had been and could be done with it opened tremendous vistas for treating the mentally ill.

In one experiment Lilly placed some 600 electrodes in various areas of a monkey's brain and found that by stimulating different cortical sections with electrical current he could provoke movements of limbs, eyes, trunk, and other parts of the animal's body. He also investigated motivational circuits in the brains of rats, cats, and monkeys and pinpointed an area that, when stimulated with an electrical current, produces a sense of well-being and another area that produces pain, anxiety, or terror.

These sensations occur naturally in human beings and animals, but apparently electrical stimulation provoked them in a much stronger

Fabian Bachrach

DR. JOHN C. LILLY

intensity than that in which they would normally occur. Lilly found that animals would often ignore primary urges like hunger, thirst, and sex to continue to receive the pleasant sensation under experimental conditions. Animals exposed to the pain sensation would become hostile and unhappy. But an irritated or ferocious animal could be made docile and happy by activating the electrodes that brought him the sense of well-being.

In his book, *Man and Dolphin* (Doubleday, 1961), Lilly reports that, in addition to being able to induce feelings of pleasure or pain, scientists can now make an animal feel hungry, thirsty, or satiated, hot or cold, regardless of actual physical conditions, merely by activating electrodes implanted in appropriate areas of the brain. He has been able to teach animals to give themselves a sensation of general well-being or to avoid a painful one by moving a mechanism that activates or shuts off the appropriate electrodes in their own brains.

The development of the "reward-stimulation" technique was important for experiments in animal learning. "These motivationally active systems in the brain, positive and negative, are extremely powerful and push an animal to learn as much as he is capable of learning within a very short period of time," Lilly observed in *Man and Dolphin*. "The method is much more powerful than any other kind of direct reward or punishment . . . and it has the convenience of immediate and definite control of intensity and timing on the part of the operator." Lilly found the method useful in his later experiments with dolphins.

In another series of experiments at the National Institute of Mental Health, designed to determine the effects of a lack of stimuli on the brain, Lilly floated face down in a tank of tepid, slowly flowing water. He wore nothing save a breathing mask, could see nothing, and could

LILLY, JOHN C.—*Continued*

hear nothing except faint water noises. Although he welcomed the quiet, homogeneous environment as restful at first, he gradually began to yearn strongly for some external stimulus, and sought even the slightest sensation like that produced by rubbing one finger against another. Eventually he experienced hallucinations. The research has implications for the treatment of the mentally ill and for military training of men who will have to endure long periods of isolation. In 1958 Lilly was chairman of a session in a sensory deprivation symposium at Harvard Medical School.

The beginning of Lilly's interest in dolphins can be traced back to 1949. Having read in the newspapers of a beached whale (of which the dolphin is a small variety), he and two friends, a neurosurgeon and an expert on whales, set out for Maine to obtain the whale's brain for examination. They failed to carry it away intact. But during the course of their conversation about whales, the size of their brains (up to six times as large as the human brain), and their seagoing life as compared with that of land mammals, Lilly became intrigued with the idea of investigating "brains really worthy of research, nothing so small as . . . cats and monkeys."

The brain of the *Tursiops truncatus,* or bottle-nosed dolphin, roughly compares with the human brain in weight (1,700 grams to 1,450 grams) and relative weight per unit of body length (200 grams to 240 grams). Sometimes erroneously called a "porpoise," this creature is a generally docile marine mammal that adapts well to captivity and learns quickly. It is the mainstay of trick acts at several oceanaria in the United States, including the Marine Studios in St. Augustine, Florida.

In the fall of 1955 Lilly and seven other scientists made a two-week visit to the Marine Studios to do pioneering neurophysiological studies of the brains of dolphins. They had intended to map areas in the brains of live dolphins that had already been mapped in smaller animals. However, the five animals provided by the Marine Studios died under general anesthesia due to the failure of their non-automatic breathing systems.

Working with monkeys, Lilly devised a method of inserting electrodes into the brain without the use of anesthesia. In October 1957 he returned to the Marine Studios to apply the method to dolphins. He soon found the reward and punishment systems in the animal's brain and discovered that, whereas a monkey needed several hundred trials to learn to stimulate his own reward system by pressing a lever, the dolphin learned after one trial. Reward, rather than punishment, proved the best inducement to the dolphin's learning.

During both that visit and one that he made in January 1958 Lilly observed a variety of dolphin vocalizations, including clicking, whistling, quacking, and "squeaking-door" noises. He noted that they seemed to be capable of mimicking human words or laughter. Dolphins vocalize both in air and water and, while they can make noises that can be heard by human beings, they have an additional, higher range that human

beings cannot hear. By stimulating the reward system in their brains at the appropriate times, Lilly was able to make the dolphins vocalize in air and in the human sound range. In January 1958 one of the dolphins with which he was working became too cold; its muscles froze and prevented it from surfacing to breathe. It uttered a distress call, and two other animals came to its rescue until it could once again swim. "This episode . . . and others gave rise to our suspicions that these animals have a very complex language and know how to use it for descriptive and predictive purposes," Lilly has said.

Lilly eventually became highly impressed with the intelligence of dolphins. He began to wonder whether they might not be capable of "long sustained chains of reasoning based on accumulation of masses of data" and whether the species might not have a language. In his book, *Man and Dolphin* (1961), he warns against making the biased assumption that man tops the evolutionary scale and that no further evolution is possible. He feels that the whale family may possess resources as complex as, though different from, man and that the capacities of these animals should not be underestimated. He feels it may be possible to establish communication with them, either by learning their language or by teaching them ours.

In 1958-59 Lilly realized his financial assets and bought and cleared some land on St. Thomas, Virgin Islands. He built a pool and a laboratory and set up his Communication Research Institute so that he could work with dolphins all year round. He later received grants from the Office of Naval Research and from the National Science Foundation. Lilly has continued to experiment with getting dolphins to vocalize and to mimic human words. Although he feels he has succeeded in this to some extent, he points out that the next, crucial step must be for the dolphins to recognize the meaning of the words that they mimic. Eventually, Lilly believes, it may be possible for human beings to speak with other species. In a chapter, "Implications," in his book, he discusses communication between interplanetary peoples and the ways in which dolphins could help to solve various marine problems of man if communication should prove feasible. In the fall of 1962 Lilly received an $80,700 one-year grant from the National Aeronautics and Space Administration for research on the possibility of establishing communication between man and other species.

Lilly, who is a Fellow of the American Association for the Advancement of Science and of the New York Academy of Sciences, belongs to many professional organizations. He has lectured at the California Institute of Technology, Harvard University, the University of North Carolina, Western Reserve University, Johns Hopkins University, the University of Cincinnati, the College of Physicians and Surgeons, the University of Southern California, the Mayo Foundation, the Cincinnati Society of Neurology and Psychiatry, the Brookings Institute, the New York Academy of Medicine, the American Academy of Neurology, and the American Philosophical Society. In 1960 he was a research professor in the department of medicine of the University of Miami Medical School.

He was on the steering committee on neurophysiology of the American Physiological Society from 1953 to 1956, on the fellowship board of the National Institute of Mental Health from 1954 to 1957, and on the scientific advisory committee for graduate schools of the National Institutes of Health in 1954. During 1957 he was an associate editor of *Psychosomatic Medicine*.

Among Lilly's helpers at the Communication Research Institute are his wife, Elisabeth Christine (Bjerg) Lilly, whom he married in 1959, and the six children in their household: Lilly and his wife have one child; two are Lilly's by a previous marriage, in 1936, and three are Mrs. Lilly's by a previous marriage. Although working with dolphins is now Lilly's principal avocation, he is an ex-radio amateur, an excellent skier, and, in his words, a fair yachtsman.

References

American Men of Science 10th ed (1960-62)

Lilly, John C. Man and Dolphin (1961)

Wide World

JOHN V. LINDSAY

LINDSAY, JOHN V(LIET) Nov. 24, 1921-
United States Representative; lawyer
Address: b. House Office Bldg., Washington 25, D.C.; h. 155 E. 72d St., New York 21

When John V. Lindsay, United States Representative of the Seventeenth Congressional District of New York was waging his first campaign for election to Congress in 1958, he was asked by interviewer Mike Wallace: "What's in it for you?" Lindsay replied that he had been brought up in an atmosphere in which the guiding principle was that "the greatest service you can give is public service," and that in his view the purpose of life is "to make some contribution to the community." "Some people's community," he continued, "is themselves; others, their family; others, General Electric; others, their law firm; others go beyond that into the state. That's for me."

Lindsay began his career in the private practice of law and served as executive assistant to the Attorney General of the United States in 1955-56. He was first elected to Congress in 1958 and re-elected by an increased majority in 1960. He is a member of the House Judiciary committee. Regarded as one of the strongest voices of liberalism in the House of Representatives and in the Republican party, Lindsay is known as a champion of constitutional rights and individual liberties.

John Vliet Lindsay was born on Riverside Drive in New York City on November 24, 1921 to George Nelson and Florence Eleanor (Vliet) Lindsay. He has a twin brother, David A. (named in 1959 a general counsel for the United States Treasury) and two other brothers, George Nelson, Jr., and Robert V.; and one sister, Mrs. Cooper Schieffelin. His father, the son of an English brick manufacturer who came to the United States from the Isle of Wight about 1881, is an investment banker and chairman of the board of the American Swiss Corporation (a subsidiary of Crédit Suisse). Lindsay received his early education at the Buckley School for Boys in New York City. For his secondary schooling

he attended St. Paul's School at Concord, New Hampshire, where he was active in rowing and other sports, and graduated in 1940. He then attended Yale University, where he majored in history and was stroke on the freshman rowing crew. He graduated with the B.A. degree in April 1943.

Entering the United States Naval Reserve as an ensign in May 1943, Lindsay served as a gunnery officer aboard the destroyer USS *Swanson* and participated in the Sicily landings. He also took part in the Seventh Fleet landings at Biak, Hollandia, and the Admiralty Islands, and served with Carrier Task Group 38.4 during the invasion of the Philippines. He earned five battle stars and held the rank of lieutenant, senior grade, when he was discharged in March 1946.

While studying at Yale University School of Law after the war Lindsay met Herbert Brownell, Jr., a noted New York lawyer active in Republican politics. Brownell was a close friend of one of the partners in the Wall Street law firm of Webster, Sheffield & Chrystie, with which Lindsay became associated after receiving the LL.B. degree from Yale in June 1948. Admitted to the New York State bar in 1949 and to the Federal bar for the Southern District of New York in 1950, Lindsay has since 1953 been a partner in what is now the firm of Webster, Sheffield, Fleischmann, Hitchcock & Chrystie.

Active in Republican politics, Lindsay became a member of the board of governors of the New York Young Republican Club in 1949. In 1951 he was one of the eleven founders of the Youth for Eisenhower movement, and in 1952 he began a one-year term as president of the New York Young Republican Club. At the Republican National Convention in the summer of 1952 Lindsay worked with Herbert Brownell as what he later described as "a legal man on the Louisiana delegate steal." His abilities impressed Brownell,

LINDSAY, JOHN V.—*Continued*

who became Attorney General in the cabinet of President Dwight D. Eisenhower in 1953.

In January 1955 Brownell invited Lindsay to Washington to serve as his executive assistant. In the same year Lindsay was admitted to the United States Supreme Court bar, and in 1956 he was admitted to the bar of the District of Columbia. As Brownell's assistant Lindsay served as the Justice Department's liaison with the White House, the cabinet, the National Security Council, and Congress. He also helped to draft legislation, including the Civil Rights Bill of 1957 and a liberalized immigration bill, and he made two trips to Europe in order to facilitate the admission of refugees to the United States. He remained in this position until he resigned in December 1956.

The Seventeenth Congressional District of New York, of which Lindsay had been a legal resident since 1948, encompasses the center of the borough of Manhattan, extending from Harlem to Greenwich Village and from the East River to the lower West Side. Because it takes in the wealthy residential areas of Fifth and Park Avenues it is known as the "silk stocking district," but it also includes the theatrical and garment districts and midtown loft and tenement areas. The only Republican-held district in Manhattan, it was represented by Frederic René Coudert, Jr., an old guard Republican from 1946 to .1958. In 1954 the Democratic candidate, Anthony B. Akers, came within 315 votes of unseating him. In 1956, after Coudert again almost lost to Akers, Lindsay contemplated taking action to bring about a reorganization of the Republican party in New York, but he was unable to do so because he was working in Washington at the time.

On April 16, 1958 Lindsay formally announced his candidacy for Coudert's seat, expressing concern about the loss of Republican strength in a traditionally Republican stronghold. "We have not seen the type of aggressive leadership needed in Congress to carry forward the Eisenhower program," he told reporters. About a month later Coudert announced that he would not run again, and the regular Republican organization threw its support to Elliot H. Goodwin. Following what was described in the New York *Times* (July 28, 1958) as "an all-out, free-swinging, old-fashioned primary battle," Lindsay defeated Goodwin by a vote of 6,129 to 4,052 in the primary on August 12, 1958. After defeating the Democratic-Liberal candidate, Anthony B. Akers, in the election of November 4, 1958 by a vote of 53,674 to 45,956, Lindsay said: "Undoubtedly it helped me a great deal to have gone through my primary fight. It proved that I am a free man, a completely free man—just as Nelson Rockefeller is a free man."

Seated in the Eighty-sixth Congress and assigned to the Judiciary Committee, Lindsay soon made his presence felt. On January 8, 1959 he announced his intention to submit to the House legislation aimed at curbing the activities of bigots against churches and integrated schools. A few weeks later he defended the United States Supreme Court against an attack by Representative Noah M. Mason of Illinois, thereby break-

ing an unwritten rule that freshmen do not publicly challenge the statements of senior colleagues. In February 1959 he told a veterans' organization that he would vigorously oppose legislation that would permit the State Department to withhold passports solely on the basis of confidential information. In September 1959 Lindsay cast the sole dissenting vote against a bill giving the Postmaster General new powers to impound allegedly obscene mail.

Early in the second session of the Eighty-sixth Congress Lindsay moved to raise the interest rate ceiling on long-term United States bonds. In April 1960 he sponsored in the House a bill for voluntary health insurance for the aged proposed by Senator Javits in the Senate as an alternative to the Forand Bill, which would make medical care part of the Social Security system. In the same month he introduced a bill to establish a federal Department of Urban Affairs within the cabinet. An advocate of an active role for the United States in international affairs, Lindsay came out in favor of repeal of the Connally Reservation to United States participation in the International Court of Justice, in a letter to the New York *Times* (July 6, 1960). His concern with the plight of refugees prompted him to refer to the refugee relief bill, passed in the House in April 1960, as "short term sedation when what is needed is major legislative surgery." In August 1960 he proposed that the former immigration center at Ellis Island be converted into an international educational exchange center to be called the "University of Freedom." In November he urged admission to the United States of Arab refugees from Palestine.

In voting on key measures in the Eighty-sixth Congress Lindsay supported, in 1959, the housing act, the mutual security act, and the Labor-Management Reporting and Disclosure act. He voted against the rural electrification loan bill and the Tennessee Valley Authority self-financing bill, and he voted to sustain the President's veto on the public works appropriation bill. In 1960 he voted for the Civil Rights Act, the School Construction Assistance Act, foreign aid appropriations, and salary increases for postal workers. He opposed the Farm Surplus Reduction Act of 1960.

Victorious over his Democratic opponent, William vanden Heuvel, by a vote of 80,048 to 53,900 in the election of November 8, 1960, Lindsay continued to serve on the Judiciary Committee in the Eighty-seventh Congress. In February 1961 he was censured by the Young Republican Club of New York for supporting the Kennedy administration's measure to enlarge the membership of the Rules Committee. In May he again supported the administration by urging passage of its bill to create seventy-three new federal judgeships. He declined consideration as Republican candidate for Mayor of New York City in the municipal election campaign of 1961, but he was named Republican campaign chairman for that election in June 1961.

Legislation embodying New York Governor Nelson A. Rockefeller's proposals for a federal program for medical care for the aged was introduced by Lindsay in April 1962 as an alternative to the administration's controversial medical care plan. In the following month, acting alone, Lindsay blocked adoption, by unanimous consent, of an anti-subversive bill, recommended by the House Committee on Un-American Activities. He felt that this legislation would deprive employees of defense industries, accused of disloyalty, of the right to confront their accusers. He repeated his stand on this issue in August 1962.

Lindsay's votes on key issues in 1961 included support of the administration's Housing Act, the Foreign Assistance Act, the public works appropriation bill, and the Peace Corps Act. In 1962 he voted for the establishment of a Department of Urban Affairs, for the setting up of a private corporation to operate a communications satellites system, and for raising the ceiling of the national debt. In June 1962 Lindsay supported the Trade Expansion Act, authorizing the President to negotiate new tariff agreements, and in July he voted for the Foreign Aid Authorization Act, including a four-year aid program for Latin America. Although he voted for the constitutional amendment eliminating the poll tax, he criticized the amendment because it failed to cover state and local elections. "If we're going to have a constitutional amendment, let's have a meaningful one," he said.

A supporter of the arts, Lindsay has introduced a number of bills designed to alleviate some of the problems facing American show business, including one that would repeal the federal tax on theater tickets. He is the co-sponsor, with Frank Thompson, Jr., Democrat of New Jersey, of the administration-supported Thompson-Lindsay bill for the creation of a Federal Advisory Council on the Arts. In May 1962 he sponsored a bill to create a President's Advisory Council on Education. To encourage interest in art, Lindsay displays paintings of contemporary American artists in his New York office.

In New York City Lindsay has occasionally come into conflict with the city-planning projects of Robert H. Moses. In the spring of 1959 he introduced a bill requiring full advance disclosure of urban redevelopment plans before they could be accepted by any federal agency. In August 1962 he urged the city administration to give up plans for an expressway that would displace about 2,000 families and 800 businesses in lower Manhattan. In the same month he countered Moses' controversial plan to build a highway on Fire Island with a bill to establish a national seashore on the island.

Although Lindsay has maintained an amicable relationship with the Kennedy administration, he criticized Attorney General Robert F. Kennedy's good-will tour around the world in early 1962. In a letter to Secretary of State Dean Rusk in February 1962 he questioned the wisdom of "free-wheeling foreign missions on the part of highly-placed amateurs." In view of continued nuclear weapons testing on the part of both the Soviet Union and the United States, Lindsay, in a speech on the House floor in June 1962, called on President Kennedy to keep the American people fully informed of the facts on contamination of milk by radioactive fallout.

Congressman Lindsay is a member of the American Bar Association, the New York State Bar Association, and the Bar Association of the City of New York (in which he has served on the executive committee). He is a member of the Council on Foreign Relations and the Citizens Committee for Children of New York City and serves on the board of directors of Freedom House. He attends the Episcopal Church. Lindsay has contributed articles and book reviews on topics of current interest to newspapers and magazines, and he often writes letters to the editors of newspapers.

On June 18, 1949 John V. Lindsay married Mary Anne Harrison, a graduate of Vassar College and a former schoolteacher. Mrs. Lindsay is active in the foster home department of the Children's Aid Society and in the women's division of the Legal Aid Society. The Lindsays have three daughters, Katharine H., Margaret N., and Anne H., and one son, John V. Lindsay, Jr. Lindsay is six feet three inches tall, weighs about 180 pounds, and has light brown hair and blue eyes. Described by Don Ross of the New York *Herald Tribune* (August 14, 1958) as "a non-television watcher of some years' standing," he is fond of reading history. During the winter months his favorite recreation is ice skating; in the summer he sails with his wife from his father's home in Oyster Bay, Long Island.

References

Look 23:58+ D 8 '59 pors
N Y Herald Tribune p1 Ag 4 '58 por; p9 Ag 14 '58 por
N Y Times p34 N 1 '60 por
N Y Times Mag p46+ O 23 '60 pors
New Yorker 36:25+ Je 15 '60

Congressional Directory (1962)
Martindale-Hubbell Law Directory (1962)
Who's Who in America, 1962-63

LIPPMANN, WALTER Sept. 23, 1889- Journalist; writer

Address: b. c/o New York Herald Tribune, 230 W. 41st St., New York 36; h. 3525 Woodley Rd., Washington 16, D.C.

NOTE: This biography supersedes the article that appeared in *Current Biography* in 1940.

Forty or more years of scholarly and interpretive journalism, on the *New Republic*, the New York *World*, and the New York *Herald Tribune*, successively, have given Walter Lippmann unquestioned claim to the title of dean of American newspapermen. Besides his thousands of columns, he has written some twenty-five books, mostly on political philosophy. His latest volume is *Western Unity and the Common Market* (1962). Since 1960 he has made four television appearances that have confirmed his reputation as a sage and well-informed critic who does not shape his opinion to agree with the popular view. In the orderly and lucid prose of "Today and Tomorrow," the column that he has been writing for the New York *Herald Tribune* since 1931, he analyzes world crises with a depth

Wide World

WALTER LIPPMANN

and breadth of knowledge that is possibly un-matched in journalism.

Lippmann has survived unsparing criticism of his shifting position on economic, political, and foreign policy issues over the years. Now his work has come to be regarded as defying stock labels; he camps neither with the liberals nor the conservatives, although from time to time he may take up the cause of one group or another. Some of his admirers find his con-sistency, and perhaps his chief virtue, in his humanism. Among the regular readers of his column in the 250 newspapers in which it ap-pears throughout the world are business leaders, statesmen (including President Kennedy and Premier Khrushchev), and other newspapermen.

The only child of Jacob and Daisy (Baum) Lippmann, Walter Lippmann was born on Sep-tember 23, 1889 in New York City. Both his parents were of German-Jewish stock; one of his grandfathers, Louis Lippmann, had moved to New York City from Germany in 1848. As a prosperous clothing manufacturer and real estate broker, his father had the means to give Walter every opportunity to develop the extra-ordinary intellectual capacity that he showed even as a boy. During vacations abroad with his parents he made an early acquaintance with European art, literature, music, and several languages.

In 1896 Walter Lippmann enrolled in Dr. Julius Sachs' School for Boys, a private school on New York's West Side. Here during the next ten years he wrote pieces for student pub-lications, distinguished himself in debating, and won a number of prizes for academic excellence. At Harvard University, which he entered in 1906, he also achieved a brilliant scholastic record and was elected to Phi Beta Kappa. He completed the requirements for his B.A. degree, *cum laude*, in three years, but graduated with his class in 1910.

Philosophy, political science, economics, and languages had been Lippmann's favorite sub-jects at Harvard. He has said that Wiliam James, whom he met at the university, was the hero of his life. In his fourth year Lippmann assisted George Santayana in a course in the history of philosophy. He also had many aes-thetic interests, but he devoted most of his free time in college to the study and discus-sion of social and economic problems. He joined the Harvard Socialist Club and served for a time as its president. Many of the articles that he wrote for *Harvard Illustrated, Harvard Advocate*, and other university periodicals re-flected the concern with social reform of the Fabian Socialists.

Briefly, while still at Harvard in 1910, Lipp-mann worked as a reporter for the Boston *Common*, a weekly devoted to social reform. Then for about a year Lincoln Steffens engaged him to help in the preparation of articles for *Everybody's Magazine* on corruption in big busi-ness, politics, and government. Believing that he would have the chance to help put into practice some of his humanitarian ideals, in January 1912 he became executive secretary to the Reverend George R. Lunn, Socialist mayor of Schenectady, New York.

After four months in Schenectady, however, Lippmann resigned, apparently having felt that the people who voted for the Socialist ticket were not prepared to accept a Socialist program. Marquis Childs pointed out in an essay in *Walter Lippmann and His Times* (Harcourt, 1959), "His was the position of the intellectual, the critic, for whom the tiresome and often dubious necessities of political life were dis-tasteful."

In the summer of 1912 Lippmann went to Maine to set down some ideas that he had been thinking about for years on the faults of the modern industrial system and the need for re-form. His first book, *A Preface to Politics* (Mac-millan, 1913), which was well received by lib-erals, gave Socialism a qualified acceptance; but a year later his *Drift and Mastery* (Holt, 1914) found increasing fault with the whole Socialist movement, especially with Marxism. In *The Good Society* (Little, 1937) he not only rejected Socialism outright, but also repudiated "free col-lectivism," which he had earlier tolerated, in favor of "liberalism." David Elliott Weingast explained Lippmann's point of view in *Walter Lippmann, A Study in Personal Journalism* (Rutgers, 1949): "True liberalism must be recog-nized as the opponent of all practices, whether of industry or labor, that restricted the free work-ing of our market economy. . . . Liberalism, he emphasized, was neither the defender of the status quo nor the friend of privilege."

A Preface to Politics, meanwhile, had recom-mended Lippmann to Herbert Croly, who in-vited Lippmann to join him in 1914 in founding the *New Republic*, a journal of liberal opinion. The progressive views of the *New Republic* often agreed with the policies of President Woodrow Wilson's government, but Lippmann has denied that the magazine was ever the organ of the Wilson administration. He was, however, in touch with top people in Washington through

Colonel Edward M. House. In 1917, after the United States had entered World War I, Lippmann served as an assistant to Secretary of War Newton D. Baker, but in the summer he was transferred, as secretary, to a research organization under House's direction that was charged with collecting ethnic, political, and geographical information for use at a peace conference at the end of the war. About a year later he was commissioned a captain in the Army Military Intelligence and was assigned to a propaganda operation on the Meuse-Argonne front. Toward the end of the war he went to Paris as a member of the American Commission to Negotiate Peace, but, disillusioned with Allied policy on several issues, he resigned.

Upon his return to New York in March 1919 Lippmann resumed his work on the *New Republic*, but soon left that magazine to write *Public Opinion* (Macmillan, 1922), in which, as in *Liberty and the News* (Harcourt, 1920), he discussed the difficulty of adequately informing the citizenry on the complex problems of contemporary society. In 1921 he accepted Herbert Bayard Swope's invitation to join the editorial staff of the New York *World*, a crusading paper noted for its attacks on corruption, poverty, and injustice. From 1923 to 1929 Lippmann was in charge of the editorial page, and from 1929 until the *World* ceased publication in February 1931, he held the title of editor.

Since much of Lippmann's work on the *World* had criticized the administrations of Presidents Harding, Coolidge, and Hoover, many of his admirers were dismayed when he took a job as columnist for the New York *Herald Tribune*, a stronghold of Republican thinking. With the appearance of his first column, on September 8, 1931, the *Herald Tribune* assured its readers that Lippmann's work would be independent, that he would "write freely upon such topics as he selects, expressing whatever opinions he holds."

"Today and Tomorrow" at first was published four times a week and later three times a week. At present Lippmann writes a twice-weekly column, which is syndicated in over 250 newspapers in the United States and some twenty-five foreign countries. Scholarship, calm appraisal, serious conviction—all the qualities that marked his work for the *World*—also distinguish his efforts on the *Herald Tribune* to serve as an interpreter of world affairs. He steers clear of sensational scoops, predictions, invective, and gossip. Although he often draws his information from people directly involved in news events, he remains a detached observer.

The early concern of Lippmann's column was the Depression. He generally disapproved of New Deal economic and financial policies and many other aspects of the Roosevelt program, although he found much to admire in Roosevelt whom he eventually came to regard as one of the greatest Presidents of the century. He backed Landon against Roosevelt in 1936 and Dewey against Truman in 1948. Again in 1952 he preferred the Republican candidate, Eisenhower, but in 1956 he supported Stevenson and in 1960, Kennedy. He has criticized both parties, and his arguments for or against a candidate are conceded to have been to a considerable degree nonpartisan and nonpersonal.

During World War II, in his column and in his books *U.S. Foreign Policy: Shield of the Republic* (Little, 1943) and *U.S. War Aims* (Little, 1944), Lippmann strongly opposed adoption of a policy of isolationism after the war. According to Joseph C. Harsch (New York *Herald Tribune*, March 19, 1961), "He was as much as any one other single person the original architect of the Atlantic Alliance." For some years he has insisted that controversies of the cold war should be settled by diplomacy, and his remark on a 1961 television program, "I don't think old men ought to promote wars for young men to fight," provoked Max Ascoli to refer to him as a "negotiation-monger" (*Reporter*, November 9, 1961).

On two occasions, in November 1958 and April 1961, Lippmann discussed with Nikita S. Khrushchev in Russia some of the crucial aspects of the East-West conflict. He published his account of the meetings in his columns and in *The Communist World and Ours* (Little, 1959) and *The Coming Tests with Russia* (Little, 1961). He also gave his impressions of the Soviet Premier, along with his own views on a wide range of other subjects, during his much-acclaimed television interviews for *CBS Reports*, the first of which was broadcast in July 1960.

"Today and Tomorrow" has earned Lippmann two Pulitzer Prizes. The first award, in 1958, was a special citation for "the wisdom, perception and high sense of responsibility with which he has commented for many years on national and international affairs." In 1962 he received a Pulitzer award for "wise and responsible international reporting." Another prize that he won in 1962 was a George Foster Peabody Award, which cited him along with *CBS Reports* for having done "the most to promote international understanding during 1961." He holds a large number of honorary degrees and several foreign decorations, including Commander of the Legion of Honor, Officer of the Order of Leopold (Belgium), and Commander of the Order of Orange-Nassau (the Netherlands).

Every winter, as part of his work, Lippmann makes a trip to Europe, South America, or some other part of the world, and it is said that foreign governments prepare for his visit as carefully as they would for the arrival of a high-ranking statesman. Also in some measure as part of his work, he leads a busy social life in Washington and, during the summer, in Southwest Harbor, Maine. His clubs include the Century, Harvard, and Coffee House in New York City; the Metropolitan, Cosmos, Army-Navy Country, and National Press in Washington; and the Faculty in Cambridge, Massachusetts. He also belongs to the National Institute of Arts and Letters and the American Academy of Arts and Letters.

Walter Lippmann married Faye Albertson on May 24, 1917; he was later divorced and on March 26, 1938 he married Helen Byrne Armstrong. Much younger in appearance than his seventy-three years, he has only recently begun to show a touch of gray in his black hair. He is five feet ten inches tall, weighs 180 pounds, and has brown eyes. Although never a sports enthusiast, he learned to play a good game of

LIPPMANN, WALTER—Continued
golf and tennis; he also enjoys carpentry among
other hobbies. His courteous and friendly, perhaps even courtly, manner is said to grow cold
in the face of bigotry or idle conversation. In a
tribute to Lippmann in Walter Lippmann and
His Times fellow journalist James Reston wrote:
"No doubt Walter Lippmann . . . would prefer
to be judged on his books on political philosophy. . . . But while philosophy may be his love,
journalism has been his mistress, and the amazing thing is that he has managed to be so faithful to both. . . . I know that he has given my
generation of newspapermen a wider vision of
our duty. He has shown us how to put the
event of the day in its proper relationship to
the history of yesterday and the dream of
tomorrow."

    References
    Look 25:100+ Ap 25 '61 por
    N Y Herald Tribune II p3 Mr 19 '61
    Newsweek 58:65+ D 18 '61 por
    Childs, Marquis ed. Walter Lippmann
        and His Times (1959)
    International Who's Who, 1961-62
    Twentieth Century Authors (1942; First
        Supplement, 1955)
    Weingast, David Elliott. Walter Lipp-
        mann (1949)
    Who's Who, 1962
    Who's Who in America, 1962-63

MACAPAGAL, DIOSDADO (mŏk-à-pà-gäl'
dē-ōs-dä'dō) Sept. 28, 1910- President of the
Republic of the Philippines
Address: Malacañang, Manila, Republic of the
Philippines

The fifth President of the Republic of the
Philippines, Diosdado Macapagal, is proving to
be one of the most resolute statesmen in the history of the young nation, which received its
independence from the United States in 1946.
After winning a resounding victory over the incumbent President Carlos P. Garcia in the elections of November 1961, the humbly born Macapagal put into action his pledge to bring decency
and prosperity to the Philippines. Carrying on
in the tradition of the late President Ramón
Magsaysay, Macapagal, who likes to refer to
himself as the "conscience of the common man,"
has taken steps to alleviate the nation's major
problems of corruption, unemployment, and poverty. On the international scene Macapagal is
an outspoken anti-Communist, and he seeks to
maintain firm ties to the United States.

A native of the town of Lubao in the province
of Pampanga, north of Manila, Diosdado Macapagal was born in a palm-frond hut on September 28, 1910. His father, Urbano Macapagal,
was a jobless poet and playwright who wrote
prose in Tagalog, the native dialect. His mother,
the former Romana Pañgan, whose parents were
poor tenant farmers, was a devout Roman Catholic, who taught the catechism to school children.
The second of four children, "Dadong" Macapagal grew up in abject poverty. During the day he
attended the village school, worked in the fields,

and tended water buffaloes; at night he went
out into the rice fields to catch frogs for food.
Named class valedictorian when he graduated
from elementary school at the head of his class
in 1925, he had to borrow a suit from a class-
mate to attend commencement exercises.

After graduating from the Pampanga high
school with the second-highest average in his
class in 1929, Macapagal entered the University
of the Philippines in Manila, working part-time
as a computer with the Bureau of Lands. He
received an associate in arts degree in 1932. For
a time he interrupted his schooling because of
lack of funds and ill health and returned to his
home province. There he and his friend Rogelio
de la Rosa (who later became a leading Filipino
film star) wrote, produced, and acted in Tagalog
operettas patterned upon the classic Spanish
zarzuelas. Macapagal continued his studies at
the University of Santo Tomas in Manila, aided
financially by the philanthropist Honorio Ven-
tura. He acquired a brilliant scholastic record,
captained a debating team, and won gold
medals for debating and oratory. He earned his
bachelor of laws degree in 1936 after passing
his bar examination at the top of the list.
Macapagal later returned to the University of
Santo Tomas, where he received a master's degree in law in 1941, a doctor of laws degree in
1947, and a doctor of philosophy degree in economics in 1957.

After his graduation from the University of
Santo Tomas Macapagal entered private law
practice. In 1941 he served briefly as a legal
assistant to Philippine President Manuel Quezon,
and later in the year he returned to the University of Santo Tomas as a professor of law.
When the Japanese invaded the Philippines he
left the university and joined the anti-Japanese
underground as an intelligence agent. After the
war Macapagal returned to his law professorship
and became senior partner in the law firm
Macapagal & Eusebio. Concurrently he worked
with the Philippine Department of Foreign Affairs; he was appointed assistant in the legal
division in 1946 and chief of the legal division
in 1947. In 1948 he served as second secretary
to the Philippine Embassy in Washington, D.C.,
and in 1949 he returned to Manila, where he
served as counselor on legal affairs and treaties
with the Department of Foreign Affairs. From
1947 to 1949 he was president of the Philippine
Lawyers Association.

Running on the Liberal party ticket as a
candidate for the first district of Pampanga
province in 1949, Macapagal was elected to the
Philippine House of Representatives. He received
20,000 more votes than his nearest opponent. In
the elections of 1953, in which the Nationalist
party won an overwhelming victory, he was the
only Liberal party member to win re-election to
the House. During his years in Congress he
served on the House committees on appropriations, commerce and industry, ways and means,
economic planning, and banks, currency, and
corporations. He was chairman of the House
committee on foreign affairs from 1950 to 1953.
He also was a member of the executive-legislative committee for the revision of the Philippine-
American trade agreement and of the committee

on Japanese reparations. A popular legislator, he was voted by the Manila press as one of the ten best congressmen from 1949 to 1953, and the best legislator in the Third Philippine Congress (1954-57).

As a Congressman, Macapagal gained a reputation on the international as well as on the domestic scene. In 1952 he was the author and sponsor of the Foreign Service Act. In 1950 he was a delegate to the Southeast Asia Conference and to the United Nations General Assembly. In 1951, while serving as chairman of the Philippine U.N. delegation, he distinguished himself in a debate with Soviet Foreign Minister Andrei Vishinsky. In the same year he was a negotiator and signer of the United States-Philippine mutual defense treaty in Washington, and of the Japanese peace treaty at San Francisco. While serving in Congress Macapagal continued to engage in the private practice of law and to teach at the university.

In the elections of November 1957 Macapagal ran for the Vice-Presidency of the republic, and he received 116,940 more votes than the total with which Carlos P. Garcia won the Presidency on the Nationalist party ticket. On December 20, 1957 he was chosen by Liberal Senators and Congressmen as the titular head of the Liberal party. Refusing President Garcia's request that he join the Nationalist party, Vice-President Macapagal remained largely an outsider in the government. He was given only ceremonial duties, was barred from cabinet meetings, and was placed at the end of all official reception lines.

In an effort to strengthen the Liberal party Macapagal toured the country, going from village to village, talking to peasants and denouncing the Garcia administration, mainly on the issues of graft and corruption. In November 1960 he visited the United States. In January 1961 he persuaded members of the Progressive party to join the Liberal party in a united opposition to the Nationalist administration of Garcia. He was nominated as the Liberal candidate for President on January 21, 1961.

Embarking on what has been described as the most extensive political campaign in the history of the Philippines, Macapagal traveled throughout the islands, reaching virtually every accessible town. "I come from the poor," he told the peasants. "Let me reap for you the harvest of the poor. Let us break the chain of poverty. Let me lead you to prosperity!" On November 14, 1961 more than 6,500,000 Filipinos went to the polls. When the final vote was tabulated Macapagal was elected President by a majority of 651,874 votes. In his inaugural speech on December 30, 1961, the new chief executive promised: "I shall be president not only of the rich but more so of the poor. We must help bridge the wide gap between the poor man and the man of wealth, not by pulling down the rich to his level as communism desires, but by raising the poor towards the more abundant life."

On the day after his inauguration Macapagal opened Malacañang, the presidential palace, to all Filipinos. He also canceled the traditional inaugural ball and called instead an outdoor dance to which the common people were invited.

DIOSDADO MACAPAGAL

Soon after he took office Macapagal issued a decree forbidding any member of his family or that of his wife to participate in any business deals with the government. He dismissed hundreds of corrupt officials and started court action against those who could not explain their sudden acquisition of wealth.

On January 21, 1962 Macapagal took a major step in the direction of restoring a free economy to the Philippines by issuing an order abolishing economic controls that had been in effect since 1948. The order devalued the Philippine peso by setting its value according to the prevailing free market rate instead of by government directive. It also provided for the lifting of foreign exchange controls and for the reduction of tariff rates on essential consumer goods.

Macapagal believes that one of the ways to alleviate the problem of unemployment is to decentralize the economy and to encourage the spread of commerce and industry into the nation's provinces. He also maintains that political decentralization, with greater powers vested in provincial and local governments, is essential to the growth of democratic institutions, and he has proposed the establishment of eight regional legislatures with power to levy taxes. To alleviate the plight of the Filipino peasant in view of vast population growth, Macapagal has instituted a public-land clearance program, making new farmlands available for immediate use.

Although he strongly supports the United States, Macapagal has maintained a high degree of independence in his foreign policies. A staunch anti-Communist, he has said that he would never recognize the Communist regime in China, regardless of what the United States or other nations might decide. In May 1962 Macapagal criticized United States support of the neutralists in Laos as "a species of sophistry that can only weaken the defense of the free world." In the same month he canceled a state

MACAPAGAL, DIOSDADO—*Continued*
visit to the United States, after the House of
Representatives had rejected a bill for payment
of $73,000,000 in Philippine war claims. (When
the United States Congress subsequently reversed
itself and passed a revised war claims bill Macapagal declared that this was "proof of the innate
sense of fairness of the American people.")
Furthermore, Macapagal designated Philippine
independence day to fall on June 12, the anniversary of the date when the Filipinos declared
their independence from Spain in 1898, instead
of July 4, when the United States granted the
islands independence in 1946. He observed that
this change "does not detract from the respect
and gratitude which the Filipino people have for
the people of the United States."

In June 1962 Macapagal came into conflict
with Great Britain by advancing a claim of
Philippine sovereignty over the British colony of
North Borneo. On July 27, 1962 Macapagal
proposed the establishment of a Greater Malayan
Confederation, including the Philippines, which
would supersede the British-sponsored plan for a
Federation of Malaysia. Such a plan, he said,
might be a step toward the ultimate establishment of a Pan-Asian union.

Diosdado Macapagal's first wife died during
the Japanese occupation of the Philippines in
World War II. Two children were born to this
marriage, Maria Cielo and Arturo. On May 5,
1946 Macapagal married Evangelina Macaraeg,
a doctor of medicine and a former queen of the
Cebu Carnival. They have two children, Maria
Gloria and Diosdado, Jr. President Macapagal is
of medium build and wears plain sport shirts
and slacks. He prefers the simple life, and he
ordered the sale of the $2,500,000 presidential
yacht shortly after taking office. For relaxation
he plays billiards. His favorite American is
Abraham Lincoln. He is regarded as a man of
incorruptible integrity, and his private and public life is said to be totally devoid of scandal.
From 1955 to 1961 he was vice-president of the
Free Enterprise Society of the Philippines. In a
news analysis in the Washington *Post and
Times Herald* (November 17, 1961) J. A. Villa-
mor described Macapagal as "a gentle, tactful,
brilliant lawyer and academician . . . who still
occasionally shows the naiveté of a 'provinciano,'
especially when pressured in the Madison Avenue
manner."

References

N Y Times p6 N 16 '61 por
Time 78:22 N 24 '61 por
Asia Who's Who (1960)
Philippines Who's Who (1957)

McNEELY, EUGENE J(OHNSON) Nov. 1,
1900- Business executive; engineer

Address: b. American Telephone and Telegraph
Company, 195 Broadway, New York 7; h. 680
Madison Ave., New York 21

After almost forty years of association with
the Bell System, Eugene J. McNeely took office as
the tenth president of the American Telephone
and Telegraph Company on August 16, 1961.

His predecessor, Frederick R. Kappel, who is now
chairman of the board and chief executive officer
of A.T. & T., said at the annual meeting of share
owners in April 1962 that McNeely's election as
president "reflects the confidence of all . . . who
have been privileged to work with him."

With more than 725,000 employees and some
2,057,000 share owners, A.T. & T. is the largest
corporation in the world. During the first year
of McNeely's presidency it took a revolutionary
step toward the development of a new global
communications system when the communications satellite Telstar was successfully launched
on July 10, 1962. Telstar, the first privately
financed space project, can receive, amplify, and
retransmit telephone calls, telecasts, pictures, and
teletype messages between continents. It has been
described as the "first practical large-scale use of
space."

Eugene Johnson McNeely was born on November 1, 1900 in Jackson, Missouri to T. E. and
Mattie (Johnson) McNeely. His paternal grandparents came to southeast Missouri from the
Carolinas in 1820; his mother was a native of
Mississippi. As a boy McNeely willingly worked
in his family's garden and milked the cows, but
he preferred to go fishing. He took an after-
school job in a canning factory for 40 cents a
day and he later worked in an axe handle factory. One summer he was employed in an abstract office in Jackson. After graduating from
high school in Jackson in 1918 he attended
Southeast Missouri Teachers College at Cape
Giradeaux. He entered the University of Missouri in Columbia in 1920 and received the
B.S. degree in electrical engineering in 1922.

In the fall of 1922 McNeely was hired by the
Southwestern Bell Telephone Company at
St. Louis as a student engineer, "running down
orders" at a salary of $25 a week. For a time
he worked as a cable splicer's helper, and later,
as an installer. From 1926 to 1929 he was division plant engineer at Kansas City and St. Louis,
and during the latter year he worked for a time
as area plant supervisor in St. Louis. McNeely
has recalled that one of the most satisfying jobs
he ever held was that of division construction
superintendent for the company in Arkansas
from 1929 to 1932, although it was demanding,
and production had to be carefully scheduled.
However, he liked the job because, as he has
said, "you could see what you were doing—your
errors as well as your progress. . . . I guess I got
to know about every country road in Arkansas."

From 1932 to 1935 McNeely served as district
plant superintendent at East St. Louis, Illinois.
He was division plant superintendent at Little
Rock, Arkansas from 1935 to 1937, and at Kansas
City, Missouri from 1937 to 1941. He returned
to St. Louis in August 1941, serving as assistant
plant personnel supervisor until May 1942, and
as general plant personnel supervisor for the
next two years. In May 1944 he became plant
superintendent of the Eastern Missouri and
Arkansas area, and from January 1947 until
March 1948 he was general plant manager for
the Southwestern Bell Telephone Company at
St. Louis.

In March 1948 McNeely was named vice-
president for personnel relations with A.T. & T.
in New York City. He served as vice-president

of operations and a director of Northwestern Bell Telephone Company at Omaha, Nebraska from January to December 1949 and was president, director, and a member of the executive committee of Northwestern Bell from December 1949 to September 1952. He then returned to New York, where he served as vice-president in charge of the personnel relations department until January 1954. In 1954-55 McNeely was vice-president in charge of the operation and engineering department of A.T. & T. He served as executive vice-president in charge of administration, director, and member of the executive committee of A.T. & T., from October 1955 until his election as president on August 16, 1961. He is A.T. & T.'s third president in a row to have risen through the ranks to the top administrative position.

The American Telephone and Telegraph Company, the headquarters company of the Bell Telephone System, was incorporated in 1885 to build and operate long distance lines between the regional telephone companies that used patents controlled by the American Bell Telephone Company (founded in 1880). In 1900 A.T. & T. took over Bell's assets and it has acquired the stock of twenty operating subsidiaries. It owns 99.8 percent of the stock of the Western Electric Company, the largest of all Bell units and the purchasing agent for the entire system. Western Electric has manufactured components for guided missiles, radar units, and experimental satellites for the United States government and it is the prime contractor for the Nike missile system. Another subsidiary of A.T. & T. is Bell Telephone Laboratories, the largest electrical engineering project in the United States, which was established to develop new technological methods of communication.

The pioneering work in space communications was done by Dr. J. R. Pierce, research director of Bell Telephone Laboratories. In co-operation with the United States government he developed the experimental data-transmitting satellite Echo I, which was launched in August 1960. Speaking at the fiftieth anniversary meeting of the Telephone Pioneers of America in Boston on September 21, 1961, McNeely expressed his confidence in his company's ability to build an effective space communications system. He said that the project would be a profitless venture in the experimental period, and that the system would be under government regulation when it begins to operate commercially.

Asked to comment on President John F. Kennedy's request to Congress on February 7, 1962 for the chartering of a private monopoly that would own and operate a communications satellite system, McNeely noted that the bill would require careful study. He expressed the hope that the bill would permit "private ownership and operation of ground stations by the communications carriers who are responsible to the customer for the quality of his service." McNeely gave the first demonstration of the practicability of the Telstar satellite at the convention of the American Newspaper Publishers Association on April 25, 1962. Using a three-foot working model, he showed that a 250-word story could be sent at the rate of 1,000 words per minute

AT&T Photo Service

EUGENE J. McNEELY

from a transmitter to a receiver on the convention stage at the Waldorf-Astoria Hotel in New York.

Telstar, which was launched by the National Aeronautics and Space Administration from Cape Canaveral, Florida on July 10, 1962, is an active, repeater-type satellite. Its purpose is to test microwave communications in outer space, to study satellite tracking techniques, and to determine the effects of radiation and of micrometeorites on satellites. It is capable of providing 600 telephone channels or one television channel, or the equivalent. Constructed of magnesium and aluminum, Telstar is thirty-four and one-half inches in diameter, weighs 170 pounds, and is powered by 3,600 solar cells. It orbits the earth every 158 minutes at a distance from the earth varying from 593 to 3,502 miles.

On the day of its launching Telstar transmitted television pictures from a station in Andover, Maine to stations in France and England. According to A.T. & T. scientists, some thirty or forty such satellites would be needed to provide continuous, world-wide coverage. In a transatlantic telephone conversation beamed over Telstar on July 13, 1962 McNeely told the French Minister of Communications, Jacques Marette: "All of us here are proud indeed of the success of the satellite, which should lead to enlarged, more flexible world-wide communications. I hope it will become a symbol of greater understanding and friendship between nations."

A.T. & T. has spent about $50,000,000 on the Telstar project, and the eventual cost may exceed three times that amount. In April 1962 McNeely said that of a total of $1,400,000,000 spent by A.T. & T. for research and development on non-military projects since the end of World War II, more than $1,000,000,000 had been for fields closely related to the development of a satellites communications system. Great Britain, France, West Germany, and Italy are partici-

McNEELY, EUGENE J.—*Continued*

pating in the Telstar program, and Japan is expected to join in 1963. In addition to A.T. & T. six other major companies are planning to build communications satellites. In August 1962 both houses of Congress passed a bill to create a privately-owned and government-controlled enterprise to operate a world-wide satellite communications system. A.T. & T. is expected to own a large part of the stock of the new corporation. In the field of telephone communications A.T. & T. spokesmen have promised a number of new services and techniques for the near future.

McNeely is a director of the Illinois Bell Telephone Company, the Southern New England Telephone Company, and the Continental Oil Company. He is a trustee of the East River Savings Bank, the Manufacturers-Hanover Trust Company, and Columbia University Teachers College, and he is a member of the executive committee of the Downtown-Lower Manhattan Association. His fraternities are Tau Beta Pi (the honorary engineering fraternity) and Eta Kappa Nu (the honor society in electrical engineering), and he belongs to the University Club of New York. In 1957 the University of Missouri conferred on him its Honor Award for Distinguished Service in Engineering.

Eugene J. McNeely married Eunice Miller on February 19, 1927. To escape from New York on weekends the McNeelys leave their Manhattan apartment for Stone Ridge near Kingston, New York, where they have a seventy-acre plot and an old house that they remodeled themselves. Described as soft-spoken and unassuming, McNeely is an energetic perfectionist who keeps in close touch with the company's operations. He keeps a golden telephone on his desk and dials his own long distance calls. Once, upon being asked his recipe for success, he replied: "Keep trying to do things better and more intelligently." He looks for employees who show a constant desire to excel. In dealing with people McNeely recalls the advice of a former employer, who said, "try to understand how the other guy is thinking."

References

N Y Herald Tribune p24 Ag 17 '61 por
N Y Times p31 Ag 17 '61 por
Newsweek 58:62 Ag 28 '61
U S News 51:24 Ag 28 '61 por
Who's Who in America, 1962-63

MARKS, SIMON, 1ST BARON July 9, 1888-
British merchant

Address: h. 47 Grosvenor Square, London, W. 1, England; Titlarks Farm, Sunningdale, Berkshire, England

One of the two peers created in 1961 by Queen Elizabeth II of England is Simon Marks, the son of a Polish immigrant who once sold pins and thimbles in a Leeds street market. The immigrant made this small business a success; his son developed it into a British institution. Simon Marks, now the first Baron Marks of Broughton, is chairman and joint managing

director of Marks & Spencer Ltd., a nationwide chain of approximately 250 stores selling clothing and some food items. The chain's unorthodox and enlightened business methods have made clothes of high quality as accessible to typists and laborers as to the rich. Lord Marks has been credited with raising the British standard of living and with weakening class barriers—which partly depend on differences in dress. His peerage was preceded in 1944 by a knighthood, and by many other honors for his services to the public, to the British government, to Israel, and to science.

Simon Marks was born on July 9, 1888 in Leeds in the county of York, England to Michael and Hannah (Cohen) Marks, who had immigrated to England from Poland four years earlier. He was educated at Manchester Grammar School, one of Britain's finest secondary schools, where he stayed until the sixth form, and subsequently spent two years in Germany and France, learning French and German and studying business methods. Lord Marks has made it clear, however, that in the development of his business philosophy, he owes more to his father than to formal study.

Michael Marks, who is commemorated in the St. Michael trademark that appears on many Marks & Spencer products, laid the foundations of the chain store in 1884, when he settled in England's industrial Midlands and set up a trestle table in the weekly market at Leeds. He hawked needles, thread, lace, thimbles, and pins with the slogan "Don't ask the price; it's a penny." This uniform price policy limited his profits but increased his sales, and its simplicity enabled him to dispense with record-keeping.

Because of these factors and Marks's insistence on quality, the tiny business prospered. In 1894, hampered by lack of capital and manpower, Michael Marks went into partnership with Thomas Spencer, a Yorkshire textile salesman who had extended him credit during his first difficult years. The partners established two policies that Marks & Spencer has followed ever since: profits were plowed back into the business and (thanks to Spencer's contacts) goods were bought directly from manufacturers, without the intervention of wholesalers. Thomas Spencer died in 1905; Michael Marks, at the age of forty-four, in 1907. By the time of Marks's death the firm owned seventy "Penny Bazaars" all over England—no longer stalls in open markets, but permanent stores in shopping centers.

When his father died, Simon Marks was nineteen and had just joined the business. In 1911 he became a director of Marks & Spencer Ltd., and in 1916 he became chairman of the company and joint managing director, positions he has held ever since. His joint managing director and vice-chairman is Israel Sieff, Marks's brother-in-law and a friend since their days in school. Sir Simon has said, "Mr. Sieff was always interested in social questions, and it was he who made me realize what a terrible part is played in people's lives by fear and insecurity, and how much people are affected by them in business."

In 1913 Marks had met Chaim Weizmann, who was then teaching biochemistry at the University of Manchester. Through his friendship with the man who was later to become the first President of Israel Marks became one of the earliest financial supporters of Zionism—a cause that for years has been one of the leading interests of his life. In 1914 Great Britain entered World War I and Marks joined the Royal Artillery as a signaler. When the British government espoused the cause of a national home for the Jews, Marks was seconded from the Royal Artillery to work with Weizmann. He established a headquarters, paying the rent out of his own pocket, and soon, still in his twenties, found himself representing Weizmann on equal terms with generals and admirals.

This experience did not mark the end of Marks's service to his government. In 1938 he helped to found the Air Defence Cadet Corps and watched it grow into a force of 250,000 cadets that in 1941 was taken over by the Air Ministry and renamed the Air Training Corps. Early in World War II he served as deputy chairman of the London and South Eastern Regional Board, concerned with production, and as honorary adviser to the Ministry of Petroleum Warfare. The Ministry was responsible for the development of the Crocodile flame-throwing tank, the Fido device for clearing fog from airfields, and Pluto, the submarine oil pipeline across the English Channel that helped to make possible the Allied invasion of Europe. During the war Marks also served as one of the first directors of British Overseas Airways, remaining on the board for four years.

But Marks & Spencer itself is Lord Marks's greatest achievement. In 1927, when the firm became a public company, its sales for the year totaled $6,334,100 and its profit before tax was $339,500. By 1960-61 sales had risen to almost $500,000,000 and net profits to $30,000,000. Food items (mostly bakery products) account for an increasingly large proportion of Marks & Spencer sales—nineteen percent in 1961-62.

With justification, Simon Marks names his father as his inspiration and the source of many of his ideas. That Marks & Spencer continues to emphasize value and quality is indicated by the fact that 6,000,000 people a week patronize the chain store and that purchasers have included the Prince and Princess of Monaco and the Duchess of Windsor. Goods marketed by the store are made to precise specifications and research goes on constantly at the firm's London headquarters to improve quality, durability, and design. Yet the most expensive item that Marks & Spencer sold in 1961 was a woman's woolen suit costing $18.20. The firm's success has forced other stores to improve the quality and lower the prices of their merchandise.

Moreover, Lord Marks has made it dramatically clear that he shares his father's predilection for simplicity in management and in record-keeping. Since 1957 he has abolished about 120 tons of forms, saving an estimated $14,000,000 in printing and labor costs, and he has eliminated time clocks. Although sales receipts are not given and customers are not permitted to try on clothes in the stores, any article bearing the firm's label is exchanged without question. Lord Marks will not allow the number of his stores to exceed 250, since he feels that this is the maxi-

British Inf. Services

LORD MARKS

mum number that can be properly supervised. During the past fifteen years he has invested some $150,000,000 in enlarging and improving existing stores, but he has spent almost no money on advertising.

The firm still buys directly from manufacturers, and it is Lord Marks's unique relationship with his suppliers that is central to the chain's success. Marks & Spencer dispenses with factories and warehouses. Goods flow into the stores as they are needed. Instead of the conventional buyers, "selectors" work with manufacturers, determining standards, planning production, passing on the results of tests and experiments made at the Marks & Spencer laboratories, encouraging industrialists to establish their own research units. Marks & Spencer usually absorbs between sixty and seventy percent of a manufacturer's product, leaving him a degree of freedom but still assuring him the advantages of planned and continuous production.

Lord Marks, who retained large holdings in Marks & Spencer shares when the firm became a public company, is an extremely rich man, but he has been lavishly generous with institutions and causes that interest him. Among them are the Royal College of Surgeons, University College in London, Manchester Grammar School, and the state of Israel. He holds an honorary D.Sc. degree in economics from the University of London for his work in promoting co-operation between science and industry. He is an Honorary Fellow of the Weizmann Institute of Science at Rehovot in Israel, of University College in London, and of the Royal College of Surgeons.

In paying Sir Simon tribute on the occasion of his being made an Honorary Fellow of the

MARKS, SIMON, 1ST BARON—*Continued*
Royal College of Surgeons, Sir Archibald Mc-
Indoe, the plastic surgeon, said: "He is among
the leaders who have brought the technicians
from the back room to the front room. He has
always fought against bureaucracy and remote
control. He has always laid great stress on the
importance of good human relationships. . . .
In this, his own field, he has produced a social
revolution entirely due to his scientific outlook."

On July 27, 1915 in Manchester, England, with
Chaim Weizmann as one of the witnesses, Simon
Marks married Miriam Sieff, a sister of his friend
and associate Israel Sieff (who is married to
Marks's sister). They have a son, Michael, and
a daughter, Hannah Olive. Once an ardent
tennis player, Sir Simon now restricts his exercise
to brisk walks between his office and his flat in
Grosvenor Square. He occasionally retreats to his
farm in Berkshire. He enjoys going to the theater
and to concerts and collects paintings by the
French Impressionists. Goronwy Rees in *The
Multimillionaires* (Macmillan, 1961) describes
Lord Marks as being small, jaunty, and active,
with graying hair, mobile features, and quick,
expressive gestures. His manner is said to be
assured but modest and unaffected, marked by a
youthful capacity for enthusiasm and spontaneity.

Yet, according to Rees, Marks has a sharp eye
and "a certain ruthlessness in judging others who
have not met his own high standards." On his
desk stands the motto: "The day is short and the
work is great and the labourers are sluggish and
the reward is much and the master of the house
is urgent." Marks thinks of his enterprise as an
experiment in industrial co-operation for the
benefit of the consumer. To Rees he appears
"half philanthropist, half artist, rather than a
man of business."

> *References*
>
> Economist 199:1310 Je 17 '61; 203:1159
>   Je 16 '62
> N Y Times p74 Ja 12 '60 por; p2 Je 10 '61
>   por
> Time 77:76 Ja 13 '61 por
> Burke's Peerage, Baronetage, and Knight-
>   age, 1959
> International Year Book and Statesmen's
>   Who's Who, 1962
> Rees, Goronwy. The Multimillionaires
>   (1961)
> Who's Who, 1962
> Who's Who in World Jewry (1955)

MORSE, ROBERT (ALAN) May 18, 1931-
Actor
Address: b. c/o General Artists Corp., 640 5th
Ave., New York 19

Robert Morse, the brilliant young star of the
Pulitzer-Prize-winning Broadway musical comedy
*How to Succeed in Business Without Really Try-
ing*, is living proof of how to succeed in show
business by trying every minute. Since making
his debut on Broadway in the Thornton Wilder
comedy *The Matchmaker* in 1955 he has given
widely praised performances in the Broadway
musicals *Say, Darling* and *Take Me Along*, and

he has appeared in motion pictures and on television. He won the Antoinette Perry (Tony)
award of the American Theatre Wing for the
best performance of the 1961-62 season, as J.
Pierrepont Finch, the conniving and Machiavel-
lian—yet charming—hero of *How to Succeed*.

The ebullient and irrepressible Bobby Morse
was born Robert Alan Morse, in Newton, Massachusetts, near Boston, on May 18, 1931. His
father, Charles Morse, managed a chain of movie
houses in New England and is now the manager of a record shop. His mother, the former
May Silver, was a professional pianist before her
marriage. He has an older brother, Richard, also
a professional actor, and a sister, Barbara, who
is a teacher. (Morse's parents now live in Emerson, New Jersey, in a house he helped them to
buy.) As a boy Morse avidly collected records of
Broadway shows, and he was greatly inspired by
such stars as Ray Bolger and Danny Kaye. One
of his first pieces of theatrical improvisation
occurred when he was scolded by his kindergarten teacher for being late. "His eyes filled
with tears," his mother recalls, "and he gulped,
'I've just come from my father's funeral.'" He
received his early education at Ward Elementary
School and Weeks Junior High School, in Newton.

At Newton High School, where he was known
as "Mousey," Morse's schoolboy antics (such as
appearing at school in catsup-stained bandages
with the explanation that his mother had hit
him with a rolling pin) left him little time for
studying, to the despair of his teachers. He was
shipped off to St. Louis, where he attended the
lower school of The Principia, a college run by
the Christian Science Church, but this had little
effect on the brash youngster, and he returned
to Newton High. His theatrical ambitions and
talents were finally recognized by Henry Lasker,
a perceptive music teacher, who was a friend of
Leonard Bernstein. Lasker let Robert Morse direct and star in a junior class production of
Walter Kerr's *Sing Out, Sweet Land,* which
proved to be a hit. Morse remembers this period
as one of the happiest in his life, and his school
grades markedly improved at the time. During
his senior year he played the role of Koko in a
school production of the Gilbert and Sullivan
operetta *The Mikado*.

Morse made his professional debut one summer as a student apprentice with the Peterborough (New Hampshire) Players, appearing
with his brother in Leonard Bernstein's musical
On the Town. After graduating from Newton
High School in June 1950 he headed for New
York City, where his brother was struggling to
gain a foothold in the theater. There Robert
Morse obtained a $12-a-week job operating a
spotlight for the Children's World Theatre,
which was touring the New Jersey suburbs. One
night he directed the spotlight away from his
brother, who was playing the Pied Piper, and he
lost his job. After working briefly as a cookie
salesman at Schrafft's, and as a Fuller Brush
salesman, he returned to Newton.

In late 1950 Morse enlisted in the Navy for a
four-year term. He served most of the time as a
sonarman on board a destroyer and made two
trips around the world. After his discharge he

returned to New York City, more convinced than ever that his future was in the theater. He moved in with his brother and enrolled in the American Theatre Wing's musical comedy course under the G.I. Bill, working at various jobs to meet expenses. While appearing as a stand-in for contestants on the television quiz show, *Name That Tune,* he was spotted by Martin Baum, a theatrical agent, who obtained a small part for him as a Marine in the film *The Proud and the Profane* (Paramount, 1956).

Returning to New York, Morse appeared for a time on *True Confessions* radio broadcasts. He was also able to arrange an appointment with the British director Tyrone Guthrie for a role in Thornton Wilder's farce, *The Matchmaker.* Without even giving him an audition, Guthrie hired him for the role of the young apprentice, Barnaby Tucker. During the out-of-town tryouts Morse nearly lost the part because of what he later admitted was his "obstreperous" and "foolish" behavior, and he was so "irritatingly erratic" that the rest of the cast signed a petition to have him dropped. Unable to find an adequate replacement, the producer David Merrick kept Morse in the role, and when the play opened on Broadway on December 5, 1955 Morse turned in a memorable performance that planted his feet firmly on the road to stardom. Morse was the only member of the original cast who appeared in the motion picture version of *The Matchmaker* (Paramount, 1958).

Morse next appeared on Broadway in *Say, Darling,* the "comedy about a musical" by Richard and Marian Bissell and Abe Burrows, which opened on April 3, 1958. The show received mixed reviews, but Morse, in a minor role, stole the show as a brilliantly comic young actor. Frank Aston wrote in the New York *World Telegram and Sun* (April 4, 1958) that Morse gave an "amazingly droll" performance as "an ineffectual, limp-wristed, over-mannered big shot of the theater world." Morse also appeared in the revival of *Say, Darling* that opened at New York's City Center on February 5, 1959.

With Jackie Gleason, Walter Pidgeon, and Eileen Herlie, Morse was assigned a starring role in the musical *Take Me Along,* based on Eugene O'Neill's *Ah, Wilderness!* After *Take Me Along* opened on Broadway on October 22, 1959 Brooks Atkinson wrote in the New York *Times* (October 23, 1959): "In a production that is not ideally cast in all the principal roles, Mr. Morse plays young Richard without a false note. He describes the bumptious innocence of a youth struggling with literary ideas that are beyond him. And he does not forget that in addition to being comic, Richard is honest and lovable. Mr. Morse does not sentimentalize a very real character."

Playing J. Pierrepont Finch, Morse achieved recognition as one of the most gifted young actors in the theater when he co-starred with Rudy Vallee in the musical *How to Succeed in Business Without Really Trying.* A satire of big business, the show is based on Edward Shepherd Mead's novel of the same title that was published by Simon and Schuster in 1952. Abe Burrows, who collaborated with Jack Weinstock, Willie Gilbert, and Frank Loesser on the musi-

ROBERT MORSE

cal, has said, "I wouldn't have written the show if we hadn't been able to get Morse."

Abe Burrows' faith was justified by the acclaim accorded the musical and its stars when the show opened on Broadway on October 14, 1961. Richard Watts, Jr., observed in the New York *Post* (October 16, 1961): "It was a triumph for many talented people and cause for an ovation to Robert Morse in its vital central role." A writer for *Newsweek* (November 27, 1961) noted that Morse "has taken over the show and the character and made them his own the way Ray Bolger did with *Where's Charley?*, the way Ethel Merman did with *Annie Get Your Gun,* the way possibly three or four other performers have done in the past twenty years." President John F. Kennedy attended *How to Succeed* on January 20, 1962 and reportedly enjoyed himself. In April 1962 the show was voted the best musical by the New York Drama Critics Circle, and in the following month it won a Pulitzer Prize. For his performance Morse received the Antoinette Perry (Tony) award of the American Theatre Wing in April 1962.

In addition to his stage performances Morse has also appeared on a number of television shows, including a production of *The Velvet Glove* with Helen Hayes, the *Play of the Week* production of Jean Anouilh's *Thieves' Carnival,* the *Shirley Temple Show,* and *Naked City.* In May 1962, he signed a four-picture contract with the film producer Otto Preminger, to begin when his $1,750 per week stint in *How to Succeed* ends in October 1963.

Five feet eight inches in height, Robert Morse has bright eyes, disorderly brown hair, and the animation of a high school cheerleader. His baritone will never take him to the stage of the Metropolitan Opera House, but its quaver is appropriate to the relaxed demands of musical comedy. A *Time* writer (November 17, 1961) has pointed out that he "seems to have been formed by a head-on collision between Mickey

MORSE, ROBERT—*Continued*

Rooney and John Fitzgerald Kennedy." Although he is not a trained dancer, he delights audiences and critics with the way he throws himself constantly about on stage, taking his inspiration from musical comedy star Ray Bolger and from his sports idol, professional basketball star Bob Cousy.

Morse has won a reputation—which he is now trying to live down—as an uninhibited cutup who kisses headwaiters, vaults into hatcheck booths, and fires away with imaginary pistols at imaginary badmen from restaurant tables. He has calmed down considerably from his early days as an irresponsible clown. He attributes his new self-discipline to his marriage and the two years he spent in psychoanalysis. "I got something I never got from my parents," he has said of his analyst. "I found a friend who knew me and did not condemn me for my outlandish behavior."

Robert Morse's wife, the former Carole D'Andrea, is a professional dancer, who appeared in the stage and screen versions of *West Side Story*. The couple has one daughter, Andrea. On May 24, 1962, Morse was named "Stage Father of the Year" by the National Father's Day Committee. Morse hopes that his wife will resume her career. "Carole's a wildly talented dancer," he told Robert Wahls in an interview for the New York *Sunday News* (May 13, 1962). "She's the reason I go home nights and watch the Late Late Show on TV."

References

N Y Sunday News II p10 My 13 '62 pors
N Y Times II p4 F 28 '60
Newsweek 58:50+ N 27 '61 pors
Time 78:78+ N 17 '61 por

MOTHERWELL, ROBERT (BURNS, 3D)
(mŭth′ẽr-wŭl) Jan. 24, 1915-   Artist; lecturer

Address: b. c/o Sidney Janis Gallery, 15 E. 57th St., New York 22; h. 173 E. 94th St., New York 28

To Robert Motherwell, for whom a painting is a vehicle of passion, phrases like "automatic abstract art" and "abstract expressionism" are unsatisfactory designations of the style of painting that he—with Mark Rothko, Hans Hofmann, and other New York artists—has helped to make predominant in American art since World War II. Some traces of the influence of Miró's automation and Mondriaan's pure intelligence, as well as of Matisse, whom he also admires, might be detected in the development of his work. But the intensity of feeling that can give vibrancy to black or paradoxical tenderness to the collision of bulky forms is entirely Motherwell's own and accounts for much of his exhilarating originality. Although his painting and collages vary considerably in size and mood, his trademark has perhaps come to be spacious and powerful canvases that monumentalize profound emotional experiences.

As his name suggests, Robert Burns Motherwell 3d is of Scottish origin on his father's side. Once when asked about his role as a spokesman

or dialectician for the abstract-expressionist group, he quipped that he was talkative because of being Irish—an attribute that he owes to the ancestors of his mother, Margaret (Hogan) Motherwell. His parents were both natives of the United States and had made their home in Aberdeen, Washington, where Robert Motherwell was born on January 24, 1915. Robert Burns Motherwell 2d was a banker and from about 1927 to his death in 1943 held the position of president of the Wells Fargo Bank in San Francisco, although Robert in early childhood was not reared in an atmosphere of wealth.

The Motherwell family moved to San Francisco in 1918, but until he was about twenty-five years old Robert Motherwell used to return frequently to Washington's coast to spend summers near Aberdeen. An early indication of talent won him a scholarship to the Otis Art Institute in Los Angeles, where he studied from 1923 to 1927. Because of chronic asthma, he was sent in 1929 to the Moran Preparatory School in the desert at Atascadero, California. There he played football and tennis and also excelled academically, graduating as valedictorian in 1932.

About this time Motherwell took a brief course in painting at the California School of Fine Arts in San Francisco. He chose philosophy as his major subject at Stanford University, which he entered in 1932, and became particularly interested in aesthetics. After receiving his B.A. degree in 1937, he studied for a year at Harvard University's Graduate School of Philosophy. In an article for *Art in America* (number 2, 1961) he remarked, "When you have a retrospective at a museum, the first thing they ask you for in your biography is where you studied, as if that counts! I always remember Rothko's stories as a Jewish immigrant student at Yale, or my own misery in the Graduate School at Harvard." From one of his Harvard professors, however, David Prall, Motherwell learned to apply the findings of relational logic to the study of aesthetics, and he has admitted, "It has helped me in the formulation of a defense of the paintings my colleagues and I do" (*Art Digest*, October 1, 1951).

During a vacation from college in the summer of 1935, Motherwell had toured western Europe with his father and younger sister. In 1938 he revisited Europe to study art in Paris and at the University of Grenoble, and before returning to the United States in July 1939, he exhibited his paintings, for the first time, in Paris. He then spent another year on the West Coast, teaching at the University of Oregon, and enjoyed his final summer at Aberdeen.

Since 1940, when he enrolled in Columbia University's Graduate School of Architecture and Art, Motherwell has been settled more or less in New York. Art historian Meyer Schapiro, with whom he studied at Columbia, encouraged his desire to paint and introduced him to Kurt Seligmann. Seligmann not only instructed him in engraving but brought him into contact with a number of surrealist painters in New York, including Yves Tanguy, Max Ernst, and Marcel Duchamps, who were exiled during World War II from Nazi-occupied Paris.

Another surrealist whom Motherwell met at this time was Matta. The two artists visited

Mexico in the summer and fall of 1941, and partly through Matta, he became interested in the surrealist theory, or technique, of automatism —a suspension of the conscious mind to release subconscious imagery. Motherwell turned from a figurative and brightly colorful style of painting, suggestive of Matisse Fauvism, to work from that time on in so-called "automatic abstract art." He joined Jackson Pollock, William Baziotes, and other artists, as well as Matta, in early experiments in automatism; and in 1942 he showed his work at the "First Papers of Surrealism" exhibition at the Whitelaw Reid Mansion in New York.

Along with Pollock and Rothko, Motherwell was among the several promising abstract expressionists whose work Peggy Guggenheim so boldly encouraged during the war years in New York. He had his first one-man show at her Art of This Century gallery in 1944. In association with Rothko, Baziotes, David Hare, and Barnett Newman, in 1947 he founded an art school, called the Subjects of the Artist, on 8th Street in Greenwich Village. The meetings there of avantgarde artists, "Friday Evenings with an Artist," became the club of the School of New York, as the movement of abstract expressionists is often called. The school on 8th Street was discontinued after one year, but in 1948 Motherwell opened his own school in a studio that he shared for a year or so with Bradley Walker Tomlin on 10th Street.

Teaching has occupied a fairly important place in Motherwell's career. In the summer of 1945 and again of 1951 he was an instructor at Black Mountain College in North Carolina. He taught at Oberlin College in Ohio in the summer of 1952 and at Colorado Springs Fine Arts Center in the summer of 1954. From 1951 to 1958 he was associate professor of art at the Graduate School of Hunter College in New York and, more recently, he taught briefly in 1962 at the University of Miami.

Like Hans Hofmann, Franz Kline, and Willem de Kooning, Motherwell belongs to the "action" painters among the abstract expressionists —painters whose initial impulses are developed in part through the act of painting itself and whose abstractions frequently take form from the artists' reaction to the texture of materials, the shape of the brush, the color of the paint. So that the viewer can respond to the gestures of the artist in the act of creating, the finished painting retains lines and forms that show the process of executing a picture.

An action painter relies greatly upon improvising, which suggests quickness in painting, and in an article for the American catalog of the São Paulo 1961 biennial Frank O'Hara wrote of the ease with which Motherwell paints and of his unerring "recognition of the perfect formal improvision, the exact spatial nuance, the specific touch which may sweep from stately calm to dizzying speed in one linear action." Yet Motherwell expands and reforms his concepts through various stages before completing a painting, often sustaining his work over a prolonged period. He once said in an interview for *Art Digest* (October 1, 1951), "Never can I paint an idea without modifying it enormously during the process."

Hans Namuth
ROBERT MOTHERWELL

Reviewing Motherwell's exhibit at the Sidney Janis Gallery in the spring of 1961, Jack Kroll commented in *Art News* (May 1961) on the artist's necessity for "an incendiary meeting of emotion and gesture." In several large paintings, including the nearly ten-foot-long *Black and White*, he observed that "the central blazoning event has been thrown off a galvanic spoor of spatters and drips that act like the sun's corona to lick the astronomer's eye into an expansive awareness of decisive occurrence . . . it is no picayune water-pistol that spurts Motherwell's automatism, but a proud big Bertha that rears its muzzle into the blank sky and asks no quarter from critics of controlled combustion."

Motherwell has, in fact, said that a painting is a vehicle of passion; through it the artist makes human contact with the viewer so that passions touch and are shared. Since Motherwell's "felt thought" and "thought feeling," as he calls it, is concrete to him, he does not think of his painting as abstract, or "remote from reality." To viewers who see no meaning or sense in nonrepresentational art, Motherwell replies that painting is much more than picture-making and story-telling: "A man is neither a decoration nor an anecdote" (John I. H. Baur, editor, *The New Decade,* Macmillan, 1955).

Some critics, however, find that Motherwell's treatment of his subject is occasionally so personal and subjective that communication is jeopardized. "The outsider is put in a difficult position here," a New York *Times* (March 15, 1959) critic wrote of Motherwell's 1959 show at the Janis Gallery. "He can justifiably admire the fastidious, almost fussy handling of oil paint and water-color; the sprightly, nervous calligraphical dots and dashes and the delicate ebb and flow of discreet color. He can tease himself into imagining meanings for the shapes. Nevertheless, for the outsider, these shapes are arbitrary and root-

MOTHERWELL, ROBERT—*Continued*

less. Their 'reality' exists for the painter alone. . . ."

Nearly always profound, mysterious and somber, the passion of Motherwell's paintings sometimes centers on love, as in *Je t'aime* (1955-57) and *Two Figures with Cerulean Blue Stripe* (1960), and sometimes on doom and melancholy and death, as in *The Little Spanish Prison* (1941) and the two series of paintings that he calls *Elegies to the Spanish Republic* and *Iberia*. The Spanish elegies, on which Motherwell has been working since 1948, are in O'Hara's opinion "one of the most important achievements in American art." He describes them as "the first American paintings to use black and white in a full symbolic sense: the white of purity, of light, of experience, which cuts into the dominating black forms of death briefly and is ultimately conquered, may be reversed in meaning because of the ritual sense of the event."

A master of the collage, Motherwell has also found creative stimulation and fulfillment in the surface and tactile effects of pasted papers, with a sensitivity to his material indicated in the titles *The Best Toys are Made of Paper* (1948) and *The Tearingness of Collaging* (1957). He is said to have been early influenced by cubist collage, and since 1941 he has given collage serious treatment in his overall contribution to American art, handling collage with a restraint and distinctive style that confirms it as an art form rather than an amusing oddity.

Motherwell's collages are more free of anxiety than his paintings. They are sometimes witty and lyrical, but complex, and often richly evocative and nostalgic. Sam Hunter, who helped to prepare the catalog for Motherwell's collage exhibit at Berggruen in Paris in 1961, sees in *The French Line,* one of many collages paying tribute to Matisse, an example of Motherwell's fondness for contrasting the cultures of America and Europe: "We find both the legend of a European product, *Gressins Labouchede,* and the vivid remembrance of another expression of European civility, the Cote d'Azur seaside. . . . The ensemble, however, has the insistent brilliance of an American billboard in a plastic statement combining violence with grace."

Since 1957 Motherwell's paintings and collages have been exhibited in biannual one-man shows at the Janis Gallery in New York. He was among the thirty-five American painters and sculptors of the postwar decade whose work was shown in the "New Decade" exhibit of the Whitney Museum of American Art in New York in the spring of 1955 (an exhibit later sent to California, Colorado, and Missouri). In 1961 he showed one of a pair of eighteen-foot paintings at the Guggenheim Museum in New York. Elsewhere in the United States, his work has been seen in an exhibit of four American artists at the Contemporary Arts Society in Houston in 1953, at a retrospective at Bennington College in 1959, and at a large retrospective at the Pasadena Art Museum in 1962.

As early as 1946, when his paintings were being shown for perhaps the first time in Chicago and San Francisco, Motherwell was included among six Americans exhibited at the

Galerie Maeght in Paris. In later years his work was shown at the Tate Gallery in London and at museums in Madrid, Brussels, Amsterdam, Moscow, and other European cities. In 1950 he contributed to the exhibit in the United States pavilion at the Venice Biennale; in the fall of 1954 he was a guest of the West German government as a member of a group representing the various arts; and in 1961 the Museum of Modern Art in New York chose a one-man show of his paintings to make up a major part of the United States exhibit at the sixth Bienal do Museu de Art Moderna São Paulo in Brazil.

Motherwell has written articles for *Partisan Review, New Republic, Art News,* and other periodicals. From 1944 to 1952 he edited a series of art books, The Documents of Modern Art, for Wittenborn and Company in New York, and in 1951 he edited a large anthology, *The Dada Painters and Poets* (Wittenborn), with texts and illustrations by Arp and others.

On April 6, 1958 Robert Motherwell married Helen Frankenthaler, who is also an artist. By a previous marriage he has two children, Jeannie and Lise. Motherwell is a Democrat and an Episcopalian and a member of the Protestant Council for Art and Culture. His club in New York is the Artists'. Looking somewhat like an athlete or sportsman, he stands six feet one inch tall and weighs 190 pounds; his eyes are gray and his hair is light brown. He likes to live near the sea. A few years after he had given up spending summers on the West Coast, he built an experimental house, designed by Pierre Chareau, in East Hampton on Long Island. In 1950 he sold the house and some six years later he bought an eighteenth-century house on Cape Cod, for summer enjoyment. He belongs to the Provincetown Yacht and Tennis Club and plays poker. Part of his summers he often gives to foreign travel.

References

Baur, John I. H. ed. The New Decade (1955)
International Who's Who, 1961-62
Who's Who in America, 1962-63
Who's Who in American Art, 1959

NASH, PHILLEO   Oct. 25, 1909-   United States government official

Address: b. Department of the Interior, Washington 25, D.C.; h. 800 4th St., S.W., Washington 24, D.C.

In appointing Philleo Nash Commissioner of Indian Affairs in July 1961, President John F. Kennedy took a step toward blazing a new trail for American Indians. An anthropologist, Nash has long had an interest in Indian affairs and minority problems; he served as a special assistant for minority affairs under President Harry S. Truman from 1946 through 1952. Nash came to his present post from his position as lieutenant governor of Wisconsin (1959-61). He is also the president of the Biron Cranberry Company, a family concern in Wisconsin Rapids, Wisconsin.

Philleo Nash was born on October 25, 1909 in Wisconsin Rapids, Wisconsin to Guy Nash, a cranberry grower, and Florence Belle (Philleo) Nash, a musician. His brother, Thomas, died in 1931. His sister, Jean Nash, manages the family business, the Biron Cranberry Company, at Wisconsin Rapids; she was formerly president of the Wisconsin Cranberry Sales Company. Nash was reared in the city of his birth and attended public schools there. He graduated in 1926 from Lincoln High School, where he was active in music, speech, debating, the student council, and the student newspaper and yearbook. He became a vice-president and member of the board of directors of the Biron Cranberry Company in 1928.

At the University of Wisconsin Nash played in the school orchestra and proved an excellent student, winning honors in his senior year. He graduated in 1932 with a B.A. degree in anthropology. Continuing his studies at the University of Chicago, he became a Fellow at the laboratory of anthropology in Santa Fe, New Mexico and was elected to the science research honor fraternity, Sigma Xi. In the year 1935-36, subsidized by a Social Science Research Council Fellowship, Nash lived among the Klamath Indians on their reservation in Oregon. His doctoral dissertation, "The Place of Religious Revivalism in the Formation of the Intercultural Community on Klamath Reservation," dealt with the Klamath Indian ghost dance of 1870, which he held to be part of the tribe's response to its initial contact with white men. He received a Ph.D. degree in anthropology from the University of Chicago in 1937.

From 1937 to 1941 Nash was a lecturer in anthropology at the University of Toronto in Canada. In 1939 he served as secretary of the Yale-Toronto International Conference on Indian Welfare. In 1941 he returned to his native state and became a special lecturer in anthropology at the University of Wisconsin and manager of the Biron Cranberry Company for one year. In 1942 he moved to Washington, D.C., where he took a post as special assistant for domestic operations to Elmer Davis, then director of the Office of War Information. He held this position until 1945, serving also as a special assistant to the Secretary of War, Henry L. Stimson, in 1943. He helped to write and edit a number of government publications on minority groups in the armed services.

Between 1946 and 1953 Nash was a special White House assistant for minority problems and acted as a liaison officer betwen the White House and the Department of the Interior. In 1946 he helped to write the final report of the President's Committee on Fair Employment Practices. From 1952 to 1953 he was an administrative assistant to President Truman. He became president of the Biron Cranberry Company in 1946.

When Dwight D. Eisenhower became President of the United States in January 1953, Nash returned to Wisconsin, where he became active in state politics and was chairman of the state Democratic party from 1955 to 1957. In the 1958 elections Nash ran for the office of lieutenant governor on the ticket of the gubernatorial candidate Gaylord A. Nelson. Both men were elected for a two-year term; they were re-elected in 1960 for another two-year period, but Nash did not

PHILLEO NASH

complete his term of office. While lieutenant governor, he was chairman of the Governor's Refugee Committee.

Nash's knowledge of and interest in Indian affairs led to his appointment as vice-chairman of the Menominee Tribal Trust in 1961. Established with a Milwaukee bank, the trust holds and invests the funds of minors belonging to the tribe. During this period, the Menominee Indians of Wisconsin reached their full independence from federal trusteeship by forming an independent state-chartered corporation to administer tribal property. The reservation was formally designated Wisconsin's seventy-second county—Menominee County—by Governor Nelson on May 5, 1961. From 1942 to 1961 Nash was a board member of the Association on American Indian Affairs.

The Office of the Commissioner of Indian Affairs was created as part of the War Department in 1824 and was transferred to the Interior Department in 1849. Called the Bureau of Indian Affairs since 1947, the agency has as its prime function the management of the affairs of about 350,000 of the 500,000 Indians who live in the United States. This has involved the promotion of health and welfare, the education of Indian children, the encouragement of Indian arts and crafts, the reclamation of land, and economic development through proper land use and the supervision of tribal funds and the settlement of Indian claims against the government.

The federal government's Indian policy has undergone many changes in the last century, leaving many Indians confused and uncertain about their status. After an era of paternalistic supervision on reservations, the General Allotment Act passed by Congress in 1897 authorized the government to subdivide tribally owned land into individual parcels without consulting the tribes affected. As a result more than half of the best Indian land holdings passed into non-Indian

NASH, PHILLEO—*Continued*
hands. In 1924 the first inhabitants of the
United States were given their citizenship; in
1934 the Indian Reorganization Act tried to aid
the now impoverished Indians by restoring tribal
authority and land ownership. Another policy
switch occurred in 1953 when Congress passed a
resolution to end the Indians' status as wards of
the government and make them subject to the
privileges and responsibilities of other citizens as
rapidly as possible. Enforcement of law and
order in Indian communities would become a
state rather than a federal responsibility whenever any state legislature voted to assume jurisdiction over the Indians. Indian tribes were not
consulted in this change of federal-state roles.
This policy, aimed at "getting the government
out of the Indian business," did much to confuse
the already complex Indian problem and to divert attention from the real needs of the Indians.

In recent years groups interested in the plight
of the Indians have tried to articulate their views
and present programs for reform. Such attempts
were consolidated at the American Indian Chicago Conference, conceived by Professor Sol Tax
of the University of Chicago's Anthropology Department and financed by the University and by
grants from the Wenner-Gren and Schwartzhaupt
foundations. Nearly 100 tribes were represented
by over 450 delegates at the conference held from
June 13 to 20, 1961.

The delegates, who took a little time out for
tribal dancing, prepared a statement of purpose
that reaffirmed the rights and duties of Indians
to maintain and build upon their spiritual and
cultural values. While affirming their loyalty to
the United States, the delegates agreed that the
federal government had an obligation to help
the Indians reach full equality of educational
and economic status before ending its role as
guardian.

President John F. Kennedy had promised the
Indians a review of their problems during his
1960 Presidential campaign. To implement this
promise Secretary of the Interior Stewart L.
Udall appointed a special task force on Indian
affairs in February 1961. Philleo Nash was
chosen one of the members. The group, headed
by W. W. Keeler, an oil executive and principal
chief of the Cherokees, sought to recommend
plans for reorganizing the Bureau of Indian
Affairs.

The Acting Commissioner of Indian Affairs,
James O. Crow, accompanied the group on field
trips, and members consulted with tribal leaders
and with experts on Indian problems. The conclusions and proposals of the task force were
presented to Secretary Udall in a seventy-seven-
page report in July 1961. Members of the task
force recommended a shift in federal policy from
termination of the trust relationship towards
greater development of human and natural resources on Indian reservations. They also suggested that eligibility for special federal services
be withdrawn from Indians, "who are as competent as most non-Indians to look after their
own affairs," and that the Social Security and
Area Redevelopment Acts be applied to Indians
as well as to non-Indians. (Some forty-seven
Indian reservations were among the depressed

areas named in November 1961 as eligible for
help under the Area Redevelopment Act.) On
July 12, 1961 Secretary Udall endorsed the report
and announced that he intended to make it the
basis for future operations in the Bureau of
Indian Affairs.

On July 31, 1961 President Kennedy named
Philleo Nash Commissioner of Indian Affairs.
The $18,500-a-year post had been vacant since
January 1961; John O. Crow had acted as Commissioner. A New York *Times* editorial writer
called Nash an excellent choice, and a reporter
for the Washington *Post and Times Herald* observed that Nash was remarkably well-qualified
and the right man for the job. When Nash was
sworn into office on September 26, 1961, Secretary Udall remarked, "Give the Indians proper
development and growth on their own lands,
and termination will take of itself."

The first conference of superintendents of
Indian reservations in twenty-three years was
held in Denver, Colorado in October 1961. Addressing the conferees, Nash discussed problems
facing the Bureau of Indian Affairs, including
the need for making better use of Indian lands
and for improving vocational training, education,
and industrial development among Indians. During 1961 the Public Housing Administration
began to plan the first low-rent public housing
project for an Indian reservation, and the Bureau
of Indian Affairs made arrangements for establishing an Institute of American Indian Arts at
Santa Fe, New Mexico, where qualified Indians
could take a high school program together with
two years of advanced study in art. The Haskell
Institute in Lawrence, Kansas, founded in 1884,
is a United States government school for Indians,
which offers a high school curriculum and post-
high school vocational training courses.

Nash is a member of the American Anthropo-
logical Association, the Washington Anthropo-
logical Society, and the Society for Applied Anthropology. He belongs to the National Capital
Democratic Club, the Cosmos Club in Washington, D.C., and Theta Delta Chi. From 1945 to
1952 he served as president of the Georgetown
Day School, and he is an honorary curator of
the Milwaukee Public Museum. He is a Congregationalist.

On November 2, 1935 Philleo Nash married
Edith Rosenfels, an anthropologist. They have
two daughters, Margaret Helen (Mrs. Eric C.
Kast) and Sally. Nash, who has been characterized as a genial and persuasive man, has white
hair and hazel eyes, stands five feet six inches
tall, and weighs 200 pounds. He likes to sing
and to play the guitar—talents that he put to
use for Senator Hubert H. Humphrey's campaign
for the Presidential nomination. In the months
preceding the Democratic national convention
Nash often appeared as Humphrey's advance
man, strumming the guitar and singing campaign songs.

References

N Y Times p22 Ag 1 '61
Washington (D.C.) Post A p4 Ag 1 '61
    por
Who's Who in America, 1962-63

NICKLAUS, JACK (WILLIAM) (nĭk'lŭs)
Jan. 21, 1940- Professional golfer
Address: b. 85 E. Gay St., Columbus, Ohio;
h. 1845 Elmwood Ave., Columbus 12, Ohio

The current "golden boy" of golf, Jack Nicklaus, is regarded by many as one of the world's greatest golfers. A devotee of golf since the age of ten, he was the National Amateur champion in 1959 and 1961. Before he turned professional in late 1961 Nicklaus had been called by sportswriters the greatest amateur golfer since Bobby Jones. In June 1962 Nicklaus defeated Arnold Palmer in the United States Open tournament—one of the most important events in professional golf. A few months later he won the most lucrative top prize in golf when he defeated Palmer and Gary Player in the first World Series of Golf exhibition.

Jack William Nicklaus was born in Columbus, Ohio on January 21, 1940 to Louis Charles and Nellie Helen (Schoener) Nicklaus. His father owns a chain of drug stores in Columbus and is a former president of the Ohio Pharmacy Board. He has a younger sister, Marilyn, who recalls that he was a "great big mischief-maker" as a boy. Jack Nicklaus was introduced to golf by his father, an athlete in his own right. Having suffered an ankle injury in a volleyball game, Charles Nicklaus was ordered by his physician to walk at least two hours a day to strengthen his ankle. He decided to take up golf, and Jack went along to keep his father company. Playing for the first time when he was ten years old, Jack Nicklaus shot a 51 for nine holes, and he has steadily improved since then.

Charles Nicklaus told a writer for *Time* (June 29, 1962): "By the time Jack was twelve I couldn't handle him any more. I remember one day I hit as good a drive as I could, maybe 260 yards. I told Jack, 'If you outhit that one, I'll buy you a Cadillac convertible.' He hit his ball 25 or 30 yards past mine and I never outdrove him again." (Jack Nicklaus never forgot the promise, but settled for a Mercury convertible when he graduated from high school.)

The potentialities of twelve-year-old Jack Nicklaus were recognized by Jack Grout, then a professional at the Scioto Country Club in Columbus, who enrolled the boy in his Friday morning class for junior club members. Grout encouraged his students to hit the ball as far as they could, as a means of stretching muscles and developing power. (He felt that they could learn control and finesse later.) Nicklaus later took private lessons from Grout and became a demonstrator in his junior class.

At the age of thirteen Nicklaus shot a 69 over the 7,095-yard course at Scioto. By the time he was fourteen he had become something of a local celebrity and was being compared to Bobby Jones by sportswriters. When he played in his first National Amateur tournament in 1955, at Richmond, Virginia, Bobby Jones was on hand to watch him perform for the first time, attesting to Nicklaus' growing reputation. However, Nicklaus was so rattled by all the attention that he played far below his capabilities and was beaten in the first round of the tournament. It was one of the few times that he sagged under pressure. The following year Nicklaus won his first major

JACK NICKLAUS

tournament—the Ohio Open—from a full field of professionals. He shot a record first round of 64 and led all the way.

During his four years at Upper Arlington High School in Columbus Nicklaus played football, baseball, basketball, and golf. In 1957, when the time came for him to graduate, he received scholarship offers from a dozen colleges. "He was talking about how much this one or that one had offered him, how good a deal he could get," Charles Nicklaus remembers. "I told him to stop thinking about the fun and money and think about the education." He estimates that he has spent more than $35,000 to finance his son's pursuit of golf. "It's the most wonderful money I ever spent," he says. "I figure it's like living my life all over again. I always wanted to be champ" (*Time*, June 29, 1962).

Guided by his father's advice, Nicklaus attended Ohio State University at Columbus without benefit of a scholarship and enrolled in a pre-pharmacy course. He earned a junior license as a pharmacist and helped out in his father's stores during vacations, but he later changed his major to business administration, with an emphasis on insurance. He became a bridge addict, and as a member of Phi Gamma Delta fraternity he served as chairman of "Hell Week." Under the guidance of Ohio State golfing coach Robert Kepler, Nicklaus became an outstanding collegiate golfer, but he failed to make much progress on the national scene. Although he won the Trans-Mississippi championship and earned a prize from the United States Junior Chamber of Commerce War Memorial Scholarship Fund by winning a Jaycee junior tournament, he made a poor showing in his first National Open tournament and in the National Juniors and the National Amateur.

The turning point came in the spring of 1959, when Nicklaus was chosen for the nine-man team of American amateurs opposing a team of British amateurs in the Walker Cup matches.

(Continued next page)

NICKLAUS, JACK—*Continued*

At Muirfield, Scotland he toured the course like a veteran. He won both his matches and helped immeasurably towards the 9-3 victory achieved by the Americans. "The goal of every amateur is to make the Walker Cup team," he said shortly afterward. "Simply being selected for it gave me a new confidence in myself. 'Here I am,' I told myself, 'playing right alongside these better players. I must be on a par with them.' Then I began to demand much more of myself, and I began to play better than I ever had. The way it seems to me, in golf you're always breaking a barrier. When you bust it, you set yourself a little higher barrier and try to break that one."

Using his Walker Cup experience as a springboard, Nicklaus went on in 1959 to acquire one of the most impressive amateur records of all time. He was defeated only once in thirty matches, losing in the semifinals of the British Amateur tournament. He won the North and South championship, added the Grand Challenge Cup at Sandwich, England, and retained his Trans-Mississippi title. Playing with the professionals on their summer tour he was the top amateur in the Gleneagles, Buick, and Western open tournaments. In September 1959 Nicklaus won the National Amateur title at Broadmoor in Colorado Springs, by defeating veteran defending champion Charlie Coe at the 36th hole.

In March 1960 Nicklaus and Deane Beman won the International Men's Four-Ball title at Hollywood, Florida, and in August of that year the two men teamed up again to defeat Canada and Mexico for the Americas Cup Amateur championship at Ottawa. In June 1960 Nicklaus placed second to Palmer in the United States Open competition. His 72-hole score of 282 was the lowest ever shot by an amateur in the national Open. In October of that year Nicklaus led the United States to a one-sided victory in the World Amateur Team championship at the Merion Golf Club in Pennsylvania by weaving together rounds of 66, 67, 68, and 68 for a total score of 269—18 strokes lower than Ben Hogan's total when he won the Open at Merion in 1950. When President Dwight D. Eisenhower met Nicklaus after the World Amateur competition, he told him: "Mr. Nicklaus, at the Augusta National Golf Club, as you know, we build bridges to commemorate the records set by top players in the Masters. The way you're going, perhaps we should stop building those bridges. You look like you'll beat all the marks."

Nicklaus defeated Jim Key in March 1961 to win the Western Amateur tournament at New Orleans. He regained the United States Amateur crown in September of that year, defeating Dudley Wysong at Pebble Beach, California. In the following month, at Monterrey, Mexico, Nicklaus was again a member of a victorious team that defeated Canada and Mexico for the Americas Cup Amateur championship.

Although a few months earlier he had been determined to remain an amateur golfer while earning his living in the insurance business, Nicklaus decided in November 1961 to become a professional. "I just decided I wanted to play golf," he said. "And I owe it to my family to give them the best possible living I can." "He's

destined to become the greatest player of all times and I'm sure he never would be able to do it as an amateur," Deane Beman said, when he moved into Nicklaus' position as the world's leading amateur golfer. Nicklaus made his debut as a professional in an exhibition match at Miami on December 30, 1961, losing to Gary Player. During his first five months as a professional Nicklaus did not win any of the tournaments he entered, although he finished in the money in all seventeen of these contests.

In June 1962 Nicklaus proved that he could more than hold his own with the best American golfers in the sixty-second United States Open tournament played at the Oakmont Country Club course in Pennsylvania. He battled the formidable Arnold Palmer to a deadlock in four rounds of superb golf, and then defeated Palmer by a score of 71 to 74 in an 18-hole playoff, becoming the youngest Open champion since Bobby Jones did so in 1923 at the age of twenty-one.

In September 1962 Nicklaus competed with Arnold Palmer and Gary Player in the first World Series of Golf television exhibition at the Firestone Country Club in Akron, Ohio. He won the $50,000 first prize in the 36-hole series with a score of 135 while Palmer and Player each scored 139. Nicklaus added another victory later in the same month, when he won the Seattle Open tournament with a 72-hole score of 265.

On the course Nicklaus concentrates completely on his game. He charts his course and always knows his distance from the pin and what club to use. He can drive a ball 300 yards or more, but his drive lacks the easy, fluid motion of some other golfers. According to a writer for *Time* (June 29, 1962): "Nicklaus' swing is pure thunder. His wide, stubby-fingered hands choke the club in an old-fashioned interlocking grip, and when he swings he looks as if he might shoot in the 90's: his arms move back stiffly, his head sometimes bobs, his right knee brutally forces his left side out of the way on the downswing, and his right elbow flies away from his body. But at the moment of impact, when all that power pours into the club head, Nicklaus hits the ball as squarely and solidly as a golf ball can be hit." Nicklaus concedes that his only weakness is in his putting.

On July 23, 1960 Jack Nicklaus married Barbara Jean Bash, whom he had met at Ohio State University. They have a son, Jack William Nicklaus 2d. On his wedding day Nicklaus and three ushers played eighteen holes of golf before the afternoon ceremony. Nicklaus is six feet tall, weighs about 205 pounds, and has blue eyes and short-cropped blond hair. Although he thinks nothing of topping a spaghetti dinner with a milk shake, he watches his weight more closely now than he did as an amateur, when his girth earned him such nicknames as "Blob-o," "Whale-man" and "Ohio Fats." Relaxed and good-natured, he has never been known to lose his temper. He likes to hunt and fish and enjoys an occasional game of basketball or handball. He belongs to the Scioto Country Club and the Athletic Club of Columbus, and the La Gorce Country Club of Miami, Florida.

In addition to playing professional golf Nicklaus hopes to continue working as an insurance salesman and intends to return to Ohio State University during off-seasons to complete the work towards his degree. Nicklaus has written articles on golf for *Sports Illustrated,* and Simon and Schuster is planning to publish his instructional book on golf. Endorsements, exhibitions, and the like, assure him a substantial income in addition to his tournament earnings. His main goal, however, is not to become a millionaire, but—in his own words—"the world's greatest golfer."

References

N Y Times p29 Je 18 '62 por
Sat Eve Post 234:24+ Ap 8 '61 pors
Sports Illus 13:45+ S 12 '60 pors
Time 79:38+ Je 29 '62 pors

O'CASEY, SEAN Mar. 30, 1880- Irish playwright
Address: Flat 3, 40 Trumlands Rd., St. Marychurch, Torquay, Devon, England

For nearly forty years the doyen of Irish playwrights, Sean O'Casey, has poured his anger, compassion, whimsey, and laughter into plays about Ireland. A common laborer until he achieved dramatic success with *Juno and the Paycock* in 1924 at Dublin's Abbey Theatre, O'Casey left Ireland after the riot that attended the Abbey's production of *The Plough and the Stars* in 1926. Self-exiled in England since then, he moved at the age of sixty into a vein of experiment in fantastic comedy that includes the play *Cock-a-doodle Dandy* (1949). A continuing nuisance to that school of dramatic criticism which likes to freeze its playwrights in predictable molds, O'Casey still rambles, singing as he pleases, through the green wilds of dramatic technique, and his voice, as Robert Hogan has said, "like William Butler Yeats and good Irish whisky, improves with age."

Sean O'Casey was born John Casey in Dublin, Ireland on March 30, 1880 to Michael and Susan (Archer) Casey. He was the youngest of a large brood of children, only five of whom grew to adulthood. In a city where the Roman Catholic majority was poor and the Protestant minority prosperous, the Caseys were both poor and Protestant. Michael Casey, a religious proselytizer, earned his living as a commercial clerk. He died when Sean O'Casey was a child, bequeathing to him an independent spirit and an antagonism to pietistic Catholicism.

A sickly child with a chronic eye disease, O'Casey grew up in tenement squalor, and it marked his life and work indelibly. He went to church mostly because of maternal pressure and read the Bible partly because he liked it as literature. Confirmed in the Church of Ireland at the age of seventeen, he was for a time active in the affairs of St. Barnabas Church, teaching Sunday school and singing in the choir. He drifted away from the church in his twenties without, however, breaking a filial bond to the Reverend Edward Martin Griffin, the rector of St. Barnabas Church.

When he was about ten years old, O'Casey discovered the dramas of Shakespeare and Dion Boucicault through the amateur theatrical activi-ties of his older brother Archie. He increasingly took part in these activities, eventually making his debut with the Townsend Dramatic Group in north Dublin. By the age of fourteen he had begun to teach himself to read and write, although he experienced considerable difficulty because of his poor eyesight. From the salary he earned as a stockboy, and later as a laborer, O'Casey managed to set aside enough money to buy used books that he coveted.

During the years 1900 to 1910 O'Casey developed a number of talents. He painted and sketched, learned to play the Celtic bagpipes (he was a founder of the St. Lawrence O'Toole Pipers Band), and amused fellow members of the St. Lawrence O'Toole Club with renditions of satiric songs he had written. Many of these were published in 1918 under the titles *Songs of the Wren* and *More Songs of the Wren.* The author was listed as Sean O'Cathasaigh, evidence of O'Casey's involvement with the Irish Revival. He also learned to speak, read, and write Gaelic fluently, and he taught it in a Gaelic League slum school. The name O'Cathasaigh was anglicized to O'Casey in 1923, when the Abbey Theatre accepted his first play.

Although O'Casey was sympathetic to two major currents of his day, the revival of Irish culture and the Irish freedom movement, he dedicated his energies and time primarily to the cause of labor. His first articles were published in labor periodicals, and he was greatly influenced by James Larkin, the labor leader who inspired Irish workers to unite and fight against their shocking living and working conditions. O'Casey joined Larkin's Irish Transport and General Workers' Union, and when the union formed the Irish Citizen Army in 1913, he became its secretary. Shortly thereafter a rival group, the Irish Volunteers, whose members were nationalistic, middle-class, and largely unconcerned with the cause of labor, began to weaken the Irish Citizen Army by infiltrating its ranks and recruiting its members. O'Casey fought to preserve the strength and independence of his group, but he failed and resigned as secretary in 1914. His *Story of the Irish Citizen Army* (Maunsel, 1919) is a short history of the organization. He also wrote *The Story of Thomas Ashe* (Fergus O'Connor, 1918) about a friend who had died in the aftermath of the great nationalist uprising of 1916.

When he was in his mid-thirties, O'Casey decided to write a play that would be produced at Dublin's Abbey Theatre, which was founded by William Butler Yeats and Lady Gregory around the turn of the century. After several years, following the rejection of three one-act plays, O'Casey's first full-length play, *The Shadow of a Gunman,* was produced at the Abbey in April 1923. Together with *Juno and the Paycock,* presented in March 1924, it has been credited with reversing the Abbey's trend toward bankruptcy. Upon receiving twenty-five pounds as his share in *Juno's* financial success, O'Casey gave up his work as a laborer and, at the age of forty-four, began to live by his pen.

O'Casey's play *The Plough and the Stars,* whose title is taken from the symbols on the Irish Citizen Army flag, was first produced at the Abbey in February 1926. *The Plough and*

SEAN O'CASEY

the Stars and the two earlier plays constitute what David Krause has called in his study Sean O'Casey (1960) a tragi-comic trilogy. In his treatment of character, of Irish life, and of war O'Casey sharply disagreed with sentimental Irish patriots who envisaged Ireland as a "queen," a bright green land of pure maidens and heroic men. His personae are Dublin's poor, with all their strengths and flaws, as he knew them from experience; his women emerge as strong and realistic, his men are sometimes cowardly, sodden with drink, and given to illusions. Sex and religion are not idealized and the Irish struggles for independence are not conventionally portrayed. The heroes are not the national fighters, but the non-combatants, especially the women who must endure the chaos of war and the loss of those they love.

The blunt realism of The Plough and the Stars, which had even offended some of the actors and which drew the epithet "sewage school of drama" from some critics, so lacerated the sensibilities of Dublin audiences that a riot broke out at the theater during the fourth performance of the play. Amidst the din William Butler Yeats spoke from the stage as he had at riots attending Synge's The Playboy of the Western World years before: "You have disgraced yourselves again. . . . Dublin has once more rocked the cradle of genius. From such a scene in this theater went forth the fame of Synge. Equally the fame of O'Casey is born here tonight. This is his apotheosis."

Convinced that he could not write freely in Ireland, unhappy in the Abbey milieu, and disillusioned with the political failure of the labor cause, O'Casey moved to London after traveling there in the spring of 1926 to receive the Hawthornden Prize and 100 pounds for his play Juno and the Paycock. In London he wrote The Silver Tassie, another play that refuses to glorify or sentimentalize war. Its heroes are the suffer-

ing infantrymen of World War I. O'Casey experimented in this play by combining his primarily realistic first and third acts with an expressionistic second act in which the characters and setting lose their identities and become symbolic. This, among other considerations, prompted Yeats to reject the play for production at the Abbey. The bitter correspondence—about the nature of drama itself as much as about the play—that ensued between Yeats and O'Casey was released to newspapers by O'Casey and received wide publicity. The Silver Tassie was first presented at the Apollo Theatre in London in October 1929. A few years later Yeats and O'Casey were reconciled, and The Silver Tassie was presented at the Abbey Theatre in 1935.

"I am out to destroy the accepted naturalistic presentation of character," O'Casey told a reporter during rehearsals of Within the Gates, his first completely expressionistic play, which opened at the Royalty Theatre, London, on February 7, 1934. He was also out to destroy the facade that the "rationally functioning" British mind had erected in front of what he considered bankrupt capitalism and unchristian Christianity. The radical message carried by the symbolic Cockney characters in a depression setting drew the fire of many London critics, led by James Agate, who called the play "pretentious rubbish." But a reviewer in the London Times wrote that O'Casey's "art purges the dross from his controversy." O'Casey answered Agate and other detractors in the essays of The Flying Wasp (Macmillan, 1937). The London production of Within the Gates ended after twenty-eight performances, but a National Theatre production in America later in 1934 was more successful. O'Casey traveled to New York to assist the National Theatre production.

Except for the one-act play The End of the Beginning, presented at the Abbey Theatre in February 1937, no new plays by O'Casey were produced during the last half of the 1930's. The End of the Beginning, with another one-acter, some early verse, and four short stories, was published in Windfalls (Macmillan, 1934), which was banned in Ireland. During this decade O'Casey derived his income more from the publication of books and plays, many of which were published before production, than from the presentation of his plays.

O'Casey's next two plays, The Star Turns Red (produced in 1940) and Oak Leaves and Lavender (produced in 1947) are didactic, anti-Fascist pieces of proletarian literature, his least satisfactory from an artistic viewpoint. Red Roses for Me, produced in Dublin in 1943, takes place during the time of the 1913 Dublin strike and also sympathizes with the struggles of workers to achieve a better life. In this piece, however, O'Casey did not allow his thesis to override his characters and action. "In the ordeals and hopes of Ayamonn, a young laborer with poetic aspirations, O'Casey has crystallized his vision of the good life," David Krause wrote in Sean O'Casey. He called the play O'Casey's most autobiographical and his most lyrical and affirmative work.

O'Casey's autobiography, written in a fiction-like form with Johnny (later Sean) Casside representing O'Casey, was published in successive volumes by Macmillan in 1939, 1942, 1946, 1949,

1952, and 1954. *I Knock at the Door* and *Pictures in the Hallway*, which contain some of his most lyrical prose, cover his childhood and adolescence and young manhood, respectively. *Drums Under the Window*, covering the years 1905 to 1916, is full of his heroes of that period and of satire, fantasy, farce, and mockery directed against the politics of Dublin's Roman Catholic clergy and the blind sanctimoniousness of Dublin's Protestant clergy. *Inishfallen Fare Thee Well*, covering the crucial decade of his life beginning with the death of his mother and ending with his self-exile (1916-26), is more tragic and ironic. *Rose and Crown* spans the years 1926 to 1934 and *Sunset and Evening Star* the years 1934 to 1953. The autobiography was published in a two-volume edition, under the title *Mirror in My House*, by Macmillan in 1956. "The self-portrait that emerges from the autobiography," David Krause has written, "is that of a proud rebel with a mighty rage for life who in the midst of tragic surroundings made himself a great comic artist. That portrait is presented with . . . remarkable integrity and vitality." Portions of the autobiography have been adapted for stage reading.

Meanwhile O'Casey had embarked on his great comic cycle of plays set in imaginary Irish villages and aimed with malice lightened by fun and free of rage at English and Irish follies, and through them at more universal vanity. *Purple Dust* opened in Boston in December 1944, four years after its publication. Chronicling the misadventures of two caricatured Englishmen in Ireland, the play succeeds in bringing together a variety of comic elements, particularly farce and satire. *Cock-a-doodle Dandy*, a satiric fantasy that is O'Casey's own favorite among his plays, pits the spirit of life and joy, symbolized by the Dionysian, magic-performing Cock, against naysaying puritanical bigotry, symbolized by Father Domineer and other crawthumpers in the Irish village of Nyadnanave (Gaelic for "nest of saints"). The first production of *Cock-a-doodle Dandy* was at the People's Theatre, Newcastle-on-Tyne, England, in December 1949. It has also been presented off-Broadway and at the Edinburgh Festival.

The Bishop's Bonfire presented the same basic conflict in a motley plot that began with farce and ended with tragic melodrama. Its première at the Gaiety Theatre in Dublin in 1955 under the direction of Tyrone Guthrie was successful despite the barrage of negative criticism that came from Dublin critics even before the play opened.

The Drums of Father Ned, also a masterly blending of various comic elements, is merrier than its predecessors, although the old conflict is here (the forces of life, joy and freedom led in this instance by the spirit of a clergyman who never appears, a spirit O'Casey modeled partly upon an actual priest "exiled to Altoona, Pennsylvania"). Scheduled for presentation at the 1958 Dublin International Theatre Festival, *The Drums of Father Ned* was withdrawn by the Dublin Tostal Council. O'Casey, not to be outdone, thereupon banned all performances of his plays in Ireland until further notice. The world première of *The Drums of Father Ned* was given by the Lafayette (Indiana) Little Theater, an amateur group, in April 1959.

One-act plays by O'Casey that have been produced include *Cathleen Listens In* (1923); *Nannie's Night Out* (1924); *Pound on Demand* (1947); *Hall of Healing, Bedtime Story*, and *Time To Go*, presented in New York City in 1952; and *Figuro in the Night* and *The Moon Shines on Kylenamoe*, scheduled for production by the Greater New York Chapter of the American National Theater and Academy (ANTA) in October 1962. His plays have been published individually and in collections by Macmillan & Company Ltd., London, the Macmillan Company, New York, and St. Martin's Press. *The Green Crow*, containing his short stories and essays, was published by Braziller in 1956.

In 1927 Sean O'Casey married Eileen Carey (née Reynolds), an Irish actress whom he had met when she was playing in the first London production of *The Plough and the Stars*. They have two children, Breon and Shivaun (who is an actress). A second son, Niall Ayamonn, died in 1956. The O'Caseys lived in Totnes, Devon, England, from 1939 until 1955, when they moved to their present residence on the Devon coast.

Sean O'Casey is loose-limbed and tall. He wears thick glasses for his weak eyes, and has had to give up reading because of failing vision. For many years he has been in poor health. A believer in communism, he has never abandoned the apparel that identifies him with the working class—turtleneck sweater and cap. As in former years, he still helps his wife with the household chores. O'Casey likes to sing and is interested in painting, trees, flowers, science, and good music.

References

N Y Herald Tribune IV p1+ My 20 '62
   por
Life 26:18 Ja 16 '62 por
Hogan, Robert. The Experiments of Sean O'Casey (1960)
Krause, David. Sean O'Casey (1960)
O'Casey, Sean. Mirror in My House (1956)
Twentieth Century Authors (1942; First Supplement, 1955)
Who's Who, 1961
Who's Who in the Theatre (1961)

PICASSO, PABLO Oct. 25, 1881- Artist
Address: "La Californie," Cannes, France

> NOTE: This biography supersedes the article that appeared in *Current Biography* in 1943.

Where Pablo Picasso will rank among the masters in the history of art may remain a controversial matter for some time, but few would question his pivotal position in twentieth-century painting. Picasso is a vigorous innovator, a skillful technician, and a versatile creative genius. By re-examining and assimilating the artistic styles of the past and present he has influenced

Wide World

PABLO PICASSO

the direction of art in his own age more extensively than any other contemporary artist. Spanish-born Picasso has lived most of his life in France, where for sixty years he has created some 5,000 paintings, drawings, etchings, lithographs, sculptures, and ceramics. In every medium and in every avant-garde or classical phase of his career, his artistic production has been definitive. Because of its variety of expression as well as the vast range of human experience that it explores, his work defies categorizing.

In Picasso's global art, the characteristics of his Spanish origin are discernible in countless forms. Pablo Ruiz Picasso was born in Málaga on the southern coast of Spain on October 25, 1881, the first of three children of Maria (Picasso Lopez) and Don José Ruiz Blasco. (When he was about twenty he began signing his paintings with his mother's family name.) He had two sisters, Lola and Concepción; the younger, Concepción, died at an early age. His paternal grandfather and several other members of his father's family were amateur painters, but only his father made art his profession. Don José taught art at the school of arts and industries in Málaga and later at Da Guarda school in La Coruña, where the family moved in 1891.

Pablo Picasso, a pupil for four years at Da Guarda, also studied art with his father at home, learning to draw and paint birds, flowers, and people, in the classical tradition. Acknowledging his son's early technical excellence, the father turned over his paints and brushes to Pablo in 1894. Don José continued, however, to teach and was on the faculty of La Llonja art school in Barcelona in 1895 when his son passed in only one day a qualifying examination that a candidate was allowed a month to complete.

One of the pictures that Picasso painted at fourteen in his own Barcelona studio, *Science and Charity*—done in a realistic manner inspired by

Velásquez and other Spanish masters—won him an honorable mention award at the Exhibition of Fine Arts in Madrid in 1897. Later in the year he was admitted to the Royal Academy of Madrid, but after a few months of study there he rejoined his Bohemian friends at Barcelona's The Four Cats cabaret, where he held his first exhibition. In his passion to paint he covered the walls of the cabaret and of his friends' rooms with portraits and caricatures and he made so many sketches on paper that he had almost enough fuel for his stove.

Drawn to Paris by his interest in the impressionists and postimpressionists, Picasso made his home there in 1904. He had first visited Paris in 1900 and a year later had seen his work exhibited for the first time in that city, at Ambroise Vollard's. Berthe Weill, who had earlier bought some of his sketches, gave him an exhibition at her gallery in 1902. In Paris he had the opportunity to study the paintings of Manet, Degas, Renoir, Vuillard, Toulouse-Lautrec, Cézanne, Gauguin, and dozens of other modernists, all of whom contributed in some degree to the development of his genius.

The several phases or periods in Picasso's career, marked by a predominant color or style, do not lend themselves to exact dating. His Blue Period began when he was still living in Spain, in late 1901 or 1902. Whether or not he chose blue for reasons of economy, as he has maintained, the color suited perfectly and heightened enormously the somber mood of his classical treatment of themes such as poverty, hunger, and mental suffering that reflected his pessimistic social outlook at that time. Some examples are *Seller of Mistletoes* (1903), *La Vie* (1903), and *The Frugal Repast* (1904). In his symbolic use of blue, a negation of realistic coloring, Picasso achieved a liberation from naturalism that suggests a genuine admiration for El Greco.

By the time that Picasso had entered upon his Rose Period, about the end of 1904, he was settled in Paris, living in a Montmartre studio that a year or so later he was to share with his model Fernande Olivier. He enjoyed the stimulating friendship of a number of writers, including Max Jacob, Maurice Raynal, and André Salmon, and before long he met the poet Guillaume Apollinaire and the painters Juan Gris, Georges Braque, André Derain, and Henri Rousseau. His brighter attitude toward life, which perhaps more than the color justifies the designation Rose Period, was also encouraged by the sale of many of his paintings to the American writer Gertrude Stein and the Russian merchant Sergei Shchukin.

In its early phase the Rose Period produced a number of thematically related works dealing with acrobats, *saltimbanques,* and other circus figures, such as *The Harlequin's Family* (1905). Picasso matched his warmer tonality in coloring with a tenderness in his feeling about his subject and a corresponding delicacy of line. Toward the end of the Rose Period, in 1906, he painted his famed portrait of Gertrude Stein. When everyone told him that the portrait did not look like Gertrude Stein, Picasso replied, "Never mind, in the end she will look like the portrait."

The herald of cubism, *Les demoiselles d'Avignon*, Picasso's major work of 1907, became a landmark both in his own career and in the history of modern art. The demoiselles typify his brief Negro Period, when he shared the enthusiasm of many other Parisian artists for African wood carving. More significantly, he was stimulated by the disregard of natural form in African masks and he tried to cope in his own way, as Cézanne had done in his, with the problems of representing the third dimension on the flat surface of the picture. After his outpouring of feeling in the Blue Period, he had grown less subjective and was ready to subordinate emotion and color to matters concerned with pure form.

Picasso's search for solutions of problems in representing volume made him a leader, along with Braque, of cubism, which breaks up natural objects into geometric forms and reassembles them according to aesthetic, rather than pictorial, values. Unlike some cubists, Picasso stopped short of abstract painting. He came close to nonobjectivism in his portrait of Daniel-Henry Kahnweiler (1910), for which, however, Kahnweiler had to sit more than twenty times. *The Card Player* (1913-14) and *Vive la France* (1914) are striking examples of his work in cubism; in another, *The Roast Goose* (1913), he experimented with the cubist auxiliary devices of collage, *trompe-l'oeil*, and printed lettering. The gay and colorful *Three Musicians* (1921) climaxed his painting in strict synthetic cubism, but he continued to use cubist techniques throughout his career.

Some years earlier Picasso had returned to naturalism in a series of portrait drawings, including a study of Max Jacob (1915). It may be supposed that his renewed interest in a classical treatment of his subject, particularly of the human form, was heightened by his visit to Italy in 1917—by the art of the past that he saw there and by his introduction to the Russian ballet. He went to Rome at the persuasion of Jean Cocteau to design the scenery and costumes for Sergei Diaghilev's production of *Parade*. He later did the costumes and scenery for several other Diaghilev ballets and designed the curtain for the Cocteau-Milhaud ballet, *Le train bleu* (1924). It was during his visit to Rome that he met Olga Koklova, a Ballet Russe dancer whom he married on July 12, 1918. During that year he painted her portrait in his then prevailing classical style.

In 1925 Picasso took part in the first surrealist exhibition in Paris. Like the cubists, the surrealists break up natural objects, but unlike the cubists, they reassemble the fragments not according to deliberate and conscious design, but according to unconscious association. Although he took full advantage of the freedom it permitted for violent distortion and rearrangement of all parts of the human body, Picasso seems to have been a comparatively indifferent experimenter in surrealism during the late 1920's and the 1930's. In his etching *Minotauromachy* (1935), however, with its surrealist-like dream symbolism, he created a powerful allegory that depicts the conflict between good and evil through a number of baffling symbols and themes.

The outbreak of the Spanish Civil War in 1936 aroused Picasso from his customary political apathy, and he became a champion of the Loyalist cause. His 1937 series of etchings *Sueño y mentira de Franco (Dream and Lie of Franco)*, which used the bull and horse symbols of *Minotauromachy*, prepared the way for *Guernica* (1937), the painting named after an undefended Basque town destroyed in an air raid in April 1937. This impassioned and compassionate indictment of violence is generally regarded as Picasso's masterpiece. "Done . . . in a frenzy of rage and grief," Stuart Preston wrote in the New York *Times* (August 12, 1962), "it ranks as an apocalyptic vision in his work as well as being one of the most emotionally charged and explosive paintings in the history of art." *Guernica* was first shown at the Paris Exposition of 1937 and is now, on extended loan from the artist, in the Picasso collection of the Museum of Modern Art in New York.

Remaining in Paris during World War II, as he had done during much of World War I, Picasso painted many landscapes (several of the city) and portraits (his favorite model at this time was Dora Maar) in which he continued to work out new formal inventions while making simultaneous use of the various stylistic means that he had already mastered. Since the end of the war he has lived for the most part in the South of France. At Antibes in 1946, he painted his charming *La joie de vivre*, in which he drew upon idyllic symbols of classic mythology to express his delight in women, music, and dance. From time to time, in another way of reinterpreting the past, he has painted his own versions of old masterpieces. In 1954-55, for example, he did a series of variations on Delacroix' *The Women of Algiers*.

Book illustration continues to occupy a fairly important place in Picasso's work. Among his notable early illustrations were those for Ovid's *Métamorphoses* (1931), Aristophanes' *Lysistrata* (1934), and Buffon's *Histoire naturelle* (1942). After the war he illustrated Gongora's *Vingt poèmes* among other books. Pepe Illo's *Tauromaquia* (1959), for which he made twenty-six sugar aquatints, was praised in the London *Times Literary Supplement* (August 10, 1962) as "one of the greatest illustrated books of all time."

Many of the favorite subjects of Picasso's painting—women, musical instruments, bulls and other animals, owls and other birds—he treated also in sculpture, in which he has occasionally worked from the first decade of the century to the present. Emily Genauer (New York *Herald Tribune*, April 29, 1962) described his recent *Standing Woman* (1961) as "a six-foot-tall painted iron construction with collage of metal screen that is so airy, so inventive, so witty, so impudent as to make most young artists' experiments with collage sculpture look heavy-handed and self-conscious." Picasso's work in ceramics dates from 1946-47, when he began to learn the rudiments of the craft at a workshop in Vallauris on the French Riviera and became interested in developing new methods and techniques to take advantage, in painting ceramics, of a dimension that does not exist on the flat canvas surface.

(Continued next page)

PICASSO, PABLO—*Continued*

London honored Picasso in the summer of 1960 with an exhibit of 269 paintings at the Tate Gallery, and in New York in the spring of 1962 nine galleries joined in a comprehensive showing of more than 300 of his paintings, drawings, and sculptures. In another observance of Picasso's eightieth birthday Harper & Brothers published in 1961 *Picasso's Picassos*, containing 532 paintings, photographed by David Douglas Duncan, from the artist's private collection. During New York's 1962 celebration Picasso was awarded the Lenin Peace Prize. This was the second Lenin award (he won the first in 1950) that the Soviet Union has bestowed on Picasso, who joined the French Communist party in 1944 and whose lithograph *Peace Dove* of 1949 was used as a symbol of the Communist World Peace Congress in Paris. Picasso has never visited either Russia or the United States.

Picasso has a son, Paulo, by his first wife, Olga Koklova Picasso, from whom he was separated in 1935 but to whom he remained married until her death in 1955. During 1935, also, Picasso's daughter, Maïa, was born; her mother was his model Marie-Thérèse Walter. He and the painter François Gilot, whom he met in 1946, are the parents of a son, Claude, and a daughter, Paloma. Françoise Gilot left Picasso in 1953, reportedly complaining that she had been living not with a man, but with an historical monument. On March 2, 1961 he married thirty-five-year-old Jacqueline Roque, who had been his model since 1954. Picasso's intimate relationships have been supremely important in his work because he so often paints his emotional reactions to subjects that attract him emotionally.

The description that Janet Flanner in *Men and Monuments* (Harper, 1957) gave of Picasso at seventy-five holds true for the octogenarian: ". . . he still functions in periodic concentrations of his remorseless energy. The black mane of his youth and that 'celebrated lock of hair that fell over one eye, like a black currant,' as an early friend described it, have long since disappeared. His large head is now an impressive, almost bare cranium, from which his bright, jet-black eyes, rather like the bold eyes of a bull, watch with unabated attention. His strong, short, muscular body hardly looks middle-aged in its flesh and proportions. . . . Excessive in himself, he has always inspired hyperbole in others as the only logical method of dealing with his special case, which is that of a phenomenal man."

References

Barr, Alfred H., Jr. Picasso: Fifty Years of His Art (1946)
Boeck, Wilhelm and Sabartés, Jaime. Picasso (1955)
Elgar, Frank. Picasso (1956)
Flanner, Janet. Men and Monuments (1957)
Penrose, Roland. Picasso: His Life and Work (1958)
Raynal, Maurice. Picasso (1953)
Who's Who, 1962
Who's Who in France, 1959-60

POMPIDOU, GEORGES (JEAN RAYMOND) (pōm'pē-dōō) July 5, 1911 Premier of France; banker

Address: h. 24 quai de Bethune, Paris 4ᵉ, France

> BULLETIN: The French National Assembly forced Pompidou to submit his resignation on October 6, 1962.

When in 1960 the Algerian nationalists demanded proof of President Charles de Gaulle's sincerity before entering peace talks that would end the Algerian struggle for independence, the President of France said: "I will send them Pompidou. His presence will be my signature." Today, as Premier of France, Georges Pompidou is more than ever de Gaulle's "signature." Although the former teacher and general director of the banking house of Rothschild had never held a seat in Parliament or any other elective post, there are few men closer than he to the President of France. The two men, who have been close friends since 1944, resemble each other both intellectually and morally and see eye-to-eye on almost every problem concerning France's future. On April 14, 1962 Pompidou was called on by de Gaulle to form the second government of the Fifth Republic of France, replacing Michel Debré as Premier.

Georges Jean Raymond Pompidou, the son of Léon and Marie-Louise (Chavagnac) Pompidou, was born on July 5, 1911 in the town of Montboudif, department of Cantal, in the mountainous Auvergne region of south-central France. His father was a professor of Spanish at the University of Clermont, and his sister and brother-in-law are in the teaching profession. Pompidou received his secondary education at the Lycée d'Albi and at the Lycée Louis le Grand in Paris. He was known as a brilliant student, and he won first prize in the Concours Général, a grand competition for the intellectual elite of all of France's lycées.

For his higher education Pompidou entered the country's top school of literary studies, École Normale Supérieure, from which the cream of the French teaching profession is recruited. After winning a first prize in Greek, he was graduated an *agrégé* in literature. He then attended, and received a diploma from, the École Libre des Sciences Politiques, a school for administrators. Pompidou began his teaching career as a professor of literature at the lycée in Marseilles, and by the outbreak of World War II he was teaching at the Lycée Henri IV in Paris.

From 1939 until the fall of France in 1940 Pompidou served as an infantry lieutenant in the French army, and during the German occupation of Paris he was active in the resistance movement. When General Charles de Gaulle set up his provisional government of France in 1944, Pompidou joined his staff as advisor on information and education policies. In the same year he served on de Gaulle's mission to Moscow. The two men became close friends, and until de Gaulle went into temporary retirement in January 1946 Pompidou was his first assistant. From 1946 until 1954 Pompidou served on the Council of State, France's top judicial body. He also was deputy director-general of tourism from 1946 to 1949. He received a diploma from the

Centre des Hautes Études Administratives in 1947.

In 1954 Pompidou joined the staff of the investment bank of Rothschild Frères, where he soon rose to the position of general director. During de Gaulle's twelve-year retirement Pompidou kept in close touch with the general at his country estate at Colombey, helping de Gaulle in the production of his memoirs, collecting documents and archive materials, and acting as his negotiator with Paris printing firms.

When de Gaulle emerged from retirement in June 1958 and returned to power as Premier, he appointed Pompidou chief of cabinet. As de Gaulle's cabinet director Pompidou was one of the few men who had the privilege of disputing the general's decisions. In January 1959, after de Gaulle had taken office as President of France and after the difficult tasks of organizing the newly established Fifth Republic had been completed, Pompidou returned to private life and resumed his duties as director of the Rothschild bank. Later in the year President de Gaulle appointed Pompidou to serve as a member of the Constitutional Council for a nine-year term of office. Under the constitution of the Fifth Republic, the council is one of the three governmental institutions, together with the two houses of Parliament, that decide the constitutionality of French legislation.

While serving on the Council, Pompidou also remained President de Gaulle's confidant and close friend. He was entrusted with several confidential missions, including the job of making the first secret contacts with the Algerian Nationalist rebel regime (FLN) in Switzerland in 1960. He prepared the basis for the truce negotiations with the FLN and held talks with FLN leaders at Switzerland and Tunisia in 1961. Shortly after his role in the negotiations became known, a plastic bomb—apparently planted by right-wing extremists—was exploded near the headquarters of the Rothschild bank, where his office was located.

On April 8, 1962 the people of France overwhelmingly approved President de Gaulle's Algerian peace settlement in a national referendum. The cease-fire agreement with the FLN won 90.7 percent of the vote. Less than a week later Premier Michel Debré resigned after serving three years and three months in the Premiership —the longest in French republican history. (Under the constitution of the Fifth Republic the Premier is directly responsible to the President rather than to Parliament, and thus governments are far more stable than had been the case in the Fourth Republic.) Debré resigned partly because of the tensions of office, and partly because he differed with de Gaulle on the strategy of calling elections.

President de Gaulle called upon Georges Pompidou to form the second government of the Fifth Republic on April 14, 1962. Upon his appointment an editorial in the New York *Times* (April 16, 1962) observed: "The new Premier is virtually unknown politically, and his banking connections are not the normal road to popularity or public office in France. His strength is that he has the full confidence of President de Gaulle, whose intimate, faithful and competent associate he had been for many years."

French Embassy, Press & Inf. Division

GEORGES POMPIDOU

Pompidou is the first civilian in modern French history to become Premier without any parliamentary experience.

Pompidou completed his cabinet selections on April 15, 1962. His cabinet was substantially the same as that of his predecessor and his principal ministries remained largely unchanged. He retained fifteen of the twenty-two ministers and four of the seven secretaries of state of the Debré government. On April 26, 1962 Premier Pompidou made his first appearance before the National Assembly. In a thirty-five-minute address covering foreign and domestic policy, he promised to "end violence in Algeria by every available means" and pointed out that France's most urgent problem was to break the hold of the right-wing terrorists in Algeria. He also emphasized a program to raise living standards, speed industrial expansion, and increase financial stability.

Reflecting much of de Gaulle's thinking in his speech, Pompidou pointed out that his government intended to go ahead with plans to modernize the French Army, including "indispensable" atomic and space programs. He also hinted at de Gaulle's determination to win a greater voice in establishing Allied policies. He indicated that France would continue to work for changes in the North Atlantic Treaty Organization to give France more influence in its administration, and he said that with equal rights France would remain a "sure, faithful" ally of the West. Pompidou received a vote of confidence of 259 to 128, with 119 abstentions. This is the lowest vote of approval received by a Premier since de Gaulle became President, and it seems to indicate increasing dissatisfaction with de Gaulle's broad presidential powers. Pompidou's support comes mainly from the Gaullist Union for the New Republic (UNR) and the Roman Catholic Popular Republican Movement

POMPIDOU, GEORGES—*Continued*

(MRP). He is opposed by the extreme right-wing elements because of his adherence to de Gaulle's conciliatory policy toward Algeria, and by the parties of the left—notably the Communists—because of his background in banking.

Pompidou faced his first cabinet crisis on May 16, 1962, when five ministers resigned in protest against President de Gaulle's attack, at a news conference, on the concept of a politically integrated Europe. The five were members of the MRP, which had long championed the idea of an integrated, supranational Europe as opposed to de Gaulle's proposals for a loose confederation of states whose sovereignty would be undiminished. Pompidou subsequently appointed four new ministers and personally took over the Ministry of Territorial Planning, which had previously been headed by Maurice Schumann. Like Pompidou, most of the ministers in the new cabinet are not politicians, but administrators and technicians loyal to de Gaulle.

Among the problems facing Premier Pompidou following the Algerian settlement was the threat of widespread labor disputes. In May 1962 Pompidou met with trade union leaders in an effort to forestall a series of threatened strikes, and in July Pompidou's cabinet streamlined and simplified the national defense organization as a result of the end of the Algerian war. The cabinet also approved a bill, to be submitted to Parliament, recognizing the status of conscientious objectors. Later in the same month Pompidou staked the life of his government on the passage of a bill for appropriations to build a nuclear striking force for France. The bill was subsequently passed by the National Assembly and a motion of censure by the left opposition failed to receive sufficient support for consideration.

On October 30, 1935 Georges Pompidou married Claude Cahour, the daughter of a Brittany physician. They have one son, Alain, who is a student of medicine. A moderately heavy-set man of medium height, Pompidou has graying black hair, a prominent nose, and heavy black eyebrows that accent his sparkling blue eyes. A chain-smoker of cigarettes, he generally appears reserved and reflective, although on occasion he has been known to be assertive in his manner and caustic in his wit. He serves on the boards of directors of several business organizations, including railroad companies. He is an officer of the Legion of Honor.

In addition to his preoccupation with business and governmental affairs Pompidou continues to cultivate his literary interests. In recent years he has published several literary works, including a study of Jean Baptiste Racine's *Brittannicus*, and studies of Hippolyte Taine and André Malraux. He is also the editor of an anthology of French poetry, published in 1961. His favorite poet is Charles Baudelaire. Pompidou speaks English fluently and is familiar with English literature. He is enthusiastic about all forms of art, particularly music, sculpture, and modern painting. The library of his Paris apartment contains thousands of books, mostly in belles-lettres. Although he is not a sportsman he likes the beach and the sea and occasionally goes sailing. He also enjoys cultivating roses in the garden of his country house in the outskirts of Paris.

References

> N Y Herald Tribune p4 Ap 15 '62 por
> N Y Post Mag p4 Ap 15 '62 por
> N Y Times p10 Ap 16 '62 por
> New Yorker 38:151+ Ap 28 '62; 38:146
>   My 12 '62
> Newsweek 59:41 Ap 23 '62 por
> International Who's Who, 1961-62
> Who's Who in France, 1961-62

SOUVANNA PHOUMA, PRINCE OF LAOS
(soo-vän'á poo'má) Oct. 7, 1901- Premier of Laos

Address: Domaine du Nongthévada, Vientiane, Laos

A "troika" government, which represents the pro-Communist, neutralist, and right-wing royalist elements of the Kingdom of Laos, is headed by the neutralist Premier Prince Souvanna Phouma, who took office on June 22, 1962, succeeding the rightist Prince Boun Oum. Widely regarded as the one man who could forge unity among the divergent Laotian factions, Souvanna Phouma is serving for the fourth time in the Premiership under the constitutional monarchy in the kingdom of the tinkling temple bells.

The Kingdom of Laos came under French protection in 1893 and was one of the states that formed the Indo-Chinese Union in 1899. With the growth of nationalism following the Japanese occupation of World War II Laos became an independent sovereign state as a result of treaties with France in 1949 and 1953. It was admitted to the United Nations in December 1955. Bounded in the north by Chinese territory, in the south by Cambodia, in the east by Vietnam, and in the west by Thailand and Burma, Laos has in recent years been a battleground in the struggle between pro-Communist and anti-Communist forces in Southeast Asia. As Premier, Souvanna Phouma seeks to maintain the freedom, independence, and neutrality of Laos in accordance with the international neutralization agreement signed in Geneva in July 1962.

Tiao Souvanna Phouma (Tiao is the Laotian term for Prince) was born in the royal capital of Luangprabang in Laos on October 7, 1901. One of five half-brothers, he is a son of the much-married Prince Ouphat Bounkhong, the viceroy of the Kingdom of Luangprabang, and of Princess Thongsy. He is a nephew of the late King Sisavang Vong. Souvanna Phouma received his early education at French schools in Hanoi (now the capital of North Vietnam), where he attended the Collège Paul-Bert and the Lycée Albert Sarraut. For his higher education he was sent to France. He received the diploma of engineer-architect from the École Spéciale des Travaux Publics et du Bâtiment of the University of Paris, and the diploma of engineer-electrician from the Institut Électrotechnique of the University of Grenoble. In 1931 he returned to his homeland and entered the Public Works Service of Indo-China.

From 1931 to 1940 Souvanna Phouma worked with the Bureau of Architecture, a division of the Public Works Service, in Vientiane, in the southern part of Laos. He was chief of the bureau from 1932 to 1935, and for a time he was director of the water and electrical services of the city. Under the auspices of the French School of the Far East, he also directed the restoration of Vat Phakeo in Vientiane. He served as subdivisional engineer of public works at Phoukhoun in 1940-41 and at Luangprabang from 1941 to 1944. During 1944-45 he was the chief engineer of the technical bureau of the territorial division of public works at Vientiane, holding the title of principal engineer of the first class with the Ministry of Public Works of Indo-China.

Following the end of World War II and the surrender of Japan Souvanna Phouma, in co-operation with his elder half-brother, Prince Pethsarath, and his younger half-brother, Prince Souphanouvong, initiated a Lao-issarak or "free Laos" movement. King Sisavang Vong was placed under house arrest for having declared allegiance to France and for having supported the restoration of Indo-China to France. Prince Souvanna Phouma briefly became Prime Minister in a provisional government of a free Laos that had been established under Chinese auspices.

When French forces returned to Laos in 1946 and reasserted control over the state, Souvanna Phouma and other members of the Lao-issarak movement went into exile in Thailand. A Franco-Laotian *modus vivendi* was signed in August 1946, and in May 1947 a constitution was promulgated by King Sisavang Vong. After France had granted Laos the status of an independent state within the French Union under a treaty signed in Paris in July 1949, Souvanna Phouma returned from exile and offered his services to the royal government. From February 1950 until November 1951 he served as minister of public works, and of posts, telecommunications, and planning. Between 1951 and 1954 he was Premier and president of the council of ministers, as well as minister of posts, telecommunications, planning, and information.

Meanwhile, Souvanna Phouma's half-brother Prince Souphanouvong, who had broken with the Lao-issarak in 1949, organized the pro-Communist Pathet Lao forces with the aid of Ho Chi Minh, the Communist leader of Vietminh forces from the neighboring state of Vietnam. In 1953 the Vietminh forces, aided by the Pathet Lao, staged several attacks upon Laos. In an "appeal to the conscience and judgment of all the free nations," on December 25, 1953, Premier Souvanna Phouma denounced the "odious aggression" and imperialism of the invading forces, and their efforts to "impose the Communist ideology upon a people which . . . will always refuse it." In early 1954 he scorned Vietminh pretensions to "liberate" Laos from French colonialism, pointing out that on the basis of a treaty with France, signed in October 1953, Laos was now a completely independent country within the French Union. He noted that the Pathet Lao regime, which had its center in northeast Laos, was of little importance and without prestige in Laos.

SOUVANNA PHOUMA, PRINCE OF LAOS

In 1954 France relinquished all control over Indo-China. The agreements signed at Geneva in July 1954 provided for the independence, sovereignty, and territorial integrity of the three Indo-Chinese states: Laos, Vietnam (divided into a northern Communist and a southern pro-Western regime), and Cambodia. An international control commission was established to make certain that the terms of the agreements were carried out. From October 1954 until November 1955 Souvanna Phouma served as deputy premier and as minister of national defense and war veterans. As acting Premier in late 1955 he was concerned with the breach of the cease-fire on the part of the Pathet Lao forces, but expressed the view that these insurgent forces could easily be held in check.

After an earlier unsuccessful attempt to form a government Souvanna Phouma was voted into office as Premier on March 21, 1956. (He retained the post of minister of national defense and war veterans, and added the ministries of foreign affairs and information.) In his investiture speech he pledged opposition to foreign interference in the internal affairs of Laos and promised a five-year economic and agricultural program. After continued negotiations between Souvanna Phouma and Souphanouvong the two half-brothers issued a joint communiqué in August 1956, expressing their intentions to end all hostilities between their respective parties. The two provinces held by the Pathet Lao were to revert to the control of the royal government, and Pathet Lao military forces were to come under the command of the crown. It was also agreed that Laos, in accordance with the Geneva agreements, would not join any military alliances or allow foreign military bases on its territory.

On visits to Communist China and North Vietnam in August 1956 Souvanna Phouma repeated his country's intention to adhere to a policy of neutrality, but declared that Laos was

SOUVANNA PHOUMA, PRINCE OF LAOS
—Continued

not ready to establish diplomatic or economic relations with either country. Further negotiations with Souphanouvong (who, Souvanna Phouma maintained, was never a Communist, but only a "misled patriot") resulted in a pact in November 1957 providing for a "national union" government, which was subsequently given unanimous approval by the National Assembly. The agreement provided for integration of part of the Pathet Lao into the government's forces, and the inclusion of two Pathet Lao leaders (one of them Souphanouvong) in the cabinet. In January 1958 Souvanna Phouma visited the United States to assure Americans of Laos' friendship for the West and to help put United States aid to Laos on a firmer footing.

When in the elections of May 1958 the pro-Communist elements showed increasing strength, Souvanna Phouma was forced to resign and a new anti-Communist coalition government, headed by Phoui Sananikone, was formed. Souvanna Phouma was named Ambassador to France and subsequently also became Laotian Ambassador to Italy. He returned to Laos to become president of the National Assembly in May 1960. A military coup by Captain Kong Le in August 1960 brought Souvanna Phouma back into power as Premier and minister of defense and of foreign affairs, in an effort to restore a neutralist policy. Denying any intention to follow a pro-Communist policy, Souvanna Phouma said in a speech on October 2, 1960 that he would respect Communism in other countries but would never allow it to rule in Laos, because it was incompatible with the traditions of the Laotian people and with the Buddhist religion.

In December 1960, following a short-lived leftist coup, which forced Souvanna Phouma into exile in Cambodia, control of the government was taken over by American-supported rightist forces led by General Phoumi Nosavan. The United States recognized the new pro-Western government of Prince Boun Oum, while the Soviet Union and Communist China continued to recognize Souvanna Phouma as the legal Premier. In an interview with a New York *Times* correspondent in Cambodia on January 19, 1961 Souvanna Phouma charged that the United States government had betrayed his neutralist regime and was responsible for the continuing bloodshed. In the following month he conferred with Pathet Lao rebel leaders, and in March 1961 he reached an agreement in principle with General Phoumi Nosavan, representing the Boun Oum government, on joint efforts to restore peace and neutrality in Laos.

In March and April of 1961 Souvanna Phouma toured world capitals, including Paris, London, New Delhi, Cairo, and Moscow, and gained considerable support for his position. He cancelled a planned visit to the United States, because he had been informed that President Kennedy would see him only as a private citizen, and not by formal appointment. Nevertheless he praised the Kennedy administration for its support of a neutral Laos as constituting a significant change from previous American policies, although he criticized what he regarded as undue intervention on the part of the United States in the affairs of

Laos. (At their meeting in Vienna in June 1962 President Kennedy and Soviet Premier Khrushchev both endorsed the concept of a neutral and independent Laos.) While visiting New Delhi Souvanna Phouma talked with United States Ambassador-at-Large, W. Averell Harriman, who reported to President Kennedy on March 29, 1961 that the Prince was an important factor in Laos, and that he was one of the personalities who would have to be dealt with if a Laotian settlement was to be achieved.

Amid continued civil strife between pro-Communist and right-wing government forces in Laos a new conference of fourteen nations opened in Geneva on May 16, 1961 to determine the future of Laos. On October 18, 1961, after extensive negotiations among the representatives of the contending factions in Laos, King Savang Vatthana designated Souvanna Phouma to head a coalition government, once an agreement was reached on the composition of a coalition cabinet. Although all three factions agreed on the Premiership of Souvanna Phouma, the dispute over the composition of the coalition cabinet dragged on for several months. Finally, on June 22, 1962, Souvanna Phouma and his eighteen cabinet members were sworn into office in a Buddhist ceremony at Vientiane. In his inaugural address the Premier outlined a projected policy of neutrality and declared that Laos would base its foreign policy on the "five principles" of peaceful co-existence established by the Asian neutralist movement. Souvanna Phouma also took personal control of the ministry of defense. The new coalition cabinet formally took over control of the government on August 27, 1962.

At Geneva a fourteen-nation agreement was signed on July 23, 1962, establishing the terms for safeguarding the neutrality of Laos and providing for the withdrawal of all foreign forces from the country. On a visit to the United States in late July 1962 Souvanna Phouma told President Kennedy that he hoped that Laos "will be able to follow in the footsteps of Austria," and predicted that "in a few years we will see a Laos which will be neutral and ready to do its bit for the peace of the world."

Prince Souvanna Phouma is a commander of the Legion of Honor of France. His decorations include the Grand Cross of a Million Elephants and the White Parasol of Laos, and he also holds the Grand Cross of the Order of the White Elephant of Thailand. He is an honorary member of the Rotary Club of Vientiane. In 1956-57 he attended the eleventh session of the United Nations General Assembly in New York City. He is the leader of the National Progressive party of Laos.

Prince Souvanna Phouma was married on August 2, 1933 to Aline-Claire Allard, who was born to a French father and Laotian mother. They have four children: Moune Anne-Marie (the wife of Count Hubert de Germiny), Mangkra Georges, Kinda Aliette, and Panya Alain. All of the children have been educated in France. Souvanna Phouma is a devout Buddhist, although his wife and children are Roman Catholics. He is fluent in French but speaks little English. Described as "a pipe-smoking, English country squire-type," he is of medium height and slightly heavy-set, and is said to look twenty years younger than he is. He enjoys hunting, gardening, and relaxing at his estate, Mong Thevada, on the Mekong River near Vientiane. Although he usually wears Western clothes, for ceremonial occasions he sometimes wears a native costume. His pleasant and charming manners are said by diplomats to cover a shrewd mind.

References

N Y Herald Tribune p14 O 9 '61
N Y Times p14 Ag 16 '60 por
Asia Who's Who (1960)
International Who's Who, 1961-62
International Year Book and Statesmen's Who's Who, 1962
Who's Who in America, 1962-63
Who's Who in France, 1959-60

STEACIE, E(DGAR) W(ILLIAM) R(ICHARD) Dec. 25, 1900-Aug. 28, 1962 Physical chemist; president of the Canadian National Research Council, 1952-62, and of the International Council of Scientific Unions, 1961-62. See *Current Biography* (January) 1953.

Obituary

N Y Times p29 Ag 29 '62

STEFANSSON, VILHJALMUR Nov. 3, 1879-Aug. 26, 1962 Explorer of, and leading authority on, the Arctic; wrote twenty-four books and many articles on this region. See *Current Biography* (October) 1942.

Obituary

N Y Times p1+ Ag 27 '62

STUART, J(OHN) LEIGHTON June 24, 1876-Sept. 19, 1962 Former United States Ambassador to China (1946-49); ordained Presbyterian minister, served most of his life as missionary and educator in China. See *Current Biography* (October) 1946.

Obituary

N Y Times p33 S 20 '62

CURRENT BIOGRAPHY—VOL. 23. NOS. 1-10

This is the index to the January-November 1962 issues. For the index to the 1961 biographies, see December 1961 issue or 1961 Yearbook. For the index to 1940-1950 biographies, see 1950 Yearbook. For 1951-1960 index, see 1960 Yearbook.

Corea, Sir (George) Claude (Stanley) obit Nov 62
Coward, Noel (Pierce) Mar 62

Dalton, (Edward) Hugh (John Neale) Dalton, Baron obit Apr 62
Darling, Jay Norwood obit Mar 62
Davies, Clement (Edward) obit May 62
Davis, Miles (Dewey, Jr.) Jun 62
Day, Dorothy May 62
Day, J(ames) Edward May 62
Dean, H(enry) Trendley obit Jul 62
Dearborn, Ned H(arland) obit Oct 62
Delaney, Shelagh Apr 62
Del Castillo (del Rey), Antonio (Cánovas) See Castillo (del Rey), A. Sep 62
Dickerson, Nancy Hanschman See Hanschman, N. Sep 62
Dickson, (Horatio Henry) Lovat Sep 62
Dobrynin, Anatoly F(edorovich) Sep 62
Dobzhansky, Theodosius (Grigorievich) Sep 62
Downey, Sheridan obit Jan 62
Drozniak, Edward Jul 62
Dryfoos, Orvil E(ugene) Jan 62
Dubuffet, Jean Jul 62
Duffy, Edmund obit Nov 62
Duke, Angier Biddle Feb 62
Dulles, Eleanor Lansing Sep 62
Dunham, Franklin obit Jan 62
Dworshak, Henry C(larence) obit Oct 62

Eady, Sir (Crawfurd) Wilfrid (Griffin) obit Feb 62
Eddy, Manton S(prague) obit Jun 62
Edwards, Vincent Oct 62
Einaudi, Luigi obit Jan 62
Eisler, Hanns obit Nov 62
Eklund, (Arne) Sigvard Jul 62
Eliot, T(homas) S(tearns) Oct 62
Ellis, Elmer Jul 62
Elvehjem, C(onrad) A(rnold) obit Oct 62

Fairless, Benjamin F(ranklin) obit Feb 62
Faulkner, William obit Sep 62
Ferguson, Elsie obit Jan 62
Ferriss, Hugh obit Mar 62
Fielding, Gabriel Feb 62
Fitch, Robert Elliot Apr 62
Fleming, Sam(uel) M. Jun 62
Foerster, Friedrich Wilhelm Jul 62
Folkers, Karl (August) Oct 62
Ford, Edward Charles See Ford, W. Apr 62
Ford, Whitey Apr 62

Forrester, Maureen (Kathleen Stewart) Jul 62
Francis, Connie Jul 62
Frische, Carl A(lfred) Oct 62
Fuchs, Joseph (Philip) Oct 62

Gardiner, James Garfield obit Mar 62
Gavin, John Sep 62
Gilmore, Voit Feb 62
Glenn, John H(erschel), Jr. Jun 62
Goodman, Benny Oct 62
Goodspeed, Edgar J(ohnson) obit Mar 62
Goossens, Sir Eugene obit Sep 62
Gordon, Lincoln Feb 62
Goulart, João (Belchior Marques) Sep 62
Goulet, Robert (Gerard) Sep 62
Gove, Philip B(abcock) Oct 62
Graham, John Oct 62
Grant, Gordon (Hope) obit Jul 62
Greenebaum, Leon C(harles) Jan 62
Gregory, Dick Jun 62
Grimes, Tammy (Lee) Jul 62
Guggenheim, Peggy Oct 62
Guggenheimer, Mrs. Charles S. See Guggenheimer, M. Oct 62
Guggenheimer, Minnie Oct 62
Guinzburg, Harold K(leinert) obit Jan 62
Guion, Connie M(yers) Feb 62

Hall, Peter (Reginald Frederick) Feb 62
Hammond, John Hays, Jr. Jul 62
Hanschman, Nancy (Conners) Sep 62
Hansen, Carl F(rancis) Oct 62
Hardenbrook, Donald J(ohnson) Jul 62
Hargrave, Thomas J(ean) obit Apr 62
Harris, Harwell Hamilton Jan 62
Harrison, James L(erlie) Oct 62
Hart, Moss obit Feb 62
Hartigan, Grace Sep 62
Hartle, Russell P(eter) obit Jan 62
Hayakawa, Sessue Sep 62
Head, Matthew See Canaday, J. May 62
Heath, Edward (Richard George) Oct 62
Heineman, Ben W(alter) Jan 62
Herbster, Ben M(ohr) Jul 62
Hesse, Hermann biog Oct 62 obit Oct 62
Hesselgren, Kerstin obit Oct 62
Hester, James M(cNaughton) Jun 62
Hillyer, Robert Silliman obit Feb 62
Hocking, William Ernest Mar 62

Hodes, Henry I(rving) obit Apr 62
Hodges, Gil(bert Ray) Oct 62
Hofstadter, Robert Oct 62
Holman, Eugene obit Oct 62
Holt, Isabella obit May 62
Houk, Ralph (George) Jul 62
Houle, Cyril O(rvin) May 62
Howe, Gordie Mar 62
Howe, Gordon See Howe, Gordie Mar 62
Hu Shih obit Apr 62
Hubbard, Bernard (Rosencrans) obit Jul 62
Hughes, Richard J(oseph) Jul 62
Husing, Ted obit Oct 62

Ives, Irving M(cNeil) obit Apr 62

Jacobson, Leon Orris Oct 62
John, Augustus (Edwin) obit Jan 62
Johnson, Harold Ogden obit Apr 62

Kahn, Herman Oct 62
Katsh, Abraham I(saac) Mar 62
Kay, Hershy Mar 62
Keldysh, Mstislav (Vsevolodovich) Feb 62
Kennelly, Martin H(enry) obit Jan 62
Khouri, Faris el- obit Feb 62
Kindelberger, J(ames) H(oward) obit Oct 62
Kingman, Dong (Moy Shu) Oct 62
Kiplinger, W(illard) M(onroe) Jan 62
Kirk, Russell (Amos) Sep 62
Klahre, Ethel S(usan) May 62
Kobak, Edgar obit Jul 62
Koestler, Arthur Jan 62
Korth, Fred (H.) Jul 62
Kovacs, Ernie obit Mar 62
Krag, Jens Otto Oct 62
Kreisler, Fritz obit Mar 62

Larson, Leonard W(infield) May 62
Lefèvre, Théo(dore Joseph Albéric Marie) Jun 62
Lehmann, Inge Nov 62
Lewis, Jerry Nov 62
Lewis, John (Aaron) Jan 62
Lilly, John C(unningham) Nov 62
Lindsay, John V(liet) Nov 62
Lipchitz, Jacques Apr 62
Lippmann, Walter Nov 62
Lober, Georg (John) obit Feb 62
Loeb, James (Isaac), Jr. Jan 62
Louw, Eric H(endrik) Mar 62
Love, J(ames) Spencer obit Mar 62
Luhan, Mabel Dodge obit Oct 62
Luthuli, Albert John Feb 62

Macapagal, Diosdado Nov 62
McCarthy, Clem obit Jul 62
McClintic, Guthrie obit Jan 62
McConnell, F(owler) B(eery) obit Feb 62
McCormack, John W(illiam) Apr 62
McCormick, Myron obit Oct 62
McCracken, Joan obit Jan 62
McNeely, Eugene J(ohnson) Nov 62
McSwigan, Marie obit Sep 62
Macy, John W(illiams), Jr. Jan 62
Mao Tse-tung May 62
Marais, Jean Apr 62
Margai, Sir Milton (Augustus Strieby) Feb 62
Marks, Simon, 1st Baron Nov 62
Martin, Edmund F(ible) Jan 62
Marvel, Mrs. Archie D. Apr 62
Marvel, Elizabeth Newell See Marvel, Mrs. A. D. Apr 62
Meerloo, Joost A(braham) M(aurits) Jan 62
Mellers, Wilfrid (Howard) Feb 62
Meštrović, Ivan obit Mar 62
Miller, Harry W(illis) Mar 62
Miller, William E(dward) Feb 62
Monroe, Marilyn obit Oct 62
Moore, Charlotte Emma See Sitterly, C. M. Jan 62
Morison, Samuel Eliot Sep 62
Morse, Robert (Alan) Nov 62
Moses, Anna Mary Robertson obit Feb 62
Mössbauer, Rudolf L(udwig) May 62
Motherwell, Robert (Burns, 3d) Nov 62
Mowrer, Edgar Ansel Jul 62
Muench, Aloisius (Joseph), Cardinal obit Apr 62
Murphy, (Eleanor) Patricia Apr 62

Nash, Philleo Nov 62
Nestingen, Ivan A(rnold) Mar 62
Newhart, Bob Mar 62
Nicklaus, Jack (William) Nov 62
Nitze, Paul H(enry) Feb 62

O'Casey, Sean Nov 62
Ochoa, Severo Jun 62
Ogburn, Charlton obit Apr 62
Olav V, King of Norway Jan 62
Osgood, Charles E(gerton) Apr 62
Ozbirn, Catharine (Freeman) See Ozbirn, Mrs. E. L. Jan 62
Ozbirn, Mrs. E. Lee Jan 62

Page, Ruth Jun 62
Parker, Cola G(odden) obit Sep 62

Peden, Katherine (Graham) May 62
Petri, Egon obit Jul 62
Pevsner, Antoine obit Jun 62
Picasso, Pablo Nov 62
Piccard, Auguste obit May 62
Pompidou, Georges (Jean Raymond) Nov 62
Portinari, Candido obit Mar 62

Rabaut, Louis Charles obit Jan 62
Ramírez, Pedro P(ablo) obit Sep 62
Randolph, Jennings Jan 62
Rayburn, Sam(uel Taliaferro) obit Jan 62
Read, Sir Herbert (Edward) Mar 62
Reischauer, Edwin O(ldfather) May 62
Reybold, Eugene obit Jan 62
Rivers, Thomas M(ilton) obit Jul 62
Robinson, Spottswood W(illiam), 3d Mar 62
Rogers, Frank B(radway) Jun 62
Rogers, Rutherford David Jun 62
Rose, (Iain) Murray Jun 62
Russell, Donald J(oseph) May 62
Russell, James S(argent) Jan 62

Sandström, (Alfred) Emil (Fredrik) obit Sep 62
Satterfield, John C(reighton) Jul 62
Savage, Augusta (Christine) obit May 62
Schoeppel, Andrew F. obit Mar 62
Scofield, Paul Mar 62
Senghor, Léopold Sédar Mar 62
Shirer, William L(awrence) May 62
Shotton, Burt(on Edwin) obit Oct 62
Shurlock, Geoffrey M. Jan 62
Sitterly, Mrs. Bancroft Walker See Sitterly, C. M. Jan 62
Sitterly, Charlotte Moore Jan 62
Slocum, (Manly) Harvey obit Jan 62
Smith, Margaret (Madeline) Chase Mar 62
Souvanna Phouma, Prince of Laos Nov 62
Spahn, Warren (Edward) May 62
Speicher, Eugene (Edward) obit Jul 62
Spottswood, Stephen Gill Apr 62
Steacie, E(dgar) W(illiam) R(ichard) obit Nov 62
Stefansson, Vilhjalmur obit Nov 62
Stelle, John obit Sep 62
Stikker, Dirk U(ipko) Feb 62
Stokes, Anson Phelps, Jr. Jul 62
Stuart, J(ohn) Leighton obit Nov 62

Suggs, Louise Jan 62
Sunderland, Thomas E(lbert) Apr 62
Swann, W(illiam) F(rancis) G(ray) obit Mar 62
Swift, Harold H(iggins) obit Sep 62
Switzer, Mary E(lizabeth) Jan 62

Taylor, A(lbert) Hoyt obit Jan 62
Teagle, Walter C(lark) obit Feb 62
Thant, U Feb 62
Thomas, Norman (Mattoon) Jul 62
Thurber, James obit Jan 62
Tillinghast, Charles C(arpenter), Jr. Feb 62
Tobias, Channing H(eggie) obit Jan 62
Turner, Ewald (Walter) May 62

Unitas, John Feb 62

Vandiver, S(amuel) Ernest Jul 62
Van Pelt, John V(redenburgh) obit Sep 62
Vertès, Marcel obit Jan 62
Viereck, George Sylvester obit May 62
Vilar, Jean (Louis Côme) Apr 62
Volpe, John A(nthony) Feb 62

Waddington, C(onrad) H(al) Apr 62
Wagner, Richard Apr 62
Wald, Jerry obit Sep 62
Walsh, Chad Feb 62
Walsh, William B(ertalan) May 62
Walter, Bruno obit Apr 62
Ward, Paul L(angdon) Mar 62
Watson, Lucile obit Sep 62
Watts, Alan (Wilson) Mar 62
Webb, James E(dwin) May 62
Welsh, Matthew E(mpson) Jun 62
Wenner-Gren, Axel (Leonard) obit Jun 62
Wesker, Arnold Feb 62
Whalen, Grover A(loysius) obit Jun 62
Whitton, Rex M(arion) May 62
Wickens, Aryness Joy Sep 62
Wilcox, Francis O(rlando) Apr 62
Wilkinson, Bud See Wilkinson, C. Apr 62
Wilkinson, Charles (Burnham) Apr 62
Wills, Royal Barry obit Feb 62
Winiarski, Bohdan (Stefan) Feb 62
Wood, Natalie Apr 62

Yamasaki, Minoru Mar 62
Young, Owen D. obit Sep 62

STATEMENT REQUIRED BY THE ACT OF AUGUST 24, 1912, AS AMENDED BY THE ACTS OF MARCH 3, 1933, JULY 2, 1946 AND JUNE 11, 1960 (74 STAT. 208) SHOWING THE OWNERSHIP, MANAGEMENT, AND CIRCULATION OF CURRENT BIOGRAPHY, published monthly except August at New York, N.Y., for October 1, 1962.

1. The names and addresses of the publisher, editor, managing editor, and business managers are:

Publisher, THE H. W. WILSON COMPANY,
    950 University Avenue, New York 52, N.Y.

Editor, CHARLES MORITZ,
    950 University Avenue, New York 52, N.Y.

Managing editor, None

Business manager, None

2. The owner is: (If owned by a corporation, its name and address must be stated and also immediately thereunder the names and addresses of stockholders owning or holding 1 percent or more of total amount of stock. If not owned by a corporation, the names and addresses of the individual owners must be given. If owned by a partnership or other unincorporated firm, its name and address, as well as that of each individual member, must be given.)

The H. W. Wilson Company, 950 University Avenue, New York 52, N.Y.;— Florence A. Arnold, 950 University Ave., New York 52, N.Y.; Mrs. Bertha M. Erickson, 733 Midland Ave., Yonkers, N.Y.; Howard Haycraft, 950 University Ave., New York 52, N.Y.; Mertice M. James, Box 1117, Chautauqua, N.Y.; Arthur and Hannah Johnson, 2471 Grand Ave., New York 68, N.Y.; Edward S. Kelley, 30 South Lawn Ave., Elmsford, N.Y.; Catherine A. Lahey, 3963 Seton Ave., New York 66, N.Y.; Mrs. Ida E. Rigg, 34-44 82nd St., Jackson Heights, N.Y.; Charles J. Shaw, 950 University Ave., New York 52, N.Y.; The H. W. Wilson Foundation, Inc., 950 University Ave., New York 52, N.Y.

3. The known bondholders, mortgagees, and other security holders owning or holding 1 percent or more of total amount of bonds, mortgages, or other securities are: (If there are none, so state.)

Thomas E. and Anna Barrett, 11370 Second St. E., Treasure Island, St. Petersburg 6, Fla.; Rupert E. Flower, Box 751, Visalia, Calif.; Mrs. Irma B. Fontana, 156 W. Waterview St., Northport, N.Y.; Bertha Joel, 5400 Fieldston Road, New York 71, N.Y.; M. Alma Josenhans, 602 East Ann St., Ann Arbor, Mich.; Ruth R. Keil, 253 Oak St., Westwood, Mass.; Edith T. Kramer, 2600 Creston Ave., New York 58, N.Y.; Gretta Smith, 122 Second Ave., Chula Vista, Calif.; Ruth B. Wallad, 35-31 85th St., Apt. 2B, Jackson Heights 72, N.Y.; The H. W. Wilson Foundation, Inc., 950 University Ave., New York 52, N.Y.

4. Paragraphs 2 and 3 include, in cases where the stockholder or security holder appears upon the books of the company as trustee or in any other fiduciary relation, the name of the person or corporation for whom such trustee is acting; also the statements in the two paragraphs show the affiant's full knowledge and belief as to the circumstances and conditions under which stockholders and security holders who do not appear upon the books of the company as trustees, hold stock and securities in a capacity other than that of a bona fide owner.

5. The average number of copies of each issue of this publication sold or distributed, through the mails or otherwise, to paid subscribers during 12 months preceding the date shown above was: (This information is required by the act of June 11, 1960 to be included in all statements regardless of frequency of issue.) 13,065

THE H. W. WILSON COMPANY
By: John Jamieson, Secretary

Sworn to and subscribed before me this 18th day of September 1962.

ETHEL NOLTE

[SEAL]

Notary Public, State of New York
No. 03-8154750
Commission Expires March 30, 1964

CURRENT
BIOGRAPHY

DECEMBER 1962
VOL. 23   NO. 11

Editor: Charles Moritz

PUBLISHED BY THE H. W. WILSON COMPANY, 950 UNIVERSITY AVE., NEW YORK

CONTENTS

ABOUT THIS PUBLICATION

Current Biography (published every month except August) presents articles on people who are prominent in the news—in national and international affairs, the sciences, the arts, labor, and industry. Sources of information are newspapers, magazines, books, and, in some cases, the biographees themselves. It should be pointed out, however, that these are objective rather than authorized biographies. At the end of the year the articles in the monthly issues are cumulated in one alphabet, revised, and printed in a single volume known as *Current Biography Yearbook*.

Authorities for biographees' full names, with some exceptions, are the bibliographical publications of The Wilson Company. When a biographee prefers a certain name form, that is indicated in the heading of the article: for example, Macmillan, (Maurice) Harold means that he is usually referred to as Harold Macmillan. When a professional name is used in the heading, as, for example, Glenn Ford, the real name, in this case Gwyllyn Samuel Newton Ford, appears in the article itself.

The heading of each article includes the pronunciation of the name if it is unusual, date of birth (if obtainable), and occupation. The article is supplemented by a list of references to sources of *biographical* information, in two alphabets: (1) newspapers and periodicals and (2) books.

References to newspapers and periodicals are listed in abbreviated form; for example, "Sat Eve Post 217:14+ S 30 '44 por" means *Saturday Evening Post*, volume 217, pages 14 ff, September 30, 1944, with portrait. For full names, see the section "Periodical and Newspaper Designations," which is included in all *Current Biography* Yearbooks and in the January issue each year. Obituary notices appear for persons whose biographies have been published in *Current Biography*.

An index to names that have appeared this year is to be found at the back of this issue.

NOTE: Authors whose biographies do not appear in *Current Biography* may usually be found in *Twentieth Century Authors*, Kunitz & Haycraft, 1942, H. W. Wilson Company, or in the First Supplement (1955). Authors of books for young people are included in *The Junior Book of Authors* (Second Edition, Revised) edited by Kunitz & Haycraft, 1951, H. W. Wilson Company. Musicians whose biographies do not appear in *Current Biography* may usually be found in *Living Musicians*, compiled and edited by David Ewen, 1940, H. W. Wilson Company, or in its First Supplement (1957).

KEY TO PRONUNCIATION

ā	āle	N	Not pronounced, but indicates the nasal tone of the preceding vowel, as in the French *bon* (bôN).	û	ûrn; French eu, as in *jeu* (zhû); German ö, oe, as in *schön* (shûn), *Goethe* (gû'tĕ)
â	câre				
ă	ădd				
ä	äccount				
ä	ärm				
à	àsk				
à	sofà			ŭ	tŭb
		ō	ōld	ṳ	circŭs
ē	ēve	ô	ôrb	ü	Pronounced approximately as ē, with rounded lips: French u, as in *menu* (mē-nü); German ü, as in *grün*
ĕ	ĕnd	ŏ	ŏdd		
ē	makēr	oi	oil		
		o͞o	o͞oze		
g	go	o͝o	fo͝ot		
		ou	out		
ī	īce				
ĭ	ĭll	*th*	*then*	zh	azure
		th	thin		
ᴋ	German ch as in *ich* (īᴋ)			′ =	main accent
		ū	cūbe	″ =	secondary accent

CURRENT BIOGRAPHY

DECEMBER 1962

BÉKÉSY, GEORG VON (bā'kĕ-shē) June 3, 1899- Physicist
Address: b. Psycho-Acoustic Laboratory, Harvard University, Cambridge 38, Mass.; h. 14 Shepard St., Cambridge 38, Mass.

The recipient of the Nobel Prize in Medicine for 1961 is the Hungarian-born physicist Dr. Georg von Békésy, a leading authority on the functioning of the ear, who has been a senior research fellow with the Psycho-Acoustic Laboratory of Harvard University since 1949. Békésy won the prize, including a $48,300 cash award, in recognition of his research on hearing: he identified the process by which sound waves are transformed in the inner ear to signals interpreted by the brain as high or low sounds, thus permitting an individual to distinguish, say, a basso from a soprano.

Georg von Békésy was born on June 3, 1899 in Budapest, Hungary to Alexander von Békésy, a member of the diplomatic service, and the former Paula Mazaly. His mother, brother, and sister still live in Budapest, where Georg grew up and attended school. He recalls that he first became fascinated with sound when he heard high-pitched gypsy music as a boy. From 1916 to 1920 he studied at the University of Bern in Switzerland. He then enrolled at the University of Budapest, where he took his Ph.D. degree in physics in 1923.

Békésy began his career as a communications engineer in the research laboratory of the Hungarian telephone system. To determine how much of a sound range a new cable should be capable of relaying, he decided to make investigations of how the human ear receives sound. Working with animals and cadavers, Békésy initially probed the functioning of the eardrum, a delicate mechanism that separates the outer ear from the middle ear. By gluing tiny mirrors to the eardrum and by beaming bright light as well as sound into the ear, he was able to observe reflections that indicated the movements of the membrane when struck by sounds. In another series of experiments he observed how the ossicles—three tiny mobile bones in the middle ear, called the hammer, anvil, and stirrup—pick up the vibrations transmitted by the eardrum and relay them to the cochlea in the inner ear.

The fact that sound travels to the inner ear had long been known, but it was not known how the ear distinguishes between various pitches. Békésy's most notable contribution lies in original research involving the cochlea, the spiral-shaped channel in the inner ear, from which nerves pick up sound signals for the brain. Békésy con-

Wide World

GEORG VON BÉKÉSY

structed models of the cochlea, and he worked with a corpse whose auditory mechanisms were stimulated by electricity. To experiment on the delicate cochlea, which is about half the size of a small fingernail and protected by liquid and hard bone, Békésy had to develop new tools and techniques.

He devised exceedingly fine drills and probes, micromanipulators that refined his almost imperceptible motions, and scissors with blades only a few thousandths of an inch long. He reached the cochlea by grinding a fine opening in the bone, thus revealing part of the basilar membrane. By substituting for the liquid inside the cochlea a saline solution containing fine aluminum and coal particles and by using stroboscopic illumination, he was able to observe and measure a phenomenon he called the "traveling wave."

The innermost ossicle, the stirrup bone, acts as a lid on an opening in the cochlea called the oval window. As sound vibrations cause the bone to move, it exerts pressure on the liquid within the cochlea, and the vibrations are transmitted to the basilar membrane, a thin partition that runs the length of the cochlea. Before Békésy completed his studies, it had been postulated that the basilar membrane contained groups of fibers that, like the strings on musical instruments, would vibrate only in harmony with the

BÉKÉSY, GEORG VON—*Continued*

specific frequencies to which they are tuned. Each group of fibers, it was thought, stimulated different nerve endings, which enabled the brain to distinguish specific notes.

Békésy established, however, that as traveling waves pass along the basilar membrane, the entire membrane vibrates. Each wave causes maximal vibration at a different section of the membrane, according to the wave's frequency. High frequency waves (high sounds) reach their peak on the part of the basilar membrane nearest the stirrup bone; low frequency waves (low sounds) attain maximum amplitude further along the membrane. Microscopic nerve cells within the cochlea detect the position of wave peaks and transmit this information to the brain, which interprets it as high or low sounds.

For his "discoveries concerning the physical mechanisms of stimulation within the cochlea," which he had been making for more than thirty years, Békésy was awarded the 1961 Nobel Prize in Medicine by King Gustaf VI of Sweden on December 10, 1961 in Stockholm. He had learned that he was to receive the prize about two months before, in October, when he was in the Waldorf-Astoria Hotel on his way to receive an achievement award from the Deafness Research Foundation. Newsmen had accosted him and asked his reactions to having won "the award." Békésy, thinking they meant the Deafness Research Foundation award, was astonished at receiving so much attention, until he understood that "the award" they were referring to was the Nobel Prize.

Békésy worked with the Hungarian telephone system for twenty-three years, from 1923 to 1946. During the same period he was also employed in the central laboratory of Siemens & Halske A.G., in Berlin (1926-27), and at the University of Budapest, where he was a lecturer from 1932 to 1939, a special professor from 1939 to 1940, and a full professor from 1940 to 1946. In 1946 he emigrated to Sweden, where he worked at the Karolinska Institute in Stockholm for a year. He held a title as research professor at the Karolinska Institute from 1947 to 1949, but did not actually assume this post in Sweden.

Since 1947 Békésy has been in the United States. From 1947 to 1949 he was a research lecturer at the Psycho-Acoustic Laboratory at Harvard University, and since 1949 he has been a senior research fellow in psychophysics there. "This lab is full of people who are interested in his work and we were able to provide complete freedom for him to do whatever he wanted," Dr. Stanley S. Stevens, director of the laboratory, has said. "A scientist likes to be in an environment where people appreciate what he does and where his work is not constrained." Békésy's work was first brought to the attention of Americans in 1938 in a book, *Hearing: Its Psychology and Physiology,* by Hallowell Davis and Dr. Stevens. Most of Békésy's numerous papers have been translated and collected in *Experiments in Hearing* (McGraw, 1960) by Ernest G. Wever.

Békésy has extended his interest in hearing to visual and tactile sensations, which he has measured and recorded. In 1958 he reported that he had devised an apparatus that allows the skin to "hear." A greatly enlarged version of the cochlea, the device is a long tube filled with fluid, with a membrane running along it. When the subject places his forearm against the membrane and when sounds are sent through the tube, the skin of the forearm feels high and low sounds in distinctly different positions on the arm, just as the nerve cells in contact with the basilar membrane in the cochlea detect the different points at which various sound waves reach their peak. Békésy's invention may at some time be adapted to enable the deaf to "hear" through tactile sensations.

Known as a scientist's scientist, Békésy is primarily interested in research, not in developing practical applications. He has, however, devised an audiometer that can determine whether deafness in individual cases is caused by damage to the ear or to the brain. Also, as Dr. Gordon D. Hoople of the Deafness Research Foundation has pointed out, "Because of his work, ear surgeons can build new eardrums of skin or vein tissue and can replace small bones of the ear with plastic substitutes." The official Nobel citation stated, "There is hardly any problem concerning the physical mechanics of acoustic stimulation to which von Békésy has not added clarity and understanding."

Békésy has lectured in the United States and Europe. In addition to the awards mentioned above, he has received the Denker Prize in Otology (1931), the Leibnitz Medal from the Academy of Sciences in Berlin (1937), the Guyot Prize for Speech and Otology from Groningen University (1939), the Academy Award from the Academy of Science in Budapest (1946), the Shambaugh Prize in Otology (1950), the Howard Crosby Warren Medal from the Society of Experimental Psychologists (1955), the Gold Medal of the American Otological Society (1957), and the Gold Medal of the Acoustical Society of America (1961). He received honorary M.D. degrees from Wilhelm University in Münster, Germany (1955) and the University of Bern (1959).

"Dr. Georg von Békésy looks like the little, pale, stoop-shouldered, anonymous man you often see hunched over a foreign-language newspaper . . . in the Automat or on the Lexington Avenue IRT," a *Sunday News* reporter (October 29, 1961) wrote. A slight man with gray hair, light blue eyes, and a small mustache, Békésy, who is now an American citizen, has an unassuming manner and retiring habits. He usually works in his laboratory from nine in the morning until ten at night, eating his lunch there and taking his evening meal at a restaurant before walking the few blocks home. Occasionally he will visit a colleague's home and get some exercise; he has sawed wood at Dr. Stevens' house. "But . . . if he uses his big muscles too much," Stevens says, "he loses the sensitivity he needs in his small muscles. He has to avoid violent exercise with his gross muscles."

Amidst the models of ears and other scientific paraphernalia in his laboratory stand many pieces of primitive art, which Békésy collects with dedication. This hobby and his work are his principal recreations, and he has been asked whether he does not indeed lead a lonely life. "I like a lonely life," he answered. "Concentration on one field is possible only if you are lonely to a certain degree. If someone is a scientist, he loves to work on some problem and my hope is to contribute to the deafness problem."

References

N Y Sunday News p94+ O 29 '61
N Y Times p14 O 20 '61 por
American Men of Science 10th ed (1960-62)
Who's Who in America, 1962-63

BEMELMANS, LUDWIG Apr. 27, 1898-Oct. 1, 1962 Writer and illustrator of books for children and adults; best known for his book *Madeline* (1939), about a small girl in Paris; also known for his paintings. See *Current Biography* (April) 1941.

Obituary

N Y Times p39 O 2 '62

BURNS, JAMES MacGREGOR Aug. 3, 1918-College professor; political scientist; writer
Address: b. Williams College, Williamstown, Mass.; h. 115 Park St., Williamstown, Mass.

JAMES MacGREGOR BURNS

A political scientist engaged in politics, somewhat in the tradition of Woodrow Wilson, James MacGregor Burns repudiates the idea of any fundamental antagonism between the thinker and the doer in American society. He sees no incompatibility between his work as professor of political science at Williams College and the role that he has played in practical politics, on behalf of the Democratic party, for example, as a candidate for Congress in 1958. His books and articles on American government and his biographies of Franklin D. Roosevelt (1956) and John F. Kennedy (1960) have been generally praised for both their engaging literary qualities and their academic integrity.

James MacGregor Burns was born on August 3, 1918 in Melrose, Massachusetts to Mildred Curry (Bunce) Burns and Robert Arthur Burns, a businessman who specialized in sales and advertising. He and his two brothers, Robert A. Burns and Charles H. Burns, grew up in a rural area of Massachusetts, in Burlington, and traveled a good deal with their parents in Europe and Mexico. Since Burlington was then too small to have a high school, James Burns attended nearby Lexington High School, where he was editor of the yearbook and a member of the tennis team.

After entering Williams College in Williamstown, Massachusetts in 1935, Burns majored in political science and at the same time laid the groundwork for his career as a writer by serving as editor in chief of the *Williams Record*, the student newspaper, and the student monthly magazine. He was also president of a nonfraternity social organization, the Garfield Club. A Phi Beta Kappa student, he won prizes for his undergraduate thesis and graduated in 1939 *magna cum laude,* receiving his B.A. degree with highest honors in political science.

The following year Burns studied at the National Institute of Public Affairs. He returned to Williams College in 1941 as an instructor in

political science. After the United States entered World War II, however, he left the campus, in 1942, to become the executive secretary of the nonferrous metals commission of the National War Labor Board. In 1943 he joined the Army with the rank of private, and during the next two years he served as combat historian with the 1st Information and Historical Service and eventually advanced to master sergeant. Assigned to the Pacific theater, he took part in the fighting at Guam, Saipan, and Okinawa and wrote accounts of the operations. He is the author of *Guam: Operations of the 77th Infantry Division* (1944) and the co-author of *Okinawa: The Last Battle* (1947).

At the end of the war Burns studied at Harvard University, which in 1947 awarded him both the M.A. and Ph.D. degrees, and in 1949 he took further graduate courses at the London School of Economics. Meanwhile, in 1947, he had resumed teaching at Williams College, as assistant professor in political science; he was promoted to associate professor in 1950 and to full professor in 1953. He has specialized in American politics, but he has also taught international politics, comparative government, and political thought.

Burns's critical approach to his subject is evident in the concern for government reform that underlies *Congress on Trial; The Legislative Process and the Administrative State* (Harper, 1949), in which he examined the pressures of conflicting local and national interests that plague Congressmen and continually threaten to delay and obstruct action in the legislature. He proposed the development of stronger, more responsible and unified parties through a reorganization of political alignment on a national scale. (It might be noted that after the Democratic National Convention of 1960, which nominated Kennedy as a Presidential candidate, Burns boldly suggested that fulfillment of the Democratic platform would require certain Congressional reforms, including the elimination of

BURNS, JAMES MacGREGOR—*Continued*

the seniority system for selecting committee chairmen, even though the changes might cause many Southerners to bolt the Democratic party.)

His writings have identified Burns with the school of political scientists in the United States who believe that the American system of government should be made more responsive to the increasing complexities of national and international needs. His *Government by the People; The Dynamics of American National Government* (Prentice-Hall, 1951), written in collaboration with Jack Walter Peltason, is a college textbook that gives the student a sense of the living and growing nature of the governmental system. S. G. Brown observed in *Annals of the American Academy of Political and Social Science* (September 1952), "The tacit assumption throughout is that big government and big power, as means for the advancement of the general welfare, are inevitable and that the administrative process is the characteristic development of modern democracy."

The vital need of the United States, as Burns sees it, is strong leadership, sustained by centralized and disciplined political parties. He emphasizes this viewpoint in *Roosevelt: The Lion and the Fox* (Harcourt, 1956), a biography of Franklin D. Roosevelt that covers the President's career from his first year in the White House through the 1940 election. Without concealing his own liberal sympathies, Burns presented a frank, objective, and scholarly detailed analysis of Roosevelt's strengths and weaknesses. A number of reviewers found it to be the best study of Roosevelt to date, and it was awarded both the Tamiment Prize (1956) and the Woodrow Wilson Foundation Award (1957).

In keeping with his views that the social scientist should take a responsible part in the practical world of government, Burns served as a staff member in Massachusetts of the so-called "Little Hoover Commission" in 1949. Believing also that good citizens have the duty to be active in political parties, Burns worked as a local and county leader of the Democratic party. He was a member of the Berkshire County delegation to the Massachusetts state convention in 1954 and a member of the Massachusetts delegation to the Democratic National Convention in 1952, 1956, and 1960.

During 1958 Burns ran, unsuccessfully, against Republican Representative John H. Heselton as the Democratic candidate to the United States House of Representatives from the heavily Republican First Massachusetts District, the westernmost district of his state. His campaign strengthened his relationship with John F. Kennedy, who was then running for re-election to the Senate. Burns had been associated with Kennedy for some years in Massachusetts politics and had taken a major part in 1955 in proposing that Kennedy seek nomination as the Democratic Vice-Presidential candidate.

In his preface to *John Kennedy; A Political Profile* (Harcourt, 1960) Burns wrote, "Following his re-election [in 1958] and my defeat, Senator Kennedy offered me a responsible position in his office, which I declined because I felt that, despite my affection and admiration for him, I did not know enough about his presidential qualifications to make the complete commitment that such a job required." While gathering material for his biography of Kennedy, however, he became more convinced of Kennedy's capacity for national leadership, and during 1960 he campaigned for Kennedy throughout the Northeast and Midwest.

John Kennedy, an election-year biography that has been described as Kennedy's authorized biography, is a factual and authentic account of the life and work of the man who became President. Sidney Hyman commented in the New York *Times Book Review* (January 24, 1960), "It is written with grace and stylistic distinction by an author who, having free access to intimate materials, seems to have been swayed by no consideration except his own perceptions."

At present Burns is writing a study of Presidential leadership that, he says, "will relate the Presidency closely to both Congress and the party system, both from a historical and contemporary standpoint." He has contributed a number of articles to the *Atlantic Monthly, New Republic,* and other magazines. In an article in the New York *Times Magazine* (August 31, 1958), "Professor in the Political Maze," which he wrote when he was running for the Democratic nomination for Congress, he argued for a place for the scholar in politics, pointing out the contributions that the political scientists can make in directing the affairs of the state.

In participating in community activities, Burns serves as chairman of the Berkshire County Council against Discrimination (a semigovernmental organization), as a member of the board of trustees of Stockbridge School, and as a member of the advisory board of the Berkshire Community College. He belongs to the American Civil Liberties Union, Americans for Democratic Action, American Legion, and the Grange. In 1960-61 he was president of the New England Political Science Association, and he is also a member of the American Political Science Association. His church is the Congregational.

James MacGregor Burns married Janet Rose Dismorr Thompson on May 23, 1942; they have four children: David MacGregor, Timothy Stewart, Deborah Edwards, and Margaret Rebecca Antonia. Mrs. Burns is a preparatory school teacher and the administrative officer of the Cluett Center for Development Economics at Williams College. Professor Burns has brown hair and hazel eyes, stands six feet tall, and weighs 175 pounds. As in his high school years, he plays tennis for recreation, and in the winter he takes advantage of New England's opportunities for skiing.

References

American Men of Science 10th ed (1960-62)
Who's Who in America, 1962-63

CANNON, CAVENDISH W(ELLES) Feb. 1, 1895-Oct. 7, 1962 First United States Ambassador to Morocco, 1956-58; during the late 1940's and early 1950's was successively United States

Ambassador to Yugoslavia, Portugal, and Greece. See *Current Biography* (July) 1957.

Obituary

N Y Times p23 O 8 '62

DE TOLEDANO, RALPH   *See* Toledano, Ralph de

PARTRIDGE, DEBORAH (CANNON)   *See* Wolfe, Deborah (Cannon) Partridge

RAWLINGS, SIR (HENRY) BERNARD (HUGHES) May 21, 1889-Sept. 30, 1962 Admiral; second in command of the British Pacific Naval Forces in 1944-45. See *Current Biography* (August) 1945.

Obituary

N Y Times p39 O 2 '62

RESOR, STANLEY B(URNET) Apr. 30, 1879-Oct. 29, 1962 Chairman (1955-61) and president (1916-55) of the advertising agency J. Walter Thompson Company; a founder and president (1923-24) of the American Association of Advertising Agencies. See *Current Biography* (July) 1949.

Obituary

N Y Times p35 O 30 '62

ROBARTS, JOHN P(ARMENTER) Jan. 11, 1917- Prime Minister of Ontario; lawyer

Address: b. Office of the Prime Minister, Parliament Bldgs., Toronto, Ontario, Canada; h. 375 St. James St., London, Ontario, Canada

The wealthiest and most populous of the provinces of Canada, but beset recently by industrial and economic problems, Ontario presents a variety of challenges to its political helmsman, John P. Robarts, who succeeded Leslie M. Frost as prime minister and leader of the provincial Progressive Conservative party on November 8, 1961. Robarts is a lawyer from London, Ontario, which he was first elected to represent in the province's Legislative Assembly in 1951. Since December 1959 he has served in the cabinet as minister of education, and he is the author of the so-called Robarts Plan for rapid construction of vocational and technical schools to counter the effects on the economy of automation and unemployment.

Born to Herbert and Florence May (Stacpoole) Robarts on January 11, 1917, John Parmenter Robarts is of Canadian-English parentage on his father's side and Canadian-Irish on his mother's. He is a native of Banff, Alberta and spent his early years in Winnipeg, Manitoba and Galt, Ontario, where he attended public grade school. In 1931, when he was fourteen, the family moved to his present home city of London. There, after graduating from high school, he entered the University of Western Ontario.

Photographic Illustrators, Toronto

JOHN P. ROBARTS

To help finance his higher education, Robarts worked summers on the lake boats. In college he majored in business administration, but by 1939, when he received his B.A. degree with honors, he had decided on law as a career. In early 1940, however, soon after he had enrolled in Osgoode Hall Law School in Toronto, he joined the Royal Canadian Navy Volunteer Reserve for World War II service. Enlisting as an ordinary seaman, he received an officer's commission in England in 1941. Before his retirement from the Navy in 1945 in the rank of lieutenant, he had served in the Atlantic, the Mediterranean, and Pacific theaters of war. For distinguished service at Salerno, Italy in 1943 he was mentioned in dispatches.

In 1947, when he had completed his course at Osgoode Hall, Robarts was admitted to the Ontario bar and began to practise law in Hamilton, Ontario. After about a year there he returned to London to become a partner in the law firm of Carrothers, Fox, Robarts and Betts. Early in 1951 he was elected an alderman on the London city council, and later in the year, at the general election of November 22, he was elected as a Progressive Conservative to represent the London riding in the Ontario Legislative Assembly in Toronto.

Under the leadership of Leslie M. Frost, who had become Ontario's prime minister in 1949, the Progressive Conservatives gained a majority in 1951 of seventy-nine seats, the largest majority ever held in the legislature, which then consisted of ninety members. At that time Ontario was the only province with a Progressive Conservative administration. Redistricting brought up to ninety-eight the total number of Ontario Legislative Assembly seats to be filled at the general election of May 26, 1955. The Progressive Conservatives won eighty-four, and of the remaining fourteen the Liberals won eleven. In the London area, which had been divided into two ridings,

ROBARTS, JOHN P.—*Continued*

Robarts was elected M.P.P. (member of the provincial parliament) for London North.

One of the assignments that Robarts held in the provincial legislature was chairman of the Select Committee on Toll Roads and Highway Financing, whose report had a substantial influence on highway policy. On December 22, 1958 Prime Minister Frost named him to his cabinet as minister without portfolio, and in 1958 Robarts also became a member of the Ontario water resources commission.

At a provincial general election in June 1959 the Frost administration was returned to power with a noticeably reduced but still overwhelming majority. The Progressive Conservatives took seventy-one of the ninety-eight Legislative Assembly seats; most of the thirten seats that they lost went to the Liberals. Robarts, who was re-elected by the London North riding, was appointed minister of education on December 17, 1959—about five weeks before the twenty-sixth legislature began its first session.

During the first and second sessions (from January to April 1960 and from November 1960 to March 1961) Robarts "confined himself to noncontroversial speeches that dealt with his own portfolio," according to John Miller in the Toronto *Globe Magazine* (November 11, 1961), "and he did rapid and extremely competent homework." Miller went on to point out, "In his 18-month term as Education Minister, he proved he can get on top of a particular assignment quickly, efficiently and, more significant, in a quiet way."

In 1960-61 the province and municipalities offered thirteen years of free education to nearly 2,600,000 Ontario pupils under only about 40,000 teachers. With the enrollment increasing at an average of 70,000 pupils a year, Education Minister Robarts induced the legislature to increase financial aid to schools by 23 percent. To overcome the teacher shortage he sponsored construction of new teachers colleges; he also introduced a program for the establishment of trade schools and for the rebuilding of the Ryerson Institute of Technology. Aid on a vastly increased scale was also provided for Ontario's eight universities serving over 30,000 students.

In Ontario, as in other Canadian provinces, the British parliamentary system of government is followed with slight variations. Executive power is nominally vested in a lieutenant governor, appointed for five years by the federal government, but is in practice exercised by the executive council (cabinet), the members of which sit in and are answerable to the legislature. The constitutional title of the prime minister, who is the leader of the majority party, is president of the council. The resignation, therefore, on August 2, 1961 of the aging Leslie M. Frost as leader of the provincial Progressive Conservative party called for the election not only of a new party leader but also, by implication, of a new prime minister, even though Frost retained temporarily the presidency of the council.

A convention of 1,780 delegates was called for October 24, 1961 in Toronto; seven candidates vied for the party leadership; and late on October 25, on the sixth ballot, Education Minister

Robarts was chosen. "The people who have put Mr. Robarts into the top party job—and indirectly into the Premier's office—were voting for the policies of Leslie Frost," commented Stanley Westall in the Toronto *Globe and Mail* (October 27, 1961), "and for the kind of image which he has portrayed successfully to the voters of the province. In every way John Robarts is a true successor."

On November 8, 1961 Robarts was sworn in to succeed Frost as prime minister and president of the council. His reorganized cabinet, which reflected his cognizance of regional sensitivities and old and new points of view, contained two of his rivals for party leadership, A. Kelso Roberts as attorney general and Robert Macaulay as energy resources minister. Robarts retained the office of minister of education. In discussing the political and economic problems that confronted Robarts, Miller called him "the man on the chopping block." He had not been elected prime minister by the voters, and until the end of the twenty-sixth legislature and a new general election he would be "living on the tail end of another man's mandate."

The new prime minister encountered trouble not long after the legislature reconvened for the fall session when the Liberal leader, John Wintermeyer, called for the appointment of a Royal Commission to investigate allegations of crime and corruption in Ontario. Robarts responded by naming the highly respected Justice Wilfred Roach to head such a commission, thereby risking the political effects of a possibly unfavorable report. Then early in January 1962 he made what seemed at the time a tactical mistake by describing five by-elections to be held later that month as "a baby general election" and a test of his administration. The Liberals retained two seats by increased majorities and won Renfrew South from the Conservatives, while the Conservatives held onto two strongholds in the Toronto area by only narrow margins. An ensuing party caucus, however, strengthened rather than diminished his status as leader. When the legislature reconvened shortly afterward Robarts announced that his government would appoint a three-member independent commission to study redistribution of electoral districts in Ontario.

In his capacity as education minister Robarts was the author of a plan to meet the requirements of a technical and vocational training agreement between the federal government and the provinces under which the federal government undertook to pay 75 percent of the cost of building and equipping new technical and vocational schools, provided such buildings were completed by March 31, 1963. Otherwise, the percentage of federal aid would fall to 50. Under the Robarts Plan, Ontario expected to complete on schedule five new trade schools, fourteen vocational high schools, additions to five institutes of technology, sixteen other schools, and fifty-six vocational high schools. In drawing up this building program Robarts was particularly concerned with preventing the labor market from being flooded by unskilled workers, both teen-aged and middle-aged.

The University of Toronto awarded Robarts an honorary LL.D. degree in June 1962. In his address on that occasion he urged the graduating class to help preserve the traditional independence of Canadian universities. Observing that increased state financial participation invariably resulted in greater state control, he said, "The health and development of our universities lies in a blending of support by the state and support by the community at large."

John P. Robarts and Norah McCormick met while both were undergraduates at the University of Western Ontario. They were married on July 7, 1944 and have two children, Robin Hollis and Timothy Parmenter. Stanley Westall of the Toronto *Globe and Mail* has described Robarts as "cautious, mild-spoken and inclined to be stubborn when he is sure he is right," and John Miller has found that his "handshake often communicates more than his speech-making." He is a member of the London Hunt and City Clubs, as well as of the Delta Upsilon fraternity and the Albany Club in Toronto, and mentions golf as his favorite recreation. An Anglican, he is a member of the Church of St. John the Evangelist in London. Robarts was created a Queen's Counsel in 1954.

References

Toronto Globe and Mail p4 O 27 '61 por
Toronto Globe and Mail Globe Mag p3+
N 11 '61 pors

Canadian Parliamentary Guide, 1962
Canadian Who's Who, 1958-60

ROBUS, HUGO May 10, 1885- Sculptor
Address: 37 E. 4th St., New York 3

The name of Hugo Robus is often linked with that of José de Creeft because both sculptors, in an age of abstractionism in art, are interested in form—especially the female form. Largely self-taught, Robus works in an idiom derived from Constantin Brancusi, but nevertheless unmistakably his own. He spent many years as a painter before he came around to his true medium, sculpture, and began to create works distinguished for their fluidity, smoothness, lyricism, simplicity, and humor. Robus was seventy before his sculpture yielded him enough income to live on and he had to wait twenty-five years before he could afford to cast his first sculpture, *Dawn*, in bronze. He believes that every great work of art must communicate a clear human meaning in plastic terms; in all his sculpture, no matter how great the deliberate distortion, the viewer can recognize human forms circulating in space. He has said, "All creative art has the same purpose—to express the essence of life."

Hugo Robus was born on May 10, 1885 in Cleveland, Ohio to Edward Robus, an iron molder, and Anne (Daniels) Robus. He has an older sister, Charlotte, who still lives in Cleveland; another older sister died many years ago. "My family were not at all sympathetic to my following the arts as my occupation," Robus has recalled. "A quite understandable attitude since the arts meant little to them and seemed a most doubtful way to economic security." But—in his own words—Robus had "a single-track mind aimed at being a fine arts student and professional" and after he

graduated from Cleveland's Central High School in 1903 he attended the Cleveland School of Art from 1904 to 1908.

Impressed by Robus' talent and dedication, Horace Potter, who was an instructor of design at the Cleveland School of Art, gave him a summer job making handwrought jewelry, tableware, and ivory carving. Out of his weekly wages of $25 Robus managed to save enough to spend the winters of 1910 and 1911 studying painting at the art school of the National Academy of Design in New York and the following two years studying in Paris. It was a spectacular feat of frugality that he was often to repeat in the years that followed.

It was an exhilarating Paris in which Robus found himself, and he met Gertrude Stein, Marsden Hartley, and Jacob Epstein, among other celebrities. He sloughed off the last vestiges of Cleveland provincialism by traveling in Italy and southern France. One winter, as an approach to the problems of form in painting, he studied sculpture under Antoine Bourdelle at the Académie de la Grande Chaumière, but when he returned to the United States in 1914 he was still dedicated to painting as his chosen medium.

A year later Robus married Irene Bogart Chubb, a fellow art student from Cleveland, and the couple settled down into a loft on Fourteenth Street, on the fringe of Greenwich Village. Although the loft was devoid of a bathtub or central heating, it was cheap and roomy, and Robus and his wife partitioned it off for their own purposes. For twenty years they made it their home during a period of economic deprivation when their income sometimes dipped to $700 a year.

For a time Robus taught at Myra Carr's modern art school and exhibited with the group known as "The Independents." Ralph Pearson, the art historian, has recalled attending the classes in modern art that Robus taught in a studio fronting on Washington Square South. Until her death in December 1958, Mrs. Robus was able to supplement the family income by helping her husband in the production of jewelry and tableware. She designed hand-dyed batik skirts and costume accessories for women, while her husband designed textiles. They somehow scraped enough out of their savings to buy a farm in New City, Rockland County, New York, where one of their neighbors, Maxwell Anderson, the playwright, once commissioned a silver tea set from Robus.

Until 1920 Robus experimented constantly in painting, varying his style with each canvas. Impressionism dominated his *Firenze* (1914); *Backyards* (1916) revealed the influence of the Futurists whom Robus had admired on his trip to Italy, especially Boccioni; *Portrait of a Room* (1919), which has as its subject the sitting room of his New City farmhouse, was cubist. Most significant perhaps was his *Bathers, or Composition of Nudes* (1917), whose curving lines and flowing forms clearly foreshadowed the style of his sculpture.

After 1920 Robus never again laid paint on canvas. For one thing, he had never been able to develop a painting style that met his

HUGO ROBUS

own exacting standards. For another, he was so fascinated by form that he found himself applying paint to canvas a quarter of an inch thick—a process so expensive that he hastened to find a medium that he could afford. Although nothing could be cheaper than the common Hudson River clay he used at first for his work in sculpture, he later used plaster, building his figures on armatures after making preliminary models or sketches. At first, Robus has said, he "sadly missed color," but "the problems of making form rhythmic, and expressive from endless viewpoints became all-absorbing." His early experiments with sculpture led him to the realization that "complete satisfaction with the result of one's efforts just cannot be achieved; the ideal advances too."

Since painting no longer held any interest for him, Robus felt obliged to give up the meager income that teaching it yielded him, but, on the other hand, he could not yet teach sculpture because, he says, "he had nothing to teach." It was not until two decades had passed that he felt sure enough of his subject to teach again. Beginning with 1942, he frequently taught sculpture at Columbia University's summer sessions, through the 1940's and into the 1950's. From 1950 to 1958 he was an instructor in sculpture at Hunter College. He was the visiting artist in 1948 at the Munson-Williams-Proctor Institute in Utica, New York, and from 1955-56 he was an instructor in sculpture at the art school of the Brooklyn Museum.

With the same modesty, patience, and self-criticism, Robus also refused to exhibit his sculpture until he felt sure of the quality of his work. Not until 1933, thirteen years after he had switched from painting to sculpture, did he finally have a show—at the Whitney Museum of American Art in New York City, which has invited him to exhibit in every sculpture exhibition that it has held since

then. Outstanding in his first exhibition was *Dawn* (1933), a female figure greeting the new day with a stretch and a yawn. His *Walking Figure* (1923) had been his first work that had really measured up to his own demanding standards, and it was not shown until the State Department chose it for the American National Exhibition in Moscow in the summer of 1959.

Among the works that Robus had executed before his first exhibition were the abstract *Despair* (1927) and *Girl Reading* (1929), now in the collection of the International Business Machines Corporation, showing a teen-aged girl in an awkward pose. A year after his first exhibition came *Song* (1934), now in the Metropolitan Museum of Art, the figure of an adolescent girl, her hands clasped in front of her, her head raised in song.

Nowhere is Robus' wit more evident than in the titles he has assigned to some of his work. To the graceful sculpture of a girl washing her hair he assigned the working title of *Soap in Her Eyes,* and he called three headless figures with vase-like necks *Three Caryatids Without a Portico* (1954). The head on his *Water Carrier* (1956) consists of a water pitcher. "Just a jughead, I guess," Robus once quipped.

Like many other American artists during the Depression, Robus worked for the Federal Art Project in New York, from 1937 to 1939. In the 1940's he gave up making the lithe and delicate forms that had become his stock in trade in favor of bulkier shapes in the agonized, quasi-cubist style of Jacques Lipchitz. After viewing one of Robus' exhibitions during this period, Henry McBride complained in the New York *World-Telegram and Sun* (February 25, 1949): "Nature has its own harmonies and rhythms, even at its most violent. Robus's recent work is just violent."

McBride may have been referring to such highly abstract and roughhewn works as *Compassion* (1949) and *Reunion* (1945), which is now owned by the Cleveland Museum of Art. In any case, Robus felt that his sleek figures were in danger of becoming too mannered and too formularized. In the 1950's there emerged out of his experiments a richer style, embodied most brilliantly perhaps in *Meditating Girl* (1958), a lyrical and poignant work that perfectly fuses form and movement.

Although abstractionism has been rampant during the 1950's and the 1960's, Robus has never turned his back on the human figure. Like his own life, his forms have always been disciplined and controlled. To Emily Genauer, writing in the New York *Herald Tribune* (May 8, 1960), they look back to "universal and impersonal concepts of youth, womanliness, innocence, despair." Even Henry McBride came away from an exhibition at the Whitney Museum of American Art with homage for Robus in *Art Digest* (May 1953): "It was a pleasure to see all the wit scintillating. . . . Robus is undoubtedly the James Thurber of sculpture." Fellow sculptor William Zorach has pointed out that much of Robus' work "is turned inward and deals with the weird, the strange, the nostalgic mysteries of our inner emotions and dreams. He conveys a feeling of strangeness and fantasy. . . . Whether one likes it or not it is always fascinating."

Hugo Robus has exhibited more often in group shows than in one-man shows. In 1939 he exhibited in a group show at the New York World's Fair. He had one-man shows at the Grand Central Galleries in New York in 1946 and 1949; at the Munson-Williams-Proctor Institute Art Gallery and School of Art in 1948; and at the Corcoran Gallery of Art in Washington, D.C. in 1958. By far the most important was the retrospective exhibition, circulated by the American Federation of Arts, under a grant from the Ford Foundation, that opened at the Whitney Museum of American Art on May 3, 1960. "My wife would have loved this show," Robus remarked at the opening of the exhibition.

His honors and awards date back to 1939, when he was chosen a member of the jury for American Art Today at the New York World's Fair. In 1942 he won the second prize at the Artists for Victory Exhibition at the Metropolitan Museum of Art. He was a member of the jury for the Shilling Fund in 1946, and a member of the jury for the sculpture show at the Metropolitan Museum of Art in 1952. In 1950 he won the Widener Gold Medal, and in 1953 the Alfred G. B. Steel Memorial Prize, both awarded by the Pennsylvania Academy of the Fine Arts. In 1957 he received a citation and grant from the National Institute of Arts and Letters.

By his marriage to Irene Bogart Chubb, Hugo Robus has one son, Hugo. The sculptor is about five feet nine inches in height, weighs 142 pounds, and has blue eyes and "gray to near white" hair. He belongs to the Sculptors Guild and the Federation of Modern Painters and Sculptors. Robus has no religious affiliation and is an independent in politics. Apart from art, contact with nature, including gardening, has yielded him the greatest pleasure.

"The artist of our time seems too concerned with reflecting the present rather than with projecting beauty and hope," Robus once wrote. "So much of present-day presentation is as sterile of human experience as any so-called academic art of the past. Interesting designs, media, textures, etc., still belong to the field of craft art and are not adequate of themselves to replace the emotions. They are a means and should not be considered an end product. We live in a period of deliberately sloppy drawing and craftsmanship. I try to be philosophic about present-day work, but I do have the optimist's hope that before much time passes, art will be returned to the care of the artist and cease to be the racket it has become."

References

Who's Who in America, 1962-63
Who's Who in American Art (1962)

ROGERS, CARL R(ANSOM) Jan. 8, 1902- Psychologist; psychotherapist; university professor *Address:* b. University of Wisconsin, Madison 6, Wis.; h. 5701 Winnequah Rd., Madison 4, Wis.

Dr. Carl R. Rogers, professor of psychology and psychiatry at the University of Wisconsin, is best known as the originator of the nondirective "client-centered" theory of psychotherapy. This prescribes a person-to-person, rather than a doctor-patient, relationship between therapist and client and allows the client to control the course, pace, and length of his own treatment. Rogers has taught at the University of Wisconsin since 1957. Before that, from 1945 to 1957, he had been professor of psychology and executive secretary of the Counseling Center at the University of Chicago. The author of many articles and several books, Carl Rogers was awarded a fellowship at the Center for Advanced Study in the Behavioral Sciences at Palo Alto, California for the year 1962-63.

Carl Ransom Rogers, the fourth of six children of Walter A. and Julia (Cushing) Rogers, was born in Oak Park, Illinois on January 8, 1902. An older brother, Lester Cushing Rogers, is a construction executive. Raised in an affectionate but strict religious atmosphere, in which the value of hard work was continually stressed, Carl Rogers was a solitary boy who spent most of his spare time reading. When Carl was twelve, his father, a prosperous businessman, bought a farm, which he operated scientifically and which became the family's home. The boy had access to many books on scientific agriculture, and he gleaned from them "a knowledge of and a respect for the methods of science in a field of practical endeavor." The Rogers children were encouraged to raise their own fowl and livestock. Carl also developed an interest in night-flying moths and became an authority on the silkworm moths found in a nearby woods, which he bred in captivity.

Rogers enrolled at the University of Wisconsin with the intention of majoring in agriculture, but after attending "some emotionally charged student religious conferences," he decided to enter the Protestant ministry. He changed his major to history, believing this would better prepare him for this calling. In his junior year he was one of a dozen American students chosen to take part in the World Student Christian Federation Conference held in China in 1922. His six-month visit to the Orient proved to be a decisive experience, as he has explained in his autobiographical essay, "This is Me," which appears in his book *On Becoming a Person* (Houghton, 1961). "I was forced to stretch my thinking, to realize that sincere and honest people could believe in very divergent religious doctrines. In major ways I for the first time emancipated myself from the religious thinking of my parents, and realized that I could not go along with them."

Elected to the honor fraternities Phi Beta Kappa and Phi Kappa Phi, Rogers graduated from the University of Wisconsin with a B.A. degree in 1924. He then entered Union Theological Seminary, one of the most liberal seminaries in the United States at that time. He was one of a group of students who obtained permission to set up and attend, for credit, an independent seminar in which they could explore their own religious doubts and questions. "This seminar was deeply satisfying and clarifying," Rogers has recalled in "This is Me." "It moved me a long way toward a philosophy of life which was my own. The majority of the members . . .

University of Wisconsin
CARL R. ROGERS

in thinking their way through questions they had raised, thought themselves right out of religious work. I was one. I felt that questions as to the meaning of life and the possibility of the . . . improvement of life for individuals would probably always interest me, but I could not work in a field where I would be required to believe in some specified religious doctrine."

Greatly interested in psychology and psychiatry courses at Union Theological Seminary, Rogers began to attend courses in these subjects at Columbia University Teachers College. He took a course in the philosophy of education under William H. Kilpatrick and did his first practical clinical work with children under Leta Hollingworth. Child guidance attracted him, and he gradually came to consider himself a clinical psychologist. He won a fellowship to the new Institute for Child Guidance, sponsored by the Commonwealth Fund, where he was exposed to a Freudian psychoanalytical viewpoint that contrasted greatly with the rigorous, objective, statistical approach with which he was familiar from his studies at Teachers College.

Continuing his education, Rogers received his M.A. degree in 1928 and his Ph.D. degree in 1931 from Teachers College. His thesis, "Measuring Personality Adjustment in Children Nine to Thirteen Years of Age," was a study of the results of tests given to fifty-two children from the Institute for Child Guidance and two groups of private and public school children. Rogers' research was published in his first book, *Measuring Personality Adjustment in Children,* by Teachers College in 1931.

In 1928 Rogers became a psychologist at the child study department of the Society for the Prevention of Cruelty to Children in Rochester, New York; he was made director of the agency in 1930. Over the next decade, as he provided diagnostic, planning, and treatment services for delinquent and underprivileged children, he came

to question the validity of certain authoritative teachings on effective clinical techniques. In particular, he rejected any approach that called for the use of preconceived categories in interpreting individual clients' problems. "I was moving away from any approach which was coercive or pushing in clinical relationships," Rogers has written in "This is Me," "because such approaches were never more than superficially effective. . . . It began to occur to me that unless I had a need to demonstrate my own cleverness and learning, I would do better to rely upon the client for the direction of movement in the [therapeutic] process."

Out of Rogers' experiences with treating problem children came his book *The Clinical Treatment of the Problem Child* (Houghton, 1939) and his lectures at the University of Rochester from 1935 to 1940. At first his courses at the university were listed under the departments of sociology and education, since the psychology department refused to regard Rogers' clinical work as psychology. Rogers recalls that, feeling himself alienated from the prevailing school of experimental psychologists who worked with rats, he was drawn to the social work profession and served as an officer in local and national social work bodies. In 1939 he helped establish the Rochester Guidance Center and became its first director.

Accepting a full professorship in clinical psychology at Ohio State University in 1940, Rogers began to teach treatment and counseling methods to graduate students. As he gave his lectures he became aware that, out of his own experience, he had developed a distinctive, unorthodox viewpoint on psychotherapy. When he presented it in a paper, "Newer Concepts of Psychotherapy," at the University of Minnesota in December 1940 he raised much heated pro and con discussion among psychologists as to its merits.

Somewhat taken aback at the vehement criticism his theories drew from some quarters, Rogers nevertheless discussed what he saw as "a more effective orientation to therapy" in his book *Counseling and Psychotherapy* (Houghton, 1942). In it he set forth his hypothesis that the individual, through a relationship with an accepting, empathetic therapist, can resolve his problems and develop the insight to reshape his own life. "We see therapy as an experience, not in intellectual terms. We treat the client as a person, not as an object to be manipulated and directed," Rogers has said. In nondirective therapy no formal guidance is given the client, nor are the client's present difficulties necessarily linked to early experiences, as in Freudian psychoanalysis. However, the therapist can, by virtue of having empathized with his client, make interpretive remarks that clarify a problem and produce insight. The divergence between Rogers' method and traditional psychoanalysis is illustrated by a brief comment by a neo-Freudian quoted in *Time* (July 1, 1957): "Rogers' method is unsystematic, undisciplined, and humanistic. Rogers doesn't analyze and doesn't diagnose. We have no common ground."

In 1944 Rogers served as psychological consultant to the Army Air Force. He was director of counseling services of the United Service Organizations during 1944-45. With John L. Wallen he wrote *Counseling With Returned Service-men* (McGraw Hill, 1946), a counselors' manual of principles and techniques to help returning servicemen adjust to civilian life.

From 1945 to 1957 Rogers was a professor of psychology at the University of Chicago and the executive secretary of the university-connected Counseling Center, which he had helped to establish, where hundreds of clients have received therapeutic help. The center provided Rogers with an opportunity to do large-scale research on the effectiveness of his counseling methods, and he has found that, of ten cases, two get no better, two show some improvement, and six are markedly improved after therapy (*Time*, July 1, 1957). A description of the research program and its results is contained in the book *Psychotherapy and Personality Change* (Univ. of Chicago Press, 1954), which Rogers edited with Rosalind Dymond. Rogers has also noted that certain attitudes of the therapist, rather than techniques *per se*, result in favorable personality changes in the client.

Rogers' theories of personality and behavior and a description of his method and its application to fields like education and administration are contained in his book *Client-Centered Therapy* (Houghton Mifflin, 1951). He expects to continue revising his theories and techniques as clinical experiences and research make such revisions necessary.

Invited to lecture at the University of Wisconsin in 1957 as Knapp Visiting Professor, Rogers later joined the permanent faculty of the university as professor of psychology and psychiatry. He has lectured widely and written many articles for general magazines and professional journals. A selection of his papers from the years 1951 through 1960 and his autobiographical essay make up *On Becoming a Person*. Rogers believes that all people, even the deeply disturbed, are capable of developing in a positive direction: toward self-actualization, toward maturity, and toward socialization. "I have come to feel that the more fully the individual is understood and accepted," Rogers has written, "the more he tends to drop the false fronts with which he has been meeting life, and the more he tends to move in a direction which is forward."

Rogers was named a Fellow of the Center for Advanced Study in the Behavioral Sciences at Palo Alto, California for the year 1962-63. He has been a visiting professor at Teachers College, Columbia University, in 1935, at the University of California at Los Angeles, in 1947, at Harvard University, in 1948, and at Occidental College, in 1950. Rogers was named to the American Academy of Arts and Sciences in May 1961. He received the Distinguished Scientific Contribution Award from the American Psychological Association in 1956 and was cited for outstanding research by the American Personnel and Guidance Association in 1955 and 1961. He was awarded the Nicholas Murray Butler Medal by Columbia University in 1955. Rogers holds an L.H.D. degree from Lawrence College (1956).

A founding member of the American Association for Applied Psychology, Rogers was chairman of its clinical section from 1942 to 1944

and its president in the year 1944-45. He served as vice-president of the American Orthopsychiatric Association in 1941-42 and as a member of the emergency committee in psychology of the National Research Council from 1943 to 1945. Rogers was the president of the American Psychological Association in the year 1946-47, and he headed the APA's division of clinical and abnormal psychology in 1949-50. Also a charter member of the American Academy of Psychotherapists, he was the academy's president in 1956-57.

Carl Ransom Rogers married the artist Helen Martha Elliott, a childhood friend, on August 28, 1924. They have two children: a son, David Elliott, who is a professor of medicine at Vanderbilt University School of Medicine, and a daughter, Natalie, now Mrs. Lawrence Howard Fuchs, whose husband is dean of faculty at Brandeis University. Rogers and his wife occasionally spend time in isolated spots in Mexico and the Caribbean, where he enjoys painting, swimming, snorkeling, and taking colored photographs. "In these spots," he has written, "where no more than two to four hours a day goes for professional work, I have made most of whatever advances I have made in the last few years."

References

Time 70:34+ Jl 1 '57 por

American Men of Science 10th ed (1960-62)

Rogers, Carl. On Becoming a Person (1961)

Who's Who in America, 1962-63

ROMBAUER, IRMA (VON) S(TARKLOFF) Oct. 30, 1877-Oct. 14, 1962 Author of best-selling cookbook *The Joy of Cooking*, later revised and published as *The New Joy of Cooking*. See *Current Biography* (December) 1953.

Obituary

N Y Times p39 O 17 '62

ROOSA, ROBERT V(INCENT) (rō'zà) June 21, 1918- United States government official; economist

Address: b. Room 3312, Main Treasury Bldg., Washington 25, D.C.; h. 5901 Searl Terrace, Washington 16, D.C.

Few positions, if any, in the federal government require a higher degree of technical knowledge and skill than that of Under Secretary of the Treasury for Monetary Affairs—the office that Robert V. Roosa has held in the Kennedy administration since January 1961. As one of two chief aides to Secretary of the Treasury C. Douglas Dillon, Roosa is responsible for the management of the country's enormous national debt and for handling such problems as curbing the outflow of gold and dollars from the United States and setting the interest rates for Treasury offerings and refunds. Widely known in domestic and international banking circles, he had been associated for almost twenty years with the Federal Reserve Bank of New York, where he was

Fabian Bachrach

ROBERT V. ROOSA

serving as vice-president for research when Kennedy appointed him to the Treasury. Senator Paul H. Douglas has called him "probably the foremost authority on the technical operation of the money market in Government securities."

Robert Vincent Roosa, who was born in Marquette, on Lake Superior in northern Michigan, on June 21, 1918, is the only son of Harvey Mapes and Ruth Elizabeth (Lagerquist) Rosa, both of Swedish descent. (His parents had changed the spelling of their name to Rosa so that it would agree with its pronunciation. Roosa used the shortened form for a time and then returned to the original.) With his sister, now Mrs. Elizabeth Lynch, he was brought up in the Detroit suburb of River Rouge, where their father was principal of the high school for twenty-five years before his retirement in 1947. Roosa was a member of the class of 1935 at the River Rouge High School and of the school's cross-country and debating teams. For two years he held a state championship for extemporaneous speaking.

Later, at the University of Michigan, Roosa was also a member of the debating team, as well as a director of the *Michigan Wolverine* and speaker of the Student Senate. He was elected to Phi Beta Kappa and was chosen for a Rhodes Scholarship, but when he graduated with the B.A. degree in economics in 1939, he was unable to take advantage of the scholarship because of the outbreak of World War II and the consequent travel restrictions.

Remaining at the University of Michigan for another year, he taught economics and studied for the M.A. degree, which he received in 1940. He later held appointments as a teaching Fellow and tutor in economics at Harvard University and as an instructor in economics at the Massachusetts Institute of Technology while carrying on research in monetary policy. In 1942 the University of Michigan awarded him the Ph.D.

degree in economics, for which he had written *The Monetary Powers of Some Federal Agencies Outside the Federal Reserve System.* He felt that academic work in his field needed to be enriched by experience, and in 1941 he had joined the research department of the Federal Reserve Bank of New York as an economist.

In 1943 Roosa entered the Army as a private and was attached for a time to the Office of Strategic Services. He then became an air target specialist on the staff of General Omar N. Bradley's 12th Army Group in Europe, where his service as an intelligence officer brought him two Bronze Stars. After he was demobilized in the rank of captain in 1946, he rejoined the research department of the Federal Reserve Bank of New York.

During the next five years Roosa published, among other articles, "Small Business and Depression" (*Harvard Business Review,* January 1948); "Postwar Credit Controls in France" (*Federal Reserve Bulletin,* April 1949); "The Problem of French Recovery" (*Economic Review,* June 1949); and "The Revival of Monetary Policy" (*Review of Economics and Statistics,* February 1951). In addition, he wrote "Interest Rates and the Central Bank" for the *Essays in Honor of J. H. Williams* (Macmillan, 1951).

The Federal Reserve Bank of New York promoted Roosa from economist to manager of its research department in 1951. Two years later he was made assistant vice-president of the research department, and then after serving from 1954 to 1956 as vice-president for the securities department, he became vice-president for the research department. His book *Federal Reserve Operations in the Money and Government Securities Markets,* published by the bank in 1956, was the first detailed account of the subject.

As W. H. Lawrence pointed out in the New York *Times* December 30, 1960), while in the post of vice-president for research, Roosa was an important spokesman for the central banking system of the United States: he "argued eloquently against forced-draft efforts to spur the country's economic growth, particularly through attempts to restrain interest rates artificially." He served as associate economist on the federal open market committee of the Federal Reserve, and for the *Banque Nationale de Belgique* bulletin of September 1959 he wrote the article "The Central Bank in a Market Economy," which was reprinted in *Fortune* in March 1961.

At the time of his nomination, by President-elect Kennedy on December 29, 1960, for the post of Under Secretary of the Treasury for Monetary Affairs, one press wire service carried the erroneous statement that Roosa had not voted for fifteen years. "Confusion," he explains, "arose from the fact that I have not registered for a particular political party for the past ten years. In fact, I have voted in all elections for which I have been eligible since reaching voting age." Roosa held the view that as an officer of the Federal Reserve Bank he was in the best tradition of a career public servant in avoiding any affiliation that could be regarded as partisan. His vote in the Presidential election of 1960 is known only by his friends.

In the hearing on his nomination by the Senate Finance Committee, however, Roosa admitted that he had been impressed by statements that Kennedy, then a Senator, had made in October to the effect that "in the area of international affairs and the balance of payments . . . it was clearly recognized that we could not solve the problem by changing the price of gold," and that in connection with the state of the domestic economy "the Federal Reserve system must remain as the controller of the money supply and that this was an essential part of solving the balance of payments problem."

Roosa was sworn in as Under Secretary for Monetary Affairs on January 31, 1961, succeeding Julian Baird. In one of several statements on the part that the Kennedy administration would play in the country's economy, he explained, "The government's role is to help assure the functioning of the checks and balances in a market economy; it helps to adjust imbalances by taking action at the margins but it never dictates the composition of the whole nor does it actually operate many of the parts" (New York *World-Telegram and Sun*, March 18, 1961). With other government officials he took part in a series of regional conferences aimed at gaining support for the administration's programs, and in Detroit in November 1961 he said that he saw no reason to doubt that federal revenues would balance expenditures by 1963, provided defense spending did not exceed expected amounts.

Among the problems that concern Roosa are those regarding the outflow of gold and the international standing of the dollar. In testimony before a House of Representatives subcommittee in June 1962 he opposed a domestic gold subsidy. "The monetary system of the entire world," he said, "is hinged to the interconvertibility which we maintain between gold and dollars [at $35 per ounce]. Any form of subsidy to American gold production would impair that relationship." Later in the same month he noted that the outflow of gold from this country in the first half of 1962 had amounted to $450,000,000 as compared with $857,000,000 in the whole of 1961. He also noted that while the United States gold supply was at a twenty-three-year low of $16,400,000,000, it still accounted for 40 percent of the non-Communist world's gold reserves.

Shortly before the September 1962 meeting of the World Bank and Monetary Fund in Washington, Roosa presented his views on solving the free world's monetary problems in an article published by the Federal Reserve Bank of Philadelphia. The Roosa Plan rejected such proposals for reform as devaluating the dollar or setting up a supranational center bank. It offered instead a scheme whereby the United States would accept certain foreign currencies, instead of gold or dollars, in payment of deficits. The United States could hold such currencies as part of its reserves or could use them, instead of dollars, to pay its debts to foreign countries. Since foreign countries would not have to use their supply of gold for payments to the United States, the dollar would be strengthened as the reserve currency of the free world. Just as important, in the opinion of some financial observers, as his work in building up world confidence in the dollar, has been the series of innovations that Roosa has used in restructuring the United States $199,000,000,000 marketable debt.

Robert Vincent Roosa and Ruth Grace Amende of Providence, Rhode Island, met during World War II when Miss Amende was a United States Foreign Service Auxiliary specialist with the American Embassy in London. Married on March 16, 1946, they have two daughters, Meredith Ann and Alison Ruth. For about ten years Mrs. Roosa taught Russian and French at Barnard College, Columbia University, and at the time of her husband's appointment to the Treasury was preparing her doctoral thesis at Columbia. Both Robert and Ruth Roosa are opera fans and travel enthusiasts: with their family they made an automobile trip through Western Europe in 1959 and toured Russia, Poland, and Czechoslovakia in the summer of 1960, traveling economy class. Swimming is also a favorite recreation of Robert Roosa, and woodworking yet another.

After Roosa was appointed to the Treasury, the family moved to Washington from Mount Vernon, New York, where Roosa had been active in behalf of the Seaburg Memorial Home. He is five feet eleven inches in height, weighs 185 pounds, and has blue eyes and brown hair. He is a Protestant. The professional organizations to which he belongs are the American Economic Association, the American Finance Association, the American Statistical Association, and the Council on Foreign Relations.

References

Am Banker p1 D 30 '60 por
Bsns W p20 Ja 7 '61 por
Democratic Digest p16 Ja-F '61
N Y Herald Tribune p22 D 30 '60
N Y Times p8 D 30 '60
N Y World-Telegram p10 Mr 18 '61 por
Washington (D.C.) Star A p5 D 29 '60
International Who's Who, 1961-62
New Frontiersmen (1961)
United States Congress. Senate. Hearing before the Committee on Finance, Ja 26 '61 (1961)
Who's Who in America, 1962-63

SCHELL, MAXIMILIAN Dec. 8, 1930- Actor

Address: b. c/o United Artists Corp., 729 7th Ave., New York 19

Actor-intellectuals, especially in motion pictures, belong to a comparatively rare breed, but the many-talented and multilingual Maximilian Schell indisputably belongs to their number. Although the Austrian-born Schell had appeared in films and on the stage in Europe for years, he was relatively unknown to American audiences when he won an Oscar from the Academy of Motion Picture Arts and Sciences in 1961 for his performance as Hans Rolfe, the German defense counsel in *Judgment at Nuremberg*. He is one of five acting Schells—two men and three women, one of whom is his famous older sister, Maria—who are rapidly becoming to the European theatrical profession what the Barrymores were to the United States.

The third of four children, Maximilian Schell was born in Vienna, Austria on December 8,

Columbia Pictures Corp.
MAXIMILIAN SCHELL

1930 to Hermann Ferdinand Schell, a poet and playwright, and Margarethe (de Noé) Schell, an Austrian actress who now runs a drama school in Berne, Switzerland. One of Maximilian Schell's great-grandfathers was French, and one of his grandfathers was a court composer, a friend of Wagner and of Liszt. His older sister, Maria, has been called the most celebrated Teutonic actress since Marlene Dietrich. His older brother, Karl, is a film actor and his younger sister acts under the name of Editha Nordberg.

The name of Hermann Ferdinand Schell was prominent on the Nazi blacklist, and in 1938 the Schell family fled from Vienna to escape from the *Anschluss*. They settled in Zurich, Switzerland, where they became naturalized Swiss citizens. Maximilian Schell looks back nostalgically to a childhood and youth spent in Zurich with books and music, surrounded by beautiful buildings. To him his Swiss citizenship is important because Switzerland proves that "different people with different languages can live together in peace," and he once interrupted a television rehearsal to announce that although he was cast as a German, he wanted to make it clear that he is Swiss.

Hermann Ferdinand Schell gently tried to keep his children from entering the theatrical profession, feeling that it was too intense an occupation to bring real happiness, but the glamour of their mother's career was a stronger influence. Brought up in a Roman Catholic family, Maximilian Schell at first entertained the childhood ambition of becoming Pope; he later dreamed of becoming a concert pianist. He began to experiment with acting when he was eight years old, wrote his first play for his preparatory school when he was eleven, and in the same year played the son of Wilhelm Tell in a professional production of Schiller's *Wilhelm Tell*.

He attended the University of Zurich and the University of Munich, studying philosophy and

the history of art—subjects chosen to please his father, who still hoped that his Max might become a university professor. Outside the classroom he was active in university dramatics and earned some of his spending money and tuition by appearing with professional theater groups. He earned additional money by playing professional soccer and was rated the European equivalent of All-American. He was also a member of a champion Swiss rowing team, and he did some sports reporting for the *Neue Züricher Zeitung* in Zurich. Schell finished his formal education when he abandoned a doctoral thesis on stage designs executed by French modernists, feeling that it was a scientific dissection rather than an artistic creation.

For the next four years Schell toured Europe as an actor, perfecting his craft and improving his knowledge of French, German, and Italian. At first he had refused to learn English at school because it held no interest for him; he later learned it only to read Shakespeare. Schell appeared on the stages of London, Vienna, Hamburg, Munich, Zurich, Berlin, and Salzburg. He served his required time in the Swiss army, in which he still holds rank, and to which he returns for three weeks of training each year.

Maximilian Schell's first screen appearance was in a small but important role in Laslo Benedek's German film called *Kinder, Mütter, und ein General* (Children, Mothers, and a General). His other German-language films include *Reifende Jugend* (Ripening Youth); *Der 20 Juli* (The Twentieth of July); *Das Mädchen aus Flandern* (The Girl from Flanders); *Die Ehe des Doktors Medizin Danwitz* (The Marriage of Dr. Danwitz); *Die Letzten werden die Ersten Sein* (The Last Shall Be First); and *Ein Wunderbarer Sommer* (A Wonderful Summer).

His knowledge of English was still a faltering one at best when he was approached in Paris by Marlon Brando and Edward Dmytryk, the film director, with an offer of the role of the Nazi lieutenant Hardenberg in Twentieth Century-Fox's screen version of Irwin Shaw's novel *The Young Lions*. "I couldn't speak English but I talked for four hours in French with Marlon Brando," Schell has recalled. "I played my part phonetically. Of course, then I had to learn English." When *The Young Lions* was released in April 1958 American critics were quick to discern the merits of Schell's performance. A reviewer for the Washington *Post and Times Herald* (April 19, 1958) observed: "Most forceful of the men is Maximilian Schell as the militaristic German. It is a crisply conceived role, smaller than the others, but there is touching truth in Schell's portrayal."

The year 1958 was also the one in which Schell made his American stage debut on Broadway, appearing in Ira Levin's *Interlock*, which starred Celeste Holm. Although the play lasted only four performances after its opening on February 6, 1958, Schell drew favorable notices for his performance as Paul, the romantic lead; Walter Kerr, for example, writing in the New York *Herald Tribune* (February 7, 1958) found him "little short of brilliant in a wavering role."

Although, after the collapse of *Interlock*, Schell underwent seven lean months, he turned down sixteen American film offers because it embarrassed him "to speak badly written words from a script that has no substance." In the meantime he began to derive more of his income from television, beginning in the United States with an appearance opposite Joan Fontaine in *Perilous* over CBS-TV on June 22, 1959. He starred in a three-hour television production of *Hamlet,* which was filmed in Munich and telecast throughout Europe. He co-starred with Julie Harris in *Turn the Key Deftly* for *Sunday Showcase* over NBC-TV on March 7, 1960, and his performance in *Child of Our Time* on *Playhouse 90* over CBS-TV in February 1959 won him a nomination for an Emmy award from the National Television Academy. Again he was nominated for an Emmy award after his appearance as Hans Rolfe, the German defense lawyer, in the original television production of *Judgment at Nuremberg* over *Playhouse 90* in April 1959, with a script by Abby Mann. He appeared in a television production of Hemingway's *The Fifth Column* over CBS-TV on January 29, 1960 and played d'Artagnan in *The Three Musketeers* over CBS-TV in November and December of 1960.

One reason that Schell fulfilled so many television engagements was his reluctance at first to make American movies. "I was deeply afraid that I would lose my identity and my feeling of unity and balance if I came to America," he has said. "I felt that experiences in America often tended to be meaningless and destructive—especially in Hollywood. But when I did come, I discovered some of the unique American qualities—warmth, openness and sincerity. I stopped being afraid." He also had reservations about repeating his original television role of Hans Rolfe for Stanley Kramer's film version of Abby Mann's *Judgment at Nuremberg,* only shortly before having seen a movie in Germany about the concentration camps. "Sometimes I will be sitting at a café table with some nice German and then I learn afterward that he did such and such," Schell once said. "Such nice people, you can't believe it. I sometimes think I won't trust anybody anymore."

Released through United Artists, *Judgment at Nuremberg* had its première in Berlin on December 14, 1961 before an invited audience of German notables, including Mayor Willy Brandt. When it opened in New York City on December 19, 1961, it was acclaimed by the critics for its content, treatment, and for the praiseworthy performances of Spencer Tracy, Burt Lancaster, Richard Widmark, Marlene Dietrich, Judy Garland, Montgomery Clift, and Maximilian Schell. A reviewer for *Time* (January 19, 1962) noted: "Schell dominates the film and easily outdoes his more celebrated co-stars. He is going to become much better known as a performer of unusual excellence and also as a frank and outspoken actor-intellectual." Sidney Skolsky in the New York *Post* (December 31, 1961) predicted that Schell would receive an Oscar nomination for his performance. In January 1962 Schell received the New York Film Critics' award as best actor of the year and on April 9, 1962 he won an Oscar from the Academy of Motion Picture Arts and Sciences for his performance in *Judgment at Nuremberg.*

Having lent his luster to an excellent film, Schell came to the rescue of an otherwise un-fortunate one when he played Walter Langer, a young German tutor, in the heavyhanded adaptation of Peter Shaffer's *Five Finger Exercise* that was released by Columbia Pictures in April 1962. His most recent film for Columbia Pictures is *The Reluctant Saint,* in which he plays the space-borne Italian Saint Joseph of Cupertino. After seeing a preview, a critic for *Show* magazine (October 1962) informed his readers: "It will be a surprise to no one that last year's Academy Award winner Maximilian Schell is an excellent actor. In the role of Desa, he manages with grace and fluidity to blend into one character two classic opposites, the ecstatic visionary of the mysteries and the underdog hero of comedy. It is impossible to imagine the picture without him." In the summer of 1962 Schell was in Hamburg, Germany, where he was co-starring with Sophia Loren in Vittorio DeSica's production of a film based on a play by Jean-Paul Sartre, with the working title of *The Prisoners of Altona.*

Meanwhile Schell continues to be as serious about his craft as ever. To the consternation of some directors he sometimes rewrites his lines, possibly to fulfill his urge to become a playwright. He is saving his money so that he can someday found a classical theater that would be modern in concept, staffed with leading players who would tour the world's capitals, acting in English. He prefers stage acting to films because he feels that the movie actor is at the mercy of the film editor. In his more despondent moods Schell considers giving up acting altogether for writing or directing on the grounds that acting uses up a man's emotions, leaving him depersonalized, and that acting is a form of prostitution in which the actor sells his emotions and mouths words that are not his own. "There are all kinds of acting," Schell has said, "from fake to first-rate. Fake acting contaminates an audience. First-rate acting transports them, makes them feel something that they have never felt before. That is what art should do. It is a sin to be false in art."

Standing six feet in height, weighing about 160 pounds, Maximilian Schell has deep brown eyes, black hair, jutting jaws, and a brooding face. Sometimes he walks with the stride of a boxer, sometimes with a dancer's grace. The shyness and dignity of his outward appearance camouflage an underlying friendliness and sense of humor. He fills the voids of his bachelor existence with playwriting, chess matches, piano playing, tennis, skiing, fencing, rowing, cycling, and swimming. He prefers intimate conversation to the babble of large parties. By October 29, 1961 he had put down enough roots in the United States to be able to tell May Okon of the New York *Daily News:* "I'm America's number one fan. . . . I like your towns, your cities, the people, the deserts, the mountains and wide spaces, and the way Americans treat one another and anyone they meet."

References

Look 26:144+ My 22 '62 por
Time 79:48+ Ja 19 '62 por
Wer ist Wer? (1962)

SCHRÖDER, GERHARD Sept. 11, 1910- Minister of Foreign Affairs of the Federal Republic of Germany
Address: b. Auswärtiges Amt, Koblenzerstr. 101, Bonn, West Germany

A new star on the West German political horizon is Gerhard Schröder, who became Minister of Foreign Affairs of the Federal Republic of Germany on November 14, 1961. Although he has made no radical changes in the foreign policy line of his predecessor, Heinrich von Brentano, or his superior, Chancellor Konrad Adenauer, he has shown an independence and a skill for diplomacy in his post that have made him a favorite candidate to succeed to the Chancellorship after Adenauer retires, as he is expected to do. Schröder, who belongs to the moderate Christian Democratic Union (CDU), was West German Minister of the Interior for eight years, from 1953 to 1961. A lawyer who helped reconstruct the West German steel and iron industries after World War II, he has been the CDU delegate from Mettmann, Düsseldorf in the Bundestag (Parliament) since 1949.

Gerhard Schröder, the son of Jan Schröder, a railroad official, and Antina (Duit) Schröder, was born in Saarbrücken, Germany on September 11, 1910. He has a brother, Adelbert, and a sister, Marie-Renate Schröder, both doctors of medicine. Gerhard Schröder attended schools in Saarbrücken, Friedberg, and Giessen and the Kaiser Wilhelm Gymnasium in Trier, from which he graduated in 1929. From 1929 to 1932 he studied law and political science at the universities of Königsberg, Edinburgh, Berlin, and Bonn, and in 1933 he received his doctor of laws degree. During the next few years he passed his first and second state law examinations. He served as an assistant at the law faculty of Bonn University and at the Institute of Foreign and International Civil Law in Berlin and as a junior barrister with a leading Berlin law firm. In 1939 Schröder was admitted to the bar of the Regional Court in Berlin and set up a law partnership with Walther Schmidt, Wilhelm and Joachim Beutner, Friedrich Kempner, and Heinz Pinner.

From 1939 to 1945 Schröder served in the German Army, attaining the rank of corporal. He had joined the Nazi party in 1933 as a means of furthering his legal career, since he believed it was the only way a young lawyer could "get on" at that time in Germany (New York *Times,* November 4, 1961), but he was expelled from it in 1941 when he married a woman of Jewish ancestry according to the Nuremberg laws. In 1938 he joined a confessional branch of the German Protestant Church that opposed the Nazis. Although political opponents have raked up Schröder's past Nazi affiliation, a postwar investigation cleared him of complicity in Nazi war crimes.

After the war Schröder became personal secretary to the president of Rhine province and then a senior counselor in the state government of North Rhine-Westphalia. He served at the same time as chairman of the German committee on electoral law under the Allied Control Commission (British section) and as deputy member of the zonal advisory council in Hamburg. He also helped to found the Society of German Voters in

Frankfurt am Main. In 1947 he resumed private law practice in Düsseldorf. He became a director of several iron and steel companies and a departmental director in the Association of Steel Trustees, and he helped to reorganize and rebuild the iron and steel industries in West Germany.

The creation of the Federal Republic of Germany, which was formed from the American, British, and French occupation zones, was proclaimed in May 1949, and elections for the first West German Parliament (Bundestag) were held in August of that year. Schröder was asked to stand for a seat by the Christian Democratic Union (CDU), a middle-of-the-road party uniting Protestants and Catholics. He was elected as a member of the first Bundestag from the constituency of Mettmann, Düsseldorf. In 1952 he served as deputy leader of the CDU-CSU parliamentary group in the Bundestag. (The Christian Social Union—CSU—is the Bavarian affiliate of the CDU.) He is a member of the central executive committee of the CDU and of the CDU's committee for the Rhineland and chairman of the Protestant working group of the CDU-CSU.

Schröder was re-elected to the Bundestag in 1953, 1957, and 1961. He was appointed Federal Minister of the Interior in October 1953 and held this post for eight years. In November 1958 he created a political stir by proposing a constitutional amendment that would give the federal government special powers in the event of a national emergency like grave internal disorder or external aggression. (The responsibility for preserving order under such conditions had remained with the former Allied occupying powers.) Schröder linked the proposal to a request for stronger police powers, saying he could not efficiently control subversive activities within West Germany unless federal authority was strengthened. The political opposition objected that the plan resembled a state-of-emergency provision of the Weimar Republic that Hitler had exploited to obtain power.

As a result of Schröder's initiative the Communist party was outlawed in West Germany in 1956. Also during his term of office, in 1960, the government set up a commission of scholars and educators to recommend methods of teaching the history of the Nazi period to West German public school students. Although he did much to ensure the internal stability and security of his country, Schröder did not confine his attention to domestic matters: he often discussed foreign policy questions in articles, speeches, and conferences. This squares with Schröder's belief that a minister should not concentrate too narrowly on the specialized demands of his job but strive to understand political developments in a number of fields.

For six years following the formation of the Federal Republic of Germany in 1949 Chancellor Konrad Adenauer reserved the portfolio of foreign affairs for himself, and from 1955 to 1961 this ministry was held by Heinrich von Brentano. After the elections of September 1961 the CDU was forced for the first time to form a coalition government; Brentano's resignation was a result of concessions the CDU made to its junior coalition partner, the Free Democratic Party (FDP). Schröder was named Minister of

Foreign Affairs on November 14, 1961, although the FDP expressed some fears that he might be "soft" on the Berlin question—that is, that he might countenance the separation of West Berlin from West Germany in a settlement between the West and the Soviet Union.

The preservation of West Berlin as a part of West Germany and the ultimate reunification of the two Germanys are goals advocated by nearly all German politicians, but the means for achieving these ends are frequently the subject of controversy. West Germany cannot muster the political strength to realize these goals independently and must therefore co-operate with the United States in negotiations with the Soviet Union, without jeopardizing West German objectives.

As Foreign Minister, Schröder has followed a flexible, pragmatic course on these questions that has sometimes led him into conflict with his predecessor, Brentano, and with Chancellor Adenauer. For instance, in the spring of 1962, both Adenauer and Brentano criticized, while Schröder approved, a United States package proposal that provided for the establishment of an international authority to oversee access routes between West Berlin and West Germany and for the establishment of Pan-German committees to discuss "technical" matters. Criticism of this particular plan, as of others, sprang from a fear that it might lead to the recognition of East Germany —to the recognition of existing divisions of German territory that could result in a permanent division of the country.

Schröder favors a gradual reconciliation with Eastern European countries like Poland, Hungary, and Czechoslovakia; in August 1962, however, he affirmed the existing "Hallstein doctrine" of his government that West Germany would sever diplomatic relations with any nation officially recognizing East Germany (except for the Soviet Union). Schröder, who is something of an Anglophile, welcomes the entry of Britain into the Common Market; he tends to rely less on France than Adenauer does. Schröder looks forward to West Germany's incorporation into a European federation. Although conflict could arise between the Foreign Minister and the Chancellor in view of the fact that Adenauer frequently speaks out on foreign policy issues himself, Schröder has managed to differ from, and yet remain loyal to, the Chancellor. He has also won friends among the coalition FDP and the opposition Social Democratic Party (SPD).

Writing in the New York *Times Magazine* (October 14, 1962), Flora Lewis pointed out that although Schröder's opportunities for making radical changes in foreign policy are limited, he has conducted the ministership in a new and striking style. According to Miss Lewis, Schröder has relied on suavity rather than on bluntness, and his imperviousness to emotion has served him well in diplomacy. "Until he became Foreign Minister," Miss Lewis wrote, "he was one of the top Christian Democratic backroom politicians, widely respected for his quick and agile

GERHARD SCHRÖDER

mind, his grasp of technique and political maneuver. Now in the limelight, he monitors his public image with meticulous care and seeks to overcome a reputation for ruthless calculation with a combination of boldness, accessibility, and ease."

Adenauer, who was eighty-six in 1962, has pledged to step down from his position as leader of the Federal Republic of Germany some time before the elections of 1965 to make way for a younger successor. Schröder is considered to have excellent prospects for becoming Adenauer's successor, since he occupies the second most important position in the government, he has won support from diverse political factions, and he has demonstrated, without exceeding his position, that he is capable of independent and sensible action. Schröder has visited the United States four times—in 1953, 1957, 1961, and 1962. In 1959 he received an honorary doctorate from the University of Maryland.

Gerhard Schröder married Brigitte Landsberg, the daughter of a banker, in 1941. They have two daughters, Christina and Antina, and a son, Jan. Schröder is five feet nine inches tall and has dark blond hair and grey eyes. For relaxation he takes long walks, swims, reads, and listens to classical music. He is the president of the German Society for Photography.

References

Christian Sci Mon p2 N 18 '61 por
N Y Times p7 N 4 '61 por
N Y Times Mag p28+ O 14 '62 por
International Who's Who, 1961-62
International Yearbook and Statesmen's Who's Who, 1962
Wer ist Wer? (1962)
Who's Who in Germany (1960)

SCHUMAN, WILLIAM (HOWARD) Aug. 4, 1910- Composer; educator; administrator

Address: b. c/o Lincoln Center for the Performing Arts, Inc., 10 Columbus Circle, New York 19

> NOTE: This biography supersedes the article that appeared in *Current Biography* in 1942.

As both an administrator and a composer, an organization man and an artist, William Schuman is ideally suited for his post as president of the Lincoln Center for the Performing Arts, which he has occupied since January 1962. Schuman has said that his mind is seething with ideas and projects for the still unfinished $142,000,000 center in New York City, the first constituent of which, Philharmonic Hall, opened its doors to the public on September 23, 1962.

Before coming to Lincoln Center, Schuman had displayed his creative and administrative talents as president of the Juilliard School of Music in New York City from 1945 through 1961, where he both revitalized and revolutionized the curriculum. From 1935 to 1945 he taught on the faculty of Sarah Lawrence College in Bronxville, New York. In announcing Schuman's recent appointment, John D. Rockefeller 3d, chairman of the Lincoln Center, said: "He brings to Lincoln Center a thorough and professional awareness of the artistic opportunities that lie before us as well as an understanding of the difficult business problems that must be surmounted."

Named for President William Howard Taft, William Howard Schuman was born on August 4, 1910 in New York City to Samuel Schuman, a businessman, and Ray (Heilbrunn) Schuman. (The family name had been modified by the father from the original "Schuhmann.") As a boy growing up on New York's upper West Side, Schuman harbored no greater musical ambition than to learn to play Beethoven's "Minuet in G," and at the age of eleven he began to study violin. At fourteen he performed MacDowell's "To a Wild Rose" and Pierné's "Serenade" in one of Blanche Schwarz's pupil recitals. "Most composers' first memory is the equivalent of hearing Mozart played in heavenly fashion," Schuman once recalled. "My first memory is of a conversation I overheard between my father and my grandfather—about a mortgage. But I also remember my mother playing Rubinstein's 'Melody in F' on the piano and my father playing the William Tell overture on the pianola loud—every morning before he went to business."

Sport was his master passion rather than music. In grade school he organized an athletic and outing club for neighborhood children, where he taught boxing, wrestling, and baseball for a small fee. "Baseball was my youth," Schuman once told an interviewer and added: "Had I been a better catcher, I might never have been a musician." At New York's George Washington High School he organized a jazz outfit known as "Billy Schuman and his Alamo Society Orchestra," in which he played piano, banjo, saxophone, and clarinet. Although Schuman gave up his orchestra at eighteen, he continued his interest in popular music by writing tunes with lyrics by Frank Loesser and Edward C. Marks, Jr. One of his collaborations with Loesser, "In

Love with the Memory of You," became a hit. He also played in night clubs and worked as a copywriter for an ad agency and as a salesman for a lithographer.

A concert by the New York Philharmonic Symphony to which he was taken by his sister on April 4, 1930 permanently resolved Schuman's conflict between athletics and music, and he plunged into the serious study of music. (He was aware that what he learned would also help him in harmonizing and scoring his popular music.) At nineteen he attended the Malkin Conservatory of Music, studying harmony with Max Persin, counterpoint with Charles Haubiel, and composition with Roy Harris. To prepare himself for the teaching of music, he entered Teachers College of Columbia University in 1933. He received his B.S. degree in 1935 and spent that summer at the Mozarteum in Salzburg, where he held a scholarship in conducting and began to compose his first symphony. Columbia University gave Schuman an M.A. degree in music in 1937.

In the autumn of 1935 Schuman joined the faculty of Sarah Lawrence in Bronxville, New York because he had heard that its teaching staff consisted of "people who actually did what they taught." At Sarah Lawrence he taught music appreciation, harmony, and choral singing, and conducted a student chorus that became good enough to perform with the Boston Symphony Orchestra at Carnegie Hall under Serge Koussevitsky. Arranging his time so that he could continue to compose, he won the first Pulitzer prize ever given for music for his secular cantata, *A Free Song*, in 1943.

When, in 1944, Schuman was offered the job of director of publications by the music publisher G. Schirmer, Inc., he was at first reluctant to accept, but Serge Koussevitsky assured him, "Villiam, through the night you vill become businessman." According to Schuman's associates at G. Schirmer, Inc., Koussevitsky was gifted with prophecy. Schuman showed his usual combination of practicality and vision, and diligently combed through 5,000 manuscripts a year. After Schuman became president of the Juilliard School of Music in 1945, he continued as special publications consultant to G. Schirmer, Inc., until 1951.

When Schuman was appointed to the presidency of the Juilliard School of Music one trustee reportedly remarked: "This will either be the greatest thing that ever happened to Juilliard or the most colossal error of our collective lives." Most observers agree that Schuman transformed the school from a nineteenth-century conservatory into a twentieth-century institution. During his presidency he amalgamated the graduate school with the regular school, established the Juilliard String Quartet, and introduced contemporary music into the curriculum and the programs of the school. He founded a department of dance and developed the literature and materials of music concept in which musical theory, composition, and history were all brought together in one program. To reach his goal of making "responsible adults out of musicians," he added such courses as sociology and race relations to the curriculum. "Musical education has to be ventilated," Schuman once said. "We must develop educated people who are musicians in order to develop music."

Since Juilliard had early agreed to become a constituent of the Lincoln Center for the Performing Arts, Schuman was involved in the initial planning of the fourteen-acre center on the West Side of New York City as a member of its council. Other constituents are the Metropolitan Opera, the New York Philharmonic Symphony, the Vivian Beaumont Theater, a dance and operetta theater, and a library-museum. Looking for an executive with professional background in the performing arts who would both be a man of creative ideas and an administrator, the members of the board of the Lincoln Center chose Schuman as a man who measured up to all their requirements. Before he accepted, Schuman made sure that he would have enough free time to compose. "You want an artist, I presume, not an ex-artist," he told the board. On January 1, 1962 he became president of the Lincoln Center for the Performing Arts, succeeding General Maxwell D. Taylor who had resigned to become military adviser to President John F. Kennedy.

At the core of Lincoln Center is a special fund of $10,000,000 to be raised through private contributions. More than half of that amount has already been raised, and Schuman hopes to augment it during his presidency. Schuman, who dreams of making Lincoln Center a dynamic and constructive force in the arts, says, "I didn't take this job to be a landlord." Among the projects he is revolving in his mind is the first of the center's summer festivals, planned for 1966, which will take in all the performing arts and will run for four weeks, and for which many new works will be commissioned. His other projects include a teachers' institute for 1966, choral groups, after-work concerts, and a children's theater. Schuman, who welcomes suggestions, says, "I am no czar at Lincoln Center."

Appropriately, the New York Philharmonic Symphony opened its 1962-63 season at Philharmonic Hall of Lincoln Center with a performance of William Schuman's recently composed Eighth Symphony. In addition to his orchestral works, Schuman has written four string quartets, works for piano, film and ballet scores, choral works, and works for band. His music is as driving, propulsive, energetic, and enthusiastic as the man himself. No avant-gardist, he is basically a traditionalist who handles advanced contemporary musical techniques. Although he once told a conductor, "It's all melody; if you can't sing my music it's because you can't sing," not all his listeners would agree. Dissonant, complex, polyharmonic, using a juxtaposition of modes, his compositions are sometimes difficult to listen to. He has never written twelve-tone music, but his music sometimes lacks key signatures. Many of his works have been recorded on the Columbia, Decca, Mercury, Louisville, RCA Victor, and Concordia labels.

William Schuman has received commissions from the Elizabeth Sprague Coolidge Foundation, the Ford Foundation, the Koussevitzky Music Foundation, the Ballet Theatre, the Philadelphia Orchestra, the Boston Symphony Orchestra, André Kostelanetz, and Martha Graham,

Carl Mydans

WILLIAM SCHUMAN

among others. He holds honorary doctorates in music from Columbia University, New York University, the University of Wisconsin, Colgate University, and other colleges, universities, and conservatories.

He has served as a member of the advisory committee on cultural information, United States Information Agency; as chairman of the board of judges of student composers' awards, Broadcast Music, Inc.; and as a member of the music panel, American National Theatre and Academy. He is a director of the Metropolitan Opera Association, the Koussevitsky Music Foundation, the Walter W. Naumburg Foundation, and the Composers Forum.

In addition to the first Pulitzer Prize for music, Schuman has won many other honors, including Guggenheim Fellowships in 1939-41; the first Town-Hall-League of Composers Award in 1940; an award from the National Institute of Arts and Letters in 1944; the New York Critics Circle Award, 1950-51; the Columbia University Bicentennial Anniversary Medal in 1957; and the first Brandeis University Creative Arts award in music in 1957. He is a Fellow of the National Institute of Arts and Letters and an honorary member of the Royal Academy of Music, in London. His clubs are the Century and the Lotos.

By his marriage to Frances Prince on March 27, 1936 William Schuman has two children, Anthony William and Andrea Frances. The music critic of the New York Times, Harold C. Schonberg, has described Schuman as "a tall, slim, bald man, impeccably dressed, with a narrow face, prominent features, a look of intelligence so pronounced it can almost be touched, a perpetually eager expression and a quality of quivering, suppressed excitement, something like that of a leashed Doberman pinscher who sees a rabbit in the distance." No matter how busy his schedule Schuman tries to sandwich in at least

SCHUMAN, WILLIAM—*Continued*

600 hours of composing a year, accompanying himself in a light baritone as he works, resorting to the piano only occasionally. His recreations are reading in bed, going to the theater and to movies, and swimming in the pool in the backyard of his thirteen-room house in New Rochelle, New York or in the swim-run dug into his basement. Still interested in baseball, he once wrote an opera, *The Mighty Casey*, about Casey at the bat.

References

> Baker's Biographical Dictionary of Musicians (1958)
> Ewen, David, ed. American Composers Today (1949)
> Ewen, David, ed. The New Book of Modern Composers (1961)
> Who's Who in America, 1962-63

SHERROD, ROBERT (LEE) (shĕr'rŭd) Feb. 8, 1909- Editor; journalist; writer
Address: b. c/o Saturday Evening Post, 666 5th Ave., New York 19; h. 570 Park Ave., New York 21

> NOTE: This biography supersedes the article that appeared in *Current Biography* in 1944.

Robert Sherrod was appointed to the editorship of the *Saturday Evening Post*, one of the key positions in the publishing world, in March 1962, at a time when its publisher, the Curtis Publishing Company, was going through a financial crisis. The future of the *Post*, which traces its origins back to the eighteenth century, may well depend on Sherrod's vision and leadership at this point in its history.

Before he was appointed editor in chief Sherrod had been with the *Saturday Evening Post* for ten years. From 1952 to 1955 he was its Far East correspondent, and from 1955 to 1962 its managing editor. From 1935 to 1952 he was a journalist and editor on the staff of Time, Inc. Out of his experiences as a war correspondent in the Pacific for *Time* magazine from 1942 to 1945 he wrote *Tarawa: The Story of a Battle* and *On to Westward: War in the Central Pacific*.

Robert Lee Sherrod was born in Thomas County, Georgia on February 8, 1909, one of five children of Joseph Sherrod, a lumberman, and Victoria Ellen (Evers) Sherrod. He graduated from the Thomasville (Georgia) High School in 1925 and then attended the University of Georgia, where he received the B.A. degree in 1929. While an undergraduate he was associate editor of the college yearbook and campus correspondent for the Atlanta *Constitution*. According to Sherrod, one factor that influenced him to take up a journalistic career was "a vast curiosity."

Between 1929 and 1935 Sherrod was a reporter for the Atlanta *Constitution*, the Palm Beach (Florida) *Daily News,* the *Hampton Chronicle* of Westhampton Beach, Long Island, and the New York *Herald Tribune* (from 1932 to 1934). In 1935 he became a Washington correspondent for *Time* magazine, and in 1942 he was made one of its associate editors. He was one of the

first *Time* correspondents to be sent overseas after the United States entered World War II; from 1942 to 1945 he was a war correspondent for *Time* in the Pacific.

Sherrod was assigned to the South Pacific in January 1942 and was aboard one of the first convoys bound for Australia. After covering General MacArthur's troops in action in Australia and New Guinea, he went on to the Aleutians in July 1943, to report on the final stages of the battle for Attu. He was one of nine correspondents commended by the United States Army for their conduct during the twenty-day fight on Attu, and he was commended by the United States Navy for his reporting of the landing on Attu.

After a brief visit to New York Sherrod was assigned to the Central Pacific in September 1943, where he covered the Wake Island raid. He then took part in the landing and battle on the Gilbert Islands atoll Tarawa, during which some 5,000 Americans and Japanese lost their lives. One of his purposes in writing *Tarawa: The Story of a Battle* (Duell, 1944) was to bring home to Americans the seriousness of the war, and in March 1944 he dedicated many lectures and radio speeches to the same end. For his reporting of the Tarawa battle Sherrod was commended by the United States Navy, and for his war reporting he received an award from the Headliners Club.

By June 1944 Sherrod was back in the Pacific theater, covering the taking of Saipan Island in 1944 and of Iwo Jima and Okinawa in 1945. His book *On to Westward: War in the Central Pacific* (Duell, 1945) outlines the course of the Pacific war between November 1943 and April 1945. In reviewing the book for the New York *Herald Tribune Weekly Book Review* (December 9, 1945) P. J. Searles commented, "Sherrod respects the Navy, gives due credit to the Air Force, somewhat grudgingly grants the Army its share of the glory, but his heart is always with the marines." After the war Sherrod reported for *Time* from the Far East. When he returned from Shanghai to the United States in 1948 he was asked by the Marine Corps to write a history of its combat aviation.

To do the job, Sherrod took a leave of absence from *Time*, but by the end of a year, despite the help he received from a translator of Japanese documents and six researchers, he realized that the work would require much more time. Returning to the Luce publications, he became the chief Pentagon correspondent for *Time* and *Life*, and spent his evenings and weekends working on the Marine history, which ultimately took him four years to complete. Covering the history of almost the entire Pacific war, Sherrod's *History of the Marine Corps Aviation in World War II* was published by the Combat Forces Press in 1952. "It was a pretty sedentary job," Sherrod recalls, "but I think I was prouder of it than anything else I have done. . . . When I was finally finished, I liked it, and I had also learned . . . that being a thorough reporter didn't necessarily qualify one to be a good historian. It was the hard way but I think it made me a better reporter." Sherrod also helped to write the text for *Life's Picture History of World War II,* which was published by Time, Inc. in 1950.

In 1952 Sherrod became a Far East correspondent for the *Saturday Evening Post.* Based in Tokyo, he traveled over a territory comprising seventeen countries and wrote about ten articles a year. Some of his *Post* articles won him two awards for foreign peacetime correspondence: the Benjamin Franklin Award from the University of Illinois, in 1954, and an award from the Overseas Press Club, in 1955. In 1955 he gave up writing to become managing editor of the *Post,* and in March 1962 he was promoted to the position of the *Post's* editor in chief.

Sherrod stepped into the top editorial position at the *Post* at a time when its publisher, the Curtis Publishing Company, was undergoing a financial crisis. In 1961, for the first time in seventy years of operation, the company ended a year in the red, sustaining a net loss of $4,193,585 despite increased circulation of all its magazines. (In addition to the *Post,* it publishes the *Ladies' Home Journal,* the *American Home, Holiday,* and *Jack and Jill.*)

A major cause of the deficit was the decline of *Post* advertising income from $104,000,000 in 1960 to $86,500,000 in 1961. The *Post,* which normally supplies more than one half of the company's annual revenues, is said to have lost advertising business to such competitors as *Life* and *Look* and to television. Other factors to which the difficulties of the Curtis Publishing Company have been attributed are old-fashioned management and the fact that the *Ladies' Home Journal* had lost out in a circulation race with its principal competitor, *McCall's* magazine.

In an effort to improve its position the Curtis Publishing Company introduced a number of sweeping changes. The *Saturday Evening Post,* which had been published weekly, was cut back to forty-five issues a year, and the *Ladies' Home Journal* and the *American Home,* reduced from twelve to ten issues a year, began to accept liquor advertising. The editorial offices of the *Post* were moved to New York in the interests of efficiency. Partly as a result of the move to New York and partly as the result of retirement the editorial staffs of the Curtis magazines were significantly changed. Matthew J. Culligan replaced Robert E. MacNeal as president of Curtis, while Sherrod succeeded Robert Fuoss, who had been editor in chief of the *Post* for only three months.

Under the editorship of Ben Hibbs, from 1942 to 1961, the *Saturday Evening Post* had built up its circulation as a light, folksy, human-interest magazine that appealed to the average reader. In an effort to modernize the publication Fuoss introduced a startling new layout for the *Post,* including a new cover design, bleeding of pictures, and the use of unusual type. The consensus was that Fuoss had gone too far in this direction, and when Sherrod took over the editorship he announced his intention of toning down this layout and combining the best of the new style with the best of the old. A symbolic instance of Sherrod's break with tradition is his replacement of George Horace Lorimer's desk with his own when he assumed the editorship. Lorimer had been editor of the *Post* from 1899 to

Philippe Halsman

ROBERT SHERROD

1936, and his desk had been used by each of Sherrod's predecessors.

Convinced that the literacy of the *Post's* readers has risen over the past twenty-five years, Sherrod hopes to improve the quality of the *Post's* editorial matter, nonfiction articles, and stories. He plans to publish "whatever in the world that interests people, whatever is good and incisive, entertaining, and accurate and decent."

Sherrod is a member of the Overseas Press Club in New York City, the National Press Club in Washington, D.C., Sigma Delta Chi, Alpha Tau Omega, and the Downtown Club of Philadelphia. He is an Episcopalian and a Democrat. Sherrod owns a library of over 1,000 books, every volume of which he has read. His other recreations are fishing, skin diving, and golf.

A soft-spoken, mild-mannered man, Sherrod is five feet eleven inches tall, weighs 165 pounds, and has brown hair and brown eyes. By his marriage in 1936 to Elizabeth Hudson, who died on December 21, 1958, Sherrod has two sons, John Hudson and Robert Lee, Jr. On May 5, 1961 he married the former Margaret Carson Ruff, who had been a public relations counselor to the Metropolitan Opera Company. Mrs. Sherrod's daughter by a former marriage, Carla Ruff, lives with them.

References

N Y Times p45 Mr 26 '62 por

Philadelphia Evening Bulletin p47 Mr 27 '62

Who's Who in America, 1962-63

SINCLAIR, UPTON (BEALL, JR.) Sept. 20, 1878- Author

Address: h. Monrovia, Calif.

"You don't have to be satisfied with America as you find it. You can change it," Upton Sinclair wrote in an article that appeared in the

UPTON SINCLAIR

San Francisco *Sunday Chronicle* (April 8, 1962).
"I didn't like the way I found America some
sixty years ago, and I've been trying to change it
ever since. I think I have succeeded in some
ways." A champion of the underdog, Upton
Sinclair has been a writer since his boyhood and
has never had any other profession. During his
career he has written more than eighty books,
some twenty plays, and hundreds of articles, in
which he has dealt with virtually every American
social problem. His works appear in some sixty
languages, and he is considered to be the most
widely read American author abroad.

The only son in a distinguished but impoverished Southern family, Upton Beall Sinclair,
Jr., was born on September 20, 1878 in Baltimore,
Maryland to Upton Beall and Priscilla Augusta
(Harden) Sinclair. His great-grandfather, Commodore Arthur Sinclair, commanded American
naval forces on Lake Huron in the War of 1812,
and his paternal grandfather was an officer in
the navy of the Confederacy during the Civil
War. His father, a wholesale liquor salesman,
viewed the world of business with aristocratic
disdain and took to drink when he failed in
business, although he remained devoted to his
family. Upton Sinclair was of delicate health as
a child, but he displayed an active mind and
taught himself to read by the time he was five.
Although he had the opportunity, at the age of
ten, to live with wealthy relatives, he chose to
share the poverty of his family and accompanied
his parents to New York City, where his father
obtained employment as a hat salesman.

In the New York public schools, where he was
known as "Chappie" by his classmates, Sinclair
skipped a grade and took part in sports. An avid
reader, he devoured the works of Shakespeare
and Milton by the time he was thirteen, and he
later studied Carlyle, Browning, Thackeray,
Goethe, and Zola. The three greatest influences
on his intellectual development were Jesus, Hamlet, and Shelley. Although he had been greatly

impressed as a child by the Episcopal services
that he had attended with his parents, he had
become a religious skeptic by the time he reached
adolescence, without abandoning the moral teachings of Christianity.

In 1892, at the age of fourteen, Sinclair entered
the College of the City of New York, where he
took courses in Latin and English literature. He
lived alone, supporting himself by writing for
comic papers, for *Argosy* and other adventure-
story magazines, and for the publishers Street &
Smith. By the time he was sixteen he was convinced that he wanted to make writing his
career.

After graduating from City College with a
B.A. degree in 1897, near the bottom of his class,
he entered graduate school at Columbia University, ostensibly with the intention of becoming a
lawyer. He enrolled as a special student, "picking and choosing courses," and taught himself
French, German, and Italian. To support himself
and his mother he continued to write, grinding
out an estimated 2,000,000 words a year.

Disillusioned with what he considered to be
the materialistic atmosphere at the university,
Sinclair moved to Quebec, Canada in the spring
of 1900, with savings of $100. Living in a shack
in the woods, he wrote his first novel, *Springtime
and Harvest*, which was privately published in
1901 with the aid of a loan from a relative, and
which sold enough copies to enable Sinclair to
repay the debt. In the next few years he wrote
the novels *King Midas* (Funk & Wagnalls, 1901);
Prince Hagen (L.C. Page, 1903), a satirical
fable; and *The Journal of Arthur Stirling* (Appleton, 1903), a partly autobiographical diary of a
disillusioned young poet. In these early novels
he expressed Socialist sentiments, which he had
arrived at independently, before he had actually
made any personal contacts with Socialists.

In 1903 Sinclair moved with his wife and son
to a shack near Princeton, New Jersey, where he
wrote *Manassas* (Macmillan, 1904), a Civil War
novel about a young Southern aristocrat who
became an abolitionist and joined the Union
army. Since his first five novels had netted him
a total of less than $1,000, Sinclair was forced to
continue with hack writing to support his family.
At the same time he propagandized for the
patronage of the arts by wealthy men. During
this period he turned down an offer of a high-
paying position as advertising manager with a
leading magazine and a similar offer of a job
as editorial writer for what he later referred to as
"America's greatest publisher of prostitute newspapers." In 1902 Sinclair joined the Socialist
party. In 1905 he and Jack London helped to
found the Intercollegiate Socialist Society, and in
the following year Sinclair was a Socialist candidate for Congress from New Jersey.

The Jungle (Doubleday, 1906), which brought
fame to Sinclair almost overnight, was the result
of observations he made in 1904, during a seven-
week stay in the packinghouse district of Chicago. The novel, centering around the life of a
Lithuanian immigrant family, became a best
seller in seventeen languages. Although Sinclair
failed in his efforts to alleviate the appalling
conditions of the packinghouse workers, his description of unsanitary conditions in the meat-

packing industry haunted the imagination of the public. President Theodore Roosevelt invited Sinclair to the White House and ordered a Congressional investigation that culminated in the passage of pure food laws. "I aimed at the public's heart, and by accident I hit it in the stomach," Sinclair later recalled.

In November 1906 Sinclair founded a cooperative community, the Helicon Home Colony, near Englewood, New Jersey, with the $30,000 that he had netted from *The Jungle*. The colony, which numbered some fifty or sixty residents, was visited by William James and John Dewey, and Sinclair Lewis, then a young reporter, tended furnaces there for a time. The colony was destroyed by fire in March 1907, possibly as a result of arson. In 1908 Sinclair founded a traveling theater company for social drama in California, and in 1909 he and his family moved to a single-tax colony in Arden, Delaware, remaining there for three years.

Meanwhile Sinclair continued to write in the crusading spirit of the muckrakers, whose exposés of social ills made a major impact on America during the Progressive era of Theodore Roosevelt. The writings of Upton Sinclair during this period included *The Industrial Republic* (Doubleday, 1907), a utopian novel; *The Metropolis* (Moffatt, 1908), an attack on New York high society; *The Moneychangers* (Dodge, 1910), an exposé of Wall Street financial interests; *Samuel the Seeker* (Dodge, 1910); and *Plays of Protest* (Kennerley, 1912). His autobiographical *Love's Pilgrimage* (Kennerley, 1911) was once described as one of America's great novels. In 1909 Sinclair issued a manifesto, addressed to Socialists and organized workers of Europe and America, calling on them to counter the danger of war with the threat of a general strike.

In 1912 Sinclair went to Holland to facilitate his divorce from his first wife. While in Europe, he wrote a novelized version of Eugene Brieux's play *Damaged Goods* (Winston, 1913), and the novels *Sylvia* (Winston, 1913) and *Sylvia's Marriage* (Sinclair, 1914). Although he considered settling in Europe, he returned to the United States in 1913 and remarried. Sinclair's continued concern with the conditions of labor prompted him to take up the cause of the striking coal miners in Colorado, and he was arrested in 1914 while picketing the New York offices of the Rockefeller mining interests. In 1915 he moved to Pasadena, California, where he wrote *King Coal* (Macmillan, 1917), a novel about the plight of the Colorado mine workers, in the same vein as *The Jungle*.

In 1917 Sinclair resigned from the Socialist party in opposition to its antiwar position. Although he had often expressed pacifist sentiments in the past, he regarded German militarism as a menace, and in February 1917 he wrote to President Woodrow Wilson, urging him to aid the Allies. From April 1918 to February 1919 he edited his own journal, *Upton Sinclair's*, which reflected Wilson's ideals. After the war Sinclair returned to the Socialist fold, having become disillusioned with Wilson's war policies, partly as a result of Allied intervention in the Soviet Union. His disillusionment is reflected in his war novel *Jimmie Higgins* (Boni & Liveright, 1919), and in *100%: The Story of a Patriot* (Sinclair, 1921). Ten years after the end of World War I Sinclair said: "If at the beginning of 1917 I had known what I know today I would have opposed the war and gone to jail with the pacifist radicals."

In the postwar years Sinclair devoted several books to the study of the relationships between moneyed interests and various American institutions. The best known of these is *The Brass Check* (Sinclair, 1919), an indictment of the venality of American journalism. In a similar manner Sinclair dealt with organized religion in *The Profits of Religion* (Sinclair, 1918); with education in *Goose Step* (Sinclair, 1923) and *The Goslings* (1924); and with the arts in *Mammonart* (Sinclair, 1925) and *Money Writes!* (Boni, 1927). His novel *Oil* (Boni, 1927), dealing with the scandals of the Harding administration and with southern California society, became immensely popular, as did *Boston* (Boni, 1929), a fictional account of the Sacco-Vanzetti case. Other books written by Sinclair during this period include *The Book of Life* (Macmillan, 1921), on the art of living; *They Call Me Carpenter* (Boni, 1922), a story of Christ; *The Wet Parade* (Farrar, 1931), a defense of Prohibition; *American Outpost* (Farrar, 1932), a personal reminiscence; and the novels *Roman Holiday* (Farrar, 1931) and *William Fox* (Sinclair, 1933). He was nominated for a Nobel Prize in 1932.

In California Sinclair was a Socialist candidate for Congress in 1920, for the Senate in 1922, and for governor in 1926 and 1930. In 1923 he was arrested for his role in a free speech fight in Los Angeles and in the same year he founded the southern California chapter of the American Civil Liberties Union. His four-act play *Singing Jailbirds* (Sinclair, 1924) is based on the persecution of members of the Industrial Workers of the World in California.

In 1934 Sinclair ran for governor of California as the candidate of the Democratic party after defeating George Creel in the primary election. His platform was based on the slogan "End Poverty in California" (EPIC) and emphasized production for use, full employment, government-owned production plants, and an elaborate pension plan. However, despite his immense popularity, he was defeated by the Republican candidate Frank F. Merriam by a vote of 1,138,000 to 879,000. His writings during the late 1930's include *What God Means to Me* (Farrar, 1936); *Co-op* (Farrar, 1936), a novel about communal life; *The Gnomobile* (Farrar, 1937), a children's story; *The Flivver King: A Story of Ford-America* (Sinclair, 1937), which was widely distributed by the United Auto Workers; and *Little Steel* (Farrar, 1938), about industrial strife in the steel industry.

In his eleven-volume *Lanny Budd* series Sinclair presented a fictionalized world history of the turbulent period from 1913 to 1949. Written from a Socialist and anti-Fascist viewpoint, the

SINCLAIR, UPTON—*Continued*

series was published by the Viking Press and includes *World's End* (1940), *Between Two Worlds* (1941), *Dragon's Teeth* (1942), *Wide is the Gate* (1943), *Presidential Agent* (1944), *Dragon Harvest* (1945), *A World to Win* (1946), *Presidential Mission* (1947), *One Clear Call* (1948), *O Shepherd, Speak* (1949), and *The Return of Lanny Budd* (1953). For *Dragon's Teeth*, which dealt with the rise of Nazism in Germany, Sinclair was awarded the Pulitzer Prize for fiction in 1943.

Other books that Sinclair has written in recent years include *Another Pamela* (Viking, 1950); *A Personal Jesus* (Evans, 1952); *Cup of Fury* (Channel Press, 1956), which deals with the evils of drink; *It Happened to Didymus* (Sagamore, 1958), a moral fable; and the satirical novel *Affectionately, Eve* (Twayne, 1961). In 1960 the University of Missouri Press published Sinclair's *My Lifetime in Letters*, including some 300 of the approximately 250,000 letters he has received over the years, which are contained in the collection of his papers at the University of Indiana library. *The Autobiography of Upton Sinclair* was published by Harcourt, Brace & Company in late 1962.

Sinclair is a member of the League for Industrial Democracy, the American Civil Liberties Union, and the American Institute of Arts and Letters. In 1962 he received the Page One Award from the New York Newspaper Guild and the Social Justice Award from the United Auto Workers. George Bernard Shaw wrote to Sinclair in 1941: "When people ask me what has happened in my long lifetime I do not refer them to the newspaper files or to the authorities, but to your novels."

Upton Sinclair's first marriage, to Meta H. Fuller in 1901, ended in divorce in 1913. He has one son, David, from this marriage. In 1913 Sinclair married Mary Craig Kimbrough, a member of a prominent Southern family, who died in April 1961. With his third wife, the former Mary Hard, whom he married in October 1961, Sinclair lives on a half acre in Monrovia, California. An agile and good-humored octogenarian, Upton Sinclair is five feet seven inches tall and weighs 130 pounds; he has white hair, a ruddy complexion, and blue-gray eyes framed by gold-rimmed glasses. He still likes to garden and keeps up with world affairs by subscribing to some fifty periodicals. A nonsmoker and teetotaler, he lives on a diet consisting largely of brown rice, fresh fruit, and celery.

Although he has consistently voted Democratic since 1934, Sinclair considers himself as much a Socialist as he ever was. He would like to see authors become more aware of the need for social justice. An anti-Communist, Sinclair believes that social change should be brought about within the framework of democratic institutions. He estimates that during the course of his career he earned about $1,000,000, most of which he spent on various causes. "I'm a religious man to the extent that I am sure this universe can't be an accident," Sinclair told Joseph Wershba of the New York *Post* (May 7, 1962). "My efforts are to find out what is righteousness in the world, to live it, and try to help others live it."

References

Dell, Floyd. Upton Sinclair: A Study in Social Protest (1927)
Kazin, Alfred. On Native Grounds (1942)
Sinclair, Upton. My Lifetime in Letters (1960)
Sinclair, Upton. The Autobiography of Upton Sinclair (1962)
Twentieth Century Authors (1942; First Supplement, 1955)
Who's Who in America, 1962-63

SKIDMORE, LOUIS Apr. 8, 1897-Sept. 27, 1962 Architect; engineer; co-founder of the firm of Skidmore, Owings & Merrill, which built Oak Ridge, Tennessee, Lever House and Chase Manhattan Building in New York City, and the Air Force Academy in Colorado Springs. See *Current Biography* (December) 1951.

Obituary

N Y Times p23 S 29 '61

SNELL, PETER (GEORGE) Dec. 17, 1938-
Middle-distance runner
Address: h. Pukekohe, New Zealand

Early in 1962 the middle-distance runner Peter Snell of New Zealand turned the track world topsy-turvy by setting five world's records in events ranging from the 800-meter to the one-mile run. The most spectacular and coveted of these records was that for the mile, which he set in Wanganui, New Zealand on January 27, 1962 with a time of 3 minutes, 54.4 seconds—one-tenth of a second better than the previous mark, set in 1958. The other four titles Snell holds are the outdoor 800-meter and 880-yard (half-mile) and the indoor 880-yard and 1,000-yard records.

Snell's achievements are all the more impressive since he had been regarded as a good but not exceptional runner. Except for winning the 800-meter run at the 1960 Olympic Games in Rome—and there were many who looked upon that victory as something of a fluke—Snell had attracted little attention beyond his native New Zealand. In fact, his record mile race at Wanganui was only the fifth of his career, and he had never before run a competition mile in under four minutes.

Peter George Snell was born on December 17, 1938 in Opunake, a small beach town on the southwestern coast of New Zealand. His father is an engineer, and he has an older brother, Jack, who is a noted cricket player. An active boy, Peter consumed large quantities of honey, probably because he needed to replenish energy quickly, and his mother bought honey sixty pounds at a time to keep him well supplied. Honey remains his dietary preference today.

In 1947 Snell's family moved to Te Aroha, where he attended elementary school and the Te Aroha District High School. He then became a boarder at Mount Albert Grammar School in

Auckland, where he went out for swimming, boxing, Rugby, cricket, tennis, and track. He was also a prefect and a noncommissioned officer in the cadet corps. The headmaster of Mount Albert once saw Snell working out on the track one evening after a full morning of playing tennis and an afternoon of playing cricket. "What are you doing, Snell?" the headmaster inquired. "I'm trying to get fit, sir," Snell answered.

Snell was the half-mile champion of Mount Albert, and in 1957 he won the 880-yard (half-mile) event at the Auckland Inter-Secondary Schools Athletic Championships in 1 minute, 59.6 seconds. After graduating from the school he joined an Auckland firm, James A. Stewart and Partners, to train as a quantity surveyor (a person who estimates amounts of materials needed for construction projects). At first undecided as to whether he should follow track or tennis, in both of which he had achieved success in school, Snell decided on track and started training with his customary zeal. At this time he was helping his parents to build a new home in Pukekohe, a town about thirty miles from Auckland. Every week, after he finished work at the surveying office, he visited Pukekohe, making the trip in both directions by bus for twenty miles and running for the last ten.

The results of Snell's strenuous training were not immediately evident. His performances were promising rather than outstanding. His fortunes changed for the better, however, when he met the famed New Zealand track coach Arthur Lydiard. A former marathon runner, Lydiard has achieved impressive results through his method of marathon training for middle-distance runners. His athletes have dominated New Zealand middle-distance running for years; twelve of them have entered international competitions, and two, Murray Halberg and Snell, are Olympic champions. Lydiard works to build up stamina rather than speed. His training regimen calls for one hundred miles of cross-country running a week over rugged terrain, the idea being that a man with enough stamina to run twenty miles daily will have little difficulty in running a single mile at a very fast pace. In Snell, Lydiard found an ideal pupil. "The first time he ran twenty miles he cried like a child for the last mile with the pain," Lydiard recalled recently. "Now he can run a marathon without turning a hair."

In 1959 Snell won the mile and half-mile titles at the New Zealand Amateur Athletic Championships, and he established an 800-meter New Zealand record of 1 minute, 51.2 seconds. He broke a leg at the beginning of the 1960 season, but within two months after he had resumed training, he ran 880 yards in 1 minute, 49.2 seconds, a record for New Zealand. In March 1960 he retained the national 880-yard title, and later that year, at the Moomba Festival meeting in Australia, he won the 880-yard event, beating the Australian runners Elliott and Blue.

When Snell went with the New Zealand team to Rome in September 1960 to compete in the Olympic Games, he was not widely known outside his own country. But at the trial heats it quickly became evident that he had reached the peak of his training. In the 800-meter final the Belgian runner Roger Moens, the pre-race fa-

PETER SNELL

vorite, held what he thought was a comfortable lead as he turned into the final stretch. Twenty meters from the tape he decided to reassure himself by stealing a glance over his right shoulder. No one was in view. But while Moens was looking to his right, Snell came bursting through on his left to win the coveted gold medal and set an Olympic record of 1 minute, 46.3 seconds for the 800-meter distance. In an interview after the race the disappointed Moens said of Snell: "He'll never get anywhere with his build; he is too heavy and his legs are too muscular."

Snell does not, in fact, have the build of a runner. Standing five feet ten and one-half inches tall and weighing 171 pounds, he is twenty pounds heavier than the famous milers and half-milers of modern times, and he is shorter than most. He gives the impression of surging strength rather than flowing speed. A writer for *Sports Illustrated* (February 12, 1962) compared the usual middle-distance runner to a Jaguar, Snell to a Sherman tank—with overdrive. After his Olympic triumph, Snell ran half-mile races in Dublin and London, winning both. Upon his return to New Zealand he was awarded the Murray Halberg trophy as the Auckland athlete who produced the year's outstanding performance.

In 1961 Snell began to concentrate on the mile run. He won a New Zealand invitational mile in the lackluster time of 4 minutes, 8.4 seconds in January. A month later, at an Auckland meet, he ran the mile in 4 minutes, 5.6 seconds, finishing second to Dyrol Burleson of the United States. Also in February he placed second in 880-yard events at Auckland and Christchurch and won a half-mile race at Wellington with a time of 1 minute, 52.4 seconds. Worn out from many months of international competition, he did not compete in the New Zealand Amateur Athletic Championships in

SNELL, PETER—*Continued*
March 1961. In May 1961 he was named "Sportsman of the Year" by New Zealand sportswriters.

In June 1961 Snell began an international tour by winning a half-mile event at Stanford University in California. He won half-mile races in London, Durham, and Dublin. An hour after he took the Dublin event in 1 minute, 47.2 seconds, he ran the fastest mile (4 minutes, 1.2 seconds) in a four-man relay race in which the New Zealanders Snell, Halberg, G. F. Philpott, and A. B. Magee lowered the world record by 1.6 seconds with a time of 16 minutes, 23.8 seconds. Also during the summer of 1961 Snell won an 800-meter event at the Finnish World Games in Helsinki, an 800-meter race in Turku, Finland, and a 1,000-meter race at Kristinehamn, Sweden.

In Ocober 1961 Snell won a "centennial mile" at Auckland in 4 minutes, 13 seconds, an extremely poor time in these days of sub-four-minute miles. Two months later, however, competing at Timaru, New Zealand, he covered the distance in 4 minutes, 1.3 seconds, setting the stage for his performance on January 27, 1962 at Wanganui, New Zealand. There he broke the world mile record with a time of 3 minutes, 54.4 seconds, one-tenth of a second better than the mark set by the Australian Herb Elliott in 1958.

The day after his record mile, Snell flew to Auckland; then he was driven to nearby Papakura, where he changed into track shorts, and ran fifteen miles to his parents' home in Pukekohe to tell them about the race. On February 3, 1962, at Christchurch, New Zealand, he set a world standard of 1 minute, 45.1 seconds for the 880-yard outdoor run, topping the 1 minute, 46.8 second mark set by Tom Courtney of the United States in 1957. En route to the 880-yard record, Snell was timed in 1 minute, 44.3 seconds for the shorter 800-meter run; this too was a new world record. Snell set a new world indoor mark at Los Angeles on February 10, 1962, by running 1,000 yards in 2 minutes, 6 seconds. On March 18, 1962, in Tokyo, he established another record by running the indoor half-mile in 1 minute, 49.9 seconds.

A pleasant, rather quiet man, Snell believes he can improve on the mile time a little. In predicting that Snell will eventually lower the mile standard to 3 minutes, 48 seconds, Coach Lydiard explains: "He is a big man. Like all big men it is very difficult for him to reach the condition of a smaller man. . . . But when you work a big man into condition he will always beat a smaller man, even in running." When Snell is in New Zealand he boards with a family in an Auckland suburb, continuing his studies for a surveying career. He plans to retire from the track after the 1964 Olympic Games in Tokyo, in which he hopes to compete. In June 1962 he was designated a Member of the British Empire.

References

N Y Times p25 Ja 31 '62 por; p36 F 8 '62 por
Sports Illus 16:48+ F 5 '62 por; 16:16+ F 12 '62 por; 16:16+ F 19 '62 por

TITOV, GHERMAN (STEPANOVICH)
(tĕ'tôv gĕr'män stĕp-än'ô-vĭch) Sept. 11, 1935-
Soviet cosmonaut
Address: c/o The Kremlin, Moscow, U.S.S.R.

The Soviet cosmonaut Gherman Stepanovich Titov became the first man to spend a day in space when he rode his spaceship, *Vostok II,* through seventeen-and-a-half orbits (over 436,000 miles) around the earth on August 6 and 7, 1961. Major Titov, a Soviet Air Force jet pilot who was twenty-five years old at the time of his flight, was preceded into space by his friend Yuri Gagarin, who completed a one-orbit trip in the *Vostok I* on April 12, 1961. Titov's record flight was later exceeded by two of his countrymen, Pavel R. Popovich and Andrian G. Nikolayev, who traveled through forty-eight and sixty-four orbits, respectively, in August 1962. Three Americans have also circled the earth in orbital flights: John H. Glenn, Jr., Malcolm Scott Carpenter, and Walter M. Schirra, Jr., who made three, three, and six global turns, respectively, in 1962.

Gherman Stepanovich Titov, the son of Stepan Pavlovich and Aleksandra Mikhailovna Titov, was born on September 11, 1935 in the Altai region of Siberia, near the southeastern border of the Soviet Union. His paternal great-grandfather, attracted by the promise of free farmland, had immigrated from European Russia to Siberia in the nineteenth century; both his grandfathers had helped to build Maiskoe Utro (May Morning), the first of the new peasants' communes that came into being in the Altai after the revolution of 1917.

"Gera" Titov and his sister, Zemfira, grew up in Polkovnikovo, a small village about twenty miles from the May Morning commune, where their father taught Russian language and literature in the village school. Stepan Titov, in addition to being a scholar, drew well and played the violin. His son has been quoted as saying "Father was my idol when I was a child and is still the person I respect and love the most."

In 1942 Stepan Titov was called to the Russian front, and his family moved for the duration of World War II to Maiskoe Utro, where Gherman enrolled at the elementary school on the commune. When his father was demobilized, the Titovs returned to Polkovnikovo, where the boy continued his schooling. Under his father's influence Titov had begun to read early, and he was a conscientious student, who took part in the activities of the literary club.

Also athletic, he had begun to ski at the age of three, and he enjoyed skating, cycling, and playing the Russian equivalents of baseball and football. Common sense and tenacity were two qualities that Titov exhibited early. He once saved the lives of five other children by leading them home in a blinding snow storm. In 1945, he collapsed and almost froze to death on a road because he refused to abandon a sack of flour, which he had carried many miles and which was badly needed at home by his family.

Martin Caidin relates in *I Am Eagle!* (Bobbs-Merrill, 1962), a biography based on interviews with the cosmonaut, that a desire to fly was aroused in Titov as the result of a visit he received in Polkovnikovo from an uncle who was an aviator. After completing his secondary education in June 1953 Titov applied to the Soviet Military Commission for acceptance as an aviation cadet. He was accepted, and that fall he was sent to Kustenai in northwest Kazakhstan for primary training as a military pilot.

Titov and his classmates were the first cadets at this installation and, after experiencing a single heady flight in a training plane, they were put to work building quarters for themselves. They attended ground training classes in the mechanical and physical aspects of flying and in the spring of 1954 were allowed to take to the air again in Yak-18's. In 1955 Titov was transferred for advanced flight training to the Stalingrad Flying Academy, where he learned to do stunts with Yak-11's and to fly the MIG jet fighters. He spent most of his spare time exercising in the gymnasium, especially trying to strengthen his arms, one of which he had broken as a boy. Once his quick temper nearly resulted in his expulsion from the school, and thereafter he worked hard to discipline his mental as well as his physical reactions.

Having obtained excellent ratings in all subjects, Titov graduated from the academy in 1957. On his twenty-second birthday he received an order ending his cadet training and designating him a lieutenant in the Soviet Air Force. He requested assignment to a combat squadron and was sent to serve in the Leningrad Military District. Titov had joined the Komsomol—the Young Communist League—in 1949. Komsomol twice honored him while he was serving in Leningrad for successes in military training and political awareness and for exemplary military discipline.

Titov spent the next year or so in honing his skills as a jet fighter pilot. One day he was called into the office of an Air Force colonel, where he was asked about his interest in jets and rocketry, and was requested to decide immediately whether he would volunteer for special training in "a new field of aviation." He accepted on the spot. Weeks of grueling medical, psychological, and physical endurance tests followed, and Titov experienced many qualms as men were winnowed out from the program.

Surviving this stage, however, he was subsequently ordered to Moscow to enter the space training program, which began with two months of constant athletic work, including running, hockey, and basketball. The attrition of candidates continued until, by the middle of December 1960, only twelve men were left to begin the second, technical training, phase of the program.

Titov received additional jump training, designed to make him an expert in parachute techniques (including free fall); at the conclusion of the training he was awarded the classification of "parachute instructor." He and his classmates studied "bio-cosmonautics," or the effects on the body of speed, centrifugal force, lack of oxygen, radiation, and other factors involved in cosmic flight. They heard lectures from astronomers, technicians, engineers, and doctors. They learned the technical aspects of rocketry and studied films of ascending rockets and of dogs and other animals that the Russians put into orbit beginning in 1957.

Wide World

GHERMAN TITOV

Transferred to an Air Force research center, they entered a new phase of the program that was directly concerned with conditions they would meet in space flight. Titov spent two weeks in a "chamber of silence," and he has said that this was one of the most difficult parts of the program to endure. Encased in a pressure suit, he was placed in a centrifuge and required to withstand forces equalling fifteen times the force of gravity. Another machine spun him simultaneously in three different planes of motion; he recalls that this initially produced a feeling of nausea, which abated as he became accustomed to the three-axis movement. He also withstood high and low temperatures in a thermal chamber, and, carried in a plane, floated for periods of up to a minute in a weightless condition.

Titov has spoken of his respect for the scientist who is chiefly responsible for designing the Soviet space program. (The Soviet Union has not revealed his name.) Inspired by the cosmonauts' first briefing from the Chief Designer, as the scientist is titled, Titov has explained, "We gained more of a feeling for what we were doing, and why, from this initial encounter than from any other single event of our entire training program."

After what seemed to the impatient Titov an interminable period of time the cosmonauts were taken to see Baikonur, a space center in Kazakhstan with a giant underground command and control network, from which the Soviet satellites and space ships were launched. They came to know intimately every detail of the *Vostok* (East) spaceship in which one of them would take man's first step beyond the atmosphere of the earth. As experienced pilots they thought of certain modifications—particularly with respect to the pilot's cabin—that they later were able to submit for consideration. Titov was the first to volunteer drawings and plans for modifications

TITOV, GHERMAN—*Continued*

to the Chief Designer, and several of his recommendations were incorporated into the design of the *Vostok*.

Titov was honored for his efforts with an appointment to the scientific and technical council for Project Vostok on an equal status level with the engineers, and he became the cosmonauts' representative at project meetings. During one meeting he conceived the germ of a new engineering concept that he hastened to elaborate in his office through the whole of that night. The next morning he presented his plans to the Chief Designer; several months later his contribution (which is still secret) brought him the Order of Lenin, one of the highest honors the Soviet government confers upon its citizens, representing a contribution to Soviet progress of the greatest importance.

The first Soviet cosmonaut, indeed the first human being, to make a space flight around the earth, was Yuri Alekseyevich Gagarin, who made a one-orbit trip in the *Vostok I* on April 12, 1961. Titov was the standby cosmonaut for Gagarin, with whom he had become close friends during the course of their space training.

The five-ton, bullet-shaped *Vostok II* that carried Titov was boosted into space at 9 A.M. Moscow time on August 6, 1961. During its flying time of twenty-five hours and eighteen minutes, it reached an apogee of 159.3 miles and a perigee of 110.3 miles. After a seventeen-and-a-half-orbit flight the spaceship landed on August 7, 1961 at 10:18 A.M. Moscow time in a field near the town of Krasnyy Kut in the Saratov region. Titov had been ejected with his seat from the falling capsule and had returned to earth under his own parachute.

Throughout the flight Titov reported on his condition via two-way radio to the ground, using the code name *Oriel*, or *Eagle*. Medical and other data were transmitted to the ground by electronic instruments. The weightless condition that he experienced for about twenty-five hours did not hinder him in the performance of assigned tasks. Twice during the flight he switched the automatic pilot system to manual control, as Gagarin had not. (The manual system provides for orientation of the capsule about a three-way axis, but not for a change in the capsule's main orbit path.) While he passed over the Soviet Union during one orbit Titov heard over the radio that he had been promoted to the rank of major.

During the third orbit he ate lunch out of tubes; spilling a little currant juice, he noticed the drops hanging like berries in the air before him until he scooped them into his mouth. Titov did physical exercises and slept about eight hours (he overslept his schedule by half an hour). He had some trouble getting to sleep because when he relaxed, his arms would float straight up in the air, but he solved this problem by confining them under his seat belt. Titov took color photographs of the earth. Varied colors of oceans and continents stood out clearly: Africa appeared to him as a yellow continent with dark green jungle spots, somewhat reminiscent of a leopard. Although he was able to carry out all his tasks with precision, Titov felt

ill on two occasions: he experienced a feeling of disorientation and vertigo immediately after he went into orbit and a feeling of dizziness and nausea during the sixth orbit. Scientists speculated, after his trip, that illness due to prolonged weightlessness might prove a major difficulty in long space flights, but subsequent, longer trips by Soviet cosmonauts have tended to demonstrate that prolonged weightlessness does not necessarily produce discomfort.

Within two hours after he landed Titov spoke by telephone to Premier Nikita S. Khrushchev in Moscow. The Premier congratulated him and said that his flight had earned him full membership in the Communist party. (Titov had become a candidate member in April 1961; the normal probation period is one year.) Titov subsequently received a hero's welcome in Moscow and was awarded the Soviet cosmonaut medal and several other decorations. His flight was certified in March 1962 by the International Aeronautical Federation.

Titov visited the United States for two weeks in April and May 1962. He attended a reception at the United Nations and then joined the American astronaut John H. Glenn, Jr., in appearing before the third International Space Science Symposium sponsored by the committee on space research of the International Council of Scientific Unions. Titov and his wife, who accompanied him, were shown around Washington, D.C. by John and Anna Glenn, and Titov met President John F. Kennedy.

Giving his impressions of the American trip, Titov wrote in *Pravda*, the Communist party newspaper, that he was delighted to discover that the Uncle Remus stories that he had enjoyed in his youth had been written by an American writer, Joel Chandler Harris. He also mentioned other American writers that he liked—Walt Whitman, Theodore Dreiser, Ernest Hemingway, and John Steinbeck—and said that he admired the pictures of Rockwell Kent, the music of George Gershwin, and the concert performances of Van Cliburn.

Gherman Titov stands five feet five inches tall, weighs about 141 pounds, and has gray eyes and fair hair. He met his wife, Tamara Vasilyevna Titov, to whom he was married on April 24, 1958, in Leningrad, where she was a cook in an Air Force cafeteria. They had one son, Igor, who died a few months after his birth. In contrast to the American astronaut John H. Glenn, Jr., who is deeply religious, Titov is an atheist. At a news conference in Seattle in May 1962 he said, "In my travels around the earth all day long I looked around and . . . I saw no God or angels. I don't believe in God. I believe in man, his strength, his possibilities, and his reason."

During the sixth orbit of his flight Titov was suddenly overwhelmed with a feeling of exhilaration, and his routine code name, *Eagle*, became a cry of joy. His account of this occurrence is given in Martin Caidin's book: "I felt elation as I had never before known in my life . . . the miracles of space before my eyes to drink in hour after hour; the realization of the most fantastic dream that men have ever dared to nourish in their minds . . . the superb performance of all my equipment. . . . And all this, this . . .

incredible sweep was mine; to see and sense and wonder, and later to carry it back to the planet with me. I felt no later reflection or regret when, feeling as I did, I replied to a call from earth with the cry: 'I am Eagle! I am Eagle!' "

References

N Y Post p4 My 2 '62
N Y Times p6 Ag 7 '61 por
N Y Herald Tribune p3 Ag 7 '61 por
Titov, Gherman and Caidin, Martin. I Am Eagle! (1962)
Who's Who in the USSR, 1961-62

TOLEDANO, RALPH DE (tō-lā-dä'nō) Aug. 17, 1916- Writer; editor
Address: b. 1319 F St., N.W., Washington 4, D.C.; h. 3315 Rowland Pl., N.W., Washington 8, D.C.

The reputation that Ralph de Toledano has acquired as one of the country's keenest political analysts rests both upon his work in journalism, formerly as associate editor of *Newsweek* and now as a nationally syndicated columnist for King Features, and upon his books and many magazine articles, which often deal with the problem of Communism. Much of his writing, such as his biography *Nixon* (1956) and *Lament for a Generation* (1960), conveys intense concern and a sense of personal involvement in the American political scene. He is also a poet and an authority on jazz.

Ralph de Toledano, who was born on August 17, 1916 in the International Zone of Tangier, is the son of Haim de Toledano, a former newspaperman, translator, and businessman, and Suzane (Nahon) de Toledano, a former correspondent for Latin-American and Moroccan newspapers. Of Spanish descent, he belongs to a family whose records go back to the fifteenth century in Spain; some of his ancestors were prominent in Morocco. His parents, who are American, brought him to live in New York when he was five years old. He has a brother, Edward, and a sister, Gladys; another brother, Henry, is deceased.

In secondary school—the Society for Ethical Culture's Fieldston School in Riverdale, New York—de Toledano took much interest in writing. He edited the school magazine, *Inklings,* and an independent weekly with some 1,000 subscribers, *Crosstown,* which he had helped to found. Upon graduating in 1934 he entered Columbia College, where he majored in literature and philosophy. His extracurricular activities included holding the managing editorship in 1936-37 and the editorship in 1937-38 of the *Columbia Jester,* which won during those years the Intercollegiate Cup as the best college humor magazine in the country. He was also associate editor of the *Columbia Review* from 1936 to 1938; managing editor of *Chimère,* the French magazine; president of Philolexian, a literary society on the campus; member of the honorary Laughing Lion Society; and a contributor to the *Columbia Daily Spectator.* His literary honors included the Boar's Head poetry award and, on two occasions, the Philolexian Prize for Poetry.

City News Bureau, Wash., D.C.
RALPH DE TOLEDANO

In June 1938, after receiving his B.A. degree, de Toledano somewhat reluctantly inaugurated his professional career by accepting the position of general editor of what he has termed a "string of rather dubious publications." He left the job two years later when offered the associate editorship of the *New Leader,* then a weekly newspaper with a strong voice of anti-Communism. At the same time de Toledano contributed music and record criticism to the *American Mercury.*

When de Toledano entered the Army as a private in March 1943, he underwent training in antiaircraft artillery to become a first-class gunner. He was later assigned to the Office of Strategic Services and sent to Cornell University for an intensive course in Italian, but he was dropped from a projected mission in Italy, reportedly for being too strongly anti-Communist. Proficient in Spanish, as well as French, he served as chief of section of the Information and Education Service in San Juan, Puerto Rico, where his duties included the editing of Army newspapers. (Called in 1954 as a witness before a Senate internal security subcommittee concerned with Communist infiltration of the Army's Information and Education Service, de Toledano testified that some of the material distributed by that agency in 1945 praised the Chinese Communists as friends of the United States.)

Leaving the Army as staff sergeant in January 1946, de Toledano returned to New York and took over the editorship of the *Standard,* published by the American Ethical Union, a federation of educational and religious societies, for which he also did publicity work. Before the year was over he had become the first manager of the anti-Communist monthly *Plain Talk,* of which he was a founder. In 1947 the International Ladies Garment Workers Union hired de Toledano as publicity director. "There was a

TOLEDANO, RALPH DE—*Continued*

great deal of turnover in that particular position," he recalls, "and I hold the all-time occupancy record of eight months."

De Toledano's next employer, *Newsweek* magazine, retained him for twelve years. Starting as assistant editor in 1948, he first covered national affairs from his office in New York City. Before two years had passed he was promoted to associate editor of the magazine. In the course of his work in journalism he developed many excellent high-level contacts and news sources throughout the country. He often scored newsworthy beats, such as the first face-to-face interview with the former Soviet code clerk, Igor Gouzenko, who after having defected in 1945, had exposed an international atomic spy ring, and had gone into hiding in Canada.

The experience that de Toledano acquired on the "subversive beat," in studying and reporting espionage, proved useful when he was assigned to the Algier Hiss trial. From his close involvement with the case emerged *Seeds of Treason* (published by Funk for Newsweek Bookshelf, 1950), which he wrote with Victor Lasky of the New York *World-Telegram and Sun*. As de Toledano himself pointed out in the preface to the revised, 1962 edition (Regnery) of his book, when *Seeds of Treason* appeared it was attacked in reviews in several important newspapers and magazines. The *Christian Science Monitor*, for example, commented that "a book like this takes its part in the stream of national thinking and emotion, weighing not just the fate of one individual named Hiss but the whole question of how this country can keep its poise and democratic integrity while at the same time dealing competently with espionage. . . . On these matters the book perpetuates darkness." Such criticism, however, was counterbalanced by praise in other publications; the book became a best seller and was brought out in British, Swedish, and Chinese editions.

In *Spies, Dupes and Diplomats* (Duell, 1952) de Toledano contends that the three categories of people named in the title—American and non-American espionage agents for the Soviet Union, misguided liberals, and assorted officials of various branches of the government—have served to further immeasurably the Russian goal of world conquest. De Toledano's first novel, *Day of Reckoning* (Holt, 1955), is the story of an American newspaperman's search for a Communist murderer whom he intends to kill, and it is based in part on events surrounding the death of Carlo Tresca, an anarchist leader who was murdered in New York in 1943. Herbert A. Philbrick, a former counterspy in the American Communist party, observed in the New York *Herald Tribune Book Review* (April 3, 1955), "Ralph de Toledano's documentary 'Seeds of Treason' read stranger than fiction. Now this able young journalist has created a novel which carries a greater impact of reality than all the official reports put together." After the book's publication de Toledano charged that some booksellers had suppressed his anti-Communist novel and that in some stores it had been placed where it would not be seen by the book-buying public.

While covering the 1952 and 1956 Presidential campaigns, de Toledano became acquainted with the nation's top leaders. "I've got good friends in the Democratic Party and in the Republican Party—in both wings of both parties," he has said. He spent his last four years with *Newsweek* in Washington, where his assignments included the activities of Vice-President Richard M. Nixon and events at the White House, the Justice Department, the Supreme Court, and the Labor Department. As both a correspondent and a friend he traveled with Nixon in 1959 on his visit to Poland and Russia.

De Toledano's friendship with the Vice-President inspired *Nixon* (Holt, 1956), a biography devoted chiefly to an account of Nixon's public career. Some reviewers felt that the book, the first Nixon biography, was too biased to offer any historical significance. W. S. White wrote in the New York *Times* (March 18, 1956), "It is best to say straightaway that this book is not quite fair either to history or to the subject upon whom Ralph de Toledano turns such an embarrassingly uncritical view." J. W. Stein, who praised the biography in *Library Journal* (March 15, 1956) as "zestful and alive," suggested that because of the diversity of attitude toward Nixon, "many readers will be made glad by this book, some sad, some mad."

It was Nixon who wrote the foreword to de Toledano's autobiographical *Lament for a Generation* (Farrar, 1960), which records the intellectual passage of a man from radicalism to conservatism and from agnosticism to faith. Like most of de Toledano's books, *Lament for a Generation* received mixed reviews. While August Heckscher described it in the New York *Herald Tribune Book Review* (July 17, 1960) as "skillfully written, ranging widely across the personalities and issues of a quarter century," Anthony Lewis complained in the New York *Times Book Review* (June 5, 1960), "The book is filled with pointlessly vindictive comments about individuals —a form of poisonous name-dropping. And the style is turgidly pseudo-poetic."

In his present position as nationally syndicated columnist for King Features, de Toledano, reporting from the nation's capital, "packs as much hard news . . . as possible" into his 750-word column called "In Washington," which appears four days each week. "I try to give my readers the feel of Washington—from the Hill to the White House to the Pentagon," he has said. When de Toledano accepted his post with the syndicated column in 1960 he was also employed as radio-TV commentator for the Taft Broadcasting Company. His association with the network ended in 1961, at which time he began another writing venture as editor of *World*, a compact weekly tabloid with a conservative slant, covering national and international news but avoiding government news. De Toledano organized *World*, trained the staff, and then, because of policy differences, left the paper.

De Toledano's free-lance work, including his poetry, has been published in *Collier's*, *Reader's Digest*, *Coronet*, *American Scholar*, *Commonweal*, *Commentary*, *National Review*, *Modern Age*, *Poetry*, and other periodicals. One of his many contributions to the *American Mercury*, "The Cult of the Conductor," an article on music, was reprinted in a collection of essays for college use as a model of English prose.

A devotee of jazz, which he learned to love while a student at Columbia, de Toledano in 1938-39 co-founded and co-edited with Eugene Williams the country's first serious jazz publication, *Jazz Information*. His work for the magazine led to his editing *Frontiers of Jazz* (Durrell, 1947; revised edition, Ungar, 1962), an anthology of articles about jazz. Virgil Thomson found that it had "an authority that few works in this field achieve," and R. B. Gehman recommended it in *Saturday Review of Literature* (May 22, 1948) as an anthology that "undoubtedly will be consulted as a reference work for some time to come."

As part of his engrossment in politics and world affairs de Toledano has made hundreds of public appearances on television and radio and before groups like the University of Virginia Public Affairs Institute, Dartmouth University's Great Issues Course, and the United States Navy seminars. While on the *Newsweek* staff he was a member of the American Newspaper Guild, and he is a present member of the National Press Club in Washington, the Washington Chapter of Sigma Delta Chi, the International Mark Twain Society, and the Dutch Treat Club in New York City. He is a sponsor of the Young Americans for Freedom and an honorary member of the Chicago Press Club. The Veterans of Foreign Wars honored him with its Loyalty Award in 1952, and in both 1950 and 1962 he won the George Washington Medal of the Freedoms Foundation.

Ralph de Toledano married Nora Romaine, an artist and writer, on July 6, 1938, almost immediately after his graduation from college. They live in Washington with their two sons, James and Paul Christopher, who share de Toledano's enthusiasm for French folk songs and for salt water fishing. His other avocations include swimming, stamp collecting, and song writing. He is five feet eleven and a half inches tall, weighs 155 pounds, and has brown eyes and jet-black hair.

In correcting some misunderstandings about his political stand, de Toledano has explained, "I have been called in print a John Bircher, a Communist, and other similar names. If I must be classified, it must be as a non-conformist conservative with general (though often critical) Republican sympathies. I derive my politics from a belief in God and the dignity of man."

References

Am Mercury 80:93+ Ap '55
Ed & Pub 93:46 Ap 16 '60 por
Lib J 80:296 F 1 '55 por
Who Knows—and What (1954)
Who's Who in America, 1962-63

TOWER, JOHN G(OODWIN) Sept. 29, 1925-
United States Senator from Texas

Address: b. Senate Office Bldg., Washington 25, D.C.; h. 1609 Sparks St., Wichita Falls, Tex.

When he took office on June 15, 1961, John G. Tower became the first Republican Senator from Texas since the 1870's and the third Republican Senator in the history of the state. He

Wide World
JOHN G. TOWER

won the Senate seat formerly held by Vice-President Lyndon B. Johnson by his victory over seventy candidates in an interim election on April 4, 1961 and by his defeat of his closest rival, the Democrat William Blakley, in a runoff election on May 27, 1961.

A former assistant professor of political science at Midwestern University in Wichita Falls, Texas, Tower belongs to the far right of the political spectrum. His unusual election victory has been interpreted by many as ushering in a revival of the two-party system in Texas. Tower has become a prominent figure in his party, and he is regarded, along with Senator Barry M. Goldwater, as one of the strongest champions of Republican conservatism. He is the author of a book, *A Program for Conservatives* (Macfadden, 1962), with a foreword by Goldwater, which outlines an eight-point program for conservatives.

John Goodwin Tower was born in Houston, Texas on September 29, 1925, the son of Dr. Joe Z. and Beryl (Goodwin) Tower. He grew up in a strongly Methodist home. His father, a minister, is executive secretary of the Texas Conference of the Methodist Church, and his grandfathers on both sides were also Methodist clergymen.

Tower graduated from high school in Beaumont, Texas in 1942. He then enlisted in the United States Navy and served three years on an amphibious gunboat in the Pacific. After his discharge he enrolled at Southwestern University in Georgetown, Texas. Majoring in political science, he finished his undergraduate work in three years and received his B.A. degree in 1948. He worked as a radio announcer in 1948 and 1949 at stations KFDM in Beaumont and KTAE in Taylor, Texas, and from 1950 to 1951 he was an insurance agent in Dallas.

Returning to academic life in 1951, he became an assistant professor of political science at Midwestern University in Wichita Falls, Texas. Meanwhile, he continued his own education at

TOWER, JOHN G.—Continued

Southern Methodist University in Dallas. In 1952 he went to England to study at the London School of Economics and Political Science; while there he did extensive field research into the organization of the Conservative party. After submitting his master's thesis, "The Conservative Worker in Britain," he received his M.A. degree in political science from Southern Methodist University in 1953. He resumed his academic duties at Midwestern University, where he remained until June 1960.

Although he was originally a Democrat, Tower changed his party affiliation during his senior year in college, in 1948. In the years that followed, he became active in the state Republican party, serving on its executive committee in the Twenty-third Senatorial District and as co-chairman and then chairman of its committee on education and research. In 1956 he was a delegate to the Republican National Convention.

In the November 1960 election Senator Lyndon B. Johnson ran for both the United States Senate and the Vice-Presidency. Tower was the Republican candidate who opposed him for election to the Senate, and, although Johnson won both offices, Tower received an impressive 41 percent of the vote. When Johnson resigned his Senate seat to take the Vice-Presidency, the governor appointed a Democrat William Blakley, to serve an interim term until an election could be held in the spring of 1961.

In the election of April 4, 1961, Tower again ran on the Republican ticket. He opposed seventy candidates of all political hues, and, although he led the field, his 31.5 percent of the vote was not enough for a clear majority. Blakley was second in the election, with 18.3 percent of the vote, and according to Texas law a runoff election was required between the two top candidates. In the election of May 27, 1961 the Republican was victorious over the Democrat by about 10,000 votes.

Actually, according to the New York Times (May 29, 1961), Tower and Blakley are both ultraconservatives who hold almost identical views, and the only real election issue was the question of party affiliation. Although Texas had voted for the Republican President Dwight D. Eisenhower in 1952 and 1956 and had almost given the victory to the Republican Richard M. Nixon in the Presidential elections of 1960, the state tradition was still overwhelmingly Democratic at the time of Tower's election. Texas then had only one Republican Representative out of twenty, and Ralph W. Yarborough, the senior Senator, is a Democrat.

Tower's election was viewed as resulting from a shift in the Democratic balance of power from the rural to urban areas, which brought about the first signs of an emergence of a genuine two-party state. His victory was also interpreted as an advance for the type of political conservatism that is identified with Senator Barry M. Goldwater. Although he has been in the Senate for little over a year Tower is already rivalling Senator Goldwater as a speechmaker and drawing card at Republican party rallies and social functions.

Upon assuming his Senate seat Tower was assigned to two major Senate committees: Bank-ing and Currency, and Labor and Public Welfare. He is also on the influential Senate Republican Policy Committee, the National Republican Senatorial Campaign Committee, and the Civil War Centennial Commission. In February 1962 he was one of six Senators appointed to the twelve-member Senate-House committee charged with drafting an affirmative statement of Republican principles.

Tower has been cited by the Americans for Constitutional Action, a conservative political organization, for showing 100 percent agreement with their 1960-61 voting index during the half of year 1961 that he was in office. Included in A.C.A.-approved voting for the years 1960 and 1961 were restriction of foreign aid programs and opposition of bills for extension of minimum wage, for area redevelopment and manpower training, for feed-grain programs, and for federal aid to housing and education.

As a new Senator in the first session of the Eighty-seventh Congress Tower supported a bill providing $958,570,000 in added appropriations for aircraft, missiles, and naval vessels to meet a possible crisis in Berlin or elsewhere. He was against reducing a military assistance authorization from $1.8 billion to $1.55 billion. He voted for a Goldwater amendment to eliminate the authority of the new United States Arms Control and Disarmament Agency to conduct and support research on disarmament, and he was against the passage of a bill to establish a disarmament agency within the Department of State.

Tower opposed an amendment to increase by $2,000,000 the funds for the United States Information Agency. He voted for the reduction of Peace Corps fiscal authorization in 1962 from $40,000,000 to $25,000,000. He was against the passage of the Educational and Cultural Exchange Act of 1961 and against permitting the President to make agreements with international organizations for sponsoring exchange programs. He favored reduction of foreign subsidies and their control in the form of annual, rather than long-term, appropriations by Congress.

On the domestic front, Tower introduced an amendment to the Small Business Act of 1961 to delete a provision requiring the Small Business Administration, the Defense Department, and the General Services Administration to approve regulations designed to provide small businesses with a greater share of government sub-contracts. He supported legislation demanding the application of antitrust laws to federations of co-operatives. Tower opposed the passage of the Manpower Development and Training Act of 1961 that authorized a four-year $655,000,000 program for training unemployed workers. He voted for reduction of agricultural conservation payments, against extending feed-grain programs, against liberalizing Social Security benefits, and against the passage of a $4.88 billion housing act. Tower opposed the establishment of a ten-year, $691,500,000 program of oceanographic and Great Lakes research and surveys. He was against a $95,000,000 authorization for construction of electric generating facilities for the new Hanford, Washington plutonium-producing reactor.

Tower vetoed the nomination of Spottswood Robinson 3d, dean of Howard University Law School, to the Civil Rights Commission. He opposed making the commission a permanent agency, although he voted to extend its authority for two years. Tower voted to kill an amendment to prohibit the payment of contract funds for airport terminal buildings containing racially segregated facilities. He opposed authorizing the Attorney General to bring civil suits for injunctions to prevent individuals from being deprived of their civil rights.

During the second session of the Eighty-seventh Congress, which began in January 1962, Tower voted for the authorization of approximately $12.9 billion for procurement of missiles, aircraft, and naval vessels. He opposed giving aid to Communist countries and allowing surplus food sales or gifts to be made to Communist countries like Yugoslavia and Poland. Tower voted against the College Academic Facilities and Scholarship Act providing about $2.7 billion for a program of federal aid to higher education. He opposed a civil rights bill requiring that anyone with at least a sixth-grade education be passed in a literacy test for voting in federal elections, and he joined with fourteen Southern Democrats in opposing a constitutional amendment banning the poll tax as a prerequisite for voting in federal elections. (Texas is one of the states that imposes a poll tax.)

Tower was one of the Senators who contributed to the defeat, 52 to 48, on July 17, 1962, of an administration-backed plan for health insurance for the aged, to be financed through the Social Security system. He had previously attacked this kind of legislation on television and in speeches in Texas cities. In May 1962 it was disclosed that Blue Cross-Blue Shield private group insurance organizations of Texas had paid for travel and hotel expenses in connection with Tower's speaking engagements. When criticized for accepting expense aid, Tower contended that payment of expenses for Congressmen fulfilling speaking engagements is a common practice.

In a speech to the Senate in March 1962, Tower offered a program of action that he called an affirmative, conservative legislative program. He asked for application of antitrust laws to what he called some monopolistic labor practices, proposed across-the-board reductions in individual and business taxes, along with mandatory budget balancing. He called for less government competition with private business and a farm program to increase gradually acreage allotments and marketing quotas, while gradually reducing the level of price supports. He also proposed that Congress declare that "victory over Communism is the aim and objective of United States foreign policy." In his book, *A Program for Conservatives*, Tower calls for a Congressional investigation of government competition with private business, a mandatory balanced federal budget, and a maximum individual and corporate income tax rate of 47 percent.

Referring to statements by the Republican Senators Jacob K. Javits and Kenneth B. Keating that radical right-wing elements seeking to infiltrate the Republican party are giving it a bad name, Tower said that he does not regard extreme right-wing elements like the John Birch Society as a menace to the Republican party. "To me the terms 'conservative' and 'extremist' are incompatible," he said. "I regard conserva-

tism as synonymous with progress. The freer people are from government interference, the more progress they are likely to make." He added that his party should not fall into the error of apologizing for its convictions, but must instead assert them confidently.

Tower is on the board of stewards of the First Methodist Church in Wichita Falls. He is a director of the Wichita Falls Symphony Orchestra and a director and past president of the Wichita Falls Civic Playhouse. He belongs to the American and international political science associations, the Southwest Social Science Association, the Texas Historical Society, the Hansard Society (British), Kappa Sigma, the Kiwanis, and the Wichita Falls Chamber of Commerce.

On March 21, 1952 John G. Tower married Joza Lou Bullington, who was a piano teacher in Wichita Falls. She is a cousin of Orville Bullington, who ran in Texas as a Republican for governor in the 1930's. The Towers have three daughters, Penelope, Marian, and Jeanne.

One of the shortest men Texans have ever elected, Tower stands five feet five and one-half inches tall and weighs less than 150, but he has been called a political giant killer. His favorite icebreaker in the Senatorial contest was, "My name is Tower—but you can see that I don't." He is genial and outgoing, smokes moderately, and takes an occasional drink. A conservative in dress as well as in politics, he is given to wearing neat, three-button suits, regimental striped ties, a breast pocket handkerchief, and a fedora hat.

References

Nation 192:491 Je 10 '61
N Y Herald Tribune p1 My 29 '61 por
N Y Times p8 My 29 '61 por
Time 77:16 Je 9 '61

Congressional Directory (1962)
Who's Who in America, 1962-63

VANCE, CYRUS R(OBERTS) Mar. 27, 1917-
Secretary of the Army

Address: b. Department of the Army, Washington 25, D.C.; h. 3060 Foxhall Rd., Washington, D.C.

At a crisis-ridden time when the Department of Defense is alerted for action in safeguarding the security of the United States, Cyrus R. Vance has been named to the important post of Secretary of the Army. A lawyer formerly engaged in private law practice, he succeeded Elvis J. Stahr, Jr., on July 5, 1962. Before his appointment, Vance helped to reorganize and modernize the defense machine as general counsel of the Department of Defense. Before that he worked with Senate committees investigating missile and space satellite programs.

Cyrus Roberts Vance was born in Clarksburg, West Virginia on March 27, 1917 to John Carl and Amy (Roberts) Vance. His father died when he was five years old; his mother still lives in Clarksburg. He has a brother who practises law in Rochester, New York. Vance attended the Kent School in Kent, Connecticut, where he was senior prefect of the student body, rowed on the crew, and played football and hockey. When he

U. S. Army Photograph

CYRUS R. VANCE

graduated from Kent School, he went on to Yale University, where he majored in economics and took his B.A. degree in 1939. At Yale he played varsity wing on the hockey team in his junior and senior years, and he belonged to the Fence Club, the Scroll and Key, and the Torch Honor Society. Going on to Yale Law School, he was student director of the Yale moot court of appeals and graduated with honors with an LL.B. degree in 1942.

After leaving Yale Law School, Vance enlisted as a midshipman in the United States Navy's V-7 program and graduated from the United States Naval Reserve on August 5, 1942 as an ensign. He served at the Prairie State Midshipmen's School in New York City as an instructor in naval ordnance until April 1943, when he was posted to the destroyer USS *Hale* as a gunnery officer. During World War II Vance served aboard the destroyer for twenty months in the Atlantic and Pacific oceans, taking part in operations at Bougainville, Tarawa, the Marshall Islands, Saipan, and Guam. In December 1944 he took a brief course in naval ordnance and operations and was assigned to the Naval Training Station at Norfolk, Virginia, where he helped to organize destroyer crews. In August 1945 he was ordered to the USS *Henderson* as a gunnery officer and he served in Hawaiian waters with the Pacific Fleet until March 28, 1946, when he was released from active duty with the rank of lieutenant, senior grade.

From 1946 to 1947 Vance was assistant to the president of the Mead Corporation, manufacturers of paper products, but he left the company in 1947 to practise law with the New York firm of Simpson, Thacher, and Bartlett. After becoming a partner on January 1, 1956, he specialized in civil litigation, usually in the preparation of cases, until he left the firm in January 1961 to become general counsel for the Department of Defense.

While practising law privately, Vance also served in government positions. In 1957 and 1958, as special counsel to the preparedness investigating subcommittee of the Committee on Armed Services of the United States Senate during its inquiry into satellite and missile programs, he helped to investigate the service programs for the Redstone, Jupiter, Thor, Titan, Atlas, and Polaris weapons systems. Also in 1958 he served as consulting counsel to the Special Committee on Space and Astronautics of the Senate during hearings on, and the drafting of, the National Space Act of 1958, which created the National Aeronautics and Space Administration (NASA) and the National Aeronautics and Space Council.

In 1959 Vance became associate counsel to the Senate preparedness investigating subcommittee and conducted preliminary hearings on the Defense Department budget and the role of the Bureau of the Budget in formulating and executing this budget. In 1960 he served as associate special counsel during hearings on missiles, space, and other defense matters, held jointly by the preparedness investigating subcommittee and the Senate Committee on Aeronautical and Space Sciences. In this position he conducted an inquiry into the comparative reliability of United States and Soviet missiles and ICBM and space satellite programming for the United States.

During the subcommittee hearings in 1957 Vance often took his turn at questioning witnesses, but little attention was focused on him. Someone who took part in the hearings recalls, "Vance was around for two weeks before many of us realized that he was there." But Vance had made a favorable impression, and when the Democrats took office in 1961 he was chosen for the job of general counsel for the Department of Defense. Having withdrawn from his law firm on January 16, 1961, he was sworn in as general counsel on January 29, 1961.

As the chief legal officer of the Department of Defense, the general counsel is responsible for giving legal advice to the Secretary and Deputy Secretary of Defense and to the chairman of the Joint Chiefs of Staff. He advises the defense establishment on problems of international and commercial law and on the function and structure of the government, including the executive-legislative relationship. He is also responsible for the close supervision of security matters within the department, for investigating unauthorized disclosures of classified information, and for the procurement of the legislative program.

In addition to carrying out his traditional duties, Vance spent about half of his time as general counsel on a new project—the office of organizational and management planning. It was set up early in 1961 on the directive of the new Secretary of Defense, Robert S. McNamara, to make recommendations for a more effective, efficient defense establishment. Often acting on preliminary suggestions from McNamara himself, the office conducted research and made proposals that resulted in dramatic changes in Pentagon organization. Among the recommendations adopted in some form have been: combining the offices of the assistant secretaries of defense for manpower, personnel, and reserve and for health and medical into an office of the assistant secretary of defense for manpower; designating the Air Force as responsible for the Defense Department's space research and development program; establishment of a defense supply agency and of a defense intelligence agency. Vance also worked with the Army on its reorganization study.

When Elvis J. Stahr, Jr., resigned as Secretary of the Army to become president of Indiana University, Cyrus R. Vance was Secretary McNamara's personal choice to succeed Stahr. Vance was sworn in as Secretary of the Army on July 5, 1962. A New York *Times* (July 6, 1962) writer said his appointment "reflected the recognition on the part of many officials that Vance, by character and accomplishment, fitted in neatly with the management criteria established by the Secretary of Defense Robert S. McNamara—precision of thought, orderliness, attention to detail." At the ceremony Vance pledged to do everything in his power "to ensure that the Army remains more than equal to any task."

Under the National Security Act of 1947 the Department of War, originally created in 1789, was designated the Department of the Army, and the Air Force was separated from it. The 1949 amendments to this act established the Department of Defense as an executive department of the government, and provided that the departments of Army, Navy, and Air Force be military departments within the Department of Defense.

In his new post Vance is confronted with a Secretary of Defense who has a tendency to centralize the decision-making process in his own office. In the past Vance worked directly with McNamara. But, as Warren Rogers, Jr., wrote in the New York *Herald Tribune* (July 24, 1962), "Vance has another client now. The Army. And since the Army and McNamara seldom see eye-to-eye on the really hard-nosed questions, like how big it should be and toward what mission it should be pointed . . . Vance has his work cut out for him. On the one hand, he must educate the Army to its opportunities and how to seize them. On the other, he must find a *modus vivendi* with a strong-willed Secretary of Defense." Secretary Vance, Rogers notes, can help the Army "march out of the shadows of the Air Force's missiles and bombers and the Navy's super-carriers and Polaris submarines." Speaking before a session of the Association of the United States Army in October 1962, Vance said that the Army in the next ten years would "move strongly into the air with its men, its doctrine, its weapons, and its equipment" to gain mobility.

Vance is a member of the bars of New York State, the United States District Court for the Southern District of New York, the United States Court of Appeals for the Second Circuit, and the United States Supreme Court. He belongs to the American Bar Association and to its associate and advisory committee of the standing committee for aeronautical law. He is a member of the New York State Bar Association and of the Association of the Bar of the City of New York, on whose joint committee on the revision of the New York Civil Practice Act he serves. He is also a Fellow of the American College of Trial Lawyers and chairman of the committee on adjudication of claims of the Administrative Conference of the United States.

Vance is on the executive committee of the Yale Law School Association, and he has served as vice-chairman of the Yale alumni fund. He belongs to the American Legion and has been a vestryman at the Church of the Heavenly Rest in New York City. He belongs to the Century Association in New York, the Metropolitan Club in Washington, and the Links Club in New York. Vance is a trustee of Kent School. He was a director and chairman of the board of the Union Settlement Association, Inc., and a trustee of the Boys' Club of New York.

Cyrus R. Vance married Grace Elsie Sloane, a painter, on February 15, 1947. They have five children: Elsie Nicoll, Amy Sloane, Grace Roberts and Camilla (who are twins), and Cyrus Roberts, Jr. Vance is a tall, slender man with graying dark hair. He is soft-spoken and calm. His recreations are playing squash, golf, and tennis, fishing, gardening, and reading.

References

N Y Herald Tribune p1+ My 21 '62 por
N Y Times p1+ My 21 '62; p7 Jl 6 '62 por
Who's Who in America, 1962-63

VON BÉKÉSY, GEORG *See* Békésy, Georg von

WHITE, BYRON R(AYMOND) June 8, 1917- Associate Justice of the Supreme Court of the United States

Address: b. Supreme Court Bldg., 1 First St., N.E., Washington 25, D.C.; h. 5174 Watson St., N.W., Washington, D.C.

Byron R. White, the first New Frontier appointee to the United States Supreme Court, is a man who, according to President John F. Kennedy, has "excelled in everything he has attempted . . . and will excel on the highest court in the land." White, the youngest member of the Supreme Court, was a college and professional football star and also achieved a brilliant scholastic record. Before he became a Supreme Court Justice on April 16, 1962 White was Deputy Attorney General under Attorney General Robert F. Kennedy for about a year; from 1947 to 1961 he practised law in Denver, Colorado.

Byron Raymond White was born on June 8, 1917 at Fort Collins, Colorado. He grew up in Wellington, Colorado, a small lumber and sugar beet farming community near the Wyoming border. His father, Alfred White, a lumber dealer and a staunch Republican, was the mayor of Wellington. His older brother, Dr. Clayton Samuel White, is the director of research for the Lovelace Foundation for Medical Education and Research in Albuquerque, New Mexico.

While attending Wellington High School, White worked in the sugar beet fields and as a railroad section hand. He graduated from high school with a straight A average and was the valedictorian of his five-member class. He nearly duplicated this record at the University of Colorado, receiving A's in all but two of his courses. At the head of his class of 267, he was elected to Phi Beta Kappa, and at his graduation in June 1938 with the B.A. degree he was the class valedictorian. White held part-time jobs as a

BYRON R. WHITE

waiter in fraternity and sorority houses. He served as president of the Associated Students (the student body) in 1937-38. During his college years, impressed with Franklin D. Roosevelt's New Deal program, he switched his political affiliation to the Democratic party.

White's scholastic achievements were matched by his prowess on the football field. A halfback on the University of Colorado's team, he was a star punter, passer, and runner, and his exploits were followed eagerly by fans throughout the United States. In 1937, during the fall semester of his senior year, "Whizzer" White led Colorado through an unbeaten season to the Cotton Bowl game in January 1938. He was the collegiate champion for scoring, rushing, and total offense for the 1937 season, and he was also the 1937 All-America selection of Grantland Rice. White was equally successful on the university's baseball diamond and basketball court.

After graduating from the University of Colorado, White intended to study law at Oxford University on a Rhodes scholarship. But the Pittsburgh Pirates (now the Steelers), a professional football team, offered him $15,800 to play one season with them, much more than any other player in the National Football League was getting. "How can I refuse an offer like that?" White asked at the time. "It will pay my way through law school." During the 1938 season with Pittsburgh he led the league in ground gaining.

White entered Oxford University in January 1939 and began to read law, but his stay at Oxford was a brief one. World War II broke out in September 1939, and he returned to the United States shortly thereafter. While he was in England he first met John F. Kennedy, whose father, Joseph P. Kennedy, was then the United States Ambassador to the Court of St. James. On his return to the United States White entered Yale University Law School and at the same time signed to play professional football for the Detroit Lions. He played for the Lions in

1940 and 1941. He was the league's top ground gainer and in 1940 was picked for the all-league team. In 1954 White was named to the National Football Hall of Fame. Eight years later, in 1962, he received a gold medal from the National Football Foundation and Hall of Fame for distinguished service and devotion to the game of American intercollegiate football.

In July 1941, while still studying for a law degree, White tried to join the United States Marines, but he was rejected because of color blindness. The following year, however, he was accepted by the United States Navy, and in May 1942 he was commissioned a lieutenant, junior grade. In 1943, as a naval intelligence officer based on the Solomon Islands in the Pacific, White again met his acquaintance of prewar England, John F. Kennedy, who had just returned to the base as a hero after his boat, PT 109, had been sunk by a Japanese destroyer. White returned to civilian life in 1946, after winning two Bronze Stars and a Presidential unit citation. He was discharged from the United States Naval Reserve with the rank of lieutenant commander in 1954.

White returned to Yale in February 1946. He graduated *magna cum laude* with the LL.B. degree in November 1946 and was elected to Order of the Coif, a legal scholastic honorary society. Previously, in 1940, he had won the Edgar M. Cullen Prize for high scholastic standing. During the 1946-47 term of the Supreme Court, White served as law clerk to Fred M. Vinson, then the Chief Justice of the United States. At this time he renewed his friendship with John F. Kennedy, then a freshman Congressman from Massachusetts, whose office was near the Supreme Court building.

In 1947 White moved to Denver, where he became an associate with the law firm of Lewis, Grant, Newton, Davis, and Henry (now Lewis, Grant, and Davis), which had a general civil practice. He later became a partner and worked mostly on corporation cases, remaining with the firm until January 1961. Until 1960 his participation in political life in Denver was limited to holding minor posts in Democratic ward politics, like those of precinct committeeman and district captain.

But as the 1960 Presidential campaign began to develop, White moved to support John F. Kennedy in his bid for the Democratic Presidential nomination. He became head of the Colorado Kennedy committee and was credited with delivering twenty-seven of the state's forty-two convention delegates' votes for Kennedy's nomination. The Colorado vote was regarded as a key to Kennedy's success in the West. "I thought it was important for a Democrat to occupy the White House," White said at the time, "and I thought of all the candidates, Kennedy was the best in terms of ability, judgment, and potential."

After the national Democratic convention in July 1960 Robert Kennedy, who was managing his brother's campaign, asked White to head the national Citizens for Kennedy organization. The group was formed to interest independents and Republicans and to provide a rallying point for volunteers. White so impressed the Kennedy brothers with his drive and ability during the election campaign that it was generally predicted that he would play an important role in the Kennedy government. On December 8, 1960 John F. Kennedy offered White a post in his administration, although no specific job was mentioned at the time. Shortly thereafter Robert F. Kennedy became Attorney General. White was appointed Deputy Attorney General on January 24, 1961. As the second-in-command at the United States Department of Justice, White supervised antitrust cases and civil rights suits and screened candidates for federal judgeships. In May 1961 he directed federal marshals who were sent to Montgomery, Alabama to quell the race riots touched off by the Freedom Riders.

On March 29, 1962 President Kennedy announced that Justice Charles Evans Whittaker would resign for health reasons from the United States Supreme Court. The following day the President named White to fill the $35,000 post. "I have known Mr. White for over twenty years," he said. "His character, experience, and intellectual force qualify him superbly for service on the nation's highest tribunal. His varied experience in legal practice, in government and in the Navy—in addition to his remarkable scholarly accomplishments and his service to Chief Justice Vinson—have given him a humane and understanding approach to people and to problems. He has excelled in everything he has attempted—in his academic life, in his military service, in his career before the bar and in the federal government—and I know that he will excel on the highest court in the land."

The American Bar Association's committee on the federal judiciary, which checks the qualifications of prospective judicial appointees, gave White its highest rating, "exceptionally well qualified," and praised his adherence to principle, his sense of fairness, and his intellectual capacities. The committee members had known White from their work together on judicial selection. Leaders of both parties in Congress also approved of White's appointment, and on April 11, 1962 his nomination was approved by the Senate in a voice vote shortly after the Senate Judiciary Committee had unanimously upheld his appointment. David Lawrence complained in the New York *Herald Tribune* (April 2, 1962) that White had had no judicial experience and that experienced and qualified judges had been passed over. An editorial writer in the New York *Times* (April 1, 1962) observed: "He has not yet achieved the scholarly legal distinction that would justify hailing his appointment as a great and inevitable one. . . . However, Mr. White's brilliant record as a student does testify to his superior intellect."

White was sworn in as an Associate Justice of the United States Supreme Court on April 16, 1962. He is the youngest Justice of the present court and the ninety-third Justice and the first native of Colorado to sit on the Supreme Court bench. He was immediately assigned the supervision of the Tenth United States Circuit, which consists of Wyoming, Utah, Kansas, Oklahoma, New Mexico, and Colorado.

Although many observers speculated as to whether White would ultimately join the liberals or the traditionalists in the court, they generally agreed that no determination of his position could be made in the few weeks remaining in the 1961-62 term when he took his seat on the bench. During that term he acted in several cases and wrote three opinions and one dissent. His dissent was delivered on June 25, 1962, the last day of the term, when he dissented from a six-man majority opinion that held unconstitutional a California law making narcotics addiction a crime. The majority said that since the statute required no proof of use and punished an illness it was a "cruel and unusual punishment." White called the invocation of the little-used "cruel and unusual punishment" clause of the Constitution "novel" and accused the majority of imposing its own philosophical predilections on legislators. The constitutionality of the statute could have been saved, he said, by interpreting it to mean that use of narcotics as well as addiction was required for a conviction.

In 1946 Byron R. White was married to Marion Lloyd Stearns, the daughter of Dr. Robert L. Stearns, a former president of the University of Colorado. They have two children, Charles and Nancy. White is an Episcopalian. A calm and modest man, he stands an inch or two over six feet, weighs about 190 pounds, and has gray hair that was once blond and green eyes. Although the days of his football triumphs are past, he still skis and plays an occasional game of squash.

References

Kansas City Times F 28 '62 por
N Y Post Mag p2 Ag 14 '60 pors; p2 Ag 1 '62 pors
N Y Times p12 Jl 21 '60 por; p10 Mr 31 '62 por
New Frontiersmen (1961)
Who's Who in America, 1962-63

WOLFE, DEBORAH (CANNON) PARTRIDGE Dec. 22, 1916- Educator; United States government consultant

Address: b. Room 430, House Office Bldg., Washington 25, D.C.; Queens College of the City University of New York, Flushing 67, N.Y.; h. 62 S. Union Ave., Cranford, N.J.; 2747 Oakman Court, Detroit 38, Mich.

The chief of education for the House of Representatives Committee on Education and Labor is Dr. Deborah Partridge Wolfe, one of the few women and also one of the few Negroes to hold a high-ranking staff position on Capitol Hill. In this position she serves as liaison between the House committee and the Department of Health, Education, and Welfare. An associate professor of education at Queens College, New York City, since 1951, Dr. Wolfe took a leave of absence from the college upon assuming the government post on January 15, 1962. Before coming to Queens College she headed the department of elementary education and was director of graduate work at Tuskegee Institute in Alabama. She has taught at several other colleges and universities. Dr. Wolfe has lectured throughout the United States and abroad; she has written a number of articles for learned journals, and she has received many honors and awards.

Deborah Cannon Partridge Wolfe was born on December 22, 1916 in Cranford, New Jersey

Queens College

DEBORAH PARTRIDGE WOLFE

to the Reverend David Wadsworth and Gertrude
(Moody) Cannon. She has a sister, Dr. Mary
Cannon McLean, a specialist in education for
the mentally handicapped in the Springfield,
Massachusetts public schools. A brother, Dr.
David Wadsworth Cannon, Jr., who had been
a professor of psychology at Virginia State College, is no longer living. Dr. Wolfe maintains
that love of children and the desire to serve
her fellow man helped to influence her to become an educator. "Having lived in the home of
a clergyman and having participated in the
activities of the church from my infancy, it
was not surprising that I enjoyed being with
people and working with them," she has said.
"Since my mother was a teacher and principal
I had watched her at work and thought I might
also enjoy this area of specialization. My older
brother was teaching in college when I was in
high school and my sister was teaching elementary school; both enjoyed their work and
influenced me."

At Cranford High School Deborah Cannon
was a member of the National Honor Society
and of the Latin and French clubs, and served
on the student council and on the editorial
board of *Spotlight*, the school's magazine. She
was a soloist with the choral group and also
took part in sports, including hockey, tennis,
track, soccer, and basketball. Following graduation from high school in 1933 she entered
New Jersey State Teachers College in Jersey
City, where she majored in education and chose
social studies and English as her minor subjects. Her extracurricular activities included participation in women's sports and on the debating
team, singing as a soloist in the glee club,
and serving as literary editor of *Tower* and
sports editor of *Tower Watch*. She was president of the history club and of the international
relations club, secretary of the psychology club,
and a member of the student council and of
the honor society. During the summer of 1935

she worked as director of the community center
of the First Baptist Church in Cranford, New
Jersey, and in the summers of 1936 and 1937
she directed a community center for migratory
workers in Hurlock, Maryland. She graduated
from the teachers college with the B.S. degree
in 1937.

In the year before her graduation from college,
Deborah Partridge Wolfe began her teaching
career at the Lincoln School in Cranford, New
Jersey, where she taught mathematics and English under the Works Progress Administration
adult education project. She later became supervising teacher, and then principal, of this program. At the same time she undertook graduate
study in education and sociology at Teachers
College of Columbia University, where she was
treasurer of the teacher education club, secretary
of the Negro education club, and a member of
the Kappa Delta Pi honor society in education.
She received the M.A. degree in 1938, after
submitting the thesis "A Background Study and
Teacher Training Program for the Education
of Migrants."

From 1938 to 1950 Deborah Partridge Wolfe
was a member of the faculty of Tuskegee Institute in Alabama, where she taught education and served as head of the department of
elementary education and director of graduate
work. During part of this period, from 1938
to 1943, she was also principal and teacher
trainer of elementary and junior high school
classes at Prairie Farms School in Tuskegee.
From 1943 to 1945 she was principal and teacher trainer at Mitchell's Mill School in Tuskegee.
Having received a two-year fellowship from the
General Education Board in 1943, she continued
her graduate studies, and in the summer of
1944 she attended Vassar College in Poughkeepsie, New York. In 1945 Columbia University
conferred upon her the degree of Ed.D., after
she had completed her doctoral study "Rede-
signing the Curriculum of Rural Laboratory
Schools of Tuskegee Institute." She took postdoctoral work at the University of Pennsylvania in 1950-51 and at the Union Theological
Seminary and the Jewish Seminary of America
in New York City in 1952.

In 1951 Dr. Wolfe became a faculty member
of Queens College in New York City, where
she served as associate professor of education
and co-ordinator of laboratory schools. During
summers she taught courses in education and
human relations at various colleges and universities: at Grambling College in Louisiana in
1946; at New York University from 1951 to 1954;
at Texas College in 1952-53; at the University of
Michigan in 1952; and at the University of
Illinois in 1956-57. She also taught classes
at Columbia University in the fall of 1954, the
spring of 1955, and the fall of 1957; and at
Fordham University in the spring of 1952. In
addition to her teaching activities Dr. Wolfe
has served on a number of faculty boards
and committees and has acted as faculty adviser
to various campus organizations.

Dr. Wolfe has traveled widely throughout
Europe, the Middle East, and the Western
Hemisphere. In 1960 and 1961 she gave over
100 lectures while traveling in the United States
and Europe. Her observations as a member of
a team of educators visiting the schools of the

Soviet Union were recorded in her articles "Education in the U.S.S.R." (*New York State Education,* April 1959) and "Student Life at Moscow State University." Over the years she has written more than twenty articles on education and human relations for such publications as *Journal of Negro Education, Understanding the Child, School Executive, Our National Family,* and *Journal of Educational Sociology.*

As an expert in the field of education Dr. Wolfe has occasionally been called upon to serve the United States government. In 1950 she received an invitation from President Harry S. Truman to the White House Conference on Children and Youth, and in 1955 she was invited by President Dwight D. Eisenhower to take part in the White House Conference on Education. She has also attended the White House Conference on the Aging. During 1959 and 1960 she served on the Citizens Advisory Committee on Youth Fitness, to which she had been appointed by President Eisenhower. She was invited to attend the inauguration of President John F. Kennedy in January 1961.

On January 10, 1962 Dr. Wolfe's appointment as education chief of the House of Representatives Committee on Education and Labor was officially announced. She was appointed by committee chairman Adam Clayton Powell, Jr., Democratic Representative of New York, to take office effective January 15, 1962. In this position Dr. Wolfe is the committee's chief educational consultant, and she is in charge of research and the drafting of legislation in the field of education. She also serves as the committee's liaison officer with the Department of Health, Education, and Welfare on educational matters. Dr. Wolfe, who is on leave of absence from Queens College, reportedly receives $17,649 a year—the highest possible salary for an employee of the House of Representatives.

Dr. Wolfe devotes much of her time to civic and organizational affairs. She has served as director of youth activities of the Second Baptist Church of Roselle, New Jersey; member of the citizens advisory committee of the board of education of Cranford, New Jersey; project chairman of the League of Women Voters; education chairman and vice-president of the National Council of Negro Women; board member and chairman of the educational advisory committee of the Lisle Fellowship; member of the leadership services committee of the national YWCA; and member of the education committee of the National Conference of Christians and Jews. She has served as vice-president of the American Council on Human Rights; secretary of the Council of National Organizations for Children and Youth; consultant to the Phelps-Stokes Fund; and member of the board of directors of the National Panhellenic Council.

Other organizations in which Dr. Wolfe has been active include the National Association for the Advancement of Colored People, the National Association of Negro Business and Professional Women, the American Association of University Women, the American Association of University Professors, the American Academy of Social and Political Science, and the Fellowship of Southern Churchmen. She also belongs to the American Teachers Association, the New York State Teachers Association, the National Education Association, the Comparative Education Society, the International Reading Association, the National Society for the Study of Education, and the Association of Childhood Education. She is international president of Zeta Phi Beta sorority and is a member of Pi Lambda Theta education sorority.

Among the honors and distinctions received by Dr. Wolfe are a citation from the National Baptist Convention for outstanding contribution to the religious and civil welfare of America (1952); the Atlantic Region Achievement Award of Zeta Phi Beta sorority (1957); the National Achievement Award of the National Association of Negro Business and Professional Women's Clubs (1958); the Woman of the Year award of Delta Beta Zeta chapter of Zeta Phi Beta sorority (1959); the Woman of the Year award of the Women of Morgan State College, Baltimore, Maryland (1959); and the Today's Makers of History Award of the Association for the Study of Negro Life and History (1959). The *Pittsburgh Courier* and Personal Products, Inc., named her one of New York's outstanding ten women in 1958, and the *Amsterdam News* designated her as an honoree in 1959. In 1957 she received an honorary membership in the National Society for the Prevention of Juvenile Delinquency, because of her contributions to this field. The board of education of Macon County, Alabama has named a school in honor of Dr. Wolfe.

On June 1, 1940 Deborah Cannon married Henry Roy Partridge, and she has one son, Henry Roy Partridge, Jr. The marriage ended in divorce in August 1950, and on August 9, 1959 she married Estemore Avis Wolfe. Dr. Wolfe is five feet three inches tall. She is a Baptist. Dr. Wolfe continues her interests in music and sports and is fond of singing, playing the piano and organ, listening to operas and concerts, and attending the theater. She still plays tennis, badminton, ping pong, billiards, and softball and also enjoys rowing. Her favorite spectator sports are football, baseball, and basketball. During her employment in Washington Dr. Wolfe frequently commutes on weekends to her home in Cranford, New Jersey, where she lives with her husband and son.

References

N Y Times p25 Ja 11 '62 por

Who's Who of American Women (1961-62)

WOODWARD, ROBERT F(ORBES) Oct. 1, 1908- Diplomat

Address: b. American Embassy, Madrid, Spain; h. 1642 Avon Place, N.W., Washington, D.C.; 3224 Harriet Ave., Minneapolis, Minn.

In seeking improvement in United States relations with Latin American republics, a goal to which the Kennedy administration has given primary importance, Robert F. Woodward was able to offer the experience of a thirty-year career in the Foreign Service devoted almost entirely to Latin-American affairs. He has represented his

Dept. of State—Whit Keith, Jr.
ROBERT F. WOODWARD

country in some ten Latin-American republics, including Costa Rica, Uruguay, and Chile, where he held the rank of ambassador. From time to time he has been called in from the field to fill administrative posts in the State Department. The most recent of these was the highly sensitive office of Assistant Secretary of State for Inter-American Affairs, which he held from June 1961 to March 1962, when he was appointed Ambassador to Spain.

Robert Forbes Woodward was born in Minneapolis, Minnesota on October 1, 1908 to Charles Emerson and Ella (Robertson) Woodward. While attending high school he worked as a part-time office boy at Lindsay Brothers Company, a Minneapolis printing firm. During his four years of study at the University of Minnesota he continued to work at Lindsay Brothers, where he rose from printer's devil, pulling proofs and dumping dead type, to part-time manager of the plant, and in 1929 to assistant editor of a farm machinery catalogue. He received his B.A. degree in 1930 and entered the Foreign Service on December 17, 1931.

In his first assignment Woodward served for a little over a year, in 1932-33, as vice-consul at the American consulate in Winnipeg, Canada. Then after a brief training period at the Foreign Service School in the State Department in Washington, he received the first of a series of appointments in South America that laid the groundwork of his career. He served as vice-consul at Buenos Aires, Argentina from 1933 to 1935, at Asunción, Paraguay briefly in 1935, at Bogotá, Colombia in 1936-37, and at Rio de Janeiro, Brazil from 1937 to 1939.

Then assigned to the State Department, Woodward spent the next three years in Washington and during part of that time, in 1941, took courses at George Washington University. He became acting assistant chief of the division of American Republics in November 1941 and assistant chief in July 1942. Later in 1942 he began another series of tours of duty in South America when he was appointed second secretary and consul at La Paz, Bolivia. In 1944 he moved to Guatemala as second secretary and the following year was promoted to first secretary. From 1945 to 1947 he was counselor of embassy at Havana, Cuba.

In March 1947 Woodward was reassigned to the State Department and named deputy director of the office of American Republics, a position that he held until mid-1949. Then for one academic year he was detailed to the National War College in Washington and in July 1950 was sent to Sweden as counselor of embassy at Stockholm. Soon after returning to duty in the State Department in the spring of 1952, he became chief of the division of Foreign Service personnel. He later acted briefly as special assistant to the Assistant Secretary of State for Inter-American Affairs and in August 1953 was promoted to Deputy Assistant Secretary of State for Inter-American Affairs.

Woodward's first ambassadorial assignment, to Costa Rica in 1954, gave him the opportunity again for on-the-spot observation of the complex problems arising from political and economic changes throughout South America. Transferred to Uruguay four years later, he presented his credentials as ambassador in Montevideo in the spring of 1958. Uruguay's President Eduardo V. Haedo praised Woodward's work in his country, saying that although the United States had sent many able diplomats before, none had "succeeded so well in defending the position of the United States while at the same time evidencing a deep comprehension of the people and problems of the Republic of Uruguay."

Early in his administration, in April 1961, President John F. Kennedy appointed Woodward to head the United States diplomatic mission in Chile. A few months later, however, on June 16, 1961, Kennedy named the ambassador to fill the long-vacant office of Assistant Secretary of State for Inter-American Affairs, one of the most important positions in the State Department. The appointment was enthusiastically endorsed in the press because of Woodward's demonstrated understanding of the enormous social and economic strains that threaten efforts toward democratic reform in Latin America.

Some commentators speculated as to whether the President would give the views of a career officer sufficient weight to enable him to carry out a policy of repairing the United States' deteriorating alliance with Latin American countries. It was reported that the reason that several candidates, approached before Woodward, had refused the appointment was that they feared that experts close to the President would go over their heads in making decisions. Senator Wayne Morse, a member of the Foreign Relations Committee said, when praising the selection of Woodward, "I consider it important that the administrative jurisdiction over Latin-American affairs be returned to the State Department and taken away from special advisers in the White House."

One of Woodward's major responsibilities as Assistant Secretary of State for Inter-American

Affairs was to push forward the Kennedy administration's Alliance for Progress program, a plan to raise the standard of living in South America through United States economic and technical co-operation with countries that demonstrated their readiness to work for social reform. The program attempted to deal with fundamental problems in agriculture, housing, education, and other problems such as Woodward himself had been pointing out in his dispatches for a long time. He was vice-chairman in August 1961 of the forty-member United States delegation to the Inter-American Economic and Social Conference at Punta del Este, Uruguay, a meeting proposed by President Kennedy to help set up a working organization for the ten-year, $20 billion alliance project.

Another of Woodward's concerns was United States relations with the Dominican Republic, where the struggle for power after the death of Rafael Leónidas Trujillo Molina in 1961, raised the question of United States intervention to help secure a popular government on the island. In November 1961 he appeared before a nine-nation Organization of American States committee to propose lifting some economic sanctions earlier imposed against the Dominican Republic by O.A.S. sister states. At the time he argued that apparently democracy was looking up in the Republic and feared that continuing coercive measures would dampen this spirit. Lifting the ban, he felt, would be a "gesture of encouragement to further progress."

As tensions continued to ease in the Republic, the O.A.S. lifted its sanctions late in December. A further result of Woodward's policy appeared in January 1962 when the United States resumed diplomatic relations with the Dominican Republic after seventeen months of official silence. Later in January, however, President Joaquin Balaguer, to whom the United States had attributed much of the island's advance toward democracy, was overthrown by a civil-military junta.

In a move intended to concentrate operational responsibility for foreign affairs in the State Department, rather than have it divided between the department and the White House, Kennedy in November 1961 had appointed Richard Goodwin, a Latin-American specialist on the White House staff, as deputy to Assistant Secretary Woodward. "It was denied, however," the New York *Times* (November 28, 1961) reported, "that Mr. Woodward had been placed on shaky ground." On March 8, 1962 the White House announced that Woodward was being reassigned as ambassador and that Edwin M. Martin would be shifted from the post of Assistant Secretary of State for Economic Affairs to the Inter-American Affairs post.

One of the best-liked officers in the Foreign Service, Woodward is industrious and unpretentious and has the reputation of not being a "yes" man. His affability, sense of humor, relaxed manner, and concern for others also probably account for his success in diplomacy. As related in a biographical sketch in the New York *Times* (June 17, 1961), a few years ago a mishap with an electric garage door resulted in the loss of one of Woodward's eyes; a secretary recalls, "It

was a terrible thing for him, yet he was worried that it would upset us. So the first thing he did was to call and try to calm us down."

Robert F. Woodward married Virginia Parker Cooke of Washington on February 20, 1943 in Lima, Peru. The Woodwards have a son, Robert Forbes, Jr., and a daughter, Mary Cooke. He is a member of the Metropolitan Club and Chevy Chase Club, both of Washington, D.C.

References

N Y Times p3 Je 17 '61 por
N Y World-Telegram p3 Je 17 '61 por
Department of State Biographic Register, 1961
Who's Who in America, 1962-63

YOULOU, FULBERT June 9, 1917- President and Premier of the Republic of the Congo (formerly French Territory of the Middle Congo)
Address: 68 rue Banda, Brazzaville, Republic of the Congo

One of the four territories that formerly made up the federation of French Equatorial Africa, then the Middle Congo and now the Republic of the Congo, was proclaimed an independent republic within the French Community at its capital city, Brazzaville, on August 15, 1960. Its President and Premier, elected for a five-year term, is a flamboyant political leader and a former Roman Catholic parish priest, Fulbert Youlou, who, despite differences with ecclesiastic authorities as to his status, still uses the title of *abbé*. His government maintains close ties with France in economic and other affairs, and he himself is strongly anti-Communistic. Youlou's republic, which has a population of about 790,000 and is slightly smaller than the state of Montana, is not to be confused with its much larger neighbor, the former Belgian possession Republic of the Congo.

A member of the Balali tribe in the Kongo ethnic group, Fulbert Youlou, whose name means "reflection," was born on June 9, 1917 at Moumboulo, not far from Brazzaville, the capital of what was then French Equatorial Africa. His father, Fulbert Bindi, was a trader; his mother's maiden name was Josephine Bilombo. After attending an elementary mission school at Brazzaville, Youlou entered a Catholic seminary at Akono in the French Cameroons and then transferred to a school in the Cameroons capital, Yaoundé, where he studied philosophy with Barthélemy Boganda, who later became Premier of the Central African Republic.

For a while Youlou taught at the seminary of M'bamou in the Middle Congo before resuming his theological studies at Libreville in Gabon. He completed his education at the Grand Seminary in Brazzaville, was ordained a priest in June 1946, and served successively as vicar of St. Joseph Parish in Brazzaville and as a parish priest in the Mindouli diocese. Interested in both vocal music and the organ, he helped to train the Brazzaville Cathedral choir. He was also the founder of a St. Vincent de Paul Conference.

The Middle Congo, an area of about 139,000 square miles, extended northward from the lower stretch of the Congo River between Stanley Pool

French Embassy Press &
Inf. Division

FULBERT YOULOU

and the Atlantic Ocean. It was made a French territory in 1903, and five years later, with the neighboring areas of Gabon, Ubangi-Shari, and Chad, it became one of the four territories of the federation of French Equatorial Africa. After the fall of France in 1940 the federation, under the leadership of Governor General Félix Eboué of Chad, rallied strongly to the Free French cause. A conference of African territories held at Brazzaville in 1944 recommended giving the peoples of the territories "an ever-larger share in the life and democratic institutions of the French community." This principle was incorporated in the new French constitution of 1946, which provided for an elected Representative Council in each territory and representation in the Chamber of Deputies and Senate in Paris.

Throughout his ten years as an officiating priest, Youlou took a growing interest in politics, especially in youth movements and in the program of the Congo Friends' Society, which had been established in Paris by the Lari chieftain Matswa in the late 1930's. Suspended from priestly functions in 1956, reportedly for having broken his sacerdotal vows, Youlou defied ecclesiastical authority by continuing to wear a white cassock and by using the title *abbé*.

Also in 1956 Youlou founded a new political party, the Democratic Union for the Defense of African Interests (Union Démocratique de la Défense des Intérêts Africains, or U.D.D.I.A.), and a weekly paper, *Cette Semaine* (This Week). Early in the year he had been defeated as a candidate for Deputy in the French National Assembly, but in November 1956 he was elected Mayor of Brazzaville, an office he still holds. In March 1957 he was elected to the Middle Congo Territorial Assembly as councilor of Djoué. At that time his U.D.D.I.A. party won twenty-two seats, but had to concede leadership to the Mouvement Socialiste Africain, headed by Jacques Opangault, which took twenty-three seats. With

a one-seat majority, Opangault became Premier, and, despite their rivalry, in May 1957 Youlou accepted the portfolio of Minister of Agriculture, Livestock, Water and Forests in Obangault's cabinet. In August 1957 his U.D.D.I.A. became affiliated with the Rassemblement Démocratique Africain (African Democratic Rally), a unifying movement of all races and religions in French West Africa.

On September 28, 1958 a referendum was held in France and her possessions on adoption of President Charles de Gaulle's constitution for the Fifth Republic, under which the overseas territories were given six months to choose between retaining their existing status or becoming either Overseas Departments or autonomous states within a French Community. The Middle Congo electorate gave a 79 percent vote for adoption. Two months later, on November 28, the Middle Congo Territorial Assembly, unanimously choosing self-government within the community, proclaimed a Republic of the Congo and transformed itself into a Legislative and Constituent Assembly.

Meanwhile, having persuaded a Socialist deputy to defect to the U.D.D.I.A., Youlou had secured a one-seat majority for his party, and on December 8, 1958 he was appointed Premier in a provisional government. In February 1959, however, after the U.D.D.I.A. majority had voted down a demand by the opposition leader, Obangault, for a new election to decide whether or not the Congo should unite with other French West African states, and the Socialists had walked out of the assembly, serious rioting broke out between tribesmen supporting Youlou and those supporting Obangault. About 100 casualties occurred in the fighting, which ended after four days with the intervention of French troops and the jailing of Obangault. On February 20 the assembly adopted several of the twelve basic laws now comprising the Constitution of the Republic of the Congo and transformed the provisional government into the first official government of the republic.

Under pressure from the French, who urged an early election even though Obangault was in prison and the Socialists were disorganized, Youlou set June 14, 1959 as the date for a legislative election. The assembly was enlarged to sixty-one seats, and with most of the new seats allotted to areas dominated by Youlou, the U.D.D.I.A. took fifty of the sixty-one seats. Now called the National Assembly, the legislature convened on June 27 to re-elect Youlou as Premier, and on July 3 he formed a coalition cabinet with himself as Minister of Justice and Foreign Minister as well as Premier. The cabinet included two Socialists, and Obangault, released from prison at that time, later also joined the government. On November 21, 1959, in accordance with the constitution, Youlou was elected by the assembly to a five-year term as President. He not only determines general policy but heads the administrative services and the armed forces and is empowered to "issue regulations."

The Republic of the Congo attained full sovereignty on July 12, 1960 when France accorded it recognition as an independent state within the French Community. Independence was formally proclaimed at Brazzaville on August 15, 1960, and on September 20 the republic was admitted to the United Nations. In a news conference as early as July 16, 1960 Youlou had warned that the civil conflict in the adjacent former Belgian possession Republic of the Congo could lead to intervention of Communist forces in Africa. He refused to receive Patrice Lumumba as an emissary to the Independence Day celebration, and although on personally good terms with President Joseph Kasavubu, he was sympathetic with the secessionist movement of Moise Tshombe of Katanga Province.

In late December 1960 Youlou charged that United Nations intervention in the former Belgian Congo was bringing "endless ruin and death" to Katanga and warned that he would bar U.N. planes from use of his country's airspace. The rift between the governments of Kasavubu and Youlou deepened, and during the following spring the river traffic between Leopoldville and Brazzaville was halted. In May 1961, after alleging that U.N. planes had buzzed Brazzaville, Youlou closed the city's airport to the United Nations.

When Youlou visited the United States in June 1961, he was entertained by President John F. Kennedy, with whom he discussed long-range economic development of the Republic of the Congo. Work had already begun on a hydroelectric project on the Kouilou River at Sounda, where the blocking of a narrow gorge is expected to generate 9 billion kilowatts of power annually, making possible the development of hydrometallurgical and hydrochemical industries. The scheme includes the creation of a lake, on whose shores bananas, rice, sugar, and jute could be grown to add to the republic's existing coffee, timber, zinc, peanuts, and palm products.

Youlou has remarked that his "life portrait fluctuates with history." He has been described in the New York *Times* (June 16, 1959) as "a short man with a round, childlike face and a nervous manner," and he is said to be suspicious and vain, but not without a sense of humor. Smith Hempstone, who visited him in Brazzaville, wrote in *Africa—Angry Young Giant* (Praeger, 1961), "The Abbé Fulbert is not above blessing the ballpoint pens of primary students, thus guaranteeing them a pass in their examinations. He . . . likes to wear the tri-coloured sash of office [of Mayor] over his white cassock topped off with a homburg and to distribute five-franc notes to enthusiastic supporters as his blue-green Pontiac takes him to work. . . . [He] is given to using colourful turns of phrase, such as 'the thirst for a better state itches us.' " He remains a bachelor. Football is his favorite sport.

References
N Y Post p57 Je 9 '61
Newsweek 59:20+ Ja 1 '61 por
Time 72:24 D 15 '58 por
U S News 49:14 Ag 29 '60 por

International Who's Who, 1961-62
Italiaander, Rolf. New Leaders of Africa (1961)
Phelps, R. H. ed. Men in the News:2 (1960)
Segal, Ronald. Political Africa (1961)
Who's Who in France, 1961-62

CURRENT BIOGRAPHY—VOL. 23. NOS. 1-11

This is the index to the January-December 1962 issues. For the index to the 1961 biographies, see December 1961 issue or 1961 Yearbook. For the index to 1940-1950 biographies, see 1950 Yearbook. For 1951-1960 index, see 1960 Yearbook.

Ford, Whitey Apr 62
Forrester, Maureen (Kathleen Stewart) Jul 62
Francis, Connie Jul 62
Frische, Carl A(lfred) Oct 62
Fuchs, Joseph (Philip) Oct 62

Gardiner, James Garfield obit Mar 62
Gavin, John Sep 62
Gilmore, Voit Feb 62
Glenn, John H(erschel), Jr. Jun 62
Goodman, Benny Oct 62
Goodspeed, Edgar J(ohnson) obit Mar 62
Goossens, Sir Eugene obit Sep 62
Gordon, Lincoln Feb 62
Goulart, João (Belchior Marques) Sep 62
Goulet, Robert (Gerard) Sep 62
Gove, Philip B(abcock) Oct 62
Graham, John Oct 62
Grant, Gordon (Hope) obit Jul 62
Greenebaum, Leon C(harles) Jan 62
Gregory, Dick Jun 62
Grimes, Tammy (Lee) Jul 62
Guggenheim, Peggy Oct 62
Guggenheimer, Mrs. Charles S. See Guggenheimer, M. Oct 62
Guggenheimer, Minnie Oct 62
Guinzburg, Harold K(leinert) obit Jan 62
Guion, Connie M(yers) Feb 62

Hall, Peter (Reginald Frederick) Feb 62
Hammond, John Hays, Jr. Jul 62
Hanschman, Nancy (Conners) Sep 62
Hansen, Carl F(rancis) Oct 62
Hardenbrook, Donald J(ohnson) Jul 62
Hargrave, Thomas J(ean) obit Apr 62
Harris, Harwell Hamilton Jan 62
Harrison, James L(erlie) Oct 62
Hart, Moss obit Feb 62
Hartigan, Grace Sep 62
Hartle, Russell P(eter) obit Jan 62
Hayakawa, Sessue Sep 62
Head, Matthew See Canaday, J. May 62
Heath, Edward (Richard George) Oct 62
Heineman, Ben W(alter) Jan 62
Herbster, Ben M(ohr) Jul 62
Hesse, Hermann biog Oct 62 obit Oct 62
Hesselgren, Kerstin obit Oct 62
Hester, James M(cNaughton) Jun 62
Hillyer, Robert Silliman obit Feb 62

Hocking, William Ernest Mar 62
Hodes, Henry I(rving) obit Apr 62
Hodges, Gil(bert Ray) Oct 62
Hofstadter, Robert Oct 62
Holman, Eugene obit Oct 62
Holt, Isabella obit May 62
Houk, Ralph (George) Jul 62
Houle, Cyril O(rvin) May 62
Howe, Gordie Mar 62
Howe, Gordon See Howe, Gordie Mar 62
Hu Shih obit Apr 62
Hubbard, Bernard (Rosencrans) obit Jul 62
Hughes, Richard J(oseph) Jul 62
Husing, Ted obit Oct 62

Ives, Irving M(cNeil) obit Apr 62

Jacobson, Leon Orris Oct 62
John, Augustus (Edwin) obit Jan 62
Johnson, Harold Ogden obit Apr 62

Kahn, Herman Oct 62
Katsh, Abraham I(saac) Mar 62
Kay, Hershy Mar 62
Keldysh, Mstislav (Vsevolodovich) Feb 62
Kennelly, Martin H(enry) obit Jan 62
Khouri, Faris el- obit Feb 62
Kindelberger, J(ames) H(oward) obit Oct 62
Kingman, Dong (Moy Shu) Oct 62
Kiplinger, W(illard) M(onroe) Jan 62
Kirk, Russell (Amos) Sep 62
Klahre, Ethel S(usan) May 62
Kobak, Edgar obit Jul 62
Koestler, Arthur Jan 62
Korth, Fred (H.) Jul 62
Kovacs, Ernie obit Mar 62
Krag, Jens Otto Oct 62
Kreisler, Fritz obit Mar 62

Larson, Leonard W(infield) May 62
Lefèvre, Théo(dore Joseph Albéric Marie) Jun 62
Lehmann, Inge Nov 62
Lewis, Jerry Nov 62
Lewis, John (Aaron) Jan 62
Lilly, John C(unningham) Nov 62
Lindsay, John V(liet) Nov 62
Lipchitz, Jacques Apr 62
Lippmann, Walter Nov 62
Lober, Georg (John) obit Feb 62
Loeb, James (Isaac), Jr. Jan 62
Louw, Eric H(endrik) Mar 62
Love, J(ames) Spencer obit Mar 62
Luhan, Mabel Dodge obit Oct 62
Luthuli, Albert John Feb 62

Macapagal, Diosdado Nov 62
McCarthy, Clem obit Jul 62
McClintic, Guthrie obit Jan 62
McConnell, F(owler) B(eery) obit Feb 62
McCormack, John W(illiam) Apr 62
McCormick, Myron obit Oct 62
McCracken, Joan obit Jan 62
McNeely, Eugene J(ohnson) Nov 62
McSwigan, Marie obit Sep 62
Macy, John W(illiams), Jr. Jan 62
Mao Tse-tung May 62
Marais, Jean Apr 62
Margai, Sir Milton (Augustus Strieby) Feb 62
Marks, Simon, 1st Baron Nov 62
Martin, Edmund F(ible) Jan 62
Marvel, Mrs. Archie D. Apr 62
Marvel, Elizabeth Newell See Marvel, Mrs. A. D. Apr 62
Meerloo, Joost A(braham) M(aurits) Jan 62
Mellers, Wilfrid (Howard) Feb 62
Meštrović, Ivan obit Mar 62
Miller, Harry W(illis) Mar 62
Miller, William E(dward) Feb 62
Monroe, Marilyn obit Oct 62
Moore, Charlotte Emma See Sitterly, C. M. Jan 62
Morison, Samuel Eliot Sep 62
Morse, Robert (Alan) Nov 62
Moses, Anna Mary Robertson obit Feb 62
Mössbauer, Rudolf L(udwig) May 62
Motherwell, Robert (Burns, 3d) Nov 62
Mowrer, Edgar Ansel Jul 62
Muench, Aloisius (Joseph), Cardinal obit Apr 62
Murphy, (Eleanor) Patricia Apr 62

Nash, Philleo Nov 62
Nestingen, Ivan A(rnold) Mar 62
Newhart, Bob Mar 62
Nicklaus, Jack (William) Nov 62
Nitze, Paul H(enry) Feb 62

O'Casey, Sean Nov 62
Ochoa, Severo Jun 62
Ogburn, Charlton obit Apr 62
Olav V, King of Norway Jan 62
Osgood, Charles E(gerton) Apr 62
Ozbirn, Catharine (Freeman) See Ozbirn, Mrs. E. L. Jan 62
Ozbirn, Mrs. E. Lee Jan 62

Page, Ruth Jun 62
Parker, Cola G(odden) obit Sep 62
Partridge, Deborah (Cannon) See Wolfe, D. Dec 62

Peden, Katherine (Graham) May 62

Petri, Egon obit Jul 62

Pevsner, Antoine obit Jun 62

Picasso, Pablo Nov 62

Piccard, Auguste obit May 62

Pompidou, Georges (Jean Raymond) Nov 62

Portinari, Candido obit Mar 62

Rabaut, Louis Charles obit Jan 62

Ramírez, Pedro P(ablo) obit Sep 62

Randolph, Jennings Jan 62

Rawlings, Sir (Henry) Bernard (Hughes) obit Dec 62

Rayburn, Sam(uel Taliaferro) obit Jan 62

Read, Sir Herbert (Edward) Mar 62

Reischauer, Edwin O(ldfather) May 62

Resor, Stanley B(urnet) obit Dec 62

Reybold, Eugene obit Jan 62

Rivers, Thomas M(ilton) obit Jul 62

Robarts, John P(armenter) Dec 62

Robinson, Spottswood W(illiam), 3d Mar 62

Robus, Hugo Dec 62

Rogers, Carl R(ansom) Dec 62

Rogers, Frank B(radway) Jun 62

Rogers, Rutherford David Jun 62

Rombauer, Irma (von) S(tarkloff) obit Dec 62

Roosa, Robert V(incent) Dec 62

Rose, (Iain) Murray Jun 62

Russell, Donald J(oseph) May 62

Russell, James S(argent) Jan 62

Sandström, (Alfred) Emil (Fredrik) obit Sep 62

Satterfield, John C(reighton) Jul 62

Savage, Augusta (Christine) obit May 62

Schell, Maximilian Dec 62

Schoeppel, Andrew F. obit Mar 62

Schröder, Gerhard Dec 62

Schuman, William (Howard) Dec 62

Scofield, Paul Mar 62

Senghor, Léopold Sédar Mar 62

Sherrod, Robert (Lee) Dec 62

Shirer, William L(awrence) May 62

Shotton, Burt(on Edwin) obit Oct 62

Shurlock, Geoffrey M. Jan 62

Sinclair, Upton (Beall, Jr.) Dec 62

Sitterly, Mrs. Bancroft Walker See Sitterly, C. M. Jan 62

Sitterly, Charlotte Moore Jan 62

Skidmore, Louis obit Dec 62

Slocum, (Manly) Harvey obit Jan 62

Smith, Margaret (Madeline) Chase Mar 62

Snell, Peter (George) Dec 62

Souvanna Phouma, Prince of Laos Nov 62

Spahn, Warren (Edward) May 62

Speicher, Eugene (Edward) obit Jul 62

Spottswood, Stephen Gill Apr 62

Steacie, E(dgar) W(illiam) R(ichard) obit Nov 62

Stefansson, Vilhjalmur obit Nov 62

Stelle, John obit Sep 62

Stikker, Dirk U(ipko) Feb 62

Stokes, Anson Phelps, Jr. Jul 62

Stuart, J(ohn) Leighton obit Nov 62

Suggs, Louise Jan 62

Sunderland, Thomas E(lbert) Apr 62

Swann, W(illiam) F(rancis) G(ray) obit Mar 62

Swift, Harold H(iggins) obit Sep 62

Switzer, Mary E(lizabeth) Jan 62

Taylor, A(lbert) Hoyt obit Jan 62

Teagle, Walter C(lark) obit Feb 62

Thant, U Feb 62

Thomas, Norman (Mattoon) Jul 62

Thurber, James obit Jan 62

Tillinghast, Charles C(arpenter), Jr. Feb 62

Titov, Gherman (Stepanovich) Dec 62

Tobias, Channing H(eggie) obit Jan 62

Toledano, Ralph de Dec 62

Tower, John G(oodwin) Dec 62

Turner, Ewald (Walter) May 62

Unitas, John Feb 62

Vance, Cyrus R(oberts) Dec 62

Vandiver, S(amuel) Ernest Jul 62

Van Pelt, John V(redenburgh) obit Sep 62

Vertès, Marcel obit Jan 62

Viereck, George Sylvester obit May 62

Vilar, Jean (Louis Côme) Apr 62

Volpe, John A(nthony) Feb 62

Von Békésy, Georg See Békésy, Georg von Dec 62

Waddington, C(onrad) H(al) Apr 62

Wagner, Richard Apr 62

Wald, Jerry obit Sep 62

Walsh, Chad Feb 62

Walsh, William B(ertalan) May 62

Walter, Bruno obit Apr 62

Ward, Paul L(angdon) Mar 62

Watson, Lucile obit Sep 62

Watts, Alan (Wilson) Mar 62

Webb, James E(dwin) May 62

Welsh, Matthew E(mpson) Jun 62

Wenner-Gren, Axel (Leonard) obit Jan 62

Wesker, Arnold Feb 62

Whalen, Grover A(loysius) obit Jun 62

White, Byron R(aymond) Dec 62

Whitton, Rex M(arion) May 62

Wickens, Aryness Joy Sep 62

Wilcox, Francis O(rlando) Apr 62

Wilkinson, Bud See Wilkinson, C. Apr 62

Wilkinson, Charles (Burnham) Apr 62

Wills, Royal Barry obit Feb 62

Winiarski, Bohdan (Stefan) Feb 62

Wolfe, Deborah (Cannon) Partridge Dec 62

Wood, Natalie Apr 62

Woodward, Robert F(orbes) Dec 62

Yamasaki, Minoru Mar 62

Youlou, Fulbert Dec 62

Young, Owen D. obit Sep 62